PENGUIN REFERENCE

The Penguin Dictionary of British Surnames

John Titford, born in Holloway Road, London, as the Second World War was nearing its end and before the post-war baby boom had taken off, was educated at Haberdashers' Aske's School Hampstead/Elstree, St John's College, Cambridge, the Sorbonne in Paris and at the universities of Newcastle-upon-Tyne and San Francisco. Formerly a teacher and lecturer in English language and literature in schools and colleges, he now lives in Derbyshire, where he works as a writer, broadcaster, researcher and genealogical bookseller. He has lectured regularly on family history, dialect and related topics throughout Britain, in the United States of America, New Zealand and elsewhere.

The author of a number of books on dialect, communication and media studies and family history, he is a liveryman of the Worshipful Company of Scriveners, Chairman of Examiners for the Institute of Heraldic and Genealogical Studies, and was elected a Fellow of the Society of Genealogists in 2004.

In what spare time he can muster, he plays guitar, melodeon and concertina, is a great lover of American blues and English folk music, sings, with his wife Heather, in the 'Rolling Stock Company' choir, based in Derbyshire, and is a magistrate.

The Penguin Dictionary of
BRITISH SURNAMES

John Titford

PENGUIN BOOKS

PENGUIN BOOKS

Published by the Penguin Group
Penguin Books Ltd, 80 Strand, London WC2R 0RL, England
Penguin Group (USA) Inc., 375 Hudson Street, New York, New York 10014, USA
Penguin Group (Canada), 90 Eglinton Avenue East, Suite 700, Toronto, Ontario, Canada M4P 2Y3
(a division of Pearson Penguin Canada Inc.)
Penguin Ireland, 25 St Stephen's Green, Dublin 2, Ireland (a division of Penguin Books Ltd)
Penguin Group (Australia), 250 Camberwell Road, Camberwell, Victoria 3124, Australia
(a division of Pearson Australia Group Pty Ltd)
Penguin Books India Pvt Ltd, 11 Community Centre, Panchsheel Park, New Delhi – 110 017, India
Penguin Group (NZ), 67 Apollo Drive, Rosedale, North Shore 0632, New Zealand
(a division of Pearson New Zealand Ltd)
Penguin Books (South Africa) (Pty) Ltd, 24 Sturdee Avenue, Rosebank, Johannesburg 2196, South Africa

Penguin Books Ltd, Registered Offices: 80 Strand, London WC2R 0RL, England

www.penguin.com

First published 2009
1

The moral right of the author has been asserted

Set in ITC Stone Sans and ITC Stone Serif
Typeset by Data Standards Ltd, Frome, Somerset
Printed in England by Clays Ltd, St Ives plc

ISBN: 978-0-141-02320-5

www.greenpenguin.co.uk

For Heather

who has been my support and my inspiration over many happy years

Contents

Introduction

Surnames: such a treasure!

The surnames we bear are more special and precious than we sometimes give them credit for. Older than almost anything else we can call our own, they can be redolent of former times and offer a tantalizing glimpse of the past, telling us at least something of interest about our far-off ancestors in a way that nothing else can.

The variety on offer is almost overwhelming. There are several hundred thousand different surnames in the British Isles, about the same number of words as can be found in the *Oxford English Dictionary*. Many of the commonest surnames within these islands are Welsh, Scottish or Irish, but the great majority of people in Britain have rare names, a paradox to which Robin McKie has drawn attention in *Face of Britain* (2006): 'It is usual to have an unusual name... We may think of ourselves as a nation of Smiths and Joneses. In reality we are distinguished by our Attenboroughs, Crabtrees and Poultons.'

A surname is that part of our full name which is truly hereditary, having passed down a male, or sometimes a female, ancestral line, or a combination of the two. Many British surnames have been handed on in this way since the thirteenth century, if not earlier, and arose originally as a result of the need to make a distinction between individuals of the same single name. If a village was full of men called 'Richard', it would be a useful ploy to separate them by calling one 'Richard Williams', another 'Richard Selby' and another 'Richard Black'. These extra names, borne by an individual during his or her lifetime, would initially have been 'bynames', specific to one person; if such bynames then became hereditary, they were metamorphosed into fully fledged surnames.

The burgeoning use (and eventually the imposition) of surnames suited the central authorities very nicely, made it easier for them to keep track of the population and to collect taxes, but the practice also became something of a necessity for those individuals who were keen to establish an uncontested title to property of one sort or another and to pass it on to their male descendants, who would bear the same surname as they did. Continuity was thus assured.

Various regions of the British Isles adopted surnames at different periods in history: the Irish were quick off the mark, while many living in the Highlands of Scotland or in Wales only opted for surnames, or had them forced upon them, in very recent times.

Illegitimacy could confuse the issue, of course, and a byname bestowed upon a foundling, commonly consisting of the name of the place in which he or she had been discovered, could then become hereditary. In 1695 a young child was found abandoned in Pickwick, Wilts, and was baptized 'Moses **Pickwick**' accordingly. His grandson Eleazer Pickwick became a wealthy stagecoach proprietor in Bath, serving as Mayor of the City in 1826, and it was the name of his cousin, another Moses Pickwick, that Dickens's character Sam Weller saw emblazoned upon a London to Bath coach in *The Pickwick Papers*.

It is the existence of surnames that allows family historians and others to trace pedigrees back through several centuries (with a bit of luck...), and the surname which you acquired at birth will tell you at least something of interest about a far-distant mediaeval ancestor – that his father's baptismal name was William, that he lived near a mill, that he came from Cornwall, that he was a smith by trade, that he had red hair – and so on.

One aspect of this process which is readily observable and intriguing, but which has not yet been fully understood, is why certain individuals acquired a surname based upon a father's first-name, some were named after a feature of the landscape or a local place-name, leaving others to be known by a name based upon an occupational term or upon some kind of nickname.

There is often a regional dimension to all this. Were we to take surname evidence alone, we might conclude that there were more bull-headed (**Bulleid/Bullied**), short/fat (**Chubb**) and clumsy/heavily built (**Clapp**) people in Devon than elsewhere in the country, and that those living in the south or south-west of England were more inclined to be stubborn (**Chiver(s)**), those in Buckinghamshire/Middlesex to be lazy (**Dormer**), those in Somerset to be greedy (**Greedy**), those in the Isle of Wight to be loyal (**Leal**), those in East Anglia to be discreet (**Secrett**), those in the West Riding of Yorkshire (**Standeven**) and in Somerset (**Standfast**) to be assertive and resolute, those in Lancashire and Yorkshire to be haughty (**Bar(r)on**), those in Cheshire and Lancashire to be cocky (**Crank**) and those in Lancashire to be prompt, quick and opportunistic (**Ready**).

Were there more simpletons (**Geach**) in Cornwall/Devon, more tricksters (**Larter**) in Norfolk/Suffolk, more fat-bellies (**Puddephat(t)/Puddefoot/Puddifoot**) in Bedfordshire, Buckinghamshire and Hertfordshire, more broad ribs (**Brodribb/Broadribb**) in Somerset, more lute-players (**Luther**) and frog-like folk (**Paddock**) in Shropshire, more dancers (**Hopper**) in County Durham, more handsome-headed people (**Fairhead**) in East Anglia, more pugilists (**Poyner**) in the West Midlands, more money-grubbers (**Winpenny/Wimpenny**) in the West Riding of Yorkshire, more shovers and pushers (**Showers**) in Somerset and more outlaws (**Outlaw**) in East Anglia?

Was it only in Sussex that people had large/ugly heads (**Tester**), and mainly in Kent/Surrey/Sussex that they had big heads (**Coppard**)? Were deformed feet (**Foot**) a speciality of southern and south-west England? Were there more births around Christmas time (**Christmas**) in East Anglia and in southern England than elsewhere? Were twins more prevalent in Essex (**Twin**) and in Cambridgeshire (**Twinn**)? Were moustaches especially popular in Wales (**Garnon**)?

These and similar questions are likely to remain merely rhetorical until further research throws more light into such dark corners.

A number of different languages have given rise to the surnames found within the British Isles. When a disparate collection of Angles, Saxons, Jutes and Frisians made their home in a country which they were to call '*England*' from the fourth century AD onwards, their own closely related languages, referred to as 'Old English' by scholars, drove the Celtic languages spoken by the indigenous population to the margins of the British Isles. I have had something to say about Celtic naming patterns used within Scotland, Wales, Ireland, the Isle of Man and Cornwall in *Searching for surnames* (2002).

Viking invaders who began arriving in the ninth and tenth centuries spoke what we now refer to as 'Old Norse', a set of languages which in time became melded with Old English without too much difficulty, but the arrival of a further group of Vikings from Normandy in 1066 posed a more serious linguistic challenge. The Normans used a variety of French which, together with written Latin, could in theory have eradicated the English language entirely during the next few centuries. Nothing of the sort happened: English promptly went underground, simplified its grammar, borrowed as many French words as it found useful, and ultimately emerged during the fourteenth century, robust and healthy, as a new hybrid which we refer to as 'Middle English', which could hold its head high as an official and literary language as well as a vernacular one. English has moved on again since then, however. We no longer pronounce the initial letter '*k*' in a word like 'knight', nor do we give the '*gh*' in such a word its full guttural force; at the time when Geoffrey Chaucer was writing *The Canterbury Tales* in the fourteenth century, a word such as 'nightingale', together with the associated surname, would have been pronounced in a manner commensurate with its spelling – as 'nichtingahleh'.

So at the time when many surnames were first beginning to appear, the English language which gave rise to them was still learning to come to an accommodation with Norman French, and was under infinitely less centralized control than it is today. This is something to think about if ever we are tempted to expect surnames to be constant and consistent throughout time and place. Some are, but many are not. The great majority of surnames were born in an era of linguistic flux and have lived through changes in fashion and usage over the centuries, yet are still with us today. Some arose from the standard language, which itself has changed dramatically over the years, while others have their roots in regional dialects which were never fully incorporated into what became known as Standard English.

Surname study, which is only partly an exact science, and which seems at times to be born out of Chaos Theory, should be tackled with a great deal of care – if at all – by those of a particularly tidy state of mind, or who are subject to any medical condition akin to Asperger's Syndrome. William F. Hoffman, author of *Polish surnames: origins and meanings* (Second edition, 1998), knows the score: 'We would like to think the formation of surnames was an orderly process, guided by rational rules... [but] these people chose names, or had names thrust upon them, as circumstances dictated, and seldom stopped to ask "Will my great-great-great-grandson be able to figure out where this name came from?". As with all things human, the process was sloppy, catch-as-catch-can, and downright chaotic. But it worked, and anything that works has method hidden somewhere in the madness.'

It is partly the need to impose some kind of order upon chaos that has led most compilers of surname dictionaries and other writers on the subject to use a simple classification system of the sort used in this dictionary.

Entries which are marked 'F' here are surnames derived from a first-name or given-name; those marked 'T' have a topographical origin – that is, they are derived from a natural or a man-made feature of the landscape; 'P' indicates a place-name origin, 'O' is used for surnames which are based upon an occupation, office or status, and 'N' for those which began as a nickname.

Surnames based upon a first-name

The practice of sons and daughters adding their father's name to their own is the oldest method used to distinguish individuals clearly one from the other. There are many variations on this theme: Russians will commonly bear three names – a first name, a second name which is patronymic (that is, the father's name, with '*vich*' added for men and '*evna*' for women) and a surname. Characters in novels like *War and Peace* will commonly refer to each other by both the first and the patronymic name, and Victor Komarovsky in *Dr Zhivago*, hoping to endear himself to a young lady, says: 'Don't call me "Mr. Komarovsky", my dear – call me "Victor Ippolotovich"' – an alternative which might not sound so mellifluous to non-Russian speakers, perhaps?

Most Welsh surnames are patronymic in origin, and many in centuries past were not hereditary surnames at all. Hugh, son of William, would be called 'Hugh Williams'; his son David would be called 'David Hughes', while David's son Evan would be called 'Evan Davies' – and so on. This has often made the tracing of Welsh pedigrees a difficult if not impossible task, alas. The Welsh prefix '*ap*' (or '*ab*' before a vowel) means 'son of'. This might be shortened so that Hugh the son of Richard would be 'Hugh ap Richard', but eventually 'Hugh Pritchard'. Surnames with this origin include **Probert**, **Pumphrey**, **Pugh**, **Powell** (ap Howell), **Pryce** (ap Rhys), **Bowen** and **Bevan**.

The Welsh are often justifiably proud of their deep ancestry, a fact clearly in evidence on a gravestone in Llanrhaiadr, Wales, which reads: 'Here/Lyeth ye body/of John/Ap Robert Ap Porth/Ap David Ap Griffith/Ap David Vaughan/Ap Blethyn Ap Griffith/Ap Meredith Ap Jerworth/Ap Llewellyn Ap Jerom/Ap Heilin Ap Cowryd/Ap Cadvan Ap Alawgwa/Ap Cadell the King of Powys/Who Departed this Life/The xx day of March/In the year of our Lord God/1642/And of his age XCV'.

Hereditary surnames based upon the first-name of a father or mother are very common among English-speaking peoples. The surname might take the first-name with no modification – so a person might be called Thomas **John** or John **Thomas**; an '*s*' might be added, giving **Williams**, **Phillips** or **Richards** (that is, 'William's son' and so on); in northern England and in the English Midlands especially, the ending '*son*' might be used, giving us **Richardson**, **Thom(p)son**, **Anderson** ('son of Andrew') and **Tennyson** ('son of Dennis').

Various pet-forms of the first-name might be used, hence: **Dick(s)/Dickson** ('son of Richard'), **Watt(s)/Watson** ('son of Walter') and **Hobb(s)/Hobson** ('son of Hob', a nickname for Robert), while diminutive suffixes help to create surnames such as **Bartlett**, **Dickens**, **Perkin**, **Philpot(t)**, **Tomkin**, **Wilkin** and the like. It's worth looking out for these and other suffixes used in combination with first-names, including: *-cock/ cox/cott*; *-et(t)(e)/ot(t)(e)*; *-ie/y*; *-in/ings/ins*; *-ken/kin*; *-mot(t)/ment/mett*; *-mough/maugh/ muff/mouth/more*.

Sometimes the permutations derived from a single baptismal name can be bewildering in their variety – as in the case of 'Richard', which has spawned the following forms:

DICK	HIGGS	RICHETT
DICKENS	HIGMAN	RICHEY
DICKENSON	HISCOCK	RICHIE
DICKSON	HITCH	RICHMAN

DIXON	HITCHCOCK	RICK
HEACOCK	HITCHISON	RICKARD
HICK	HITCHMOUGH	RICKEARD
HICKIN	HIX	RICKETT
HICKMAN	RECKETT	RICKETTS
HICKMOT	RICARD	RICKMAN
HICKOX	RICH	RICKS
HICKS	RICHARD	RICKSON
HICKSON	RICHARDS	RITCHARD
HIGGINS	RICHE	RITCHIE
HIGGINSON	RICHER	RIX

Even a cursory glance at surnames featured in this dictionary under the headings of **Peter**, **Robert**, **Roger**, **Simon** and the like will make it clear that different surname variants derived from a single first-name can have a strikingly varied pattern of distribution within Britain.

Entries in the present dictionary which feature surnames derived from a group of similar, if related, first-names have been the hardest of all to control; at times the challenges posed by clusters such as **Ralf**, **Relf**, **Roland**, **Rolf**, **Rowe**, **Rowland** and **Ryland** have seemed almost insuperable.

Sometimes matters can be slightly more complex than we might think: the surname **Martin**, derived from a first-name, can be of English origin, but it is also one of the commonest surnames in France, and is found in Spain and elsewhere.

We should never discount the possibility that a surname might have been based upon a female name – that of a mother, rather than that of a father.

The female first-name *Maud* has given rise to surnames like **Moule**, **Mould** and **Ma(u)lt**, while its variant form *Matilda* is the origin of **Tillet(t)**, **Tilson** and **Tilletson**; *Annis*, a variation on *Agnes*, has given us surnames such as **Anness**, **Annas**, **Annott** and **Annison**, and *Catlin*, a form of *Catherine*, has provided us with **Cattlin**, **Catling**, **Catt**, **Cat(t)on**, **Cattell** and others. The first-name *Margaret* is unusual, in that the surname **Margaret** itself hardly exists, though variants derived from pet-forms such as *Mogg(e)* and *Pogg(e)* are easy enough to find.

In Scotland, Ireland and the Isle of Man '*Mac*' or '*Mc*' means 'son of'; in some cases the '*Ma*' is suppressed, giving us surnames such as the Irish **Keegan** (*Mac Aodhagain*) and the Manx **Clucas** (*Mac Lucas*). Irish *O'* (an Anglicization of '*ua*'), means 'grandson', so **O'Brien** was Brien's grandson. Several families that settled in Ireland soon after the Norman Conquest bore a name beginning with the element '*Fitz*', from the French *fils* ('son'). On occasions *Fitz*- can indicate illegitimacy – certainly in the case of a surname such as **Fitzroy** (*Fils Roi* – 'son of the King').

Surnames with a topographical origin

Topographical surnames were used originally as a way of describing a person who lived at/near some natural feature of the landscape such as a wood, a hill or a heath, or in/beside a man-made edifice such as a mill, a hall, a bridge or a church. Regional variations have given us **Coomb(e)(s)** (a valley), **Thwaite** (a meadow or clearing), **Burn(s)** (a stream), **Clough** (a slope or ravine) and many others, and at times it can be difficult if not impossible to decide whether a person called **Clough**, for example, had an ancestor who lived near a slope/ravine, or whether he hailed from a specific place by the name of *Clough*, with the same meaning. In principle, the surname **Armitage** could have been borne in the first instance by anyone who lived in or near any old hermitage (for the important relationship between *-ar-* and *-er-* here, see **Armistead** in this dictionary), but George Redmonds has shown that most, if not all, present-day **Armitage**s have their origins in a single identifiable place called *Hermitage Bridge* in Almondbury, near Huddersfield, West Riding of Yorkshire.

The spelling of many topographical surnames has changed over time or according to locality, so **Bridge(s)/Brigg(s)** and **Gate(s)/Yate(s)** are essentially the same names in varying forms.

Many topographical surnames are not at all scarce, and it should be clear that not all individuals called **Wood**, **Hill** and **Heath** are necessarily related.

Those who lived at, or had arrived from, the north, south, east or west of any given settlement could acquire surnames such as **Norris**, **Southern/Sotheran/Sutton**, **East(man)** and **Weston**.

Some surnames have retained a preposition, or the rudiments of one, as their first syllable, a process known as metanalysis. Men who lived at or near a ridge, a wood or a tree could acquire the bynames or surnames **Attridge**, **Attwood/Underwood** and **Attree**, and a person who dwelt beside a river, stream, lake or pond could be known as **Bywater**. Someone who dwelt near a spring or a well could be known as **At(t)well**, and this in turn could be shortened to **Twells**. It was once a common practice to change the preposition *at* to *atten* when the following word began with a vowel, so William who lived near an ash tree would be known as *William* **atten ash**, while his neighbour Thomas, who preferred to set up home near an oak tree, would be *Thomas* **atten oak**. Over time, William's byname or surname would eventually be shortened to **Nash**, and Thomas's to **Noake(s)**. For similar examples, see surnames such as **New**, **Noad**, **Noar**, **Nye**, **Tash**, **Tee** and **Troake** in this dictionary.

Surnames with a place-name origin

If a surname which interests you is clearly based upon a specific place-name rather than a general topographical feature, then you may feel that you have a satisfying 'fix' as to your ancestral roots. You won't be alone: within the English-speaking world, more surnames owe their origin to a place-name than to any other source. Why not put this to the test some time? My own surname of Titford has a place-name origin, as does my wife's maiden name of Flockton, and so do the surnames of many of our closest friends.

A man with a byname or surname such as **Morley** may have been wealthy enough to own land in a village of that name, or he may only have acquired **Morley** as a second-name when he moved somewhere else, his place of origin at that stage being a useful way of identifying him.

Caution is advised, however: we know that some place-names have given rise to surnames, but it's worth remembering that a number of surnames have themselves been used as the names of places. Chickens and eggs. There is a minor place called 'Titford' in western Wiltshire, but it doesn't represent the origin of my own surname – rather, it acquired its name from the fact that a small-time yeoman called Richard Titford was farming there in the early seventeenth century.

In general terms, do be conscious of the fact some surnames will have their origin in an abandoned or alternative form of a place-name. Armed with the knowledge that the town of *Brighton* on the south coast of England was known as *Brighthelmestone* until the late eighteenth century, you would not be tempted to assume that the surname **Brighton** had its origins there. In the event, it comes from a place called *Breighton* in Yorkshire. Matters are even more difficult when it comes to a surname such as **Rawnsley**, which has its origins in a locality in Barkisland, West Riding of Yorkshire, formerly called *Rawnsleycliffe*, but now known simply as *Cliff*. No modern gazetteer could help us with that one... Alternatively, the place in question might simply have disappeared from the map over the years. The surname **Insole/Insoll/Insull** comes from a lost place-name in Elmley Lovett, Worcestershire, and **Iredale/Iredell** from a lost farm in Cumberland, once situated between Loweswater and Fangs Brow.

Sometimes surnames are user-friendly enough to reflect the usual pronunciation of a place-name, regardless of its present-day spelling, as in: **Wooster** (*Worcester*), **Bister** (*Bicester*), **Ensor** (*Edensor* in Derbyshire), **Pomfret** (*Pontefract*), **Norridge** (*Norwich*) and **Bro(m)mage** or **Bromidge** (*Bromwich*).

Other places have a nasty habit of being generally known by dialectal variants. Jedburgh in the lowlands of Scotland is called '*Jeddart*' or '*Jethart*' by the locals, and a village near to my home in Derbyshire which is formally named 'Horsley Woodhouse' is only ever spoken of as '*Ossly Woodus*'. Local knowledge can be vital here. The fact that I happen to know that '*Bonser*' is a commonly used pronunciation of the Derbyshire village of *Bonsall* puts me in a strong position to be able to doubt the accepted wisdom that the local surname **Bonser** is from Old French *bon sire* ('good sir').

Many place-names – too many, we may say – are all-too-similar to others, making it difficult to sort out which surnames emanate from which places. So although **Leyton** in Essex clearly gave rise to a related surname, the existence of other place-names and surnames such as **Laughton**, **Lawton**, **Layton** and **Leighton** serves only to confuse matters.

Very often a single surname, with or without known variants, can have come from any one of a number of similar place-names. So surnames in the group **Caudle/Caldwall/Caldwell/Calwell/Caudwell/Cauldwell/Cawdle/Chadwell/Chardle/Chardwell/Coldwell** can take us back to one of the following place-names: *Caldwell* (Derbyshire, North Riding of Yorkshire, Warwickshire); *Caldwall* (Worcestershire); *Cauldwell* (Bedfordshire, Nottinghamshire); *Caudle Green* (Gloucestershire); *Caudle Ditch, Cawdle Fen* and *Chardle Ditch* (Cambridgeshire); *Chadwell* (Essex, Hertfordshire, Leicestershire, Wiltshire); *Chardwell* (Essex). In Scotland, **Caldwell** and **Coldwell**, formerly pronounced '*Carwall*', are from *Caldwell*, Renfrewshire.

'Place-name' is perhaps rather too specific a term to be using here. Various surnames of the sort we are examining within this grouping have their origin in the name of a town or village, but others are from the name of a country within the British Isles (**England/English**, **Ireland/Irish**), or further afield (**France/French**, or **Pettingill** – a man from Portugal), or are based upon an English county name (**Cornwall**, **Westmorland** – yet **Derbyshire** and **Hampshire** are not always what they seem, and the surname **Somerset** is most commonly found in the West Riding of Yorkshire...).

The most insignificant of hamlets (some of them now lost), and even small farmsteads, have given rise to surnames. Indeed, you are more likely to come across a person with a surname such as **Davenport** or **Priestley**, based upon the names of comparatively insignificant settlements in Cheshire and Yorkshire respectively, than you are to meet someone called **London**, **Colchester** or **Canterbury**. Migration, in the past as in the present, was commonly from the country into the towns, which is probably why so many surnames have their origin in the kind of small rural settlements from which such migrants hailed.

Do watch out, however, for the names of major towns dressed up in an unfamiliar form: **Bristow** is clearly derived from Bristol, but more obscure are surnames such as **Burmicham**, **Glasscowe** and **Edenbrow**, which will have referred originally to men who came from Birmingham, Glasgow and Edinburgh.

Just as there were plenty of woods, hills and heaths in the landscape which gave rise quite independently to surnames, so there was no lack of places called Langley, Horsley, Smalley and the like, each of which spawned surnames borne by individuals who bore no blood relationship to each other. Not only that, but a number of unrelated individuals from any one of these Langleys, Horsleys or Smalleys could have acquired this place-name as a hereditary surname.

By contrast, a considerable number of surnames with a place-name origin are known to have been used by only one single family throughout the centuries. Such is the case with my own surname of **Titford**. It's worth remembering that the process whereby surnames have changed their form and spelling over the years has also been at work with place-names. The place now called (North) Tidworth in Wiltshire was 'Todeworth' and then 'Tuddewurth' in the thirteenth century (a not-uncommon development), just as the surname Titford was formerly **Totford** and later **Tutford** in the same county. In other words, place-names have changed over time, and so have surnames; if we struggle to make sense of it all, we're shooting at not one, but two moving targets.

Many surnames which are now very familiar to us within the British Isles have their origin in a place-name across the seas, particularly in mainland Europe. Some have been modified to suit English tastes, so **Bullen/Boleyn** refers to a person from *Boulogne*, and many **Cullens** came originally from *Cologne* (*Köln*) in Germany. And just as surnames such as **Nash** and **Noake(s)** carry the remnants of a lost preposition, so a truncated form of the French preposition *de* is observable in names such as **Daltry** [d'Hauterive], **Dangerfield** [d'Angerville], **Danvers** [d'Anvers], **Darcy** [d'Arcy], **Darell/ Dorrell** [d'Airel], **Devereux** [d'Evreux] and **Dando** [d'Aunou].

Another feature to be on the lookout for, both in place-names and in surnames, is the process known as metathesis, whereby letters in a word change places. The place-name *Althorp*, in Northamptonshire, was formerly *Aldrop* and the like, and a surname such as **Thrupp** is a metathetical variant of **Thorp(e)**, and **Purdham** of **Prudhomme**.

No name dictionary can include every known surname with a place-name origin, and disappointed readers should seek help from a detailed gazetteer – the Victorians produced many fine examples of these, and others are available on the internet, including works such as Samuel Lewis's *Topographical dictionaries* for England, Wales and Scotland. For an immensely detailed listing of places large and small, I always turn to a work entitled *General Register Office: Census 1951: England and Wales: Index of place names* (1955), though there are similar publications for other census years. Here thousands of place-names are provided, arranged alphabetically and accompanied by information presented in columns, as follows: place-name; description (civil parish, ecclesiastical parish, 'locality', etc.); administrative county in which situated; borough, urban district or rural district in which situated; number of registration district in which situated; population in 1951.

Just as it took Dr Johnson's *Dictionary*, published in the eighteenth century, to create a general respect for the standard spelling of words, so it was the introduction of the Ordnance Survey in 1790 that began the process whereby place-name spellings became standardized. If you want to examine earlier or alternative forms of any given place-name in England, then turn to the county volumes steadily being published by the English Place-name Society. The *Concise Oxford Dictionary of English Place-names* (first published in 1935) takes a not-dissimilar approach, in much less detail, but at least it covers a selection of places from the whole of England. The fine, scholarly *Cambridge Dictionary of English Place-names* by Victor Watts (2004) can also be immensely useful, but you'll practically need to take out a mortgage if you wish to buy your own copy.

As to ancient and modern dialectal versions of a number of place-names, it's worth taking a look at *A pronouncing dictionary of English place-names including local and archaic variants* by K. Forster (1981) and at *A glossary of dialectal place-nomenclature* by R. C. Hope. A reprint of the second edition of this book was published by Gale Research Company of Detroit in 1968, and it is arranged both alphabetically by place-name and also by county. Here you will find – to your amazement, maybe? – that a village in Devon with the official name of *Woodfardisworthy* is known locally as *Oolsery*. Few people, it seems, relish the thought of expending enough breath to pronounce a multi-syllable place-name or surname in full, so *Woodfardisworthy* is shortened in everyday speech to make it more manageable. And so it is with surnames – **Wolstenholme** being reduced in some cases to **Woosnam, Worsman, Worsnop** and **Worsnip**. One family of Sheffield cutlers, originally called **Wolstenholme**, adopted the surname **Wostenholm** (dropping the first '*l*' and the final '*e*') in order to create a name which was more convenient for stamping on their knives.

For an international listing of the names of places and of geographical features, you should try to find a copy of *The Times index-gazetteer of the world* (1965) which includes many thousand entries. At approximately one thousand pages, with each entry presented in small print, it is a very substantial work indeed.

Do please note, by the way, that the element 'field' as found in a place-name/ surname has changed its meaning over the years. Old English *feld* (like Dutch *veldt*) referred to a large tract of unenclosed land, not to a neat little parcel of ground surrounded by hedges or by dry-stone walls.

Surnames from occupations, office or status

Surnames based upon an occupation can afford a fascinating insight into social history, since alongside the familiar **Baker, Butcher, Carpenter, Cook, Mason, Miller, Smith, Taylor** and the like, it's not difficult to spot references to trades that are long-since defunct: **Byron** can refer to a cowman, **Chapman** to an itinerant trader, **Chaucer** to a shoemaker, **Crerar** to a sievewright, **Culpeper** to a spicer or herbalist, **Earwaker** to one who watched over wild boars, **Falder** to a shepherd, **Hansard** to a maker of cutlasses or daggers, **Jagger** to a man in charge of packhorses, **Keeble** to a maker or seller of cudgels, **Lorimer** to a harness maker, **Parmenter** to a maker of lace and trimmings, **Runciman** to a man in charge of work-horses known as *rouncies*, and **Threadgold** to someone who practised embroidery using gold thread.

Different regional terms can be used to describe even some of the most basic trades or occupations throughout the British Isles, and each may have given rise to a related surname. Several names bear witness to the vital importance of the wool trade in earlier centuries: a person whose job it was to full cloth would be known as a *fuller* in the eastern counties of England, as a *walker* in the north and as a *tucker* in southern and western areas. All three terms have coined surnames which survive to the present day.

Regional variations of the surname **Thatcher** include **Theaker** (Yorkshire), **Thacker** (West Midlands) and **Thaxter** (a feminine or dialectal form, found mainly in Norfolk). Millers were also essential to the economy, but in this case slight variations on the same word have produced a set of related surnames: there is **Miller** itself, but also **Millward** (more commonly found in the south and west of England and the Midlands), **Milner** (mostly found in the north and east of England and in the Scottish Lowlands) and **Millar** (a Scottish spelling of the word *miller*). The spelling **Meller** may also be found, though the similar-looking surname **Mellor** comes from one of a number of place-names in the north of England and the Midlands.

The Wiltshire surname **Pothecary/Potticary** comes from an occupational term for a spicer, druggist, apothecary, from Greek via Old French. Such a person, in the immortal words of Shelley Klein, author of *The concise dictionary of surnames* (2004), would have been a 'Keeper of a drug store'.

Other occupationally based surnames which exhibit a similar loss of an initial letter include **Jenner** (an engineer) and **Stroulger/Strow(l)ger** (an astrologer).

The surname **Farmer** is not as common as one might suppose, considering how many English people farmed for a living. In fact such a name was usually applied to a person who collected ('farmed') taxes and revenues, and paid for the privilege.

The manorial system threw up its fair share of occupational terms, many of which gave rise to surnames: a **Parker** and a **Forester** looked after the parks and forests respectively; a **Woodward** tended the woods, a **Woodruff** ('wood reeve') was responsible for policing such areas, and a **Warner** (warrener) was in charge of the rabbit warrens.

A 'herd' was a man responsible for tending animals, so we have related surnames such as **Shepherd** (sheep), **Cowherd** (cows), **Goddard** (goats), **Stoddard** (stud of horses), **Oxnard** (oxen), **Colthard/Colthart** (colts), **Gossard/Gossart** (geese), **Hoggard** (hogs), **Lambert** (lambs) and **Geldard** (geldings).

Smith (from a person who would 'smite' or strike with a hammer) is not only the commonest surname in England – it is also prolific in Scotland, the United States and elsewhere. The Latin for a smith is *Faber*, so in English we have **Farrer/Ferrar**, in German **Faber** (as well as **Schmidt**), and in French there is the very common surname **Lefevre**. The Celtic term for a smith gives us **Goff/Gough**, **Govan**, **Gow** and **Gowan**, while the Cornish **Angove** is literally '*the* smith'.

But beware: **Goodwright** might appear to be a trade-name, but in reality it is a variant on the first-name *Godrich*.

Some surnames are derived from occupational terms which were once applied specifically to females, though which were later used for practitioners of both sexes: a *baxter* was a female baker, a *brewster* a female brewer and a *webster* a female weaver. A *spinster*, of course, stayed at home spinning while her contemporaries upped and got married. A *hollister*, sad to relate, once referred to a female brothel-keeper or whore-monger; *hollier* was the male equivalent. Cottle wryly remarks: 'There is no evidence to save the face of this surname by relating it to an occupational term for a female haulier, or to a word used for a hiding-place oʀ *heolstor*, or a nickname for a big, awkward man (northern dialect *hulster*), or some Norse-settled village ending in *-ster*'.

Bearers of surnames such as **Hollister** and **Hollier** benefit from the fact that the original term which gave rise to them has long-since passed out of use. Less fortunate are those whose surname is derived from what was once a perfectly innocuous occupational term: a *crapper* was a picker of vegetables or fruit, a reaper of corn, or a man who polled cattle, and *raper* was a northern dialect word for a rope-maker.

In principle, churchmen were supposed to be celibate, though not all were, but surnames such as **Abbot**, **Bishop**, **Chaplin**, **Clerk**, **Deacon**, **Dean**, **Friar**, **Monk**, **Parsons**, **Priest**, **Prior** and **Vicars** were often applied to a servant of a clergyman rather than being used for the offspring of the man himself. A *summoner*, meanwhile (giving us the surname **Sumner**), would summon parishioners to attend the dreaded ecclesiastical court, while a **Palmer** could well have returned from a pilgrimage to the Holy Land, bearing palm leaves.

Several surnames are derived by way of a process known as 'metonymy', whereby an object or substance used in a particular trade has become a term used to describe the craftsman himself. So the occupation of goldsmith can give rise to the surname **Gold**, just as **Wool** can have its origins in a wool-worker and **Bacon** be applied to a pig butcher.

A related class of surnames is derived from a person's social status (**Francom(b)(e)/ Frankham** was a free man, while a **Tennant** held land subject to feudal dues being forthcoming), or from the office he held (**Chamberlaine**, **Marshall**, **Reeve**, **Steward**). Some surnames which sound so fine, however, such as **Knight**, **King** and the rest, will in most cases have come from an individual who played such a role in a pageant or in a mediaeval miracle or mystery play.

For details concerning a wide range of occupations, some of them now unfamiliar, see *A dictionary of old trades, titles and occupations* by Colin Waters (1999). The website *www.rmhh.co.uk/occup/index.html* tackles the same subject, and provides links to other sites.

Surnames from nicknames

Nicknames, like bynames and surnames, very often serve the purpose of distinguishing between individuals of the same name – perhaps nowhere more so, within the British Isles, than in Wales, where 'Jones the Bread' is the baker, 'Jones the Meat' is the butcher and 'Jones the Post' is the postman. Occupational nicknames, then, in this case.

Many nicknames, however, refer to a person's physical appearance, mode of dress, manner of speech, or to some distinctive character trait.

Not all nicknames pulled their punches, and some of our ancestors must have been a rum-looking bunch, judging by the surnames they acquired: **Foljambe** (afflicted with a crippled leg), **Bunyan** (suffering from a bunion or similar bodily lump, though it can also refer to a baker of fruit tarts), **Hamill** (a scarred or maimed person – though in Scotland and Northern Ireland it can alternatively be derived from a French place-name), **Puddephat** (shaped like a barrel), **Oliphant** (as large and ungainly as an elephant).

It is particularly gratifying to find that so many Scottish surnames are signally lacking in euphemism, giving the impression, for example, that a whole host of people living north of the border were crippled in one way or another, having bow legs (**Cruickshank**), broken bones (**Brisbane**), a twisted nose (**Cameron**) or a crooked mouth (**Campbell**). The Irish, too, can be fond of no-punches-pulled surnames: **Kennedy** means 'ugly head'.

Some individuals must have reminded their friends and family of a variety of animals – hence surnames such as **Tod** (a fox) and **Brock** (a badger). Bird-names have given us **Crow(e)/Corbett**, **Duck**, **Peacock**, **Wildgoose**, **Woodcock** and **Wren**. East Anglia in particular abounds in game-bird surnames such as **Partridge**, **Pheasant** and the rest, but what can it have been about the original Mr **Starling** that led to his unusual nickname/byname/surname? Did he love brightly coloured clothes, did he have an ungainly waddling gait, or was he possessed of a greedy, squabbling temperament? Humans have repaid their debt to the birds: just as humans have acquired bird-names, so birds have acquired human ones: there's *Tom Tit*, *Robin Redbreast*, *Jack Daw*, *Jenny Wren*, *Mag Pie*, *Polly Parrot* – and even *Margery Daw* and the dialectical *Nettle Peggy* (green finch).

Fishy surnames are more rarely found: Mr **Pike** and Mr **Tench** may have borne some passing resemblance to such denizens of the deep, though the surname of Mr **Salmon** would have come from the first-name *Solomon*.

Other pleasant nickname-surnames celebrated the fact that an individual resembled a rose or a lily, though it's perhaps a relief to learn that there is no evidence of anyone being nicknamed 'Cauliflower' because of a cauliflower ear...

Hair-colour (even lack of hair) and complexion frequently gave rise to associated surnames, though particular care will sometimes need to be taken: two separate Old English adjectives, *blæc* ('black', of hair or complexion) and *blac* ('fair') have given rise to the surname **Black**. In other words, on occasions black really can be white. In similar vein, the surname **Blacker**, from the Middle English verb *blaken*, referred to a bleacher. So an occupational term which looks as if it might refer to a blackener was actually used for a whitener.

A very large number of surnames have their origin in an adjective used to highlight the original bearer's character or personality, and it's no surprise to find that complimentary names such as the following have survived more readily than critical ones: **Bligh** (cheerful); **Car(e)less** (ebullient, without a care in the world); **Curtis** (courteous, refined); **Douce/Douche/Duce/Dowsett** (sweet, pleasant); **Hendy** (pleasant and affable); **Jolly/Jolliffe(e)** (jolly, cheerful); **Lawty/L(e)uty** (trustworthy); **Prowse** (brave, valiant).

However, the use of irony can never be ruled out: Mr **Sweet** might have been pleasant and kind, or no such thing; Mr **Bellamy** could have been a fine friend – or quite the opposite.

Various other surnames in this dictionary have been deemed to be nicknames because that is the category which most closely defines their nature.

The meaning of the surname **Child** is generally clear enough – not that many children would have founded a family line while still in infancy – though the term could also refer to a young man waiting to be elevated to the status of a knight.

Gamble, with its variants **Gambell**, **Gammell**, **Gemmell**, and the rest, comes from a word used for an old man, and **Oldknow** means *old enough* ('*enow*').

Eame was a term used for a maternal uncle, and a man who took care of his nephews and nieces once their parents had died might have acquired this as a surname. *Mine eame* ('my uncle') could be divided in such a way as to give the surname **Neame**, though this can also be a nickname for a short person. **Neve**, by contrast, means '*nephew*' – perhaps referring to someone who was raised by an uncle, or whose uncle was famous in some way. **Soane** is from Middle English *sone* ('*son*'), and was used for someone who shared the same personal name as his father. Cottle points out with glee that **Soan(e)s** means 'son of the son'.

The word *cousin* was once a notoriously imprecise term for a relative of almost any degree of closeness, and the surname **Cousin(s)/Cussen/Cozen(s)/Cushing** could have been applied to anyone who was kin to a person of some importance. Similarly, the brother of a person of some social standing could simply have been named **Brother**. **Od(h)am(s)**, from a word meaning *son-in-law*, could be applied to a man who had acquired a wealthy or influential father-in-law by making an advantageous marriage. **Ayer** or **Eyre** is simply what it sounds like – an heir to a title or fortune – and a man called **Heritage** would have inherited his land from an ancestor rather than having acquired it in any other way. **Bairnsfather/Barnsfather**, a surname chiefly found in northern England and Scotland, was used for the father or alleged father of an illegitimate child.

People born at Christmas could have acquired a surname such as **Christmas**, **Noel** or **Y(o)ule**; Easter babies could be **Pask(e)** and the like, a January child could be **January**, and one born at Whitsuntide could be **Pentecost**. The surname **Loveday** comes from a day set aside in mediaeval times for the settling of disputes, while **Hockaday** is based upon an important term-day, the second Tuesday after Easter Sunday, on which rents were due.

An intriguing class of surnames consists of those which indicate that a man was particularly fond of using certain clichés, oaths or modes of expression.

A person who used the phrase *good sir* to excess could acquire **Goodsir** as a byname/ surname, though this could also be a nickname for a venerable old man. **Debney** is said to be derived from a French phrase meaning *God bless*; **Purd(e)y** is from Old French *pour Dieu* (by God), **Pardoe** is from *par Dieu* and **Purefoy** is from *par foi* (by my faith). **Godbe(a)r/Godbeher** can be *may God be here* (though there are other possible origins, including, prosaically enough, *good beer*); **God(s)help** is from *by the help of God*; **Goodby** is from *God be with you*; **Go(o)dsave** is from *for God's sake*; **Godsname** is from *in God's name*; and **Goodspeed** is from *may God speed you*. **Mordew/Mordey** is from the oath *mort dieu* (literally, *death of God*), and in theory **Mothersole/Mothersill** could be a corruption of *on my mother's soul*, though a toponymic origin – from *Moddershall* in Staffordshire – is perhaps more likely.

Self-help

The fact that no dictionary such as this one can include every surname that has ever existed was one of the reasons why I wrote *Searching for surnames* (2002), which is intended to be a self-help guide for those who need to interpret a variety of names from first principles. I shan't repeat here what I said there, but can offer a few hints and pointers to those for whom surname study may be a new and unfamiliar discipline.

With surnames, as with place-names, it's important to attempt to isolate and to make sense of separate elements, and to think of these as building blocks which make up the whole.

Be on the lookout for first-names as an initial element, and be aware that these can take several forms and might acquire patronymic, diminutive or other suffixes: *Adam*, for example, lies at the root of surnames such as **Atcheson**, **Acheson** and **Atkinson**, and the servant of man called *Bartholomew* might have acquired the charming surname of **Batman**.

Place-names have given rise to a great number of surnames, so it's worth taking note of tell-tale place-name elements, including references to trees such as ash, oak and beech, or to crops such as beans and barley. The final element in a place-name, be it from Old English, Old Norse or one of the Celtic languages, may be particularly distinctive, so be on the lookout for *-ford*, *-ham*, *-hurst*, *-ley*, *-thwaite*, *-ton*, *-wick* and the like. You might find it helpful to refer to the list of place-name prefixes and suffixes which appears in *Searching for surnames*. Do take care, however, when attempting to divide a place-name up into its various elements: a hill on the east side of Lake Windermere called *Gunnershow* is not '*Gunner show*', but '*Gunner's how*' (the mound of a man called *Gunner*).

We need to be flexible in our thinking, aware that several surnames, like place-names, have taken different forms over the centuries, that they have been borne by many individuals who were illiterate or who had strong regional accents (speech impediments, even), and were more often than not written down by clerks whose own education left much to be desired. It was not until the nineteenth century and the advent of compulsory education within Britain that surnames achieved some real, though limited, degree of stability.

Expect to find a surname such as **Bentall** spelt **Bendall** and **Fenn** spelt **Venn**, the only difference in each case being that between an unvoiced consonant (*-t-* and *F-*) and a voiced one (*-d-* and *V-*). You may find **Hemery** as **Emery**, **Sheriff** as **Sherriff**, **Sherborn** as **Sherbourne** – and **Parkes** as **Perkes**, since vowels within surnames are notoriously unstable. For the relationship between the *-er-* of a surname such as **Sherman** and the *-ar-* of **Sharman**, see the entry for the surname **Armistead** in this dictionary. Some names can take a bewildering variety of forms, such as **Annable/Hannable/Hannibal/Honeyball/Hunnable/Hunneyball/Hunneybell/Hunnibal/Hunnibell**, and among the more striking cross-references you will find in this dictionary are '**Hurr(e)y, see Woolrich**' and '**Lenfestey, see Vaisey**'.

Local accents and dialects can make a difference: **Axtell**, a variant of **Ashkettle/(H)askel(l)/Astell/Astill**, reflects the common regional pronunciation whereby *-sk* is rendered as *-x* (*ask* becoming *axe*).

Certain families who like to keep themselves at arm's length from *hoi polloi* can make life more difficult for the rest of us by insisting that their surname be pronounced in a way that you would hardly guess at from the way in which it is spelt. This is especially true of surnames with a French origin: **Fiennes** is pronounced *Fines*, **Grosvenor** is *Grovenor*, **Beauchamp** is *Beecham* and **Villiers** is *Villers*. The **Waldegrave**s prefer to be known as *Waldgrave*; the **Cholmondeley**s favour the pronunciation *Chumly*, and the double-barrelled **Leveson-Gower**s are *Looson Gore*. The longest surname in the English-speaking world, **Featherstonehaugh**, is (mercifully) shortened in everyday speech to *Fanshaw*.

Things are no easier in Scotland, where **Menzies** is *Mingis*, **Dalziel** is *Deeyell*, **Auchinleck** is *Affleck* and **Marjoribanks** is *Marchbanks*.

Astle might look different to **Astell** on the printed page, but both are pronounced in an identical fashion and merely represent different spellings of the same surname. And so it is with **Bale/Bail**, **Askwith/Asquith** and many others.

When it comes to surnames (and place-names) which have changed their shape or spelling significantly over the years, it's worth mentioning a process which is commonly called 'folk etymology'. Whether an individual or a family stayed put in one place or moved around a lot, they may have found that their surname caused problems to their neighbours, who might then have re-shaped the name to suit their own purposes, forcing it to conform to a word in everyday use, a local place-name or a surname or personal name with which they were already familiar. I once researched a family by the name of **Petticoat**, who would appear to have been **Pennicott**s (a surname with a place-name origin) before a man so-called moved from England to Maryland, USA, in the seventeenth century and had his named changed for him whether he liked it or not.

A significant number of surnames can have more than one possible origin (firstname, place-name, occupation, etc.), and you'll find in any case that surname scholars often disagree on which (if any) of a number of explanations are applicable (see, for example, **Camel**). Eve McLaughlin makes the point firmly and with a touch of humour by using the surname of **Cock** as an example: 'A Cock could be a cook, a watchman (getting up early), a hill dweller, an arrogant person (strutting like a cock), rather randy, a small boatman, a diminutive of Isaac, or just a young lad'.

For examples of multiple origins at work in surnames included in this dictionary, see **Beck**, **Clare**, **Gale**, **Hook**, **Idle**, **Pike** – and **Kay(e)/Keay/Key(e)(s)**, which could be from an occupational term for a maker of keys/a key-bearer, or a dweller by a wharf, or a nickname from some resemblance to a jackdaw, or a nickname for a left-handed/footed person, or from a Middle English first-name of Welsh or Breton origin – not forgetting a Manx origin, from **Mac Aodha/Aoidh** ('son of *Aodh*').

On occasions fairly minor differences in the spelling of a surname can create variants which are found in markedly different locations.

This can be true of a surname with a topographical origin: **Frain** (dweller by an ash tree) belongs mainly to Lancashire, **Frane** to Lancashire and Leicestershire, **Frayn** to Cornwall and Devon and **Frayne** to Devon.

Thorneycroft, with a topographical or place-name origin (dweller at an enclosed piece of land in the thorns, or from a place-name with the same meaning) is found mainly in the West Riding of Yorkshire, **Thorncroft** in Middlesex and Kent, **Thornicroft** in Warwickshire and **Thornycroft** in Cheshire.

Keat, which has a nickname origin (from some resemblance to the bird of prey, the kite) is encountered mainly in Cornwall, **Keate** in Lancashire, **Keates** in Staffordshire, **Keats** in Dorset and **Keyte** in Gloucestershire and Warwickshire. **Peascod** (possibly an occupational term for a seller of peas, or a nickname for a person of little worth) is found chiefly in Cumberland, **Peasgood** in Lincolnshire, **Peasegood** in the West Riding of Yorkshire, **Pescod** in County Durham.

The same can apply to surnames with an occupational origin: **Shovel** (a maker or user of shovels) is at its strongest in Devon, **Shovell** in Cornwall, **Shoveller** in Surrey and surrounding areas, **Shouler** in Buckinghamshire, **Showler** in Lincolnshire and **Showell** in Warwickshire.

Not what they seem

A final word of warning: self-help is all very well, but not all surnames are what they seem.

What may look like a surname with a place-name origin might be derived from a first-name: **Edridge** is from *Edrich* or *Ederick*, **Gumbley** from *Gumbald*, **Gutt(e)ridge** from *Goderiche* or *Cuterich*, **Rickwood** from *Richold* or *Richward*, **Ottoway** and **Ottewell** from *Otoïs* or *Otewi*, **Catton** from *Catlin*, **Sibley** from *Sibley* (Latin *Sibilla*, Greek *Sibylla*), **Utteridge/Outridge/Uttridge** from *Uhtric* and **Rigden** from *Richard*.

The original Mr **Stallwood/Stal(l)worthy** (variants of **Stallard**) was valiant, Mr **Pedley** was stealthy, Mr **Grealey/Gredley** was pock-marked, Mr **Sealey** was happy/blessed, Mr **Belham** was handsome, Mr **Bonham** was good and Mr **Gulliford** was a glutton (from Old French *goulafre*). **Beveridge**, from the Middle English *beverage*, has a connection with the practice of buying drinks to seal a bargain, and **Telford** comes from an occupational term for a cleaver or cutter of iron. Not a place-name in sight...

Beware false assumptions, then: **Attack** refers to a dweller 'by the oak'; **Bible** is from the first-name *Bibby* (*Isabel*); **Bream** can be from a place so-called in Gloucestershire; **Broomhead** refers to a dweller on a hilltop with broom-bushes, or is from a place-name with the same meaning; **Fidget** is a variant of **Fitch**, a surname of unknown origin; a **Flasher** dwelt beside a pond or marsh; **Forward** is a term for a swineherd; **Hattrick** (nothing to do with cricket...) is a variant of **Arkwright**; **Hidden** is from a place-name in Berkshire and **Irons** from *Airaines*, Somme; **Large** was a nickname for a generous person, rather than a corpulent one; **Lax** is an occupational term for one who caught, or in some way resembled, a salmon; **Looney** is an Anglicized form of Irish Gaelic **O'Luanaigh**; **Mutter** was used for one who spoke at a moot; a **Nutter** was a keeper of oxen; **Overall** refers to a dweller at the upper hall; a **Panther** was an official in charge of a pantry; **Parrot** is from *North Perrot* (Somerset) or *South Perrott* (Dorset); **Pester** is an occupational term for a baker; **Ponder** is a dweller by a pond; **Prestige** is from *Prestwich* in Lancashire; **Quarrell** can be from an occupational term for a maker of crossbows/bolts/arrows; **Stocking** means 'dweller at ground cleared of tree-stumps', or is from a place-name with the same meaning; **Tickle** is from *Tickhill* in the West Riding of Yorkshire; **Tipple** is from a diminutive form of the first-name *Theobald*; **Waistcoat** is from one of a number of places in southern England called *Westcot*, *Westcott* or *Westcote*.

As for **Virgin** – strange to relate, it would appear to mean exactly what it says, though we might argue that a lack of virginity was a necessary prerequisite for procreation and the subsequent continuation of a hereditary surname. But perhaps (grasping at straws...) we might guess that such a name was applied to a man who had played the Blessed Virgin in a mystery play (there being no actresses), or was used ironically for a lecherous person, one who was far from being a virgin?

A new edition of The Penguin Dictionary of Surnames

A hiding to nothing

Every compiler of a surname dictionary is on a hiding to nothing. No such work can be totally comprehensive; each will necessarily be something of a surface-skimmer, consisting more often than not of an amalgam of material, a good deal of which has been published before in one form or another.

As a result, some readers will be disappointed – affronted, even – to discover that a cherished surname of theirs has not been included, while others, ardent researchers themselves, will find that a name which interests them *is* featured, but that they know more about its meaning, its origin, its variant forms and its distribution than the hapless compiler, whose focus has had to be wide-ranging as well as specific. That's good news in its way, of course: gone are the days when gentleman scholars with time on their hands, a smattering of etymological expertise and a vivid imagination, ruled the surname roost; these days an army of amateur scholars, many of them family historians with access to a range and depth of relevant data which earlier researchers could only have dreamed of, can make a major contribution of their own, can help to widen yet further the billowing skirts of surname knowledge. In an age when digital information, and even DNA analysis (see, for example, the entry for **Brooking** in this dictionary), are so readily available, surname study finally belongs to the people, to the many rather than the few, and is much richer as a result.

Nature and scope of this book

My own involvement with the present dictionary followed the publication of *Searching for surnames* (2002), a book in which I attempted to help readers interpret a range of surnames from a number of first principles, regardless of whether these appeared in an existing 'dictionary' or not.

The present task has been to produce a new edition of *The Penguin Dictionary of Surnames*, originally compiled by Basil Cottle in 1967. That, at any rate, was the theory. In the event, the thirty years which have passed since Cottle's revised edition of 1978 saw the light of day have been witness to so many developments in the field of surname study that I've ended up, willy-nilly, producing a fish of a very different colour.

Basil Cottle was a remarkable man: a polymath who had been (of all things...) head of the Albanian section of the code-breakers at Bletchley Park during the Second World War, and a Reader in Mediaeval Studies at Bristol University thereafter. He also had a sharp wit, and could exhibit a wicked sense of humour on occasions. I've preserved a smattering of his more zany and quirky remarks in my text, within inverted commas, and have also quoted him verbatim on occasions when he has had something so apposite and eloquent to say that any modification would have seemed both unnecessary and churlish. Here he is in full flow, talking about the ubiquitous surname **Smith**: 'The primate and patriarch of our surnames... It is a frequent victim of hyphenation, either in a sincere effort to avoid ambiguity or in an insincere one to sound distingué; and it has recently gathered to itself many changed foreign surnames. Yet it remains primitive: a smith *smites*, and his honoured name rings down the ages like an anvil.'

At other times Cottle can be delightfully eccentric – '**Rasmussen**: Scandinavian version of "son of Erasmus [= 'beloved']" Greek, the saint whose bowels were wound out on a windlass in Diocletian's persecution. This exotic surname is included because the saint doesn't get a look-in in British nomenclature...' – or has clearly given in to the temptation to go to town on an exotic surname which is certainly fascinating, but which can hardly, if ever, be found in a British context – '**Rounsivell** [Place-name] "Roncesvalles" (once Basque *Rozabal*, second element *zabal* "extensive"; wrongly associated with "dewy/spear/sorrel/nags" + "valley" Latin), Place-name-name in Navarre, north Spain, where traditionally Charlemagne's rear-guard was attacked by Saracens and Roland was killed; its priory had as a cell a hospital at Charing Cross (dedicated to Our Lady of Rouncevale)...'

The main skills that Cottle brought to bear were those of a linguist and a historian. My own approach has necessarily been rather different, arising out of my experience as an amateur dialectician and as a professional genealogist.

It has been a privilege to work on Cottle's text, to share his joys, his frustrations, his certainties and his uncertainties, though such an exercise has been not a little spooky on occasions: as the original text was nearing its end I could feel his growing exhaustion (matched, indeed, by my own...), could empathize with him as the sureness of his touch began to desert him and he was clearly working under pressure, hurrying along with an uncharacteristic tendency to be inconsistent, repetitive and incomplete.

Here, in summary, are the ways in which the present book is both similar to, yet different from, Cottle's original:

Cottle preserved

The surnames included here are essentially those which appeared in Cottle's original book. He clearly applied a selection process of some sort – as much idiosyncratic as logical, perhaps – and in general I've followed his lead.

A range of English, Scottish, Welsh and Irish surnames is featured, including examples from Cornwall and from the Isle of Man, but I have not attempted to emulate the ambitious task which Patrick Hanks and Flavia Hodges set themselves in *A dictionary of surnames* (1988), of incorporating surnames of European and Jewish origin, together with others from across the world.

Cottle amended

Despite having used Cottle's text as a foundation, I've modified it as I've gone along, attempting to make certain entries more concise or more comprehensible, and have done my best to achieve a greater degree of consistency in the way in which the surnames featured are presented and cross-referenced.

I've also omitted a number of surnames which seem not to have survived in any significant numbers into modern times. Here I've placed a heavy reliance upon a CD produced by Steve Archer of Archer Software, entitled *The British nineteenth century surname atlas* (2003). This splendid resource has been my secret weapon, providing, as it does, both maps and distribution figures for over 400,000 surnames which appeared in the British population census for the year 1881.

As a result, out have gone certain scarce surnames featured by Cottle, by Hanks and Hodges in *A dictionary of surnames* (1988) and by others, such as the very rare **Bellmain** (only eight examples in 1881, all in Scotland, with one lone **Belmaine** in Herts) and **Howgrave** (borne by only one person in 1881), together with **Chiselhurst**, **Clarewood**, **Fernilee**, **Finesilver**, **Foxeth**, **Horsmanden**, **Icemonger**, **Jennifer** and many others, which would appear to have disappeared completely by 1881.

It might have seemed reasonable and obvious enough for Cottle to suppose that a surname such as **Liss** must be derived from the place-name in Hampshire, but by 1881 only six individuals were so-named, and all lived in Lancashire. **Canonbury**, a surname which gives every appearance of being derived from the place so-called in Middlesex, is not only absent from the 1881 census – it even fails to appear in major listings of parish register entries for the United Kingdom from the sixteenth century onwards.

On occasions I have made exceptions, nevertheless, and couldn't resist including practically extinct surnames such as **Whitgift**, made famous thanks to John **Whitgift**, Archbishop of Canterbury and founder of a school in Croydon, Surrey, which bears his name, and **Mompesson**, which has passed into history thanks to William Mompesson, the Anglican clergyman who heroically succeeded in confining an attack of bubonic plague within the limits of his parish of Eyam, Derbyshire, in 1665.

If there has been one thing above all others which has proved to be a bugbear to compilers of surname dictionaries up to and including Hanks and Hodges, it has been the absence of reliable evidence as to the distribution pattern of names within the United Kingdom and beyond. In an age of readily available digital information, such a problem has all but vanished: a few keystrokes will bring up material from decennial British censuses from 1841 to 1911, while the *International Genealogical Index*, offered free of charge by the Church of Jesus Christ of Latter-day Saints, includes millions of name entries, chiefly taken from parish registers, and provides a deeper historical perspective.

When it came to the distribution of surnames he chose to feature, Cottle was forced, *faute de mieux*, to rely heavily upon a book by H. B. Guppy entitled *The homes of family names in Great Britain* (1890) – a fine and fascinating work in its way, but one in which the author relied chiefly upon lists of farmers as they appeared in contemporary printed directories in order to arrive at his conclusions. Sometimes Guppy's statements about the preponderance of a surname in a particular locality accord with evidence now available from the 1881 census; more often than not, alas, they do not.

It is good fortune, then, rather than any innate wisdom, which has allowed me to question and to correct countless statements made by Cottle regarding the occurrence of particular surnames in certain parts of the country.

A mere handful of examples of cases in which Cottle has proved to be far adrift when it comes to surname distribution will suffice here. He says that Guppy found **Bowser** only in Lincolnshire, though in the 1881 census it is three times more common in County Durham than in Lincolnshire, and he further states that the surname **Wroe**, a Lancashire/West Riding of Yorkshire variant of **Wray**, was 'counted by Guppy only in Devon'. We are told that **Wager** is chiefly a Derbyshire surname (in fact it is restricted to Essex, Gloucestershire and Middlesex), that **January** belongs to Dorset and Somerset (it's a Cambridgeshire surname) and that **Weatherhogg** is 'chiefly a northern and Scots surname' (though it was almost entirely restricted to Lincolnshire in 1881). At times Cottle's reliance upon Guppy can betray his own best instincts: speaking of the surname **Wharton**, which he says is derived from such a place-name found in Cheshire, Herefordshire, Lincolnshire and Westmorland, he writes: 'Guppy's count of the surname in only Norfolk–Suffolk adds to the confusion'. If there is confusion, then Guppy has unwittingly been responsible for it: in the event, the 1881 census indicates that **Wharton** has a healthy presence in the place-name-source counties of Cheshire and Westmorland, though it is less common in Herefordshire and Lincolnshire.

Information provided by the 1881 census can be vital in other ways, too. Many surnames with a place-name origin are still found in significant numbers in the county or region where that place is situated. Several of our British ancestors moved around the country more readily and more regularly than we might ever have supposed, but many others stayed put in the same neighbourhood, or made only short journeys away from home.

So if the 1881 census shows that a large number of individuals bearing a place-name-type surname are clustered in a particular county or within a limited geographical area, warning bells should start ringing. If established surname dictionaries have suggested a place-name origin far from the epicentre of the surname in 1881, there may be a rat to be smelt, some accepted wisdom to be questioned.

So it is with a surname such as **Horsham**. Cottle and others have tumbled straight into the trap awaiting anyone who has even a nodding acquaintance with the place so-called in Sussex (though there is also a *Horsham* in Norfolk) – this, surely, is the point of origin? Not so. The 1881 census tells a different story: **Horsham** is predominantly a Devon surname, and in most if not all cases the two settlements called *Horsham* in that county will probably have given rise to the surname.

Cottle would seem to have had a particular blind-spot when it comes to surnames derived from Devon place-names, despite the fact that the two volumes which comprise *The place-names of Devon* (English Place-name Society, 1931/1932) by J. E. B. Gover, A. Mawer and F. M. Stenton are available in many academic libraries.

The point is, of course, that without information from the 1881 census or other such sources to alert them to a possible Devon connexion, Cottle and others would have had no reason to pay particular attention to that county and its place-names.

When it comes to the surname **Grendon**, Cottle is happy enough to refer to places so-called in Berkshire, Herefordshire (two such), Northamptonshire and Warwickshire; yet this is a Devon surname, and there are no fewer than four places called *Grendon* in that county. Other surnames with a Devon place-name origin have foxed earlier scholars, including: **Liverton** (Reaney and Cottle refer to *Liverton* in the North Riding of Yorkshire, but there are two places called *Liverton* in Devon) and **Sloley** (Cottle mentions such a place-name in Norfolk and Warwickshire, but the origin must be *Sloley*, in Shirwell, Devon). As to **Hingston**, both Hanks and Hodges (who would derive the surname from an apparently non-existent place-name in Cornwall) and Cottle (who refers to a place in Cambridgeshire – *Hinxton*, presumably) are uncharacteristically wide of the mark. This, too, is a Devon surname, and as such is almost certainly derived from the place-name *Hingston*, in Bigbury.

At times Cottle suggests a general topographical source for a surname, ignoring the fact that a place-name with the same meaning might have been the origin in many if not most cases. So although **Langmead** can refer to a dweller in any long meadow, as a Devon surname it is just as likely to have arisen specifically from the place-name *Langmead* in Sampford Courtenay.

The place-names of Kent, like those of Devon, seem to have been all-too-often ignored by surname scholars. An explanation here might lie in the fact that the English Place-name Society has not yet produced any volumes relating to the county, and researchers will need to lay their hands on a copy of *The place-names of Kent*, a fine work by J. K. Wallenberg, published in Uppsala, Sweden, in 1934, which is not so easy to find. A companion volume, *Kentish place-names*, also by Wallenberg, had appeared in 1931.

The surname **Lindridge**, Cottle informs us, is derived from a place-name in Worcestershire; but this is primarily a Kent surname, and the two places called *Lindridge* in that county (one in Lamberhurst, the other in Staplehurst) will almost certainly be the point of origin in most cases. So it is, too, with Kent surnames such as **Kingsford** (Cottle mentions places in Warwickshire and Worcestershire), **Kingswood** (Cottle speaks of place-names in Gloucestershire, Surrey and Warwickshire) and **Quarrington** (Cottle favours place-names in County Durham and in Lincolnshire), all of which reflect known Kent place-names.

We might very happily assume that the surname **Greenstreet** referred originally to a dweller at any old green highroad, but the 1881 census shows that this was also then a Kent surname, and Wallenberg's *Place-names of Kent* usefully provides the information that there is a place called *Greenstreet* in Teynham. Sydney Greenstreet (1879–1954), the Hollywood actor known for his performances in films such as *The Maltese Falcon*, was born in Sandwich, Kent.

To understand the surname **Queenborough**, however, we'll need to leave Kent far behind and look elsewhere. Cottle makes reference to the place-name *Queenborough*, Kent, but this scarce surname is chiefly found in Leicestershire, where the origin is likely to be the settlement called *Queniborough* (OE 'The Queen's borough').

The distribution pattern of some surnames which might not appear at first glance to have a place-name origin can provide us with food for thought. Both Reaney and Cottle believe that **Kippen** was originally a nickname for a fat or tubby person (OE *cypping*), but the fact that in the 1881 census it is restricted almost entirely to Scotland leads us to look elsewhere – to a place called *Kippen* (Gaelic *ceaopan* 'little stump'), near Stirling.

On occasions we might wish that Cottle had gone the extra mile in his thinking. He derives **Cundy** from an Old French word for a conduit, waterpipe, pump, fountain, and says that it is 'found in Yorks in 1379, but Guppy counted it only in Cornwall'. Indeed, it is found principally – though not exclusively – in Cornwall in 1881, where it is from Cornish *cun dy* 'house where dogs were bred'. Similarly, Cottle is aware of the fact that Guppy found the surname **Paynter** mainly in Cornwall, but failed to investigate further, and limited himself to grouping **Paynter** together with **Painter**, which has an occupational origin. **Paynter**, as found in Cornwall, is from Cornish *pen-dyr*, 'Dweller at an end of land'.

Some earlier surname scholars – notably C. W. Bardsley – are fond of lamenting the fact that although they are convinced that a particular surname has a place-name origin, they 'cannot find the spot'. These days, finding such 'spots' is much easier than it used to be, but one can't help feeling on occasions that a dictionary compiler has given up without a fight. When it comes to the surname **Swansborough**, Cottle is pleased to point out that in the legend of King Havelock the Dane, his little sister is called *Swanborough*, but neither he nor Hanks and Hodges can identify a likely place-name origin here. Yet this is very largely a Wiltshire surname, and the source will almost certainly be *Swanborough Tump* in Manninford Abbots, Wiltshire, the former meeting place for the Hundred of Swanborough.

To avoid the elephant trap which lies in wait for all unsuspecting researchers, it is vital not to claim that a surname is derived from a place-name which only came into existence in fairly recent times. It's all very well to say that **Winterbottom** has its origins in one of two places called *Winterbottom* in Cheshire, one in Goostrey-cum-Barnshaw, the other in Mere, but the first recorded references to each of these only date from as late as the nineteenth century, and in any case such places are probably named from a former owner who bore the **Winterbottom** surname. Cottle, alas, falls headlong into another Cheshire trap. Speaking of the surname **Hazelgrove**, he refers to *Hazel Grove*, a settlement on the outskirts of Stockport, which only acquired its name in the nineteenth century, having formerly been known as Bullock Smithy. As it happens, the surname is found almost exclusively in Sussex, where it would seem that the place called *Hazel Grove* in that county could well be the principal place of origin.

Cottle augmented

There are some ways in which I have enlarged the original *Penguin Dictionary of Surnames*.

On a number of occasions I have used phrases such as 'chiefly found in...' and the like, in which case it has generally been the occurrence of a surname in the 1881 census which I have used as my evidence. Clearly some surnames could, and did, move around a great deal with the families which bore them, both before and after the closing decades of the nineteenth century, but many others have remained rooted to the spot over several centuries, and I hope that the frequent snapshots I have provided as to the location of names in 1881 will prove to be a useful addition to this dictionary.

I've also included a number of mini-biographies, highlighting a well-known person (sometimes more than one) who has borne a particular surname, especially if it is unusual or distinctive. In such cases I have made no distinction between, say, William Shakespeare and David Beckham – all are grist to the surname mill. Incidentally, George Redmonds impishly points out that the footballers David Beckham and Teddy Sheringham carry surnames derived from neighbouring places in Norfolk: East and West Beckham lie cheek-by-jowl with the coastal town of Sheringham.

On occasions it has been satisfying to find that the subject of a biography has come from a county in which his or her surname is known to have originated, or where it has been most prolific. William and James **Horlick**, after whom the famous bedtime drink is named, emigrated to the USA from Gloucestershire, the principal home of their unusual surname. The cricketer Mike **Atherton**, whose surname is derived from a place-name in Lancashire, was born in that county in 1968. **Knapman** being a Devon surname, it's gratifying to discover that Roger Knapman, former leader of the United Kingdom Independence Party (UKIP), is a Devonian by birth. **Plowden** is from a place-name in Shropshire, and although Edwin Noel Auguste Plowden, Baron Plowden (1907–2001), compiler of the Plowden Report on primary school education, was born in Strachur, Argyll, his Plowden ancestors had long been established in Shropshire. **Plowright**, from an occupational term for a plough-maker, is strongest in Lincolnshire, which is where the actress Dame Joan Plowright was born in 1929. And Joseph Malaby **Dent** (1849–1926), the founder of the publishing company J. M. Dent, was born in County Durham, which is where most **Dent**s hail from.

Sometimes we have to travel back through several generations of the family of a well-known person in order to arrive at a locality which accords with the known source of the surname. **Waugh** is a surname of unknown origin which is strongest in Northumberland and in Roxburghshire, Scotland. The writer Evelyn Waugh (1903–1966) was born in West Hampstead, London, but his father Arthur Waugh, from Midsomer Norton, Somerset, was the great-grandson of the Scottish divine Dr Alexander Waugh (1754–1827), from Berwickshire.

One chance discovery I made while compiling these short biographies surprised and intrigued me, though others will probably have noticed it long before I did. The fact is that one of the major qualifications for success in life is to have had a sickly childhood. Delicacy of constitution marked out men such as Edward Lear (epilepsy, asthma, bronchitis and short-sightedness), Horace Walpole, Sabine Baring-Gould, Charles Babbage, Lord Kitchener, Charles Kingsley (sickly, stammering), William Wilberforce (precocious but frail as a child), Philip Doddridge (a consumptive), Gerald Scarfe (asthmatic), Charles Wolfe (an extremely delicate child), John Flamsteed (subject to rheumatic disorders and consumption), Sir Stamford Raffles ('a frail, diffident youth') and several others. The lesson is clear: illness can be good for you...

I've never been deliriously happy at including surnames for which the only honest explanation is 'origin unknown', but sometimes needs must. On occasions I've given up without much of a fight, and have compiled a tame enough entry such as that for **Blunden**: 'Origin uncertain: blond or grizzled hair OE? The fact that the *-den* ending makes this look like a place-name is probably a red herring'. Yet I felt that I could hardly have omitted a surname borne by one of England's better-known poets, Edmund Blunden. The Scottish surname of Andrew Motion, Poet Laureate, gets fuller treatment, though no definite conclusions have been reached, for all my efforts.

From time to time (like Basil Cottle before me) I've found the temptation to include little extra snippets of information, many of which perhaps interest me more than they do the reader, impossible to resist. So it is that I've mentioned the fact that Orson Welles and Marilyn Monroe share a common ancestor, a cooper on board the *Mayflower* by the name of John Alden, and that the chat-show host Jerry Springer was born in 1944 inside East Finchley station on the London Underground network. When the going gets tough, mildly irreverent comments are likely to trip off the editor's typewriter fingers all too easily: '**Gulliver**. Nickname for a glutton. In so far as he was any kind of a glutton, Jonathan Swift's Lemuel Gulliver, hero of the travels which bear his name, was a glutton for punishment at the hands of little men, big men and other assorted oddities. There were compensations: at least he got to slide down the ample bosoms of giant ladies in the land of the Brobdingnagians...'

I've also occasionally included the odd gem or two such as the fact that the birth of a child called '*Windsor* **Castle**' was registered in Radford, Nottingham, in 1876. I gratefully acknowledge a marvellously irreverent little book, *Potty Fartwell and Knob* by Russell Ash (2007), as the source for this and similar surrealist treasures.

Then there are the surnames – some of them fairly common ones such as **Col(e)gate** and **Haworth/Howarth** – which Cottle had failed to include for some unaccountable reason, and which I've added to the pot.

I have also paid special attention to a number of names which had been side-stepped or given short shrift in earlier dictionaries, such as **Copledick/Copledike/ Cobeldyk**, and **Dorricott/Dadecote/Dallicot(e)/Dallicott/Derricott/Doddicott**; in the latter case I was assisted (as were Hanks and Hodges in much of their work) by research already carried out by those for whom this is an ancestral surname. On occasions, recently published research has improved our knowledge significantly: of **Goulty/ Golty**, Hanks and Hodges say that 'no forms have been found before 1544, when Robert **Golty** was married at Debach, Suffolk', but that fails to take account of William **Gowty**, vicar of West Bilney, Norfolk, whose will was proved in the Consistory Court of Norwich in 1403, and of several other fifteenth- and early sixteenth-century testators featured in *Goulty wills and administrations* by George A. Goulty, published in 1994.

I also confess to having made a special effort to feature surnames, no matter how rare, borne by friends, acquaintances and former students, especially if they have posed something of a daunting challenge. Hence there are entries for **Bavister**, **Behagg**, **Palethorpe**, **Pincott**, **Spowage**, **Stonhold**, **Todkill**, **Tolliday**, **Wathall**, **Wilderspin**, **Woodiwiss** and others. Some of these have been dealt with in more detail in my book *Searching for surnames* (2002), or in articles published in *Family Tree Magazine*.

Then there are those surnames such as **Cattermole** and **Plimsoll** which scholars have anguished over long and hard. I've normally tried my best to add my tuppenceworth in such cases – though no doubt with varying degrees of success...

Dwarfs on giants' shoulders

What of earlier surname dictionaries, many of them still highly regarded and useful within their limits?

It is perhaps all too easy to patronize former workers in the surname field, even to sneer at their achievements. Many were giants in their own way, and those of us who have arrived on the scene late in the day are in many ways simply dwarfs on giants' shoulders. Serious students of surnames would do well to have a range of relevant books on their shelves, the old (Lower, Bardsley, Harrison, Weekley, Ewen, Reaney/ Wilson and the rest) alongside the new (McKinley, Hanks and Hodges, Redmonds, Hey), not forgetting the various volumes in the *English surnames series*, the result of work carried out as part of the English Surnames Survey at the University of Leicester, published during the period 1973–1998.

Most books on surnames bear more than a passing resemblance to the legendary curate's egg, being good in some parts, but unpalatable if not positively indigestible in others.

A number of early scholars were frequently too imaginative for their own good, or were too literal in their interpretations. Some were prepared to assume, for example, that the Derbyshire surname **Purs(e)glove** might have been a nickname applied to a person who wore a glove with a purse in it, whereas such a name will almost certainly have arisen when folk etymology, favouring the familiar word 'glove', got to work on a place-name such as *Purslow* in Shropshire. Similarly, the oh-so-simple explanation for the origin of the surname **Spendlove** – that it was a nickname for a person who spread love around, or who wasted it by over-use – ignores the fact that the county of Derbyshire, where the surname is particularly in evidence, has place-names such as *Spellow* and *Le Spenelowe*, which could well have been the origin in many cases.

Three classic surname dictionaries in particular have stood the test of time and stand head and shoulders above the rest. These, in effect, have proved to be the giants...

C. W. Bardsley's *Dictionary of English and Welsh surnames* was first published in 1901 but has been reprinted many times since. The author is thorough and thoughtful in his own way, and his book is still extremely useful, but surname study has moved on and conquered new heights since his work first saw the light of day, and he can now seem rather old-fashioned both in his choice of names and in some of his explanations.

P. H. Reaney's *Dictionary of British surnames* first appeared in 1958; later editions with corrections and additions by R. M. Wilson bear the more strictly accurate title of *A dictionary of* **English** *surnames*, and you can now purchase one of these in paperback at a very affordable price. Reaney was a dedicated student of the subject, and he offers a number of very helpful examples of surnames being used in early written records. Modern scholars have had reservations about some of his work, however, since he appears not to have taken sufficient account of the fact that many early surnames died out when a family or families which bore them failed to produce male offspring, or fell victim to the Black Death, which ravaged the country during the fourteenth century, or to similar but less severe outbreaks of plague and other fatal diseases.

George Redmonds, while admitting that Reaney can be useful as a compendium of mediaeval surnames, has reservations which he expresses in *Surnames and genealogy: a new approach* (new edition, 2002): 'The truth is that without some sort of genealogical evidence it can be unwise to link modern surnames with those found in mediaeval sources... His [Reaney's] insistence on the value of early examples of surnames is revealing, for it emphasizes that his real concern was to explain the meaning of mediaeval surnames, whether or not they became hereditary and, perhaps more importantly, whether or not they survived into modern times...'

The point is well made. When it comes to a surname such as **Boss(e)y**, Reaney quotes twelfth- and thirteenth-century examples, and gives the meaning as 'hunchbacked'. Yet by the time of the 1881 census, the surname scarcely exists in England and Wales. Both Reaney and Cottle list **Bookbinder**, the derivation of which is obvious enough, and Reaney provides examples of its use in mediaeval times. Yet in the 1881 census there are only two people bearing this name in England and Wales,

Meyer and Morris Bookbinder, both living in Islington but born in the Netherlands, both in the diamond trade, and both, we may suppose, of Jewish origin.

P. Hanks and F. Hodges' *A dictionary of surnames* (1988) is a substantial and scholarly work, and I am only too happy to acknowledge the fact that I have found it to be of immense value in compiling this present book. Its arrangement has something of the inspirational about it: surnames with the same or very similar meanings (like **Baker**, **Bacher** and **Baxter**) are grouped together for the purpose of explanation, and access to all the names included can be gained by way of an index at the back.

By the time Hanks and Hodges published their dictionary in 1988, surname studies had moved on a great deal since Bardsley and Reaney, so that many convincing new meanings and origins are included, and a number of old myths laid to rest. The compilers also had the good sense to enlist the help of a number of professional and amateur family historians as they moved towards publication.

A genealogical approach

So we move to the significance of genealogy for surname study.

Families and surnames are inextricably related; the study of one must involve a study of the other, and to gain a full understanding of any surname you'd be well advised to pay close attention to its behaviour and its distribution in a historical context, to give as much consideration to the families who have carried it down through the generations as to the name itself in isolation.

We can take it as an article of faith that the further back in time we are able to take a surname, the greater the chance of our being able to determine more precisely where it might have originated and what it means. This is especially true, for example, of surnames based upon the name of a place, be it large or small, where a journey back in history may well bring us ever closer to the place-name origin. Not only that, but even the most basic of research programmes which moves us back through the generations should throw up variant forms and spellings of a surname which might offer a clue as to its meaning.

Modern surname scholars such as George Redmonds have emphasized precisely this point, and his book *Surnames and genealogy: a new approach*, originally published by the New England Historic Genealogical Society in 1997 with a new printing in 2002, is a seminal work which I cannot recommend too highly. *The surname detective* by Colin Rogers (1995) and *Family names and family history* by David Hey (2000) also adopt a genealogical approach, and make entertaining and stimulating reading.

One of the major failings of older surname dictionaries has been that they have tended to treat surnames out of context, as some kind of linguistic challenge unrelated to genealogical evidence. This has worried George Redmonds not a little: 'Surnames could change fundamentally in the course of two or three generations... The fact that they could, in the process, become identical with other surnames and, more confusingly, with place-names and personal names with which they had no real connexion, will at the same time emphasize how important genealogical methods are in matters of origin and meaning.'

It is with this in mind (hedging my bets, if you like) that I have frequently used the formula 'Readily confused with/a variant of' in the present dictionary.

Significant developments in the field of DNA analysis have enabled George Redmonds to find that his own theories of surname development, based upon meticulous research into early written records, were often confirmed thanks to evidence from 'Y' chromosome samples taken from living people who bore similar but not identical surnames, and who were indeed proved to be distantly related, as George had presumed – and hoped – that they would be. Studies into mitochondrial ('MT') DNA, which is transmitted down the female line, are also gaining momentum and producing some exciting results. Old and new technologies are thus coming together, answering some existing questions but also posing a whole host of fresh ones.

Not all surnames yield up their meaning without a fight, and more often than not it is a genealogical approach which will pay dividends. By way of an example, let's finish off with a fairly detailed look at the innocuous-seeming surname of **Ayckbourn**.

The name of Alan Ayckbourn conjures up images of finely crafted plays performed, above all, in Scarborough, Yorkshire. The playwright's surname, surely, must take us deep into the English countryside and a place bearing the same name? It would be tempting to suppose so, and Hanks and Hodges, in *A dictionary of surnames* (1988) were clearly thinking along these lines when they wrote: '**Ayckbourn** N English: habitation name from a place, not now identifiable, deriving its name from ON *eiki* oak + OE *burna* stream...'

This is as far as an orthodox approach can take us, though we can search in vain for the elusive settlement bearing the name 'Ayckbourn'. It *ought* to exist – but it doesn't, and probably never did.

In this case, only a genealogical approach can force the surname to yield up its origins.

Alan Ayckbourn was born in London in 1939, son of Horace and Irene Maud (née Worley). The 1881 census for England and Wales reveals just how rare a surname this is: there are only five examples of Ayckbourn, all in Middlesex, together with seven Ayckburns in Kent and six Ackbourns in Surrey. The International Genealogical Index, which at times features entries as far back as the sixteenth century and beyond, only offers us seven Ayckbourns, all from the nineteenth century, living in Surrey, Cheshire, Hampshire and London. Three such entries are for men with the middle name of Harman. All of this gets us no further back than the year 1846, not a promising start. A family cannot suddenly materialize from nowhere in the early nineteenth century; they must either have come to England from abroad, or changed their name, or both.

One or two Ayckbourns can be glimpsed in various records as they flit by, such as Augustus H. Ayckbourn, surgeon of Wendover, Bucks, in commercial directories for 1830 (Pigot's) and 1839 (Robson's), and Harman Ayckbourn, parliamentary reporter, whose name is referred to in connexion with the political papers of Sir William Jolliffe, dated 30 August 1859 (Somerset Archives, ref.DD/HY/24/16/136).

Here we have the 'Harman' name again, one which will prove to be the vital clue as we move on a further stage. London directories for London in the years 1774, 1779, 1780 and 1781 carry references to: 'Aychbowm, Herman and Dederick', cut-glass manufacturers of 9 New Road, Ratcliffe. This provides the vital connexion between the name Herman/Harman and the name Aychbowm/Ayckbourn. Failing other evidence, we will probably be safe in assuming that a Mr Aychbowm married a daughter of his partner Mr Herman/Harman, changed his name to Ayckbourn and had descendants with the middle name of Harman, leading eventually to

Edward Harman Ayckbourn, who married in Surrey in 1870, and Robert Harman Ayckbourn, who married in London in 1855 and again in 1861. Holden's London directory for 1790 includes a 'J. Ayckbown', china man, at 9 Great Surrey Street, Blackfriars Row, and this same spelling variant appears thirty years later in Dublin, at which time M. Ayckbown & Co, china and glass merchants, are listed in an 1820 directory at 16 Grafton Street, right in the heart of the city.

So the English-sounding surname of Ayckbourn would seem to be derived from the German-sounding Aychbowm/Ayckbown. As if to reinforce the point, the 1861 census for Chorley in Cheshire lists a lady by the name of Emily Harriet E. Ayckbourn, a 24-year-old clergyman's daughter, born in Heidelberg, Germany; in the census taken thirty years later she was in London, listed at the Orphanage of Mercy, Paddington, 'Emily H[arriet] E. Ayckbowm, aged 54, born in Heidelberg'. Allowing for a certain indistinctness in the handwriting of the census enumerator, we have proof positive here that the surnames Ayckbowm and Ayckbourn are one and the same.

Correspondence on the internet (http://people.bath.ac.uk/ccsdc/genealogy/ct/224.html) provides a further glimpse of the Aychbowm/Ayckbown/Ayckbowm surname, in the form of a letter from Gustaf Eichbaum, whose own surname means 'oak tree': 'As a German oaktree I'm always interested in what other oak trees did in the past. Today I had a look (at) the Reverend Frederick Ayckbowm, whom I know as Frederick Eichbaum, son of Johann Diederich [N.B.] Eichbaum, 1748–1807, who was married to Mary Barnes, 1754–1831. The oldest known Eichbaum in that line was Johann Heinrich Eichbaum and Margarethe Lahmann/Lohmann. He probably went to Dublin one day... maybe the father worked as a glassmaker... I'm interested... because I was asked about the family of the foundress of the Community of the Sisters of the Church (CSC), Emily Ayckbowm or better Eichbaum... [H]er brother, Rev. Frederick Albert Grosvenor Eichbaum (1840–1909), Chester, kept that name all his life.'

We return, then, to the indomitable Emily Ayckbown, also known as Ayckbourn and as Eichbaum. Born on 14 November 1836 in Heidelberg, she was the daughter of Frederick Ayckbown and Mary Ann Hutchinson, who had married on 13 February 1833 in Onchan, Isle of Man. Frederick's origins were in Ireland: he was born in 1793 in Dublin, son of John Diedrich Ayckbown and Mary Barnes, and when he entered Trinity College, Dublin, on 4 July 1810, he was said to be the son of John Dedrich Ayckbown, glass-maker (*Alumni Dublinenses* by G. D. Burtchaell and T. U. Sadleir, 1924). Graduating in 1816, he chose to enter the church, and was made rector of Holy Trinity Church, Chester, in 1825. Quite why Frederick and Mary Ann's daughter Emily was born in Heidelberg is unclear: perhaps Heidelberg was where Frederick's ancestral roots lay? In any event, she was baptized at her father's church in Chester on 17 October 1837, as her sister Mary Constance had been two years earlier, to be followed by her sister Gertrude Dorathea [sic] in 1838. Gertrude's birth was registered at Great Boughton, Cheshire, under the surname of Ayckbourn. Frederick remarried in 1846, his new wife being Charlotte Spens, and he died on 23 August 1862. Eight years later his daughter Emily, having left Chester for London, founded the Community of the Sisters of the Church (commonly called the Kilburn Sisters) and so established a movement which would have an international reach as time went by. An account of her life is given in *A valiant Victorian: the life and times of Mother Emily*

Ackbowm, 1836–1900 of the Community of the Sisters of the Church (Sisters of the Church, 1964). Emily died in Thanet, Kent, on 5 January 1900.

So we can forget the search for a place-name in England called 'Ayckbourn'. The principal family of **Ayckbourn**s within the British Isles started life as protestant Germans surnamed Eichbaum/Aychbowm/Ayckbowm/Ayckbown, and their earliest male-line ancestor probably lived near an oak tree.

Thus, I hope we may say, a genealogical approach to surname study is vindicated. So much more work remains to be done...

Further research

Printed works

The subject of names in general and of surnames in particular has generated a vast amount of related literature, written in a wide variety of languages. The 'further reading' list which follows consists mainly of standard works on surnames; each has its own story to tell, and has something positive to contribute to the overall fund of knowledge.

Addison, Sir William *Understanding English surnames*. 1978.

Anderson, W. *Genealogy and surnames*. 1865.

Ashley, L. R. N. *What's in a name?* 1989.

Barber, H. *British family names*. Second edition, 1903.

Bardsley, C. W. *A dictionary of English and Welsh surnames*. Originally published in 1901, reprinted several times.

Bardsley, C. W. *English surnames, their sources and significations*. Originally published in 1873, reprinted 1969.

Bardsley, C. W. *Romance of the London Directory*. Originally published in 1879, reprinted 1971.

Baring-Gould, S. *Family names and their story*. 1910.

Bell, R. *The book of Ulster surnames*. 1988.

Black, G. F. *The surnames of Scotland*. Originally published in 1946, reprinted several times.

Bowditch, N. I. *Suffolk surnames*. 1857. Suffolk, Massachusetts, not Suffolk, England.

Bowman, W. D. *What is your surname?* 1932.

Charnock, R. S. *Ludus patronymicus; or, the etymology of curious surnames*. 1868.

Charnock, R. S. *Patronymica Cornu-Britannica*. Originally published in 1870, reprinted 2000.

Cole, J. and J. S. Titford *Tracing your family tree: the comprehensive guide to discovering your family history*. Fourth edition, 2003.

Cottle, Basil *The Penguin Dictionary of Surnames*. Second edition, 1978.

Dauzat, A. *Dictionnaire étymologique des noms de famille et prénoms de France*. 1951.

De Breffny, B. *Irish family names: arms, origins and locations*. 1982.

Dolan, J. R., et al. *English ancestral names*. 1972.

Dorward, D. *Scottish surnames*. 1995.

Dunkling, L. *Dictionary of surnames*. 1998.

Dunkling, L. *The Guinness Book of Names*. 1974.

Dyson, T. *Place names and surnames, their origin and meaning, with special reference to the West Riding of Yorkshire*. 1944.

Ewen, C. L'Estrange *A guide to the origin of British surnames*. 1938.

Ewen, C. L'Estrange *A history of surnames of the British Isles*. 1931.

Ferguson, R. *Surnames as a science*. Second edition, 1884.

Freeman, J. W. *Discovering surnames: their origins and meanings*. Second edition, 1973.

Guppy, H. B. *The homes of family names in Great Britain*. 1890.

Hanks, P. *Dictionary of American family names*. 2003.

Hanks, P. and F Hodges *A dictionary of surnames*. 1988.

Harrison, H. *Surnames of the United Kingdom: a concise etymological dictionary*. 1912–18, reprinted 1992.

Hey, D. *Family names and family history*. 2000.

Hook, J. N. *Family names: how our surnames came to America*. 1982.

Hughes, J. P. *How you got your name*. Revised edition, 1961.

Hughes, J. P. *Is thy name Wart?* 1965.

Johnston, J. B. *The Scottish Macs: their derivation and origin*. 1922.

Kelly, P. *Irish family names*. 1976.

Kneen, J. J. *The personal names of the Isle of Man*. 1937.

Lasker, G. W. and C. G. N. Mascie-Taylor *Atlas of British surnames*. 1990.

Long, H. *Personal and family names*. 1883, reprinted 1968.

Lower, M. A. *English surnames: essays on family nomenclature*. 1842.

Lower, M. A. *Patronymica Britannica*. 1860.

Mac Giolla Domhnaigh, P. *Some Ulster surnames*. New edition ?1974.

McKinley, R. A. *A history of British surnames*. 1990.

McLaughlin, Eve *Surnames and their origins*. 1997.

MacLysaght, E. *The surnames of Ireland*. Sixth edition, 1985.

Matheson, R. E. *Varieties and synonymes of surnames and Christian names in Ireland*. 1901.

Matthews, C. M. *English surnames*. 1966.

Miller, G. M. *BBC Pronouncing Dictionary of British Names*. 1971.

Mills, Halford Lupton ['A Smardonian'] *The family names of the Weald of Kent*. 1901.

Moore, A. W. *The surnames and place-names of the Isle of Man*. 1890.

Morgan, T. J. and P. *Welsh surnames*. 1985.

[No author named] *The Norman People and their existing descendants in the British Dominions and the United States of America*. 1874, reprinted 1975, 1989.

Payton, G. [revised by J Paxton] *The Penguin Dictionary of Proper Names*. 1991.

Pine, L. G. *The story of surnames*. 1965.

Quilliam, L. *Surnames of the Manks*. 1989.

Reaney, P. H. *The origin of English surnames*. 1967.

Reaney, P. H. and R. M. Wilson *A dictionary of English surnames*. Third edition, 1995.

Redmonds, G. *Surnames and genealogy: a new approach*. 1997, republished 2002.

Redmonds, G. *Yorkshire surnames series*. Part one: Bradford (1990); Part two: Huddersfield (1992); Part three: Halifax (2001).

Rogers, C. D. *The surname detective*. 1995.

Rogers, K. H. *Vikings and surnames*. 1991.

Room, A. *Dictionary of proper names*. 1994.

Room, A. *Dictionary of trade name origins*. Revised edition, 1982.

Room, A. *Naming names: a book of pseudonyms and name changes with a 'Who's who'*. 1981.

Rosenthal, E. *South African surnames*. 1965.

Rowlands, J. and S. *The surnames of Wales*. 1996.

Scollins, R. and J. S. Titford *Ey up mi duck: dialect of Derbyshire and the East Midlands*. First published 1976–7, new edition 2000.

Seary, E. R. *Family names of the Island of Newfoundland*. 1977.

Smith, E. C. *American surnames*. 1969, 1986.

Smith, E. C. *New dictionary of American family names*. 1956, 1973.

Smith, E. C. *The story of our names*. 1950, 1970.

Titford, J. S. *Searching for surnames*. 2002.

Titford, J. S. *Succeeding in family history: helpful hints and time-saving tips*. 2001.

Titford, J. S. *The Titford family 1547–1947*. 1989.

[Various editors]: seven volumes in the *English surnames series*, the result of work carried out as part of the English Surnames Survey at the University of Leicester, 1973–1998.

Verstappen, P. *The book of surnames: origins and oddities of popular names*. 1980.

Weekley, E. *The romance of names*. 1914.

Weekley, E. *Surnames*. 1916.

Weekley, E. *Words and names*. 1932.

White, G. P. *A handbook of Cornish surnames*. Third edition, 1999.

Wilson, S. *The means of naming*. 1998.

Woulfe, Rev. P. *Irish names and surnames*. 1923. Reprinted several times.

For the present work I have also made use of snippets of information culled from the following books:

Ash, R. *Potty Fartwell and Knob*. 2007.

Ash, R. and Lake, B. *Fish who answer the telephone and other bizarre books*. 2006.

Morris, D. *The pioneering emigrants*. 2006.

Digital sources

CD-ROMs

Surnames:

- *The British nineteenth-century surname atlas* is a fully interactive CD-ROM product that provides distribution maps for all of the surnames and forenames found in the 1881 census of England, Scotland and Wales. For further details, see Steve Archer's website: *www.archersoftware.co.uk* Also useful as a way of determining the distribution of surnames in more recent times are the various editions of the *UK Info Disk* on CD-ROM, which include names and addresses gleaned from telephone directories and electoral rolls.
- *Grenham's Irish surnames* is the title of a CD-ROM, first developed with Eneclann in 2003, which aims to provide a resource for anyone interested in the history of Irish surnames, or in starting Irish genealogical research. For further details, see John Grenham's website: *www.johngrenham.com/software/surnames.shtml*

Biographies:
Who's Who 1897–1996: one hundred years of biography. A CD-ROM published by A. & C. Black, Ltd.

Genealogy:
- *National Burial Index for England and Wales*. An essential complement to the baptism and marriage entries featured on the *International Genealogical Index [IGI]* (see below). The second edition was published by the Federation of Family History Societies in 2004, and many of the entries featured are also available on a pay-per-view basis on the Federation's website at *www.familyhistoryonline.net*

Websites

The Internet is positively awash with information which is of use to anyone conducting research into family history or into the meaning and origins of surnames. There is a host of family history sites, some free-of-charge and some demanding fees; not only that, but you can use your favourite search engine to obtain information on a given surname – especially if it is unusual and distinctive.

The usual caveat applies, however. Some information which is offered on the Internet is well researched and reliable, but much, alas, is utter drivel.

Surnames:
- *www.nationaltrustnames.org.uk* This National Trust website presents the findings of a project based at University College London (UCL) which is investigating the distribution of surnames in Great Britain, both current and historic. It allows users to search the databases so far created, and to trace the geography and history of family names. This project has expanded its remit to provide distribution and statistical information on surnames worldwide. For results of this research, see *www.publicprofiler.org/?page_id=8*
- *www.spatial-literacy.org* In time it is expected that this website will expand the existing Great Britain Surname Profiler, examining surnames on a global scale.
- *www.nameswell.info* The website of Rosalind Moffatt of Nameswell Surname Research, who has used her own experience as a speech and language therapist to good effect in surname study, and has written a fascinating series of relevant articles in *Family Tree Magazine*.
- *www.genuki.org.uk/big/eng/DBY/NamesPersonal/index.html* An index to a selection of detailed and scholarly articles from *The Peak Advertiser* featuring the derivation of surnames, with special emphasis on their occurrence in Derbyshire, reproduced with the permission of their author, Desmond Holden.
- *www.unusualsurnames.com* A website featuring unusual surnames. A Google search will readily throw up similar sites, including a listing provided by Sheila Francis at: *http://freepages.genealogy.rootsweb.ancestry.com/~sheilafrancis/unusualsurnames.htm*
- *www.last-names.net* A listing enabling researchers to find the ethnic origin and meaning of a number of Irish, German, English, French, Italian and Jewish last names.
- *www.nameseekers.co.uk/surname.htm* 'Your surname can tell you much about your family history. Here is an A-Z of the more common surname meanings'.

- *www.namethesaurus.com/Thesaurus/Search.aspx* A useful listing of known surname variants.
- *www.northeastengland.talktalk.net/Surnames%20of%20North%20East%20England. htm* Features surnames from County Durham and Northumberland.
- *http://homepages.newnet.co.uk/dance/webpjd* Philip Dance's website is devoted to the resources available for the study of the distribution, incidence and statistical analysis of the surnames of Britain, mainly post 1837, and primarily as a mass phenomenon. It does not concern itself with the history or etymology of individual surnames.
- *www.snsbi.org.uk* Website of the Society for Name Studies in Britain and Ireland, which was formally inaugurated in November 1991. The Society publishes the journal *Nomina*, and organizes annual conferences and day schools.
- *www.gen-find.com/resources/surname_origins_history.html* An article on surnames.
- *www.spub.co.uk/surnames.pdf* A challenging article on surnames by Peter Christian.
- *www.users.uswest.net/~butchmatt/WelshNames&Surnames.htm* An article on Welsh surnames by J. B. Davies of Cardiff.
- *www.namethesaurus.com* A site which uses NameX technology to identify variants of over three million distinct surnames.
- *http://surnamedb.com* A very interesting and useful website, but something of a curate's egg: detailed and scholarly in parts, but sometimes paying scant attention to the distribution patterns of certain surnames which it features.

Biographies:
- *www.wikipedia.org* An evergreen but also ever-growing collection of biographies, international in scope.
- *www.oxforddnb.com* The Dictionary of National Biography. Impressive in the depth of its coverage, though only deceased British men and women are featured. Access to this site is often provided free of charge by virtue of an arrangement between the publishers and a number of public libraries.

Genealogy:
- *www.familysearch.org* A remarkable website, provided free to users by the Church of Jesus Christ of Latter-day Saints (Mormons), and containing, among other things, information from the 1881 British Census (available thanks to a project jointly undertaken by the Genealogical Society of Utah and the Federation of Family History Societies) and the *International Genealogical Index* (*IGI*). The *IGI*, developed over many years by the church, which has a special interest in genealogical matters, provides information about literally millions of individuals throughout the world. Britain is strongly represented; a certain amount of miscellaneous information from various sources is included, but the essential core of the British index is its collection of baptism and marriage entries taken from parish registers, some from as early as the sixteenth century, and most pre-dating the advent of national civil registration of births, marriages and deaths in England and Wales in 1837. The *IGI* is only a 'finding aid', not a primary source, but can be of immeasurable value for family historians and others, and can provide dedicated researchers outside the world of academia with an opportunity to make a real contribution to surname studies.

- *www.ancestry.co.uk; www.thegenealogist.co.uk* Just two of a number of such websites which offer researchers pay-per-view access to a range of genealogical data, including information from general registration records of birth, marriage and death within England and Wales, and from the British decennial censuses, 1841–1901. Note that the 1881 census can be accessed free of charge at *www.familysearch.org* (see above).
- *www.nationalarchives.gov.uk* Several record offices throughout Britain have their own website, but the one provided by the National Archives (TNA) is of particular value, including, as it does, access to various military records, probate records of the Prerogative Court of Canterbury, Domesday Book, 'Access to Archives' (A2A) and much else.

Acknowledgements

Very many people have contributed to this book in various ways, whether they have been aware of it or not, and I beg the forgiveness of those whom I may inadvertently have failed to mention here.

George Redmonds of Lepton, near Huddersfield, has been an entertaining and inspirational friend, as always. His knowledge of surnames is unsurpassed, and I only hope that I have not misunderstood or misinterpreted any of his hard-won findings. Books on surname study written by George and by his friend David Hey have inspired so many of us in recent years, and I happily acknowledge the debt which I owe to them both.

Other friends and correspondents who deserve a particular mention here include Steve Archer, Duncan Harrington and Cecil Humphery-Smith, together with two dear departed mates, Don Steel and Nick Vine Hall.

I have had assistance with specific surnames from Jim Beardsley (Beardsley), Danny Corns (Corns), Peter Dewar (Dewar), Mrs C. Doughty (Arkinstall), Linda Edwards (Dorricott), Terry Hart-Jones (Dax), David Hawkings (Paxman), Derek Palgrave (Eustace), Rosemary and Thorsten Sjolin and Andrew James (Brooking), Robert Albert Snowball (Snowball), John Spendlove (Spendlove), Roy Stockdill (Stockdill), Bob Trubshaw (Trubshaw), John Twistleton (Twistleton) and Michael Walker (Spowage).

This book would never have seen the light of day were it not for the secretarial and editorial help I have received from my dear friend Gwen Jones, from her niece Angela Cooke and from Richard Williams. They lightened the load for me and kept me sane when the task in hand threatened to overwhelm me.

My wife Heather, whose main interests in life – thank goodness – are rather different from my own, has nevertheless always taken a keen interest in my work and in surname study in particular. She has proved to be a font and a fountain of knowledge, as ever, and not for the first time I owe her my deepest gratitude for all the support and encouragement she has given me while this book has been in the making.

John Titford
2009

List of abbreviations

Classification of surnames

F = first-name
N = nickname
O = occupational
P = place-name
T = topographical

Language sources

ME = Middle English
OE = Old English
OF = Old French
ON = Old Norse
OW = Old Welsh

Counties

Beds = Bedfordshire
Bucks = Buckinghamshire
Cambs = Cambridgeshire
Chesh = Cheshire
Co Durham = County Durham
Cumbd = Cumberland
Derbys = Derbyshire
ERYorks = East Riding of Yorkshire
Gloucs = Gloucestershire
Hants = Hampshire
Herefords = Herefordshire
Herts = Hertfordshire
Hunts = Huntingdonshire
Lancs = Lancashire

Leics = Leicestershire
Lincs = Lincolnshire
Middx = Middlesex
Northants = Northamptonshire
Northd = Northumberland
Notts = Nottinghamshire
NRYorks = North Riding of Yorkshire
Oxon = Oxfordshire
Salop = Shropshire
Staffs = Staffordshire
Warwicks = Warwickshire
Westmd = Westmorland
Wilts = Wiltshire
Worcs = Worcestershire
WRYorks = West Riding of Yorkshire

Note: Original/historic English, Scottish and Welsh county names have been used throughout.

THE PENGUIN
DICTIONARY OF
BRITISH SURNAMES

Abbatt, *see* Abbot.

Abberley P Place-name in Worcs OE *'Ealdbeald*'s clearing'.

Abbett, *see* Abbot.

Abbey/Abdey/Abdie T/O A person who lived near/worked at an abbey, Latin *abbatia*.

Abbiss T Dweller near an abbey.

Abbot(t)/Abbatt/Abbett/Labbett O/N A person employed by an abbot, or who acted like one. From Aramaic *abba* (father), via Latin and OE. **Abbott** is the commonest spelling; the *L-* element in **Labbett** (very much a Devon surname) is an abbreviation of the French definite article *Le*. Cottle informs us that 'George **Abbot** (died 1633) was the only Archbishop of Canterbury ever to shoot a gamekeeper…'

Abdey/Abdie, *see* Abbey.

Abel(l)/Able F From the Hebrew first-name *Hevel*, borne by the first murder victim mentioned in the Old Testament, who was killed by his brother Cain. **Abel** is a commoner surname spelling than **Abell**. **Ablett**, **Ablitt** and **Ablott** are diminutives, and **Aplin/Applin** (Dorset/Somerset surnames) are double diminutives ('Ab-el-in'), via *Ab*, a pet-form of *Abel*.

Abercrombie/Abercromby P Place-name *Abercrombie*, Fife, Scotland. Scots Gaelic 'mouth of the crooked stream'.

Abernethy P Place-name in Perth and Inverness, Scots Gaelic and British 'mouth/confluence of the *Nethy*'. Most common in southern Scotland and Munster, Ireland. *The Abernethy Biscuit was named after Dr John Abernethy (born 1764), surgeon at St Bartholomew's Hospital in London.*

Able/Ablett/Ablitt/Ablott, *see* Abel.

Abraham/Abram/Abrams/Abramson F From the Hebrew first-name *Avraham*, 'father of a multitude'. *Abraham* (originally *Abram*, 'high father') was the first Jewish patriarch, and both Jewish and gentile families have used *Abraham* as a first-name.

Absalom/Absolom/Absolon/Absolum F From the Hebrew first-name *Avshalom*, 'father of peace'. *Absalom* was the third son of King David, and was killed when his hair became entangled in a tree. **Ashplant**, a strange variant arrived at by folk etymology, is found mainly in Devon.

Acheson, *see* Adam.

Ackerman/Akerman O A farmer, manorial ploughman (compare **Ackers**). Also a Jewish surname, from German *acker* ('field').

Ackers/Acres/Akers T Dweller near a plot of arable land ME *acker* ('field'). The initial letter '*A*' of **Acres** and **Akers** is pronounced long, unlike the '*A*' in surnames such as **Ackerman**. **Ackers** is found chiefly in Lancs and **Acres** in southern counties of England; **Akers**, scattered, is strong in both Oxon and WRYorks.

Acklam P Place-name in ERYorks and NR Yorks OE 'at the oak woods/clearings', exhibiting the use of a dative plural after a lost preposition.

Ackland/Acland P Places-name *Acland* (OE *'Acca*'s lane') *Barton*, Devon, or from other places similarly named. Found chiefly in the west of England, especially Devon. *Joss Ackland, actor, was born in 1928 in North Kensington, London.*

Ackroyd/Acroyd/Akroyd/Aykroyd T Dweller in a clearing within an oak wood OE. Commonest in WRYorks.

Acland, *see* Ackland.

A'Court T/O Dweller at, or worker at, a (manorial) court OF.

Acres, *see* Ackers.

Acroyd, *see* Ackroyd.

Acton P Place-name in several counties OE 'place at the oaks'. Found chiefly in north-west England.

Adair, *see* Edgar.

Adam/Adams F From a first-name, originally Hebrew ('red', from a red skin colour), very popular in England in mediaeval times. Has given rise to many surnames beginning in *Ad-* and *At-* (**Adamson, Addey, Addie, Addis, Addison, Atkin, Atkins** [chiefly Midlands], **Atkinson** [chiefly northern]). Scots forms include **Aiken(s), Aiker(s), Aikin(s), Aitken(s)** and **Aitkin(s).** **Adcock** consists of a diminutive of *Adam*, plus the familiar suffix *-cock*. **Acheson,** a Scots and Border form of **Atkinson** (as are **Atcheson** and **Atchison**), is the family name of the Earls of Gosford.

Adamson/Adcock/Addey/Addie/ Addis/Addison, *see* Adam.

A'Deane T Dweller in or near a valley ME *dene*. A southern English surname.

Adlam/Adlum F From an OF version of the Germanic first-name *Adalhelm* ('noble helmet'). Commonest in the West Country, especially Wilts and Somerset.

Adlard/Allard/Allart/Hallet(t) F From an OF first-name *Adelard* ('noble hard').

Adlington P Place-name in Chesh and Lancs OE 'the place/farm of a family called *Adling* ("prosperity wolf")'. The surname is found mainly in Notts/Derbys. *Rebecca Adlington, the freestyle swimmer who won two gold medals at the Beijing Olympics in 2008, was born in 1989 in Mansfield, Notts.*

Adlum, *see* Adlam.

Adorian, *see* Doran.

Adrian F First-name found in several languages, from Latin *(H)adrianus*, used of a person from the Adriatic Sea. The name of a Roman Emperor and of several popes, including Nicholas Breakspear (Adrian IV).

Affleck/Auchinleck P Scots Gaelic placenames, *Affleck/Auchinleck* ('field of the [flat] stone'), in Ayrshire and Angus, Scotland. *Ben Affleck (Benjamin Geza Affleck), film actor, producer, writer and director, born in 1972 in Berkeley, California, has Scottish and English ancestry on his father's side of the family… Field Marshall Sir Claude (John Eyre) Auchinleck (born in Aldershot, Hants, 1884, died in Marrakesh, Morocco, 1981), was considered by Rommel to be one of the greatest generals of the Second World War.*

Agar/Algar/Alger/Auger/Augur/ Elgar F From the ME first-name *Alger* ('noble/elf/old spear') or ON 'elf spear'. **Agar** is the family name of the Earls of Normanton. *Sir Edward William Elgar (1857–1934), composer and conductor, was born in Broadheath, Worcs, though his father, William Elgar, was a native of Dover in Kent.*

Agate T Dweller by the gate OE. Found chiefly in south-east England.

Agg/Agget(t) F Diminutive of the female first-name *Agace* (Latin *Agatha*,'good').

Agnes/Annis(s) F From a first-name popularly associated with Latin *agnus* (lamb).

Agnew N/P/F Nickname for a meek (lamb-like) person OF *agneau* (lamb); or from the place-name *Agneaux* in La Manche; Irish: Anglicized form of Gaelic **O'Gnimh**, 'descendant of *Gniomh* ("Action")'. Found chiefly in north-west England and Scotland.

Agutter T Dweller near a gutter/drain/watercourse ME. Strongest in south midland counties of England. *The actress Jennifer Ann ('Jenny') Agutter was born in Taunton, Somerset, in 1952.*

Ahern(e)/Hearn(e) F Irish: Anglicized form of Gaelic **O'** [descendant of] hEachthighearna. Commonest in southwest Ireland. *Bertie Ahern, former Irish Taoiseach, was born in 1951 in Dublin.*

Aiken(s)/Aiker(s)/Aikin(s), *see* Adam.

Ailmark, *see* Hallmark.

Ailwyn, *see* Alwin.

Aimes, *see* Ames.

Ainsley/An(ne)sley/Aynsley P Place-names: *Annesley*, Notts OE 'solitary ("one") clearing' or '*An*'s clearing'; *Ansley*, Warwicks OE 'hermitage clearing'. Readily confused with/a variant of **Ainslie**.

Ainslie P Scots surname found mainly in the Borders, from an unidentified place. Readily confused with/a variant of **Ainsley**.

Ainsworth P Place-name in Lancs OW and OE '*Ewan*'s enclosure'.

Aish, *see* Ash.

Aistrope P Place-name *Aisthorpe* in Lincs OE and ON 'eastern settlement'. Readily confused with/a variant of **Astrop**.

Aitken(s)/Aitkin(s), *see* Adam.

Aizlewood, *see* Hazelwood.

Akehurst P Place-name *Akehurst Farm* in Hellingly, Sussex OE 'oak hill/wood', and a Sussex surname.

Akerman, *see* Ackerman.

Akers, *see* Ackers.

Akroyd, *see* Ackroyd.

Alabaster O Corruption by folk etymology of OF *arblaster*, a crossbowman. See **Ballaster**.

Al(l)an/Allen/Alleyn(e)/Alline/Allyn F From an ancient Celtic first-name, especially popular as a first-name in Lincs, where many of William the Conqueror's Breton followers settled. Early Breton stem suggests an origin in Germanic tribal *Alemann* ('all men'), as in the French name for Germany, *Allemagne*. Compare **Alman**. *Edward Alleyn (1566–1626), born in the parish of St Botolph Bishopsgate, London, one of the leading actors of his day, founded Dulwich College and Alleyn's School in south-east London... Rev. Simon Aleyn, who held the living of the thirteenth-century church at Bray, Berks, from 1540 to 1588, and was famous for his religious inconstancy, was the original 'Vicar of Bray'.*

Alban/Albone/Allebone/Allibon(d)/Allibone F/N From the first-name *Alban*, derived from one of the Roman cities of Italy and Gaul named *Alba* (Latin *alba*, 'white'), often used in honour of St Alban, the first British martyr. **Albin/Aubin** could be a variant of **Alban**, or be derived from the Latin word *albus* (white), used for a person of white hair or complexion.

Albert/Allbright/Aubert F From a Germanic first-name, 'noble bright' (compare Modern German *Albrecht*).

Albin/Albone, *see* Alban.

Al(l)cock F A diminutive form of various first-names beginning with *Al-* (*Alban*, *Albert*, etc.) and *cock* ('young lad'). Readily confused with/a variant of **Alcott**.

Alcott T A person living near a cottage OE 'old cottage/hut'. Readily confused with/a variant of **Alcock**. *Louisa May Alcott (1832–1888), author of* Little Women, *was the daughter of Amos Alcott, who had changed his surname from* **Alcox***. The family had English origins: George Alcock, probably from Leics, was an early settler of Massachusetts.*

Alden/Auden F From the first-name *Aldine* ME 'old friend'. Readily confused with/a variant of **Haldane**. *The fondly held belief of the family of the poet and writer W(ystan) H(ugh) Auden (1907–1973) that* *their surname had Icelandic origins would seem to be without foundation.*

Al(l)der/Alderson/Older F/T From OE first-names, *Ealdhere* or *Aethelhere*, or dweller near an alder tree OE. **Older** acknowledges the rounding of *Al-* in southern speech. **Alder** is most commonly found in Northd, **Alderson** in Yorks and Co Durham, and **Older** in the south-east of England.

Alderman O Status term for an elder OE *ealdorman*. Found chiefly in Bucks.

Alderson, *see* **Alder**.

Alderton P Place-name in a number of counties: Salop, Suffolk OE 'farm in the alders'; Gloucs, Northants, Wilts OE 'farm of *Ealdhere*'s people'; Essex OE '?Farm of *Aethelwaru*'s people'. Found chiefly in East Anglia and in the south-east of England.

Al(l)dis/Aldous F/P A pet-form of one of a number of OE first-names beginning with *Ald* (old); or from a place-name in Renfrewshire, Scotland. **Aldis** is most commonly found in Norfolk, **Alldis** in Surrey, **Aldous** in Suffolk.

Aldred/Aldritt/Eldred F/T From the ME first-name *Aldred* ('old counsel') or dweller near alder trees OE. Chiefly a Lancs surname.

Aldrich F From an OE first-name meaning 'old/elf/noble-rule', or a variant of **Aldridge** or **Oldridge**.

Aldridge/Eldridge P Place-name *Aldridge*, Staffs OE 'dairy-farm in the alders', or a variant of **Aldrich** or **Oldridge**.

Aldritt, *see* **Aldred**.

Alefounder O Occupational term for an official appointed by a manorial court to establish the quality of ale, known as an ale-founder or as an ale-conner. Also occasionally found as a first-name.

Alexander/Sander(s)/Sanders(on)/ Sandison/Saunders(on) F From the Greek first-name *Alexander* ('defender of men'), a byname used by Paris, son of King Priam of Troy in Homer's *Iliad*, but also made famous by Alexander the Great. Popularized in the Middle Ages by the spread of apocryphal Alexander Romances. Much favoured in Scotland (where it is commonly shortened to *Sandy*) after the English-born Queen Margaret named a son '*Alexander*'. **Alexander** is the family name of the Earls of Caledon. *See also* **Sandeman**, **Sands**, **Sandy**. *Nicholas Saunderson (c.1683–1739), who was blinded by smallpox at a young age, nevertheless rose to become Professor of Mathematics at Cambridge University. Born in Thirlstone, near Penistone, WRYorks, he reputedly learned to read by tracing out letters on gravestones with his fingers.*

Alford/Alvord P Place-name in a number of English counties OE 'old ford' or OE '?*Ealdgyth*'s ford', or from *Alford* in Aberdeenshire. Found chiefly in western counties of England, especially Devon.

Alfred F From the ME first-name *Alvred/ Alured* ('elf counsel'), most famously borne by King Alfred the Great (849-899).

Algar/Alger, *see* **Agar**.

Alice, *see* **Alis**.

Al(l)is(s)/Alice/Allatt/Allott F From the ME female first-name *Alis* (originally *Adalhaid[is]*, represented by the modern name *Adelaide*). **Al(l)ison** is a Scots diminutive of the same name.

Al(l)ison, *see* **Alis**.

Allan, *see* **Alan**.

Allard/Allart, *see* **Adlard**.

Allatt, *see* **Alis**.

Allbright, *see* **Albert**.

Allcock, *see* **Alcock**.

Allder, *see* **Alder**.

Alldis, *see* **Aldis**.

Allebone, *see* **Alban**.

Allen, *see* **Alan**.

Allenby P From one of two Cumbrian

place-names: *Allonby* and *Ellonby* ON *'Agyllun/Alan's* farm', but chiefly a Lincs surname. *Field-Marshal Viscount (Edmund Henry Hynman) Allenby of Megiddo (1861–1936) was born on the estate of his maternal grandfather, at Brackenhurst, near Southwell, Notts.*

Allerton P Place-name in Lancs, WRYorks, Somerset OE 'place in the alders'. Found chiefly in WRYorks and Lancs.

Alleyn(e), *see* Alan.

Allibon(d)/Allibone, *see* Alban.

Alline, *see* Alan.

Allmark, *see* Hallmark.

Allnutt/Allnatt F From the OE first-name *Aethelnoth*.

Allott, *see* Alis.

Allport P Derbys place-name *Alport* OE 'old market town'. Chiefly a Staffs surname.

Allright/Allwright F From an OE first-name *Aethelric*. Found chiefly in south-eastern counties of England.

Allsop(p), *see* Alsop.

Allston(e), *see* Alston.

Allward, *see* Aylward.

Allwright, *see* Allright.

Allyn, *see* Alan.

Almack, *see* Hallmark.

Alman P A person from Germany, Anglo-Norman French *Aleman* ('all the men'). Compare the Modern French name for Germany, *Allemagne* and the surname **Alan**. Readily confused with/a variant of **Almond**.

Almond F From the OE first-name *Aethelmund* ('noble protection'). Readily confused with/a variant of **Alman**. Chiefly a Lancs surname.

A(l)lsop(p) P Place-name in Derbys, *Alsop en le Dale* OE *'Aelle's* valley': '…the only place-name in the country which could have given rise to this surname' (David

Hey). Chiefly a Derbys/Notts/Staffs surname. *Kenneth Allsop (1920–1973), print and television journalist and author, was born in Yorkshire.*

Al(l)ston(e) F/P From the ME first-name *Alstan*; or from one of a number of place-names, such as as: *Alston* in Cumbd OE *'Halfdan's* farm/village'; *Alston* in Staffs OE *'Aelfweard's* farm/village'; *Alstone* in Gloucs OE *'Aelfsige's* estate'. There are a number of settlements called *Alston* in Devon, with various meanings, such as OE *'Aelfbeorht's* farm/village'/OE *'Aethelnoth's* farm/village'.

Altham P Place-name in Lancs OE 'river-meadow with swans', and most commonly found in that county.

Alton P Place-name found in several counties OE 'old/stream-source' or OE *'Aelfa/Aella/Eanwulf's* place'. Chiefly a Midlands and Northern surname.

Alveston P Place-names: *Alvaston* OE *'Alwald's* farm' in Chesh and Derbys; *Alveston* OE *'Aelfwig's* stone' in Gloucs; *Alveston* OE *'Eanwulf's* farm' in Warwicks.

Alvin, *see* Alwin.

Alvord, *see* Alford.

Alwen, *see* Alwin.

Alwin/Ailwyn/Alvin/Alwen/Alwyn/ Aylwin/Elvin/Elwin/Elwyn F From the ME first-name *Al(f)win*. **Alwin** (scarce) is found mainly in Kent, **Aylwin** in Sussex.

Ambler O/N Occupational name for an enameller, or applied to a walker (ME *ambler*), sometimes used for a person who ambled like a slow horse. In the Prologue to *The Canterbury Tales*, Chaucer makes a point of mentioning the Wife of Bath's horse: '…Up-on an *amblere* esily she sat…' Principally a WRYorks surname. Bizarrely enough, an Irish equivalent is **McCambridge**.

Ambrose F From a mediaeval first-name, from Greek ('immortal'), made popular thanks to St Ambrose, a fourth-century Bishop of Milan and teacher of St Augustine. *Emrys* is a Welsh form. Most commonly found in Cambs and Essex.

Amery/Amory/Emberson/Ember(r)y/ Embry/Em(m)erson/Emery/Emory/ Empson/Emson/Hemery F From a Germanic first-name, *Amalric*. **Amery** and **Amory** are found chiefly in the West Country. **Emmerson** ('son of…') is the commonest of the group. For the family name Heathcoat Amory, see **Heathcote**. *Ralph Waldo Emerson (1803–1882), American essayist and poet, was born in Boston, Massachusetts, the son of a Unitarian minister.*

Ames/Aimes/Amey/Amis(s)/Amos F/N From an OF first-name or nickname, *Amis*, from Latin *amicus* ('friend'). **Amos** was the name of a minor prophet; *Amos* was not used as a first-name in England before the Reformation, and has never been common. *The English writer Kingsley Amis (1922–1995) was born in Clapham, South London, the son of a mustard clerk; his marriage to Hilary Bardwell produced a son, Martin Amis, born in 1949, who is now a well-known novelist in his own right.*

Amey/Amis(s), *see* **Ames**.

Ammon/Amond, *see* **Hammond**.

Amor F/N From a mediaeval first-name or nickname meaning 'love', or a nickname for a person who was exceedingly amorous.

Amory, *see* **Amery**.

Amos, *see* **Ames**.

Ancliff, *see* **Antcliff**.

Anderson, *see* **Andrew**.

Andrew F Originally from the Greek *Andreas* ('manly'), the name of the first of Jesus' disciples. His bones were brought from Saint Regulus to Scotland, of which he is patron saint. Many varieties of the surname exist throughout the Christian world. Although the first-name *Andrew* is a favourite among Scots, as a surname **Andrew** is found chiefly in Cornwall, Devon and Lancs. **Andrew(e)s** is a far more common surname than **Andrew**, and **Anderson** ('son of *Andrew*'), mostly

found in Scotland and in the north of England, is the family name of the Viscounts Waverley. *See also* **Drew**, **Tancock** (mainly found in Devon) and **Tandy** (mainly found in Worcs). *Rob Andrew, England's most capped rugby union fly-half and the highest point-scorer in English rugby history, was born Christopher Robert Andrew in 1963 in Richmond, Yorks.*

Andrewartha P From a Cornish placename *Trewartha*, formerly *Andrewartha*, which has no connexion with the name *Andrew*, the meaning being 'the upper homestead'; *an* is the Cornish (and also Scots Gaelic) definite article (compare **Angove**). Commonest in south-west Cornwall.

Angel(l) N Nickname for an angelic person, from OF *angel* (Latin *angelus*), or for a person who played an angel in a mystery play.

Angove O Cornish, *an* and *gove* 'the smith'. Compare **Goff**.

Angus F/P Scots and Irish: from the Gaelic first-name *Aonghus* ('one choice'); or from the Scottish county of that name, called after an eighth-century Pictish King.

Anker(s) ?F/N A surname of uncertain origin. There is a French first-name *Anchier*, and an 'anchorite' is a recluse. Yet the surname, found in Chesh and elsewhere, is also very prominent in Cambs, and could well have been brought to Hatfield and Sandtoft, Yorks, thence to Whittlesey and Thorney, Cambs, by one or more families originally named **Hancar**, **Hanchor** or **Anchor**, who worked on the drainage of the fens alongside Cornelius Vermuyden. The similar French surname **Hancard** is from a pet-form of *Je(han)* with a double suffix *-ek* and *-ard*.

Ann(e) F/P From the first-name *Hanna(h)*, Hebrew '(God) has favoured me', said in an apocryphal gospel to be the Blessed Virgin's mother. The first-name *Ann* is not recorded in England until the 1200s, so the surname could be a diminutive of *Agnes*. Or from a place called *Ann* (named after a local brook) in Hants.

Annable/Hannable/Hannibal/ Honeyball/Hunnable/Hunneyball/ Hunneybell/Hunnibal/Hunnibell F

From the first-name *Annable*, a corruption of *Amable/Amabel* (Latin *amabilis*, 'lovable', French *aimable*, English *amiable*). Compare the female first-names *An(n)abell(a)*, *Arabell(a)* and *Mabel*. **Annable** is a Derbys surname; the classical-sounding **Hannibal**, very scarce, is found mainly in Lancs.

Annesley, *see* Ainsley.

Annett F Diminutive of the first-names *Agnes/Ann/Annis*. Chiefly a Northd surname.

Annis(s), *see* Agnes.

Ansell/Anselm F From a Germanic first-name, brought to France and England by St *Anselm*. Chiefly an East Anglian and south-east-of-England surname. A man bearing the extraordinary name of 'Percy *Stonehenge* W. **Ansell**' was born in 1874 – not in Wilts, but in the parish of St Olave, Southwark, London. *Ansell's Brewery, noted in its later years for its unpalatable fizzy beer, was founded in 1857 by Joseph Ansell, hopmaster and maltster, at Aston Park, Birmingham.*

Ansley, *see* Ainsley.

Anslow P Place-name in Staffs OE '*Eanswith*'s wood/clearing'. Found mainly in Staffs and Salop.

Anstey/Anstee/Anstie P Place-names: *Anstey* (Leics, Herts, Hants, Dorset, Devon), *Ansty* (Warwicks, Wilts, Sussex, Dorset). From OE *anstiga* ('one path', that is, a road with a fork at both ends). Principally West Country surnames. Readily confused with/variants of **Anstice**.

Anstice/Ansteys/Anstis F From the ME first-name *Ansta(y)se* or the female *Anastasie* (Greek: 'resurrection'). Popularized by the female Saint *Anastasia*, rather than the male Saint *Anastasius*. Readily confused with/variants of **Anstey**. The European surnames **Nastase/Nastasi** have the same origin.

Anstie, *see* Anstey.

Anstis, *see* Anstice.

Anstruther P Place-name in Fife, Scotland, Scots Gaelic: 'the stream' (*an* being the definite article, as in Cornish: compare the surnames **Andrewartha**, **Angove**).

Antcliff(e)/Ancliff P Place-names: *Arnecliff*, *Ingleby*, *Arncliffe* (NRYorks); *Arncliffe* (WRYorks) OE: 'eagle's cliff'. Found chiefly in WRYorks.

Ant(h)ony F From the first-name, derived from Latin *Antonius*. Many varieties exist throughout Europe, with or without the intrusive letter 'h'. *Saint Anthony's fire* (erysipelas) is derived from an Egyptian hermit of that name.

Antrobus P Place-name in Chesh ON '*Eindrithi/Andrithi*'s bush'.

Anyan/Anyon, *see* Onion.

Aplin, *see* Abel.

Appelbe(e), *see* Appleby.

Apperley P Place-name in Gloucs, Northd, WRYorks OE 'wood-clearing with apple trees'. Chiefly a Herefords surname.

Appleby/Appelbe(e) P Place-name in Westmd, Leics, Lincs OE and ON 'apple farm'. Chiefly a Northd and Co Durham surname.

Applegarth/Applegate/Applegath P Place-name *Applegarth* in Cumbd, ERYorks, NRYorks ON 'apple enclosure, orchard'. Chiefly a Co Durham surname. *Robert Applegarth (1834–1924), the prominent trade unionist and fighter for working-class causes, was born in Hull… Adam Applegarth, born in Sunderland in 1962, was Chief Executive Officer of the Northern Rock Bank at the time when it suffered a severe financial crisis in the year 2007.*

Appleton P Place-name in Chesh, Norfolk, NRYorks, Berks, Lancs, Suffolk OE 'apple farm'. Chiefly a Yorks/Lancs surname.

Applewhite P Place-names in Cumbd and Westmd, and a lost village in Suffolk OE and ON 'clearing with apples'. Found chiefly in Lincs.

Appleyard T/P Dweller at an apple orchard OE, or from a place-name in WRYorks, with the same meaning. Found chiefly in WRYorks.

Applin, *see* Abel.

Apps T/N Dweller near an aspen tree OE, or a nickname for a timid person who is wont to tremble like the leaves of such a tree. Found in south-eastern counties of England, especially Kent.

April/Averell/Averill/Everill N Nickname for a person born or baptized during the month of April, or who was spring-like and youthful, or changeable, like the weather in April T. S. Eliot's 'cruellest month' in *The Waste Land*). Not generally known as a first-name.

Aram/Arram P Place-names: *Arram* ERYorks ON 'at the shielings'; *Averham* Notts ('?settlement at the floods'). Found chiefly in Midland counties of England.

Arbury/Arber(r)y T/P Dweller by the earthworks OE; or from a place-name *Arbury*, with the same meaning, in Herts and Lancs – though these are chiefly West Country surnames.

Arbuthnot(t) P Scottish place-name *Arbuthnott*, near Aberdeen, Scots Gaelic 'mouth of the little holy/healing stream'.

Archbald/Archbell/Archbo(u)ld/Archbutt/Archibald F English and Scots, from a Norman first-name *Archambault* ('precious-bold'). As a surname, commonest in Scotland, and much favoured as a first-name by the Douglas and Campbell families.

Archdeacon O Occupational term for a bearer of the ecclesiastical office of 'chief deacon' to a bishop OE, from Latin. Such a man should have been celibate, but his servants could have acquired the name by association. Found chiefly in Lancs.

Archer O A professional or amateur bowman, famed for his archery skills OF *arch(i)er*.

Archibald, *see* Archbald.

Arden P Place-name *Arden* in Warwicks (hence the connexion with Shakespeare's mother, Mary **Arden**) and NRYorks OE 'dwelling place'. One branch of the **Arden** family can trace its origins back to a time before the Norman Conquest – a very rare accomplishment. By the late nineteenth century **Arden**, together with **Ardern** and **Hardern** (apparently variant forms), was chiefly found in Chesh, and settlements in that county bearing names such as *Arden* and *Ardern* probably acquired them from family names, rather than vice versa. **Hardern** is readily confused with/a variant of **Harden**.

Ardern, *see* Arden.

Argall, *see* Arkell.

Argent N/O Nickname for a person of wealth, of silver hair colour, or who worked in the silver trades OF *argent* ('silver'). Found chiefly in East Anglia.

Arkell/Argall/Arkill/Arkle F From an ON first-name *Arnkell* ('eagle cauldron'). **Arkell** is most commonly found in the West Midlands, **Arkle** in Northd. *Arkle (1957–1970), the famous Irish racehorse, was named after Arkle, a mountain in the Scottish highlands.*

Arkenstall, *see* Arkinstall.

Arkill, *see* Arkell.

Arkinstall/Arkenstall/Artin(g)stall P Bardsley supposes that a place called *Artinstall* must be the origin here, but adds: 'I do not know the precise spot, nor can I say whether it is in Lancashire or Cheshire'. He quotes examples of the surname in use, indicating its development from **Artonstall** (1578) to **Arstall** and **Artenstall** (both these latter variants having died out in the British Isles by the time of the 1881 census). In the event we can say with some degree of certainty that the origin lies in the now-lost place-name *Alretunstall* in Timperley, Chesh OE 'alder tree farm'. A family history researcher, Mrs C. Doughty of Co Durham, has found no fewer than fifteen variants of such a surname: **Arkinstall, Arkinstal, Applestone, Appleston, Arkinstone, Arkinston, Ardinshaw, Ardinstow, Apleston, Appestone, Appliston, Apliston, Arkenstall, Harkinstall, Harkinstal.** Arkinstall and **Arkenstall** (very scarce) are mainly found in Staffs, **Artinstall** and **Artingstall** in Lancs.

Arkle, *see* Arkell.

Arkwright O Occupational term for a maker of chests OF *arc*. Most common in Lancs. The scarce Chesh variant **Hattrick** has no connexion with the game of cricket... *Sir Richard Arkwright (1732–1792), pioneer of the Industrial Revolution, was born in Preston, Lancs.*

Arlet(t)(e), *see* Arlott.

Arley P Place-name in Chesh, Lancs, Warwicks, Worcs OE 'eagle wood'. An exceptionally scarce scattered surname.

Arlott(e)/Arlet(t)(e) N Nickname for a fellow, chap, rogue, rascal, wandering entertainer ME. 'Harlot', for a lady of easy virtue, was a later development. *The Hampshire accent of (Leslie Thomas) John Arlott (1914–1991), sports commentator, born in Basingstoke, was once said to be 'the sound of summer' during the English cricket season.*

Armatrading, *see* Armitread.

Armer, *see* Armour.

Armetriding, *see* Armitread.

Armistead/Armitstead T Dweller near a hermit's cell, OF and OE 'hermit's place'. Until the late eighteenth century, the spelling 'er' was commonly rendered as 'ar' in spoken English – *serve* being pronounced *sarve*, etc. – and certain words which are currently spelt with an *er* formerly used an *ar* spelling to reflect this earlier pronunciation. This older pronunciation persists in the case of *clerk, Berkshire, Derby*, etc. Compare the surnames **Armitage** (hermitage) and **Farmery** (infirmary). **Armistead** is chiefly a Cumbd/Lancs/Westmd surname.

Armitage/Armytage T/P A person who lived by a hermitage (compare **Armistead**) OF. But not just any old hermitage – George Redmonds has shown that most, if not all, present-day **Armitage**s have their origins in *Hermitage Bridge* in Almondbury, near Huddersfield WRYorks. The surname **Hermitage**, very scarce, belongs mainly to Kent. The will of John **Hermitage**, alias **Armitage**, mariner aboard HMS *Pembroke*, was proved in London in 1750.

Armitread/Armatrading/Armetriding P Place-name *Armetriding* in Lancs ME 'hermit clearing'. Exceptionally scarce northwest of England surnames. *Joan Armatrading, born in 1950 in Basseterre, St Kitts, West Indies (but whose family moved to Birmingham in 1958), was the first black female singer-songwriter based in Britain to compete on equal terms with white singers.*

Armitstead, *see* Armistead.

Armour/Armer/Larmo(u)r O Occupational term for a maker of arms and armour OF.

Armstrong N Nickname for a person who was strong in the arm OE. Very much a surname from the English/Scottish border (along with **Kerr, Elliot**, etc.).

Armytage, *see* Armitage.

Arnaud, *see* Arnold.

Arnold/Arnaud/Arnot(t) F/P From a Norman personal name meaning 'Eagle Power', or from places called *Arnold* in Notts/ERYorks. **Yarnold**, chiefly a Worcs surname, is said to be an early corruption of **Arnold**. *Thomas Arnold, headmaster of Rugby School, was born at East Cowes, Isle of Wight, in 1795; his son Matthew Arnold, the well-known poet, was born at Laleham, Middx (where his father was then the parish priest) in 1822... Sir Malcolm Arnold (1921–2006), born in Northampton to a family of well-to-do shoemakers, was a musician of eclectic tastes who was the first British composer to win an Oscar – for his* *musical score to the film* Bridge on the River Kwai.

Arram, *see* Aram.

Arrindell, *see* Arundel.

Arrington P Place-name in Cambs OE 'the place of the *Earningas*', or a variant of **Harrington**. A very scarce scattered surname.

Arrowsmith O Occupational term for an arrow-maker OE. **Arrowsmith** is found chiefly in Lancs, Chesh and Staffs; **Harri-smith** is a very scarce NRYorks variant.

Arthur F From a Celtic first-name, popular since mediaeval times thanks to the legend of King Arthur, a British leader who repelled the Saxon invaders and was pre-sumably a romanized Briton with a first-name derived from a Latin family name *Artorius* – though Celtic sources have also been suggested.

Artin(g)stall, *see* Arkinstall.

Arundale, *see* Arundel.

Arundel(l)/Arrindell/Arundale P/N Place-name in West Sussex OE 'horehound valley'; or a nickname for a person resem-bling a swallow OF *arondel* (Modern French *hirondelle*).

Asch(e), *see* Ash.

Ascombe, *see* Ashcomb.

Ascot(t) P Place-names in several counties, including *Ascot* (Berks) and *Ascott* (Bucks) OE 'eastern cottage/hut'.

Ascroft, *see* Ashcroft.

Ash(e)/Aish/Asch(e)/Aysh T/P Dweller by an ash-tree OE, or from one of a number of place-names with the same meaning. The source of surnames like **Dash**, **Nash**, **Rash**, **Tash**. *See also* **Aske** and **Esh**. *Claudius Ash (1792–1854), goldsmith and dental manu-facturer, was the first person to manufacture a set of viable modern dentures, made of porcel-ain and gold. Although he was born in Bethnal Green, London, his male-line ancestry can be traced back to a family of yeomen living around Cannock Manor in Staffs.*

Ashbee, *see* Ashby.

Ashbridge T/P Dweller near the ash trees, or a corruption of *Ashridge*, Herts OE 'ash tree ridge' – though this is a surname prin-cipally found in north and north-east Eng-land.

Ashbrook P There is such a place-name in Gloucs OE 'eastern brook', but the surname is mainly found in Chesh (where there flows the *Ash Brook* OE 'ash-tree brook') and Lancs.

Ashburner O Occupational term for a burner of ashes, one who made potash by burning ashes of wood, weeds, or straw OE. Chiefly found in Furness and the Lake Dis-trict.

Ashby/Ashbee P Place-name in various counties, chiefly in the English Midlands, the most significant being *Ashby de la Zouch* in Leics ON 'ash tree farm'.

Ashcomb(e)/Ascombe P Place-name *Ash-combe* in Devon and Somerset OE 'ash tree valley'.

Ashcroft/Ascroft P From an unidentified place-name OE 'ash paddock/enclosure'. The first known reference to *Ashcroft*, Berks, only dates from the mid sixteenth century. Chiefly a Lancs surname in both spellings. *Dame Peggy (Edith Margaret Emily) Ashcroft (1907–1991), highly acclaimed actress, was born in Croydon, Surrey.*

Ashdown P Place-names: *Ashdown (Forest)*, Sussex, and *Ashdon* Essex OE 'ash-tree hill'. *Ashdown* is the former name of the Berk-shire Downs OE '?*Aesc*'s/ash-tree hill'. Found chiefly in south-eastern counties of England, especially Kent. *Paddy (Jeremy John Durham) Ashdown, former leader of the Liberal Democrat Party, was born in New Delhi, India, in 1941, where his father was a Captain in the Indian Army. Having been brought up chiefly in Northern Ireland, he acquired the nickname 'Paddy'.*

Ashe, *see* Ash.

Ashenden T/P Dweller in a valley in which ash trees grow, or from the place-names

Ashendon in Bucks OE 'hill covered with ash trees', or even *Ashington*, Northd. Found chiefly in south-eastern counties of England, especially Kent.

Ashfield P Place-name in Suffolk, Herefords, Hants, Suffolk, Notts OE 'open land with ash trees'.

Ashford P Place-names in several counties, including *Ashford*, Kent, and *Ashford-in-the-Water*, Derbys OE 'ash tree ford'.

**Ashkettle/(H)askel(l)/Astell/Astill/
Astle/Eskell/Haskin(g)** F From the ON first-name *Asketill* ('God-sacrifical cauldron'). The variation **Axtell** exhibits the common regional pronunciation whereby *-sk* is rendered as *-x* (also in evidence when the word *ask* becoming *axe*). Readily confused with/a variant of **Astle**. **Ashkettle** itself is exceptionally scarce; **Astill** is found mainly in Leics and Notts.

Ashley P Place-name in several counties OE 'ash tree wood/glade/clearing'.

Ashman O/T Occupational term for a sailor, pirate OE; or a dweller by an ash-tree. Chiefly a Somerset surname.

Ashmead T/P Dweller by an ash-tree meadow OE, or from a place-name in Gloucs with the same meaning. Chiefly a Gloucs surname.

Ashmore P There is such a place-name in Dorset OE 'ash-tree pool', but the surname is found chiefly in Derbys, and also in Worcs (where it is probably derived from *Ashmoor Common* in Kempsey OE 'eastern marsh-land').

Ashplant, *see* **Absalom**.

Ashton P Place-name in many counties OE 'ash-tree farm/place', including *Ashton-under-Lyne* near Manchester. Found chiefly in Lancs, Chesh and WRYorks

Ash(h)urst P Place-name in Kent, Surrey, Sussex OE 'ash tree hill/wood'. Found chiefly in Lancs (and derived there from *Ashurst Beacon*, Wigan?).

Ashwell P Place-names in Herts, Rutland, Somerset OE 'stream/string in the ash trees'. Chiefly a Herts surname.

Ashwin F From an OE first-name *Aescwine* ('spear friend'), borne by a King of Wessex in the seventh century.

Ashwood T/P Dweller by an ash-tree wood OE, or from a minor place-name with the same meaning (such as the one in Staffs).

Ashworth P Place-names in Lancs and elsewhere OE 'enclosure in the ash trees'. Chiefly a Lancs/WRYorks surname.

Ask(h)am P Place-names in Notts, WRYorks, Westmd OE 'homestead in the ash trees'. Found chiefly in WRYorks.

Aske P/T Place-name in NRYorks ON 'ash tree', or a variation of **Ash**. *The Askes were a prominent family with origins in the North Riding of Yorkshire, to which belonged: Robert Aske (1500–1537), leader of the Pilgrimage of Grace, who was executed for treason at York in 1537; Robert Aske (1619–1689), City of London merchant, who is chiefly remembered for his charitable foundations, including the Haberdashers' Aske's schools; and John Aske, regicide.*

Askel(l), *see* **Ashkettle**.

Askew/Askey/Ayscough/Haskew/Haskey P Place-name *Aiskew* in NRYorks ON 'oak wood'. *The much-loved comedian Arthur (Bowden) Askey (1900–1982) was a native of Liverpool.*

Askham, *see* **Askam**.

Askwith, *see* **Asquith**.

Aspinal(l)/Aspinell/Aspinwall P Place-name *Aspinwall* in Lancs OE 'spring/stream/well in the aspens (trembling poplars)'.

Asquith/Askwith P Place-name *Askwith*, WRYorks ON 'ash tree wood'. *Herbert Henry (universally known as 'H.H.') Asquith, First Earl of Oxford and Asquith (1852–1928), who served as Liberal Prime Minister of the United Kingdom, 1908–1916, was born in Morley, WRYorks, son of Joseph Dixon Asquith and Emily (Willans).*

Astell, *see* **Ashkettle** and **Astle**.

Asterley P Place-names: *Asterley* in Salop and *Asterleigh* in Oxon OE 'eastern clearing'. Found chiefly in Montgomeryshire, Wales.

Astill, *see* **Ashkettle**.

Astle/Astel(l) P Place-name *Astle* in Chesh OE 'eastern hill'. Readily confused with/a variant of **Ashkettle**.

Astley P Place-name in Warwicks and elsewhere OE 'eastern wood/clearing'. Chiefly a Warwicks surname. Family name of the Barons Hastings.

Aston T/P Dweller near a large stone (ME 'at stone'), or from a place-name found in over a dozen English counties, of which ten are in Salop OE 'eastern place'. Found chiefly in Staffs.

Astrop P Place-name in Northants OE and ON 'eastern settlement'. Readily confused with/a variant of **Aistrope**.

Astwood P Place-name in Bucks, Worcs OE 'eastern wood'.

Atcheson/Atchison/Atkin(s)/Atkin-son, *see* **Adam**.

Atherton P Place-name in Lancs OE '*Ather*'s place'. *Mike Atherton, who captained the England cricket team in more test matches than any other player, was born in Failsworth, near Oldham, Lancs, in 1968.*

Athol(l) P Place-name in Scotland, Scots Gaelic 'New Ireland'. **Atlay/Atlee/Atley**, *see* **Attlee**.

Attack T Dweller at an oak (OE *ac*) tree. A scarce surname, with a presence in WRYorks.

Attenborough T A dweller at the manor house ME *atte* and *burh*. Found chiefly in Notts and Derbys, though the place in Notts, which was not a village in the Middle Ages, is neither the origin, nor of the same derivation, being *Adda's burh*. *The Attenborough brothers, Richard [Samuel] (born 1923, Cambridge) and David [Frederick] (born 1926, London), were the sons of Frederick Attenborough, Principal of University College,* *Leicester. Richard became famous as a film and stage actor, director and producer, and David as a much-loved presenter of natural history TV programmes and a television executive. Their grandfather ran a corner shop in Stapleford, Notts, near the village of Attenborough.*

Atthill T Dweller at the hill ME. A long-established Norfolk surname.

Attlee/Atlay/Atlee/Atley/Attley T Dweller at the meadow, pasture ME, the second -*t*- being the remains of the definite article (*the*). A rare surname in all spellings: **Attlee** and **Atlee** can be found in Surrey, **Atlay** in NRYorks, **Atley** in Co Durham and WRYorks, **Attley** in Co Durham and Northants. Compare **Lee**. *The male-line ancestry of former Prime Minister Clement [Richard] Attlee, Earl Attlee, can be traced back to Ralph Attlee, son of John, who was buried in Cobham, Surrey, in 1619.*

Attridge, *see* **Etheredge**.

Attwater, *see* **Atwater**.

Attwick T Dweller at the dairy-farm OE. A very scarce Sussex surname.

Attwill, *see* **Atwell**.

Attwood, *see* **Atwood**.

Attwool(l), *see* **Atwell**.

At(t)water T Dweller at the water ME.

At(t)well/At(t)will/Attwool(l)/Twell(s) T Dweller at the well or stream ME. **Atwell** is mainly found in Somerset, **Attwell** in Middx, **Atwill** in Devon/Somerset, **Attwill** (very scarce) in south and south-western counties of England, **Attwool** in Hants and Somerset, **Attwooll** in Dorset, **Twell** in Lincs and **Twells** in Notts. One prominent **Twells** family can trace its origins back to Godfrey **Twells**, born in Nottingham, who married Margaret Rogers of Chesterton, Cambs, and moved to Cambridge in 1620. *Winifred Atwell (1914–1983), accomplished player of both ragtime and classical piano, was born in Trinidad and ended her career in Australia.*

At(t)wood T Dweller at the wood OE. Chiefly found in Kent.

Atyeo T Dweller by the river OE, a south-west dialect form. Principally a Somerset surname. *John Atyeo (1932–1993), Portsmouth, Bristol City and England footballer, was born in Dilton Marsh, Wilts.*

Aubert, *see* Albert.

Aubin, *see* Alban.

Aubray/Aubrey/Aubry/Avery/Awber(r)y F From the Germanic first-name *Alberic*, via ME/OF *Aubri*. **Avery** is chiefly a south-of-England surname.

Auchinleck, *see* Affleck.

Auckland P Place-name in Co Durham, originally said to be Celtic; possibly a form of *Alclyde* (the former name of *Dumbarton*), meaning 'cliff/rock on the Clyde'. There are records of the surname being used in Yorks as early as the thirteenth century; by the late nineteenth century it could mostly be found in Lincs and WRYorks. *In 1840 Captain William Hobson, first Governor of New Zealand, named the town of Auckland in honour of his patron, Lord Auckland, then Viceroy of India, whose family name was Eden.*

Auden, *see* Alden.

Auger, *see* Agar.

Aughton P Place-names in Lancs, Wilts, ERYorks and WRYorks OE 'place in the oaks'.

Augur, *see* Agar.

Augustine, *see* Austin.

Auld/Ault T/N Dweller at a hill, from Welsh *allt* (pronounced 'olt' in England); or from a Scottish form of the adjective 'old'. **Auld** is found mainly in Scotland, **Ault** in the English Midlands, especially Derbys.

Austin/Augustine/Austen F From the ME/OF first-name *Austin*, a vernacular form of Latin *Augustinus*. *St Augustine* of Hippo (354–430) and *St Augustine* of Canterbury (died c.605) were well-known and respected saints. *Jane Austen (1775–1817), the novelist, was born at the rectory in Steventon, Hants, the daughter of Rev. George Austen (from a Kentish family) and Cassandra (née Leigh).*

Avent N/F Nickname for a fitting, handsome person OF *avenant*, used also as a first-name. Chiefly a Devon surname.

Averell/Averill, *see* April.

Avery/Awber(r)y, *see* Aubray.

Awre P Place-name in Gloucs ?OE 'alder tree', and found almost exclusively in that county.

Axtell, *see* Ashkettle.

Aychbowm/Aychbown, *see* Ayckbourn.

Ayckbourn T From the German surname *Eichbaum* (oak tree), via **Aychbowm/Aychbown/Ayckbowm/Ayckbown**. Emigrants from Germany brought this name to Ireland in the eighteenth century, thence to England in the nineteenth century. For further details, see pages 27–29. *Alan Ayckbourn, the English dramatist closely associated with the town of Scarborough, Yorks, was born in London in 1939.*

Ayckbowm/Ayckbown, *see* Ayckbourn.

Ayer(s)/Ayre/Eyre(s)/Hair N/P Nickname for a person known to be the heir to a title or a significant inheritance ME from OF; or, in Scotland, from the place-name *Ayr*. One branch of the **Eyre** family from Wilts can trace its origins back to a crusader, Humphrey **Le Heyr**. The **Eyres** also prospered in Derbys and elsewhere. When Enos Rose married a woman bearing the first-names Mary Ann in Allington, Wilts, in 1859, her surname was spelt in three different ways on the marriage certificate: her surname, and that of her father, is shown as **Eyres**, but Mary Ann signed her name as **Ayres**, and a family witness signed as **Ayers**.

Aykroyd, *see* Ackroyd.

Ayler O Occupational term for a garlic-seller OF. A south-of-England surname.

Ayliff(e) F From the ME female first-name *Ayleve/Aylgive* or the ON byname *Eilifr*. There would appear to be no connexion with the village of *Aycliffe*, Co Durham. Found chiefly in southern counties of England.

Aylmer/Aylmore F From the ME first-name *Ailmar*. Readily confused with/a variant of **Elmar** or **Elmore**. *Sir Felix Aylmer (1889–1979), the distinguished actor, was born in Corsham, Wilts.*

Aylward/Allward F From a Germanic first-name OE *Aethelweard*. Found chiefly in southern counties of England, especially Hants. *Gladys Aylward, born in London c.1902, the daughter of a postman, became a missionary in China; her life there formed the basis of the film* Inn of the Sixth Happiness.

Aylwin, *see* **Alwin**.

Aynsley, *see* **Ainsley**.

Ayre, *see* **Ayer**.

Ayscough, *see* **Askew**.

Aysh, *see* **Ash**.

B

Babb(s)/Babbage F From the female first-name *Babb*, a pet-form of *Barbara*, or from the OE first-name *Babba*. **Babcock** and **Bab(b)it(t)(s)** are diminutives; some USA **Babbitt**s claim descent from a settler named **Bobet**. **Babbage** is probably from the same source, though Bardsley wonders whether it might not be derived from an unidentified Devon place-name with the *Babb-* element (as in *Babbacombe*). *See also* **Bebb**. *Charles Babbage (1791–1871), inventor of the first calculating-machine/computer, is said to have been born near Teignmouth, Devon, though he was baptized at St Mary Newington, Surrey, the son of a London banker with Devon origins. He is buried at Kensal Green Cemetery, London.*

Babbington, *see* Babington.

Babbit(t)(s), *see* Babb.

Babcock, *see* Babb and Badcock.

Babington/Babbington P Place-names: *Babbington* (Notts); *Babington* (Somerset), *Bavington* (Northd) OE '*Babba*'s settlement'. Widespread in both spellings. Readily confused with/a variant of **Bebbington**. *The historian Thomas Babington (or Babbington) Macaulay (1800–1859) was born in Leicestershire… The Babington Plot, a doomed plan to assassinate Queen Elizabeth I and to install Mary Queen of Scots on the throne, was named after Anthony Babington (1561–1586), a young Roman Catholic gentleman who was born at Dethick Manor, Derbys, in 1561.*

Babit(t)(s), *see* Babb.

Bacchus, *see* Backhouse.

Bach(e) T Dweller by a stream ME *bache*. Scattered surnames, **Bache** having a distinctive presence in Staffs. **Bach** is also well known, of course, as a German surname.

Ba(t)chelor/Batchelar/Batchelder/ Batcheldor/Batchel(l)er/Batchel(l)or/ Batchelour O Status/occupational term for a young knight, novice in arms ME, OF *bacheler*, which eventually acquired the meaning of an unmarried man.

Back T/F/N Dweller by a ridge or hill OE; or from the OE first-name *Bacca*; or a nickname for a hunchback OE. **Bax** is 'son of **Back**'.

Backhouse/Bacchus/Backus T/O Dweller at, or worker at, a bake house OE *boechus*. The surname of a well-known family of Quaker bankers from the north of England.

Bacon O/F Occupational term for a bacon seller, pork butcher OF; or from the Germanic first-name *Bacco/Bahho* (compare **Bagg**). **Bagot** and **Bagehot** are diminutive forms; the trio of characters known as Bushy, **Bagot** and Green appear in Shakespeare's play *Richard II*.

Badcock F Diminutive from the first-names *Bartholomew* (via *Bad/Bat*) or *Badda* OE, plus *cock* ('little lad'). Sometimes corrupted to **Babcock**. **Badcock** is found chiefly in Berks, Devon and Somerset, where there is a *Badcox Lane* in the town of Frome.

Badder, *see* Bather.

Badman F Servant of *Bartholomew* (*Badd*, *Batt*), just as **Jackman/Jakeman** means 'servant of *Jack*', and so on. Chiefly a Somerset surname.

Badrick/Batt(e)rick/Betteridge F From the OE first-name *Beaduric*. **Badrick** can be found in Bucks; **Batterick** and **Battrick** are Dorset variants; **Betteridge** is strongest in Hants, Oxon and Warwicks.

Bagehot, *see* Bacon.

Bagg(e) O/F Occupational term for a maker of bags, or from the Germanic first-name *Bacco/Bahho* (see **Bacon**). **Bagg** is chiefly a Dorset/Somerset surname; **Bagge** is strongest in Middx and Norfolk.

Bagley/Baggaley/Bag(g)uley P Place-names: *Bagley* in Berks, Salop, Somerset, WRYorks; *Baguley* in Chesh, all OE '?*Bacga*'s wood/bag-shaped animal's wood'.

Bagot, *see* Bacon.

Bagshaw P Place-name in Derbys OE '*Bacga*'s wood', and a surname mainly found in that county.

Baguley, *see* Bagley.

Bail(e)/Bale(s)/Bayle(s) T Dweller near the outer-court wall of a castle (as in *motte and bailey*) ME *bail(e)*.

Bailey/Baillie/Baylie(s)/Baylis(s)/Bayl(e)y/ O/T/P Occupational term for a bailiff, a crown official, a king's officer in a county, hundred or town, keeper of a royal building or demesne, sheriff's deputy, or even an agent/factor ME *bail(l)i*. A Scots alderman is still referred to as a *bailie*. Or (as in **Baile**), a dweller near the outer wall of a castle (compare the Old *Bailey*, London). Or from the place-name *Bailey* in Lancs OE 'berry wood/clearing'. The surname exhibits a wide range of spellings. **Bailey** is the family name of the Barons Glanusk.

Bain(e)/Bayne(s) O/N Occupational term for an attendant at a public bath-house of *baine* ('bath'); or a nickname for a tall skinny man (from 'bone', as in 'all skin and bone'), or for someone who was direct, obliging, hospitable ON *beinn* ('straightforward, direct'); Scots: nickname for a fair-haired person, Gaelic *ban* ('white').

Bainbridge P Place-names: Co Durham, WRYorks ON 'straight/direct/handy bridge', NRYorks ON 'bridge over the river *Bain*'. Unsurprisingly, a north-of-England surname. *Dame Beryl Bainbridge, the English novelist with a special interest in her own family's history, was born in Liverpool in 1934 and raised in nearby Formby.*

Baine, *see* Bain.

Bainton, *see* Baynton.

Baird O Scots: occupational term for a poet/minstrel, Gaelic *bard*. Family name of the Viscounts Stonehaven. *John Logie Baird (1888–1946), television pioneer, was born in Helensburgh, Argyll, Scotland, where an impressive bust created in his memory can now be seen.*

Bairstow/Baistow/Barstow/Bastow P Place-name *Bairstow* WRYorks OE 'place where berries grow'. Most commonly found in WRYorks, especially in Bradford, where it is first recorded in the thirteenth century. Subject to a range of variant spellings and misspellings, and readily confused with/a variant of **Burstall** and **Burstow** (see **Bristow**). *Stan Barstow, the English writer whose works include the well-known novel* A kind of loving *(1960), was born in 1928 in Horbury, Yorks.*

Baisbrown(e) P Place-name in Westmd ON 'cowshed edge'.

Baistow, *see* Bairstow.

Baker O Occupational name for a baker ME *bakere*, who worked in the kitchens of a large house, or who was in charge of a communal oven. Found as a surname all over England, though rarer in the north.

Bakewell P Place-name in Derbys OE '*Badeca*'s stream/spring'. The surname **Bakewell** is found chiefly in the Midland counties of Derbys, Leics and Staffs, while the variants **Balkwell** and **Balkwill** are most commonly encountered in Bucks and Gloucs. *Robert Bakewell (1725–1795), agricultural pioneer and stock breeder, was born at Dishley (otherwise Dixley), near Loughborough, Leics… The television presenter Joan Bakewell (once* described by Frank Muir as 'the thinking man's crumpet') was born Joan Dawson Rowlands in Stockport, Chesh (near the border with Derbys), in 1933, and acquired the Bakewell surname when she married Michael Bakewell.

Balch, *see* Belch.

Balderston(e)/Bolders(t)on P From one of two places called *Balderston(e)* in Lancs OE '*Bealdhere*'s farm', or from a place in West Lothian, Scotland, with the same etymology.

Balding, *see* Baud.

Baldock P Place-name in Herts, so-named in the twelfth century by the Knights Templars, who held the manor, in honour of the city of *Baghdad* ME/OF *Baldac*. A surname principally found in Kent.

Baldrick/Baldree/Baldr(e)y/Boldero(e) F From a Germanic personal name, meaning 'bold ruler'. Found chiefly in East Anglia. *To those whose understanding of mediaeval times has been conditioned by the television series Blackadder, the name Baldrick will forever be associated with the character of that name, a former dung-shoveller played by Tony Robinson, who acted as sidekick and punchbag to Edmund Blackadder.*

Baldwin F From a Germanic first-name, meaning 'bold friend', borne by various Crusader Kings of Jerusalem.

Bale(s), *see* Bail.

Balfe N Irish: nickname for a stammering, dumb person, Gaelic *Balbh*.

Balfour P There are several places so-called in the Highlands of Scotland, Scots Gaelic *Bail(e)puir* 'village with pasture'. Traditionally pronounced Bal*four*, but more commonly Bal*four* (the opposite being the case with the Scots surname **Lamont**, L*amont* in Scotland, L*amont* once Anglicized). Family name of the Barons Kinross and the Barons Riverdale. *Arthur James Balfour, First Earl of Balfour (1848–1930), British statesman and Prime Minister, was born at Whittingehame, East Lothian, Scotland.*

Balhatchet O Occupational term for an executioner OF (literally 'give the axe'). A rare surname, found principally in Devon and Cornwall, with a few examples in Worcs. R. S. Charnock, in *Patronymica Cornu-Britannica* (1870), derives this surname, as found in Cornwall, from *bal* (a parcel of tin works) and *valas* (to dig), but says that 'Gilbert gives the local name *Ballachize*... but he is probably speaking of Ireland'.

Balkwell/Balkwill, *see* Bakewell.

Ball(s) N/T/F Nickname for a fat ball-shaped person ME, or referring to a bald person, or to someone who lived by a bulbous-looking hill, or from the ON first-name *Balle*. **Ball** is principally found in Lancs, and **Balls** in Norfolk and Suffolk. **Ballard**, an associated surname, may have referred to its initial bearer's fatness or baldness (or both?), and is found mostly in the south-east of England and in the South Midlands. An individual named 'Bertram *Cannon* **Ball**' was born in Stourbridge, Worcs, in 1875, and long before the footballer David Beckham acquired any such nickname, a boy named '*Golden* **Balls**' was baptized at Aylsham, Norfolk, on 26 September, 1813. He had a son similarly named: '*Golden* **Balls**, Junior'. *Alan Ball (1945–2007), who was certainly short, but was neither fat nor bald in his heyday, was the youngest member of the victorious England soccer team in the 1966 World Cup. Born in Farnworth, Bolton, Lancs, he was the son of Alan Ball senior, a footballer and manager... The Labour Party politician and cabinet minister Edward Michael ('Ed') Balls was born in Norwich, Norfolk, in 1967.*

Ballamy, *see* Bellamy.

Ballantyne/Ballenden/Ballendine/Ballentine/Bellenden P Scots: apparently derived from *Bellenden*, Roxburghshire and Selkirk, Gaelic *baile an deadhain* ('the dean's farmstead'). A family of **Ballenden** was formerly prominent in the Orkney Islands, and Ballantyne's Hospital, Edinburgh, was founded by Robert **Bellentyne** or **Bellenden**, Abbot of Holyrood. **Ballendine** is a variant found in Northern Ireland.

Ballard, *see* Ball.

Ballaster/Ballester/Ballister O Occupational term for a maker of crossbows, or a person armed with a crossbow ME, OF *baleste* (compare *ballistics*). The related Channel Islands surname *Larbalestier* and the French surnames *Larbalette/Larbalétier* include the definite article, *L'*. **Alabaster** is a corruption by folk etymology.

Ballenden/Ballendine/Ballentine, *see* Ballantyne.

Ballester, *see* Ballaster.

Ballinger, *see* Beringer.

Ballister, *see* Ballaster.

Balls, *see* Ball.

Balmer O Occupational term for a seller of spices or ointments ME, OF *basme*, *balme*, *baume* ('balm'). Principally a Co Durham/Lancs surname.

Balsden/Balsdon P Place-name *Balsdean* in Sussex OE 'Bold's valley'. **Balsdon** is chiefly a Devon surname, and is probably derived from *West Balsdon* in Cornwall.

Balshaw P Place-name in Lancs OE 'rounded/smooth wood'.

Bamford P Place-name in Derbys and Lancs OE 'ford with a footbridge' (literally a 'beam').

Bampfylde P Place-name *Bampfylde Lodge* in Poltimore, Devon (originally recorded as *Benefeld* – 'bean field'). A scarce Devon surname, borne by the Barons Poltimore.

Bance, *see* Bone.

Bancroft/Bencroft P There are one or two minor place-names in various counties that could in principle have given rise to such surnames, such as *Bencroft Farm*, Northants, which was *Banecroft* in the thirteenth century, and *Bancroft* in the fourteenth century OE 'bean paddock'. Cottle speaks of a place-name in Cambs, but the first known reference to *Bancroft(e) Field* in that county dates from as late as 1364. In the event, while **Bencroft** is a scarce and scattered surname, **Bancroft** is found chiefly in the north of England, being especially strong in WRYorks, where it has been recorded as early as the fifteenth century. George Redmonds favours the idea that an unidentified place-name in East Lancs might be the source of the surname as found in WRYorks. *Anne Bancroft (1931–2005), the Academy Award-winning actress, born in New York, was originally named Anna Maria Louisa Italiano, but in 1952 changed her surname to Bancroft, because she felt that it sounded so 'elegant'.*

Banfield P From a place-name not yet identified, with the meaning of 'bean field'. The surname is found mainly in western and south-eastern counties of England.

Banham P Place-name in Norfolk OE 'homestead where beans grow'.

Ban(n)ister O Occupational term for a basket-maker, Anglo-Norman French *banastre* ('basket'). The use of *ban(n)ister* for the hand-rail of a stair dates from as late as the seventeenth century, and is a corruption of *baluster* (compare *balustrade*), referring to a pillar made in the shape of a curve (from resemblance to a wild pomegranate flower, Greek *balaustion*). *Sir Roger Bannister, born to a family of modest means in Harrow, Middx in 1929, was the first person to run a mile in under four minutes, a feat which he achieved in Oxford on 6 May 1954.*

Banker, *see* Banks. No connexion with any financial institution.

Bankes, *see* Banks.

Bankhead T/P Dweller at the top of a hill or bank, though there are several places called *Bankhead* in Scotland. The name is most commonly found in Northern Ireland, from where emigrants took it to the south-eastern states of North America in the eighteenth century. *Tallulah Bankhead (1902–1968), actress and bonne vivante, was born in Huntsville, Alabama, to a Methodist father (William Brockman Bankhead, Speaker of the US House of Representatives, a Democrat) and an Episcopalian mother (Adelaide Eugenia Sledge), who died at her birth.*

Bank(e)s/Banker T Dweller on a bank or hillside ME/ON. A person by the name of

Piggy **Banks**, born in Kimmeridge, Dorset, appears in the 1851 census for Stonehouse, Devon.

Banner/Bannar/Bannerman O Occupational term for a standard/flag/banner-bearer OF *baniere*. **Banner** is very strong in Worcs; **Bannar** is a scarce Staffs/WRYorks surname; **Bannerman** belongs to Scotland, and a family of this name features a banner on its armorial bearings. *Sir Henry Campbell-Bannerman (1836–1908), Liberal statesman, was the first person to be styled 'Prime Minister' (as opposed to 'First Lord of the Treasury') when he held that office from 1905 to 1908. Born at Kelvinside House in Glasgow, Scotland, he added Bannerman to his surname in 1871 as a condition of inheriting an uncle's estate at Hunton Court, Kent.*

Baragwanath/Baragwaneth O/N Cornish: occupational term for a baker of high-grade loaves made from wheat, Cornish *bara* ('bread') and *gwaneth* ('wheat'); or a nickname for a fastidious person who would eat only wheat bread. Now a widely spread name in Cornwall.

Barbary F From the popular mediaeval first-name *Barbara*, which has its origins in Latin and Greek words for a foreigner/barbarian – 'the kind of foreigner who could make only un-Greek noises like *ba-ba*' (Cottle).

Barber O Occupational name for a barber OF *barbier*, a man whose skills would usually encompass not only haircutting and shaving, but also surgery and dentistry, and who would be likely to display a striped red-and-white pole outside his premises accordingly. The surname is widespread, but is most commonly found in Chesh, Lancs, WRYorks and Norfolk. **Barbour** is a Scots variant. The intriguingly named '*Ali Barber*' was baptized at Iversk with Musselburgh, Midlothian, Scotland, on 29 August 1731.

Barbour, *see* Barber.

Barcham, *see* Bircham.

Barclay/Berkeley P Place-names: *Berkeley*, Gloucs; *Berkley*, Somerset, and *Barklye*, Sus-

sex OE 'birch wood'. Now chiefly a Scots surname, thanks to descendants of a **Berkeley** from Gloucs who settled north of the border during King David I's reign. *In 1690 two Quakers, Thomas Gould and John Freame, established a banking house in Lombard Street, London. In 1736 James Barclay joined them as a partner, conferring on the bank the name which it still bears. James Barclay's grandfather, born at Gordonstoun, Morayshire, Scotland, in the 1640s, was the famous Quaker writer and 'apologist' Robert Barclay. Robert's son David migrated to London, where he became a rich linen merchant. His first marriage to Ann Taylor produced James Barclay, the eldest son, and his second wife was Priscilla Freame, daughter of the banker John Freame. When James Barclay then married Priscilla's younger sister Sarah in 1733, complex family relationships were established. James's sister-in-law Priscilla was the wife of his own father, and James was not only John Freame's step grandson, but also his son-in-law.*

Bardell, *see* Bardolph.

Barden P Place-name in NRYorks and WRYorks OE 'barley valley'.

Bardolph/Bardell F From the Germanic first-name *Bertolf*. 'Now tainted by its disreputable connection with Falstaff' (Cottle).

Bardsley P Place-name in Lancs OE '*Beornred*'s clearing'. Some confusion can arise with the surname **Beardsley**, which has its origins in the Midlands. *Rev. Charles Wareing Bardsley, one-time vicar of Ulverston, Lancs, and honorary canon of Carlisle Cathedral, wrote a number of books on surnames, of which the most famous is his Dictionary of English and Welsh surnames, published in 1901 and several times reprinted. The son of Rev. James Bardsley of Burnley, Lancs, he had several brothers who also bore the middle name of Wareing, one of whom, John Wareing Bardsley, became Bishop of Carlisle.*

Barfoot/Barefoot N Nickname for a person who (from poverty or from choice) was in the habit of going about his daily life without footwear.

Barford P Place-name (OE 'barley ford') in various counties, including Northants, where the surname is most commonly found. There is also a place called *Barforth* in NRYorks.

Barham P Place name in Hunts, Suffolk OE 'hill homestead' and Kent OE '*Biora/Beora*'s homestead'.

Baring, *see* Bear.

Bark(e), *see* Barker.

Barker/Bark(e)(s) O Occupational name for a barker, who stripped bark from trees and tanned leather with it, or for a shepherd, from Anglo-Norman French *bercher* (modern French *berger*). For the relationship between -*er*- and -*ar*-, see **Armistead**. **Barker** is a very common surname in Yorks; **Bark** is strongest in Lincs, **Barke** and **Barks** in Notts, **Barkes** in Co Durham.

Barkham P Place-names in Berks, Sussex OE 'river meadow with birches'. Principally an East Anglian surname.

Barks, *see* Barker.

Barksby, *see* Barsby.

Barkway P Place-name in Herts OE 'track through birches'. Principally an East Anglian surname.

Barlow(e) P Place-name in various counties, especially in Derbys, Lancs, WRYorks OE 'barley hill'. **Barlow** is chiefly a Chesh/Lancs/Notts surname; **Barlowe**, a scarce variant, can be found in Lancs/WRYorks.

Barmby, *see* Barnaby.

Barn(e)(s) T/O/P Dweller near, or worker at, a barn (literally a 'barley house') ME; or the offspring or servant of a *barne* (mediaeval term for a person of high social status), or from *Barnes* in Surrey OE 'the barns'. **Barnes** is the family name of the Barons Gorell.

Barnaby/Barmby/Barnby F/P From a vernacular ME form of the first-name *Barnabus*, or from one of a number of places called *Barmby*, *Barnaby* or *Barnby* in all three of the old ridings of Yorks, including *Barnaby*

NRYorks OE '*Beornwald*'s settlement'. *Nicholas Jonathan ('Nick') Barmby, midfield player for the England soccer team, was born in Hull in 1974.*

Barnard, *see* Bernard.

Barnby, *see* Barnaby.

Barne(s), *see* Barn.

Barnet(t) P/F Place-name *Barnet* in Herts and Middx OE 'place cleared by burning'; or from the first-name *Bernard*. Also favoured as a surname by the Jewish community.

Barnfather, *see* Bairnsfather.

Barnfield P There are minor places so-called in various counties OE 'barn (barley house) field'. Predominantly found in Gloucs and in other South Midlands counties.

Barnham/Barnum T/O/P Dweller at, or worker at, a number of barns; or from a place-name in Norfolk, Suffolk, Sussex OE '*Beorn(a)*'s homestead'. *The American showman P[hineas] T[aylor] Barnum (1810–1891), born in Bethel, Connecticut, the son of an innkeeper, claimed descent from an English titled family of Barnham. Perhaps he was thinking of the Barnham family of Boughton Monchelsea, Kent, whose baronetcy became extinct in 1728?*

Barns, *see* Barn.

Ba(i)rnsfather N Nickname for the alleged father of an illegitimate child ME *bairn* ('child').

Barnstable/Bastable P Place-name *Barnstaple* OE '?*Bearda*'s staple/post' in Devon, which is almost indistiguishable from 'Barnstable' in its pronunciation, and is referred to as *Barstable* in the sixteenth century and as *Bastable* in the seventeenth. **Barnstable** is mainly a Somerset surname; **Bastable** is found chiefly in southern counties of England, especially Dorset.

Barnum, *see* Barnham.

Barnwell P Place-names in Cambs and Northants OE 'the stream by the burial-mound', though the surname is strongest in Warwicks.

Bar(r)on O/N/F From the rank or title of a Baron ME/OF, or for someone who acted in a haughty Baron-like fashion; or from service in a baronial household; or from the courtesy title of certain freemen of the Cinque Ports, London and York; or from the OF first-name *Baro*. Mainly found in Lancs, but also in Yorks.

Barraby/Barrowby P Place-name *Barrowby* in Lincs and WRYorks ON 'farm on the hill'. **Barraby** is a scarce surname, found in the 1881 census mainly in Carmarthenshire, alongside a few scattered examples of **Barrowby**.

Barraclough/Barrowclough P From a place-name OE 'dell with a grove'. Reaney and Cottle say that such a place-name cannot be identified, and Hanks and Hodges speak of *Barrowclough* near Halifax, WRYorks. George Redmonds deals with the complexities of the surname, saying that it is most commonly found in Southowram, and that one possible source is therefore the 'deserted mediaeval settlement beside... Barrowclough Lane', referred to by S. A. Moorhouse and M. Faull in *West Yorkshire: an archaeological survey* (Leeds, 1981).

Barrat(t)/Barret(t) F/N From a Germanic first-name; or a nickname for a cantankerous or untrustworthy person ME *baret*, *barat* ('strife, deceit') or a nickname derived from OF *barette*, meaning 'cap'. **Barrett** is by far the commonest form. An individual named '*Faith Hope and Charity* **Barratt**' was born in Exeter, Devon, in 1846.

Barrell O/N Occupational term for a cooper, who made barrels OF *baril*, or a nickname for someone as fat as a barrel, or having the capacity of a barrel; or a variant on **Barwell**, or a corruption of the Huguenot surname **Beharell**.

Barret(t), *see* Barrat.

Barrie, *see* Barry.

Barringer, *see* Beringer.

Barrington P Place-name in Cambs OE '*Bara*'s settlement', Gloucs OE 'the settlement of *Beorn*'s people', Somerset and Northd. Readily confused with/a variant of **Berrington**. **Barrington** is chiefly found in Lancs and Somerset, and is also borne by an extended family of Irish Quakers. *Jonah Barrington (born in Ireland in 1941) is regarded as having been one of the world's finest-ever squash players; his namesake Sir Jonah Barrington (1760–1834) was a well-known judge in the Irish Court of Admiralty.*

Barron, *see* Baron.

Barrow T/P Dweller by a grove or hill OE; or from one of a number of related place-names, most with the meaning 'at the grove/hill/mound'. *Barrow in Furness*, formerly an island, was named after *Barra* in the Outer Hebrides ON '*St Barr*'s Island'. The surname is mainly found in Lancs.

Barrowby, *see* Barraby.

Barrowclough, *see* Barraclough.

Barry/Barrie/Dubarry T/P/F Dweller by a rampart, Anglo-Norman French *barri* (so Madame Dubarry is 'of the rampart'). Scots: from one of a number of places called *Barry*, the one in Angus being possibly from Gaelic *borrach* ('grassy, rough hill'). Welsh: *ab Harry* (son of *Harry*, a variant of *Henry*), or from one of several places called *Barry* OW *barr* ('summit'). Irish: Anglicized form of Gaelic **O'** [descendant of] **Beargha** ('robber') or **O'** [descendant of] **Baire**.

Barsby P Place-name in Leics ON '*Barn*'s/ child's farm', and chiefly a Leics surname. **Barksby**, probably a variant, is a rare surname found in Derbys and elsewhere.

Barson, *see* Bartholomew.

Barstow, *see* Bairstow.

Bart, *see* Bert.

Bartelot, *see* Bartholomew.

Barter N Nickname for a person known for bartering or squabbling OF. A surname of the south and south-west of England.

Bartholomew F From a mediaeval first-name with Aramaic roots. Principally found in South Midlands and southern counties of England (especially Kent), it has spawned many other surnames when shortened to *Bat-* and the like. **Bartle**, a shortened form, is found mainly in WRYorks, and **Beattie/Beatt(e)y** in Scotland and Cumbd/Westmd, whereas the double-diminutive variants **Bartlet(t)**, **Bart(t)elot** and **Bertalot** are chiefly encountered in southern counties of England, especially Devon, Dorset, Somerset and Surrey. **Barson** is 'son of *Bartholomew*'. *See also* **Beaton**. Several generations of a family bearing the surname **Bartholemew** were clockmakers in Sherborne, Dorset, in the seventeenth and eighteenth centuries.

Bartle/Bartlet(t), *see* **Bartholomew**.

Bartley P Place-name in Hants, Worcs OE 'birch wood/clearing'.

Barton P Place-names in a very large number of counties OE 'barley farm'. The word *barton*, meaning a 'farmyard', is still in local use.

Bartram/Bartrum, *see* **Bertram**.

Bart(t)elot, *see* **Bartholomew**.

Barwell P Place-name in Leics OE 'boar stream'. *See also* **Barrell**.

Barwick/Berwick P Place-names: *Barwick* in Norfolk, Somerset, WRYorks and elsewhere; *Berwick* in Dorset and elsewhere, including *Berwick-upon-Tweed*, Northd, all OE 'barley/corn farm, grange'. For the relationship between *-er-* and *-ar-* (**Berwick/Barwick**), see **Armistead**. **Barwick** is sometimes pronounced *Barrick*, and **Berwick** is usually pronounced *Berrick*.

Baseley, *see* **Basil**.

Basil(l) F From a mediaeval first-name *Basil*, ultimately from Greek *Basileios* ('kingly'). **Baseley**, **Bazell(e)**, **Bazel(e)y** and **Bazley** are from feminine forms of *Basil*.

Baskerville/Basketfield/Baskwell P From the place-name *Boscherville* in Eure, Normandy. Chiefly found in Chesh and

also in Devon, the home of Sir Arthur Conan Doyle's dreaded Hound of the Baskervilles. *John Baskerville (1706–1775), born in Wolverley, near Kidderminster, Worcs, is best known as a printer who gave his name to a font which is still much favoured today.*

Bass(e) N/P Nickname for a short, dwarfish man, or one of lowly origins, or one who resembled a fish of this name (how?) ME/OF. In Scotland, from a place-name in Aberdeenshire, ?Gaelic *bathais* ('front, forehead'). *William Bass, who owned a carrier business transporting goods between London and Manchester, founded a brewery in Burton-on-Trent, Staffs, in 1777. The company is now owned by Coors, and its once-familiar high-quality bitter is but a distant memory.*

Bassingthwai(gh)te P Place-name *Bassenthwaite*, Cumbd ON '*Bastun*'s clearing'.

Bastable, *see* **Barnstable**.

Bastard N A no-holds-barred surname meaning precisely what it says, from ME, OF *bastard*. The name formerly carried less opprobrium than it does today, but several bearers of such a surname will have chosen more euphemistic alternatives over the years. A surname which is particularly in evidence in Devon. When a lady called Mary **Madcap** married a man called John **Bastard** in 1782, she may have felt that she had jumped from the frying-pan into the fire?

Basten/Bastian/Bastien/Basti(o)n, *see* **Sebastian**.

Bastow, *see* **Bairstow**.

Batchelar/Batchelder/Batcheldor/ Batchel(l)er/Batchel(l)or/Batchelour, *see* **Bachelor**.

Bate F/O From the first-name *Bartholomew*, via ME *Batte*; or an occupational term for a boatman OE *bat* (compare **Bateman**).

Bateman O Servant of *Bate* (*Bartholomew*), or a boatman OE *bat* (compare **Bate**).

Bath P/O From the place-name in Somerset, or from a man who worked at a bath house.

Found mainly in southern counties of England, and in Cornwall.

Bather/Badder/Batho F Welsh: 'son of *Atha*' (*ab Atha*). **Bather** is found mainly in Salop and Chesh, and **Batho** in English counties bordering Wales and in the north-west.

Batman F Servant of **Bate/Batt** (*Bartholomew*).

Batt(s) F Of many possible origins, and no doubt sometimes a diminutive of the first-name *Bartholomew*. Found mainly in southern counties of England.

Batten F Diminutive of the first-name *Bartholomew*. Found mainly in southern counties of England. Hence **Batterson** ('son of *Batten/Batty*').

Batterick, *see* Badrick.

Batterson, *see* Batten.

Battey/Battie/Batty(e) F A pet-form of *Bartholomew*, via *Batt*. A WRYorks surname. Poor John **Battey**, born in Derbys c.1879 (but in the 1901 census for Cudworth, Yorks) was given the middle name of 'Moron'.

Battrick, *see* Badrick.

Batts, *see* Batt.

Batty(e), *see* Battey.

Baud/Balding/Bo(u)lding/Boocock/ Boulting/Bowcock F/N From the Germanic first-name *Baldo*, or a nickname for a sprightly, cheerful person OF *baud*.

Bavister O This may look like a (female) occupational surname, but is a late development of the surname **Vavaso(u)r**, via **Vavister**. Chiefly found in East Anglia and Beds.

Bawdon, *see* Bowden.

Bax, *see* Back.

Baxendale/Baxenden P Place-name *Baxenden* in Lancs OE 'valley where the bakestones are found'. These surnames have a particularly strong presence Lancs, though the very scarce variant **Baxendine** is found mainly in Midlothian, Scotland.

Baxendine, *see* Baxendale.

Baxter O Occupational name for a baker, especially a female baker. Compare *webster* (a female weaver), *brewster* (a female brewer), and so on.

Bayle(s), *see* Bail.

Baylie(s)/Baylis(s)/Bayl(e)y, *see* Bailey.

Bayne(s), *see* Bain.

Baynton/Bainton/Bayntun P Place-names: *Bainton* in ERYorks OE 'the settlement of *Baga*'s people', Northants OE 'the settlement of *Bada*'s people', Lincs and Oxon; *Baynton*, Wilts OE 'the settlement of *Bæga*'s people'.

Bazalgette P Place-name in Lozère, France. *The first evidence of a person of this surname settling permanently in England is an Act of Denization dated 18 October 1792, granted in respect of Louis Bazalgette (1750–1830), a tailor of Grosvenor Street, Grosvenor Square, London, who had been born in Ispagnac, Lozère. Louis and his wife Catherine Metivier had a son, Captain Joseph William Bazalgette RN, who married Theresa Philo Pritton in 1816 and in turn had a son also named Joseph William, who would achieve fame as Sir Joseph Bazalgette (1819–1891), the civil engineer who gave London its extensive sewer network and built the Embankment. Peter Bazalgette, author and pioneer of television 'reality' shows, founded the TV production company named Bazal.*

Bazell(e)/Bazel(e)y/Bazley, *see* Basil.

Beach/Beech/Beecher/Beechman T Dweller by a beck or stream ME *beche* or by a beech wood, ME *beche* 'beech tree'.

Beacham, *see* Beauchamp.

Beacon T Dweller by a hilltop beacon OE. Found principally in southern counties of England, especially in Kent.

Beadel/Beadell/Beadle/Beedell/ Biddle O Occupational term for a beadle, town-crier, apparitor ME *bedele*. **Beedell** is a variant chiefly found in Devon; **Biddle** is widespread, with a strong presence in Warwicks.

Beagle, *see* Beharel.

Beak(e), *see* Beck.

Beal(e)/Beel N/P Nickname for a handsome or beautiful person OF *bel* ('fair'); or from *Beal* in Northd OE 'hill with bees', or *Beal* in WRYorks OE 'nook by loops (of the river Aire)'.

Beaman(d)/Beament, *see* Beamont, Beeman.

Beamer O Occupational term for a trumpeter OE *biemere*. A rare surname, marginally most common in Chesh and Lancs.

Beamish P From a place-name *Beaumaris-sur-Dire* in Calvados, Normandy, or from various places in France named *Beaumetz*; or from *Beamish* OF 'beautiful dwelling' in Co Durham, a place well known for its industrial museum – though this scattered surname is found mainly in south-east England.

Bea(u)mont/Beaman/Beamand/Beament/Beeman/Belmont/Beman(d)/ Bement P/F From one of a number of places called *Beaumont* OF 'beautiful hill' in Normandy and elsewhere, but there are also places so-named in England. Welsh: 'son of *Edmond*' (*ab Edmond*). Chiefly found in Yorks. Family name of the Viscounts Allendale.

Bean O/N/F Occupational term for a seller or grower of beans OE *bean*; or a nickname for person of little value ('not worth a bean...'), or who is pleasant, kindly ME *bene*; or (in Scotland) an Anglicization of the Gaelic first-name *Beathan* ('life'). Hence **McBain**, **McBean**.

Bear(e)/Baring N/F Nickname for a person who resembled a bear (ME *bere*) in some way; or from an abbreviated form of a Germanic first-name. Readily confused with/a variant of **Beer**. The **Baring** family of Hants are descended from John **Baring**, an eighteenth-century settler in Devon, who was the son of a Lutheran minister from Bremen. For the family of **Baring-Gould**, see **Gould** (under **Gold**).

Beard N/P Nickname for a man who sported a beard – and would thus be distinctive, since for several generations after the Conquest men were generally cleanshaven; or from the place-name *Beard* OE *brerd* 'brim, bank' in Derbys. The surname is widespread in southern and Midland counties.

Beardsley P Bardsley and Reaney yoke this surname together with **Bardsley**, and indicate that both are derived from *Bardsley* in Lancs, but an unidentified place-name in Derbys or Notts is more likely as an origin for **Beardsley**, given the preponderance of the surname in both these counties, and especially in the town of Ilkeston in the former Derbys coalfield. There are also a significant number of **Beardsley**s in the USA. *Aubrey (Vincent) Beardsley (1871–1898), author and illustrator, was born in Brighton, Sussex, far removed from any possible Derbys or Notts origins. His father Vincent Paul Beardsley, son of Paul Beardsley, a Clerkenwell goldsmith, had dissipated an inherited fortune and was forced to live within very modest means.*

Beare, *see* Bear.

Beaton/Beaten/Beeton/Bethune/Betton P/F Place-name *Béthune*, Pas-de-Calais, France; or from the mediaeval first-name *Be(a)ton*, a short form of *Beatrice* or (in Scotland) *Bartholomew*. **Beaton** is most commonly found in Scotland, which is also home to the surname **Bethune**, pronounced 'Beeton'. **Betterson** and **Betti(n)son** are 'son of **Beaton**'. *See also* **Betton**. *In 1856 a London woman named Isabella Mary Mayson (1836–1865) married a publisher by the name of Samuel Orchard Beeton, and shortly thereafter achieved fame as the author of* Mrs Beeton's *book of household management. Following the birth of her fourth child in January 1865, she died of puerperal fever at the age of 28.*

Beattie/Beatt(e)y, *see* Bartholomew.

Beauchamp/Beacham/Beecham P
From one of several place-names in France, with the meaning of 'lovely field'. Generally pronounced 'Beecham' in all spellings. *Sir Thomas Beecham (1879–1961), musician and conductor, was born at St Helens, Lancs, the son of Joseph Beecham; his grandfather Thomas Beecham was the original manufacturer of Beecham's Pills.*

Beauclerk N Nickname, literally 'fair clerk' OF, whether 'clerk' be a member of the clergy or a writer of neat scripts. Family name of the Dukes of St Albans, descendants of King Charles II and Nell Gwyn.

Beaufort/Belfort P From one of various places called *Beaufort* OF 'beautiful fortress' in France. One **Beaufort** family, illegitimate descendants of John of Gaunt and Catherine Swinford, who adopted a portcullis for their armorial bearings, held great sway in England during mediaeval times. Lady Margaret Beaufort, Countess of Richmond and Derby, married Edmund Tudor, by whom she had a son who became King Henry VII. *The Beaufort Scale, which measures wind velocity, was named after the English admiral Sir Francis Beaufort (1774–1857), whose origins were Huguenot.*

Beaulieu, *see* **Bewley**.

Beausire, *see* **Bowser**.

Beauvoir, *see* **Beaver**.

Beavan/Beaven, *see* **Bevan**.

Beaver/Beauvoir/Beever/Belvedere
P/N Place-names: *Beauvoir* in France, *Belvoir* in Leics OF '(with a) beautiful view'; or a nickname for a person bearing some resemblance (industrious?) to a beaver OE *beofor*. *Belvoir Castle*, in the *Vale of Belvoir* (both pronounced 'Beever'), is the family seat of the Dukes of Rutland.

Beavis/Be(e)vis/Bovis N/P A nickname from OF *bel filz*, literally 'handsome/dear son'; or from *Beauvais* (capital of the Gaulish tribe *Bellovaci*) or from various other places in France named *Beauvois* OF 'lovely sight'.

Bebb F From one of two OE first-names: *Bebba* (masculine) or *Bebbe* (feminine). The town of *Bamborough*, Northd, is named after Queen *Bebbe*, wife of King Æthelfrith. However, Bardsley claims that the name is a variant of **Babb**, derived from the first-name *Barbara*. Found chiefly in Wales and in north-west counties of England.

Bebbington P Place-name *Bebington* in Chesh OE '*Bebbe*'s settlement'. A Chesh/Lancs surname. Readily confused with/a variant of **Babington**.

Beck T/P/O/N A dweller by a stream, northern ME *bekke*; or from one of a number of places called *Bec* in France; or an occupational term for a maker of pickaxes OE *becca*; or a nickname for a person with a large nose OF *bec* 'beak'. Strongest in WRYorks. *See also* **Becket**.

Becket(t) N/P Diminutive of **Beck**, thus used of a person with a small nose OF *bec* 'beak', rather than a large one; or from the place-name *Beckett*: in Berks OE 'bee shelter' or in Devon OE '*Bicca*'s shelter'. **Beckett** is the family name of the Barons Grimthorpe. *The spurious arms attributed to St Thomas a Becket, Archbishop of Canterbury 1162–1170, which feature three Cornish choughs, otherwise referred to as 'beckits' or 'becquets', are an example of punning or canting arms, and form part of the officially granted armorial bearings of the City of Canterbury… Samuel Beckett (1906–1989), Irish novelist, poet and dramatist, came from a family (Beckett/Becquet) which is said, with little supporting evidence, to have Huguenot origins.*

Beckford P Place-name in Gloucs OE '*Becca*'s ford'. A surname of south and south-east England. *William Beckford (1709–1770), whose family had made a fortune in the sugar industry in Jamaica, was a well-known eighteenth-century politician who twice became Lord Mayor of London. His only legitimate son William (Thomas) Beckford (1760–1844), notorious novelist, art critic and eccentric, dissipated that fortune in building Fonthill Abbey in Wilts, which was eventually reduced to a ruin as funds ran out.*

Beckham P Place-name in Norfolk OE '*Becca*'s homestead'. The 1881 census indicates that this is a rare surname, such **Beckhams** as there are being found chiefly in Norfolk itself and in Middx (where some individuals bearing the surname had been born in Norfolk), and this could be a surname with a single-family origin. An individual with the unusual name of 'John Sidney Six **Beckham**' was born in Norwich, Norfolk, in 1860. *David (Robert Joseph) Beckham, well-known and influential international footballer, was born in Leytonstone, East London, in 1975, the son of Ted Beckham, a kitchen fitter, and Sandra (née West), a hairdresser from a Jewish family.*

Beckles P Place-name *Beccles* in Suffolk OE 'stream meadow'. A very scarce Sussex surname.

Beckwith P Place-name in WRYorks OE and ON 'beech wood'. Chiefly found in WRYorks, but also in Co Durham and Essex.

Bedale P Place-name in NRYorks OE '*Bede*'s nook'.

Beddoe(s)/Beddow(e)(s) F From the Welsh first-name *Meredith*, via the diminutive *Bedo*. Chiefly found in Wales and in west and north-west counties of England.

Bedford P Place-name in Beds and Lancs OE '*Bede*'s ford'. The surname occurs in both counties, but is predominantly found in WRYorks.

Bedser P From a now-lost place-name, which Reaney says was probably near Bexhill, Sussex. A rare surname, found principally in Surrey. *Sir Alec (Victor) Bedser and his twin brother Eric (Arthur) were born just minutes apart on 4 July 1918 in Reading, Berks, where their father was stationed with the Royal Flying Corps. The family soon moved to Woking in Surrey, a county which both men represented as first-class cricketers. Alec, who became chairman of selectors for the England team, was widely regarded as one of the greatest cricketers of his generation. As twins the two men were inseparable, and neither married.*

Bedward F Welsh, 'son of *Edward*' (*ab Edward*).

Bedwell P Place-name in Essex, Herts, Middx OE 'spring/stream with a bucket/butt'. Readily confused with/a variant of **Bidwell**.

Beech, *see* **Beach**.

Beecham, *see* **Beauchamp**.

Beecher, *see* **Beach**.

Beechey P From a minor place-name with the meaning of 'beech-hedge/enclosure' ME *beche* ('beech'). Strongest in Oxon.

Beechman, *see* **Beach**.

Beedell, *see* **Beadel**.

Beel, *see* **Beal**.

Beeman/Beaman(d)/Beament/ Beman(d)/Bement O/P Occupational term for a beekeeper OE; or a variation of **Beamont**.

Beer/Bere P Place-name *Beer* in Devon, Dorset, Hants, Somerset OE *beara* (the dative case of OE *bearu* 'grove, wood'). Readily confused with/a variant of **Bear**. The charmingly named 'Christopher Strong **Beer**' was baptized in Stoke Damarel, Devon, on 17 April 1768.

Beeton, *see* **Beaton**.

Beever, *see* **Beaver**.

Beevis, *see* **Beavis**.

Behagg N An Anglicized spelling of **Behague**, a variant of the Flemish surname **Behaguel**, with its roots in the Middle Dutch word *bagen*, used for a likeable man who is eager to please (Marie-Thérèse Morlet, *Dictionnaire étymologique des noms de famille* [1991]). Ernest Weekley's half-hearted contention, in his book *Surnames*, that **Behagg** is derived from a dialectal term for a hedge or enclosure is far wide of the mark. A Huguenot family of **Behaggs** was settled in Whittlesey and Thorney, Cambs, as early as the 1650s, and this has long been a Cambs/Hunts surname, probably identical with the surname **Beharrel**.

Behaghel/Behar(r)all, *see* Beharel.

Beharel(l) N Huguenot immigrants bearing the name **Beharell/Behaghel** (and also **Behar, Beharé, Beharet** and **Beharey**) initially settled in Canterbury in the 1500s, but made their way to Sandtoft in Lincs during the seventeenth century, at a time when the Fenland was being drained, thence to Thorney, Cambs – a pattern of settlement which reinforces the idea that they are the same family as that known as **Behagg** (see above for an explanation as to meaning). Principal variants are **Behar(r)all**, **Behar(r)el(l)** and **Beharrill**, while folk etymology is no doubt responsible for **Barrell** and **Beagle**. Predictably enough, **Beharell** is found mainly in Cambs, Hunts and ERYorks, but also has a presence in Lancs.

Beharrill, *see* Beharel.

Belch/Balch N Nickname 'for a man given to eructation' (Cottle), or used for a person displaying pride or arrogance, or one who was stout, built like a beam OE *balca*. **Balch** is found mainly in Somerset. *See also* **Belcher**.

Belcher/Bewsher N Nickname for a person with a pleasant face or manner OF *beu/bel* and *chere*; or a variant of Belch. **Belcher** is most commonly found in Berks; **Bewsher**, a rare variant, in north-west England. Compare **Bowser**. *Jonathan Belcher (1681/2–1757), who was governor of Massachusetts and New Hampshire, USA, from 1730 to 1741, was born in Cambridge, Massachusetts.*

Beld(h)am/Beldom N Nickname from Anglo-French, literally 'fine lady', but can be used in a sneering way for an old hag. Surnames of south-east England and East Anglia.

Belfort, *see* Beaufort.

Belgrave P Place-name in Leics and Warwicks OE 'marten grove', but a scarce surname mostly found in south-east England.

Belham N Despite appearances, not a place-name but a nickname for a handsome man OF *beu/bel* and *homme*. Strongest in Norfolk and in Surrey.

Belitha/Belither, *see* Billiter.

Bell O/T/F Used of a person having a connexion with bells – a bell-maker or bell-ringer, or one who lived at the sign of the bell or near the town bell; or from the mediaeval first-name *Bel* (a shortened form of *Isobel*), used for both males and females. The surname is frequently found in Scotland, where it can be an Anglicized form of the Gaelic **Mac Giolla Mhaoil**. *Arthur Bell of Perth in Scotland began selling his newly developed blended whisky in 1825, though it was not until 1904 that his company's name appeared on the label, to be followed in 1929 by the catch-phrase, 'Afore ye go'… Alexander Graham Bell, inventor of the telephone, was born in Edinburgh on 3 March 1847, son of Alexander Melville Bell and his wife Eliza Grace (née Symonds). When his parents emigrated to Canada in 1870, he accompanied them.*

Bellamy/Ballamy N Nickname for a 'fine/handsome friend', used either literally or ironically ('a fine friend you turned out to be…') OF *beu/bel* and *ami*. **Bellamy** is strongest in northern counties of England; **Ballamy** is found mainly in Devonshire.

Bellasis P From one of a number of place-names: *Belasis, Bellasis* (Co Durham), *Bellasis* (Northd), *Bellasize* (ERYorks) or *Belsize* (Herts, Northants), all from OF 'lovely site'. A rare surname, found mainly in north-western counties of England.

Bellchamber(s) O Occupational term for a man who tended or rang church bells, rather than someone who lived in a church tower among the bells… Both **Bellchamber** and **Bellchambers** are most commonly found in south-eastern counties of England.

Bellenden, *see* Ballantyne.

Bellerby P Place-name in NRYorks ON '*Bag*'s farm'. A surname of the north of England.

Bellinger, *see* Beringer.

Bellis(s) F Welsh, 'son of *Ellis*' (*ab Ellis*). Compare **Bliss**.

Bellringer, *see* **Beringer**.

Belmont, *see* **Beamont**.

Belt N/O A wearer or maker of belts OE. Found mainly in Yorks.

Belvedere, *see* **Beaver**.

Beman(d)/Bement, *see* **Beamont**, **Beeman**.

Benbow/Benbough O Occupational term for an archer OF (literally 'bend-bow'). Found mainly in the West Midlands, the north-west, and Wales (especially Montgomeryshire). *Admiral John Benbow (1653–1702), son of a tanner from Shrewsbury, is perhaps at least as famous for the songs composed in his honour as for his undoubted prowess as a naval commander. Abandoned by mutinous captains under his command during an engagement in the West Indies during the War of the Spanish Succession, he was left to fight the French unaided, and eventually died of wounds in Jamaica on 4 November 1702.*

Bence, *see* **Benn**.

Bench ?T A surname of uncertain origin: one who sat on a bench, or lived near an earth bank ME *benche*?

Bencroft, *see* **Bancroft**.

Bendall/Bendell, *see* **Bentall**.

Bendix, *see* **Benedict**.

Bendle, *see* **Bentall**.

Benedict F From the mediaeval first-name *Benedict* (Latin 'blessed'), made popular thanks to St *Benedict* (c.480-550), founder of the Benedictine order of monks. The diminutive **Ben(n)et(t)** is far more commonly met with as a surname, and is the family name of the Earls of Tankerville. **Bennison** ('son of **Bennet**'), which has a pleasing flavour of 'benison' (blessing) about it, is found mainly in northern counties of England, especially in Lancs and NRYorks. **Bendix** is a very scarce variant. **Benskin**, probably a diminutive variant, has a certain presence in Leics. *See also* **Benn**. *The expression 'Gordon Bennett', uttered by sensitive souls who wish to avoid full-on blasphemy, has its origins in the outrageous and iconoclastic James Gordon Bennett (1841–1918), one-time proprietor of the* New York Herald... *William Bendix (1906–1964), the radio, TV and film actor, was born in New York on 14 January 1906, son of Oscar Bendix, a musician... The Bendix Corporation, famous for manufacturing washing machines and much else, was founded in 1924 by the inventor Vincent Bendix... Benskin's Watford (Herts) Brewery, based upon a business originally developed by members of the Dyson family, was bought from them by Joseph Benskin, a retired hotel owner, in 1867.*

Benet, *see* **Benedict**.

Benfield T/P Dweller by a bean field OE; or from the place-name *Benefield*, Northants, or from one of a number of minor place-names in Dorset and Sussex, all with the same meaning. *See also* **Banfield**. Most common in southern England and the South Midlands.

Benger, *see* **Beringer**.

Benion, *see* **Beynon**.

Benjamin F From a Hebrew first-name 'son of the south', that of the youngest of Jacob's sons in the bible. A fairly rare but widespread surname in England and Wales, not confined to Jews.

Benn/Bence F From the ME first-name *Benne*, developed in part from *Benedict*. *See also* **Benson**.

Bennet(t), *see* **Benedict**.

Benneworth/Benniworth P Place-name *Benniworth*, Lincs OE 'the enclosure of the *Be(o)nningas*'. A scarce surname.

Bennion, *see* **Beynon**.

Bennison/Bennitt, *see* **Benedict**.

Benniworth, *see* **Benneworth**.

Benskin, *see* **Benedict**.

Benson F/P Son of *Benne* (see **Benn**), or from *Benson* (formerly *Bænesingtun*) Oxon OE '*Benesa*'s farm'. Found in the English

Midlands and the north, especially in Lancs and WRYorks.

Benste(a)d/Binste(a)d P Place-names in various counties, such as *Banstead*, Surrey OE 'place where beans are grown'. **Bensted**, **Binsted** and **Binstead** are found mainly in the south of England; **Benstead** is more widespread.

Bentall/Bendall/Bendell/Bendle/ Benthall P Place-name *Benthall*, Salop OE 'bent-grass nook', but there is also a *Benhall* OE 'place where beans are grown' in Suffolk (see **Benwell**).

Bentley P Place-name in a widely-scattered range of counties OE 'clearing covered with bent-grass'.

Benton P There are villages called *Benton* in Northd OE 'bean/bent-grass settlement', though the surname is widely spread, and is most commonly found in Staffs.

Benwell/Bennell P Place-names: *Benwell* Northd OE 'inside the wall' and *Banwell Farm* in Sussex OE 'spring by which beans grow'. **Bennell** is a variant, and there is a *Benhall* OE 'place where beans are grown' in Suffolk (see **Bentall**).

Benyon, *see* Beynon.

Bere, *see* Beer.

Beriman, *see* Berryman.

Beringer/Ballinger/Barringer/Bellinger/Bellringer/Benger F From a Germanic first-name. *Beringar* was one of Charlemagne's Twelve Paladins. The feminine form *Berengaria* was the name of Richard I's Queen and also a well-known liner. **Bellringer** is a variant brought about by folk etymology. **Beringer** is found mainly in Cornwall, **Ballinger** in Gloucs, **Bellringer** in Somerset, and **Benger** in Wilts.

Berkeley, *see* Barclay.

Berkenshaw, *see* Birkenshaw.

Bernard/Barnard F Germanic first-name *Bernhard*. A name much favoured by the Normans, used long before it was made even more popular thanks to Saint *Bernard* of Clairvaux (c.1090–1153). **Bernard** is the family name of the Earls of Bandon. **Barnard** is most commonly found in Essex, Norfolk and Suffolk, while **Bernard** is more widespread. *Dr Thomas (John) Barnardo (1845–1905), founder of Dr Barnardo's Homes for destitute children, was born in Dublin. His mother was English, and his Jewish father, who came from Hamburg, had family roots in Spain.*

Berridge, *see* Beveridge.

Berrington P Place-name in Salop, Worcs OE 'place attached to a fort/manor', and in Northd OE 'hill with a (prehistoric) camp'. Readily confused with/a variant of **Barrington**.

Berry, *see* Bury.

Berryman/Beriman O Occupational term for a servant at a manor ME *buri*. **Berryman** is most commonly found in the West Country, especially Cornwall; **Beriman** is a very scarce variant.

Bert/Bart/Birt/Burt F From a Germanic first-name such as *Berthold*, via *Berto*. *See also* **Bright**.

Bertalot, *see* Bartholomew.

Bertenshaw, *see* Birkenshaw.

Bertram/Bartram/Bartrum/Bertrand F From the Germanic first-name *Bertram*, brought to England by the Normans and common as a first-name in France during the Middle Ages. For the relationship between -*er*- and -*ar*- (**Bertram/Bartram**), see **Armistead**.

Berwick, *see* Barwick.

Bes(s)ant/Besent, *see* Bezant.

Bessemer O Occupational term for a maker of besoms/brooms ME *besem*, 'broom'. The German and Dutch surname **Besemer** has the same meaning. The **Bessemer** surname is only in evidence in England from the late eighteenth century onwards. It is said that Sir Henry **Bessemer** (1813–1898), inventor of the famous

Bessemer converter, who was born near Hitchin in Herts, came from a family with Huguenot roots which had formerly spelt its name **Bassemer**. If this is so, it would seem likely that the original immigrants who carried the surname to England had their roots in the Low Countries – rather than in France, for example, where there is little or no evidence of its being used. No such name is featured in dictionaries of French surnames.

Best O/N Occupational term for a person who tended beasts, or a nickname for one who resembled a beast in some way (savage, stupid?) ME, OF *beste*, 'beast'. A very widespread name throughout England. Family name of the Barons Wynford. *George Best (1946–2005), born in Belfast, Northern Ireland, is widely regarded as having been one of the greatest footballers of all time. His star shone most brightly while he was playing for Manchester United FC.*

Betchley P Place-names: *Beckley* Sussex OE '*Becca*'s clearing', or *Beachley* Gloucs OE '*Betti*'s clearing'. Found chiefly in southern and south-eastern counties of England.

Bethel(l)/Bithell F From the first-name *Elizabeth*, via the diminutive *Beth*. Welsh: son of (*ab-*) *Ithel*. **Bethell** is the family name of the Barons Westbury.

Bethune, *see* **Beaton**.

Betteridge F Despite appearances, not from a place-name. See **Badrick**.

Betterson/Betti(n)son F Son of **Beaton**.

Betton P Place-names in Salop: *Betton Abbots* and *Betton in Hales* OE 'stream/beech-tree settlement'; or a form of **Beaton**.

Bevan/Beavan/Beaven F Welsh: son of (*ab-*) *Evan*. See also **Bevin**. *Aneurin ('Nye') Bevan (1897–1960), the well-known Labour Party politician who began working life as a coal-miner, was born of Nonconformist parents in Tredegar, Monmouthshire.*

Beveridge/Berridge N Nickname derived from ME *beverage*, connected with the buying of drinks used to seal a bargain. **Bever-idge** is found mainly in the north of England and in Scotland, especially Fife, while **Berridge** is a South Midlands name, commonest in Leics. *Sir William Beveridge (1879–1963), known chiefly for his role in establishing the post-World War II welfare state in Britain, was born in Bengal, India, the son of a judge in the Indian Civil Service.*

Beverley P Place-name in ERYorks, named at a time when the beaver (OE *beofor*) still found a home in the British Isles. Used in more recent times as a female first-name.

Bevin N/F Nickname for a wine-drinker (compare Modern English slang, *bevvy*, a drink), from OF *bei(vre)*, *boi(vre)* and *vin* (drink-wine); or a variant of **Bevan**. *During the Second World War, Bevin Boys worked in coalmines under the terms of an act passed in 1940 at a time when Ernest Bevin (1881–1951) was Minister of Labour. Bevin was born at Winsford, Somerset; his mother's former husband was called William Bevin, but the identity of Ernest's father is unknown.*

Bevis, *see* **Beavis**.

Bew N Nickname for a handsome, beautiful person OF. Readily confused with/a variant of **Bewes**.

Bewes F/P Welsh, son of (*ab-*) *Hugh*, with an extra 's' added for good measure; or from *Bayeux* in Calvados, home of the famous tapestry. Found chiefly in Devon. Readily confused with/a variant of **Bew**. *Rodney Bewes (born 1938), television actor well known for his role as Bob Ferris in* The Likely Lads, *was born in Bingley, West Yorkshire, but was raised mainly in Luton, Beds.*

Bewick P Place-name in Northd and East Yorks OE 'bee-farm'. A Co Durham/Northd surname.

Bewley/Beaulieu P From one of a number of places in France called *Beaulieu* OF *beu/bellieu* 'beautiful place'; or from *Bewley* in Co Durham, Kent, Westmd, or from *Beaulieu*, Hants. Generally pronounced 'Bewley' in both spellings. **Bewley** is strongest in Cumbd and Lancs; **Beaulieu** is very scarce as an English surname.

Bewsher, *see* Belcher.

Bexley P Place-name, Kent OE 'box-tree wood clearing'. A rare Surrey surname.

Beynon/Ben(n)ion/Benyon F Welsh: son of (ab-) *Einion*. See **Onion**. **Beynon** is chiefly found in South Wales, **Benion** and **Bennion** in Chesh/Lancs, and **Benyon** in Lancs.

Bez(z)ant/Besant/Besent O/N A *besant* ME was a gold coin of a type first minted at *Byzantium*, and in heraldry is the name for a golden roundel. A person so-called might have worked as a coiner, or have been famed as a money-bags. The surname **Bezant** is widely scattered; **Besant** is found mainly in southern counties of England, and **Besent** is predominantly a Dorset name. *Sir Walter Besant (1836–1901), novelist and historian, was born in Portsmouth to a mercantile family.*

Bibb(e)y/Bibb/Bible F From the mediaeval first-name *Isabel* (ultimately from *Elizabeth*), via *Bibbe*. **Bibby** is found chiefly in Lancs, and **Bibb** in the West Midlands. **Bible** is a much rarer variant.

Bickerstaff(e)/Bickersteth/Biggerstaff P Place-name *Bickerstaff* in Lancs OE 'bee-keepers' staithe/landing-place'.

Bickerton P Place-name in Chesh, Northd, WRYorks OE 'beekeepers' place'. Most commonly found in Chesh, Lancs and Staffs.

Biddick P/F Reaney derives this from *Biddick*, Co Durham OE 'by the ditch', and says that it can alternatively refer to a dweller by a ditch. Its strong presence in Cornwall has to be accounted for, however, and G. Pawley White gives its origin as the Cornish first-name *Budik*, though it could in principle be a shortened form of **Bidlake**.

Biddle, *see* Beadel.

Biddlecombe P Place-name *Bittiscombe* in Somerset OE '?*Bitel*'s valley'. Chiefly a Hants surname, though a well-known family of clockmakers called *Biddlecombe* was settled at Stourton Caundle in Dorset during the eighteenth century.

Biddulph P Place-name in Staffs OE 'by the digging/mine'.

Bidlake P Place-name in Devon OE '*Bid(d)a*'s streamlet' and *Bidlake Farm* in Dorset. By the late nineteenth century the surname could be found in limited numbers in Gloucs, Surrey and elsewhere. See also **Biddick**.

Bidwell P Place-name *Bidwell*, Beds OE '*Byda*'s spring'. Readily confused with/a variant of **Bedwell**.

Bigg(s) N/P Nickname for a big, strong person ME *bigge*, though some early forms are preceded by *de*, which suggests a place-name origin.

Biggerstaff, *see* Bickerstaff.

Biggin(g)(s) P Place-names: *Biggin* in Derbys, Essex, Warwicks, WRYorks; *Biggins* in Westmd, all ME from ON *bigging* (building). *Newbiggin* is a place-name commonly found in the north of England, but *Biggin Hill* in Kent is of too recent date to have given rise to a surname.

Biggs, *see* Bigg.

Bill/Billing(s) F/O From a shortened form of a Germanic first-name such as *Billaud* or *Billard*; or an occupational term for a maker of swords OE *bil*, or pruning hooks. '*Bill*' as a shortened form of *William* was too late a development to have affected surnames. **Bill** is a Midlands surname, found mainly in Staffs; **Billing** is widespread, with a strong presence in Cornwall; **Billings** is evenly spread throughout England, being strongest in Staffs.

Billing(s)hurst P Place-name in Sussex OE '*Billing*'s hill/wood'.

Billings, *see* Bill.

Billingshurst, *see* Billinghurst.

Billingsley P Place-name in Salop, of uncertain etymology: possibly OE 'clearing near a hill shaped like a sword'. Chiefly a Staffs/Warwicks surname.

Billiter O Occupational term for a bell-founder OE. *Billiter Lane* in the City of London was home to men practising this craft. Reaney has much to say about this surname, and quotes examples of its use from the thirteenth to the sixteenth centuries. It made its way to North America in due course (a Joseph **Billiter** arrived in Maryland in 1671), but in England it may sometimes be found masquerading as **Belitha/Belither** or a number of associated names, and eighteenth-century probate indexes for the Prerogative Court of Canterbury include examples of individuals called '**Belitha** alias **Belitho**', '**Belitha** alias **Bolitha**' and '**Belither** alias **Bolithar**'. These references stop just short of identifying such surnames with the Cornish **Bolitho**. The modern French noun *belître*, incidentally, refers to a cad or bounder.

Binch, *see* **Binks**.

Bindless/Bindloes/Bindloss O 'Probably a wolf-trapper OE/OF' (Reaney). A very rare surname whatever the spelling. **Bindless** is found in Lancs, and **Bindloss** in Westmd.

Bindon P Place-name in Dorset OE 'inside the hills'. A family of this name first settled in Co Tipperary, Ireland, in 1580, though in more recent times the surname has been associated with Co Clare.

Bing/Byng A simple-looking surname, though its origin is uncertain; from an OE clan-name? **Bing** is found mainly in Kent, while **Byng** is more widespread. *Admiral John Byng (1704–1757), born in Beds, was the son of George Byng, First Viscount Torrington, also a highly regarded admiral. In the early years of the Seven Years' War, John Byng was court-martialled and executed for 'failing to do his utmost' during the Battle of Menorca. Voltaire remarked wryly in* Candide *that such a draconian act was needed pour encourager les autres.*

Bingham P Place-name in Notts OE 'the homestead of *Binningas*, descendants of *Binna*' or 'manger-homestead'. **Bingham** families settled in Dorset and in Ireland, including the Earls Lucan, are said to have Notts origins. The surname is still found in Notts and in neighbouring Derbys, but the greatest concentration of **Bing-**

hams is in WRYorks. *Richard John Bingham, Seventh Earl of Lucan (born 1934), a professional gambler, spectacularly disappeared in 1974 after his children's nanny was found murdered in London. Pending a more conclusive outcome, Earl Lucan's son cannot inherit his father's title, and is known by his courtesy title, Lord Bingham.*

Bingley P Place-name in WRYorks OE 'clearing with a hollow' or 'clearing of *Binningas*, descendants of *Binna*' (compare **Bingham**).

Binks/Binch T Dweller at a raised bank, or *bink* (northern equivalent of ME *bench*). **Binch** is a Notts variant.

Binn(s) F/T/O From the ME first-name *Binne*; or a dweller at the bin/manger/stall in a hollow area known as a *binn*; or a maker of bins or mangers. **Binns** is by far the commoner spelling, found chiefly in Lancs and in WRYorks. John *Wheeler* **Binns** was born in Wellington, Salop, in 1874 – long before the introduction of the ubiquitous Wheelie Bins.

Binste(a)d, *see* **Bensted**.

Bir(k)beck P From a minor place-name. Reaney derives the surname from *Birkbeck Fells* in Westmd; although the first known reference to this place only dates from 1669, the nearby river known as *Birk Beck* ON 'birch stream' was so-called as early as the thirteenth century. **Birkbeck** is most commonly found in WRYorks, and **Birbeck** in Co Durham. *Birkbeck College, University of London, can trace its origins back to 1823, when the London Mechanics' Institution was founded by George Birkbeck (1776–1841), who was born into a Quaker family in Settle, NRYorks.*

Birch/Birk/Burch T Dweller by a birch tree OE *birce*. **Birk** is a northern form. Sometimes corrupted to **Burge**. See also **Birkett**.

Birchall/Burchall P From a lost place-name in the parish of Eccles, Lancs, according to Hanks and Hodges. *Birchall* OE 'birch nook' in the Manchester area was *Birchehalgh* in 1295 and had become *Birchall* by 1601-2. Reaney suggests that the surname comes from either *Birchill* in Derbys or *Birchills* in Staffs. The latter, lying one mile north-west of Walsall, may only have acquired this name as recently as the sixteenth century, but the place now known as *Birchill (Farm)* near Hassop, Derbys, appears in the Domesday Book, where it is referred to as *Berceles*. Both **Birchall** and **Burchall** are chiefly found in Lancs.

Bircham/Barcham/Burcham P From one of a group of villages called *Bircham* in Norfolk OE 'newly-broken-up land homestead'. For the *-ar* element in **Barcham**, see **Armistead**. Chiefly a Norfolk surname in all spellings.

Bircumshaw, *see* **Birkenshaw**.

Bird/Burd/Byrd O/N Occupational term for a bird catcher, or a nickname for a person resembling a bird in some way OE. **Burd** can also have the meaning of 'girl, maiden', or even '?sempstress'; the diminutives **Burdekin/Burdikin** are scarce variations, found mainly in Derbys, but also in Lancs and WRYorks. There is an oft-quoted example of a tombstone on which a father, mother and their four children are listed as **McEneaney, McAneany, McAneny, McEnaney, McEneany** and **Bird**, the last based on the mistaken notion that the surname has something to do with Gaelic *ean* 'bird'.

Birdseye/Birdesey/Birdsaie/Birdsay(e) /Birdsey/Budsey ?P The well-known frozen food company *Bird's Eye* is named after its founder, Clarence (*'Bob'*) **Birdseye** (1886–1956) of Brooklyn, New York, who made the extraordinary claim that his unusual name (which was originally written as two words, not one) came from an English ancestor, a page at the royal court, who was nicknamed *Bird's Eye* by the Queen after having shot a diving hawk through the eye with an arrow. It's easy enough to mock such a suggestion, but proof that a name of this ilk could indeed have been used as a nickname, and even by way of a byname which may have passed down through several generations of a family, is provided by George Redmonds, who quotes sixteenth-century examples from

Yorks of a number of men bearing the common surname of **Hartley** who all bore the distinguishing alias of '*Byrdye*' (that is, '*Birdeye*'? '*Birdie*'?). To confuse matters even further, Redmonds has found the Holmfirth, Yorks, surname **Beardsell** spelt as **Bardsaye** and **Berdsay** in the sixteenth century, neither of which is so very far removed from **Birdseye**. It would appear that **Beardsell** has its origin in a place in Rochdale, Lancs, now known as *Buersill* OE '?*Bugered/Buered*'s hill'. Could the village called *Bardsey* near Leeds, WRYorks OE '?*Beornred*'s island' (*Berdesei* in 1086), and/or *Bardsea*, Lancs (*Berdeseye* in the thirteenth/fourteenth centuries), which would seem to share exactly the same origin, have given rise to **Birdseye**-type surnames, by a process of folk etymology? For the relationship between *-ar*, *-er* (and *-ir*) in such placenames and surnames, see **Armistead**. **Bardsey** as a surname is scarcely featured in the 1881 census for England and Wales, but there are a handful of **Birdseys** in Beds and elsewhere. Bardsley is certainly in favour of a place-name origin: 'Local, of Birdsey, I cannot find the place... But the meaning seems clear: the "Birdseye", i.e., the islet or eyot in the stream frequented by birds'. The **Birdseye** surname crops up from time to time in south-east England: on 18 April, 1908, Richard Jacob Chambers, bachelor, and Rosina Frances **Birdseye**, spinster, were married at the church of St Andrew, Lambeth.

Birk, *see* **Birch**.

Birkbeck, *see* **Birbeck**.

Birkby P Place-name in Yorks and Cumbd ON 'Britons' farm'. The surname is most prolific in WRYorks.

Birkenshaw, etc... P Place-name *Birkenshaw* in WRYorks OE 'birch-tree shaw'. A surname which comes in a bewildering number of variants, as listed by Reaney: **Birkenshaw, Birkinshaw, Bircumshaw, Birtenshaw, Berkenshaw, Bertenshaw, Burkenshaw, Burkinshaw, Burkinshear, Burkimsher, Burtinshaw, Burtonshaw, Buttanshaw, Buttenshaw, Buttonshaw,**

Brigenshaw, Briggenshaw, Briginshaw, Brigginshaw, Brockenshaw, Brokenshaw, Brokenshire, Bruckshaw. **Bottomshaw** is yet another version.

Birkett/Birkitt/Burchett/Burkett T Dweller by birch trees OE. Sometimes, by metathesis, **Brickett**. Readily confused with/a variant of **Burchard**. See also **Birch**.

Birkin/Burkin P Place-name *Birkin* in WRYorks OE 'birch grove'. **Birkin** is most commonly found in Derbys/Notts/Staffs, and **Burkin** in Kent/Middx/Surrey.

Birkinshaw, *see* **Birkenshaw**.

Birkitt, *see* **Birkett**.

Birley P There are various places so-called in Derbys OE 'clearing with a byre/cow-shed', and also in Herefords OE 'clearing by a fort/manor'.

Birmingham/Bermingham P Place-name *Birmingham* in Warwicks OE '*Beorn-mund*'s homestead'.

Birstall, *see* **Burstall**.

Birt, *see* **Bert**.

Birtenshaw, *see* **Birkenshaw**.

Birtle(s) P Place-names *Birtle/Birtles* in Lancs, Chesh OE 'birch hill'. The surname occurs most frequently in Lancs, Yorks and Westmd.

Birtw(h)istle P From the name of a now-lost place near Padiham, Lancs OE 'fledg-ling's (river) fork'. *Sir Harrison Birtwistle, controversial modern musical composer, was born in Accrington, Lancs, in 1952.*

Bish, *see* **Bush**.

Bishop/Bisp O/N Derived, we may hope, from a bishop's servant rather than from the nominally celibate prelate himself. Or a person with the appearance or bearing of a bishop, or who took such a part in a play. Compare **Levick** and **Veck**. **Bishop** is mostly a southern surname; **Bisp** is very rare, and confined almost exclusively to the village of Winterbourne, near Bristol.

Bishton P Place-name in Staffs, Monmouthshire OE 'Bishop's farm/manor'.

Bisp, *see* **Bishop**.

Bispham P Place-names in Lancs OE 'Bishop's homestead', in which county most occurrences of the surname **Bispham** can be found.

Biss/Bisset(t) N Nickname for a person whose complexion or clothing was dingy ME/OF *bis* ('murky'). The surname **Bizet** is a French equivalent. *The British actress Jacqueline Bisset (Winifred Jacqueline Fraser-Bisset) was born in 1944 in Weybridge, Surrey, daughter of Max Fraser-Bisset and Arlette Alexander. Her mother was French, and she has Scottish ancestry on her father's side… Georges Bizet (1838–1875), famed for his opera* Carmen, *was a native of Paris.*

Bissell, *see* **Bushell**.

Bisset(t), *see* **Biss**.

Bithell, *see* **Bethel(l)**.

Black/Blake N Nickname for a black(-haired), dark-complexioned person OE *blæc*; or – confusingly – for a fair, pale person OE *blac. Blac* pronounced with a short and a long vowel meant 'black' and 'pale' respectively. The surnames **Black** and **Blake** prove that black can indeed be white… *William Blake (1757–1827), poet, painter and mystic who lived and died in poverty, was born in London, son of James Blake, a hosier.*

Blackadder P River and place-name in Berwickshire, Scotland. No connexion with snakes: the place-name is known to have been pronounced and written as 'Black-water', which probably indicates its true origins.

Blackburn(e)/Blackbourn(e) P Place-names with related spellings exist in various counties; there are places called *Blackburn* in Lancs OE 'black stream', Co Durham and WRYorks.

Blackden/Blagden/Blagdon P Place-names: *Blackden* in Chesh OE 'dark valley';

Blagdon in Devon, Dorset, Somerset OE 'black hill' and Northd OE 'black valley'.

Blacker/Blaker/Blatcher/Blecher O Occupational term for a bleacher ME *blaker*. So what looks like a blackener is actually a whitener… Compare the surname **Black**. The surname **Blaxter** (most commonly found in Norfolk) has its origins in a word that was originally used for a female bleacher, but which was also applied to males (compare **Baxter**).

Blackford P Place-name in Cumbd, Lancs, Salop and Somerset OE 'black ford'. Found mainly in southern, south-western and Midland counties of England.

Blackley/Blacklee/Blakeley P From one of a number of places called *Blackley* (one such being in Lancs OE 'black clearing/wood', pronounced 'Blakeley'), or *Blakeley*.

Blacklock/Blakelock N Nickname for a person with black hair OE *blæc* ('dark') and *locc* ('lock' [of hair]). **Blacklock** is strongest in northern England and in the Scottish Lowlands, **Blakelock** in Co Durham/NRYorks/WRYorks. *Thomas Blacklock (1721–1791), the poet and writer who lost his sight from smallpox in early infancy, was born in Annan, Dumfriesshire, Scotland, the son of John Blacklock, a bricklayer from Cumbd, and his wife Ann Rae.*

Blackman/Blakeman/Bleakman N Nickname for a black-haired/dark man OE. Also once used as a first-name.

Blackmore/Blakemore P Place-names: *Blackmore*: Herts OE 'black mere', Essex OE 'black moor'; *Blackmoor*: Dorset OE 'black moor/forest', Hants OE 'black mere'; *Blakemere*: Herefords OE '*Blaeca*'s mere'; *Blakemore*: Devon OE 'black moor'. **Blackmore** is most commonly found in Devon, **Blakemore** in Staffs. *Richard Doddridge ('R. D.') Blackmore (1825–1900), author of* Lorna Doone, *who was born in Berkshire but had his schooling in Somerset and Devon, is said to have done for Devonshire what Sir Walter Scott did for the Highlands of Scotland. His namesake, Sir Richard Blackmore (1654–1729), born at Corsham in Wilts, had*

the unenviable reputation of being a poet of mind-numbing dullness, though he was also a very competent physician.

Blackshaw P Place-name in WRYorks OE 'black wood'. Principally a Lancs/Chesh surname.

Blackwell/Blackwall P Place-name in many counties OE 'black spring/stream'.

Blackwood P Place-name in ERYorks, WRYorks, Monmouthshire and Scotland OE 'black wood'.

Blagden/Blagdon, *see* **Blackden**.

Blagrave/Blagrove P Place-names: *Blagrave* (Berks), *Blagrove* (Devon) OE 'black grove'.

Blake, *see* **Black**.

Blakeley, *see* **Blackley**.

Blakelock, *see* **Blacklock**.

Blakeman, *see* **Blackman**.

Blakemore, *see* **Blackmore**.

Blaker, *see* **Blacker**.

Bla(y)mire ?P A northern English surname of uncertain origin. The place called *Blamires* in WRYorks was probably named after a **Blamire** family, rather than vice versa. George Redmonds says that there is no evidence of this surname having Yorkshire origins, and highlights the significance of Reaney's own evidence that a family of this name was living in Cumbd in 1250. Jonas **Blamires**, a Nonconformist minister, was buried at Durham in 1708. A scarce surname overall, met with principally in Lancs, Westmd and WRYorks.

Blampey, *see* **Blampied**.

Blamphin, *see* **Pamplin**.

Blampied/Blampey N Nickname for a person who (in some way) had a 'white foot' OF.

Blanchard N/F Nickname for a person of white appearance OF; or from a Germanic first-name, meaning 'shining/beautiful-strong'. 'It was even the first-name of the Arthurian Sir Launfal's horse' (Cottle).

Blanchflower/Branchflower N Nickname for a person of white appearance OF. 'The heroine of a swooning medieval romance with young Floris; mocking when applied to males' (Cottle). Chiefly found in Norfolk, but also in Lancs. *Robert Dennis ('Danny') Blanchflower (1926–1993), twice voted Footballer of the Year in England, was raised in Belfast, Northern Ireland.*

Bland P Place-name in WRYorks, of doubtful etymology, perhaps with the meaning of 'windy place'. 'The gentle, coaxing adjective arrived far too late to form a surname' (Cottle). A widespread surname, strongest in WRYorks. The Derbys/Notts/Staffs surname **Blant** is probably a variant of **Bland**.

Blandford P The name of more than one place in Dorset OE 'ford where blays/gudgeons could be fished'. 'Even if the story be true that many unclaimed orphans were so named after the total destruction of Blandford by fire in 1731, the meaning of the surname is unchanged' (Cottle).

Blant, *see* Bland.

Blatcher, *see* Blacker.

Blatherwick P Place-name in Northants (etymology uncertain: OE 'blackthorn/bladderwort settlement'?), but very much a Notts surname.

Blaxter, *see* Blacker.

Blaymire, *see* Blamire.

Bleakman, *see* Blackman.

Bleasdale P Place-name in Lancs OE 'valley with a white/bare spot', and found most commonly in that county. *Alan Bleasdale, creator of the TV series Boys from the Blackstuff, was born in Liverpool in 1946.*

Blecher, *see* Blacker.

Blencow(e)/Blincow(e) P Place-name *Blencow* in Cumbd, of which the etymology is uncertain: perhaps British/ON 'top hill'. **Blencowe** is the most common variant, but

in all spellings this is now a South Midlands surname.

Blen(n)erhasset(t)/Blennerhassit P Place-name in Cumbd, Welsh *blaen* 'top' and ON *heysætre* 'hay shieling'. 'Oddly dismembered by US scholar Roland Blenner-Hassett' (Cottle). This is a rare surname within the United Kingdom, originating in Cumbd but now randomly spread. Members of the **Blennerhassett** family were MPs for Carlisle from the fourteenth to the seventeenth century, and Sir Rowland **Blennerhassett** of Kerry, created a Baronet in 1809, was a direct descendant of Alan **de Blenerhayset**, who was Mayor of Carlisle in 1382. Irish denization acts dated 17 April 1702 in respect of Jon and Robert **Blener Hasset** [sic] probably represent the first arrival of men of this name in Ireland, at which time the family settled in Fermanagh and Kerry. Canon James *Blennerhassett* Leslie (1865–1952), the author of a highly acclaimed series of published works featuring succession lists of Irish clergy, acquired his middle name from his mother Mary Ann, a descendant of the **Blennerhassetts** of Ballyseedy, Co Kerry.

Blenkinsop(p)/Blenkinship P Place-name *Blenkinsopp* Northd (etymology uncertain: the second element is OE *hop* 'dry land in a fen', and the first could be a personal name or the Welsh word *blaen* 'top').

Blenkiron P Place-name *Blencarn* in Cumbd, Welsh *blaen-carn*, 'hilltop with a cairn', but the surname is generally found further east, in Co Durham and NRYorks. Matthew **Blenkiron**, a lead-miner from the Yorkshire Dales, emigrated to America in 1839 aboard the ship *Roscius*.

Blessed/Blisset N/F Nickname for a blessed, fortunate person, but also used in mediaeval times as a female first-name. *Brian Blessed, the actor once described as 'the loudest man alive', pronounces his surname 'Blessèd'; he was born in Mexborough, Yorkshire, in 1937, the son of a coal-miner.*

Blewett/Blewitt/Bluett N Nickname for one who has blue eyes, or favours blue clothing ME. **Blewett** is principally a Cornish and West Country surname, while **Blewitt** is more widespread.

Bligh/Blight/Bly(e)/Blythe(e) N Nickname for a cheerful person OE. **Blyth** is commonly pronounced '*Bly*'. **Bligh** is most commonly found in Kent, but as a Cornish surname it is derived from *blyth* ('wolf'). **Blight** is chiefly a Cornwall/Devon surname. **Bligh** is the family name of the Earls of Darnley. *Vice-Admiral William Bligh (1754–1817) of* Bounty *fame, who eventually became Governor of New South Wales, was born in Plymouth of a family once well established in Cornwall.* For William Jefferson **Blythe** III ('Bill Clinton'), see **Clinton**.

Blighton, *see* Blyton.

Blincow(e), *see* Blencow.

Bliss N/P/F Nickname for a joyful person ME, but Reaney also takes it back to the place-name *Blay* (formerly *Bleis*) in Normandy. A surname of southern England and the South Midlands. Welsh: son of (*ab-*) *Ellis* (compare **Bellis**). *Philip Bliss (1787–1857), antiquary, book-collector and sub-librarian at the Bodleian Library, Oxford, was born in Chipping Sodbury, Gloucs.*

Blisset, *see* Blessed.

Blom(e)field, *see* Bloomfield.

Blondell, *see* Blunt.

Blood O/N From OE *blod* ('blood'), and so probably used for a person who drew blood (a physician), or for a blood-relative.

Bloodworth/Bludder/Bludworth P From *Blidworth*, Notts (local pronunciation: *Bliddeth*). Sir Thomas **Bludworth**, who was Lord Mayor of London at the time of the Great Fire of 1666, is described by Pepys as being something of a clueless nincompoop. It was long supposed that he was the son of Sir Thomas **Bludder** of Hanchford, Reigate, Surrey, until someone thought to check the apprenticeship records of the Vintners' Company of London, of which he eventually became Master. When he was apprenticed to Martin Linton, vintner, on 7 July 1635, he is described unequivocally as Thomas, son of Edward **Bludworth** of Heanor, Derbys – a town which lies not so very far from *Blidworth* itself. Members of the **Bludworth/Bloodworth** family live in Heanor to this day, though the surname is most commonly found in Gloucs.

Bloom O Occupational term for an iron worker, from ME *blome* ('iron ingot') – also the origin of the surname **Bloomer** – but more commonly encountered as a Jewish name of the 'ornamental' variety, derived from Yiddish *blum* (flower). *Claire Bloom, British film and stage actress, was born in London in 1931 to parents with eastern European Jewish ancestry: her father was Edward Blume (from a family originally known as Blumenthal) and her mother was Elizabeth Grew (originally Griewski)… Mrs Amelia Jenks Bloomer, wife of Dexter Bloomer of New York, was responsible for the popularity of the ankle-length garments that acquired her (married) name… Steve Bloomer (1874–1938), the first football superstar, played for Derby County and captained England during the Victorian era.*

Bloomer, *see* Bloom.

Bloomfield/Blom(e)field P Place-name *Blonville-sur-Mer* in Calvados, France. Chiefly an East Anglian surname, whatever the spelling. *Francis Blomefield (1705–1752), author of a definitive history of the county of Norfolk, was born at Fersfield in that county.*

Bloor(e)/Blore P Place-name *Blore* in Staffs OE *blor* 'blister, swelling' (that is, 'hill') or 'bare spot'; but although **Bloor** and **Bloore** are most commonly found in Staffs, **Blore** is chiefly a Lancs surname. *Edward Blore, architect, artist and compiler of* The monumental remains of noble and eminent persons *(1826), was born in Derby on 13 September 1787, son of Thomas Blore (1764–1818), a native of Ashbourne in Derbys, who was the author of* The history of Rutland.

Blount, *see* Blunt.

Blox(h)am P Place-names: *Bloxham*, Oxon; *Bloxholm*, Lincs OE '*Blocc*'s homestead'.

Bludder/Bludworth, *see* Bloodworth.

Bluett, *see* Blewett.

Blundell, *see* Blunt.

Blunden ?N A surname of uncertain meaning: maybe a nickname for a person with blond or grizzled hair OE, with the adjectival ending *-en*, as in *wheaten*. Compare **Blunt**. The fact that the *-den* ending makes this look like a place-name is probably a red herring. Mainly confined to southern counties of England. *Edmund Blunden (1896–1974), poet, author and Professor of Poetry at Oxford, was born in London. In his early life, having taken part in the battles of Ypres and the Somme, he was awarded the Military Cross.*

Blunt/Blount N Nickname for a blond, fair-headed person (Anglo-Norman French *blunt*), or a nickname for a stupid person (ME *blunt/blont*, dull). Compare **Blunden**. **Blondell** and **Blundell** are diminutive forms.

Bly(e)/Blyth(e), *see* Bligh.

Blyton/Blighton P Place-name *Blyton* Lancs OE '*Blitha/Blih*'s settlement'. *Enid (Mary) Blyton (1897–1968), born in East Dulwich, London, the daughter of a cutlery salesman, was a hugely popular children's writer. Twice married, she retained her maiden name as an author.*

Boar/Boor/Bore N Nickname for a person bearing some resemblance to a boar OE *bar*. **Boar** and **Bore** are rare surnames, found mainly in Suffolk; **Boor** is strongest in Lincs.

Boatswain O Occupational term for a boatman ON. Also used as a first-name. Presumably the surname, like the occupational term itself, is pronounced 'bosun'? A rare surname, found mainly in Dorset.

Boatwright O Occupational term for a boat builder OE. A rare East Anglian surname.

Boddie, *see* Body.

Boddington P Place-name in Gloucs and Northants OE 'the farm of *Bota*'s people'.

Widespread, but found particularly in Warwicks and Northants. *In 1853 Henry Boddington, who had worked for many years in the brewery owned by Caister and Fry in Strangeways, Manchester, became the sole proprietor of the company. The Boddington family has run the business ever since.*

Boddy, *see* Body.

Bodel(l) F/P From an OF first-name *Bodo*, followed by the diminutive suffix *-ell*; also found in France as a form of *Bodeau*, with variants *Bod(e)let*, *Bodelin* and *Bodelot*. In Scotland (and Ulster), a corruption of **Bothwell**, which itself is derived from the lordship of that name in Lanarkshire, which in mediaeval times is referred to as *Boduel*. *Jack (John Geoffrey) Bodell, British heavyweight boxing champion and former coal-miner, was born in Newhall, South Derbys, where he is known to many locals as 'Jackie Bodle'.*

Bodenham P Place-name in Herefords and Wilts OE '*Boda*'s homestead'. Chiefly found in Salop, Worcs and Gloucs.

Bodicoat, *see* Bodycote.

Bod(d)y/Boddie N/O/T Nickname for a person of corpulent or striking physique OE *bodig*; or an occupational name for a messenger ME *bode*. As found in Cornwall, 'probably from *bod-dy*, as a special kind of house in a dwelling-place or settlement' (G. Pawley White).

Bodycoat, *see* Bodycote.

Bodycote/Bodicoat/Bodycoat/Bodycott P There is a place called *Bodicote* in Oxon OE 'cottage of *Boda/Boda*'s people', though the surname is almost entirely restricted to the county of Leics, whatever the spelling.

Bol(l)am/Bollom P Place-name *Bolam* in Co Durham and Northd OE 'at the tree trunks/planks'. A Northd surname.

Bolan, *see* Hayling.

Bol(l)and/Bowland P Place-names: *Bowland* in Lancs, ERYorks and WRYorks; *Bolland* in Devon OE '?land by a river bend'.

Bold N/T/P Nickname for a bold or brave person ME; or used for someone who lived at a specific dwelling house OE *bold* ('hall, house') or from a place-name *Bold* in Lancs, Salop OE 'house, palace'. Largely a Lancs surname.

Boldero(e), *see* Baldrick.

Bolders(t)on, *see* Balderston.

Bolding, *see* Baud.

Boleyn, *see* Bullen.

Bolingbroke P Place-name in Lincs OE 'brook of *Bul(l)a*'s people'. Commonly pronounced '*Bolingbrook*'. *Henry Bolingbroke, son of John of Gaunt, Duke of Lancaster, who deposed King Richard II and ascended the throne as King Henry IV, acquired his name from the fact that he had been born at Bolingbroke Castle, Lincs.* **Bollinger**, *see* Pollinger.

Bolitho P There are various places so-called in Cornwall, Cornish '?dwelling with dairies'. Despite certain similarities, probably not a variant of **Belitha** (see **Billiter**).

Bolland, *see* Boland.

Bollen, *see* Bullen.

Bollom, *see* Bolam.

Bolt/Boult O/N Occupational term for a maker of bolts/missiles/arrows OE *bolt* (as in the bolt of a crossbow), or who bolted or sifted flour OF (hence also **Bolter/Boulter**); or a nickname for a person as strong and stocky as a bolt OE, or who was especially bold OE. **Bolt** belongs mainly to Devon, and **Boulter** to Leics; **Boult** is more widespread. *Robert (Oxton) Bolt (1924–1995), the English dramatist who twice married the actress Sarah Miles, was born and educated in Manchester… Sir Adrian (Cedric) Boult (1889–1983), born in Chester, became a very successful orchestral conductor.*

Bolter, *see* Bolt.

Bolting, *see* Baud.

Bolton/Boulton P There are various places called *Bolton* in England, in particular the one in Lancs OE 'place with groups of houses/centre of a village'.

Bompas, *see* Bumpas.

Bomphrey, *see* Bumphrey.

Bonar, *see* Bonner.

Bond/Bound(s)/Bound(e)y/Bund(e)y O Occupational term for a husbandman, peasant farmer ME *bonde*, from OE/ON. At one time carried the meaning of a bound serf. Very widespread as a surname. The cleverly named '*Honour* **Bound**' was buried in St Pinnock, Cornwall, in 1783.

Bondfield, *see* Bonfield.

Bone/Bunn N Nickname for a good person OF *bon* – or for a bony one OE *ban*. **Bone** is strongest in Hants and Middx, **Bunn** in Norfolk. It was perhaps a trifle unkind of Mr and Mrs **Bone** to name their daughter '*Nora* (**Bone**)' when she was born in South Stoneham, Hants, in 1902. Reaney regards **Bunce** as being a variant of **Bunn**, and indeed it could simply be '**Bunn**'s (son)'. Either that, or there may be a nickname origin – but while Rosalind Moffitt notes (in *Family Tree Magazine*, March 2007) that '*bunce*' can be a dialectal term for a 'bonus' ('that's bunce!'), she admits that such a usage is mainly restricted to Lancs, Scotland and Ireland, whereas **Bunce** as a surname belongs to southern England. A muster roll for Bucks in 1522 includes the names of Henry **Bunce** of Leckhamstead and John and Thomas **Bunce** of Dinton, and there are two people called **Buns** in such a roll for West Berks in the same year. Alternative spellings for **Bunce** might include **Bounce/Bunts** (both very scarce) and **Bance** (strongest in Kent, Middx, Surrey).

Bon(d)field P From one of the places called *Bonneville* in Normandy. **Bonfield** is a Herts surname; **Bondfield**, much rarer, is chiefly found in Somerset.

Bongard/Bongars N Nickname for a trusted servant OF *bon* and *gars*.

Bonham/Bonhomme N/O/P Nickname for

a good man OF *bon homme* – there was a religious order of *Bonshommes*, who had a fine priory at Edington, Wilts; or an occupational term for a peasant farmer; or from an unidentified place-name. Chiefly a Bucks/Northants name. *The firm of Bonham's, auctioneers, was founded in 1793 by Thomas Dodd, an antique print dealer, and Walter Bonham, a book specialist.*

Boniface F From a mediaeval first-name, never very popular in England, but used by no fewer than nine popes. Chiefly a Sussex surname.

Bonithan/Bonithon, *see* Bonthron.

Bonner/Bonar N Nickname for a gentle, gracious, courteous person OF. **Bonar** is very much a Scottish surname, found particularly in Lanarkshire. *Andrew Bonar Law (1858–1923), Conservative Prime Minister, was born in New Brunswick, Canada, of Scots-Irish and Scots descent.*

Bonser N/P Generally supposed to be derived from OF *bon sire*, used for a fine gentleman (or ironically for a less-than fine one), or for a man who habitually used such a phrase in everyday speech, but a much more likely origin must be the town of *Bonsall* OE '*Bunt*'s nook of land' in Derbys, known locally as 'Bonser'. While it is found in Derbys itself, the surname is principally associated with the adjoining counties of Leics and Notts.

Bonthron(e) T/P Scots: a surname mainly found in Fifeshire in both spellings, for which G. F. Black gives no source, though he believes that it has developed in some cases from **Bontavern**. In Cornwall matters are slightly more complicated: **Bonthron** and **Bonythorn** (very scarce) refer to a dweller on a promontory or headland, Cornish *bo'n-i-tron*, while the not-dissimilar surnames **Bonithan**, **Bonithon** and **Bonython** (all extremely scarce) are from *Bonithon/Bonython*, later *Bonithin*, an estate in the parish of Cury, Cornish *bo'n'y-y-thon* 'the furzy dwelling' or *bos Nectan* 'dwelling of *Nectan/Nighton*'.

Bonython/Bonythorn, *see* Bonthron.

Boocock/Bowcock, *see* Baud.

Boodle T/P Dweller near a large house OE *bothl/botl*, or from a place-name with similar meaning, such as *Buddle* in Hants, Somerset, or *Budle* in Northd. *Boodle's Club in London was founded by Edward Boodle, third son of John Boodle of the Three Tuns, Oswestry, Salop, who was baptized in that town on 14 May 1722.*

Booker O Occupational term for a writer or a binder of books, or for a bleacher ME *bouken*.

Bool, *see* Bull.

Boon/Bown N/P Nickname for a good person OF *bon*, or from the place-name *Bohon* in La Manche. **Bown** has an odd distribution, being comparatively strong in Derbys, but also in Somerset. *The famous American frontiersman Daniel Boone (1734–1820) came from a Quaker family; his paternal grandfather, a weaver, had emigrated from Exeter in Devon to Philadelphia in 1717.*

Boor, *see* Boar.

Boorman, *see* Bower.

Boosey/Boosie T/O/P Dweller at, or worker at, a cow-shed ME *bos(e)*; or from the place-name *Balhousie* in Fife, Scotland, though there are very few examples of individuals in Scotland having borne such a surname in either of its principal spellings. *The firm of Boosey & Company, originally a lending library, was founded by John Boosey, whose family, cloth spinners of Franco-Flemish origin, had settled in Essex in the early fifteenth century. In 1930 Boosey & Company joined with Hawkes & Son to form Boosey and Hawkes, a partnership which at one time dominated the music industry.*

Boot(e) O Occupational term for a maker or seller of boots ME/OF *bote*. A Midlands surname, chiefly found in Notts, but also in Derbys and Staffs. A man named '*Jack* **Boot**' was born in Uxbridge, Middx, in 1899, and '*Wellington* **Boot**' first saw the light of day in Linton, Cambs, in 1869. *John Boot (1815–1860), born in Radcliffe on Trent, Notts, was the founder of Boots the*

Chemists, a company which his son Jesse Boot turned into a retail outlet known throughout the United Kingdom.

Booth/Boothman T/O Dweller by, or worker at, a hut or bothy ME *both(e)*. A northern surname, found mainly in Chesh. *There is no lack of well-known people bearing the Booth surname. Booth's Dry Gin was first distilled by a family of that name in 1740; 'General' William Booth (1829–1912), founder of the Salvation Army, was born in the splendid-sounding Notintone Place, Nottingham; Richard Booth, 'King of Hay', is a famous Hay-on-Wye bookseller; Cherie Booth/Blair is both a prominent lawyer and the wife of a former Prime Minister; John Wilkes Booth (1838–1865), a native of Maryland whose parents had moved to the USA from England in 1821 and named him after the British revolutionary John Wilkes, achieved notoriety by assassinating President Abraham Lincoln after the American Civil War.*

Boothby P Place-name in Lincs, Cumbd ON 'farm with huts/sheds'.

Boothman, *see* Booth.

Boothroyd P Place-name in WRYorks ON and OE 'clearing with huts/sheds'. *Betty Boothroyd, a former Tiller Girl who became the first female speaker of the House of Commons, was born in Dewsbury, Yorks, in 1929.*

Bootle/Boutle P Place-name *Bootle* in Cumbd and Lancs OE 'house, dwelling'. **Bootle** is found chiefly in Lancs, but **Boutle**, a rare surname, belongs mainly to East Anglia and south-east England, and may have a different origin.

Borland P Place-names *Bor(e)land* and *Bordland* in Scotland OE and ON 'land held on the rental of a food supply'. Found chiefly in Lanarkshire and Ayrshire.

Borley P Place-names: *Borley*, Essex (with a much-haunted rectory); *Boreley*, Worcs OE 'boar wood'. The surname **Borley** is mostly found in south-east England and East Anglia, being strongest in Essex.

Borman, *see* Bower.

Borthwick P From the old Barony of *Borthwick*, lying beside *Borthwick Water* in Roxburghshire, Scotland OE 'board/table/fort village'. A Scottish/Northd surname. Readily confused with/a variant of **Borwick**.

Borton, *see* Burton.

Borwick P Place-name in Lancs OE 'demesne farm'. A surname found mainly in north-west England. Readily confused with/a variant of **Borthwick**. *Borwick's Baking Powder, 'the best in the world', was invented by a bored vicar who succeeded in making his family very wealthy. George Borwick, baking powder manufacturer, served as Member of Parliament for North Croydon, 1918–1922.*

Boscawen P From one of various place-names in Cornwall, Cornish 'house by the elder tree'. Family name of the Earls Falmouth.

Bostock P Place-name in Chesh OE '*Bota*'s place'. One fairly grand family of **Bostocks** descend from the twelfth-century Sir Gilbert of **Bostock**. Rather less grand, but still worthy, bearers of this name can be found in some profusion in the Derbys town of Ilkeston, where Jonathan **Bostock** (1807–1889) was once the town crier and bill poster. He was known as 'Derby Trot' because he had once trotted from Ilkeston to Derby and back three times – a distance of sixty miles – but a contemporary remarked that 'the style of his dress would lead some to imagine that measurement was a thing unknown, and buttons extremely scarce'.

Boston P Place-name in Lincs OE '(St) *Botolph*'s (preaching) stone/stone house'. St Botolph's church, Boston, with a tower 272 feet high, is famously known as the *Boston Stump*.

Bosworth P Place-names in Leics: *Husbands Bosworth* OE '*Boar*'s enclosure' and *Market Bosworth* OE '*Bosa*'s enclosure'. A Midlands surname.

Botham, *see* Bottom.

Bothwell, *see* Bodel.

Bott F/N From an OE first-name; or a nickname for a person who bore some resemblance to a toad OE *bot*. Chiefly a Midlands surname, strongest in Staffs.

Bottom(s)/Botham T Dweller in the broad valley OE *botm* ('valley bottom'). 'Stress on the second syllable is a hapless attempt to conceal a perfectly respectable meaning' (Cottle). **Bottom** is found mainly in WRYorks; **Botham** is a Midlands surname, strongest in Derbys. *Ian Botham, English Test cricketer, was born in 1955 in Heswall, Chesh, though his greatest contribution to county cricket was as a player for Somerset CCC.*

Bottomley P Place-name in WRYorks OE 'clearing in a dell'. Sometimes softened to **Bothamley**. *Horatio Bottomley (1860–1933), a prominent journalist, Member of Parliament and swindler, who was once described as 'irredeemably, utterly, psychotically corrupt', was born in Bethnal Green, London.*

Bottomshaw, *see* Birkenshaw.

Boucher, *see* Butcher.

Bough O/N Occupational term for someone who worked with bulls, Norman French *boeuf* ('bull'), or a nickname for a person who looked like a bull; or a variant of **Bow**. **Bough** can be pronounced to rhyme with 'cow', or to rhyme with 'cough'.

Boughton P Place-name in Kent, Chesh OE 'place in the beeches'; and also in Northants, Norfolk, Notts, Chesh, Beds (some with the meaning of OE '*Bucca*'s place'). A widespread surname, strongest in southern counties of England.

Boulding, *see* Baud.

Boult/Boulter, *see* Bolt.

Boulting, *see* Baud.

Boulton, *see* Bolton.

Boumphrey, *see* Bumphrey.

Bounce, *see* Bone.

Bound(s)/Bound(e)y, *see* Bond.

Bourke, *see* Burke.

Bourn(e)/Burn(e)(s)/Burness T/P Dweller by a stream OE *burna/burne*; or from a place-name with the same meaning, such as *Bourn*, Cambs; *St Mary Bourne*, Hants; *Bourne* Lincs. The word *burn* is now generally found only in the north of England and in Scotland, but *burn* and *bourn(e)* were once common in the south, being used eventually to refer to an intermittent stream, especially one flowing only in winter (though *brook* is a common southern alternative). So it is that there are places in the south of England called *Burnham*, *Bournemouth* and *Wimborne*, and the surname **Bourn(e)** can be found throughout northern and southern counties of England. *The family of the Ayrshire poet Robert/ Rabbie Burns (1759–1796), formerly Campbells from Burnhouse in Taynuilt, had originally carried the surname Burness. It was Robert and his brother who decided to adopt the spelling 'Burns'.*

Bourton, *see* Burton.

Boutle, *see* Bootle.

Bouverie T/O Dweller by, or worker at, an ox farm OF *boverie*. Rare in England. Sometimes found as a Huguenot surname, and is also borne by the family of Pleydell-Bouverie, Earls of Radnor, whose ancestry can be traced back to Laurence Des Bouveries, born in 1542, who moved from his home in Lille, Flanders, to Canterbury in 1568.

Bouvier, *see* Boyer.

Bovey P Place-names *Bovey Tracy* or *North Bovey*, Devon, which take their name from the river *Bovey*. Chiefly a Devon surname.

Bovis, *see* Beavis.

Bow(e)/Bough O/T/P Occupational term for a maker of bows ME *bow*, from OE *boga*; or a dweller near a bridge OE *boga* (describing the bow-shape of an arched bridge); or from such a place-name in various counties.

Bowater T Dweller on ground above a stretch of water ME *buven* ('above') and *water*. Mainly a Staffs/Worcs surname. *William Vansittart Bowater (1838–1924), founder of the famous paper-manufacturing company which bore his name, came from an ancestral line which can be traced back to John Bowater of Whitley, Coventry, Warwicks, who was known to have been alive and active in the 1630s.*

Bowcher, *see* Butcher.

Bowcott P/F From some minor place-name, possibly *Boycott* in Bucks, Salop, Worcs OE '*Boia*'s cottage' (compare **Boycott**); or from the first-name *Baldwin* with the addition of *cock* ('little lad').

Bowden/Bawdon/Bowdon P There are places called *Bowden* in various counties OE '*Buga*'s hill' or '*Bofa*'s settlement', and also *Bowden Edge*, Derbys, and *Bowdon*, Chesh OE 'arched/rounded hill'.

Bowe, *see* Bow.

Bowell(s), *see* Bowles.

Bowen F Welsh: son of (*ab-*) *Owen*. Chiefly a South Wales and Welsh/English border surname.

Bower(s)/Bo(o)rman/Bowerman/Bowra(h)/Bowring T/O/P Dweller in a small cottage OE *bur*; or a house servant; or from a minor place-name such as (*East & West*) *Bower*, Somerset; *Bowers Gifford*, Essex OE 'cottage'. Readily confused with/a variant of **Bowyer**. Bowring is largely a Dorset surname. *John Boorman, English film-maker, was born in Shepperton, Surrey, in 1933.*

Bowes P Place-name in NRYorks (now in Co Durham) ME 'arched bridge', and the surname is most commonly found in that area of England. *Queen Elizabeth the Queen Mother, mother of Queen Elizabeth II, was born Elizabeth Angela Marguerite Bowes-Lyon, daughter of the fourteenth Earl of Strathmore and Kinghorne. The family surname dates from the marriage of John, ninth Earl of Strathmore, to Mary Eleanor Bowes, daughter of George Bowes of Streatlam Castle and Gibside, Co Durham, in 1767.*

Bowie N Nickname for a yellow-haired person, Scots Gaelic *buidhe*. The surname is generally confined to Scotland and Northd. *The American Bowie Knife was invented by Colonel James Bowie (1795–1836), who died during the Battle of the Alamo, and whose adventurous life inspired the English singer, songwriter and actor David Robert Jones (born in Brixton, London, in 1947) to change his name to David Bowie (which he pronounces to rhyme with 'Joey').*

Bowker, *see* Butcher.

Bowland, *see* Boland.

Bowler O/N Occupational term for a maker or seller of bowls, or a nickname for a hard drinker ME *boller* (a drinking vessel). Found mainly in the Midlands, especially Derbys, but also has had a significant presence in Bucks.

Bowles/Bowell(s) P/F Place-name *Bouelles* in Seine Maritime; Welsh: son of (*ab-*) *Howell*. Most commonly found in Kent.

Bowley T/P Dweller in/near a bullock-pasture OE, or from a place-name with the same meaning in Herefords. A south-of-England and Midlands surname, commonest in Leics. *The name of Al (Albert Alick) Bowlly (1899–1941), world-renowned South African crooner, sounds almost quintessentially English, but not quite. He was born in Mozambique to a Greek father, Alick Pauli, and a Lebanese mother. The Pauli surname was first written as 'Bowlly' in error when the couple emigrated to South Africa from Australia.*

Bowmaker O Occupational term for a maker of bows OE. A scarce surname, found mainly in Northd and Co Durham.

Bowman O Occupational term for an archer (one who used a bow) OE, as opposed to the surname **Bowyer** (one who made bows).

Bown, *see* Boon.

Bowness P Place-name in Cumbd ON 'rounded headland' and Westmd ON 'bulls' headland'. The surname is most frequently found in these two counties, and also in Lancs. *William Bowness (1809–1867), portrait painter, was born in Kendal, Westmd.*

Bowra(h)/Bowring, *see* **Bower**.

Bowser/Beausire N/T/P Accepted wisdom has it that the surname **Bowser** arose by way of a nickname for someone who frequently used the phrase *beau sire* ('fair sir'), though Reaney suggests that it might perhaps have been applied to a dweller in a place planted with bushes, from French *bussière*. Yet 'Bowser' is a well-established and still-used dialectal term for the town of *Bolsover* in Derbyshire, and there is an example from the seventeenth century of an individual involved in a legal case in London who bore the surname 'Bolsover alias Bowser'. Compare **Belcher**. **Bowser** is most commonly found in Co Durham, **Beausire** (scarce) in Chesh. *The confectionery firm of Callard and Bowser, once known for products such as Creamline Toffee, was established in Finchley, North London, in 1837 by Daniel Callard and his brother-in-law J Bowser.*

Bowyer/Boyer O Occupational term for a maker or seller of bows. Readily confused with/a variant of **Bower**.

Box T/P Dweller by a box-tree OE, or from a place-name with the same meaning in Gloucs, Herts, Wilts.

Box(h)all P From a lost place-name in Sussex, *Boxholte* OE 'box-tree holt'. *John Boxall (1524/5-1571), state administrator and churchman under the Tudors, was born at Bramshott, Hants… Sir Charles Gervaise Boxall (1851-1914), army officer and promoter of rail-mounted artillery, was born at Delves House, Ringmer, Sussex.*

Boxley P Place-name in Kent OE 'box-tree wood/clearing'. A scarce scattered surname.

Boxwell P Place-name in Gloucs OE 'spring/stream in the box-trees', and chiefly a Gloucs surname.

Boyce/Boy(e)s T/N/F Dweller in or near a wood OF *bois*; or a nickname for a youth/servant ME *boy*; or from a Germanic first-name *Boia*. **Boys** and **Boyce** are widespread surnames; **Boyes** is strongest in Lancs and Yorks.

Boycott P From some minor place-name, possibly *Boycott* in Bucks, Salop, Worcs OE '*Boia*'s cottage', see **Bowcott**. A scarce surname, mainly associated with the county of Salop. *Geoffrey Boycott, English Test cricketer, was born in Fitzwilliam, Yorks, in 1940… The brutal tactics of Captain Charles Boycott (1832–1897), the Norfolk clergyman's son who was estate agent for an absentee landlord in County Mayo, Ireland, led in 1880 to his ostracism and to the use of his surname in everyday speech, both as a noun and as a verb.*

Boyd ?P/N Scots and Irish. Origin disputed. From the island of *Bute*? Nickname for a yellow-haired person, Scots Gaelic *buidhe* ('yellow')? Family name of the Barons Kilmarnock.

Boyer/Bouvier O Occupational term for a herdsman OF *bouvier*. **Boyer** can be a variant of **Bowyer**. *Jacqueline Lee Bouvier (born 1929), daughter of John Vernou Bouvier III, stockbroker, and his wife Janet Lee, married John Fitzgerald Kennedy in Newport, Rhode Island, in 1953 and became America's First Lady, 1961–1963.*

Boyes, *see* **Boyce**.

Boyle F/P Irish: Anglicized form of Gaelic **O'** [descendant of] **Baoighill**; Scots: from the place-name *Boyville*, near Caen, France. Family name of the Earls of Glasgow, Shannon and Cork and Orrery.

Boys, *see* **Boyce**.

Brabazon/Brabbin/Brabbyn/Braben/ Brabham/Brabin/Brabner P Used to refer to a man from *Brabant* (Belgium/Netherlands). 'The surname may be disreputable; thirteenth-century Brabançons were thuggish mercenaries who beat up French provinces' (Cottle). Family name of the Earls of Meath. *Jack Brabham (Sir John Arthur Brabham), Formula One motor-racing champion, a second-generation Australian who was the son of a grocer, was born in Sydney in 1926.*

Bracegirdle O Occupational term for a

maker of belts for holding up breeches OE *brec* and *gyrdel*. Chiefly a Chesh/Lancs surname. *Timothy Bracegirdle or Bracegir, Perpetual Curate of Holy Trinity, Minories, in the City of London, was conducting a thriving and profitable business in irregular or clandestine marriages there in the 1640s… John Bracegirdle (died 1614), clergyman and poet, was reputedly the son of John Bracegirdle, vicar of Stratford-upon-Avon, and (also reputedly) was born in Chesh… Anne Bracegirdle (1671–1748), actress and singer, was born in Northants.*

Brach/Bra(t)cher/Breach/Bre(a)cher T Dweller by an opening, a spinney left as a boundary, newly broken/tilled land OE. Readily confused with/a variant of **Brack**.

Brack O/N Occupational term for a master of hunting dogs, Middle High German *bracke*, or a nickname for someone who resembled such a dog. Also found as a surname in Germany, and in France (**Braque**). Readily confused with/a variant of **Brach**.

Brackenbury/Brackenborough P Place-name *Brackenborough* OE 'hill covered with bracken' in Lincs. Very much a Lincs surname in both spellings, though there is a place called *Breckenbrough* (with the same meaning) in NRYorks.

Brackenridge/Breckenridge P Place-names: *Brackenrigg*, Cumbd; *Brackenrig*, Lanarkshire, Scotland OE 'ridge overgrown with bracken'. Both variants are most commonly found in Ayrshire and Lanarkshire. The prominent American family of **Breckenridge** traces its ancestry back to Alexander **Breckenridge**, a Scottish covenanter who fled to America on the restoration of the Stuarts.

Bradbourn(e)/Bradburn(e) P Place-name in Derbys and Kent OE 'broad stream'. **Bradbourn(e)** (scarce) is found mainly in Staffs; **Bradburn**, a Lancs surname, is much more prolific.

Bradbrook P From a minor place-name OE 'broad brook'.

Bradburn(e), *see* Bradbourn.

Bradbury P Place-name in Co Durham OE 'fortified place built of boards', but mainly a Lancs/Yorks surname. A certain 'P. George Hopeless **Bradbury**' was born in Sheffield, Yorks, in 1874.

Braddock T/P Dweller by the broad oak, or from a minor place-name such as *Braddock*, Cornwall, with the same meaning. The surname occurs mainly in Chesh and Lancs. *Bessie Braddock (1899–1970), the British Labour Party politician who was born Elizabeth Bamber in Liverpool, married John 'Jack' Braddock in 1922. She served as MP for Liverpool Exchange from 1945 to 1969.*

Bradfield P Place-name in many counties OE 'broad open land'.

Bradford P Place-name in many counties, including the town in WRYorks and the village of *Bradford on Avon*, Wilts OE 'broad ford'. *William Bradford (1589–1657), a prominent Pilgrim Father, was born in Austerfield, WRYorks.*

Bradgate P Place-name *Bradgate* in WRYorks and Leics OE 'broad gate/gap'. A scarce surname, mainly found in Lancs.

Bradley/Broadely/Broadley T/P Dweller at the broad wood/clearing OE; or from one of the many places called *Bradley* in England and Scotland, with the same meaning. **Broadley** is found mainly in WRYorks, Lancs and Lanarkshire, Scotland.

Bradman N Nickname for a broad man OE. Chiefly found in Suffolk. *Sir Donald Bradman (1908–2001), the Australian cricketer widely regarded as the best batsman of all time (with a Test batting average of 99.94 runs), was born in Cootamundra, New South Wales, son of George Bradman and Emily Whatman. The Bradman family had arrived in Australia in the year 1852.*

Bradnam P Place-name *Bradenham* in Bucks and Norfolk OE 'at the wide river-meadow/homestead'. A surname most commonly found in Suffolk.

Bradshaw/Brayshaw/Brayshay P Place-name *Bradshaw* in various counties, including Derbys, Lancs, WRYorks OE 'broad wood'. **Bradshaw** is most commonly found in Lancs, **Brayshaw** and **Brayshay** in WRYorks.

Bradstreet ⊤ Dweller on or near a broad street OE *brad stræt*, such as a Roman highway. Chiefly found in Suffolk.

Bradwell P Place-name in Bucks, Derbys, Essex, Somerset, Suffolk and elsewhere OE 'broad stream'.

Bragg(e) N Nickname for a lively, brisk, brave, possibly proud or arrogant person ME *bragge*. The *-e* ending of **Bragge** could indicate the use of a weak adjective after a lost definite article.

Braham P/F Place-names: *Braham* and *Bramham*, WRYorks OE '?meadow covered with broom'; *Braham Farm*, Cambs OE '? bramble meadow'; *Brantham*, Suffolk OE '*Brant/Branta*'s village' (for the loss of the letter *-n-*, compare the way in which the surname **Graham** can be derived from *Grantham*, Lincs). Also found as a Jewish surname, a shortened form of **Abraham**. **Bream/Breem**, not fishy surnames, can be a variant of **Braham**.

Brailsford/Brelsford P Place-name *Brailsford* in Derbys OE 'ford at the burial/tumulus'. **Brailsford**, predictably, is mainly a Derbys, Notts and WRYorks surname, while **Brelsford** is associated with the county of Lancs.

Braithwaite P Place-name in Cumbd, NRYorks, WRYorks ON 'broad clearing'.

Brake ⊤ Dweller by a thicket or a clump of bracken (the word *brake* in ME could carry either meaning). Chiefly a Dorset/Somerset surname.

Brakspear, *see* Breakspear.

Bramah/Bram(h)all/Brummell ⊤/P
Dweller in a remote spot where broom grows OE; or from a place-name with the same meaning, such as *Bramhall*, Chesh, or *Bromhill*, Sussex. **Bramah** (a scarce surname), **Bramall** and **Bramhall** (more common) are found chiefly in Lancs and WRYorks; **Brummell**, also scarce, is found in Cambs and Surrey. *See also* **Brambell**

and **Bramwell**. *The famous dandy George Bryan ('Beau') Brummell (1778–1840) was born in Downing Street, London, where his father was private secretary to the Prime Minister, Lord North.*

Brambell/Bramble N/⊤ Nickname for a person as prickly as a bramble OE *bræmel*; or (less likely, as the name is scarcely if ever found with a preposition attached) a dweller in a place overgrown with brambles. Or a variant of **Bramah/Bramhall**. **Brambell** is a very scarce surname; **Bramble** is found mainly in the south of England, especially Hants and Kent. *Wilfrid Brambell (1912–1985), alias Wilfred Brambell/Wilfred Bramble, a Dublin-born actor, achieved fame thanks to his role in the TV series* Steptoe and Son. *On screen, Alfred Steptoe (Wilfrid Brambell) and his son Harold (Harry H. Corbett) had a tumultuous relationship; off-screen matters were even worse – the two actors loathed each other.*

Bramford P Place-name in Suffolk OE 'ford by the broom-bushes'. A scarce surname, strongest in Lincs.

Bramhall, *see* Bramah.

Bramley P Place-name in Derbys, Hants, Surrey, Yorks and elsewhere OE 'clearing/field overgrown with broom'. Mainly a Midlands/North of England surname.

Brampton P Place-name found throughout England OE 'place where broom grows'.

Bramwell P From an unidentified place-name OE 'broom spring/well'. A surname of the North of England. *See also* **Bramah/Bram(h)all**.

Branaghan, *see* Branigan.

Branch ?N Presumably some kind of a nickname from ME, OF *branche*, from Latin *branca* ('paw, foot'), but precisely why it would have been used as a surname is not clear. Might it suggest 'descendant, offspring'? The surname is concentrated in the south-east and south-west of England, but not in Wilts, where there is a Hundred named '*Branch and Dole*' (*Branch*, which was *Brencesberge* in 1086, is OE '?*Braenci*'s hill/barrow'). *Brenchley* in Kent OE *'Braenci*'s wood/clearing' was *Branchlee* in 1254. A child called '*Olive* **Branch**' was born in West Ham, Essex, in 1880.

Branchflower, *see* Blanchflower.

Brand/Braund F From the Germanic first-name *Brando*, 'sword, torch, firebrand'. **Brand** is a widespread surname, found chiefly in south-eastern counties of England and in Scotland; **Braund** is chiefly found in Devon. *Marlon Brando (1924–2004), American actor, was born in Omaha, Nebraska, son of Marlon Brando senior and Dorothy (née Pennybaker).*

Brandon P Place-name in Co Durham, Northd, Norfolk, Suffolk, Warwicks and elsewhere OE 'hill covered with broom', though the first element of the Lincs *Brandon* may be the river *Brant* OE 'steep(-sided)'. In Ireland, the origin may be *Brendan* ('stinking hair').

Brandreth P Place-name *Brandred (Farm)*, Kent OE 'burnt clearing', though the surname is strongest in Lancs. Compare **Brend**, **Brent**. *Gyles Brandreth, cheerful television celebrity, former Conservative MP for Chester and first-class Monopoly and Scrabble player, was born at a British Forces Hospital in Germany; his family moved to London when he was three years old.*

Brangwyn/Brangwin ?F English and Welsh: possibly from the Welsh female first-name *Branwen* ('white/fair raven'), which was borne by two ladies in Celtic legend, one of whom had the risky job of being Isolde's maid.

Bran(n)igan/Branaghan/Brannan/ Brannon F Irish: Anglicized form of Gaelic **O'** [descendant of] **Branagain** ('raven').

Branthwaite/Branwhite P Place-name in Cumbd (two such) OE 'clearing overgrown with broom'.

Brasher/Brasier/Brasseur/Brazier O Occupational term for a brewer OF *brasser*, or for a brassfounder OE *broesian*.

Bratcher, *see* Brach.

Bratton P Place-name in Devon, Somerset, Wilts OE 'newly cultivated/broken-up farm' and in Salop, Somerset OE 'place on a brook'. A scattered surname, strong in Staffs. Readily confused with/a variant of **Bret(t)on** (see **Brett**).

Braund, *see* Brand.

Bray P Place-name in Berks OF 'marsh' and Devon, Cornish 'hill'.

Braybrook(e) P Place-name in Northants OE 'broad brook'.

Brayer O Occupational term for a maker or seller of pestles OF. A very scarce scattered surname.

Brayshaw/Brayshay, *see* Bradshaw.

Brayton P Place-name in Cumbd, WRYorks ON/OE 'broad place'.

Brazier, *see* Brasher.

Breach/Breacher, *see* Brach.

Breakspear N Nickname for a fine warrior in battle or tournament, or – ironically – for a clumsy one ME/OE ('break spear'). *Nicholas Breakspear, born in Langley, Herts, was England's only pope, Adrian IV (1154-9).*

Bream/Breem P/N Place-names: *Bream*, Gloucs ME 'rough ground' or OE 'broom'; *Braham/Bramham*, ERYorks OE 'broom/gorse homestead'; *Brantham*, Suffolk OE '*Brant*'s homestead'; or a nickname for an energetic person ME *brem(e)/brim(me)*. Only a fanciful imagination would make any connexion with the coarse fish, the bream, much loved by anglers. *See also* **Braham.**

Brearley, *see* Brierly.

Brecher, *see* Brach.

Breckenridge, *see* Brackenridge.

Brede/Breed(e) P From a minor place-name in various counties, such as *Brede* in East Sussex OE 'broad place'.

Breem, *see* Bream.

Breen P/F Place-name *Brean* in Somerset, etymology uncertain (Welsh *bre*, a hill?);

Irish: Anglicized form of Gaelic **O'** [descendant of] **Braion** ('moisture'). Within England, the surname is strongest in Lancs.

Breese/Breeze N/F Nickname for an irritating person OE *breeze* ('gadfly'); Welsh: son of (*ab-*) *Rhys/Rees*. **Breese** is most commonly met with in Montgomeryshire, but also occurs in Norfolk; **Breeze** is more widespread, but can also be found in Montgomeryshire as well as Lancs, Norfolk, Salop and Staffs.

Brelsford, *see* **Brailsford**.

Bremner/Brimner P A name applied to a settler from *Brabant* in the Low Countries (early Scots *Brebner/Brabanare*). These are Scottish surnames: **Bremner** is most in evidence in Aberdeenshire and Caithness; **Brimner**, much scarcer, can be found in Angus. *William John ('Billy') Bremner (1942–1997), the footballer best known for his captaincy of Leeds United during the 1960s and 1970s, was born in Stirling, Scotland… Rory Bremner, highly acclaimed impressionist and comedian, was born in Edinburgh in 1961.*

Brend N/T Nickname for a person branded, 'burnt', as a criminal OE; but Reaney shows that it has sometimes been used for a person living in a land cleared by burning OE (compare **Brent** and **Brandreth**). A Devon surname.

Brennan(d) F/O/N Irish: Anglicized form of Gaelic **O'** [descendant of] **Braonain**; or an occupational term for an official who branded criminals ('burn-hand'), or a nickname for one who suffered such a punishment ('burnt-hand') ME.

Brent T/P/N Dweller at a high place or one cleared by fire ME *brent*; or from the place-name *Brent* in Devon and Somerset OE 'steep'/Celtic 'hill'; or a nickname for a criminal who had been branded, 'burnt' (compare **Brend** and **Brandreth**).

Brereton/Brierton P Place-names: *Brereton*, Chesh OE 'briar settlement' and Staffs OE 'briar hill'; *Brierton*, Co Durham OE 'briar-valley and farm'. The prominent American family of **Brereton** came from Malpas, Chesh; the surname is most commonly found in that county, but also in Lancs and Staffs.

Bretherton P Place-name in Lancs OE/ON and OE 'the brothers' farm'. *See also* **Brotherton**.

Brett/Bret(t)(on)/Britt(on)/Brittain/Brittan/Britten P/N A native of Brittany OF *Bret*. A number of Celts were driven from south-west England to north-west France in the face of Anglo-Saxon invasions, and many Bretons, in turn, settled in East Anglia following the Norman Conquest. Bretons, alas, had a reputation for being stupid, and the surname may have this meaning on occasions. Or from one of a number of place-names: *Monk Bretton* and *West Bretton*, WRYorks; *Bretton*, Derbys OE 'freshly broken land'. **Bret(t)on** can also be confused with, or be a variant of, **Bratton**. **Brett** is the family name of the Viscounts Esher. *Vera Brittain, highly regarded poet and author of the autobiographical work* Testament of youth, *was born in Newcastle-under-Lyme, Staffs, in 1893, the daughter of a paper manufacturer.*

Brew O Irish: Anglicized form of **O'** [descendant of] **Brughadha**; Manx: **MacVriw** ('son of the judge'). The surname is strongly represented in recent times in the Isle of Man, and also in Lancs.

Brewer/Brewster/Bruster O/P Occupational term for a brewer OE. The suffix *-ster* (as in **Webster**, etc.) is theoretically one which is applied to female practitioners of the trade, but was also used extensively for men. **Brewer** can alternatively be a Norman name, describing a person from *Bruyère* in Calvados, and in some cases **Bruster** can refer to a female (or male) embroiderer ME *broudestere*. *William Brewster, Pilgrim Father (1567–1644), would appear to have come from Scrooby, Notts.*

Brian/Brine/Bryan/Bryant/Bryne F From the Celtic first-name *Brian*. Some Breton '*Brian*'s who arrived in England at the time of the Norman Conquest found their way to Ireland, where a variety of the name already existed. *Brian Boru* was King of Ireland in 1002, and today **O'Brien** is one of the commonest Irish surnames. **Brine** is mainly a Dorset/Somerset surname. The *-t* of **Bryant** (found chiefly in south-west England and in Glamorgan) is a parasitic dental of the sort found in the surname **Hammon (d)** and the word *varmin(t)*.

Briar(s)/Brier(s)/Bryer(s) T Dweller in a place covered in brambles OE.

Brice/Bryce F From a Celtic first-name, of unknown meaning. St *Brice* (died 444) was successor as Bishop of Tours to the ever-popular St Martin. Now, alas, he is remembered as the saint on whose day the Danes were massacred.

Brickett, *see* Birkett.

Bridewell T/P Dweller at a spring/stream where birds proliferated OE, or at a spring dedicated to St Bridget. The Bridewell in London, named after St Bridget, became a prison too late to be the origin of a surname. The surname is scarce, and is confined almost exclusively to Wilts, so the place-name in that county, *Bridewell Springs* OE 'bride's spring' (possibly a fertility spring), which was simply *Brudewelle* in the fourteenth century, could be the source of the surname. See also **Bridle**.

Bridge(s)/Bridger/Brigg(s) T/O/P Dweller by a bridge; or an occupational term for a bridge-keeper (compare **Bridgman**). **Brigg/ Briggs** are ON versions found chiefly in the former Danelaw, though **Bridge** is very much a Lancs surname. Cottle says that the Lincs town of *Brigg* is of too late a formation to be the origin, but a reference to it (as '*Glaunford Brigge*') can be found as early as 1318. An alternative origin is the Flemish town of *Bruges/Brugge* ('bridges'). **Delbridge** OF/OE 'of the bridge' is a known variant, found in Cornwall and Devon. **Bridges** has the meaning of 'at/of/by' the bridge, rather than being a plural.

Bridgeford P Place-names: *Great* and *Little Bridgeford* in Staffs; *East* and *West Bridgford* in Notts OE 'ford by a bridge'.

Bridger, *see* Bridge. There is no evidence that it refers to a bridge-builder.

Bridg(e)man T/O Dweller at a bridge, or an occupational term for a bridgekeeper OE; maintenance of a bridge often devolved upon a hermit – or the 'bridgeman' could be a tollkeeper. Compare **Bridge**. **Bridgeman** is the family name of the Earls of Bradford, who have long favoured 'Orlando' as a first-name.

Bridg(e)water P Place-name *Bridgwater*, Somerset. The 'water' element is deceptive: it refers to the fee of *Walter* de Dowai. The first-name 'Walter' was formerly pronounced as 'Water', and abbreviated to 'Wat' (as in the village of *Whatstandwell*, Derbys, named after Walter Stonewell); dropping the *-l-* in the name of the Somerset town is therefore a good example of folk-etymology. **Bridgwater** and **Bridgewater** are widespread surnames, strongest in the Midlands.

Bridg(e)wood T Dweller at a wood situated near a bridge OE, or at a birch wood OE. Both spellings of the surname are commonest in Staffs.

Bridle O/P Occupational term for a maker of bridles OE *bridel*, or from a minor place-name such as *Bridwell*, Devon, or *Bridewell Springs*, Wilts OE 'bride-spring' (perhaps a location for fertility rituals). Possibly also a corruption of **Brightwell**. See also **Bridewell**.

Brierl(e)y/Brearley/Briley P There are places called *Brierl(e)y* in Staffs, WRYorks and elsewhere OE 'clearing with briars'. A very Lancs surname, whatever the spelling. *John Michael ('Mike') Brearley, former England cricket captain, was born in Harrow, Middx, in 1942, son of a master at the City of London School. He now works as a psychoanalyst and psychotherapist.*

Brier(s), *see* Briar.

Brierton, *see* Brereton.

Brigenshaw, *see* Birkenshaw.

Brigg(s), *see* Bridge.

Briggenshaw/Brigginshaw, *see* Birkenshaw.

Brigham P   Place-name in Cumbd and ERYorks OE (Scandinavianized) 'homestead by a bridge'. *Brigham Young (1801–1877) was the Second Prophet and President of the Church of Jesus Christ of Latter-day Saints (Mormons).*

Brighouse P   Place-name in WRYorks ON and OE: 'houses by a bridge'.

Bright N/F   Nickname for a person who was bright, handsome OE; or a shortened form of an OE first-name beginning *beorht*. Another form, with -*r*- in its original place, after the vowel, is seen in names such as **Birt/Burt** and **Bert/Bart**. *Richard Bright (1789–1858), a leading medical practitioner of his day, gave his name to Bright's Disease.*

Brighton P   Of too early a date of origin to be from the contracted place-name of *Brighton*, Sussex (originally *Brighthelmstone*, OE '*Beorhthelm*'s settlement'), this surname is derived from *Breighton*, ERYorks OE 'farm by a bridge' – yet it is most commonly found (oddly enough) in Norfolk.

Brightwell P   Place-name in Berks, Oxon, Suffolk OE 'bright spring/stream'. *See also* **Bridle**.

Briginshaw, *see* **Birkenshaw**.

Briley, *see* **Brierly**.

Brill P   Place-name in Bucks and Cornwall; tautological, being British 'hill' and OE 'hill'. The surname is strongest in Bucks and Surrey, very rare in Cornwall.

Brimble/Brim(m)ell T   Dweller by a bramble, blackberry-bush OE. **Brimble** is chiefly a Somerset surname; **Brimmell** is more common in Gloucs.

Brimblecombe P   Place-name in Devon OE 'bramble valley', and a Devon surname.

Brim(m)ell, *see* **Brimble**.

Brimner, *see* **Bremner**.

Brind P   There is a place so-called in ERYorks OE 'burnt place, place cleared by burning', but this is a southern English surname, strongest in Berks and Middx.

Brindley P   Place-name in Chesh OE 'burnt wood/clearing'. Very much a Staffs surname, and there are places in that county named *Brindley Ford* and *Brindley Heath. The engineer James Brindley (1716–1772) was born in Derbys, but spent most of his life in neighbouring Staffs.*

Brine, *see* **Brian**.

Brisbane N   A nickname of uncertain meaning. From OF and OE 'break-bone', it could refer to a crippled person with broken bones, or a thug who broke other people's bones? Very much a Scottish surname, found particularly in Lanarkshire; it can't be, can it, that Scotland had more than its fair share of cripples or pugilists? The first Scot known to have borne such a surname is William **Brisbone**, whose name appears in a list of archers sent from Berwick to Roxburgh in 1298 (Black, *The surnames of Scotland*). The Queensland city was named after a Scots baronet, Sir Thomas **Brisbane**.

Brisco(e) P   Place-names: *Briscoe*, Cumbd ON 'Britons' wood'; *Brisco*, Cumbd; *Briscoe*, NRYorks ON 'birch wood'. **Brisco** (found mainly in Cumbd and Lancs) is much scarcer than **Briscoe** (Chesh, Lancs, Salop).

Brisley P   Place-name in Norfolk OE 'wood/clearing full of gadflies', but almost exclusively a Kent surname.

Brison, *see* **Bryson**.

Bristol(l) P   Place-names: *Birstal* (WRYorks); *Birstall* (Leics); *Burstall* (Suffolk, ERYorks) OE 'fort site'. *Bir/Bur* has mutated to *Bri* by metathesis, no doubt corrupted by the familiar city-name. Cities rarely give surnames, the citizens tending to stay put – but see **Bristow**. An uncommon surname, found mainly in the English Midlands.

Bristow(e) P   Place-name, the city and county of Bristol (originally *Bristow*) OE '(assembling) place at the bridge'. The inhabitants of Bristol still famously pronounce an '*l*' at the end of certain words ending in a vowel, especially an '*a*', thus being named *Veronical, Normal* or *Eval*, spending a night at the *operal*, suffering from *influenzal* or *pneumonial*, and visiting

Africal, Americal or *Russial*. Interpretations of the city name as '(St) *Brig* (sister of St *Brendan*)'s place', 'bright place', 'breach/ gorge place' are seemingly frivolous. **Bristow** is found mainly in south-east England. **Burstow** (readily confused with/a variant of **Bairstow/Burstall**) could be a variant of **Bristow** as a result of metathesis, but it is most common in Sussex, and probably has its origins in the Surrey place-name *Burstow* OE 'fortified place'.

Britt(on)/Brittain/Brittan/Britten, *see* **Brett**.

Broad N 'Broad, stout' OE.

Broadbent P Minor place-name in Lancs OE 'broad with bent grass' (compare **Bentley**). A WRYorks and Lancs surname. *Jim Broadbent, the English actor who won an Academy Award for his portrayal of John Bayley in the film* Iris *(2001), was born in Lincs in 1949.*

Broadely, *see* **Bradley**.

Broadfoot N Nickname for a person with a broad foot OE. Mainly a Scottish surname, but also found in Lancs and elsewhere.

Broadhead T/N Dweller by a wide headland/hilltop ME/OE, or a nickname for a person with a broad head ME/OE. Chiefly a WRYorks surname.

Broadley, *see* **Bradley**.

Broadribb, *see* **Brodribb**.

Broadrick, *see* **Broderick**.

Broadwater P Place-name in Essex and Sussex OE 'wide stream'.

Broadway P Place-name in various counties, including Dorset and Worcs OE 'wide road'.

Broadwood P Place-name in Devon and Somerset OE 'wide wood'. A scarce surname, widely scattered. *John Broadwood (1732–1812), founder of Broadwood & Sons, the oldest piano company in the world, was born in Oldhamstocks in East Lothian, Scotland, from where he walked to London as a young man and started work as a harpsichord maker.*

Broatch, *see* **Brooch**.

Broben/Brobin/Brobyn F Welsh: son of (*ab-*) *Robin*.

Brock N Nickname for a person resembling a badger in some way, the word *brock* being one of the very few Celtic words to have survived the Anglo-Saxon linguistic take-over which began in the fourth century AD. In mediaeval times badgers were regarded as unpleasant, smelly creatures rather than as fascinating, charming ones. Or a variant on **Brook**. **Brock** is particularly strong in Devon.

Brockenshaw, *see* **Birkenshaw**.

Brockhurst P Place-name in Salop and Warwicks, Celtic and OE 'badger hill/ wood' (compare **Brocklehurst**). A scarce surname, confined to the south of England and the Midlands.

Brocklehurst P Place-name in Lancs, Celtic and OE 'badger hill/wood' (compare **Brockhurst**). In more recent times the surname **Brocklehurst** (most commonly found in Chesh, Derbys and Lancs) has been borne by a prominent silk-manufacturing family in Macclesfield, Chesh. What can have been in the mind of the parents of a child born in Prestwich, Lancs, in 1877, who was given the name of '*Foetus* **Brocklehurst**'? Did the child survive?

Brocklesby P Place-name in Lincs ON '*Broklauss*'s farm' (*Broklauss* meaning literally 'Trouserless'), and most commonly found in that county.

Brockless/Brockliss N Nickname for a person having no breeches ON (compare **Brocklesby**). A rare surname in both spellings, **Brockless** occurring most frequently in Bucks. Men and women in other counties, we may suppose, were more able to hold on to their trousers?

Brockton P Place-names: *Brockton*, Salop and *Brocton*, Staffs OE 'place on a brook'. A very scarce surname.

Brockus

92

Brockus, *see* Brookhouse.

Brockway T Dweller at a road by a brook OE. Found mainly in southern counties of England.

Broderick/Broadrick F Welsh: son of (*ab-*) *Roderick*.

Brodribb/Broadribb N Nickname for a person with broad ribs OE. *Given the fact that the surname Brodribb is found mainly in Somerset, it's no surprise to find that John Henry Brodribb (1828–1905), the stage actor knighted in 1895 as Sir Henry Irving, was born in Keinton Mandeville in that county.*

Brogden P Place-name in WRYorks OE 'brook valley'.

Broke, *see* Brook.

Brokenbrow P Place-name *Brokenborough* in Gloucs and Wilts OE 'broken/uneven hill'. A scarce surname, found mainly in these two counties.

Brokenshaw, *see* Birkenshaw.

Bromage, *see* Bromwich.

Brome, *see* Broom.

Bromfield, *see* Broomfield.

Bromhall/Broomhall P Place-names: *Bromhall*, Berks; *Broomhall*, Chesh OE 'broom nook'.

Bromham P Place-name in Beds OE 'homestead where broom grows'.

Bromhead, *see* Broomhead.

Bromley P Place-name in various counties, including Kent OE 'broom wood'.

Brommage, *see* Bromwich.

Brompton P Place-name in Middx, Salop, ERYorks OE 'settlement where broom grows'. Chiefly a surname of the English Midlands and the north.

Bromwich/Brom(m)age P Place-name *Bromwich* OE 'broom farm' in various parts of the West Midlands, where the surname is still generally located.

Brooch/Broatch O Occupational term for a maker of brooches, from an OE word meaning 'brooch, pin, lance'. **Brooch** is a very scarce surname; **Broatch**, slightly less scarce, is found mainly in Cumbd, Staffs and Dumfries, Scotland.

Brook(e)(s)/Broke T/P Dweller by a brook OE *broc*. **Broke**, which is closer to the original spelling, is nevertheless usually pronounced 'Brook' (as with the Lords Willoughby **de Broke**). In theory such a surname could be expected to have as many origins as there are streams, and place-names in Kent, Rutland and Norfolk may have contributed. However, **Brook(e)** is mostly found in WRYorks, especially around Huddersfield, and George Redmonds points out that the name has far fewer origins than is generally assumed. The spelling **Brooke** is evidence of the dative case following a lost preposition, while **Brook(e)s** is 'at the brook', rather than a plural, *-es* being the older form of our genitive *'s*. **Brooks** is the family name of the Barons Crawshaw. *Arthur Brooke (1845–1918), born in Ashton-under-Lyne, Lancs, the founder of the tea company known as 'Brooke, Bond' and later simply as 'Brooke Bond', opened his first shop in Manchester in 1869. There never was a Mr Bond, but 'it seemed so well' that it was added to 'Brooke' to make the company name… Sir James Brooke (1803–1868), naval officer and first Rajah of Sarawak, was born in Secrore, India, the son of a Chief Judge of the East India Company's court at Moorshabad.*

Brooker T Dweller at the brook OE. Compare **Brook**. The *-er* element, so often associated with an occupation (carpenter, tinker, weaver) is used here in a way that is exemplified in words such as cottager or villager. A south/south-east of England surname.

Brookhouse/Brockus T Dweller in a house by a brook OE. An uncommon surname, found chiefly in Notts/Staffs.

Brooking(s) ?T/P/O A surname which has yet to yield up its meaning satisfactorily. Known variants include: **Brewkins, Broa-**

coon, **Brocan**, **Brochan**, **Brocken**, **Brockon**, **Brokan**, **Brokenge**, **Brokens**, **Broking**, **Bro-kinge**, **Brokyn**, **Brokynge**, **Broocking**, **Broo-kan**, **Brookeing**, **Brooken**, **Brookhan**, **Brookin**, **Brookinge**, **Brookings**, **Brookins**, **Brookling**, **Brookyn**, **Browkinge**, **Bruckyn**. To suppose that such a surname refers to a dweller by the stream, from OE *broc* ('brook'), as Reaney and Hanks and Hodges do, is seductively simple, but fails to explain the -*ing* element. This is predomin-antly a Devon surname; no references to it appear in the lay subsidy for that county in 1332, but there are a good number of **Bro-kyng**s in the 1524-7 Devon subsidy (and a William **Brokyng** in the contemporary sub-sidy for Sussex), and a John **Brokyng** served on the Common Council of Plymouth in 1452. We might be safer in suggesting an unidentified place-name with the meaning '*Brocca*'s people', though the *Broc*- element in the Devon place-names *Brockham*, *Brock-hill*, *Brockhole* is from an OE (from Old Brit-ish) word for a badger. The hamlet in Devon called *Brooking*, off the A385 near Totnes, may have taken its name from a family of **Brooking**s living there, rather than vice versa. An extensive study of the surname undertaken by the Brooking Fam-ily History Society, using DNA and other evidence, has established the existence of one major branch of the family (which even includes Thomas **Brookens**, born in 1782 in Ireland, who emigrated to America), along with several further branches. Given the fact that members of the **Brokynge/** **Brooking** family in Devon conducted a sig-nificant amount of business overseas, it has even been suggested that the surname could be derived from the ME word 'broker'. Perhaps the early **Brokynges** earned a living by broking…? **Brooking** is not the only sur-name of its kind to elude capture; **Brock-ington**, which also has a significant presence in Devon, is similarly elusive. *Sir Trevor Brooking, football player, manager and pundit, was born in Barking, Essex, in 1948… Charles Brooking (1723–1759), marine artist, was born within the dockyard area of Deptford in Kent, the son of a man of the same name… The Brookings Institution, which devotes itself*

to analysing public policy issues in the USA, was named in honour of one of its early leaders, a businessman from St Louis by the name of Robert Somers Brookings (1850–1932). Families of Brookings are known to have been living in both New England and Virginia from as early as the seventeenth century.

Brooks, *see* **Brook**.

Brooksbank P From a minor place-name OE 'brook bank'. One branch of the **Brooks-bank** family from Warley (Halifax, WRYorks) settled in South Crosland in about 1500 (George Redmonds).

Broom(e)/Brome T/P Dweller by the broom (bush) OE; or from a place-name with the same meaning in Beds, Co Dur-ham, Norfolk, Salop, Suffolk, Worcs and elsewhere. Compare **Brougham**.

Brooman N Nickname for a brown-skinned or brown-haired man OE. A sur-name of south-east England.

Broomfield/Bromfield P Place-names *Broomfield* and *Bromfield* in a number of counties OE 'open country where broom grows'. Widespread in both spellings, **Broomfield** being strongest in Hants.

Broomhall, *see* **Bromhall**.

Broomhead/Bromhead T/P Dweller on a hilltop with broom-bushes OE; or from *Broomhead Hall*, WRYorks. Not, mercifully, a description of physical appearance. **Broomhead** is chiefly found in Derbys, Lancs and WRYorks, **Bromhead** in Leics and Notts.

Brother(s) N/F Nickname for a brother (or even a younger son/kinsman) of a person of note; or a guild-brother (fellow-guilds-man); or from the ON first-name *brothor*.

Brotherton P Place-name in Suffolk and WRYorks ON and OE 'farm belonging to a brother, or to a person named *Brother*'. Chiefly found in Lancs. *See also* **Bretherton**.

Brough P Place-name in Derbys, Yorks and elsewhere OE 'fortress/ancient camp'. Usu-ally pronounced '*Bruff*', and chiefly a sur-name of the English Midlands.

Brougham P Place-name in Westmd OE 'homestead by the fort' – the fort in this case being the Roman station *Brocavum*. Usually pronounced '*Broom*' or '*Brooham*', so see also **Broom**. *The four-wheeled horse-drawn carriage known as a* brougham *was invented by Henry Brougham, First Baron Brougham and Vaux (1778–1868), a nineteenth-century Lord Chancellor.*

Broughton/Brutton P *Broughton* OE 'place on a brook' or 'place on a hill/mound' is a very common place-name. **Broughton** is usually pronounced '*Brawton*'.

Brown(e) N/F Nickname for a person with brown hair or a brown complexion, or favouring brown clothes ME *brun*; or from the OE first-name *Brun*, with the same meaning. The -*e* in **Browne** is sometimes added in an attempt to add distinction to this most common of surnames, but can also indicate the use of a weak adjective after a lost definite article. **Browne** is the family name of the Marquesses of Sligo and of more than one Baron.

Brownhill P Place-name in various counties (Chesh, Staffs, Yorks) OE 'brown hill'. Most commonly found in Chesh, Lancs and WRYorks, and many present-day bearers of this surname are descended from a family which was settled at *Brownhill* near Sale, Chesh, in the thirteenth century.

Browning F From the ME/OE first-name *Bruning*. There is no evidence that the -*ing* element has the familiar meaning of 'family/folk of'. Found mainly in the south and south-west of England. *The male-line ancestry of the poet and playwright Robert Browning (1812–1889), who was born in Camberwell, London, had long-established roots in Dorset.*

Brownjohn N Nickname: 'brown-haired/brown-skinned John' OE. Bardsley says that this surname, like **Prettijohn** and **Littlejohn**, arose as a way of distinguishing between various bearers of the common font-name *John*. A scarce surname, found mainly in the south of England.

Brownlee/Brownlea/Brownlie T/P Dweller at a brown clearing OE; or from the place-name *Brownlee* in Ayrshire and in Lanarkshire, Scotland. **Brownlee** is strongest in Lanarkshire; **Brownlea** and **Brownlie** are much scarcer variants.

Brownsmith O Occupational term for a copper/brass smith OE. A very scarce surname.

Broxholm(e) P Place-name in Lincs, Old Danish and ON 'island in a brook'. A Lincs surname in both spellings.

Bruce P Scots surname, from some place in Normandy; various scholars have suggested *Brix* (Cherbourg), *Le Brus* (Calvados) and *Briouze* (Orne). One of the commonest surnames in Scotland, and the family name of the Earls of Elgin and of other peers.

Bruckshaw, *see* **Birkenshaw**.

Brudenell N Norman nickname, *Bretonell* ('little Breton'), a patronizing if not derogatory term. Belongs to the same class of surnames as **Brett**, etc. Family name of the Earls of Cardigan.

Brummell, *see* **Bramah**.

Brundish P Place-name in Suffolk OE 'park/pasture/estate on a stream'. Occurs almost exclusively in Suffolk and Norfolk.

Brunker F From an OE first-name with the meaning 'brown/burnished spear'. A scarce surname, most commonly found in Wilts.

Brunskill P From an unidentified place-name ON '*Brunn*'s ravine'. A surname found almost exclusively in the north of England, though one Yorkshire Dales family named **Brunskill** emigrated to the Mississippi region of North America aboard the ship *Washington* in 1833.

Brunton P Place-name in Northd and Wilts OE 'place on a stream'. Found mainly in the north of England and Scotland, but also in Norfolk.

Bruster, *see* **Brewer**.

Bruton P Place-name in Somerset OE 'farm on the river *Brue*'. Commonest in nearby Gloucs.

Brutton, *see* Broughton.

Bryan/Bryant, *see* Brian.

Bryce, *see* Brice.

Bryceson, *see* Bryson.

Bryer(s), *see* Briar.

Bryne, *see* Brian.

Bryson/Brison/Bryceson F Son of *Brice*, a first-name (probably of Celtic origin) borne by a fifth-century saint who was Bishop of Tours; Irish: Anglicized form of **O'** [descendant of] **Briosain** ('flame'). *The much-loved American author William McGuire ('Bill') Bryson was famously born in Des Moines, Iowa, USA ('Well, somebody had to be…'), the son of William and Mary Bryson.*

Buchan P Place-name in Aberdeenshire and Kirkcudbrightshire, Scotland, possibly derived from Gaelic *baogh* (cow) followed by the diminutive suffix *-an*. *John Buchan (1875–1940), first Baron Tweedsmuir, the popular novelist and former Governor-General of Canada, was the son of John Buchan, senior, a Scottish Free Church minister.*

Buchanan P Place-name in Stirlingshire, Scotland, Gaelic 'house of the canon'. But the surname of some American **Buchanans** represents an Anglicized form of the German name **Buchenhain** ('beech wood').

Buck N/F/O/T Nickname for a person bearing some resemblance to a he-goat in character or appearance OE *bucc(a)* (also found as a first-name), or who worked with such creatures; or a dweller near a beech tree OE *boc*.

Buckden/Bugden P Place-name *Buckden*, Hunts OE 'stag valley'. The Bishops of Lincoln very much favoured the village of Buckden, which marked a halfway point on their frequent journeys to London, and built an imposing palace there.

Buckingham P Place-name in Bucks OE 'river-meadow of *Bucca*'s followers'. A surname of the south, south-west and South Midlands of England, with a particular presence (for some reason) in Cornwall and Devon.

Buckland P Several settlements in the south of England and in the Midlands are called *Buckland*, as was a now-lost village in Lincs OE 'land held by charter' (literally, 'book-land').

Buckleigh, *see* Buckley.

Buckler O Occupational term for a buckle-maker OF, or possibly used to describe a fencer armed with a 'sword and buckler'. It has even been suggested that such a surname, which can be found as **Bokeler**, **Buckeler**, **Buclier** and **Bucler**, might be related to **Bacheler** and **Backeler**, and be derived from the office of *Bachelerii Regis*. A rarer surname than might be supposed; by the late nineteenth century it was fairly widespread, having a noticeable presence in Warwicks, but most **Buckler**s who have left their mark on society are connected with a family first known to have been living in Dorset in the fifteenth century. *Andrew Buckler of Weymouth, who was in Jamestown, Virginia, in the early seventeenth century alongside John Smith and others, belongs to this family branch, as does Rev. Edward Buckler, formerly one of Oliver Cromwell's chaplains, who was ejected from his living at Calbourn in the Isle of Wight during the Restoration; he was a direct ancestor of John Buckler of Calbourn (1770–1851) and his son John Chessell Buckler, noted architects and water-colour artists.*

Buckley/Buckleigh P/O Place-names *Buckley* and *Buckleigh* in Somerset and elsewhere OE 'buck (male deer) clearing', or from *Bulkeley*, Chesh OE 'bullock clearing'. Irish: Anglicized form of **O'** [descendant of] **Buachalla** ('cowherd'). **Buckley** is the family name of the Barons Wrenbury.

Buckman O Occupational term for a goat/stag-keeper OE or for one who studies/writes/binds books OE.

Buckminster/Buckmaster P Place-name *Buckminister*, Leics OE '*Bucca*'s church/minster'. **Buckminster** was often corrupted to **Buckmaster** (compare the **Kittermaster** surname, from *Kidderminster*), as it was in the case of James **Buckminister**, one of the proprietors of Sudbury, New England, in the 1640s. Thomas **Buckminster**, also known as **Buckmaster**, published an *Almanacke for the Yeare of Our Lord God 1595*. **Buckminster** is a very scarce name in the British Isles; **Buckmaster**, less scarce, is found mainly in south-eastern counties. *Richard Buckminster Fuller (1895–1983), an American visionary, inventor and author, was born to a family of Nonconformists in Milton, Massachusetts, on 12 July 1895.*

Bucknall/Bucknell/Bucknill P Place-names: *Bucknall* in Lincs, Staffs OE '*Bucca*'s nook'; *Bucknell* in Herefords, Oxon, Salop OE '*Bucca*'s hill'. **Bucknall** is a widespread surname, strongest in Staffs; **Bucknell**, scarcer, is mainly found in Devon; **Bucknill**, just as scarce, is also mainly a Staffs surname.

Buckton P Place-name in Herefords, Northd, ERYorks OE '*Bucca*'s/stag/goat farm'.

Budd N From an OE byname *Budde*, used for a plump, tubby person, though Reaney speaks of a connexion with OE *budda*, a beetle. Mainly a south and south-west of England surname. *The former Olympic athlete Zola Budd, who was granted British citizenship on the grounds that her grandfather was British, was born in Bloemfontein, South Africa, in 1966. She was as far from being 'plump, tubby' as it's possible to get, and could outrun most beetles.*

Budgen N Nickname for a person much prone to using the phrase 'Bon Jean' (Anglo-Norman French, 'Good John'). Chiefly a Sussex surname.

Budsey, *see* Birdseye.

Buffard N Nickname for a person liable to puff up with pride or anger OF. A scarce surname, limited almost entirely to Sussex (not, surely, a county known for its puffed-up people?).

Bugby P Probably a corruption of the place-name *Buckby*, Northants OE and ON '?*Bucca*'s/stag/goat farm'. A Northants surname.

Bugden, *see* Buckden.

Bugg N Uncomplimentary nickname for a person who had something of the bogy, spectre, hobgoblin or scarecrow about him ME; or from the ON byname *Buggi* ('fat man'). The surname is strongest in Suffolk.

Bulger O Occupational term for a wallet/bag-maker OF.

Bulkeley P Place-name in Chesh OE 'bullock pasture'.

Bull N/O Nickname for a man as powerful or aggressive as a bull; or an occupational term for one who tended bulls, or who worked at a house or inn bearing the sign of a bull ME. Mainly a southern English surname.

Bullas/Bullus O/P In principle such a surname could refer to a man who worked at any bull-house OE, situated anywhere, but David Hey notes that all the evidence points to an origin from two specific place-names, one in the West Midlands and one (*Bullhouse*) in Penistone, WRYorks.

Bulleid/Bullied N Nickname for a person who was bull-headed in appearance or character OE. Very much a Devon surname. *Oliver Vaughan Snell Bulleid, an influential engineer and locomotive designer with the Southern Railway, was born in New Zealand in 1882 and died in Malta in 1970.*

Bullen/Boleyn/Bollen/Bullin P Place-name, the French port of *Boulogne* (Latin *Bononia*, Gaulish *bona*, 'foundation'). *Most famously the name of Anne Boleyn, one of Henry VIII's ill-fated wives, who – according to Stanley Holloway – walks the Bloody Tower with her head tucked underneath her arm, planning revenge on her cruel husband.*

Bullied, *see* Bulleid.

Bullin, *see* Bullen.

Bullinger, *see* Pillinger.

Bullock N Nickname for a spirited young man, one who was as lively as an uncastrated steer OE.

Bullus, *see* Bullas.

Bullworthy P Place-names in Devon: *Bul-worthy* (two such) OE '*Bula's*/bull farm'; *Bulkworthy* OE '*Bulca's* farm'. A scarce surname, largely confined to Devon.

Bulmer P Place-names in Essex, NRYorks OE 'bulls' lake'. Chiefly a Durham/Lancs/Yorks surname. *Bulmer's Cider was founded in 1887 by Percy Bulmer, the 20-year-old son of Charles Henry Bulmer, rector of Credenhill, Herefords, whose family had been in that county for several generations.*

Bulpin T/O A dweller by, or worker at, a bull-pen OE. Chiefly a Somerset name.

Bumpas/Bompas N Nickname for a swift walker OF *bon pas* ('good pace').

B(o)umphrey F Welsh: son of (*ab-*) *Humphrey*. Yet by the late nineteenth century **Bumphrey** and **Boumphrey**, both scarce, were chiefly found in Norfolk and Chesh/Lancs respectively.

Bumstead/Bumpstead P Place-names *Helion Bumpstead* and *Steeple Bumpstead*, Essex OE '?reedy place'. The surname **Bumstead** is most commonly found in southern counties of England and East Anglia, especially Sussex and Suffolk; **Bumpstead**, of rare occurrence, is also mainly a Suffolk name.

Bunce, *see* Bone.

Bunclarke N/O Nickname/occupational term for a 'good clerk' OF.

Buncombe/Bunkham/Bunkum P From an unidentified place OE 'reed valley'. In America, the political claptrap of the member for Buncombe County, North Carolina, in the mid nineteenth century, propelled the word *bunkum* into everyday use.

Bund(e)y, *see* Bond.

Bunkham/Bunkum, *see* Buncombe.

Bunn, *see* Bone.

Bunn(e)y N/P A nickname for a person having a noticeable lump or swelling ME; though early forms using the preposition *de* are lacking, there may in principle sometimes be a place-name origin from *Bunny* in

Notts OE 'reed island'. *Bunny* is most commonly found in Cornwall, while *Bunney*, more widespread, occurs in both Cornwall and Leics.

Bunting N Nickname from a bird so-called, etymology unknown. A widespread surname, strongest in Derbys. *Jabez Bunting, English Wesleyan Methodist writer and thinker, born in Manchester in 1779, was a minister of the gospel for no fewer than fifty-seven years.*

Bunts, *see* Bone.

Bunyan N/O Nickname for a person who was disfigured by a bunion OF, or an occupational term for one who made 'buns' OF or other pastry. The surname is very localized, being limited in the main to Beds and Herts, and most bearers of it, including John **Bunyan** (1628–1688), the Beds-born author of *Pilgrim's progress*, are members of a single family.

Burbage/Burbidge/Burbridge P Place-name *Burbage* in Derbys, Wilts OE 'fort/manor brook' and Leics OE 'fort/manor ridge'. **Burbridge** is a misspelling. **Burbage** is most commonly found in Leics, **Burbidge** in Wilts, **Burbridge** in Kent.

Burch, *see* Birch.

Burchall, *see* Birchall.

Burcham, *see* Bircham.

Burchard/Burchatt F From an OE first-name meaning 'fort-hardy'. Both forms are exceptionally scarce. Readily confused with/a variant of **Birkett**.

Burchett, *see* Birkett.

Burd/Burdekin, *see* Bird.

Burden/Burdon F/N/P From an OF first-name *Burdo*; or a nickname for a person carrying a pilgrim's staff ME/OF *bourdon*; or from place-names: *Burdon* in Co Durham (two such), one being OE 'valley with a byre/cowshed', and another OE 'forthill'; *Burden Head* in WRYorks OE 'fort-hill'.

Burdge, *see* Burge.

Burdikin, *see* Bird.

Burdon, *see* Burden.

Burfitt/Burfoot/Burford P Place-name *Burford* in Oxon and Salop OE 'ford by a fort/manor'.

Burfoot/Burford, *see* Burfitt.

Burgan/Burgin/Burgoin/Burgon/Burgoyne P A person from *Burgundy* in France OF *Bourgogne*.

Burge/Burdge T Dweller by a bridge OE *brycg*, by process of metathesis. Chiefly a Somerset/Dorset surname. *See also* **Birch**.

Burgess/Burgis O Status term for a citizen, freeman, inhabitant of a borough ME. Most common in Lancs and Chesh.

Burgh, *see* Burke.

Burghley/Burleigh/Burley P Place-names: *Burley* in various counties from Hants to WRYorks; *Burghley*, Northants OE 'wood/clearing belonging to the fort/manor'. *Burghley House*, Northants, home of the Marquesses of Exeter, is on the outskirts of the town of Stamford, most of which (that portion lying on the far side of the river Welland) lies in the county of Lincs.

Burgin, *see* Burgan.

Burgis, *see* Burgess.

Burgoin/Burgon/Burgoyne, *see* Burgan.

Burk(e)/Bourke/(De) Burgh/De Burca T/P Dweller at the fort/manor OE *burh*; or from a place-name *Burgh*, with the same meaning, in various counties, including Cumbd and Suffolk. Exported to Ireland by a twelfth-century Norman knight from *Burgh* in Suffolk who became Earl of Ulster, **Burke** is now mainly an Irish surname, associated particularly with Edmund **Burke** (1729–1797), the Dublin-born political writer and thinker, and the **Burke** family of heralds and genealogists. *See also* **Burrough(s)**. *Chris De Burgh, the Irish musician and songwriter known particularly for his rendition of* Lady in Red, *was born in 1948 in Buenos Aires, Argentina, to Charles Davison,*

a British diplomat, and Maeve Emily De Burgh. Once he embarked on a performing career, he adopted his mother's distinctive maiden name as his own.

Burkenshaw, *see* Birkenshaw.

Burkett, *see* Birkett.

Burkimsher, *see* Birkenshaw.

Burkin, *see* Birkin.

Burkinshaw/Burkinshear, *see* Birkenshaw.

Burl(e) O Occupational term for a cupbearer, butler OE.

Burleigh/Burley, *see* Burghley.

Burlington T/P 'Dweller at *Bret*'s farm' OE; or (by metathesis) from the place-name *Bridlington*, ERYorks. Scarce as a surname, widespread, but moderately more common in Surrey. *Burlington has been widely used as a place-name in the USA... Burlington Arcade, off Piccadilly, London, runs beside Burlington House, built for the first Earl of Burlington (Bridlington) in 1668... Burlington Bertie (from Bow), who famously rose at ten-thirty, was the creation of William Hargreaves, who first sprang this would-be toff upon an unsuspecting music-hall public in the year 1914.*

Burman O Occupational term for a servant in a bower (chamber), or a descriptive term for a townsman, burgess (from 'borough'). A scattered surname, most common in Lincs.

Burnaby/Burnby P Place-name *Burnby* in ERYorks ON 'farm by a spring/well'. Scarce in either spelling: **Burnaby** can be found in Kent, and **Burnby** in Lancs and WRYorks. *Robert Burnaby (1828–1878), born in Leics, settled as a pioneer in British Columbia, where a town was named in his honour.*

Burnage P Place-name in Lancs OE '?brown hedge', but a scarce surname, marginally more common in Beds.

Burnby, *see* Burnaby.

Burn(e), *see* Bourn.

Burnel(l) N Nickname for a person with brown hair or skin OF (diminutive).

Burnes/Burness, *see* Bourn.

Burnet(t) N/O/T/P Nickname for someone with brown hair or complexion OF; or an occupational term for a seller of brown cloth OF; or a dweller near a place cleared by burning; or from the place-name *Burnett* in Somerset. Found as a surname in England and also in Scotland, where it is pronounced with a strong stress on the '-ett' element.

Burnham P Place-name in Bucks, Essex, Norfolk OE 'homestead on a burn/stream', and in Somerset OE 'meadow on a burn' and in Lincs (two such) OE '?at the springs', exhibiting the use of a dative plural after a lost preposition.

Burnley P Place-name in Lancs OE 'clearing on a stream', or OE 'clearing on the river *Brun*'.

Burnside T/P Dweller by a burn or stream, or from a Scottish or English place-name – sometimes with the meaning 'bank of a stream' OE, though in Westmd the meaning is 'hill belonging to *Brunwulf*'. Found mainly in Co Durham and Lanarkshire, Scotland. *Ambrose Everett Burnside, a US Union General during the Civil War, sported the kind of mutton-chop whiskers which were eventually known, from a twisted version of his surname, as 'sideburns'.*

Burrell/Burrill N A nickname derived from OF 'coarse woollen cloth' or, as an adjective, 'reddish-brown', but it came to mean 'coarse, unlettered'. A thirteenth-century landowner by the name of Peter **Burel** gave his name to *Langley Burrell*, Wilts.

Burrough(s)/Burrow(s) T Dweller by a hill OE *beorg*, or at a bower house OE *bur hus*. Readily confused with/variants of **Burke** and **Bury/Berry**, which are derived from OE *burh*, a fort.

Burstall/Birstall P Place-names: *Burstall* in Staffs, Suffolk, ERYorks; *Birstal* in WRYorks; *Birstale* in Leics; *Boarstall* in Bucks OE 'site of a fort'. *Borstal*, part of the City of Rochester in Kent, famous for its young offenders' institution, has the meaning OE 'place of refuge' or 'pathway up a

steep hill'. Readily confused with/a variant of **Bairstow**, **Burstow** (see **Bristow**).

Burstow, *see* Bristow.

Burt, *see* Bert.

Burtinshaw, *see* Birkenshaw.

Burton/Bo(u)rton P There are dozens of places in England called *Burton*, the commonest meaning being OE 'fort/manor-house enclosure', or even 'fortified farm/farm near a fort'; in a couple of cases (especially the Staffs town) the first element is genitive, 'belonging to the fort', but *Burton Bradstock*, Dorset, is Celtic and OE 'place/farm on the river *Bredy*'. *Burton* in Sussex is OE '*Budeca*'s place', and *Burton Salmon*, WRYorks, is ON and OE 'broad place'. It is tempting to suppose that the surname **Bo(u)rton**, which can be a variant of **Burton**, could also be derived from the Gloucs settlements of *Bourton-on-the-hill* or *Bourton-on-the-water*. *At least two well-known Burtons were not born with that surname. Richard Burton, the Welsh actor, abandoned his surname of Jenkins when he was adopted by a local schoolmaster, Philip H. Burton... When Montague Burton, famous for his tailors' shops, was born in 1885 in the Russian province of Kovno (later Lithuania), his name was Meshe David Osinsky. It is said that he adopted the Burton surname while aboard a train that stopped at Burton-on-Trent in Staffs.*

Burtonshaw, *see* Birkenshaw.

Burwash P Place-name in Sussex OE 'ploughland by a fort/manor'. A very scarce surname.

Bury/Berry T/P Dweller at the fort/manor OE, the *-y* representing a dative after a lost preposition; or from a place-name with the same meaning: *Bury*, Lancs; *Bury St Edmunds*, Suffolk; *Berry Pomeroy*, Devon. **Berry** (the family name of the Viscounts Camrose and the Viscounts Kemsley) is by far the commoner spelling, but both are predominantly Lancs surnames. See also **Burrough**.

Busby P Place-name in NRYorks ON 'bush/shrub farm'. Readily confused with/a variant of **Bushby**. *The surname is most com-*

monly found in England, though the former Manchester United football manager Sir Alexander Matthew ('Matt') Busby (1909–1994), was born in Orbiston, North Lanarkshire, Scotland.

Bush(e) T Dweller at a bush ON (?and OE), possibly showing the use of the dative after a lost preposition. A girl bearing the unforgettable name of 'Rose **Bush**' was born in Shoreditch, London, in 1864. George Walker ('Dubya') Bush (born in Connecticut, 6 July 1946), forty-third President of the United States, is a seventeenth cousin of Prince William of Wales and a distant cousin of John Kerry, whom he defeated in the presidential election of 2004.

Bushby P Suggested place-name origins include Bushby in Leics ON 'Butr's homestead' and Bushbury in Salop OE 'Bishop's manor', though neither properly accounts for the fact that such a surname would seem to have its origins in northern counties of England. By the time of the 1881 census it had a particular presence in Sussex. Readily confused with/a variant of **Busby**.

Bushe, see Bush.

Bushell/Bissell O Occupational term for one who measured out corn in bushels, or who made baskets used for this purpose OF. Very much a Kentish surname.

Bushen T Dweller at the bushes ON (?and OE), a dative plural after a lost preposition. Chiefly a Devon/Somerset surname.

Buss O/N Occupational term for a cooper OF; or a nickname for someone shaped like the sort of barrels which coopers made. Chiefly a Kent surname. Miss Frances Buss (1827–1894), suffragette and founder headmistress of the North London Collegiate School, came from a family based in Holland but with English roots.

Butcher/Boucher/Bowcher/Bowker O Occupational term for a butcher OF.

Butler O Occupational term for a butler/ wine-steward/head servant OF (compare the word 'bottle'). In royal households, a high office epitomized by Archbishop Hubert Walter's brother, the first Pincerna

of Ireland, and in the **Butler**s, Dukes of Ormond. Still the family name of a number of Irish peers.

Butlin N A nickname meaning literally 'hustle the churl' OF boute-vilain, suggesting an ability to herd the common people. Chiefly a Northants surname. Sir William Heygate Edmund Colborne ('Billy') Butlin (1899–1980), founder of the holiday camps that bear his name, was born in Cape Town, South Africa, of a family from Leonard Stanley, Gloucs; his paternal grandfather was a clergyman, while his mother's family were travelling showmen.

Butner O Occupational term for a buttonmaker OF. An exceptionally scarce surname.

Butt N/F/T Nickname for a stumpy, short person ME, or from a ME first-name But(t), of unknown origin, but possibly carrying the same meaning; plenty of men in East Anglia and the south of England had But as a first-name from William I's time onwards. Or a dweller near a place used for archery practice ME but. A West Country surname.

Buttanshaw/Buttenshaw, see Birkenshaw.

Butter(s) O/N Occupational term for a person who produced butter/worked in a buttery; or a nickname for a man who bore some resemblance (a booming voice?) to a bittern OF butor. Principally found in Norfolk and Lincs, but also in Staffs.

Butterby P Place-name in Co Durham OE 'beautiful find' – no connexion with butter... A very scarce surname.

Butterfield T Dweller at a dairy farm (a field where butter is produced) OE; the various places called Butterfield in WRYorks are probably of too recent a date to be the origin of such a surname. A Yorks/Lancs surname.

Butters, see Butter.

Butterwick P Place-name in Dorset and in six northern counties OE 'butter (dairy) farm'. Chiefly a NRYorks surname.

Butterworth P Place-name in Lancs OE

'enclosure where butter is produced'. Very much a Lancs surname. *Peter Butterworth (1919–1979), the English comic actor who starred in no fewer than sixteen* Carry on *films, was born in Bramhall, Chesh.*

Buttery O Occupational term for a worker in/manager of a larder or liquor-store OF. Mainly found in the Midlands and in northern counties of England.

Button O Occupational term for a button-maker OF.

Buttonshaw, *see* Birkenshaw.

Buxton P Place-names in Derbys OE 'rock-ing-stones/logan-stones' and Norfolk OE '*Bucc*'s place'. Commonest in Derbys and other Midland counties.

Buzzard N Nickname for a person bearing some resemblance to a buzzard OF, the no-good hawk that couldn't be used for falconry; hence someone stupid and futile.

Byard/Byatt T Dweller by the yard/enclosure OE. **Byatt** is more likely to be used of a person living near a gate OE *yat(e)/geat*.

Bye T Dweller by a bend in a river OE, or 'at the *by*' (village) ON, exhibiting the use of the dative after a lost preposition (compare '*by(e)-laws*'). A scattered surname, strongest in southern England and East Anglia.

Byers T/P Dweller at the byres/cowsheds OE (compare **Byrom**) or from a place-name: *Byers Green*, Co Durham or *Byres*, East Lothian, Scotland.

Byfield P Place-name in Northants OE 'open land in a river-bend'.

Byfleet P Place-name in Surrey OE 'by the stream' (as in *Fleet Street*, London).

Byford T/P Dweller by a ford, or from a place-name in Herefords OE 'ford by the bend or where commerce took place'.

Bygrave(s) T/P Dweller by the trench/ditch/grove OE; or from *Bygrave*, Herts, with the same meaning. Most commonly found (without the final 's') in the Home Counties and East Anglia. *Walter William ('Max') Bygraves, popular singer and song-writer, was born in Rotherhithe, South London,*

in 1922, son of a professional boxer known as 'Battling Tom Smith'.

Byng, *see* Bing.

Bynorth T Dweller to the north (of some place or other) OE. A scarce surname of south-east England.

Byrne(s) F Irish: Anglicized form of **O'** [descendant of] **Broin** (probably from *Bran*, a raven). *Bran*, a son of the King of Leinster, died in Cologne in 1052.

Byrom/Byron T/O/P Dweller at, or worker at, the byre/cowsheds OE (originally *-um*, being an OE dative plural after a lost preposition) – compare **Byers**; or from a place-name with the same meaning: *Byrom*, Lancs/*Byram*, WRYorks. *George Gordon, Lord Byron (1788–1824), English poet and man of letters, was born in London, the son of 'Mad Jack' Byron and Catherine Gordon. The title of Baron Byron had been granted to John Byron, one of Charles I's officers in the Civil War. Byron the poet bore several names during his lifetime: born George Gordon Byron, he inherited the family title at the age of ten, becoming George Gordon (Byron), Baron Byron; later, in accordance with a stipulation expressed in the will of his mother-in-law, he became George Gordon Noel, Lord Byron.*

Bysouth T Dweller to the south (of some place or other) OE. A scarce south-east England surname.

Bythesea T Dweller by the sea/pool/water-course OE. Casual visitors to Trowbridge, Wilts, may ponder as to the existence of a 'Bythesea Road' in this inland town. In fact it was named after Samuel **Bythesea**, whose relation John **Bythesea** was awarded the Victoria Cross in 1857 for his bravery during the Crimean War. **Bythesea** families were once prominent in Trowbridge itself, and also in Axbridge, Somerset. A very scarce surname.

Bytheway T Dweller by the road OE. Mainly a Salop surname.

Bywater(s) T Dweller by the water(s) OE.

Bywood T Dweller by the wood OE.

C

Caborne/Cabourn P Place-name: *Cabourne* Lincs OE 'stream with jackdaws'.

Cadbury P Place-names in Somerset (*Cadbury*, near Bristol; *North* and *South Cadbury*, near Wincanton) and Devon OE '*Cada*'s fortress'. *The famous chocolate company of this name was founded by John Cadbury, who began selling tea, coffee and chocolate in Bull Street, Birmingham, in 1824.*

Caddick/Caddock N Nickname for a decrepit, epileptic person, one afflicted with falling sickness OF.

Caddow N Nickname for a person bearing some similarity to a jackdaw ME *cad(d)aw*, *cad(d)owe*. Compare **Coe**, **Daw**. A very scarce surname, mainly confined to Scotland.

Cadogan/Cadwgan F From an OW first-name, comprised of *cad* ('battle'), followed by a suffix to make it adjectival. *See also* **Dugan**.

Cadwal(l)ad(e)r/Cadwalladar F A glorious four-syllable surname derived from an OW first-name: *cad* ('battle') and *gwaladr* ('leader'), known to have been in use since at least as early as the seventh century.

Cadwgan, *see* **Cadogan**.

Caesar N A nickname. The Roman leader's family had borne this name long before he was born by Caesarian section, so it doesn't derive from the Latin stem *caes* ('cut'); the meaning, from Latin, is '?fleece, head of hair'/'?bluish-grey'. *John Caesar of Ballahick, Kirk Malew, Isle of Man, was a member of the Keys during the seventeenth century... Sir Julius Caesar (1557/8–1636), English judge and politician, was born in Tottenham, Middx, the son of Giulio Cesare Adelmare, physician to Queen Elizabeth I, who was descended in the female line from the Dukes of Cesarini.*

Caffin/Caffyn N A nickname, from a diminutive of an Old Norman French word for 'bald'; or a variant of **Coffin**.

Caffyn, *see* **Caffin**.

Cage/Cager O/T Occupational term for a maker of cages OF, or for one living or working at a cage for petty criminals. *Nicholas Cage (born 1964), Academy Award-winning actor, has Italian ancestry on his father's side, and English and German on his mother's. He was born Nicholas Kim Coppola, but to avoid any charge of nepotism as a result of his being the nephew of the director Francis Ford Coppola, he assumed the name of Cage, inspired by a* Marvel *comic character named Luke Cage, an African-American super-hero.*

Cahill F Irish: Anglicized form of Gaelic O' [descendant of] **Cathail** ('powerful in battle').

Cain(e)/Cane/Kane N/P/F Nickname for a man as thin as a reed OF *cane*; or from *Caen*, a Gaulish place-name in Calvados; or from an OW female first-name meaning 'beautiful'. Manx: a contraction of the patronymic **Mac Cathain** (Irish *cath*, Manx *cah*: 'battle'). *See also* **Cains** and **O'Kane**. For the actor Sir Michael **Caine**, *see* **Micklewhite** (under **Micklethwait**).

Cain(e)s/Keynes T/P Dweller by juniper-trees OF; or from place-names such as

Cahagnes and *Cahaignes* in Calvados, Eure, France. A family called **Keynes** owned *Combe Keynes*, Dorset, in the fourteenth century, and many Wilts estates later. Hugo **de Cayenes** held land in the *Milton Keynes* area of Bucks in 1227. Mainly a Dorset surname. *See also* **Cain.**

Caird O Occupational term for a craftsman, smith, Scots Gaelic.

Caister/Caistor P Place-name in Norfolk, Lincs OE (from Latin) 'Roman site'.

Cake O Occupational term for a maker of cakes, flat buns ON.

Cakebread O Occupational term for a maker of fine flat loaves, griddlecakes ON and OE.

Calcott/Cal(l)cut(t) P From places with such names in various counties, some with the meaning of 'cold cottage/hut' OE, but *Calcott* in Berks and Wilts are OE '?*Cela*'s cottage'.

Calcraft T Dweller at the cold croft OE. A scarce surname, with a limited presence in Notts. Readily confused with/a variant of **Chalcraft**. *The public executioner William Calcraft (1800–1879), a quiet and respectable-looking man whose hobby was breeding rabbits, but whose work as a hangman was incompetent beyond belief, was born at Baddow, near Chelmsford, Essex.*

Calcut(t), *see* **Calcott.**

Caldbeck P Place-name in Cumbd 'cold stream' ON.

**Caldecot(t)/Caldecote/Caldecourt/
Caldicot(t)/Cal(l)icot(t)** P Place-names *Caldecote/Caldicot* in many English counties and in Monmouthshire OE 'cold cottage(s)/hut(s)'. *Randolph Caldecott (1846–1886), well known principally as an illustrator of children's books, was born in Chester, the son of a local businessman.*

Calder P British river-name; place-name in Cumbd, Lancs, WRYorks OW and Old British 'hard/violent stream'. Principally a Scottish surname, but found also in northern England.

**Calderon/Caudron/Cauldron/Caw-
dron** O Occupational term for a cauldron-maker OF.

Calderwood/Catherwood P Scots: From the place-name *Calderwood* in Lanarkshire, named after the river *Calder*, plus ME wood. **Calderwood** and **Catherwood** are also Northern Irish surnames, the former being particularly strong in Co Antrim.

Caldicot(t), *see* **Caldecot.**

Caldwall/Caldwell, *see* **Caudle.**

Cal(l)f(e) O/N/F Occupational term for a man who tended calves, or who resembled them in some way OE; or from an ON first-name *Kalfr.*

Calicot(t), *see* **Caldecot.**

Calladine/Cannadine P Presumably derived from an unidentified place-name. Possibly related to **Carwardine/Carden.** **Calladine** is very much a Derbys surname; **Cannadine** is exceptionally scarce.

Callard, *see* **Collard.**

**Callaway/Calloway/Kellaway/Kelle-
way** P Place-name *Caillouet* in Eure, France OF 'pebbly place'. A family from there must have established *Tytherington Kellaways*, Wilts. **Callaway** is found in southern counties of England, principally in Hants; **Callo-way** is widespread; **Kellaway**, found in Dorset, is very scarce, as is **Kelleway**, which belongs chiefly to the Isle of Wight.

Callcut(t), *see* **Calcott.**

Callicot(t), *see* **Caldecot.**

Callow P Place-name in various counties, most with the meaning (from OE) of 'bald-topped hill', 'cold hill'; *Calow* in Derbys is 'bald nook'. In Derbys, where the name is most common, it is usually pronounced '*Cayloe*' – possibly to avoid any association with the meaning of 'inexperienced' (a '*callow* youth').

Calloway, *see* **Callaway.**

Calpin, *see* **Culpin.**

Calthrop/Calthorp(e) P Derived by

metathesis from *Calthorpe*, Norfolk and Oxon ON and OE '*Kali*'s settlement' or 'charcoal/colt/cabbage settlement'. But a 'caltrap/caltrop' is a four-spiked metal ball intended to hobble horses in battle… **Calthorpe** is commonly pronounced '*Cawlthorp*'. A scarce Lincs surname; one **Calthrop** family of Gosberton in that county claim descent from Walter **de Calthrop**, a thirteenth-century Bishop of Norwich. The Barons **Calthorpe** are of *Calthorpe*, Norfolk.

Calton P Place-name in Derbys, Staffs, WRYorks OE 'calf farm'.

Calver P Place-name in Derbys (pronounced '*Carver*') OE 'ridge for grazing calves'. Almost exclusively an East Anglian surname.

Calverd, *see* Calvert.

Calverley P Place-names: *Calverley*, WRYorks OE 'clearing/pasture for calves'; *Calverleigh*, Dorset OE 'clearing in a bare wood'. A WRYorks surname.

Calvert/Calverd O Occupational term for a calf-herd OE. **Calvert** is a WRYorks/Lancs surname; **Calverd** is exceptionally scarce. **Calvert** is the surname of the former Barons Baltimore.

Calwell, *see* Caudle.

Cam(m)/Came P/N Place- and river-name *Cam* in Gloucs, British '?crooked' (compare **Cambridge**); or from the place-name *Caen* in France. Scots Gaelic: nickname for a crooked/cross-eyed person (compare 'gammy' or 'game' leg).

Cam(m)amile/Camomile N/O Blossoms of camomile OF, from Latin, from Greek 'earth apple' smell like apples, and are used in pharmacy, but why precisely camomile should give rise to a surname is not clear; perhaps a nickname for a sweet-smelling person, or an occupational term for a herbalist? Rare, whatever the spelling: **Camamile** is marginally more common in Notts, while **Camomile**, widespread, is found mainly in the Midlands and the North. A strangely elusive surname: there is a mere handful of **Camamile**s/**Camomile**s in Notts from the early seventeenth century, in Treswell and South Wheatley, but almost nowhere else. It has much of the flavour of a French surname, but M. T. Morlet's *Dictionnaire étymologique des noms de famille* (1991) only features **Camail(le)** and **Chamaillé/Chamaillet/Chamaillon**. There is no evidence of a Huguenot origin.

Camborne/Camburn P Place-name *Camborne* in Cornwall, Cornish 'crooked hill'.

Cambridge P Place-name in Gloucs, British and OE 'bridge over the river *Cam*' (compare **Cam**). The university city of *Cambridge* was once 'bridge over the *Granta*'. Found in Gloucs, Surrey and Scotland.

Camburn, *see* Camborne.

Came, *see* Cam.

Cam(m)el(l) N/F/P Possibly a nickname for a camel-like person. The imagination boggles: lugubrious? lumbering? grumpy? 'Camel' comes from Greek via Latin, ultimately Semitic. Bardsley, linking **Camel** with **Gamel**, will have none of it: 'No connexion with the animal… Baptismal name, "the son of *Gamel*"… "G" constantly becomes "C" in English nomenclature…'. A place-name origin is a possibility, though the source or sources of the Somerset place-names *Queen Camel* and *East/West Camel* have long exercised scholars. Cottle says that both are 'doubtful claimants to be the site of Camelot', but James Hill in *The place-names of Somerset* (1914) considers a range of other possibilities: *Camlas* is a Welsh word for a trench or ditch, *cymle* is a common field for cattle, and *cinmael* is a retreat, but Hill favours a river-name origin: *Cam* ('bent, crooked') is an element in numerous river-names, including the *Camel* which rises near Maperton and joins the Yeo on which East and West Camel stand. More prosaically, **Camel** can be an alternative pronunciation of the surname **Campbell**. A scarce widespread surname. *The well-known shipbuilding company of Cammell Laird came into existence as a result of the merger of Laird, Son and Co. of Birkenhead and Johnson Cammell & Co. of*

Sheffield (founded by Charles Cammell and Henry and Thomas Johnson).

Cameron N/P Scots Gaelic: nickname for a person with a crooked/hook nose (compare **Campbell**, 'crooked mouth'); or from one of a number of places in the Scottish Lowlands so-called, Gaelic 'crooked hill'. *The Conservative Party politician David Cameron (born in 1966), who descends on his father's side from King William IV and his mistress Dorothea Jordan, would seem not to have inherited the prominent nose of his supposed forefathers…*

Camm, *see* **Cam**.

Camomile, *see* **Camamile**.

Camp(s) N/O A nickname or occupational name for a warrior ME *kempe*, OE *cempa*, Latin *campus*, 'field (of battle)'. Compare **Kemp**. Found mainly in Essex, Herts and Middx.

Campbell N Scots Gaelic 'crooked mouth' (compare **Cameron**, 'crooked nose'). A very common surname in Scotland and Ireland. Family name of the Dukes of Argyll and of other Scots peers. See also **Camel**.

Campin T/P Dweller at open country, fertile land OF; or from places called *Campagne* in Oise, Pas-de-Calais, or from the *Champagne* region. A widespread but rare surname.

Campion, *see* **Champion**.

Camps, *see* **Camp**.

Campton P Place-name in Beds, British and OE 'place on the crooked (stream)'. Widespread but rare.

Can(n)ard N Nickname for a sluggard, wastrel OF. An inn-sign at *Cannard's Grave* near Shepton Mallet, Somerset, once displayed a hanged man. **Canard** is an extremely rare surname; **Cannard**, somewhat less scarce, is found mainly in the south and south-west of England.

Candler, *see* **Chandler**.

Cane, *see* **Caine**.

Cann O/T/P Occupational term for a maker or seller of cans, pots, buckets or jars OE *canna* ('can'); or a dweller in a deep valley, from the same OE source; or from a place so-named in Dorset. Very much a Devon surname.

Cannadine, *see* **Calladine**.

Cannan F Irish: **O'** [descendant of] **Cano**. An Anglicized spelling of two different Irish septs, and often rendered as **Cannon**.

Cannard, *see* **Canard**.

Cannel(l) O/F Occupational term for a seller of cinnamon OF. There are no known *atte-* or *de-* forms to suggest that the origin may be OF 'channel, river-bed, gutter, ditch'. Or a shortened version of Manx **McConnal**. **Cannel** is a scarce surname, found mainly in north-west England; **Cannell** is very much a Manx surname.

Cannington P Place-name in Somerset, Celtic and OE 'farm by the Quantock Hills'.

Cannon O Occupational term for a canon, a member of a communal house of clergy, Old Norman French. **Channon** is an OF version. But see **Cannan**.

Cansick ?P Perhaps from the place-name *Kenswick*, Worcs OE '*Kech*'s dairy farm'. The related surname **Kensick**, very scarce, can be found in Lancs and Worcs.

Cant, *see* **Chant**.

Cantel(l)o(w) N/P Nickname from the OF word *Canteloup/Canteleu* ('song of the wolf'), and used to refer to anything which people dreaded; or from places so-called in Calvados/Seine-Maritime in France. *Cantaluppi*, near Rome, was the place where cantaloup(e) melons were first grown. *St Thomas de Cantelupe (died 1282) was Bishop of Hereford.*

Canter O Occupational term for a singer, Old Norman French. A *cantor* (related to the office of precentor) was in charge of a cathedral choir.

Cantle T/?P Dweller at a nook, corner, angle of land, Old Norman French; but some lost place-name with the element *-hill/-well/ -hall/-haugh* may be concealed here. Strongest in Gloucs/Somerset.

Capel/Caple T/P/N Dweller at a chapel, Old Norman French; or from places called *Capel* or *Caple* in various counties; or a nickname for a person bearing some resemblance to a horse or nag ME, from ON, ultimately from Low Latin.

Capern, *see* **Caperon**.

Caperon/Capern/Capron O/N Occupational term/nickname for a maker of/ wearer of a distinctive hood or cap, Old Norman French *caprun* (compare the French word *chapeau*, 'hat').

Caple, *see* **Capel**.

Capon O/N Occupational term for a breeder or seller of capons (neutered cockerels) OE; or a nickname for a cuckold (well and truly neutered, as it were, in a metaphorical sense).

Capper O/N Occupational term/nickname for a maker or wearer of caps or hats OE.

Capron, *see* **Caperon**.

Capstack/Capstick, *see* **Copestake**.

Card(er) O Occupational term for a carder/ teaser of wool OF. Long before the development of digital data storage, a girl named '*I.D.* Card' was born in Portsmouth, Hants, in 1908. A man by the name of *Valentine Card*, born in 1913, died in Chelmsford, Essex, in 1993.

Carden, *see* **Carwardine**.

Carder, *see* **Card**.

Cardew P Place-names in Cornwall and Cumbd, Celtic 'black fort'. A scarce surname, found mainly in Cornwall and Devon.

Careless, *see* **Carless**.

Carey, *see* **Cary**.

Carless/Careless N Nickname for a person deemed to be free from worry/responsibility OE (rather than distracted, clumsy).

Carleton, *see* **Carlton**.

Carli(s)le P Place-name *Carlisle* in Cumbd; the Romano-British name meant 'belonging to *Lugovalos* ["strong as the celtic god *Lugus*"]'; to this the OW word for 'fort/city' has been prefixed.

Carlton/Carleton P Place-name used in at least a dozen counties, from Beds to Yorks ON and OE 'settlement of the common man'. The name is a Scandinavianized version of *Charleton* (compare **Charlton**). **Carleton** is the family name of the Viscounts Dorchester.

Carman F/O From an ON first-name *Kar(l)-mathr* ('male person') (compare *Charles*); or an occupational name for a carter, Anglo-Norman French and Middle Low German. The City of London Livery Company known as the Worshipful Company of Carmen was established in the year 1668.

Carmichael P Scots: from the place-name *Carmichael*, Lanarkshire, British *ker* (fort) plus the first-name *Michael*, where a family of this name held land as early as the twelfth century and in which county the surname has long lingered. *The English actor Ian Carmichael was born in Hull, Yorkshire, in 1920 ... The American musician Hoagland Howard 'Hoagy' Carmichael (1899–1981) was born in Bloomington, Indiana.*

Carnegie P Scots: place-name in Angus, Gaelic *cathair an eige* 'fort at the gap'. *Andrew Carnegie (1835–1919), the American industrialist and philanthropist, was born in Dunfermline, Scotland... Dale (Breckenridge) Carnegie (1888–1955), formerly 'Carnagey', the author of books such as* How to win friends and influence people, *was born to a poor farming family in Maryville, Missouri, USA.*

Carpenter O Occupational term for a carpenter, Anglo-Norman French. Colin Rogers in *The surname detective* (1995) makes the telling point that this surname is conspicuous by its absence in the north of England, where a carpenter was commonly known as a 'wright'.

Carr T/P Dweller at a marsh, wet ground overgrown with brushwood ON. *Carr* is also a frequent place-name element, especially in the Danelaw, and **Carr** principally a northern surname. **Kerr** (also **Ker**), a form of the surname which belongs principally to Scotland and the north of England, is generally pronounced '*Carr*' – a ploy, perhaps, to avoid any association with the word '*cur*' (a worthless dog, cowardly fellow)? For the relationship between -*ar*- and -*er*- in such names, see **Armistead**. *The* **Kerr** *family of the Scottish borders, Marquesses of Lothian and Barons Teviot, have long been been predominantly left-handed. When Sir Andrew* **Kerr** *returned from the Battle of Flodden in 1513, he trained his followers to use their weapons with their left hand, just as he did, and the* **Kerr***s' border castle of Ferniehirst has a famous 'left-handed' staircase. A common Border dialect expression for 'left-handed' is 'kerry/kerrie-handed' (or 'cairy/carrie/carrie/corrie/corry-handed/fisted'), though there might well have been confusion thanks to the fact that the Gaelic word cearr means 'wrong/left-handed'. Deborah* **Kerr** *(1921–2007), Scottish actress, originally Deborah Jane Kerr-Trimmer, was born in Helensbugh, near Glasgow.*

Carruthers P Scots: place-name in Dumfries, British '?*Rhydderch*'s fort'. One local pronounciation is '*Kridders*'. In the thirteenth century the **Carruthers** were stewards of Annandale under the Bruces, and from then until the seventeenth century at least, the surname has been spelt in a variety of ways.

Carslake/Karslake/Ke(a)rslake ?P Surnames of uncertain origin, though they give every appearance of being derived from an unidentifiable place-name with the meaning of OE 'watercress stream'. Principally Devon surnames.

Carsley/Cassley P Place-names: *Keresley*, Warwicks; *Kearsley*, Lancs and Northd, OE '*Cenhere*'s clearing', or OE 'clearing with cress'. **Carsley**, a scarce surname, can be found in Salop and elsewhere; **Cassley**, also scarce, is chiefly associated with Lancs.

Carswell T/P Dweller near a spring/stream where cress grows OE; or from such a place-name in Berks and Devon, with the same meaning.

Carter O/F Occupational term for a maker or driver of carts ME from Anglo-Norman French. Manx: a shortened form of **McArthur**.

Carthy, *see* **McCarthy**.

Cartledge/Cartlidge T/P Dweller by a stream in rough, stony ground ON and OE, or from *Cartledge*, Derbys, with the same meaning. Strong in Derbys in either spelling.

Cartwright O Occupational term for a maker of carts OE.

Carus T/P Dweller in a house on wet ground/by the brushwood ME and OE; or from the place-names *Carhouse*, Lincs, or *Car House*, WRYorks, with the same meaning. Compare **Bullas** ('bull-house') and the like. However, the surname, which is scarce, is marginally more common in Lancs than elsewhere.

Carver O Occupational term for a sculptor OE, or for a ploughman, Anglo-Norman French *caruier* ('plough').

Carwardine/Carden P Place-name *Carden* (formerly *Cawardyn*), Chesh OE 'enclosure by a rock'. The place-name element -*war-dine* can be found in many settlements on the English side of the border with Wales; -*worthy* can be found in many other place names, and the Sussex town of *Worthing* may even owe its origin to -*wardine*. See *also* **Calladine**.

Cary/Carey P Place-names in Somerset, derived from a river-name: *Castle Cary, Cary Fitzpaine, Lytes Cary, Babcary*, Celtic 'pleasant stream'. **Cary**, chiefly a Somerset surname, is much scarcer than **Carey**, which has a strong presence in Lancs. **Cary** is the family name of the Viscounts Falkland. *George Carey, the 103rd Archbishop of Canterbury, was born in the East End of London in 1935… Carey Street, a London thoroughfare, was named after Nicholas Carey, who had houses there in the seventeenth century.*

Casbolt N Nickname for a bald-headed person ME *casbalde*, a term of reproach. Very scarce, with a presence in Cambs.

Case O Occupational term for a maker of boxes or cases, Anglo-Norman French *cas(s)e*. But see also **Cass**. A widespread surname, most common in Lancs.

Casement F Irish: 'son of *Osmund*'; Manx: ON 'son of *Asmundr* ["fee of the gods"]'. Apart from its presence in Ireland, the surname can be found in Lancs and the Isle of Man. *The British diplomat Sir Roger Casement (1864–1916), whose male-line ancestry can be traced back to the Isle of Man, had a deep belief in Irish nationalism, and was hanged for treason by the British during the First World War.*

Cash, *see* **Cass**.

Cashen/Cashin N/F Irish: nickname for a crooked person; Manx: a shortened form of **Mac Caisin** ('son of *Caisin*').

Cass/Cash F A diminutive of *Cassandra* (of unknown origin), a feminine form of *Alexander*. The unfortunate Trojan princess so-named was able to foretell the future accurately, but her predictions were always disbelieved. Her story made *Cassandra* a popular first-name in the Middle Ages. **Cass** is found mainly in the north of England, but also has a presence in the southeast; **Cash** is mainly a Midlands and northern surname; **Casson** ('son of **Cass**') is strongest in Lancs, WRYorks and Cumbd. *See also* **Case**. *Sir Hugh Casson (1910–1999), architect and designer, nephew of the actor Sir Lewis Casson, came from a Welsh family.*

Cassley, *see* **Carsley**.

Casson, *see* **Cass**.

Casterton P Place-name in Rutland, Westmd OE 'place by a Roman site'. A scarce surname, found in Lincs, Notts and Rutland.

Castle T/O Dweller at, or worker at, a castle, Anglo-Norman French *castel*. Most commonly found in Kent, but also in WRYorks and elsewhere. Surprise, surprise: the birth of a child called '*Windsor* **Castle**' was registered in Radford, Nottingham, in 1876. *Roy Castle (1932–1994), multi-talented entertainer and television performer, was born near Holmfirth in Yorkshire.*

Castleton P Place-name in five counties, most famously in the High Peak of Derbys OF and OE 'place by a castle'.

Caswall/Caswell P Place-names in ten counties, originally spelt more like *Carswell*, but also *Crasswell*, *Cresswell*, *Carsewell*, *Kerswell* OE 'spring/stream where cress grows'.

Catcheside P Place-name in Northd OE and OF and OE 'cold-cheer hill'. A scarce surname, found mainly in north-eastern counties of England.

Catchpole/Catchpoll/Catchpool(e) O Occupational term, literally 'chase-fowl' OF (compare the word '*poultry*', '*pullet*') for one who seized poultry in lieu of debts, a tax-gatherer, a sheriff's official arresting on warrant for debt. A surname with a conspicuous presence in Norfolk and Suffolk.

Cater/Cator/Chater O Occupational term for a person who buys OF (compare Modern French *acheter* 'to buy'), and so used for a caterer, a purveyor for a household.

Catford P Place-name in Kent OE '(wild) cats' ford'.

Cathcart P Scots: place-name near Glasgow (*Katkert/Ketkert* in the twelfth century). The second element refers to the river *Cart*, while the first could be derived from a British word meaning 'battle', or ('*ker*') 'a fort'.

Catherwood, *see* **Calderwood**.

Catley P Place-name in four counties OE '(wild) cats' wood/clearing'. Strongest in both the south-east and north-west of England.

Catlin(g)/Catt/Cattell/Cattle/Catton F From the mediaeval female first-name *Cat(e)lin(e)*, an Anglo-Norman French form of *Catherine*. Popularized thanks to the legendary martyr *St Katherine* of Alexandria, one of the fourteen Holy Helpers.

Catmore P Place-name in Berks OE '(wild) cats' lake', or the lake (mere) of a man whose first-name had the meaning of 'cat'. A scarce surname, found in southern counties of England and in East Anglia.

Cator, *see* Cater.

Catt N/F Nickname for a person who bore some similarity to a cat OE; or a shortened form of **Catlin**, with its origins in the name *Catherine* (and *St Catharine's* College, Cambridge, is referred to familiarly as '*Cat's*').

Cattanach/Cattenach F Scots: from a Gaelic first-name, meaning 'of the clan (**Chattan**) descended from the devotee of *St Catan* ("little cat")'.

Cattell, *see* Catlin.

Cattenach, *see* Cattanach.

Catterall/Catterell/Catterill/Catteroll P Place-name *Catterall* in Lancs ON '?cat's-tail' – a long strip of land'). Ekwall quotes *Katterall*, Norway, as having the same meaning. **Catterall**, the most commonly found of these alternative spellings, is very largely a Lancs surname.

Catterick P Place-name in NRYorks, possibly derived originally from Latin *cataracta*, 'waterfall, cataract', Celticized. A surname of northern and north-eastern counties of England.

Catterill, *see* Catterall.

Cattermole The exact meaning of this surname has long been a subject of debate, with no positive conclusion being reached. Walter Rye, in *Norfolk families* (1911), speculates that 'this unusual surname may be a corruption for **Kakermol**, Thomas **Kakermol** occurring on the Subsidy Roll for 6 Edward III (1332/1333) at Tivetshall'. Bardsley says: 'I find no early traces; perhaps an immigrant from the Low Countries', a theory picked up by Reaney, who remarks that the surname's late arrival in Suffolk suggests a possible Dutch or Flemish origin. Yet the 'arrival in Suffolk' – and in the neighbouring county of Norfolk – is not

as late as Reaney implies. Probate records for the Archdeaconry of Suffolk include John **Cakemol** of Ringsfield (1454), together with various seventeenth-century testators bearing the surnames **Cattermoll**, **Catermole** and **Cattamol**; in similar records for the Archdeaconry of Sudbury, Suffolk, we find Thomas **Catywold** of Cockfield (1483), Richard **Cadywold** of Bury St Edmund's (1548) and John **Cadywold** of Long Melford (1610). When the will of Richard **Cattermole** of Dickleburgh, Norfolk, was proved in the Norwich Archdeaconry Court in 1565, his name was also spelt **Kakyrmolle**. Vital records show that a **Cattermole** family had a continuous presence in this same parish of Dickleburgh from least as early as the mid sixteenth century onwards. Not only that, but John **Catermoll** of 'Stokeaysche' is listed in a Suffolk Subsidy Return for 1524 ('in wages, £1'), and there is even a stray **Katermould** in Kent in 1613. Once we consider the possibility – as Rye clearly did – that this name could begin with the element *Ca(c)k* as opposed to *Cat(t)*, new possibilities emerge; perhaps *Cac(k)* had too many scatological associations and was abandoned by some family groups? *Cac(k)*-type surnames abound in Suffolk and Norfolk from the late sixteenth century onwards, appearing in a bewildering variety of forms: **Cacamole**, **Cacamool**, **Cacamoule**, **Cackamole**, **Cackamoul**, **Cackelmoul**, **Cackermold**, **Cackermole**, **Cackymole**, **Cakamole**, **Cakamould**, **Cakamoule**, **Cakemoole**, **Cakermole**, **Cakermoule**, **Cocamold**, **Cockermole**, **Cockymole**, **Kakemoll**. The most charming first-name bestowed upon a person bearing such a surname must be that of *Alsaints* **Kakemole**, son of Robert, who was baptized on 1 November 1627 at Surlingham, Norfolk.

Catteroll, *see* Catterall.

Cattle, *see* Catlin.

Catton P Place-name in various counties, including: Northd OE '(wild) cats' valley'; Derbys, Norfolk, ERYorks, NRYorks OE and ON and OF 'cat's cheerful's place' (from an owner's name). *See also* Catlin.

**Caudle/Caldwall/Caldwell/Calwell/
Caudwell/Cauldwell/Cawdell/
Cawdle/Chadwell/Chardle/
Chardwell/Coldwell/Colwell/Colwill**

P/N   Place-names: *Caldwell* (Derbys,
NRYorks, Warwicks); *Caldwall* (Worcs);
Cauldwell (Beds, Notts); *Caudle Green*
(Gloucs); *Caudle Ditch* and *Cawdle Fen*
(Cambs); *Chadwell* (Essex, Herts, Leics,
Wilts); *Chardwell* (Essex); *Chardle Ditch*
(Cambs); *Colwell* (Northd and Isle of
Wight; *Colwall* (Herefords, which was *Cole-
welle* in Domesday Book, 1086), all OE 'cold
well or stream'. *Colwell*, Devon, is British
and OE 'river Coly (literally "narrow")
stream', and there is a *Colwill* in the same
county. **Colwell** is a widespread surname;
Colwill is very much in evidence in
Devon. In Scotland, **Caldwell** and **Coldwell**,
formerly pronounced *'Carwall'*, are from
Cladwell, Renfrewshire. Cottle notes that
Caudle can also be derived from a name
for a sweet, spiced gruel OF, an invalid beverage which might have given rise to a nickname and then a surname, 'for some
mocking reason'. *Sir Alexander Caldwell
(1763–1839), army officer in the East India
Company, was the son of William Caldwell
by his third wife Isabella Clark, of Inverness.*

Caudron, *see* **Calderon**.

Caudwell, *see* **Caudle**.

Cauldron, *see* **Calderon**.

Cauldwell, *see* **Caudle**.

Causey T Dweller by the causeway OF (compare modern French *chausée*, a roadway),
meaning 'surfaced with limestone'. The
-way ending is the result of folk etymology.
'Causey' is still commonly used in midlands and northern dialect for a pavement:
'Eh fell off t'causey inter th'oss-road' (a
nasty accident which once befell an inebri-
ated Derbyshireman...).

Cavanagh, *see* **Kavanagh**.

Cave/Cavel(l) N/P Nickname for a bald
man OF *chaufe/chauve* (*see also* **Chaff**); or
from place-names in ERYorks, *North* and
South Cave, named after a river so-called,
from OE *caf* ('swift'). **Cavel(l)** (readily con-

fused with/a variant of **Cavil(l)**) is a diminutive. **Cave** is a widespread surname, strong
in Lancs. The baronet family of **Cave-
Browne-Cave** has a male-line ancestry
stretching back to an eleventh-century
landowner named Wyamarus **De Cave** of
North and South Cave, Yorks. *Edith Louisa
Cavell (1865–1915), nurse and war heroine, was
born in Swardeston Vicarage, Norfolk, where
her father was the parish priest.*

Cavendish P Place-name in Suffolk OE 'pasture of *Cafna*' (a byname with the meaning
'bold'/'bold-daring'). The **Cavendish** family, Dukes of Devonshire, traces its origin
back to a sixteenth-century Suffolk gentleman, Sir William **Cavendish**. The **Cavendish** surname is also borne by the Dukes of
Newcastle and Portland.

Cavill P Place-names *Cavil/Cavile* in
ERYorks OE 'jackdaw field'. Readily confused with/a variant of **Cavel(l)** (*see* **Cave**).

Cawdell/Cawdle, *see* **Caudle**.

Cawdron, *see* **Calderon**.

Cawood P Place-name in Lancs, WRYorks
OE 'jackdaw wood'.

Cawthorn(e) P Place-names *Cawthorn/
Cawthorne* in WRYorks, NRYorks OE 'cold/
bleak/exposed thorn-bush'.

Cawton P Place-name NRYorks OE 'calf
farm'.

Cecil F From the OW first-name *Seisylt*, a
corruption of the Latin *Sextilius* ('sixth'),
the spelling modified by association with
the Latin name *Caecilius* (from *caecus*,
'blind'). The surname is commonly pronounced *'Sissel'*. The **Cecils**, Marquesses of
Exeter and of Salisbury, trace their origins
back to William **Cecil**, Lord Burghley
(1520–1598), who came from Welsh gentry
stock. **Saycell** and **Saysell**, found chiefly in
Lancs and Gloucs respectively, are variants.

Chad(d)away, *see* **Chataway**.

Chadderton/Chatterton P From a place-
name *Chadderton* in Lancs, British and OE
'place by a hill', and a predominantly
Lancs surname. *The male-line ancestors of*

the poet Thomas Chatterton (1752–1770), sextons to the church of St Mary Redcliffe in Bristol through several generations, had been known originally as 'Chadderton'. Chatterton the poet, only seventeen years old when he died in Brooke Street, London, was long supposed to have committed suicide; in the event it would appear that his death was caused by an accidental overdose of arsenic and laudanum.

Chadwell, *see* **Caudle**.

Chadwick P Place-name *Chadwick*: one in Warwicks and another in Worcs OE '*Ceadel*'s dairy farm'; another in Lancs, and a second one in Worcs OE '*Ceadda*'s dairy farm'. *Ceadda* was the name borne by *St Chad*, an Anglo-Saxon bishop.

Chafer T/O Dweller at, or worker at, a lime-kiln OF *chauffour*. Strongest in Lincs.

Chaff(e)/Chaffin N Nickname for a bald man OF *chaufe/chauve*, with a weak adjective after a lost definite article. *See also* **Cave**. **Chaffin** is a diminutive. **Chaff** is a scarce surname, limited mainly to Devon; **Chaffin**, even scarcer, may principally be found in Somerset and Dorset.

Chainey, *see* **Chesnay**.

Chalcraft/Chalcroft T/P Dweller at the calves' paddock OE, or from the place-name *Chalcroft* in Hants, which presumably has the same origin and meaning. Readily confused with/a variant of **Calcraft**.

Chalcroft, *see* **Chalcraft**.

Chalice, *see* **Challis**.

Chalk(e)/Chalker T/P/O Dweller on or near chalk-soil OE; or from a place-name with the same meaning, such as *Chalk*, Kent, or *Chalke*, Wilts; or an occupational term for a *chalker*, who worked with chalk or whitewash. **Chalker** is predominantly a Wilts surname.

Chalker, *see* **Chalk**.

Challen(s)/Challener/Challenor/Chawner P/O Place-name *Châlons-sur-Marne* in France (named after a Gaulish tribe, the

Catalauni); or an occupational term for a maker or seller of shalloons (blankets), which were commonly made there; or from *Châlon-sur-Saône* OF (from Gaulish *Caladun-*) in Saône-et-Loire. See also **Challenger**.

Challener, *see* **Challen**.

Challenger O From a term used for a plaintiff, challenger, accuser OF; or, by folk etymology, for **Challener/Challenor** (see **Challen**). **Challenger** has an uneven scattered presence, being strongest in WRYorks, Somerset and Monmouthshire.

Challenor, *see* **Challen**.

Challis(s)/Chalice/Shallis P Place-name *Escalles*, in Pas-de-Calais, France OF 'ladder, abrupt drop' (compare Modern French *échelle* [ladder], *escalier* [flight of stairs]). **Challis** is found mainly in south-east England and in East Anglia; **Challiss** (WRYorks), **Chalice** (Devon) and **Shallis** (Somerset) are all scarce.

Chalmers, *see* **Chambers**.

Chalton P Place-name in Hants OE 'place on the chalk' and (two such) in Beds OE 'calf farm'.

Chamberlain(e)/Chamberlayne/Chamberlin O Occupational term for a private attendant of a king or lord, one charged with control of private rooms; eventually used for a steward, and even for a kind of male head chambermaid at an inn OF form of Latin *camera* ('room') and Germanic -*ling* (as in dar*ling*, hire*ling*, change*ling* and other – often contemptuous – words). Compare **Chambers**.

Chamberlayne, *see* **Chamberlain**.

Chamberlin, *see* **Chamberlain**.

Chambers O Occupational term for a servant within private, rather than public, rooms. Less grand than a **Chamberlain**. **Chalmers** is a Scots variant. *The television presenter Judith Chalmers was born in Manchester in 1936.*

Champion/Campion O/N Occupational

term for a person whose profession it was to fight for another in wager of battle; or a nickname for an athlete, especially a boxer or wrestler OF, from Latin *campus* ('field', 'arena'). Bears comparison with **Champness**. **Champion** is found mainly in south and south-west counties of England; **Campion**, a Norman form, is commonest in Lancs.

Champness/Champney(s) P From the French province of *Champagne* OF from Latin, 'plain; flat country'. **Champness** is a scarce surname, found in Middx and elsewhere; **Champney** is strongest in WRYorks; **Champneys**, also scarce, has a limited presence in Surrey.

Champney(s), *see* **Champness**.

Chancellor O/N Occupational term for a worker in a chancery, archivist, secretary OF; or a nickname for a person exuding an air of learning, whether or not he had the qualities to back it up.

Chandler/Candler O Occupational term for a maker or seller of candles OF. The broader meaning of the word to describe a seller of many articles, as a ships' chandler would do, is a later development. **Chandler** is found mainly in south/south-east counties of England; **Candler**, a Norman form, is widespread but uncommon.

Chaney, *see* **Chesnay**.

Channon, *see* **Cannon**.

Chant/Cant O Occupational term for a professional or amateur singer OF. **Chant** is mainly a Somerset surname; **Cant**, a Norman version, can be found in Essex, but also in Scotland.

Chantr(e)y O/P Occupational term for one who sang masses in a chantry-chapel; or from a place-name near Frome, Somerset, with the same meaning. Found mainly in Midland counties, and strong in Lincs. *The English sculptor Sir Francis Leggatt Chantrey (1781–1841), son of Francis Chantrey, a tenant farmer and carpenter, was born in Norton, Derbys, where a pub was named in his honour.*

Chaplain/Chaplin(g) O Occupational term for a chantry-priest, chaplain OF. *Sir Charles Spencer ('Charlie') Chaplin (1889–1977), film actor and director, was reputedly born on 16 April 1889 in Walworth, Surrey, though no birth certificate for him has been found. His father Charles, a successful music-hall performer, left him and his brother Sydney to be brought up in abject poverty by their mother Hannah Harriett Pedingham Hill (stage name: 'Lily Harley').*

Chaplin(g), *see* **Chaplain**.

Chapman O Occupational term for a merchant, trader OE *ceap* ('barter/bargain'), which is found as an element in place-names such as *Chipping* Norton, Oxon, and *Chep*stow, Monmouthshire, and also occurs in street-names such as *Cheap*side in London. Burns' famous poem *Tam o' Shanter* begins: 'When *chapman* billies leave the street…'. 'A universal occupation and surname' (Cottle).

Chappel(l)/Chapple T/O A dweller near, or one who officiated at, a chapel OF. *Gregory Stephen ('Greg') Chappell (born 1948) has been one of Australia's finest cricketers. He and Ian Chappell are the only brothers to have made centuries in each innings of the same test match, a feat achieved at Wellington in 1974.*

Chapple, *see* **Chappel**.

Chard/Chart P Place names: *Chard* in Somerset and *Chart* in Kent OE 'house in a chart or rough common'. **Chard** is found mainly in south-western counties; **Chart**, a scarce surname, is located mainly in Surrey and Sussex.

Chardle/Chardwell, *see* **Caudle**.

Charity N/T/O Nickname for a person full of Christian love OF; or a dweller/worker at a house of refuge, a hospital. An East Midlands surname.

Charles F/O From the Germanic first-name *Carl* ('man'), Latinized as *Carolus* and popular thanks to the Charlemagne stories; or a status term for a villein, serf, peasant OE *ceorl*, which also gives us the adjective *churlish*.

Charleston ?F/P There are places called *Charlestown* in various English counties, but they are of too recent a foundation to have given rise to such a surname. **Charleson**, 'son of Charles', is a more likely origin, the intrusive '*t*' bearing comparison with **Johnston(e)/Johnson**. It would also be tempting to think that on occasions **Charleston** might be a variant on **Charlton**, which does have a place-name origin. A scarce surname with an unusual distribution: it can be found in places as far apart as Lancs, Cornwall and West Lothian.

Charley P Place-name in Leics, British and OE 'wood/clearing by a cairn/rock' (compare nearby *Charnwood* Forest).

Charlton P Fifteen or more counties have places of this name (there are seven in Somerset alone) OE 'place of the free-peasants/villeins'. A decidedly north-east of England surname. *See also* **Carlton** and **Chorlton**.

Charlwood P Place-name in Surrey, OE 'wood of the villeins'.

Charnell O Occupational term for a gravedigger, or a custodian of a charnel-house, mortuary chapel, cemetery OF. A scarce surname, with a presence in Staffs and Warwicks.

Charney P There is such a place-name in Berks, British and OE 'island on the (river) *Chain*', but this is a scarce Lancs surname, and as such is possibly an abbreviated form of **Charnock**, which emanates from that county.

Charnock P Place-names *Charnock Heath* and *Charnock Richard*, Lancs OW *carn* ('rock'). Richard **Chernok** is mentioned in Lancs Assize Rolls in 1246, and in time various members of the **Charnock** family made their home in Beds and elsewhere. See also **Charney**.

Chart, *see* **Chard**.

Charteris P A Scots and English surname, from the cathedral city of *Chartres* (seat of the Gaulish tribe, the *Carnutes*), Eure-et-Loir, France, or, less romantically, from the Fenland town of *Chatteris*, Cambs (etymology uncertain). Commonly pronounced '*Charters*' (and *Chartres Street* in the French Quarter of New Orleans is referred to as '*Charter Street*'). See also **Chatteris**. Family name of the Earls of Wemyss and March. *Leslie Charteris (1907–1993), writer of mystery fiction and creator of Simon Templar, 'The Saint', was born in Singapore to a Chinese physician father and an English mother. Originally named Leslie Charles Bowyer-Yin, in 1926 he changed his name legally to Charteris in honour of Francis Charteris (1672–1732), a Scottish aristocrat and notorious rake who had acquired the unfortunate nickname of 'The Rape-Master General'.*

Chase O Occupational term for a skilled huntsman OF *chasseur*. Early forms do not support the theory that the surname might be derived from '*chase*', meaning 'unenclosed hunting-ground' (as in *Enfield Chase*, *Cannock Chase*, etc.). *The main claim to fame of model and actress Lorraine Chase (born in Deptford, London, in 1951) rests on her appearance in a Campari advertisement in which she is asked if she was 'wafted here from paradise'. Her unabashed Cockney reply was: 'Nah! Luton Airport…'*

Chaston T Dweller by a chestnut tree OF. Principally a Norfolk/Suffolk surname.

Chat(t)away/Chad(d)away P From an unidentified place, possibly called *Chadway* ('*Chad*'s road'); the development of the surname could be from **Chadway** to **Chad(d)away** to **Chat(t)away**. Both **Chaddaway** and **Chataway** are scarce surnames, marginally more in evidence in Warwicks than elsewhere. *Christopher Chataway (born 1931), son of J. D. P. Chataway of Woking, Surrey, has had a varied career which has included being a champion athlete, a news broadcaster and a Member of Parliament. Gravestones commemorating members of the Chataway family related to him can be seen in the churchyard of Peckleton, Leics.*

Chater, *see* **Cater**.

Chatteris P Place-name in Cambs, British

and OE 'strip of woodland'. A very scarce surname. See also **Charteris**.

Chatterley P Place-name in Staffs, the first element of which is probably from a British word meaning 'chair/dominant hill'.

Chatterton, *see* **Chadderton**.

Chaucer O Occupational term for a maker of hose/breeches/leg-armour/boots/gaiters OF. *The English poet Geoffrey Chaucer (c.1343–1400), the son and grandson of London vintners with family origins in Ipswich, Suffolk, was known by several other bynames during his life, including 'De Malin' and 'De London'.*

Chawner, *see* **Challen**.

Cheadle P Place-name in Chesh and Staffs, comprised (tautologically) of British *ceto-* ('wood') and OE *leah* ('wood, clearing').

Cheater O Occupational term for an escheator OF, whose duty was to look after the king's escheats (the lapsing of heirless land to the Crown) in the county of his appointment. Opportunities for shady dealing being rife when such revenue was involved, the verb 'to cheat' in the sense of 'to swindle' eventually acquired its later meaning. A surname mostly found in Hants.

Cheatham, *see* **Chetham**.

Checkley P Place-name in Chesh OE '*Ceaddica*'s clearing'; Herefords, Staffs OE '*Ceacca*'s clearing'. A widespread surname, with a significant presence in Warwicks.

Chedzey/Chedzoy/Chidgey/Chidzey P Place-name *Chedzoy* in Somerset OE '*Cedd*'s island', and most commonly found in that county.

Cheek N Nickname for a person with some distinguishing mark affecting a cheek or jawbone. Mostly found in Essex and Middx.

Cheese/Cheeseman/Cheese(w)right O Occupational term for a maker or seller of cheese OE. *John Cleese, actor and comedian, was born in Weston-super-Mare, Somerset, in 1939, the son of Reginald Francis Cleese, who had changed his surname from 'Cheese' when*

he joined the army in 1915. In the event, 'Cleese' is a surname in its own right, though a very rare one.

Cheetham, *see* **Chetham**.

Cheever(s), *see* **Chever**.

Chegwidden/Chegwin T/P Cornish: dweller by, or in, a white house, or from the place-name *Chegwidden*, Constantine, with the same meaning. Found in mid and west Cornwall.

Chenevix O Occupational term for a grower or seller of hemp-seed OF – presumably for the purpose of making sacks, ropes, nets and coarse cloth, rather than for its mind-changing or medicinal qualities as cannabis. Surname of a distinguished Huguenot family from Lorraine, who fled to Ireland and elsewhere after the revocation of the Edict of Nantes in 1685. Philip **Chenevix** was one such refugee; his grandson became Bishop of Killaloe in 1745, and his great-grandson Richard **Chenevix Trench** was Archbishop of Dublin. Anthony **Chenevix-Trench** (1919–1979) was headmaster of Eton. The **Chenevix-Trench** surname came into existence following the marriage of Richard Trench and Melesina **Chenevix** in Paris in 1803.

Cheney, *see* **Chesnay**.

Chenhall/Chenhalls P Cornish. *Chynhale* ('house on the moor') is a place-name found in Wendron and Perranzabuloe parishes; *Chenalls* ('house on the cliff or shore') is in St Erth.

Chenoweth/Chynoweth P Place-name in many Cornish parishes, with the meaning of 'new house'.

Cheriton/Charrington/Cherrington P Place-names *Cherington/Cheriton/Cherrington* in several counties, some with the meaning, from OE, of 'settlement by the river bend', others being 'church settlement'. **Cheriton** is mainly a Devon surname; **Charrington**, quite scarce, can be found in Surrey and Middx, and **Cherrington**, widespread, has a significant presence in Staffs. *John Charrington (1739–1815) and his* *brother Henry acquired full ownership of a brewery in Mile End Road, London, in 1783, and turned it into a hugely successful business venture… The firm of Charrington's, coal and coke merchants of London, founded in 1731, was headed by five generations of men named John Charrington.*

Chermside/Chernside/Chirnside P The place-name *Chirnside* OE 'hill shaped like a churn' in Berwickshire, Scotland, has clearly given rise to the surname **Chirnside** as found north of the border and in Northd, though **Chermside/Chernside**, both scarce surnames, are more commonly found in the south and south-west of England, in Devon and elsewhere. *Sir Robert Alexander Chermside (1792–1860), who had been at the battle of Waterloo and was later physician to the British Embassy in Paris, was born at Portaferry, Co Down; his grandson Sir Herbert Charles Chermside (1850–1929), a brilliant scholar and athlete, achieved particular eminence as an army officer.*

Cherrington, *see* **Cheriton**.

Cherry T/O A person who lived near, or who cultivated, cherry trees ME.

Cheshire P Named after the county of *Cheshire*. Found as a surname in a broad band stretching from the Home Counties to the north-west of England. *Appropriately enough, (Geoffrey) Leonard Cheshire, Baron Cheshire VC (1917–1992), Air Force officer and Founder of the Cheshire Homes, was born in Hoole, Chester, in the county of Cheshire.*

Chesnay/Chainey/Chaney/Cheney/ Chesney T/P Dweller at an oak grove OF, or from one of a number of places in France called *Chenay, Chenoy, Chesnoy* and *Quesnay*.

Chesney, *see* **Chesnay**.

Chester P Place-name *Chester*, the county town of Cheshire OE 'Roman site' or from smaller places so-named in Chesh, Derbys and Co Durham. *'Cheeky' Charlie Chester (1914–1997), popular stand-up comedian and radio and television presenter, was born Cecil Victor Manser in Eastbourne, Sussex.*

Chesterfield P Place-name in Derbys OE 'open land by a Roman site'. Oddly enough, a strongly Cornish surname. Might coal- or lead-miners from Derbys have travelled south-west to the tin mines of Cornwall?

Chesterton P Place-name in various counties OE 'place by a Roman site'. An uncommon surname, found in Leics and elsewhere. *Gilbert Keith ('G.K.') Chesterton (1874–1936), English writer, was born in Campden Hill, Kensington, London.*

Chestnut T Dweller by a chestnut-tree OF and OE. A very scarce surname, found in the Scottish counties of Lanarkshire and Renfrewshire.

Che(e)tham/Cheatham P Place-name in Lancs, British and OE 'homestead by a wood'. **Cheatham** is a scarcer surname than **Cheetham**, but both are predominantly in evidence in Lancs. **Chetham**'s Library (pronounced 'Cheetham'), Manchester, founded in 1653 according to the terms of the will of Humphrey **Chetham**, is the oldest public library in the English-speaking world. It was here in 1843 that the **Chetham** Society, dedicated to the publication of 'remains historical and literary connected with the Palatine Counties of Lancashire and Cheshire', held its first meeting.

Chettle T/P Dweller in a deep valley locked in hills OE (literally 'kettle, cauldron'); also a place-name in Dorset, though the surname is mostly found in Northants and Notts.

Chetwode/Chetwood P Place-name in Bucks, British and OE, tautologically 'wood wood'.

Che(e)ver(s)/Chiver(s) N/O Nickname for someone as stubborn (or as nimble) as a nanny-goat OF, or a goat-herd. **Chevers**, a very scarce surname, has a presence in Middx; **Chivers**, much more prolific, is found in southern and south-western counties, being strongest in Somerset. *The company of Chivers, famous above all for its jam, was established by John Chivers at a factory near Histon, Cambs, in 1873.*

Chick/Chicken O/N Occupational term for

a person who worked with poultry, or a nickname or term of endearment OE 'chicken'. Cottle says: 'Bardsley in 1901 feared that **Chicken** was extinct, but five were in the London telephone directory in 1963'. Quite so. Bardsley was even then far off the mark, the surname having had a presence in Co Durham and elsewhere at the time of the 1881 census. Present-day published authors such as John C. **Chicken**, Stephen **Chicken**, H. **Chicken**, Edward **Chicken** and Andrew H. **Chicken** would not thank us for claiming that their surname was extinct.

Chidgey/Chidzey, *see* **Chedzey**.

Chilcote/Chilcott P Place-names: *Chilcote* in Leics and Northants OE 'cottages of the children/young nobles/princes'; *Chilcott* in Somerset OE '*Ceola*'s cottages'. **Chilcott** is chiefly a surname of the south-western counties of England; **Chilcote**, much scarcer, is mainly to be found in Somerset.

Child(e)(s) O Status term for a minor, a youth awaiting knighthood, a page OE. Compare Byron's *Childe Harold* and Browning's *Childe Roland*. *Francis James Child (1825–1896), a Harvard professor who was born in Boston, Massachusetts, achieved international fame thanks to his scholarly work on English and Scottish ballads, published as* The English and Scottish popular ballads *(1882–1898).*

Chilton P Place-name in several counties OE 'children's farm/manor'. The first element may mean variously 'princes, young nobles, youths awaiting knighthood, retainers, young monks'. But *Chilton-upon-Polden*, Somerset, is OE 'chalk/lime-stone hill farm' and *Chilton*, Isle of Wight, is OE '*Ceola*'s farm'. Reaney shows how one thirteenth-century bearer of the surname/byname was from *Chilhampton*, Wilts OE 'children's village'.

Chilver(s) ?F Seemingly from an OE first-name *Ceolfrith* ('ship-peace'). An East Anglian surname in both spellings.

Chin(n) N Nickname for a person with a chin which was worthy of note in some way

OE, though plenty of Chinese people bear the name **Chin/Chen**. Both **Chin** and **Chinn** are very much in evidence in Cornwall, though **Chinn** is strongest in Warwicks.

Chippendale/Chippindale/Chippindall P An earlier form of the place-name *Chipping*, Lancs OE 'market (town) valley'. *Chipping* was often added to the names of towns that held a market – see **Chapman** and **Chipping**. Whatever the spelling, such surnames are strongest in Lancs and WRYorks. *Thomas Chippendale (1718–1779), cabinet-maker and furniture designer, was born at Farnley, near Otley, WRYorks.*

Chipping P Place-name in various counties OE 'market'. See **Chippendale**.

Chirnside, *see* **Chermside**.

Chisholm P Place-name *Chisholme* in Roxburghshire, Scotland OE 'meadow good for cheese'. Members of the **Chisholm** clan had moved north to the Highlands by the mid fourteenth century.

Chislett P Place-name *Chislet* in Kent OE 'gravel place'. Strongest in south-western counties of England, especially Somerset.

Chisnall P Place-name in Lancs OE 'gravelly nook'.

Chiswick P Place-name in Cambs, Essex, Middx OE 'cheese farm'. An ON version of the same place-name can be observed in *Keswick*, Cumbd.

Chitty N/P Nickname from a ME word for a whelp, pup, cub; or from a place-name in Kent OE '?*Citta*'s island'. Strong in Surrey, but also in Middx.

Chiver(s), *see* **Chever**.

Cholmondeley/Chum(b)ley P Place-name *Cholmondeley* in Chesh OE '*Ceolmund*'s wood/clearing'. Usually pronounced '*Chumley*', and is the family name of the Barons Delamere.

Chorley P Place-name in several counties OE 'wood/clearing of the villeins'.

Chorlton P Place-name in Chesh, Lancs

and Staffs OE 'enclosure of the villeins'. Compare **Carlton** and **Charlton**.

Christey, *see* **Christian**.

Christian F From the OF first-name *Christian*, used for both males and females in the Middle Ages. **Christie** and **Christ(e)y** are diminutive forms, found in both England and Scotland; **Christison** ('son of **Christian**') is strongest in Angus, Scotland. *One family named Christian had a notable presence on the Isle of Man, and Fletcher Christian (1764–1793), the Bounty mutineer, though he was born near Cockermouth, Cumbd, had Manx origins… Agatha Christie, the crime novelist (1890–1976), born Agatha Mary Clarissa Miller in Torquay, Devon, to an American father and an English mother, married Colonel Archibald Christie of the Royal Flying Corps in 1914… In 1953 John Reginald Halliday Christie (1898–1953), originally from Halifax WRYorks, was found guilty of the murder of his wife, whose body he had hidden under the floorboards of their house at 10 Rillington Place, Notting Hill, alongside the corpses of seven other females. All had been strangled… On a happier note, the firm of Christie's, the oldest fine-art auctioneers in the world, was founded by James Christie (1730–1803), who first established his salerooms in 1766. His portrait was painted in oils by his friend Thomas Gainsborough in 1778.*

Christie/Christison, *see* **Christian**.

Christmas N Nickname for a person born or baptized at Christmas, or having a special connexion with that time of year OE. Mainly found in Cambs, Sussex and Middx, with East Anglian origins.

Christopher/Christophers(on)/ Chrystal(l)/Cristal/Kid/Kitson/Kitt(s)/ Kitto/Kittow F From a mediaeval first-name with Greek origins; the literal meaning, 'bearer of Christ', 'once a declaration of personal witness', had foisted on to it the handsome and preposterous legend of the giant's ferrying the Christ-Child – whence the belief in *Saint Christopher* as a protector against accidents, and the motorists' trinkets' (Cottle). In principle the surnames **Kitt**, **Kitto**, **Kittow** (chiefly Cornish) and

Kitts (chiefly found in Lancs) can alternatively be derived from the female first-name *Katherine*. **Chrystal(l)/Cristal** are Scots forms of the surname. **Christophers(on)** and its many European equivalents carry the meaning 'son of Christopher'. *See also* **Kid**. *Kris Kristofferson, singer-songwriter and actor, was born in Brownsville, Texas in 1936, the son of an Air Force general. He shares with former US President Bill Clinton and former Prime Minister of Australia Bob Hawke, among others, the distinction of having been a Rhodes Scholar at Oxford University.*

Christy, *see* **Christian**.

Chrystal(l), *see* **Christopher**.

Chubb N Nickname derived from the name of the fish, the *chub* ME, a member of the carp family much-beloved of anglers, short and fat in appearance, with coarse flesh and sluggish habits, given to hovering in the sun or deep below roots. Thoreau says it tastes 'like brown paper salted'. So *Chubb* became a nickname for a fat, lazy, doltish, spiritless or awkward person. The term 'chubby' is a more modern development, though lacking the pejorative overtones. The surname is mostly found in the south-west of England, particularly in Devon. Family name of the Barons Hayter. *Charles Chubb, originally a ship's ironmonger in Winchester, Hants, moved to Portsmouth in 1804, and finally to Wolverhampton in 1818, where he was joined by his brother Jeremiah. From such modest beginnings would arise the world-famous company of Chubb Locks, known for its high-security locking systems.*

Chum(b)ley, *see* **Cholmondeley**.

Church T/O Dweller near a church OE; or an occupational term for a person who bore duties such as those of verger or sexton. Related surnames (all with OE roots) include: **Churcher** (connected with the church), **Churchman/Churchward** (kept the church, like a modern sexton or verger), **Churchouse** (lived near a church or minded it), **Churchyard** (maintained the churchyard). *Charlotte Church, singer and television presenter, was born Charlotte*

Maria Reed in Llandaff, Cardiff, in 1986, but acquired her present name when she was legally adopted by her mother's second husband, James Church.

Churcher, *see* Church.

Churchill P Place-name in various counties OE 'church hill'. The surname of the famous Churchill family, Dukes of Marlborough, has Somerset origins. The first-name *Winston*, famously borne by Sir Winston Churchill (1874–1965), who was born in the family's ducal country seat of Blenheim Palace, comes from neighbouring Gloucs.

Churchman/Churchouse/Churchward/Churchyard, *see* Church.

Churley P There is apparently now no village so-called, but the meaning of 'villeins' wood/clearing' OE is unequivocal enough. Possibly a corruption of **Chorley**, though there was an Adam **Churleye** in Somerset in 1327, and an Edward and a John **Churley** in a Somerset Subsidy, 1581–1582. A scarce surname, latterly found mostly in Devon, the same county in which a William **Churley** is listed in a Subsidy of 1543 in Beer, Uplowman.

Churton P Place in Chesh, OE 'church farm'.

Chynoweth, *see* Chenoweth.

Cinnamon(d) N Cottle derives this surname from the fragrant spice cinnamon OF, pointing out that it was perhaps used mainly as a term of endearment, and that Absolon calls Alisoun 'sweet cinnamon' in Chaucer's *The Miller's Tale*. Reaney might be nearer the mark, however, in his listing for **Cinnamond/Sinnamon**: '… from *Saint-Amand* (Cotentin)'. G. F. Black (*Surnames of Scotland*, 1946) gives **Cinnamond** as a variant of **Kininmonth**, derived from either of two places so-named in Fife. There is also a *Kyninmonthe* (later *Kinmouth*) in Banffshire. **Cinnamon** is a very scarce surname, found mainly in north-western counties of England, while **Cinnamond**, similarly scarce, was limited to the Scottish county of Lanarkshire by the late nineteenth century.

Clachar O Occupational term for a stone-mason, Scots Gaelic. *See also* **McClacher**.

Clanc(e)y F Irish: Anglicized form of Gaelic **Mac Fhlannchaidh** ('son of Ruddy Warrior').

Clapcott P Place-name *Clapcot* in Berks OE '?hillock cottage(s)', though the present settlement of that name is not so situated. See **Clapp**. A very scarce Dorset/Hants surname.

Clapham P Place-name in Beds, London, Sussex, WRYorks OE 'hillock homestead'.

Clapp N Nickname for a clumsy or heavily-built person OE, as in the various *Clap-/Clop-* element in place-names with humps and hillocks. Very much a Devon/Somerset surname. *Jerome Clapp, father of the writer Jerome K. Jerome, changed his name to Jerome Clapp Jerome. Jerome junior then altered his middle name to Klapka, in honour of the exiled Hungarian general Gjörgy Klapka.*

Clapton P Place-name in six counties (three in Somerset) OE 'hillock farm'. A widespread surname. *By the time the well-known musician Eric Clapton was born on 30 March 1945 in Ripley, Surrey, his unmarried mother Molly Clapton had been abandoned by Eric's soldier father, Edward Walter Fry. Eric was brought up by his grandmother Rose and her second husband, Jack Clapp, believing for many years that they were his parents, and that his mother was his older sister. The similarity between the surnames Clapton and Clapp is purely coincidental.*

Clare/Clear(e) F/P/O From the first-name *Cla(i)re* (usually borne by females) ME, OF from Latin *Clara* ('famous'), made more popular by *St Clare* of Assisi (died 1253) – *see also* **Sinclair**. Or from *Clare*, Oxon OE 'clay slope' or *Clare*, Suffolk, so-called from a British river name ('?bright'). Or an occupational term for a worker in clay/(wattle and) daub OE. **Clare** is a widespread surname, very strong in Lancs. *John Clare (1793–1864), the self-educated 'Northamptonshire Peasant Poet' and musician, was born at Helpston, near Peterborough, the son of a farm labourer.*

Clarges O Occupational term for a servant of (or even a son of?) a clergyman OF. Compare **Clark**. An exceptionally rare south-of-England surname.

Claridge F From the female first-name *Clarice*, based on the Latin *claritia* ('brightness'). Bardsley found a lady called alternately *Claricie* and *Clarugge* in Cambs in 1273. The surname can be found in a wide belt stretching from London to the English Midlands. *Richard Claridge (1649–1723), Quaker minister, schoolmaster and author, was born in Farmborough, Warwicks; his contemporary Samuel Claridge (1631–1704/5) was a Quaker activist who accompanied Cromwell to Ireland in 1651... In 1854 William Claridge and his wife Marianne, both of whom had formerly been in service, extended their hotel premises in Brook Street, London, by purchasing the adjacent Mivart's Hotel. In time Claridge's Hotel became something of an English institution – for those who could afford to stay there.*

Clark(e)/**Clerk**(e) O Occupational term for a cleric, scholar, clerk, secretary OF, especially a cleric in minor orders and therefore not necessarily celibate. For -*er* and -*ar* spellings and pronunciations see under **Armistead**. **Clerk**(e) is a rare original form. **Clarke** and **Clerke** are commonly found surnames throughout the British Isles. See also **Clery** and **McChlery**.

Clary, *see* **Clery**.

Clatworthy/Clotworthy P Place-name *Clatworthy* in Somerset OE 'enclosure where burdock/goosegrass grows'. A Devon/Somerset surname.

Clavering P Place-name in Essex OE 'clover field', but a very scarce surname, located for the most part in Co Durham and Northd.

Clay T/O A dweller in an area with clay soil; or an occupational term for a worker in a clay pit. *Cassius Marcellus Clay (1810–1903), American abolitionist, a second cousin of the famous politician Henry Clay, was born in Madison County, Kentucky. His namesake Cassius Marcellus Clay, junior (son of Cassius Marcellus Clay, senior), the world heavyweight boxing champion who chose in 1964 to be known as Muhammad Ali, was also born in Kentucky, in Louisville.*

Claybrooke P Place-name in Leics OE 'clayey brook'. A very scarce surname, found in Salop and elsewhere.

Claydon P Place-name in Bucks (four such), Oxon, Suffolk OE 'clay(ey) hill'.

Claypo(o)le P Place-name *Claypole*, Lincs OE 'clayey pool'.

Clayton P Place-name in four counties, in particular Lancs (five) and WRYorks (three) OE 'place in the clay/place with good clay for pottery'. Found mainly in Chesh, Lancs and WRYorks.

Cleak(e) A surname of unknown origin; perhaps from a misspelling of **Clerk**(e), or from the name of a piece of land near Ermington, Devon, now called *Clickland*, formerly *Clekeland(e)* OE '?boundary-stone territory' (Hanks and Hodges). A rare surname of the south of England. A family of West Country clockmakers named **Cleak** can be traced back to Ezekiel **Cleak** of Exeter, Devon, who died in 1709.

Cleal(e)/**Cleall**/**Cleel**(e)/**Cleell**/**Clehill**/**Clele**/**Cleyil** T Dweller at the clayey hill OE. **Cleal** is a surname of southern and south-western counties of England, especially Dorset.

Clear(e), *see* **Clare**.

Cleary, *see* **Clery**.

Cleave(s)/Cleeve(s)/Cleve(s)/Cliff(e)/Clifft/Clift/Clive T/P Dweller at the cliff, slope, river-bank OE, or from *Cleeve* in Gloucs, Somerset, Worcs, with the same meaning. **Clive** exhibits the use of a dative after a lost preposition, with a 'v' for 'ff' between vowels (compare *life* and *alive*). *See also* **Cleaver**. **Cleave** is a Devon and Cornwall surname. In 1802 the second Earl of Powis changed his family's surname from **Clive** to **Herbert** by Royal Licence. *Robert Clive, First Baron Clive of Plessey (1725–1774), born at Styche Hall, Moreton Say, Salop, was a key figure in the establish-*

ment of British India... The American actor (Edward) Montgomery Clift (1920–1966) was born in Omaha, Nebraska, the son of a banker.

Cleaveland, *see* **Cleveland**.

Cleaver o Occupational term for a butcher, or for a person skilled at splitting logs into planks OE. Can also be a variant of **Cleave**.

Clee T/P Dweller at a fork in a road or river, from an OE word for a claw or cloven hoof; or from a place-name such as *Clee*, Lincs or *Clee/Cleobury*, Salop, of uncertain etymology.

Cleel(e)/Cleell, *see* **Cleal**.

Cleese, *see* **Cheese**.

Cleeve(s), *see* **Cleave**.

Clegg P Place-name in Lancs ON '(haystack-shaped) hill', and found mainly in that county, as well as in WRYorks.

Cleghorn P Place-name in Lanarkshire, Scotland OE 'clay house'. The surname is found in Northd and in Scotland.

Clehill/Clele, *see* **Cleal**.

Clement/Clemas/Clemence/Clemens F From an OF male first-name *Clement*, with the meaning 'mild, merciful', borne by *St Clement*, a disciple of St Paul, to whom forty-odd churches in England are dedicated, and by a number of popes. Also readily confused with the separate male/female first-name *Clemence*. **Clemo(w)** is a Cornish variant; **Clemson** ('son of *Clem*', a diminutive of *Clement*) is found chiefly in the English Midlands.

Clemo(w)/Clemson, *see* **Clement**.

Clench, *see* **Clinch**.

Clennell P Place-name in Northd OE 'clean hill' – that is, a hill free from weeds/thorns.

Clent P Place-name in Worcs OE 'rock, hill'.

Clerk(e), *see* **Clark**.

Clery/Clary/Cleary o Irish: Anglicized form of Gaelic **O'** [descendant of] **Clery** ('clerk'). *See also* **McChlery**. *The well-known*

camp comedian Julian Clary was born in Teddington, Middx, in 1959.

Cleve, *see* **Cleave**.

Cleveland/Cleaveland P English region in NRYorks OE 'cliff/hilly district'. **Cleveland** has a wide distribution; **Cleaveland**, very scarce, is found in the south of England. *(Stephen) Grover Cleveland (1837–1908), who served two separate terms as US President, was born in Caldwell, New Jersey. His male-line ancestry can be traced back to Moses Cleveland, who emigrated to Plymouth, Massachusetts, from Ipswich, Suffolk, in 1635, accompanied by his brother Aaron.*

Cleveley/Cleverley P Place-names: *Cleveley*, Oxon; *Cleveley/Cleveleys*, Lancs OE 'wood/clearing on a cliff'. The intrusive 'r' in **Cleverley** was probably introduced thanks to its association with the complimentary adverb 'cleverly'.

Cleves, *see* **Cleave**.

Clew(e), *see* **Clough**.

Clewer P Place-name in Berks, Somerset OE 'cliff/slope dwellers' (a tribal name).

Clewes, *see* **Clough**.

Clewlow/Cluelee/Cluly/Cluelow/Clu-low P Place-name *Cleulow* in Chesh OE '?ball-shaped mound'.

Cleyil, *see* **Cleal**.

Cliff(e), *see* **Cleave**.

Clifford P Place-name in Gloucs, Herefords, WRYorks OE 'ford at a cliff'. 'Its use as a first-name is late and strange; and "the little girl who was called Precipice after her Uncle Cliff" is even less funny than it looks' (Cottle). Family name of the Barons Clifford of Chudleigh.

Clifft/Clift, *see* **Cleave**.

Clifton P Place-name in over two dozen counties, from Dorset to Northd OE 'place on a cliff'; '*Clifton*' is also the usual pronunciation of *Cliveden*, Berks OE 'valley among the cliffs'.

Clinch/Clench T/P/O Dweller at the ravine,

crevice OE (North Country *clink*); or from a place-name *Clench* in Wilts OE 'lump, mass, hill'; or an occupational term for a maker of clinches/big nails/rivets OE (see **Clink**).

Clink(er) O Occupational term for a riveter OE. See **Clinch**. **Clink** is a scarce Scottish surname; **Clinker** can be found in southern and south-western counties of England.

Clinton P Place-names: *Glympton*, Oxon, ?British and OE 'settlement on the (river) *Glyme*', which was *Clinton* in 1199, or *Glinton*, Cambs (Northants) OE '?fence/enclosure settlement', which was *Clinton* in 1060. One family of **Clinton**s were Earls of Lincoln, and **Pelham-Clinton** is the surname of the Dukes of Newcastle-under-Lyme. *William Jefferson ('Bill') Clinton, the forty-second President of the USA, was born William Jefferson Blythe III in Hope, Arkansas, in 1946. His father died three months before he was born, and following his mother's remarriage to Roger Clinton, young Bill ('Billy' as he was then known) eventually took his stepfather's surname as his own.*

Clitheroe/Clitherow P Place-name *Clitheroe*, Lancs OE and ON 'hill/mound of loose stones' (compare dialectal *clider/clither*: gravel, debris). *James Robinson ('Jimmy') Clitheroe, 'The Clitheroe Kid' (1921–1973), the all-round entertainer who was only four feet three inches tall as an adult, was born in Clitheroe, Lancs, but raised in Blacko, near Nelson.*

Clive, *see* **Cleave**.

Clooney/Cloney F Irish: Anglicized form of Gaelic **O'** [descendant of] **Cluanaigh** ('deceitful/flattering'). **Cloney** is a Co Wexford surname; in Co Down **Clooney** can alternatively be a form of **MacLoonie**. *According to the 1880 American census, the great-great-grandfather of the actor George Clooney was an immigrant from Ireland who became a jeweller; his son Andrew Clooney was Mayor of Maysville, Kentucky, and campaigned with the help of George's two aunts, Rosemary and Betty, both of whom were singers and radio stars.*

Clopton P Place-name in four counties OE 'hill/hillock place'.

Close T/N Dweller by an enclosure OF, or a nickname for a discreet, reserved person ME.

Clothier O Occupational term for a cloth-worker or a seller of cloth OE with the agent suffix *-er*. Very largely a Somerset surname, where clothiers were much in evidence during the heyday of the wool trade.

Clotworthy, *see* **Clatworthy**.

Cloud T Dweller by a hill or crag OE (as in *Temple Cloud*, Somerset). No connexion with clouds in the sky.

Clough/Clew(e)(s)/Clow/Cluff T/P Dweller by a ravine, deep valley OE. A common place-name element in the north of England, and the surname **Clough** is found chiefly in Lancs and WRYorks. **Clew** is scarce and scattered. *Brian (Howard) Clough (1935–2004), outspoken and highly successful football manager, was born in Grove Hill, Middlesbrough.*

Cloutman O Occupational term for a codger, cobbler, patcher OE (compare: 'Ne'er cast a clout till May be out', or the dialectal 'dish clout' for 'dish cloth').

Clow, *see* **Clough**.

Cluelee/Cluelow/Clulow, *see* **Clewlow**.

Cluff, *see* **Clough**.

Clunes F/P Anglicized form of Gaelic **Mac Gluin** ('son of *Glun*'); place-name in Inverness and Perthshire, Scots Gaelic 'meadow stance/resting-place'.

Clutterbuck Origin uncertain. The name looks as though it could be Dutch in origin, but it could be a corruption of an English place-name ending in *-brook/-beck*, such as *Clitherbeck* in NRYorks OE and ON 'stream at the debris/quarry', or *Clouter Brook* in Chesh OE '?noisy/clumsy brook'. Yet this is a Gloucs surname (also found in neighbouring Somerset) from at least as early as the sixteenth century. Members of a **Clutterbuck** family, said to have escaped from persecution in the Low Countries in the

1500s, were Mayors of Gloucester in the sixteenth and seventeenth centuries, and left their name at *Clutterbuck Farm* in that county. *Robert Clutterbuck (1772–1831), author of* The history and antiquities of the county of Hertford *(published 1815–1827) was born and baptized at Watford House, Watford, in that county.*

Clutton P Place-name in Chesh, Somerset OE 'rocky hill place'.

Coady, *see* **Cody**.

Coaley/Coley P Place-names: *Coaley* in Gloucs OE 'clearing/wood in a recess'; *Coley* in Berks OE 'charcoal clearing' and in Somerset OF and OE 'the hill meadow' and in WRYorks OE 'cold, bleak clearing'. **Coaley** is a scarce Lancs/Warwicks surname; **Coley** is mostly found in the English Midlands.

Coat(e)(s), *see* **Cote**.

Cobbeldick/Cobbledick/Coppledick/ Coppledike P From an unidentified place-name, presumably in Lincs OE '*Cobbold*'s ditch/dike', in which county there was a *Coppledyke* manor at Freiston. There are individuals bearing the **Copledike/Copuldyke/Copeldick** surname in Heralds' Visitation records for Cambs and Norfolk; the Suffolk Visitation of 1561 includes a **Copledike** family of Horham, and there is a reference to 'the manor of Brodocks late *Copledyke* in Horham', purchased by Simon Brodock in 1541. The **Copledick/ Copledike/Cobeldyk**s of Harrington, Lincs, including a long succession of knights, can be traced back to Roger **Copledick**, who married Elinor, daughter of Ralph Spalding, in the thirteenth century. The arms borne by the Suffolk **Copledike**s being identical to those of the **Copledick**s of Harrington, it would probably be fruitless to look for yet another possible Suffolk place-name origin, such as *Copdock* OE 'copped oak'. Many variant spellings are known, including **Cobbledick**, **Cobbleditch**, **Cobledike**, **Copeldick**, **Copleditch**, **Couppleditch** and **Cuppleditch**. In principle the *Cob-* and *Cop-* spellings, indicating a difference only in a single voiced/ unvoiced consonant, should represent the same surname, but whereas **Cobbledick** was a distinctively Cornish and Devon surname by the late nineteenth century (and had been there since at least the early 1600s), the surname **Coppledick**, by then transformed into **Coupleditch**, clung tenaciously to the county of Lincs.

Cobbett, *see* **Cobbold**.

Cobbledick, *see* **Cobbeldick**.

Cobbold/Cobbett F From a ME first-name *Cutebald*, meaning 'famed bold'. **Cobbold** is very much a Suffolk surname. *Thomas Cobbold founded a brewing business at Harwick, Essex, in 1723, later moving to Ipswich, Suffolk, in 1746. In 1957 Tollemache and Cobbold, two family-run breweries, merged to form 'Tolly Cobbold'… William Cobbett (1763–1835), essayist, politician and agriculturalist, was born in Farnham Surrey, son of George Cobbett, a publican and farmer.*

Cobden P Place-name in Devon, Derbys OE '*Cobba*'s hill', but in *Cobdenhill*, Herts, the first element is OE 'lopped/polled thorn'. *Richard Cobden (1804–1865), a manufacturer and politician whose name is frequently linked with that of the Lancastrian Quaker John Bright (1811–1889), was born to a long-established farming family near Heyshott, Sussex.*

Cobham P Place-name in Kent, Sussex OE '*Cobba*'s homestead' and Surrey OE '?*Cofa*'s homestead'. For all that, the surname is most commonly found in Lancs.

Cobleigh/Cobley P Place-name *Cobley* in Lapford and East Worlington, Devon OE '*Cobba*'s clearing'. The Devon worthies Bill Brewer, Jan Stewer, Peter Gurney, Peter Davy, Dan'l Whiddon, Harry Hawke and 'Old Uncle Tom **Cobley/Cobbleigh**', famously featured in the folk song *Widecombe Fair*, collected by Sabine Baring-Gould, may have been real people, or just a charming fiction. The parish churchyard in Spreyton, twelve miles north of Widecombe in the Moor, contains the grave of a Tom **Cobley** (possibly the nephew of the song's 'Uncle Tom **Cobley**'), and of a 'Bill Brewer', and a family named Pearce lived nearby. But Jean Harrowven in *The origins of rhymes, songs and sayings* (1977) points out that the parish register for Crediton in Devon features a Tom **Cobbley**, who was baptized there in the late seventeenth century, and includes the surnames of some of Tom's mates: **Pearce**, **Stuer**, **Davy** and **Hawke**.

Cobner, *see* Copner.

Coburn, *see* Cockburn.

Cochran(e) P Place-name, ?British 'red brook', in Renfrewshire, Scotland. Family name of the Earls of Dundonald.

Cock/Cox(e) T/O/N A surname in which many possibilities meet, mostly jests. One rare but real origin is OE 'hillock, heap' (as in *haycock*); or 'at the (sign of the) Cock'; or '(person responsible for a) ship's boat' OF; or a 'cook'. But above all it is a nickname, from 'cockerel' OE, or meaning 'fatty' OE (if it be from the OE first-name *Cocca*), or applied to a person with red hair or complexion, Welsh *coch*. The strutting barnyard fowl became a generic term for pert lads, and was attached as a suffix to diminutive forms, as in **Hitchcock** ('son of *Richard*'). **Cocks** (the family name of the Barons Somers), meaning 'son of **Cock**', is more commonly found in the form **Cox** (sometimes even **Coxe**). **Coxon** is also 'son of **Cock**', while **Cocking** can be 'son/descendant of **Cock**', or from the place-name *Cocking* in Sussex OE '*Cocca*'s people'.

Cockayne N Nickname for someone living in cloud-cuckooland ME *cokayne*, a dreamer. Ashbourne church, Derbys, contains impressive tombs commemorating members of the **Cockayne** family, which traces its origins back to the twelfth-century John **Cockayne**. *Sir William* **Cockayne**, *son of William* **Cockayne** *of Baddesley Ensor, Warwicks, was Lord Mayor of London, 1619–20; the eminent genealogist George Edward* **Cokayne** *('G.E.C.'), who was appointed Clarenceux King of Arms in 1894, was born George Edward Adams, but adopted the* **Cokayne** *surname in 1873, according to a stipulation laid down in his mother's will.*

Cockbaine N Nickname for a person having legs like a cockerel, strutting OE (compare **Langbain**, literally 'long bones'). Most commonly found in Cumbd. Readily confused with/a variant of **Cockburn**.

Cockbill N Nickname from OE: 'cockerel's bill'. There was a Ralph **Cokkebill** in Warwicks in 1332. A Warwicks/Worcs surname.

Cockburn/Coburn P Place-name in Berwickshire, Scotland OE '*Cocca*'s/cock stream'. Usually pronounced '*Coburn*' in both spellings. **Cockburn** is most commonly found in Co Durham/Northd and in Midlothian, Scotland; **Coburn**, much scarcer, is strongest in Lancs. Readily confused with/a variant of **Cockbaine**. *The Oscar-winning actor James (Harrison) Coburn (1928–2002) was born in Laurel, Nebraska, USA but grew up in Compton, California.*

Cockcraft/Cockcroft, *see* Cockroft.

Cocker(h)am/Cockram P Place-name *Cockerham* in Lancs, Celtic and OE 'homestead on the river *Cocker* ("crooked")'.

Cockfield P Place-name in Suffolk OE '*Cohha*'s field' and in Co Durham OE '*Cocca*'s field'.

Cocking, *see* Cock.

Cockram, *see* Cockerham.

Cockroft/Cockcraft/Cockcroft T/P Dweller at the cockcroft, or from a place so-called in Rishworth, WRYorks OE 'cock (a domestic cock, the woodcock, or even a haycock) paddock'. George Redmonds makes mention of a Richard de **Cocckecroft**, living in Sowerby in 1296. *Sir John (Douglas) Cockcroft (1897–1967), the eminent nuclear physicist, was born in Langfield, Yorks.*

Codrington P Place-name in Gloucs OE '*Cuthere*'s farm'. Mainly a Gloucs surname, but since the seventeenth century **Codringtons** have had a significant presence in Antigua, Barbados and elsewhere in the British West Indies.

Co(a)dy F Irish: Anglicized form of Gaelic **O'** [descendant of] *Cuidighthigh* ('helpful') or of *Mac Oda* ('son of *Oda*'. A personal name of unknown origin). A Kilkenny name. *William Frederick Cody (1846–1917), better known as 'Buffalo Bill', was born in the Iowa Territory of the USA. One legenad has it that he is a direct descendant of Milesius, King of Spain, whose three sons founded the first dynasty in Ireland (dream on…).*

Coe N Nickname for a person bearing some resemblance to a jackdaw ON and OE, or from a Norfolk dialect word for an 'odd old fellow'. Fairly charming, either way. Principally an East Anglian surname. Compare **Kay**. *Sebastian Newbold ('Seb') Coe, Baron Coe, athlete and politician, was born in 1956 in Chiswick, London, but was brought up in Sheffield.*

Coen, *see* **Cohen**.

Coffey/Coffee F Irish: Anglicized form of Gaelic **O'** [descendant of] **Cobhthaigh** ('victorious').

Coffin O Occupational term for a maker of baskets, coffers OF. The modern-day meaning of the word 'coffin' reflects a later specialized usage. A family bearing this surname is responsible for the place-name *Thorne Coffin*, Somerset, and Hugh **Coffin** held *Coffinswell*, Devon, in 1185. *But* **Coffin** *may sometimes be a variant of* **Caffin**. *A Devon surname, one taken to America by Tristram, son of Peter* **Coffin** *of Brixton in that county, who settled in New England in 1642. Members of the Coffin family were numbered among the Loyalists of Massachusetts during the American War of Independence. In 1797 Rev. John Pine of East Down Manor in Devon assumed by Royal Licence the additional surname of Coffin, thus establishing the wondrously named Portledge family of 'Pine-Coffin'.*

Cogswell/Coxwell P Place-names: *Coxwell*, Berks OE '*Cocc*'s spring'; *Coggeshall*, Essex OE '*Cogg*'s hall'. For all that, **Cogswell** is a scarce surname mainly found in Scotland; **Coxwell**, also uncommon, can be found scattered across south-east and south-west counties of England.

Cohen/Coen/Cohn/Cowen/Kaplan O Principally a Jewish surname, from the Hebrew *kohen*, a priest, though not all Jews so-called belong to the priestly caste, some families having adopted the surname during the days of the Russian empire. **Cohen/Coen** can also be an Irish surname, an Anglicized form of the Gaelic **O'** [descendant of] **Cadhain**.

Coker P Name of three places in Somerset, British 'crooked [river]', one of which, *East Coker*, was used by T. S. Eliot as the title of a poem in his *Four Quartets* collection.

Colborn(e)/Colb(o)urn(e) P Possibly from the place-name *Colburn* in NRYorks OE 'cool stream'. **Colborn** and **Colborne**, uncommon surnames, are mainly found in southern and south-western counties of England; **Colbourn** is mainly a Staffs surname; **Colbourne** is scattered throughout the south and the South Midlands.

Colby P Place-name in Norfolk and Cumbd ON and OE '*Cole*'s farm/village'.

Colclough P Place-name *Cowclough* in Lancs OE '*Cola*'s ravine'. Commonly pronounced '*Cokely*'.

Coldham P Place-name in Cambs OE 'cold homestead'.

Coldstream P Place-name in Berwickshire, Scotland OE 'cold stream' (the Tweed), where the Coldstream Guards were first recruited. A very scarce surname, encountered mainly in Midlothian.

Coldwell, *see* **Caudle**.

Cole(s)/Coll(s) F/T A pet-form of the ME first-names *Nicolas* or *Cola* ('coal-black, swarthy'). Where a byname/surname is recorded as **atte Cole/Colle**, the meaning is probably OE 'hill'. Or an Anglicized form of the Scottish **Mac Gille Chomhghaill** or the Irish **Mac Giolla Chomhghaill** ('son of the servant of *St Comhghall*'). **Cole** is the family surname of the Earls of Enniskillen. **Coles** ('son of Cole') is commonly found in the south-west.

Colebrook(e) P Place-names *Colebrook/Colebrooke* in Devon, presumably OE 'cool brook'. Also used in Winchester, Hants, for an area once containing the city's washing-place. Mainly a Hants surname.

Colefax/Colefox, *see* Colfax.

Colegate, *see* Colgate.

Coleman/Colman F/O From a first-name: either Germanic, with the sense of 'coal-black/swarthy man', or a diminutive of *Nicolas*, with -**man** added to mean 'servant'; or Irish *Columbán* (a derivative of the first-name of Saint *Columba*), which became **Colman** and was brought from Ireland by Vikings (*see also* **McCallum**); or, in the Weald of Kent/Sussex in particular, an occupational term for a charcoal-burner ME. **Coleman** is found mainly in Kent, Middx and Surrey; **Colman** is very much a Norfolk surname. *The Colman family, mustard and starch manufacturers of Norwich, Norfolk, can trace its origins back to Jeremiah Colman (1777–1851), a one-time flour miller at Bawburgh.*

Coleridge P Two place-names in Devon OE 'ridge where charcoal is burnt'. *The poet and critic Samuel Taylor Coleridge (1772–1834) was born in Ottery St Mary, Devon, where his father (who died when Samuel was only eight years old) was vicar and schoolmaster.*

Coles, *see* Cole.

Coley, *see* Coaley.

Colfax/Colefax/Col(e)fox N Nickname based upon some resemblance to a coal-fox, brant-fox OE, 'a melanistic type – Chaucer tips its tail and ears with black; from some nasty trait' (Cottle). A very scarce surname, whatever the spelling.

Col(e)gate P Place-names: *Colgate* in West Sussex, *Colgates* in Kent OE '?*Col(l)a*'s/charcoal/rounded hill gate'. A scarce surname, mainly found in Kent in both spellings. *Colgate toothpaste, manufactured by the Colgate-Palmolive Company, has its origins in a soap and candle maker named William Colgate (1783–1857), who opened a factory on Dutch Street, New York, in 1806. William was born in Hollingbourn, Kent; his father Robert Colgate (1758–1826), a supporter of the American War of Independence, emigrated* *from Shoreham, Kent, to Baltimore, Maryland, in 1798.*

Col(l)in/Collard/Collen/Collet(t)Collins/Coll(s)/Colling(e)(s)/Cowlin(g) F Double diminutives of the first-name *Nicolas*, via *Coll*. *See also* **Cowlin** and **Nichol**. Or possibly from another meaning of *Cole/Coll*. Variants ending in -*s* or in -*son*, such as **Collins** or **Col(l)inson**, mean 'son of Colin', but the surname of most of the **Collins**es in Ireland is derived from **O'** [descendant of] **Cullane**. **Collen** is a Cambs surname.

Col(l)inson, *see* Colin.

Coll, *see* Cole and Colin.

Collard F/P It is frequently claimed that **Collard** is derived from the first-name *Col(l)in*, though Bardsley speaks of its having its roots in a Gloucs first-name *Collard*. Yet there is a Devon place-name *Callard*, in Burrington, giving rise to a family described in the 1620 heralds' visitation of Devon as '**Callard** of *Callard*'. There are three ancient gentry families named **Collard** (formerly **Callard** by all accounts), and it is implied in visitation and subsequent records that they all spring from the same root, settling in Essex and Kent, and also in Devon, where the line can be traced back to John **Callard** of *Callard*, living in 1498. By the late nineteenth century, **Collard**s could mostly be found in Kent, Middx and Somerset, while **Callard** was still a predominantly Devon surname.

Colledge P/T Place-names: *Colwich*, Staffs; *Colwick*, Notts OE 'farm where charcoal is burnt'; in neither case is the -*w*- sounded. 'The meaning "college (of priests/canons/students)" OF is barely possible' (Cottle). Alternatively, M. A. Lower suggests that in the north of England any court or group of cottages having a common entrance at the street is called a '*college*'. **Colledge** is a widespread surname, strongest in Warwicks; **College**, very much scarcer, has a limited presence in Co Durham.

College, *see* Colledge.

Collen/Collet(t), *see* Colin.

Colley N Nickname for a coaly, dusky, swarthy person OE.

Collier/Col(l)yer O Occupational term for a charcoal burner or seller OE. **Collier** is more commonly found than **Collyer**, which is predominantly a Surrey surname. **Collier** is the family name of the Viscounts Monkswell.

Collin/Colling(e)(s), *see* Colin.

Collingwood P Place-name in Staffs OF and OE 'challenge/dispute wood' (i.e. a wood the ownership of which is disputed), but the surname is found most often in Co Durham. *Both the first-name and the surname of Admiral Cuthbert Collingwood, Baron Collingwood (1748–1810), bear witness to his north-east-of-England origins. He was born in Newcastle-upon-Tyne to an old-established but impoverished Northd family.*

Collins/Collinson/Collis, *see* Colin.

Collishaw, *see* Cowlishaw.

Collison, *see* Colin.

Collop O 'Probably a name for a cook-house keeper' (Reaney); literally 'fried meat; bacon and eggs' OE. Found in Essex and Middx.

Colls, *see* Cole and Colin.

Collyer, *see* Collier.

Collyshaw, *see* Cowlishaw

Colman, *see* Coleman.

Colmer/Collymore/Cullimore/Culmer P Surnames with place-name origins: there is a *Colemore* in Salop, and also in Hants (*Colemere* in 1086, *Culemere* in 1196) OE 'the cool pond'; *Colmer* in Devon is OE '*Cola*'s moor' and *Court Culmore* (formerly *Caldemor[e]*) in Montgomeryshire, Wales, is OE 'cold moor'. **Collymore**, a scarce surname, belongs mainly to Devon; **Colmer** is found in that county, and also in Cornwall and Somerset; **Cullimore** is most commonly encountered in Gloucs, and **Culmer** in Kent. There were **Collymore**s in Jamaica in the late nineteenth century, at which time Ren Philip **Collymore** was Registrar

of Marriages and Clerk of the Parochial Board for St James' parish. *Stanley Victor ('Stan') Collymore, the English footballer who rose to fame in the 1990s, was born in Stone, Staffs, in 1971.*

Colpepper, *see* Culpeper.

Colquhoun P Scots: from a place-name in Aberdeenshire, Gaelic '?narrow nook/wood'. The usual pronunciation is '*Kohoon*'.

Coltard, *see* Colthard.

Colthard/Colthart/Coultard/Coulthart O Occupational term for a colt-herd OE. Compare **Stodart**, etc. **Colthard**, a rare surname, can be found in Co Durham and Cumbd; **Coltard**, also rare, belongs to WRYorks; **Coulthard**, by far the most frequently encountered spelling, is found in the north, especially Co Durham and Cumbd.

Coltman O Occupational term for a colt-keeper OE. Found in Co Durham and in Leics.

Colvill(e) P From the place-name *Colleville* in Seine-Maritime, France ON and OF '*Koli*'s settlement'. The mining town of *Coalville* in Leics, usually pronounced (with a certain degree of delicacy) with the stress on the second syllable, was created in the nineteenth century within *Whitwick*, and can have no relevance here. The surname **Colvill** is found mainly in southern England, **Colville** in Scotland. It's hard to imagine that the poor unfortunate called '*Not Wanted James Colvill*', born in Lambeth, London, in 1861, could have found his set of first-names anything but a blow to his self-esteem.

Colwill, *see* Caudle.

Colyer, *see* Collier.

Combe/Coom(be)(s)/Cumbes T/P Dweller in a small valley, a valley in the flank of a hill, a short valley running up from the sea OE. The OE word is usually derived from Welsh *cwm*, but this may not be the whole story; the *-e* may show a dative after a lost preposition. Or from a place-name *Co(o)mb(e)* with the same meaning, of which there are many in the south of England – nine in Somerset, six in Devon, and six in other counties. The associated surnames are mainly south-western. A person charmingly called *'Honey* **Coombes'** was born in Stratford-upon-Avon, Warwicks, in 1880.

Comber/Comer/Coom(b)er T/O Dweller in a *Combe* (valley); or possibly an occupational term for a comb-maker OE, with an *-er* suffix.

Comfort N/P Nickname from a ME/OF word meaning 'encouragement, support', so presumably used of a person who offered the same. Or from a now-lost place, possibly in Kent or Surrey, in which counties the surname is most commonly found. Formerly known to have been a Cornish surname, related to **Comeford**, **Comerford** and **Commerford**, from the place-name *Comfort* in Gewnnap, Cornish *cym-vor*, 'the great valley' (the adjective coming second). *Alex Comfort (1920–2000), physician, poet, novelist and anarchist, who was best known (much to his chagrin, it would seem) for his books on human sexuality, was born in Edmonton, Middx.*

Comley N/T Nickname for a comely, handsome, admirable person OE. But in view of the *-ley* suffix, the surname could possibly refer to a dweller in a clearing in a combe/valley OE. There is a place called *Combley* in the Isle of Wight.

Commin(s)/Comming(s), *see* **Cummin**.

Compton P Place-name OE 'place in a combe/valley' in a dozen West Midland and southern counties, from Devon to Staffs, including eight in Somerset, and also one in WRYorks. Frequently pronounced *'Cumpton'*. Family name of the Marquesses of Northampton. *Denis (Charles Scott) Compton (1918–1997), who had the rare distinction of playing both cricket and football for England, was born in Hendon, Middx.*

Comyns, *see* **Cummin**.

Congreve P Place-name in Staffs OE 'grove in a combe/valley'. An uncommon surname, found particularly in Lincs and WRYorks. *William Congreve (1670–1729), playwright and poet, was born in Bardsey Grange, Yorkshire, though his father was from Youghal in Ireland, and he was educated at Kilkenny School and Trinity College, Dublin.*

Conibear, *see* **Conybear**.

Coningsby/Conisbee P Place-name *Coningsby*, Lincs ON 'King's farm'. A rare surname in either spelling, **Conisbee** being found mainly in southern counties of England. *Benjamin Disraeli's novel* Coningsby, *about an orphan child of that name, younger son of Lord Monmouth, was published in 1844. He also had a nephew named Major Coningsby Disraeli.*

Connell, *see* **O'Connell** (under **McConnal**).

Conner O Occupational term for a 'conner' (an ale-conner), an inspector of weights and measures OE. Readily confused with/a variant of **Conor**.

Conning N/O Nickname based upon some resemblance to a rabbit OF; or an occupational term for a clever, skilled person OE (compare the word *cunning*). Widespread in both England and Scotland.

Connolly F Irish: Anglicized form of Gaelic **O'** [descendant of] **Conghalaigh** ('valiant').

Con(n)or(s) F Irish: Anglicized form of Gaelic **O'** [descendant of] **Conchobhair** (literally 'dog'/'desiring'). Common Irish surnames, readily confused with/variants of **Conner**. *See also* **O'Conor**. *The world-class American tennis player James Scott ('Jimmy') Connors was born in East St Louis, Illinois, in 1952.*

Considine, *see* **Constantine**.

Constable O Occupational term for the chief executive officer of a king's court, a castle governor, a justice of the peace, or a parish constable OF (literally 'count of the stable'). A widespread surname, found particularly in south-east England. *John Constable (1776–1837), landscape painter and draughtsman, was born in East Bergholt,*

Suffolk, the son of a mill owner and gentleman farmer named Golding Constable and his wife Jane (née Brickbeck).

Constantine/Considine F From a mediaeval given name, from Latin *Constantinus*, meaning 'steadfast, constant'. Made popular thanks to *Constantine* the Great, the first Christian ruler of the Roman Empire after whom Constantinople (formerly Byzantium) was named. *See also* **Costain**.

Conway P/F Welsh: place-name *Conwy*, North Wales (from a British river-name), garrisoned by Edward I with his Englishmen. Hardly any Welsh place-names have given rise to surnames, whereas thousands of English places have. Scots: from *Conway*, in the parish of Beauly, Gaelic 'free quartering, billeting'. Irish: Anglicized form of various Gaelic names, such as **Mac Conmhaigh**.

Conybear(e)/Conibear/Cunneber T Dweller by a rabbit burrow/warren OF and OE. A strongly Devon surname in all spellings.

Conyers P Place-names *Cogners/Coignières* OF 'quince-trees' in Sarthe/Seine-et-Oise, France. A WRYorks surname, though scarcely in evidence, if at all, in France itself.

Conyngham, *see* **Cunningham**.

Cooch, *see* **Couch**.

Cook(e) O Occupational term for a cook OE. 'A good old surname that ought not to have the snobbish -*e*; Guppy found that sturdy farmers mostly did without it, and the national figures are usually 3 **Cook**:1 **Cooke**, but in parts of the north Midlands the position is reversed' (Cottle). *See also* **Lequeux**. A person bearing the unfortunate name of '*Sexy* **Cook**' died in Bedminster, Somerset, in 1848, while '*Humiliation* **Cook**' died in Ipswich, Suffolk, in the same year.

Cooksey P Place-name in Worcs OE '*Cucu*'s island'. Strongest in Staffs.

Coom(be), *see* **Combe**.

Coomber, *see* **Comber**.

Coombes, *see* **Combe**.

Coomer, *see* **Comber**.

Cooms, *see* **Combe**.

Coop(e), *see* **Cope**.

Cooper/Couper/Cowper O Occupational term for a maker or repairer of wooden tubs/casks/buckets ME, from Germanic and Low Latin. A common surname everywhere save in the north of England. **Couper**, a Scots form, can alternatively be from the place-name *Coupar* (etymology unknown), one in Angus, one in Fife. *See also* **Copper**. *William Cowper (1731–1800), English poet and hymnodist, who was born in Berkhamsted, Herts, pronounced his surname as 'Cooper'.*

Cooperthwaite, *see* **Copperthwaite**.

Coot(e) N Nickname for a bald person, or for one who was as daft as a coot, a proverbially dim-witted bird ME.

Cope/Coop(e)/Coup(e) O/N Occupational term for a maker of capes/copes/cloaks OE, or a nickname for a person who habitually wore such a garment.

Copeland/Copland/Coupland P Place-names: *Copeland*, Cumbd; *Coupland*, Northd ON 'bought land' (that is, land which had been purchased, not held by feudal tenure). *Aaron Copland (1900–1990), American composer, was born in Brooklyn, New York, of Lithuanian Jewish descent. His father had Anglicized his original name of 'Kaplan' to 'Copland' while stopping off in England en route to America.*

Copestake/Capstack/Capstick O Occupational term for a woodcutter OF and OE (literally 'cut-stake'). **Copestake** is a Derbys/Staffs surname; **Capstick** is mostly found in Lancs/WRYorks.

Copland, *see* **Copeland**.

Copleston(e), *see* **Copplestone**.

Copley P Place-name in several counties (ten such being in WRYorks) OE '*Coppa*'s/

hilltop clearing', though the Cambs place is OE 'round tumulus'.

Copner N/P Nickname for an illicit lover, adulterer, paramour OE; or from the place-name *Copnor* in Hants OE '*Coppa*'s landing-place'.

Copp T/N Dweller at the hilltop OE; or a nickname for someone with a large head (the crown of which was large as a hilltop).

Coppard N Nickname for a 'Big-head' OE and OF, referring to either a physical or a personality trait (or both?). A Kent/Surrey/Sussex surname.

Copper O Occupational term for a worker in copper (an element named after the island of *Cyprus*, via OE), or a variant of **Cooper**. *Members of the Copper family of Rottingdean, Sussex, have long been famous for their knowledge of folk music and tradition. The surname of James Copper (1845–1924), son of a Rottingdean farmworker, gave rise to his nickname of 'Brasser'. In the event, the surname belongs as much to Kent as to Sussex.*

Coppersmith O Occupational term for a worker in copper OE.

Copperthwaite/Cooperthwaite/ Copperwheat/Copperwhite/ Cowperthwaite/Cowpertwait P Place-name in NRYorks ME 'the cooper's field'.

Coppledick/Coppledike, *see* **Cobbeldick**.

Copplestone P Place-name: two such in Devon OE 'logan stone/rocking stone', and a lost place in Suffolk. An uncommon West Country surname, strongest in Devon.

Corbet(t), *see* **Corbin**.

Corbin/Corbet(t)/Corp(e)/Corps N
Nickname for a person who bore some resemblance to a crow or raven OF (modern French *corbeau* 'crow'; *grand corbeau* 'raven') – perhaps having black hair, or being noisy/raucous. The diminutive form **Corbett** is very common in Gloucs/Herefords/Salop/Warwicks/Worcs, but was also taken to Scotland during the twelfth century. **Corp** is found mainly in Somerset;

Corps mainly in Hants. **Corbett** is the family name of the Barons Rowallan.

Corbishley/Curbishley/Curbishly P
Place-name in Chesh OE 'cur-bitch clearing', where there is a reference to an Adam de **Curbicheley** in the early fourteenth century. **Curbishley** and **Curbishly** are predominantly Chesh surnames, while **Corbishley**, by far the commonest variant, can also be met with in Lancs and Staffs. *Llewellyn Charles Curbishley, commonly known as Alan Curbishley, a successful football player and manager who was once in the running for the role of England manager, was born in 1957 in Forest Gate, East London.*

Corcoran N Irish: nickname for a red/purple-faced person. Also **O'Corcoran**, **McCorcoran**.

Cordeaux An elusive surname, rare and scattered, which would seem at first sight to be French in origin, or to be an English name which has been 'Frenchified'. There is a French surname **Cordeix**, a variant of **Corne**, which itself has several different meanings, and '*corbeau*' is a French word meaning 'crow'. Yet within England **Cordeaux** would appear to have started life in Yorks as **Cordukes** (the commonest spelling), **Curdox(e)**, **Curdix**, **Curdex**, **Cordeux**, **Cordox** and **Curdax**, just as the apparently French surname **Prideaux**, from the place-name *Pridias* in Cornwall, would originally have been pronounced '*Priddux*'. So we have a surname which may have been French in origin, pronounced and spelt by the English as they heard it, or it may have had an English origin in the first place, only acquiring a touch of French gloss later in its life. More mundanely, could **Cordeaux** simply be a Frenched-up variant of **Corder**, or from a Yorks place-name such as *Cawder*? The variant **Cordeux**, also scarce, can be found in the 1881 census in both Surrey and WRYorks.

Corden, *see* **Cordiner**.

Corder O/N Occupational term for a maker of cord or string, or a nickname for one who wore fancy ribbons of some sort OF. Strongest in Essex. Compare **Cordeaux**.

Corder(e)y/Corderoy N Nickname for a proud man OF *coeur de roi* ('heart of a King'). **Corderey** is a very scarce surname; **Corderoy**, rather less scarce, belongs to Berks, Middx and Surrey.

Cordeux, *see* **Cordeaux**.

Cordiner/Corden/Cordon O Occupational term for a cordwainer, leatherworker, shoemaker OF, originally a person who worked with fine leather from the Spanish city of *Córdoba*. **Cordiner** is mostly found in Aberdeenshire, Scotland.

Corfe P There are places so-called in Dorset (two such) and in Somerset OE 'a pass or cutting', though this is chiefly a surname of Chesh and surrounding counties.

Cork/Corker O Occupational term for a supplier or user of a purple dye prepared from lichens ME.

Corlett F Manx: 'son of *Thor*'s People' ON (the initial 'C' being the remains of **Mac**, 'son of'). One Manx family of **Corlett**s settled in England and became **Collet**s.

Corley P Place-name in Warwicks OE 'wood with cranes/herons'. Chiefly a Lancs surname.

Cormack, *see* **McCormack**.

Cornelius F From a Roman family name, perhaps derived from *cornu* 'horn'; the devout centurion in Acts x.1 was so-called, as were several martyred popes. Not used as a first-name in mediaeval England, it was introduced partly from the Low Countries and partly (to render names like *Conchubhar*) from Ireland. Chiefly a south-of-England surname, but can also be found in South Wales.

Cornell/Cornwall/Cornwallis/ Cornwell P Place-names: the county of *Cornwall* (consisting of the tribal name *Kernow* and OE *wealas*, meaning 'foreigners', as in *Wales/Welsh* and surnames such as **Walsh**, **Wallace**, etc.); *Cornall*, a lost place in Lancs; *Cornhill*, Northd OE 'crane/heron enclosure'; *Cornhill*, London OE 'hill where corn is sold'; *Cornwell*, Oxon OE 'crane/

heron stream'. **Cornwallis** refers to a man from *Cornwall*. In principle, **Cornell** can alternatively be a shortened form of **Cornelius**.

Corner T/O Dweller at a corner OF; or an occupational term for a horn-player OF. A northern surname, found particularly in Co Durham.

Cornes, *see* **Cornish**.

Corney P Place-name in Cumbd and Herts OE 'island with corn/cranes'; or a lost place in Lancs OE 'nook with cranes'.

Cornford/Cornforth P Place-names: *Cornford* in Dorset and *Cornford* (now lost) near Fairford, Gloucs OE 'mill ford' or 'ford where querns were to be got'; *Cornforth*, Co Durham OE 'ford with cranes'. **Cornford** is a Sussex/Kent surname; **Cornforth** belongs to the north – to Co Durham and NRYorks in particular.

Cornish P A man from *Cornwall* (see **Cornell**); not surprisingly, a Devon/Somerset surname. **Corns** and **Cornes**, variants from OF *corneis*, are found in Staffs and in Chesh/Staffs respectively. In the nineteenth century, when pig-iron was much in demand during the Franco-Prussian war, Stanton Iron Works near Ilkeston, Derbys, placed advertisements in Salop and Staffs newspapers in an attempt to recruit workers; among the families which heeded the call and duly arrived by canal at Gallows Inn, Ilkeston, were those bearing the surname **Corns**.

Corns, *see* **Cornish**.

Cornwall/Cornwallis/Cornwell, *see* **Cornell**.

Corp(e)/Corps, *see* **Corbin**.

Corrick N Nickname for a person resembling a dwarf/elf, Cornish and Breton. Still a surname of the south-west of England.

Cosh/Coysh T Dweller in a hut, cabin, cottage, hovel ?Celtic. Appears as a surname in Essex from 1248 onwards, but in more recent times can be found in places as far apart as south-west England and Wigtownshire, Scotland.

Costain F Manx: 'son of *Augustine*', the initial 'C' being the remains of **Mac**, 'son of'; or a diminutive of **Constantine**.

Costello F Irish: probably a shortened form of **Mac Costello** ('son of *Jocelyn*'). MacLysaght says that this surname exhibits the first recorded instance of a Norman family assuming a **Mac** name. Readily confused with/a variant of **Gostelow**. *The musician and songwriter Declan Patrick MacManus (born in London, of Irish ancestry, in 1954) eventually opted for the stage-name Elvis Costello, a sublime/ridiculous combination of Elvis Presley's first-name and his own mother's maiden-name.*

Coster O Occupational term for a grower or seller of *costard* apples ME (as sold originally by a *costermonger*). A surname of the south of England.

Cote(s)/Coat(e)/Coates T/P Dweller in a cottage, hut, (sheep-) cote OE; or from a place-name (*Cote, Cotes, Coat, Coate, Coates*) found in thirteen English counties. *Eric Coates (formerly Frank Harrison Coates) (1886–1957), English composer, was born in Hucknall, Notts, the son of William Harrison Coates, a surgeon, and Mary Jane Gwynne (née Blower).*

Coton, *see* **Cotton**.

Cottam T/P Dweller at the cottages OE (exhibiting a dative plural *-um* after a lost preposition); or from a place-name: *Cottam* in Notts, ERYorks; *Cotham* in Notts and in Bristol.

Cottenham P Place-name in Cambs OE '*Cot(t)a*'s homestead'.

Cotter/Cottier O/F Status name for a cottager, a villein holding a 'cot' through labour service OF. Irish and Manx (originally from ON): **Mac Oitir**, the 'Ma' element being suppressed. The Manx **Cottier** is pronounced *Cotcher*.

Cotterell/Cotterill/Cottrel/Cottrill O Status name for a cottager OF, diminutive;

compare **Cotter**. Mainly a Midlands surname.

Cottier, *see* **Cotter**.

Cottingham P Place-name in Northants and ERYorks OE 'homestead of *Cott(a)*'s people', though by the late nineteenth century the surname was found mostly in Lincs and Sussex. By then some **Cottingham**s – such as one family from Gunnerside in the Yorkshire Dales who settled in Iowa in the 1830s – had decided to emigrate.

Cottle O/P Occupational term for a maker of chain-mail, Anglo-Norman French, or for a cutler OF. Cornish: from the place called *Cotehele* ('wood by the estuary'), embowered in trees in a horseshoe bend of the river Tamar. There were **Cottel**s at *Cotehele* in the 1200s, and in 1120 Sir Robert **de Cotel** held the manor of Camerton, Somerset. A surname found in north Cornwall, and borne by the esteemed first editor of the *Penguin Dictionary of Surnames*.

Cotton/Coton T/P Dweller at the cottages/ huts OE (exhibiting a dative plural after a lost preposition); or from a place so-called, found in at least a dozen counties. In the year 2002 a marriage took place in Rochdale, Lancs, between Gary J. W. **Needle** and Samantha L. **Cotton**.

Cottrel/Cottrill, *see* **Cotterell**.

Couch/Cooch/Coucher/Couchman O/N Occupational term for a maker of beds, couches, pallets, mattresses, upholstery OF *couche*; or a nickname for a bed-ridden or lazy person (the original 'couch potato'?); Cornish: a nickname for a red-haired man, Cornish *cough*, 'red'. The Welsh surname **Gough** can have the same meaning. **Couchman** was a surname found mainly in mid-Kent until recent times. *Sir Arthur Thomas Quiller-Couch (1863–1944), the writer and critic known universally simply as 'Q', and something of a professional Cornishman, pronounced the second element in his surname 'Cooch'. Sir Arthur's grandfather was the doctor-naturalist Jonathan Couch (1789–1870). See also* **Quiller**. *For a detailed study of the* surnames Couch and Quiller, see *Searching for surnames* by John Titford (2002).

Coulson, see Nichol.

Coulthard/Coulthart, see Colthard.

Coulton P Place-name in NRYorks OE 'Cole's place', or 'place with charcoal-burning/colts'.

Counter O Occupational term for a treasurer, one who keeps accounts OF (Norman dialect).

Coup(e), see Cope.

Couper, see Cooper.

Coupland, see Copeland.

Coupleditch, see Cobbeldick.

Courage N Nickname for a person exhibiting heartiness, spirit, courage OF. *Courage & Co, the well-known firm of London brewers, was founded in the late eighteenth century by John Courage, an Aberdonian of Huguenot ancestry.*

Court T/O/N Dweller at, or worker at, a court, manor, castle OF; or a nickname for a short person OF.

Courtauld N Nickname for a short person OF. A surname famously borne by a Huguenot family which settled in England and has made a major contribution to its commercial and artistic life.

Courtenay N/P Nickname for a man with a short nose OF; or from the place-name *Courtenay* in Loiret or Gâtinais. 'A magnificent family that provided three emperors of Constantinople and the long line of the Earls of Devon' (Cottle). *Tom Courtenay (pronounced 'Cortney'), English stage and film actor, was born in Hull, Yorkshire, in 1937.*

Courtier O Occupational term for a judge (working in a *court* of law), or for a man working at a manorial (rather than a royal) court OF. A Devon surname.

Courtnell P Place-name *Courteenhall* (pronounced 'Cortnell'), Northants OE 'Curta's enclosure'. A scarce surname, found mainly in Hants, but also in Norfolk.

Cousen(s)/Cousin(s)/Couzen(s)/Cushing/Cushion/Cussen(s)/Cussin(s)/Cusson(s) N Nickname for a cousin (once a very general term used to indicate a family relationship), relative, nephew OF. *Peter Cushing (1913–1994), the English actor known particularly for his appearances in Hammer films, was born in Kenley, Surrey… Cussons' Imperial Leather Soap owes its name to a man named Thomas Cussons who opened a chemist shop in Manchester in 1869.*

Coutts P Scots: place-name *Cults*, Aberdeenshire, Gaelic *coillte* ('woods'), with the addition of the English plural marker *-s*. *A Montrose branch of this family gave rise to* **Coutts** *the bankers, which has had offices in the Strand, London, since 1692.*

Couzen, see Cousen.

Cove P Not used for a dweller at a cove in a general sense, but (as relevant family records make clear) from place-names with this meaning, *North* and *South Cove*, Suffolk OE.

Cowan, see McOwen.

Coward/Cowherd O Occupational term for a cow-herd OE (compare **Shepherd**, **Stodart**, etc.). **Cowherd**, 'a fine old bucolic surname made to look craven' (Cottle), is much rarer than **Coward**. *Sir Noël (Peirce) Coward (1899–1973), playwright and composer, was born in Teddington, Middx, to parents who both had a special interest in music.*

Cowder(o)y/Cowdray/Cowdrey P Place-name *Cowdray* in Sussex OF 'hazel copse'. *(Michael) Colin Cowdrey, Baron Cowdrey of Tonbridge (1932–2000), English cricketer and cricket administrator, was born in Ootacamund, India. His parents ensured that his full initials, 'M.C.C.', would echo those of the famous Marylebone Cricket Club.*

Cowen, see McOwen and Cohen.

Cowgill P Place-names (five such) in WRYorks, meaning variously 'ravine with cows/coal/a dam', or '*Kalli's* ravine', both from ON and OE.

Cowherd, see Coward.

Cowley P/F Place-names in: Gloucs OE 'cow pasture'; Derbys, Lancs OE 'charcoal wood/ clearing'; Bucks, Devon, Oxon, Staffs '*Cufa*'s pasture'; Middx OE '*Cofa*'s pasture'. Manx: a variant on **Kewley**, from **McAulay** or **McAuley**, the 'Ma' element being suppressed.

Cowlin(g) N/F Place-name *Cowling* in WRYorks OE or ON 'place by (a hill called) *Coll*'; or a double diminutive of *Nicolas* (see **Colin**).

Cowlishaw/Collishaw/Collyshaw/ Cowlinshaw P Place-name *Cowlishaw* in Derbys, Lancs OE 'charcoal wood'.

Cowmeadow T/P Dweller at a meadow with cows OE. A distinctive and scarce surname, found in Gloucs.

Cowpe P Place-name in Lancs OE 'cow valley', and a Lancs surname.

Cowper, *see* **Cooper**.

Cowperthwaite/Cowpertwait, *see* **Copperthwaite**.

Cowslade T Dweller at a dell with cows OE. The separation of elements is *Cow/slade* (compare the place-name *Chapmanslade*, Wilts: *Chapman/slade*). 'A Newbury, Berks, family said to have become extinct in 1931' (Cottle). A mere smattering of **Cowslade**s was also in evidence in the 1881 census for the Isle of Wight.

Cox(e), *see* **Cock**.

Coxeter O Occupational term for a cocksetter, one who set the cocks in cock-fighting OE. A very scarce surname, with a presence in Berks.

Coxon, *see* **Cock**.

Coxwell, *see* **Cogswell**.

Coy N Nickname for a quiet, shy, coy person OF.

Coysh, *see* **Cosh**.

Crab/Crabb(e) N Nickname for a person as sharp as a crab-apple ME, or having a funny walk or a spiteful, crabby temper, ME *crabbe*. George Crabbe (1754–1832), poet

and clergyman, was born in Aldeburgh, Suffolk; his father had originally lived at Norton, near Loddon, Norfolk.

Crabtree T Dweller by a crab-apple tree ME and OE. A distinctive Lancs/WRYorks surname. *Crabtree and Evelyn, a company which has natural health stores on many a high street and in many a shopping mall, and which sounds English to the core (as it were…), was founded in 1973 in Cambridge, Massachusetts. 'Crabtree' is a tribute to the health-giving properties of the Wild Apple, and 'Evelyn' is used in honour of John Evelyn, the seventeenth-century diarist, who was an early convert to the conservationist cause.*

Crad(d)ock/Cradick F Welsh: from the first-name *Caradawg* 'amiable'. See also **McCarthy**.

Crafton P Place-name in Bucks OE 'place where (wild) saffron grows'. Yet this scarce surname is mainly found in Essex and Lancs.

Cragg/Craig T Dweller at a crag, a steep rock, Scots Gaelic or OW. **Craig**, a Scots and Northd form, is the family name of the Viscounts Craigavon.

Craigie P Scots: place-name in a number of Scottish counties, all derived from Scots Gaelic 'crag, rock'.

Cranage P Place-name in Chesh OE 'stream with crows'. Found in the north and in the Midlands, especially Staffs.

Crandon P Place-name in Somerset, possibly OE 'hill with cranes', or, because it was spelt *Grenedon* and *Grandon* in 1086 and 1212, OE 'green hill'. A Somerset surname.

Crane N Nickname for a person who resembled the bird, the crane, in some way (skinny and long-legged?) OE.

Cranfield P Place-name in Beds OE 'crane pasture'.

Cranford P Place-name in Devon, Essex, Middx, Northants OE 'crane ford'.

Cranham P Place-name in Essex OE 'headland with crows'.

Crank N Nickname for a high-spirited, cocky person ME. A Chesh/Lancs surname.

Crankshaw/Cranshaw/Crenshaw/ Cron(k)shaw P Place-name *Cranshaw* in Lancs OE 'wood with cranes'. Not to be confused with **Crawshaw** and its variants. *Sir Eric Norman Spencer Crankshaw (1885–1966), soldier and one-time Assistant Secretary to Winston Churchill in the War Department, was born in Donegal, Ireland… Edward Crankshaw (1909–1984), writer and commentator on Soviet affairs, was born in London.*

Cranley P Place-names: *Cranley*, Suffolk; *Cranleigh*, Surrey OE 'clearing with cranes'.

Cranmer P Place-name in Norfolk OE 'lake with cranes'. Largely an Essex surname. *Thomas Cranmer (1489–1556), who was Archbishop of Canterbury at the time of the Reformation and who was burned for heresy in 1556, was born to a minor gentry family in Aslockton, Notts.*

Cranshaw, *see* **Crankshaw**.

Cranwell P Place-name in Lincs OE 'spring with cranes'.

Crapp/Crapper, *see* **Cropper**.

Crarer, *see* **Crerar**.

Crashaw, *see* **Crawshaw**.

Cross N Nickname for a fat person OF. Found in Co Durham and Northd. *See also* **Craze**.

Craster P Place-name in Northd OE 'Roman site with crows'; the surname, a scarce one, is found mainly in that county.

Crathorn P Place-name in NRYorks ON '?thorntree in a nook' or ?'corncrake thorntree'. A scarce surname, found in Warwicks.

Craven P Place-name: a district of WRYorks, probably from Welsh *craf* 'garlic'. 'No reference, we are glad to say, to cowardice' (Cottle).

Crawcour N/P Nickname for a heartbreaker OF (literally 'break-heart'). Or from the place-name *Crèvecour* in Calvados, Oise,

Nord, etc. A very scarce scattered surname. **Crocker** can occasionally be a variant.

Crawford P Place-name in Lancs, Dorset, and Lanarkshire, Scotland OE 'ford with crows'. Largely, but by no means exclusively, a Scots/North Country surname. For Joan **Crawford**, actress, see **Le Sueur**.

Crawhall P In principle, the origin here should be an OE place-name meaning 'enclosure with crows', but no such place is now known. A very scarce Co Durham name.

Crawley P Place-name in nine counties OE 'wood/clearing with crows', but the place-name in Northd is OE 'hill with crows'. Mainly found in the south-east corner of England.

Crawshaw/Crashaw/Crawshay/ Croshaw/Crowsher P Place-name *Crawshaw Booth*, Lancs OE 'wood with crows'. Not to be confused with **Crankshaw** and its variants.

Craze N/T Nickname for a fat person OF (see also **Crass**). In Cornwall, where the surname is most commonly found, the source lies elsewhere: *Chrease* and *Chyrease* are words meaning 'the middle house'; *Creis* and *Creiz* mean 'force, strength', and *cres* is 'peace, quiet, rest'.

Creagh N Irish: an adjective derived from a word meaning 'branch', the family so-named having reputedly carried boughs in a battle against Norsemen at Limerick. Commonly pronounced '*Cray*'.

Crearer, *see* **Crerar**.

Crease/Crees(e) N Nickname for a person who was elegant, dainty OE (so not to be confused with the similar surnames **Crass** and **Craze**, meaning 'fat'). Generally West Country surnames.

Crebbin, *see* **Cribben**.

Creech P Place-name in Dorset, Somerset, British 'hill'.

Crees(e), *see* **Crease**.

Creighton/Crichton P Place-names:

Creighton, Staffs OW and OE 'rock/cliff place'; *Crichton*, Midlothian, Scotland, Scots Gaelic and OE 'border/boundary place'. In either spelling, the usual pronunciation is '*Cr-eye-ton*'. **Creighton** is especially strong in Lancs, **Crichton** in Scotland. Members of the **Crichton** family have been Earls of Erne, Earls of Caithness and Viscounts Frendraught. *The Admirable Crichton, a comedy written in 1902 by J. M. Barrie, was named in honour of fellow-Scot James Crichton, a sixteenth-century athlete and all-round genius.*

Crenshaw, *see* **Crankshaw**.

Crerar/Crearer/Crarer O Occupational term for a sievewright, Scots Gaelic *criathrar*. The **Crerar**s were originally a small sept settled in the Strathspey and Lochtay-side areas, and the surname is well known to bibliophiles thanks to the fact that John **Crerar** (1827–1889), a Scotsman by birth, endowed a public library which bears his name in Chicago, USA.

Cres(s)well P Place-name in Derbys, Northd, Staffs and Pembrokeshire OE 'spring/stream where cress grows' OE. **Creswell** is a widespread surname, found in Staffs and elsewhere; **Cresswell** belongs mainly to Derbys and Staffs.

Crew(e) P Place-name in Chesh, OW 'ford, stepping-stones'.

Cribb O Occupational term for a person who worked in a manger/stall for cattle OE.

Cribben(s)/Crebbin/Cribbin/Gribben/Gribbin F Irish and Manx: Anglicized form of *Mac Roiban/MacRoibin*, from the Anglo-Norman French first-name *Robin*, a diminutive of *Robert*. *Bernard Cribbins, English character actor, was born in 1928 in Oldham, Lancs.*

Cribbin, *see* **Cribben**.

Crichton, *see* **Creighton**.

Cricket(t) P There are two places called *Cricket* in Somerset, Celtic with an OF suffix 'little hill', but the surname **Cricket** is found

mainly in Cumbd, and **Crickett** in Kent. Both are scarce.

Crippen/Cripps, *see* **Crispin**.

Crisp(e) N Nickname for a man with curly hair OE; or a shortened from of **Crispin**.

Crispin/Crippen/Cripps F From the ME/OF first-name *Crispin* ('curly-haired'); compare **Crisp**. *St Crispin*, patron saint of shoe-makers, was martyred at Soissons, c. AD 285. **Cripps** (arrived at by metathesis) is the family name of the Barons Parmoor. *Dr Hawley Harvey Crippen (1862–1910), notorious murderer, was born at Coldwater, Michigan, USA, the only son of of Myron Augustus Crippen, a local storekeeper, and his wife Andresse Skinner. His colourful and brutal career ended on 23 November 1910, when he was hanged at Pentonville Prison for murdering his wife… Sir (Richard) Stafford Cripps (1889–1952), politician and lawyer, was born at Elm Park Gardens, London; his father was a Member of Parliament, and his mother was a sister of Beatrice Webb (née Potter).*

Cristal, *see* **Christopher**.

Critchley/Crutchley P From a place-name *Critchley*, now lost but probably once in Lancs, Celtic and OE 'hill-hill', and still mainly a Lancs surname. *Sir Julian Critchley (1930–2000), a Conservative Party politician of heterodox views, was born at the Royal Northern Hospital, Holloway Road, London (as indeed, some years later, was the editor of the present edition of the* Penguin Dictionary of British Surnames…*).*

Croasdale, *see* **Crossdale**.

Crocker/Croker O Occupational term for a crockery-maker, potter OE. Or a form of **Crawcour**.

Crockett N/F English and Scots: nickname for a person who favoured a particular hair-style ME *croket* ('large curl'); Scots: an Anglicized form of **Mac Riocaird** ('son of *Richard*'). A surname widely scattered throughout England and Scotland. *Davy Crockett (1786–1836), the so-called 'king of the wild frontier' best known for his stand at* the Alamo, was born near Rogersville, Tennessee. His ancestry can be traced back to Joseph Louis Crocketagne, who was born in Co Donegal, Ireland, in 1676.

Crockford P Place-name *Crockford Bridge* Surrey, of uncertain etymology. **Crockfords** are located chiefly in the south and south-east of England. **Croxford**, found mainly in the south and the Midlands, may be a variant of **Crockford**, but may also be from an unidentified place-name with the meaning of ON and OE *'Krokr's* ford'. Crockford's Clerical Directory *was founded in 1858 by the London-based printer and publisher John Crockford (?1823–1865), whose origin and parentage remain obscure, though his marriage certificate states that his father was John Crockford, schoolmaster.*

Croft(s) P Place-name in Herts, Lancs, Lincs, NRYorks OE 'arable enclosure adjoining a house'; and in Leics OE 'machine, engine, mill' (compare the word *craft*). **Croft**, a widespread surname, is strong in Lancs; **Crofts** can be found mainly in the Midlands and in WRYorks.

Crofton P Place-name in several counties OE 'place with a croft'; but the place in Kent was once *Cropton* OE '?hump/hillock place', and the place in Lincs is OE '?saffron place'.

Crofts, *see* **Croft**.

Croker, *see* **Crocker**.

Cromer P Place-name in Norfolk OE 'mere/pool with crows'.

Crompton P Place-name in Lancs OE 'place in a stream-bend'.

Cromwell P Place-name in Notts, WRYorks OE 'winding stream'. *'Crumwell'* would formerly have been a common pronunciation of such a surname. **Cromwell** is not common anywhere, and is widely scattered. *The family of Oliver Cromwell (1599–1658), Lord Protector of England, had achieved a significant degree of wealth and influence in Huntingdonshire by the time he was born in its county town in the year 1599. His great-grandfather Morgan Williams, from Glamorgan, had married the elder sister of Henry VIII's minister* Thomas Cromwell, and in the next generation Morgan's son Richard duly changed his surname to Cromwell. The Protector himself, son of Robert Cromwell, occasionally referred to himself as 'Williams, alias Cromwell'.

Cron(k)shaw, *see* **Crankshaw**.

Crook(e)(s) F/N/T/P From the first-name *Krokr* ON 'hook, crook'; or a nickname for a hunchback or twister; or a dweller by a nook/bend; or from place-names such as *Crook* in Co Durham, or *Crookes* in WRYorks, with the same meaning.

Crookdale P Place-name in Cumbd ON 'crookèd-oak valley', and a Cumbrian surname.

Crooks, *see* **Crook**.

Croom(e) T/P Dweller at the nooks/side-valleys OE, exhibiting a dative plural after a lost preposition; or from a place-name such as *Croom* in ERYorks OW 'crooked stream', or *Croome* (three such) in Worcs. A scarce surname in either spelling; **Croom** is found mainly in southern counties of England, **Croome** in Gloucs.

Cropp, *see* **Cropper**.

Cropper/Crapper O Occupational term for a picker of vegetables or fruit, a reaper of corn, or a man who polled cattle, from a ME word meaning 'to pick, pluck'. As to **Crapper**, David Hey says: 'It is not clear what the early bearers of this name were cropping. It could have been iron or it could have been cloth'. The surnames **Crapp** and **Cropp** can have the same derivation as **Cropper/Crapper**, though **Cropp** can also refer to a dweller at a hilltop ME *cropp*, and **Crapp** as found in Cornwall may be from *crapya* ('to grip'), or be a variant of **Greep**, from *gryb* ('crest/ridge'). A monumental inscription once extant in Mylor churchyard, Cornwall, read: 'Joseph **Crapp**: Alas Frend Joseph/His End was Allmost Sudden/As thou the mandate came/Express from heaven/his foot it slip, And he did fall/help help he cries & that was all'. **Cropper** is principally a Lancs surname; **Crapper** belongs mainly to WRYorks, **Cropp** to Hants and **Crapp** to Cornwall.

Thomas Crapper (1837–1910), famous as a manufacturer of water closets, whose name has directly or indirectly influenced the development of the verb/noun 'crap', was born in the Yorkshire hamlet of Waterside and was taken for baptism at the parish church of Thorne on 28 September 1836. For a more detailed study of Thomas Crapper, see Searching for surnames by John Titford (2002).

Crosby/Crosbee/Crosbie P Place-names: four in Cumbd (where *Crosscanonby* was once *Crosby-Canonby*), and others in Lancs, Lincs, Westmd, Yorks (all in the Scandinavian area) ON 'village/farm with cross(es)'. ON *kross* is from Irish, and ultimately from Latin. *Harry Lillis 'Bing' Crosby (1903–1977), singer and actor, was born in Tacoma, Washington State, the son of an English-American father and an Irish-American mother from County Mayo. His seventeenth-century English-born ancestors include Thomas Prence and Patience Brewster, who was related to William Brewster from Notts, a passenger aboard the* Mayflower.

Croshaw, *see* **Crawshaw**.

Cross T Dweller by a market/roadside cross, or even at a crossroads ON *kross*. The same meaning, therefore, as the surname **Crouch**. Particularly strong in Lancs. The unfortunately named '*Chris* **Cross**' was born in Trull, Somerset, on 1 November 1598.

Crossdale/Croasdale P Place-name in Cumbd ON 'valley with crosses'. Lancs surnames.

Crossley P Place-name in WRYorks (two such) OE 'clearing with a cross'. Family name of the Barons Somerleyton.

Crosthwaite P Place-name in Cumbd, Westmd, NRYorks ON 'clearing with a cross'.

Croston P Place-name in Lancs OE 'place with a (market) cross'.

Crouch/Croucher/Crutch T/P Dweller by a market/roadside cross, or even a crossroads ON *kross*. The same meaning, therefore, as the surname **Cross**. The Crutchèd

Friars, so-called from their bearing or wearing a cross, gave their name to a thoroughfare in the City of London. Or from the place-name *Crutch* in Worcs, Celtic 'hill', which was *Cruchia* in 1285 and *Crouch(e)* in 1538 – though **Crouch** is overwhelmingly a surname of the south of England. *Peter Crouch, the English international footballer known for launching into a jerky robotic dancing routine to celebrate the scoring of a goal, was born in Macclesfield, Chesh, in 1981, though brought up mainly in London.*

Croughton P Place-name in Chesh, Northants OE 'saffron/river fork farm'. A scarce scattered surname.

Crow(e) N Nickname for a person bearing some resemblance to a crow OE. *Russell Crowe, Academy Award-winning film actor, was born in New Zealand in 1964. One of his great-great-great-grandmothers was a Maori, and he also has Norwegian, Scottish and Welsh ancestry.*

Crowcombe P Place-name in Somerset OE 'crow valley', and a Somerset surname.

Crowder, *see* **Crowther**.

Crowe, *see* **Crow**.

Crowhurst P Place-name in Surrey OE 'wooded hill with crows'.

Crowl(e) P Place-names: Lincs OE 'curly (like the *crulle* locks of Chaucer's Squire), winding', named after a now-lost river; Worcs OE '?clearing at the bend/nook'. But this is principally a Cornish surname, where it is possibly derived from *crow(le)*, a cottager.

Crowley P/F Place-name in Chesh, Lancs OE 'wood/clearing with crows'. Irish: Anglicized form of Gaelic **O'** [descendant of] **Cruadhlaoich** ('hard hero'). *The English writer, occultist and would-be Antichrist Aleister Crowley (1875–1947) was born Edward Alexander Crowley in Leamington, Warwicks, and raised in a Plymouth Brethren family.*

Crowsher, *see* **Crawshaw**.

Crowther/Crowder O/N Occupational term/nickname for a person who played on a mediaeval stringed instrument known as a *crowd* ME *crouth*, *croude*; Welsh *crwth*, with an *-er* suffix. **Crowther** is mainly a Lancs and WRYorks surname; **Crowder**, much scarcer, is found in both the Midlands and the north. *Leslie Crowther (1933–1996), English comedian and television presenter, was born in Nottingham, son of Leslie Crowther, senior... Samuel Adjai Crowther (c.1806–1891), born in the Egba group of the Yoruba people in what is now Nigeria, was the first black African Anglican bishop. Captured by slave raiders, he escaped to Sierra Leone, where he was converted to Christianity and in 1825 was baptized under his new name.*

Croxall P Place-name in Staffs ON '*Hook*'s hall'.

Croxford, *see* **Crockford**.

Croydon P Place-name in Cambs, Surrey and Somerset OE 'saffron valley'/'hill with crows'/'valley with crows'. Oddly distributed, with a particular presence in both Devon and Staffs.

Crozier O/T Occupational term for a person who carried a bishop's crozier or cross in processions OF; near a cross, or who sold crosses.

Crudgington P Place-name in Salop, British and OE '?hill-hill enclosure'. Susan Holmes has traced a family of this name back to the 1430s, at which time they were living north of Bridgnorth, Salop; from there some individuals moved to Worcs and (in 1770) to the East End of London.

Cruickshank N/T Scots: nickname for a man with a crookèd leg or legs ON; or from the place-name *Cruik*, Kincardineshire, with the addition of *shank*, meaning the projecting point of a hill. *The actor Andrew (John Maxton) Cruickshank (1907–1988), remembered in particular for his role as Dr Cameron in the television series* Dr Findlay's casebook, *was born in Aberdeen, the son of Andrew Cruickshank senior, a hall porter, and his wife Ann Morrison Cadger, a stocking knitter.*

Cruise, *see* **Cruse**.

Crump N Nickname for a crooked, stooping person OE. Found mainly in English counties on the border with Wales.

Cruse/Cruise N/P Nickname for a ferocious person ME; or (sometimes in the form **Cruwys**), from a place-name *Cruys-Straëte* in northern France. For the actor Tom **Cruise**, *see* **Mapother**.

Crutch, *see* **Crouch**.

Crutchley, *see* **Critchley**.

Cubbin, *see* **McGibbon**.

Cuckoo/Cuckow N Nickname for a person bearing some resemblance to a cuckoo OF 'perhaps for promiscuity' (Cottle). A Kent surname in both spellings. *See also* **Goakes**. For some odd reason a Surrey-based family bearing the surname **Cookoe/Cuckow/ Cuckoo** favoured 'Nightingale' as a male first-name throughout the eighteenth and early nineteenth centuries. Everything kept neatly within the bird family, then.

Cudbird/Cudding/Cuddy, *see* **Cuthbert**.

Cudlipp N/P 'This can hardly be anything but "cut/cleft lip, hare-lip" OE, though early forms are lacking' (Cottle). *Cudlippstown* in Petertavy, Devon, was *Codelip(p)* in 1238: OE 'the leap (over a stream) belonging to *Cudda*'. *Hubert Kinsman ('Hugh') Cudlipp, Baron Cudlipp (1913–1998), journalist and publishing executive, was born in Cardiff, the son of a commercial traveller.*

Cuerden P Place-name in Lancs OW 'ashtree'.

Cuff(e) O/N/F Occupational term/nickname for a person who made or wore fine gloves ME *cuffe* 'glove'. Irish: Anglicized form of **Mac Dhuibh** ('son of the black one'). **Cuff/Cuffe** was the surname of two noble Irish families: the Earls of Desart (originally from Somerset and Northants, title extinct in 1934) and the Barons Tyrawley (emigrants from Somerset to Ireland in the seventeenth century, title extinct in 1821).

Culcheth P Place-name in Lancs ow 'recess in a wood'. An exceptionally scarce surname, found in Leics and Warwicks.

Culham/Cullum P Place-name *Culham* in Berks OE 'river-meadow with a kiln' and Oxon OE '*Cula*'s enclosure'. A man at Oxford in 1570 was called William **Culhame** or **Colham** or **Culme**.

Cullen P From the German Rhineland city of *Cologne* (literally, 'colony') OF from Latin; Scots: from *Cullen*, Banffshire, Scots Gaelic 'little nook'. Or a form of **Culling**.

Culleton P Place-name *Colyton*, Devon, Celtic and OE 'farm on the narrow river'.

Culliford P Place-name *Colyford*, Devon, Celtic and OE 'ford on the narrow river'.

Cullimore, *see* Colmer.

Culling F From a ME first-name, from OE *Cula/Ceola*. Principally a Norfolk surname. *See also* Cullen.

Cullum, *see* Culham.

Culmer, *see* Colmer.

Culpan, *see* Culpin.

Culpep(p)er/Colpepper O Occupational term for a spicer OE (literally 'coal/black pepper'). *Nicholas Culpeper (1616–1654), physician, astrologer, author of* The complete herbal *and a member of a very eminent Kent and Sussex family, was baptized on 18 October 1616 at Ockley, Surrey, the parish at which his father had been the rector until his untimely death nineteen days previously. Nor was this the only tragedy to afflict Nicholas Culpeper: in 1634 a young lady from Sussex with whom he planned to elope was struck dead by lightning on her way to their secret rendezvous.*

Culpin/Calpin/Culpan/Culpon T/P/N Established surname dictionaries give a wide berth to such surnames. **Calpin**, **Culpan** and **Culpon** (all scarce) belong to Yorks, while **Culpin** can be found over a wide geographical area in both Britain and Ireland. George Redmonds focuses upon **Culpan/Culpon**, saying that the most likely origin lies in the ME word *colpan*, which refers to 'a

piece cut off' and has given us the modern English word *coupon*. What seems to have been cut off at the time when the name **Culpan/Culpon** first appears was a strip of land: in 1307 John **Culpon** paid twelve pence for a half-acre of land at Mytholmroyd WRYorks which had originally been cut off from the waste, and being the man who had acquired the *colpan*, he no doubt acquired his freshly-coined by-name/surname as a result. The not-dissimilar surnames **Culpey/Culpie/Culpye** can be found in Cambs from at least as early as the sixteenth century. Some researchers would link **Culpin** and the like with the surname **Kilpin**, or connect it with similar German surnames derived from *kulpe*, the German word for a carp (the fish); a Johans **Kulpin** is known to have been living in Stralsund in the fourteenth century.

Culpon, *see* Culpin.

Culver T/O/N Dweller at, or one employed at, a dovecote OE; or a nickname for someone resembling a dove in some way (mild of character?). **Culver** is mainly found in Kent, while the variant **Culverhouse** ('dovehouse') is a scattered surname.

Culverhouse, *see* Culver.

Culverwell P From a place-name meaning OE 'spring/stream frequented by doves'. No such place is now recorded, but this is a south-western surname, and there is a place called *Culverswell* (with the same meaning) in Devon.

Cumberbatch P Place-name *Comberbatch* in Chesh OE '*Cumbra*'s stream', or 'stream of the Britons'.

Cumberland P Formerly an English county OW and OE 'land of the Britons/Cymry'. A scattered surname, with a particular presence in Notts.

Cumberledge/Cumberlege/Cumberlidge P Probably from an unidentified place meaning OW and OE 'Welshman's/Welshmen's ridge/bank'. **Cumberledge**, a scarce scattered surname, has something of a presence in Staffs; **Cumberlege** is scarcer still. *Many publications of the Oxford Uni-*

versity Press over the years carried the title-page legend: 'Geoffrey Cumberlege at the University Press'. The publisher in question, Geoffrey Fenwick Jocelyn Cumberlege (1891–1979), was born at Walsted Place, Lindfield, Sussex, the son of a local landowner… Eighteenth-century records of Quakers arriving in Philadelphia include the name of Rachel Cumberlidge, 'from London, England, received 4 month 26, 1702'.

Cumberworth P   Place-name in Lincs, WRYorks OE 'Welshman's/Welshmen's enclosure'.

Cumbes, *see* Combe.

Cumine/Cuming(s), *see* Cummin.

Cummin(e)(s)/Commin(s)/Comming(s) /Comyns/Cumming(s) F   From a Breton first-name meaning 'crooked', 'bent', originally brought to eastern areas of England by Breton settlers. A seventh-century Abbot of Iona was named *Cumin*. Robert **Cumin**, a companion of William the Conqueror, was an ancestor of Bruce's enemy the **Red Comyn**. Forms in *-ng* are mostly Scots.

Cundall/Cundell/Cundill P   Place-name *Cundall* in NRYorks OE and ON 'valley-valley' (tautologically).

Cundy T   Cottle derives this from 'conduit, waterpipe, pump, fountain' OF, and says that it is 'found in Yorks in 1379, but Guppy counted it only in Cornwall'. Indeed, it is found principally – though not exclusively – in Cornwall, where its meaning is 'house where dogs were bred', Cornish *cundy*. During the nineteenth century, various members of a **Cundy** family were highly regarded architects in London and elsewhere.

Cunneber, *see* Conybear.

Cunningham/Conyngham P/F   Place-name *Cunningham* in Ayrshire, Scotland, British, of uncertain origin, formerly *Cunegan*; the modern spelling, with its *-ham* suffix, is the work of an Anglicized scribe. Irish: Anglicized form of Gaelic **O'** [descendant of] **Cuinneagain**, a diminutive of the Old Irish personal name *Conn* ('leader', 'chief').

Elizabeth Conyngham (1769–1861), née Denison, who was the openly acknowledged mistress of King George IV for ten years, married an Irish peer named Henry Conyngham, Viscount Conyngham, in 1794.

Curbishley/Curbishly, *see* Corbishley.

Curley F   Irish: heavily abbreviated Anglicized form of **Mac Toirdhealbhaigh** ('Thorlike').

Curling N   A nickname, 'little curly' ME (by metathesis from Germanic *crulling*). Found as **Crullyng** in thirteenth-century Sussex. In the main, a Kent surname.

Curnow, *see* Kernow.

Curran F   Irish: Anglicized form of Gaelic **O'** [descendant of] **Corraidhin**, a diminutive of *corradh*, 'spear'. Chiefly a Co Waterford surname, but now spread evenly through the four provinces of Ireland.

Currie P/F   Place-name *Corrie* in Dumfries, Scotland, Scots Gaelic 'cauldron/ravine/ glen'. Not, apparently, from the place named *Currie* (Scots Gaelic dative 'wet plain') in Midlothian. Alternatively, possibly an Anglicization of **McVurich** 'son of *Murdoch*'.

Curry P/F/O   Place-name: settlements in Somerset, named after the river *Curry*, etymology unknown; Cornwall: Cornish 'corner place'; Scotland (see **Currie**, above); Irish: Anglicized form of Gaelic **O'** [descendant of] **Comhraidhe** or **O'Corra**. Or from an OF word for 'kitchen' – used, presumably, for one who worked in one.

Curtain/Curtin N/F   Nickname for a short person OF. Irish and Scots: an Anglicized form, by metathesis, of Gaelic **Mac Cruitin** ('son of hunchback').

Curthoys, *see* Curtis.

Curtin, *see* Curtain.

Curtis/Curthoys/Curtois N   Nickname for a courteous, educated, well-bred person OF, or used ironically for someone who signally lacked such qualities; or a nickname for a short person, or one who wore short stockings or breeches ME (compare the surname **Shorthouse**). There is nothing to suggest that the origin might be an abbreviated form of 'court-house' OF and OE. The variant **Curthoys** is a scarce Gloucs surname, and **Curtois** has a significant presence in Lincs. *The surname of Michael Reginald Harry Carttiss, a former Conservative MP who was born and brought up in Great Yarmouth, Norfolk, resulted in his being referred to, rather unkindly, as a 'walking spelling mistake'.*

Curwen P/F Place-name *Colvend* (formerly *Culwen*) in Kirkcudbrightshire, Scots Gaelic '?at the back of the hill'. Manx: an abbreviated form of **Mac Eireamhain**, the initial 'C' being an abbreviated form of **Mac**, 'son of'. Mainly a Lancs surname.

Curzon P/N From the place-name *Notre-dame-de-Courson* in Calvados, Normandy, from the Gallo-Roman personal name *Curtius* ('short'). Or a nickname for a shortish person OF. A Chesh/Derbys surname, one borne by a number of peers. *George Nathaniel Curzon, First Marquess Curzon of Kedleston, Derbys (1859–1925) crowned a glittering career by becoming Viceroy of India. While he was a student at Oxford, he was the inspiration for a piece of doggerel which found its way into national folklore: 'My name is George Nathaniel Curzon,/I am a most superior person…'.*

Cushing/Cushion, *see* **Cousen**.

Cuss O Occupational term for a maker of thigh-armour OF. A Gloucs/Wilts surname.

Cussen(s)/Cussin(s)/Cusson(s), *see* **Cousen**.

Custance F/P The usual English form of the female name *Constance* (Latin, 'steadfastness'), or a male name with the same meaning. But Reaney found that some were from *Countances*, in Manche, named after the Emperor *Constantius Chlorus*, who fortified it in AD 305–6. Generally an East Anglian surname.

Cutbirth, *see* **Cuthbert**.

Cuthbert/Cudbird/Cudding/Cuddy/Cutt(s)/Cutting F From a ME first-name

Cudbert, OE 'famous-bright'. Popularized thanks to *St Cuthbert*, the seventh-century Bishop of Lindisfarne and notorious misogynist, whose cult held sway chiefly in north England and south Scotland. Pet-forms such as *Cutt* have given rise to related surnames, as has *Cudd(y)*, which helps to disentangle the meaning of the Scottish place-name *Kirkcudbright* (pronounced '*Kirkoobree*'), which is 'St Cuthbert's church'. **Cuthbertson** (a surname of north-east England and Scotland) is 'son of *Cuthbert*', and **Cutting** is 'son of *Cutt*' (the -*ing* suffix indicating a patronymic, as so often). The surname **Cuthbert** is found mainly in northern counties of England and in Scotland, **Cudbird** and **Cudding** in Norfolk, **Cuddy** in Lancs, **Cutt** in the Orkney Islands, **Cutts** in WRYorks and **Cutting** in East Anglia.

Cuthbertson, *see* **Cuthbert**.

Cutlack, *see* **Gullick**.

Cutler O Occupational term for a maker/vendor/sharpener of cutlery OF.

Cutlock, *see* **Gullick**.

Cutt(s), *see* **Cuthbert**.

Cutter O Occupational term for a craftsman who cut various things, especially a tailor or barber, or else a wood/stone-cutter ME. 'Painfully apt surname of Ephraim Cutter, eminent USA physician and surgeon' (Cottle).

Cutteridge, *see* **Godrich**.

Cutting, *see* **Cuthbert**.

Cutts, *see* **Cuthbert**.

Cypher N A nickname derived from a cypher in the sense of 'zero' OF from Arabic (ultimately from a verb meaning 'to be empty'). The term had reached England by 1400, but its application as a surname is ambiguous; there is certainly no evidence that we might be talking of an encoder or cryptanalyst. A very scarce surname, found in Gloucs and Wilts.

D

Dabb(s)/Dabinett, *see* **Robert**.

Dabney, *see* **Daubeny**.

Dack F Seemingly derived from an OE first-name or byname *Doecca*, of uncertain origin. Bardsley contents himself with describing it as 'a curious Norfolk surname'. **Dax** (strongest in Salop) is probably a patronymic form ('son of *Dack*'), though it can be found as a French surname, originating in the place-name *Dax* (alias *Ax*/*Aqs*) in Landes, a corruption of *Civitas aquensis*, 'the city of waters', or else with the meaning '*D'Ax [-les-Thermes]*', from a place in Ariège. Some connexion with the German surname **Dachs**, used for a person who resembled a badger in some way (compare *dachshund*, a 'badger-dog') should probably not be ruled out in some cases.

Dacre P Place-name in Cumbd, Celtic 'dropping/trickling stream'.

Dadecote, *see* **Dorricott**.

D'Aeth, *see* **Death**.

Daff(e)y, *see* **David**.

Daft N Nickname for a meek, gentle person OE, though the less complimentary meaning is mediaeval, too. Chiefly a Notts/Lincs surname, where it is usually pronounced with a short 'a'.

Dagg/Dagger O/N Occupational term for a maker of daggers, or a nickname for a person who conspicuously carried one. *Dagger* is a ME development of the OF *dagg*. The word '*dagg*' was also used to refer to an ornamental scallop on a garment, or a pointed slash to show a brighter colour

through. **Daggeberd** is a 1310 byname/surname for a man with a pointed beard.

Daintith/Dainty, *see* **Dentith**.

Daish, *see* **Dash**.

Dakin(g), *see* **David**.

Dalby/Dolby P Place-name *Dalby* in Leics (three such), Lincs, NRYorks ON 'valley farm'. **Dalby** has a particularly strong presence in WRYorks; **Dolby** is more commonly found in Lincs and Northants. *Ray Dolby, founder of Dolby Sound Systems, was educated at Stanford University, California, and later at Pembroke College, Cambridge. Dolby Laboratories, initially based in London, moved to its headquarters in San Francisco in 1976.*

Dale T Dweller in a valley, dale OE and ON (compare **Dall**). A frequently-found and scattered surname, commoner than the number of present-day *dales* would suggest.

Dall T/N Dweller in a dale, valley ON/OE (compare **Dale**), or a nickname derived from a ME word meaning 'hand, paw'. An uncommon surname, at its strongest in Fifeshire, Scotland.

Dallas P Place-name in Moray and Ross, Scots Gaelic 'meadow stance/resting-place' (both elements ?from British). *The identity of the person after whom Dallas, Texas, is named remains a mystery. John Neely Bryan, who founded the city in 1841, claimed that it was named after 'my friend Dallas'. Former US Vice-President George Mifflin Dallas is one candidate for the honour.*

Dallicot(e)/Dallicott, *see* **Dorricott**.

Dallimore, *see* De la Mare.

Dalling P Place-name in Norfolk OE '*D(e)alla*'s people'. A scattered surname, most common in Devon.

Dallison P Said to be from the place-name *Alençon*, Orne, Gaulish via OF, though it looks suspiciously like a patronymic of some sort. Chiefly a surname of the English Midlands.

Dalton/Daton/Daughton/Dawton P From one of a number of places called *Dalton*, found in typical dale country in Co Durham, Lancs, Northd, Westmd, Yorks OE 'dale farm'. The spelling **D'Alton** is likely to be a mere affectation. The **Daton** and **Daughton** families of Co Kilkenny were originally Norman, from *Autun* in Seine-et-Loire, named after *Augustus*. No connexion with *Alton*, Hants. The surname **Dalton** is most commonly found in Lancs.

Daltry/Dawtr(e)y/Hawtr(e)y P Place-name *Hauterive* in Orne OF 'high bank'. **Daltry** and **Dawtr(e)y** contain the fused preposition *de*. *Roger Daltrey, a member of The Who rock band, was born in Hammersmith, London, in 1944… Sir Charles Hawtrey (1858–1923), stage actor and director, was born at Eton College, Bucks, where his father was a master. An English comedy actor named George Hartree (1914–1988) took the stage name of Sir Charles Hawtrey; he once claimed that he was the son of the theatrical knight of that name, believing that it would bring him work.*

Dalwood P Place-name in Devon OE 'wood in a valley'.

Dalyell, *see* Dalziel.

Dalziel(l)/Dalyell P Place-name *Dalziel* in Lanarkshire, Scotland, originally spelt *Dalyell*, *Daliel* and *Dallel*. Johnston (*Place-names of Scotland*, 1970) poetically suggests that the meaning is 'field of the sungleam', from Scots Gaelic; 'white field' is another possibility. The spelling **Dalziel**, like that of the surnames **McFadze(a)n** and **Menzies**, might seem to be part of a plot to confuse Sassenachs and others. The ME symbol known as a 'yogh', which resembles a letter 'z', was eventually written as such, but plays no part in the pronunciation of the surname, which is 'Dee-ell'. *Sir Thomas Dalyell of the Binns, 11th Baronet (born 1932), known as 'Tam Dalyell' was a fiery and independent Labour Member of the House of Commons from 1962 to 2005 – famously, the 'Member for West Lothian'. He inherited his baronetcy through his mother, but never uses the title. The army officer 'Bloody Tam Dalyell' of the Binns was a distant ancestor.*

Dam(m)ant/Damment/Damont/Dayman/Dayment/Daymond/Diamond/Diment/Dimond/Dimont/Dyment/Dymond/Dymont O/T/N These surnames would appear to form a cohesive group, though different origins may be at work. One source will be an occupational term for a 'dayman', a dairyman/herdsman OE (compare **Day**); most variants exhibit an excrescent dental *-t-* or *-d-*, just as the French word *paysan* has been converted into the English *peasant*. Dauzat suggests that **Damont** may refer to a person dwelling in a place 'upstream (from other houses)' OF; this is perhaps a more satisfactory explanation for those variants containing the short *-a-* vowel than the family tradition that the surname comes from a nickname OE *Daegmund*, with the meaning of 'day protector'. The **Dammant** group is said to have had its heartland at *Dallinghoo* in Suffolk. So the precious stone may not figure at all as the origin of the surname **Diamond**, which is widespread, most commonly found in Lancs and in Lanarkshire, Scotland.

Damerall/Damerell P Place-name *Aumale*, Seine-Maritime OF 'white marl'. Seen in fuller form in the English title of the Duke of *Albemarle* and in the Shakespearean character *Aumerle*. These are scarce Devon surnames, and the manor of *Stoke Damarel*, Devon, was held by Robert de **Albamarla** in 1086.

Damerham P Place-name in Hants, formerly a Royal manor OE 'river-meadow belonging to the judges'.

Damment/Damont, *see* Damant.

Dampier P From one of a number of places called *Dampierre* in France, named in honour of *St Peter*, the first element being ultimately Latin *dominus* 'master'. A scarce surname, found mainly in southern and south-western counties of England. *William Dampier (1651–1715), English sea captain, buccaneer and explorer, was born at East Coker in Somerset.*

Damson N A nickname for the son of a lady/noblewoman/prioress/ abbess OF and OE – though *dame* was used, with mock respect, of *any* woman. A very scarce scattered surname.

Danby P Place-name: three such in NRYorks ON 'Danes' farm'. A Yorks and Co Durham surname.

Dance/Dancer O Occupational term for a (professional) dancer OF. **Dance** is a widespread surname, found principally in southern counties of England and on the Welsh border; **Dancer**, fairly scarce, has a presence in Bucks. One can only assume that the father of a man calld 'Robert *Morris* Dancer', born in Prescot, Lancs, in 1903, danced the Morris… *The English actor Charles Dance was born in 1946 in Redditch, Worcs.*

Dando P Place-name *Aunou* in Orne, Normandy OF 'alder-tree', with the addition of the *D'* prefix. A Somerset surname, borne by one Norman immigrant who gave his name to the village of *Compton Dando* in that county. The surname is apparently not derived from an oath 'God's tooth!' (*dent-Dieu*), as some have suggested. *Jill Dando (1961–1999), the much-loved television presenter who was born in Weston-super-Mare, Somerset, was murdered on her doorstep in London in April 1999.*

Dane, *see* Dean, and **Dench** (under **Denis**).

Dangerfield P Place-name *Angerville* in Calvados, Eure, Seine-Maritime, Seine-et-Oise ON and OF '*Asgeirr*'s settlement'. Strongest in Gloucs and Staffs.

Daniel(l) F From the first-name *Daniel* (Hebrew 'God is my judge'), a major prophet whose experiences in the lion's den made his name a popular one.

Danvers P From *Anvers*, a French version of the name of the Belgian town of *Antwerp* ('at the wharf').

Darben N A nickname for a dear child/ bairn OE. An unusual and scarce surname, found in Bucks and a few other counties.

Darbishire, *see* Derbyshire.

Darby/Derby P Place-names: *Derby*, Derbys; *West Derby*, Lancs ON 'deer settlement', both of which are commonly pronounced 'Darby'. This could refer to 'deer' in its modern restricted sense, or to wild animals in general (the 'mice and rats and such small deer' of *King Lear*). But the *Darby* of *Darby and Joan* is a first-name, a pet-form of Irish *Dermot/Diarmuid* ('free from envy'). **Darby** is at its strongest in Staffs, **Derby** in Lancs. *Abraham Darby (1678–1717), the Quaker industrialist who was the first of three generations of men so-named, was born near Sedgley, Staffs. His grandmother Jane was the illegitimate daughter of Edward Sutton, Fifth Baron Dudley… John Nelson Darby (1800–1882), who gave his name to the religious sect known as the Darbyites (Exclusive/ Plymouth Brethren), was born in Westminster; his father, who came from Sussex, also inherited an estate in Ireland.*

Dargan/Dorgan F Irish: Anglicized form of Gaelic **O'** [descendant of] **Deargain**. **Dargan** belongs to Leinster; **Dorgan** is a Munster version.

Dark(e) N Nickname for someone with dark hair or a dark complexion OE. Found mainly in Devon and Gloucs, but also with a presence in Scotland.

Darley P Place-name in Derbys and elsewhere OE '(wild) animal/deer wood/clearing'.

Darling N Nickname, 'darling' (literally 'little dear') OE. Commonly found in Scotland, where it could be a translation of the surname **Farquhar**.

Darnell P/N Place-name in WRYorks OE 'hidden nook'. Alternatively, possibly derived from the plant *darnel* OF, the consumption of which was thought to make a person tipsy.

Dart P/O A rarity, in being derived from a river name – that of the *Dart*, apparently derived from a British word meaning 'oak' (as are the names of the rivers *Darwen* and *Derwent*). Alternatively, an occupational term for a maker of arrows ME *dart*.

Darton P Place-name in WRYorks OE 'deer enclosure'.

Darwen/Darwent/Darwin/Derwent
P/F From a place-name: *Darwen* in Lancs, derived from a small stream so-called, or *Derwent* near Hathersage, Derbys. Until the late eighteenth century the spelling '-*er*' in many English words and names was pronounced as '-*ar*' (as is still the case with 'clerk' and 'Derby', for instance); consequently, the names of the rivers *Darwen* and *Derwent* are essentially the same, derived from a British word meaning 'oak' (compare the name of the river *Dart*, in Devon). Surnames in the **Darwen** group can also come from a first-name *Deorwine* OE 'dear friend'. **Darwen** is a Lancs surname; **Darwin** and **Darwent** are strongly present in WRYorks; **Derwent**, fairly scarce, also belongs to the northern counties. *Charles (Robert) Darwin (1809–1882), the eminent English naturalist, was born in Shrewsbury, Salop. He had a fine head-start in life, being the grandson of Erasmus Darwin on his father's side, and of Josiah Wedgwood on his mother's. Darwin married his first cousin, a course of action which particularly appealed to him because it would ensure that he had fewer relatives to visit.*

Dash/Daish/Daysh T Dweller at an ash tree OF 'de', followed by 'ash'. The surname **Dash** can be found scattered across southern counties of England; **Daish**, very scarce, has a presence on the Isle of Wight; **Daysh**, also scarce, is a Hants surname.

Dashwood T/P Dweller at an ash wood OE 'ash' and 'wood', preceded by the OF prefix 'de', or at a place so-named, with the same meaning. Principally a surname of southern England.

Daton, *see* **Dalton**.

Dauben(e)y/Dabney/Daubney P Place-name *Aubigny*, found in three départements of Normandy, from the Gallo-Roman first-name *Albinius*, from Latin *albus*, 'white'. **Daubney** is a Lincs surname; **Daubeney** is much scarcer, as is **Dabney**, which has a presence in Berks. Readily confused with/a variant of **Debney**.

Dauber O An OF occupational term for a person who completed the 'wattle and daub' process, with clay/roughcast/plaster/whitewash. A Lancs surname.

Daubney, *see* **Daubeney**.

Daughton, *see* **Dalton**.

Davenport P/F Place-name in Chesh OE and Celtic 'market town on the river *Dane*'. Irish: Anglicized form of Gaelic **O'** [descendant of] **Donndubhartaigh**. Chiefly a Chesh/Lancs surname.

Davey, *see* **David**.

David(s)/Daff(e)y/Dav(e)y/Davidge/
Davi(e)(s)/Dowd F From the Hebrew first-name *David*, meaning 'beloved', the popularity of which stems less from the Old Testament king than from the patron saint of Wales and two Scots kings. The surname **David** can be found with some frequency in South Wales, and **Davie/Dav(e)y** chiefly in Cornwall and Devon. **Davidge** would appear to be a misspelling of **Davids**. **Dawkins** (a surname of southern/south-eastern counties of England) and **Dawson** (found mainly in the north, especially Lancs) are both 'son of *David*', via *Daw*. **Dakin(g)** and **Daykin** (a Notts and Derbys surname) are double diminutive forms. The predominantly Welsh **Davies** (son of *David*) is easily the commonest surname of the **David** family; **Davis** is the English spelling of the same name. **Davidson** belongs mainly to Northd, Cumbd, Westmd, Co Durham and – especially – Scotland, while **Davison** is more common in the north-east of England. **Davies** is the family name of the Barons

Darwen, and **Davison** of the Barons Brough-shane. See also **Daw**, **Day** and **Dodd**. *Thomas Daffy or Daffie (son of Giles Daffie of Abingdon, Berks), a seventeenth-century rector of Harby and of Redmile, Leics, produced a cure-all potion that would achieve fame as 'Daffy's Elixir'... Elizabeth David (1913–1992), one of the best-known cookery writers of the twentieth century, was brought up in Sussex, but was of Welsh ancestry. Born Elizabeth Gwynne, she married Lieut.-Col. Tony David.*

Davidge/Davie(s), *see* **David**.

Davin, *see* **Devin**.

Davis/Davison/Davy, *see* **David**.

Daw(e)(s)/Dow F/N A diminutive of **David**, but probably linked in the popular mind with the jackdaw ME, a loud, handsome, thieving but foolish bird. How clever of Mr and Mrs **Dow** to have had a child called '*Win* **Dow**' (get it?), born in Maldon, Essex, in 1886; and what of a man in the 1901 census for Bermondsey, London, who gloried in the name of '*Jack* **Daw**'?

Dawkins, *see* **David**.

Dawlish P Place-name in Devon, Celtic 'black stream'.

Daws, *see* **Daw**.

Dawson, *see* **David**.

Dawton, *see* **Dalton**.

Dawtr(e)y, *see* **Daltry**.

Dax, *see* **Dack**.

Day F/O From the ME first-name *Day(e)/Dey(e)*; or a diminutive of **David**; or an occupational term for a dairymaid, dairyman, servant OE. This is a surname which positively invites comical combinations of first and last names, rendering genuine examples such as: *Any* **Day**, *Christmas* **Day**, *Lucky* **Day**, *May* **Day**, *Time of* **Day**...

Daykin, *see* **David**.

Dayman/Dayment/Daymond, *see* **Damant**.

Daysh, *see* **Dash**.

Deacon/Deakin O Occupational term for a deacon OE, ultimately from Greek, meaning 'servant'; this dignitary, next below a priest, was nominally celibate. **Deakon** is a very scarce variant.

Deadman/Debenham/Debnam P Place-name *Debenham*, Suffolk OE 'deep(-river) homestead'. **Debenham** and **Debnam** have a strong presence in East Anglia, but **Deadman** belongs to the south/south-east of England.

Deakin/Deakon, *see* **Deacon**.

Deal T/P Dweller in a valley OE; or from a place so-called in Kent.

Dean(e)/Dane T/P/O/N Dweller in a valley ME *dene*, or in a place so-called; or an occupational term for a man who worked for a cathedral dean, or a nickname for a person who behaved grandly like a dean. **Dane** can also be a variant of **Dench** – see **Denis**. **Deane** is rare, but is the family name of the Barons Muskerry. *James (Byrom) Dean (1931–1955), the American actor whose iconic status rests upon his appearance in only three films, was born in Marion, Indiana, though he was raised in Santa Monica, California.*

Dear(e)/Deer(e) F/N From a first-name *Dere* ME 'beloved', or a nickname for someone who behaved like a wild or fierce beast, from a ME adjective *dere*, which was eventually restricted in meaning and used as a noun to give the modern word *deer*.

Deare, *see* **Dear**.

Dearden P Place-name *Dearden Clough* in Lancs OE 'beast/deer valley'. A Lancs surname in either spelling. Readily confused with/a variant of **Durden**. *Basil Dearden (1911–1971), film director, was born Basil Clive Dear in Southend-on-Sea, Essex.*

Dearman N Nickname for a dear person OE. Strongest in Herts and Middx.

Death/D'Aeth/D'Eath/De Ath N/O/P Nickname for a gloomy person, or one who had played the part of Death in pageants and plays ME; or an occupational term for a person who gathered kindling wood ME *dethe*. There is a place called *Ath* in Belgium, which could in principle have led to a surname, '**D'Ath**', though several bearers of the surname have no doubt bestowed an apostrophe on it in order to soften its hard edges. Pronunciations such as '*Deeth*' and '*Dee-ath*' can also achieve a degree of such softening.

Deathridge/Detheridge ?O A surname of uncertain origin. Reaney derives it from an occupational term for a person who chopped timber ME *Dethewright*; Cottle toys with the idea that it might mean 'executioner, murderer' (from two OE stems), but seems not to be very convinced by his own theorizing here. Both variants look seductively like surnames derived from a place-name. **Deathridge** is a rare surname, found in Warwicks and elsewhere; **Detheridge**, also scarce, occurs in Staffs and Worcs.

Deayton, *see* **Deighton**.

Debenham/Debnam, *see* **Deadman**.

Debney N Nickname for a person who was forever exclaiming 'God bless!' OF. A scarce surname, with a presence in Staffs. Readily confused with/a variant of **Daubney**.

De Burca/De Burgh, *see* **Burk**.

Decourc(e)y P Place-name *Courcy* OF '*Curtius*'s place' in Calvados, Manche, Loiret, Marne. Very scarce surnames within England.

Deeping P There are four places so-called in Lincs OE 'deep place/fen'.

Deeprose, *see* **Diprose**.

Deer(e), *see* **Dear**.

Deighton/Deayton/Ditton P Place-names: *Deighton* in ERYorks, NRYorks, WRYorks; *Ditton* in various counties OE 'place with a dike/ditch around'. *Len Deighton (pronounced 'Dayton'), the British author of spy fiction and historical novels, was born in London in 1929… Deighton, Bell and Co, the antiquarian bookshop which acquired its name in 1854, when the publisher* *George Bell acquired the firm of J. & J. J. Deighton, always favoured the pronunciation 'Dye-ton'. Founded in 1778, it finally closed its corner shop premises in Trinity Street, Cambridge, in 1998… (Gordon) Angus Deayton (born 1956), English comic actor and television presenter, was brought up in Surrey.*

De la Bere T Dweller at swine-pasture OF and OE. A very scarce surname, found in Gloucs and elsewhere.

Delafield, *see* **Field**.

De la Hay(e)/Delahay(e), *see* **Hay**.

De la Mare/Dallimore/Delamar(e)/ Delamer(e)/Delamore P Place-name *Delamere* in Chesh OF and OE 'of the lake'. The third element could be OE 'mere/moor/ marsh', though many places in France are called *La Mare* OF 'lake, pond'. *Walter (John) de la Mare (1873–1956), poet and writer, was born in Charlton, near Woolwich, London. His Delamare forebears were Huguenot silk merchants, and Walter (alias 'Jack' or 'W.J.') restored the French manner of writing his surname.*

Delamar(e)/Delamer(e)/Delamore, *see* **De la Mare**.

Delane, *see* **Delany**.

Delan(e)y P/F Place-name in Normandy OF 'alder grove'. Irish: Anglicized form of Gaelic **O'** [descendant of] **Dubhshlaine**.

De la Rue/Delarue T Dweller in a street, in a house giving onto the highway OF. *The De La Rue Company, famous for its security printing and for its design and production of playing cards, was founded in London in 1821 by Thomas De La Rue, who was born in Forest, Guernsey, on 24 March 1793.*

Delbridge, *see* **Bridge**.

Delf/Delph/Delve P Place-name *Delph/ Delves* in various counties OE 'digging, ditch, quarry, pit'.

Dell/Dellar/Deller T Dweller in a dell OE. **Dell** is mainly found in Herts, Middx and Surrey, **Dellar** in Cambs, and **Deller** in Surrey.

Delph/Delve, see Delf.

Dempsey F Irish: Anglicized form of Gaelic O' [descendant of] **Diomasaigh** ('proud'). *William Harrison 'Jack' Dempsey (1895–1983), world-class American heavyweight boxer, was born in Manassa, Colorado, of a family with both Irish and Choctaw Indian roots.*

Dempster O Occupational term for a judge, arbiter OE, originally used for females, as with **Brewster**, **Baxter**, etc. Compare *deemsters* in the Isle of Man, and the former *dempsters* in Scotland. A mainly Scottish surname.

Denby P Place-name in Derbys, WRYorks ON 'Danes' farm' (which might suggest that Danes were distinctive, thin on the ground, in the places in question?).

Dench, see Denis.

Denford P Place-name in Berks, Northants OE 'ford in a valley' OE, yet chiefly a Devon surname.

Denham P Place-names: one such in Bucks (near Uxbridge) and the one in Suffolk are OE 'valley homestead'; another in Bucks (near Quainton) is OE 'hill of the family/folk of *Dunn*' or 'hill of the hill people'.

Den(n)is(e)/Dench/Denness/Dennet(t) /Dennish/Denniss F/P From the first-names *Denis* (male) and *Denise* (female), originally referring to a follower of *Dionysus/Bacchus*, the Greek god of wine. Alternatively, **Denis** and **Dench/Dane** can refer to a person from Denmark ME *den(s)ch*. **Dennet(t)** is a diminutive form. *See also* **Denison**, and for **Dennish** see also **Devenish**. *Dame Judith Olivia ('Judi') Dench, Academy Award-winning actress, was born in 1934 into a York-based family of Quakers.*

Den(n)ison/Denson/Tennison/Tennyson F/N Patronymics, 'Son of *Denis*' (see Denis); but **Den(n)ison** can be a nickname for a denizen OF, one living in a city with all its attendant privileges, and **Denson** can be 'son of the Dean' (see **Dean**). **Denison** is the family name of the Barons Londesborough. **Tennyson** *is principally a surname of the north*

of England, but the poet Alfred, Lord Tennyson (1809–1892), was born in Somersby rectory, Lincs.

Denley T/P Dweller at a a clearing/wood in a valley OE, or from a place so-called (possibly *Delly*, Oxon, which was *Denleghe* in the fourteenth century?). Principally a Devon/Gloucs surname.

Denman T Dweller in a valley ME *dene*.

Denmead P Place-name in Hants OE 'meadow in a valley'.

Denness, see Denis.

Dennet(t), see Denis.

Dennish, see Denis and Devenish.

Dennison, see Denison.

Denniss, see Denis.

Denson, see Denison.

Dent N/P Nickname from 'tooth' OF *dent* – suggesting some peculiarity or distinctiveness of dentition; or from a place-name in Cumbd and WRYorks (possibly from a British name meaning a 'hill'). Strongest in Co Durham. Family name of the Barons Furnivall. *Joseph Malaby Dent (1849–1926), the founder of the publishing company J. M. Dent, well known for its* Everyman's Library *series of books, was born in Darlington, Co Durham.*

Dentith/Daintith/Dainty/Denty N Nickname derived from OF 'pleasure, speciality' OF, from Latin stem *dignitas-* (worth, value), or, as an adjective, 'smart, handsome'. **Dainteth** and **Daintith** are both Lancs surnames, the latter also having a presence in Chesh. **Dainty** belongs mainly to Staffs/Northants; **Denty**, much scarcer, can be found in Somerset. *William Hooper Frank John ('Billy') Dainty (1927–1986), a RADA-trained comedian and pantomime star, was born at Dudley in the West Midlands.*

Denton P Place-name in several counties OE 'valley place', though *Denton*, Northants, is OE 'the place of *Dudda*'s people'.

Denty, see Dentith.

Denver P Place-name in Norfolk OE 'Danes' crossing/ferry'. *John Denver (1943–1997), American singer and songwriter, was born Henry John Deutschendorf, Jr, in Roswell, New Mexico. He adopted his new surname in honour of Denver, Colorado, his favourite city, which itself was named after James W. Denver, Governor of Kansas.*

Derby, *see* Darby.

Derbyshire/Darbishire P Such surnames are as likely to have been applied to a person from *West Derby*, Lancs (and the surrounding area once known as *Derbyshire*) ON 'deer farm', as from the Midlands county of *Derbyshire*. Principally a Lancs surname in either spelling.

Derrick F From the Dutch first-name *Derrick*, more familiar as *Derek* ('people rule'). Mainly a Somerset/Gloucs surname.

Derricott, *see* Dorricott.

Derwent, *see* Darwen.

Desborough P Place-name: Berks OE 'hill where pennyroyal grows' and Northants OE '*Dear*'s fort/manor'. A Midlands and East Anglia surname, found especially in Northants.

Desmond P Irish: Anglicized form of Gaelic **O'** [descendant of] **Deasmhumhnaigh** ('the man from south Munster').

Detheridge, *see* Deathridge.

Devane, *see* Devin.

Devenish P 'A man from the county of Devon' OE (from a British tribe, the *Dumnonii*). The surname is most commonly found in Essex. **Dennish** is a very scarce variant (*see also* **Denis**).

Deverall, *see* Deverell.

Dever(e)aux/Devereu(x)/Deverose/ Deveroux P Place-name *Evreux*, Eure OF, from the Celtic tribe *Eburovices* 'dwellers on the (river) *Ebura*', from the Gaulish for 'yew'. A surname taken to Ireland at the time of the Anglo-Norman invasion. Members of the extended **Devereux** family, who pronounce their name *Deverix*, have long been key participants in the unique carol-singing tradition in Kilmore, Co Wexford, which dates back to at least as early as the mid eighteenth century. *Saint Devereux*, a place-name in Herefords, is a corruption of *St Dyfrig's*. The **D'Evereux** family were once Earls of Salisbury; **Devereux** was famously the surname of the Earls of Essex, and is now borne by the Viscounts Hereford. *See also* **Everest**.

Deverell/Deverall/Deverill P Place-names: *Deverill*, Wilts, *Deveral*, Cornwall, Celtic 'river-fertile upland'. West Country surnames.

Devereu(x), *see* Deveraux.

Deverill, *see* Deverell.

Deverose/Deveroux, *see* Deveraux.

Devin(e)/Davin/Devane/Devinn N/F Nickname for a person who was perfect in every way ME, or used ironically for someone who signally lacked such a quality. Irish: Anglicized form of Gaelic **O'** [descendant of] **Damhain** or of **O'Dubhain**. **Davin** is a County Tipperary variant.

Devinn, *see* Devin.

Dewar N/P Scots: the Highland Dewars take their name from the Gaelic *Deoir/Deoradh*, meaning a pilgrim, a stranger (compare **McIndeor**), or a person having custody of a saint's relics – in this case the five relics of St Fillan, and in particular his crozier, which was present at the Battle of Bannockburn. Also from the Highlands come the whisky Dewars, headed by Baron Forteviot. The Lowland Dewars of that Ilk derive their name from the farm of *Dewar* (Gaelic, of uncertain etymology; maybe also from a word meaning 'relic') in the parish of Heriot, Midlothian, from which Thomas and Piers de Dewar rendered homage to King Edward I in 1296. This family has now been recognized by the Lord Lyon King of Arms as Chief of the name and arms of Dewar. *The firm of John Dewar & Sons, Ltd, whisky distillers of Perth and London, was founded in 1846.*

Dewdney F/P From an OF first-name meaning 'God-given', though Bardsley is persuaded that the origin is a place-name *Dowdney*, which he was unable to locate. The surname belongs to the south of England.

Dewhurst/Dewhirst P Place-name in Lancs OE 'wet wood', and chiefly a Lancs surname.

Dewsall P Place-name in Herefords, Welsh (*Dewi*) and OE '(Saint) *David*'s well/spring'. An exceptionally scarce surname.

Dewsbury/Jewsbury P Place-name *Dewsbury*, WRYorks (the second element is OE 'fort/manor', the first element is OE '?water, stream (literally "dew")'.

Dexter O Occupational term for a dyer OE. Originally a female occupational term (compare **Brewster/Brewer**), but eventually used more generally. A Midlands surname, with a strong presence in Leics. *Edward Ralph ('Ted') Dexter, English cricketer, was born in Milan, Italy, in 1935... Colin Dexter, famous for his Inspector Morse novels, was born in Stamford, Lincs, in 1930.*

Diamond, *see* **Damant**.

Dibb(s)/Dibble, *see* **Theobald**.

Dibden/Dibdin P Place-name *Dibden* in Hants, Kent OE 'deep valley'.

Dible/Diboll, *see* **Theobald**.

Diccox, *see* **Richard**.

Dick/Dicken(s)(son)/Dick(s)(son), *see* **Richard**.

Dicker O/T/P Occupational term for a digger of ditches, or for a person living near a ditch OE; or used for a person who came from an iron-working area of East Sussex called 'the Dicker', so-named, it is said, from a rent paid by a bundle of ten iron rods ME 'unit of ten'. For all that, this is chiefly a Devon surname.

Dickin(s)(son), *see* **Richard**.

Didcock P Place-name *Didcot* in Berks/ Oxon OE '*Dudda*'s cottage(s)'. A scarce Berks surname.

Diddle F Possibly a pet-form of the first-name *Dudda* OE (compare **Didcock**), to which Tengvik ascribes the meaning of 'rounded/lumpish, deceiving/rascally, cropped/hairless' (take your pick...). Certainly not 'cheat' as in current slang, though some bearers of the surname may have changed it over the years because of its negative associations. An exceptionally scarce surname, with something of a presence in Surrey.

Digby P Place-name in Lincs ON 'farm at a ditch/drain'.

Diggens/Diggins/Diggle(s), *see* **Richard**.

Digweed O Occupational term for a digger-up of weeds ?OE. An unusual and scarce surname, found in southern counties, with a particular presence in Berks and in Hants.

Dillon F From the Germanic first-name *Dillo*. Irish: Anglicized form of Gaelic **O'** [descendant of] **Duilleain**.

Dillwyn, *see* **Dilwyn**.

Dilworth P Place-name in Lancs OE 'enclosure where dill grows'.

Dil(l)wyn P Place-name *Dilwyn* in Herefords OE 'at the shady/secret places' (exhibiting the use of a dative plural after a lost preposition).

Dimblebee/Dimbleby P Place-name *Dembleby* in Lincs ON '?pool/?gorge farm'. *Richard (Frederick) Dimbleby (1913–1965), the radio and television broadcaster who was practically a British institution in his own right, was born in Richmond, Surrey. Two of his sons, David and Jonathan, have followed in his journalistic footsteps.*

Diment, *see* **Damant**.

Dimmock, *see* **Dymock**.

Dimond/Dimont, *see* **Damant**.

Dingle P Place-name in Lancs, Warwicks OE 'dingle/dell'.

Dingley P Place-name in Northants OE 'wood/clearing in a dingle/dell'.

Dingwall P Place-name in Ross and Cromarty ON 'parliament field'. Compare *Ting-*

wall (Orkney), *Tingwall* (Shetland), the *Tynwald* (Isle of Man) and the Icelandic *Thingvellir* – all in areas of Scandinavian settlement and administration. A north-of-Scotland surname.

Dinham P Place-names: *Dinham* in Monmouthshire; *Dinan* in Brittany, Gaulish 'sacred valley'.

Dinmore P Place-name in Herefords OW 'big hill' (the adjective following the noun).

Dinsdale P Place-name of a settlement partly in Co Durham, partly in NRYorks OE '*Deighton*'s nook/recess'. Various members of a **Dinsdale** family from the Yorkshire Dales emigrated to America during the 1830s and 1840s.

Dinwiddie/Dinwiddy/Dunwoody P Place-name *Dinwoodie* in Dumfries, Scotland, of uncertain etymology ('hill with the shrubs'?). *Gwyneth Dunwoody (1930–2008), outspoken Member of Parliament, was born Gwyneth Patricia Phillips in Fulham, London. Her father Morgan Phillips was General Secretary of the Labour Party from 1944 to 1962; her mother Norah Phillips was a life peer, and her former husband, John Elliot Orr Dunwoody, was a Labour MP from 1966 to 1970.*

Diplock T Dweller by the deep stream OE. A Kent/Sussex surname. *Jury-less 'Diplock courts' were introduced by the British Government in Northern Ireland in 1972 in response to a report by Lord (Kenneth) Diplock (1907–1985), who was born in Croydon, Surrey, the son of a local solicitor.*

Dipple, *see* **Theobald**.

Diprose P Said to be a corruption of **De Préaux**, from one of several places in Normandy called *Préaux*. Chiefly a Kent surname. **Deeprose** is a Sussex variant.

Disley P Place-name in Chesh, near Stockport OE, of uncertain etymology. 'Dusty clearing' and 'clearing with a mound' have been suggested by A. H. Smith and by Gillis Kristensson respectively. The *Dis-* element is of uncertain origin: a personal name?

Disney P Place-name *Isigny* in Calvados, from the Gallo-Roman personal name *Isinius*. A widespread surname. *Walter Elias ('Walt') Disney (1901–1966), Chicago-born film producer and animator, came from a family with roots in Gowran, County Kilkenny, Ireland.*

Diss P Place-name in Norfolk OE (Normanized) 'ditch/dike'.

Ditchett P Place-name *Ditcheat* in Somerset OE 'gate in the dike' (i.e., in the Fosse Way).

Ditton, *see* **Deighton**.

Diver O/N Occupational term for a rope-dancer, tight-rope walker, funambulist? Or possibly a nickname for a person bearing some resemblance to a diving bird ME *dive*. Strongest in Cambs.

Dix/Dixey/Dixie/Dixon, *see* **Richard**.

Dobb(s/Dobb(i)e/Dobbin(g)(s)/ Dobbi(n)son/Dobby(n), *see* **Robert**.

Dobell/Doble N Nickname for a twin OF (that is, a 'double'). **Dobell** belongs mainly to the south-east and south-west of England, but is also found in Chesh and Lancs; **Dobel**, very scarce, has a presence in the south-west.

Dobois, *see* **Dubois**.

Dobson, *see* **Robert**.

Docherty/Doherty/Dougharty F Irish: O' [descendant of] **Dochartaigh** ('unlucky/ hurtful'). Also taken to Scotland by immigrants. *Thomas Henderson ('Tommy') Docherty, former footballer and football manager, was born in the Gorbals, Glasgow, in 1928.*

Dockeray/Dockery/Dockray/Dockree P/F There are four places in Cumbd called *Dockray* OE/ON '?nook with dock/sorrel'. The intriguing-looking **Docwra** is an older spelling. Irish: Anglicized form of Gaelic **O'** [descendant of] **Dochraidh** ('unlucky/hurtful'). *Sir Thomas Docwra (died 1527), Prior of the Knights of St John of Jerusalem in England, came from an old Westmd family… William Dockwra or Dockwray (c.1635–1716), born in*

London, established a system of penny postage as early as 1680.

Docwra, *see* Dockeray.

Dod(d)(s) F From a ME first-name *Dodde/ Dudde*. Various meanings have been suggested, all Germanic in origin: 'fat/ dowdy/dishonest/close-cropped'. The dialectal *dod* 'rounded hilltop' would seem at first sight to be a likely alternative source, but early examples of such surnames are not preceded by *de* or *at*.

Doddicott, *see* Dorricott.

Doddridge, *see* Dodridge.

Dod(d)s, *see* Dod.

Dodge/Dodgeon/Dodgin/Dodgshun/ Dodg(e)son, *see* Roger.

Dod(d)ridge/Dudbridge/Dudderidge/ Duddridge P Place-name *Dudbridge* in Gloucs OE '*Dudda*'s bridge'. These are West Country surnames: **Doddridge** is most common in Devon, and **Dudderidge** and **Duddridge** in Somerset. **Dudbridge**, scarce, can be met with in both Somerset and Gloucs.

Dodson, *see* Roger.

Dodwell P Place-name in Warwicks OE '*Dodda*'s stream/spring'. A widespread surname, found in its county of origin, but also in Bucks and Gloucs.

Doe N/P Nickname from an OE word for a doe – presumably for a person of mild or gentle disposition; or '**D'Eu**', from the place-name *Eu* in Seine-Maritime, 'city of *Augustus*', which was originally *Augusta*. Chiefly an Essex/Middx surname.

Doggett N Nickname for a person bearing some resemblance to a dog OE *docga*; the second element could indicate a diminutive, or be derived from OE *heafod*, 'head'. Probably not an affectionate or complimentary nickname in either case. A scarce surname in England, found mainly in East Anglia (Cambs in particular), but one which is known to have been used in the Irish province of Leinster since the thirteenth century. *Thomas Doggett, actor and theatre manager, left money in his will to pay for the establishment of a rowing race on the river Thames in which participants still compete annually for the famous 'Doggett's Coat and Badge'. The exact date of Doggett's birth in Dublin is a matter of some dispute, but he was buried on 27 September 1721 in the churchyard of St John the Evangelist, Eltham, Kent.*

Doherty, *see* Docherty.

Doidge, *see* Roger.

Doig F Scots: from a first-name, Gaelic from OW, meaning '(devotee of Saint) *Cadoc*'. Strongest in the county of Angus.

Dolbear P Place-name *Dolbeare* in Ashburton, Devon OE '*Dola*'s grove'; the surname is found principally in that county.

Dolby, *see* Dalby.

Donaghy, *see* McDonaugh.

Donald F From a Scots Gaelic first-name meaning 'world mighty'. **Donaldson** ('son of **Donald**') is also primarily a Scottish surname.

Donaldson, *see* Donald.

Donat F From a first-name, with the literal meaning of 'given' (Latin past participle *donatus*), popular in mediaeval times because it was used by various martyrs, as well as a schismatic, a mediaeval Latin grammarian, and a South Wales St *Dunawd*, whose name gave rise to two places called *St Donat's* in Glamorgan. An exceptionally scarce English and Scottish surname. *Robert Donat (1905–1958), stage and screen actor, was born in Withington, Manchester, the son of Ernst Emil Donat, a civil engineer of Polish origin.*

Doncaster P Place-name in WRYorks OE and Celtic 'Roman site on the (river) *Don*'. A Midlands and northern surname.

Donkin, *see* Duncan.

Donle(a)vy F From an Irish first-name meaning '?brown mountain'. *See also* **Dunlop**. *It once suited Hollywood film bosses to create the fiction that the actor Brian Donlevy*

(1901–1972) came from Portadown, County Armagh. The more prosaic truth was that he was born in Cleveland, Ohio.

Donn(e), *see* Dunn.

Donnelly F Irish: Anglicized form of Gaelic O' [descendant of] **Donnghaile** ('brown valour').

Donoghue/Donohue/Dunphy F Irish: O' [descendant of] **Donnchadha** (*Duncan*).

Donovan, *see* O'Donovan.

Doolan F Irish: O' [descendant of] **Dubhlainn** ('black defiance').

Dooley F Irish: O' [descendant of] **Dubhlaoich** ('black hero'). *The North Carolina folk song* Tom Dooley, *in which the eponymous central character was to lay down his head and die, featured the fate of Tom Dula, an impoverished Confederate veteran who was hanged for the murder of a girl named Laura Foster in Wilkes County in 1868. The lyrics were written by Thomas C. Land, a local poet. In Appalachian speech, the final letter 'a' of a word or name was commonly replaced by a 'y' sound – hence 'Grand Ole Opry'; so it was that Dula's surname was pronounced 'Dooley'.*

Doolittle N A nickname for someone who did little, a lounger, idler OE. A scarce surname, found in north-western counties of England, but also in Worcs, where it figures splendidly in the firm of **Doolittle** and Dalley, estate agents of Kidderminster.

Doorbar A surname of unknown origin. Cottle says: 'The compound (both elements OE) exists in ME, but makes little sense as a surname. Perhaps a corruption of **Dauber**'. Chiefly found in Staffs.

Doran F Irish: O' [descendant of] **Deoradhain** ('exile/stranger'). The variant **Adorian** is found in County Down, while **Dorian** belongs to County Donegal.

Dorchester/Dossetter P Place-name *Dorchester*: in Dorset, Celtic/OE 'Roman site where ?fist-play/boxing was held'; Oxon, Celtic/OE 'bright/splendid Roman

site'. A very scarce surname, found in Beds and Middx.

Dore P Place-names: *Dore*, Derbys OE 'door (i.e., pass)'; *Abbey Dore*, Herefords, from a Celtic river-name meaning 'water, stream'. Yet the surname is strongest in the Isle of Wight, and also has a presence in Hants, Middx, Oxon and elsewhere.

Dorgan, *see* Dargan.

Dorian, *see* Doran.

Dormer N Nickname for a sleeper, lazybones OF. A Bucks and Middx surname.

Dorricott/Dadecote/Dallicot(e)/Dallicott/Derricott/Doddicott P An intriguing surname exhibiting a wide range of variants, but one which appears not to have excited the interest of compilers of surname dictionaries. We should clearly be looking for a place-name origin. In Devon there is *Dodscott* (*Dodecota* in Domesday Book) and three settlements called *Darracott* (one in Georgeham, one in Welcombe, and *Higher Darracott* in Great Torrington), all of which were *Doddecote* or *Dodecote* OE '*Dod(d)a*'s cottage' in the thirteenth and fourteenth centuries. There is also a *Darracott* in Cornwall. In Chesh, *Dodcott Farm* (*Doddecote* in the twelfth century) also has the meaning of '*Dod(d)a*'s cottage', while *Didcote* is OE '*Dydda*'s cottage'. *Didcot*, Berks, (now in Oxon) is OE '*Dudda*'s cottage'. There is also a *Darlingscott* OE '*Deorling*'s cottages' in Worcs. Present-day researcher Robert **Derricott** has recorded no fewer than 169 spelling variations of the family name, and his own direct male-line ancestry includes an Isaac **Daricote**, a John **Dadecote**, a John **Dallicote**, a William **Dallicott**, a William **Dodicott**, a John **Dodicote**, a Roger **Dodycote**, a Roger **Dedicote** and a Humfrey **Dedycote**. He focuses upon a Saxon tithing named *Dydicot* or *Dudecote*, recorded in Gloucs in the year 757, and speaks of family migration from that county into Berks by 1208, and then into Devon, Salop and Worcs by c.1500.

Dorrington P Place-name: in Lincs and

Salop (near Woore) OE 'farm of *Dear*'s followers' OE; another in Salop (near Condover) OE 'farm of *Dodda*'s followers'. An Essex and Middx surname.

Dorton P Place-name in Berks OE 'place in a door (i.e. pass)'. A scarce surname found in a few counties in southern England.

Dorward/Dorwood/Durward O Scots: occupational term for a doorkeeper OE. To be door-ward to the King, a great honour, was once hereditary in the family of De Lundin, but the **Dorward**s of Arbroath were probably involved in the more humble task of being doorkeepers to the local Abbey. **Dorward** is most commonly found in the county of Angus, **Durward** in Aberdeenshire. Sir Walter Scott's novel *Quentin Durward* was published in 1823.

Dossetter, *see* **Dorchester**.

Doubtfire N A nickname with the literal meaning of 'put out the fire' OE. A scarce surname with an odd distribution (Middx, Surrey, WRYorks), but one which is familiar to cinema-goers thanks to Robin Williams's portrayal of Mrs Euphegenia **Doubtfire** in the 1993 comedy film *Mrs Doubtfire*. Clearly the makers of the film, and the author of the novel on which it was based, believed that the **Doubtfire** surname itself would prompt a chuckle.

Douce/Douche/Dowse/Duce N/F Nickname for a sweet, affable person OF; also once used as a female first-name. **Dowse** is a Lincs surname.

Dougal(l)/Dougill/Doyle F Scots and Irish: from a first-name meaning 'dark stranger/foreigner', originally applied to dark-haired Danes, as opposed to blond Norwegians.

Dougharty, *see* **Docherty**.

Doughty/Dowty N Nickname for a tough, valiant person OE.

Dougill, *see* **Dougal**.

Douglas(s) P Place-name in Lanarkshire, Scotland, Gaelic 'black water, dark stream'. Other possible places of origin include *Dou-*glas, Isle of Man; *Dawlish*, Devon; *Dowlais*, Glamorgan. A surname of lowland Scotland and northern England, and the family name of several peers.

Dovaston P Place-name in Salop OW/OE '*Dufan*'s farm'. A scarce surname, found in Lancs and in Salop itself.

Dove N/O/F Nickname for a person as gentle as a dove or who kept doves OE/ON; also once used as a first-name for both men and women. In Scotland, a variant of **Duff**.

Dover P Place-name in Kent, Celtic 'waters'. As a surname, more common in the north of England than in the south.

Dow, *see* **Daw** and **Duff**.

Doward P Place-names in Herefords OW 'two hills'. A scarce surname, found in Gloucs, Lancs and Middx.

Dowd F Irish: Anglicized form of Gaelic O' [descendant of] **Dubhda** ('black'). Also a ME form of **David**.

Dowdeswell P Place-name in Gloucs OE '*Dogod*'s stream/spring' (compare **Dowding**), and found predominantly in that county.

Dowding F From an OE first-name *Dogod* (compare **Dowdeswell**). A West Country surname. *Hugh Caswall Tremenheere Dowding, First Baron Dowding (1882–1970), Air Force officer and (later) committed spiritualist, was born in Moffat, Dumfriesshire, where his father, a native of Devizes in Wilts, was the founder and headmaster of St Ninian's Preparatory School.*

Dowler O Occupational term for a maker of dowels (a peg or bolt with no head) and similar objects ME.

Down(e)(s) T/P Dweller by a down, hill OE *dun*, or from a place-name with such an element. **Down(e)s** is a plural or a possessive, and the *-e-* of *Downe(s)* could reflect the use of a dative after a lost preposition. Or a variant of **Dunn**.

Downend P Place-name in Berks, Cornwall, Gloucs, Isle of Wight, Somerset OE 'end of the hill' or 'lower end'. Two of the three places in Gloucs so-called have the second meaning.

Downham P Place-name in: Cambs, Essex, Norfolk, Suffolk OE 'hill homestead'; Lancs, Northd and (*Downholme*) NRYorks OE '(at) the hills'. Exhibiting the use of a dative plural following a lost preposition.

Downing F From the first-names *Down/ Dunn*, with the familiar -*ing* ('family of') suffix OE. A widespread surname, found from Cornwall to Lancs. *See also* **Dunning**. *Downing Street, London, was named after the soldier and diplomat Sir George Downing (1632–1689), First Baronet, whose legacy later allowed his grandson, the third Baronet, to provide the financial wherewithal for the foundation of Downing College, Cambridge.*

Downton P Place-name in Herefords, Salop, Wilts OE 'hill farm'.

Dowse, *see* **Douce**.

Dowsett N Nickname for a sweet person OF, diminutive. An Essex/Middx surname.

Dowty, *see* **Doughty**.

Doyle, *see* **Dougal**.

D'Oyl(e)y P Place-name *Ouilly*, of which there are five in Calvados, France, preceded by a shortened form of the preposition *de*. The 'non-U' *doily* (never, ever found in the 'best households') was named from a maker with a similar surname. *Richard D'Oyly Carte (1844–1901), theatrical impresario, was born in Greek Street, Soho, London, the son of Richard Carte (formerly Cart) and Eliza Jones, whose ancestors had been D'Oylys.*

Drake N/F/O From an OE byname meaning 'snake/dragon', also used as a first-name; or a dweller at a house bearing such a sign; or an occupational term for a battle-standard bearer ME. 'Unlikely ever to mean *male duck*' (Cottle). *Charlie Drake (1925–2006), English comedian, was born Charles Edward Springall in the Elephant and Castle, Southwark, London. 'Drake' was his mother's maiden name.*

Drane N Nickname for a drone (as in a beehive), lazybones OE. Chiefly an Essex/ Norfolk surname.

Draper O Occupational term for a (woollen) cloth-maker/seller OF. **Drapper** is a scarce Kent/Surrey variant.

Drapper, *see* **Draper**.

Drawbridge T Dweller at the drawbridge OE. A Kent surname.

Drawer O Occupational term for a carrier, dragger, puller, transporter, a drawer of things that get drawn (such as wire) OE. A very scarce Devon surname.

Drax P Place-name in WRYorks OE 'portage' (overland between the rivers Ouse and Aire). Compare the word *drag*, and the surnames **Dray**, **Draycott** and **Drayton**. The **Drax** element in the charming multi-barrelled surname of Admiral Sir Reginald **Plunkett-Ernle-Erle-Drax** (1880–1967) is derived from a Yorks family which also held estates in Barbados, where *Drax Hall* may still be seen. Latterly **Drax** has been a scarce ERYorks surname.

Dray O/T Occupational term for a person who made or operated a dray or a sled OE. Ekwall claims that the surname could alternatively be derived from a topographical term meaning 'portage, place for drawing/ dragging boats overland, a hill requiring extra pull'. Compare **Drax**, **Draycott** and **Drayton**. A Kent surname.

Draycott P Place-name in Berks, Derbys, Oxon, Somerset, Staffs, Wilts and Worcs OE 'shed for keeping drays/sleds'. Compare **Drax**, **Dray** and **Drayton**.

Drayton P Place-name in a great number of Midland and southern counties OE 'portage/slipway/sled-track/steep hill' plus 'farm' OE. Compare **Drax**, **Dray** and **Dracott**.

Drew/Druce F/N/P An abbreviated form of the first-name *Andrew*; or from the first-name *Drogo*, Germanic '?ghost, phantom'); or a nickname for a lover, sweetheart OF (compare **Drury**). **Druce** can alternatively be from one of various places called *Dreux* in Eure-et-Loir, from Gaulish *Durocasses* or can be a nickname for a sturdy, stocky person OF. **Dreweatt**, **Drewett** and **Drewitt** are pet forms. **Drew** is a widespread surname, with a strong presence in Devon and Middx; **Druce** is found mainly in the south-east of England.

Dreweatt/Drewett/Drewitt, *see* **Drew**.

Drew(e)ry, *see* **Drury**.

Driffill P Place-name *Driffield* in Gloucs, ERYorks OE 'dirt/manure field'. A scarce Lincs surname.

Dring N/O Nickname/occupational or status term for a young man, servant; later, a free tenant holding by service and rent and military duty ON. **Dreng** (the rarer and more-or-less obsolete original form of the surname) has become **Dring**, just as the OE word *streng* became *string*. **Dring** is most often encountered in Lincs.

Drinkale/Drinkall N Nickname for a person who was fond of exclaiming 'Drink health!' or 'Drink luck!' OE, the reply to 'Wassail!'. The surname **Drinkale** has become so scarce as to be almost obsolete; **Drinkall**, also scarce, can be found in Lancs and in Lincs.

Drinkwater N A nickname, literally 'drink water' OE, used either for a person in extreme poverty who could not afford ale, or, sarcastically, of a drunkard. 'A correspondent has suggested to me that some bearers may have been, long before the discovery of insulin, diabetics with voracious unnatural thirsts' (Cottle). *John Drinkwater (1882–1937), poet and playwright, was born at Leytonstone, Essex.*

Driscoll F Irish: Anglicized form of Gaelic **O'** [descendant of] **hEidirsceoil** ('messenger').

Driver O Occupational term for a drover, or a driver of a team/vehicle, OE plus an occupational *-er* suffix. In ploughing, a driver urged oxen on with a lash, either at their side or by walking backwards in front of them, whereas the 'holder' OE actually held the plough-handles.

Druce, *see* **Drew**.

Drummond P There are various places bearing this or a similar name in Scotland, Scots Gaelic *drommain* ('ridge'). Family name of the Earls of Perth.

Drury/Drew(e)ry N A nickname derived from an OF word meaning 'love-affair, love-token, sweetheart'. Compare **Drew**. *Drury Lane, London, acquired its name in the sixteenth century when Sir William Drury built a house at its south end.*

Drysdale P Place-name *Dryfesdale*, Dumfriesshire, Scotland, so-called from the river *Dryfe* plus OE 'valley'.

Dubarry, *see* **Barry**.

Dubois/Dobois T Dweller at ('of') a wood OF. A Huguenot surname. The name of the Bristol costumiers **Dobois** has been pronounced *Doughboys* by locals.

Duce, *see* **Douce**.

Duck O/N Occupational term for a breeder or seller of ducks OE, or a nickname for a duck-like person (ungainly? noisy?). A widespread surname. *See also* **Duckett**. Readily confused with/a variant of **Duke**.

Duckett N/F A diminutive of a number of ME and OF words meaning variously 'duck' (compare **Duck**), or 'owl' or of a ME first-name such as *Ducca* or *Duke*. Bardsley showed that **Duckett**, in WRYorks especially, is a diminutive of the first-name *Marmaduke*, but there are other more opaque origins in Reaney to account for its high incidence in Somerset. In the event, it is at its strongest in Lancs.

Duckham P Dweller by a river-meadow/homestead ?with ducks or ?belonging to *Ducca* OE. Has a strong presence in Devon. *Sir Arthur McDougall Duckham (1879–1932), gas engineer, was born in Blackheath, London; his brother Alexander founded the well-known Duckham oil company.*

Duckworth P The name of two places in Lancs (in Oswaldtwistle and Bury), presumably OE '*Ducca*'s enclosure'. Very much a Lancs surname.

Dudbridge, *see* Dodridge.

Dudden P Place-name *Duddon* in Chesh OE '*Dudda*'s hill'.

Dudderidge/Duddridge, *see* Dodridge.

Dudgeon, *see* Roger.

Dudley P Place-name in Worcs OE '*Dudda*'s clearing'.

Duff/Dove/Dow N Irish and Scots: a nickname for a black, dark person, Gaelic *dubh* ('black'). Compare **Gilduff, McDuff**. Duff is the family name of the former Dukes of Fife.

Duffey/Duffie/Duffy F From an Irish and Scots Gaelic first-name meaning 'black man of peace'.

Duffield P Place-name in Derbys, ERYorks OE 'open country with doves'.

Duffy, *see* Duffey.

Dufton P Place-name in Westmd OE 'place with doves'. Chiefly a WRYorks surname.

Dug(g)an F Irish, Scots and Manx: **O'** [descendant of] *Dubhagain* (double dim of 'black, dark'). Welsh: shortened form of **Cadogan**.

Dugdale P Place-name: probably *Dagdale*, Staffs OE '*Ducca*'s valley', but chiefly a Lancs surname. *Although Sir William Dugdale (1605–1686), antiquary and herald, was born at Shustoke Rectory in Warwicks, his father was a native of Clitheroe, Lancs.*

Duggan, *see* Dugan.

Duguid N Scots: nickname for a person who meant well OE 'do good'.

Duke N/O Status term for a duke, captain of an army OF, but often used as a nickname for a person exhibiting arrogance; or an occupational term for a someone who worked in a ducal household. In Yorkshire the first-name *Marmaduke* was shortened to '*Duke*'. In principle the surname **Duke** could be confused with **Duck**, though its location is generally different, being found mostly in Sussex and Dorset. Family name of the Barons Merrivale.

Dulwich P Place-name in London OE 'dill meadow'. A very scarce surname, more-or-less confined to London itself.

Dummer P Place-names: *Dummer*, Hants and *Dimmer*, Somerset OE 'pool/mere by a hill'. Strongest in Hants and Sussex.

Duncalf(e) T/N Bardsley admits that he is guessing when he gives the putative meaning of this surname as 'at the dun croft', lamenting the fact that 'a proved solution of the surname is beyond my reading'. For Reaney and Cottle it is 'grey-brown/dun calf' OE. At least the geographical origin of such a name is not in doubt: the first known reference to the **Duncalfs** of Foxwist, Chesh, dates from 1306. The surname also occurs in Staffs in the seventeenth century, but a Chesh origin seems certain.

Duncan/Donkin/Dunkin F Scots and Irish: Anglicized form of Gaelic **Duinnchinn** ('brown warrior'). The diminutive form **Donkin** is a surname of the north-east of England, whereas **Dunkin** is strongest in Kent.

Dungworth P Place-name in WRYorks OE 'enclosure with an underground room/house' (perhaps one lined with dung?).

Dunham P Place-name: Chesh, Norfolk OE 'hill homestead'; Notts OE '*Dunna*'s homestead'.

Dunhill T/P/F Very few surname dictionaries choose to feature this innocuous-looking name. It could refer generally to a dweller near a brown [OE *dun(n)*] hill, though it seems to cry out for a place-name origin. Confusingly, OE *dun* can also mean a hill, giving us 'hill-hill', though it could represent an OE first-name. There is a *Dunhill* near Waterford, Ireland, but **Dunhill** is predominantly a WRYorks surname. *Dunkhill* and *Dunghill Syke*, near Idle in WRYorks, might seem to offer a slight ray of hope here, with their apparently unimpeachable OE origin ('dung hill'), but the first known references to such places date from as late as the nineteenth and eighteenth centuries respectively. *Alfred Dunhill (1872–1959), manufacturer of the pipes and* *tobacco which bear his name, was born in Hornsey, Middx.*

Dunkerton P Place-name in Somerset OW/OE 'hill fort-rock farm', and a Somerset surname.

Dunkin, *see* Duncan.

Dunkley P A surname of uncertain origin, though clearly a place-name is involved: Hanks and Hodges tentatively suggest *Dinckley*, Lancs (which was *Dunkythele* in 1246), British and OE '?fort wood wood/clearing', but by the late nineteenth century this had become predominantly a Northants surname, and the origin there could well be the village of *Dingley*, Northants OE '?wood/clearing marked by one or two valleys' or '*Dynni*'s clearing'.

Dunlop P Scots: place-name near Kilmarnock, Gaelic 'muddy fort'. In Ireland, sometimes a version of **Donle(a)vy**. English speakers tend to stress the first syllable in the surname, while Scots generally render it as 'Dun**lop**'. *John Boyd Dunlop (1840–1921), the inventor of the pneumatic inflatable tyre, was born in Dreghorn, Ayrshire. The first Dunlop tyre factory opened in Dublin in 1889.*

Dunmow P Place-name in Essex OE 'hill meadow', famous for its 'flitch' ceremony, and an Essex surname.

Dunn(e)/Donn(e) N/P Scots/Irish: nickname for a brown, dark, swarthy person, Gaelic *donn*. Scots: from the place-name *Dun*, Angus, Gaelic *dun* ('fort'). English: nickname for a person with dark hair or a dark complexion ME *dunn*. *See also* **Down**. *The metaphysical poet and clergyman John Donne (1573–1631) pronounced his surname as 'Dun'. His family had originated in Radnor, Wales, where the form of their name was originally 'Dwynn'.*

Dunning N/P/F From *Dunn*, used as a first-name or as a nickname, originally applied to a person with dark hair or a dark complexion ME, plus the familiar OE -*ing* ('family of') suffix. Scots: from the place-name *Dunyn* in Perthshire, Gaelic *dunan* ('fort'). Irish: Anglicized form of Gaelic **O'** [descendant of] **Duinnin** ('brown/dark'). But

Desmond Holden points out that in 1432 the sheriff of Norwich was referred to as 'John **Dunning** or **Downing**' (see **Downing**).

Dunnsford, *see* Dunsford.

Dunphy, *see* Donoghue.

Dunscombe P From an unidentified place-name in south-west England OE '*Dunn*'s valley'. A widespread surname, with a significant presence in Glamorgan.

Dun(n)sford P Place-names: *Dunsford*, Devon; *Dunsforth*, WRYorks OE '*Dunn*'s ford'.

Dunsheath N A scarce surname found in Scotland and in Northern Ireland (in Co Tyrone and Co Antrim since the seventeenth century), possibly a variant of the Scottish surname **Dunsleve** ('brown of the hill'). There is a place called *Dunseith* in South Dakota, USA.

Dunstall P Place-name in Lincs, Staffs OE 'homestead', with the same meaning as **Tunstall**, and readily confused with it. Chiefly a Kent/Sussex surname, but also found in Lincs/Staffs. *See also* **Dunster**.

Dunstan/Dunston(e) F/P From the first-name *Dunstan* ME 'hill/dark stone', made popular thanks to St Dunstan, Archbishop of Canterbury (died 988). Or from *Dunstone*, Devon OE '*Dunstan*'s settlement', or from a number of places in various counties with similar names (*Dunstan, Dunston*) but different etymologies.

Dunster P Place-name in Somerset OE '*Dunn*'s tor/hill'. Yet the surname's significant presence in Kent suggests that its origin there might be *Dunstall Wood* OE 'downplace'. See **Dunstall**.

Dunston(e), *see* Dunstan.

Dunwoody, *see* Dinwiddie.

Duparc(q) T Dweller at ('of the') park OF.

Dupont T Dweller at ('of the') bridge OF. *The internationally known Dupont Company was founded in 1802 as a gunpowder mill in Wilmington, Delaware, by Eleuthère Irénée du*

Pont, two years after he and his family had left France in the wake of the French Revolution.

Dupuy T Dweller at ('of the') isolated peak OF.

Duran(d)/Dur(r)an(t) N Nickname for a steadfast or obstinate person OF. Known as a Huguenot name. *The band Duran Duran, formed in 1978, was named after Dr Durand Durand, a character in Roger Vadim's science-fiction film* Barbarella.

Durden N A nickname, literally 'hard-tooth' OF. A scattered surname, strongest in Lancs. Readily confused with/a variant of **Dearden**.

Durham P Place-name in the county of that name (formerly *Dunholm*) OE and ON 'hill peninsula'. Surprisingly widespread as a surname.

Durley P Place-names: *Durley*, Hants; *Durleigh*, Somerset OE 'wild beast wood/clearing'.

Durnford P Place-name in Wilts OE 'hidden/secret ford'.

Dur(r)an(t), *see* Duran.

Dursley P Place-name in Gloucs OE '*Deorsige*'s clearing'.

Durston P Place-name in Somerset OE '*Dear*'s farm' OE, and a Somerset surname.

Durward, *see* Dorward.

Dwell(e)y N Nickname from an OE word meaning 'misled, erring, doting, in heresy'.

Dwerrihouse/Dwerryhouse P Place-name in Lancs OE 'dwarf's house' (a superstitious name for some odd natural feature?). One family of this name migrated from Garston to London in the eighteenth

century, setting up business as high-class clock and watch makers.

Dyball/Dybell/Dyble, *see* Theobald.

Dyce/Dyes P Scots: place-name *Dyce*, Aberdeenshire, Gaelic *deis* 'to the south'. The first recorded instance of a person bearing such a surname (which has continued to be located mainly near its place of origin) is John de *Diss*, admitted burgess of Aberdeen in 1467. *Later* **Dyce**s *include Alexander* **Dyce** *(1798–1869), Shakespearean scholar, William* **Dyce** *(1806–1864), Pre-Raphaelite painter, and General Alexander* **Dyce** *of the Madras Infantry.*

Dye F From the mediaeval female first-name *Dennis* or *Dionysia* (feminine of *Dionysius*). The fanciful suggestion that the origin might be **D'Eye** ('of *Eye*' OE 'island', the Suffolk place), is given at least some credence by the presence of the surname in nearby Norfolk. **Dyson**, chiefly a WRYorks/Lancs surname, is 'son of **Dye**'. *See also* **Tyson**.

Dyer O Occupational term for a dyer OE. The surname **Lister** has the same meaning.

Dyes, *see* Dyce.

Dyke T Dweller by the dike/ditch OE.

Dyment, *see* Damant.

Dymock/Dimmock/Dymoke P Place-name in Gloucs, possibly OW 'pigsty'. **Dymock** and **Dimmock** are both scattered surnames, the former with a presence in Scotland as well as England. The **Dymoke** family of Scrivelsby, Lincs, have been hereditary King's Champions for many generations.

Dymond/Dymont, *see* Damant.

Dyson, *see* Dye.

E

Eachus T Pronounced to rhyme with *teach us*, this gives the appearance of having originally been a house name, perhaps with a first element related to OE 'addition, increase'. Principally a Chesh surname, recorded in the field-name *Eachus Plan* in Minshull Vernon.

Ead(e)(s)/Eakin/Ede(s)/Eed(s) F From a ME female first-name *Eda*, from *Edith*, meaning 'prosperity, happiness'; or (in the north of England and Scotland in particular) from a ME short-form of *Adam*. For **Ede** and Ravenscroft, robe-makers, see **Ravenscroft**.

Eager(s), *see* Edgar.

Eakin, *see* Ead and Richard.

Eames N Nickname derived from an OE word for an uncle (originally a *maternal* uncle only), presumably one who was charged with the upbringing of an orphaned niece or nephew. A south-of-England and Midlands surname. **Yemm**, from a Forest of Dean dialect version of the same word, is mainly a Gloucs surname.

Eardley P Place-name in Staffs OE 'dwelling-place clearing'.

Earl(e)/Hurl(e) O/N Occupational term for a person employed in an earl's household, or a nickname for one who had all the swagger of a person of noble birth, or who played the part of an earl in a pageant. During the first few centuries following the Norman Conquest of 1066, the title of *earl* was applied to a high-ranking official, rather than to a nobleman as such, but the impact of the Conquest can be judged by the fact that the title of an earl is the only one in the peerage which comes from an OE word, the others being French/Latin in origin. *See also* **Earley**. The surnames **Earl** and **Earle** are widespread, as is **Hurl** (which Cottle refers to as 'a thoroughly illiterate' variant); **Hurle** can mostly be found in the south-west.

Earley/Early P Place-name *Earley* in Berks OE 'ploughing-field'. Corrupted to **Early**, though this could alternatively be a variant of **Earl**. On hearing the news that a child born in Wandsworth, London, in 1899 was named '*Gladys Rose* **Early**', contemporaries must have been tempted to remark: 'I'm glad to hear it…'.

Earnshaw/Hearnshaw/Yearnshaw P Place-name *Earnshaw* in Lancs OE 'grove with eagles', though Redmonds says that the **Earnshaw**s of Holmfirth, Yorks, may have had their roots in Chesh. It is not uncommon to find that surnames beginning with the letter 'E' acquire an initial 'Y' both in pronunciation and spelling.

Earwaker/Earwicker F From the ME first-name *Erewaker* ('wild-boar watchman'). Usually pronounced '*Urracker*' or '*Erraker*'. *John Parsons Earwaker (1847–1895), antiquary and author of* East Cheshire, past and present *and other topographical works, was born in Manchester, the son of a local merchant.*

Easdale, *see* Esdaile.

East T A name applied to a newcomer from the east, or to a dweller to the east of a village or town OE.

Eastabrook/Easterbrook T Dweller to

the east of a brook OE. Chiefly a Devon surname in either spelling.

Easter T/P/N Dweller to the east of a village or town ME; or from places so-called in Essex OE 'sheepfold'; or having a particular connexion (time of birth/baptism, etc.) with the festival of Easter, which has an OE pagan name derived from a Germanic goddess of the *east* or dawn, whose festival was at the vernal equinox.

Easterbrook, *see* **Eastabrook**.

Eastham P Place-names in Chesh, Somerset, Worcs OE 'eastern homestead/river-meadow'. Largely a Lancs surname.

Easthaugh T/P Dweller by the eastern enclosure OE, or from a place so-called in Norfolk, with the same meaning. A scarce Suffolk surname.

Easthope/Eastop P Place-name *Easthope* in Salop OE 'eastern valley'.

Eastman/Eastment T/F Dweller to the east of a village or town ME; or from the OE first-name *Eastmund* ('grace protector'), which Thackeray helped to revive in its derivative form *Esmond*. *George Eastman (1854–1932), founder of the Eastman Kodak Company and the inventor of roll film, was born in Waterville, Oneida County, New York.*

Easton P Place-name in a dozen or so English counties. Normally OE 'eastern/east-facing place', or 'to the east of the farm/village'; but *Easton*, Devon, is OE '*Ælfric*'s place'; Great and Little *Easton*, Essex, are OE 'stone(s) by the island', and *Easton* Neston, Northants, is OE '*Eadstan*'s place'.

Eastop, *see* **Easthope**.

Eastwell P Place-name in Kent, Leics OE 'eastern spring/stream'.

Eastwood P Place-names in a number of counties, such as Essex OE 'eastern wood' and Notts (D. H. Lawrence's birthplace) OE 'eastern clearing'.

Easy ?N/P/F A nickname, but of uncertain meaning: ?carefree (ME). Alternative suggestions have included: a place-name such as *Essé*, Ille de Vilaine, France, *Eisey*, Wilts, or *St Issey*, Cornwall; or a corrupted form of the first-name *Isaiah*. A scarce surname, mainly found in Cambs.

Eaton P There are thirty or so places called *Eaton* in about fifteen counties OE 'river/island farm'; *Eton*, Bucks, is OE 'settlement on the river Thames'. Readily confused with/a variant of **Eyton**. Eaton is the family name of the Barons Cheylesmore.

Eave(s)/Eavis, *see* **Eve**.

Ebbetts, *see* **Isabell**.

Eccles P English and Scottish place-name found in Kent, Lancs, Norfolk, Berwick, Dumfries OW/Irish (from Latin) 'church'.

Eccleston(e) P Place-name in Chesh, Lancs (four such) OW/Irish (from Latin) and OE 'church farm' (compare **Eccles**). **Eccleston** is very much a Lancs surname. **Ecclestone**, strongest in Staffs, is less common. *Bernard Charles ('Bernie') Ecclestone, Formula One supremo and Labour Party donor, was born in 1930 near Bungay in Suffolk, though his family moved to Bexleyheath, Kent, when he was a small child.*

Ecott P From an unidentified place-name, the element *-cott* being normally OE 'cottage(s)'. Very scarce, with a limited presence in Gloucs.

Eddis/Edds/Edison/Edson F Derived from a diminutive of one of a number of first-names beginning with *Ed-*. *Thomas Alva Edison (1847–1931), American inventor, was born in Milan, Ohio. His father, a native of Marsalltown, Nova Scotia, came from a family with Dutch origins.*

Eddolls F From an OE first-name with the meaning of 'prosperity/happiness-wolf'. A scarce surname of the south-west counties of England.

Edds, *see* **Eddis**.

Ede, *see* **Ead**.

Eden F/P From the ME first-name *Edun*, with the meaning of 'prosperity-bear cub'; or from a place-name such as *Castle Eden* or

Eden Burn in Co Durham, derived from a British river-name. *Sir Anthony Eden (1897–1977), whose time as Prime Minister of the United Kingdom (1955–1957) was cut short by the Suez Crisis, was a member of the Eden family of Windleston Hall, near Eden Burn in Co Durham, which acquired a baronetcy in 1672.*

Edenbrow P From the place-name *Edinburgh*, Scotland, said to be from the Brythonic *Din Eidyn* ('fort of *Eidyn*'); but alternatively derived from, or confused with, the surname **Attenborough**. Such a surname appears in a number of Lincs parish registers, spelt in a variety of ways: **Edenbrow**; **Edinburgh**; **Eddingborrow**; **Eden Borrough**; **Edenbarugh**; **Edenborough**; **Edenborow**; **Edenborrough**; **Edenborrow**; **Edenburgh**; **Edinbergh**; **Edinborough**; **Edinbourrugh**; **Edinbrough** and **Edinbrow**. Yet although a banns register for Leasingham, Lincs, includes the names of William Allett and Mary **Edenborough**, when the couple married on 29 November 1791, the bride's surname is spelt **Attenborough**. For a detailed study of such surnames, see *Searching for surnames* by John Titford (2002).

Edes, *see* Ead.

Edgar/Eager(s)/Odger(s) F From the OE first-name *Eadgar* ('prosperity/happiness-spear'). **Adair** is a Scots variant. **Edgar** is strong in Scotland, **Eager** in Sussex and **Odger/Odgers** in Cornwall.

Edge T Dweller by a crest, ridge, steep hill OE.

Edge(r)ley, *see* Edgley.

Edgerton, *see* Egerton.

Edgeworth, *see* Edgworth.

Edg(e)(r)ley P Place-name *Edgeley* in Chesh, Salop OE 'park/pasture clearing'.

Edgoose/Etgoose F/N/T A variant on the first-name *Edgar*; or possibly a nickname for a person who enjoyed a nice goose dinner at Michaelmas ('eat-goose')? But did Edward **Edfox** of St John Timberhill, Nor-wich, exempt from paying the Hearth Tax there in 1673/4, really eat foxes? Leslie Dunkling (*Dictionary of surnames*, 1998) contends that **Edgoose** is derived from *edgehouse* (corner house). A late fifteenth-century chancery case involving the executors of William **Edgoos** of Bulwick, Northants, would seem to be the earliest known reference to this surname, but from the early sixteenth century it is most in evidence in Pinchbeck, Lincs, where the splendidly named Goodozia **Edgoose** was baptized in 1617. In more recent times the surname has become settled in Norfolk. Historical variant spellings include **Edgoos**, **Edgoss**, **Edgose**, **Edgoose**, **Edggoose** and **Eatgoose**.

Edg(e)worth P Place-name in Gloucs, Lancs OE 'enclosure on an edge'.

Edington P Place-names: Wilts (with its glorious priory) OE 'wasteland hill'; Somerset OE '*Eadwine*'s place'; Northd OE 'the settlement of *Ida*'s people'; Berwickshire, Scotland OE '?*Hading*'s village' (*Haedentun* in the eleventh century, so compare the Scottish place-name *Haddington*). Principally a surname of northern England and Scotland.

Edison, *see* Eddis.

Edman(s)/Edmand(s), *see* Edmund.

Edmead(e)s/Edmett N Nickname for a good-hearted, humble-minded, gentle person OE. **Edmead** and **Edmett** are both scarce surnames; the former is found mainly in Middx and Surrey, the latter in Kent.

Edmund/Edman(s)/Edmands/ Edmond(s)/Edmondson/Edmunds(on) F/O From the ME first-name *Edmund* ('prosperity/happiness-protector'). *St Edmund* the Martyr, King of the East Angles (841–869), and two other popular Anglo-Saxon kings, gave the first-name an early currency, which *St Edmund* of Abingdon (c.1174–1240) prolonged. Forms with -*o*- are of an OF type; those incorporating the element -*man*- may indicate 'servant of' someone whose first-name began with *Ed*-. **Edmunds/Edmundson** are 'son of

Edmund'. **Edmondson** and **Edmundson** are found chiefly in Lancs. **Edmondson** is the family name of the Barons Sandford.

Edrich/Edridge F From the ME first-name *Edrich/Ederick* ('prosperity/happiness-powerful').

Edson, *see* **Eddis**.

Edward(e)(s)/Edwardson F From the ME first-name *Edward* ('prosperity/happiness-guardian'). Popular thanks to *Edward* the Martyr (962-979) and to *Edward* the Confessor (1004–1066), who preceded St George as patron saint of England. **Edward(e)s** (very common in Wales) and **Edwardson** are 'son of **Edward**'. **Edwardes** is the family name of the Barons Kensington. *See also* **Ewart**.

Edwin(g) F From the ME first-name *Edwine* 'prosperity/happiness-friend'.

Eed(s), *see* **Ead**.

Efford P Place-name in Cornwall, Devon (three such), Hants OE 'ford usable at ebb-tide'. Chiefly a Devon surname.

Egan, *see* **Richard**.

Egerton/Edgerton P Place-name *Egerton* in various counties OE '*Ecghere/Ecgheard*'s place'. *Edgton*, Salop, is 'hill with an edge or brow'. **Egerton** is the family name of the Dukes of Sutherland, the former Dukes of Bridgewater and the Earls of Wilton.

Eggin(g)ton P Place names: *Egginton*, Derbys OE 'the settlement of *Ecga* or his people'; *Eggington*, Beds OE 'oak hill/*Ecca*'s hill'.

Eggleston P Place-name in Co Durham OE '*Ecgwulf*'s settlement'. *See also* **Eggleton**.

Eggleton P Place-name in Herefords OE '*Ecgwulf/Ecgel*'s settlement'. A south-of-England surname, but also found in Norfolk. *See also* **Eggleston**.

Eglinton P Scots: place-name in Ayrshire OE '?*Ægelwine*'s settlement'. A scarce scattered surname, with a presence in Lanarkshire.

Eisda(i)le/Eisdell, *see* **Esdaile**.

Eke P Place-name *Eyke* in Suffolk ON 'oak'. Principally a Norfolk surname.

Eland P Place-name in Northd OE 'island'. A surname of the northern counties of England.

Eld N Nickname for an old person OE *eald*, in south-western dialect, though the surname, a scarce one, is found mainly in the Midlands.

Elder N Nickname for a elder, senior person OE. No connexion with the elder tree.

Eldred, *see* **Aldred**.

Eldridge, *see* **Aldridge**.

Eley F Diminutive of the first-name *Elijah/Elias*. Readily confused with/a variant of **Ely**. Mainly a Derbys surname.

Elford P The place-name *Elford* as found in Northd and Staffs OE '*Ella*'s/elder-tree ford' may be a red herring. *Yelverton* in Devon was formerly *Elleford* (with the same meaning as *Elford*), and the surname is most commonly found in that county and also in Dorset.

Elgar, *see* **Agar**.

Elias/El(l)iot(t)/Elkin(s)/Ellis/Ellison F From the first-name *Elias*, a Greek form of the Hebrew first-name *Elijah* ('Yahweh is God'). The vogue of the first-name was perhaps spread by Crusaders who had been to Mount Carmel. **Eliot(t)** and **Elliot(t)** can be diminutives of **Elias/Ellis**, or of the ME English and Scots first-name *Elyat/Elyt*, or, in Scotland, an Anglicized version of the surname **Elloch/Eloth**, Gaelic *eileach* ('mound, bank'). The **Eliot** family, along with the **Kerrs** and others, were key players in many an English/Scottish border war. **Elliott** is far commoner than **Elliot**, but both are evenly spread throughout England. **Elias**, mainly found in Wales and in Lancs, is much scarcer than **Ellis(s)**, which is a ME variant also popular in Wales, perhaps by fusion with a first-name such as *Elised* (from the Welsh *elus* 'charitable, benevolent'). **Elkin** is found mainly in the south of England, especially Wilts; **Elkins**, more widely scattered, is strongest in the Midlands, especially Staffs. **Elliot** is the family name of the Earls of Minto; **Eliot** is the family name of the Earls of St Germans. *The poet Thomas Stearns ('T. S.') Eliot (1888–1965), born in St Louis, Missouri, was a descendant of Andrew Eliot, a shoemaker from East Coker, Somerset, who emigrated to Boston, Massachusetts, in 1670.*

Eliot(t)/Elkin(s), *see* **Elias**.

Ellen/Ellin(s)/Ellings F From a mediaeval form of the first-name *Helen*, Greek, '?bright'. *St Helen, who is said to have found the True Cross, was the mother of Constantine the Great, and according to legend was the daughter of Old King Cole of Colchester; all this was enough to ensure her a cult in England.*

Ellerbeck P Place-name in NRYorks ON 'alder brook'.

Ellerker P Place-name in ERYorks ON 'alder marsh'.

Ellerman, *see* **Elliman**.

Ellerton P Place-name: ERYorks and NRYorks ON and OE 'alder place'; Salop OE '*Æthelheard*'s place'. Strongest in Staffs.

Ellery ?P/F Cornish: perhaps from the manor of *Elerky* in Veryan, Cornish *elerchy* ('swan's house'); or a variant of **Hilary**.

Elliman/Ellerman O Occupational term for an oil-maker/seller OE. *An appropriate surname, we might say, to be borne by James Elliman, who developed his famous embrocation (still manufactured to this day) while he was running a drapery business in Slough, Bucks, in the 1840s.*

Ellin(s)/Ellings, *see* **Ellen**.

Elliot(t)/Ellis(s)/Ellison/Elloch, *see* **Elias**.

Elm(e)(s) T/P Dweller by the elm-tree OE, or from the place-name *Elm* in Cambs, Somerset, with the same meaning. Compare **Nelms**.

Elmar/Elmer/Elmore P Place-name *Elmer* in Sussex OE 'eel mere/pool'. Readily confused with/a variant of **Aylmer** or **Elmore**.

Elme, *see* **Elm**.

Elmer, *see* **Elmar**.

Elmore P Place-name in Gloucs OE 'riverbank with elms'. Readily confused with/a variant of **Aylmer** or **Elmar**.

Elms, *see* **Elm**.

Eloth, *see* **Elias**.

Elphick F From an OE first-name composed of the elements 'elf/fairy' and 'high'. An uncommon surname, found in Kent, Middx and Surrey. *St Elphick, the Archbishop of Canterbury who was martyred by Danes at Greenwich in 1012, was called 'Alphege' by the Normans.*

Elshaw David Hey recounts a fascinating story as to the origins of this Sheffield surname. He reports that Geoffrey Austin has traced all **Elshaw**s back to William **Elshaw** of the Foundling Hospital in Ackworth, Yorks, an orphan child from London, born on 4 April 1758. Originally named William Collins, he was given the surname **Elshaw** – for reasons that are now lost to us.

Elstob/Elstub P Place-name *Elstob* in Co Durham OE 'elder-tree stump'. *Elizabeth Elstob (1683–1756), the first female scholar to make a major contribution to the study of Anglo-Saxon, was born in Newcastle-upon-Tyne, the daughter of a local merchant.*

Elston P/F Place-name in several counties, including Lancs OE '*Ethelsige*'s farm'; Notts OE '*Ailaifr*'s farm'; Wilts '*Elias (Giffard)*'s farm'. Or from an OE first-name with the meaning of 'old/temple-stone'. A widespread surname, strongest in Devon.

Elstub, *see* **Elstob**.

Elvey F From an OE first-name with the meaning of 'elf-gift'. Chiefly a Kent surname.

Elvin, *see* **Alwin**.

Elward F From an OE first-name with the meaning of 'elf/noble-guard'.

Elwell P Place-name in Dorset OE 'wishing

(literally omen, good luck) well', but most commonly found in Staffs and Worcs.

Elwes F From the OF female first-name *Eloïse*, Germanic 'hale/healthy-wide'. *Héloïse* was the doomed love of Abélard. *John Elwes (c.1730–1789), Member of Parliament and nephew of Sir Harvey Elwes, was the best known of a family of notorious misers who had made their fortune in the brewing business in Southwark, London. He walked everywhere in all weathers, slept under hedges, ate maggot-infested meat and wore a manky wig that had reputedly been thrown into a ditch by a beggar.*

Elwin, *see* Alwin.

Elwood F From an OE first-name with the meaning of 'elf-ruler'.

Elwyn, *see* Alwin.

Ely P Place-name in Cambs (the former Isle of Ely) OE 'eel district'. Readily confused with/a variant of **Eley**.

Em(m)anuel F From a Hebrew first-name meaning 'God with us'. A rare scattered surname in either spelling, with a presence in South Wales. *When it was deemed appropriate that the dress worn by Diana Spencer at her wedding to the Prince of Wales in 1981 be designed in the Principality itself, the task was entrusted to David Emanuel (born in Bridgend in 1952) and his wife Elizabeth.*

Emberson/Ember(r)y/Embry/Emerson/Emery, *see* Amery.

Emm(s)/Emmet(t)/Emmot(t)/Imm(s)
F/P From *Emma*, a Germanic feminine first-name cut down from some double-name with a first element *ermin-* or *irmin-* ('whole/universal'). Popularized by the daughter of Duke Richard I of Normandy, wife of King Ethelred the Unready, and later of King Canute. **Emmet(t)** and **Emmot(t)** are diminutives, though **Emmot(t)** can also be from a place-name in Lancs OE 'stream-meeting, confluence'. There are references to an **Emmott** family in the Colne area of Lancs as early as the thirteenth century (Redmonds).

Emmanuel, *see* Emanuel.

Emmerson, *see* Amery.

Emmet(t)/Emmot(t)/Emms, *see* Emm.

Emory/Empson/Emson, *see* Amery.

Endacott/Endicott P Place-name in Devon OE 'beyond the cottages'.

Enfield P Place-name in Middx OE 'open country with lambs'. *Harry Enfield, British comedian, was born in Sussex in 1961; his father, Edward Enfield, is also something of a media star in his own right.*

England P From England OE 'the country of the Angles' (and the Saxons, etc., for that matter), who came from an *angle*-shaped area of Holstein. 'A curiously uninformative surname for use in England' (Cottle). A widespread surname, with a strong presence in WRYorks.

Englefield P Place-name in Surrey OE '*Ingweald*'s field'. A surname of the southern counties of England.

English/Inglis(h) P 'English' OE; formerly referring to Angles as opposed to Saxons, but by surname times denoting an Englishman living among borderers (Welsh, Strathclyde Welsh, Scots), or in the old Scandinavian areas of the north, or in intensely Normanized districts; or one who had returned from being so-nicknamed in France or elsewhere. As to **Inglis(h)**, Cottle says: 'Scots form of **English**, with Scots disregard of any English sensibility about the initial; a far better spelling, since *eng* had by surname times turned into *ing* (as in *string* for earlier *streng*); **Inglis** is frequent for unaccented **Inglish** in Scots'. In the event, while **Inglis** is a surname found principally in Scotland, **Inglish** (very scarce) belongs mainly to England itself. **English** is a widespread surname, particularly in evidence in Co Durham and Northd.

Ennion, *see* Onion.

Enright/Enwright F Irish: Anglicized form of Gaelic **Indreachtach** ('attacker').

Enwright is a variant made to look like a 'wright' (craftsman).

Ensor P Place-name *Edensor* (pronounced 'Ensor') on the edge of the Chatsworth House estate in Derbys OE 'Eadhun's ridge'. The surname has a presence in Derbys, but is most commonly found in Warwicks.

Entissle, *see* Entwisle.

Entwis(t)le P Place-name *Entwisle*, Lancs OE 'land at a river-fork with waterhens/ ducks'. Found in Ireland as **Entissle**.

Enwright, *see* Enright.

Equall N Nickname for an equable person, an equal/peer, Latin *aequalis*. A very scarce surname, with a presence in Gloucs.

Erith P Place-names: *Erith*, Kent and *Earith*, Hunts OE 'gravelly landing-place'.

Erridge P Place-name *Eridge*, Sussex OE 'eagle ridge'.

Erskine P Place-name in Renfrewshire, Scotland. Etymology (Celtic) uncertain; said by Johnston to be 'projecting height'. A surname long borne by aristocratic Scottish families.

Erwin, *see* Irvin.

Esbester, *see* Isbister.

Escombe P Place-name in Co Durham OE 'at the parks/pastures', exhibiting the use of a dative plural after a lost preposition.

Escott P Place-name *Escot*, Devon OE 'eastern cottage'.

Esdaile/Easdale/Eisda(i)le/Eisdell/ Esdale/Eskdale/Isdale/Isdell P Place-names: *Eskdale*, Dumfries; *Eskadale*, Inverness, Celtic and OE 'dale of the river *Esk* (literally "water"; compare the rivers Exe, Axe and Usk, and the word *whisk(e)y*). 'Not likely to be from *Easdale* in Argyllshire' (Black). Just to confuse matters, a male-line ancestor of Sir James **Esdaile**, Lord Mayor of London in 1778, was a French Protestant who fled to England following the revocation of the Edict of Nantes in 1685.

Esdale, *see* Esdaile.

Esh P Place-name in Co Durham OE 'ash tree'; or a variant of **Ash**. A scarce Co Durham/Yorks surname.

Eskdale, *see* Esdaile.

Eskell, *see* Ashkettle.

Eskridge/Eskrigg P Place-name *Eskrigg* in Lancs, or possibly *Escrick*, NRYorks. George **Eskridge**, a wealthy early eighteenth-century Virginia lawyer in whose honour George Washington was reputedly named, came from a family named **Eskrigg** which had long been settled in the village of Over Kellet, Lancs. The surname is now very rare in England, but still has its main presence in Lancs.

Esmond(e), *see* Eastman.

Espley P There is a place in Northd called *Epsley Hall* OE 'aspen wood/clearing', which was *Es(s)peley/Aspele* in the thirteenth century, but the place-name *Espley* in Salop, with the same meaning, is more likely to be the source of this predominantly Staffs surname in most cases.

Essam, *see* Isham.

Essex P From the English county of *Essex*, the area where the East Saxons originally lived OE. The surname is most commonly found in Gloucs and Warwicks.

Esslemont P Place-name in the parish of Ellon, Aberdeenshire, a Scots Gaelic version of British '?low hill' (the hill in question being 219 feet high) or '?spell/incantation hill'.

Etheredge/Attridge/Etheridge F From an OE first-name meaning 'noble-rule'.

Etheridge, *see* Etheredge.

Eubank, *see* Ewbank.

Euden P Place-name in Co Durham, Northd OE 'yew valley'.

Eustace/Eustice/Eustis F From a first-name derived from Greek, meaning 'fruitful'. The more famous of two *Saints Eustace* is a patron saint of hunters, having been converted by a stag with a crucifix in its horns. England nearly had a *Bad King Eustace*, Stephen's son, but 'Christ would not have it that he should rule long', says the Peterborough chronicler. The genealogist Derek Palgrave has pointed out that the first element in a name like **Eustace** can appear as *Eue, Ewa, Ew, Ewe, You, Yow, Eau, U, Ui, Yoi, Yu* and *Yui*. Your current editor and his wife live in a house called *Yew Tree Farm*, but get letters addressed to *Ewe Tree Farm* and *U Tree Farm*, so I know what he means. **Eustace** is widely scattered; **Eustice** belongs to Cornwall, and **Eustis** is a very rare Glamorgan surname.

Evans F '(Son) of *Evan*', one of the Welsh forms of **John** (another of which gave rise to the equally popular surname **Jones**). It is possible that *Evan* sometimes absorbed the Romano-British first-name *Eugenius* 'well-born'. See **John** and **Heaven**.

Evatt, *see* Evett.

Eve(s)/Eave(s)/Eavis F/T Adam called his wife *Eve* 'because she was the mother of all living', says the Book of Genesis, but her name may have meant either 'lively' or 'serpent' in Hebrew. **Eves** and **Eaves** can be 'son of *Eve*', but either form could refer to a dweller near a rim, edge or border (compare the 'eaves' of a house) OE *efes*, used especially for the skirts of a wood. Each spelling of the surname has its own distinctive pattern of distribution, being found chiefly in the following counties: **Eve** (Essex, Middx); **Eves** (Kent); **Eaves** (Lancs); **Eavis** (scarce, widespread). *Trevor Eve, the English television and film actor, was born in Birmingham in 1951.*

Eve(r)le(i)gh/Everl(e)y P Place-names: *Everleigh*, Wilts OE 'wild-boar wood' OE; *Evelegh* (a now lost place in Broad Clyst), Devon OE 'ivy wood'. *Isaac Donald ('Don') Everly (born in Brownie, Kentucky, in 1937) and Phillip ('Phil') Everly (born in Chicago, Illinois, in 1939), who achieved fame in the world of popular music as the 'Everly Brothers', spent their formative years in Iowa.*

Evemy/Ivimey F From a female Greek first-name, meaning 'auspicious speech'. In the apocryphal *Acts of Peter*, *Euphemia* is one of Agrippa's four concubines, converted and martyred; a saint of the name was martyred in Bithynia in the fourth century. Scarce in either form: **Evemy** can be found in Dorset/Hants and **Ivimey** in Essex. *Joseph Ivimey (1773–1834), Baptist minister and historian, was born in Ringwood, Hants.*

Everard/Everatt/Everett/Everhard/Everitt F From a Germanic first-name *Everhard*, with elements meaning 'wild-boar' and 'hard'. Mostly introduced into England after 1066, but an OE form may have contributed. **Everett**, the commonest spelling within this group, is mainly found in East Anglia, and is particularly strong in Essex and Middx. *Everard's Brewery in Leics acquired its name in 1849, when Thomas and William Everard joined Thomas Hull in leasing Southgate Brewery, Leicester, from Wilmot & Co.*

Everatt, *see* Everard.

Everden(e) T/P Dweller at a wild-boar hill OE; or from the place-name *Everdon*, Northants OE 'wild-boar valley'. *Bathsheba Everdene was the heroine of Thomas Hardy's novel* Far from the madding crowd.

Everest P From the place-name *Evreux* in Normandy (compare **Deveraux**). The famous surname has travelled from Normandy to Nepal via Britain.

Everett, *see* Everard.

Everhard, *see* Everard.

Everill, *see* April.

Everitt, *see* Everard.

Everl(e)y, *see* Evelegh.

Evershed N Nickname from OE 'boar's head' – perhaps for a person who lived at a dwelling bearing such a sign. A scarce surname, with a presence in Sussex.

Everton P Place-name in Berks, Lancs, Notts OE 'wild-boar place'.

Eves, *see* Eve.

Evett/Evatt/Evitt F A diminutive of the first-name *Eve*.

Ewan/Ewen F The exact origin here has been much argued over. Most probably from a Greek first-name meaning 'well-born', and thus equivalent to *Owen* and the Arthurian knight *Ywain*; the Greek original was much transformed in its passage through Celtic, whence emerge Scottish, Irish and Welsh forms. Can sometimes (?) be from a Welsh form of **John** (as are **Evans**, **Jones**, etc.). **Youens** is 'son of **Ewan**'.

Ewart F/O/P From an OF version of the first-name *Edward*, or an occupational name for a shepherd ME *ewehirde*, or from a place-name in Northd OE 'enclosure on a river'.

Ewbank/Eubank T Dweller at a hillside with yews OE. *Christopher Livingstone ('Chris') Eubank, the lisping and fashion-conscious former boxing champion, who was born in Dulwich, London, in 1966, spent his early years in Jamaica. He dropped the final 's' of his Eubanks surname when he signed for Barry Hearn in 1989.*

Ewen, *see* **Ewan**.

Ewer(s) O Occupational term for a water-bearer OF (compare French *eau*), the servant who brought basins of water for guests to wash at table between courses. **Ewer** is most commonly found in Herts and Middx, **Ewers** in Essex and Middx.

Ewhurst P Place-name in Hants, Surrey, Sussex OE 'yew wood'.

Excell, *see* **Exell**.

Exelby P Place-names: *Exelby*, NRYorks; *Asselby*, ERYorks ON '*Askell*'s farm'. Principally a Yorkshire surname, it had nevertheless reached Cornwall by the 1600s – and stayed there.

Ex(c)ell P There are two places named *Exhall* in Warwicks OW and OE 'church nook'. **Excell** is principally found in Kent; **Exell** is widespread, with a particular presence in Gloucs.

Ex(t)on P Place-name *Exton* in: Rutland OE '?ox farm'; Hants OE 'East Saxons' place'; Devon OE and Celtic 'place on the (river) *Exe*'.

Eye P Place-name in several counties OE 'island'. A very scarce widespread surname.

Eynon, *see* **Onion**.

Eyre(s), *see* **Ayer**.

Eyton P There are two places so-named in Salop OE 'place on a river'. Readily confused with/a variant of **Eaton**.

Ezard, *see* **Isard**.

F

Faber O Occupational term for a smith, from Latin. Reinforced in England by the arrival of persecuted Huguenots from the late seventeenth century onwards.

Fabian F From a Roman family name derived from Latin, with the meaning of 'bean', and the name of a sainted third-century pope. An uncommon surname, strongest in Hants.

Facey, *see* **Vaisey**.

Facitt, *see* **Fawcet**.

Fage N Nickname derived from a ME word meaning 'flattery, coaxing, deceit'. A very scarce surname, found in Middx.

Fagg O? A surname of uncertain origin; a fishmonger or baker? Very much a Kent surname.

Fahey/Fahy F Irish: Anglicized form of Gaelic **O'** [descendant of] **Fathaigh**. Readily confused with/a variant of **Fay**. *John (Aloysius) Fahey (1939–2001), the influential guitarist and composer, was born in Washington DC, USA. His main inspiration came not from his Irish roots, but from American blues and folk music.*

Fair N Nickname for a handsome, pretty person OE.

Fairbairn(e) N Nickname for a lovely child OE, but possibly also a variant of **Freeborn**. Readily confused with/a variant of **Fairbourn**.

Fairbank(s) P From a minor place-name found in various counties OE and ON 'lovely/fern hillside(s)'. **Fairbank** is found mainly in WRYorks; **Fairbanks** is strongest in Staffs. Readily confused with/a variant of **Firbank**. *Douglas Fairbanks (1883–1939), the American actor, director and producer, was born Douglas Elton Ullman in Denver, Colorado, of a part-Jewish father and a Roman Catholic mother, Ella Adelaide Marsh. Fairbanks was the surname of his mother's first husband and of his half-brother, John Fairbanks.*

Fairbourn/Fairburn P Place-names: *Fairbourne*, Kent; *Fairburn*, WRYorks OE 'stream in the ferns'. *Fairburn*, Ross and Cromarty, Scotland (*Ferburny* in 1527) is Gaelic 'over the wet place'. Readily confused with/a variant of **Fairbairn**.

Fairbrass, *see* **Firebrace**.

Fairbrother/Farebrother N Nickname for a person who was considered to be the fairer/fairest of brothers, or who had a fair or handsome brother. Even, sometimes, 'father's brother' (that is, an uncle who was responsible for the upbringing of his deceased brother's children) OE. **Fairbrother** is chiefly a Lancs surname; **Farebrother**, much scarcer, can be found in Surrey.

Fairburn, *see* **Fairbourn**.

Fairchild N Nickname for a handsome child OE.

Faircliff(e)/Faircloth/Fairclough T/P Dweller at a pleasant ravine OE, or from an unidentified place-name with the same meaning. **Fairclough** is common in Lancs, and most if not all bearers of this surname would seem to belong to a family group which held land in Ormskirk as early as the fourteenth century. '**Faircloth** occurs aptly as the surname of a draper at Stromness, Orkney' (Cottle).

Fairfax N Nickname for a person with lovely (but not necessarily blond) hair OE. *Thomas Fairfax, third Lord Fairfax of Cameron (1612–1671), the parliamentary army officer, was born in Denton, Yorks, and educated – like many a northern gentleman of his generation – at St John's College, Cambridge.*

Fairfield T/P Dweller in a beautiful field OE, or from a place-name with this meaning in Derbys. *Fairfield* in Worcs is OE 'pig field' (compare the word 'farrow'). Strongest in Warwicks. For Cicily Isabel **Fairfield** (Dame Rebecca West), see **West**.

Fairford/Fairfoot N/P Nickname for a person with a handsome foot OE; or (in principle) from the place-name *Fairford* in Gloucs OE 'clear ford' – though the surname **Fairford**, surprisingly scarce, is found mainly in Lancs. **Fairfoot**, also scarce, can be found in WRYorks.

Fairfoul(l)/Fairfull N Nickname from OE 'pretty bird'. Scarce Scottish surnames.

Fairhead N Nickname for a person with a handsome head OE. An Essex/Norfolk surname.

Fairhurst T/P Dweller in a pleasant copse/wooded hill OE, or from a place in Lancs with this meaning.

Fairlie/Fairlee/Fairless/Fairley P In *The surnames of Scotland* G. F. Black deals separately with the surnames **Fairley** and **Fairlie**, but it would seem likely that these are one and the same, derived from the place-name *Fairlie* in Ayrshire OE 'beautiful wood/clearing'. A Scots family named De Ros acquired the surname **Fairlie** when they were granted land in that place by Robert Bruce. The fact that there is a *Fairlie* in the Isle of Wight with this meaning may well be an irrelevance. **Fairlee** is very scarce and scattered; **Fairley** and **Fairlie** belong principally to Scotland, and **Fairless** is almost exclusively a Co Durham/Northd surname. Confusion with the surname **Farley** should perhaps not be discounted?

Fairman N Nickname for a handsome man OE; but can be confused with **Farman**.

Fairweather N Literally 'bright, calm weather' OE; perhaps used to describe a person's temperament, or from a greeting he was fond of using. Compare **Merryweather**. A scattered surname, strongest in Angus, Scotland. *The guitarist and songwriter Andy Fairweather Low, a founder member of the British pop band Amen Corner, was born in 1946 in Ystrad Mynach, Hengoed, Wales.*

Faithful(l) N Nickname for a devout, sincere, loyal person OF and OE. Very much a Hants surname in either spelling. *A significant contingent of Faithfulls from Hants and Berks served as officers in the Bengal Army in the early nineteenth century… Marianne Faithfull, singer and actress, born in Hampstead, North London, in 1946, is the daughter of a Major Robert Glynn Faithfull, military officer and college professor, and Baroness Eva Erisso, originally from Vienna, who had both Jewish and noble roots from the Hapsburg Dynasty.*

Falcon O/N Occupational term for a falconer OF, or a nickname for a person who resembled a falcon in some way. Compare **Faulkner**, and see **Falk**.

Falconar/Falconer, *see* **Faulkner**.

Falder/Faulder/Folder O Occupational term for a person who worked at (sheep-)folds or pens OE. Readily confused with/a variant of **Faldo**, to which it is related etymologically. **Falder** (a scarce surname found in places as far apart as Cumbd and Herts) retains the long *ā* of OE, while **Folder** (even more scarce, with a slim presence in Cumbd) has a long *ō*. **Faulder** is a Cumbd/Westmd variant.

Faldo P Place-name in Beds OE 'promonontory of land with a fold upon it'. Formerly a Beds surname, and a taxation return for Higham and Faldo in that county made in 1297 includes the name of Andrew de Fald(o), who was assessed for half a quarter of wheat (20d), two bushels of beans and peas (9d), one mare (4s) and one heifer (3s). Families called **Faldo** living in Goldington and Oakley, Beds, are featured in Heralds' Visitations of the seventeenth century, though by the late nineteenth century this had become a very scarce surname, with a presence in Kent and Surrey. Readily confused with/a variant of **Falder**, to which it is related etymologically. *Nicholas Alexander ('Nick') Faldo, the English golfer (originally a carpet fitter), was born in 1957 in Welwyn Garden City, Herts.*

Falk/Faulk(e)s/Faux/Fawk(e)s/ Fewkes/ffolkes/ffook(e)s/ffoulk(e)(s)/ Fo(a)kes/Folk(e)(s)/Fook(e)(s)/ Foulk(e)(s)/Fowke(s)/Fulk/Fulkes/ Fulks/Voak/Voke(s)/Vokins/Volk(e)s F From a Norman first-name which took forms such as *Fulco, Fouques,* etc. ('folk, people'). Whence many surnames, including some with *F-* voiced to *V-,* and even the Welsh first-name *Ffwc.* Some variants may be derived from a Germanic first-name, through OF *Fauques* ('falcon'), or have been applied to a falconer. As to **ffolkes/ ffooks/ffoulkes** and the like (the '*ff*' sometimes represented by '*Ff*'), Cottle says: 'There is nothing superior about the typographical absurdity of putting *ff* for initial *F,* an old mediaeval manuscript habit'. *Peter (Michael) Falk, the American actor with one glass eye, best-known for his portrayal of Columbo, the detective whose shabby clothes and awkward manner masked a razor-like mind, was born to a Jewish family in New York City in 1927... Guy Fawkes (c.1570–1606), Gunpowder Plot conspirator, was born in York, where the Fawkes family had long had a strong presence.*

Falkiner/Falk(e)ner/Falknor, *see* **Faulkner**.

Fa(u)lk(i)ner/Fa(u)lconar/Fa(u)lconer/ Fa(u)lkiner/Fa(u)lk(e)ner/Fa(u)lknor/ Fawkner O Occupational term for a hawker, falconer, keeper/trainer of falcons OF. The *-l-* is a pedantic restoration from Latin, and is not pronounced. 'Cranedriver' is another possible meaning here; Reaney cites a 1257 carpenter who made a *faucon* ('crane/windlass') to be worked by *falconarii. The American novelist William Faulkner (1897–1962), born in Mississippi, came from a family called Falconer, from Inverness, Scotland, who changed their surname to Faulkner and then to Falkner. The novelist resurrected the extra letter 'u' for his own use.*

Fall(s)/Faull T/N 'Dweller by a waterfall, a fall in the ground, a place with felled trees' OE. **Faull** is mostly found in Cornwall, where it might alternatively be a nickname from Cornish *fall* ('fail, fault, deficiency'), or refer to a dweller at a place where beeches grow (Cornish *faw-la*).

Faller P Place-name *Fawler* in Berks, Oxon OE 'tessellated (Roman) pavement', one such having been found in a Roman villa near *Fawler,* Oxon, in 1865. A widespread but scarce surname, found in Lancs, Middx and elsewhere.

Fallon F/O Irish: Anglicized form of Gaelic O' [descendant of] **Fallamhain** ('leader'); or a variant of **Fuller**.

Fallow(e)(s) T/N Dweller by newly cultivated land OE; or a nickname for a person with tawny hair ME *fallow*.

Fallowfield P Place-name in Lancs, Northd OE 'ploughed/harrowed/fallow/brownish field'. A northern surname, commonest in Lancs and Westmd.

Fance, *see* **Venn**.

Fane N Nickname for a glad, eager, well-disposed person OE. **Vane** is a south-of-England form, with the *F-* voiced. 'An Old English lexicon will reveal no initial *V-,* and any word or name in Modern English beginning with *V-* will be either an importation (mostly from French and Latin) or a southern (including south-western and south-eastern) dialect form of this kind' (Cottle). **Fane** is the family name of the Earls of Westmorland, and **Vane** of the Barons Barnard.

Fann, *see* **Venn**.

Fant/Faunt N Nickname from the OF word *enfant* (English *infant*), with the first element omitted. A scarce surname, with a presence in Lancs, Lincs and Middx. The '*u*' in **Faunt** goes some way towards imitating the French nasal sound.

Farebrother, *see* **Fairbrother**.

Farenden, *see* **Farrington**.

Farewell, *see* **Farwell**.

Fargher, *see* **Farquar**.

Faringdon, *see* **Farrington**.

Farleigh, *see* **Farley**.

Farley/Farleigh P Place-name in several counties OE 'clearing with ferns'. See also **Varley**. Farley is widespread; **Farleigh**, much scarcer, belongs to Devon, where there is more than one settlement of this name. Potentially confused with **Fairlie** and its variants? *Farley's rusks were originally developed in the 1850s as a nutritious biscuit for the children of poor families by Edwin Farley, who had a baker's shop in Plymouth, Devon.*

Farlow P Dweller at a fern hill OE. An uncommon but widespread surname.

Farman O Occupational term for a traveller, hawker, pedlar ON. Chiefly a Norfolk/Suffolk surname. Readily confused with **Fairman**.

Farmborough P Place-name in Somerset OE 'fern mound/hill'; or a variant of **Farnborough**. A scarce Middx/Surrey surname.

Farmer O Occupational term for a tax-collector, steward, bailiff OF – not an English word, and 'not of the present sturdy meaning' (Cottle). **Fermor** is a Kent/Sussex variant.

Farnall, *see* **Farnill**.

Farnborough P Place-name in Berks, Hants, Kent, Warwicks OE 'fern mound/hill'; or a variant of **Farmborough**. A very scarce Bucks/Middx surname.

Farncombe P Place-name in Surrey, NRYorks OE 'fern valley'. A scarce Gloucs surname.

Farndon, *see* **Farrington**.

Farnell, *see* **Farnill**.

Farnes T/P Dweller by the ferns, bracken OE, or from an unidentified place with this meaning. No apparent connexion with the seventeen Farne Islands off the Northd coast. A scarce Sussex surname.

Farnham P Place-name in seven counties OE 'homestead/river-meadow in the ferns'; but *Farnham* in Northd is OE '(at) the thorns' (dative plural).

Farnill/Farnall/Farnell T/P Dweller at a fern hill OE, or from a place-name (*Farnhill*, *Fernhill*) with the same meaning in eight counties. There are places called *Farnell* in Kent and Wilts.

Farnley P Place-name (two such) in WRYorks OE 'clearing with ferns'.

Farnorth, *see* **Farnworth**.

Farnworth/Farnorth P Place-name *Farnworth* (two such) in Lancs OE 'fern enclosure'. A Lancs surname in both spellings.

Farqu(h)ar N Scots Gaelic: 'very dear one'. **Farqu(h)arson** is 'son of **Farqu(h)ar**'. **Fargher** is a Manx form.

Farqu(h)arson, *see* **Farquar**.

Farr N Nickname derived from an OE word meaning a 'bull', used for a sturdy or fierce man. A widespread surname, strongest in Middx.

Farrah, *see* **Ferrar**.

Farran/Farrance, *see* **Farrant**.

Farrant(s)/Farran/Farrance/Farren/ Farrin N/F Nickname for a person with grey hair, or who wore grey clothes OF *ferrant*; or from the mediaeval first-name *Fer(r)ant*, probably an OF version of *Ferdinand*. But *Hill Farrance*, Somerset, is named after a Norman landowner *Faron* OF 'pilferer, ferret'.

Farrar, *see* **Ferrar**.

Farren, *see* **Farrant**.

Farrer/Farrey, *see* **Ferrar**.

Farrin, *see* **Farrant**.

**Farrington/Farenden/Far(r)ingdon/
Farndon** P These apparently similar surnames can have their origins in different
place-names: *Farrington Gurney* OE 'farm in
the ferns' in Somerset; *Farringdon* OE 'fern
hill' in Devon; *Faringdon* OE 'fern/bracken
hill' in Berks, Dorset, Hants, and Oxon (*Little Faringdon*); *Farndon* OE 'fern hill' in
Chesh, Notts and Northants (two such).
Farringdon in London, originally the Ward
of Ludgate and Newgate, was named after
two successive Aldermen, William **de Farndon** (1278–1293) and Nicholas **de Farndon**
(1293–1334).

Farrow, *see* Ferrar.

Farthing N/F Nickname for a person who
paid a farthing OE in rent, or who occupied a
quarter ('fourth thing') of a virgate of lane –
that is, up to thirty acres OE; or from an ON
first-name *Farthegn* ('traveller').

Farwell/Farewell P/N Place-name *Farewell*
in Staffs OE 'beautiful spring/stream'; or a
nickname for a person who fared well (prospered), or whose favourite exclamation was
'Fare (thee) well!'. **Farwell** is found principally in Dorset; **Farewell**, much scarcer, has
a presence in Kent.

Fatheringham, *see* Fotheringham.

Fat(t) N A nickname (simple, unequivocal)
for a fat person OE. **Fat** is a very scarce surname; **Fatt**, slightly less scarce, can be
found in Middx.

Faucett, *see* Fawcet.

Faulconar/Faulconer, *see* Faulkner.

Fauld(s), *see* Fold.

Faulder, *see* Falder.

Faulk(e)s, *see* Falk.

Faull, *see* Fall.

Faunt, *see* Fant.

Faux, *see* Falk.

Fa(u)vel(l)/Favill N Nickname for a person
with a tawny, fawn complexion OF, or for
one who was given to flattery, insincerity or

intrigue OF *favele*, from Latin *fabella* 'little
yarn, fable'.

**Fawcet(t)/Facitt/Faucett/Fawcit(t)/
Forsett/Fossett** P Place-name *Fawcett* in
Westmd OE 'varicoloured hillside'. The
place-name *Facit*, near Rochdale, Lancs
(with the same meaning?), may be too
late to have given rise to a related surname.
The dialectal and American word *faucet* (a
tap) would appear to have no relevance
here. These are predominantly northern
surnames, **Fawcett** being the commonest
variant; **Facitt**, very scarce, can be found
in Lancs.

Fawdon P Place-name (two such) in
Northd OE 'varicoloured hill', and a Northd
surname.

Fawkes, *see* Falk.

Fawkner, *see* Faulkner.

Fawks, *see* Falk.

Fawn N Nickname derived from OF 'cub,
young fallow deer'. Chiefly a Lincs surname.

Fay/Fey T/P/N/F Dweller by a 'beech-tree'
OF, or from a place-name in France with
that meaning; or a nickname for a person
with supernatural powers OF *faie* ('fairy') or
who was reliable, trustworthy OF *fei* ('loyalty'). Irish: from **O'** [descendant of] **Fay**
('raven'). Readily confused with/a variant
of **Fahey**.

Faza(c)kerley/Phizacklea P Place-name
Fazakerley, Lancs OE 'border-field-wood';
for the '*a(c)ker*' element, compare the
word *acre*.

Feak(e)s, *see* Fitch.

Fear(s) N Nickname for a person who was
proud ME *fere* ('proud') or sociable ME *fe(a)re*
('comrade'). No real connexion with the
present-day word 'fear'. **Fear** is found
mainly in Gloucs, **Fears** in Sussex.

Fearing, *see* Fearon.

Fearn(e), *see* Fern.

Fearnehough, *see* Fernyhough.

Fearnley, *see* **Fernley**.

Fearnyhough, *see* **Fernyhough**.

Fearon/Fearing O Occupational term for a smith OF. Compare **Faber**, **Feaver**, **Ferrar**. **Fearon** is a Cumbd surname; **Fearing** is a very scarce variant.

Fears, *see* **Fear**.

Feather(s) N/O/P Nickname for a lightweight person (in body or character) – or even one who chose to wear feathers?; or an occupational term for someone who traded in feathers OE. An abbreviation of the surname **Featherstone** is not beyond the realms of credibility, and some Yorkshire **Feathers** even choose to believe that their name is derived from *Feizor* in the West Riding ON '*Fech*'s shieling' (*Fech* may have derived his name from Irish *Fíach*, whence, ultimately, the French word for a cab, *fiacre* – since Paris hackney-men first parked their cabs outside the church of *St Fiacre*). *Victor Grayson ('Vic') Feather (1908–1976), Baron Feather, trade union leader, was born in Bradford, Yorks.*

Featherston(e) P Place-name *Featherstone* in Northd, Staffs, WRYorks OE 'cromlech, tetralith' (literally 'four-stone': three uprights and a capstone). *See also* **Featherstonhaugh**.

Featherston(e)haugh P Original form of the place in Northd now called simply *Featherstone* (see **Featherstone**), the 'haugh' element carrying the meaning of 'nook'. One of the longest of all English surnames, commonly pronounced '*Fanshaw*'.

Feaver O Occupational term for a smith OF *fevre*. Compare **Faber**, **Fearon/Fearing**, **Ferrar** and **Offer**, and French surnames such as **Le Fever** and **Lefe(b)vre** (commonly pronounced '*Lefever*' in England), which were often brought to England by Huguenots. Chiefly a Kent surname.

Feilden, *see* **Fielden**.

Feilding, *see* **Fielding**.

Felgate, *see* **Fieldgate**.

Felix F From a mediaeval first-name derived from Latin 'lucky, fortunate'. A name used by popes and by the apostle of the East Angles. 'The surname may also owe something to the feminine version *Felicia*; but the male first-name was killed by a film cat' (Cottle). A scarce Middx/Surrey/Cardiganshire surname.

Fell T/O Dweller by a fell, mountain ON. Chiefly a northern surname (found especially in Lancs), but in other areas it could be derived from OE 'skin, hide', used as an occupational term for a person who dealt in such products (a fellmonger) – compare the word 'pelt'. Chiefly a Lancs surname. *Dr John Fell (1625–1686), Bishop of Oxford, born in Longworth, Berks, was immortalized in the ditty which begins: 'I do not love thee Dr Fell…'*

Fellow(e)s N Nickname for a partner, companion ON, or for a fellow/member of a trade guild. Reaney also refers to an intermediate form **Fel(t)house** (still in existence as a scarce Staffs surname) from **Fieldhouse**. **Fellowes** is the family name of the Barons Ailwyn and de Ramsey.

Felste(a)d P Place-name *Felsted*, Essex OE 'site in a field'; the surname **Felsted** is mostly found in that county, but **Felstead** is more common in Leics and Middx.

Feltham P Place-name in Somerset OE 'hay meadow' and in Middx OE 'field homestead'. Strongest in Wilts.

Felthouse, *see* **Fellowes** and **Fieldhouse**.

Felton P Place-name in various counties OE 'place in a field'.

Femister/Phemister/Phimister O Occupational term for a 'fee-master' OE and OF – that is, a shepherd, cowherd. A scarce Scottish surname in all spellings.

Fenby P Place-name in Lincs OE and ON 'fen farm'. *Eric Fenby (1906–1997), the musicologist who spent five years of his life working in the capacity of an amanuensis to the blind and paralysed composer Frederick Delius, was born in Scarborough, Yorks.*

Fender O Occupational term/nickname for

a defender OF; compare the 'fender' which 'defends' a fire and the American 'fender', which protects an automobile. A surname which is widespread throughout England, Wales and Scotland, strongest in Lancs and Northd.

Fenelon, *see* Fenlon.

Fenemore/Fenimore, *see* Finnemore.

Fen(e)lon F/P Irish: Anglicized form of Gaelic **O'** [descendant of] **Fionnalain** (the first element meaning 'white, fair'). A family of this name were chiefs in Co Westmeath before the 1100s, but the name is now found mostly in Co Carlow and Co Wexford. Bearers of this surname who are of English stock may be descendants of Huguenots called **Fénelon** who fled France following the revocation of the Edict of Nantes in 1685, and were named from a place so-called in the Dordogne.

Fenn, *see* Venn.

Fennell O Occupational term for a grower or seller of fennel OE, a plant used in medicine and cookery. But Reaney also shows that a couple of landowners called **Fitzneal** ('son of *Neal*') were respelt as *Fennel* and the like.

Fenner, *see* Venn.

Fennimore, *see* Finnemore.

Fenton P Place-name in several counties OE 'place in a fen'. *See also* **Venton**.

Fenwick P Place-name in Northd (two such), WRYorks and Ayrshire, Scotland OE 'dairy-farm in a fen'. Usually pronounced '*Fennick*'. One Northd border family of **Fenwick**s had its own repeated slogan or rallying-cry '*A Fenwyke!*', and a hectic record of fray and reprisal against the Scots. The surname **Phoenix** is simply **Fenwick** dressed up in unfamiliar garb – just as **Pharaoh** is a variant of **Ferrer**.

Ferber, *see* Frobisher.

Fergus(s)/Fergus(s)on F Irish and Scots Gaelic first-name with the meaning 'man force'. **Fergus(s)on** is 'son of *Fergus*'.

Fermor, *see* Farmer.

Fern/Fearn(e) T Dweller at the fern(s), bracken OE.

Ferneyhough, *see* Fernyhough.

Fernley/Fearnley P Place-name *Fernley* in WRYorks OE 'clearing with ferns'.

Fern(e)yhough/Fearnehough/Fearny-hough/Fernihough T/P Dweller at a hollow with bracken OE, or from *Fernyhalgh* OE 'bracken enclosure' in Fulwood, Lancs.

Fernival, *see* Furnival.

Ferrar/Farrah/Farrar/Farrer/Farrey/Farrow/Ferrer/Pharaoh/Varah O Occupational term for a smith, ironworker OF; compare the surnames **Faber**, **Fearon/Fearing** and **Feaver**, the French word *fer* ('iron') and the English word *farrier*. See also **Ferrier** and **Ferry**. **Varah** is a surname of WRYorks. **Pharaoh** (very scarce, with a presence in Hants and Lancs) is perhaps as exotic a variant of **Ferrar** as **Phoenix** is of **Fenwick**. *The American actress Mia Farrow (Maria de Lourdes Villiers-Farrow), born in Los Angeles, California, in 1945, is the daughter of John Farrow, an Australian film director, and the Irish actress Maureen O'Sullivan… Kathleen Mary Ferrier (1912–1953), well-known contralto, was born in Walton-le-Dale, Lancs.*

Ferrier O Occupational term for a ferryman ON (with an *-er* suffix); or a variant of **Ferrar** or **Ferry**.

Ferry T Dweller at a ferry ON, or a variant of **Ferrar** or **Ferrier**. Mainly a Co Durham surname. *The singer and songwriter Bryan Ferry, who achieved fame as lead vocalist with Roxy Music in the 1970s, was born in Washington, Co Durham, in 1945.*

Fettiplace O Occupational term for an usher, one who would shout: 'Make room! Give place!' OF. A scarce Notts surname.

Fewkes, *see* Falk.

Fewsdale/Fusedale P Place-name *Fusedale* in Westmd ON 'cattle-shed ("fee-house") valley'. Examples of both **Fewsdale** and

Fusedale spellings can readily be found in parish registers over several centuries, and such records suggest that these have been mainly Yorks surnames. By the time of the 1881 census, however, although **Fewsdales** can be found in WRYorks, there was a mere handful of **Fusedale**s, recorded only in Middx.

Fewster O Occupational term for a maker of saddletrees OF. Or a variant of **Forster**. A north-of-England surname.

Fewtrell O Possibly from an occupational term for a keeper of hounds, or for one who managed them in the chase ME *veuterer* from OF. A surname found mainly in Salop.

Fey, *see* **Fay**.

ffinch, *see* **Finch**.

ffisk(e), *see* **Fish**.

ffitch, *see* **Fitch**.

ffolkes/ffook(e)s, *see* **Falk**.

fforde, *see* **Ford**.

ffoulk(e)(s), *see* **Falk**.

ffrench, *see* **French**.

ffytche/Fick, *see* **Fitch**.

Fiddes P Place-name in Aberdeenshire, Scotland, Scots Gaelic 'wood stance/resting-place', and chiefly an Aberdeenshire surname.

Fiddian, *see* **Vivian**.

Fiddler, *see* **Fidler**.

Fiddy, *see* **Fido**.

Fidge, *see* **Fitch**.

Fidgeon, *see* **Fitzjohn**, **Fitch** and **Vivian**.

Fidget(t), *see* **Fitch**.

Fid(d)ler O/N Occupational term or nickname for a fiddle-player OE. Readily confused with/a variant of **Vidler**.

Fido(e)/Fiddy N Nickname for a person fond of exclaimimg 'Son of God!' OF 'fitz Dieu'. **Fido** (now hopelessly compromised

by its association with a 'pet'-name for a dog?) is widespread, found particularly in Somerset and Wilts; **Fidoe** is a scarce West Midlands surname; **Fiddy** belongs mainly to Norfolk.

Field(s) T Dweller at a field, cultivated land, but especially open country OE, a common place-name element in areas that had been wooded. Compare **Fielden**, **Fielder** and **Fielding**. **Delafield** OF and OE 'of the field' is a known variant. It had to happen: a child born in West Derby, Lancs, in 1908, gloried in the name of *'Paddy* **Fields***'*.

Fielden/Feilden T Dweller in open country, in the fields OE dative plural in -*um* after a lost preposition. Compare **Field** and **Fielder**. **Fielden** is by far the commoner spelling, but both are Lancs surnames. Readily confused with/a variant of **Fielding**.

Fielder T/O Dweller in the fields/open country OE, or one who worked in such a place. Compare **Field**, **Fielden** and **Fielding**. Found chiefly in coastal counties of southern England.

Fieldgate/Felgate T/P Dweller at a gate OE or on a road ON into a field/open country. *Felgate* is a place-name in Worcs; *Fell Gate*, possibly ON 'fell, hill', is in Co Durham. Far-from-common East Anglian surnames, **Fieldgate** being found mainly in Essex, **Felgate** in Suffolk.

Fieldhouse/Felthouse T Dweller in a house in a field/open country OE. A Staffs surname in both spellings, though **Fieldhouse** (much the commoner of the two) is strongest in WRYorks.

Fielding/Feilding T A field-dweller OE. Compare **Field** and **Fielder**. Chiefly surnames of the north of England. Readily confused with/variants of **Fielden**. *Henry Fielding (1707–1754), the novelist, is descended from a family originally named Feilding/Fieldeng/Fyilding, Earls of Denbigh and Desmond.*

Fields, *see* **Field**.

Fiennes P Place-name in Pas-de-Calais, Germanic plus a suffix: 'flat open country'. Generally pronounced *'Fines'*. The **Fiennes**

ancestry of the family of Twistleton-Wykeham-**Fiennes** (Barons Saye and Sele) reputedly extends back to Giles **Fiennes** of *Fiennes*, Artois, who settled in England during mediaeval times. The explorer Sir Ranulph **Fiennes**, third baronet (born 1944) belongs to this family, as do the actor brothers Ralph **Fiennes** (born 1962) and Joseph **Fiennes** (born 1970).

Fife, *see* **Fyfe**.

Filer O Occupational term for a person who files or makes files OE *fil* plus *-er* suffix; or a spinner OF *fil* ('thread'). By the seventeenth century the word had come to mean 'pickpocket'. Chiefly a Somerset surname.

Fillary/Fillery N Nickname for a royal bastard, or for a person adopting royal manners above his station OF 'son of the King'. Compare **Fitzroy**. Kent/Surrey/Sussex surnames.

Fillingham P Place-name in Lincs OE 'homestead of *Fygla*'s people'.

Filmer/Fil(l)more, *see* **Finnemore**.

Finbow P Place-name *Finborough* in Suffolk OE 'woodpecker hill', and a Suffolk surname.

Finch/ffinch/Fink N/O Nickname for a person bearing some resemblance to a finch OE, a bird which had a reputation for stupidity in the Middle Ages; or an occupational term for a person who caught finches and sold them as song-birds or to make up a (modest) pie. In Chaucer, *to pull a finch* meant 'to swindle a simpleton', and this may suggest one meaning for the nickname. In mediaeval times a London family called **Finck** left their name in both St Benet **Fink** church and **Finch** Lane, but more recently the surname **Fink** has been brought to Britain by German Jews. **Finch** is a widespread surname, strongest in Lancs, Middx and Surrey. *See also* **Pink**. *Peter (Frederick George) Finch (1916–1977), actor, was born in Cromwell Road, London. At his birth registration his father was named as Captain George Ingle Finch, an Australian scientist, but it emerged later that Peter was the son of Major Wentworth 'Jock' Campbell, whom his mother*

married following a divorce from George Finch in 1920.

Fincham P Place-name in Norfolk OE 'homestead frequented by finches'.

Finchley P Place-name in Middx OE 'clearing/wood with finches'. A very scarce scattered surname.

Findlater/Finlater/Finlator P Scots: place-name *Findlater* in Banffshire, Gaelic 'white hillside'. The *-d-* in **Findlater** is excrescent, and **Finlater** is nearer the original. 'A preposterous family belief exists that it denotes former holdings as far as the "world's end" (French *fin de la terre*)' (Cottle).

Findlay/Findley/Findlow, *see* **Finlay**.

Findon P Place-name in Sussex OE 'woodpile hill'.

Fine N Nickname for a refined, delicate person OF.

Finer O Occupational term for a refiner of precious metals ME.

Fink, *see* **Finch**.

Finlater/Finlator, *see* **Findlater**.

Finlay/Findlay/Findley/Findlow/Finley/Finlow F From the Scots first-name *Fionnlagh*, meaning 'fair hero'. The *-d-* in **Findlay/Findley/Findlow** is excrescent, but Reaney shows that it was used in Scotland as early as c.1060. **Finlayson** is 'son of **Finlay**'.

Finley/Finlow, *see* **Finlay**.

Finn F English: from the ON first-name *Finnr*; Irish (also **Finnegan**): Anglicized form of Gaelic **O'** [descendant of] **Fionn** ('white/fairheaded').

Finnegan, *see* **Finn**.

Finnemore/Fenemore/Fe(n)nimore/Filmer/Fil(l)more/Finnimore/Fyn(a)more/Phillimore/Phin(n)imore F From a Norman personal name, *Filimor*, Germanic *filu* and *mari* 'very famous'. The surname has taken a bewildering range of forms over the years, no fewer than 122 of which are listed in *Memorials of the family of Fynmore* (1886), compiled by the well-known genealogist W. P. W. Phillimore. A family group of **Phillimore**s, descendants of the advocate Joseph **Phillimore** (1775–1855), became well known in London legal circles from the early nineteenth century onwards. *James Fenimore Cooper (1789–1851), the prolific American writer, was born in Burlington, New Jersey, the twelfth son of William Cooper, a judge and member of Congress, and his wife Elizabeth (née Fenimore), who had married in Burlington on 12 November 1774.*

Firbank T/P Dweller at a woodland hill OE; or from a place-name with this meaning in Westmd. Strongest in Co Durham. Readily confused with/a variant of **Fairbank**.

Firebrace/Fairbrass N A nickname for a man with a proud/fierce arm OF *fier bras*. **Firebrace** is an exceptionally rare surname; the 1881 census features only two individuals with such a name, one in Kent and one in Surrey. Yet it survived: during the Second World War, Sir Aylmer Newton George **Firebrace** (1886–1972), born in Southsea, Hants, was director of London's fire-fighting brigades. **Fairbrass** is a slightly less scarce surname, found mainly in Kent. *Henry Firebrace (1619–1690/1), a loyal supporter of the Stuart kings Charles I and Charles II, and who eventually became a member of the latter's royal household, lies buried in the Lady Chapel of the parish church of Stoke Golding, Leics.*

Firminger, *see* **Furminger**.

Firth T Dweller in woodland OE. Reaney shows how the OE word (which should in principle have developed into *firghth*) was corrupted through misspelling of its spirants, and metathesis of the *-r-*, into such forms as **Freak(e)**, **Fright**, **Frith**, **Fryd** (a very scarce Lancs surname) and **Thrift**.

Fish/ffisk(e)/Fisk(e) O/N Occupational term for a catcher or seller of fish OE; or a nickname for a person bearing some (far-fetched?) resemblance to a fish. **Fisk(e)/ffiske** are ON forms. **Fish** is a widespread surname, strongest in Lancs. *Michael Fish, the*

popular television weather forecaster who in 1987 famously failed to predict a hurricane which duly arrived and devastated southern counties of England, was born in Eastbourne, Sussex, in 1944.

Fishbourne/Fishburn(e) P Place names: *Fishburn* (Co Durham), *Fishbourne* (Sussex, Isle of Wight) OE 'fish stream'. A rare surname, whatever the spelling; **Fishbourne** is widespread, **Fishburn** is found mainly in the north of England.

Fisher O/T Occupational term for a fisherman OE with an *-er* suffix. But the surname is found everywhere, even inland, and references can be found to individuals bearing the name '**de** or **atte Fisher**' which must suggest a fishery of some sort.

Fisherton P Place-name (two such) in Wilts OE 'fishermen's place'.

Fishlock T Dweller at a fish-garth or fish-weir OE, an enclosed piece of river for the easy taking of fish. A south-of-England surname, commonest in Wilts.

Fishwick P Place-name in Lancs OE 'dairy-farm where fish was sold'. 'The effect on the milk is not recorded' (Cottle).

Fisk(e), *see* **Fish**.

Fison/Fyson F Bardsley takes such a surname to mean 'Son of *Fye*', which he suggests could be a pet form of the popular female first-name *Felicia*, though to Rev. Henry Barber it is derived from *Fusi*, a diminutive of *Vigfus*. Very few other compilers of surname dictionaries feature **Fison** or **Fyson** at all. A strongly Cambs/Suffolk surname. *The Fison family, millers and manufacturers of fertilizers and chemicals, traces its origin back to James Fison (1735–1806), born at Langham, near Bury St Edmunds, Suffolk, who began life as a baker.*

Fitch/Feak(e)s/ffitch/ffytche/Fick/ Fidge/Fidgeon/Fidget(t)/Fitchet(t) ?O The exact meaning of this surname has long been a subject of debate. It probably has some connexion with an OF term meaning 'point, lance, spear', and may refer to a man whose job involved the use of an iron-pointed tool of some sort. Reaney rejects the long-held theory that the origin was the English word *fitch*, meaning a fitchew or polecat, since such a term is not known to have been used until the sixteenth century. Early evidence of the surname's existence suggests an East Anglian origin. **Fidget(t)**, **Fidgeon** and **Fitchet(t)** are diminutive forms.

Fitchew, *see* **Fitzhugh**.

Fitter ?O Possibly an occupational term for someone who set things up, made them ready; even a joiner or carpenter. Not a known ME word, and even the verb *to fit* is very late, but persons are called *le fittere* in the twelfth and thirteenth centuries in Warwicks, Glos and Cambs. The jury is still out on this one. In more recent times, a Warwicks surname.

Fitz- It is a common misconception that surnames beginning with **Fitz-** indicate the founder's illegitimacy. Such is not the case, though the prefix does distinguish recent royal bastards.

Fitzgerald F 'Son (OF) of *Gerald*'. *Gerald*, Constable of Pembroke, married Nest, Princess of Wales; their line settled in Ireland, where the surname multiplied, and is the family name of the Dukes of Leinster.

Fitzgibbon F 'Son (OF) of *Gibbon*'. A common Irish surname.

Fitzhugh F 'Son (OF) of *Hugh*'. **Fitchew** is a very scarce Surrey variant.

Fitzjames F 'Son (OF) of *James*'. The principal family bearing this surname is descended from an illegitimate son of King James II.

Fitzjohn/Fidgeon F 'Son (OF) of *John*'. It is a common misconception that this and several other **Fitz-** surnames indicate the founder's illegitimacy. Such is not the case, though the prefix does distinguish recent royal bastards.

Fitzmaurice F 'Son (OF) of *Maurice*'.

Fitzpatrick F 'Son OF of *Patrick*'; or rather, 'son of the devotee of (Saint) **Patrick**' (as also with **Kilpatrick**).

Fitzroy N 'Son of the King' OF; if meant seriously, this must imply illegitimacy. Compare **Fillary/Fillery**. **Fitzroy** is the family name of the Dukes of Grafton, who are descended from a liaison between King Charles II and Barbara Villiers, Duchess of Cleveland and so qualify, alongside many others, as 'Right Royal Bastards'.

Fitzsim(m)on(s) F 'Son (OF) of *Simon*'.

Flack ?N A surname of unknown origin, though it is sometimes said to be a variant of **Flagg**. It may refer to a person who 'flacked' or 'flapped' about, being dressed in scruffy clothes. An East Anglian surname.

Flagg P Place-names: *Flagg*, Derbys and *Flags*, Notts OE *flage*/ON *flaga* ('slab') or ON *flag* ('turf, sod, peat-cutting') – though the surname, which is scarce, can be found in Somerset and elsewhere, but not in Midland counties.

Flaherty F Irish: Anglicized form of Gaelic **O'** [descendant of] **Fhlaithbheartaigh** ('bright ruler'). Compare **Laverty** and see **McLarty**.

Flamstead/Flamsteed/Flamstede P
Place-name in Herts OE 'refuge place'. The surname had established a modest but significant presence in both Northants and Warwicks during the sixteenth century, and can be found in Derbys in the early 1600s. By the late nineteenth century, **Flamstead** and **Flamsteed** had become very scarce surnames, while **Flamsted** was effectively non-existent. *John Flamsteed (1646–1719), the first Astronomer Royal, was the son of a Derby maltster, but was born in the neighbouring village of Denby, whence his family had moved during the Civil War.*

Flanagan F Irish: Anglicized form of Gaelic **O'** [descendant of] **Flannagain** ('Ruddy'). *Bud Flanagan (1896–1968), the comedian and singer best known for his partnership with Chesney Allen, was born Chaim Reuben Weintrop in Hanbury Street, London, the son of Polish immigrants.*

Flanders P A person from *Flanders* OF, from Flemish 'submerged land'. *Michael (Henry) Flanders (1922–1975), the actor and lyricist known principally for his musical partnership with Donald Swann, was born in Hampstead, London. His daughter Stephanie Flanders (born 1968) is a television presenter with a particular expertise in economics.*

Flann(er) O Occupational term for a flan/pancake/custard-pie maker OF; a German surname **Pfannkucher** ('pancakemaker') is known to exist. A very scarce Warwicks surname.

Flannery F Irish: Anglicized form of Gaelic **O'** [descendant of] **Flannghaile** ('red-valour').

Flash/Flasher/Flashman/Flask T Dweller by a pond, marsh ME, from OF or Dutch.

Flatman/Flatt T/O Dweller on level ground OE. The fact that a Norfolk village is named Newton *Flotman* OE *flotman* 'ferry-man, sailor, pirate' might be food for thought here, though *Floteman* appears as a personal name in Domesday Book, 1086. A Norfolk and Suffolk surname.

Flaxman O Occupational term for a dresser or seller of flax OE.

Fleet P/N Place-name in various counties OE 'creek, estuary'; or a nickname for a swift runner ('fleet of foot') OE (compare **Flett**).

Fleetwood P From an unidentified place-name OE 'wood on a stream/estuary' – but not the town in Lancs, which acquired its name in 1836 from its founder, Sir Peter Hesketh **Fleetwood**.

Fleming/Flemming P A Fleming, a man from *Flanders* OF, Normanized. Various places as far apart as Canterbury and South Pembrokeshire were home to Flemish weavers and the like, but the surname has a healthy presence in Lancs, and is fairly common in Scotland, especially in Lanarkshire.

Flesher O Occupational term for a butcher, a flesh-hewer OE. Cottle notes: 'Still the nor-mal word for *butcher* on Scots facias; the English mincingly prefer *meat purveyor* (is 'mincingly' an intended pun?). Readily confused with/a variant of **Fletcher**.

Fletcher O Occupational term for a maker or seller of arrows OF. Readily confused with/a variant of **Flesher**. Particularly common in Lancs and WRYorks, but also in Derbys and Notts (where there would have been plenty of business opportunities for fletchers in Sherwood Forest…).

Flett P/N A surname of the Orkneys, seemingly from a place-name in Delting, Shetland ON 'strip of arable land'; or a nickname for a person who was swift of foot ON (compare **Fleet**). A scarce Banffshire/Orkney surname.

Fletton P Place-name in Hunts OE 'place on a river' (the Nene).

Flinn, *see* **Flynn**.

Flint T/P Dweller near a flint outcrop OE; or from the place-name *Flint*, in the old Welsh county of that name.

Flintham P Place-name in Notts OE 'flinty homestead'.

Flintoff/Flintoft P From an unidentified place OE and ON 'house-site where flints are found'. The surname is found above all in the Yarm district of NRYorks; the surname **Flinton**, from the place of that name in ERYorks OE 'flint farm/village', which occurs with some frequency in the same area, may be a variant. *Andrew Flintoff MBE, the England cricketer known as 'Freddie' because of perceived similarities between his surname and that of Fred Flintstone, was born in Preston, Lancs, in 1977.*

Flinton, *see* **Flintoff**.

Flippance, *see* **Philip**.

Flitton P Place-name in Beds OE '(on) the streams', exhibiting the use of a dative plural after a lost preposition.

Floater O Occupational term for a mariner OE *flota* ('boat, fleet') with an added suffix. A very scarce ERYorks surname.

Flockton P Place-name near Huddersfield, WRYorks ON and OE *'Floki*'s settlement'. Very largely a WRYorks surname, with a strong presence at Rothwell; migration has carried it to Chesh/Lancs, Sheffield, Derbys and London. The very limited number of **Flocktons/Flogdens** found throughout the centuries in Norfolk probably derive their name from a settlement which lies west of Ipswich, Suffolk; originally *Flochetuna* (1086) and *Floketon(e)* (1201–1357), it eventually lost its guttural and became *Flowton*. Listed together with the nearby settlement of Somersham in the 1327 Subsidy Returns for Suffolk as *Floketone*, it was proably responsible for the surname/byname borne in that year by Nicholao **de Floketon**, who was then living in Sudbury.

Flood T Dweller by a stream or gutter OE; or a variant of the Welsh **Lloyd**. In Ireland, often a translation of **Tully**.

Flook/Fluck/Flux F From an ON first-name *Flōki* ('outspoken'). Yet why would a surname with ON origins be most commonly found in Gloucs? A stray Mr **Fluck** ran a small provisions shop at the bottom end of Portugal Place, Cambridge, in the 1960s. *Diana Dors (1931–1984), the voluptuous actress, was born Diana Mary Fluck in Swindon, Wilts.*

Flower O/N Occupational term for an arrow-maker OE *flā*, plus an *-er* suffix; or for a miller, a maker of flour ME (*flower* and *flour* having once been the same word); or a nickname from ME *flo(u)r* ('flower, blossom'), commonly used as a term of endearment. Strong in the West Country, especially Somerset. Family name of the Viscounts Ashbrook. A man with the unfortunate name of '*Colly* Flower' was married to Rebecca Block at St George, Hanover Square, London, on 1 September 1796.

Flowerdew/Flowerday The exact origin of these Norfolk surnames remains a mystery. Bardsley believes that **Flowerday** could be a nickname, or of local origin, possibly introduced from the Low Countries.

Given the fact that the name *Floure-dieu* appears in Norfolk records in 1541, it is hardly surprising that other scholars have toyed with the idea that the origin may be *fleur de dieu* OF 'flower of God' – an odd expression which may not get us very far. Cottle is not happy with such theories, nor with the idea of 'dew on flowers', nor, really, with his own suggestion that there might be a connexion with Modern French *à fleur d'eau* 'at water level', despite the fact that so much of Norfolk can be thus described.

Floyd, *see* **Lloyd**.

Fluck, *see* **Flook**.

Fludger An uncommon surname of uncertain meaning, which by the late nineteenth century was restricted mainly to Kent. Possibly a variant of **Fulcher/Fulger**, by metathesis? Or of the Scottish surname **Fledger**? Or of **Floodgate**, a dweller by, or keeper of, a flood-gate OE *flodgeat* (a Kent/Middx/Surrey surname)?

Flunder N Nickname from a flatfish, flounder ME; 'a ship was so named in 1319, but it is hard to see why a person should be' (Cottle). A very scarce Beds/Kent surname.

Flux, *see* **Flook**.

Flynn/Flinn F Irish: Anglicized form of Gaelic **O'** [descendant of] **Flhoinn** ('ruddy'). Compare **Lynn**. *Errol Flynn (1909–1969), the actor best known for his starring role in many a swashbuckling movie, was described by the Hollywood publicity department as a 'Mad Irishman', an 'Elegant Englishman' and a 'Bold American'. In fact he was an Australian, born in Hobart, Tasmania, where his father was a university professor.*

Foakes, *see* **Falk**.

Foden/Fowden P From a now-lost placename *Fodon* in Chesh OE 'colourful/variegated hollow'; common in Chesh as a place-name element and in Chesh and Lancs as a surname. *The Foden Truck Company, which was first established in Sandbach, Chesh, in 1856, was founded by Edwin Foden.*

The company produced its last truck in July 2006.

Fogarty/Gogarty F Irish: Anglicized form of the Gaelic first-name *Fogartach* ('banished').

Fogg T/O/N Dweller by rank, tall grass ME (probably of ON origin); or an occupational term/nickname for a person who grazed cattle on grass of this kind. Found as a surname in Norfolk in the sixteenth century, but now belonging chiefly to Lancs.

Fokes, *see* Falk.

Fold(e)(s)/Fauld(s) T/O Dweller at, or worker at, an animal fold or pen OE.

Folder, *see* Falder.

Foldes/Folds, *see* Fold.

Foley F Irish: Anglicized form of Gaelic **O'** [descendant of] *Foghladha* ('pirate, plunderer'). Readily confused with/a variant of **Folly**.

Foljambe N Nickname for a person with a withered or crippled ('foolish') leg OF. Usually pronouced *'Fullgerm'*. Family name of the Earls of Liverpool.

Folk(e)s, *see* Falk.

Foll N Nickname for a foolish person OF; **Follet(t)** and **Folli(o)tt** are diminutives ('little fool'). *Gilbert* **Foliot**, *Bishop of London (c.1110–1187) was Becket's arch-enemy.*

Follet(t), *see* Foll.

Folley, *see* Folly.

Folli(o)tt, *see* Foll.

Folly/Folley ?P Cottle toys with the idea that this surname might refer to a folly (some capricious building or plantation) OF, and is here following Bardsley, who makes reference to Henry, Roger and Richard **de la Folye** of Wiltshire, featured in the Hundred Rolls, 1273. However, given the fact that the surnames **Folly** and **Folley** both belong mainly to Cornwall, in some instances the origin may well be the place-name *Fowey* in that county, named after the river (Old Cornish 'beech river')

on which it stands. Admittedly, the fact that early forms of the place-name, such as *Fowy* (1301), do not correspond with 'Folly', and that the usual pronunciation of the place-name is *'Foy'* doesn't serve to advance the case… Readily confused with/ a variant of **Foley**.

Fook(e)s, *see* **Falk**.

Foord, *see* Ford.

Foot N Nickname for a person suffering from some deformity of the foot OE or ON. Sufferers so-named seem to have lived chiefly in south and particularly south-western counties of England, especially Dorset. *Michael Foot, English politician and former leader of the Labour Party, was born in 1913 in Plymouth, Devon; his father, Isaac Foot, had been Liberal Member of Parliament for Bodmin, Cornwall.*

Footman O Occupational term for a servant on foot, a pedestrian (who couldn't afford a horse), or a foot-soldier OE. A scarce Middx/Surrey surname.

Forbes P/F Scots: place-name in Aberdeenshire, Gaelic 'field' with Pictish suffix *-ais*. The place-name is pronounced with two syllables, as was the surname (compare *Fettes*, *Geddes*) until more recent times. Irish: Anglicized form of Gaelic **Mac Fearbhisigh** ('man-prosperity'). **Forbes** is the surname of the family holding the premier Scottish barony, and of the Irish Earls of Granard.

Ford(e)/fforde/Foord/Forder/Forth T/P Dweller by a ford OE; there are many places simply called *Ford*, and *'ford'* is an element in several English place-names. **Forde** exhibits the use of a dative after a lost preposition. As to **Forth**: the development from *-rd* to *-rth* is in general late ME and north-country, and there would appear to be no connexion here with the Scots river so-named. Why does it come as no surprise to learn that a member of a **Forth** family, born in Eye, Northants, in 1847 or so, was called *'Sally* **Forth**'? *Gerald Rudolph Ford (1913–2006), thirty-eighth President of the United States, was born in Omaha, Nebraska.*

Originally named Leslie Lynch King, Jr, he later acquired the name of his stepfather, Gerald Rudolff [sic] Ford; young Gerald was only informed of the true circumstances of his birth when he was seventeen years old, and didn't change his name legally until 1935… Henry Ford (1863–1947), founder of the Ford Motor Company, was born on a farm near Detroit, Michigan, the son of an American mother with Belgian origins and a father from County Cork, Ireland.

Fordham P Place-name in Cambs, Essex and Norfolk OE 'homestead by a ford'.

Fordyce P Place-name in Banffshire, Scotland, Gaelic 'land to the south'.

Foreman, *see* Forman.

Forest/Forrest T/O Dweller/worker/official in a forest OF, a wooded area reserved as a royal hunting-ground. **Forest** (uncommon) and **Forrest** (much more common) are both widespread surnames, but particularly strong in Lancs.

Forest(i)er/Forrester O Occupational term for a forester, gamekeeper OF, or an official in charge of a forest (a wooded area reserved as a royal hunting-ground). Reaney cites the perquisites of one *forestarius* – Christmas log, wind-felled timber, and acorns/mast for his pigs. Or a variant of **Forster** or **Foster**.

Forman/Foreman O/N Occupational term/nickname for a keeper of pigs, a swineherd OE (compare **Forward**); or a leader of a group OE 'front man' (compare the modern term *foreman*).

Formby P Place-name in Lancs ON 'old farm' or '*Forni*'s farm'. *George Formby, Jr (1904–1961), the music-hall entertainer who was born George Hoy Booth in Wigan, Lancs, took his father's stage name and made it his own.*

Forrest, *see* Forest.

Forrester, *see* Forester.

Forsdick/Forsdyke, *see* Fosdick.

Forse, *see* Foss.

Forsett, *see* Fawcet.

Forsey, *see* Fursey.

Forster T/O A dweller/worker in a forest OE; or an occupational term for a shearer, cutler, scissors-maker OF, or a worker in wood OF. Or a variant of **Fewster**, **Forester** or **Foster**. Principally found in the northeast of England.

Forsyth F/P Scots: from a Gaelic first-name meaning 'man of peace'. But there was also a place of approximately this name, evidenced by people called *de Forsith* in the fourteenth century.

Fortescue/Fortesquieu N Nickname for a valiant warrior OF (literally 'strong shield'). Compare the word *escutcheon*.

Forth, *see* Ford.

Fortman N Nickname for a man with strong hands OF. A very scarce scattered surname.

Fortnam/Fortnum N Nickname for a person whose physical prowess exceeded his intelligence OF (literally 'strong young donkey'). A scarce surname, found in Herts and Northants. *By the early eighteenth century a family of Fortnums, originally from Oxford, had established themselves as high-class builders in London, benefiting from the aftermath of the Great Fire of 1666. William Fortnum took a post as footman to Queen Anne, and in 1705 became a lodger in a house owned by Hugh Mason, who had a small shop in St James's Market. Two years later the two men established the well-known firm of Fortnum and Mason.*

Forty P Place-name in Middx, Wilts, Worcs OE 'projecting island, peninsula' (usually in marshy ground). Mainly a Gloucs surname.

Forward/Forwood O Occupational term for a swineherd OE; note that a sow giving birth to a litter of pigs is said to be *farrowing*. Compare **Forman**.

Fosbery/Fosbury P Place-name *Fosbury* (two such) in Wilts OE 'fort on a roof-like hill' or 'chieftain's fort'. *Richard Douglas ('Dick') Fosbury, the American high-jump* *champion who gave his name to the 'Fosbury flop', was born in Portland, Oregon, in 1947.*

Fosdick/Forsdick/Forsdyke/Fosdyke P Place-name *Fosdyke* in Lincs ON (or OE) and '*Fot*'s ditch' OE.

Foss(e)/Forse/Voss P From a place called *Foss(e)* OE, or which included this element. Places called *Foss(e)* in Warwicks (four such), Wilts (two such) and Lincs are near the Roman road called the '*Fosse* Way' OE, from Latin; others are named after the river *Foss* in Yorks. No connexion with ON *fors/foss*, a waterfall, has been established. **Foss** is a surname found chiefly at the south-west end of the Fosse Way; **Fosse**, very scarce, has a presence in Jersey, and **Voss**, scattered, is strong in Leics.

Fossett, *see* Fawcet.

Foster N/O Nickname for a foster-child/foster-parent OE; or a variant of **Forester** or **Forster**. But **Foster** Lane, in the City of London, commemorates *Saint Vedast/Vaast*, Bishop of Arras.

Fothergill P Place-name in WRYorks ON 'ravine where fodder could be got'.

Fotheringham/Fatheringham P Place-name *Fothringham* in Angus, Scotland, which was called *ffodryngay* in 1261, and is apparently named after *Fotheringhay*, Northants, which is probably OE 'island for foddering/grazing'. A Scottish surname in both spellings.

Foulk(e)(s), *see* Falk.

Fountain T/P Dweller at a fountain, spring OF, or from one of a a number of a place-names in France, variously spelt.

Fouracre/Foweraker T Dweller on a four-acre holding of land OE. A scarce surname in both spellings; **Fouracre** can be found in Somerset, and **Foweraker** in WRYorks.

Fowden, *see* Foden.

Foweather N Nickname from OE 'dirty weather', applied to a person with a sullen temperament, or to one who used such a term as a favourite greeting. **Fouweather,**

listed by Cottle, seems not to have survived into modern times; **Foweather**, very scarce, can be found in WRYorks.

Foweraker, *see* Fouracre.

Fowke(s), *see* Falk.

Fowle/Fuggle(s)/Vowell(s)/Vowels/Vowles N/O Nickname for a person who resembled a bird in some way, or an occupational term for one who caught birds OE. The surname **Fuggle(s)** (compare the German word for a bird, *vogel*) is closer to the OE form.

Fowler O/N Occupational term/nickname for a bird-catcher, fowler OE with an -*er* suffix; *fowl* denoted a bird of any kind, not just the barnyard and game types.

Fox N Nickname for a person resembling a fox OE (sly, red-haired?). There is no evidence for its having its origins in a sign-name. **Fox** would also seem to have assimilated surnames of the **Faulk(e)s** or **Foulk(e)(s)** variety. Strongest in Lancs. *Charles James Fox (1749–1806), Whig politician, was born in London; his distinctly Stuart first-names bear witness to the fact that through his mother he was a direct descendant of King Charles II... George Fox (1624–1691), founder of the Religious Society of Friends ('Quakers') was born in Drayton-in-the-Clay (later Fenny Drayton), Leics.*

Fox(h)all/Foxell P Place-names: *Foxhall* in Suffolk and *Foxhale* (now lost) in Salop OE 'fox burrow'. **Foxall** and **Foxhall** are both scarce surnames, found principally in the West Midlands. **Foxell**, very rare, can be found in Berks and Middx.

Foxcroft P Bardsley notes that this surname was first fixed on the Yorks border of north Lancs, and in recent times it has had a strong presence in Lancs. George Redmonds describes it as being a 'very difficult' surname, one which is clearly derived from a minor place-name somewhere in or about Thornton in Lonsdale, possibly just over the border in Westmd. Cottle is persuaded that such a place-name origin must be OE 'enclosure infested with foxes', but Redmonds says that a 'fox' has no part in such a name, and that an OF personal-name *Fulco* is much more likely to have given rise to the *Fox* element. One family of **Foxcrofts** arrived in Halifax in the late fifteenth century, and enjoyed considerable status there in the century which followed. An immigrant named George **Foxcroft** had arrived in New England by at least as early as 1629.

Foxell, *see* Foxall.

Foxlee/Foxley P   Place-name *Foxley* in Norfolk, Northants, Wilts OE 'fox wood/clearing'.

Foxton P   Place-name in: Cambs, Leics, NRYorks OE 'place infested with foxes/fox hill'; Co Durham, Northd (both originally *Foxden*) OE 'fox valley'.

Foxwell P   From an unidentified place OE 'stream/spring with foxes'. Chiefly a Somerset surname.

Frain/Fra(y)ne/Frayn(e)/Frean(e)/Freen T   Dweller by an ash tree OF. **Frain** is found mainly in Lancs; **Frane** (scarce) in Lancs and Leics; **Frayn** in Cornwall and Devon; **Frayne** (scarce) in Devon; **Frean** and **Freane** (scarce), scattered; **Freen** (very scarce) in Middx. *In 1857 James Peek (1800–1879), the son of a farm labourer from Devon, joined forces with his nephew by marriage, George Hender Frean, a flour miller and engineer, and established a biscuit manufactory known from the start as Peek Frean – later to become a household name… Michael Frayn, English dramatist and columnist, was born in the suburbs of London in 1933, and grew up in Ewell, South London.*

Frampton P   Place-name in various counties, each taking its name from the river *Frome* OW 'fair/brisk', but the places so-called in Gloucs and Lincs have the first-name of an original owner as the first element. Strongest in Dorset/Hants.

Francis F   From a mediaeval first-name, originally meaning 'Frenchman' OF. Made popular thanks to *St Francis* of Assisi (1181–1226).

Francom(b)(e)/Frankham N/O   Nickname/status term for a free man OF *fran-*

chomme. The spelling of **Frankcom(b)(e)** has been altered over the years to give the appearance of a place-name with the final element *-com(b)(e)*. **Frankham** also resembles a place-name, with a different final element. Surnames of the **Francom(b)(e)** type are chiefly found in Gloucs; **Frankham** is more widely spread.

Frane, *see* Frain.

Frank(s) F/N   From the Norman first-name *Franc*, originally used for a Frank, Frenchman OF, from Germanic; or a nickname for a man who was free, freeborn (not a serf), or was liberal, generous OF. Certainly not a diminutive of *Francis*.

Frankham, *see* Francom.

Frankland O   Status term for one who occupied a piece of land free from any obligation to pay rent or to offer service to a feudal lord. A northern surname, found in most profusion in Lancs and WRYorks.

Franklin(g)/Franklen/Franklyn O   Status term for a franklin, free citizen, a gentleman who held a rank in society below the nobility but within striking distance of knights, esquires and serjeants-at-law OF. Chaucer's Franklin, a prosperous and wholesome pilgrim, offered such wonderful hospitality that it 'snewed' in his house of meat and drink.

Franks, *see* Frank.

Fraser/Frazer/Frizzell/Frizzle   Scots: a surname of uncertain origin, recorded in the mid twelfth century as **de Frisselle**, **de Freseliere**, **de Fresel**, as if from a place-name in France beginning with the elements *Fris-* or *Fres-*. Sir Simon **Fraser** (executed 1306) is referred to as 'Simond Frysel'. The first element could be from an OF word for an ash-tree, perhaps modified with the addition of the *-er* suffix to make it **Fraissier** – a 'strawberrier', a gatherer of strawberries. Certainly the armorial bearings of the Fraser clan include three silver cinquefoils or *fraises*. **Frazer** is a less Jacobite form of **Fraser**. In Ireland, *-s-* and *-z-* interchange in these surnames. **Fraser** is the family name of the Barons Lovat, Saltoun and Strathalmond.

Frater O A man in charge of the monastic refectory OF. Found mainly in the north-east of England, and in Scotland.

Frayn(e), *see* **Frain**.

Frazer, *see* **Fraser**.

Freak(e) N/P Nickname for warrior, hero; or, as an adjective, 'bold, brave, zealous' OE. Or a variant of **Firth**. **Freak** is a scarce Dorset/Gloucs surname.

Frean(e), *see* **Frain**.

Frear, *see* **Frere**.

Frederick(s) F From a Germanic first-name meaning 'peace-rule', made popular in central Europe thanks to the fact that it was borne by many members of the Hohenstaufen royal dynasty.

Free N Nickname for a free (or noble, generous) person OE. An East Anglian surname. Compare **Fry**.

Freebody O Status term for a freeborn man, a freeman OE. A scarce south-of-England surname, found particularly in Berks and Surrey. *In 1851 William Debenham, who had a drapery business in both London and Cheltenham, took his son William and his brother-in-law Clement Burgess Freebody (born in Hurley, Berks, in 1815) into partnership, thus creating the well-known firm of Debenham, Son and Freebody.*

Freeborn O Status term for a man who was born free, not a serf OE. Once popular as a first-name. Possibly also a variant of **Fairbairn**. The surname has a significant presence in Northern Ireland.

Freeborough T Dweller in a free borough or corporate town OE. A fairly scarce Midlands surname.

Freegard F From a Germanic first-name meaning 'peace-spear'. A very scarce Wilts surname.

Freeland O Status term for a tenant of land with no rental or service ties attached OE. A scattered surname, strong in Surrey.

Freelove F From an OE first-name meaning 'peace-survivor', but elements seen in **Free** and **Leaf** are possibly involved in some cases. A rare surname, found in the south-east of England.

Freeman O Status term for a freeborn man, a freeman OE.

Freen, *see* **Frain**.

Freer, *see* **Frere**.

Fre(e)mantle P From one of a number of minor places in France called *Fromentel* OF 'cold cloak' – that is, a wood seen as the only covering a poor man could expect as shelter; or from *Freemantle* in Hants, named in imitation of them. **Fremantle** is the family name of the Barons Cottesloe. *The port city of Fremantle, Western Australia, which was the first settlement of the Swan River colonists in 1829, was named after Charles Fremantle, an English naval officer who first established a camp at the site. The city is known familiarly as 'Freo'.*

French/ffrench P/N Ethnic name for someone from France, or for one who adopted French airs. Some Irish bearers assert that it is from a place-name meaning 'ash-tree(s)' OF. Family name of the Earls of Ypres and the Barons De Freyne.

Frere/Frear/Freer/Fryer O Occupational term for a friar OF. Friars, like abbots, were nominally celibate, but the offspring of their servants might have acquired the surnames **Frere/Frear/Freer** and **Abbott**. **Frere**, scarce, is found in Middx and Norfolk; **Frear**, also scarce, belongs to the Midlands and the North; **Freer**, widespread, has a significant presence in Leics; **Fryer**, widespread, can be found particularly in Lancs and WRYorks.

Freshwater O/T/P Occupational term for a seller of fresh water OE; or a dweller near a healthy water supply; or from the place-name *Freshwater* in the Isle of Wight OE 'stream with fresh (not salty) water'. An Essex/Middx/Surrey surname.

Freston P Place-name in Suffolk OE 'place of the Frisians' ('immigrants, not cows', Cottle). A scarce East Anglian surname. Readily confused with/a variant of **Friston**.

Frew P Scots: from the *Fords of Frew*, ?British 'stream', on the river Forth.

Frewen/Frewin(g)/Frowen F From *Frewine*, an OE first-name meaning 'generous friend'. A seventeenth-century Archbishop of York bore the charming name '*Accepted Frewen*'. **Frewen** is a scarce Middx/Oxon surname.

Frewin(g), *see* **Frewen**.

Friend N Nickname for a friend – or relation OE. Strongest in Devon and Kent. *George Taylor Friend OBE (1881–1969), highly acclaimed artist and bookplate designer, was born in Bloomsbury, London, the son of Robert and Mary Friend.*

Fright, *see* **Firth**.

Frisby P Place-name (three such, one now lost) in Leics ON 'Frisians' homestead'.

Friskney P Place-name in Lincs OE 'at the fresh-water river', the -*n*- indicating the dative of the adjective in the 'weak' position after the lost preposition and definite article. A long-established Lincs surname, but scarce.

Friston P Place-name in Suffolk OE 'place of the Frisians' and in Sussex OE '*Frige*'s settlement' or 'furze hill'. A scarce Suffolk surname, readily confused with/a variant of **Freston**.

Frith, *see* **Firth**.

Frizzell/Frizzle, *see* **Fraser**.

Frobisher/Furber/Ferber O Occupational term for a furbisher/polisher/burnisher of armour/swords, etc. OF. The surnames **Furber** and **Ferber** are the same as **Frobisher** without the OF -*iss*- infix. **Frobisher** is a WRYorks surname; **Furber** is found in western counties of England from Chesh to Devon; **Ferber**, scarce, has a presence in Lancs. *Sir Martin Frobisher (?1535–1594), privateer and naval commander,* *was born at Altofts, near Normanton in Yorkshire. The Frobishers of Yorkshire descend from John Frobisher, a thirteenth-century Scot who was granted lands in Denbighshire, Wales; in the century following, the family settled in West Yorshire and acquired the manor of Altofts by marriage.*

Frome/Froom(e) T/P Dweller near one of five rivers with this name ?OW 'brisk, fine'; or specifically from *Frome* in Somerset. The spelling **Froom(e)** represents the usual pronunciation of both the rivers and of the town. **Frome** is a scattered surname with a particular presence in Surrey; **Froom** belongs principally to Devon, and **Froome** to the south of England, especially Hants.

Frost N Nickname for a person with a frosty character, or who had white hair or a white beard, or was born during a notoriously cold spell OE.

Froud(e)/Frowd(e)/Frude F From an OE personal name *Frod(a)*, meaning 'wise, prudent' OE. Commonly pronounced '*Froode*'. **Froud**, **Froude** and **Frowd** are all south-of-England surnames; **Frowde**, very scarce, is more scattered. *Henry Frowde (1841–1927), the publisher to the University of Oxford who used India paper to great effect in several of the books for which he was responsible, was born at Southsea, Hants; the Frowde family originated in Devon, and claimed – without any evidence – that they were related to the historian James Anthony Froude.*

Frowen, *see* **Frewen**.

Frude, *see* **Froud**.

Fry(e) O/N Status term/nickname for a freeborn or noble, generous person OE (the variant **Frye** possibly exhibiting the use of a weak adjective after a lost definite article); or a nickname for a little person, child, offspring ON (as in the *fry* of a fish). **Fry** is a surname of the south and south-west of England; **Frye**, quite scarce, can be found in Essex. *Christopher Fry (1907–2005), the English dramatist who wrote* The Lady's Not for Burning, *was born in Bristol, son of Christopher John Harris and Emma Marguerite Hammond (daughter of Emma Louise Fry);*

he adopted his maternal grandmother's surname as his own… Elizabeth Fry, née Gurney (1780–1845), prison reformer and philanthropist, came from a prominent family of Quakers who were bankers in Norfolk; in 1800 she married Joseph Fry, also a banker, whose business interests included dealing in colonial wares… Stephen John Fry, British comedian, actor and author, was born in Hampstead, London, son of Alan Fry and Marianne Neumann, an Austrian of Jewish descent, but spent his childhood in Booton, near Reepham, Norfolk.

Fryd, *see* **Firth**.

Frye, *see* **Fry**.

Fryer, *see* **Frere**.

Fudge, *see* **Fulcher**.

Fuggle(s), *see* **Fowle**.

Fulbrook P Place-name in Bucks, Oxon, Warwicks OE 'dirty/muddy brook'.

Fulcher/Fudge/Fulger/Fullager F From a Germanic first-name OF *Foucher* ('people-army'). **Fulcher** belongs chiefly to East Anglia; **Fudge** is a south-west-of-England surname; **Fullagers** have long lived in Kent.

Fulford P Place-name in various counties OE 'dirty/muddy ford'. A widespread surname, with a significant presence in Devon.

Fulger, *see* **Fulcher**.

Fulk/Fulkes/Fulks, *see* **Falk**.

Fullager, *see* **Fulcher**.

Fullalove/Fulleylove N Nickname for a person who was 'full of love' OE. A scarce Lancs surname.

Fullarton, *see* **Fullerton**.

Fuller/Fallon/Voller O Occupational term for a dresser of cloth, one who would trample it in water to thicken it OE *fullere* and OF *foleur*. Compare **Tucker** and **Walker**. The surname **Voller** belongs to the south of England, especially to Hants, Surrey and Sussex. **Fallon** is found mainly in Lancs.

Fullerton/Fullarton/Fulton P From one of a number of Scots and English place-names: *Fullerton*, Ayrshire; *Foulertoun*, Forfarshire; *Fulton*, Roxburghshire; *Fullerton*, Hants OE 'bird-catchers' place'.

Fulleylove, *see* **Fullalove**.

Fullwood, *see* **Fulwood**.

Fulshaw T/P Dweller at the dirty/muddy grove OE; or from the place-name *Fulshaw*, with the same meaning, in Chesh, WRYorks. A scarce scattered surname.

Fulthorp(e) P Place-name *Fulthorpe*, near Grindon, Co Durham OE 'dirty/muddy hamlet'. Scarce in both spellings, found mainly in Co Durham and Northd. **Fulthrope**, a metathetic form listed by Cottle, appears to have become extinct in the United Kingdom by the late nineteenth century.

Fulton, *see* **Fullerton**.

Fulwell P Place-name in Co Durham, Oxon OE 'dirty/muddy stream'.

Ful(l)wood P Place-name in Lancs, Notts OE dirty/muddy wood'.

Furber, *see* **Frobisher**.

Furlong T Dweller at a furlong of land OE – literally 'furrow-long', a word which eventually came to be used to refer to a measure of one eighth of a mile. A scattered surname, found in Lancs and also in Ireland.

Furminger/Firminger O Occupational term for a cheese-maker/seller OF (compare modern French *fromage* 'cheese'). Surnames of south-east England.

Furnace/Furnass/Furneaux/Furness/Furnish/Furniss T/P Dweller at the furnaces OF; or from various places in France called *Fourneaux*; or from the *Furness* district of Lancs ON 'headland near the island called Rump'. Investigations as to whether minor place-names in the Peak District of Derbys might be the point of origin in some cases are ongoing. *Richard Furness (1791–1857), poet and hymn-writer (and much else, in an eventful life…), was born in the* *village of Eyam, Derbys, the son of a small farmer… David Furnish, the Canadian filmmaker who is the civil partner of the musician Elton John, was born in Toronto in 1962.*

Furnass, *see* **Furnace**.

Furneaux, *see* **Furnace**.

Furnell T/P Dweller at the furnace OF (*Fourneaux* being the plural, so compare **Furnace/Furneaux**); or from places called *Fournel*, *Fournal*, in Normandy. Strongest in Wilts.

Furness/Furnish/Furniss, *see* **Furnace**.

Furnival(l) P Place-names in France: *Fournival* (Oise) and *Fourneville* (Calvados), Gallo-Roman and OF *'Furnus's* valley/ town'. Gerard **de Furnival** from *Fournevilla* in Normandy, after fighting in the Crusades under King Richard I, came to England and married Maud de Lovetot, from whom he acquired land in Hallamshire in WRYorks. The former *Furnival's Inn* (one of the so-called Inns of Chancery) in the Holborn area of London was founded in 1376 by Gerard **de Furnival's** descendant Sir William **Furnival** (1326–1383). By the late nineteenth century the surname **Furnival** could be found chiefly in the Midlands and the north-west of England, while **Fernival** (scarce), like **Furnival** itself, had a distinctive presence in Staffs.

Fursdon P From one of several minor places in Devon OE 'gorse hill', and a Devon surname.

Furse(man)/Furze(man) T Dweller in an area covered in gorse OE. Compare **Fursey**. Chiefly Devon surnames.

Fursey/Forsey T Dweller at an enclosure covered in gorse. Compare **Furse**. **Fursey**, a scarce surname, is found in Devon; **Forsey** belongs to the south of England, especially Dorset, where there is no lack of minor place-names containing the elements *Furze/Furzey/Furzy*.

Furze(man), *see* **Furse**.

Fusedale, *see* **Fewsdale**.

Fyfe/Fife/Fyffe P From the county-kingdom of *Fife* in Scotland, probably named after *Fib*, one of the seven sons of Cruithne, legendary father of the Picts. *The firm of Fyffes, fruit importers, famed above all for its bananas, was established in England in 1888 as E. W. Fyffe Son & Co Ltd. The founder, Edward Wathen Fyffe (1853–1935), was born in Woodchester, Gloucs, the son of a tea importer who had a business in London. It was when his wife Ida was ill with tuberculosis that the family moved to the warmer climate of the Canary Islands, where he was able to expand his business.*

Fyn(a)more, *see* **Finnemore**.

Fyson, *see* **Fison**.

G

Gabb N Nickname for a liar, deceiver OF. A surname found mainly in Gloucs.

Gabriel F From a Hebrew first-name, meaning 'God is a strong man'; the Archangel of the Annunciation.

Gadd O/N Occupational term for a driver of cattle; or a nickname for an irritating person ON (literally 'goad, sting'). A widespread surname, most commonly found in Middx and Surrey, but also as far north as Lancs.

Gadsby P Place-name *Gaddesby* in Leics ON 'the farm of *Gaddr*' (a first-name meaning literally 'goad/sting', as in the surname **Gadd**).

Gadsden/Gadsdon P Place-name *Gaddesden* in Herts OE '*Goete*'s valley' OE. Scarce, whatever the spelling; **Gadsdens** are found mainly in Beds, **Gadsdons** in Middx.

Gaffikin, *see* **Gavigan**.

Gail, *see* **Gale**.

Gaillard, *see* **Gaylord**.

Gailor(d), *see* **Gaylord** and **Gayler**.

Gain(e)(s) N Nickname for a crafty or ingenious person, from an OF word meaning 'ingenuity, trickery'.

Gainford P Place-name in Co Durham OE 'direct ford' (the first element Scandinavianized). A scarce Cumbd surname.

Gains, *see* **Gain**.

Gaitskell/Gaitskill/Gaskell/Gaskill P Most surname dictionaries derive these surnames from *Gatesgill* in Cumbd ON 'shelter for goats', though *Gaisgill*, Westmd ON

'wild-goose valley', must also be a possible source? **Gaitskell** and **Gaitskill** are Cumbd surnames. **Gaskill** is rarer than **Gaskell**, but both are found mainly in Lancs. *Hugh Gaitskell (1906–1963), one-time leader of the Labour Party, was born in Kensington, the son of Arthur Gaitskell of the Indian Civil Service and Adelaide Mary Jamieson, the daughter of a former consul-general in Shanghai.*

Galbraith P A Scots Gaelic term, literally 'stranger Briton', used originally for a Welshman who had settled among Scots Gaels and had never become fully integrated. Compare **Gall**. Family name of the Barons Strathclyde.

Gale/Gail N/F/T/O Nickname for a jolly person OF, or for one who was wanton, licentious OE; or from a Germanic first-name *Gal(l)on*; or one who dwelt near a gaol, was a gaolbird, or a gaoler OF. The British retain the spelling *gaol*, while Americans prefer *jail*, which more readily represents the pronunciation. For all that, both **Gale** and **Gail** are pronounced with a hard '*g*'. Problems can arise: a man carving the word *gaol* in a courthouse in the centre of Nottingham had originally rendered this as *goal* in error. A stonemason's hapless 'correction' can be seen to this day.

Gall N Nickname of Celtic origin meaning 'foreigner, stranger'. Scottish highlanders would apply such a term to those from the Lowlands, or to Vikings, and in Ireland it would be used for English and Welsh settlers following the Norman Conquest of 1066. Compare **Galbraith**. *Sandy Gall, television presenter and newsreader, was born in Penany in 1927, and educated in Scotland.*

Galla(g)her/Gallacher F Irish: Anglicized form of Gaelic **O'** [descendant of] **Gallchobhair** ('foreign help'). **Gallagher** is by far the commonest spelling.

Galley/Gallie O/N Occupational term for a sailor, one who served on a 'galley' – a vessel with sails and oars, or a large rowing-boat (as on the Thames) OF; or a nickname for a pilgrim who had been to Galilee in the Holy Land. **Galley** has a particularly strong presence in both Co Durham and Essex; **Gallie** is largely a Scottish surname.

Galloway P From the area so-called in Scotland, Gaelic 'stranger/foreigner Gael', which for many years was a province of English Northumbria. *The Scottish politician George Galloway, 'Gorgeous George' to some, and a dangerous radical to others, was born in Dundee in 1954.*

Galpin O Occupational term for a galloper, errand-boy; but also a turnspit, scullion OF. The surnames **Gilpin** and **Kilpin** have a different origin to **Galpin**, though all three can potentially be confused. **Galpin** is mainly a Dorset surname.

Galsworthy/Goldsworthy/Goldworthy/Golsworthy P Place-names: *Galsworthy*, Devon OE '?bog-myrtle/sweet-gale slope'; *Goldsworthy*, Devon OE '*Gold*'s enclosure'; *Goldsworthy*, Cornwall, Cornish '?field-fair/market' (a field in which fairs/ markets were held). Of such surnames **Goldworthy**, very scattered, is perhaps the scarcest. *John Galsworthy (1867–1933), English novelist and playwright, was born in Surrey.*

Galton P Place-name in Dorset OE 'tribute/ rent-farm' (that is, one occupied on payment of a rent). *Sir Francis Galton (1822–1911), geneticist and eugenicist, a grandson of Erasmus Darwin, was born in Birmingham.*

Galvin F Irish: Anglicized form of Gaelic **O'** [descendant of] **Gealbhain** ('bright-white').

Gamage P Place-name *Gamaches* in Eure and Somme, France OF, from Gaulish '?winding-water'. A scarce widespread surname. *Gamages, the now-defunct London*

department store, was founded in 1878 by Arthur Walter Gamage, the son of a Herefords farmer.

Gamble/Gambell N Nickname for an old person ON. *See also* **Gamlin**. **Gamble** belongs mainly to the English North and Midlands, but also to the Ulster counties of Antrim, Down and Derry. **Gambell**, very much scarcer, can be found in Kent.

Gamblin(g), *see* Gamlin.

Gambrill N Nickname for a person built like a crooked stick (or who carried one?) OF. A very scarce Kent surname.

Game N Nickname for a sporty person, or for one given to jokes and jests OE *gamen*. The scarce variants **Games** and **Gameson** ('son of **Game**') are mainly found in South Wales and in Warwicks/Monmouthshire respectively.

Games(on), *see* Game.

Gamlin/Gamblin(g) N Nickname for a little old man (diminutive of **Gamble/Gambell**) ON, with an OF suffix. Yet *Gamelyn* was the lusty and agreeable young hero of a mediaeval tale and (via Lodge's *Rosalynde*) the precursor of Orlando in *As You Like It*. A scarce surname in any spelling; **Gamlin** can be found in Somerset, and **Gamblin** in Hants.

Gammon N Nickname for a lame person, one with a 'gammy' or 'game' leg, Old Norman French (compare a *gammon* of bacon, and the modern French word for a leg, *jambe*); or a variant of **Game**. A surname of the south of England.

Gand(e)y ?O/?P Plausible explanations as to the origin of this Norman surname include: a wearer of gloves or a glove-maker OF *gant*; a person from a place so-named in France, or from *Ghent* in Flanders. The likelihood of a place-name origin in at least some cases is reinforced by the fact that a Hugh *de* **Gandy** was High Sheriff of Devon in the twelfth century, though in more recent times the surname is mostly encountered in Lancs and Chesh. A lady bearing the euphonious name of '*Sandy* **Gandy**' married John Evans at Davenham, Chesh, on 31 October 1814.

Gant, *see* **Gaunt**.

Gape N Nickname for a weak, feeble person OF. A very scarce surname, found in Dorset and Glamorgan.

Garbett F From a Norman first-name meaning 'spear-bold/bright'. Readily confused with/a variant of **Garbutt** or **Gobbett**. An uncommon surname, found in Worcs.

Garbutt F From one of two first-names: Germanic *Geribald* ('spear-brave/bold'); Norman *Geribodo* ('spear-messenger'). Readily confused with/a variant of **Garbett** or **Gobbett**. Very much a northern surname, found especially in Co Durham and WRYorks.

Gard O Occupational term for a watchman, warder, guard OF. A Devon and Somerset surname.

Garden/Gardener, *see* **Gardner**.

Gardham P Place-name in ERYorks ON '(at the) fences/enclosures', exhibiting the use of a dative plural after a lost preposition. A very scarce ERYorks surname.

Gardner/Gardener/Gardiner/Garden/ Jardine T/O Dweller in/worker at a garden OF (Norman), though **Jardine** (found in north-west England and Scotland) is from Parisian French *Jardin*. **Gardner** is the most frequently found spelling. *See also* **Garner**.

Garfitt P A scarce WRYorks surname, presumably derived from the place-name *Garforth* OE '*Gæra*'s ford'.

Garland O/T/P Occupational name for a maker of garlands, chaplets OF; or a dweller at the sign of the garland; or from a minor place-name, possibly *Garland*, Devon OE 'triangular piece of land'. Chaucer mentions a dog called *Garland* (meaning '?barking, croaking', from *grailler* OF). A widespread surname, strongest in the south-west of England, and found especially in Gloucs and Somerset.

Garlic(k) O/N Occupational term for a grower or seller of garlic, or a nickname for person fond of eating garlic OE. The surname **Garlic**, scarce, can be found in Northants; **Garlick**, much more common, is much in evidence in Lancs.

Garman, *see* **German**.

Garmston P Place-name in Salop OE '*Garmund*'s farm'. A Gloucs/Salop surname.

Garner T/O Dweller at/worker at a granary OF; or a variant of **Gardner**.

Garnet(t) O/F The usual explanations for this surname – that it refers to a seller of pomegranates OF or to a maker/seller of hinges OF – seem not a little far-fetched. George Redmonds is suitably sceptical; pointing out that this is chiefly a surname of the north-west of England and that it may have a connexion with Benedict **Garnet**, chief forester of Lancaster during the reign of Richard I, he believes that a first-name origin is more likely. **Garnett** is principally a Lancs surname; **Garnet** features strongly in that county, but also in WRYorks.

Garnham P From an unidentified place-name OE '*Gara*'s homestead', probably in East Anglia. Mainly a Suffolk surname. Can be confused with **Garnon**.

Garnon(s) N Nickname for a person who wore a moustache OF – an oddity among the clean-shaven Normans. Compare the first-name *Algernon*, which means 'with a moustache'. A very scarce surname, found in Glamorgan and Pembrokeshire, Wales. Can be confused with **Garnham**.

Garra(r)d/Garratt, *see* **Garrett**.

Garraway P/F Place-name *Garway* in Herefords OW '(church of Saint) *Guoruoe*'; the first-name recurs in the *Book of Llandaf*. But Reaney also instances early forms without *de* and far from Wales, which are from the OE first-name *Gārwīg* ('spear-war'). A scattered surname, found mainly in the south of England.

Garrett/Garra(r)d/Garratt/Garred/ Garritt/Garrod/Ger(r)ard/Gerald/ Gerratt/Gerred/Gerrett/Girard(et)/ Girardot/Jarra(r)d/Jarratt/Jarraud/ Jarred/Jarrett/Jarritt/Jarro(l)d/ Jarrott/Jerratt/Jerreat(t)/Jerred/ Jerrett/Jerrold F From *Gerald* ('spear-rule') or *Gerard* ('spear-brave'), Germanic first-names introduced by the Normans. Some of these variants can take a final 's', indicating 'son of'. The **Garrett**-type variants are pronounced with a hard *G-*, the others with a soft *G-* ('*J-*'). **Girard(et)** and **Girardot** are found in England as Huguenot surnames. **Jarrett** is a distinctively Kent surname. *Garrard, one of the oldest jewellery houses in the world, was originally founded in the early eighteenth century by George Wickes; in 1802 Robert Garrard took sole control of the firm.*

Garth T Dweller at an enclosure, garden, paddock ON.

Garton P Place-name (two such) in ERYorks ON 'fenced farm'.

Garve P Scots: place-name in Ross and Cromarty, Gaelic 'rough (place)'.

Gascoign(e)/Gascoin(e)/Gascoyne/ Gaskin P Used of a Gascon, from the province of Gascony OF, from Latin: 'land of the Basques'. The variant **Gaskin** has no connexion with *(galla)gaskins*, an old form of breeches. *(Arthur) Bamber Gascoigne (born in London, 1935), author, television presenter and all-round intellectual, had some fascinating forebears and relations, to say the least. Captain Terence O'Neill, former Prime Minister of Northern Ireland, was his uncle (his mother's brother), and his Gascoigne ancestry can be traced back to William Gascoigne, who bought land in Harewood, Yorks, in 1364. The ancestral line includes two earlier Bamber Gascoignes, both of whom were members of Parliament during the eighteenth century.*

Gask P Cottle, following Black, derives **Gask** from a place-name in Perthshire, Scotland (Scots Gaelic 'point of land running out from a plateau'), and there is a reference to Galfridus **de Gaisk** in Scotland in the early thirteenth century – but by the late nineteenth century this had become a very scarce Leics surname.

Gaskell/Gaskill, *see* Gaitskell.

Gaskin, *see* Gascoign.

Gatacre/Gataker P Place-name *Gateacre* in Lancs and *Gatacre* in Salop OE 'field by a gate'. An exceptionally scarce surname, whatever the spelling.

Gatchell/Getchell ?P Perhaps from an unidentified place-name with the OE elements 'goat' or 'gate' and 'hill'. **Gatchell**s are much in evidence in parish register entries for Somerset from the sixteenth century onwards, but the surname has migrated considerable distances: to Ireland, where Quaker **Gatchell**s made glass in Waterford, and to North America. The American musician John Fahey composed and played a much-loved guitar piece called 'Beautiful Linda Getchell'. The 1881 census includes no **Getchell**s; **Gatchell**, very scarce, can be found in Lanarkshire, Scotland, and elsewhere.

Gatcomb(e)/Gatcum P Place-name *Gatcombe* in Gloucs, Isle of Wight, Somerset and Wilts OE 'goat/gap valley'. **Gatcombe** is a scarce Somerset surname; **Gatcum**, even scarcer, can be found in Surrey.

Gate(s) T/O/N Dweller by a main road ON or by a gate OE; or from an OE word for a goat – and thus used as an occupational term for a goat-herd or as a nickname for an obstinate or smelly person; or an occupational term for a watchman OF. Sometimes a variant of **Geddes**?

Gatehouse T Dweller at a gate-house OE, a house at the entrance of a castle, monastery, etc. A scattered surname, found principally in WRYorks. *Major-General Alexander Hugh Gatehouse (1895–1964), born in Coventry, was a highly decorated tank commander in both the First and the Second World Wars.*

Gateley P Place-name in Norfolk OE 'clearing with goats'. Yet this is chiefly a Staffs/Warwicks surname, readily confused with/ a variant of **Gatley**.

Gates, *see* **Gate**.

Gatley P Place-name in Herefords OE 'clearing in a pass/goat clearing' and in Chesh OE 'goats' cliff'. Chiefly a Chesh/Lancs surname. Readily confused with/a variant of **Gateley**.

Gatward O Occupational name for a gatekeeper OE, or for a goatherd OE. Most in evidence in the Home Counties, especially Herts.

Gaukro(d)ger, *see* **Gawkroger**.

Gauld T A Lowlander, Scots Gaelic.

Gaunt/Gant P/N/O A person from *Ghent* in Flanders (French *Gand*); or a nickname for a person who was gaunt, lean, haggard ME; or an occupational term for a a glove-maker OF. Shakespeare's John **of Gaunt** has great fun making puns on his own surname. Very strong in WRYorks.

Gavigan/Gaffikin/Gavaghan F Irish: Anglicized form of Gaelic **O'** [descendant of] **Eachagain**. **Gavaghan** is largely found in Mayo and Roscommon, **Gaffikin** in Co Down.

Gavin F From the first-name *Gawain* OF and ME (ultimately from OW *Gwalchmai*), borne by King Arthur's nephew, who in earlier romances was the foremost of his knights. An English/Scottish surname, very strong in Lancs. *See also* **Gawn** and **Walwin**.

Gawkro(d)ger/Gaukro(d)ger P The temptation to believe that this distinctive Yorkshire surname means 'stupid/clumsy *Roger*' has proved irresistible to most compilers of surname dictionaries, but such an explanation has done those that bear it a great disservice. Certainly 'gawk' can mean 'clumsy' dialectally, but George Redmonds has shown that the surname is derived from a minor place-name near Sowerby (*Gaukrocher* in 1351), meaning 'cuckoo rock'.

Gawn(e) F/O A form of the first-name *Gawain* (see **Gavin**); but in the Isle of Man, from Manx **Mac y Ghaauin**, 'son of the smith'.

Gay(e) N/P Nickname for a gay, cheerful person OF; or from a place in Normandy called *Gaye*. **Gay**, widespread, belongs principally to the south-west of England; **Gaye**, much scarcer, is mainly a Devon surname. *John Gay (1685–1723), poet and playwright, was born in Barnstaple, Devon.*

Gaydon P Place-name in Warwicks OE '?*Gæga*'s hill'. Compare **Gayton**

Gaye, *see* **Gay**.

Gaylard, *see* **Gaylord**.

Gayler/Gailor(d)/Gaylor O Occupational term for a gaoler, Old Norman French. Readily confused with/a variant of **Gaylord**.

Gaylord/Gaillard/Gailor(d)/Gaylard N/F Nickname for a brisk, high-spirited person OF; or from *Gailhard*, a Germanic firstname ('joyous-strong'). Folk etymology has replaced the element -*lard* with -*lord*. Readily confused with/a variant of **Gayler**, **Gillard** (see **Gill**).

Gayton P Place-name in Chesh, Lincs (two such) OE 'goat farm'; the places called *Gayton* in Norfolk, Northants and Staffs may have the same meaning, or be OE '*Gæga*'s farm' (compare **Gaydon**).

Gazeley P Place-name in Suffolk OE '*Gægi*'s clearing'. Principally a Home Counties surname.

Geach/Jex N/F Nickname for a simpleton, fool ME *geche/geck*. **Jex** can be 'son of (a) geach' or 'son of *Jack*'. **Geach** is particularly strong in Cornwall and Devon; **Jex** is principally a Norfolk surname. *Sophia Jex-Blake (1840–1912), the physician and campaigner for women's rights who founded the London School of Medicine for Women, was born in Hastings, Sussex. Her mother, Maria Emily Cubitt, came from a Norfolk family, and her brother Thomas became headmaster of Rugby School.*

Geary/Gear/Gearing/Geering/Gerrish N/F Nickname for a giddy, capricious, fickle person ON; or from a Germanic first-name *Geric* (derived from *geri*, a spear); Irish:

Anglicized form of Gaelic **O'** [descendant of] **Gadhra** ('hound').

Geddes P   Scots: place-name in Nairn, Gaelic '?mountain ridge'. Sometimes a variant of **Gates**? Readily confused with **Geddie/Giddy**? *In the film* Citizen Kane, *Boss Jim W. Geddes famously uses every underhand trick in the book to score a political victory over Charles Foster Kane.*

Geddie   A Scots surname of unknown origin, early examples being found in Arbroath. Readily confused with **Geddes/Giddy**?

Gedge N   Nickname for a 'loose/flighty girl, wench; bloke' OF (so says Cottle, who also regards **Gigg** as being a variant). Chiefly found in Norfolk.

Gedling, *see* **Gelding**.

Gedye, *see* **Giddy**.

Gee   A surname of uncertain origin, mainly found in Chesh and Lancs. W. G. Hoskins tackles it head-on, pointing out that its variants in Leics include **Jee**, **Jay**, **Jees** and **Jeyes**. Whereas place-names such as *Gee* in Chesh or *Jay* in Salop have been suggested as points of origin, Hoskins is convinced that in Leics, **Gee** was originally **Joye** (a surname which is also mentioned in the thirteenth-century Hundred Rolls for Bucks, Cambs, Hunts, Norfolk and Oxon). See **Joy**.

Geering, *see* **Geary**.

Geldard/Geldart/Gelder O   Occupational term for a man who tended the sterile cattle (literally 'geld-herd') ON and OE. Chiefly WRYorks surnames, though they also have a significant presence in Lancs.

Gelding N/P/O   Usually said to be a nickname derived from 'gelding, eunuch' ON. Possibly an unlikely origin for a hereditary surname, unless perhaps it originally referred to a man who *tended* geldings. Though one which might be borne out by its scarcity, a few instances being found in Middx, and also in Notts, where in principle it could be derived (by metathesis) from the place-name *Gedling* OE '(the settle-

ment of) *Gedel/Gedla*'s people'. The surname **Gedling** also scarce, can be found in Cumbd and Co Durham.

Geldof, *see* **Gilduff**.

Gell F   Often a variant of **Julian**, but as a Manx surname it is derived from **Mac an Ghaill**, meaning 'son of the foreigner' (i.e., a Norseman or an Englishman). One prominent **Gell** family was long settled in Hopton, near Wirksworth, Derbys, their surname being immortalized in a nearby road known as the *Via Gellia*.

Gelsthorpe P   Place-name *Gelsthorpe*, WRYorks ON '?*Geili*'s outlying farmstead'. A scarce surname, chiefly found in Derbys and Notts. **Giltrap**, apparently a variant and also scarce, is principally in evidence in eastern counties of Ireland, where it is of fairly recent occurrence. **Gelthorpe**, **Gilstrap**, **Gilthorpe** and **Giltrop** are even rarer variants. *The English guitarist Gordon Giltrap, whose playing reflects a wide variety of musical styles, was born in 1948 in Brenchley, Kent.*

Gelthorpe, *see* **Gelsthorpe**.

Gent/Gentle N   Nickname for a person who was well born, noble and courteous – or neat and shapely OF. Sometimes used ironically.

Gentleman O/N   Status term for a man of gentle birth OF and OE, or a nickname for one who was not 'gentle' in that sense, but behaved as if he were. A scarce surname.

Geoffrey, *see* **Jeffrey**.

Geoghegan F   Irish: Anglicized form of Gaelic **Mag Eochagain** ('son of ?horseman'). Commonly pronounced '*Gaygan*'.

George F   From a Greek first-name meaning 'farmer'. The fact that *George* (quite an obscure personage) was the patron saint of England helped to popularize the name to some extent, but the arrival of the Hanoverian Kings in the eighteenth century began its long vogue as a first-name. For Roman Catholics its use has now declined again, since Pope John XXIII demoted *St George* (at the same time declaring that St

Philomena never existed at all). Mainly a south-of-England surname, but also found in South Wales. Readily confused with/a variant of **Gorge**.

Gerald/Gerard, *see* **Garrett**.

German/Garman/Germany/Jarma(i)n /Jerman/Jermin(e)/Jermyn P/O/F A person from, or who traded with, Germany; also used as a first-name in various forms. *German* was a name given to people from that region by the Gauls (Celtic words meaning either 'neighbour' or 'battle-cry' have been proposed), just as the *Welsh* OE 'foreigner' had to suffer the indignity of being so-called by the invading Angles, Saxons, Jutes, Frisians and the rest. The popularity of the great *Saint German*, Bishop of Auxerre in the fourth and fifth centuries, helped to make the form *Garmon* a favourite in Wales. For the *-ar* element in **Jarma(i)n**, *see* **Armistead**. **German** is a widespread surname, strong in Devon but also in Lancs; **Garman**, scarce, is found chiefly in Surrey and Sussex; **Jarman** is widespread; **Jerman** has a presence in Devon, but is particularly strong in Montgomeryshire. **Germany** (readily confused with **Jeremy**?) belongs mainly to East Anglia and Kent. *Jermyn Street, London, was built on land granted by the King to Henry Jermyn in 1661. Raised to the peerage by Charles I as Baron of St Edmundsbury, Suffolk, in 1643, Jermyn was created Earl of St Albans by Charles II in 1660.*

Gerrard, *see* **Garrett**.

Gerratt/Gerred/Gerrett, *see* **Garrett**.

Gerrish, *see* **Geary**.

Gervis, *see* **Jervis**.

Getchell, *see* **Gatchell**.

Gethin(g) F From an ow first-name meaning '?dusky, swarthy'. *See also* **Gittins**.

Getty F Irish: Anglicized form of Gaelic **Mag Eitigh**, found as a surname chiefly in Northern Ireland. *Jean Paul Getty (1892–1976), the American industralist, was born in Minneapolis, Minnesota; in due course the Getty family made significant investments in the Republic of Ireland, and in 1999 J. P. Getty's grandson, John Paul Getty III, along with several other members of his family, were granted Irish citizenship.*

Gibb(e)(s)/Gibbard/Gibben(s)/Gibberd/Gibbin(s)/Gibbing(s)/Gibbon(s)/ Gibby/Gibson, *see* **Gilbert**.

Giddings P Place-names *Great, Little* and *Steeple Gidding* in Hunts OE '*Gydda*'s people'. Readily confused with/a variant of **Gittins** – or even of **Giddy**.

Giddy/Gedye N Many surname dictionaries favour a derivation from an OE word meaning 'insane, crazy' (originally 'possessed by a *god*'), or even toy with the idea that **Giddy** might be a pet-form of the first-name *Gideon*, but given the fact that such surnames are found principally in Devon and Cornwall, the Old Cornish word *gedyer* ('leader') very probably accounts for most instances of the surname. In Scotland, readily confused with **Geddes/Geddie**, and in England with **Giddings**?

Giffard/Gifford/Jefford/Jefford N/F Nickname for a bloated, puffy-cheeked individual OF. The Conqueror granted the Norman family of **Giffard** over a hundred manors in England, whence its wide distribution. Or from a Germanic first-name *Gebhardt*, meaning 'gift-hardy'. **Gifford** in East Lothian probably takes its name from the family, rather than vice versa. **Giffard** (pronounced '*Jiffard*') is the family name of the Earls of Halsbury.

Gigg, *see* **Gedge**.

Gilasbey, *see* **Gillespey**.

Gilbert/Gibb(e)(s)/Gibbard/Gibben(s) /Gibberd/Gibbin(s)/Gibbing(s)/ Gibbon(s)/Gibby/Gibson/Gilbertson/ Gipp(s)/Gipson F Ultimately derived from a Germanic first-name *Gislebert* 'pledge/ hostage-bright'. Brought to the British Isles by the Normans, its popularity spread thanks to *St Gilbert* of Sempringham (who reputedly lived from 1085 to 1189), founder of the only English monastic order. In Scotland it absorbed *Gilbride*. The source of many surnames, especially via the pet-form *Gibb*, which in the Middle Ages was also a familiar term for a cat, especially a tom. **Gibson**, the commonest surname of the **Gilbert** group (though it is comparatively rare in the south of England), is the family name of the Barons Ashbourne. **Gibbs** is the family name of the Barons Aldenham and the Barons Wraxall. Both **Gibbard** (widespread) and **Gibberd** (much scarcer) are found in Oxon. *See also* **Cubbin** (under **McGibbon**), **Kipps** (under **Kipping**). In a census return for 1881, Bertha **Gibson**, the 31-year-old daughter of Jane **Gibson** of 34 Bedford Square, Brighton, Sussex, was described in the following deprecating terms: 'Supposed to be a lady'.

Gilbertson, *see* **Gilbert**.

Gilbride F Scots Gaelic first-name meaning 'devotee of (Saint) *Bridget*'. *See also* **Gilbert**, **McBride**.

Gilchrist/Gilk(e)s F Scots: from the Gaelic first-name *Gille Criosd* ('servant/devotee of Christ'). In Scotland, a *gillie*, originally a Highland Chief's retainer, will accompany hunting parties. Compare **Gill**. **Gilk(e)s** can also be a diminutive of the first-name *William*.

Gildea/Kildea F Irish: Anglicized form of Gaelic *Mac Giolla Dhé* ('son of the devotee/servant of God'). A Tirconnell surname, more recently found in Connacht and Clare.

Gilder O Occupational term for a gilder OE.

Gildersleeve N Nickname for a person with a liking for ostentatious clothes, literally 'golden sleeve' OE. A very scarce surname, found in the south of England.

Gilduff/Kil(l)duff N Irish: Anglicized form of **Mac Giolla Dhuibh** ('son of the servant of the black-haired boy'). Compare **Duff**, **McDuff**. *It might be tempting to suppose that the surname of the Irish musician and political activist Bob Geldof (born in Dun Laoghaire, Dublin, in 1951) represents a mutant form of 'Gilduff', but in the event his paternal grandfather was an immigrant from Belgium. The German surname 'Geldolf' is derived from a now-obsolete first-name or from one of a number of place-names.*

Giles F From a mediaeval first-name meaning 'kid, young goat', originally Latin *Aegidius* from Greek, whence OF *Gide*, *Gire*, *Gile*. The name of a miracle-working sixth-century saint who modestly escaped publicity by moving from Athens to France; associated with cripples, beggars, hunted creatures. *See also* **Gillard**.

Gilfoil, *see* **Guilfoyle**.

Gilford P Place-name *Guildford*, Surrey (still pronounced '*Gilford*') OE 'ford where (golden) marsh marigolds grow', though the surname, a scarce one, is found chiefly in Scotland. The North family are Earls of Guilford.

Gilfoyle, *see* **Guilfoyle**.

Gilhespy, *see* **Gillespey**.

Gilk(e)s, *see* **Gilchrist**.

Gill/Gillet/Gillet(t)(e) F/T/O From a first-name such as *Giles*, *Julian* or *William*. In **Gill** the initial '*G*' is pronounced hard, as in *gag*, but in the diminutive **Gillet(t)(e)** it is soft, as in *gem*. Or a dweller by a ravine ON. In Scotland, from an occupational term for a devotee or servant, Scots Gaelic and ON – compare the Scots word *gillie*. There is no evidence that **Gill** might be a diminutive of the first-name **Gilbert**. **Gilliard**, **Gilliart** and **Gilliat(t)** could be variants of **Gill**, via **Gillett(e)**, or of **Gillard**. **Gill** is a widespread surname, strongest in Lancs and WRYorks. *King Camp Gillette (1855–1932), of safety razor fame, was born in Fond du Lac, Wisconsin, USA, and raised in Chicago.*

Gillam, *see* **William**.

Gillanders F Scots Gaelic: 'servant/devotee of (Saint) *Andrew*'. An unusual and distinctive surname, found mainly in Aberdeenshire and in Ross and Cromarty.

Gillard F With the initial '*G*' pronounced hard, as in *gag*: OF form of the Norman first-name *Willard*; with the initial '*G*' pronounced soft, as in *gem*: a diminutive of *Giles* (see **Giles**). Or possibly a variant of

Gaylord, **Gilliard**, **Gilliart** and **Gilliat(t)** can be variants of this surname, or of **Gill**/**Gill-ette**. **Gillard** is mainly a Devon/Somerset surname. Readily confused with/a variant of **Giller**.

Gillem, *see* **William**.

Giller T Dweller at a ravine ON with suffix. An uncommon scattered surname. Readily confused with/a variant of **Gillard**.

Gillespey/**Gilasbey**/**Gilhespy**/**Gillespie** O Anglicized forms of Scots Gaelic **Mac Gille Easbuig** and Irish Gaelic **Mac Giolla Easbuig** ('son of the servant of the Bishop').

Gillet(t)(e), *see* **Gill**.

Gillham/**Gilliam**, *see* **William**.

Gillian, *see* **Julian**.

Gilliard/**Gilliart**/**Gillia(t)t**, *see* **Gill** and **Gillard**.

Gillibrand F From a Norman first-name *Gillebrand* ('hostage-sword'). A scarce Lancs surname.

Gillick, *see* **Gullick**.

Gillie(s) F From a Scots Gaelic first-name *Gilla Iosa* ('devotee of Jesus').

Gillingham P Place-name in Dorset and Norfolk (the initial '*G*' pronounced hard, as in *gag*); and in Kent (the initial '*G*' pronounced soft, as in *gem*) OE 'homestead of *Gylla*'s followers'. Chiefly a Dorset surname.

Gillow P Place-name in Herefords OW 'retreat at the pool'.

Gillum, *see* **William**.

Gil(l)man, *see* **William**.

Gilmartin/**Kilmartin** F Irish: Anglicized form of Gaelic **Mac Giolla Mhartain** ('servant/devotee of [Saint] *Martin*'). Also found in Scotland and (rarely) in northern England.

Gilmer/**Gilmor(e)**/**Gilmour**/**Kilmore** F/P Anglicized forms of Scots Gaelic **Mac Gille Mhoire** and Irish Gaelic **Mac Giolla Mhuire**

('servant/devotee of (the Virgin) Mary'), compare **Murray**; or from a place-name *Gillamoor* in NRYorks OE 'moor belonging to the village of Gilling'.

Gilpatrick/**Kilpatrick** F/P Irish: Anglicized form of Gaelic **Mac Giolla Phadraig** ('son of the servant of [Saint] *Patrick*'); or, Irish and Scots, from one of various place-names with the meaning 'church of (Saint) *Patrick*'.

Gilpin F Irish: Anglicized form of Gaelic **Mac Giolla Fionn** 'son of the fair-haired boy'. In England this surname can be found in south Westmd from the thirteenth century onwards, but the river *Gilpin*, first recorded in the seventeenth century, is probably named after a family, rather than vice versa. In more recent years the surname can be found mainly in Devon, but also in WRYorks. Potentially confused with/a variant of **Galpin** and **Kilpin**. The fact that John Gilpin, 'a trainband captain…of famous London town' featured in the poem by William Cowper, was a galloper 'upon his nimble steed' brings us coincidentally close to one meaning of the surname **Galpin**, 'galloper'.

Gilroy/**Kilroy** F Irish and Scots: Anglicized form of Gaelic **Mac Giolla Ruaidh** 'servant of the red-haired boy'. *Robert Kilroy-Silk, the controversial television presenter and politician, was born in Birmingham in 1942, the son of William Silk and the stepson of John Kilroy… The well-known graffiti catchphrase 'Kilroy was here' is of uncertain origin, though an elaborate story concerning chalk marks made by James J. Kilroy, an American shipyard inspector during the Second World War, has long been in circulation.*

Gilstrap, *see* **Gelsthorpe**.

Gilthorpe, *see* **Gelsthorpe**.

Giltrap, *see* **Gelsthorpe**.

Giltrop, *see* **Gelsthorpe**.

Gingell/**Gingle**/**Jingle** A surname of uncertain origin. Well-established surname dictionaries either omit it (Reaney), or state that its meaning is not known (Hanks and

Hodges). Bardsley claims that it comes from an unidentifiable place-name, *Gingdale*, in Wilts or Gloucs, and backs up his claim with a reference dated 1273 to a Michael de **Gingedale** of Wilts. The surname has continued to be limited almost exclusively to the counties of Wilts and Gloucs (particularly Bristol), and given the fact that the place-name *Bristol* evolved from *Bristow*, and that Bristolians are famous to this day for closing off certain words with an 'l' sound (suffering from *influenzal*, taking their holidays in *Americal* or *Africal*), **Gingell** might conceivably be a variant of the surname **Ginger** (see **Ginger**). Roger **Gingiure** can be found in Assize records for Gloucs in 1221. **Jingle**, which is both scarcer and more widespread than **Gingell**, could possibly share the same origin. *Hanks and Hodges link the surname Gingold with Gingell, though it is exceptionally scarce within Britain; the actress Hermione Gingold (1897–1987) was the daughter of James Gingold, an immigrant from Austria who claimed not only Viennese but also Turkish amd Romanian ancestry, and his Jewish wife, Kate Walter.*

Ginger O/N Occupational term for a seller of ginger OE (from the East, via Latin), or (therefore) a nickname for a hot-tempered person. No proof exists of its use as a nickname for a ginger-haired person. A Home Counties surname. See also **Gingell**.

Gingle/Gingold, *see* Gingell.

Ginn O/N Occupational term for a trapper of animals, or a nickname for a cunning person OF 'snare'.

Gipp(s)/Gipson, *see* Gilbert.

Girard(et)/Girardot, *see* Garrett.

Girdler O Occupational term for a maker of belts or girdles OE.

Girle N Nickname for a youth, young person, girl ME *girle/gurle/gerle*, probably from a lost OE form with *y*. 'The *-e* is not swank, but organic' (Cottle). A very scarce Hants surname.

Girton P Place-name in Cambs, Notts OE 'gravelly farm' (compare the word *grit*).

Gitsham P Place-name *Gittisham* in Devon OE '*Gyddi*'s homestead'. A scarce Devon surname.

Gittin(g)s F From the Welsh first-name *Gutyn* or *Guto*; or a variant of **Gethin**. **Gittins**, the commonest form, is strongest in Salop; **Gittings** is mainly found in Staffs. Readily confused with/a variant of **Giddings**.

Glad, *see* Gladden.

Gladden/Glad(d)ing N/F Nickname for a glad, cheerful person, or from a first-name with the same meaning OE. Chiefly East Anglian surnames; **Glad** is a very scarce variant.

Gladman N/F Nickname for a cheerful man, or from a first-name with the same meaning OE.

Gladwin N/F Nickname for a glad friend, or from a first-name with the same meaning OE.

Glaisher/Glaysher/Glayzer/Glaze/Glazier O Occupational term for a glazier, glass-maker OE. Compare **Glass**. Or a variant of **Glaister**.

Glaister ?P A Scots surname of uncertain origin, possibly from a place-name such as *Glaister* or *Glacester*, Angus, or from a place-name element. See also **Glaisher**.

Glanvill(e) P Place-name *Glanville*, Calvados, Germanic and OF '*Gland*'s domain'.

Glas(s)cock/Glas(s)cote/Glascott P Place-name *Glascote* in Warwicks OE 'hut where glass is made'.

Glascoe, *see* Glasgow.

Glascote/Glascott, *see* Glascock.

Glasgow/Glascoe P From the place-name *Glasgow*, the city in Lanarkshire, Scotland, or from two minor settlements so-called in Aberdeenshire ?British 'green/blue hollow'.

Glass O/F Occupational term for a glass-maker OE (compare **Glaisher**). Scots and

Irish: Anglicization of a number of surnames containing the Gaelic element *Glas* 'green, grey, blue'. *William Glass, a Royal Artillery Driver born at Kelso, Scotland, in 1787, was one of the first British settlers on the South Atlantic island of Tristan da Cunha.*

Glassbrook, *see* Glazebrook.

Glasscock/Glasscote, *see* Glascock.

Glasson T/P Dweller by a grass plot, Cornish *glesyn*; or from the place-name *Glasson*, of which there is one in Lancs OE '?bright/shining spot' and one in Cumbd, Celtic '?green/blue river'. A widespread surname, but found especially in Cornwall.

Glastonbury P Place-name in Somerset, Celtic and OE 'fort/mound of the people of the place where ?woad grows'. A very scarce surname, with a limited presence in Gloucs.

Glaysher/Glayzer, *see* Glaisher.

Glazebrook/Glassbrook P Place-name *Glazebrook* in Lancs OW and OE 'blue/green brook'. A widespread surname, but strongest in Lancs. M. A. Lower, in *Patronymica Britannica* (1860) claims that **Glazebrook** is a 'recent southern corruption of **Grazebrook**', a surname derived from *Gresbrooke*, Yorks, but H. Sydney Grazebrook, who is well used to the two spellings becoming confused, makes a sharp distinction between the Lancs **Glazebrook**s and the Yorks **Grazebrook**s. *See also* **Grazebrook**.

Glazer/Glazier, *see* Glaisher.

Gleave(s) O/N Occupational term from a seller or maker of lances, bills or swords OF, or a nickname for one who was an expert in wielding such weapons. A Lancs surname.

Gleed N Nickname derived from the name of the bird of prey, the kite OE. Strongest in Kent and Middx.

Glen(n)/Glyn(n)/Glynne T/P Scots: dweller in a valley, or from a place-name with the same meaning, Gaelic *gleann*; English: place-names: *Glen Parva* (home of a well-known Young Offenders' Institution)

and *Glen Magna*, Leics, possibly from the British *glenno* ('valley'); or from the river *Glen*, Northd, British *glano* ('clean, holy, beautiful').

Glenister ? O A scarce surname of uncertain meaning, though it could well be an occupational term for a gleaner OF, possibly used originally for females (compare **Brewster**, **Webster** and the like). Theories that the surname might be Scottish take little account of the fact that it belongs almost entirely to the Home Counties of England. Records of the bede rolls of the Gild of St Mary (1282–1349), held at Corpus Christi College, Cambridge, include a reference to William **Glenester**. A certain Robert **Glenister**, aged 25, was transported from London to Virginia aboard the ship *Safety* in 1635. *The actor brothers Robert and Philip Glenister were both born in the London area, in 1960 and 1963 respectively.*

Glew N Nickname for a sensible, sagacious, cautious person OE. **Glew** is found mainly in Lincs and WRYorks; **Glow** is a very scarce variant.

Glossop P Place-name in Derbys OE '*Glott*'s valley'. Mainly found in Derbys itself, and in the neighbouring counties of Lancs and WRYorks.

Gloster P Place-name: the city of *Gloucester* (pronounced as the spelling of the surname indicates), Celtic and OE 'bright/splendid Roman site'. A scarce surname, most common in Warwicks.

Glover O Occupational term for a glove maker/seller OE. A widespread surname, particularly strong in Lancs. In the 1861 census for Harthorne, Derbys, Dinah **Glover** (aged 46), the wife of Thomas **Glover**, is listed as: 'Wife, idle woman'.

Glow, *see* Glew.

Glyn(n)/Glynne, *see* Glen.

Goacher N Nickname for a person with a good/nice/happy face OE and OF (compare the word *cheer*). Very much a Sussex surname.

Goakes/Gook(s) N **Goakes**, which belongs to Cambs and Hunts, would seem to be a seventeenth-century variant on one or more of a number of surnames known to have been in existence from at least as early as the previous century, such as: **Gooke(s)** (Lincs and Norfolk); **Gootes** (Cambs); **Goat/Goats/Gotes/Gottes** (Cambs); **Goates** (Norfolk). Of these, **Gooke(s)** would perhaps be the most likely source for many **Goakes** families, but although Reaney derives such a surname from *gaukr*, an ON word for a cuckoo ('perhaps for promiscuity' adds Cottle), the thirteenth- and fifteenth-century examples he quotes are from Yorks, not East Anglia. For a study of these surnames, see *Searching for surnames* by John Titford (2002). See also **Cuckoo**.

Goatman O Occupational term for a man who tends goats OE. A very scarce Gloucs surname.

Gobbett ?N Possibly a nickname from OF *gobet* ('lump, morsel') or meaning 'go better' (compare **Golightly**). A scarce East Anglian surname, readily confused with/a variant of **Garbett**, **Garbutt**, **Godbert**.

Godbear/Godbe(e)r/Godbehere N Nickname for a person whose favourite greeting was 'God be here!' OE, 'mingled with "good beer" OE' (Cottle). Compare **Godsafe**, **Goodspeed**. Or a variant of **Godbert**. **Godber** is very much a Derbys/Notts surname.

Godbert F From a mediaeval first-name *Godebert* OE 'God/good-bright'. Readily confused with/a variant of **Godbear** or **Gobbett**.

Godbold F From a Norman first-name *Godebald* OE 'God/good-bold' OE.

Goddard/Goodhard F From a Germanic first-name *Godhard* 'God/good-hard/brave'. Made popular thanks to *St Goddard*, an eleventh-century bishop who founded a hospice on the borders of Switzerland and Italy.

Godfrey/Godfery/Godfray/Godfree F From a Norman first-name *Godefrei/Godefroi(s)* 'God-peace'.

Godley P Place-names: *Godley* in Chesh, Devon, Surrey, Sussex and WRYorks; *Goodleigh*, Devon OE '*Goda*'s wood/clearing', or simply 'good clearing'.

Godman, *see* **Goodman**.

Godney P Place-name in Somerset '*Goda*'s island', though the surname, very scarce, is found mainly in ERYorks.

Godrich/Cutteridge/Godrick/ Godridge/Gooderick/Gooderidge/ Goodrich/Goodrick(e)/Goodridge/ Goodwright/Gutteridge F/P From the ME first-name *Goderiche* (OE *Godric*), meaning 'good-power', or ME *Cuterich* (OE *Cuthric*), meaning 'famous-power'. The Normans used *Godric* as a nickname for an Englishman, calling Henry I and his wife *Godric* and *Godiva* as a result of his alleged English sympathies and her English lineage. The *-ridge* element in certain variants of this surname gives them a spurious resemblance to a place-name, though *Goodrich* in Herefords (*Castellum Godrici* '*Godric*'s Castle' in the twelfth century) may be the origin in some cases. **Godrich** (found in Hants), **Godrick** and **Godridge** (found in Surrey) are all very scarce; **Goodrich**, a scattered surname, belongs mainly to Middx; **Goodrick**, also scattered, can be found principally in the north of England; **Goodwright**, scarce, belongs to Kent and Surrey; **Gutteridge**, widespread, is found mainly in the south and the Midlands; **Cutteridge** is a very scarce Cambs surname.

Godsafe/Godsa(l)ve N Nickname for a person whose favourite greeting was '(for) God's sake!' OE. Surnames of south-east England. Compare **Godbear**, **Goodspeed**.

Godsal(l)/Goodsall N Nickname for a good soul, 'decent chap' OE. Or a variant of **Godsell**. **Godsall** is a scarce Herefords surname; **Goodsall**, also scarce, can be found in Kent and Surrey.

Godsa(l)ve, *see* **Godsafe**.

Godsell P Place-names *Gadshill*, *Godshill*,

Godsell in Hants, Isle of Wight, Kent and Wilts. OE 'God's hill'. Or a variant of **Godsal**. A widespread surname.

Godsmark N Nickname for a person bearing a mark of the plague, known as 'God's mark' OE. A scarce Kent and Sussex surname.

Godwin/Goodwin F From an OE first-name meaning 'good friend/protector', 'illustrated neither by William **Godwin** the atheist nor by **Godwin**, Harold II's father, who blinded Prince Alfred between Guildford and Ely' (Cottle).

Goff(e)/Gooch/Goodge/Gotch/ Gough/Gudge/Gutch O/N English: occupational term for a smith, Celtic (compare Cornish **Angove**); following the Norman Conquest, Breton settlers took the name into East Anglia and elsewhere. Welsh: nickname for a red-headed/red-faced man, Welsh *goch*, but with the *-ch* sound made into *-ff*. **Gutch** is a very scarce variant, found in the south and south-west of England. *Goodge Street, London, is named after a carpenter named John Goodge who acquired land in the area in 1718.*

Gogarty, *see* **Fogarty**.

Golbo(u)rn(e) P Place-name *Golborne* in Chesh, Lancs OE 'marsh marigold stream'.

Gold/Golding/Goold/Gould/Goulding O/N/F Occupational term for a worker in gold OE; or a nickname for a golden/yellow-haired person OE; or from a first-name *Golda* (male)/*Golde* (female) OE 'gold, precious, rich'. **Golding** developed from *Golda*, and the spelling **Gould(ing)** represents an earlier pronunciation of the word '*gold*'. **Gold** is also a component in a large number of European surnames. **Golding** belongs mainly to south-eastern counties of England, and **Gould** to south-western counties; **Goold**, widespread, can be found in places as far apart as Middx and Lanarkshire, Scotland; **Goulding**, also widespread, has its strongest presence in Lancs. *The novelist Sir William (Gerald) Golding (1911–1993) was born in his maternal grandmother's house at St Columb Minor, Cornwall.*

He was told that his great-grandparents were so quarrelsome that one part of the family changed the spelling of its name so as not to be confused with the others… Rev. Sabine Baring-Gould (1834–1924), hymn-writer and folk-song collector, inherited family estates at Lew Trenchard, Devon, where he presented himself to the rectorship in 1881. His Gould ancestors had originally come from Seaborough, Devon, near the Somerset border.

Gold(s)b(o)rough P Place-name *Goldsborough* in NRYorks OE '*Golda*'s fort' and in WRYorks OE '*Godhelm*'s fort'. **Goldborough** is a very rare Yorks/Durham surname; **Goldsborough** is less scarce.

Golding, *see* **Gold**.

Goldsb(o)rough, *see* **Goldborough**.

Goldsmith O Occupational term for a goldsmith OE; reinforced within the United Kingdom by Jewish immigrants who have Anglicized the German/Ashkenazic **Goldschmid(t)**.

Goldstone F/P From an OE first-name *Goldstan* ('gold stone'); or from a place-name such as *Goldstone* in Salop OE '*Golda*'s stone' or *Goldstone*'s farm, Kent OE '*Goldstan*'s settlement [*tun*]'.

Goldsworthy, *see* **Galsworthy**.

Goldthorpe P Place-name in WRYorks OE '*Gold*'s hamlet'.

Goldworthy, *see* **Galsworthy**.

Golightly O/N Occupational term/nickname for a man/messenger who sped quickly OE. A northern surname, found particularly in Co Durham and WRYorks.

Golley, *see* **Gully**.

Golsworthy, *see* **Galsworthy**.

Golty, *see* **Goulty**.

Gomer/Gummer/Gummerson F From a ME first-name *Godmer* 'God/good-famous'. *John Selwyn Gummer (born 1939), British politician, the son of an Anglican clergyman, was educated at Holy Trinity Primary School, Brompton, London; at King's School, Roche-*

ster, Kent; and (appropriately) at Selwyn College, Cambridge.

Gomersall P Place-name *Gomersal* in WRYorks OE '*Godmær*'s nook'.

Gomm(e) N Apparently a nickname from OE *guma* ('a man'); found (with an intrusive *-r-*) in *bridegroom*. **Gomm** and **Gomme** are both scarce surnames, the former found in Bucks, the latter in Oxon. *Sir (George) Laurence Gomme (1853–1916), famous for the work on folklore he carried out with his wife Alice (née Merck, 1853–1938), was born in Stepney, London.*

Gooch, *see* Goff.

Good(e)/Gooding N/F Nickname for a good person OE; or from a mediaeval firstname, from OE *Goda* ('good/God'), or the first element of a double name beginning thus. The *-e* in **Goode** can indicate a weak adjective after a lost definite article. **Good** is a widespread surname; **Goode** is strongest in Warwicks. Some **Good(e)** families in North America are descended from Northern Irish ('Scotch Irish') immigrants who originally settled on the eastern seaboard in the eighteenth century.

Goodall/Goodale/Goodell P/O Place-names: *Gowdall*, WRYorks OE 'marigold nook', *Goodale House* (now lost), ERYorks OE 'house where good ale is brewed'; or an occupational term for a brewer or a seller of good ale OE. **Goodall** is strongest in WRYorks; **Goodale**, scarce, is mainly found in East Anglia.

Gooday, *see* Goodday.

Goodbairn/Goodban(d)/Goodborn/ Goodbourn/Goodburn/Goodbun N Nickname for a 'good child' OE; typical of the counties where *bairn* remains in use.

Goodban(d), *see* Goodbairn.

Goodbody N Nickname for a good person OE. There have been **Goodbody**s in Ireland since the 1630s, and the surname has since been borne by a number of Quaker families. A book published in 1983 under the title of *Illustrated history of gymnastics* was written

(appropriately enough) by John **Goodbody**.

Goodborn/Goodbourn/Goodburn/ Goodbun, *see* Goodbairn.

Goodchild N/F Nickname for a 'good child' ME, or from a mediaeval first-name with the same meaning; or used for the godchild OE of a prominent member of the community.

Goodday/Gooday F/N From an OE firstname *Goddoeg* ('good-day'), or a nickname for a person whose favourite greeting was 'Good day!' OE. Scarce East Anglian surnames. Compare **Godbear**.

Goode, *see* Good.

Goodell, *see* Goodall.

Goodenough/Goodenow/Goodnough N Nickname, literally 'good enough' OE, perhaps used of a person easily satisfied, or whose achievements in life were merely 'good enough', and no more; but possibly sometimes absorbing the expression 'good knave' ('good boy/servant') OE. **Goodenough** is mainly a south-of-England surname; **Goodnough** is exceptionally scarce, while **Goodenow**, practically extinct in England and Wales by the late nineteenth century, exhibits the archaic and dialectal word *enow*.

Gooder F From a ME first-name *Godere* ('good-army').

Gooderick, *see* Godrich.

Gooderidge, *see* Godrich.

Goodeve/Goodey/Goodison F/N From a ME female first-name *Godeve* ('God/good gift') – compare Lady *Godiva*, and see **Goodliff**. **Goodey** can also be a nickname for a widow, or a woman of independent means ME *goodwife*. **Goodeve** and **Goodey** are chiefly found in the south of England; **Goodison** ('son of **Goodeve/Goodey**'), like most surnames ending in *-son*, belongs to the north.

Goodfellow N Nickname for a good companion/associate, a popular man OE and ON.

A widespread surname in both England and Scotland.

Goodge, *see* Goff.

Goodger, *see* Goodyear.

Goodhard, *see* Goddard and Goodhart.

Goodh(e)art/Goodhard N Nickname for a person with a good heart OE.

Goodhew F/N From an ON first-name meaning 'battle-spirit', or a nickname for a good servant, a trusted member of a household OE. Occurs most prominently in Kent. *Duncan Alexander Goodhew MBE, former captain of the England swimming team and Olympic gold medallist, was born in 1957, the son of Donald F. Goodhew of Yapton, West Sussex, and Dolores (née Venn).*

Gooding, *see* Good.

Goodison, *see* Goodeve.

Goodlad/Goodlet N Nickname for good lad/servant OE. Chiefly found in Scotland and the north. *Lord (Sir Alastair) Goodlad, a Member of Parliament who served as British High Commissioner in Australia (2000–2005), was born in 1943. His father, John Fordyce Robertson Goodlad, a doctor living in Lincoln, was born in Lerwick, Shetland, in 1907, and graduated from Aberdeen University.*

Goodley P There are two places called *Goodleigh* in Devon: one is OE '*Goda*'s wood/clearing', but the settlement in Uffculme may be OE 'good clearing'. Yet the surname is mainly found in East Anglia and the East Midlands.

Goodliff(e) F From an OE first-name meaning 'good/God dear (sweetheart)', a form of *Godiva* (see **Goodeve**). **Goodliffe**, found in the Midlands and the north, is more common than **Goodliff**.

Goodman/Godman N/F Nickname for a good man OE, or a householder OE; or from a ME first-name *Godeman*, with the same meaning, or from an OE first-name *Guthmund* ('battle-protection'), the ON form being *Guthmundr*. Also a surname adopted by a significant number of Ashkenazic Jewish families.

Goodnough, *see* Goodenough.

Goodrich/Goodrick(e)/Goodridge, *see* Godrich.

Goodrum F From an ON first-name *Guthormr* ('battle-dragon/snake'). King Alfred's great enemy is now usually styled *Guthrum*. A Norfolk surname.

Goodsall, *see* Godsal.

Goodson N/F A nickname for a good son, or from an OE first-name *Godsunu*, with the same meaning. Or 'son of **Good**'. 'But not *godson* – every boy was a godson in our Middle Ages' (Cottle).

Goodspeed N Nickname for a person whose favourite greeting was '(May) God prosper (you)!' OE, *speed* being in this case being subjunctive, and having no sense of quickness. Compare **Godbear**, **Godsafe**. **Goodspeed** is a very rare surname in the British Isles, being found in small numbers in Middx and Surrey, but a family of **Goodspeed**s, said to be from Wingrave, Bucks, was well settled in Massachusetts, USA, by the late seventeenth century. *Charles Elliot Goodspeed, who belonged to a Cotuit, Massachusetts, family, founded a bookshop bearing his name which was once a favourite haunt of bibliophiles. When the shop on Beacon Street, Boston, closed in 1995, there were those (the present author amongst them) who said that a certain glory had passed from the earth…*

Goodwin, *see* Godwin.

Goodwright, *see* Godrich.

Goodyear/Goodger N Perhaps a nickname for a person who was fond of exclaiming 'Good year!' OE, a New Year's greeting. Charmingly enough, in some parts of the English-speaking world, including the Caribbean, people speak of *Old Year's Night* rather than *New Year's Eve*. Compare **Godbear**. **Goodyear** is a widespread surname, strongest in WRYorks. *The Goodyear Tire and Rubber Company,* *founded in 1898, was named in honour of Charles Goodyear (born in New Haven, Connecticut in 1800, died in New York, 1860), the inventor of vulcanized rubber.*

Gook(s), *see* **Goakes**.

Goold, *see* **Gold**.

Goord, *see* **Gourd**.

Goosey P Place-name in Berks OE 'goose island'. A scarce Northants surname.

Gordon P/F Place-names: *Gordon* in Berwickshire and Kincardineshire, apparently from Scots Gaelic 'spacious fort'; *Gourdon* in Saône-et-Loire, France, from a Gallo-Roman first-name *Gordus*, plus a suffix. Irish: Anglicization of **Mag Mhuirneachain** ('son of beloved'). The variants **Gourdon/ Gurden/Gurdon** can also be diminutives of **Gourd**. **Gordon** is the family name of the Dukes of Richmond and of the Marquesses of Aberdeen and of Huntly.

Gore P Place-name in various counties, including Kent and Wilts OE 'triangular (originally spear-shaped – compare *garlick*) plot of ground' – that is, land left over after oblong plots had been allocated, shaped like a dress-maker's *gore*. Compare **Gorham** and **Gorman**. Or 'dirt/dung' OE may be involved – compare **Gorton**. Family name of the Earls of Arran. *Albert Arnold ('Al') Gore, forty-fifth Vice-President of the United States and environmentalist, was born in Washington DC in 1948. His room-mate while he was a student at Harvard College was the actor Tommy Lee Jones.*

Gorge P There are various places so-called in England and France OF 'gorge'. One family so-called bore a *gurge* (a whirlpool) as an armorial charge. A scarce scattered surname. Readily confused with/a variant of **George**.

Gorham T/P Dweller by a dirty/triangular homestead/river-meadow OE? *Gorhambury*, Herts, was referred to as 'Goram' or 'Gorham' in mediaeval times. A **Goreham** family had a strong presence in New England: John **Gorham** (born 1619/20) died in Swansea, Massachusetts, in 1675/6. Compare

Gore and **Gorman**. Principally a south-of-England/East Anglia surname, strongest in Kent.

Gorman F/T From the ME first-name *Gormund* ('spear-protection'); or a dweller on a triangular piece of land. Compare **Gore** and **Gorham**. Irish: Anglicization of Gaelic **Mac Goromain** ('son of Blue').

Gorton P Place-name in Lancs OE 'dirt/ dung place'.

Gosden P From an unidentified place-name. There is a *Gosden House* in Bramley, Surrey, but that would appear to have acquired its name from John **Gosden**, referred to in feet of fines records in 1364, and the origin may be *Gosden Hill* OE 'goose valley' in Send-with-Ripley in the same county. A scarce surname found mainly in the south of England, including the Isle of Wight.

Gosford P Place-name in Devon, Oxon and Warwicks OE 'goose ford'.

Goslin(g) N/F Nickname from 'gosling' a young goose, ME from OE *gōs*; or a variant of **Jocelyn** (*see also* **Goss**).

Goss(e) F A shortened form of a name such as **Jocelyn**, **Joyce** or **Gosling**.

Gossage P There is a place called *Gorsuch*, in Lancs OE 'goose ford', and several named *Gussage* OE '?gush-of-water, watercourse' in Dorset, but this scarce surname is found mainly in Warwicks and Worcs. *William Gossage (1799–1877), born in Burgh in the Marsh, Lincs, developed a cheap but high quality soap, and the factory on the Mersey which manufactured this product became the largest of its kind in England. Advertisements for 'Gossage's Dry Soap' became a familiar sight throughout the country, but Gossage's eventually became subsumed within Unilever.*

Gossard O Occupational term for a gooseherd, a keeper of geese OE, 'a pretty simple task' (Cottle). A very scarce surname, with a limited presence in Derbys. *In 1901 Henry William Gossard founded a company bearing his name in Chicago; specializing in the pro-*

duction of high-class lingerie, it soon became a household name around the world.

Gosse, *see* Goss.

Gostelow P There is a place called *Gorstella* in Chesh OE 'gorsy mound' or 'mound at a gorse-hill', though this is chiefly a Lincs surname. Readily confused with/a variant of **Costello**.

Gotch, *see* Goff.

Gotham P Place-name in Notts (pronounced '*Goatam*') OE 'homestead with goats', a village which was famously the home of the 'Wise' or 'Mad' Men of Gotham, who allegedly built a stockade fence to prevent a cuckoo from escaping… Strongest in Staffs.

Gotobed N Nickname from OE 'go to bed', probably given to an early bearer of such a surname who was lazy, being 'more than ordinarily attached to his couch', as M. A. Lower puts it, just as the scarce Dutch surname **Komtebedde** appears to mean simply 'come to bed'. Kinder scholars have toyed with the idea that the origin may be Old German *Gott-bet* 'pray to God', and Bardsley is convinced that the meaning is 'son of *Godbert*'. This is a scarce Cambs surname; graveyards in that county contain an abundance of **Gotobed** tombstones, but living **Gotobed**s are thinner on the ground, many having changed their surname to something altogether safer.

Gough, *see* Goff.

Goulborn/Golborne P Place-name *Golborne* in Chesh, Lancs OE 'stream with (golden) marsh marigolds'. **Goulborn** and **Golborne** are scarce surnames; both can be found in Lancs, but **Goulborn** also in Herts.

Gould/Goulding, *see* Gold.

Goulty/Golty East Anglian surnames of unknown origin. Hanks and Hodges say that 'no forms have been found before 1544, when Robert **Golty** was married at Debach, Suffolk', but that does not take account of William **Gowty**, vicar of West Bilney, Norfolk, whose will was proved in

the Consistory Court of Norwich in 1403, nor several other fifteenth- and early sixteenth-century testators featured in *Goulty wills and administrations* by George A. Goulty (1994). These have continued to be scarce Norfolk/Suffolk surnames, probably with a single-family origin.

Goundry, *see* Grundy.

Gourd/Goord N/O Uncomplimentary nickname for a coarse, dull, lumpish person OF; or perhaps an occupational term for a bottle/flask-maker OF, with reference to the dried shell of the gourd. Both **Gourd** (Cornwall/Devon/Hants) and **Goord** (Kent/Sussex) are scarce surnames. The variants **Gourdon/Gurden/Gurdon** can also be diminutives of **Gordon**.

Gourdon, *see* Gordon and Gourd.

Gow O Occupational term for a smith (Scots Gaelic). Compare **McGowan**.

Gowan(s)/Gowen, *see* McGowan.

Gower P/F From one of a number of places in northern France called *Gouy*, or from the region north of Paris known in OF as *Gohiere*; or from the Norman first-name *Go(h)ier* ('good-army'). Welsh: from the *Gower* peninsula, Welsh *Gwyr*. The surname is frequently pronounced '*Gore*', though not in Wales. *David (Ivon) Gower, former captain of the England cricket team, was born in Tunbridge Wells, Kent, in 1957.*

Grace(y)/Gracie N/F Nickname for a gracious person ME; or a Latinized form (under the influence of *gratia*) of a Germanic/OF female first-name, possibly meaning 'grey'. **Gracie** is mainly a Scottish surname.

Gradidge P Place-name *Graddage* in Devon OE 'big ditch'. A scarce surname, found mainly in Hants. *The Gradidge Company, famous for making cricket bats and golf clubs, was founded by Harry Gradidge in 1870… (John) Roderick Warlow Gradidge (1929–2000), British architect, had Cornish ancestry on his father's side.*

Grady F Irish: **O'** [descendant of] **Grada** ('noble').

Grafham P Place-names: *Grafham*, Hunts and *Graffham*, Sussex OE 'homestead by a grove'. A scarce South of England surname.

Grafton P Place-name in many counties OE 'farm by a grove'.

Graham/Grayham P Place-name *Grantham* in Lincs OE '*Granta*'s homestead', or OE 'gravelly homestead', recorded in Domesday Book as *Graham*. The loss of *-nt-* is due to Norman influence. The name **Graham** was taken to Scotland early in the twelfth century by a Norman baron called William de **Graham**, who had estates in Lincs, and as a surname is now found mainly in Scotland and Northern Ireland. Compare the Scottish families of **Lindsay** (from *Lindsey*, Lincs) and **Ramsay** (from *Ramsey*, Hunts). The use of *Graham* as a first-name is a more recent developmemt. Family name of the Dukes of Montrose.

Grainge(r), *see* **Grange**.

Grand, *see* **Grant**.

Grandfield, *see* **Grenville**.

Grange(r)/Grainge(r) T/O Dweller at/ worker at a grange, granary, barn OF. **Grange** and **Granger** are very widespread surnames, found in England and Scotland; **Grainger**, also widespread, is strongest in Staffs, and **Grainge** in WRYorks. *Percy (Aldridge) Grainger (1882–1961), composer and folklorist, was born in Brighton, Victoria, Australia.*

Grant/Grand N/F Nickname for someone who was tall/large, or was the elder/eldest person within a family OF; or from a mediaeval first-name, possibly from OE *Granta* (compare **Graham**). **Grant**, very strong in Scotland, is the surname of the Barons de Longueuil and the Barons Strathspey.

Granville, *see* **Grenville**.

Grason, *see* **Graveson**.

Gratian/Gration, *see* **Graveson** and **Gratton**.

Gratrix, *see* **Greatorex**.

Grattan, *see* **Gratton**.

Grattan, *see* **Gratton**.

Gratton/Grattan P Place-name *Gratton* in Devon and Derbys OE 'big hill' (though the latter may be OE 'big farm'). Given the preponderance of the surname **Gratton** in Derbys, a connexion with **Gratian/Gration** should perhaps not be discounted.

Grave(s) O/F Occupational term for a steward, the manager of property ON; an ON first-name *Greifi* ('count, earl') is sometimes also involved. Readily confused with/a variant of **Greave**, **Grieve** and **Grove**. See also **Graveson**. There is no evidence to suggest a connexion with a place-name meaning 'sandy/ pebbly soil' OF, or with *grave* in the sense of a tomb.

Gravel(l) T Dweller at a gravelly place OF. Both **Gravel** (Lincs) and **Gravell** (Carmarthenshire) are scarce surnames.

Gravener, *see* **Gravenor**.

Graveney P Place-name in Kent OE 'stream of the ditch/trench'. *This is a scarce surname found mostly in the south of England, but Tom Graveney, the Gloucestershire, Worcestershire and England cricketer, who was born in Northd in 1927, doesn't fit the mould.*

Gravenor/Gravener O Occupational term for a 'great hunter' OF (the first element being OF *grand*). Scarce in either spelling; **Gravenor** is found mainly in Wales and in neighbouring English border counties; **Gravener** has a limited presence in Kent.

Graves, *see* **Grave**.

Graveson/Grason/Graveston/Gratian/ Gration/Grayshan/Grays(h)on/Grayston(e) O 'Son of the steward' (see **Grave**). **Gratian** and **Gration**, scarce Derbys surnames, give the appearance of having been Latinized, but see also **Gratton**. **Grason** (WRYorks), **Graveston** (Lancs, Westmd) and **Grayshan** (Lancs, WRYorks) are also scarce. *Larry Grayson (1923–1995), camp comedian and gameshow host, was born William White in Banbury, Oxon; his parents were unmarried, and he was adopted by a family of coal-miners in Nuneaton, Warwicks.*

Graveston, *see* Graveson.

Gray, *see* Grey.

Grayham, *see* Graham.

Grayshan/Grays(h)on, *see* Graveson.

Grayston(e) T/P/O Dweller by a grey stone OE; or from a place-name with the same meaning; or a variant of **Graveson**.

Grazebrook P H. Sydney Grazebrook, author of *The heraldry of Worcestershire* (1873), has this to say about his family name: 'This family claims to represent the ancient family of Gresbrooke, which came originally from Gresbrooke [also Gersebroc, Greysbrook], co.York, but which was seated, from the thirteenth to the commencement of the eighteenth century, at Shenstone, in Staffordshire, and at Middleton, in Warwickshire'. Latterly the **Grazebrooks** were settled at Stourbridge, Worcs, and this has become a scarce localized surname. Writing to a correspondent (J. Paul Rylands) in 1878, the year in which his book *Genealogical memoranda relating to the family of Grazebrook* was published, H. Sydney Grazebrook says: 'Our name is constantly miswritten & mis-called "Glazebrook". I constantly receive letters (from strangers) so addressed; and in the neighbourhood of Stourbridge people invariably call us "Gl...". I have never met with an instance of any one of our family writing his name with an "l", but as the extracts from the Oldswinford registers prove, it was so written by the parsons & clerks almost constantly'. *See also* **Glazebrook**.

Greag(g), *see* Gregory.

Grealey/Gredley/Greely N Nickname for a person who was pock-marked, pitted (literally 'hailstone-marked') OF. A scarce surname in all spellings; **Grealey** can be found in Lancs and **Gredley** in Essex; **Greely** is widely scattered. Readily confused with/a variant of **Greasley/Gresley**.

Greasley, *see* Gresley.

Greathead N Nickname for a person with a big head OE. A widely spread surname, strongest in Co Durham.

Greatorex/Gratrix/Greatrex/Greatrix P From some minor place-name such a *Great Rakes*, meaning 'large track' OE. Reaney gives *Greterakes* in Derbys as the point of origin, though no such place can readily be found. *Rake* is a term used in the Derbys lead-mining industry to refer to a vertical vein of ore, though there is also a place named *Great Rocks* near Wormhill in the same county. *Gratrix* Lane, in Ashton on Mersey, Chesh, is named after a family of this name. **Greatorex**, by far the commonest form, is predominantly a Derbys surname; **Gratrix**, **Greatrex** and **Greatrix**, all comparatively scarce, are found mainly in Staffs and Warwicks.

Greave(s)/Greeve(s)/Greve(s) T Dweller at a grove. Readily confused with/a variant of **Grave**, **Grieve** and **Grove**. **Greaves** is the family name of the Earls of Dysart.

Grebbin, *see* Cribben.

Grebby P Place-name in Lincs ON 'stony/gravelly farm'. A Derbys/Lincs surname.

Greedy N Nickname for a greedy, gluttonous person OE. A scarce Somerset surname.

Greel(e)y, *see* Grealey.

Green(e) N/T Originally used of a person who wore green clothes, or who played the part of the Green Man in a May Day pageant, or who lived at or near a village green OE. 'The -*e* is justified – the OE word had it, or it could show a dative after a lost preposition' (Cottle). **Green** is a very common surname; **Greening** is a diminutive. Just as Jews arriving in America frequently had their names 'Americanized', so the reverse could sometimes happen, as with Mr Benjamin **Green**, who emigrated to Israel, where he became Mr 'Ben Gurion'. In the 1881 census for Wootton Wawen, Warwicks, the occupation of poor John Green, aged 30 but still living with his parents, is given as 'Scarecrow'.

Greenacre T Dweller at a patch of green

cultivated land OE. A scarce Norfolk surname.

Greene, *see* **Green**.

Greenfield T/P Dweller at a green field OE, or from a place-name (found in six counties) with the same meaning; or an Anglicization of a surname such as **Grenville**. Found in Surrey and Sussex, but also in the north of England.

Greengrass T Dweller at a place where luxuriant green grass was known to grow OE and ON. A Norfolk/Suffolk surname.

Greenhalf/Greenhalge/Greenhalgh/ Greenhall P Place-name *Greenhalgh*, Lancs OE 'green enclosure', now pronounced '*Greena*'. Invites confusion with **Greenhow**.

Greenham/Grinham P Place-name *Greenham*, Berks OE 'green river-meadow'.

Greenhead P The place so-called in Northd OE 'green top/hill' might seem to be a likely origin here, but this scarce surname is found mainly in Surrey.

Greenhill T/P Dweller at a green hill OE, or from one of a number of places so-called, though *Greenhill* in Worcs is OE 'hill of the spectre/goblin'. Despite a family tradition of Huguenot ancestry, the Gloucs/Worcs surname **Grinnell** is a variant of **Greenhill**.

Greenhow(e)/Greenhoff/Greenough P Place-names: *Greenhow*, WRYorks, NRYorks; *Gerna*, Lancs OE 'green mound/ hill' (or ON, if second element be from *haug*). **Greenough** is usually pronounced '*Greenuff*'. Invites confusion with **Greenhalf**.

Greening, *see* **Green**.

Greenleaf/Greenleaves P A reference to John **de Grenelef** (Yorks, 1379), quoted by Bardsley, suggests a place-name origin, though no such place (*Greencliff* OE?) is readily identifiable. In more recent years, **Greenleaf** has established itself as a scarce south-east-of-England surname. **Greenleaves**, even scarcer, can be found in Chesh and Lancs.

Greenough, *see* **Greenhow**.

Greenslade T/P Dweller in a green valley/ glade, or from a place-name in Devon with the same meaning. Chiefly a Devon surname.

Greensmith O Occupational term for a worker in copper OE, from the colour of its patination. A surname of the English Midlands and WRYorks.

Greenstreet T/P Dweller at the green highroad OE, or from a place-name in Teynham, Kent, with the same meaning. A scarce Kent surname. *Sydney Greenstreet (1879–1954), the Hollywood actor known for his performances in films such as* The Maltese Falcon, *was born in Sandwich, Kent, the son of a leather merchant.*

Greenwell P Place-name in Cumbd and Co Durham OE 'grassy spring/stream'. A Co Durham surname.

Greenwood T/P Dweller by a green wood OE, or from a place-name with the same meaning. Potentially confused with **Grimwood**? George Redmonds says that this 'spectacularly prolific' Calder Valley (WRYorks) surname could well have just one, not many, points of origin, being derived from a hamlet now known as *Greenwood Lee* near Heptonstall. For all that, Nathaniel **Greenwood**, a mid seventeenth-century emigrant to New England, came not from Yorks but from Norwich in Norfolk.

Greer, *see* **Gregory**.

Greet T/P/N/F Dweller on gravelly soil OE (compare *grit*); or from a place-name with the same meaning in Gloucs, Salop, Worcs; or a nickname for a large, fat person OE (compare *great*); or ? a diminutive of the first-name *Margaret*. The surname is very strong in Cornwall, where the origin is most likely to be the place-name *Parc and Gret*, St Ives, Cornish *grug* ('mound, barrow').

Greetham P Place-name in Lincs and Rutland OE 'gravelly homestead/river-meadow'. Most commonly found in Lincs.

Greeve(s), *see* Greave.

Greg(g)(s), *see* Gregory.

Gregor, *see* Gregory.

**Gregory/Greag(g)/Greer/Greg(g)(s)/
Gregor/Gregson/Greig/Gricks/Grier/
Grierson/Grig(g)(s)/Grig(g)son/Grix**
F/N From the first-name *Gregory*, from Greek
('watchful'). The name of at least three
great saints – *Gregory* Nazianzen and *Gregory*
of Nyssa (among the Fathers of the Eastern
Church) and Pope *Gregory* the Great, who
sent St Augustine to Britain. **Grig(g)** could
alternatively be a nickname for a dwarf-like
person ME, or can be derived from Cornish
gregga ('to cackle'). **Gregory** is very strong in
Lancs, and has a significant presence in
Derbys and Middx. **Gricks** (scarce) and
Grix are mainly East Anglian surnames.
Greer, **Grier** and **Greig** are Scots forms of
the diminutive, the latter being one of the
surnames adopted by those members of the
Clan MacGregor who migrated to Aberdeenshire, 1580–1600. *The surname of the
Norwegian composer Edvard Grieg
(1843–1907) is often misspelled Greig, which
was in fact the original surname of his Scottish
great-grandfather, who settled in Norway in
about 1770.*

Grendon P The fact that there are places
called *Grendon* in Berks, Herefords (two
such), Northants and Warwicks OE 'green
hill/valley' may, *pace* Cottle, be of little or
no relevance. The fact is that this is predominantly a Devon surname, and there
are no fewer than four places called *Grendon*
in that county.

Grenville/Granville/Grenfell P There are
half-a-dozen places called *Grainville* in Normandy OF '*Warin*'s domain'. **Grenville** is a
scarce Lancs surname; **Granville** is widely
scattered; **Grenfell**, scarce, has a significant
presence in Cornwall. The variant **Grandfield** is chiefly found in Gloucs and Somerset. *Joyce Grenfell (née Phipps, 1910–1979),
actress, broadcaster and lifelong Christian Scientist, was born in London of an English father
and an American mother, Nora Langhorne,
who was the sister of Nancy Astor, the first
woman to take her seat in the House of Commons. In 1929 she married Reginald Pascoe
Grenfell, a man possessed of two distinctively
Cornish names.*

Gresham P Place-name in Norfolk OE
'grass/grazing homestead'.

Gresley/Greasley P Place-names: *Gresley*
(two such) in Derbys; *Greasley* in Notts OE
'gravel/pebble clearing'. Many varieties are
known to exist, and such surnames could
in principle be confused with **Grealey**. *Sir
(Herbert) Nigel Gresley (1876–1941), railway
engineer, though he was born in Edinburgh,
was the son of Rev. Nigel Gresley, rector of
Netherseale, Leics, and the grandson of Sir William Nigel Gresley, ninth baronet, of Drakelow,
Derbys.*

Gresty P Place-name in Chesh OE 'badger-
run'. A Chesh/Lancs surname.

Gretton P Place-name in Gloucs, Salop OE
'stony/gravelly place'.

Greve(s), *see* Greave.

Grew N Nickname from an OF word for a
crane (the bird), used presumably for a person with long legs. Because diagrammatic
family trees once used a crane's foot symbol
to mark succession (or because they were
once presented in such a way as to resemble
a crane's foot?), they became known as
*pedigree*s (French '*pied de grue*'). A scarce
widespread surname.

Grey/Gray N/P Nickname for a grey-haired
person, or even a pale-faced one OE. **Gray** is
the most commonly found form, and
Americans still use this spelling to describe
the colour. Those who were **de Gray** had
their origins in a place called *Graye* in Calvados. **Grey** is the family name of the Earls
of Stamford.

Greygoose N Nickname for a person bearing some resemblance to a grey/wild goose
OE. A very scarce scattered surname.

Greystock P Place-name *Greystoke* in
Cumbd OW and OE 'monastery/place on
the (river) *Cray*'. A very scarce Lancs surname.

Gribben/Gribbin, *see* Cribben.

Gribble T Cottle suggests that this surname refers to a dweller near a blackthorn/crab-apple tree (from a Dorset/Devon/Cornwall dialect term), and cites examples from Devon such as *Gribble Lane* in Rockbeare, *Gribble Inn* in Little Torrington, *Gribbleford Bridge* in Hatherleigh, *Grybbelparke* on Dartmoor (1386), and a man named Walter *atte Gribbele* in Crediton (1330). In the event the surname probably refers to a dweller near a distant ridge, Cornish *cryb-a-bell*.

Grice N/O Nickname for a grey-haired man OF; or an occupational term for a swineherd ON – or from some resemblance to a pig… Chiefly a Midlands/northern surname.

Gricks/Grier, *see* Gregory.

Grief, *see* Grieve.

Grieve(s) O Occupational term for an overseer, manager, bailiff, steward OE (Northumbrian) *groefa*. A northern and Scots surname. Readily confused with/a variant of **Grave**, **Greave** and **Grove**. **Grief** is a scarce Norfolk variant.

Griffin F/N A diminutive of **Griffith**; or a nickname for a fierce person ME *griffin* (gryphon, a heraldic beast); Irish: Anglicized form of Gaelic **O'** [descendant of] **Griobhtha** ('gryphon'). **Griffing** is a scarce scattered variant.

Griffing, *see* Griffin.

Griffis, *see* Griffith.

Griffith(s) F/N From the OW first-name *Gruffydd*, where the *-ydd* element means 'lord'. A supposed connexion with the Latin *Rufus* 'red-haired' is not proven. **Griffis** is a scarce scattered variant. *See also* **Griffin**.

Grig(g)(s), *see* Gregory.

Grill(s)/Gryll(s) N Nickname for a fierce, cruel person OE (from a verb meaning 'to gnash the teeth'). **Grylls** is a strongly Cornish surname, where it is possibly derived from *gryll*, a cricket.

Grime(s) F From an ON first-name meaning 'mask, helmet'. Both **Grime** and **Grimes** are Lancs surnames, though the latter is more widely scattered.

Grimley P Place-name in Worcs OE 'spectre/goblin wood/clearing'.

Grim(m)ond, *see* McCrimmon.

Grimsditch P There were several earthworks of this name OE 'the Masked One's dyke' in Anglo-Saxon England – in south Wilts, Herts, Middx, and in the Hundred of Bucklow, Chesh. The last of these is very probably the origin of this very scarce Chesh/Lancs surname.

Grimshaw P Place-name (two such) in Lancs OE '*Grimm*'s wood', and a Lancs surname.

Grimsley P From an unidentified place-name, OE '*Grimm*'s wood/clearing'. A scattered surname, found mainly in Leics, Oxon and Warwicks.

Grimstead/Grimsteed P Place-name *Grimstead* in Wilts OE 'green homestead'. A very scarce surname in either spelling, with a presence in Somerset.

Grimston(e) P Place-name found in various northern and eastern counties of England ON and OE '*Grime/Grimm*'s place'. An uncommon Yorks surname in either spelling. **Grimston** is the family name of the Earls of Verulam.

Grimwade/Grimwood F From a Norman first-name *Grimward* ('mask-guardian'). Predominantly East Anglian surnames, **Grimwood** being by far the commoner variant. Potentially confused with **Greenwood**?

Grindal/Grindell/Grindle P Place-names: *Grindle*, Salop; *Grindale*, ERYorks OE 'green valley/hill'. **Grindal**, very scarce, can be found in Cumbd/Westmd; both **Grindell** and **Grindle** have a presence in Gloucs, but also in Yorks (**Grindell**, ERYorks; **Grindle**, WRYorks).

Grindley P Place-name in Staffs OE 'green wood/clearing', though the surname is strongest in Lancs.

Grindrod P Place-name in Lancs OE 'green clearing'.

Grinham, *see* **Greenham**.

Grinnell, *see* **Greenhill**.

Grinstead P Place-name *Grinstead* (two such) in Sussex OE 'green place/site'. A south-east-of-England surname.

Grinton P There is a place so-named in NRYorks OE 'green place', but by the late nineteenth century this scarce surname could chiefly be found in Fifeshire and Midlothian, Scotland.

Gris(e)dale P Place-names: *Grisdale*, WRYorks; *Grisedale/Grizedale* (two such), Lancs ON 'valley with pigs'. North-west-of-England surnames.

Grisenthwaite P From an unidentified place-name ON 'pigs' clearing' – presumably in the north-west of England, where this scarce surname can mainly be found.

Grisewood P From an unidentified place-name ON and OE 'wood with pigs' – possibly in the north-east/north-west of England, where this scarce surname can mainly be found. *Frederick Henry ('Freddie') Grisewood (1888–1972), well-known broadcaster with the BBC, was born in Daylesford, Worcs, the son of Rev. Arthur George Grisewood (originally from Finchley, Middx), who was rector there.*

Grissom/Grisson N Nickname for a 'greyish' person (complexion? clothing?) OF. Both variants are exceptionally scarce. *Virgil Ivan ('Gus') Grissom (1926–1967), United States pilot and astronaut, born in Mitchell, Indiana, was killed during a training exercise for the Apollo One space mission.*

Grist ?O A surname of unknown origin, perhaps an occupational term for a miller, based upon OE *grist*, from *grindan* ('grinding'), though '*grist*' was not used to describe corn ready to be ground until the fifteenth century. A surname of southern England. In 1824 the *Morning Herald* was happy to report that a dressmaker in Bath had four female assistants in her employ, whose names were **Grist**, **Miller**, **Meal** and **Flour**.

Griswold P Place-name in Warwicks OE 'gravelly/pebbly woodland'. Very scarce in the British Isles, but with a significant presence in North America; Edward **Griswold**, born in Kenilworth, Warwicks, in 1607, was an early New England immigrant.

Grix, *see* **Gregory**.

Grocock, *see* **Groocock**.

Gronow F Anglicized version of the Welsh first-name *Goronwy* OW *Guorgonui*. An uncommon surname, found mainly in Glamorgan. *Rees Howell Gronow (1794–1865), writer, soldier and Member of Parliament for Stafford, the son of a landowner from Court Herbert, Glamorgan, is mainly remembered for his four-volume autobiographical work entitled* Reminiscences of Captain Gronow *(1861).*

Groocock/Grocock/Growcock/Growcott N Nickname, literally 'crane-cock' OF and OE, perhaps for someone with legs as long as such a bird. There are small clusters of **Groocock**s in the Midlands (especially Leics) and the north; **Grocock** has a distinctive but modest presence in Notts, and **Growcott** in Salop and Staffs; **Growcock**, much scarcer, can be found in Lincs.

Groom O Occupational term for a servant, attendant, farm worker, shepherd ME. A widespread surname with a strong presence in East Anglia.

Groombridge P Place-name in Kent ME and OE 'grooms'/servants' bridge'.

Grose, *see* **Gross**.

Groser O Occupational term for a wholesaler OF (compare *grocer*). A scarce scattered surname.

Gross/Grose N/T Nickname for a fat, large person OF. European immigrants of German origin have brought surnames such as **Gross** into the British Isles in more recent times. **Grose** has a very strong presence in Cornwall, where it is derived from Cornish *an grows* ('the cross').

Grosvenor O Occupational term for a 'great/chief huntsman' OF. **Grosvenor**s claim descent from an uncle of Rollo, founder of Normandy. The first **Grosvenor** settler in England was Gilbert le **Grosvenor**, kinsman of the Conqueror. Commonly pronounced '*Grovener*'. A scattered surname with a significant presence in Staffs. Family name of the Dukes of Westminster and the Barons Ebury.

Groundwater P From the name of a farm in Orphir, Orkney, on the Loch of Kirbister ON 'shallow lake', and an Orcadian surname.

Grout O/N Occupational term for a dealer in groats, porridge, coarse meal OE, or perhaps a nickname for a person whose favourite food this was. Reaney points out that there was a nickname of the same meaning in ON. Many a meal in the southern states of the USA is accompanied by *grits*, rather than *groats*. A surname found principally in the south-east of England, especially Essex.

Grove(s)/Grover T Dweller at a grove, copse, thicket OE. The -*es* of **Groves** could indicate the use of the genitive case, or could be a plural ending. Readily confused with/a variant of **Grave**, **Greave** and **Grieve**.

Growcock/Growcott, *see* **Groocock**.

Grubb N/O Nickname for a small person ME *grub* ('midget'); or an occupational term for a digger, grubber ME, from Germanic. *Sarah Grubb (née Tuke, 1756–1790), Quaker minister and author, born in York, married Robert Grubb (1743–1797) in Clonmell, Co Tipperary, Ireland, in 1782.*

Grundy/Goundry F From a Germanic first-name *Gondri/Gundric* 'battle rule'; or, and also by metathesis, a variant of the Cornish surname **Gundry**. **Grundy** can be found in the English Midlands and the north, especially Lancs; **Goundry** is a scarce Co Durham surname. *Mrs Grundy, the notorious prude, first appeared in Thomas Morton's play* Speed the Plough *(1798)… The name of Solomon Grundy, made familiar thanks to a nineteenth-century children's rhyme ('Born on a Monday… buried on Sun-*

day') is said to be derived from an English/French salad meal known as salmagundi.

Gryll(s), *see* **Grill**.

Guard O Occupational term for a watchman, guard OF. Strongest in Devon.

Gudge, *see* **Goff**.

Guest N Nickname for a guest, stranger, traveller ON. A widespread surname, strong in Lancs, Staffs, WRYorks. Family name of the Viscounts Wimborne.

Guiatt, *see* **Guy**.

Guild O Status/occupational term for a member of a fraternity, trade/craft guild OE and ON, or for one who had duties at a guildhall. Largely a Scottish surname, particularly strong in Angus.

Guilfoyle/Gilfoil/Gilfoyle/Kilfoyle F Irish: Anglicized form of Gaelic **Mac Giolla Phoil** ('son of the devotee of (St) *Paul*').

Guin(n)ess F Irish: abbreviated form of **McGuinness**, Anglicized form of Gaelic **Mag Aonghuis**, from the first-name *Aonghus* (*Angus*). **Guinness** is the family name of the Earls of Iveagh (descendants of the brewer Arthur Guinness) and the Barons Moyne. *Arthur Guinness (1725–1803), a member of a Protestant family with Roman Catholic roots, established the St James's Gate Brewery in Dublin in the year 1759… The actor Alec Guinness (1914–2000) was born in Paddington, London, the son of Agnes Cuffe, who married David Daniel Stiven when the young Alec was five years old. Nine years later he was told that although he was then known as Alec Stiven, his real father's name was Guinness, a surname which he then adopted.*

Guise P From the district in France so-called; or a variant of **Guy(s)**. A widespread surname, strongest in Worcs.

Gullett T Dweller by a water-channel, ravine, gully ME from OF *goulet* (a diminutuve of throat; compare the *gullet* of a fowl). Cottle says: 'A south Devon surname originating in *Gullet Farm* and thereabouts, on Southpool Creek (I am grateful to Mr John R.

Lyall of Ivanhoe, Australia, for his splendid documentation of all this)'.

Gullick/Cutlack/Cutlock/Gillick F From a ME first-name *Gullake/Gudloc*, meaning 'battle-sport' (compare the northern dialectal verb 'to lake', meaning 'to play'). 'Yet one famous *Guthlac* was a hermit saint in the Fens' (Cottle). **Gullick** (uncommon) is found in Gloucs and Somerset; **Cutlack** (scarce) has a presence in Cambs, and **Cutlock** (very scarce) in Norfolk; **Gillick** (scarce) can be found in both England and Scotland.

Gulliford/Gulliver N Nickname for a glutton OF. **Gulliford** is chiefly a Somerset surname; **Gulliver** is more common and widespread. In so far as he was any kind of a glutton, Jonathan Swift's Lemuel **Gulliver**, hero of the travels which bear his name, was a glutton for punishment at the hands of little men, big men and other assorted oddities. There were compensations: at least he got to slide down the ample bosoms of giant ladies in the land of the Brobdingnagians.

Gully N Nickname for a giant man ME from the Hebrew first-name *Golyat* (*Goliath*). Strongest in Devon. Family name of the Viscounts Selby.

Gumbley F Such a surname might look as if it has a place-name origin, but it is derived from a diminutive of a Norman first-name *Gumbald* ('battle-bold'). Other surnames with a similar derivation, such as **Gumball**, **Gumbel**, **Gumbold** and even **Gumboil** (sic), appear to have faded into obscurity. **Gumbley** is most commonly found in Warwicks.

Gummer/Gummerson, *see* **Gomer**.

Gun(n)/Gunning/Gunson F/O/N From an ON first-name *Gunnr* ('battle'), or from its feminine form *Gunne*, which gave rise to the word *gun* in its ballistic sense; or from other compound first-names containing this element; or an occupational term for a person who operated a cannon; or a nickname for a forceful person ME. **Gun** can be found scattered across England and Scotland, strongest in Kent; **Gunn**, much com-

moner, is very strong in Caithness, Scotland, where its origin is the Scots Gaelic name **Mac Gille Dhuinn** ('son of the brown one's servant'). **Gunning**, which contains the diminutive element *-ing*, is widely scattered, strongest in Somerset. **Gunson** ('son of **Gunn**') is a northern surname. *The Thompson submachine gun, designed by John T. Thompson during the period 1917–1919, was known as a 'Tommy Gun', yet a boy called 'Tommy **Gun**' was born in Evesham, Worcs, in 1838. The Anglo-American poet Thom Gunn (1929–2004) was born in Gravesend, Kent.*

Gundry T/F Dweller at a homestead on the down, Cornish *gun-dre*; or, by metathesis, a variant of **Grundy**. A scarce south-of-England surname, found principally in Cornwall.

Gunning/Gunson, *see* **Gunn**.

Gunter F From a Norman first-name meaning 'battle-army'. Strongest in Gloucs and Monmouthshire. *Raymond James ('Ray') Gunter (1909–1977), trade union leader and politician, was born in Llanhilleth, Abertillery, Monmouthshire.*

Gunthorpe P Place-name in various counties ON '*Gunn*'s hamlet'; but the place in Notts, home to a signficant bridge across the river Trent, is '*Gunnhildr*'s hamlet'. An uncommon surname belonging principally to the Midlands and the north.

Gunton P Place-name in Norfolk and Suffolk ON and OE '*Gunn*'s place'. An East Anglian surname, strongest in Norfolk.

Guppy P Place-name in Dorset OE '*Guppa*'s enclosure'. Principally a south-west-of-England surname. *Guppy* has become a twenty-first-century slang term for a 'gay yuppie' – one who wants to maintain a reputation as a slick, modern urbanite. *Henry Brougham Guppy (1854–1926), born in Falmouth, Cornwall, is principally known as a botanist and biologist with wide experience of the flora and fauna of the Pacific and the West Indies, but surname enthusiasts remember him above all for his book* Homes of family names in Great Britain *(1890), with its early attempts to localize such names… Darius Guppy, the*

Eton-and-Oxford-educated fraudster, close friend of Earl Spencer and grandson of an Iranian ayatollah, who was convicted in 1993 of having staged a false £1.8m jewellery robbery in New York and then claimed on the insurance, is a descendant of Robert John Lechmere Guppy (1836–1916), a naturalist with a particular expertise in the palaeontology of the West Indies, after whom the fish called the guppy *is named.*

Gurden, *see* **Gordon** and **Gourd**. A scarce Oxon surname.

Gurdon, *see* **Gordon** and **Gourd**. A scarce Essex/Middx surname.

Gurney P From one of several places called *Gournai/Gournay* in Normandy, based on a Gallo-Roman F *Gordinus* with the addition of a suffix. The **Gurneys** were a famous Quaker family based principally in Earlham and Keswick, Norfolk.

Gutch, *see* **Goff**.

Guthrie P/F Scots: place-name near Forfar, Gaelic 'windy place'; or an Anglicized form of Gaelic **Mag Uchtre** (of uncertain origin). Irish: Anglicized form of Gaelic **O'** [descendant of] **Flaithimh** ('prince').

Gutteridge, *see* **Godrich**.

Guy(e)/Guise/Guys/Gye/Gyte F/O From the Germanic first-name *Wido*, of uncertain origin, introduced into the British Isles by the Normans in forms beginning *W-* (hence **Whyatt**, **Wyatt**, **Wyard** and **Wye**), while Parisian French gave forms beginning *G-*. *Guy* as a first-name achieved

notoriety thanks to Guy Fawkes. Or an occupational name for a guide OF *gui*. **Guiatt**, **Guyat(t)**, **Guyon** and **Guyot(t)** are diminutives. *Sir Thomas Wyatt (c.1503–1542), poet and ambassador, the son of Sir Henry Wyatt and grandson of Richard Wyatt of Yorkshire, was probably born at Allington Castle, Kent; his son, Sir Thomas Wyatt (c.1521–1554), leader of a rebellion which bears his name, was beheaded in 1554.*

Guyat(t)/Guye, *see* **Guy**.

Guyler N Nickname for a deceitful person, from ME verb *guylen*, 'to deceive'. A scarce Notts surname, with a limited presence in Lancs and elsewhere. *Deryck Guyler (1914–1999), versatile English actor, was born in Wallasey, Chesh, and brought up in Liverpool.*

Guyon/Guyot(t)/Guys, *see* **Guy**.

Gwatkins, *see* **Walter**.

Gwilli(a)m, *see* **William**.

Gwyn(n)(e)/Gwin(n) N Welsh: nickname for a person with white/fair hair or a pallid complexion OW. The descendants of a family of Welsh origin named **Gwynn** which settled in Ireland in the sixteenth century have had a strong connexion with Dublin University. *See also* **Winn**.

Gwyther F From an OW (from Latin) first-name meaning 'victor'.

Gye, *see* **Guy**.

Gyte, *see* **Guy**. A Derbys/WRYorks surname.

H

Hack/Hake N Nickname for a person with a hooked nose or hunched body, or from *Haki*, an ON byname with this meaning. The diminutive form **Hackett** is found mainly in the West Midlands and in north-west England.

Hacker O Occupational term for a butcher, or for a wood-cutter, a maker of hacks/hoes/mattocks/picks/bills, ME from Germanic. Strongest in Gloucs and Wilts.

Hackett, *see* Hack.

Hackwood ?O/?P Origin uncertain. Either an occupational term for a man who 'hacked wood', or from a place-name such as *Hackwood*, Hants OE 'haw[thorn] wood' or *Hackwood*, Northants ME and OE '? hacked/cut wood'. A scarce Staffs surname.

Haddon P Place-name in Derbys, Dorset, Northants OE 'heathery hill'. Or a variant of **Howden**.

Hadfield P Place-name in Derbys OE 'heathery field'.

Hadley P Place-name *Hadley/Hadleigh* in Essex, Middx, Suffolk, Sussex OE 'heathery clearing/field'.

Hagan F Irish: Anglicized form of Gaelic **O'** [descendant of] **hAgain** ('young'). In England the surname can be derived from a Germanic first-name meaning 'thornbush, fence, protector'. A connexion with a Germanic word for a tomcat, to denote virility, has also been suggested.

Haggis P Scots: from one of various Lowland places so-called ON and OE 'clearing-house'. Probably no connexion with the tasty food of this name, Burns's 'Chieftain o' the puddin' race'.

Hagley P Place-name in various counties OE 'haw wood/clearing'.

Hague, *see* Haig.

Haig(h)/Hague T/P Dweller near a fenced enclosure OE or ON, or from a place-name *Haigh* with the same meaning in Lancs and WRYorks (two such). Scots: from one of a number of place-names in northern France, such as *La Hague* ON 'enclosure', in Manche. 'In the case of the Earls **Haig** the origin is **Haighton**, a place-name in Lancs OE *Haugh* "settlement in a nook recess"' (Cottle).

Hail(e)y/Hall(e)y/Hal(e)y P Place-name in Bucks, Herts, Oxon OE 'hay clearing/field'. *Edmond Halley (1656–1742), the English astronomer who gave his name to a comet, was born in Haggerston, London, the son of a wealthy soapboiler... The pop singer Bill Haley [pronounced 'Hay-lee'] (1925–1981), born in Michigan but raised in Pennsylvania, was only too delighted, given his surname, to name his backing group 'The Comets'.*

Haim(e), *see* Hammond.

Hain(e)(s)/Hanes/Hayne(s) F/P/N From a ME first-name *Hain* ('hawthorn'); or from a place-name element such as *Hayne(s)*, found in *Haynes*, Beds, but particularly in evidence in Devon OE 'enclosure'; or a nickname for humble, mean, niggardly person OE. The '-*e*-' element in certain variants indicates the use of a weak adjective after a lost definite article. *John Haynes (?1594–1653), the first Governor of Connecticut, was originally from Essex, England; his name-*

sake, the well-known Fulham and England footballer John Norman ('Johnny') Haynes (1934–2005), was born in the Kentish Town area of North London.

Hair, *see* **O'Hair** and **Ayer**.

Hake, *see* **Hack**.

Haldane/Halden/Haldin F Scots: From the ON first-name *Halfdanr* (OE *Healfdene*) – literally 'half Dane', for a person of mixed parentage. Readily confused with/a variant of **Alden**. *Richard Burdon Haldane, Viscount Haldane (1856–1928), Lord Chancellor, who was born in Edinburgh, belonged to a family with roots in Gleneagles, Perthshire.*

Hale/Haugh/Hallows/Heal(e)/Hele T/P/F Dweller in a nook, side-valley, retreat, or on alluvial land OE *halh*; or by a hedge, enclosure OE *haga*; or from one of several place-names such as *Hale, Hales, Haw, Hawes, Heale, Hele*, with the same meaning; or from a ME first-name (OE *Hoele* or *Hoegel*). **Haw** and **Hawes** can be variants of **Hale** or be from a Norman female first-name *Haueis*, from Germanic *Haduwidis* 'battle-wide'. See also **Hawk**.

Haley, *see* **Haily**.

Halford P Place-name in Devon, Salop, Warwicks OE 'ford in a nook'. *The firm of Halfords, known for selling car and bicycle parts, had its origins in a shop opened in the early twentieth century in Halford Street, Leicester.*

Halfpenny N Nickname for a person of little value, or short in stature, or who paid a half-penny rent. A very scarce surname. Although there is such a surname in Ireland (an Anglicized form of Gaelic **O'** [descendant of] **hAilpin**), the famous *Halfpenny Bridge* over the Liffey in Dublin (opened in 1816 as the Wellington Bridge) is so-called because of the charge originally levied on pedestrians who used it. Do bearers of the surname pronounce it 'hayp'ny'?

Hal(l)ifax P Place-name *Halifax* in WRYorks OE 'holy (i.e. church-owned) flax (-field)' OE, with loss of *-l-*; or OE 'holy rough grass' – a town which uses the punning

'holy head (of hair)' of Saint John the Baptist as its armorial bearings.

Hal(l)iwell/Hallawell/Hallowell P From one of a number of place-names such as *Halwell, Halwill, Holwell, Holywell*, including *Halliwell*, Lancs, with the meaning OE 'holy well'.

Hall T/O Dweller at, or worker at, a large house OE/ON. A common surname.

Hallam T From *Hallamshire*, a district of WRYorks around Sheffield OE 'stone, rock'; or from *Kirk Hallam, Little Hallam* or *West Hallam*, near Ilkeston, Derbys OE 'nook, recess'.

Hallawell, *see* **Haliwell**.

Hallet(t), *see* **Adlard**.

Halley, *see* **Haily**.

Halliday/Hallidie, *see* **Holiday**.

Hallifax, *see* **Halifax**.

Halliwell, *see* **Haliwell**.

Hallmark/Ailmark/Allmark/Almack N Nickname for a person who paid a 'half-mark' OE, worth six shillings and eight pence (one third of a pound), in rent. **Hallmark** is a scarce Lancs/Staffs surname.

Hallowell, *see* **Haliwell**.

Hallow(e)s P Place-names: *Hallow* in Worcs; *Hallows* in Lancs OE 'of (at) the nook'. Mainly a Lancs surname. See also **Hale**.

Hally, *see* **Haily**.

Halse P Place-name in Somerset, Northants OE 'neck' (of land). Largely a Devon surname.

Halste(a)d/Hasted P Place-names: *Halstead* in Essex, Kent, Leics; *Hawstead* in Suffolk OE '(strong)hold/shelter site'. **Halsted** and **Halstead** are mainly Lancs surnames; **Hasted** (readily confused with/a variant of **Halstead/Halsted**) has historically belonged mainly to Suffolk and to Hants, though Edward **Hasted** (1732–1812), historian of Kent, came from a family settled in that county. Compare **Horstead**.

Halton P Place-name in various counties OE 'settlement in a nook'.

Haly, *see* Haily.

Ham/Hamm/Hammer T Dweller at a river-meadow OE. **Ham** is very much a West Country surname; **Hammer**, scarce, has a presence in Cornwall and elsewhere; **Hamm**, even scarcer, is more widely scattered.

Hamblen, *see* Hamlin.

Hambleton, *see* Hamilton.

Hamblett, *see* Hammond.

Hamblin(g)/Hambly, *see* Hamlin.

Hambrook P Place-name in Gloucs OE 'rocky/stony brook', though this is predominantly a Kent surname.

Hame, *see* Hammond.

Hamerton/Hammerton P Place-names: *Hamerton* in Hunts and *Hammerton* in WRYorks (several such) ON and OE. The second element is 'place/farm' OE; the first element could be '(hammer-shaped) crag' or 'hammer(-smithy)' or a plant-name 'hammer-sedge/-wort'.

Hamilton/Hambleton P The town called *Hamilton* in Lanarkshire, Scotland, was so-named in the thirteenth century after an Englishman from a now-deserted place called *Hamilton* in Leics OE 'scarred/crooked hill'. In principle the **Hamilton** surname could be derived from either place, or from *Hambleton* in Lancs, Rutland, North Yorks; *Hambledon* in Hants, Surrey, Dorset; *Hambleden* in Bucks; or *Hameldon*, Lancs. A common surname in Scotland, one borne by the Dukes of Abercorn and by five other peers.

Hamlen, *see* Hamlin.

Hamlet(t)/Hamley, *see* Hammond.

Hamlin(e)/Hamblen/Hamblin(g)/Hambly/Hamley/Hamlyn F From an Anglo-Norman French first-name *Ham(b)lin*, a double diminutive of *Hammond* (see **Hammond**). Most variants belong mainly to Cornwall and the West Country. The *-b-* in **Hamblen/Hamblin(g)/Hambly** is added to ease pronunciation (compare **Hamblett**, a variant of **Hammond**). *In 1760 William Hamley, from Bodmin in Cornwall, founded the 'Noah's Ark' toy shop in High Holborn, London; it eventually acquired his surname, and at one time was the largest toy shop in the world... (Lord) Paul Hamlyn (1926–2001), Jewish publisher and philanthropist, was born Paul Bertrand Wolfgang Hamburger in Berlin; he moved to London with his family in 1933.*

Hamm/Hammer, *see* Ham.

Hammerton, *see* Hamerton.

Hammon, *see* Hammond.

Hammond/Ammon/Amond/Haim(e)/Hamblett/Hame/Hamlet(t)/Hamley/Hammon/Hamnet(t)/Hamon F From a Norman first-name *Hamo(n)* (already found in OF with excrescent *-d*); or from one of two ON first-names, *Hamundr* ('high-protection') or *Amundr* ('ancestor-protection'). Compare **Hamlin**. Variants ending in *-ett* are diminutives. Of **Hamlet**, Cottle says: 'No connection with a small village or the Prince of Denmark'. Shakespeare's son *Hamnet* was named after a godfather. The *-b-* in **Hamblett** is added to ease pronunciation (compare **Hamblen/Hamblin(g)/Hambly**, variants of **Hamlin**).

Hamnet(t)/Hamon, *see* Hammond.

Hampden P Place-name in Bucks OE 'homestead valley'. *John Hampden (1594–1643), parliamentary opponent of Charles I in the period before the Civil War, was the son of William Hampden of Great Hampden, Bucks.*

Hampshire/Hamshaw P From one of two place-names. *Hampshire*, the county in the south of England, which was *Suthampton-scir* c.1050, but *Hamtesira* in the thirteenth century, was named after *Hamtun*, the old name for *Southampton*. The abbreviated form *Hants* comes from OE *Hamtunscir* (*Hantescire* in Domesday Book, 1086). The county itself was long known as *Southampton(shire)*, though a map published by William Camden in 1637 bears the title '*Hamshire*', and *New Hampshire*, on the eastern seaboard of North America, was first named and settled as an independent colony in the year 1623. The area known as *Hallamshire* in the Sheffield area of South Yorks also gave rise to the **Hampshire** surname, and the surname is at its strongest in that part of the world. *John ('Jackie') Hampshire, Yorkshire and England cricketer and umpire, was born in 1941 in Thurnscoe, Yorks... Susan Hampshire OBE, the English film and television actress and campaigner on dyslexia issues, was born in London in 1942. Upon her marriage to Sir Eddie Kulukundis in 1981 she became Lady Kulukundis.*

Hampton P Place-name in nine contiguous southern and Midland counties OE 'homestead farm'/'chief manor'/'place in a river-meadow'/'(at the) high place' – not forgetting the towns of *South*hampton and *North*hampton.

Hanbury P Place-names: *Hanbury* in Staffs, Worcs OE '(at) the high fort/mound/manor' (the *-n-* indicating the weak dative of the adjective after a lost preposition and definite article); *Handborough*, Oxon OE '*Hagena*'s hill'. *The pharmaceutical company Allen and Hanbury had its origins in the early nineteenth century, when the prominent Quaker William Allen (1790–1859), who had a flourishing business in Plough Court, London, took on three partners, including his nephew Cornelius Hanbury (1796–1869), son of Capel Hanbury of Ware, Herts.*

Hancock/Hancox, *see* Hann.

Hand(s) N/F Nickname for a person with a deformed or missing hand OE. Irish: an Anglicized form of Gaelic **O'** [descendant of] Flaithimh.

Handcock, *see* Hann.

Handford/Hanford/Hannaford P Place-names: *Hannaford*, Devon; *Hanford*, Staffs; *Handforth*, Chesh OE 'ford where there were cocks', or '*Cock*'s ford'; *Hanford*, Devon,

may be OE 'stone/rock ford'. Readily confused with/a variant of **Hansford**.

Handley/Hanl(e)y P Place-names: *Handley* in Chesh, Derbys, Dorset; *Hanley* in Staffs, Worcs OE '(at) the high wood/clearing'. Both **Handley** and **Hanley** are surnames of the Midlands and the north, particularly strong in Lancs. *Thomas Reginald ('Tommy') Handley (1892–1949), comedian, was born at Toxteth Park, Liverpool.*

Hands, *see* Hand.

Hanes, *see* Hain.

Hanford P see Handford.

Hankin(g)(s)/Hanks, *see* Hann.

Hanl(e)y, *see* Handley.

Hann/Hancock/Hancox/Handcock/Hankin(g)(s)/Hanks/Hanson F From the mediaeval first-name *Han(n)*, usually a shortened form of *Johan* (*John*), though sometimes demonstrably derived from *Henry*, and even *Randolph*. Variants ending in *cock/cox* are diminutives (see **Cock**); the *-kin* suffix in **Hankin(g)** is from Flemish. **Hann** is a Dorset and Somerset surname, while **Hanks** is found mainly in Gloucs. *See also* **John**. *Anthony John ('Tony') Hancock (1924–1968), the English comedian who found fame as the fictitious Anthony Aloysius St John Hancock, the charming but bumbling occupant of 23 Railway Cuttings, East Cheam, was born at Small Heath, Birmingham... Thomas Jeffrey ('Tom') Hanks, American film actor and producer, was born in 1956 in Concord, California; his father Amos Mefford Hanks was a relation of President Abraham Lincoln's mother, and his earliest known male-line ancestor was Thomas Hanks, who died in Gloucester County, Virginia, in the late seventeenth century.*

Hannable, *see* Annable.

Hannaford, *see* Handford.

Hannah F/P From the mediaeval female first-name *Hannah*, from the Hebrew *Chana* ('God has favoured me [with offspring]'); or from the place-name *Hannah* in Lincs OE 'island full of (wild) cocks'/

'*Cock*'s island'; Irish: Anglicized form of Gaelic **O'** [descendant of] **hAnnaigh** ('iniquity').

Hannibal, *see* **Annable**.

Hansard o Occupational term for a maker or seller of cutlasses, daggers OF. Chiefly a Lincs surname. *Luke Hansard (1752–1838), from Norwich in Norfolk, began producing a series of printed reports of parliamentary proceedings which still bears his name.*

Hansford P From an unidentified place – possibly *Ansford*, Somerset OE '*Ealhmund*'s ford'. Largely a Dorset surname. Readily confused with/a variant of **Handford**.

Hanson, *see* **Hann**.

Harbisher o Occupational term for a 'shelterer' or lodginghouse-keeper OE and OF (from Germanic). Related to the rare surname **Herbage**, with the familiar change from *-ar-* to *-er-* (see **Armistead**). A very scarce NRYorks and WRYorks surname.

Harborn(e)/Harbourn(e)/Harburn P Place-name *Harborne* in Staffs, Warwicks OE 'dirty stream'.

Harbottle P Place-name in Northd OE 'hirelings' dwelling'. A Co Durham/Northd surname.

Harbourn(e)/Harburn, *see* **Harborn**

Harbutt, *see* **Herbert**.

Harcourt P Place-names in Salop: one near Cleobury Mortimer OE 'hawker's/falconer's cottage', another near Wem OE '?harper's cottage'/'?cottage at a salt-harp' (for sifting salt). Or from more than one place-name in Calvados and Eure, France (the second element meaning 'court, manor' OF, from Latin), whence the prominent English and French families of **Harcourt** derived their surname. Commonly pronounced '*Harkut*'.

Hardcastle P Place-name in WRYorks OE and OF (Norman) 'cheerless dwelling'. *William ('Bill') Hardcastle (1918–1975), journalist and radio broadcaster, was born in Newcastle-upon-Tyne.*

Harden P There are places so-called in

WRYorks OE 'grey/grey-stone (i.e. boundary)/hare valley' and in Staffs OE '?high enclosure', but this is very largely a Kent surname. Readily confused with/a variant of **Arden**.

Hardern, *see* **Arden**.

Hardie/Hardiman, *see* **Hardy**.

Harding(e) F From an OE first-name meaning 'brave man/warrior/hero'; also possibly absorbing *Hardwin*, Germanic ('bold friend'), brought to the British Isles by the Normans. **Hardinge**, a scarce variant, is commonly pronounced '*Harding*'.

Hardman O/F Occupational term for a herdsman; or from the OE first-name *Heardmann* ('brave/strong man'). Predominantly a Lancs surname. Readily confused with **Hardiman/Hardyman**.

Hardwick P Place-name in over fifteen counties OE '(dairy-)herd farm/sheep farm'. For the relationship between *-ar-* and *-er-* see **Armistead**. *Hardwick in Derbys was not only the geographical term used to identify the famous English noblewoman Bess of Hardwick (?1527–1608); it was also her maiden surname.*

Hardy/Hardie/Hardiman/Hardyman

N/F Nickname for a bold, tough, daring man OF, originally Germanic. **Hardie** is a rare form. **Hardiman** (readily confused with **Hardman**) can also be Irish in origin, an Anglicized form of Gaelic **O'** [descendant of] **hArgadain** ('silver'). *(James) Keir (formerly Kerr) Hardie (1856–1915), founder of the Labour Party, was born in Legbrannock, Lanarkshire, the illegitimate son of a farm servant named Mary Kerr, who married David Hardie in 1859.*

Hare N/F Nickname for a hare-like person (swift of foot, timorous) OE; or a variant of Irish **O'Hair**.

Harewood, *see* **Harwood**.

Harfoot N Nickname for a fast runner ON and OE ('harefoot'). A Cornish surname.

Harford P Place-name in Gloucs OE 'harts'

ford' and in Devon OE 'army ford'. A widely scattered surname, strongest in Gloucs.

Hargr(e)ave(s) P Place-name *Hargr(e)ave(s)* in Chesh, Lancs, Northants, Suffolk OE 'grove with hares/grey grove'.

Harland/Harlan P Place-name in NRYorks OE 'cairn/rock/tumulus land'. Chiefly a Co Durham and Yorks surname. An American family named **Harlan** can trace its origins back to George **Harland**, a Quaker immigrant from Durham. *The Belfast shipyard of Harland and Wolff was founded in 1861 by Gustav Wilhelm Wolff and Edward James Harland (1831–1895, later Sir Edward Harland, Bart), son of a physician from Scarborough, Yorks.*

Harley P Place-name in Salop, WRYorks OE 'wood/clearing with hares' (though OE 'grey wood' is possible). *William S. Harley, born in Milwaukee in 1880, joined forces with a childhood friend, Arthur Davidson, to produce the first Harley-Davidson motorcycle in 1903… Harley Street, London, was built in the mid eighteenth century on land which the Duke of Portland had inherited from his wife, the former Lady Margaret Cavendish Harley.*

Harlock/Horlick/Horlock N Nickname for a person with grey hair/'locks' OE. **Harlock** is a scattered surname, found mostly in Hunts; **Horlick**, scarce, is predominantly a Gloucs surname; **Horlock** can be found in southern counties of England, especially Dorset. *Horlicks, the well-known malted milk drink, takes its name from two brothers, William and James Horlick, who emigrated from Gloucs to the USA and founded the J. & W. Horlicks company in Chicago in 1873. Perhaps predictably, 'Horlicks' has become a euphemistic term for 'bollocks' ('a load of old Horlicks'/'they made a complete Horlicks of it'); company sales appear not to have suffered as a result.*

Harlow P Place-name in Essex and elsewhere OE 'army/people mound (Hundred meeting-place)'.

Harmon F From an OF (from Germanic) first-name meaning 'army man, warrior'. A scattered surname.

Harmsworth P Place-name *Harmondsworth*, Middx OE '*Heremund*'s enclosure'. Family name of the Viscounts Rothermere, the first of whom, Harold Sidney Harmsworth, was born in Hampstead, Middx.

Harold, *see* **Harrod**.

Harper/Harpur O Occupational term for a maker/player of harps OE. The **Harpur-Crewe** family was long settled at Calke Abbey in Derbys.

Harrad, *see* **Harrod**.

Harral(d)/Harrall, *see* **Harrod**.

Harrap, *see* **Harrop**.

Harrel(l), *see* **Harrod**.

Harrie(s), *see* **Harris**.

Harriman O Occupational term for a servant of a man named *Harry*. Strongest in Leics.

Harrington P/F Place-name in: Cumbd OE 'place/farm of *Hoefer*'s people'; Lincs OE '?settlement on stony ground'; Northants OE '?place of the heath-dwellers' (compare **Hetherington**). Irish: Anglicized form of Gaelic O' [descendant of] hArrachtain ('powerful'). *See also* **Arrington**.

Harris/Harrie(s)/Harris(s)on/Harry F From the first-name *Henry*; not so much a diminutive, rather its regular ME pronunciation. **Harris** vastly outnumbers **Harries** everywhere save in South Wales, where the latter slightly predominates. **Harris** is the family name of the Earls of Malmesbury, but has also commonly been adopted by Jewish immigrants.

Harrismith, *see* **Arrowsmith**.

Harris(s)on, *see* **Harris**.

Harrod/Harold/Harrad/Harral(d)/Harrall/Harrel(l)/Harrold/Herauld F/O From an OE first-name *Hereweald* (ON *Haraldr*), meaning 'army power'; or a variant of **Harwood**; or an occupational term for a herald OF *herau(l)t*. For the relationship between -*ar*- and -*er*- see **Armistead**. *Harrods department store was founded in Stepney, East*

London, in 1834 by Charles Henry Harrod; the move to Knightsbridge took place fifteen years later.

Harrop P Place-name in WRYorks and elsewhere OE 'hares' valley'. Chiefly a Chesh/Lancs/WRYorks surname. **Harrap** is a scarcer variant.

Harrow P Place-names: *Harrow*, Middx; *Peper Harrow*, Surrey OE 'heathen temple'. A scarce surname, strongest in Middx.

Harry, *see* **Harris**.

Hart/Hartigan N/F Nickname for a person bearing some resemblance to a hart or stag ME *hert*. For the relationship between *-ar-* and *-er-* see **Armistead**. The popular idea that this might be a sign-name is not borne out by early forms. Irish: Anglicized form of Gaelic **O'** [descendant of] **hAirt** ('bear'); **Hartigan** and **O'Hartigan** are variants. A surname which has also commonly been adopted by Jewish immigrants. It was a man called Lemon **Hart**, a Jewish wine and spirit merchant working in Penzance in the late eighteenth century, who first sold spirits under his own full name – and *Lemon Hart* rum still adorns the shelves of off-licences and supermarkets to the present day. **Hort** is a scarce variant, found particularly in Gloucs; **Hurt** belongs to Derbys, Notts and WRYorks. *The actor John Hurt, son of a clergyman, was born in Chesterfield, Derbys; his namesake (Mississippi) John Hurt, known for his delicate and incisive performances as a blues singer and guitarist, was born in Carroll County, Mississippi, in 1892.*

Hartfield P Place-name in Sussex OE 'field with stags', and chiefly a Sussex surname.

Hartford P Place-names: *Hartford* in Chesh and Northd, *Hertford* in Herts OE 'stag ford'; *Hartford* in Hunts OE 'army ford'.

Hartigan, *see* **Hart**.

Hartill P Place-name *Harthill* in Chesh, Derbys, West Yorks OE 'hill with stags'. A scarce surname which belongs chiefly to the West Midlands, especially Staffs.

Hartland P Place-name in Devon OE 'island (peninsula) with stags'.

Hartley P Place-name in several counties OE 'stag wood/clearing'; Northd OE 'stag hill'; Westmd OE 'wood claw (tongue of land between streams)'. Most commonly found in Lancs and WRYorks.

Harton P Place-name in Co Durham OE 'hill with stags' and in NRYorks OE '?stony/stoneheap farm'. A scarce scattered surname.

Hartshorn(e) P Place-name in Derbys OE 'headland with stags'.

Hartwell P Place-name in Bucks, Northants, Staffs OE 'stags' spring/stream'.

Harvey/Harvie/Hervey F From a Breton first-name *Aeruiu/Haerviu*, meaning 'battle/carnage-worthy'. Normanized as *Hervé* and introduced into England by Breton followers of William the Conqueror. The spelling **Hervey**, the family name of the Marquesses of Bristol, is older and much rarer; for the relationship between *-ar-* and *-er-* see **Armistead**. **Harvie** is a Scots variant.

Harwell P Place-name in Berks OE 'stream from the grey (hill)'. A scarce surname, with an oddly scattered presence in England, Scotland and Wales.

Harwich P Place-name in Essex OE 'army camp'. An exceptionally scarce surname.

Harwood/Harewood P Place-names: *Harwood* in Lancs, Northd, NRYorks; *Harewood* in Hants, Herefords, WRYorks OE 'grey/hares' wood'. The Lascelles family, Earls of **Harewood**, pronounce their title as '*Harwood*'. Readily confused with/a variant of **Horwood**. *See also* **Harrod**.

Hasel- For surnames beginning thus, *see* **Hazel-**.

Haskel(l), *see* **Ashkettle**.

Haskew/Haskey, *see* **Askew**.

Haskin(g), *see* **Ashkettle**.

Haslam T/P Dweller by the hazels OE, or from a place-name in Lancs with the same meaning, exhibiting a dative plural following a lost preposition. Chiefly a Lancs surname.

Hasle- For surnames beginning thus, *see* Hazel-.

Hasler P Place-names: *Haselor*, Warwicks; *Haselour*, Staffs OE 'hazel slope', but a scarce Essex/Middx surname.

Haslip/Haslop/Haslup, *see* Heslop.

Hasted, *see* Halsted.

Haswell P Place-name in Co Durham and in Somerset OE 'spring/stream in the hazels'. A scattered surname, strong in Co Durham.

Hatch/Hatcher T/P Dweller by a gate OE or from places so-named in Beds, Hants, Somerset, Wilts OE 'gate, forest-gate, floodgate, sluice'. Both **Hatch** and **Hatcher** are well-established in southern counties of England, but **Hatch** also has a presence in Lancs. *The Hatch family of Ulcombe, Kent, were well known as bellfounders from the sixteenth century onwards.*

Haterley/Haterly, *see* Hattersley.

Hatfield/Hatfull P Place-names *Hatfield* in various counties OE 'field overgrown with heather'. The bizarre variant **Hatfull**, very scarce, can be found in Kent, Middx and Surrey.

Hatherleigh/Hatherley P Place-names: *Hatherleigh* in Devon, *Hatherley* in Gloucs OE 'hawthorn wood/clearing'. In the event, these are chiefly Devon surnames in either spelling.

Hatherton P Place-name in Chesh OE 'hawthorns/?heather settlement' and in Staffs OE 'hawthorn hill'. A scarce surname, found mainly in northern counties.

Hatrly/Hatterlay/Hatterley/Hatterly, *see* Hattersley.

Hattersley P Place-name in Chesh, of uncertain etymology, perhaps OE 'deer/stag's clearing'. Known variants include **Haterley, Haterly, Hatrly, Hatterlay, Hatterley, Hatterly. Hattersley** is principally a WRYorks surname. *Roy (Sydney George) Hattersley, Baron Hattersley, former deputy leader of the Labour Party, was born in 1932 in Sheffield, WRYorks, of which city his mother Enid Hattersley was Lord Mayor in 1981–82.*

Hatton P Place-names in several counties OE 'place on a heath'.

Hattrick, *see* Arkwright.

Haugh, *see* Hale.

Haughton P Place-name in six counties OE 'settlement in a nook'; but the place-name in Notts is OE 'settlement on the spur of a hill'.

Hauxwell P Place-name in NRYorks OE 'spring/stream with hawks' or *'Hafoc'*s spring/stream'. A scarce NRYorks surname.

Havelock F From an ON first-name *Hafleikr*, meaning 'sea-play/sport'. A Co Durham/Northd surname. *General Sir Henry Havelock (1796–1857), hero of the Indian Mutiny of 1857, was born at Ford Hall, near Sunderland, the son of William Havelock, a shipbuilder, and his wife Jane (née Carter). Many a public house is named in his honour.*

Havercroft P Place-name in WRYorks ON and OE 'oat croft', but principally a Lincs surname.

Haverfield T/P Dweller at an oat field ON and OE, or from an unidentified place with this meaning. A scarce scattered surname.

Haw/Hawes, *see* Hale.

Hawk(e)(s) O/N/T Occupational term for a keeper of hawks OE, or a nickname for one who paid a hawk by way of rent, or for a person resembling a hawk in some way (rapacious? sharp-eyed?). But where such a surname was originally preceded by the prepositions *de* or *atte*, and for **Haw** and **Hawes**, *see* Hale. **Hawke** is a strongly Cornish surname. **Hawkett** is a very scarce Kent/Middx diminutive form. See also **Hawkin**. *Robert James Lee ('Bob') Hawke, former Rhodes Scholar at Oxford University and Prime Minister of Australia, was born in Bordertown, South Australia, in 1929; both his parents were of*

Cornish extraction... The male-line ancestry of the noted American film director Howard Hawks (1896–1977) can be traced back to John Hawks of Hadley, Massachusetts and Windsor, Connecticut, said to be the brother of Adan Hawks, a member of the famous Winthrop fleet of immigrants which arrived in the New World in 1630.

Hawkett, *see* **Hawk**.

Hawkin(g)(s) F Diminutive of *Hal*, a pet-form of the first-name *Harry* (which itself is a diminutive of *Henry*); or a diminutive of **Hawk**. **Hawkins** is a widespread surname; **Hawkings**, much less common, belongs mainly to Devon and Somerset.

Hawkridge P There are places so-called in Berks and Somerset OE 'ridge with hawks', but this is mainly a WRYorks surname.

Hawks, *see* **Hawk**.

Hawksworth P Place-name in WRYorks OE 'Hafoc's enclosure' and Notts 'Hoc's/Hauk's enclosure'. Mainly a WRYorks surname.

Haworth P In principle this surname is derived from the place-name *Haworth* in WRYorks OE 'hedge enclosure', though George Redmonds has found evidence in Yorkshire of a John **Hayward**, also known as **Hayworth** and **Haworth** in Kirkburton (1548–1562) and a William **Haworthe**, alias **Hayward**, in Saddleworth (1603). In short, **Haworth** belongs to a set of surnames such as **Haywood**, **Hayworth**, **Heywood**, **Heyworth**, **Howard** and **Howarth**, which are readily confused and can in principle be variants of each other.

Hawthorn(e) T/P Dweller at a hawthorn OE bush, or from a place-name with the same meaning, of which there are several. The *-e* in **Hawthorne** could indicate the use of a dative after a lost preposition. **Hawthorn** is widely scattered throughout England and Scotland, but **Hawthorne** is less common; both have a significant presence in Staffs. *The American novelist Nathaniel Hawthorne (1804–1864), born in Salem, Massachusetts, is descended from William Hathorne, who was an immigrant from England in 1630. It is said that the shame of discovering that this*

William's son John was a judge at the Salem witch trials caused Nathaniel to add a 'w' to his surname shortly after leaving college.

Hawton P There is a place so-called in Notts OE 'settlement in a hollow', though this is chiefly a West Country surname.

Hawtr(e)y, *see* **Daltry**.

Hay/Hey T/P/N/F Dweller by a fence, enclosure, hedge OE; or from a place-name with the same meaning in various counties; or from *La Haye/Les Hayes* in Normandy; or a nickname for a tall ('high') person; or from the mediaeval first-name *Hay* (also with the meaning of 'tall'). George Redmonds points out that the difficulty with the surname **Hey** is that there were two similar words in OE meaning 'enclosure' (leading to place-names such as *Hey* and *Haigh*, and thus to related surnames), and that they are almost impossible to separate. One **Hey** family in WRYorks had its origins in a 'hey' or enclosure in Scammonden. Other variants of the surname include **De la Hay(e)** and **Delahay(e)**. **Hay** is principally a surname of Scotland and the north of England, and is the family name of the Marquesses of Tweeddale and the Earls of Erroll and of Kinnoull. Readily confused with/a variant of **Hays**.

Hayden, *see* **Haydon**.

Haydock P Place-name in Lancs OW 'barley/corn place', and principally a Lancs surname.

Haydon/Hayden P Place-names: *Haydon*: Kent OE 'heather(-grown) hill'; Dorset, Somerset, Wilts OE 'hay/enclosure hill'; Northd (three such) OE 'hay valley' – and there are further places so-named in Gloucs, Herts and Surrey; *Hayden*: Gloucs OE 'enclosure hill'. **Hayden** is a scattered surname; **Haydon** is found mainly in Devon, Middx and Surrey. Readily confused with/a variant of **Heydon**.

Hayes, *see* **Hays**.

Hayho(e)/Hayhow/Heyhoe T/P Dweller at a high hillspur OE, or from a minor place-name with the same meaning. East

Anglian surnames, except for **Hayho**, which is very scarce and scattered.

Hayling P/F Place-name *Hayling* in Hants OE '*Hoegel*'s people'. Welsh: from the first-name *Heilyn* ('cup-bearer'); **Bolan** and **Palin** are Welsh 'son of *Heilyn*' (*ab Heilyn*) – though none of these surnames seems to have taken root in the Principality itself. **Hayling**, uncommon, is found in Gloucs and Worcs; **Bolan** is strongest in Lancs, and **Palin** in Chesh. In principle **Pelling** could also be a variant of *ab Heilyn*, but being a very scarce Sussex surname, it is almost certainly derived from the minor place-name *Peelings* in that county (*Pellinges* in Domesday Book) OE '?(the home of) *Pydel*'s people'. *The stage surname of singer/songwriter Marc Bolan (1947–1977) would be entirely a red herring here. Born with the name Mark Feld into a Jewish family in Hackney, he originally chose to call himself Toby Tyler, but when the Decca record company arbitrarily renamed him Marc Bowland, he asserted at least some authority by opting for the alternative Bolan… Michael Palin, comedian, actor, writer and television presenter, was born in Sheffield, Yorks, in 1943.*

Hayne(s), *see* **Hain**.

Hay(e)s P/F There are places called *Hayes* in Devon and Dorset OE 'of (at) the enclosure', and in Kent OE 'brushwood'. Irish: Anglicized form of Gaelic **O'** [descendant of] **hAodha** ('fire'). Readily confused with/a variant of **Hay**.

Haythornthwaite/Haythornwhite P Place-name *Hawthornthwaite* in Lancs ON 'clearing with hawthorns'. A surname which has been subject to a bewildering variety of spellings over the centuries. A calendar of wills proved in the Archdeaconry of Richmond includes no fewer than thirteen such spellings from 1561 to 1680: **Hathenthwait; Hathernett; Hathernwhate; Hathornthwait; Hathornthwaite; Hathornthwat; Hathornthwayt; Hathornthwayte; Hathernthwaite; Hawthornthate; Hawthornewhaite; Hathornwaite; Hathornwat**. There have also been **Hathronwhett**s and **Heathornwight**s, and

when John, son of John **Hatharnethawight** was apprenticed to Richard Eskrige of the Brewers' Company of London on 27 January 1572/3, the enrolling clerk no doubt did his best to spell this very exotic northern surname as he heard it pronounced.

Hayton P Place-names in several counties OE 'hay/enclosure/hedge farm'.

Hayward O Occupational term for an official who supervised the Lammas lands enclosed for corn and controlled straying cattle, a bailiff OE 'fence/hedge/enclosure guardian'. Readily confused with/a variant of **Haworth**, **Haywood**, **Hayworth**, **Heywood**, **Heyworth**, **Howard** and **Howarth**.

Haywood P Place-name in several counties OE 'fenced/enclosed wood'. Readily confused with/a variant of **Haworth**, **Hayward**, **Hayworth**, **Heywood**, **Heyworth**, **Howard** and **Howarth**.

Hayworth/Heyworth P Place-name *Hayward's Heath*, Sussex, which was *Hayworthe* in 1261 OE 'hedge/hay enclosure'. Readily confused with/a variant of **Haworth**, **Hayward**, **Haywood**, **Heywood**, **Howard** and **Howarth**. *The Hollywood actress Rita Hayworth was the daughter of Eduardo Cansino and Volga Haworth [sic], a Ziegfeld Follies dancer who was said to be related to the distinguished American actor, Joseph Haworth (1855–1903). Rita Hayworth was a cousin by marriage of the actress and dancer Ginger Rogers; both married five times.*

Hazel(l)/Hessel T Dweller at a hazel tree OE. *Phoebe Hessel, famed for having fought for many years as a private soldier in the fifth regiment of foot, was born in Stepney and died (reputedly at the age of one hundred and eight) in Brighton, Sussex, in 1821.*

Hazeldeane/Hazelden(e)/Hazeldine/ Hazeldon/Hes(s)eldine/Hes(s)eltine P Place-names (*Hasel-*, *Hesel-*, *Hesle-*, *Hasling* + *-den*, *-don*) OE 'valley of hazels'. Readily confused with/a variant of **Hazelton/Hazeltine**.

Hazelgrave/Hazelgrove T/P Dweller in a hazel grove, or from one of a number of place-names with the same meaning, including: *Hazel Greave, Hazle Greave, Hez-zlegreave, Hazelgrove, Hazel Grove*, WRYorks; *Hazel Grove*, NRYorks. Cottle makes reference to *Hazel Grove* in Chesh, but this settlement on the outskirts of Stockport acquired its name in the nineteenth century, having formerly been known as Bullock Smithy. **Hazelgrave**, a very scarce surname, has a limited presence in Staffs and in WRYorks. Given the fact that **Hazelgrove**, slightly less rare, is found almost exclusively in Sussex, it would seem that the place called *Hazel Grove* in that county could well be the principal place of origin.

Hazelhurst P Place-name in Lancs OE 'wooded hill with hazels'.

Hazell, *see* **Hazel**.

Hazelrigg P Place-name in Cumbd, Lancs, Northd ON 'ridge covered with hazels'.

Hazelton/Hazeltine P Place-name in Gloucs (two such) OE 'place in the hazels/hazel valley'. Readily confused with/a variant of **Hazeldeane** and its variants.

Hazelwood/Aizlewood P Place-names *Hazelwood/Hazlewood* in various counties OE 'hazel wood'. **Aizlewood** is chiefly found in WRYorks.

Hazle- For surnames beginning thus, *see* **Hazel**.

Head T/N Dweller at the head or top of a valley OE, or a nickname for a person with some peculiarity of the head (from the same OE word). A prolific surname in south-east England in particular.

Headlam P Place-name in Co Durham OE '(at) the heathery clearings', exhibiting the use of a dative plural after a lost preposition. A Co Durham and NRYorks surname.

Headley/Hedley P Place-names *Headley* and *Hedley* in various counties OE 'heathery clearing'.

Heal(e), *see* **Hale**.

Healey/Healy/Heel(e)y P/F Place-name *Healey* in Lancs and elsewhere in the north of England OE 'high wood/clearing'.

Irish: an anglicized form of Gaelic **O'** [descendant of] **hEilidhe** ('the claimant') or of **O'hEalaighthe** ('ingenious'). *Denis (Winston) Healey, Baron Healey, Labour politician and Chancellor of the Exchequer, whose paternal grandfather was a tailor from Enniskillen in Northern Ireland, was born in Mottingham in Kent in 1917, but moved with his family to Keighley WRYorks when he was five years old… Austin-Healey cars, based upon a model developed by Donald Mitchell Healey, first went into production in the 1950s… Austin (Sean) Healey, Leicester Tigers and England rugby player [his naming can hardly have been an accident…], was born in 1973 in Wallasey, Chesh.*

Heard, *see* **Herd**.

Hearn(e), *see* **Hern**. But sometimes a variant of Irish **Aherne**.

Hearnshaw, *see* **Earnshaw**.

Heath T/P Dweller on a heath, or from a place-name with the same meaning, found in several counties OE 'heath' – that is, land commonly covered in heather. *Sir Edward Richard George ('Ted') Heath, former Prime Minister of the United Kingdom, was born in Broadstairs, Kent. His father was a carpenter and his mother a maid… Johnny Kidd (1935–1966), the singer and songwriter who named himself after the notorious pirate Captain Kidd and had a backing group called The Pirates, was born Frederick Heath in Willesden, North London.*

Heathcote/Heathcoat/Heathcott P Place-name in Derbys, Warwicks and elsewhere OE 'cottage on a heath'. Chiefly a Derbys surname, and commonly pronounced '*Hethket*'. *Sir John Heathcoat Heathcoat-Amory, MP for Tiverton, Devon, the son of Samuel Amory and the grandson of the man who invented the lace machine, assumed the additional surname of Heathcoat in 1874.*

Heathfield P Place-name in Somerset, Sussex OE 'field with heather'.

Heatley P Place-name in Chesh, Staffs, Salop OE 'heathery clearing'. A Midlands/northern surname.

Heaton P Place-names in Lancs, Northd and WRYorks OE 'high place'.

Heaven(s) F Welsh: a corruption of the first-name *Evan* as a result of folk etymology (see **Evans**).

Hebble(th)waite/Hebblewhite/Hepplewhite P Place-name *Heblethwaite*, WRYorks OE 'clearing by a plank-bridge (dialectal)'. *George Hepplewhite (?1727–1786), cabinet and chair maker, was probably born in Ryton, Co Durham; he served an apprenticeship in Lancaster before moving to London, where he established a flourishing business.*

Hebborn/Hebb(o)urn, *see* Hepburn.

Hebden P Place-name in WRYorks OE 'valley where hips grow'. A Yorks/Lancs surname.

Hector F The great Trojan hero *Hector*'s name (Greek: '?holding fast') was spread by mediaeval romances, and took root in Scotland as a convenient rendering of the Scots Gaelic first-names *Eachdonn* ('brown horse') and *Eachann* ('horse': see **McKechnie**). **Hector** is not a common surname, but has a significant presence (oddly?) in the West Country as well as in Scotland.

Hedge(s)/Hedger T Dweller at a hedge OE. *The firm of Benson and Hedges, cigarette manufacturers, was founded in 1873 by Richard Benson and William Hedges. Noel Gallagher, member of the pop group Oasis, not only smoked Benson and Hedges cigarettes – he also named his two dogs 'Benson' and 'Hedges'.*

Hedgecock/Hedgecoe, *see* Richard.

Hedger/Hedges, *see* Hedge.

Hedghog(g) F An exceptionally scarce surname which Bardsley is happy enough to regard as a nickname based upon the little bristly animal – a quite extraordinary proposition? **Hedghog(g)** will presumably be nothing more than a development of **Hedgecock/Hedgecoe**, variants of **Richard**, by a process of folk etymology? In 1608 a man described as George **Hedghogge**, gent, of Warwicks was a co-defendant in a case

proceeding through the Court of Star Chamber, and on 2 March 1618/19 a licence was issued by the Bishop of London in respect of the forthcoming marriage of Dominick Vanoutwick and Barbara **Hedghogg**, widow of John **Hedghogg**.

Hedley, *see* Headley.

Heel(e)y, *see* Healey.

Hegarty F Irish: an Anglicized form of Gaelic **O'** [descendant of] **hEigceartaigh** ('unjust').

Hele, *see* Hale.

Helliar/Hellier/Hilliar/Hillier/Hillyer O Occupational term for a roofer, tiler, slater OE. All variants are most commonly found in the West Country.

Hemery, *see* Amery.

Hem(m)ingway P From an unidentified minor place in WRYorks ON and OE '*Hemming*'s way/path'. *Ernest Hemingway (1899–1961), American author and journalist, was named after his maternal grandfather, Ernest Hall, an English immigrant and Civil War veteran who lived with the Hemingway family in a house he owned in the suburbs of Chicago.*

Hemming(s) F From an ON first-name *Hemmingr* (the first element meaning 'home'). **Hemming** is a West Midlands surname; **Hemmings** is rather more widely spread.

Hempstead P Place-name *Hempstead/ Hempsted*: Essex, Herts OE 'homestead'; Gloucs, a contraction of OE 'high homestead'; Norfolk OE 'place where hemp grows'. East Anglian surnames.

Henderson, *see* Henry.

Hendon P Place-name in Middx OE '(at) the high hill', the *Hen-* element being a weak dative adjective after a lost preposition and the definite article. *Hendon* in Co Durham OE 'valley with hinds (female deer)' may or may not have given rise to such a surname, but by the late nineteenth century **Hendon** had become limited mainly to the counties of Middx and Surrey.

Hendra P From one of a number of place-names in Cornwall, Cornish *hendre* 'winter homestead'. A Cornish surname.

Hendr(e)y/Hendrie, *see* Henry.

Hendy N Nickname for a courteous, courtly, kind person ME. Mainly a south-west-of-England surname.

Henfrey F A Norman version of a Germanic first-name meaning 'home peace'. A scarce surname, found mainly in the Midlands and the North.

Henham P Place-name in Essex, Suffolk OE '(at) the high homestead' (with *Hen-* as in **Hendon**), but mainly a Kent surname.

Henley P Place-name in several counties; OE '(at) the high wood/clearing' (with *Hen-* as in **Hendon**), but the place-name in Salop is OE 'bird wood' (compare the word *'hen'*).

Hennes(s)(e)y F Irish: Anglicized form of Gaelic **O'** [descendant of] **hAonghusa** (*Angus*). **Hennessy** is the family name of the Barons Windlesham. *The company which produces Hennessy cognac takes its name from its founder, Richard Hennessy (born 1720), who left Co Cork in Ireland to make his home in France.*

Henry/Hendr(e)y/Hendrie F From a Norman version of a Germanic first-name meaning 'home power'. The first-name of eight Kings of England. Found as a surname mainly in the north of England and in Scotland, and is the source of many other surnames in *Han-/Hen-/Harr-/Herr-*. **Hendr(e)y** and **Hendrie** are Scottish forms, as is **Henderson** ('son of *Henry*'), which is the family name of the Barons Faringdon.

Henshaw P Place-name in Northd OE '*Hethin*'s nook' and in Chesh ME 'hen wood'. **Henshaw**s migrated far and wide: though the surname is mostly found in northern and Midland counties, one family of that name living in Billingshurst, Sussex, had its origins in William **Henshaw** of Worth in that county, who died in 1587.

Hensman O Occupational term for a groom, squire, carrier OE (literally 'stal-lion-man'). A scarce surname, found chiefly in Middx and Northants.

Henstridge P Place-name in Somerset OE 'ridge where stallions were kept'. The first element occurs in the virile name of *Hengist*, who began the expulsion of the Britons from England. A scarce surname, found chiefly in Hants and Wilts.

Henthorn(e) P Place-name in Lancs OE 'thorn-bush/-spinney with birds', and a Lancs surname.

Henton P Place-name in Oxon OE '(at) the high place' (with *Hen-* as in **Hendon**) and in Somerset OE '?hen farm', though the surname is most commonly found in Notts.

Henwick P Place-name in Northants, Worcs OE 'monks' dwelling', but a very scarce Sussex surname.

Henwood P Place-name in Warwicks OE 'nuns' wood' and in Cornwall OE 'bird wood'. Principally a Cornish surname.

Hepburn/Hebborn/Hebbo(u)rn P Place-names: *Hepburn*, Co Durham and *Hebburn*, Northd OE 'high burial-mound/tumulus'. *Katharine (Houghton) Hepburn (1907–2003), American film, stage and television star, was born in Hartford, Connecticut; she counts the* Mayflower *immigrant William Brewster as one of her ancestors… Audrey Hepburn (1929–1993), Anglo-Dutch film and stage actress, was born Audrey Kathleen Ruston in Elsene, Brussels, Belgium, the daughter of an English father (Joseph Victor Anthony Ruston, who eventually appended the surname of his maternal grandmother Kathleen Hepburn to his own), and a Dutch aristocratic mother (Baroness Ella van Heemstra). Audrey Hepburn's ancestors include King Edward III of England and James Hepburn, Fourth Earl of Bothwell, from whom Katharine Hepburn may also be descended.*

Heppenstall, *see* Heptonstall.

Hepple P Place-name in Northd OE 'nook where hips grow'. A Co Durham/Northd surname.

Heptonstall/Heppenstall/Heptinstall/
P Place-name *Heptonstall* in WRYorks OE
'stall/stable where hips grow'.

Hepworth P Place-name in Suffolk and
WRYorks OE 'enclosure where hips grow'.
An uncommon WRYorks surname. *Dame
Barbara Hepworth (1903–1975), British sculp-
tor, was born in Wakefield, WRYorks.*

Herapath T Dweller by a military road,
highway OE (literally 'army path'). 'A
resounding old surname, which must
have been applied early, before the *word*
itself left our vocabulary' (Cottle). A scarce
surname, found in places as far apart as
Middx and Glamorgan.

Herauld, *see* **Harrod.**

Herbage, *see* **Harbisher.**

Herbert F A Germanic first-name brought
to Britain by the Normans, meaning 'army-
bright'. **Harbutt** represents what would
have been an earlier pronunciation of **Herbert**, later modified by the familiar move
from *-ar-* to *-er-* (see **Armistead**). **Herbert**
is the family name of the Earls of Carnar-
von, Pembroke and Montgomery, and
Powis, and of two Barons. A widespread surname throughout England and Wales.

Herd/Heard O Occupational term for a
herdsman OE.

Hermitage, *see* **Armitage.**

Hern(e)/Hearn(e)/Hurn T/P Dweller by a
nook, bend, corner, spit of land, curving
valley OE, or from the place-name *Herne*,
with the same meaning, in Kent; *Herne* in
Beds is OE '?(at) the stoneheaps', exhibiting
the use of a dative plural after a lost preposition. The spelling **Hurn** uses a West Midland and southern *-u-* for a south-eastern *-e-*
(OE West Saxon *-y-*).

Herrick F From an ON first-name *Eirik*,
meaning 'mercy/peace-power'. The initial
H- is parasitic. Most commonly found in
Lincs by the late nineteenth century. *Sir
William Herrick or Heyricke (?1557–1652),
Elizabethan financier and royal jeweller,
came from a noted Leicester family. His son*

*Henry Herrick is known to have been living in
Salem, Massachusetts, as early as 1629, and
the poet Robert Herrick (1591–1674), the son
of Nicholas Herrick and grandson of Thomas
Ericke, came from the same Leics family.*

Herring O/N Occupational term for a person who sold herring, or who fished for
them OE; or a nickname for a person of little
value (there is evidence from as early as the
thirteenth century of the phrase 'not worth
a herring' being in common use). A widespread surname which is found in not a few
coastal counties.

Herst, *see* **Hurst.**

Hervey, *see* **Harvey.**

Hes(s)el- For surnames beginning thus, *see*
Hazel-.

Hes(s)eldine/Hes(s)eltine, *see* **Hazeldeane.**

Hesketh/Heskett P Place-name *Hesketh* in
Lancs, NRYorks ON 'horse-track, race-
course'; but *Hesketh Newmarket*, Cumbd, is
ON and OE 'ash-tree hill', with a a parasitic
H-.

**Heslop/Haslip/Haslop/Haslup/Hislop/
Hyslop** P From an unidentified place-name
in the north of England with the meaning
of 'hazel valley' OE. **Heslop** is found chiefly
in Co Durham and Northd; **Hislop** is mainly
a Scottish surname. *Ian Hislop, editor of the
satirical British magazine* Private Eye *and
once the most sued man in England, was
born in 1960 in Swansea, South Wales, to a
Scottish father and a mother from the Channel
Islands.*

Hessel- For surnames beginning thus, *see*
Hazel-.

Hesseldine/Hesseltine, *see* **Hazeldeane.**

Heston P Place-name in Middx OE 'place in
the brushwood', though this scarce surname is mainly found in Lancs.

Hetherington P Place-name in Northd OE
'?place of the heath-dwellers'. Strongest in
Cumbd. Compare **Harrington**.

Hett P Place-name in Co Durham OE

'hat(-shaped hill)'. Mainly a surname of the English Midlands and north.

Heugh P Place-name in various counties, including Co Durham OE 'hill-spur' (compare **Hough**).

Hever P Place-name in Kent OE 'high edge'. A scarce Kent surname.

Hewat, *see* **Hugh**.

Hewer O Occupational term for a stone-/wood-cutter OE. Chiefly a Gloucs surname.

Hewet(t)/Hewetson, *see* **Hugh**.

Hewick P Place-name in WRYorks OE 'high dwelling'. Chiefly a Yorks surname.

Hewish/Huish P Place-names: *Hewish* in Somerset; *Huish* in Devon, Somerset and Wilts OE 'hide of land' (enough to support a family/household). From the same stem as **Hyde**. A West Country surname in both spellings.

Hewit(t)/Hewitson/Hewlett/Hewlitt/ Hewson, *see* **Hugh**.

Hext N Nickname for the 'highest, tallest' person OE. Chiefly a Devon surname.

Hey, *see* **Hay**.

Heydon P Place-name in Cambs/Norfolk OE 'hay valley/hill'. A scarce and scattered surname, strongest in Oxon. Readily confused with/a variant of **Haydon**.

Heyhoe, *see* **Hayho**.

Heysham P Place-name in Lancs (pronounced '*Heesham*') OE 'homestead in the brushwood'. A scarce surname which (oddly) is strongest in Devon.

Heywood P Place-name in Lancs/Wilts OE 'high/enclosed wood'. Readily confused with/a variant of **Haworth**, **Hayward**, **Haywood**, **Hayworth**, **Heyworth**, **Howard** and **Howarth**.

Heyworth, *see* **Hayworth**.

Hick(s), *see* **Richard**.

Hickey F Irish: Anglicized form of Gaelic **O'**

[descendant of] **hIcidhe** ('healer/physician').

Hickinbotham/Higginbotham/Higginbottam/Higginbottom P Place-name in Lancs OE 'valley with oaks', now known as *Oakenbottom*.

Hickmott/Hickson, *see* **Richard**.

Hidden P Place-name in Berks OE 'valley with a landing-place', but a scarce Kent/Lancs/Middx surname.

Higgen(s)/Higgin(s), *see* **Richard**.

Higginbotham/Higginbottam/Higginbottom, *see* **Hickinbotham**.

Higgins, *see* **Richard**.

Higgs, *see* **Richard**.

Higham P Place-names in several counties OE 'high homestead'.

Higson, *see* **Richard**.

Hil(l)ary F From a mediaeval first-name, from Latin 'cheerful' (compare *hilarious*). Saint *Hilary* of Poitiers (died AD 368) made it popular as a male first-name, but **Hilary** can also be a perversion of the first-name *Eulalia*, Greek 'sweetly speaking', the name of a female patron saint of Barcelona, which early acquired an *-r-* for the second *-l-*. **Hilary** and **Hillary** are mostly found in the north of England. *See also* **Ellery**. *Sir Edmund (Percival) Hillary, mountaineer and explorer, was born in Tuakau, near Auckland, New Zealand, in 1919; his Yorkshire grandparents had settled in northern Wairoa in the mid nineteenth century.*

Hildebrand F From a Germanic first-name meaning 'battle-sword', an appropriate name for the most militant of all popes. A scarce scattered surname within England.

Hilder T Dweller at a slope OE plus *-er* suffix. A Kent/Sussex surname.

Hill(s) P/F Dweller at the hill OE; or, very rarely, from the pet-form of some Germanic first-name beginning *Hild-* ('battle'). A very common surname, the family name of the Marquesses of Downshire and the Barons Sandys.

Hillam P Place-name in WRYorks OE '(at) the hills', exhibiting the use of a dative plural after a lost preposition. Principally a WRYorks surname.

Hillary, *see* Hilary.

Hilliar/Hillier/Hillyer, *see* Helliar.

Hills, *see* Hill.

Hilton P Place-name in Derbys, Hunts, Staffs, NRYorks OE 'place/farm on a hill'; but the place-name in Westmd may have the ON first element 'shed', and the place-name in Dorset may have the OE first element '?slope/?tansy'.

Hind(e)(s)/Hynd(e)(s) N Nickname for a person bearing some resemblance (timidity?) to a hind, a female deer OE. Readily confused with/a variant of **Hine**.

Hindley P Place-name in Lancs and Northd OE 'wood/clearing with hinds (female deer)'.

Hinds, *see* Hind.

Hine(s)/Hyne(s) O Occupational term for a servant OE (later *hind*, with parasitic -*d*). **Hine** and **Hyne** are strongest in Devon, but **Hines** and **Hynes** in Lancs. Readily confused with/a variant of **Hind**.

Hingston P Both Hanks and Hodges (who would derive this surname from an apparently non-existent place-name in Cornwall) and Cottle (who refers to a place in Cambs – *Hinxton*, presumably) are uncharacteristically wide of the mark when it comes to **Hingston**. Given the fact that it is a Devon surname, it is almost certainly derived from *Hingston*, in Bigbury in that county OE 'hind's stone' (possibly some local boundary mark).

Hinton P Place-name in several counties, including Berks, Dorset, Gloucs, Hants, Herefords, Somerset (four such), Wilts OE '(at) the high place/farm', with *Hin-* as *Hen-* in **Hendon**; also in Cambs, Dorset, Gloucs, Herefords, Northants, Salop, Somerset, Suffolk, Wilts OE 'monks'/nuns' farm'; where no monastic ownership can be proved, the first element may mean 'domestics'/household's'.

Hird, *see* Herd.

Hirst, *see* Hurst.

Hiscock(s)/Hiscoke/Hiscott/Hiscox/ Hiscutt/Hiskett, *see* Richard.

Hislop, *see* Heslop.

Hitch/Hitchcock/Hitchcoe/Hitchcott/ Hitchcox/Hitchmough/Hix/Hix(s)on, *see* Richard.

Hoad/Hoath T/P Dweller on a heath OE *hath*; or from a place-name *Hoath*, with the same meaning, in Kent. Both forms belong to the southern counties of England, **Hoad** being strongest in Sussex. *Lewis Alan ('Lew') Hoad (1934–1994), champion tennis player, was born in Glebe, New South Wales, Australia.*

Hoadl(e)y P Place-name *Hoathley* in Sussex OE 'heath wood/clearing'. Kent/Sussex surnames.

Hoar(e) N/T Nickname for an old man, or one with grey hair OE; or a dweller by a slope/shore OE. Both **Hoar** and **Hoare** belong principally to southern counties of England. *Sir Richard Colt Hoare (1758–1838), though he was born in Surrey, inherited the Stourhead estate in Wilts, and is best known for his published works on the history of that county. Both his parents, who were first cousins, belonged to the prominent banking family of Hoare.*

Hoath, *see* Hoad.

Hobart, *see* Hubert.

Hobb(e)(s)/Hobbins/Hobbis(s), *see* Robert.

Hobday O Servant of *Hobb* (*Robert*), or a servant named *Hobb*; compare **Day**. A scattered surname with a particular presence in Kent and Warwicks.

Hobson, *see* Robert.

Hockaday N Nickname for a person born

or baptized on the second Tuesday after Easter ME, a rent-day/term-day as important as Michaelmas, and eventually a popular festival. Compare surnames such as **Pentecost** and **Christmas**. Principally a Devon surname.

Hockham P Place-name in Norfolk OE 'homestead where hocks/mallows grow' (compare holly*hock*) or '*Hocca*'s homestead'. A rare south-east of England surname.

Hockold P Place-name *Hockwold* in Norfolk OE 'woodland where mallows grow', but a very scarce Staffs/WRYorks surname.

Hodge(s)/Hodgkin(s)/Hodgki(n)son/ Hodgkiss/Hodgson, *see* **Roger**.

Hodnett P Place-name *Hodnet* in Salop OW 'pleasant valley/stream', and found as a surname principally in that county.

Hodson, *see* **Roger**.

Hogarth/Hoggard/Hoggart/Hog-garth/Hoggett O Occupational term for a hog-herd OE. **Hogarth** and **Hoggarth** can alternatively be from an unidentified place-name ending in northern ME -*garth* (enclosure). **Hogarth** is found mainly in northern counties of England and in Scotland; **Hoggard**, very scarce, has a presence in ERYorks; **Hoggarth** belongs principally to Lancs, NRYorks and Westmd; **Hoggett**, scarce, can be found principally in Co Durham. *William Hogarth (1697–1764), painter and engraver, was born in Smithfield, London, the son of a schoolmaster and author, Richard Hogarth (said to be from the Vale of Brampton, Westmd), and his wife Anne Gibbons.*

Hogg O/N/F Occupational term for a swineherd, or occasionally a nickname for a person resembling a hog or pig in some way OE. Scots and Irish: an Anglicization of Gaelic **Mac an Bhanbh** 'son of the hog'. Most commonly found in Scotland and in northern counties of England.

Hoggard/Hoggart/Hoggarth/Hog-gett, *see* **Hogarth**.

Hoghton P Place-name in Lancs OE 'settle-

ment on the spur of a hill'. A rare surname found almost exclusively in that county. Readily confused with/a variant of **Houghton/Hutton**.

Hogsflesh O Occupational term for a seller of hogs' flesh OE. A very scarce surname, confined in the main to Surrey and Sussex, and known in some cases to be pronounced (euphemistically?) as *Hooflay/Hoofley*. A small contingent of **Hoofley**s was living in Kent at the time of the 1881 census.

Holbech(e)/Holbeach P Place-name *Holbeach* in Lincs OE 'brook in a ravine' (a hole, hollow). **Holbeche** is a very scarce West Midlands surname; **Holbech** and **Holbeach**, equally scarce, are rather more widespread.

Holbeck P Place-name in Lincs, Notts and WRYorks, carrying the same meaning as *Holbeach* (see **Holbech**), but incorporating an ON (or OE scandinavianized) hard '*k*' sound. A very scarce surname, as much southern as northern within England.

Holbert/Holbird/Hulbert/Hulburd F From a Germanic first-name meaning 'gracious bright'. **Holbert** (Lancs) **Holbird** (Surrey) and **Holburd** (Essex, Kent, Sussex) are all very scarce; **Hulbert** is most commonly encountered in Gloucs and Wilts. Readily confused with/a variant of **Hurlbatt**.

Holborn/Holbourn(e) P Place-names *Holborn/Holburn* in London and elsewhere OE 'hollow brook' (that is, running in a deep ravine). Not a common surname in either spelling anywhere in England or Scotland.

Holbrook P Place-name in Derbys, Dorset, Gloucs, Suffolk, Sussex and Warwicks OE 'brook in a ravine'. Commonest in Midland and northern counties, Gloucs and Somerset.

Holcomb(e) P Place-name in six counties (three such in Devon) OE 'hollow/deep valley'. Principally a West Country surname.

Hol(d)croft P Place-name in Lancs OE 'piece of enclosed land in a hollow'.

Holden P Place-name in Lancs, WRYorks

OE 'hollow/deep valley'. Most commonly found in Lancs.

Holder, *see* **Driver**.

Holderness P Place-name in ERYorks ON 'the land of a (high-ranking) yeoman' (-*er*- being from an ON genitive singular -*ar*-). A surname of the Midlands and the North.

Holeman, *see* **Holman**.

Holford P Place-name in Somerset (three such) and Sussex OE 'ford in a hollow/ravine'.

Holgate P Place-name in WRYorks and elsewhere OE and ON 'road in a hollow'.

Holiday/Halliday/Hallidie/Holliday N Nickname for a person born or baptized on a holy day/religious festival OE. The long -*o*- of *holy* is shortened as the first syllable of a trisyllable; northern forms such as **Halliday** commonly keep the -*a*- of OE and do not change it to -*o*-, though -*o*- forms do occur even in Yorks. **Holladay** (oddly, perhaps?) is mainly found in Kent.

Holker P Place-name in Lancs OE and ON 'marsh with hollows', and a surname belonging principally to that county.

Holladay, *see* **Holiday**.

Holland P/F Place-name in Essex, Lancs (*Upholland/Downholland*) and Lincs OE 'land at a spur of a hill'; but the place-name in Hunts is ON 'hedged-off sacred grove'; or from *Holland*, Middle Low German 'sunken land', originally part of the Holy Roman Empire in the Netherlands. Irish: Anglicized form of Gaelic surnames such as **Mulholland**. Readily confused with/a variant of **Hoyland**.

Holliday, *see* **Holiday**.

Hollier/Hollyer/Hullyer O/T Occupational term for a whoremonger or brothel-keeper OF; or '?dweller in the hollies' OE. **Hollier** is a surname of the south-west and the Midlands; **Hollyer** belongs to the south-east of England, and **Hullyer** to Cambs.

Holliman, *see* **Holyman**.

Hollington P Place-name in four counties OE 'place in the hollies'; a very scarce surname with a presence in Worcs and elsewhere.

Hollingworth P Place-names in Chesh, Lancs OE 'enclosure in the hollies'. Found almost exclusively in a band across the North Midlands and the north.

Hollister O Occupational term for a female brothel-keeper, debauchee OF with an OE suffix. The feminine of **Hollier**, with the familiar -*ster* element found in **Brewster** and **Webster**. 'There is no evidence to save the face of this surname by relating it to an occupational term for a female haulier, or to a word used for a hiding-place OE *heolstor*, or a nickname for a big, awkward man (northern dialect *hulster*), or some Norse-settled village ending in -*ster*' (Cottle). A scarce surname found mainly in Gloucs.

Holloway T/P Dweller at or near a hollow/sunk/artificially-cut road OE, or from a place-name in several counties with the same meaning.

Hollowbread O Occupational term for a maker or carrier of holy bread OE. An extremely scarce Essex surname.

Hollyer, *see* **Hollier**.

Hollyhock/Hollyhoke, *see* **Holyoak**.

Holm(e)(s)/Home/Hulme(s)/Hume T/P Dweller by a holly tree OE or at a river flat, an island in a fen ON; or from a place-name including such an element, especially in the former Danelaw. *The Scottish family of Home (pronounced 'hyoom'), which acquired an Earldom in 1605, derives its name from Home in Berwickshire; the fourteenth Earl, who disclaimed his peerage in 1963, became Prime Minister of the United Kingdom as Sir Alec Douglas-Home… The Scottish philosopher David Hume (1711–1776), son of Joseph Home of Ninewells, Berwickshire, was related to the Earls of Home, but decided to change the spelling of his surname to 'Hume', in line with its usual pronunciation… The American* *author Oliver Wendell Holmes (1809–1894) was descended from a sawmill owner named John Holmes, who emigrated from England to Massachusetts in the late seventeenth century.*

Holman/Holeman T Dweller in a hollow OE, by a holly tree or on an island OE. Readily confused with/a variant of **Holyman**. **Holman** is especially strong in Devon; **Holeman**, very scarce, has a presence in Surrey.

Holme, *see* **Holm**.

Holmer P Place-names: *Holmer* in Bucks, Herefords; *Homer* in Devon OE 'pool in a hollow', or 'dweller at the *holm*' (in any of its senses – see the surname **Holm**); or a variant of **Homer**. A scarce scattered surname.

Holmes, *see* **Holm**.

Holmwood, *see* **Homewood**.

Holohan, *see* **Houlihan**.

Holt T/P Dweller in a wood or copse OE, or from one of the many place-names with the same meaning. Very strong in Lancs.

Holton P Place-name in Dorset, Lincs (three such), Oxon and Somerset OE 'place at a hollow'; the two places called *Holton* in Suffolk may have had an Anglo-Saxon owner's name such as *Hola* as the first element.

Holyman/Holliman N Nickname for a holy man OE, but no doubt often used sarcastically for a person full of humbug, or a hypocrite. Readily confused with/a variant of **Holman**. **Holyman** is a very scarce scattered surname, with something of a presence in Kent and in Staffs; **Holliman**, also scarce, belongs to the Home Counties.

Holyoak(e)/Hollyhock/Hollyhoke/ Holyoke T/P Dweller by an oak tree with some religious significance, a 'gospel-oak' where the gospel for the day was read during the beating of the parish bounds at Rogationtide; or from the place-name *Holy Oakes* in Leics OE 'holy oak', which was formerly singular (*Halyok* in 1396). **Holyoak** and **Holyoake**, significantly, are surnames found chiefly in Leics; exceptionally scarce variants include **Hollyhock** (Sur-

rey; given a charming botanical flavour by folk etymology), **Hollyhoke** (Oxon) and **Holyoke** (Kent, Warwicks). *The great-grandparents of Keith Jacka Holyoake (1904–1983), Prime Minister and Governor-General of New Zealand, first settled in Riwaka, near Motueka, in 1843.*

Home, *see* **Holm**.

Homer O Occupational term for a helmet-maker OF; or a variant of **Holmer**. Chiefly a West Midlands surname.

Homewood/Holmwood P Place-name *Holm(e)wood/Homewood* in various counties OE 'homestead/holly wood', though *Holmwood* in Surrey is OE 'wood in a river-meadow'. The surname **Homewood** belongs to the south-east of England; **Holmwood**, scarce, can be found in Sussex.

Homfray, *see* **Humphrey**.

Honeen, *see* **Houneen**.

Honeyball, *see* **Annable**.

Honeybone/Honeybourne/ Honeybu(r)n/Hunnybun P Place-names: the *Honeybourne* element OE 'stream where honey could be gathered' in the neighbouring villages of *Church Honeybourne*, Worcs, and *Cow Honeybourne*, Gloucs, is pronounced *Hunnybun*. One family of **Honeybones** were prominent clockmakers; originating in Wanborough, Wilts, they migrated to Gloucs and then to other parts of the country, including Essex, Notts and Leics. *Gloucestershire clock and watchmakers* by Graham Dowler (1984) includes a list (p.43) of known variants on the **Honeybone** name, in chronological order from 1692–1849: **Honniburne**; **Honniborne**; **Honnibone**; **Hunniborne**; **Hunnibone**; **Honeybourn**; **Honybourn**; **Honnybone**; **Huniborne**; **Honybone**; **Honeybone**. The surname **Honeybone**, scattered, belongs to southern counties of England; **Hunnybun**, scarce, is also found in the south, but also in East Anglia.

Honeycombe P Place-name in Calstock, Cornwall OE 'pleasant valley/honey valley'. The story of the ancestry of the well-known newsreader, actor, author and playwright Gordon **Honeycombe** (born in Karachi, India, in 1936) was recounted in 1979 in a series of television programmes, supported by a book entitled *Discovering your family history* by Don Steel (1980). **Honeycombe**s (originally **Honicombe**s) settled in various parts of the British Isles, one branch becoming well established on Jersey, but their eighteenth-century roots lay in St Cleer and other parishes in Cornwall, with an ultimate point of origin in Calstock, near to the place called *Honeycombe* which gave the family its distinctive and charming surname.

Honley P Place-name in WRYorks OE 'stony clearing'. A scarce WRYorks surname.

Hooflay/Hoofley, *see* **Hogsflesh**.

Hook(e) O/T/P/N A surname with various possible origins: an occupational term for a maker or seller of hooks OE *hoc* ('hook'); a dweller near a 'hook' of land; or from such a place-name in various counties; or a nickname for a crook-backed, hook-nosed person OE.

Hooker O Occupational term for a maker or seller of hooks; or a person who lived near a 'hook' of land (for both of which, compare **Hook**). Principally a surname of southern and south-east England. *John Lee Hooker (1917–2001), influential blues singer and songwriter, was born near the quintessential delta town of Clarksdale, Mississippi, the son of a sharecropper who was also a Baptist preacher... Richard Hooker (1554–1600), Anglican theologian and author of* Of the lawes of ecclesiastical politie, *was born in Heavitree, Exeter, Devon... H. Richard Hornberger (1924–1997), author of the* M*A*S*H *series of books, adopted the pseudonym of* Richard Hooker.

Hoole P Place-name in Chesh and Lancs OE 'hut, shed'; but another place-name in Chesh is OE '(in) the hollow', exhibiting the use of a dative after a lost preposition. Not a common surname, found mainly in Chesh, Lancs and WRYorks.

Hoolohan, *see* **Houlihan**.

Hoon P Place-name in Derbys ON '(at) the hillocks/burial-mounds', exhibiting the use of a dative plural after a lost preposition. An uncommon Derbys/Staffs surname. *Geoff Hoon (born 1953), former Defence Secretary and Leader of the House of Commons, went to school in Nottingham and represents a Notts constituency (Ashfield).*

Hooper O Occupational term for one who makes/fits hoops on casks or barrels OE plus an -*er* suffix. Very much a West Country surname, extending up into Gloucs.

Hooton P Place-names in Chesh and WRYorks (three such), with the same meaning as **Houghton**. Chiefly a Lancs/Notts surname.

Hope T/P Dweller in an enclosed valley, a little blind valley opening out of the main dale OE, or on a piece of enclosed land rising from a fen OE. A place-name with the same meaning(s) can be found in several counties. Principally a surname of northern England and Scotland. Family name of the Marquesses of Linlithgow and the Barons Rankeillour. *Leslie Townes ('Bob') Hope (1903–2003), the American entertainer who lived to be a hundred years old, was born in London, England, though his father, William Henry Hope, was from Weston-super-Mare in Somerset and his mother, Avis Townes, was Welsh.*

Hopkin(s)/Hopkinson, *see* **Robert**.

Hopper O/N Occupational term/nickname for a leaper or dancer OE plus -*er* suffix. Largely a Co Durham surname.

Hopson, *see* **Robert**.

Hopton P Place-name in various counties (six such in Salop) OE 'place in a valley', but the place-name in the fen country of East Suffolk is OE 'piece of enclosed land rising from a fen' (compare **Hope**).

Hopwood P Place-name in Lancs and Worcs OE 'wood in a valley' (compare **Hope**). Strongest (by far) in Lancs. Family name of the Barons Southborough.

Horabin, *see* **Horobin**.

Horden P Place-name in Co Durham OE 'dirty valley'. An uncommon surname, marginally more numerous in Lancs. Readily confused with/a variant of **Hordern**.

Horder O Occupational term for a treasurer, one charged with looking after a valuable hoard (and sometimes a cellarer) OE. 'A *hoarder* did not then mean one who keeps tins of peaches under a mattress in time of war' (Cottle).

Hordern P Place-name in Lancs OE 'storehouse'. A scarce surname, found principally in Lancs and Staffs. Readily confused with/a variant of **Horden**. *Sir Michael Hordern (1911–1995), English actor, was born in Berkhamsted, Herts, the son of Captain Edward Hordern of the Royal Indian Marines and Margaret Emily Murray, whose family had invented Milk of Magnesia.*

Horley P Place-name in Oxon OE 'wood/clearing in/on a horn-shaped hill, gable, pinnacle, corner, land in a river-bend, peninsula' (compare **Horn**), but the place-name in Surrey is OE '?wood/clearing belonging to *Horne*'.

Horlick/Horlock, *see* **Harlock**.

Horn(e) O/T/P Occupational term for someone who made small articles out of horn (compare **Horner**); or one who played a musical instrument made of horn (compare **Hornblower**); or a dweller at a horn-shaped piece of land, or from a place-name in Rutland, Surrey and elsewhere, derived from one of two OE words meaning variously 'horn-shaped hill, gable, pinnacle, corner, land in a river-bend, peninsula' (compare **Horley**).

Hornblow(er) O Occupational term for a horn-blower, one who originally blew an instrument made of horn OE; among this dignitary's duties was the summoning of workmen by the equivalent of our factory hooter. A scarce scattered surname.

Hornby P Place-name in various counties in northern England (where the surname is mostly found), including Lancs ON '*Horni*'s settlement', and NRYorks ON '*Hornbothi*'s settlement'. Readily confused with/a variant of **Hornsby**. *Frank Hornby (1863–1936), inventor and politician, who developed and produced famous brands of toys such as Meccano, Hornby Model Railways and Dinky Toys, was born in Liverpool, Lancs.*

Horncastle P Place-name in Lincs OE 'Roman site on a tongue of land' (compare **Horn**). A scarce surname, with a presence in WRYorks.

Horne, *see* **Horn**.

Horner O Occupational term for a maker of horn objects (combs, spoons, and even window 'glass') OE plus *-er* suffix (compare **Horn**). Mainly a Yorks surname, though the **Horner** family of Mells in Somerset was once prominent in that locality, and gave rise to the real-life Little Jack **Horner**.

Hornsby P Place-name in Cumbd ON '*Ormr*'s settlement'. Found principally in Co Durham and in Scotland. Readily confused with/a variant of **Hornby**.

Horobin/Hor(r)abin N/F Reaney believes that such surnames originated by way of a nickname based upon a first-name, literally 'grey *Rabin/Robin*' OE, *Rabin/Robin* being diminutives of *Robert*, and 'grey' perhaps referring to hair of that colour. Desmond Holden has examined **Horobin/Hor(r)abin** in considerable detail. He says that it was once thought that the origin was a now-lost field-name near Taxal, Whaley Bridge, Derbys (formerly in Chesh), but that this was probably a case of a surname being used for a place, rather than vice versa. Although **Horobin** had become chiefly a Staffs surname by the late nineteenth century, and **Horabin** and **Horrabin** are mainly found in Lancs at that time, Holden suggests that a Devon origin might be at work, and refers to a 'Henrie **Horerobyn**' living in that county in 1596. We might add that Henry **Horobyn** (the same man?), a feltmaker, was made a freeman of Exeter in August 1578, but no such surname appears in the 1332 lay subsidy for Devon. In any event, Holden returns to Reaney's original 'grey Robin' definition in the end, and the wheel has come full circle.

Horrel(l) P Place-name *Horrel* in Devon OE 'dirty hollow'. Principally a Devon surname, whatever the spelling, and the fact that there is a place called *Horrell* in Cumbd OE 'felon hill, hill where felons were hanged', may be a red herring…

Horridge, *see* Horwich.

Horrocks P Place-name in Lancs ON 'piles of rubbish/stones' (North Country dialect *hurrock*). *General Sir Brian Gwynne Horrocks (1895–1985), army officer and television presenter, was born at Ranniken in India, the son of Sir William Heaton Horrocks, a medical doctor who was a graduate of Victoria College, Manchester.*

Horsenail(l)/Horsenell/Horsnail(l)/ Horsnall/Horsnell O Occupational term for a horseshoenail-maker, or a shoer of horses OE. All variants of this surname are scarce: there is a mere handful of **Horsnails**, **Horsnaills**, **Horsenaills**, **Horsnells** and **Horsenells** in the south-east of England, **Horsenails** in Staffs and **Horsnalls** in a few scattered counties.

Horsey P Place-name in Norfolk, Somerset and Sussex OE 'horse island'. A surname which can be found spread across southern counties of England, with a particular presence in Somerset.

Horsford P Place-names: *Horsford*, Norfolk and *Horsforth*, WRYorks OE 'ford that can be crossed on horseback'. A scattered surname, commonest in southern counties of England and well established in Devon. *General Sir John Horsford (1751–1817) of the Bengal Army, born in Middx, originally enlisted in the East India Company Artillery under the name of John Rover; his true identity was eventually discovered.*

Horsham P Cottle derives this surname from *Horsham* in Norfolk or Sussex, but the fact that it is found predominantly in Devon would suggest that the two settlements so-called in that county OE 'horse homestead/river-meadow' must be prime contenders as the source.

Horsler, *see* Ostler.

Horsley P Place-names in various counties OE 'horse-pasture'. A widespread surname, most commonly found in the Midlands and the north.

Horsnail(l)/Horsnall/Horsnell, *see* Horsenail.

Horstead P Place-names: *Horstead* in Norfolk and Sussex, *Horsted* in Kent OE 'horse farm'. **Horstead** is strongest in Lincs and Norfolk; **Horsted** is a scarce variant. Compare **Halsted**

Horsted, *see* Horstead.

Hort, *see* Hart.

Horton P Place-name in several counties OE 'muddy place', but *Horton* in Gloucs is OE 'stag hill'.

Horwich/Horridge P Place-name *Horwich* in Lancs OE 'grey wych (elm)'. Both variants are found principally in Lancs, though **Horwich** is exceptionally scarce.

Horwood P Place-name in Bucks OE 'muddy wood' and Devon OE '?grey wood'. Chiefly a Bucks/Oxon surname. Readily confused with/a variant of **Harwood**.

Hoseason F Scots: from the first-name *Hosea*. A Shetland surname. *The fact that this surname appears – wrongly – to contain the element 'season' may (or may not?) add charm to the name of the travel company, Hoseasons Holidays.*

Hos(e)good, *see* Osgood.

Hosmer, *see* Osmer.

Hotchkin(s)/Hotchkiss, *see* Roger.

Hotham P Place-name in ERYorks OE '(at) the shelters', exhibiting the use of a dative plural after a lost preposition. An ERYorks surname.

Hotter O Occupational term for a basket-maker OF. A very scarce scattered surname.

Hough T/P Dweller at a steep/slight rise OE, or from a place-name with the same meaning in Chesh, Derbys and elsewhere. Usually pronounced '*Huff*'.

Houghton P Place-name in various counties, from Northd to Hants, with a range of different OE origins: 'place on a hill-spur'; 'place in an enclosure' (Lancs, WRYorks); 'place where ale-hoof (ground-ivy) grows' (ERYorks); in some cases the first element could be the name of an Anglo-Saxon owner, *Hofa*. Readily confused with/a variant of **Hoghton/Hutton**.

Houlihan/Holohan/Hoolahan F Irish: Anglicized form of Gaelic **O'** [descendant of] hUallachain ('proud, arrogant'). Possibly the origin of the word *hooligan*, named after a rowdy London Irish family. **Houlihan** belongs to Munster, **Holohan** to Co Kilkenny and **Hoolahan** to Co Clare and Mid-Leinster.

Houneen/Honeen F Irish: Anglicized form of Gaelic **O'** [descendant of] hUainin ('green'); several Co Clare families with this surname have chosen to be known as **Greene**.

Hounslow P Place-name in Middx OE '*Hund*'s burial-mound'. A surname most commonly found in Oxon.

House T/O Dweller in, or worker at, a great house or a religious establishment OE. Readily confused with/a variant of **Howes** or **Hughes**.

Housto(u)n/Huston P Scots: place-name *Houston* in Renfrewshire OE '*Hugh*'s settlement' (referred to as *Villa Hugonis* in the early thirteenth century), though the scarce surname **Huston**, apparently a variant, is as much in evidence in England (especially in Lancs) as in Scotland. *Houston, the largest city in the state of Texas, USA, was founded in 1836 and named after Virginia-born General Sam Houston (1793–1863), commander at the battle of San Jacinto.*

Hove P Place-name in Sussex OE 'hood' ?from the shape of a hill, or 'shelter'. A scarce surname with an uneven, scattered presence in England and Wales.

Hovenden, *see* **Ovenden**.

How(e)(s) T/P Dweller by a hill, hillock, burial-mound ON, or from a place-name with the same meaning in Norfolk, NRYorks, WRYorks, and a common place-name element in the Danelaw. **Howes** can readily be confused with, or be a variant of, **House** or **Hughes**.

Howard F From the Germanic first-name *Huard/Heward* 'brave spirit', introduced by the Normans; or from the ON first-name *Haward* ('high/chief warden'). Readily confused with/a variant of **Haworth**, **Hayward**, **Haywood**, **Hayworth**, **Heywood**, **Heyworth** and **Howarth**. **Howard** is the family name of the Dukes of Norfolk and the Earls of Carlisle, Effingham, and of Suffolk and Berkshire.

Howarth P Place-name *Howarth* or *Haworth*, Lancs OE 'mound enclosure'. Readily confused with/a variant of **Haworth**, **Hayward**, **Haywood**, **Hayworth**, **Heywood**, **Heyworth** and **Howard**.

Howden P Place-name in ERYorks ON and OE 'head valley'. Scots: place-name *Howdean*, Roxburghshire OE '?nook-valley'. Or a variant of **Haddon**.

Howe, *see* **How**.

Howel(l)(s) F/P From the Welsh first-name *Hywel* ('eminent'), borne by a great law-giving Welsh king; or from *Howell*, Lincs OE '?*Huna*'s stream/the stream of the cubs' – though the surname is not prolific in that county. *See also* **Powel**. **Howell** and **Howells** are very common in South Wales; Norfolk **Howell**s probably descend from Breton settlers who arrived after 1066.

Howes, *see* **How**.

Howett, *see* **Hugh**.

Howick P Hanks and Hodges refer to places so-called in Lancs OE 'dairy-farm on a spur of a hill' and in Northd OE '?high dairy-farm', but this is very largely a surname of southern and south-east England, where the origin is likely to be *Howicks* in Surrey OE '?dairy-farm on a spur of a hill'. *Howick Farm* in Lodsworth, Sussex, home to William **de Howike** in 1327, appears with the local dialectal spelling of '*Hoick*' (compare *Hawick* in the Scottish Borders, also com-

monly pronounced as '*Hoick*') in Greenwood's map of 1823, and there is a slight
spur of land near *Howick Farm* (*Howich* in
1166) in Rudgwick, Sussex.

Howitt, *see* Hugh.

Hoyland P Place-name in WRYorks OE
'land on the spur of a hill'. Readily confused
with/a variant of **Holland**.

Hoyle T Dweller at a hole or hollow OE,
reflecting Lancs and Yorks dialectal pronunciation. *Sir Fred Hoyle (1915–2001),
astronomer, was born in Gilstead, Yorks.*

Hubert/Hobart/Hubbard/Hubbart/
Hubbert F From a Germanic first-name
meaning 'heart/mind-bright', popularized
by Saint *Hubert*, Bishop of Liège, patron of
hunters (died AD 727). **Hobart** and **Hubbard**
belong mainly to East Anglia; **Hubbart** and
Hubbert, both scarce, can be found in
Lincs; **Hubert**, also uncommon, has a presence in south-east England, but also
(thanks to French influence) in Jersey. **Hub-**
bard is the family name of the Barons
Addington. *Hobart, Tasmania, (originally
Hobart Town or Hobarton) was named after
an early nineteenth-century colonial secretary,
Lord Hobart, who in 1804 succeeded his father
as fourth Earl of Buckinghamshire. He was
born in Nocton, Lincs, to a family which pronounced its surname 'Hubberd'.*

Hucker O Occupational term for haggler,
bargainer, petty trader, huckster ME. Largely
a Somerset surname.

Hudd/Hudson F From the mediaeval first-
name *Hudde*, which appears to have pre-
dated the Norman Conquest (as *Huda*),
and to have been subsumed into the
name *Hugh* (and, according to Reaney,
into the name *Richard*). **Hudd** is found
chiefly in south-west England, especially
Gloucs; **Hudson** is much more common
and a great deal more northerly, being present in great numbers in Lancs and
WRYorks. *Roy Hudd, British radio and television actor and music-hall singer, was born in
Croydon, Surrey, in 1936. His name is sometimes confused with that of the comedian Rod
Hull (see **Hull**).*

Huffington P The original form of the surname would appear to have been **Uffing-**
ton, and the most likely source will be the
place-name *Uffington* in Berks, Lincs, Salop
OE '*Uffa*'s farm' (the -*en*- from the genitive of
the first-name having become confused
with -*ing*- in some cases). Richard **Huffing-**
ton or **Hovington** is known to have
migrated to Virginia, USA, in or about
1672, and in a book entitled *Huffington family history* (1968), J. M. Huffington of Sugar
Land, Texas, traces the family story down
to the texas oil man and former ambassador
Roy M. **Huffington** (born 1917) and his son,
the millionaire former congressman
Michael **Huffington** (born in 1947), who
married the author and columnist Ariana
Stassinopoulos, the founder of The **Huf-**
fington Post, an online news and commen-
tary website. Within the British Isles,
Huffington had become a scarce ERYorks
surname by the late nineteenth century,
while the possible variants **Huffton** and
Huffonson were to be found mainly in
Lancs.

Huffonson/Huffton, *see* Huffington.

Huggin, *see* Hugh.

Hugh(e)(s)/Hewat/Hewet(t)/Hewet-
son/Hewit(t)/Hewitson/Hewlett/
Hewlitt/Hewson/Howett/Howitt/
Huggin(s)/Hughson/Hull/Hutchence/
Hutchens/Hutcheon/Hutche(r)son/
Hutchi(n)son F/P From an OF first-name
introduced to Britain by the Normans,
meaning 'heart/mind/spirit'. Popularized
by Saint *Hugh* of Lincoln (1140–1200),
who founded the first Carthusian monastery in England. Variants beginning with
Hutch- are derived from the OF form *Huchon*.
Hughes (son of *Hugh*), which occurs in
great numbers in North Wales and Lancs
– though it is also found in Scotland and
Ireland – can readily be confused with, or be
a variant of, **House** or **Howes**. **Hewat** is a
scarce Scottish variant. An alternative origin for **Hewit(t)** is one of two places named
Hewitts in Kent OE 'cutting, cleared place'
(compare the verb *to hew*). See also **Pugh**.
Hewitt is the family name of the Viscounts
Lifford, and **Huggins** of the Viscounts Mal-

vern. *William Howitt (1792–1879), the travel writer and poet who shared his literary fame with his wife Mary (née Botham), was born in Heanor, Derbys, the son of a Quaker colliery manager... Michael Hutchence (1960–1997), born in Sydney, Australia, achieved fame not only thanks to his role as lead singer in the rock band INXS, but also as a result of his amorous liaisons with Kylie Minogue, Helena Christensen and Paula Yates, with whom he had a daughter named Heavenly Hiraani Tiger Lily Hutchence.*

Huish, *see* Hewish.

Hulbert/Hulburd, *see* Holbert.

Hull T/P/F Dweller at a hill OE, or from a place-name with the same meaning in Chesh, Somerset, Worcs; rarely, perhaps, the ERYorks town of Kingston upon *Hull* (a British river-name); or a pet-form of the first-name *Hugh*. A widely scattered surname, strong in Lancs, but also in Middx. *Rod Hull (1935–1999), a comedian rarely seen without his irritable and highly aggressive arm-puppet 'Emu', was born in the Isle of Sheppey, Kent. His name is sometimes confused with that of the comedian Roy Hudd (see Hudd).*

Hullyer, *see* Hollier.

Hulme(s), *see* Holm.

Hulse P Place-name in Chesh OE 'hollows', and very much a Chesh surname.

Hulton P Place-names in Lancs, Staffs OE 'place on a hill'. Very much a Lancs surname.

Humble N Nickname for a meek, humble person ME from OF *(h)umble*. R. S. Charnock, in *Ludus Patronymicus* (1868), has great fun playing with other possibilities: a corrupted form of **Humboldt**; from the place-name *West Humble* in Mickelham, Surrey; from old Danish names *Humbl* or *Humbli*, from ON *Humall*, the hop plant. For any theory to be convincing, it has to take account of the fact that this is a surname of north-east England, strongest in Co Durham and Northd.

Hume, *see* Holm.

Humphrey(s)/Homfray/Humfrey/ Humpherson/Humphery/ Humph(e)ries/ Humphris(s)/ Humphry(es)/Humphrys F From the OF first-name *Humfrey* ('bear cub-peace'), brought to Britain by the Normans. Newer forms with -*ph*- are much commoner than those with an -*f*-, **Humphreys** being easily the commonest of the group, though each spelling has its own distinctive regional spread, including: **Humphrey** (south-east England); **Humphreys** (south-east and north-west England, and Wales); **Humpherson** (Warwicks); **Humphris** (Gloucs, Oxon); **Humphriss** (Oxon, Warwicks); **Humphrys** (Cornwall). See also **Bumphrey**.

Hungerford P Place-name in Berks OE 'ford near unproductive land'. A scarce, scattered surname.

Hunnable/Hunneyball/Hunneybell/ Hunnibal/Hunnibell, *see* Annable.

Hunnybun, *see* Honeybone.

Hunt/Hunter O/N Occupational term/ nickname for a hunter of game, large and small OE. **Hunt** is a widespread surname, but less common in the far north of England and Scotland, which is precisely where **Hunter** takes over as the dominant variant.

Huntingdon P Place-name in Hunts OE 'huntsman's hill', though this is more a surname of the north of England than of the south. Readily confused with/a variant of **Huntington**.

Huntingford P Place-name in Dorset, Gloucs OE 'huntsmen's ford'. A scarce south-of-England surname, most commonly found in Surrey.

Huntington P Place-name in Herefords, Salop OE 'huntsmen's farm', and in Chesh, Staffs, NRYorks OE 'huntsmen's hill'. A northern surname, most commonly found in Lancs and WRYorks. Readily confused with/a variant of **Huntingdon**. *Henry Edwards Huntington (1850–1927), born in Oneonta, New York, who founded the internationally famous Huntington Library and Art Gallery in San Marino, California, was* the nephew of a self-made railway magnate, Collis Potter Huntington (1821–1900), whose widow he married. These Huntingtons can trace their ancestry back to a seventeenth-century immigrant from England – as can another American family of Huntingtons with roots in Great Sampford, Essex, of which Samuel Huntington (1731–1796), one of the signatories of the Declaration of Independence, was a member.

Huntley/Huntly P Place-names: Huntley, Gloucs and Huntlie, Berwickshire, Scotland (a now-lost place after which Huntly in Aberdeenshire, which appears not to have given rise to a related surname, was named) OE 'huntsman's wood/clearing'. Neither surname has had a massive presence in Scotland; both are most in evidence in the south and in the north-east of England.

Hunton P There are places so-called in Hants OE 'place with hounds' and in Kent OE 'the huntsman's estate' (Huntindune/Huntingtune in the twelfth century), but the most likely place of origin for this predominantly Co Durham surname must be Hunton in NR Yorks OE 'Huna's settlement'.

Hurl, see Earl.

Hurlbatt/Hurlbert/Hurlbut(t) N 'From a game of throwing short iron-spiked bats ME (from Germanic) and OF; even a USA **Hulbert** claimed this origin' (Cottle, following Bardsley and Reaney). Can it be? All variants are scarce: **Hurlbatt** can be found in Surrey, and **Hurlbert/Hurlbut/Hurlbutt** in Leics. Readily confused with/a variant of **Holbert**.

Hurle, see Earl.

Hurley P/F Place-names in Berks, Warwicks OE 'corner in a wood/clearing', but a surname with an odd scattered distribution, not centred upon either of these counties. Irish: Anglicized form of Gaelic **O'** [descendant of] **hIarfhlatha** ('[feudal] underlord'). Elizabeth Jane ('Liz') Hurley, English actress and fashion model, born in Basingstoke, Hants, in 1965, was the daughter of an Army major of Irish descent.

Hurn, see Hern.

Hurr(e)y, see Woolrich.

Hurst/Herst/Hirst T/P Dweller by the copse, hill, wooded hill OE hyrst, or from one of a number of places in various counties called Hirst or Hurst, with the same meaning. **Hurst** is by far the commonest of the group.

Hurt, see Hart.

Husband O Occupational term for a householder, farmer, husbandman ME. Strongest in places as far apart as Cornwall and NRYorks. Compare **Younghusband**.

Huss(e)y O/N/P/F Occupational term for a housewife OE, a mistress in her own household – Hussey had no pejorative connotations in early years. A less reduced form is seen in the sewing-compendium known as a hussive. Or a nickname for a person known for wearing a particular kind of trunk-hose or boots OF. Or from the place-name Houssaye in Seine-Maritime, France OF hous ('holly'). Irish: Anglicized form of Gaelic **O'** [descendant of] **hEodhusa**. **Hussey** is a widespread surname within England, but uncommon in the far north; **Hussy**, much scarcer, has a patchy distribution. Marmaduke Hussey, Baron Hussey of North Bradley (1923–2006), one-time Chairman of the Board of Governors of the BBC, a war hero who had had a leg amputated by a German surgeon on the battlefield at Anzio, was the son of Eric Hussey (1885–1958), educationist and Olympic athlete, the grandson of Rev. James Hussey (1846–1920) of Dorset and the great-grandson of James Hussey of Bath, Somerset.

Husthwaite, see Hustwayte.

Huston, see Houston.

Hustwayte/Husthwaite/Hustwitt/ Huthwaite P Place-names: Husthwaite NRYorks ON 'clearing with a house on it'; Huthwaite, Notts and WRYorks ON 'clearing on a spur of land'. The distribution of the variant surnames (all fairly scarce) makes interesting reading: **Hustwayte** (Notts); **Husthwaite** (NRYorks); **Hustwitt** (WRYorks); **Huthwaite** (Lincs and Notts).

Hutchence/Hutchens/Hutcheon/ Hutche(r)son/Hutchin(s)/ Hutchings(on)/Hutchi(n)son, *see* Hugh.

Huthwaite, *see* Hustwayte.

Hutton P English and Scots: place-name in various counties OE 'settlement on the spur of a hill'. Found chiefly in Lancs, WRYorks, and Scotland. Readily confused with/a variant of **Houghton/Hutton**. *Sir Leonard ('Len') Hutton (1916–1990), Yorkshire and England cricketer, was born into a Moravian family in Fulneck, near Leeds, Yorks, the place to which his ancestor Benjamin Hutton, a tailor, had migrated from Scotland during the eighteenth century.*

Huxley P Place-name in Chesh OE. The second element means 'clearing'; the first element is either the name of an Anglo-Saxon owner *Hucc*, or comes from an OE word meaning 'ignominy, mockery' – perhaps referring to inhospitable ground. Chiefly a Lancs surname. *The continuing success of the Huxley family of writers and teachers can be explained in part by the intellectual qualities added to their gene pool by the women they married. The author Aldous (Leonard) Huxley (1894–1963) was the son of Leonard Huxley, assistant master at Charterhouse School, who was the son of Thomas Henry Huxley, biologist, who himself was the grandson of Thomas Huxley, an innkeeper and farmer from Coventry, Warwicks.*

Huxtable P Place-name in Devon (*Hokestaple* in 1330) OE 'post on a spur of land', and chiefly a Devon surname.

Huyton P Place-name in Lancs OE 'landing-place farm', and a Lancs surname.

Hyde T Dweller on a hide of land (anything between 60 and 120 acres, enough to support a sizeable family) OE; from the same stem as **Hewish**.

Hynd(e)(s), *see* Hind.

Hyne(s), *see* Hine.

Hyslop, *see* Heslop.

Hythe T/P Dweller at a landing-place OE, or from a place-name with the same meaning in Kent.

I'Anson, *see* John.

**Ibbetson/Ibbett/Ibbitson/Ibbitt/
Ibbotson/Ibbott/Ibbs/Ibell/Ible/
Ibson**, *see* Isabell.

Ick(e)(s), *see* Richard.

Ide F From the Germanic first-name *Ida*, meaning 'labour', originally used for both men and women. **Ide** belongs very largely to Sussex, and **Ideson** ('son of *Ida*') to Lancs/WRYorks.

Iden P Place-name in Kent and Sussex OE 'woodland pasture in the yews'. A very scarce Kent/Surrey surname.

Idle N/T/F/P Nickname for an empty, vain, lazy person OE; or a dweller on an island (from Norman dialect); or from an OW first-name *Ithel* ('lord bountiful'); or from the place-name *Idle* in WRYorks OF 'uncultivated/profitless (land)' – this being perhaps the most usual source of the surname, given its strong presence in that county. *Eric Idle, English comedian and actor, was born in South Shields, Co Durham, in 1943.*

Ifield P Place-name in Kent, Sussex OE 'field with yews'. A very scarce Kent surname. *Francis Edward ('Frank') Ifield, country music singer, was born in Coventry, England, to Australian parents in 1937; the family moved to Sydney when he was still young, but he returned to the UK in 1959.*

Ifould P Place-name *Ifold* in Sussex OE 'fold in river-land'. A very scarce Hants surname.

Iggulden/Igglesden P Place-name *Ingleden* in Kent OE 'the pasture of *Igwulf*'s people'. A Kent surname in either spelling. *Sir Charles Igglesden (1861–1949), known principally for his authorship of books such as* A saunter through Kent with pen and pencil, *was born in Ashford in that county.*

Iles T Dweller at the island OF. Chiefly a Gloucs surname.

Illing(s)worth P Place-name *Illingworth* in WRYorks OE 'enclosure of *Illa*'s people'. *Ray Illingworth, Yorkshire and England cricketer, was born in 1932 in Pudsey, Yorks... For Harry Illingsworth ('Harry Worth'), see* **Worth**.

Ilsley P Place-names *East* and *West Ilsley* in Berks OE '*Hild*'s clearing'. Most commonly found in Berks and Hants.

Imm(s), *see* Emm.

Imp(e)y T/P Dweller at an enclosure for saplings/orchard-trees/grafted trees OE, or from a minor place-name with the same meaning. Very scarce surnames, commonest in Beds.

Ince P Place-name in Chesh, Cornwall, Lancs OW 'island, river-meadow'. Largely a Lancs surname.

Ing F/P From the OE first-name *Ing(a)*, of uncertain origin; or from the place-name *Ing* in Essex OE '*Giga*'s people'. Most commonly found in Bucks.

Ingall, *see* Ingle.

Inger/Inker F From the ON first-name *Ingvarr* ('*Ing* [see **Ing**]-guard'). As to **Inker**, no use of the word for an 'ink-maker' is recorded in ME. **Inger** is a scarce Derbys/

Notts surname; **Inker**, also scarce, has a limited presence in Gloucs, Surrey and Monmouthshire.

Ingersall/Ingersoll/Ingerson, *see* **Inkersall**.

Ingham P/N Place-names in Lincs, Norfolk, Suffolk OE '*Inga* [see **Ing**]'s homestead'; or a nickname for a person known for his craftiness or 'ingenuity' OF *engaine*. *Benjamin Ingham (1712–1772), the evangelist and former Methodist after whom the Inghamite sect was named, was born in Osset, Yorks, the son of a farmer and hatter… Sir Bernard Ingham, fiery journalist and former Labour Party supporter who became Margaret Thatcher's Chief Press Secretary, was born in 1932 in Halifax, Yorks, the son of cotton weavers.*

Ingle/Ingall F/P From the ON first-name *Ingialdr* ('*Ing* [see **Ing**]-tribute'); or from the place-name *Ingol* in Lancs OE '*Inga* [see **Ing**]'s hollow'. **Ingle** is found principally in WRYorks, but also in Cambs and Lancs; **Ingall**, much scarcer, is mainly a Lincs surname.

Ingleby P Place-name in Derbys, Lincs, NRYorks (three such) ON 'Englishmen's farm'.

Inglis(h), *see* **English**.

Ingpen, *see* **Inkpen**.

Ingram F/P From a Germanic first-name *Angilramn/Ingilramn*, adopted in OE (*Enguerran* in OF); the first element is 'angel' or *Ingil* (see **Ing**); the second element is 'raven'. Or from a place-name in Northd OE 'pastureland homestead/river-meadow'. A widespread and scattered surname in England, Wales and Scotland.

Inker, *see* **Inger**.

Inkersall/Ingersall/Ingersoll/Ingerson P Place-name *Inkersall* in Derbys OE '*Wyrcen/Wyrhtena*'s hill'. All variants of the surname are very scarce in the British Isles (though **Ingerson** has a limited presence in Devon), yet the surname has flourished in the USA, thanks to the descendants of John **Ingersall/Ingersoll/Ingerson/Inkersall**, an immigrant from England who arrived in Hartford, Connecticut in the 1650s and later moved to Westfield, Massachusetts. He was baptized at St Werburgh's, Derby, in 1626, son of Thomas **Inkersall**, shoemaker and town crier, and his wife Margery (née Eaton). A member of this family, Thomas **Ingersoll** (1749–1812), also from Westfield, founded the town of *Ingersoll*, Ontario, Canada; his daughter Laura Secord (1775–1868), achieved fame as a Canadian heroine of the War of 1812 – and even had a chocolate company named in her honour. In 1892 Robert Hawley **Ingersoll** (born in Delta, Michigan, in 1847) and his brother Charles founded the watch manufacturing company which still bears their name; by 1919 they had sold over seventy million of their famous 'dollar watches'.

Inkpen/Ingpen/Inkpin P Place-name *Inkpen* in Berks OE and Celtic '?hill hill', tautologically. Chiefly a Kent surname.

Inman O Occupational term for an 'inn/lodginghouse-keeper' OE.

Inskip(p)/Inskeep P Place-name in Lancs OW and OE 'island with a ?kipe (basket for catching fish)'. The distribution of the variants of this surname, all of which are scarce to some degree, is unusual, given the place of origin: **Inskip** and **Inskeep** are found principally in Staffs, while **Inskipp** belongs mainly to Kent, Surrey and Sussex.

Insole/Insoll/Insull P From a lost place-name in Elmley Lovett, Worcs, called *Insoll* in 1642, OF (from Germanic) and OE '*I(s)nard*'s hill'; this twelfth-century *I(s)nard* also leaves his first-name at *Innerstone*, Redmarley, Worcs. Both **Insoll** and **Insull** are principally found in Worcs, though **Insole** has a presence in Lincs.

Inwood T Dweller by the 'in wood' (near the manor) as opposed to the 'out-wood' OE. Chiefly a Middx and Surrey surname.

Irby P Place-name in Chesh, Lincs, NRYorks ON 'Irishmen's farm'. A very scarce surname, the family name of the Barons Boston.

Iredale/Iredell P From *Iredale*, a now-lost farm in Cumbd, between Loweswater and Fangs Brow ON 'Irishmen's valley'. Largely a Cumbd surname.

Ireland/Irish P From the island of *Ireland* OE and ON, derived from Irish *Eriu*; a name applied in the Middle Ages indiscriminately to both Scots and Irish Gaels.

Iremonger/Ironmonger O Occupational term for an ironmonger OE. **Iremonger** is found mainly in southern counties of England; **Ironmonger** is more widesprerad.

Ireton P There are places called *Kirk Ireton* and *Little Ireton* in Derbys OE 'Irishmen's farm', but the surname is mostly found in Herts and Lancs.

Irish, *see* Ireland.

Ironmonger, *see* Iremonger.

Irons P Place-name *Airaines*, Somme. Folk etymology has given the name its current form in imitation of the metal. A widespread, though not common, surname found throughout England (especially Northants) and Scotland (especially Angus). *Jeremy Irons, the English actor, was born in the Isle of Wight, though his great-great-grandfather Thomas Irons, a policeman and later a Chartist agitator, had moved to London from Dundee, Angus.*

Ironside P Cottle derives such a surname from a nickname used for an armoured warrior OE, 'or one as doughty as if he had iron flanks', but it belongs to Aberdeenshire, and has its origins in *Ironside* OE '?eagle hill-side, New Deer, in that county. The temptation for those bearing such a surname to name their sons 'Edmund' in honour of Edmund **Ironside**, eleventh-century King of England (who was certainly doughty with 'iron flanks', though didn't bear Ironside as a *surname* as such) has proved irresistible. Edmund **Yrinside** witnessed a quit-claim in Drumkarauch in 1260 (and may have acquired his surname from *Earnside* near Newburgh); Edmund **Ironside** (1805–1840) of the Bengal Army was the son of Ralph Anthony **Ironside** of Tennockside, Lanarkshire; and (William)

Edmund, first Baron **Ironside** (1880–1959), born in Edinburgh, the son of a surgeon-major in the Indian Army, belongs to a family with roots in Aberdeenshire. One family of **Ironside**s produced a Lord Mayor of London, Edward **Ironside**, banker of Lombard Street and Twickenham, who died during his mayoralty in 1753.

Irvin(e)/Erwin/Irving/Irwin(e)/Urwin P/F Place-names in Scotland: *Irvine*, Ayrshire; *Irving*, Dumfries, Celtic '?green/fresh river'; or from the ME first-name *Irwyn* or *Erwyn* ('wild boar-friend'); Irish: Anglicized form of Gaelic O' [descendant of] hEiremhoin. **Irvine** is more predominantly Scots than **Irvin**, which is particularly strong in Co Durham and Lancs; **Irwin** is mainly a Lancs surname, but can be found in Devon and elsewhere; **Irwine**, very scarce, has a presence in Lancs; **Erwin** is widely scattered, and **Urwin** belongs to Co Durham and Northd.

Isaac(s)/Isaacson F From the Hebrew first-name *Yitschak* 'He [God] may laugh' (that is, smile favourably upon), borne by the son of Abraham. A name used even by non-Jews in the Middle Ages. **Isaacs** is the family name of the Marquesses of Reading.

Isabell F Spanish and southern French form of the Hebrew first-name *Elizabeth* 'my God (is) satisfaction'. Made popular thanks to Saint John the Baptist's mother rather than through Aaron's wife. **Isabell** (found principally in Cornwall and Devon) is much scarcer as a surname than **Ebbetts**, **Ibbett**, **Ibbitt**, **Ibbott**, **Ibell**, **Ible** and **Niblett**, which are double diminutive forms via *Eb/Ib/Nib*. **Ibbs**, **Ibson** and **Nibbs**, together with the double diminutives **Ibbetson**, **Ibbitson** and **Ibbotson**, are 'son of *Ib/Nib*'.

Isard/Ezard/Issard/Issatt/Issett/ Issit(t)/Issott/Iz(z)ard/Izat(t)/Izod/ Izzet(t) F From a Germanic female first-name meaning 'ice-battle'; latinized as *Isolda*, OF *Iseut/Isaut*. Perhaps Isolde's behaviour with Tristram in the romance makes this first-name a rather risky choice? Variants such as **Izatt** and **Izzett** belong mainly to Scotland; **Ezard** is a surname of the north of England, and **Isard** and **Izard** of the south-east. *Edward John 'Eddie' Izzard, British comedian and actor, was born in Aden in 1962; his family later moved to Northern Ireland, then to Wales, and finally to Sussex. His family's spelling of this surname is exceptionally scarce… One prominent family of Izards settled in South Carolina, USA, traces its ancestry back to an Englishman named Ralph Izard, who arrived in Charleston on 3 October 1682.*

Isbister P Place-name in Orkney and Shetland ON 'estuary/more-easterly/outermost farm-settlement'. A typical Orkney and Shetland surname, one borne by the first civilian casualty of the Second World War. For some reason the variant (?) **Esbester** has something of a foothold in Bristol.

Isdale/Isdell, *see* Esdaile.

Isgar F From an OE first-name meaning 'iron spear'. A scarce Somerset surname.

Isham P Place-name in Northants OW and OE 'homestead on the (river) *Ise*' – literally 'water', the old name of the river Nene. **Essam**, another Northants surname, is probably a variant.

Islip P Place-name in Northants OW and OE 'slippery place on the (river) *Ise*' (see **Isham**) and in Oxon OE 'slipway/portage on the (river) *Ight*'. Chiefly a surname of the English Midlands.

Issatt/Issett/Issott, *see* **Isard**.

Ive(s)/Ivatt F From the Norman and Breton first-name *Ivo*, derived from a word meaning 'yew (bow)'. The saints of Cornwall and Hunts so-called are respectively local and legendary. **Ive** is a scarce scattered surname, strongest in Middx; **Ives** is mostly found in the south-east of England and East Anglia, but also in WRYorks; **Ivatt** is a scarce Cambs surname. *Henry Alfred Ivatt (born in Cambs in 1851, the son of a clergyman) and his son Henry George Ivatt (born in 1886) were both highly successful railway engineers.*

Ivers(on), *see* **Ivor**.

Ivimey, *see* **Evemy**.

Ivor/Ivers(on)/MacIvor/McIver/McIvor F From the ON first-name *Ivarr*, of uncertain origin (possibly meaning 'yew-army' – compare **Ive**), used from earliest times by the Irish, Scots and Welsh, but only later and less often by the English. Compare Saint Patrick's contemporary, Saint *Ivor*. **Ivor** is exceptionally scarce; **MacIvor** belongs to Caithness, and **McIver** to Ross and Cromarty; **McIvor** is more widely spread within Scotland. **Iverson** is found mainly in Kent.

Iz(z)ard/Izat(t)/Izod/Izzet(t), *see* **Isard**.

J

Jack(s)/Jacklin/Jackman/Jackson/ Jaggard/Jago(e)/Jakeman/Jakes/ Ja(c)ques/Jeacock F From the first-names *John* or *James* (OF *Jacques*). See also **Jacob, James, Jaggard** (under **Jagger**). **Jacklin** (mainly Lincs) and **Jaggard** (mainly Cambs) are diminutives, and **Jackman/ Jakeman** is *'Jack*'s servant'. **Jack** belongs principally to Scotland, **Jackson** (very common) to England; **Jacks** is primarily a Salop surname; **Jago** is a Welsh and Cornish form of *James* – compare Othello's tormentor *Iago*, or the famous pilgrimage destination of *Santiago* de Compostela. Of **Jakes**, Cottle says that it is 'not a popular surname, in view of its also meaning "privy"', though it is not particularly scarce, and is widespread; of **Ja(c)ques** he says: 'either a frenchifying of **Jakes**, or a late (Huguenot etc.) introduction of [the] French [first-name] meaning *James*'. **Jackson** is the family name of the Barons Allerton.

Jacob(s)/Jacobi/Jacobson/Jacoby F From the Hebrew first-name *Yaakov* (meaning 'heel', since Jacob in the Old Testament is said to have been born holding onto the heel of his twin brother Esau), which became Latin *Jacobus* (whence *Jacob, Jacques, Jago*) and later also *Jacomus* (whence *James* and pet forms *Jim/Jem*). An ancient Bristol church is dedicated to Saints Philip and *Jacob* (that is, James the Less). **Jacobi/ Jacoby** preserves the *-i* of the Latin genitive. *See also* **Jack** and **James**. W. & R. Jacob, the biscuit-making company famous for its Cream Crackers, was founded in Waterford, Ireland, by two Quaker brothers, William and Robert Jacob, in 1851... William Wymark ('W. W.') Jacobs (1863–1943), short-story writer and novelist, was born in Wapping, East London... Sir Derek Jacobi, English actor and director, was born in Leytonstone, London, in 1938, the son of a sweet-shop owner and tobacconist; his paternal great-grandfather had immigrated to England from Germany during the nineteenth century.

Jacques, *see* **Jack**.

Jaggard, *see* **Jack** and **Jagger**.

Jagger(s) O/F Occupational term for a carter, hawker, chapman, pedlar ME (from Yorks dialect); or possibly a corruption of **Jaggard** (see **Jack**). *Jagger is a WRYorks surname, and although musician, actor and songwriter Sir Michael Phillip ('Mick') Jagger of Rolling Stones fame was born in Dartford, Kent, in 1943, a step-by-step examination of his male-line ancestry leads back inexorably to Yorks. His father Basil Fanshawe Jagger (1913–2006), a teacher, was born in Wickham Bishops, near Maldon in Essex, the son of David Ernest Jagger, also a teacher, who was born in Whitehaven, Cumbd, in 1880, and married Harriett Fanshawe from Eckington, Derbys, in 1908; David Ernest's father David Jagger, a printer compositor who settled in Whitehaven and married there no fewer than three times, had been born in Morley, WRYorks – a county which is the epicentre of the Jagger surname. According to George Redmonds, most Yorks Jaggers are descended from John Jagger, a tenant of Wakefield manor in the fourteenth century... Joseph Hobson Jagger (1830–1892), born in Shelf near Bradford, Yorks, said to be a distant relation of Mick Jagger, was an engineer who noticed that one of the roulette wheels in the casino at Monte Carlo had a distinct bias which could be exploited, and who won a vast* amount of money as a result. *Fred Gilbert's music-hall song of 1892,* The man who broke the bank at Monte Carlo, *is said to be based, not upon Jagger, but upon another successful casino gambler from England named Charles Wells.*

Jago(e)/Jakeman/Jakes, *see* **Jack**.

James/Jameson/Jami(e)son F A form of the first-name *Jacob*, popularized by the two Apostles called *James* in the Authorized Version of the New Testament (in contrast to *Jacob* in the Old Testament). See also **Jack** and **Jacob**. James is common as a surname in South Wales and along the English/Welsh border; **Jameson/Jami(e)son**, common forms found in Scotland and northern England, are sometimes pronounced *'Jammy-son'*. James is the family name of the Barons Northbourne. *Jesse (Woodson) James (1847–1882), infamous for operating alongside his brother Alexander Franklin ('Frank') James as a desperado, was born near Kearney, Missouri. The brothers' male-line ancestry can be traced back to William James, who was born in England and died in Goochland, Virginia, at the age of fifty-one.*

Jane(s)/Janson, *see* **John**.

January N/P Nickname for a person born during, or having some special connexion with, the month of January (from the god *Janus*, with his two heads looking both forwards and back, or from the Latin *janua*, meaning a door/gate); or referring to a Genoese ME (via OF) *Janaway*, a man from *Genoa*, a great Mediterranean seaport in mediaeval times, from which many merchants and others found their way to England and elsewhere. January is a Cambs surname; **Jennaway** is a scarce Leics variant. *The firm of Cambridge-based estate agents which went by the name of January was eventually taken over by the more mundane-sounding Black Horse Agency.*

Jaques, *see* **Jack**.

Jardine, *see* **Gardner**.

Jarma(i)n, *see* **German**.

Jarra(r)d/Jarratt/Jarraud/Jarred/Jarrett/Jarritt/Jarro(l)d/Jarrott, *see* **Garrett**.

Jarvis, *see* **Jervis**.

Jasper/Jaspar F From the first-name *Gaspar/Caspar*, from a Persian word meaning 'treasure'. The supposed name of one of the Three Kings (though the bible makes them neither kings nor three). The surname was further popularized thanks to its resemblance to the precious stone *jasper*. Many allied variants exist throughout Europe, but within the British Isles this is mainly a Cornish surname in both spellings, **Jaspar** being very scarce.

Jay(e)(s) N Nickname for a person resembling the bird of this name OF. 'The bird is beautiful, chattering, and (from man's point of view) wicked; the second is the likeliest cause of the nickname, though a Middle English poet said his girl friend was as pretty as a jay' (Cottle). *See also* **Gee**.

Jayne(s), *see* **John**.

Jays, *see* **Jay**.

Jeacock, *see* **Jack**.

Jeavons/Jevon(s) N/F Nickname for a young person OF from Latin *juvenis* (compare modern French *jeune*, young); or from the Welsh first-name *Ieuan*, an earlier form of *Evan* (John). Principally Staffs surnames, whatever the spelling. *See also* **John**.

Jebb, *see* **Jeffrey**.

Jee(s), *see* **Gee**.

Jeeves F From the female first-name *Genevieve* OF ('?race/people-woman'), introduced into England by the Normans – though it sounds much more mellifluous in its original French form *Geneviève* than in the Anglicized version, which is all too reminiscent of a vintage motor-car featured in a film of that name. St Geneviève is the patron saint of Paris. Mainly a Beds/Herts surname. The intriguing first-name bestowed upon a child called '*Offspring Jeeves*', born in Biggleswade, Beds, in 1876, gives no clue as to gender, alas. *The*

novelist and short-story writer P. G. Wode-
house has said that he named Bertie Wooster's
valet (Reginald) Jeeves after a Warwickshire
cricketer named Percy Jeeves (1888–1916),
who was born near Dewsbury, Yorks.

Jeff/Jeffares/Jeffcoat(e)/Jeffcock/ Jeffcote/Jeffcott, *see* Jeffrey.

Jefferd/Jefford, *see* Giffard.

Jeffrey(s)/Geoffrey/Jebb/Jeff/ Jeffares/Jeffcoat(e)/Jeffcock/ Jeffcote/ Jeffcott/Jefferis(s)/Jeffers(on)/ Jeffer(e)y(s)/Jeffray/Jeffree/Jeffress/ Jeff(e)ries/Jeffry(es)/Jeff(e)s/ Jephcoat(e)/Jephcott/Jepson F From a

Norman first-name, ME *Geffrey* ('district/tra-
veller/pledge-peace'), or from one of a
number of related first-names. **Geoffrey** is
exceptionally scarce as a surname;
Jefferson and **Jepson** (in common with
many *-son* names) are most common in
the north of England; most of the other
variants are from further south (**Jeffreys**
being the most popular form), but those
ending in *-coat/-cott* are from the Midlands
or the South Midlands, especially Warwicks. The odd-looking **Jeffress**, with its
abundance of consonants, is a very scarce
Co Durham variant. *Thomas Jefferson*
(1743–1826), third President of the United
States of America, was born in Shadwell,
Goochland County, Virginia; his earliest
known male-line ancestor in America, also
named Thomas Jefferson, settled in Virginia
and was the owner of a plantation in Henrico
County in the late seventeenth century…
Arthur Stanley Jefferson (1890–1965), born in
Ulverston, Lancs, achieved worldwide fame as
the comedian Stan Laurel, a name suggested to
him by his common-law wife Mae Dahlberg. It
was in the 1920s that he first teamed up with
his long-term comedy partner, Oliver Hardy.

Jehu F From the Hebrew '*Yahweh* (God) is
he'. A rare scattered surname within England.

Jekyll/Jewell/Joel/Jolson/Joule(s)/ Jowell/Jowle/Juggins/Juke(s) F From a
Celtic (Breton/Cornish) first-name *Iudicael*
('lord/chief generous'), borne by a seventh-
century saint and hermit of Ponthieu. 'The

fictional unreliability of Dr **Jekyll** is happily
balanced by the real worth of the great gardener Miss Gertrude **Jekyll**' (Cottle). The
surname **Jekyll** as found in Cornwall and
Devon is of native origin, but its presence
further east in England can be accounted
for by Breton immigrants who arrived following the Norman Conquest. The scarce
surnames **Jowell**, **Jowle** and **Juke** have a
limited presence in WRYorks and elsewhere; **Joule** is mainly found in Derbys
and Lancs, while **Joules** is scarce and scattered; **Juggins** is in evidence in the Cotswolds and on the south coast of England,
and **Jukes** in the West Midlands, especially
Staffs. **Jolson**, a rare surname in the British
Isles, has a limited presence in Northd. **Joel**
as a Jewish surname is from the Hebrew
male first-name *Yoel*. Al *Jolson (1886–1950),*
the highly acclaimed American singer and
actor, was born in Lithuania, the son of a
rabbi. His real name was Asa Yoelson, though
the family had originally used the surname
Hesselson… Jimmy Jewel (1909–1995), com-
edian and actor, was born James Arthur Tho-
mas Marsh in Sheffield; he and his cousin Ben
Warriss became Britain's leading comedy
double-act during the 1940s and 1950s…
The electrical unit known as the 'joule' gets
its name from the English physicist James Pre-
scott Joule (1818–1889), who was born in Sal-
ford, Lancs, the son of a local brewer.

Jenckes/Jenkin(g)(s)/Jenki(n)son/ Jenks/Jenkyns, *see* John.

Jennaway, *see* January.

Jenner o Occupational term for an engin-
eer, military engineer, architect OF. Most
commonly found in the south-east of England. *Edward Jenner (1749–1823), pioneer of*
smallpox vaccination, was born in Berkeley,
Gloucs, where his father (also a Gloucs man
born and bred) was a local clergyman.

Jennett/Jennin(g)s, *see* John.

Jephcoat(e)/Jephcott/Jepson, *see* Jef-
frey.

Jeremy/Jeremiah/Jermy F From the
Hebrew first-name *Jeremiah/Yirmeyahu*
('may Yahweh [God] exalt'), borne by the

lugubrious prophet. Readily confused with certain variants of **German**? **Jeremiah** and **Jeremy** are restricted mainly to South Wales; **Jermy** is a Norfolk surname.

Jerman/Jermin(e)/Jermy/Jermyn, *see* **German**.

Jerome F From the Greek first-name *Hieronumos* ('sacred name') via OF; but the surname has sometimes absorbed a first-name such as the Germanic/Norman *Gerram* ('spear raven'). A scattered surname, particularly in evidence in Hants. *Jerome K[lapka] Jerome (1859–1927), novelist and playwright, was born in Walsall, Staffs, where his father,* (originally named Jerome **Clapp**) *was a coalmine owner and Nonconformist lay preacher.*

Jerratt/Jerreat(t)/Jerred/Jerrett/Jerrold, *see* **Garrett**.

Jervis/Gervis/Jarvis/Jervois(e) F/P From the Norman first-name *Gervase*, the first element of which means 'spear'. But those descended from the Yorks family of *de Gervaux* are from *Jervaulx* in NRYorks, an OF version of Celtic and OE *Ure dale* (*Ure* being a Celtic river-name). For the *-ar* element in **Jarvis**, *see* **Armistead**. **Jervis** is commonly pronounced as *'Jarvis'*, and **Jervois(e)** as *'Jervis'*. **Jervis** is the family name of the Viscounts St Vincent.

Jesper, *see* **Jasper**.

Jessi(e)man/Jessamine P/N A Scottish surname, though it is reputedly derived from the English settlement of *Jesmond*, Newcastle-upon-Tyne, which was *Gesmond* in 1414 and *Jessemond* in 1449 OE 'mouth of Ouse burn'. And yet the shrub *jasmine* is alternatively known as *jessamine*, so perhaps a nickname is at work here? Such surnames are found almost exclusively in Aberdeenshire, particularly in and about the town of Huntly.

Jessop(p)/Jessup, *see* **Joseph**.

Jevon(s), *see* **Jeavons**.

Jewell, *see* **Jekyll**.

Jewett/Jewitt, *see* **Julian**.

Jewsbury, *see* **Dewsbury**.

Jex, *see* **Geach**.

Jeyes, *see* **Gee**.

Jingle, *see* **Gingell**.

Jinkin(s)/Jinkinson/Jinks, *see* **John**.

Job/Jobbins/Joblin(g)/Jobson/Jope/Joplin/Jopp/Jubb/Jupe/Jupp F/N/O From a Hebrew first-name meaning 'persecuted, hated' – the fate meted out to *Job* in the Old Testament by God as a means of testing his faith; or a nickname for a wretched person OF *job/joppe*; or an occupational term for a maker or seller of either a woollen garment known as a *jube* or *jupe* OF (compare modern French *jupe* 'skirt'), or a four-gallon liquor vessel known as a *jubb* ME. **Job** is most commonly found in Cornwall; **Jobbins** in Gloucs; **Jobson**, **Jobling** and **Joplin** in Co Durham and Northd; **Joblin** in Co Durham and ERYorks (but also in the Isle of Wight…); **Jope** in Devon and Cornwall; **Jopp** in Aberdeenshire; **Jubb** in WRYorks; **Jupe** in Hants; **Jupp** in Sussex. Hobson-Jobson: a glossary of colloquial Anglo-Indian words and phrases, *a book first published in 1886, took its catchy title from a British soldiers' corruption of 'Ya Hasan! Ya Hosain', a ceremonial cry used by Muslims at the time of the Remembrance of Muharram… Janis Joplin (1943–1970), vivacious and influential rock musician and songwriter, was born in Port Arthur, Texas.*

Jocelyn/Joslin(g)/Joslyn/Josolyne/Josselyn F From *Gauzelin*, a Germanic first-name Normanized, meaning 'little Goth'. **Jocelyn**, a scarce surname mainly confined to southern and western counties of England, is the family name of the Earls of Roden. **Joslin** and **Joslyn** (together with the very scarce variants **Josolyne** and **Josselyn**) are mainly Essex surnames; **Josling** is principally found in south-east England. Most varieties have at least something of a presence in Devon. *See also* **Gosling** and **Goss**.

Joel/Jo(e)lson, *see* **Jekyll**.

John/I'Anson/Janson/Jayne(s)/Jea-vons/Jenckes/Jenkin(g)(s)/Jenks/Jen-kyns/Jennett/Jennin(g)s/Jevon(s)/Jin-kin(s)/Jinkinson/Jinks/Johncock/John-son/Johnston(e)/Jones/Joynes/Joy-nson/Junkin F From the Hebrew first-name *Yochanan* ('Jehovah has favoured [me with a child]'/'may Jehovah favour [this child]'), becoming (via Greek) Latin *Johannes*. 'Not even the worst English king could unpopularize the first-name, which (probably through the Baptist more often than the Evangelist) remained almost the favourite name at the font' (Cottle). The name took a variety of forms throughout Europe: *Sean* (Irish); *Ia(i)n* (Scottish); *Evan/Ieuan/Ioan* (Welsh); *Jean* (French); *Jan* (Dutch, Flemish, Czech); *Juan* (Spanish); *Giovanni* (Italian); *Joao* (Portuguese); *Johann/Hans* (German); *Ioanni* (Greek). *Ivan* is the Russian equivalent, and when the will of a mariner named John Nicholo 'of Ganno, Turkey' was proved in the Prerogative court of Canterbury in 1750, one of the beneficiaries was 'Stephen Ivanofsky alias Johnson'. A number of variants, some of them pet-forms, including *Jan, Jen, Jon* and *Han(n)* existed within the British Isles during mediaeval times, and gave rise to related surnames. Forms such as *Joan, Jean* and *Jane* were at one time not exclusively female, as they later became. **Johnson** is the commonest form in England (and in the USA and elsewhere); **Jones** belongs to Wales, **John** and **Jayne** to South Wales, and **Johns** to southwest England; **Jane** is commonly found in Cornwall, unlike **Janes**, which is scattered throughout southern counties of England; **I'Anson**, derived from **Janson**, reflects the fact that the upper-case letters '*I*' and '*J*' once had the same form. **Joynes** is mainly in evidence throughout the Midland counties of England, but **Joynson** is found mainly in Chesh and Lancs. Although **Jenkins** is so thoroughly a Welsh surname, its elements *Jen-* and *-kin* (Flemish in origin, but soon acclimatized) are not at all so. Cottle describes **Jenkyns** as being 'a swankification of **Jenkins** – unless the *-y-* was for manuscript clearness next to a minim letter'. **Jennings**, from the OF diminutive *Jea-nin*, with an intrusive *-g-*, is far commoner than **Jennins**. *See also* **Evans, Hann, Jack, Jeavons, Johnston, Jones**. *John Frederick Thomas ('Fred T.') Jane (1865–1916), founding editor of the publishing house specializing in books on warships and aircraft which still bears his name, was born in Richmond, Surrey, where his father was then curate (before moving on to incumbencies in Cornwall and Devon)… (John) Augustus (Edwin) John (1878–1961), artist, was born in Tenby, Pembrokeshire, of a Welsh father and an English mother.*

Johncock/Johnson, *see* John.

Johnston(e) P/F Scots: from one of a number of places called *Johnston/Johnstone*, including *Johnstone*, Dumfries ME *'John's* settlement' and the town formerly known as *Saint Johnston*, Perth (immortalized in the name of the football team); or a variant of **Johnson** (see **John**).

Joiner/Joyner O Occupational term for a joiner, a maker of wooden furniture OF. **Joiner** is strongest in Kent and Middx, **Joyner** in Gloucs.

Jolly/Jolley/Jollie/Jolliff(e)/Joly N Nickname for a cheerful, lively, attractive person OF (compare modern French *joli*, 'pretty'). **Jolliffe**, a surname most commonly found in Dorset, Hants and the Isle of Wight, is the family name of the Barons Hylton.

Jolson, *see* Jekyll.

Joly, *see* Jolly.

Jones F From the first-name *Ioan*, one of the Welsh forms of the first-name *John* (others being *Evan*, whence the surname **Evans**, and *Ieuan*, one source of **Jeavons/Jevon(s)**), with the addition of a genitive *-s*. Cottle gleefully points out that, anomalously, there is no *J* in the 'excellent Welsh alphabet'. **Jones** is the commonest surname in Wales (something approaching ten per cent of the rural population in 1890), the second commonest (after **Smith**) in England and Wales, and the sixth commonest in the USA (as of 1939). See **John**.

Jope/Joplin/Jopp, *see* Job.

Jordan/Judd/Judson/Jutson/Jutsum F
From the font-name *Jordan*, derived from
the famous river of that name, Hebrew
Yarden ('flowing down'). Crusaders often
brought back *Jordan* water for their children's baptism. Variants beginning with
Jud/Jut can alternatively be derived from
the first-name *Jude*. The surname **Jordan** is
widely scattered throughout England. **Judd**
belongs principally to the south and the
South Midlands, **Judson** to northern counties, especially WRYorks, **Jutson** (scarce), to
Devon and Kent, and **Jutsum** (very scarce)
to Devon. The fact that a child born in
Stoke-on-Trent, Staffs in 1860 carried the
full name of '*River* **Jordan**' may be just too
predictable?

Jose, *see* Joyce.

Joseph(s)/Jessop(p)/Jessup F From the
Hebrew first name *Yosef*, meaning 'may
God add (a further son)'. The Old Testament *Joseph* was the son of Jacob; the
New Testament *Joseph* was the husband of
the Virgin Mary. Many, but not all, mediaeval bearers of the name *Joseph* were Jews,
and **Joseph** is frequently a Jewish surname.
Jessop(p) (found mainly in WRYorks) and
Jessup (most common in southern and
south-east England, especially Kent) represent the usual pronunciation of the name
in mediaeval times.

Joshua F From a Hebrew first-name meaning 'God is generous'; *Jesus* is a variant of
the same name. A scarce surname, found
mainly in South Wales.

Joslin(g)/Joslyn/Josolyne/Josselyn, *see*
Jocelyn.

Joule(s)/Jowell, *see* Jekyll.

Jowett/Jowitt, *see* Julian.

Jowle, *see* Jekyll.

Joy N/F Nickname for a person of a joyful,
cheerful disposition, or from a first-name
(usually female) with the same meaning
OF. Found as a surname in southern coun-

ties of England, but also in WRYorks and
elsewhere. *See also* **Gee**.

Joyce/Jose F From the Breton first-name
Iodoc, a diminutive of *Iudh* ('Lord'), borne
by a prince and saint who had a hermitage
at what is now St Josse-sur-Mer (*Josse* being
a Norman form of *Iodoc*); or from a feminine version of this, mixed with 'joy' and
'joke' OF. But *Burton Joyce* in Notts is named
after a Norman family from *Jort* in Calvados. **Jose** is Cornish, and **Goss(e)** is also a
variant. **Joyce** is widely spread throughout
England and Scotland, but is particularly
common in Ireland, where it was introduced by Norman immigrants from Wales
in the twelfth century. *The writer James
(Augustine Aloysius) Joyce (1882–1941), born
in Dublin, was reputedly descended from
Thomas de Jorce… The fascist propagandist
and broadcaster William Brooke Joyce
(1906–1946), known as 'Lord Haw-Haw'
because of his plummy accent, was born in
Brooklyn, New York; his father, a naturalized
American citizen, came originally from County
Mayo, Ireland.*

Joyner, *see* Joiner.

Joynes/Joynson, *see* John.

Jubb, *see* Job.

Judd, *see* Jordan.

Jude F From the Hebrew first-name *Yehuda*,
of unknown meaning ('?God leads'/'?He
will be confessed'). Widely known thanks
to *Jude* the Apostle, *Judas* Maccabaeus and
Judah the fourth son of Jacob and Leah,
though *Judas* Iscariot will have done little
to popularize the name. For **Judd/Judson/
Jutson/Jutsum**, which can in principle be
derived from *Jude*, see also **Jordan**.

Judge O/N Occupational name for a judge
OF, or a nickname for one who behaved
with the kind of solemnity associated
with such an officer of the law. Found principally in both south-eastern and northern
counties of England.

Judson, *see* Jordan.

Juggins/Juke(s), *see* Jekyll.

Julian/Gillian/Jellicoe/Jewett/Jewitt/Jowett/Jowitt/Julien/Jull/Juson F From the ME first-name *Julian*, with its origins in the Latin *Iulianus*, said – without evidence – to be from Greek *ioulos* ('downy'). Popularized thanks to *St Julian* the Hospitaller, the patron of wayfarers; *St Juliana* was martyred in Nicomedia, but her bones were laid to rest over the Channel, so her name became well known in England. *Julian* was used in the Middle Ages as both a male and a female first-name – though *Juliana* also existed, and *Gillian* – which gave rise to the word *gill* (a flirt) – is a later female variant. *See also* **Gell**. The surname **Julian** is uncommon everywhere except in Cornwall; **Jellicoe** is found mainly in Chesh, **Jull** (scarce) in Kent, **Juson** (very scarce) in Bucks, and the diminutives **Jowett/Jewett/Jewitt/Jowitt** in northern counties of England. *Admiral John Rushworth Jellicoe, First Earl Jellicoe (1859–1935), naval officer, was born in Southampton, the son of a captain in the Royal Mail Steam Packet Company… Benjamin Jowett (1817–1893), who achieved fame as a reforming Master of Balliol College, Oxford, was born in Camberwell, London.*

Juniper F/T From the female first-name *Jennifer*, from OW *Gwenhwyfar* ('white-smooth-large'), borne by King Arthur's Queen *Guinevere*. The fact that *Jennifer* was once a particularly popular first-name in Cornwall doesn't help to explain the distribution of the surname **Juniper**, which seems to arrive in Sussex and elsewhere in the late seventeenth century – as if from nowhere – and by the time of the 1881 census was restricted to south-east England, particularly Essex. Various instances of surnames such as **Janivier/Jennever/Jenniver/Ginnifer/Ginniver/Ginnaver** are in evidence in Notts and elsewhere from the late seventeenth century onwards, and there was what looks like a single family known as **Geniver/Jenever/Jeniver** living in the Selsey area of Sussex from as early as the thirteenth and fourteenth centuries. Two apparently related entries from the parish register of Cuckfield in Sussex are of more than passing interest here: '29 September 1686: baptized, Frances **Juniper**, son of Francis **Juniper** and Mary Collins' and '8 May 1691: baptized, Edward **Jinnifer**, son of Francis and Mary **Jinnifer**'. The possibility that the surname might have been applied in some cases to a dweller near a juniper tree should perhaps not be discounted totally, and the French word for such a tree, *genévrier*, has certainly given rise to related surnames in that country. *'Jennifer Juniper'* ('…lives upon a hill… sitting very still…') *is the title of a song by Donovan.*

Junkin, *see* **John**.

Jupe/Jupp, *see* **Job**.

Jury T Dweller in a jury/jewry OF *ju(ie)rie*, a Jewish quarter or ghetto of the kind found in English cities before the expulsion of the Jews by King Edward I in 1290. **Jury**, much the commonest spelling of such a surname, occurs most strongly in Devon and Kent; **Jewry**, much scarcer, has a limited presence in Kent and Middx.

Juson, *see* **Julian**.

Justice O/N Occupational term for a judge, an officer of justice OF, or a nickname applied to a fair-minded person. A surname widely spread throughout the United Kingdom. *James (Norval) Robertson Justice (1907–1975), actor, was born in Lewisham, London, the son of a mining engineer.*

Jutson/Jutsum, *see* **Jordan**.

K

Kane, *see* **Cain** and **O'Kane**.

Kaplan, *see* **Cohen**.

Karslake, *see* **Carslake**.

Kavanagh/Cavanagh F Irish: Anglicized form of the Gaelic first-name *Caomhanach*, 'follower of *Caomhán* (gentle/tender)' – a name borne by no fewer than fifteen Irish saints.

Kay(e)/Keay/Key(e)(s) O/T/N/F Occupational term for a maker of keys or a key-bearer OE *coeg* ('key'); or a dweller by a wharf OF *kay(e)* ('quay'); or a nickname from some resemblance to a jackdaw ON *ka* (with *-a-* retained in northern dialect, as opposed to **Coe** further south); or a nickname for a left-handed/footed person, Danish dialect *kei* ('left') – in Lancs the charming term '*kay/kei podder*' for a left-handed person has survived into modern times; or from a ME first-name of Welsh or Breton origin (compare *Sir Kay*, King Arthur's foster brother), probably from Latin *Caius/Gaius* ('rejoicing'). In the Isle of Man **Kay** is derived from **Mac Aodha/ Aoidh** ('son of *Aodh*' – a first-name which takes two different genitive forms). 'Thus the meaning of this delightfully ambiguous surname will depend partly on ultimate place of origin – [a first-name from] the Welsh Border or Breton-settled East Anglia, [a nickname from] the North' (Cottle). *The surname of Norwich-born John Caius (1510–1573), scholar and physician, is variously spelt Keys or Kees, and the college in Cambridge of which he was a benefactor and the third founder is still pronounced 'Gonville and Keys'.*

Keach, *see* **Keech**.

Keal P Place-name (several such) in Lincs ON 'ridge'. Principally a Lincs surname, readily confused with/a variant of **Keele**.

Kearn(e)y F Irish: Anglicized form of Gaelic **O'** [descendant of] **Ceithearnaigh** ('soldier'). Frequently pronounced '*Karney*'.

Kearslake, *see* **Carslake**.

Keat(e)(s)/Keyte/Kite N Nickname from some resemblance (greed/rapacity) to the bird of prey, the kite OE *cyta*. **Keat** is found mainly in Cornwall, **Keate** in Lancs, **Keates** in Staffs, **Keats** in Dorset and **Keyte** in Gloucs and Warwicks. *John Keats (1795–1821), the poet, was born in London, the eldest of five children of an inn manager whose family name would appear to have had its origins in Cornwall or Devon.*

Keay, *see* **Kay**.

Ke(e)ble/Kibble O/N Occupational term for a maker/seller of cudgels ME *kibble*, or a nickname for someone built like a cudgel or who behaved aggressively. **Keble** and **Keeble** are surnames of south-east England and East Anglia; **Kibble**, more widely scattered, is strong in Gloucs. *The Anglican clergyman and poet John Keble (1792–1866), a member of the Oxford Movement in whose honour Keble College, Oxford, was named, was born in Fairford, Gloucs, to a family with deep roots in the eastern Cotswolds.*

Kedge N Nickname for a lively, brisk person ME (?from ON). A south-east-of-England and East Anglia surname. **Ketch** is scarce scattered variant. *See also* **Ketcham**. *Bio-*

graphical details concerning John ('Jack') Ketch (died 1686), the London-based public executioner, are notoriously hard to come by, though it would seem likely that on occasions his surname was spelt 'Catch'.

Kedgley P A challenging surname which looks as if it must have a place-name origin, though no place called *Kedgley* has yet come to light. The most likely point of origin is a small settlement called *Ketley*, Sussex OE '?kite's wood', situated near Etchingham, where sixteenth-century marriage records include the names of Margery **Ketchlawe** in 1586/7 and Jane **Ketchley** (sister of Margery?) in 1592. By 1881 Kedgley was a very scarce surname, borne by a mere handful of individuals with their origins in London, Essex, Hants, Kent and Surrey. Compare **Kedglie**.

Kedglie P A Scots surname with a place-name origin; possibly *Kedslie*, Roxburghshire OE '*Cade*'s meadow'. There are **Kedglies** in Scotland from at least as early as 1608, and the surname appears in South Leith, Midlothian, Clackmannan, Dunfermline and elsewhere. Compare **Kedgley**.

Keech/Keach/Keetch O/N Occupational term for a butcher ME (literally, a lump of animal fat) – Shakespeare calls Wolsey this, with reference to his parentage; or a less-than-complimentary nickname for an obese person. Surviving portraits of the well-known Baptist minister Benjamin **Keach** (1640–1704), who was born in Stoke Hammond, Bucks, suggest no such obesity on his part.

Keegan F Irish: Anglicized form of Gaelic **Mac Aodhagain** ('son of fire') or of **Mac Thadhgain** ('son of poet'). *Kevin Keegan, former manager of the England football team and European Footballer of the Year (twice), was born in 1951 in Armthorpe, Doncaster, Yorks.*

Keele P Place-name in Staffs OE 'cows' hill'. Readily confused with/a variant of **Keal**.

Keeling F English surname of uncertain origin; possibly derived ultimately from a shortened form of one of a number of OE names containing the element *ceol* ('keel,

ship'). Strongest in the Midlands and the north.

Keen(e) N/F Nickname for a brave, astute person OE; or from the first element of one of a number of OE names containing the elements *cene* ('brave, astute') or *cyne* ('Royal').

Keep T/O Dweller at, or guardian of, a castle keep, its innermost tower ME (from an OE verb).

Keetch, *see* **Keech**.

Keevil P Place-name in Wilts OE '?clearing in a hollow' (literally 'tub') or '?wood where timber for tubs was got' or '?*Cufa*'s wood'. A Wilts surname.

Kegworth P Place-name in Leics ON and OE '?*Kaggi*'s enclosure'. A very scarce WRYorks surname.

Keigwin T/N From the Cornish *ky gwyn* 'white hedge'/'white dog'.

Keiller/Kellar/Keller P Scots: from the lands of Easter and Wester *Keilor*, Angus, Gaelic '?clayey river'. *Kelour* is known to have been used as a first-name in Moray. *In 1797 a grocer from Dundee named James Keiller bought a job-lot of Seville oranges; it was his wife Janet's idea to turn these into marmalade, a product which the firm of James Keiller still makes to this day.*

Kelby P Place-name in Lincs ON '?ridge farm' (compare **Keal**). A scattered surname.

Kelham P Place-name in Notts ON 'at the ridges', exhibiting the use of a dative plural after a lost preposition.

Kellar/Keller, *see* **Keiller**.

Kellet(t) P Place-names *Nether* and *Over Kellet* in Lancs and *Kelleth* in Cumbd ON 'slope with a spring'. A Lancs and WRYorks surname, also carried to the Irish counties of Cavan and Meath.

Kelleway, *see* **Callaway**.

Kelley, *see* **Kelly**.

Kellogg N Occupational term for a slaughterman ME and OE (literally 'kill hog'). Originally an Essex surname, but one which had practically died out in England by the late nineteenth century. *Will Keith ('W. K.') Kellogg (1860–1951), son of John Preston Kellogg of Livingston County, Michigan, is best known for the pioneering work he carried out with his brother John Harvey Kellogg in the development of what became known as 'corn flakes'. Another prominent family of Kelloggs in the USA is descended from Joseph Kellogg (1626–c.1707), from Bocking, Essex, England, who died in Hadley, Massachusetts.*

Kelly/Kelley P/F Place-name *Kelly* in Devon OE '*Cena's* clearing', or from Welsh/Cornish *celli* 'wood, grove'. Irish: Anglicized form of Gaelic **O'** [descendant of] **Ceallaigh** ('troublesome'/'bright-headed'); *Kelly* is now one of the commonest of all Irish surnames. Scots: from one of a number of place-names, such as *Kelly*, Angus, or *Kellie*, Fife, Gaelic 'wood, grove'.

Kelton P Place-name in Cumbd OE 'calf farm'. A scarce surname, found in Cumbd itself, and also in Lanarkshire, Scotland.

Kember O Occupational term for a comber of flax or wool OE. Chiefly a Kent surname. Readily confused with/a variant of **Kimber**. Compare **Kempster**.

Kemble/Kimball/Kimbell F/P English: from the ME first-name *Kimbel/Chimbel*, from OE *Cynebeal(d)* 'royal-brave'; Welsh: from an OW first-name *Cynbel* 'chief-war' (compare Shakespeare's *Cymbeline*); or from a place-name: *Kimble*, Bucks OE 'Royal (compare the word '*king*') bell/bell-shaped hill' or *Kemble*, Gloucs (a British name derived from *Camulos*, a Celtic god?). A widely scattered surname. *The earliest in a long line of Kembles (both male and female) celebrated for their acting ability was Roger Kemble (1722–1802), son of a Herefords barber who came from a family with Wilts origins and a strong tradition of adherence to the Roman Catholic faith. Roger's actor children by his wife Sarah Ward included Sarah ('Mrs Siddons'), born in Brecon, Wales, and John Philip Kemble (1757–1823), born in Prescot, Lancs.*

Kemmis/Kemeys N Nickname for a snub-nosed person ME *cammus, camois*. The original spelling **Camois/Camoys** would appear to have died out over time; a family known originally as **Camois** and then **Kemeys**, with its early origins in Surrey, Sussex and Pembrokeshire, eventually achieved Baronet status, while members of the related **Kemeys-Tynte** family would include Charles John **Kemeys-Tynte**, a nineteenth-century Member of Parliament for Cefn Mably, Glamorgan. **Kemmis** and **Kemeys**, both very scarce, can be found in Gloucs and in Herefords/Mid Wales respectively.

Kemp(e)/Kempson O Occupational term for a champion (in the jousts, or an athlete) ME *kempe*, OE *cempa*, Latin *campus* 'field (of battle)'. 'A resounding *old* name, since the word soon passed out of the vocabulary and must therefore have been applied and fixed early' (Cottle). **Kemp** is a very widely scattered surname, particularly strong in Kent and Middx; **Kempe**, much scarcer, can be found in both Devon and in WRYorks; **Kempson** is strongest in Staffs. **Kemp** is the family name of the Barons Rochdale. Compare **Camp**. *Rachel Kempson (1910–2003), actress and wife of Sir Michael Redgrave, was born in Dartmouth, Devon, where her father was headmaster of the Royal Naval College.*

Kemplay/Kempley P Bardsley derives **Kemplay** from the place-name *Kempley*, Gloucs OE '?*Cenepa's* wood/clearing', but both variants belong primarily to the north of England, and a more likely point of origin must be *Kempley [Beck]*, WRYorks OE '*Cempa's* wood/clearing'.

Kempson, *see* **Kemp**.

Kempster O Occupational term (predominantly female – compare **Brewster**, **Webster**, etc.) for a comber of flax or wool OE. A scattered surname, strongest in Bucks. Compare **Kember**.

Kendal(l)/Kendell/Kendle P Place-name *Kendal*, Westmd, Celtic and OE 'valley of the (river) *Kent*'.

Kendrick, *see* **Kenrick**.

Kennard/Kenward/Kenwood F From an
OE first-name *Cyneweard*, ME *Keneward*
'Royal (compare the word *King*)-brave'.
The *-weard* element can also mean
'guard', as it does in the surname **Kenward**.
Kenwood may share the same origin in
some cases, but given the fact that it is so
much a Devon surname, and that four men
bearing the surname or byname of **de Kene-
wode** are listed in the Devon Lay Subsidy of
1332, we might be safe in assuming that the
place named *Kenwood* in that county (getting its name, in principle, from the river
Kenn, though that is at some distance) is the
origin in such cases. **Kennard** and **Kenward**
are most commonly found in Kent and Sussex.

Kennedy N Irish: Anglicized form of Gaelic
O' [descendant of] **Cinneidigh** ('helmeted/
ugly head'). A far cry from President John
and Senators Robert and Edward, the handsome sons of 'Joe' Kennedy (1888–1969),
former US Ambassador to the United Kingdom, whose grandparents had arrived in
America in the mid 1840s, fleeing the
Irish famine. **Kennedy** is the family name
of the Marquesses of Ailsa. Also a Scottish
surname.

Kennet(t) P Place-names in Wilts *East* and
West Kennet; a Celtic hill-name (?) has been
applied to the river *Kennet* and to the settlements on its banks. The surname is most
commonly found in Kent, in either spelling.

Kennington P Place-name in Kent OE
'royal farm' and in Berks, Surrey OE 'the
farm of *Cena*'s people'. And yet the surname has long been well established in
Lincs in particular, in which county there
is a *Kennington* Farm, Willoughton, first
referred to in a written record of the sixteenth century, which the place-name
scholar Kenneth Cameron believes could
be a transferred name from *Kennington* in
Surrey.

Kennish/Kinnish F Manx: contraction of
Mac Enys/Mac Inesh ('son of *Anghus*'). *William Kennish was the first person to submit a
practical scheme for the construction of a canal*

*to link the Atlantic and Pacific Oceans by way
of the Isthmus of Panama.*

Kenny F Scots: Anglicized form of the
Gaelic first-name *Cionaodha* ('?Respect-
Aodh [pagan fod of fire]'); Irish: Anglicized
form of the Gaelic **O'** [descendant of] **Coin-
nigh**, after whom *Kilkenny* is named. *See
also* **McKenna**.

Kenrick/Kendrick F English: from the OE
first-name *Cyneric*, via ME *Cenric* 'Royal-
power'; Welsh: from the OW first-name
Cyn(w)rig/Cynfrig 'chief man/hero'; Scots
and Irish: an abbreviated form of **McKendrick**. A fairly widespread surname in the
Midlands and the north of England in
either spelling (though scarce in Wales);
Kenrick is found chiefly in Lancs, **Kendrick**
in Staffs.

Kensick, *see* **Cansick**.

Kent P From the county name, Celtic in
origin but of uncertain meaning ('?rim,
border'/'?host, party'). A very scattered surname. *Bruce Kent, British political activist and
former Roman Catholic priest, was born in
London in 1929.*

Kentish P A person from the county of
Kent, Celtic, with an OF suffix. An uncommon surname, found in south-east England.

Kenton P Place-name in Devon, Celtic and
OE 'place on the (river) *Kenn*'; in Northd,
Suffolk OE 'Royal manor'; and in Middx OE
'*Cempa*'s settlement'.

Kenward, *see* **Kennard**.

Kenway F From an OE first-name meaning
'brave/Royal war' (compare **Kennard**). A
scarce surname, found mainly in Dorset.

Kenwood, *see* **Kennard**.

Kenworthy P Place-name in Chesh OE
'?*Cyna*'s enclosure'. A Lancs/WRYorks surname.

Kenyon P Place-name in Lancs, of uncertain etymology, possibly OW *cruc Enion*
('*Ennion*'s mound'); a Bronze Age barrow

once stood there. Predominantly a Lancs surname.

Ker, *see* **Carr**.

Kermode F Manx: abbreviated form of **Mac Dhiarmada** ('son of *Dermott*', a freeman). Pronounced with the stress on the first syllable. *The English literary critic Sir (John) Frank Kermode was born on the Isle of Man in 1919… The film critic Mark Kermode (real name Mark Fairey), born in 1963, was at Haberdashers' Aske's School, Elstree, at the same time as the comedian Sacha Baron Cohen (aka 'Ali G' and 'Borat') and the actor Jason Isaacs.*

Kernan, *see* **Tiernan**.

Kernow P Place-name: from the Cornish-language term for the county of *Cornwall*. **Curnow** is a later version.

Kerr, *see* **Carr**.

Kersey P Place-name in Suffolk OE 'watercress island' – the village that perhaps gave its name to the coarse woollen cloth.

Kershaw P Place-name *Kirkshaw*, Lancs ON and OE 'church grove'. *Andy Kershaw, the British broadcaster best known for his enthusiasm for world music, was born in Rochdale, Lancs, in 1959.*

Kerslake, *see* **Carslake**.

Kerswell P Place-names in Devon OE 'watercress spring'.

Keswick P Place-name in Cumbd, Norfolk, WRYorks OE 'cheese dairy-farm' (Scandinavianized, unlike the southern place-name *Chiswick*). Found chiefly in Cumbd.

Ketch, *see* **Kedge**.

Ketcham/Ketchum ?P/N Such surnames have become very rare within the British Isles, but as early as the sixteenth century they had a significant presence in East Anglia. Similar surnames are known to have existed in both France and Germany. In *Dictionary of American surnames* (1956) E. C. Smith includes a listing for '**Ketchum**, Ketcham. English. One who comes from *Caecca*'s homestead'. If there is a place-

name so-called, it cannot presently be identified. Or **Ketcham/Ketchum** could be variants of **Ketch** (see **Kedge**) or of **Ketchen** (see **Kitchen**)? N. I. Bowditch, in *Suffolk [Massachusetts] surnames* (3rd edition, 1861) enters the realms of fantasy by assuming that surnames such as **Nabb** and **Ketchum** ('*catch 'em*') were used to describe those who apprehended malefactors. He adds: 'It is said that, on one occasion, Mr Timothy Wiggin of Boston and Messrs Preserved Fish and Hiram **Ketchum** of New York applied for passports from England to France; and the official was indignant, thinking that it was an attempt to impose upon him by fictitious names'.

Ketchen, *see* **Kitchen**.

Ketchum, *see* **Ketcham**.

Kettel(l), *see* **Kettle**.

Ketteringham P Place-name in Norfolk OE 'homestead of the followers of *Cytringa*'. A scarce Norfolk surname.

Kettle/Kettel(l) F From an ON first-name *Ketill* '(sacrificial) cauldron', also commonly found as an element in longer names.

Kettleband ?P A very scarce Leics/Notts surname, of unknown origin, though there are places called *Kettleburn* in Northd ON '?*Ketill*'s stream' (see **Kettle**) and *Ab Kettleby* in Leics ON '(*Abbe/Abba/Abbi*'s) *Ketill*'s village'. The surname frequently appears in Notts and neighbouring counties as **Kettleburn(e)/Kettlebo(u)rn**, and Thomas **Kettleborne** of Elton appears in a subsidy list for Notts in 1689. Ann **Kettleband** 'or Alvey' married John Allen in Keyworth, Notts, in 1845. Leo Alphonsus Milligan, an army sergeant-major who made his career in India and was the father of the comedian Spike Milligan, married Florence **Kettleband**. She reputedly came from Sligo, Ireland, but the first-name '*Florence*' was much favoured during the nineteenth century by a **Kettleband** family from Notts.

Kettleburn(e)/Kettlebo(u)rn/Kettleborne, *see* **Kettleband**.

Kew O/P Occupational term for a cook, Anglo-Norman French *k(i)eu* (compare the surname **Lequeux**); or from the place-name *Caieu*, Pas-de-Calais; or from *Kew*, Middx, OE 'key/projection slope'. A widespread surname.

Kewish F Manx: abbreviated form of **Mac Uais** ('the noble's son').

Kewley, *see* Cowley.

Key(e)(s), *see* Kay.

Keymer P Place-name in Sussex OE 'cow pool', but chiefly a Norfolk surname.

Keynes, *see* Cains.

Keys, *see* Kay.

Keyte, *see* Keat.

Keyworth P Place-name in Notts OE 'enclosure made with ?poles'. Most commonly found in Lincs and WRYorks.

Kibble, *see* Keble.

Kid(d)/Kidder/Kidman/Kidson/Kydd N/O/F Nickname for a person bearing some resemblance (frisky?) to a kid, a young goat ME (?from ON); or (including **Kidman**) an occupational term for a seller of kids, or of faggots ME *kidde*; or from a Scots variant of **Kit** (*Christopher*). **Kid** and **Kidd** are found mainly in northern England and in Scotland, though the latter has a wider distribution within England; **Kidder**, scarce, has a presence in Lincs; **Kidman** is mainly a Cambs surname; **Kidson** is found mainly in the English Midlands and the north, and **Kydd** is mainly restricted to the Scottish county of Angus. *For Johnny Kidd, singer and songwriter, see* Heath… *Sam Kydd (1915–1982), British character actor, was born in Belfast, Northern Ireland… The surname Kidman is particularly well known in Australia, thanks to the wealthy landowner Sir Sidney Kidman ('The Cattle King'); Nicole (Mary) Kidman, Academy Award-winning actress, was born in Hawaii to Australian parents.*

Kiddell/Kiddle T Dweller by a fish weir or dam OF. **Kiddle** and **Kiddle** are at their strongest in both Norfolk and Somerset.

Kidder, *see* Kid.

Kiddle, *see* Kiddell.

Kidman/Kidson, *see* Kid.

Kieran F Irish: Anglicized form of the Gaelic first-name *Ciaran* ('dark/black'), borne by several Irish saints.

Kiernan, *see* Tiernan.

Kilborn/Kilbourn(e)/Kilburn(e) P Place-name *Kilburn* in Derbys and NRYorks OE 'stream by a kiln'. *Kilburn* in Middx would seem not to have been the source of a related surname. **Kilborn** is mostly found in Northants, **Kilbourn** and **Kilbourne** in Leics, and **Kilburn** in WRYorks. **Kilburne** is a scarce variant.

Kilby P Place-name in Leics OE and ON 'farm of the young nobles/gentlemen' (compare the word *child*; an ON *K-* appears here in place of the OE sound *ch-*). Strongest as a surname in Leics, but widespread.

Kildea, *see* Gildea.

Kilfoyle, *see* Guilfoyle.

Kilham P Place-name in ERYorks and Northd OE '(at) the kilns', exhibiting the use of a dative plural after a lost preposition. *Alexander Kilham (1762–1798), a founder of the Methodist New Connexion, was born at Epworth, Lincs, the place where John Wesley's own father had once been the parish priest.*

Killduff, *see* Gilduff.

Killer O Occupational term for a worker at a kiln, or for a killer of beasts (rather than humans…) ME *killere*. Compare **Kilner**. Principally a Derbys surname, particularly in evidence in the former lead-mining town of Wirksworth in that county.

Killip F Manx: a contraction of **Mac Phelip** ('son of *Philip*').

Kilmartin, *see* Gilmartin.

Kil(l)mister/Kil(l)minster/Kittermaster P Place-name *Kidderminster*, Worcs OE '*Kydder*'s monastery', which was *Kedeleministre* in the thirteeenth century. **Kilmister**, **Kilminster** and **Killminster** are Gloucs surnames; **Killmister**, very scarce, can be found in Somerset and **Kittermaster**, also scarce, in Salop.

Kilmore, *see* **Gilmer**.

Kilner O Occupational term for a worker at a kiln, a lime-burner OE. Mostly found in WRYorks. Compare **Killer**.

Kilpatrick, *see* **Gilpatrick**.

Kilpin P Place-name in ERYorks OE 'calf pen' – yet principally a Bucks/Middx/Northants surname. Readily confused with/a variant of **Culpin**, **Galpin** and **Gilpin**.

Kilroy, *see* **Gilroy**.

Kilsby P Place-name in Northants OE and ON 'farm of the child/young nobleman'. A Northants surname.

Kimball/Kimbell, *see* **Kemble**.

Kimber F From an OE female first-name *Cyneburh*, meaning 'Royal fortress', made popular in mediaeval times thanks to its being borne by a daughter of a seventh-century King of Mercia who founded an abbey and was venerated as a saint. A surname found in southern counties of England, particularly strong in Hants. Readily confused with/a variant of **Kember**. *William Kimber (1872–1961), born in Headington Quarry, Oxon, met the folk-music collector Cecil Sharp on Boxing Day 1899 while he was playing concertina for the local morris men. Both men would eventually achieve fame in the world of folk music and dance as a result of this chance meeting and their subsequent collaboration.*

Kimberl(e)y P From one of a number of place-names in Norfolk, Notts, Warwicks, derived from a variety of OE first-names with the addition of OE *leah* ('wood, clearing'). The surname exhibits a narrow pattern of distribution, being found chiefly in Midland counties of England, especially Staffs, Warwicks and Worcs.

Kimble, *see* **Kemble**.

King O/N Occupational term for a person who worked in a Royal household, or a nickname for one who played the king in a pageant or other festivity, or who was kingly or swaggering in his manner OE *cyning*. Common in England, scarcer in Scotland, scarcer still in Wales. The family name of the Earls of Lovelace. *See also* **Ray**.

Kingsbury P Place-name in Middx, Somerset OE 'King's fort/manor', and in Warwicks OE '*Cynesburh*'s fort'. A surname found mainly in a band stretching across southern counties of England.

Kingsford P Cottle derives this surname from the place-name *Kingsford* as found in Warwicks OE 'king's ford', or Worcs OE 'the ford of *Cena*'s people'; yet the surname is mostly found in Middx and especially in Kent, where there is a place called *Kingsford Street* in Mersham (*Kyngesfeld* in the thirteenth century). For a similar confusion/error, see **Kingswood**.

Kingsley P Place-name in Chesh, Hants and Staffs OE 'King's wood/clearing'. Readily confused with/a variant of **Kinsley**. *Charles Kingsley (1819–1875), novelist and Anglican clergyman, was born in Holne vicarage, Devon, where his father – a country gentleman from an established Hants family – was working as a curate.*

Kingston P Place-name in several counties, including *Kingston-on-Thames*, Surrey and *Kingston upon Hull* OE 'King's farm/manor'.

Kingswood P Cottle derives this surname from the place-name *Kingswood* as found in Gloucs (two such), Surrey and Warwicks OE 'Royal chase'; yet the surname is mostly found in Lincs and especially in Kent, where there are places of ancient origin called *King's Wood* in both Broomfield and in Wye. For a similar confusion/error, see **Kingsford**.

Kington P Place-names in various counties OE 'Royal farm/manor'. Strongest in Somerset and Wilts.

Kininmonth P From one of two places so-called in the Kingdom of Fife, Scotland (though there is also a *Kininmonth* in Aberdeenshire), Scots Gaelic 'head of the white hill'. Latterly a very scarce surname, found almost exclusively in Fife.

Kinnersley P Place-names: *Kinnersley* in Herefords, Worcs, and *Kinnerley*, Salop OE '*Cyneheard*'s wood/clearing'; *Kinnersley*, Salop OE '*Cyneheard*'s island [with an intrusive -*l*-]'. There is also a *Kinnersley* in Surrey OE '*Cyneweard*'s wood/clearing', though the surname is found chiefly in Herefords, Staffs, Worcs and Glamorgan.

Kinnish, *see* **Kennish**.

Kinnoch/Kinnock F Scots: from the Gaelic first-name *Coinneach* (*Kenneth*). *Neil Kinnock, Baron Kinnock, former leader of the British Labour Party, was born in Tredegar, Wales, of Scottish ancestry… By contrast, George Kynoch (1834–1891), whose family origins lay in Peterhead, Aberdeenshire, sat as a Conservative Party Member of Parliament for Aston Manor, Birmingham, from 1886 to 1891.*

Kinsey F From an OE first-name, meaning 'Royal victory'. Chiefly a Chesh and Lancs surname. *Alfred Kinsey (1894–1956), author of the Kinsey Report on human sexuality, was born into a fervently Methodist family in Hoboken, New Jersey, USA.*

Kinsley P Place-name in WRYorks OE '*Cyne*'s wood/clearing'. A north-of-England surname. Readily confused with/a variant of **Kingsley**.

Kipling P Place-names: *Kiplin*, NRYorks OE '(settlement of) *Cyppel*'s people' and *Kipling Cotes*, ERYorks OE '?cottage(s) associated with *Cybbel*'. Readily confused with/a variant of **Kipping**? *The writer (Joseph) Rudyard Kipling (1865–1936), born in Bombay, India, and named 'Rudyard' after the lake in Staffs where his parents had first met, came from a Kipling family with Yorks origins. In a letter to a correspondent (J. S. Speight) dated 5 May 1895, Rudyard's father John Lockwood Kipling (1837–1911) says that he believes his own male-line ancestors to have been farmers living somewhere near Bedale or Richmond, NRYorks: 'My great-grandfather's grave is at Lythe near Whitby, but that was not his native region. I have been in India for the greater part of my life and really know very little about it'.*

Kippen P Reaney and Cottle derive this surname from a nickname for a fat or tubby person OE *cypping*, but the fact that it is restricted almost entirely to Scotland leads us to look elsewhere. The origin is a place called *Kippen*, Gaelic *ceaopan* 'little stump', near Stirling. But see **Kipping**.

Kipping/Kipps N Nickname for a fat or tubby person OE *cypping* (unlike **Kippen**, above, which would seem to be derived from a Scottish place-name). Alternatively, Bardsley is persuaded by the idea that **Kipps** might be a variant of **Gilbert**, via **Gipps**. **Kipping** and **Kipps**, both very scarce, belong mainly to south-eastern counties of England. **Kipping** could perhaps be readily confused with, or be a variant of, **Kipling**.

Kirby/Kirkby P From one of a number of places in the old Danelaw called *Kirby* or *Kirkby* ON 'church farm/village'.

Kirk T English and Scots: a dweller by a church. It's easy to assume that *kirk* is a Scottish word, because it has lingered in use in that country; in the event it's nothing more than an ON equivalent of the OE *church*, and can be found in countless place-names in the old Danelaw area of England. A common surname, both in the Midlands and north of England, and in Scotland.

Kirkbride P From one of a number of place-names in the north of England ON 'church of (St) *Bridget*' (compare the surname **McBride**, or the church of *St Bride's*, Fleet Street, in London). Strongest in Cumbd.

Kirkby, *see* **Kirby**.

Kirkham P Place-name in Lancs and ERYorks OE (Scandinavianized) 'church homestead/village'.

Kirkland T/P Dweller on land belonging to the church ON and OE, or from a place-name with the same meaning in Cumbd, Ayrshire, Dumfries, Lanarkshire. *Kirkland* in Lancs is ON 'church wood'.

Kirkley P Place-name in Northd, British and OE 'hill-hill', tautologically. A surname of north and north-east England.

Kirkpatrick P Scots and Northern Irish: from one of a number of place-names meaning 'church ON of (St) *Patrick*'.

Kirkup P A Durham/Northd surname, presumably derived from an unidentified place-name in that part of England ON and OE 'church valley'.

Kirkus T Dweller at the 'church house' ON and OE/ON, based upon local pronunciation. A very scarce ERYorks surname.

Kirkwood T/P Dweller at the 'church wood' ON and OE, or from one of a number of place-names with the same meaning in the Scottish counties of Ayr, Dumfries and Lanarkshire. The first-known reference to *Kirk Wood* in Oxspring, WRYorks (Cottle's favoured place of origin) dates only from the late sixteenth century.

Kirtland P Cottle states that **Kirtland** is a corruption of **Kirkland**, though its pattern of distribution – it belongs principally to the south of England, and to Oxon in particular – would suggest that this might be wide of the mark. A more likely place of origin would be *Kirtlington*, Oxon OE '*Cyrtla*'s farm', which was *Curtlint* in the thirteenth century.

Kirton P Place-name in Lincs, Notts, Suffolk and elsewhere OE (Scandinavianized) 'church farm/village', but chiefly a Co Durham surname.

Kislingbury P Place-name in Northants OE 'fort of the followers of *Cysela*'. A very scarce Berks/Surrey surname.

Kiss/Kisser O Occupational term for a maker of thigh-armour OF *cuisse*. Very scarce Surrey surnames.

Kissack F Manx: **Mac Issak** ('son of *Isaac*').

Kisser, *see* **Kiss**.

Kitchen/Ketchen/Kitchener/Kitchi-ner/Kitchin(g) O Occupational term for someone who worked in a kitchen OE. **Kitchen**, **Kitchin** and **Kitching** are found mainly in the north of England; **Ketchen** (scarce) in Midlothian, Scotland; **Kitchener** in the South Midlands and the South;

Kitchiner in Beds and Herts. *See also* **Ketcham**. *Horatio Herbert Kitchener, Earl Kitchener of Khartoum (1850–1916), army officer, was born in Listowel, Co Kerry, Ireland; his father, Lt. Col. Henry Horatio Kitchener, was English rather than Anglo-Irish, and had been baptized at St Luke's, Old Street, London, in 1805 under the surname 'Kitchner'.*

Kite, *see* **Keat**.

Kiteley, *see* **Kitley**.

Kitley P Place-name *Kitley* in Devon OE 'wood with kites'. There is a *Kitleigh* in Cornwall. Chiefly a Somerset surname. **Kiteley** could be a variant, though its distribution (West Midlands) is different.

Kitson/Kitt, *see* **Christopher**.

Kittermaster, *see* **Kilmister**.

Kitto/Kittow/Kitts, *see* **Christopher**.

Knape O Occupational term for a servant, lad OE (compare a *knave* in a pack of cards). A very scarce Lancs surname.

Knapman, *see* **Knapp**.

Knapp T/P Dweller at a hilltop OE, or from a place-name with the same meaning in Devon, Hants, Sussex. **Knapp** is found throughout southern counties of England, though rarely in the south-west; the variants **Knapman** and **Knapper** (very scarce) belong to Devon and Staffs respectively. *Roger (Maurice) Knapman, former leader of the United Kingdom Independence Party (UKIP), was born in Crediton, Devon, in 1944.*

Knapper, *see* **Knapp**.

Knapton P Place-name in NRYorks (two such) and Norfolk OE '*Cnapa*'s farm' or OE 'young boy's farm'.

Knatchbull O Occupational term for a slaughterer/butcher ME (literally 'knock out the bull'; compare a *knacker*'s yard). A very scarce surname of the south and south-west of England. The family name of the Barons Brabourne.

Kneebone P A scarce Cornish surname derived from the place-name *Carnebone* in

Wendron, Cornish '*Ebwen*'s rock-pile'. Other suggested (fanciful?) derivations include: a topographical feature resembling a kneebone; a nickname for a person with knobbly knees; or the Cornish word *carnebol* 'colt corral'.

Knell/Kneller, *see* Knoll.

Knight(s)/Knevet(t)/Knivett O Occupational/status term for a youth, soldier, knight, feudal tenant bound to serve as a mounted warrior, or a servant in a knight's household OE. Also used as a first-name before the Norman Conquest. **Knevet(t)/Knivett** reflect the Anglo-Norman French pronunciation, at a time when the initial '*K*' would have been given its full force. **Knight** is a very common surname throughout England as far north as Yorks, but much scarcer in Wales and Scotland; **Knights** is found principally in Norfolk; **Knevett**, scarce, can be found in small pockets in southern counties of England and East Anglia; **Knevitt**, even scarcer, has a presence in Cornwall. *The literary scholar L. C. (Lionel Charles) Knights (1906–1997) was born in Grantham, Lincs.*

Knighton P Place-name in several counties (four such in Dorset) OE 'farm of the knights/retainers/youths'. Found mostly in Derbys, Northants and Notts.

Knightsbridge P Place-name in Middx OE 'bridge of the knights'. A very scarce Essex/Middx surname.

Knill, *see* Knoll.

Knipe P Place-name in Westmd ON *gnipa* 'steep/overhanging rock'. There is also a hill called *Knipe* in Ayrshire, Scotland, Gaelic and Welsh *cnap* 'knob/little hill'. During the eighteenth century, when a Rev. Mr **Knipe** (from Newcastle on Tyne) was minister at the Presbyterian Chapel in Maling's Rigg, Sunderland, his surname was commonly spelt 'Knip' in the registers. Predominantly a Lancs surname, also found in the Irish counties of Armagh and Cavan since the seventeenth century.

Knivett, *see* Knight.

Knock T/P Dweller by the hill OE *cnocc*. Or from a place-name with the same meaning: there is a *Knock Hatch* (*La Knocke* in 1267) in Sussex and a *Knock Farm* (*Cnocke* in 1194) in Kent, but given the fact that this is very much an East Anglian surname, strongest in Suffolk, Cottle's references to places called *Knock* in Scotland and Westmd may well be of little relevance.

Knoll/Knell/Kneller/Knill/Knollys/ Knowles T/P/N Dweller on a hilltop OE *cnoll*; or from any one of a number of places called *Knole/Knowle* and the like (including *Knill*, Herefords), with the same meaning; or from a nickname for a person as stout (and round?) as a hilltop. **Knoll** is a scarce scattered surname; **Knell** is found mainly in Kent, **Kneller** in Hants, **Knill** in Devon (but also in Herefords and elsewhere). **Knollys** is a very scarce scattered surname; **Knowles** is both widespread and common, especially strong in Lancs.

Knott N/T/F Nickname for a thickset person OE *cnotta* ('knot'); or a dweller by a hill ME *knot*; or from the ON first-name *Knutr*, well known thanks to King *Canute* (1016–1035). A common and scattered surname, particularly strong in Lancs. Readily confused with/a variant of **Nott**.

Know(e)lden P Place-name *Knowlton*, Kent OE 'hill settlement'. A scarce surname centred in Kent in either spelling. There is also a surname **Knowlton**, which is almost entirely restricted to Hants.

Knowles, *see* Knoll.

Knowlton, *see* Knowlden.

Knox T/P Scots, Northern Irish and northern English: dweller on a hilltop OE *cnocc*; or from any one of a number of places called *Knock* in Scotland and the north of England. Family name of the Earls of Ranfurly. *There is no lack of eminent Scotsmen bearing the name John Knox, the most famous of whom, John Knox (c 1514–1572) the religious reformer, was born at Giffordgate in Haddington.*

Knoyle P Place-names *East* and *West Knoyle* in Wilts OE 'knuckle', from the shape of the ridge nearby. A very scarce surname with something of a presence in South Wales.

Kydd, *see* **Kid**.

Kynaston P Place-names in Herefords: *Hentland Kynaston* OE *'Cyneheard*'s settlement' and *Kynaston* in Much Marcle OE *'Cyneweard*'s settlement'; also in Salop: *Kynaston* OE *'Cynefrith*'s settlement'. Chiefly a Salop surname.

Labbett, *see* Abbot.

Lachlan/Laughlan(d)/Laughlin P Scots and Irish: from a Gaelic first-name *Lochlann* (literally 'lake/fjord land', used for a person from Scandinavia, a Viking).

Lackford P Place-name in Suffolk OE 'ford where leeks are grown'. A scarce surname.

Lacock P Place-name *Lacock* or *Laycock*, Wilts OE '?streamlet', though this scarce surname is mainly encountered in Norfolk. Readily confused with/a variant of **Laycock**.

Lac(e)y P Place-name *Lassy* in Calvados, from the Gaulish first-name *Lascius*, plus suffix. Well-established **Lacey** families are fond of depicting a pike (the fish, alternatively known as a *luce* OF) on their armorial bearings in a canting or punning fashion – though the **Lacy**s, Earls of Lincoln, favoured a shield with a purple rampant lion on a gold field. Both **Lacy** and **Lacey** are widely scattered surnames, though neither is common in the far north of England or in Scotland.

Ladd O Occupational term for a lad, servant ME. Many Americans who bear this surname are descended from Daniel **Ladd**, who emigrated from London to Ipswich, Massachusetts, in 1634, though the film actor Alan (Walbridge) **Ladd** (1913–1964), was born in Hot Springs, Arkansas, the son of English immigrants.

Ladel(l) O Occupational term for a ladle maker OE. Chiefly a Norfolk surname in either spelling.

Lafferty, *see* Laverty.

Laimbeer, *see* Langabeer.

Laing, *see* Long.

Laird, *see* Lord.

Lake T/P Dweller by a stream OE; or from such a place-name in Wilts and Devon. The use of the word *lake* to refer to a stretch of water (OF from Latin *lacus*) is a fairly recent development. **Lake** is found principally in Devon, Middx and Norfolk; **Lakeman**, with the same meaning, is a scarce Devon surname.

Lakeman, *see* Lake.

Laker T/O/N Dweller at a stream (see **Lake**); or an occupational term/nickname for a player, actor, sportsman ON. The verb *to lake*, meaning *to play*, is still used in the north of England, and 'the grave, industrious peasants of the English Lake District referred to early holiday-makers there as *Lakers*' (Cottle). *Freddie Laker (1922–2006), pioneer of affordable airline flights, came from Canterbury, Kent… James Charles ('Jim') Laker (1922–1986), English cricketer, was born in Bradford, Yorks.*

Lalonde, *see* Lund.

Lalor, *see* Lawlor.

Lamb(e) O/T/N/F Occupational term for a tender of lambs OE; or a dweller at a building bearing the sign of the Paschal Lamb; or a nickname for a lamb-like person or a diminutive of the first-name *Lambert* (see **Lambert**). Commoner in the English Midlands and the north (especially Lancs) than in the south. **Lamb** is the family name of the Barons Rochester; **Lampson** ('son of

Lamb') is the family name of the Barons Killearn.

Lambern, *see* **Lamborn**.

Lambert/Lambrick/Lampard/Lamperd F/O From a Germanic first-name meaning 'land bright', popularized by the Flemings after St *Lambert*, a seventh-century Bishop of Maestricht (*see also* **Lamb**); or an occupational term for a shepherd ('lamb-herd') OE. **Lambert** is chiefly a WRYorks surname; **Lampard** is especially in evidence in Wilts; **Lamperd** is a rare surname of southern England; **Lambrick** is a very scarce variant found in Cornwall. Readily confused with/a variant of **Lampet** or **Lombard**. *Frank (James) Lampard, Jr, a footballer with West Ham and Chelsea and a member of the England squad, was born in 1978 in Romford, London. His father, Frank, Sr, played full-back for England, and the Lampards are related to another footballing family, the Redknapps.*

Lambeth P Place-name on the Surrey side of the Thames in London OE 'lamb landing-place'. A uncommon surname belonging mainly to southern counties of England.

Lambley P Place-name in Northd, Notts OE 'lambs' pasture'. Strongest in Lincs.

Lamborn(e)/Lambourn(e)/Lamburn(e) P Place-names: *Lambourne*, Essex and *Lambourn*, Berks OE 'loamy/clayey stream' or 'stream for washing lambs'. Not common in any spelling; **Lambern** is a very scarce Somerset variant.

Lambrick, *see* **Lamb**.

Lambton P Place-name in Co Durham OE 'lamb farm'. Made famous thanks to the local song *The Lambton Worm*, and the family name of the Earls of Durham.

Lamburn(e), *see* **Lamborn**.

Lamerton P Place-name in Devon OE 'farm on a lamb(-washing) stream' (the stream is still called *Lumburn*).

Lamont/Lamond O Scots: occupational term for a lawman/law-giver, Gaelic from ON. See also **McLamon**. **Lamond** is primarily an Angus surname; **Lamont** is well known in the Shetland Islands, the birthplace of the former Conservative Party Chancellor of the Exchequer (1990–1993) Norman Lamont, created a life-peer in 1998, who runs counter to the usual Scots practice by pronouncing his surname with the stress on the second syllable (compare, by contrast, **Balfour**).

Lampard/Lamperd, *see* **Lambert**.

Lampet/Lampitt/Lamputt T/O Dweller by, or worker at, a claypit OE (compare the word *loam*). Very scarce in any spelling, readily confused with/a variant of Lambert.

Lampl(o)ugh P Place-name *Lamplugh*, Cumbd ow 'church of the parish'. Both spellings of the surname are found chiefly in ERYorks.

Lamport P Place-names *Lamport* and *Langport* in various counties OE 'long market-place'. An uncommon surname, found particularly in Surrey and Hants.

Lampshire P A Cornish surname; a variant of **Lancashire**?

Lampson, *see* **Lamb**.

Lamputt, *see* **Lampet**.

Lancashire/Lankshear P Place-name, the county of *Lancashire* OE and Celtic 'Roman fort on the river *Lune*', plus 'shire'. **Lancashire** is not a common surname (mainly found, predictably, in Lancs), and nor is **Lankshear** (chiefly restricted to Dorset). See also **Lampshire**.

Lancaster/Lankester P Place-name *Lancaster*, Lancs OE and Celtic 'Roman fort on the (river) *Lune*'. **Lancastle** and **Landcastle** are scarce variants.

Lancastle, *see* **Lancaster**.

Lance F From a Norman version of the Germanic first-name *Lanzo*, which contains the element 'land'.

Lanchester P Place-name in Co Durham OE 'long Roman site'. An uncommon scattered surname, strongest in Norfolk. *Frederick William Lanchester (1868–1946), the engineer* *and inventor after whom the Lanchester Motor Company of Birmingham was named, was born in London.*

Land T/P Dweller on 'land' OE – in various senses of the word, such as a selion, an arable strip between two furrows when an open field is divided, a basic unit of plough-ing – as opposed to a town-dweller; or dweller at a glade OF, or from the place-name *Launde*, Leics, with this meaning. A surname particularly in evidence in WRYorks.

Landcastle, *see* **Lancaster**.

Lander(s), *see* **Lavender**.

Landseer T Dweller at a landmark, bound-ary OE. However, the surname is so excep-tionally scarce in England that a foreign derivation might be suspected. A compar-able French surname, **Landsheer** or **Land-herr**, is derived from the Middle High German word *lantherre*, used for a seigneur with significant estates. Sixteenth-century records for the Walloon church in Canter-bury, Kent, include individuals bearing the surnames **Landsheer(e)** and **Landshear(e)**. *Sir Edwin (Henry) Landseer (1802–1873), Eng-lish painter best known for his animal studies, was born in London, the son of Lincoln-born engraver and antiquary John George Landseer.*

Landsell, *see* **Lonsdale**.

Lane T/F Dweller at a lane OE. A widespread surname, particularly strong in Gloucs and Middx. In Ireland such a surname can be derived from Gaelic **O'** [descendant of] **Laighin** ('javelin'), **O'Luain** ('warrior') or **O'Liathain/Lehane** ('grey').

Lang, *see* **Long**.

Langabeer P From one of two place-names in Devon, one in Hatherleigh, the other in Sampford Courtenay OE 'long grove/pas-ture'. **Laimbeer** may well be a corruption of the same surname and it, like **Langabeer**, is chiefly found in Devon.

Langcake O ?Occupational term for a baker of 'long cakes' OE. A distinctive and

scarce surname, found in very limited num-bers in Cumbd and NRYorks.

Langdale P Place-name in Westmd OE and ON 'long valley'.

Langdon P Place-name in several counties OE 'long hill'. Very much a West Country surname. Readily confused with/a variant of **Longden**.

Langford P Place-name in several counties (three such in Somerset) OE 'long ford'.

Langham P Place-name in several counties OE 'long homestead'; but *Langham* in Essex is 'homestead of *Lawa*'s people'; and *Lang-ham* in Lincs OE is 'long river-island'. The surname has a particularly strong presence in Leics. *Langham Place* in London was built in the 1820s around the boundaries of a large house belonging to Sir James **Lang-ham**.

Langley P Place-name in sixteen counties from Northd to Wilts OE 'long wood/clear-ing'. Readily confused with/a variant of **Longley**.

Langmaid/Langmead P Cottle suggests that these surnames were applied in a gen-eral way to a dweller in a long meadow OE, but given the fact that **Langmead** is a Devon surname and that **Langmaid** is found principally in Cornwall and Devon, the specific origin is likely to be the place-name *Langmead* in Sampford Courtenay, Devon.

Langridge T/P Dweller at a long ridge OE, or from a place-name with the same meaning, including the now-lost *Langridge* in Hal-ling, Kent. A surname belonging almost exclusively to southern counties of Eng-land.

Langrish P Place-name in Hants OE 'long rush-bed', and chiefly a Hants surname.

Langslow P Place-name *Longslow* in Salop (*Walanceslau* in 1086) OE '*Wlanc*'s tumulus'. A very rare Herefords/Salop surname. *Cap-tain Richard Langslow (1786–1863) of the Ben-gal Army was baptized at St Lawrence, Ludlow, Salop, on 10 March 1786; his eldest son was* *born in Africa, the second in Asia, the third in North America, and the fifth at Halton House, Middx.*

Langston(e) P Place-names: *Langstone* in Devon and Hants, and *Llangstone* in Monmouthshire OE 'long (standing-)stone, a menhir'. **Langston** is chiefly a Bucks surname; **Langstone** is found in both Bucks and Worcs.

Langthorne P Place-name in NRYorks OE 'tall thornbush'. An uncommon Lancs/Yorks surname.

Langton P Place-name in six counties OE 'long place/farm'; but *Langton* in Co Durham is OE 'long hill'. Readily confused with/ a variant of **Longton**.

Langtree/Langtr(e)y P Place-name in Devon, Oxon and Lancs OE 'tall tree'. The surnames **Langtree** and **Langtry** are found principally in Lancs. *Lillie Langtry (1853–1929), the beautiful actress known as the 'Jersey Lily', who became the mistress of Edward, Prince of Wales, was born Emilie Charlotte Le Breton, and was the daughter of William Corbet Le Breton, Dean of Jersey. In 1874 she married Edward Langtry, son of a Belfast shipowner.*

Lank N Nickname for a lanky, skinny person OE. An uncommon surname, found mainly in Essex, Lincs and Rutland.

Lankester/Lankshear, *see* **Lancashire**.

Lansdell, *see* **Lonsdale**.

Lanyon P Place-name in Cornwall, *Lyn yeyn* 'cool pool or lake'.

Lapham P From an unidentified place-name, probably OE '*Læppa/Hlappa*'s homestead/river-meadow', comparable with place-names such as *Lapford*, *Lapley* and *Lapworth*. An uncommon surname, found mainly in southern and south-western counties of England.

Lappin(g) N/O Nickname for a person bearing some resemblance to a rabbit OF (modern French *lapin*), or an occupational term for a dealer in rabbits. A scarce surname,

unevenly scattered throughout England, Scotland and Wales.

Lapthorne P From one of two places called *Lapthorne* in Devon, one in Modbury, the other in Dittisham OE 'lopped/polled thorn'. A Devon surname.

Larbalestier, *see* **Ballaster**.

Larcombe P From one of two places called *Larcombe* in Devon, one in Diptford OE 'wild iris valley', the other in Blackawton OE 'lark valley': 'a pretty choice' (Cottle). A surname chiefly found in Somerset and Dorset.

Larder/Lardner O Occupational name for an official in charge of the larder, specifically responsible for pig food (acorns, mast) in the forest OF (from a word for bacon fat – compare *lard*). **Larder** is chiefly found in Lincs, **Lardner** in Middx and Oxon.

Large N Nickname for a generous person OF, one known for his *largesse*, rather than for his corpulence. A scattered surname.

Lark/Laverack/Laverick/Laverock
N/O/F Nickname for a person bearing some resemblance (fine singer? early riser?) to a lark OE, or one who caught and sold larks for the pot, they being a popular delicacy; or a variant on the first-name *Lawrence*. **Lark** is most commonly found in Norfolk, **Laverack** in Yorks, **Laverick** in north-east England, and **Laverock** (scarce) in north-west England and Scotland.

Larkin(g)(s) F English: a diminutive of the first-name *Lawrence* (see **Lawrence**). Irish: Anglicized form of Gaelic **O'** [descendant of] *Lorcain* ('fierce, cruel'). Within England, **Larkin** is chiefly a Kent surname, and is found in every province of Ireland. *Philip (Arthur) Larkin (1922–1985), English poet and writer, was born in Coventry, Warwicks; his father came originally from Lichfield, Staffs.*

Larmo(u)r, *see* **Armour**.

Larnach P Scots: regional name for a man from *Lorne*, the district of Argyllshire named after *Loarn* ('fox'), first King of the

Dalriadic Scots in the sixth century. A scarce scattered surname within Scotland.

Larner O Occupational term for a teacher/instructor, *or* for a pupil/student/scholar. The ME verb *lernen* (from OE) meant both 'to learn' and 'to teach', a surrealist confusion which has persisted into modern times in folk speech, hence: 'I'll larn 'im!'. For the relationship between *-ar-* and *-er-* see **Armistead**. A scattered surname.

Larry, *see* **Lawrence**.

Larter N ?Nickname for a deceiver, trickster, cheat, with the OE verb stem *lyrt-*, though possibly of French Huguenot or German origin. A Norfolk/Suffolk surname.

Lascelles P Place-name *Lacelle* in Orne OF ('the cell/hermitage'). Strongest in the north of England, but also found in the south-east. **Lazell**, chiefly an Essex surname, is very probably a variant. **Lascelles** is the family name of the Earls of Harewood.

Lashford, *see* **Latchford**.

Last O Occupational term for a maker of shoes, or specifically of lasts used by shoemakers OE. An East Anglian surname, very strong in Suffolk.

Latcham P Place-name in Wedmore, Somerset OE 'homestead/river-meadow at a stream', where a family so-called are known to have been living for many generations.

Latchford/Lashford P Place-name *Latchford* in various counties, including Chesh, Oxon OE 'stream ford'.

Latham/Lathom/Leed(h)am P Place-name *Latham* in various northern counties, including WRYorks and Lancs ON '(at) the barns', exhibiting the use of a dative plural after a lost preposition. **Latham**, **Lathom** (very scarce) and **Leedam** are predominantly Lancs surnames; **Leedham** is more widely spread throughout the north and the Midlands.

Latimer/Lattimer/Lattimore O Occupational term for a a clerk, a keeper of records in Latin, or an interpreter OF. The place called *Latimer* in Bucks was named after a family of this name during the fourteenth century. Mainly a north-of-England surname. *Hugh Latimer (c.1485–1555), Bishop of Worcester and Protestant martyr, was born in Thurcaston, Leics.*

Laton, *see* **Laughton**.

Latter O/N Occupational term for a lath-maker/-worker, or a nickname for a man as thin as a lath OE. Chiefly a Kent surname. *General Robert James Latter (1780–1855) of the Bengal Army, present at many battles and sieges in the subcontinent during the early nineteenth century, was born in Marylebone, London.*

Lattimer/Lattimore, *see* **Latimer**.

Latton, *see* **Laughton**.

Lauder P Scots: place-name in Berwickshire, Gaelic 'grey water' or British 'ditch'. *Sir Henry ('Harry') Lauder, music-hall artist, was born in Edinburgh.*

Laughlan(d)/Laughlin, *see* **Lachlan**.

Laughton P Place-name in various counties, including Leics, Sussex and WRYorks OE 'leek enclosure', but the place-name in Lincs is OE 'enclosed farm'. **Laughton** is found mainly in the English Midlands and the north. **Laton** and **Latton**, both scarce, are probably variants, though in general some confusion with the surnames **Lawton**, **Layton**, **Leighton** and **Leyton** would seem to be inevitable.

Launder form of **Lavender**.

Laurance/Laurence/Laurenson/Laurie, *see* **Lawrence**.

Lavender/Lander(s)/Launder O Occupational term for a washer-man/woman, a launderer, or one who washed wool OF (compare the modern French verb *laver*, to wash). No connexion with the fragrant herb. Compare **Laver**. **Lavender** is strongest in the south-east of England, **Lander** and **Launder** in the south-west.

Laver O Occupational term for a washer-man/woman OF. Strongest in Essex and Somerset. Compare **Lavender**. *Rodney George ("Rod") Laver, internationally famous tennis player, was born in Rockhampton, Australia, in 1938.*

Laverack/Laverick/Laverock, *see* **Lark**.

Laverton P Place-name in Gloucs and Somerset OE 'place with larks' or OE 'place in the irises/rushes'; but the place-name in WRYorks is Celtic and OE 'place on the (river) *Laver*'. A Gloucs/Somerset surname, with an additional limited presence in north-west Scotland.

Laverty/Lafferty F Irish (chiefly Ulster): Anglicized form of Gaelic **O'** [descendant of] **Fhlaithbheartaigh** ('valiant prince'). Compare **Flaherty**.

Law(e)(s) F/T Diminutive of **Lawrence**; but where such a name is preceded by the prepositions *de/atte*, the origin is 'hill, (burial-) mound' OE (compare **Low**). A Scots/north-of-England surname. Family name of the Barons Coleraine and the Barons Ellenborough. *Denis Law, Manchester United and Scotland football player, was born in 1940 in Aberdeen, Scotland, the son of George Law, a fisherman, and his wife Robina.*

Lawford P Place-name in various counties, including Essex and Warwicks OE '*Lealla*'s ford'. Strongest in southern counties of England, but also found in WRYorks and elsewhere. *Peter (Sydney) Lawford (1928–1984), Hollywood actor and brother-in-law of President J. F. Kennedy, was born in London, England, the son of the First World War hero Sir Sydney Turing Barlow Lawford and his wife May Somerville Bunny.*

Lawler, *see* **Lawlor**.

Lawless N Nickname for a law-breaking, licentious person ME. Strongest in Lancs.

Lawlor/Lalor/Lawler P Irish: Anglicized form of Gaelic **O'** [descendant of] **Leathlobhair** ('half-leprous'/'fairly ill').

Lawman O Occupational term for a law-man, lawgiver ON. Mainly a southern/South Midlands surname.

Lawrence/Larry/Laurance/Laurence/ Laurenson/Laurie/Law(e)(s)/Lawrance/Lawrenson/Lawrey/Lawrie/ Lawry/Lawson/Low(e)/Lowrence/ Lowrie/Lowrison/Lowr(e)y/Lowson F From a ME and OF first-name *Lorens/Laurence*, Latin *Laurentius*, referring to a man from the *Laurentum*, the Italian town named from its bay trees (compare the word *laurel*). Name of a saint and deacon, horribly martyred on a gridiron at Rome in AD 258. **Lawrence** is the commonest surname derived from such a first-name, especially in the south of England, and is the family name of the Barons Oaksey and the Barons Trevethin. **Laurie** is the normal Scots pet-form of the first-name, and Annie/Anna **Laurie** of the old Scottish song *Maxwelton's Braes* was a real person (the daughter of Robert **Laurie**, First Baronet of Maxwelton, who was loved by William Douglas (1672?-1748), author of the original poem on which it is based. **Lawson**, 'son of *Law(rence)*', a firmly established northern/south Scotland surname, is the family name of the Barons Burnham. **Lawrenson** is a Lancs surname. *See also* **Lark**, **Larkin**, **Low** and **Lowman**. *Laurence Stephen ('L.S.') Lowry (1887–1976), English painter, was born in Stretford, Manchester.*

Laws, *see* **Law**.

Lawson, *see* **Lawrence**.

Lawton P Place-name in Chesh, Herefords OE 'place on a hill'. Most commonly found in Chesh. Readily confused with/a variant of **Laughton**, **Layton**, **Leighton** and **Leyton**.

Lax O/N Occupational term for one who caught, or in some way resembled, a salmon ON. Chiefly found in Co Durham and in WRYorks.

Lay, *see* **Lee**.

Laycock P Place-name in WRYorks OE '?streamlet', and a WRYorks surname. Readily confused with/a variant of **Lacock**.

Laye, *see* **Lee**.

Layer ?N/O/P Reaney suggests that such a surname could have developed from a nickname for an heir OF, or from an occupational term for one who was a 'layer (of masoned stones)' OE, but given the fact that this is a very scarce Essex surname, the origin would seem to lie in the Essex place-names *Layer Breton* and *Layer De La Haye* – *Layer* being derived from a Celtic river-name, cognate with the *Loire*, but of unknown meaning (compare the surname **Lear**).

Layland, *see* **Leyland**.

Layton P Place-name in various counties, including Lancs OE 'water-course' and NRYorks OE 'leek settlement'. Readily confused with/a variant of **Laughton**, **Lawton**, **Leighton** or **Leyton**.

Lazell, *see* **Lascelles**.

Lazenby P Place-names: *Lazenby* in NRYorks (two such) and *Lazonby* in Cumbd ON 'freedman's farm' (the first element, ON *Leysing*, having also been used as a first-name or a byname). *George Lazenby, the actor who played James Bond in the film of* On Her Majesty's Secret Service *in 1969, was born in 1939 in Queanbeyan, New South Wales, Australia; before turning to acting he had been the highest-paid male model in the world.*

Lea, *see* **Lee**.

Leach, *see* **Leech**.

Leadbeat(t)er/Leadbetter/Leadbitter/ Lidbetter O Occupational term for a leadbeater, a worker in lead OE. Surnames which belong, predictably, to the Midlands and the north. *See also* **Liberty**.

Leader O Occupational term for a lead driver of horses, a carter OE; or for a leadworker OE.

Leaf(e)/Leaves/Leavis/Luff F/T From the OE first-name *Leofa* ('dear, loved'); or a dweller in a leafy area ME. **Leaf** has a strong presence in Yorks; **Leaves** and **Leavis**, both scarce, are found mainly in Somerset and Leics respectively; **Luff** belongs mainly to Hants and Surrey. *Frank Raymond ('F.R.') Leavis, influential literary critic, was born in Cambridge, the son of parents who had rural Cambs origins.*

Leah P Cottle suggests that this Chesh/ Lancs surname 'is **Lear** made to look biblical (though the lady's name unfortunately meant "cow" in Hebrew)', but, if pronounced '*Lee*', it could well be a variant of **Lee**.

Leahy F Irish: Anglicized form of Gaelic **O'** [descendant of] **Laochdha** ('hero').

Leak(e)/Leek T/P/O/N Dweller by a stream ON, or from a place-name with the same meaning, such as *Leak* (NRYorks), *Leake* (Lincs), *Leek* (Staffs), *Leck* (Lancs); or an occupational term/nickname for a grower or seller of leeks OE. **Leaker** was a leek-seller OE plus suffix.

Leaker, *see* **Leak**.

Leal N Nickname for a loyal person OF. Strong in the Isle of Wight – though it could have arrived there with immigrants from Spain or Portugal, where the surname is also found?

Leaman/Leman/Lemon N/F Nickname for a dear person, a sweetheart, a lover (male or female) OE; or from a ME firstname *Lefman* ('dear man'). **Leaman** is especially strong in Devon. The variant **Loveman**, listed by Reaney, had all but died out in England by the late nineteenth century. See also **Leeming**. *Jack Lemmon (1925–2001), the American actor and comedian whose real name was John Uhler Lemmon III, was born in a hospital elevator in Newton, Massachusetts, USA, the son of the president of a doughnut company.*

Lean(e) N/F Nickname for a lean, thin man OE (the -*e* existed in the Old English adjective). Scots: an abbreviated form of **McLean**. *David Lean (1908–1991), English film director and producer, was born in Croydon, Surrey, to Quaker parents.*

Leaper O Occupational term for a basketmaker OE; or for a runner, jumper, dancer? **Leapman** is a scarce Surrey variant. Readily confused with/a variant of **Leopard** and **Lepper**.

Leapman, *see* **Leaper**.

Lear P From one of a number of place-names in northern France containing the Germanic element *lar* ('clearing'); or from *Leire*, Leics, derived from a Celtic river-name, cognate with the *Loire*, but of unknown meaning (compare the surname **Layer**). **Lear**, a scattered surname, strong in Devon, has no connexion with the mythical King of Britain. *Edward Lear (1812–1888), landscape painter, writer, and compiler of nonsense verse, was born in Upper Holloway, London, the twentieth of twenty-one children. Lear himself claimed, falsely, that his male-line ancestry was Danish.*

Learmonth/Learmont P Place-name *Learmonth* in Berwickshire, Scotland, of uncertain etymology. Readily confused with/a variant of **Learmouth**. *Romantically enough, the Russian writer Mikhail Yurievich Lermontov (1814–1841) was the descendant of George Learmont, a Scot who had served as a mercenary in Poland in the early seventeenth century, and who later settled in Russia.*

Learmouth P Place-name in Northd OE 'mouth of the (river) *Lever*', and a Northd surname. Readily confused with/a variant of **Learmonth**.

Leary F Irish: Anglicized form of Gaelic **O'** [descendant of] **Laoghaire** ('calf-keeper'). The Irish port town of *Dun Laoghaire* (pronounced '*Dunleary*') was named after a fifth-century king.

Lease T Dweller at a pasture OE. A scarce scattered surname.

Leat P Place-name in Devon OE 'watercourse, pipe, conduit', and mainly a Devon surname.

Leather O Occupational term for a leather-worker/seller OE. A surname of the north and north-west of England, especially Lancs.

Leatherbarrow P Place-names *Latterbarrow* in Crook and in Witherslack, Westmd ON *látr* and OE *beorg* 'grove with an animal's lair'. A Lancs surname.

Leatherby, *see* **Lethaby**.

Leaver, *see* **Lever**.

Leaves/Leavis, *see* **Leaf**.

Ledbury P Place-name in Herefords, Celtic and OE 'fort/manor on the (river) *Leadon*'. A scarce surname found mainly in the south-west and along the English/Welsh border.

Ledger/Ledgard/Lidgard F/N From a Germanic first-name meaning 'people-spear', brought to England as *Legier* by the Normans; well known thanks to the excruciating martyrdom of *Saint Léger*, Bishop of Autun (died 678). Or, less fortunately, a euphemistic respelling of the surname **Letcher** ('lecher') – see **Leech**. **Ledger** and **Ledgard** have a distinctive presence in WRYorks, while **Lidgard** is a Lincs surname. **Ledgard** and **Lidgard** are perhaps readily confused with/variants of **Liddiard**?

Lediard, *see* **Liddiard**.

Ledsham P Place-name in Chesh OE '*Leofgeat/Leofede*'s settlement' and in WRYorks, Celtic and OE 'settlement belonging to *Leeds*' (the place-name in WRYorks). A Chesh surname.

Lee/Lay(e)/Lea/Legg/Legh/Leigh/Ley/Lye T/P/F Dweller by a meadow, an area of arable land OE; or from one of many place-names derived from OE *leah* ('wood, clearing'), such as *Lee* in Bucks, Essex, Hants, Kent, Salop, *Lea* in Chesh, Derbys, Herefords, Lancs, Lincs, Wilts, *Leigh* in Lancs or *Lye* in Herefords, Worcs. Thomas Gray's 'lowing herd' wound 'slowly o'er the *lea…*'. **Lee**, the commonest of these surname spellings, can alternatively be Irish in origin, an Anglicized form of Gaelic **O'** [descendant of] **Laoidhigh** ('poet'). **Legh**, the family name of the Barons Newton, is the nearest to the original OE *leah*, with *-gh* substituted for *-h* and with the diphthong simplified. In some cases **Lay(e)** may be derived from one of the places in France called *Laye*, originally *La Haie* 'the hedge' OF. See also **Attlee**, **Leah** and **Legg**.

Leech/Leach/Leitch O/N Occupational term for a doctor, physician OE; the bloodsucking insect got its name from the doctor, not vice versa. In rarer instances such a surname, like **Ledger/Letcher**, can originally have been a nickname for a lecher. **Leitch** is a Scottish variant.

Leed(h)am, *see* **Latham**.

Leeds P The place-name *Leeds* in WRYorks, Celtic '(district of) the people living beside the river *Lat* (the *Aire*)' would seem to be an obvious source here, but **Leeds** is a surname found mainly in Kent, Norfolk and Surrey, which makes *Leeds* in Kent OE '(settlement on the) ?loud stream' an equally likely candidate.

Leek(e), *see* **Leak**.

Leeming P/N From one of two places so-called in WRYorks, based upon an OE river name, meaning 'sparkling'; or a variant of **Leaman**. Principally a Lancs/WRYorks surname – though Jan **Leeming**, British television presenter and newsreader, was born in 1942 in Kent.

Lees(e) T/P/F A plural form of the surname **Lee**; or from a place-name such as *Lees* or *Leece*, both in Lancs OE 'pasture'; or from a mediaeval female first-name *Lece*, a contraction of *Lettice*. **Lees**, widespread, is strong in Lancs; **Leese**, very scarce, belongs to Staffs; **Leeson** ('son of *Lece*') is found mainly in the Midlands and in the north. One **Leeson** family held the Irish Earldom of Milltown (dormant since 1891), which could trace its lineage back to William **Leeson** of Cullworth, Northants.

Le Fever/Lefe(b)vre, *see* **Feaver**.

Legat(t)/Legate/Leggat(t)/Leggate/Legget(t)/Leggitt/Leggott O/N Occupational term for a legate, head of a legation, ambassador, deputy OF; or a nickname for a person who had played the part of a foreign legate in a pageant. **Leggat** is primarily a Scots surname; **Leggett** belongs to East Anglia and the south-east of England.

Legg(e) N Nickname for a person with a distinctive, long or deformed leg ON; or a variant of **Lee/Leigh**. Found mainly in the south and south-west of England, and very strong in Dorset. **Legge** is the family name of the Earls of Dartmouth.

Leggat(t)/Leggate, *see* **Legat**.

Legge, *see* **Legg**.

Legget(t)/Leggitt/Leggott, *see* **Legat**.

Legh, *see* **Lee**.

Lehane, *see* **Lane**.

Leicester/Lessiter/Lester P Place-name *Leicester* in Leics, from the OE tribal name *Ligore* (originally a British river-name) and OE *coester* '(Roman) fort'. **Leicester** is a Chesh/Lancs surname; **Lessiter** and **Lester** are more widespread.

Leigh, *see* **Lee**.

Leighton P Place-name in various counties, most of which are OE 'leek settlement', though *Leighton* in Northd is OE 'bright/light-coloured hill'. A surname which is scattered throughout England and Scotland, strong in Co Durham. Readily confused with/a variant of **Laughton**, **Lawton**, **Layton** or **Leyton**.

Leitch, *see* **Leech**.

Leleu/Leleux, *see* **Low**.

Leman/Lemon, *see* **Leaman**.

Lench P Place-name in Worcs OE '?hill'. A scarce surname, commonest in Worcs.

Lenfest(e)y, *see* **Vaisey**.

Leng, *see* **Long**.

Lennard, *see* **Leonard**.

Lennox P Scots and Northern Irish: from a district so-called near Dumbarton, Gaelic 'people of the district round the (river) *Leven*', with an English plural -*s*.

Lenthall P Place-names *Leinthall* in Herefords, Celtic and OE 'nook on the (river) *Lent*'. Found in both the West Country and the English Midlands.

Leonard/Lennard F From a Norman first-name meaning 'lion-hardy', borne by the patron saint of prisoners. **Lennard** is a later spelling.

Leopard/Leppard N/T Nickname for a person exhibiting leopard-like qualities, or who dwelt at/near the sign of the leopard OF, or who bore a coat-of-arms featuring a leopard. '*Not*, probably, from having spots such as acne' (Cottle). **Leopard** belongs to the south-east of England, while **Leppard** has a definitive presence in Sussex. Readily confused with/a variant of **Leaper** and **Lepper**. *Raymond Leppard, British conductor and harpsichordist, was born in London in 1927.*

Lepper N Nickname for a leper OF, ultimately from the Greek, meaning 'scaly'. Doubtless other skin diseases in mediaeval England were wrongly diagnosed as leprosy. Chiefly a Kent surname. Readily confused with/a variant of **Leaper** and **Leopard**.

Lequeux O Occupational term for a cook OF (see **Kew**). 'This downright yet elegant surname could also indicate a cooked-meat seller or eatinghouse-keeper' (Cottle).

Leslie/Lesley P Scots: place-name in Aberdeenshire, originally *Lesslyn* (the place-name in Fife being named after it). The first element is British or Scots Gaelic 'court/garden'; the second is Scots Gaelic 'by the pool' or 'of hollies'. Both *Leslie* and *Lesley* have more recently become popular as first-names, the latter being the spelling usually adopted for girls. **Leslie** is the family name of the Earls of Rothes.

Lessiter/Lester, *see* **Leicester**.

Le Sueur O Occupational term for a shoemaker OF. Both a French and a Channel Islands surname. *Lucille Fay LeSueur was the real name of the Hollywood actress Joan Crawford (1905 [or 1908]-1977), who was born in San Antonio, Texas, USA. Her father was from Tennessee, and her great-great-great-great-grandparents, David LeSueur and Elizabeth Chastain, were French Huguenots who had left London, England, for Virginia during the early years of the eighteenth century.*

Letby, *see* **Lethaby**.

Letcher N/T Nickname for a lecher, a profligate person OF (*see also* **Ledger** and **Leech**), but sometimes used for a person who lived at a *latch* OE 'wet place, stream'. A Cornish surname, studiously avoided by most compilers of dictionaries of Cornish surnames.

Lethaby/Leatherby/Lethby/Letherby T/P The idea that such surnames may be derived from a place-name is a seductive one, and is pursued by Bardsley ('I do not know where the place is'), by Harrison ('Belonging to *Leatherby* (ON *by-r*), estate, &c... It is not unlikely that some *Leatherby*s were originally *Leatherbarrows*'), by Cottle (who takes the meaning of such a putative place-name to be OE and ON: 'tough-soiled farm') and by Hanks and Hodges ('probably a habitation name from an unidentified place in Northern England'). Certainly the *-by* ending would suggest a Danish place-name origin, and yet the distribution of such surnames militates against such a theory, and knocks Harrison's *Leatherbarrow* theory firmly on the head: the truth is that **Lethaby** and **Lethby** are chiefly found in Devon, **Letherby** in Somerset, and **Leatherby** in both these counties. We could say that G. Pawley White comes to the rescue: pointing out that there were one hundred and forty **Lethaby/Lethby** marriages in Cornwall during the seventeenth and eighteenth centuries, he suggests that the origin of such surnames might be the Cornish *leth-va*, meaning 'milk-place, dairy'. This may be as close as we get to a satisfactory explanation of these intriguing surnames, unless we take the view that **Lethaby**-type surnames, which are not recorded in Devon in fourteenth-century Lay Subsidies, might have been brought to that county by sea or by land from Yorks by settlers bearing the surname **Letby**, which comes from *Leckby*, NRYorks (*Letteby* in 1301) ON '*Let*'s farm'. Either that, or they could be variants of the Devon surname **Lethbridge**, the origin of which is also unknown – perhaps a stream-name lies behind such surnames?

Lethbridge/Lethby/Letherby, *see* **Lethaby**.

Letheren N ?Nickname for a 'rogue, thief' ME *led(e)ron* from OF. A very scarce Devon surname.

Letsom/Letson/Lett/Lettey, *see* **Lettice**.

Lettice/Lett(e)y F From a female first-name *Lettice*, Latin *Laetitia*, meaning 'joy, gladness'. **Lett** (leading to **Lett(e)y**) is a diminutive, and **Letts**, **Letson** and **Let(t)som** are 'son of **Lett**'. *John Coakley Lettsom (1744–1815), physician and philanthropist, was born in the Virgin Islands, son of a Quaker plantation owner whose family came originally from Chesh.*

Letts/Lettsom/Letty, *see* **Lettice**.

Leuty/Lewty/Luty N Nickname derived from an OF word for 'loyalty'. 'A surname of rare abstract type' (Cottle). **Leuty** is principally a WRYorks surname, but with a presence in Cornwall; **Lewty** is found chiefly in Lancs, WRYorks and Staffs, and **Luty** in WRYorks. Readily confused with/a variant of **Lutey**.

Lever/Leaver T/P/N Dweller in a rushy spot OE *loefer* ('rush/reed/wild iris'), or from *Great* or *Little Lever* in Lancs, with the same meaning; or a nickname for a person as speedy as a hare OF *levre*, or who hunted hares, a harrier. Legend has it that there was once a man who intended to hunt hares with greyhounds for a bet, but who was so totally incompetent at what he was doing that he acquired the byname/surname **Mauleverer** ('an inept hunter of hares'); thereafter members of a family so-named (fact, not legend) bore three running greyhounds on their coat-of-arms. Both the surnames **Mauleverer** and **Leverer** would seem to have died out over time. **Lever** and **Leaver** are chiefly Lancs surnames. *William Hesketh Lever (1851–1925), soap manufacturer and philanthropist, was born in Bolton, Lancs; in 1874 he married Elizabeth Ellen Hulme, and when he was elevated to the peerage in 1917 he combined his own surname with that of his wife, becoming the First Lord Leverhulme.*

Leveridge/Loveridge F From an OE first-name *Leofric*, meaning 'dear/loved-ruler'.

Leveridge is found chiefly in Norfolk, **Loveridge** in Devon.

Leveson N Nickname for a dear/loved son OE *leofsunu*. **Leveson-Gower**, the surname borne by the Earls Granville, is pronounced '*Looson Gore*'. **Leveson** is a scarce surname, found in both Lancs and Surrey.

Levett/Levitt/Livett N/P/F Nickname, from a diminutive of Anglo-Norman French *leu* ('wolf'); or from one of the place-names in Normandy called *Livet*; or from an OE first-name *Leofgeat* ('dear/beloved', plus the tribal-name '*Geat*'). See also **Levick**. **Levett** and **Livett** are found mainly in south-east England and in East Anglia; **Levitt** belongs principally to Yorks.

Levick ?O/F To derive such a surname from OF *L'Eveske* (*L'évêque*, 'the Bishop') might be too far-fetched (compare **Bishop** and **Veck**); it could alternatively have arisen from an OE first-name *Leofeca* ('dear/beloved'), but in any event David Hey points out that **Levick** is simply the Sheffield pronunciation of **Levett/Levitt**. See also **Lucas**.

Levitt, *see* **Levett**.

Levy F Principally a Jewish surname, Hebrew *Levi* ('pledged'), but if of English origin, it is from the OE first-name *Leofeca* ('beloved warrior'). A surname with a significant presence in Lancs, as well as London.

Lew P Place-name in Oxon OE 'hill, mound'. A very scarce south-of-England/Midlands surname.

Lewell P There is a place so-named in Dorset OE 'spring/stream at a shelter' or 'sheltered/sunny spring', but this scarce surname is most commonly found in Norfolk.

Lewes P Place-name in Sussex OE 'hills, mounds'. Chiefly a south-east-of-England and East Anglia surname. Readily confused with/a variant of **Lewis**.

Lewin/Luen F From an OE first-name *Lefwine* ('dear/loved friend'); Manx: a contraction of **Mac Giolla Eoin** ('son of the devotee/servant of (Saint) *John*'.

Lewis F From a Germanic (Normanized) first-name meaning 'renowned/famous-battle', being the name of King *Clovis*. Early a popular first-name in Wales (as a sort of translation of **Llewelyn**), it has become a very common Welsh surname. Scots: from the name of the Hebridean island of *Lewis* (?ON 'silent/sad/song house'); Scots and Irish: Anglicized form of Gaelic **Mac Lughaidh** ('son of brightness'). Family name of the Barons Merthyr. Readily confused with/a variant of **Lewes**. See also **Loos**.

Leworthy P From one of three such place-names in Devon (at Bratton Fleming, Clawton, and Woolfardisworthy) OE '*Leofa*'s enclosure', and a Devon surname.

Lewton, *see* **Luton**.

Lewty, *see* **Leuty**.

Ley, *see* **Lee**.

Leyland/Layland P Place-name *Leyland* in Lancs OE 'untilled/fallow land'.

Leyton P Place-name in Essex, Celtic and OE 'settlement on the (river) *Lea*'. Readily confused with/a variant of **Laughton**, **Lawton**, **Layton** or **Leighton**.

Libby F From a pet-form of the first-names *Elizabeth* or *Isabell*.

Liberty A surname of unknown origin. In principle the abstract noun 'liberty' could be involved, as could the Germanic first-name *Albert*. Bardsley suggests a connexion with **Leadbeater**; M. A. Lower favours 'dweller at a liberty' (a group of manors, or an area outside borough jurisdiction). There is a place called *Liberty* in Fife, Scotland, but this scarce surname is found mainly in Herts, Middx and Surrey. *Sir Arthur Lasenby Liberty (1843–1917), fabric maker and founder of the famous Liberty store in Regent Street, London, was born in Chesham, Bucks, though his father, a draper and lacemaker, originally come from Nottingham.*

Lichfield/Litchfield P Place-name *Lichfield* in Staffs, Celtic and OE 'grey-wood-field' (no connexion with corpses, as in *lychgate*). Chiefly a Midlands/South Midlands surname in either spelling, which makes *Litchfield*, Hants, a much less likely source.

Lickerish/Lickorish/Licquorice/Licquorish N Nickname for a lecherous, wanton person OF. Bardsley is fairly kind in his interpretation of this surname: 'One dainty, or nice in his palate', though alternatively 'greedy or gluttonous'. Reaney doesn't mince his words: 'wanton, lecherous (ME *likerous*)'. **Lickerish** and its variants are not common, but are chiefly found in the following counties, according to the 1881 census: **Lickerish** (Northants); **Lickorish** (Warwicks); **Licquorice** (Cambs); **Licquorish** (Middx, Surrey); **Liquorice** (Leics, Northants, Surrey); **Liquorish** (Leics, Middx, Northants, Rutland: the most popular spelling). The 1881 census features Thomas **Licquorice**, a farmer of seventeen acres, his wife Ellen and their children, living at Wisbech St Mary, Cambs. A pair of gravestones commemorating two of their sons who died in their twenties can be seen in the churchyard of the now-disused chapel of ease at Guyhirn, between Wisbech and March.

Lidbetter, *see* **Leadbeater**.

Liddel(l)/Liddle P English and Scots: place-name *Liddel* in the Scots Borders and in Cumbd OE 'valley of the (river) *Hlyde*'. **Liddell** is the family name of the Barons Ravensworth.

Liddiard/Lediard/Lydiard P Place-names: *Lydiard*, Wilts and *Lydeard*, Somerset. The first element in such place-names is obscure; the second is OW *garth* ('hill'). Perhaps readily confused with **Ledgard/Lidgard** (see **Ledger**)?

Liddicoat P Place-names in Cornwall: *Lidcott*, *Lydcott*, *Ludcott*, *Lidcutt*, Cornish 'grey wood'.

Liddington P Place-name in Rutland and in Wilts OE 'farm on the (river) *Hlyde*'. Generally a South Midlands surname.

Liddle, *see* **Liddel**.

Lidgard, *see* Ledger.

Lidgate/Lidgett P Place-names *Lidgate*, *Lidget(t)* and *Lydgate* in various counties OE 'swing-gate' (compare **Lydiate**). **Lidgate** is mainly found in Northd and in Midlothian, Scotland, **Lidgett** in Lincs.

Lidiard, *see* Liddiard.

Light/Lyte N/T Nickname for a person who was cheerful OE *leoht*, or active/bustling/nimble OE *lioht*, or small of stature OE *lyt*. Reaney suggests that early forms preceded by *de/atte* refer to a dweller at a light place/glade OE. **Light** is chiefly a Hants surname. The surname spelling **Lyte** has all but died out, but a family called **Lyte** gave its name to *Lytes Cary* in Somerset, and Henry Francis **Lyte** (1793–1847) wrote the well-known hymn 'Abide with Me'. 20 February 1760 saw the baptism of a child named *'Fan Light'* at West Wittering, Sussex.

Lightbody N Scots and northern English: nickname for a small person, or for a cheerful one OE. For meanings and origins of the *light-* element, see **Light**. Strongest in Lanarkshire, Scotland.

**Lightborn(e)/Lightbound/
Lightbourn(e)/Lightbown(e)** P From a stream-name such as *Lightburne* in Ulverston, Lancs, OE 'bright stream'. A Lancs surname, whatever its spelling.

Lightfoot N Nickname for a fast runner, nimble or light of foot OE. Compare **Light** and **Lightbody**. A northern surname, strong in Lancs.

Lilley, *see* Lilly.

Lillicrap(p)/Lillicrop/Lillycrap/Lillycrop N/P Nickname for a person with white hair, a head like a lily OE. The village of *Lillicrapp* in Devon is said to be so-called thanks to a derogatory field-name OE 'little crop/yield/profit', though it could have been named after Peter **Liliecrop**, who is known to have been living there in 1330. These are principally Devon surnames, except for **Lillycrop**, which has a very limited presence in Kent.

Lill(e)y P/F/N Place-name *Lilley* in Herts OE 'flax clearing' and in Berks OE '*Lilla*'s clearing'; or a diminutive of the first-name *Elizabeth*; or a nickname for a person with fair skin or hair OE. **Lilly** is particularly strong in Lancs; **Lilley** is widespread.

Lillycrap/Lillycrop, *see* Lillicrap.

Lillywhite N Nickname for a person whose skin (or hair?) was white as a lily OE. A surname which belongs to the south of England, especially Sussex, the county of origin of James **Lillywhite** (born 1825) who founded both *Lillywhite's Cricketer's Annual* and also the chain of sports shops which bear the **Lillywhite** name. Given the geographical concentration of the **Lillywhite** surname, suggestions that it might be derived from a place-name such as *Litelthwaite*, with an ON second element, must be wide of the mark.

Limbrick P Place-name in Heath Charnock, Lancs OW and OE '?lime-tree slope'; the surname belongs chiefly to Gloucs, though **Lymerykes** in Cranham, and **Limbricks** Farm in Bisley, in that county are named after former owners, not vice versa.

Limer O Occupational term for a limeburner, whitewasher OE. Chiefly a Staffs surname.

Linacre/Lineker/Liniker T/P Dweller in or near a field where flax was grown OE; or from a place-name *Linacre* in Cambs (now lost) and Lancs, with the same meaning. **Linacre** and **Liniker** (scarce) are strongest in Lancs; **Lineker** is found mainly in Notts. *Gary Lineker, English football player and sports presenter, was born in Leicester in 1960.*

Linch, *see* Lynch.

Lincoln P Place-name in Lincs, Celtic and Latin '(Roman) colony at the pool/water'. The surname is found in Lincs itself, but is strongest in Norfolk. *Abraham Lincoln (1809–1865), sixteenth President of the USA, was descended from Samuel Lincoln, from Hingham in Norfolk, who emigrated to Massachusetts in the 1630s. There is a Lincoln* memorial in the north aisle of Hingham church.

Lind T Dweller by a lime-tree (the linden, not the citrus-fruit tree) OE. A surname unevenly scattered throughout England and Scotland.

Lindall/Lindell P Place-name *Lindal* in Lancs OE 'lime-tree valley'. Surnames found mainly in the north of England.

Lindfield P Place-name in Sussex OE 'lime-tree field', and very largely a Sussex surname.

Lindley/Linley P Place-names: *Lindley* in WRYorks (two such); *Linley* in Salop and Wilts OE 'flax field'; *Lindley* (near Otley) WRYorks (and maybe *Lindley*, Leics) OE 'lime-tree clearing/wood'.

Lindridge P Cottle refers to a place-name in Worcs, but this is primarily a Kent surname, and the two places called *Lindridge* in that county (one in Lamberhurst, the other in Staplehurst) OE 'lime-tree ridge' will almost certainly be the point of origin here.

Lindsay/Lindsey P/F Place-name *Lindsey* in Lincs, British and OE '*Lincoln* island', the original home of the great Scottish family which includes the Earls of Crawford, who descend from the Norman noble Sir Walter de **Lindissi**, from Lincs, who settled in the Scottish lowlands during the twelfth century. Compare the Scottish families of **Graham** (from *Grantham*, Lincs) and **Ramsay** (from *Ramsey*, Hunts). Or from a place-name *Lindsey* in Suffolk OE '*Lelli*'s island'. Irish: an Anglicized form of various Gaelic surnames, such as **O'** [descendant of] **Loinsigh** ('mariner'). For Robert **Lindsay**, the actor, see **Stevenson** (under **Stephen**).

Lindsell P Place-name in Essex OE 'huts among the lime-trees', and an Essex surname.

Lindsey, *see* Lindsay.

Lineker, *see* Linacre.

Ling/Lyng P Place-name *Lyng* in Norfolk OE 'the terrace-way'; the fact that **Ling** is so strongly an East Anglian surname makes

Lyng in Somerset an unlikely source. **Lyng** is a very scarce scattered surname.

Lingen P Place-name in Herefords, Welsh *llyn-gain*, '?clear water' (probably the former stream-name). In principle **Lingham** could be a variant of this surname, given an OE makeover, and Bardsley notes that there was a Richard **Lingam**, or **Lingen**, of Stoke Edith, Herefords, in 1542; but **Lingham** is primarily a Kent surname.

Lingham, *see* Lingen.

Liniker, *see* Linacre.

Linklater/Linkletter P Place-names (two such) in the Orkney Islands ON 'heath-covered rocks'. *Gordon Arthur Kelly, born in 1912 in Saskatchewan, Canada, was adopted by John Linkletter, an evangelical preacher, and Mary his wife; he later achieved fame in the USA as Art Linkletter, television show host.*

Linley, *see* Lindley.

Linthwaite P Place-names: *Linthwaite*, WRYorks and *Linethwaite*, Cumbd OE and ON 'clearing where flax is grown' – though this is chiefly a surname of the Midland counties of England.

Linton/Lynton P English and Scots: from the place-name *Linton* in several counties. Most are OE 'flax/lime-tree/torrent/hill place', according to whether they come from OE *lin/lind/hlynn/hlinc*. Other etymologies include: Celtic and OE 'settlement on the (river) *Lyne*' (Northd); OE '*Lilla*'s people's settlement' (Kent). In East Lothian, Peebles and Roxburghshire the first element is from a Scots Gaelic word meaning 'pool'. **Linton** is primarily a Scottish/northern English surname; **Lynton** is very scarce and scattered.

Linwood P Cottle makes reference to a place-name in Hants and Lincs (two such) OE 'lime-tree wood', but this is primarily a Cambs surname, and *Linwood Wood* in that county could well be the point of origin in many cases.

Lippiatt/Lippiett P Place-names *Lypiatt*, *Lypiate*, *Lipyeate*, *Leapgate* in Gloucs, Somerset, Wilts, Worcs OE 'leap-gate' (one that deer and horses can leap, but not sheep). Gloucs/Somerset surnames.

Lipton P The place-name *Lipton* in East Allington, Devon OE '?settlement by a chasm/crossing place' is probably of too late a date to have given rise to a surname; in any case, neither it nor *Lepton*, WRYorks (?with the same meaning) nor *Lupton*, Cumbd OE '*Hluppa*'s settlement' can readily be related to the scattered occurrence of the surname, with its small clusters in places as far apart as Kent, Lancs and Lanarkshire. *Sir Thomas Lipton, Baronet (1850–1931), the yachtsman and grocer who gave his name to Lipton's Tea, was born in a tenement house in Crown Street, Glasgow.*

Liquorish, *see* Lickerish.

Liscombe P Place-names in Somerset OE 'pigsty valley' and in Bucks OE 'valley with an enclosure'. A scarce surname, mostly found in the south-west.

Lisle/Lyle T/P Dweller on an island OF; or from the French town of *Lille*, with the same meaning. **Lisle** is strongest in Northd, **Lyle** in Lanarkshire and Renfrewshire, Scotland. Readily confused with **Lyal**. *Abram Lyle (1820–1891), sugar refiner of 'Tate and Lyle' fame, was born in Greenock, Renfrewshire, Scotland, where the Lyle family had been shipowners for five generations.*

Lister O Occupational term for a dyer OE plus *-er* suffix. Originally a female term, like **Baxter**, **Brewster**, etc. A surname found mainly in the north of England, especially Lancs and WRYorks. Scots: an Anglicized form of Gaelic **Mac an Fleisdeir** ('son of the arrow-maker'). *Joseph Lister, Baron Lister (1827–1921), the surgeon who first made extensive use of antiseptics, was born in Upton, Essex. His male-line ancestors were Quaker businessmen who had migrated to London from Yorks. 'Listerine' mouthwash, first developed in the 1870s, was named after Joseph Lister without his knowledge or permission.*

Litchfield, *see* Lichfield.

Lithgow P Place-name (now *Linlithgow*) in West Lothian, Scots Gaelic from British 'wet hollow'. **Lithgow** belongs to Scotland, yet the apparent variant **Lythgoe** is strongly a Lancs surname; **Lythgo**, scarce, can be found in both Essex and Lancs.

Littell, *see* Little.

Litten, *see* Litton.

Little/Littell N Nickname for a short person (alternatively used sarcastically for a tall one?) or for the younger of two brothers bearing the same first-name (which was a not uncommon practice in earlier times) OE. **Little** is widespread but particularly strong in Cumbd; **Littell**, very scarce, has a presence in Kent and Surrey.

Littleboy N/O Nickname for a little lad, boy, servant ME. An uncommon surname, strongest in Norfolk. A tombstone in Hornsey Cemetery, London, reads: 'To the memory of Emma & Maria Littleboy, the twin children of George and Emma Littleboy of Hornsey who died July 16th 1837. Two littleboys lie here yet strange to say these *little boys* are girls'.

Littlebury P Place-name in Essex OE 'little fort'. Uncommon, found in Essex, Middx and Surrey.

Littlechild N Nickname for a little youth OE. A Home Counties/East Anglia surname.

Littlefield T Dweller at a little field OE. Chiefly a Hants surname (and so may be connected with *Litchfield* in that county?).

Littlejohn N Nickname, 'little *John*' OE and Hebrew; 'a valid joke, whether applied to Titch or Lofty' (Cottle) – and *Little John/John Little* of the Robin Hood legend was a huge man. Could also have been used to distinguish the younger of two men called *John*. An Aberdeenshire surname. *Colonel Peter Littlejohn (1762/3-1834) of the Bengal Army was the son of William Littlejohn, Merchant Burgess of Aberdeen.*

Littler P/N There could be a place-name origin here (*Littleover*, Derbys OE 'little ridge') but this Chesh/Lancs surname could represent a comparative form of the adjective *little*?

Littleton/Lyttelton P Place-name in Dorset, Gloucs, Hants, Middx, Somerset, Wilts and Worcs OE 'little place/farm'. **Littleton** is the family name of the Barons Hatherton, and **Lyttelton** of Viscounts Chandos and Cobham. *Humphrey ('Humph') Lyttelton (1921–2008), jazz musician and broadcaster, was born at Eton College, where his father (son of the eighth Viscount Cobham) was a housemaster.*

Littlewood P Place-name in various counties, particularly in WRYorks OE 'little wood'. A surname belonging mainly to the north of England, especially WRYorks.

Littleworth P Place-name in Berks OE 'little enclosure' and Bucks OE 'enclosure of *Lytel*'s people'. A very scarce surname, with a limited presence in Devon and elsewhere.

Littley P/N A place-name origin would seem likely here, and there is a *Littley* Green in Essex OE 'little enclosure' and a lost settlement so-called in WRYorks (with the same meaning), but Cottle, quoting Reaney, draws attention to a twelfth-century reference to **Littley** as a nickname for a person with 'piggy eyes' OE. A scarce surname, found in Devon but also in Staffs and Warwicks.

Litton/Litten P Place-name *Litton* in various counties, including Derbys OE 'hillside farm/village', NRYorks OE '?settlement at the slope' and Somerset OE 'settlement on the river *Hlyde*'. **Litton** and **Litten** are both predominantly Devon surnames.

Livermore P Place-name *Livermere* in Suffolk OE 'rush/reed or liver-shaped/coagulated lake'. Chiefly an Essex/Middx surname.

Liversedge/Liversidge P Place-name *Liversedge* in WRYorks OE '*Leofhere*'s ridge'.

Liverton P Reaney and Cottle's belief that **Liverton** is derived from a place-name in NRYorks OE 'farm on a stream with thick/clotted water' must be wide of the mark. This is a Devon surname, and the point of its

origin will almost certainly be one of two *Liverton*s in that county – one in Ilsington OE '*Leofa*'s farm', the other in Littleham OE '?*Leofwaru*'s farm'.

Livesey/Livsey P Place-name *Livesey* in Lancs OE 'island with a shelter'. A Lancs surname in either spelling.

Livett, *see* **Levett**.

Livings F From an OE first-name *Leofing/Lyving* ('dear'). Chiefly an Essex surname.

Livingston(e) P/F Scots: place-name in West Lothian OE '*Levin*'s place'; Irish: Anglicized form of Gaelic **O'** [descendant of] **Duinnshleibhe** and **Mac Duinnshleibhe** ('brown-mountain'). One branch of the **Livingston** family in Scotland held the titles of Earls of Linlithgow and of Callendar. *Philip Livingston (1716–1778), grandson of Robert Livingston (1654–1728), who had emigrated from Scotland to America in 1673, signed the Declaration of Independence… The explorer David Livingstone (1813–1873) belonged to a branch of the McLeay family of Appin; the settlement of Blantyre in Malawi (formerly Nyasaland) was named after his birthplace in Lanarkshire… Ken Livingstone, former Mayor of London (2000–2008), was born in Lambeth, South London, the son of a ship's master with Scottish origins.*

Livsey, *see* **Livesey**.

Llewellin/Llewel(l)yn/Llewhel(l)in F From an OW first-name *Llywelin* (the first element of which is Welsh *llyw* 'leader'), borne by the last reigning Prince of Wales, and still firmly a South Wales surname. The initial *Ll-* (which counts as one letter in the Welsh alphabet) is very easy to pronounce (see **Lloyd**), but Shakespeare played safe by rendering this surname as *Fluellen*.

Lloyd N Nickname for a person with grey hair, Welsh *llwyd* ('grey'). Sometimes Anglicized to **Loyd**, **Floyd**, or even **Flood**. The initial *Ll-* counts as one letter in the Welsh alphabet, and 'The best rule for saying *Ll-* is the advice of the bilingual nineteenth-century Dean of St David's to the new English-speaking Bishop, that he should press the tip of his episcopal tongue against the roof of his apostolic mouth and hiss like a goose' (Cottle). Chiefly a Welsh surname, but with a strong presence in English counties bordering Wales.

Loade, *see* **Loader**.

Loader/Load(e)s/Loder T/O Dweller at a road/watercourse/ferry/drainage-channel OE plus suffix; or an occupational term for a carrier, ferryman OE plus suffix. **Loader** and **Loder** (the family name of the Barons Wakehurst) belong mainly to southern counties of England; **Load** (scarce) is found in Gloucs and Herefords, **Loade** (very scarce) in Gloucs and Warwicks and **Loads/Loades** in Norfolk. See also **Lodder**.

Loads, *see* **Loader**.

Loasby P Cottle refers to a place-name *Lowesby* in Lancs ON 'farm on a slope', but this is a Northants surname and is probably a variant of **Loseby**.

Lobb P Place-name in Devon OE '?steep hill' (apparently the sense is of a heavy, clumsy mass). Given the fact that this is predominantly a Cornwall/Devon surname, any connexion with the place called *Lobb* in Oxon seems unlikely. *John Lobb (1829–1895), a shoemaker born near Fowey in Cornwall, walked to London to seek his fortune; the company which he founded, now situated in fashionable St James's, London, still bears his name.*

Lochhead/Lockhead T/P Dweller at the head of a loch, Scots Gaelic plus OE, or from the former Scottish place-name *Lochhead* (now *Campbeltown*), Argyll, with the same meaning. Chiefly a Lanarkshire surname in both spellings. Potentially confused with/a variant of **Lockhart** or **Lockett** [see **Lucas**]? *The Lockheed Corporation, originally founded in the USA in 1912 as the Loughead Aircraft Manufacturing Company by brothers Allan and Malcolm Loughead, eventually had its name changed to reflect the normal pronunciation of the surname. In the event, the spelling 'Loughead' is a scarce one, found in the late nineteenth century in Lancs, rather than in Scotland, while*

the invented 'Lockheed' is a very scarce (if not non-existent) variant within the British Isles.

Lochore T/P Dweller at the grey loch, Scots Gaelic, or from a place-name with the same meaning in Fife.

Lock(e) O/T/N/F Occupational term for a locksmith OE *loc* ('lock'); or dweller near an enclosure (a place that could be locked up) OE *loca*; or nickname for a person with fine hair OE, from Old High German *loc* ('lock of hair'); or a variant of **Luke** (see **Lucas**). **Lock** is found mainly in the south and south-west of England, though **Locke** extends further north.

Locket(t), *see* **Lucas**.

Lockh(e)art F/O A Scots surname of uncertain origin, possibly from a Germanic first-name meaning 'lock-strong', though Cottle derives it from an occupational term for a sheep/cattle-fold herdsman OE. Potentially confused with/a variant of **Lochhead** or **Lockett** [see **Lucas**]?

Lockhead, *see* **Lochhead**.

Lockheart, *see* **Lockhart**.

Lockley P From an unidentified place-name, possibly *Lockleywood*, Salop OE 'enclosure in a wood, clearing'. Chiefly a Salop surname, so the place-name *Lockerley* in Hants OE 'folder's/shepherd's clearing' might be something of a red herring. Readily confused with/a variant of **Loxley**.

Lockton P Place-name in NRYorks OE 'place in an enclosure', though the surname is found mainly in the English Midlands.

Lockwood P Place-name in WRYorks OE 'enclosed wood'. A WRYorks surname, prolific in the Huddersfield area.

Lockye(a)r O Occupational term for a lockmaker, locksmith OE. Chiefly a surname of the south and south-west of England.

Locock/Lowcock F A diminutive form of the OE first-name *Lufa* ('love'). **Locock** belongs to Devon and Somerset; **Lowcock** to Lancs and Yorks.

Lodder O/N/P 'Occupational' term/nickname for a beggar OE; or a variant of **Loader**. But this south-of-England surname is particularly evident in Dorset, where there are place-names *Loders* and *Uploders* (once *Lodre*, a stream-name of Celtic origin).

Loder, *see* **Loader**.

Lodge T/O Dweller in a hut/cottage or in a masons' lodge OF (and so possibly used as an occupational term for a mason). Especially strong in WRYorks.

Loft T Dweller in an upper-room, attic ON. Found chiefly in the north and in the south-east of England, especially in Kent.

Lofthouse/Loftus P Place-names: *Lofthouse* in WRYorks and *Loftus* in NRYorks ON 'house with an upper floor' (that is, quite a substantial dwelling). **Loftus** is the family name of the Marquesses of Ely. *Nathaniel ('Nat') Lofthouse, the English footballer who played for Bolton Wanderers throughout his career, was born in Bolton in 1925.*

Logan P Place-name in four Scottish counties, Gaelic 'little hollow'.

Loman, *see* **Lowman**.

Lomas/Lomax P Lost place-name *Lomax* in Lancs OE 'nook/recess by the pool'.

Lombard/Lumbard/Lumber P/O English and Irish: a person from *Lombardy* in Italy, Germanic ('long beards'); or, because people from this place were known for practising usury, an occupational term for a moneylender or banker. A scarce scattered surname within England. Readily confused with/a variant of **Lambert**.

London P Place-name of British origin, perhaps based on a pre-Roman and pre-Anglo-Saxon first-name, applied to a person who came from *London*, or who had visited the capital. Surnames based upon large cities such as London are uncommon. A scattered surname, found mostly in the south-east of England and in East Anglia. *The American writer Jack London (1876–1916), born in San Francisco, California, was probably born John Griffith Chaney; in 1876 his mother, Flora Wellman, married a civil war veteran called John London… The real name of the English boxer and businessman Brian London (born 1934), who came from Blackpool, Lancs, was Brian Sidney Harper.*

Long/Laing/Lang/Leng N Nickname for a long, tall person OE. **Long** is very widespread; **Lang** can be found mostly in Lancs and in Lanarkshire, Scotland, but also, as an outlier, in Devon; **Laing** is chiefly Scottish, while **Leng** (a comparative form, 'longer') belongs mainly to Co Durham and Yorks.

Longbottom/Longbotham T/P Dweller in a long valley OE, or specifically from a place of this name and meaning in Warley, near Halifax, WRYorks. **Longbotham** is a euphemistic form. It was perhaps rather unkind of Mr and Mrs **Longbottom** to lumber their son with the combination of names '*Iva* **Longbottom**' when he was born in Balby, Yorks, in 1899?

Longden/Longdon P There are various places so-called, including *Longden* in Salop, *Longdon* in Staffs and in Worcs, and *Longdon* on Tern in Salop OE 'long hill'; there is also a place called *Longdendale* in Derbys. Readily confused with/a variant of **Langdon**.

Longfellow N Nickname for a tall man OE and ON. A scarce WRYorks surname. *The American poet Henry Wadsworth Longfellow (1807–1882) was born in Portland, Maine, USA. His maternal grandfather Peleg Wadsworth had been a general in the American Revolutionary War, and his Longfellow ancestors had arrived in America from Yorks in the year 1676.*

Longfield T/P Dweller at a long, extensive piece of land OE, or from a place-name with the same meaning, of which there are several in WRYorks, where this surname is mostly found. Cottle's reference to *Longfield* in Kent is probably of little relevance. See also **Longville**.

Longhurst/Longhirst P From one of various places so-called, including *Longhirst* in

Northd OE 'long wooded hill'. **Longhurst** belongs to the south-east of England; **Longhirst**, very scarce, is found chiefly in Northd. *Henry (Carpenter) Longhurst (1909–1978), the writer and commentator on golf who was briefly (1943–1945) a Member of Parliament for Acton, West London, was born in Bromham, Beds.*

Longland T Dweller at a long, extensive piece of ground OE. A widespread surname, particularly strong in Northants.

Longley T/P Dweller at a long wood/clearing OE, or from a place-name with the same meaning in Salop, Worcs and WRYorks (several such). Chiefly a WRYorks surname, readily confused with/a variant of **Langley**.

Longman N Nickname for a tall man OE. Especially strong in Hants. *The publishing company of Longman was founded in 1724 by Thomas Longman (1699–1755), the son of Ezekiel Longman of Bristol, who had been apprenticed to a London bookseller.*

Longmire P Place-name in Westmd OE and ON 'long marsh/bog', and a Westmd surname.

Longmoor/Longmore/Longmuir P Dweller at a long, extensive moor OE. **Longmoor** is found chiefly in Northd, **Longmore** in Staffs and **Longmuir** in Scotland.

Longsden, *see* **Longsdon**.

Longsdon P Place-names: *Longsdon* in Staffs and *Longstone* in Derbys OE '?hill of the long (ridge)', yet this scarce surname is as much in evidence in the south of England as in the Midlands. The variants **Longsden** and **Longston** are more concentrated, being found chiefly in Chesh/Lancs and Warwicks respectively.

Longstaff O/N Nickname for a man who carried a long staff – for personal use, or as a badge of office as a tipstaff/bailiff/constable/catchpole; or for one who was tall and thin, or who was known for being sexually well endowed OE. Found chiefly in the north-east of England, especially Co Durham.

Longston, *see* **Longsdon**.

Longton P Place-names *Longton* and *Longtown* in several counties OE 'long farm'. Readily confused with/a variant of **Langton**.

Longville P Place-name in Salop, with the same meaning as **Longfield**, given a French appearance. A scarce surname found mainly in Herefords.

Longworth P Place-name in various counties, including Berks and Lancs OE 'long enclosure'; but the place-name in Herefords is OE 'long ford'. Overwhelmingly a Lancs surname.

Lonsdale P Place-name in Lancs and Westmd, Celtic and OE 'valley of the (river) *Lune*' (compare **Lancaster**). In principle, **Landsell** and **Lansdell** could be variants, though their distribution (south-east of England and Norfolk) might make this unlikely. Hugh Cecil Lowther, Fifth Earl of Lonsdale, a noted sportsman in his own right, founded the British boxing trophy known as the *Lonsdale Belt* in 1909.

Look, *see* **Lucas**.

Looney F Irish: Anglicized form of Gaelic **O'** [descendant of] **Luanaigh** ('warrior'). Strongest in Counties Cork and Kerry.

Loos(e) P There are place-names *Loose* in Kent and *Lose* in Suffolk OE 'pigsty', the latter of which is more likely to have given rise to these predominantly Norfolk surnames, though they could well be variants of **Lewis**.

Loosel(e)y/Loosley P Place-names: *Loosley* in Bucks and *Loseley* in Surrey OE 'wood/clearing with a pigsty'. Surnames of southern England.

Loosemore P Place-name *Loosmoor* in Devon OE 'pigsty moor'; a scarce surname found in Devon – but also in Lancs.

Loosley, *see* **Loosely**.

Lord/Laird N/O Nickname for a person who behaved like a lord, lived like a lord, worked for a lord, or played the part of

'Lord of Misrule' during Christmas festivities. The OE word *Lord* originally meant 'loaf-ward, breadwinner'. The Scots and Northern Irish surname **Laird**, with the same origin, was commonly applied to a substantial landowner.

Lorimer O Occupational term for a maker or seller of bits, spurs, and other metal attachments to a horse's harness OF. Found in many parts of Scotland, and in northern England. The Worshipful Company of *Loriners* of the City of London had adopted an alternative spelling of the trade-name by the late seventeenth century; its original ordinances date from 1261.

Loring, *see* **Lorraine**.

Lorraine/Loring P Regional name for a man from the province of *Lorraine* in north-east France OF from Germanic, named after its King *Lothar* (died AD 869). **Lorraine** occurs mainly in the north of England and in Scotland; **Loring** belongs to Devon, Middx and Surrey.

Loseby P Place-name *Lowesby*, Leics ON '?*Lauss/Lausi*'s village/farm', and chiefly a Leics surname. **Loasby** is probably a variant.

Louch N Nickname for a cross-eyed, squinting person OF. Chiefly an Oxon surname.

Loud N/T/P Nickname for a loud-mouthed, noisy person OE; or dweller by a roaring stream/river OE; or from a place-name with this meaning, such as *Lyde* in Herefords and Somerset; or from the place-name *Louth*, Lincs OE '(settlement on the river) *Lud*' ('loud'). A surname most commonly found in Devon. Compare **Louth**.

Lougher P Place-name *Loughor* in Glamorgan OW 'muddy place', and a South Wales surname.

Loughlin, *see* **McLoughlin**.

Lound/Lount, *see* **Lund**.

Louth P Place-name in Lincs OE 'loud/babbling (stream)' – though the stream is now called the *Lud*. Principally a Lincs surname. Compare **Loud**.

Lovat(t)/Lovett/Lovitt N/P English: nickname from an Anglo-Norman French word for a wolf-cub. Scots **Lovat(t)**: place-name *Lovat* in Inverness, Gaelic 'rotting/putrefying place' – though the surnames **Lovat** and **Lovatt** are more commonly found in England, especially in Staffs and WRYorks, than in Scotland. **Lovett** is widespread within England; **Lovitt**, scarce, is unevenly scattered.

Love F/N From OE first-names *Lufua* (male) and *Lufu* (female), meaning 'love'; or a nickname for a person bearing some resemblance to a she-wolf OF – though used in a far-from-derogatory sense. A widespread surname in both England and Scotland. See also **Lucking**.

Loveband, *see* **Lovibond**.

Loveday F/N From an OE female first-name meaning 'dear day'; or a nickname from an OE term for a day set apart for reconciliation and concord between litigants and feuders, the day of the court leet, settlement-day – the surname perhaps referring to an arbitrator. A scattered surname.

Lovejoy N Nickname for a person who took joy in love (can this have been so unusual?) OE and OF. Bardsley remarks: 'A pretty sobriquet. Just the surname to be handed down. No fear of any male member of the family trying to get rid of it'. To a generation of television viewers, the name **Lovejoy** will be forever associated with a likeable but roguish antiques dealer played by Ian MacShane. A scarce Home Counties surname.

Lovelace/Loveless N Nickname for a loveless person OE – possibly a philanderer who made love without feeling love (in which case, **Lovelace** is a euphemistic alternative); or even from 'love lass/love the girls' OE? Yet the temptress in *Sir Gawain and the Green Knight* gave Gawain her girdle as a *luf-lace*, and the meaning may sometimes be 'keepsake, love-token', in the form of a belt. Both **Lovelace** and **Loveless** are found chiefly in southern counties of England, especially Dorset. **Lowless** is a scarce variant found in Pembrokeshire, Wales. *Richard Lovelace (1618–1657), poet and army officer,* *the son of Sir William Lovelace of Woolwich, Kent, came of a family which had been settled at Bethersden in that county since the fourteenth century.*

Lovel(l)/Lowell N Nickname for a person bearing some resemblance to a wolfcub, a little wolf OF (compare **Low**); Reaney quotes William called *Lupellus* because his father had acquired the name *Lupus* through his violent temper (so a sort of 'Wolf Junior'). A widespread surname.

Loveland P Place-name in Langtree, Devon '*Love*'s land'. A Middx/Surrey surname.

Loveless, *see* Lovelace.

Lovell, *see* Lovel.

Lovelock N Nickname for a dandy, one who wore artificial curls/lovelocks OE. A south-of-England surname.

Loveman, *see* Leaman.

Loveridge, *see* Leveridge.

Lovering F From an OE first-name meaning 'dear-army'. Chiefly a Devon surname.

Lovett, *see* Lovat.

Lovibond/Loveband N Nickname from an OE word meaning 'bond/chain of love'; Bardsley records a Nicholas **Loveband** in Norfolk at the end of the thirteenth century. **Lovibond** is a Somerset surname; **Loveband** is also found in a handful of other counties.

Lovitt, *see* Lovat.

Low(e)(s) F/T/N Diminutive of **Lawrence**; but where such a name is preceded by the prepositions *de/atte*, the origin is 'hill, (burial-)mound' OE (compare **Law**). Or a nickname for a low, short person ON, or for one who bore some resemblance (dangerous, crafty?) to a wolf OF (**Leleu** and **Leleux** being French forms) – compare **Lovel**. The final *-e* in the variant **Lowe** exhibits the use of a dative after a lost preposition. **Low** is found chiefly in Scotland, **Lowe** in the Midlands and the north and **Lowes** ('son of **Low**') in the north-east.

Lowcock, *see* Locock.

Lowder, *see* Lowther.

Lowe, *see* Low.

Lowell, *see* Lovel.

Lowes, *see* Low.

Lowless, *see* Lovelace.

Lowman/Loman O/P Occupational term for *Lawrence*'s servant; or from place-names *Uplowman*, *Craze Loman*, *Chieflowman* on the river *Loman* in Devon, Celtic 'elm river'. **Lowman** is found across southern England, **Loman** chiefly in Devon and in Lancs.

Lowndes T Dweller at the groves, woods ON; a Chesh/Lancs/Staffs surname.

Lowrie/Lowrison/Lowr(e)y, *see* Lawrence.

Lowson, *see* Lawrence.

Lowther/Lowder P Place-name *Lowther* in Westmd, on the river so-called (of unknown etymology, possibly British). Family name of the Earls of Lonsdale and the Viscounts Ullswater.

Lowton P Place-name in Devon OE '?warm/sunny hill' and in Lancs OE 'hill farm'. A surname found principally in these two counties.

Loxley P Place-name in Staffs, Warwicks, and WRYorks (two such) OE '*Locc*'s clearing'. Chiefly a WRYorks surname. Readily confused with/a variant of **Lockley**.

Loyd, *see* Lloyd.

Lubbock P From *Lübeck*, Wendish *Liubice* ('lovely'), the north German port town that headed the Hanseatic League. A Norfolk surname, the family name of the Barons Avebury.

Lucas/Locket(t)/Look/Luck/Luckes/Luckett/Luke/Lukey F From the Latin first-name *Lucas*, a form of the Greek *Loucas*, referring to a man from *Lucania* in Italy. 'The third Evangelist, beloved physician, and reputed limner of the Blessed Virgin'

(Cottle). It may sometimes have absorbed **Levick**. The diminutive **Lockett** can be readily confused with or be a variant of **Lochhead** or **Lockhart**. **Luckman** and **Lukeman** are '*Luke*'s servant'. **Lucas** and **Locket** are strongest in Lancs, **Lockett** in Staffs, **Luck** in Kent, **Luckett** in Oxon and **Luke/Lukey** in Cornwall, where the first-name *Lywci* appears in the Bodmin gospels. **Look** and **Luckes**, scarce, belong to Somerset. See also **Lock(e)** and **Lucking**.

Luce, *see* Lucey.

Lucey/Luce P/F From one of a number of place-names in Normandy and northern France derived from the Latin first-name *Lucius*; or from the mediaeval female first-name *Lucie* (Latin *Lucia*), rather than the male *Lucius*, though both are derived from Latin *luc-* 'light'. *Lucia* was a virgin martyred at Syracuse; *Lucius* was a less spectacular saint and pope who died in AD 254. An uncommon surname within the British Isles, in either spelling.

Luck/Luckes/Luckett, *see* Lucas.

Luckham P Place-name *Luccombe* in Somerset and Wilts OE '*Lufa*'s valley', or 'valley where courting takes place'. Strongest in Devon.

Luckhurst P Some surname dictionaries make unnecessarily heavy weather of this surname. Hanks and Hodges say that it is of uncertain origin and that 'it is found principally in Kent and may be a habitation name from a place in the parish of Mayfield, Sussex, recorded in 1553 as *Lukkars Croche*'. The etymology of such a place-name is uncertain – Cottle suggests that it might be derived from an early owner whose OE name meant 'dear spear', and that the whole may have been made to look like a *hirst* place-name. All this could be true and relevant enough, but because this is a Kent surname, another likely source is the settlement in that county called *Luckhurst* (in Stone cum Ebony), which is of equally dubious etymology: Wallenberg says it might be named after a Richard Le Lokiere (1292) and be 'a manorial, genitival name in disguise'.

Luckin(g) F A diminutive of **Luke** (see **Lucas**) or of **Love**. Very largely an Essex surname.

Luckman, *see* Lucas.

Lucksford, *see* Luxford.

Ludbrook P There is such a place-name in Devon OE 'loud/babbling brook', though by the late nineteenth century the **Ludbrook** surname was to be found principally in south-east England, East Anglia and WRYorks.

Ludford P Place name in Salop OE 'ford over the loud/babbling (river Teme)' and in Lincs OE 'ford on the way to *Louth*'. By the late nineteenth century the **Ludford** surname could be found mainly in Warwicks.

Ludlow P Place-name in Salop OE 'hill by the loud/babbling (river Teme)'. Compare **Ludford**. A widespread surname.

Ludwell P Place-names in various counties OE 'loud/babbling stream'. A very scarce surname, found principally in Gloucs.

Luen, *see* Lewin.

Luff, *see* Leaf.

Lugg O/N/P Possibly an occupational term/nickname derived from a ME word for a stick, staff, pole, but chiefly a Cornish surname, with its roots in a place-name such as *Trelugga*, Cornish *lugh* ('calf'), a farm where calves were bred.

Luke/Lukeman/Lukey, *see* Lucas.

Lumb P Place-name in Lancs, WRYorks OE 'pool'. A WRYorks surname.

Lumbard/Lumber, *see* Lombard.

Lumby P Place-name in WRYorks ON 'wood/grove farm'.

Lumley P Place-name in Co Durham OE 'wood/clearing by the pool' and in WRYorks OE 'long wood/clearing'. The surname has its strongest presence in these two counties. Family name of the Earls of Scarbrough.

Lumsden P Place-name in Coldingham, Berwickshire, Scotland OE '?valley of the pool'. Chiefly found in the north-east of England and in Scotland.

Lund/Lound/Lount/Lunt T/P Dweller by a grove ON, or from one of a number of place-names with the same meaning, such as *Lund* and *Lunt*, Lancs, *Lund*, ERYorks and WRYorks, *Lound*, Notts and Suffolk and *Lount*, Leics. **Lund** also became a common surname in Sweden, with the same meaning. The related surname **Lalonde** is derived from one of four places called *La Londe* in Normandy OF and ON 'the grove'; very scarce in England, it has a limited presence in Somerset. **Lund** and **Lunt** are principally Lancs surnames; **Lound** is found chiefly in Lincs and WRYorks, and **Lount** in Leics.

Lunt, *see* Lund.

Luscombe P Place-name (several such) in Devon OE 'pigsty valley', and chiefly a Devon surname.

Lusher O Occupational term, 'the usher' OF. Found mainly in Norfolk.

Lushington P From an unidentified place-name – probably *Lustinton* OE '?the settlement of *Lust*'s people' in Kent, the county in which this very scarce surname is mostly found. Early allegations for marriage licences in Kent include: Henry **Lushington**, alias **Lussenton**, of Knowlton, Kent (to marry Alice **Lussenton** of Alkham, widow), 1592, and John **Lushenden** of Barham (to marry Ann Abbott of Great Mongeham), 1612. In 1637 John **Lushenton** married Susan Pitcher in Canterbury, and Thomas **Lustington** was baptized in Milton, Kent, in 1694. The surname of John **Lashenden** of Rye, who requested a licence to marry Alice Bett of Elmstead in 1605, is probably derived from *Lashenden* OE '?muddy stream pasture' in the Kent Hundred of Barclay.

Lutey T Cornish: dweller at the calf-house. Almost entirely a Cornish surname. Readily confused with/a variant of **Leuty**.

Luther O Occupational term for a lute-player OF. Strongest in Salop.

Lutley P There is such a place-name in Staffs and Worcs OE 'little wood/clearing', but this is chiefly a Devon/Somerset surname, and could in principle be derived from *Lustleigh* in Devon OE '?*Luvesta*'s clearing', though this place-name would seem always to have been spelt with an '*s*'.

Luton/Lewton P Place-name *Luton* in Beds, British river-name and OE 'farm on the river *Lea*'; in Devon (two such) OE '*Leofgifu*'s farm'; in Kent OE '*Leofa*'s farm'. Yet this is principally a Gloucs surname in either spelling.

Lutton P Place-name in Lincs OW and OE 'pool farm'; in Northants OE '*Luda*'s farm'; in ERYorks OE 'farm on the loud river'. By the late nineteenth century this was a widely-scattered surname within England and Scotland, not strongly related to any of these counties, but also had a significant presence in Northern Ireland.

Luttrell O/N Occupational term/nickname for a hunter of otters OF, or a nickname for a person bearing some resemblance to such a creature. A surname borne by a family famous for its tenure of Dunster Castle, Somerset, and of the manor of nearby East Quantoxhead, since mediaeval times. The illuminated manuscript known as the *Luttrell Psalter* was made for the **Luttrell** family of Irnham village in Lincs during the fourteenth century. An Irish family of **Luttrells** became Earls of Carhampton in 1785.

Luty, *see* Leuty.

Luxford/Lucksford P From an unidentified place-name, presumably in the southeast of England OE '*Luck/Luke*'s ford'. **Luxford** is a Kent/Sussex surname; **Lucksford** is a much scarcer variant.

Luxon/Luxton P Devon place-names: *East Luxton* in Winkleigh, and *Luxton* in Upottery ME and OE '*Lugg*'s farm'. Devon surnames.

Lyal(l) F Possibly from an ON first-name *Liulfr* (second element: 'wolf'), or a diminutive of **Lyon**. Readily confused with **Lisle/ Lyle**.

Lydford P Place-name in Devon and Somerset (two such) OE 'ford over the loud/babbling (stream)'. A Dorset/Somerset surname.

Lydiard, *see* **Liddiard**.

Lydiate/Lydiatt P Place-name *Lydiate* in Lancs and Worcs OE 'swing-gate' (compare **Lidgate**). **Lydiate** and **Lydiatt** are both Lancs surnames, the latter also having a presence in Warwicks.

Lydiatt, *see* **Lydiate**.

Lye, *see* **Lee**.

Lyford P Place-name in Berks OE 'ford where flax grows' (compare the word *linen*), and a Berks surname.

Lyle, *see* **Lisle**.

Lyn(h)am/Lyn(e)ham P/F Place-name *Lyneham* in Devon, Oxon and Wilts OE 'homestead/river-meadow where flax grows'. Irish (also **Linehan**): Anglicized form of Gaelic O' [descendant of] **Laidhghneian** ('?snowflake/snow birth'). Within England, **Lynam** is a Derbys surname; **Lynham** is strongest in Lancs and Somerset. *Desmond Michael ('Des') Lynam, sports presenter and talk-show host, was born in 1942 in Ennis, Co Clare, Ireland, but moved to Brighton, Sussex, with his family in 1949.*

Lynch/Linch T/P/F Dweller at a hillside OE *hlinc*, or from place-names such as *Lynch* in Somerset or *Linch* in Sussex, with the same meaning. Irish: Anglicized form of Gaelic O' [descendant of] **Loingsigh** ('sailor'), or of **Linseach** (Anglo-Norman French **de Lench**), of unknown origin. *Thomas Lynch (1749–1779), an American of Irish ancestry, was a signatory of the Declaration of Independence… The surname of the American General Charles Lynch (1736–1796), who meted out harsh justice in Virginia, gave rise to the expressions 'Lynch law' and 'Lynch mob'.*

Lyndhurst P Place-name in Hants OE 'lime-tree hill/wood'. An exceptionally scarce surname. *Nicholas Lyndhurst, best known as a television actor, was born in Emsworth, Hants, in 1961.*

Lyndon P There is such a place-name in Rutland OE 'lime-tree hill', but the surname is strongest in Warwicks, where a settlement now called *Lyndon End* (formerly *Lyndon*, with the same OE meaning) is likely to be the point of origin.

Lyneham, *see* **Lynam**.

Lyng, *see* **Ling**.

Lynham, *see* **Lynam**.

Lynn P/F There are various places so-called in Norfolk, of which the best known is now called *King's Lynn*, probably named from a Celtic word meaning 'lake, pool'. Irish: Anglicized form of Gaelic O' [descendant of] or **Mac** [son of] **Fhloinn** ('ruddy'). Compare **Flynn**.

Lynton, *see* **Linton**.

Lyon N/F/P Nickname for a fierce fighter, brave as a lion OF; or from the first-name *Leo(n)*, from Latin *Leo* ('lion'), much favoured by Jews in the Middle Ages, though there were no fewer than thirteen popes called *Leo*; or from the place-name *Lyon* in central France OF, from Gaulish '?raven/crow hill/fort' (often referred to as *Lyons* in Modern English), or from *Lyons-la-Forêt* in Eure. See also **Lyal**. **Bowes-Lyon** is the family name of the Earls of Strathmore and Kinghorne.

Lyte, *see* **Light**.

Lyth(e) T/P/N Dweller at a hillside OE/ON, or from place-names such as *Lyth* in Salop and Westmd or *Lythe* in NRYorks, with the same meaning; or a nickname for a gentle person OE. A surname of the north of England in either spelling.

Lythgo(e), *see* **Lithgow**.

Lyttelton, *see* **Littleton**.

M

Mabb/Mapp F From the mediaeval first-name *Mab(be)*, a short form of ME/OF *Amabel*, from Latin *amabilis* ('lovable'). Diminutive forms include **Mabbett**, **Mabbitt**, **Mabbott**, **Mabbutt** and **Mappin**. **Mabbs**, **Mabson**, **Mapson** and **Mobbs** are 'son of *Mabb*'. **Mabley** and **Mably** would appear to be Cornish variants; the not-dissimilar surname **Mablin** is said to be from Cornish *map-lyen* ('clerk/clergyman'). *Early generations of Mappins in Sheffield were cutlers or bakers. Jonathan Mappin established a silversmith workshop in the town in 1774, and in 1849 the first Mappin shop was opened in London. Nine years later John Newton Mappin invited his brother-in-law George Webb to join the business; in course of time Mappin & Webb, jewellers, would achieve a worldwide reputation.*

Mabbett/Mabbitt/Mabbott/Mabbs/ Mabbutt/Mabl(e)y/Mabson, *see* Mabb.

Mac- For surnames beginning with *Mac-*, *see* Mc-.

Mace(y)/Macy F From a mediaeval first-name ?OE *Moessa*, also used as a pet-form of *Matthew* (and of *Thomas*?). **Macey** and **Macy** are readily confused with/a variant of **Maisey** and **Massey**. **Mace** has a strong presence in Kent and in Norfolk; **Macey** and **Macy** are generally surnames of southern and south-west England. *The founder of the American department store chain called Macy's was Rowland Hussey Macy (1822–1877), a Quaker businessman born on Nantucket Island, Massachusetts.*

Machen(t)/Machin/Machon, *see* Mason.

Mack F Scots: from the ON first-name *Makkr*

(*Magnus*). Mostly found in northern England and in Scotland, but with a significant presence in Norfolk.

Macy, *see* Mace.

Madden F Irish: Anglicized form of Gaelic O' [descendant of] **Madaidhin** ('hound').

Maddison, *see* Maddy.

Maddock(s)/Maddick(s)/Maddox F From the OW first-name *Madoc* ('fortunate, goodly'). **Maddock** and **Maddocks** are strong in Chesh and Lancs, **Maddox** in Salop and Staffs, but **Maddick** and **Maddicks** in Cornwall.

Maddy F From the mediaeval female first-names *Madde/Maud* (see **Maud**) or *Magdalen* (see **Maudling**). Or could the first-name *Matthew* be involved? **Maddy** is chiefly a Herefords surname; **Mad(d)ison** ('son of *Madde/Maud/Magdalen*') is strongest in Co Durham in either spelling. *James Madison (1751–1836), fourth President of the USA, was descended from John Madison, a ship's carpenter from Gloucester, who was receiving land grants in Virginia from the 1650s onwards.*

Madeley P Place-name in Salop and Staffs OE '*Mada*'s wood/clearing'. A Salop surname. Readily confused with/a variant of **Madley**. *Richard Madeley, co-presenter with his wife, Judy Finnigan, of the TV show 'Richard and Judy', was born in Romford, Essex, but has Shropshire ancestry on his father's side.*

Madge F From the first-names *Margaret* (see **Magg**) or *Margery* (see **Margery**). **Madge** is found mainly in Devon. **Megson**

and **Meggison** ('son of *Margaret/Margery*') are northern forms, and as to double diminutives, **Meggett** and **Meggitt** are chiefly found in the north, **Madgett** in Norfolk, and **Matchett** across much of the English Midlands and the north.

Madgett, *see* Madge.

Madison, *see* Maddy.

Madle, *see* Male.

Madley P Place-name in Herefords OW 'good place' and in Worcs OE 'maidens' wood/clearing'. Readily confused with/a variant of **Madeley**. The surname **Madley** is especially strong in Monmouthshire.

Maffey N Nickname from OF *malfé* ('ill-omened, devil'). An unusual surname, most commonly found in Hants and Surrey.

Magee, *see* McGee.

Magennis, *see* McGenis.

Magg(s)/Mogg F From the mediaeval female first-name *Mag(ge)*, a pet-form of *Margaret*, from Latin *Margarita* ('pearl'). The usual ME form was *Margerie* (see **Margery**). 'St Margaret of Antioch, said to have been martyred in the third century after quelling a dragon, was invoked in childbirth and as one of the fourteen Holy Helpers, with added lustre to the first-name through the sainted Queen of Scotland (died 1093)' (Cottle). **Magson**, **Megson** and **Meggison** ('son of *Mag*') are northern forms, while **Mogg** is strongest in Somerset. The Devon surname **Mudge** can be a variant of **Magg**, though Cottle wonders whether it might not sometimes be a nickname derived from a south-western dialect word for a midge or gnat, from West Saxon OE *mycg*. See also **Madge** and **Moxon**.

Maginnis, *see* McGenis.

Magnus F From the Scandinavian first-name *Magnus*, originally from Latin ('great'), borrowed from the much-admired Charlemagne, *Carolus Magnus*, as the first-name of *Magnus I*, King of Norway and Denmark (died 1047); thence taken to Norse parts of Ireland and Scotland. The cathedrals of Orkney and Faeroe are dedicated to *Saint Magnus the Martyr*, Earl of Orkney. For all that, this has become a scarce surname within the United Kingdom. See also **Manson** (under **Man**).

Magson, *see* Magg.

Maguire, *see* McGuire.

Maher/Meacher/Meagher F Irish: Anglicized form of Gaelic **O'** [descendant of] **Meachair** ('hospitable').

Mahon(e)(y)/Mohan F Irish: Anglicized form of the Gaelic first-name/byname *Mathghamhain* ('Bear'); or an Anglicized form of Gaelic **O'** [descendant of] **Mochain** ('early, in good time'). See also **Maughan** and **Vaughan**. 'The real name of Father Prout, the lapsed Jesuit who heard the bells of Shandon, was **Mahony**' (Cottle).

Maiden N Nickname for an effeminate, maiden-like man OE. Strongest in Lancs and Salop. *See also* **Makin**.

Maidman, *see* Maidment.

Maidment O Occupational term for a servant employed by a young woman/maiden OE. Thus the variant **Maidman** reflects the original meaning better than **Maidment**, with its parasitic *-t* (compare **Machent**, a variant of **Mason**). South/south-west-of-England surnames.

Maidwell P Place-name in Northants OE 'maidens' spring/stream'. A Norfolk/Suffolk surname.

Maile(s), *see* Male.

Main(e), *see* Mayne.

Mainprice/Mainprise/Mainprize N From a term used to describe one who acts as a surety for the appearance in court of a bailed prisoner at the specified time OF (the Modern French words involved are *main* and *prendre*). Rare surnames in any spelling; **Mainprice** can be found in Cambs, **Mainprise** and **Mainprize** in ERYorks.

Mainstone P Place-name in Salop OE 'big

rock'; Hants OF and OE *'Mahieu/Matthew*'s farm'; Herefords OF and OE *'Mayne/Maena*'s farm'. A scarce Gloucs surname.

Mainwaring/Mannering P From a now-lost place-name OF *'Warin*'s manor'. Pronounced as *'Mannering*', whatever the spelling, and known to have scores of variant forms. **Mainwaring** is mostly found along the Welsh/English border, **Mannering** in Kent.

Maisey P Place-name *Maisy* in Calvados, France OF, from the Latin first-name *Masius* plus a suffix. One such family gave its name to *Meysey Hampton*, Gloucs, and this is predominantly a Gloucs surname. Readily confused with/a variant of **Macey/Macy** (see **Mace**) and **Massey**.

Maitland ?P/N A surname of uncertain meaning and origin. Possibly from a *Mautalant*, a place-name in Manche, France OF ('?inhospitable/unproductive [soil]'). Chiefly a Scots surname, but in England it could be a nickname for a discourteous, rude person, from Anglo-Norman French. Family name of the Earls of Lauderdale, who have Anglo-Norman origins.

Major, *see* **Mauger**.

Makepeace N Nickname for a peacemaker, arbiter OE and OF. Also misspelt as **Makepiece**. A Co Durham surname in both these spellings.

Makepiece, *see* **Makepeace**.

Maker T/P Dweller by the ruin/old walls, Cornish *magor* (from Latin *maceries*), or from a place of this name in the county, with the same meaning. Chiefly a Cornwall/Devon surname, but also found in Lancs and elsewhere.

Makin/Maykin/Meaken/Meakin(g)(s)/Meekins F/N From a first-name *May*, a diminutive of *Matthew*; or a variant of **Maiden**. **Makin** is strongest in Lancs, **Maykin** (scarce) in WRYorks, **Meakin** in the English Midlands, **Meaking** in Staffs and Worcs, **Meakins** in Northants and **Meakings/Meekins** in Suffolk. **Meaken** is scarce and scattered.

Malco(l)m/Malco(l)mson F Scots: from a Gaelic first-name *Mael-Colum* ('devotee of [Saint] *Columba*').

Malden/Maldon P Place-names in Surrey and Essex OE 'hill with a sign/monument/cross'. Compare **Meldon** and **Melton**.

Male(s)/Madle/Maile(s) N Nickname for a manly, virile man OF. **Male** is strongest in Somerset, **Males** in Herts, **Madle** in Essex, **Maile** in Hunts and **Mailes** in Herefords.

Mal(l)et(t) F/N/O From a mediaeval female first-name *Malet*, a diminutive of *Mal(le)*, pet form of *Mary* (compare **Malin**, **Marriott**, **Moll** and **Mule**); or a diminutive of a male first-name *Malo/Maclou*, borne by a sixth-century Welsh monk named *Maclovius*. Or a nickname for a cursed, unfortunate person OF, or for someone with a strong, hammer-like personality OF (compare **Martel**); or an occupational term for a maker of hammers, a smith OF *ma(i)let* ('hammer'; compare *mallet*). Readily confused with/a variant of **Mallard**.

Malham/Mallam P Place-name *Malham* in WRYorks ON 'at the stony/gravelly place' (dative plural). **Malham** is strongest in WRYorks, **Mallam** in Co Durham.

Malin(s)/Malkin/Malyn/Maul(e)/Maull F From a mediaeval female first-name *Malin*, a diminutive of *Mall(e)*, a pet form of *Mary*, Hebrew '?wished-for child'. Compare **Malet**, **Marriott**, **Moll** and **Mule**. **Malleson**, **Malins** and **Mallinson** are 'son of *Mall(e)*'. *Malkin* as a first-name was also used to mean 'slattern, slut'. Chaucer gives the old widow in *The Nun's Priest's Tale* a sheep called *Malle*.

Maliphant N Nickname from OF, literally a 'bad/naughty child' (*mal enfant*). A scarce Glamorgan, South Wales, surname.

Malkin, *see* **Malin**.

Mallalieu P Place-name *Malleloy* in Meurthe-et-Moselle, France ('place with medlar trees'). Within England this is a Huguenot surname, most commonly found in Lancs and WRYorks, especially in Saddleworth, WRYorks, where it can be found (as **Malelu**, **Mallalew**, etc.) from at least as early as the 1630s. George Redmonds says that **Mellodew** (chiefly found in Lancs) can be a variant of **Mallalieu** – and this might also be true of **Melledew**, also a Lancs surname, unless either or both are variants of **Merridew** (see **Meredith**)? *The Huguenot ancestry of the Mallalieus of Saddleworth by D. F. E. Sykes was published in 1920. Frederick William Mallalieu (1860–1932), Member of Parliament for Colne Valley, was born in Delph, Yorks, and was the father of Sir (Joseph Percival) Mallalieu MP (1908–1980), whose daughter Baroness (Ann) Mallalieu is an independent-minded Labour Party member of the House of Lords.*

Mallam, *see* Malham.

Mallard F/N From an OF first-name *Malhard* ('council-brave'); or a nickname for a person deemed to resemble a drake or male wild duck in some way OF. Strongest in Northants. Readily confused with/a variant of **Malet**.

Mallender/Mallinder A surname of uncertain origin. Cottle makes suggestions: *malander* is a dry, scabby eruption behind a horse's knee OF; *malandrin* was a highwayman OF; *malantari* was a leper hospital, from Low Latin; *malandre* is a medicinal plant of the Lychnis species ME from OF, and the surname might refer to one who mixed or sold herbs. Another suggested source is the Norman French word *Molinière*, referring to a corn miller. **Mallender** is a Derbys/Notts/WRYorks surname; **Mallinder** is strongest in Derbys and WRYorks.

Mallery, *see* Mallory.

Malleson, *see* Malin.

Mallet(t), *see* Malet.

Mallinder, *see* Mallender.

Mallinson, *see* Malin.

Mallory/Mallery/Malory N Nickname for an unlucky, unfortunate person OF. **Mallory** is an uncommon surname, chiefly found in the three Ridings of Yorks; **Mallery**, also scarce, has a presence in Beds,

Lancs and Surrey, while **Malory**, scarcer still, is a scattered surname. *Sir Thomas Malory (c.1415–1471), best-known as the author of Morte D'Arthur, was the son of John Malory, Member of Parliament for Warwicks, who also held land in Leics and Northants, and his wife Philippa (née Chetwynd).*

Malone F Irish: Anglicized form of Gaelic O' [descendant of] **Maoil Eoin** ('devotee of [Saint] *John*').

Malpas(s) P From one of a number of place-names in Chesh, Cornwall, Monmouthshire and elsewhere OF 'bad passage/crossing'. Compare **Maltravers**. Found in Staffs in both spellings, **Malpas** also featuring strongly in Chesh.

Maltby P Place-names *Maltby* in Lincs, NRYorks and WRYorks, and *Mautby* in Norfolk ON '*Malti*'s farm', either of which could in principle also have given rise to the surname **Mawby**. **Maltby** is a surname of the English Midlands and the north, strongest in Notts; **Mawby** is most commonly found in Leics.

Malter O/T Occupational term for a maltster OE, or a dweller on bad/unproductive ground OF. An exceptionally scarce scattered surname.

Malthouse/Malthus T/O Dweller at a malt-house, or an occupational term for a brewer, who worked at one OE. **Malthouse** is a scattered surname, strong in WRYorks; **Malthus**, exceptionally scarce, has a presence in Gloucs and Surrey. *(Thomas) Robert Malthus (1766–1834), the political economist best known for his writings on population, was born in Wotton, Surrey. He is commonly referred to as 'Thomas', though his preferred name was 'Robert' or 'Bob', and the usual pronunciation of his surname as 'Mall-thuss' gives little enough of a clue as to its 'malthouse' origins.*

Malton P Place-name in NRYorks OE (Scandinavianized) 'middle place'.

Maltravers ?P/N Apparently from an unidentified place OF 'bad passage/crossing' (compare **Malpas**), but no such place-name in France is known, and *de* forms are lacking, so it may be a nickname in the sense of 'obstacle, trouble-maker'. In any event, this is a very scarce surname which apparently has no fixed home, though the variant **Matravers** belongs mainly to Somerset.

Malvern P Place-name in Worcs ow 'bare hill'. Strongest in Gloucs, Lancs and Warwicks.

Malyn, *see* **Malin**.

Man/Mann/Manning/Manson N/O/F Nickname for a strong or manly man – 'very much a man', as it were OE; or an occupational term for a servant, vassal, bondman OE; or from a Germanic first-name OE *Manna*. The form **Mann**, which retains the double '*n*' of OE, is common and widespread; **Man** is scattered and less frequently found; **Manning** is strongest in Devon; **Manson** belongs very largely to Scotland, where it can alternatively mean 'son of *Magnus*'.

Manby P Place-name *Maunby* in NRYorks and *Manby* in Lincs, both ON '*Magni*'s farm'.

Manchester P Place-name *Manchester* in Lancs, British and OE '*Mamucio* (breast-shaped hill)-fort'. A Lancs/WRYorks surname.

Mander ?P/O A surname of unknown origin; possibly from the place-name *Mandres* in Eure, Seine-et-Oise, etc. OF 'huts, stables'; Cottle believes that 'traditional connections with *basket*, *Maundy*, *commander*, *beggar* are unlikely'. A widespread surname, strongest in Warwicks. **Maunder** is a Devon variant.

Manderfield, *see* **Mandeville**.

Mandeville P Place-names in France, such as *Mann(e)ville*, Germanic and OF '*Manno*'s settlement', or *Magneville* OF 'great settlement'. One branch of the **Mandeville** family were Earls of Essex. The surname **Manderfield** could well be a corruption of **Mandeville** (compare **Turberville/Turberfield**). **Mandeville** is mainly a Surrey surname; **Manderfield** (scarce) can be found in Leics and Notts.

Manfield P Place-name in NRYorks OE '?common/communally-owned field'. An oddly distributed surname, in evidence in the West Country but also in NRYorks. Readily confused with/a variant of **Mansfield**.

Mangnall/Mangold O Occupational term for a person who operated a catapult/siege engine OF *mangonelle*. **Mangnall** is almost exclusively a Lancs surname. **Mangold** is a very scarce variant found in the south of England, though not all bearers of it may be of English ancestry: *Mangold*, a Germanic first-name ('much-rule') much favoured in knightly circles in Germany in the Middle Ages, has given rise to a related surname, and Hans Carl Friedrich **von Mangoldt** (1854–1925) was a German mathematician; not only that, but a *mangold wurzel* (from German, 'beet-root') is a root vegetable.

Manley N/P Although such a surname could be from a nickname for a manly, brave, independent, upright person OE, a place-name origin would be very much on the cards. Judging by the distribution of the surname – clustered in both Chesh/Lancs and Devon – two places could have been the source: *Manley* in Chesh, and *East* and *West Manley* in Devon, all from OE 'communal wood/clearing'. The distribution of the variant **Manly** is not dissimilar.

Manly, *see* **Manley**.

Mann, *see* **Man**.

Mannering, *see* **Mainwaring**.

Manners P Place-name *Mesnières* in Seine-Maritime, France OF, from the Latin verb *manere* 'to abide, remain'. Family name of the Dukes of Rutland, who are now associated with the Vale of Belvoir, but were formerly of Northd. The surname is still found in significant numbers in neighbouring Co Durham. See also **Menzies**.

Manning, *see* **Man**.

Mannington P There are places so-called in Norfolk (two such) and in Dorset OE 'farm of *Manna*'s people', though this is mainly a Sussex surname.

Mannix, *see* **McNeice** (under **McGenis**).

Mansell/Maunsell P/O From a place-name in France, such as *Le Mans* (originally the capital of the Gaulish tribe of *Ceromanni*) or *Maine* (the province) OF; or a status term for a feudal tenant, a *mansel* OF, who lived in a *manse* (consisting of enough land to keep a single family). Compare **Manser**. **Mansell** is a scattered surname, being found in pockets from Surrey to Lancs; **Maunsell**, much scarcer, has a presence in Middx and Somerset. *Nigel Mansell, the British racing driver who won the world championship in both Formula One and CART, was born at Upton-upon-Severn, Worcs, in 1953.*

Manser O/F Occupational term for a maker of handles for domestic and agricultural tools OF; or from a Hebrew first-name *Manasseh* ('he who causes to forget'), borne by Christians as well as Jews; or from *mansier* OF, a term used to describe the tenant of a *manse* (see **Mansell**). Cottle is careful to point out the suggested origins for the surname which do *not* hold water: 'Readers of Kingsley's *Hereward* should note that *mamzer* "bastard" (Low Latin from Hebrew) is not extant in ME, and cannot figure here; nor does the (southern) distribution allow the place-name *Mansergh* in Westmorland ON "*Man*'s shieling"'. Cottle is right about the geographical distribution of the surname: it belongs to Kent, Surrey and Sussex.

Mansergh P Place-name in Westmd ON '*Man*'s shieling'. By 1881 this surname was chiefly to be found in Lancs, though one prominent **Mansergh** family of Co Cork and Co Kilkenny, Ireland, had fifteenth-century roots in Barwicke Hall, Yorks.

Mansfield P Place-name in Notts, Celtic and OE 'field by the hill called *Mam* ("breast")'. Family name of the Barons Sandhurst. Chiefly found in the English Midlands and the south, also in Ireland. Readily confused with/a variant of **Manfield**. *Michael Mansfield QC, the English barrister known for his robust advocacy on behalf* of high-profile clients, was born in Finchley, London, in 1941.

Manson, *see* **Man**.

Manton P Place-name in Notts, Rutland and Wilts OE 'farm held in common', and in Lincs OE 'farm with sandy soil'. The surname is strongest in Warwicks.

Manwood T/P Dweller in a communally owned wood OE. There is such a place-name in Wilts, yet this very scarce surname can only be found in significant numbers in Lancs.

Mapledoram P Place-name *Mapledurham* in Oxon OE 'maple-tree homestead'. A very scarce Devon surname.

Mapleton P Place-names in Derbys and Kent OE 'place in the maples'. A very scarce scattered surname.

Mapother/Mapowder P Place-name *Mappowder* in Dorset OE 'place at the maple tree'. Over the centuries the surname **Mapowder** can be found mainly in Devon and Cornwall, while the alternative **Mapother** is in evidence in County Roscommon, Ireland, as early as the seventeenth century. *This is a surname which seems not to have pleased Thomas Cruise Mapother IV (born in Syracuse, New York, in 1962), who has chosen to be known throughout his film-acting career simply as Tom Cruise. Genealogists have linked him to Dylan Henry Mapother, a Welshman who emigrated to Kentucky in 1850.*

Mapp, *see* **Mabb**.

Mapperley P There are places so-called in Derbys and Notts OE 'maple wood/clearing', though this exceptionally scarce surname only has a significant presence in Suffolk.

Mappin, *see* **Mapp**.

Mapplebeck P Place-name *Maplebeck*, Notts, OE and ON 'brook in the maples'. Chiefly a WRYorks surname.

Mapplethorp(e) P Place-name *Mablethorpe* in Lincs, Germanic and ON '*Malbert*'s outlying farm'. A Lincs surname in either spelling.

Mapson, *see* **Mabb**.

Mapstone P Place-name in Devon OE '*Mætta*'s pan-stone [the big haystack-like granite block that the road has to bend around]'. Chiefly a Somerset surname.

March T/P/N Dweller at a boundary OE, more particularly in the Marches which separate England from Wales or from Scotland; or from the place-name *March* (from the locative case of OE *mearc*) in the Isle of Ely (now Cambs); or applied to someone who was born or baptized in the month of March ME, Latin *Martius*, from the Roman God *Mars*. A widespread surname, unevenly scattered. Readily confused with/ a variant of **Marks**, **Marsh** and **Murch**. *The American actor Frederick March (1897–1975) was born Ernest Frederick McIntyre Bickel in Racine, Wisconsin; his stage surname is a shortened version of his mother's maiden name, 'Marcher'.*

Marcham P Place-name in Berks OE 'homestead where smallage (wild celery) grows'. A Berks/Middx surname.

Marchant/Merchant O Occupational term for a merchant, trader OF. For the *-ar* element in **Marchant**, see **Armistead**. **Marchant** is strong in south-east England; **Merchant** is more widespread. **Marquand** is a Channel Islands form.

Marchbank(s), *see* **Marjoribanks**.

Marden/Mardon P/F Place-names: *Marden* in Kent, Sussex, Wilts and Herefords OW and OE 'mare pasture'/'boundary hill'/'boundary valley'/'?plain/?stone valley'; *Mardon* in Devon OE 'boundary hill'. There is also a French first-name *Mardon*, an oblique case of *Mard*, a form of *Médard*, Germanic 'strength hard'.

Marfleet P Place-name in ERYorks ON and OE 'fen/marsh stream'. Principally a Lincs surname.

Margary/Marger(i)son, *see* **Margery**.

Margery/Margary/Margrie F From the first-name *Margerie/Marjorie*, a diminutive of *Margaret* (see **Magg**) in OF forms. A popular saints' name, and at times fancifully connected with the herb *marjoram*. **Marger(i)son**, **Margesson**, **Margetson** and **Margetts** are 'son of *Margery/Margaret*'. **Margary**, unlike **Margery**, is commonly pronounced with a hard *-g-* sound. See also **Madge**.

Margesson/Margetson/Margetts/ Margrie, *see* **Margery**.

Marian/Marion F Diminutives of the first-name *Mary* (see **Marriott**).

Mar(r)in F/O From an OF first-name *Marin*, from *Marie*; or an occupational term for a mariner, sailor OF (compare **Marner**).

Marion, *see* **Marian**.

Marjoram N Apparently a nickname from the herb marjoram OF, from Low Latin *majorana* (of uncertain meaning); probably bestowed as a surname in tribute to sweetness and aroma, and no doubt wrongly linked with the first-names *Margery* and *Margaret*.

Marjoribanks/Marchbank(s) P A Scottish surname, adopted in the sixteenth century, it is said, by the family of **Johnston** when they acquired lands called *Marjoribanks* in Renfrew which had been granted by King Robert Bruce in 1316 to his daughter *Marjorie* (see **Margery**) when she married Walter the Steward, ancestor of the Royal Stewarts. **Marjoribanks** is commonly pronounced '*Marchbanks*'.

Mark(e) F/T/P From the Latin first-name *Marcus*, ultimately from *Mars*, the god of war. *Mark* was the author of the second gospel in the New Testament, but *Mark* was never as popular a first-name in England in mediaeval times as it was on the continent. Or a dweller on some boundary or other OE *mearc*, or from one of several places so-called, with the same meaning, such as *Mark* in Somerset. There is a place called *Marck* in Pas-de-Calais, France. **Marks** (son of *Mark*) is now chiefly thought of as a Jewish surname, though is readily confused with/a variant of **March** and **Marsh**.

Markby P Place-name in Lincs ON '*Marki*'s farm'. A very scarce Essex/Middx surname.

Marke, *see* Mark.

Marker T/O/F Dweller by a boundary of some sort (between counties, countries?) OE *mearc* (compare **Mark**). Additionally, Cottle suggests that **Marker** could be an occupational term for an embroiderer OE plus *-er*; Hanks and Hodges state that it can be a late development of the surname **Mercer**; Reaney derives it from a Germanic first-name *Markere* '?boundary army'.

Markham P Place-name in Notts OE 'homestead on the boundary'.

Markland/Martland P Cottle seems to have found a place called *Markland* in Lancs OE 'boundary lane', but maybe he was thinking of *Marland*? **Markland/Martland** could readily be confused with, or be variants of, the surname **Marland**. In any event, **Markland** and **Martland** are both Lancs surnames; for spelling variation (-*k*- and -*t*-), compare **Marklew/Martlew** and **Markley/Martley**.

Marklew/Martlew P Probably from an unidentified place-name OE '?boundary hill', but readily confused with/a variant of **Markley/Martley**? For spelling variation (-*k*- and -*t*-), compare **Markland/Martland** and **Markley/Martley**. **Marklew** is found mainly in Staffs and Warwicks, **Martlew** in Lancs.

Markley, *see* Martley.

Marks, *see* Mark.

Marland P Cottle mentions places so-called in Devon OE 'land on a mere/lake' and in Sussex OF and OE 'land fertilized with marl', but this is almost exclusively a Lancs surname, and the origin there must be *Marland*, Lancs OE 'land on a mere/lake'. Readily confused with/a variant of **Markland/Martland**.

Marlborough P Place-name in Wilts OE '?*Maeria*'s/gentian barrow'. A scarce surname, found in scattered pockets in Co Durham, Herts and Middx.

Marler T/O Dweller in an area of clay soil ME, or who worked there. Strongest in Middx/Norfolk.

Marley P Place-name in Devon OE 'boundary wood/clearing', Kent OE 'pleasant wood/clearing' and WRYorks OE 'marten (weasel) wood/clearing'. A scattered surname, strongest in Co Durham. Readily confused with/a variant of **Marlow**. *In the early 1920s Owen Aisher, a builder from Harrietsham, Kent, began making concrete roofing tiles, and founded the Marley Tile Works, which was subsequently a great commercial success… The Jamaican singer and songwriter Robert ('Bob') Marley (1945–1981) was the son of Norval Sinclair Marley, a white marine officer who came from Liverpool, Lancs, and his black Jamaican wife Cedella Booker.*

Marlow(e) P Place-name in Bucks OE 'at the leavings of a mere' – that is, that which is left after a pond has been drained. Readily confused with/a variant of **Marley**. *The playwright and poet Christopher ('Kit') Marlow (1564–1593), born in the same year as William Shakespeare, was baptized at St George's church, Canterbury, Kent. Both Christopher and his father John (a shoemaker from Ospringe, Kent) spelt their surname as 'Marley', and it can also be found as 'Morley' and 'Marle'.*

Marment/Marmont P Place-name *Marmont* in Lot-et-Garonne OF 'black/bad hill'. A Gloucs surname in both spellings.

Marmion N Nickname from an OF word meaning 'brat, monkey, grotesque', and borne by an ancient Norman family. In more recent years, a scarce Lancs surname.

Marmont, *see* Marment.

Marner O Occupational term for a mariner, sailor OF. Compare **Marin**. Strongest (predictably) in the coastal counties of Hants, Kent, Lancs and (especially) Sussex.

Marple P Place-name in Chesh OE 'boundary stream'. The surname is strongest in Derbys.

Marquand, *see* Marchant.

Marr P English: place-name in WRYorks ON '?marsh, pool'; Scots: place-name in Aberdeenshire, with a similar (uncertain) etymology. *Andrew (William Stevenson) Marr, journalist and television presenter, was born in 1959, son of William Donald Marr of Longforgan, Dundee; both father and son were educated at Loretto School, Musselburgh.*

Marrable F From a female first-name, from Latin *Mirabel* ('wonderful'). A scarce Essex/Middx surname.

Marrick P Place-name in NRYorks ON '?horse (compare *mare*) ridge'. A scarce scattered surname.

Marries/Marris T/P Dweller at a marsh, or from a place-name *Marais*, with the same meaning, in Calvados, Eure. A church in York is called 'St Saviour in the *Marishes*'. Marries is scarce and scattered; Marris is found chiefly in Lincs.

Marrin, *see* Marin.

Marriott F From the mediaeval first-name *Mariot*, a diminutive of *Mary* OF, ultimately from Aramaic *Maryam* ('?wished-for child'). Strongest in the East Midlands. Readily confused with/a variant of **Merritt**. Compare **Malet**, **Malin**, **Moll** and **Mule**. *Captain Thomas Marryat (1792–1848), naval officer and novelist, was born in London to a family with Huguenot origins. His surname is very rare in England in this spelling.*

Marris, *see* Marries.

Marrow ?N Possibly derived from a nickname, a 'marrow' or 'marra' being a mate/chum (northern dialect) or a spouse/sweetheart ME. A favourite Tyneside song begins: 'As me and me *marra* was gannin' to work…'. The surname is strongest in Lancs.

Marryat, *see* Marriott.

Marsden P Place-name in Gloucs, WRYorks OE 'boundary valley'; or from one of two places so-named in Lancs OE 'boundary mark valley'. Strongest in Lancs/WRYorks. Readily confused with/a variant of **Marston**.

Marsh T Dweller on marshy land OE *mersc*.

For the relationship between *-er-* and *-ar-*, see **Armistead**. Readily confused with/a variant of **March** and **Marks**. **Marshman** is a Hants/Wilts variant.

Marshall/Mascall/Maskall/Maskell O Occupational term, OF *maresc(h)al*, from Germanic, originally used for a man who cared for horses (or specifically, for mares) – a farrier, shoeing-smith, groom, horse-doctor – but later used to describe a wide range of functions, including a marshal in charge of a household and rising in status to a high officer such as the Earl Marshal. *Dan Maskell (1908–1992), tennis player and broadcaster, was born in Fulham, London.*

Marsham P Place-name in Norfolk OE 'homestead by a marsh'. Family name of the Earls of Romney.

Marshfield T/P Dweller in a field by a marsh OE, or from a place-name with the same meaning in Chesh, Gloucs, Monmouthshire. Strongest in Gloucs and Somerset.

Marshman, *see* Marsh.

Marson, *see* Marston.

Marston P Place-name in many counties OE 'marsh settlement'. Readily confused with/a variant of **Marsden**. Of the variant **Marson** Cottle says: 'The tempting guess of a first-name "*Mary*"'s son" is virtually impossible – Mary was a very rare name in mediaeval England, as if too good for mere mortal girls'.

Martel(l) O/N/F Occupational term for a maker or user of hammers OF or a nickname for a person with a strong, hammer-like personality (compare **Malet**); or a variant of **Martin**. **Martel(l)** and its variants are also popular surnames within continental Europe.

Marten(s), *see* Martin.

Martin F From a first-name, ultimately from Latin *Martinus* (from *Mars*, the pagan God of war). A popular name in many European countries thanks to *St Martin* of Tours, one of the greatest apostles of the West; or from the place-name *Martin* in several counties OE 'boundary settlement' (compare **Marton**). **Martyn** is a Cornwall/Devon variant, but Cottle has his own views on a related topic: '*Martin* used as a first-name is nowadays often spelt affectedly as *Martyn*, which is to be deplored'. **Martel(l)** can be a double diminutive form (but see **Martel**). **Martens** (very scarce, Co Durham), **Martins** (Norfolk) and **Martinson** (Lincs) are 'son of *Martin*'. **Martin** is a very common and widespread surname, while **Marten** is mainly found in south-east England. The 1841 census for Warminster, Wilts, includes the name of a thirty-year-old man whose name (with more than a touch of *lèse-majesté*) was '*Thomas Alias Christ* Martin'.

Martindale P Place-name in Westmd, Latin and OE '*Martin*'s valley'. Strongest in Lancs. *Sir Gabriel Martindale (1734/5-1831), also know as Martindall and Martindell, an army officer in the East India Company, was born in India, of a family said to have its roots in Worcs.*

Martland, *see* **Markland**.

Martlew, *see* **Marklew**.

Martley P Place-name in Worcs OE 'marten (weasel) wood/clearing', which was *Markleghe* in 1234, so the surname **Markley** is probably a variant; for such a spelling variation (-*k*- and -*t*-), compare **Markland/Martland** and **Marklew/Martlew**. Martley is mainly found in Lancs, **Markley** in Northants and Warwicks.

Marton P Place-name in several counties (nine in Yorks) OE 'place by a mere/lake', though the first element may sometimes be OE 'boundary' (compare **Martin**). Chiefly a WRYorks surname.

Martyn, *see* **Martin**.

Martyr N Nickname for a weasel-like person OF *martre* (compare the [pine-] *marten*), spelt so as to make it look infinitely nobler. A scarce surname, with a presence in Berks, Kent and Surrey.

Marvel(l) N/P Nickname for a person considered to be miraculous/marvellous in some way (appearance? accomplishments?) OF *merveille*, or used ironically for an utterly mundane person. Or from one of a number of places called *Merville* in France, including one in Nord OF 'smaller settlement' and one in Calvados, the first element of which is probably derived from a Germanic first-name element. Strongest in WRYorks in both spellings. *Andrew Marvell (1621–1678), though he was a Member of Parliament for Hull, ERYorks, the place of his upbringing, is best remembered as a fine poet. His father, Andrew Marvell, senior (c.1584–1641), had been born at Meldreth, Cambs, where the family had lived for several generations.*

Marvin, *see* **Mervin**.

Marwick P Place-name in the Orkneys ON 'sea/lake/marsh bay', and an Orcadian surname. *James Marwick, born in Edinburgh, Scotland, in 1862, was the son of Sir James David Marwick, an Orcadian who had once held the office of town clerk of both Glasgow and Edinburgh. In 1897 James Marwick and Roger Mitchell, formerly fellow students at Glasgow University, established an accountancy business in New York City; following several mergers over the years, KPMG (Klynveld, Peat, Marwick and Goerdeler) was created in the first mega-merger of accountancy firms, making it one of the so-called 'Big Eight'.*

Marwood P/N Place-name in Co Durham OE 'bigger wood' (compare *more*, Scots *mair*), in Devon OE 'boundary wood' and in Kent OE '?*Meora*'s enclosure'; or a nickname for someone able to cast the 'evil eye' on his enemies OF. Chiefly a surname of the north and north-east of England, but with a presence in Devon and elsewhere. *The public executioner William Marwood (1820–1883), the inventor of the 'long drop' method of dispatching his hapless customers, was born in Horncastle, Lincs.*

Mascall/Maskall/Maskell, *see* **Marshall**.

Maskery/Maskrey O Occupational term for a butcher OF (compare the word *massacre*). Strongest in Derbys and Staffs in both spellings.

Maslen/Maslin F/O From the mediaeval first-name *Masselin* OF from Germanic, sometimes used as a diminutive of *Matthew*, or from a feminine equivalent, *Mazelina*, orginally a diminutive of *Matilda* (see **Maud**); or possibly an occupational term for a maker of maplewood bowls OF. Strongest in Wilts in both spellings.

Mason/Masson O Occupational term for a (stone-)mason OF. A surname found throughout the United Kingdom, as masons themselves once were. The family name of the Barons Blackford. Norman spellings of the surname include: **Machen**, **Machin** and **Machon**, all strong in Yorks, together with **Meacham** (Staffs/Worcs), **Meacheam** (very scarce, Warwicks), **Meachem** (Staffs), **Meachim** (scarce, southwest England), **Meachin** (Chesh/Lancs), **Meecham** (Gloucs/Somerset, also Lancs) and **Meechem** (very scarce, Devon/Somerset). **Machent** (with a parasitic -*t*, as in *varmint* [*vermin*]), much scarcer, can be found in Derbys and Notts. **Masson** is chiefly an Aberdeenshire surname. See also **Musson**.

Massey/Massie F/P A diminutive of **Matthew**; or from one of a number of places in northern France, named from the Gallo-Roman first-name *Maccius*, with the addition of a local suffix. The surname/byname of Hamo **de Masci**, who in 1086 held *Dunham Massey*, Chesh, was derived from a Normandy place-name. Readily confused with/a variant of **Macey/Macy** (see **Mace**) and **Maisey**. **Massey** is strongest in Lancs, **Massie** in Aberdeenshire, Scotland.

Massingham P Place-names *Great* and *Little Massingham* in Norfolk OE 'homestead of *Mæssa*'s people'. A scarce Hants/Kent/Sussex surname.

Masson, *see* **Mason**.

Master(s) O/N Occupational term for someone who was a master at his craft OF, or who lived and/or worked at the house of a school master/trade master; or a nickname for a person who behaved as if he were master of all he surveyed. In Scotland the elder sons of Barons were called 'Master', as in R. L. Stevenson's novel *The Master of Ballantrae*.

Matchett, *see* **Madge**.

Mather O Occupational term for a mower OE (compare the word *aftermath*), one who reaped hay. Principally a Lancs surname. *In 1635 Richard Mather (1596–1669), who was born in Lowton, Lancs, decided to emigrate to Boston, Massachusetts, where he became a Congregational minister, thus establishing a Mather dynasty in the colony. Richard's son Increase Mather (1639–1723) followed in his father's footsteps as a minister and became president of Harvard College in 1685, and Increase's son Cotton Mather (1663–1728), a polymath who was considered to be the widest-read man in English America, famously became involved in New England witchcraft trials.*

Matherson/Matheson/Mathew/Mathews/Mathewson/Mathias/Mathieson/Matkin, *see* **Matthew**.

Matlock P Place-name in Derbys OE 'moot-oak, an oak where meetings are held'. A scarce surname, mainly found in Leics.

Maton, *see* **Matthew**.

Matravers, *see* **Maltravers**.

Matte(r)son/Matson, *see* **Matthew**.

Matthew/Mathew/Mat(t)hias F From the ME first-name *Mathew*, originally Hebrew *Matityahu* ('gift of God'). The Authorized Version of the Bible uses *Matthew* for the publican and the Greek/Latin *Matthias* for the thirteenth Apostle, but the two forms have become intermingled. **Mathew** and **Matthew** are found chiefly in Aberdeenshire and Angus, Scotland, while **Mathias** and **Matthias**, both Welsh surnames, belong to Pembrokeshire and Denbighshire respectively. Double diminutive forms include: **Matkin** (Derbys, Lincs), **Maton** (Hants, Wilts), **Mattin** (Suffolk), **Maycock** (Northants, Warwicks), **Mayhew** (Suffolk) and **Mayo** (chiefly Gloucs, though it is also the name of an Irish county). Patronymic forms, some featuring diminutives/double diminutives, include: **Mather-**

son (a form of **Matheson**, chiefly found in Lancs, and sometimes used as a variant of **McMathan**), **Matheson** (Inverness, and Ross and Cromarty, Scotland), **Mathews** and **Matthews** (widespread in England and Wales), **Mathewson** (Angus and Fifeshire, Scotland), **Mathieson** (Lanarkshire, Scotland), **Matson** (Kent), **Matterson** (WRYorks), **Matteson** (Lancs), **Matthewson** (Northd), **Mattinson** (Cumbd and Lancs) and **Mattison** (Lancs). See also **Mace, Madison, Makin, Maslen, Massey** and **May.**

Matthews(on)/Matthias/Mattin(son)/Mattison, see Matthew.

Mattock(s), see Maddock.

Maud(e)/Mault/Mo(u)ld/Mole/Moule/Moull/Moult/Mowle(s) F/N/O/T/P From a ME (from Germanic) female first-name *Ma(ha)lt/Maud/Mauld*, a diminutive of *Matilda* ('strength-battle') – King Henry I's daughter was known as both *Matilda* and *Maud*; or a nickname for a bald man OE. In some spellings, surnames in this group could alternatively be derived from an occupational term for a maltster OE. **Mole** can be a variant belonging to this group, but could be a nickname for a person with a distinguishing mole or blemish OE, and since Bardsley found two men referred to as *de Mol(e)* in Gloucs in the late thirteenth century, a topographical/place-name could also be a point of origin in some cases. The use of the word *mole* to mean a jetty, causeway, embankment OF is probably of too recent a date to be relevant here. See also **Maddy, Maslen, Mowat, Mudd, Mule** and **Till. Maude** is the family name of the Viscounts Hawarden. *Edward Walker ('Ted') Moult (1926–1986), the much-loved radio and television personality, was also a farmer in Ticknall, Derbys, where he originated the concept of 'pick your own strawberries'.*

Maudling F From a ME first-name *Maudeleyn*, from the Greek *Magdalene* ('woman from *Magdala* [on the Sea of Galilee]'). Hence, from St Mary *Magdalen*'s tears, the adjective *maudlin* (the pronunciation still used by *Magdalen* College, Oxford and Mag-

dalene College, Cambridge). See also **Maddy.** *Reginald Maudling (1917–1979), Conservative party politician and former Chancellor of the Exchequer and Home Secretary, was born in North Finchley, London.*

Maud(e)sley, see Mawdesley.

Mauger/Major F From the Norman first-name *Malg(i)er/Maug(i)er*, from Germanic 'council spear'. **Major** is perhaps a surprising variant. **Mauger** is a Channel Islands surname; **Major** is widespread throughout England. *The former British Prime Minister Sir John Major was born in 1943 in Carshalton, Surrey, the son of a music hall performer by the name of Tom Major-Ball, who at one time ran a business selling garden gnomes. John Major used his middle Christian name 'Roy' until the early 1980s.*

Maughan/Maugham P/F Scots: place-name in Lanarkshire, once called *Machan*, now known as *Dalserf*, Gaelic; '(river) plain'; Irish: Anglicized from Gaelic O' [descendant of] **Mochain** ('early, in good time'), *see also* **Mahon**; Welsh: from one of two place-names in Monmouthshire: *(St) Maughan* OW *Llanfocha* 'church of *St Mochan*' or *Machen* OW 'place of *Cain*'. **Maughan** and **Maugham** are both strong in Co Durham and Northd. *The author and playwright (William) Somerset Maugham [pronounced 'Morn'] (1874–1965) was born into a family known for producing eminent lawyers, which had its male-line roots in the north of England.*

Maul(e)/Maull, see Malin.

Mault, see Maud.

Maund P Place-name in Herefords OW 'plain/rocks'. A Herefords/Salop/Worcs surname.

Maunder, see Mander.

Maundrell/Maundrill Surnames of unknown origin. The word *mandrel/maundrel* is well established as a dialect term for a miner's pick, but this is one putative source for such surnames which Cottle discounts. He is equally unimpressed by other possibilities, such as: 'The superb baboon *man-*

drill or a lost -*hill* place-name or even a mysterious ME measure of capacity *mandrel*'. Instead, he offers one outside possibility: '*Maunder* "beggar" OF (or Romany), though first instanced late (1609), may have had a diminutive form, plus OF suffix -*el*'. Others have suggested a first-name origin: Old German *Mandel* or OE *Man(n)* **Maundrell** is commonest in Somerset and Wilts, **Maundrill** (scarce) in both Somerset and WRYorks.

Maunsell, *see* **Mansell**.

Maurice, *see* **Morris**.

Maw F/N/T From the first-name *Mawa* OE ?*moew* 'sea-mew' or ?*mawan* 'to mow'; or a nickname for someone who was a relative, by blood or by marriage, of an important person ME *maugh/maw* (compare **Hitchmough** (under **Richard**) and **Watmore/Watmough**); or a dweller at a meadow ?OE *mawe*. Strongest in Lincs and Yorks. Readily confused with/a variant of **Mew**.

Mawby, *see* **Maltby**.

Mawditt N Nickname for a badly educated person OF, from Latin. A scarce Gloucs surname.

Mawd(e)sley/Maud(e)sley P Place-name *Mawdesley* in Lancs OE '*Maud*'s wood/clearing'. A Lancs surname in all spellings.

Mawle, *see* **Malin**.

Maxey P Place-name in Northants, Irish and OE '*Maccus*'s island'. Strongest in Beds and Lincs.

Maxted P Place-name in Kent OE 'dungy/filthy site', and a Kent surname.

Maxton P Scots: from a place-name in Roxburghshire, Gaelic and OE '*Maccus*'s farm'.

Maxwell P Scots: place-name in Roxburghshire, Gaelic and OE '*Maccus*'s spring/stream'. *The former publisher, Member of Parliament, military hero and fraudster (Ian) Robert Maxwell (1923–1991) was born Jan Ludvok Hoch in Czechoslovakia, but adopted his new name during the Second World War.*

May(es) N/F Nickname for a youth, girl, virgin, demure young man ME, or from some connexion (birth/baptism?) with the month of May OF, from Latin; or from a diminutive of **Mayhew** (see **Matthew**). **Mease** may be a variant of **Mayes**, or of **Meese**. See also **Mee**.

Maybank N Apparently a nickname composed of *may* OF 'ill, badly' and *bank* (origin unknown: '*bench*'?). A Norman family named *Malbedeng, Malbeenc, Melbanc* (1084/1086), had land in *Clifton Maybank*, Dorset, and in *Nantwich*, Chesh. Chiefly a Kent/Surrey surname.

Maycock, *see* **Matthew**.

Mayer(s)/Meyer(s) O/N Occupational term for a mayor OF, or a nickname for someone who behaved like one. Also a popular German surname, brought to Britain by Ashkenazi Jews. Readily confused with/a variant of **Myer**.

Mayes, *see* **May**.

Mayfield P Place-name in Sussex and Staffs OE 'field with mayweed/madder'. Strongest in Notts.

Mayhew, *see* **Matthew**.

Maykin, *see* **Makin**.

Mayland P Place-name in Essex OE '(at) the island', where the -*m*- of the dative of the definite article after a lost preposition has become wrongly attached. A scarce surname, found in both Middx and WRYorks.

Maynard F From a Germanic first-name *Mainard* ('strength-hardy'); compare **Mayne**. Chiefly found in south-east England.

Mayne/Main(e) F/N/P From a Germanic first-name *Maino/Meino*, found as the first element in many compound names, and meaning 'strength' (compare '*might and main*'); or a nickname for a large person, Anglo-Norman French *magne/maine*, from Latin *magnus*; or applied to a person whose hands were distinctive in some way OF *main* ('hand'); or from a French place-name or region name, such as *Maine* or *Mayenne*.

Maynell, *see* Meynell.

Mayo, *see* Matthew.

McAdam F Scots Gaelic: **Mac Adaim** 'son of *Adam*'. *John Loudon McAdam (1756–1836), the builder and administrator of roads after whom* tar macadam *is named, was born in Ayr, Scotland.*

McAlaster, *see* McAllister.

McAleese F Irish: **Mac Giolla Iosa** 'son of the servant/devotee of Jesus'.

McAleevy F Irish: 'son of *Donlevy*'.

McAlery, *see* McChlery.

McAllister/McAl(l)aster F Scots Gaelic: **Mac Alasdair** 'son of *Alasdair/Alexander*'.

McAlonie F Scots Gaelic: **Mac Gill Onfhaidh** 'son of the servant of Storm'.

McAlpin(e) F Scots Gaelic: **Mac Ailpein** 'son of *Alpin* (of unknown meaning)'.

McAndrew F Scots Gaelic: **Mac Aindreis** 'son of *Andrew*'.

McAra F Scots Gaelic: **Mac Ara** 'son of Charioteer'. A Perthshire surname.

McArdle F Irish: **Mac Ardghail** 'son of Height-Valour'.

McArthur/McArtney/McCartney F Scots Gaelic: 'son of *Arthur*'. **McCarter** is a misspelt variant.

McAsgill/McAskie/McCaskie F Scots Gaelic: **Mac Asgail** 'son of *Askell/Asketill* ("sacrificial cauldron of the *Anses*/Gods")'.

McAteer, *see* McIntyre.

McAulay/McAuley/McAuliffe F Scots Gaelic and Irish: forms of ON 'son of *Olaf* ("Relic of the gods")'. A Hebridean and Irish group.

McAuslan(d)/McAuslane/McCausland F Scots Gaelic and Irish: **Mac Ausalain** 'son of *Absalom*'.

McAvaddy F Irish: **Mac an Mhadaidh** 'son of ?Dog'.

McAvoy/McEvoy F Irish: Mac Fhiodhb-huilde 'son of ?Woodman' or Mac Giolla Bhuide 'son of Yellow-haired Lad'. Compare **McKelvey**.

McBain/McBean F Scots Gaelic: **Mac Bheathain** 'son of *Betahan/Bean* ("Life")'. Compare **McBeth** and **McIlvain**, and *see also* **Bean**.

McBe(a)th F Scots Gaelic: **Mac Beatha** 'son of Life'.

McBradden F Scots Gaelic: **Mac Bradain** 'son of Salmon'.

McBrayne F Scots Gaelic: **Mac a' Bhriuthainn** 'son of the judge'.

McBride F Irish: **Mac Giolla Bhrighde** 'son of the devotee of (Saint) *Bridget*'; compare **Gilbride**.

McCabe F Irish: **Mac Caba** 'son of Cap/Hood'.

McCafferty/McCafferky F Irish: **Mac Eachmharcaigh** 'son of Horse Rider/Knight'. Readily confused with/a variant of **McGaffrey**.

McCaffray/McCaffrey, *see* McGaffrey.

McCaig F Scots Gaelic: **Mac Thaidhg** 'son of the poet/philosopher'.

McCall/McKail F Irish: **Mac Cathmhaoil** 'son of Battle Chief'.

McCallum F Scots Gaelic: **Mac Giolla Cholium** 'son of the devotee of (Saint) *Columba*' (see also **Coleman**).

McCambridge F Scots Gaelic: **Mac Ambrois** 'son of *Ambrose*', 'fatuously respelt' (Cottle).

McCann F Irish: **Mac Cana** 'son of Wolfhound'.

McCarlich, *see* McCarlish.

McCarlish/McCarlich F Scots Gaelic: **Mac Thearlaich** 'son of *Charles*'.

McCarter, *see* McArthur.

McCarthy F Irish: **Mac Carthaigh** 'son of *Craddock* ("Amiable")'; see **Cradock**. A very common Irish surname, also found in the form **Carthy**.

McCartney, *see* McArthur.

McCaskie, *see* McAsgill.

McCausland, *see* McAuslan.

McCaw F Scots Gaelic and Irish: **Mac Adhaimh** 'son of *Adam*'.

McChlery/McAlery/McCleary/ McCleery F Irish: **Mac Giolla Arraith/ Mac an Chleirigh**; Scots Gaelic: **M'a'Chleirich** 'son of the clerk/cleric'. *See also* **Clery** and **Clark**. McChlery is said to be the oldest hereditary surname in Europe.

McChruiter, *see* McWhirter.

McClacher F Scots Gaelic: **Mac Clachair** 'son of the mason'. See also **Clachar**.

McClan(n)achan/McClanaghan F Scots Gaelic: **Mac Gillie Onchon** 'son of the devotee of (the Irish Saint) *Onchu* ("Wolfhound")'.

McCleary/McCleery, *see* McChlery.

McCleish, *see* McLeish.

McClellan(d) F Scots Gaelic: **Mac Gille Fhinnein** 'son of the devotee of (Saint) *Fillan* ("Wolf")'.

McClements, *see* McLamont.

McClenaghan, *see* McClanachan.

McClintock F Scots Gaelic: 'son of the devotee of (Saint) *Findan* (a diminutive of *Finn*, "white")'.

McCloy F Scots Gaelic: **Mac Lughaidh** 'son of *Lewis*'.

McClumpha F Scots Gaelic: **Mac Gille Iomchadha** 'son of the devotee of (Saint) *Imchad*'.

McClung F Scots Gaelic: **Mac Luinge** 'son of *Long* (ship)'.

McComb(e)/McCombie/McComie/ McOmie F Scots Gaelic: **Mac Thom** 'son of *Thomas*'.

McConachie/McConachy/ McConagh(e)y, *see* McDonaugh.

McConnal/McConnel(l) F Scots Gaelic: **Mac Dhomhnuill** 'son of *Domhnall*' (*see also* **McDonald**); Irish: **Mac Conaill** 'son of *Conall*'. Also appears in the forms **Connell** and **O'Connell**.

McCorkill/McCorkle, *see* McCorquodale

McCormack F Scots Gaelic and Irish: **Mac Cormaic** 'son of *Cormaic* ("Chariot lad")', the name of a sixth-century seafaring saint.

McCorquodale/McCorkill/McCorkle F Scots Gaelic/Irish and ON: **Mac Corcadail** ('son of *Thurkettle/Thorketill/Torquil*'). See **Thurkettle**.

McCosh F Scots Gaelic: **Mac Coise** 'son of the footsoldier/courier'.

McCoy, *see* McKay.

McCreath, *see* McRaith.

McCrimmon F Scots Gaelic and ON: **Mac Ruimein** 'son of *Hrothmundr* ("Famed protector")'. **Grim(m)ond** is a Perthshire variant. *Joseph ('Jo') Grimond (1913–1993), leader of the Liberal Party from 1956 to 1967, was born in St Andrews, Fife, Scotland.*

McCrindell/McCrindle F Scots Gaelic: **Mac Raonuill** 'son of *Ronald/Ronald*'.

McCristal/McCrystal F Scots Gaelic: 'son of *Christopher*'.

McCrossan F Scots Gaelic and Irish: **Mac an Chrosain** 'son of the rhymer'.

McCruddan/McCrudden F Irish: **Mac Rodain** 'son of *Rodan* ("Spirited")'.

McCrum(m) F Scots Gaelic: **Mac Chruim** 'son of *Crum* ("the bent one")'.

McCrystal, *see* McCristal.

McCulloch F Scots Gaelic and Irish: **Mac Cullach** 'son of Wild Boar' or **Mac Cu-Uladh** 'son of Hound of Ulster'.

McCurtin/McKeurtan F Scots Gaelic: **Mac Artan** 'son of *Artan*' (diminutive of the old Irish first-name *Art*).

McCusker F Irish and ON: **Mac Oscair** 'son of *Asgeirr* ("God-Spear/Champion")'.

McCutcheon F Scots Gaelic: **Mac Uisdein** 'son of *Hutcheon*'.

McDade, *see* **McDaid**.

McDaid/McDade/McDevitt F Irish and Hebrew: **Mac Daibheid** 'son of *David*'.

McDa(i)rmid/McDearmid/McDermaid/McDerment/McDermid/McDermit/McDermot(t) F Scots Gaelic and Irish: **Mac Dhiarmaid(e)** 'son of *Dermid* ("Unenvious")'.

McDevitt, *see* **McDaid**.

McDonald F Scots Gaelic: **Mac Dhomhnull** (pronounced '*Mac Oonil*') 'son of *Donald*'. George F. Black maintains that 'properly speaking there is no such surname as **Mac-Donald**. MacDhomhnuill means "son of (a particular) *Donald*"; all others of the name are simply **Domhnullach**, "one of the *Donald*s"'. Be that as it may, **MacDonald** was the second commonest surname (after **Smith**) in Scotland in 1858, dropping to third (after **Smith** and **Brown**) by 1958. *See also* **McConnal**. **McDonnell**, a variant of **MacDonald** borne by a prominent Irish family with Argyllshire origins, is the family name of the Earls of Antrim.

McDonaugh/McConachie/McConachy/McConagh(e)y/McDonough F Scots Gaelic: **Mac Donnchaidh** 'son of *Duncan*'. Donaghy is an Ulster variant of **McDonaugh**.

McDonnell, *see* **McDonald**.

McDonough, *see* **McDonaugh**.

McDougal(l)/McDowall/McDowell F Scots Gaelic and Irish: **Mac Dhughaill** 'son of *Dougal*'.

McDuff(ie) F Scots Gaelic: **Mac Dubh**, 'son of *Dubh/Duff(ie)* ("Dark/Black")'. Compare **Duff**, **Gilduff**. **McDuffie** was also corrupted to **McFee** and **McPhee**.

McEachan/McGachan/McGachen F Scots Gaelic: **Mac Eachainn** 'son of Horse Lord'.

McElder(r)y F Irish: **MacGiolla Dorcha**, 'son of the dark youth'. The version of the surname with a double -*r*- is perhaps preferable, since it indicates the correct stress on the second -*e*-.

McElfrish F Scots Gaelic: **M'Gille Bhris** 'son of the devotee of (Saint) *Bricius*'.

McEl(l)istrim/McEl(l)istrum F Irish: **Mac Allastrum** 'son of *Alexander*'.

McElligott F Irish: **Mac Uileagoid** 'son of *William*' (using a double diminutive).

McElroy, *see* **McIlroy**.

McElwee, *see* **McKelvey**.

McEvoy, *see* **McAvoy**.

McEwan/McEwen/McEwing F Scots Gaelic: **Mac Eoghainn** 'son of *Ewan/Ewen*'.

McFadden/McFadye(a)n/McFadze(a)n F Scots Gaelic: **Mac Phaidein/Phaidin** 'son of *Patrick*'. The -*z*- in **McFadze(a)n** represents the obsolete letter *yogh* (shaped like a '*3*' and sounding like *gh*); compare **Dalziel** and **Menzies**.

McFail/McFall, *see* **McPhail**.

McFarlan(d)/McFarlane/McPartland F Scots Gaelic and Irish: **Mac Pharlain/Pharthalain** 'son of *Parthalan (Bartholomew)*'.

McFarquhar F Scots Gaelic: **Mac Fearchair** 'son of *Farquhar* ("Man-Dear")'.

McFate/McFeat F Scots Gaelic: **Mac Phaid** 'son of *Pate (Patrick)*'.

McFee F Scots Gaelic: **MacDhubhshith**, 'son of *Dhubhshith* ("Black-Peace")', which George F. Black calls 'one of the oldest and most interesting personal names we possess'. **McPhee** can be a variant, but see **McDuffie** (under **McDuff**).

McFetridge F Scots Gaelic: **Mac Phetruis/Pheadrius** 'son of *Peadrus (Peter)*'.

McGachan/McGachen, *see* **McEachan**.

McGaffrey/McCaffray/McCaffrey F Scots Gaelic/Irish and ON: **Mac Gafraidh** 'son of *Godfrey* ("God-Wise")'. Readily confused with/a variant of **McCafferty/McCaf-ferky**.

McGarrigle F Irish: **Mag Fhearrgail** 'son of *Fearghal* ("Man-Valour")'.

McGee/Magee F Irish: **Mac Aoidh** 'son of *Aodh*' (rendering *Hugh*). Compare **McKay**, **McHugh** and **McKee**. **McGhee** and **McGhie** are Scottish forms.

McGenis/Magennis/Maginnis/ McGuin(n)ess/McKinness F Irish: **Mag Aonghusa/Aonghuis** 'son of *Angus*'. **McInnes** is a Scots form, and **McNeice** (of which **Mannix** is a variant) an Ulster form. See also **Guiness**. *The writer (Frederick) Louis MacNeice (1907–1963) was born in Belfast, Northern Ireland, to a clergyman father who was a Galway man.*

McGeorge, *see* **McIndeor**.

McGhee/McGhie, *see* **McGee**.

McGibbon/McKibbin/McKibbon F Scots Gaelic: 'son of *Gibbon*'. See **Gibbon** (under **Gilbert**). **Cubbin** is a Manx variant.

McGilchrist F Scots Gaelic: **Mac Gille Chriosd**, Irish: **Mac Giolla Chriost** 'son of *Gilchrist* ("Devotee of Christ")'.

McGill Scots Gaelic: **Mac an Ghoill** 'son of the stranger/lowlander'; Irish: **Mac an Ghaill** 'son of the stranger' or **Mac Giolla** 'son of the servant'.

McGillivray F Scots Gaelic: **Mac Gille Bhrath**, Irish: **Mac Giolla Bhraith** 'son of Servant of Judgment'.

McGilp, *see* **McKillop**.

McGlashan F Scots Gaelic and Irish: **Mac Glasain** 'son of *Glasan* ("Grey/Sallow Lad")'.

McGoldrick F Irish: **Mac Ualghairg** 'son of *Ualgharg* ("?Proud-Fierce")'.

McGorman F Irish: **Mac Gormain** 'son of *Gorman*'.

McGovern F Irish: **Mag Shamhr(adh)ain** 'son of *Samhradhan* ("Summer")'.

McGowan/McGowing/McGown F Scots Gaelic: **Mac Gobhann**, Irish: **Mac Gabhann** 'son of the smith'. Also appears in the forms **Gowan(s)** and **Gowen**.

McGrath, *see* **McRaith**.

McGraw, *see* **McRaith**.

McGregor F Scots Gaelic: **Mac Griogair** 'son of *Gregory*'.

McGuinness, *see* **McGenis**.

McGuire/Maguire F Irish: **Mag Uidhir** 'son of *Odhar* ("Sallow")'.

McHardie/McHardy F Scots Gaelic: **Mac C(h)ardaidh** 'son of Sloe'.

McHendrie/McHenry F Scots Gaelic: **Mac Eanruig** 'son of *Henry*'.

McHugh F Irish: **Mac Aodha** 'son of *Aodh*' (rendering *Hugh*). Compare **McGee**, **McKay** and **McKee**.

McHutchin F Scots Gaelic: 'son of *Hutchin*'.

McIlraith/McIlwraith/McIlwrick F Scots Gaelic: **Mac Gille Riabhaich**, Irish: **Mac Giolla Riabhaigh** 'son of Brindled Lad'.

McIlroy/McElroy F Scots Gaelic and Irish: **Mac Giolla Rua** 'son of Red-haired Lad'.

McIlvain(e)/McIlwain(e) F Scots Gaelic: **Mac Gille Bheathain** 'son of the devotee of (Saint) *Beathan* ("Life")' – compare **McBain**, **Melvin**. Irish: **Mac Giolla Bhain** 'son of White/Fair Lad'.

McIlvany/McIlvenna/McIlwain(e) F Irish: **Mac Giolla Mheana** 'son of *Mhean* ("Gentle")'. Readily confused with/a variant of **McIlveen**, **McIlvain**.

McIlveen F Irish: **Mac Giolla Mhin** 'son of the servant of *Min* ("Gentle")'. Readily confused with/a variant of **McIlvany**, **McIlvain**.

McIlvenna/McIlwain(e), *see* **McIlvany**.

McIlwraith/McIlwrick, *see* **McIlraith**.

McIndeor/McGeorge/McKinder/ McKindewer F Scots Gaelic: **Macindeoir** 'son of the *dewar* (pilgrim/stranger)'. Compare **Dewar**. **McJarrow** and **McJerrow** are very scarce variants.

McInerny F Irish: **Mac an Airchinnigh** 'son of the *erenagh* (steward of church lands)'.

McInnes, *see* **McGenis**.

McInroy F Scots Gaelic: **Mac an Ruaidh** 'son of Red Man' or *Iain ruaidh* 'Red John/John Roy'. The **McInroys** were a sept of Clan **Donnchaidh** or **Robertson**.

McIntosh/McKintosh F Scots Gaelic: **Mac an Toisich** 'son of the chieftain'. **Toshach** and **Toshack** are shorter variants; the prime minister of Eire is referred to as the *Taoiseach*, and in Welsh *tywysog* is 'Prince'. *Mackintosh waterproofs were invented by Charles Macintosh [sic] (1766–1843), who was born in Glasgow, as was his namesake Charles Rennie Mackintosh (1868–1928), the art nouveau architect, designer and painter... John Toshack, the Welsh international footballer and football manager, was born in Cardiff, South Wales, in 1949.*

McIntyre/McAteer F Scots Gaelic and Irish: **Mac an t-saoir** 'son of the carpenter/mason'. **Tear(e)** is a Manx version of the same surname.

McIver/McIvor, *see* **Ivor**.

McJarrow/McJerrow, *see* **McIndeor**.

McKail, *see* **McCall**.

McKay/McKie F Scots Gaelic and Irish: **Mac Aodha** 'son of *Aodh*' (rendering *Hugh*). Commonly pronounced '*Mac-eye*'. Compare **McGee**, **McHugh** and **McKee**. **McKay** is the family name of the Earls of Inchcape and the Barons Reay. **McCoy** is an Irish variant. *The origins of the phrase 'The real McCoy' (the 'real thing') would seem to be lost in obscurity, unless it be a reference to Norman Selby, a succesful American boxer (born in 1873), who had changed his name to Charles 'Kid' McCoy but wished to distinguish himself from a lesser fighter called Al McCoy. But long before that a well-known brand of Scotch whisky had been referred to as 'The real MacKay' (pronounced 'Mac-eye').*

McKechnie F Scots Gaelic: **Mac Eacharna** 'son of *Eachann/Eachdonn* ("Horse")'. See also **Hector**.

McKee F Irish: **Mac Aoidh** 'son of *Aodh*' (rendering *Hugh*). Compare **McGee**, **McHugh** and **McKay**. Some individuals called **Mac an Chaoich** (Irish: 'son of Blind One') are known to have changed their surname to **McKee**.

McKeith F Scots Gaelic: **Mac Shithich** 'son of *Sithech* ("Wolf")'.

McKellar F Scots Gaelic: **Mac Ealair** 'son of *Hilary*'.

McKelvey/McKelvie F Scots Gaelic: **Mac Shealbhaigh** 'son of *Sealbhach* (*Edmond*)'; Irish: **Mac Giolla Bhuidhe** 'son of Yellow-haired Lad' (compare **McAvoy**). **McKelvey**, an Ulster surname, is ten times as common as **McKelvie**. **McElwee** is possibly a variant.

McKendrick F Irish: **Mac Eanraic** 'son of *Eanrac* ("Home-Rule")'. See also **Kenrick**.

McKenna F Scots Gaelic: **Mac Cionaodha**, Irish: **Mac Cionaoith** 'son of *Cionaodh* ("?Respect-*Aodh* [pagan god of fire]")'. See also **Kenny**.

McKenzie F Scots Gaelic: **Mac Coinnich** 'son of *Coinneach* ("Comely")'. Family name of the Earls of Cromartie and the Barons Amulree.

McKeone F Irish and Hebrew/Celtic (from Greek) *Mac Eoghain/Eoin* 'son of *John/Owen*'.

McKeown, *see* **McOwen**.

McKeurtan, *see* **McCurtin**.

McKibbin/McKibbon, *see* **McGibbon**.

McKie, *see* **McKay**.

McKillop/McGilp F Scots Gaelic: **Mac Fhilib** 'son of *Philip*'.

McKim(mie) F Scots Gaelic: **Mac Shim** 'son of *Sim(on)*'.

McKinder/McKindewer, *see* **McIndeor**.

McKinlay/McKinley F Scots Gaelic: **Mac Fhionnlaigh** 'son of *Finlay*'.

McKinnawe F Irish: **Mac Conshnamha** 'son of Swim-Hound'.

McKinness, *see* **McGenis**.

McKinnon F Scots Gaelic: **Mac Fhionghuin** 'son of Fair-born/Beloved Son'.

McKintosh, *see* **McIntosh**.

McKissack/McKissock F Scots Gaelic: **Mac Iosaig** 'son of *Isaac*'.

McLachlan F Scots Gaelic: **Mac Lachlainn** 'son of *Lachlan*'. See also **McLaughlin** and **McLoughlin**. *Victor McLaglen (1886–1959), famous for portraying Irishmen in films directed by John Ford, was born in London, the son of an Anglican clergyman who later became a bishop. His son, Andrew V. McLaglen became a noteable film director.*

McLaine, *see* **McLean**.

McLamon(t) F Scots Gaelic, from ON: **Mac Laomuinn** 'son of *Lamond/Lamont* ("law giver")'. See also **Lamont**. **McClements** is an odd corruption.

McLane, *see* **McLean**.

McLaren F Scots Gaelic: **Mac Labhruinn** 'son of *Laurence*'. Family name of the Barons Aberconway.

McLarty F Irish: **Mac Fhlaith Bheartaich** 'son of Bright Ruler'. See **Flaherty**.

McLaughlin F Irish: **Mac Lachlainn** 'son of *Lachlann*'. See also **McLachlan** and **McLoughlin**.

McLay/McLeay F/O Scots Gaelic: **Mac Dhuinnshleibhe** '?son of Brown Mountain', or *Mac an Leigh* 'son of the physician'; Irish: *Mac Giolla Eain* 'son of *Ean (John)*'.

McLean/McLaine/McLane F Scots Gaelic: **Mac Gille Eoin** 'son of the devotee of (St) John'. Commonly pronounced '*Mac-lane*' in all spellings.

McLeay, *see* **McLay**.

McLehose F Scots Gaelic: **Mac Gille Thomhais** 'son of the devotee of (Saint) *Thomas*'.

McLeish/McCleish F Scots Gaelic: **Mac Gille Iosa** 'son of the devotee of *Jesus*'.

McLennan F Scots Gaelic: **Mac Gill'innein** 'son of the devotee of (Saint) *Finnan*'.

McLeod F Scots Gaelic and ON: **Mac Leoid** 'son of *Ljotr* ("Ugly")'. Pronounced '*McCloud*'.

McLoughlin F Irish version of **McLachlan** (*see also* **McLaughlin**); but also (for a name formerly spelt **O'Melaghlin**): 'descendant of the devotee of (Saint) *Secundinus*'.

McMahon F Irish: **Mac Mathghamhna** 'son of Bear'.

McManus F Irish: **Mac Maghnuis** 'son of *Magnus*'.

McMartin F Scots Gaelic: **Mac Mhartainn/Mhartuinn** 'son of *Martin*'.

McMaster F Scots Gaelic: **Mac a' Mhaighstir** 'son of the master', approximated to the English form, itself from OF. In Scotland, *master* is a courtesy title used for barons' eldest sons and lords' uncles, or for a schoolmaster.

McMathan F Scots Gaelic: **Mac Mathgamhuinn** 'son of Bear'. See also **Matherson** (under **Matthew**).

McMichael F Scots Gaelic: **Mac Micheil** 'son of *Michael*'.

McMillan F Scots Gaelic: **Mac Maolain** 'son of the bald-head/tonsured man'. **Mullan(e)** (readily confused with/a variant of **Mullin**) and **McMullan** are Irish forms. Compare **Mulligan**.

McMinn/McMyn(n) P Scots Gaelic: **Mac Meinn** 'son of *Menzies*'. See **Menzies**.

McMorran F Scots Gaelic: **Mac Mugh-ron** 'son of Seal's Slave'.

McMorrough/McMorrow/(Mc)Murchie/Murchison F Irish: Anglicized form of Gaelic **Mac Murchadha** ('son of Sea Warrior'). Compare **Morrow** and **Murphy**. McMorrough was the name of the royal house of Leinster.

McMullan, *see* **McMillan**.

McMurchie, *see* **McMorrough**.

McMyn(n), *see* **McMinn**.

McNab F Scots Gaelic: **Mac an Aba** 'son of the abbot', 'a somewhat irregular beginning excusable by making the early chiefs *lay* abbots of Glendochart' (Cottle).

McNaboe F Irish: **Mac Anabadha** 'son of *Anabaidh* ("Premature")'.

McNaghten/McNaughton F Scots Gaelic: **Mac Neachdainn** 'son of *Neachdan*' – of uncertain origin, though the name has been linked with that of the Roman sea-god *Neptune*; Hartland Church, Devon, and a chapel in Cheddar Church, Somerset, are dedicated to St *Nectan*. See also **Naughton**. *The McNaughten rules, governing pleas of insanity in English legal cases, take their name from Daniel McNaughten, who was acquitted of murder in 1843.*

McNair F Scots Gaelic: **Mac Iain Uidhir** 'son of sallow *John*', or **Mac an Oighre** 'son of the heir/stranger', Irish **Mac an Mhaoir** 'son of the steward'.

McNally F Irish: **Mac an Fhailghigh** 'son of the poor man'. The **MacNallys** of Ulster are often called **Mac Con Ulaidh** 'son of the Hound of *Ulidia* (Eastern Ulster)'.

McNamara F Irish: **Mac Conmara** 'son of Hound of the Sea'.

McNaughton, *see* **McNaghten**.

McNeice, *see* **McGenis**.

McNevin/McNiven F Irish: **Mac Cnaimhin** 'son of ?bones/thin man' or **Mac Naoimhin** 'son of Saint'. See also **Neven**.

McNic(h)ol F Scots Gaelic: **Mac Neacail** 'son of *Nicol(as)*'.

McNid(d)er F Scots Gaelic: **Mac an Fhigheadair** 'son of the weaver'.

McNiven, *see* **McNevin**.

McNulty F Irish: **Mac an Ultaigh** 'son of the Ulsterman'.

McOmie, *see* **McComb**.

McOmish F Scots Gaelic: **Mac Thomais** 'son of *Thomas*'.

McOwen/McKeown F Scots Gaelic: **Mac Eoghain**, Irish: **Mac Eoghain** (Connacht) or **Mac Eoin** (Ulster) 'son of *Ewan/Owen*

(John)'. Many other variant spellings are known to exist.

McPartland, *see* **McFarlan**.

McPhail/McFail/McFall F Scots Gaelic: **Mac Phail**, Irish: **Mac Phoil** 'son of *Paul*'.

McPhee, *see* **McDuffie** (under **McDuff**) and **McFee**.

McPherson F Scots Gaelic: **Mac a' Phearsoin** 'son of the parson'. Family name of the Barons Strathcarron.

McPhie, *see* **McDuffie** (under **McDuff**).

McQuarrie F Scots Gaelic: **Mac Guaire** 'son of Proud/Noble'.

McQueen F Scots Gaelic: **Mac Shuibhne** 'son of *Suibhne* ("Pleasant")'; or, in Skye, Scots Gaelic and ON: 'son of *Sveinn*' (see **Swain**).

McQuillan/McQuillen F Scots Gaelic: **Mac Cailein**, Irish: **Mac Uighilin/MacCoilin** 'son of *Colin*'.

McQuillen, *see* **McQuillan**.

McQuilly F Scots Gaelic and Irish: **Mac an Choiligh** 'son of Cock'.

McQuistan/McQuisten/McQuistin/McQuiston F Scots Gaelic: **Mac Uisdein** 'son of *Hutchin*'.

McRae, *see* **McRaith**.

McRaith/McCreath/McGrath/McGraw/McRae/McRaw F Scots Gaelic and Irish: *Mag Raith* 'son of *Rath* ("Good Fortune")'.

McRaw, *see* **McRaith**.

McRobb F Scots Gaelic: 'son of *Robert*'.

McRory F Scots Gaelic and Irish: **Mac Ruairidh** 'son of *Ruadhri* ("Red King")'. *Rory* is often used as an equivalent of *Roderick*.

McRuer F Scots Gaelic: **Mac Grudaire** 'son of the brewer'.

McSorley F Scots Gaelic: **Mac Somhairle** 'son of *Summerlad*' (see **Summerland**).

McSporran F Scots Gaelic: **Mac an Sporain** 'son of the purse'.

McTaggart/McTaggert F Scots Gaelic: **Mac an t-Sagairt** 'son of the priest' (though marriage within priests' orders was illegal and invalid after the twelfth century). Compare **McVicar**.

McTaggert, *see* **McTaggart**.

McTague/McTeague/McTigue F Irish: **Mac Taidhg** 'son of *Tighe/Teague* ("Poet/Philosopher")'.

McTavish F Scots Gaelic: **Mac Tamhais** 'son of *Tammas* (Lowlands Scots for *Thomas*)'.

McTeague, *see* **McTague**.

McTigue, *see* **McTague**.

McTurk F Scots Gaelic: **Mac Tairc** 'son of *Torc* ("Boar")'.

McVarish F Scots Gaelic: **Mac Bharrais/Mac Mharais** 'son of *Maurice*'.

McVicar F Scots Gaelic and Latin: **Mac Bhiocair/Mac a'Bhiocair** 'son of the vicar'. Compare **McTaggart**.

McWatters F Scots Gaelic: 'son of *Walter*'. A Caithness surname.

McWhirter/McChruiter F Scots Gaelic: **Mac Chruiteir** 'son of the harper' (often a hereditary office).

McWilliam F Scots Gaelic: **Mac Uilleim** 'son of *William*'.

Meacham/Meacheam/Meachem, *see* **Mason**.

Meacher, *see* **Maher**.

Meachim/Meachin, *see* **Mason**.

Mead(e) T/O Dweller at a meadow OE (the *-e* of **Meade** could indicate the use of a dative after a lost preposition); or an occupational term for a maker or seller of mead, the alcoholic honey beverage OE. **Meade** is the family name of the Earls of Clanwilliam.

Meaden T ?Dweller in the meadows OE, the second element being possibly derived from the dative plural *-um*. Chiefly a West Country surname.

Meadow T Dweller at a meadow OE (from a dative case of OE *moed*). **Meadows** is 'of/at the meadow', not a plural.

Meadows, *see* **Meadow**.

Meager N Nickname for a lean, skinny person OF (compare *meagre*). A surname of the south of England, strong in Cornwall.

Meagher, *see* **Maher**.

Meake, *see* **Meek**.

Meaken/Meakin(g)(s), *see* **Makin**.

Meaney/Mooney F Irish: Anglicized form of Gaelic **O'** [descendant of] **Maonaigh** ('Rich').

Mear(e)/Mere T/P Dweller by a pond OE *mere*, or by a boundary OE *(ge)moere*; or from one of a number of places called *Meare/Mere*, found in several counties, with one or other of these meanings. **Mear(e)s** is 'of/at the pool/boundary'.

Meares, *see* **Mear**.

Mearns P Scots: place-name in Renfrewshire, Scots Gaelic *maiorne* (describing the province of a *mair*/beadle); or from a region called *The Mearns*, more or less identical with the county of Kincardine. The surname is strongest in Aberdeenshire.

Mears, *see* **Mear**.

Mease, *see* **May** and **Meese**.

Measham P Place-name in Leics OE 'homestead on the river *Mease*'. Mainly a Derbys surname. Compare **Measures**. **Messum** (scarce, found in Hants/Surrey) would appear to be a variant.

Measures Surname scholars are at sixes and sevens on this surname. Weekley suggests that it could refer to a dweller at 'hovels, tumbledown dwellings' OF *masure*; Cottle says that 'the French surname *Mesureur* (surveyor) suggests that something more elegant is possible'. Given the fact that such a surname is most commonly found in Leics, some connexion with the Leics place-name/surname **Measham** and the local river *Mease* might not be beyond the realms of possibility?

Medcalf(e), *see* Metcalf.

Meddon P There is such a place-name in Devon OE 'meadow hill', but this is a very scarce Chesh/Lancs surname.

Medley P Place-name in Oxon OE 'middle island'.

Medlicott/Middlecoat/Middlecott T/P Dweller at the 'middle cottage(s)' OE; or from a place-name such as *Medlicott* in Salop or *Middlecott* in Devon, with the same meaning. **Medlicott** is strongest in Salop, **Middlecoat** (scarce) in Cornwall and **Middlecott** (scarce) in Gloucs.

Medwin F From an OE first-name 'reward/meadow/mead (the drink)-friend'. A scarce Surrey surname.

Mee As an English surname (most commonly found in Lancs and in the English Midlands), never satisfactorily explained: a variant of **May**? From the first name *Matthew*? From the French town of *Mee*? Irish: Anglicized form of Gaelic **O'** [descendant of] **Miadhaigh** ('honourable') – compare **Meehan** – or of **MacConmidhe** ('son of Hound of Meath'. *Arthur Henry Mee (1875–1943), children's writer and creator of the popular* King's England *series of topographical books, was born in Stapleford, Notts.*

Meece, *see* Meese.

Meecham/Meechem, *see* Mason.

Meehan F Irish: Anglicized form of Gaelic **O'** [descendant of] **Miadhachain** ('honourable'). Compare **Mee**.

Meek(e)/Meake N Nickname for a meek, humble, gentle person ON. The *-e* of **Meeke** and **Meake** could indicate the use of a weak adjective after a lost definite article.

Meekins, *see* Makin.

Meese T/P Dweller in a mossy place OE; or from the place-name *Meece* in Staffs, with the same meaning. **Meese** is a Staffs surname. **Meece** is a scarce variant, and

Mease may be a variant of **Meese**, or of **May(es)**.

Meggett, *see* Madge.

Meggison, *see* Magg.

Meggitt, *see* Madge.

Megson, *see* Magg.

Meikle/Mickle N Scots: nickname for a big man, dialectal *meikle/mekill*, from ON/OE.

Meiklejohn/Micklejohn N Nickname, literally 'big John', for the larger or elder of two men called *John*. See **Meikle**.

Melbourn(e) P Place-names: *Melbourne* in ERYorks OE 'middle stream'; *Melbourne* in Derbys OE 'mill stream'; *Melbourn* in Cambs OE ('?milds [the plant variously known as *Atriplex, Chenopodium*, fat-hen, wild spinach, orach] stream'. **Melburn** is a scarce Lancs/Northd variant.

Melburn, *see* Melbourn.

Meldon P Place-name in Devon OE 'multicoloured hill' and in Northd OE 'hill with a sign/monument/cross' (compare **Malden** and **Melton**). A surname found both in Devon and Lancs.

Meldrum P Scots: place-name in Aberdeenshire, Scots Gaelic 'noble ridge'. Strongest in Fifeshire.

Melford P There is such a place-name in Suffolk OE 'ford by the hill', but in most cases this very scarce surname is likely to be a variant of **Milford**.

Melhuish/Meluish P Place-name *Melhuish* in Devon OE 'multicoloured hide of land'. Commonly pronounced '*Mellish*'. **Melhuish** and **Meluish** are Devon surnames; the variant **Mellish** is more widely spread.

Mellanby P Place-name *Melmerby* in Cumb and NRYorks ON '*Melmor* [Irish *Maelmuire*: "devotee of (St) *Mary*"]'s settlement/sandy soil settlement'.

Melledew, *see* Mallalieu and Meredith.

Mellersh P Place-name in Surrey, now *Mel-

lersh's Farm OE 'multicoloured ploughland/ stubble-field', and a Surrey surname.

Mellis F/P Scots and Irish: from the Gaelic first-name *Maol Iosa* 'devotee of Jesus'; the place-name *Mellis* in Suffolk OE 'mills' is unlikely to have given rise to this predominantly Scottish surname (strongest in Aberdeenshire).

Mellish, *see* Melhuish.

Mellodew, *see* Mallalieu and Meredith.

Mellor(s) P Place-name *Mellor* in Chesh, Derbys, Lancs, British 'bare hill'. **Mellor** is strongest in Midland and northern counties of England. **Mellors**, much scarcer, is found chiefly in Notts – appropriately enough, since D. H. Lawrence, the creator of the fictional Lady Chatterley and her lover Oliver **Mellors** the gamekeeper, was born in that county.

Mells T/P Dweller by the mills OE; there are places called *Mells* in Somerset and Suffolk, with the same meaning, though this fairly scarce surname is found principally in Hants and Lincs.

Melrose P Scots: place-names in Roxburghshire, British, 'bare moor'. Strongest in Midlothian.

Melton P Place-names: *Melton* in Leics, Lincs, Norfolk, Yorks (three such) OE (Scandinavianized) 'middle farm'; *Melton*, Suffolk OE 'mill settlement'; *Melton Constable*, Norfolk OE 'hill with a sign/monument/ cross [belonging to the constable]'. Compare **Malden** and **Meldon**.

Meluish, *see* Melhuish.

Melville P/F Scots: from one of the various places in Normandy called *Malleville*, from Latin 'bad settlement'. Strongest in Fifeshire. Irish: Anglicized form of Gaelic **O'** [descendant of] **Maoil Mhichil** ('devotee of (St) *Michael*'). *The American author Herman Melville (1819–1891) was born in New York City, the third son of Allan and Maria Gansevoort Melvill, and grandson of Major Thomas Melvill, a survivor of the Boston Tea Party.*

Maria added a final -e to the surname after her husband's death.

Melvin F Scots: Anglicized form of Gaelic **Mac Gille Bheathain** ('son of the servant of (St) *Beathan* ["Life"]') – compare **McIlvain**. Strongest in Aberdeenshire. Irish: Anglicized form of Gaelic **O'** [descendant of] **Maoil Mhin** ('devotee of [St] *Min* ["Gentle"]').

Membry/Memory, *see* Mowbray.

Mendham P Place-name in Suffolk OE '*Mynda*'s homestead'. A Norfolk/Suffolk surname.

Menheneott/Menhenett/Menhenitt/ Menhennett/Menhinick P Place-name *Menheniot* in Cornwall, Cornish *meneghy-Niet* 'sanctuary of *St Neot*'. Scarce Cornwall/Devon surnames in all spellings.

Menmuir P Place-name in Angus, Scotland, of which the second element is OE 'moor', the first being doubtful (Welsh, 'stone'/Scots Gaelic, 'little'?). An Angus surname.

Menzies P A Scots form of **Manners**. The *-z-* represents the obsolete letter *yogh* (shaped like a '*3*' and sounding like *gh*) – compare **Dalziel** and **McFadze(a)n** – and **Menzies** is correctly pronounced *Mingis*. See **McMinn**, which is a patronymic form.

Mepham P Place-name *Meopham* in Kent (pronounced '*Meppam*') OE 'homestead of *Meapa/the Meapas*'. Principally a Surrey/ Sussex surname.

Mercer O Occupational term for a merchant, especially a dealer in luxury fabrics OF. Strongest in Lancs, but also strong in Kent. See also **Marker**. *The English football player and manager Joe Mercer (1914–1990) was born in Ellesmere Port, Chesh… The American songwriter and singer John Herndon ('Johnny') Mercer (1909–1976) was born in Savannah, Georgia. His male-line ancestors included the Confederate General Hugh Weedon Mercer and the Revolutionary War General Hugh Mercer, a Scottish soldier and physician who died at the Battle of Princeton.*

Merch, *see* **Murch**.

Merchant, *see* **Marchant**.

Mercy ?N Possibly a nickname for a person who was quick to show mercy/compassion OF – though 'abstract' surnames of this sort are rare, and their meaning is often disputed. A scarce Bucks/Middx surname.

Mere, *see* **Mear**.

Meredith F Welsh: from the first-name *Meredydd* or *Maredudd* OW *Morgetiud* (?'splendour-lord'). Usually pronounced with the accent on the second syllable. Common in Wales and on the Welsh/English border. **Merridew/Merriday** are English versions, and have also found their way to Ireland. **Melledew** and **Mellodew** might be variants of **Merridew** (with an obvious attempt to make them mean 'honeydew', from Latin *mel*), or of **Mallalieu**.

Mer(r)ivale P Place-names *Merevale*, *Merrivale*, *Merryvale* in Devon, Herefords, Leics, Warwicks OE 'pleasant field (open land)'. Yet the surname is very rare in all these counties, being at its strongest in Northants in both spellings.

Merrall(s)/Merrell(s), *see* **Muriel**.

Merrett, *see* **Merritt**.

Merrick/Meyrick F/P English: from an OF personal name, composed of the Germanic elements *meri/mari* and *ric* (fame, and power); Welsh: from a Welsh first-name *Meuric*, a variant of *Maurice*; Scots: from a place-name *Merrick*, Kirkcudbrightshire, Gaelic *meurach* 'fork of a road/river'. **Merrick** is a widespread surname, found chiefly in Gloucs, Herefords, Lancs and Staffs; **Meyrick** occurs most frequently in Salop and Glamorgan. As to the Welsh **Merrick**, Cottle has some contentious views: 'Preceded by Welsh *Ap* "son of", it is the probable origin of the name *America*, since, when John Cabot returned to Bristol after his second transatlantic voyage in 1498, the king's pension of £20 was handed to him by the two collectors of customs for Bristol, the senior being Richard **Ameryk** (also appearing in the Customs Roll as **Amerik** and **Ap Meryke**), who was "probably the heaviest investor" in the expedition. He lived at Lower Court, Long Ashton, Somerset, from 1491, and his daughter Joan Brook is buried beneath a brass in St Mary Redcliffe, Bristol. (See especially B. Dunning in *Country Life*, 20 June 1963.) His title to be the eponym of the continent is surely stronger than the frivolous claim of the Italian Amerigo Vespucci'. *Joseph Carey Merrick (1862–1890), born in Leicester to Joseph Rockley Merrick and his wife Mary Jane, achieved an unenviable degree of fame as a result of the extreme deformity of his body. Early biographies, together with the 1980 film* The Elephant Man, *incorrectly refer to him as* 'John *Merrick'*.

Merridan P Place-name *Meriden* in Warwicks OE 'pleasant valley'. A very scarce scattered surname.

Merridew/Merriday, *see* **Meredith**.

Merrifield P There are places called *Merryfield* in Cornwall and Devon OE 'pleasant field', and since this surname is predominantly found in these two counties, we can probably discount the place-name *Mirfield* in WRYorks as a possible source.

Merrill(s), *see* **Muriel**.

Merriman, *see* **Merry**.

Merriott, *see* **Merritt**.

Merrison, *see* **Merry**.

Merri(o)tt/Merrett P Place-name *Merriot* in Somerset OE 'boundary gate'. Readily confused with/a variant of **Marriott**.

Merrivale, *see* **Merivale**.

Merriweather, *see* **Merryweather**.

Merry N Nickname for a cheerful, amusing, pleasant person OE. Readily confused with/a variant of surnames from the **Murray** group. **Merriman** and **Merryman** are quite literally 'cheerful/amusing/pleasant man' OE. All these are widely scattered surnames, though **Merrison** ('son of **Merry**'), very scarce, is mainly found in Norfolk.

Merryman, *see* **Merry**.

Merryweather/Merriweather N Nickname, literally 'nice weather' OE, for a person with a sunny personality – or even for one whose favourite expression was something like 'Nice weather for the time of year'? Compare **Fairweather**. Or might OE *wether/wedder* 'ram' be involved in some way? Several variant spellings are known; **Merryweather** has a strong presence in the north of England; **Merriweather**, also a northern surname, is very scarce. Such surnames are also to be found in the West Country.

Merton P Place-name *Merton* in Devon, Norfolk, Oxon, Surrey OE 'place by a lake'. Readily confused with/a variant of **Murton**. *Walter de Merton (c.1205–1277), Chancellor of England, Bishop of Rochester and founder of Merton College, Oxford (originally established in Malden, Surrey), was the son of William Cook of Basingstoke, Hants, and in his early years was known as 'Walter de Basingstoke'.*

Mervin/Marvin/Mirfin/Murfin F From an OE first-name meaning 'famous friend'. Since **Mervin** is a scarce Kent surname, and **Marvin** is found mainly in Leics, any connexion with the Welsh *Myrddin* (the *Merlin* of the Arthur story) is perhaps doubtful. **Mirfin** and **Murfin** are variants chiefly met with in WRYorks and Derbys respectively. For the relationship between *-ar-* and *–er-* (**Marvin/Mervin**), see **Armistead**. *Hank B. Marvin, lead guitarist of The Shadows (formerly The Drifters), was born Brian Robson Rankin in 1941 in Newcastle-upon-Tyne.*

Messenger/Messinger O Occupational term for a messenger OF *messag(i)er*. 'The *-n-* is a slovenly adenoidal English insertion' (Cottle) – as in **Pottinger**. Scattered surnames, **Messenger** being strong in places as far apart as Cumbd and Surrey.

Messum, *see* **Measham**.

Metcalf(e)/Medcalf(e) A surname of uncertain origin, perhaps some kind of a nickname from 'meat-calf' (a calf fattened up for food) OE, applied to a fat man. Some scholars have suggested 'mead or meadow calf', and Sir Anthony Wagner favours a hill called the 'Calf' as a possible source. Principally a Yorks surname in all spellings. A society studying the history and genealogy of families bearing such surnames is a particularly active one. *The road builder and surveyor John Metcalf (1717–1810), also known as 'Blind Jack of Knaresborough', who was blinded by smallpox at the age of six, was born in Knaresborough, WRYorks.*

Metford T ?Dweller at a ford with a meadow OE, or from a minor place-name so-called. Cottle suggests alternatives such as 'convenient/excellent/mediocre ford'. Chiefly a Somerset surname – so might *Mudford* OE 'muddy ford' in that county possibly be the source?

Methley P Place-name in WRYorks OE (Scandinavianized) 'middle wood/clearing', and a WRYorks surname.

Methuen/Methven P Place-name *Methven* in Perthshire, Scotland, ?British 'mead (the drink) stone' or ?Scots Gaelic 'middle river-plain'. *The publisher Sir Algernon Methuen Marshall Methuen, Baronet (1856–1924) was born with the surname Stedman in Southwark, London, but became 'Algernon Methuen' in the late 1890s.*

Meux P There is a place-name *Meaux* in ERYorks ON (remodelled on the French place-name *Meaux*) 'sandbank lake', but this very scarce surname is found mainly in the south of England. The fact that the **Meux** family of brewers, active from the mid eighteenth century to the early twentieth century, had its origins in the Isle of Wight, might suggest that **Meux** is probably a variant of **Mew**, which has a strong presence on the island. The surname **Meux** is commonly pronounced 'Mews'.

Mew O Occupational term for a man in charge of a hawks' cage OF *mue* (used when the hawks were 'mewing' or moulting). On the site where the royal hawks were kept at Charing Cross were built the royal stables called *mews*, eventually demolished to make way for Trafalgar Square. **Mew** is a surname of the south of England, especially strong in the Isle of Wight, so see **Meux**. Readily confused with/a variant of **Maw**.

Meyer(s), *see* Mayer.

Meynell/Maynell T/O/P/F Dweller in an isolated dwelling, or a dweller at/worker at a fortified manor house; or from one of a number of place-names in France OF *mesnil* 'abode/(nobleman's) domain' (compare *mansion*, of which this is a diminutive); or from a Norman female first-name meaning 'strength-battle'. **Meynell** is commonly pronounced *'Mennell'*. These are surnames of the English Midlands and the north. *Hugo Meynell (1735–1808), huntsman and politician, born in Bradley Park, Derbys, is sometimes described as 'the father of modern English foxhunting'.*

Meyrick, *see* Merrick.

Miall, *see* Michael.

Michael F From the ME first-name *Michael*, ultimately from Hebrew *Micha-el* 'Who is like God?', borne by several biblical characters and by the Archangel *Michael*, Captain of the Heavenly Host. **Michael** itself, a widely scattered surname which is particularly in evidence in Glamorgan, South Wales, is exceeded in popularity in some areas by forms (from OF) beginning with *Mitch-* (see **Mitchel**). **Miall** (scarce, Middx and Surrey), **Miell** (scarce, Hants and Somerset) **Myall** (Dorset and Essex) and **Myhill** (Norfolk) are known variants, via ME/Anglo-Norman French *Mihel*. The diminutive **Michie** belongs to Scotland, being very strong in Aberdeenshire, while **Michaels** and **Michaelson** ('son of *Michael*') are rare forms. See also **Miles**.

Michell, *see* Mitchel.

Michelmore P From an unidentified place-name OE 'large moor', very probably located in Devon, where this surname is chiefly found. *Arthur Clifford ('Cliff') Michelmore, British television presenter and producer, was born in Cowes, Isle of Wight, in 1919.*

Michie, *see* Michael.

Mickle, *see* Meikle.

Micklejohn, *see* Meiklejohn.

Micklem P Place-name *Mickleham* in Sur-

rey OE 'big homestead/river-meadow'. A very scarce Berks/Surrey surname.

Micklethwait(e) P From one of a number of places called *Micklethwaite* in Cumbd and WRYorks ON 'large clearing'. **Micklewhite**, *an exceptionally rare variant, is the surname originally borne by Maurice Joseph Micklewhite, junior, better known as the actor Sir Michael Caine. Born in Rotherhithe, London, in 1933, the son of a fish market porter, Michael Caine took his stage name as a result of glancing at a poster advertising the film The Caine Mutiny.*

Micklewhite, *see* Micklethwait.

Mickley P Place-name in several counties OE 'large clearing'. A rare surname, found in Essex and Northants.

Middle T/N/P Dweller in the middle (of a village) OE; or a nickname for a person of middle height; or perhaps from the place-name *Myddle* in Salop OE '?enclosure at the junction of two roads'. The surname can certainly be found in Salop, though it is strongest in Somerset.

Middlebrook T/P Dweller at the 'middle brook' OE. Largely a WRYorks surname, and possibly derived from *Middle Brook*, Clayton, in that county, though the first-known reference to this place-name dates from as late as 1588.

Middlecoat/Middlecott, *see* Medlicott.

Middledi(t)ch P From a minor place-name OE 'middle ditch'. There are field-names in Chesh so-called, but this is largely an Essex/Suffolk surname.

Middlehurst P Possibly from the place-name *Middleforth* in Lancs OE 'middle ford', the elements *forth/ford* and *hurst* often being confused in surnames. A Lancs surname.

Middlemas(s)/Middlemiss/Middlemist/Middlemost P District-name *Middlemass* in Kelso, Scotland ME 'middlemost'. Surnames of Scotland and north-east England, some variants being very scarce.

Middlemore P Place-name *Middlemoor* in

WRYorks and Devon OE 'moor set in the middle'. A very scarce Gloucs/West Midlands surname.

Middlemost, *see* Middlemas.

Middleton P Place-name found in counties as far apart as Devon and Northd – usually OE 'middle place/farm', though *Middleton on the Hill* in Herefords is OE 'large farm', and *Middleton Baggot* and *Middleton Priors* in Salop are OE 'confluence field farm'.

Middleweek/Middlewick P There is a place-name *Middlewich* in Chesh OE 'the middle salt-works', and places called *Middlewich/Middlewick* in Essex, but these are predominantly Devon surnames, and the origin there is likely to be a place now called *Middlewick Barton* OE 'middle farm' in that county.

Middlewood P There are places so-called in Cornwall, Devon and Herefords OE 'middle wood', but this scarce surname is mainly found in ERYorks and WRYorks, and the place of origin is likely to be *Middlewood* in WRYorks.

Midgley P There are several places so-called in Chesh and WRYorks OE 'wood/clearing infested by midges (gnats)'. Chiefly a WRYorks surname.

Midwinter N Nickname for a person born or baptized at Christmas, midwinter OE. A scattered surname, strongest in Gloucs.

Miell, *see* Michael.

Milborrow F From an OE feminine first-name, meaning 'mild/gentle-fortress', often used in honour of St *Mildburh*, a seventh- and eighth-century princess, abbess of Much Wenlock. A very scarce Surrey surname.

Mil(l)bourn(e)/Mil(l)burn P Place-names with various spellings in five counties OE 'mill stream'. *John Edward Thompson ('Jackie') Milburn (1924–1988), Newcastle United and England footballer, was born in the Northd mining village of Ashington.*

Mildmay N A nickname, usually pejora-

tive, for an innocuous person, as gentle as a maiden OE (compare **Maiden**). A surname borne by several eminent men and women over the centuries, but now very scarce.

Mileham P Place-name in Norfolk OE 'homestead with a mill', and mainly a Norfolk surname.

Miles/Myles F/O From the Germanic/Norman first-name *Milo*, of uncertain etymology (connected with Old Slavonic *milu* 'merciful'?), brought to England by the Normans as *Miles*. Since the usual ME form was *Mile*, the byname/surname **Miles** would probably have originally carried the sense of '*Mile*'s son/servant'. Or a general term for a servant, from Latin *miles* ('soldier'). Or a contracted form of **Michael**, perhaps via **Myhill**. Readily confused with/a variant of **Mills** (see **Mill**). **Millett** is a diminutive form. **Milson** ('son of Miles' – *see also* **Milsom**) is chiefly a Lincs surname.

Milford P Place-name in several counties OE 'ford by a mill'. Strongest in Devon. Readily confused with/a variant of **Melford**.

Milk N/O A nickname of some description OE. Reaney suggests that it could have been used for a looked-down-on milk-drinker, or for someone with white hair, but it could perhaps be a reference to an albino – or even an occupational term for some kind of milk producer or seller? A Norfolk surname. **Milkins** ('son of [diminutive of] **Milk**') is a scarce Somerset variant. *Harvey Bernard Milk (1930–1978), the first openly gay man to be elected to public office in California, was born in New York to Lithuanian-Jewish parents.*

Milkins, *see* Milk.

Mill(s)/Millen/Milln(s)/Miln(e)(s) T/O/F Dweller by a water/wind mill OE *mylen(e)* (compare Modern French *moulin*); or an occupational term for one who worked at a mill, even a miller himself (see **Miller**); or, when not preceded by prepositions such as *de* or *at*, some variants can be from a first-name such as *Miles* or *Millicent*. **Mill** itself is a fairly scarce surname, mostly found in south-west England and north-east Scotland. Variants include: **Mills** (widespread, commonest in Lancs, and readily confused with/a variant of **Miles**); **Milnes** and **Milns** (both strongest in Lancs and WRYorks, and sometimes pronounced '*Mills*'), which are 'of/at the mill' (rather than a plural), or else 'son of **Mill**'; **Miln** (scarce, found mainly in Angus, Scotland); **Milne** (most common in Lancs and in north-east Scotland); and **Millen**, which features a glide-vowel to ease pronunciation (Kent). **Milln** and **Millns** (the latter found in Lincs) are scarce variants. See also **Mullin**. **Mills** is the family name of the Barons Hillingdon. *The philosopher and economist John Stuart Mill (1806–1873) was born in London, though his father James Mill was a Scot, and his paternal grandfather had been a village shoemaker in Forfarshire… The writer Alan Alexander ('A. A.') Milne (1882–1956) was born in Kilburn, North London.*

Millar/Millard, *see* **Miller**.

Millen, *see* **Mill**.

Miller/Millar/Millard/Millier/Millman/Millward/Milner/Mullinar/Mullin(d)er/Mullinger O Occupational term for a miller. The word 'miller', from northern ME and ON, is an altered later form of the Old and early Middle English word 'milner'. Both have given rise to surnames, as has 'millward', an English Midlands equivalent. **Millwood**, a scattered surname, can be a variant of **Millward**, but could in principle sometimes be derived from a place-name such as *Millwood* in WRYorks. **Miller** is a ubiquitous surname, stronger in the south-east and the far north of England (and in Scotland), than in the Midlands, which is where **Millward** comes into its own; **Millar** is a Scots form; **Millard** is most common in Gloucs and Somerset, **Millier** (possibly a variant of **Miller**?) in Somerset alone, **Millman** in Devon, **Milner** in WRYorks; **Millers** and **Millerson** ('son of the miller') in Lancs and Kent respectively, **Mullinar** in Lancs, **Mulliner** in Lancs, Salop and Staffs, **Mullinder** in Lancs, Northd and Staffs, and **Mullinger** in Hants, Norfolk and Suffolk. See also **Mullin**.

Millerchip, *see* **Millichap**.

Millers, *see* **Miller**.

Millership, *see* **Millichap**.

Millerson, *see* **Miller**.

Millett, *see* **Miles**.

Millham P From a minor place-name OE 'river-meadow/homestead with a mill', such as (possibly) *Mileham* in Kent. A scarce Kent/Sussex surname.

Millican, *see* **Mulligan**.

Millicha(m)p/Millerchip/Millership/Millicheap/Millichip/ Millichope/ Millinship P Place-name *Millichope* in Salop OE 'valley by the mill hill'. A distinctive set of surnames, restricted in the main to Salop and the Welsh/English border.

Millier, *see* **Miller**.

Milligan/Milligen/Milliken/Millikin, *see* **Mulligan**.

Millington P Place-name in Chesh and ERYorks OE 'mill farm'.

Millinship, *see* **Millichap**.

Millman, *see* **Miller**.

Milln(s), *see* **Mill**.

Millward/Millwood, *see* **Miller**.

Miln(e), *see* **Mill**.

Milner, *see* **Miller**.

Milnes, *see* **Mill**.

Milnthorp(e) P Place-name in Notts, Westmd, ERYorks OE and ON 'settlement with a mill'. A scarce Yorks surname in both spellings.

Milsom F From the OE female first-name *Milde* ('mild'); or a variant of **Milson** (see **Miles**). Chiefly a Gloucs surname.

Milson, *see* **Miles**.

Milste(a)d P Place-name in Kent OE 'middle place'. A Kent surname in both spellings.

Milton P From any one of a great number of places so-called, some of which are OE 'middle farm', others being OE 'mill farm'. A ubiquitous surname, at its strongest in Devon and Somerset. *John Milton (1608–1674), widely regarded as one of England's greatest poets, was born in Bread Street, London.*

Milverton P Place-name in Somerset and Warwicks OE 'mill-ford farm'. A scarce Devon/Dorset/Somerset surname.

Milward, *see* Millward.

Minchin N Nickname from an OE word for a nun. 'Some disreputable joke lurks' (Cottle). Strongest in Gloucs.

Minchin(g)ton P Place-name *Minchington* in Dorset OE 'nuns' farm'. Rare in both spellings, mainly found in Somerset.

Miner(s)/Minor(s) O Occupational term for a man who built, or who worked in, a mine of various sorts (coal, lead, tin) OF, or a (military) sapper. **Miner**, not a common surname, can chiefly be found in Lancs, Somerset and Staffs; **Miners** ('son of **Miner**'), found in greater numbers, belongs to Cornwall; **Minor** is most common in the English Midlands and the north-west; **Minors**, scarce, has a presence in both Cornwall and Staffs.

Minett, *see* Minn.

Mingay F From a Breton first-name, *men-ki* 'stone dog', introduced into England by settlers who followed in the wake of William the Conqueror. **Mingay** is strongest in Suffolk; **Mingey** is a scarce variant.

Minn(s) F/N From the mediaeval first-name *Minne*, probably from Germanic *minna* ('love'), or a shortened form of *Wilhelmina*. Diminutive forms (some of which Cottle contends can alternatively be from a nickname for a dainty, delightful person OF) include **Minnie**, a scarce scattered surname; **Minett** and **Mynett**, both strongest in Gloucs (though **Minett** is also a well-known Huguenot surname); **Minnitt**, found in Lincs, Notts and WRYorks; and **Mynott**, a Cambs surname. Cottle adds:

'John **Mynot** held Carlton **Miniott** in NRYorks in 1346; of this family was the savage and jingoistic fourteenth-century poet Laurence **Minot**'. **Minns** ('son of **Minn**') is strongest in Norfolk, and **Minnis** (which would seem to carry the same meaning) in Lancs.

Minnie/Minnis/Minnitt/Minns, *see* Minn.

Minogue F Irish: Anglicized form of Gaelic O' [descendant of] **Muineog** ('monk'). Compare **Molony**, **Monahan**, **Monk** and **Moyne**. *Kylie Minogue, the Australian singer, songwriter and actress, was born in Melbourne in 1968, the daughter of Ron Minogue, an accountant, and Carol Jones, a former dancer from Maesteg, Wales.*

Minor(s), *see* Miner.

Minshall/Minshull P Place-name (*Minshull*) of two villages on either side of the river Weaver in Chesh OE '*Mann*'s shelf/ledge of land', and chiefly Chesh surnames.

Minskip P Place-name in WRYorks OE (Scandinavianized) 'land held in common'. A scarce WRYorks surname.

Minter O Occupational term for a moneyer, coiner OE. Chiefly a Kent surname.

Mintern(e) P Place-name *Minterne* in Dorset OE 'house where mint grows'. **Mintern** is mainly a Dorset/Somerset surname; **Minterne** is a much scarcer variant.

Minto P Place-name in Roxburghshire, Scotland, British and ME 'hill ridge/hill'. Chiefly a Co Durham surname. *Scott Christopher Minto, former footballer and TV football pundit, was born in 1971 in Heswall, Chesh.*

Minton P Place-name in Salop, British and OE 'mountain enclosure', and a Salop surname.

Minty P Place-name *Minety* in Wilts OE 'island with mint', and a Wilts surname.

Mirfield P Place-name in WRYorks OE 'pleasant field', and a WRYorks surname.

Mirfin, *see* **Mervin**.

Miskin N Nickname for a young man, or for the junior of two men bearing the same name OF. Sometimes used in a derogatory way, for someone deemed to be paltry or stingy. Mainly a Kent surname.

Missenden P Place-names *Great* and *Little Missenden*, Bucks OE '?*Myssa*'s/river *Mysse*/water-lily valley'. A scarce Bucks surname.

Missing ?P A Cambs/Kent surname of unknown origin, possibly from a place-name such as *Messing* in Essex OE 'settlement of the people of *Mæcca*', or even from *Messines* in Belgium (Flemish *Meesen*). *Chris Missing, an antiquarian bookdealer living in Essex, has put his surname to good effect by using the delightful trade name 'Missing Books'.*

Misson P There is a place so-called in Notts OE '?water-lilies', but this is chiefly a Cambs/Kent/Middx surname. See also **Musson**.

Mitcham/Mitchem P Place-name in Surrey OE 'large homestead'. **Mitcham** is a widely scattered surname, found mainly in southern counties of England; **Mitchem** is strongest in Dorset and Somerset.

Mitchel(l)/Michell F/N From a popular form of the first-name *Michael* (see **Michael**); or a nickname for a big person OE (compare the word *much* and dialectal *mickle*). **Mitchel** and **Mitchell** can be found throughout England and Scotland, at their strongest in WRYorks; **Michell** is primarily a Cornish variant. **Mitchelson**, **Mitchellson**, **Mitchenson** and **Mitchinson** ('son of **Mitchell**') are, predictably, chiefly northern forms.

Mitchel(l)son, *see* **Mitchel**.

Mitchem, *see* **Mitcham**.

Mitchenson, *see* **Mitchel**.

Mitchinson, *see* **Mitchel**.

Mitford P Place-name in Northd OE 'ford at the confluence'. A Co Durham/Northd surname. *The well-known family of Mitford,*

Barons Redesdale, which includes the 'Mitford sisters' (Nancy, Pamela, Unity, Diana, Jessica and Deborah), can trace its descent in the male line back to Sir John Mitford (died 1409) of Mitford, Northd.

Mitten, *see* **Mitton**.

Mitton P Place-name in Lancs, Staffs, Worcs and WRYorks OE 'farm at the confluence'. Cottle is persuaded that '**Mitten** is a version of this, not a garment', but whereas **Mitton** is a Lancs/WRYorks surname, **Mitten** belongs to the south-east of England, especially Sussex. Readily confused with/a variant of **Mutton** or **Myton**.

Miz(z)en P Hanks and Hodges derive such a surname from *Misson* in Notts, Germanic 'marshy place', but that hardly explains why **Mizen** is a Wilts surname and **Mizzen** is restricted to Essex and Middx. Perhaps the word *mission* is involved in some way?

Mobbs, *see* **Mabb**.

Moberl(e)y/Mobl(e)y P Place-names: *Mobberley* in Chesh and Staffs OE 'moot-/assembly-mound clearing', and *Mobley* in Gloucs OE 'maple-tree clearing'. These are fairly scarce surnames, and in some cases their distribution pattern bears little relationship to their supposed points of origin: **Moberly** can be found in Kent, **Moberley** in Hants and Worcs, **Mobly** in Northants and **Mobley** in Oxon and Warwicks. Readily confused with/a variant of **Moverley**.

Mockler N Nickname for a bad scholar or cleric OF *mauclerc*. A scarce, scattered surname.

Mockridge, *see* **Mogridge**.

Moffat(t)/Moffett/Moffitt P Scots: place-name in Dumfriesshire, Gaelic '?long field' (the adjective coming second). Surnames of Scotland and of northern England, especially Lancs.

Mogford/Mugford P Devon surnames, presumably from an unidentified place-name OE '*Mogga/Mugga*'s ford' in that county (by analogy with **Mogridge**). Possibly confused with **Mudford**?

Mogg F From the female first-name *Madge/ Margaret* (see **Magg**); or from an OE male first-name such as *Mogga* (see **Mogford/ Mogridge**).

Mog(g)ridge/Mockridge/ Mugg(e)ridge/Mugridge P Place-name *Mogridge* in Devon OE '*Mogga*'s ridge'. The distribution pattern of such surnames might appear to confound expectations in some cases: **Mogridge** is found chiefly in Devon, **Moggridge** in Devon and Somerset, **Mockridge** in Dorset, Gloucs and Somerset, **Muggridge** and **Muggeridge** in Kent, Surrey and Sussex, **Mugridge** in both Devon and Sussex. *(Thomas) Malcolm Muggeridge (1903–1990), journalist and broadcaster, was born in Croydon, Surrey.*

Mohan, *see* Mahon.

Moir, *see* Moor.

Mold, *see* Maud.

Mole, *see* Maud.

Molesworth P Place-names: *Molesworth* in Hunts OE '*Mul*'s enclosure', and *Mouldsworth* in Chesh OE 'hilltop/crown of the head enclosure'. The surname is strongest in Warwicks and Worcs. In the year 1716 Robert **Molesworth**, former ambassador to the court of Denmark, was raised to the peerage of Ireland as Baron of Philipstown and Viscount **Molesworth**; his family's male-line lineage can be traced back to John **Molesworth** of Helpeston, Northants, escheator of Rutland, who died in 1542, and beyond that, it is said, to Sir Walter **Molesworth**, an eminent soldier during the reign of King Edward I.

Molineux, *see* Molyneux.

Moll F From the mediaeval female first-name *Moll(e)*, a pet form of *Mary*, famously borne by the fictional character *Moll* Flanders. Compare **Malet**, **Malin**, **Marriott** and **Mule**. **Mollet(t)** and **Mollitt** are diminutives; **Mollison** is 'son of *Moll*'.

Molland P Place-name in Devon, Welsh *moel* and OE 'land by a bare hill' and a Devon surname.

Mollet(t)/Mollison/Mollitt, *see* Moll.

Molloy F Irish: Anglicized form of Gaelic **O'** [descendant of] **Maolmhuaidh** ('chieftain-venerable'); or **O'Maol Aodha** ('descendant of the devotee of [St] *Aedh*'); or **O'Maol Mhaodhog** ('descendant of the devotee of [St] *Moodhog*').

Molon(e)y F Irish: Anglicized form of Gaelic **O'Maol Dhomhnaigh** ('descendant of the devotee of the church'); or **Mac Giolla Dhomhnaigh** ('son of the devotee of the church'). Sometimes used, in an uncamouflaged way, for the illegitimate offspring of priests (compare **Minogue**, **Monahan**, **Monk** and **Moyne**).

Molton P Place-names in Devon, *North* and *South Molton* OE 'estate at, or called, *Mol* (Welsh *moel*?)'. A scarce surname, strongest in Suffolk. Readily confused with/a variant of **Moulton**.

Molyne(a)ux/Molineux P/O From one of a number of places called *Moulineaux* in Seine and Seine-Maritime, France OF 'little mills'; or an occupational term for a miller OF. Chiefly Lancs surnames in all spellings, and commonly pronounced '*Molneuks*'. **Molyneux** is the family name of the Earls of Sefton.

Mompesson P There are places called *Montpinçon* OF '?finch/chaffinch hill' in Calvados, Manche (though Norman French *pinçon* means 'pincers'). This surname, which formerly had a presence in Dorset/ Hants/Wilts, but also in Yorks, has all but died out in the British Isles. *William Mompesson (1638/9–1709), the Anglican clergyman who heroically succeeded in confining an attack of bubonic plague within the limits of his parish of Eyam, Derbys, in 1665, was born in Yorks.*

Mona(g)han F Irish: Anglicized form of Gaelic **O'** [descendant of] **Manachain** ('monk'). Might illegitimacy be supposed? Readily confused with **Moynihan**. Compare **Minogue**, **Moloney**, **Monk** and **Moyne**.

Monckton, *see* Monkton.

Moncrieff(e) P Scots: place-name *Moncrieff*

in Perthshire, British and Scots Gaelic, 'hill of the ?tribal tree'.

Monday/Munday/Mundy F/N From the ON first-name *Mundi*; or a nickname for a person born on a Monday OE ('day of the moon'), or having some particular connexion with that day of the week. Reaney suggests that such surnames might relate to a holder of 'Mondayland', held by a tenant who worked for his lord on Mondays.

Money N/O/F/P Nickname for a man with plenty of money, or an occupational term for a moneyer OF. Irish: Anglicized form of Gaelic **O'** [descendant of] **Maonaigh** ('rich'). Cottle adds: 'Bardsley's choice of a place-name in Orne OF *Monnai* (Latin first-name *Modinnus* plus suffix), and an occupational term for a monk OF *moigne*, etc., with *de* and *le* forms to support it, seems reasonable'. A surname of south-east England and East Anglia. Compare **Moneypenny**. *In 1905 Methuen published a book called* Riches and poverty, *written (appropriately) by L. G. Chiozza Money.*

Moneypenny N Probably a nickname for a man with plenty of money, or for a miser OE ('many a penny'). Compare **Money**.

Monger O Occupational term for a seller, trader OE, as in cheesemonger, fishmonger, ironmonger and costermonger (who originally sold costard apples). To *scaremonger*, of course, is to trade in 'scares'. A southern English surname.

Monk O/F Occupational term for a monk OE, 'in scandalous jest, or from service at a monastery' (Cottle). Irish: Anglicization of the surnames **Minogue** and **Monag(h)an**. Compare **Molony** and **Moyne**.

Monkhouse T/O/P Dweller in, or worker at, a house owned by a monastery OE; or from a place-name in Staffs, with the same meaning. Chiefly a Cumbd/Co Durham surname. *The comedian Bob Monkhouse (1928–2003) was born in Beckenham, Kent, to a family which ran a custard-making company known as Monk and Glass.*

Monkton/Monckton P There are places called *Monkton* OE 'monks' place/farm' in several English counties. The male-line ancestry of the Viscounts **Monckton** of Brenchley (Kent) and of the Viscounts Galway can be traced back to a family living in Cavil, Yorks, in the fifteenth century.

Monro(e), *see* Munro.

Montacute, *see* Montagu.

Montagu(e) P/F Place-names *Montagu* and *Montaigu* in France OF 'pointed hill'. The principal family bearing this surname derives it from a place-name in Manche. Irish: Anglicized form of Gaelic **Mac Taidhg** 'son of the poet/philosopher' (compare **Teague**, **McTague**). **Montagu** is the family name of the Dukes of Manchester and Earls of Sandwich. **Montacute**, from a place so-called in Somerset, with a conical hill above it, represents a Latinized version of **Montagu**, and is chiefly a Somerset surname.

Montgomerie/Montgomery P From *Montgomery* in Calvados OF and Germanic '*Gumaric*'s hill'. The surnames **Montgomerie** and **Montgomery** (frequently pronounced '*Mungummery*'), which are at their strongest in Ayrshire and Lanarkshire, Scotland, though also much in evidence in Northern Ireland, have been borne by several peers and baronets. *Bernard Law Montgomery, first Viscount Montgomery (1887–1976), the army officer universally known as 'Monty', was born in London to a family with roots in Moville, near Londonderry.*

Montrose P Place-name in Angus, Scotland, Gaelic 'moor on the cape'. A very scarce surname, strongest in Co Durham.

Monument A scarce Norfolk surname of uncertain derivation. Bardsley supposes that it might be a corruption of *Monemute* (1191) or of some other early spelling of the place-name *Monmouth*, Welsh *Mynwy* (now styled in English *Monnow*) and OE 'mouth of the little Wye'.

Moodey/Moodie, *see* Moody.

Mood(e)y N Nickname for a bold, proud, passionate person OE. **Moodie** is principally a Scots variant.

Moon(e)/Munn P/N/F Place-name *Moyon* in Manche OF, from the Gallo-Roman first-name *Modius* plus a local suffix; or a nickname for a monk-like person, Anglo-Norman French *moun*. Cornish: nickname for a slender person, Cornish *mon*. Irish: Anglicized form of Gaelic **O'** [descendant of] **Mochain** ('early/timely'). **Moon** is especially strong in Lancs and **Munn** in Kent; **Moon(e)** is scarce and scattered.

Mooney, *see* **Meaney**.

Moor(e)/More T/P/N/F When originally preceded by *at* or *de*: dweller on a moor or fen OE *mor* (**Muir** in Scotland), or from one of a number of place-names with the same meaning, such as *More* in Chesh and Salop (the *-e* of **Moore** indicating the use of the dative after a lost preposition); or a nickname for a person of dark, negroid, Moor-like appearance OF *more*, Latin *Maurus* (compare **Morrant**, **Morrell**, **Morris**); or from a first-name with this same meaning, borne by a number of Saints. Irish: Anglicized form of Gaelic **O'** [descendant of] **Mordha** ('proud'). Scots (also **Moir**): nickname for a large man, Gaelic *mor* ('great, big'). The very scarce Berks and Surrey surname **Moorcock** can be a diminutive form of **Moor(e)**, or of **Morris**, with the addition of the familiar suffix *-cock*, ('little lad'). **Moor** is very much a north-of-England variant. **Moore** is the family name of the Earls of Drogheda.

Moorby/Mor(e)by P Place-name **Moorby** in Lincs ON 'moor/fen farm'. **Moorby** is a Lancs/WRYorks surname; **Morby** and **Moreby**, more scattered, are strongest in Oxon.

Moorcock, *see* **Moor**.

Moorcraft, *see* **Moorcroft**.

Moorcroft T/P Dweller in a croft/paddock in a moor/fen OE, or from one of a number of places called *Moorcroft* in WRYorks, with the same meaning, or from a now-lost place-name *Morcroft* in Lancs. Chiefly a Lancs surname. **Moorcraft**, a scarce surname, looks at first sight as if it could be a variant, though it is mainly found in Kent.

Moore, *see* **Moor**.

Moor(e)head T/P Dweller at the top/edge of a moor/marsh OE, or from a place-name with a similar meaning in Northd, WRYorks.

Moor(e)house/Morehouse T/P Dweller at a house in a moor/fen OE, or from a place-name (including *Moorhouses*) with a similar meaning in Cumbd, Notts, WRYorks. Chiefly a Yorks surname.

Moorman T Dweller in a moor or fen OE. A scarce surname, strongest on the Isle of Wight.

Moorwood T/P Dweller in a wood on a moor OE, or from a place-name with the same meaning, for example in Derbys. A scarce WRYorks surname.

Moralee P Place-name *Morralee* in Northd OE 'swampy clearing'. A Co Durham/Northd surname.

Moran F Irish: Anglicized form of Gaelic **O'** [descendant of] **Morain** ('great/large'). Readily confused with/a variant of **Morant**.

Morant F/N From an OF first-name of uncertain etymology, maybe 'steadfast'? Chiefly a Hants surname, as is **Morrant**, which Cottle takes to be a nickname for a person of darkish appearance OF *morant* (compare **Moore**, **Morrell**, **Morris**), while Reaney favours a derivation from OF *(de)-morant*, a 'visitor who stays on'. Readily confused with/a variant of **Moran**. *Harry Harbord 'Breaker' Morant, aka Edwin Henry Morant (1864–1902), horseman, poet and soldier, who emigrated to Australia in 1883 and is regarded as an Australian folk-hero, was born in the union workhouse in Bridgwater, Somerset, the son of the workhouse master (likely?) or – according to the many legends that grew up around this romantic but elusive figure – of Admiral Sir George Digby Morant of the Royal Navy (unlikely?). Having been court-martialled for summarily executing a number of Afrikaner prisoners during the Boer War, he was himself executed by the British Army in 1902.*

Morby, *see* **Moorby**.

Morcom/Morcomb, *see* **Morcombe**.

Mor(e)combe P Place-names: *Morecombe*, Devon OE 'valley in a moor', and *Morecombelake* (*Mortecumbe* in the thirteenth century), Dorset OE '?*Morta*'s valley'. In any event, not from *Morecambe*, Lancs, which was first so-called in the late eighteenth century. **Morecombe** and **Morcombe** are Devon surnames. **Morcom**, **Morcomb** and **Morcum**, derived from Cornish *mor-cumb*, could have been used to describe a dweller in a valley leading to the sea.

Morcum, *see* Morcombe.

Morda(u)nt N Nickname for a person with a biting, vehement, sarcastic manner, from the present participle of the OF verb *mordre* 'to bite'. One family of **Mordaunts**, formerly Earls of Peterborough, had their origins in Beds, but by the late nineteenth century this was a scarce surname in either spelling, **Mordants** being found in Hants and Warwicks, **Mordaunts** in Lancs and Middx.

Mordecai F From a Babylonian first-name meaning 'devotee of *Marduk* (the Babylonian supreme God)', respelt by Jews. As a surname, mainly found in Glamorgan, South Wales.

Morden P Place-name in Cambs, Dorset, Surrey OE 'hill in a moor/fen'.

More, *see* Moore.

Moreby, *see* Moorby.

Morecombe, *see* Morcombe.

Morehen N Nickname for a person bearing some resemblance to a moorhen OE. Whatever can that resemblance have been? A scarce Northants surname.

Morehouse, *see* Moorhouse.

Moreland, *see* Morland.

Moreton, *see* Morton.

Morfee/Morfey/Morphew/Morphey N Nickname for a person who was ill-omened, devil-like OF *malfé/malfeu*. **Morfee** and **Morfey** are scarce Sussex surnames; **Morphew** and **Morphey** are strongest in Suffolk.

Morgan F Welsh, Scots and Irish: from a Celtic first-name meaning 'sea-bright' or 'great defender', still found abundantly as a surname and first-name in South Wales in particular.

Moriarty O Irish: Anglicized form of the Gaelic first-name *Muircheartach* 'sea-skilled' (skilful mariner/navigator).

Morice, *see* Morris.

Morison, *see* Morris.

Mor(e)land P There are various places called *Morland* or *Moreland* in northern England and in Scotland OE 'moor/fen land'. **Morland** is found chiefly in Co Durham and Lancs, **Moreland** in Lancs.

Morley P Place-names: *Morley* in Chesh, Derbys, Co Durham, Norfolk, WRYorks, and *Moreleigh* in Devon OE 'fen/moor clearing'. A widely distributed surname, but uncommon in the far north of England, Scotland and Wales.

Morpeth P Place-name in Northd OE 'murder path'. 'The police station there is an ancient monument' (Cottle). Chiefly a Northd surname.

Morphew/Morphey, *see* Morfee.

Morrant, *see* Morant.

Morrell F From the mediaeval first-name *Morel*, a diminutive of *More* (see **Moor**). A Yorks surname. Compare **Morrant**, **Morris**.

Morrice/Morrish/Morrison/Morriss, *see* Morris.

Morris/Maurice/Mor(r)ice/Morrish/Morriss/Morse F/N From the OF first-name *Maurice*, meaning 'Moorish, swarthy', borne by several minor saints and brought to Britain by the Normans. *Maurice* is still the usual form of the first-name, but the surname is most commonly spelt **Morris**. Or a nickname for a person of a dark or swarthy complexion, compare **Moor**, **Moorcock**, **Morrant**, **Morrell**. Morris is a widespread surname, strongest in Lancs; **Maurice** (much scarcer) is chiefly found in Chesh, **Morice/Morrice** in Aberdeenshire,

Morriss in the English Midlands and the north, and **Morison/Morrison** ('son of *Morris*') in Scotland. **Morrish**, very scarce, 'as vulgar as saying *liquorish*' (Cottle) and **Morse** can be found in Gloucs and elsewhere. **Morris** is the family name of the Barons Killanin, and **Morrison** of the Viscounts Dunrossil. *Samuel Finley Breese Morse (1791–1872), co-inventor with Alfred Vail of the Morse Code, was born in Charlestown, Massachusetts… In 1899 an egg and butter merchant called William Morrison established a business in the local market in Bradford, Yorks. From such humble beginnings grew the well-known chain of Morrison supermarkets.* For Marion Robert/Michael **Morrison**, see 'John Wayne' (under **Wain**).

Morrissey F Irish: Anglicized form of Gaelic **O'** [descendant of] **Muirgheas** ('seataboo'). But the Norman family *De Marisco* (Low Latin 'of the marsh'), became **Mac-Muiris** and later **Morrissey**.

Morrough, *see* **Morrow**.

Morrow T/P/F Dweller at a row of houses on a moor OE, or from such a place-name with the same meaning in Cumbd and elsewhere. Found chiefly in Co Durham, Lancs, and Lanarkshire, Scotland. Irish (also in the forms **Morrough/Murrough**, and connected with **Murray**): Anglicized form of the Gaelic first-name *Murchadh* ('sea warrior'). Compare **McMorrough** and **Murphy**. **Murrow** can be a variant of **Morrow**, or from the place-name *Murrow* in Cambs OE 'row (of dwellings) in a moor/ fen'. **Morse**, *see* **Morris**.

Mort ?N/F A Lancs surname of uncertain origin: perhaps a nickname for a 'stumpy' person ME dialect *murt*, from Germanic; or from some similarity to a young salmon ME *mort*; or from OF *mort* ('dead'), perhaps for someone with a death-like pallor? Or from an OE first-name *Morta*?

Mortimer/Mortimor(e) P Place-name *Mortemer* in Seine-Maritime, France OF 'dead sea' (in the sense of a stagnant lake). Typically a Devon surname in all spellings. **Mortimer** was the name of a

powerful Anglo-Norman family which settled in the Welsh marches.

Mortlock P Place-names: *Mortlake* in Surrey, *Mortelake* in Herts and *Mortlocks* in Essex ME and OE 'young salmon stream'. Strongest in Essex, Middx and Suffolk.

Morton/Moreton P From one of a large number of places in England and Scotland called *Mor(e)ton* OE 'moor/fen farm'. In northern place-names, the first element could originally have been ON. **Moreton** is the family name of the Earls of Ducie.

Mosedale P Place-name in Cumbd ON 'moss/bog valley'. Strongest in Derbys, Lancs, Staffs.

Moseley/Mosley/Mozley P From one of a number of places called *Mos(e)ley* in various English counties OE 'marsh/bog clearing' or 'field-mouse clearing', or '*Moll*'s clearing'. Surnames of the English Midlands and the north. Some American **Moseley**s are descended from a seventeenth-century settler called John **Maudesley**. *The English fascist leader Sir Oswald Ernald Mosley (1896–1980) was the grandson of Sir Oswald Mosley, fourth baronet, of Rolleston-on-Dove, Staffs.*

Moses F From the name of the Israelite leader *Moses*, Hebrew *Moshe* (of unknown meaning, possibly Egyptian in origin?), sometimes used by mediaeval Christians, and favoured by Puritans and by the Welsh after the Reformation. As a surname, **Moses** is found chiefly in Monmouthshire, Wales. The surnames **Moyes** and **Moyse**, both of which have a significant presence in East Anglia, reflect the usual mediaeval spellings of **Moses**, and there is a *Moyse's Hall* in Bury St Edmunds, Suffolk. See also **Moss** and **Mossman**. *Henry Moyes (1749/50-1807), born in Kirkcaldy, Fife, Scotland, though he was blinded by smallpox before the age of three, achieved fame as a lecturer on natural philosophy.*

Mosley, *see* **Moseley**.

Moss T/P/F Dweller at a marsh, swamp OE, or from a place-name with the same meaning in WRYorks and elsewhere; or a diminutive form of **Moses**. See also **Mossman**.

Mosscrop P Place-name in WRYorks OE '?hill in a bog'. 'But it is also an archaic word for the "tufted clubrush", which must be regarded as just coincidental' (Cottle). A Lancs surname.

Mossman O/T Occupational term for a servant of **Moses**. Cottle says that Guppy counted it only in Beds, and that this weighs against any supposed northern word meaning 'man who lives in a swamp' OE and ON, but in reality the surname exists in pockets in south-east and north-east England, the north of England and Scotland, so such a derivation is still a possibility. Compare **Moss**.

Mostyn P Place-name in Flintshire, Welsh *maes-ddin* 'field of the fortress'. Chiefly a Denbighshire/Lancs surname.

Mothersill/Mothersole P/N Place-name *Moddershall* in Staffs OE '*Modred*'s recess'; or possibly (by way of folk etymology) a nickname for a person who commonly used the oath 'by my mother's soul'. **Mothersill** is a scarce NRYorks surname; **Mothersole** is strongest in Suffolk.

Motion A Scots surname which most compilers of surname dictionaries neatly sidestep, either by omitting it, or by saying that its origin is unknown. The word *motion*, perhaps used of a man who seemed always to be on the move, is rather a sophisticated term to have given rise to a surname, and its first recorded use post-dates the main period of surname formation. **Motion** as a surname is found almost exclusively in the Kingdom of Fife, Scotland, where it is known to have been used since at least as early as the seventeenth century. The origin could be a nickname for a person as docile as a sheep, French *mouton*, or from the topographical term *motte*, meaning a prominent mound of earth (as in *motte and bailey*). **Motton** and **Mottin** would seem to be variants of the same name. *Although the surname is rare, Andrew Motion, Poet Laureate (born 1952, raised in Stisted, Essex), is not the only person to have been so called over the years. His great-grandfather Andrew Motion, from a family of Fife bakers, had grown up in the East End of London. The 1881 census features four Andrew Motions, three of whom were living in Fife itself (a sailor, a ploughman's son and a causeway layer's son). Another Andrew Motion, a London-born distiller's collector, was visiting a family in Croydon, Surrey, in 1881, but later moved to Oxon, where he became a Justice of the Peace and Lord of the Manors of Upton and Ratley.*

Motley P There is a place-name so-called in Kent OE 'moot/assembly field', but this is mainly a Lincs surname. A certain Thomas **de Motlawe** is known to have been living in Yorks in 1379. There would appear to be no connexion with the motley (mottled) garb worn by jesters.

Mottershead P Place-name, now lost, in the parish of Mottram, Chesh OE '*Motere*'s hill'. Chiefly a Chesh/Lancs surname.

Motton/Mottin, *see* **Motion**.

Mottram P Place-names in Chesh, Welsh *mochdre* '(at) the pig farms', given an OE dative plural after a lost preposition. Chiefly a Chesh/Lancs surname.

Mouat(t), *see* **Mowat**.

Mould/Moule/Moull/Moult, *see* **Maud**.

Moulton P Place-name in Chesh, Lincs, Norfolk, Northants, NRYorks, Suffolk OE '*Mula/Moda*'s farm' or 'farm with mules'. Chiefly a Chesh surname. Readily confused with/a variant of **Molton**.

Mouncey/Mounsey/Munsey P Place-names in France: *Monceaux* in Calvados and *Monchaux* in Seine-Inférieure OF 'little hills'. **Mouncey** and **Mounsey** are surnames of the north of England, but **Munsey** is most commonly found in southern counties, especially Beds.

Mount T Dweller by a hill OF. Chiefly a Kent surname.

Mountain P Chiefly a WRYorks surname; there is such a place-name in that county OF 'mountain', but it is apparently of late formation. Cottle points out that 'most of

England's real mountains are called by the locals "fells"', and suggests that 'the name could perhaps be for *Mounton*, localities in Lancs, Mon, and Pembs'.

Mountjoy P Place-name *Montjoie* in Manche OF. A *montjoie* was a cairn set up to mark a victory – especially the spiritual one won by St Denis at the site of his martyrdom; the *Montjoie Saint-Denis* was the old war-cry of the French (even in Charlemagne's time, according to the *Song of Roland*). Chiefly a Devon/Gloucs surname.

Moverley P Place-name just over the Lancs border from Todmorden, WRYorks, of uncertain etymology (the last element being OE 'clearing'). Readily confused with/a variant of **Moberley**.

Mowat(t)/Mouat(t) F/O/P From a mediaeval first-name *Mohaut*, a variation of *Mau(l)d* (see **Maud**); or an occupational term for a man in charge of communally held pasture land OE *mawe-weard* ('meadow guardian'); or from one of a number of places in France called *Mon(t)haut* OF 'high hill'. Cottle says: 'When I was last in Unst, the furthest north innkeeper in Britain was a **Mouat**'. Chiefly Scottish surnames in all spellings; **Mouat** belongs to the Shetland Islands; **Mouatt**, very scarce, can be found in Angus. **Muat** is a rare variant.

Mowbray P Place-name *Montbrai* in La Manche OF 'hill' and Gaulish 'mud/slime'. The surname **Mowbray** is mainly found in Co Durham; variants include: **Membry** (Somerset), **Memory** (Devon/Leics) and **Mummery** (Kent). Thomas **Mowbray** was created first Duke of Norfolk in 1397, a title which eventually passed to the Howard family.

Mowle(s), *see* Maud.

Moxham, *see* Moxon.

Moxon F 'Son of *Mog*', a diminutive of *Margaret*, see **Magg**. Strongest in WRYorks. **Moxham**, apparently a variant, found in counties as far apart as Lancs and Somerset, has been given a place-name appearance.

Moyes, *see* Moses.

Moyle N Cornish: nickname for a bald person, Cornish *moyl*.

Moyne O Occupational term for a monk OF. See **Monk**. A scarce scattered surname. Compare **Minogue**, **Molony** and **Monahan**.

Moynihan P Irish: Anglicized form of Gaelic **O'** [descendant of] **Muimhneachain** 'Munsterman'. Readily confused with **Monahan**?

Moyse, *see* Moses.

Mozley, *see* Moseley.

Muat, *see* Mowat.

Much/Mutch N Nickname for a big person OE (as in a place-name such as *Much Wenlock*). Chesh/Lancs surnames, though **Mutch** has a very strong presence in Aberdeenshire, Scotland, and George and John **Mutch** were in the Jacobite Army in 1745.

Mucklestone P Place-name in Staffs OE '*Mucel*'s farm'. A very scarce scattered surname.

Mudd F/T/O From a mediaeval first-name, a variant of *Maud* (see **Maud**); or from an OE male first-name, a short form of various names beginning with *Môd-* ('heart, courage'); or a dweller at a muddy spot ME *mud*; or an occupational term for one who worked with mud, perhaps making houses of wattle and daub. Strongest in the north and north-east of England.

Mudford P Place-names: *Mudford*, Somerset, and *Mudeford*, Dorset OE 'muddy ford'; *Muddiford*, Devon OE '*Moda*'s enclosure'. A Devon/Somerset/Surrey surname in the main. Possibly confused with **Mogford/Mugford**?

Mudge, *see* Magg.

Mugford, *see* Mogford.

Muggeridge/Mugridge, *see* Mogridge.

Muir, *see* Moor.

Muirhead T/P Dweller at the top of a moor, Scots dialect of OE; or from one of a number of places in southern Scotland so-called, with the same meaning.

Mulcahy F Irish: Anglicized form of Gaelic **O'** [descendant of] **Maolchathaigh** ('devotee of [St] *Cathach*').

Mulcaster, *see* Muncaster.

Mule(s) F/N/O From a mediaeval first-name, possibly *Mul* OE 'mule, half-breed' OE, also known as an element in place-names; or from the female first-name *Mulle/Molle*, a pet-form of *Mary* (compare **Moll**, **Malet**, **Malin** and **Marriott**); or readily confused with/a variant of **Mole/Moule/Moull/Mowle** (see **Maud**); or a nickname for a person as stubborn as a mule; or an occupational term for one who worked with mules OE *mul*/OF *mule*. **Mule** is exceptionally scarce; **Mules** is mostly found in Cornwall and Devon.

Mulhe(a)rn F Irish: Anglicized form of Gaelic **O'** [descendant of] **Maoilchiarain** ('devotee of [St] *Ciaran*').

Mulholland F Irish: Anglicized form of Gaelic **O'** [descendant of] **Maolchalann** ('devotee of [St] *Calann*'). An Ulster surname.

Mullan(e), *see* McMillan.

Mullarkey F Irish: Anglicized form of Gaelic **O'** [descendant of] **Maoilearca** ('devotee of [St] *Earc*').

Mullen(s), *see* Mullin.

Mullery F Irish: Anglicized form of Gaelic **O'** [descendant of] **Maolmhuire** ('devotee of the *Blessèd Virgin Mary*'). Found mainly in Roscommon and in neighbouring areas of Connacht; scarce within the United Kingdom, with a very limited presence in both the north-west and the south-east of England. *Alan Patrick Mullery, Tottenham Hotspur and England footballer, was born in Notting Hill, London, in 1941.*

Mulligan/Millican/Milligan/Milligen/Milliken/Millikin F Irish: Anglicized form of Gaelic **O'** [descendant of] **Maolagain** ('shaveling/bald-head/tonsured'). Compare **Mullan(e)** (see **McMillan**). *Terence Alan ('Spike') Milligan (1918–2002), comedian and author, was born in Ahmednagar, India,* where his father, Leo Alphonso Milligan (born in Co Sligo, Ireland, in 1890), was serving as a soldier. It is said that the family surname had previously been 'Mulligan' (see also **Kettleband**).

Mullin(s)/Mullen(s) T/O/P Dweller by, or worker at, a mill or mills OF (*see also* **Mill**, **Miller**); or from a place-name in France such as *Moulin(s)* OF 'mill(s)'. Readily confused with/a variant of **Mullan** (see **McMillan**).

Mullinar/Mullin(d)er/Mullinger, *see* **Miller**.

Mullins, *see* Mullin.

Mullock P Many surname dictionaries side-step **Mullock**. Bardsley believes that to derive such a surname from the first-name *Mulloc* 'seems to be the only natural conclusion'; Harrison is happy enough with something similar, and speaks of the OE name-stem *Mul*, with the addition of the diminutive suffix *-oc*, but also suggests a topographical origin, with the meaning 'dweller at the summit, hilltop' (Gaelic and Irish *mullach*). Yet at least as likely an origin must lie in the place name *Mullock* in Pembrokeshire, Wales OE 'mill hook' (there being a well-marked spur of land nearby), the earliest-known references to which date from the thirteenth century. Chiefly a surname of Chesh, Lancs and Staffs.

Mulren(n)an F Irish: Anglicized form of Gaelic **O'** [descendant of] **Maoilbhreanainn** ('devotee of [St] *Brendan*').

Mulvihil(l) F Irish: Anglicized form of Gaelic **O'** [descendant of] **Maoilmhichil** ('descendant of the devotee of [St] *Michael*'). Changed to **Mulville** and **Melville** in Clare and Galway, and to **Mitchell** in Ulster.

Mumby P Place-name in Lincs ON '*Mundi*'s settlement' and a Lincs surname.

Mumford P Place-names: *Mundford* in Norfolk OE '*Munda*'s ford' and *Montfort* in Normandy, France OF 'strong hill'. A scattered surname, strong in Essex and Middx.

Mummery, *see* Mowbray.

Muncaster/Mulcaster P Place-name *Muncaster* in Cumbd (formerly *Mulcaster*) OE/ON and OE *'Mula/Muli*'s (Roman) fort'. Chiefly a Lancs surname. John Pennington (c.1741–1813), army officer and politician, became the first Baron **Muncaster**. *The birth-name of the landscape and marine painter Claude Grahame Muncaster (1903–1974), who was born near Pulborough in Sussex, was (Oliver) Grahame Hall. In 1922 he adopted his Cumbrian maternal grandmother's surname of Muncaster and the first-name (a touch of* lèse-majesté*?) of the French landscape painter Claude Lorrain. Martin Muncaster, radio and television broadcaster, wrote a biograpy of his father Claude Muncaster in 1978.*

Muncey, *see* Mouncey.

Munday, *see* Monday.

Munden/Mundon, *see* Munton.

Mundy, *see* Monday.

Munn, *see* Moon.

Munro(e)/Monro(e)/Munrow P Place-name in Co Londonderry, Irish 'mouth of the (river) *Roe/Rotha*'; the Gaelic *Bun-* ('river mouth') has become *Mun-* after a preposition. The surname travelled with its bearers to the north of Scotland in the eleventh century. *James Monroe (1758–1831), fifth President of the United States, is descended from the Scottish baronial house of Munro of Foulis.*

Munsey, *see* Mouncey.

Munton/Munden/Mundon P Place-names: *Mundon*, Essex OE '?*Munda*'s hill' and *Munden* and *Great/Little Munden*, Herts OE '*Munda*'s valley'/'protection valley'. **Munton** is chiefly found in Lincs and in South Midlands counties; **Munden** is at its strongest in Dorset and Hants, and **Mundon**, scarce, is also a surname of the south of England.

Murch N Nickname for a short person, a dwarf ME. A Devon surname. **Merch** is a very scarce Lancs variant. Readily confused with/a variant of **March**.

Murchie/Murchison, *see* McMorrough.

Murcott P Place-names *Murcott/Murcot* in Northants, Oxon, Wilts, Worcs OE 'moor/fen cottage(s)'. A scarce surname, strongest in Warwicks.

Murdoch F/O Scots: Anglicized form of the Gaelic first-name *Muire(adh)ach*, derived from *muir* ('sea'). So Cottle also takes it to be an occupational term for a sailor. **Murdock** is a Northern Irish variant. *(Keith) Rupert Murdoch, powerful and controversial media tycoon, was born in Melbourne, Australia, in 1931, the son of Sir Keith Arthur Murdoch (1886–1952), newspaper proprietor, whose father Rev. Patrick John Murdoch, born at Pitsligo, Aberdeenshire, in 1850, was a Presbyterian minister who made his career in Australia.*

Murfin, *see* Mervin.

Murgatroyd P From a now-lost place-name near Halifax, WRYorks, usually taken to be OE '?*Margaret*'s clearing', though George Redmonds suggests that the first element could be 'moor-gate', referring to a gate (OE) or to a highway (ON). The 'now lost' place in question is perhaps the settlement currently known as *Hollins* in Warley.

Muriel F From a Celtic female first-name meaning 'sea-bright'. **Muriel** itself is a scarce surname, but has given rise to a number of variants, several of which are more prolific, such as **Merrall(s)**, **Merrell(s)** and **Merrill(s)** (all of which could perhaps alternatively be topographical surnames for a dweller by a pretty/pleasant hill OE), and also **Murrell(s)** and **Murrill(s)**.

Murph(e)y F Irish: Anglicized form of Gaelic **O'** [descendant of] **Murchadha** ('sea warrior'). Compare **Morrow** and **McMorrough**. The **Murphey** spelling is much rarer than **Murphy**, which is the commonest surname in Ireland, and which Irish immigration has carried into Scotland and elsewhere in the English-speaking world.

Murray/Murrey/Murrie/Murry P/F
Scots: from the county-name *Moray*, Gaelic (from British) 'seaboard settlement'; Irish: Anglicized form of the Gaelic patronymics **Mac Muire(adh)aigh** (derived from *muir* ['sea'] – compare **Murdoch**) and **Mac Giolla Mhuire** ('servant/devotee of [the Virgin] *Mary*' – compare **Gilmer**). Readily confused with/a variant of **Merry**. See also **Morrow**. **Murrey** and **Murry** are strongest in Lancs, scarce in Scotland. **Murray** is the family name of the Dukes of Atholl.

Murrell(s), *see* Muriel.

Murrey/Murrie, *see* Murray.

Murrill(s), *see* Muriel.

Murrough/Murrow, *see* Morrow.

Murry, *see* Murray.

Murton P There are places so-called in four northern counties OE 'moor/fen settlement' (compare **Morton**), yet the surname is strongest in Kent and Suffolk. Readily confused with/a variant of **Merton**.

Muscat/Muscott, *see* Muskett.

Muscroft P A WRYorks surname from an unidentified place-name OE 'enclosed land infested with mice'.

Musgrave/Musgrove P Two villages called *Musgrave* OE 'wood infested with mice' in Westmd (rather than similar place-names found in Somerset) will usually be the source of these predominantly northern surnames.

Muskett/Muscat/Muscott P/N Reaney derives such surnames from the place-names *Muscott*, Northants OE '?mice's (humble) cottages' or *Muscoates*, NRYorks OE '*Musi*'s/mouse-infested cottages'; Cottle favours a nickname, from OF 'male sparrow-hawk': 'it was proper for a holy-water clerk when hawking'. **Muskett** is at its strongest in Norfolk; **Muscat** and **Muscott**, both very scarce, can be found in Sussex and North-ants respectively.

Musson ?P/F A surname of the English Midlands, especially strong in Lincs, which

Bardsley maintains is a corruption of **Muston** or **Misson**, while Hanks and Hodges favour some kind of (unspecified) patrony-mic. *Masson* in Derbys, now the name of a hill above the Derwent OE '?*Maesa*'s valley', but formerly used of the river valley itself, may be involved here, though the first recorded references to *Le Masseden/Mas-den/Masson* date from as late as the fifteenth century. See also **Misson**, and **Masson** (under **Mason**).

Mustard O/N Occupational term for a mus-tard dealer OF, though Reaney would like to add a nickname meaning, for one with a sharp tongue. Strongest in Co Durham and in the north of Scotland.

Mustell/Mustill N Nickname for a weasel-like person OF. A scarce surname in either spelling: **Mustell** has a limited presence in Northants, **Mustill** in Cambs.

Musters P Place-name *Les Moutiers-Hubert* (*Mostiers* in 1155) in Calvados, France OF 'churches' (compare *monastery*). A very scarce scattered surname, though the fam-ily of **Chaworth Musters** has long been well established in Derbys and Notts.

Mustill, *see* Mustell.

Musto(e)/Mustow T Dweller at a place used as the formal meeting-place for a hun-dred (literally 'moot-stow') OE (compare **Mutlow**). A scarce Gloucs surname in both spellings.

Muston P Place-name in Leics OE 'mouse-infested farm' or '?muddy farm'; the place-name in ERYorks may have a similar origin, or might have had an owner with the ON name *Músi*. Strongest in Leics and other Midlands counties. See also **Musson**.

Mustow, *see* Musto.

Mutch, *see* Much.

Mutlow P Place-name in Chesh OE 'moot/assembly mound' (compare **Musto**), though the surname is strongest in Here-fords.

Mutter O Occupational term for one who speaks at the moot, a public-speaker OE; a good example of the dangers of guessing at etymologies. Strongest in Devon.

Mutton o/n Occupational term for a shepherd, or a nickname for a docile, sheep-like person, or one who resembled a sheep in other ways oe. Readily confused with/a variant of **Mitton** or **Myton**.

Muxworthy P Place-name in Devon oe 'dungy enclosure', and chiefly a Devon surname.

Myall, *see* Michael.

Myer(s) t/o Dweller at a marsh on; or an occupational term for a physician oe. Readily confused with/a variant of **Mayer**.

Myerscough P Place-name in Lancs on 'marshy/boggy wood', and a Lancs surname.

Myhill, *see* Michael.

Mylchreest F A distinctive and charming Manx surname, a contraction of **Mac-Giolla/MacGuilley Chreest** 'son of Christ's servant'.

Myles, *see* Miles.

Mynett/Mynott, *see* Minn.

Myt(t)on P Place-names: *Myton*, Warwicks and *Mytton*, Salop oe 'confluence (of streams or rivers) enclosure'. Readily confused with/a variant of **Mitton** or **Mutton**.

N

Nabb(s), *see* **Robert**.

Nairn(e) P Place-name in Scotland. The town and county (*Nairn*) take their name from the river *Nairn*, a Celtic word.

Naisbett/Naisbitt, *see* **Nesbit**.

Naish, *see* **Nash**.

Naismith O Occupational term for a knife-smith, cutler OE. Found mainly in Lanark-shire, Scotland. **Nesmith** is a very scarce variant.

Nancarrow P Cornish place-name meaning 'stag valley'.

Nance P Place-name in Illogan, Cornwall, meaning 'valley'.

Nancekivell/Nankivell P Place-name *Nankivell* in Cornwall, meaning 'horse valley'.

Napier/Napper O Occupational term for a seller of table linen or for a naperer (a table-linen-keeper in a great household) OF. Compare the word *napkin* and also *apron*, which has lost its initial *n-* to the indefinite article, having formerly been '*a napron*'. **Napier** is principally a Scottish surname; **Napper** can be found across southern England.

Napton P Place-name in Warwicks OE 'place on a bowl(-shaped hill)'.

Narracott P Place-name in Devon OE 'northern cottage(s)', and a Devon surname.

Narramore P Place-name in Devon OE 'north of the moor', and a Devon surname.

Nash/Naish T/N Dweller at the ash tree OE.

The ME *at them* (consisting of a preposition followed by the masculine dative singular of the definite article) became *atten* and later simply *n-*, which then became attached to the word *ash*. Compare **Nelms, New, Noad, Noake, Noar** and **Nye**, and see **Ness**. But there may sometimes be confusion with the OE word *nesh* ('soft, timid, delicate'), still used in Midland counties of England to describe someone who is particularly susceptible to the cold. **Nash** is most commonly found in the south of England and in Ireland, while **Naish** belongs primarily to Gloucs/Somerset/Wilts.

Nathan/Nation F From the Hebrew first-name *Natan* ('gift'), borne by the Prophet. A post-Reformation or immigrant surname. Folk etymology has given rise to the variant **Nation**, most commonly found in the south-west of England, especially Somerset. *Col Stephen Nation (1780–1828) of the Bengal Army was born in Dulverton, Somerset.*

Nation, *see* **Nathan**.

Nat(t)ras(s)/Nat(t)res(s)/Nat(t)ris(s) P Place-name *Nattrass* in Cumbd ON '*Nate*'s/nettle brushwood', though the surname was more conspicuous in the north-east of England by the late nineteenth century. A Yorkshire Dales family of **Nattrass** emigrated to Wisconsin in the early 1840s.

Naughtie, *see* **Naughty**.

Naughton P/F Place-name in Suffolk OE 'depression/navel settlement'. Irish: Angli-cized form of the Gaelic first-name *Neach-dan* (?from Latin Neptune, the Roman God of the sea). See also **McNaghten**. Within

England, chiefly a Lancs surname (the result of Irish immigration?). Readily confused with/a variant of **Naughty** and **Norton**.

Naughty/Naughtie P A surname of Aberdeenshire, Scotland, probably derived from the place-name *Nochty* in Strath Don. Readily confused with/a variant of **Naughton**. *James Naughtie, BBC radio journalist, born in Milltown of Rothiemay, Banffshire, in 1952, pronounces his surname 'Nochty' (in keeping with its origins) rather than 'Naughty'.*

Naunton P There are places so-called in Gloucs and Worcs OE 'at the new settlement', but the surname belongs principally to East Anglia.

Nayland P Place-name in Suffolk OE '(at) the island'. A very scarce Essex/Lancs surname.

Naylor/Nayler O Occupational term for a nail-maker OE.

Neal(e)/Neall/Neil(d)/Neill/Nell/Niall F From a first-name *Niall*, brought to England by Scandinavian settlers from Ireland, and by the Normans, meaning 'champion'. A Latin form was made for it (whence the first-name *Nigel*), as if it were connected with the Latin word *niger* ('black, dark'). **Neilson** is 'son of *Neil*' and **Nelson** is 'son of *Nell*'. One hapless registrar of births, marriages and deaths in Chesterfield, Derbys, had the irksome task of recording details of the birth of a young girl, born on 31 December 1985, whose full registered name was as follows: Tracy Mariclaire Lisa Tammy Samantha Christine Alexandra Candy Bonnie Ursula Zoe Nichola Patricia Lynda Kate Jean Sandra Karren Julie Jane Elizabeth Felicity Gabriella Jackie Corina Constance Arabella Clara Honor Geraldine Giona Erika Fillippa Anabel Elsie Amanda Cheryl Alanna Louise Angie Beth Crystal Dawn Debbie Eileen Grace Susan Rebecca Valerie Kay Lena Margaret Anna Amy Carol Bella Avril Ava Audry Andrea Daphne Donna Cynthia Cassie Christable Vivien Wendy Moira Jennifer Abbie Adelaide Carissa Clara Anne Astrid Barbara Clarissa Catalina Bonny Dee Hazel Iris Anthea Clarinda Bernadette Cara Alison Carrie Angela Beryl Caroline Emma Dana Vanessa Zara Violet Lynn Maggie Pamela Rosemary Ruth Cathlene Alexandrina Annette Hilary Diana Angelina Carrinna Victoria Sara Mandy Annabella Beverley Bridget Cecilia Catherine Brenda Jessica Isabella Delilah Camila Candice Helen Connie Charmaine Dorothy Melinda Nancy Marian Vicki Selina Miriam Norma Pauline Toni Penny Shari Zsa Zsa Queenie **Nelson**.

Neam(e) N Nickname for a short person OF *nain* ('dwarf') or for an uncle OE *eame*, from *mine/thine eame*: 'my/your uncle', with the *n-* detached (just as *an ewt* became *a newt* in common speech). A Kent surname. *Ronald Neame, the British cinematographer who produced the much-loved film* Brief Encounter *(1945) and many others, was born in London in 1911.*

Neap(e), *see* **Neep**.

Neat(e) O Occupational term for an ox-/cow-(herd) OE (compare *neat's-foot-oil* and the surname **Nutter**).

Neave, *see* **Neve**.

Neck N Nickname for a person with some distinguishing oddity of the neck OE. Chiefly a Devon surname.

Needham P Place-name in Derbys, Norfolk, Suffolk OE 'hardship/poverty homestead' – the kind of 'misery farm' it would be good to see the back of, presumably. A surname of the English Midlands and the north. Family name of the Earls of Kilmorey.

Needle(r) O Occupational term for a maker or user of needles OE. **Needle** is most common in Warwicks, **Needler** in ERYorks.

Neep/Neape O/N Occupational term for a grower or seller of turnips OE (as in modern Scots 'neep'), or perhaps – could it be? – a nickname for a turnip-looking person? **Neep** is found mainly in Norfolk, **Neape** (very scarce) in Staffs.

Neeve(s), *see* **Neve**.

Negus ?T A surname of uncertain origin,

perhaps referring originally to a dweller in a house situated near a large settlement OE *neah hus* ('near house'). In the sixteenth and seventeenth centuries it can be found spelt **Negose** and **Neghouse**, and the Protestation Oath Roll for the parish of Willesden in Middx (1641-2) includes the name of Edward **Negoose**. **Negus** is primarily a surname of the Home Counties, Beds and Cambs, so G. Pawley White's contention that it might be from Cornish *know-gos* ('nut grove') or *neghys* ('denied') would seem to be wide of the mark in most cases. *The popular antiques expert and broadcaster Arthur George Negus (1903–1985) was born in Reading, Berks; his father (of the same name) was a cabinet maker from Hunts.*

Neighbour N Nickname for a neighbour OE, or perhaps for a neighbourly person. A south-east-of-England surname.

Neil(d)/Neill/Neilson/Nell, *see* Neal.

Nelm(e)s T Dweller at the elms OE, where the N-, representing the -m- of the dative plural of the definite article after a lost preposition, has become attached to the following word (so compare **Nash**, **New**, **Noad**, **Noake**, **Noar** and **Nye**). See also **Elm**. Principally Gloucs surnames in either spelling.

Nelson, *see* Neal.

Nepean T Dweller at the little valley, Cornish *nan-pean/nan-vean*. A very scarce surname, with a particular presence in Devon.

Nesbit(t)/Naisbett/Naisbitt/Nisbet(t)/Nisbit P Place-names *Nisbit/Nesbit(t)* in Co Durham and in English counties bordering on Scotland, where such surnames are mostly to be found OE 'bend like a nose' (literally 'nose bight'), describing the appearance of a piece of land.

Nesfield P Place-name in WRYorks OE 'open land for cattle'. An ERYorks/NRYorks surname. Compare **Neat**.

Nesmith, *see* Naismith.

Ness T/P Dweller at a headland, projecting ridge ON, or from one of a number of place-names with the same meaning in various counties; or a corruption of **Nash**. A surname of north-east England and Scotland. *Eliot Ness (1903–1957), famous as an American prohibition agent, was born in Chicago to Norwegian parents.*

Nethercoat/Nethercot(e)/Nethercott T/P Dweller in a cottage at the lower end of any given settlement OE, or from a place-name with the same meaning in various counties. **Nethercoat** is a very scarce Essex surname; **Nethercote** is scarce and scattered, and **Nethercot** and **Nethercott** belong mainly to the West Country.

Netherton P Place-name in many counties OE 'lower place'. Mainly a Cornwall/Devon surname.

Netherwood T/P Dweller at the lower wood OE, or from a minor place so-named. This is mainly a WRYorks surname, and George Redmonds believes that families called **Netherwood** in Bradford, Airedale and Huddersfield probably had their origins in a place called *Netherwood* in Whalley, Lancs.

Netley P There is such a place-name in Salop OE 'clearing with nettles', but this is overwhelmingly a Sussex surname, so its origin is more likely to lie in one of two places in the neighbouring county of Hants: *Netley* OE 'wood/clearing where laths are obtained' or *Netley Marsh* OE 'wet clearing'.

Nettlefold P From a minor place-name such as *Nettlefold*, Surrey OE 'nettle enclosure'. A surname of south-east England, but which also has a presence in Warwicks. *Joseph Henry Nettlefold (1827–1881), the manufacturer of screws whose surname would be perpetuated in the firm of Guest, Keen and Nettlefold, was born in London.*

Nettleship T ?Dweller at an enclosed valley with nettles OE, or from a now lost place named *Nettlesthope* or same such. Mainly a WRYorks surname.

Nettleton P The place-name *Nettleton* in Lincs OE 'place in the nettles' is more likely to be the origin of this mainly WRYorks surname than a settlement with the same name in far-off Wilts.

Neve/Neave/Neeve(s) N Nickname for a nephew (of a famous person, or a boy brought up by his uncle) OE. **Neve** belongs mainly to Kent, **Neave** to Norfolk; **Neeve**, much scarcer, can be found in both these counties. 'Ethel Le Neve, who eloped, disguised as a youth, with Dr Crippen, represents a Gallic refinement of this' (Cottle). *The famous antiquaries Peter Le Neve (1661–1729), son of Francis Neve and Avis Wright, and his kinsman John Le Neve (1679–?1741), son of John Le Neve and Amy Bent, were both born in London.*

Neven/Nevin F Irish: Anglicized form of Gaelic **Mac Cnaimhin** ('son of ?bones/thin man') or of **Mac Naoimhin** ('son of saint'). Found in Ireland, Scotland and northern England. See also **McNevin**. **Niven** is a Scots variant. *David Niven (1910–1983), actor and author, though he was born in London, claimed in his autobiographies that his birthplace was Kirriemuir in Scotland.*

Nevett N 'A really defeatist Norman spelling of **Knight** (the French shy away from consonant-clusters)' (Cottle). Commonest in Salop.

Nevill(e)/Newell/Newill P From a place-name in France, such as *Neuville* ('new town') in Calvados; but the great Durham family of **Nevilles** were from *Néville* in Seine-Maritime. Family name of the Barons Braybrooke and of other peers.

Nevin, *see* Neven.

New N/T Nickname for a newcomer OE; or a dweller at the yew-tree OE *atten ew* (compare **Nash, Nelms, Noad, Noake, Noar** and **Nye**). A south-of-England surname. **Newson** 'son of **New**' is readily confused with/a variant of **Newsom**.

Newall, *see* Newhall.

Newark P Place-name in Northants, Notts and Surrey OE 'new building', though in more recent times the surname can rarely be found in any of these counties.

Newbald, *see* Newbold.

Newbegin, *see* Newbiggin.

Newber(r)y, *see* Newbury.

Newbiggin/Newbegin P Place-names in various northern counties OE and ME (from ON) 'new building'. Scarce north-east-of-England surnames.

Newbo(u)ld/Newbald/Newbolt P Place-name *Newbold* in various contiguous Midland and northern counties OE 'new building'. **Newbold** is a surname belonging mainly to these counties; **Newbald** and **Newbolt**, scarce, are more scattered.

Newbury/Newber(r)y P Place-name *Newbury* in various counties OE 'new market-town/fort'. **Newbury** is found throughout the south of England; **Newbery** and **Newberry** both belong to Devon.

Newby P Place-name in Cumbd, Westmd and Yorks OE and ON 'new farm'. A surname of the north of England, especially Lancs.

Newcomb(e)/Newcome/Newcomen N Nickname for a newly-come/arrived person, a newcomer OE. The intrusive *-b-* in **Newcomb(e)** is by analogy with the familiar place-name suffix. **Newcomen** is from the past participle *cumen* ('having come'). **Newcomb, Newcome** and **Newcomen** are scattered surnames within England; **Newcombe** belongs mainly to Devon – where its origin may be a now-lost place-name, after all? *Thomas Newcomen (1664–1729), inventor of the atmospheric steam-engine, was born in Dartmouth, Devon.*

Newcomen, *see* Newcomb.

Newell, *see* Nevill.

Newhall/Newall T/P Dweller at the new hall/manor house OE or from a place-name *Newhall*, with the same meaning, in Chesh, Derbys, Herts, Warwicks, WRYorks. Surnames of the north of England.

Newham/Newnham/Ninham P Place-names *Newham* and *Newnham* in various counties OE 'new homestead'. The *-n-* of **Newnham** is a relic of the weak dative adjective after a lost preposition and definite article. **Newham** belongs to the English north and Midlands (especially Notts), **Newnham** to the south-east and **Ninham** (very scarce) to Norfolk. *Newnham College, Cambridge, was not named after a person, but after the Cambs village of Newnham.*

Newhouse/Newiss T Dweller at a new house OE. **Newhouse** is a scarce Lancs surname; **Newiss**, even scarcer, can also be found in Chesh and in WRYorks.

Newill, *see* Nevill.

Newington P Place-name in various counties OE 'at the new farm/settlement', but found as a surname almost exclusively in Kent and Sussex.

Newiss, *see* Newhouse.

Newland(s) T/P Dweller at newly acquired or cultivated land OE, or from one of a number of place-names with the same meaning. **Newland** is a south-east-of-England surname; **Newlands** belongs to Scotland.

Newman N Nickname for a person newly arrived or settled in a particular place OE. Widespread, but found particularly in the southern half of England.

Newnham, *see* Newham.

Newport P Place-name in many counties OE (from the Latin) 'new town' (especially one with market rights).

Newsom(e)/News(h)am/Newsholme P Place-names *Newsome*, *Newsham* and *Newsholme* in various northern counties OE '(at) the new houses', exhibiting the use of a dative plural after a lost preposition. Mainly Yorks surnames. Readily confused with/a variant of **Newson** (see **New**).

Newson, *see* New.

Newstead P Place-name in Lincs, Northd, Notts, NRYorks OE 'new monastery/site/farmstead'. Most commonly found in Norfolk.

Newton P Place-name found throughout England Wales OE 'new place/homestead/farm/village'; said to be the commonest place-name in England, so sources for the surname are legion.

Niall, *see* Neal.

Nibbs/Niblett, *see* Isabell.

Nichol(d)(s)/Nicholas(s)/Nichole(tt)s/ Nicholl(s)/Nichols(on)/Nickal(ls)/ Nickel(l)(s)/Nicklas(s)/Nickle(ss)/ Nickol(l)(s)/Nickold(s)/Nickson/ Nicol(s)/Nicolas/Nicoll(s)/Nicolson/ Nixon F All variants are forms of the first-name *Nicholas*, Greek *Nikolaos* 'victory people', borne by the patron saint of children, mariners, pawnbrokers and wolves. Also the first-name of a number of Russian tsars. See also **Colin**. **Nicholls** is the commonest English surname from the group, and those ending in *-son/xon* ('son of') are northern forms, as usual. Of **Coulson** ('son of *Nicolas*'), Cottle says: 'Chiefly a surname of Northd/Co Durham/Yorks/Lincs, so places *Coulston* (Wilts) and *Coulsdon* (Surrey) are not involved'. *The film actor Jack Nicholson, born in New York City in 1937 to a showgirl named June Frances Nicholson, is descended from an Englishman called Joseph Nicholson, who married Bridget Derrig (from Sligo, Ireland) in Kent in 1854.*

Nightingale N Nickname for someone with a voice as sweet as that of a nightingale (literally 'night-singer') OE, though *Nightingale Lane* in East Smithfield, London, was formerly *Cnihtena Guild Lane*, named after the knight's guild. The modern pronunciation of the word 'nightingale' may seem pleasant enough to modern ears, but bears little resemblance to the way in which such a word would have been pronounced in mediaeval times. To Chaucer (who describes the Squire in *The Canterbury Tales* in the following terms: 'So hote he loved, that by Nightertale/He slept no more than doth a nightingale'), it would have been mellifluous in a different way, being pronounced something like 'nichtin-gahleh'. *Florence Nightingale (1820–1910), famous for her radical and reforming approach to the practice of nursing, was born (unsurprisingly) in Florence, the daughter of William Edward Shore and his wife Frances Smith.*

Her father had changed his surname to Nightingale on inheriting the Derbys estates of his great-uncle Peter Nightingale. It was to Florence's advantage that she bore a particularly pleasant set of names; might the public have warmed to her so readily had she been called Gertrude Rackenblucher or some such?

Ninham, *see* Newham.

Nisbet(t)/Nisbit, *see* Nesbit.

Niven, *see* Neven.

Nixon, *see* Nichol.

Noad(e) T Dweller at the pyre/ash-heap/pile OE; a result of a misdivision of ME *atten oade* ('at the heap') – compare **Nash**, **Nelms**, **New**, **Noake**, **Noar** and **Nye**. A surname of the south of England, strongest in Somerset.

Noake(s)/Noke(s) T Dweller at the oak(s) OE; a result of a misdivision of ME *atten oke(s)* ('at the oak[s]') – compare **Nash**, **Nelms**, **New**, **Noad**, **Noar** and **Nye**. **Noake** can be found in the Midlands and the south of England; **Noakes** belongs to the southeast, **Noke** to the Midlands and the north, **Nokes** to the Midlands and the south-east.

Noar T Dweller at the bank/slope OE; a result of a misdivision of OE *atten ora* ('at the slope') – compare **Nash**, **Nelms**, **New**, **Noad**, **Noake** and **Nye**. A scarce Lancs surname.

Nobb(s), *see* Robert.

Noble N Nickname for a notable, noble person OF, either used literally, or ironically (for a humble/ignoble person). Found throughout England and Scotland. The diminutive **Noblet(t)** (sometimes alternatively derived from *Robert* via *Nob*) is a scarce Lancs variant.

Noblet(t), *see* Noble.

Noel/Nowell N Nickname for a person born or baptized during the Christmas season OF. Of **Nowell**, Cottle says: '...this English version of the OF word even meant "Hurrah!" – as when Henry V was welcomed back to London after Agincourt –

or "news", French *nouvelles*'. **Noel** is the family name of the Earls of Gainsborough.

Noke(s), *see* Noake.

Nolan F Irish: Anglicized form of Gaelic **O'** [descendant of] **Nuallain** ('famous').

Noon N Nickname for a cheerful person ME *none* ('noon', the time of maximum sunshine), from Latin *nona*, referring to the ninth hour after sunrise, three o'clock or so having been the original time of 'noon'; or a variant of **Noone**. Long before Gary Cooper had been forced to confront a bunch of villains and a group of pusillanimous townspeople in a famous Western of 1952, a child named '*Hi* Noon' was born in Radford, Nottingham, in 1878.

Noone F Irish: Anglicized form of Gaelic **O'** [descendant of] **Nuadhain** (from the name of one of a number of Celtic gods called *Nuadha*). Or a variant of **Noon**.

Norburn T Dweller at a northern stream OE. A Lancs/WRYorks surname.

Norbury P Place-name in various counties OE 'northern fort/manor-house'. Chiefly a Chesh/Lancs surname.

Norcott, *see* Northcott.

Norgate T Dweller at the north gate (of a walled town or of a castle) OE. A Hants/Norfolk surname.

Norgrove T Dweller at the northern grove OE. Chiefly a Salop surname.

Norman(d) N/F Nickname for a Northman/Viking from Scandinavia or from Normandy OE. *Norman* was also used as a first-name by 1066, though 'the present vogue of the first-name is recent and apparently non-U' (Cottle). **Norman** is widespread throughout England, and particularly strong in Devon – far from the original Viking invasions. **Normand** is a scarce Scottish variant.

Norris(h) T/O A term used for a person who had arrived from the north (be it within England, from Scotland, or from Scandinavia), or who lived on the northern edge of a settlement OF (compare **North**); or an occupational term for a nurse or foster mother OF. **Norris** is strongest in Lancs, **Norrish** in Devon.

North T A newcomer from the north, or a dweller to the north of a settlement (compare **Norris**) OE. Family name of the Earls of Guilford. *Marine Colonel Oliver Laurence ('Ollie') North, a key player in the US 'Iran-Contra' scandal during the presidency of Ronald Reagan and who had as many detractors as supporters, was born in San Antonio, Texas, in 1943.*

Northam P Place-name in Devon and Hants OE 'northern river-meadow'. Principally a Devon surname.

Northcliffe T/P Dweller at the northern cliff, or from a place-name with the same meaning in ERYorks OE. Chiefly a (scarce) WRYorks surname. *When Dublin-born Alfred Harmsworth (1865–1922), newspaper proprietor, was raised to the peerage in 1905, he chose to be known as Baron Northcliffe of the Isle of Thanet. He later became Viscount Northcliffe.*

Northcote/Norcott/Northcott P Place-names: *Northcott* in Devon, Cornwall, Middx and elsewhere; *Norcott* in Gloucs and Herts OE 'northern cottage'. **Northcote** is a Devon surname; **Norcott** is found in the Home Counties and in Lancs, and **Northcott** in Cornwall and Devon. **Northcote** is the family name of the Earls of Iddesleigh.

Northern T A person from the north OE. A scarce Midlands/Lincs surname.

Northfield T/P Dweller at a northern field OE, or from a place-name *Northfield* in several counties with the same meaning. A scarce Cambs/Hunts/Surrey surname.

Northmore T/P Dweller at a northern moor/fen OE, or from the place-name *Northmoor* in several counties wih the same meaning. A Devon surname.

Northorpe P Place-name in Lincs ON 'northern settlement'. A scarce surname, found mostly in ERYorks.

Northover P Place-name in Somerset OE 'northern river-bank' (of the Yeo). As a surname, chiefly found in neighbouring Dorset.

Northwood/Norwood P Place-names *Norwood* and *Northwood* in several counties OE 'northern wood' or 'north of the wood'.

Norton P Place-name found in most English counties OE 'northern/north-facing place/farm/village' or 'north of the village'. The surname is widespread, but more common in the Midlands and the north. Family name of the Barons Grantley and Barons Rathcreedan. Readily confused with/a variant of **Naughton**.

Norwell P Place-name in Notts OE 'northern spring/stream'. A surname of Leics and Notts, but also found in Perthshire, Scotland, where it may have a different origin.

Norwood, *see* **Northwood**.

Notley P Place-name in Bucks, Essex and Herts OE 'nut wood'. Mainly an East Anglian surname.

Nott N Nickname for a bald man or for one with very short hair OE. Strong in Devon and Gloucs. Readily confused with/a variant of **Knott**.

Nottingham P Place-name in Notts OE '*Snot*'s family's homestead'. Strongest in Lancs.

Notton P Place-name in Dorset, Wilts, WRYorks OE 'wether-sheep/cattle farm'. A very scarce Gloucs surname.

Nourse, *see* **Nurse**.

Nowell, *see* **Noel**.

Noy/Noyce/Noyes F From the Hebrew first-name *Noah* ('long-lived'), via ME *Noye*, sometimes applied to a person who had acted such a part in a miracle play. **Noyce/Noyes** is 'son of *Noy*'. **Noy** has an unusual distribution, being found chiefly in Cornwall (where it can be derived from *noy*, the Cornish word for a nephew) and Suffolk. **Noyce** is found mainly in Hants, and **Noyes** across southern England.

Nunn N/O Nickname for a particularly pious man, or an occupational term for someone who worked at a nunnery OE. Cottle puts it rather more brutally: '…either recording some scandal, or describing a demure and prissy man'. An East Anglian surname. *Trevor Nunn, English theatre and film director, was born in 1940 in Ipswich, Suffolk.*

Nunney P Place-name in Somerset OE 'nuns' island'. A scarce surname, found in Gloucs and elsewhere.

Nurse/Nourse O Occupational term for a nurse OF. **Nurse** is chiefly a Norfolk surname; **Nourse** is less common and more widely scattered.

Nutbeam/Nutbeem T/P Dweller by a nut-tree OE, or from a place-name *Nutbane* in Hants, with the same meaning. A Hants surname in both spellings.

Nutcombe P There are places so-called in Devon (several such) and in Surrey OE 'valley with nuts'. There is a memorial in Exeter Cathedral to the Rev. Nutcombe **Nutcombe**, yet this very scarce surname was found only in Gloucs by the late nineteenth century.

Nuthall, *see* Nuttall.

Nutley P Place-name in Hants and Sussex OE 'wood/clearing with nuts'. A south-of-England surname.

Nutt O/N Occupational term for a man who gathered or sold nuts OE, or a nickname for someone resembling a nut in some way (brown complexion/bald head?). Predictably enough, there was once a girl called '*Hazel* **Nutt**', who was born in Holborn, London, in 1894.

Nuttall/Nuthall P Place-names: *Nuttall*, Lancs, and *Nuthall*, Notts OE 'nook/recess where nuts are found'. **Nuttall** is found in northern England, especially Lancs; **Nuthall** is more unevenly spread, with a presence in Norfolk, Surrey and elsewhere.

Nutter O Occupational term for a keeper of oxen ME *nowt* ('beast'), compare **Neat**; or for a clerk, scribe ME *notere* (compare the word *notary*). A Lancs/WRYorks surname.

Nye T/P Dweller at the river or island OE, or from a place-name in Somerset; a result of a misdivision of ME *atten (e)ye* ('at the river/island') – compare **Nash**, **Nelms**, **New**, **Noad**, **Noake** and **Noar**. A Kent/Middx/Surrey/Sussex surname.

O

**Oade/Oat(t)en/Oates/Oddie/Oddy/
Ott** F/T From a ME first-name *Ode*, with its
origin in a number of different earlier
names, including Germanic *Odo/Otto*
('riches'); or a dweller by a pyre/ash-heap
OE, the -*e* being evidence of the use of a
dative after a lost preposition. **Oade,
Oates** and **Oddy** are found chiefly in
WRYorks, **Oaten** in Somerset, **Oddie** in
Lancs and **Ott** in Surrey. **Oatten**, very
scarce, has a presence in Cornwall. *Titus
Oates (1649–1705), infamous for having
made false accusations of a 'Popish plot'
aimed at Protestants, was born in Oakham,
Rutland… Lawrence Edward Grace Oates
(1880–1912), the explorer who perished in an
Antarctic blizzard, was born in Putney, Lon-
don, the son of an Essex landowner… The
actor, writer and ornithologist William Edgar
('Bill') Oddie was born in 1941 in Rochdale,
Lancs.*

Oak(e)(s) T/P Dweller at an oak tree OE, or
from a place-name such as *Oake* in Somerset, with the same meaning. The -*e* of
Oake(s) is evidence of the use of a dative
(singular or plural) after a lost preposition.

Oakden, *see* **Ogden**.

Oakeley, *see* **Oakley**.

Oakey T Dweller at an oak copse OE. A scattered surname, strongest in Gloucs.

Oakford P Place-names: *Oakford* in Devon
and *Okeford* (three such) in Dorset OE 'ford
at the oak(s)'.

Oak(e)ley P From one of a number of
places called *Oakley* OE 'oak wood/clearing',
but readily confused with/a variant of **Oat-**

ley. **Oakley** is found mainly in the English
Midlands, the north-west and the south-
east; **Oakeley** is much scarcer and even
more widely scattered.

Oaten/Oates, *see* **Oade**.

Oatley P Place-name *Oteley* in Salop OE
'clearing/field where oats are grown', but
readily confused with/a variant of **Oakley**.

Oatten, *see* **Oade**.

Oborne P Place-name in Dorset OE 'winding stream'; chiefly found in Somerset.

O'Brien F Irish: descendant of **Brian** (see
Brian). Family name of the Barons Inchi-
quin, legitimist Kings of Ireland.

O'Cahan, *see* **O'Kane**.

O'Connell, *see* **McConnal**.

O'Con(n)or F Irish: descendant of **Conchobhair**, a name borne by one of the
Kings of Ulster. *See also* **Conor**.

Odam(s)/Odham(s) N/P Literally 'son-in-
law', used for a person who had prospered
by marrying the daughter of a prominent or
wealthy man; or from the place-name
Odham in Devon (*Wodeham* in 1281) OE
'wood homestead'. Scarce scattered surnames; **Odam** has its strongest presence
in Devon, **Odams** in Hunts and Leics;
Odham and **Odhams** are very scarce variants. *The British publishing firm Odham's
Press Ltd began as a newspaper group in the
1890s.*

Oddie/Oddy, *see* **Oade**.

Odell P Place-name in Beds OE 'hill where woad grows', and chiefly a Beds surname.

Odger(s), *see* **Edgar**.

Odham(s), *see* **Odam**.

Odiam P Place-name *Odiham* in Hants OE 'wooded homestead'. A very scarce Hants/ Surrey surname.

O'Donnell F Irish: descendant of **Donald**.

O'Donovan N Irish: descendant of **Donndubhain** ('dark brown').

Offer O Occupational name for a goldsmith OF. Compare **Feaver**. A south-of-England surname.

Offord P Place-names *Offord Cluney* and *Offord Darcy* in Hunts OE 'upper ford'; chiefly an East Anglian surname, it can readily be confused with, or be a variant of, **Orford**.

Ogborn(e)/Ogbourn(e)/Ogburn P Place-names *Ogbourne St George* and *Ogbourne St Andrew* in Wilts OE '*Oc(c)a*'s stream'. Scarce scattered surnames.

Ogden/Oakden P There are minor places called *Ogden* in various counties, including Lancs and WRYorks OE 'oak valley'. **Ogden** is found chiefly in Lancs, **Oakden** (much scarcer) in Derbys.

Ogg N Nickname used to distinguish the younger of two people bearing the same name, Scots Gaelic *og* ('young'). Strongest in Aberdeenshire.

Ogilvie/Ogilvy P Place-name *Ogilvie* in Angus, probably OW *uchel* and Gaelic *bheinn*, 'high hill'. **Ogilvy** is the family name of the Earls of Airlie.

O'Hagan F Irish: descendant of **hAgain** ('young').

O'Hair(e)/O'Hare/O'Hear F Irish: descendant of **hAichir** ('sharp/angry'). See also **Hare**. Readily confused with **O'Hara**?

O'Hara F Irish: descendant of **hEaghra** (of uncertain origin). Readily confused with **O'Hair**?

O'Hare/O'Hear, *see* **O'Hair**.

O'Kane/O'Cahan F Irish: descendant of **Cathain** ('warrior'). An Ulster surname from early times. See also **Cain**.

Oke, *see* **Oake**.

O'Keef(f)e F Irish: descendant of **Caoimh** ('gentle/tender').

Old(s) N Theoretically **Old** and **Olds** are derived from OE *eald* ('old', senior'), used to distinguish the elder of two people bearing the same name, but in Cornwall, where such surnames are mostly found, the origin is likely to be Cornish *als* ('cliff/shore/ strand').

Oldacre/Oldaker T Dweller at the old ploughland OE. Scarce in either spelling; **Oldacre** is mainly found in Staffs, **Oldaker** in Warwicks.

Oldbury P Place-name in various counties OE 'old fort'. A Midlands surname.

Older, *see* **Alder**.

Oldfield P Place-name in various counties OE 'long-/formerly-cultivated field'. Strongest in WRYorks. *The musician Mike Oldfield of* Tubular Bells *fame was born in Reading, Berks, in 1953.*

Oldham P Place-name in Lancs OE and ON 'long-/formerly-cultivated river flat (*holm*)'.

Oldland P Place-name in Gloucs, probably OE 'neglected arable land', and chiefly a Gloucs surname.

Oldreive/Oldreave O Occupational term used to describe an old reeve (official/steward/sheriff) OE. These are Devon surnames, though **Oldreave** is very scarce.

Oldridge P Place-name in Devon OE '?*Wealda*'s ridge', and found chiefly in that county; but readily confused with/a variant of **Aldrich** or **Aldridge**.

Oldroyd P From one of a number of minor place-names in the north of England OE 'old clearing'.

Olds, *see* **Old**.

O'Leary, *see* **Leary**.

Ol(l)iff(e) F From an ON first-name *Olaf* ('relic of the gods'). Popularized thanks to *St Olaf/Olav II*, eleventh-century King of Norway, who brought Christianity to his country and after whom the London churches of *St Olave*, Hart Street, *St Olave*, Silver Street and *St Olave*, Southwark, were named. Compare **Umpleby**. Or a variant of **Olive**. A scarce south-east-of-England surname, whatever the spelling.

Oliphant N/O/T Nickname derived from ME *olifant* ('elephant'), used perhaps for a large ungainly person '...the clumsy adversary of Chaucer's Sir Thopas was Sir Olifaunt' (Cottle); or an occupational term for a dealer or worker in ivory; or a dweller at the sign of the elephant. A surname more commonly found in Scotland than in England.

Olive F From the Latin feminine first-name *Olive*, borne by two saints, or a variant of **Olliff**. Largely a Lancs surname, but also found in southern counties of England.

Oliv(i)er F From the OF first-name *Olivier* ('?olive tree'), brought to England by the Normans. Made popular because it was borne by one of Charlemagne's peers, the friend of Roland, who was featured in several romances. Being the first-name of *Oliver* Cromwell it fell out of favour in England during the Restoration, but was later revived.

Ollerenshaw/Ollerearnshaw P Place-name *Ollerenshaw* in Derbys OE 'wood with alders'. **Ollerenshaw** is strongest in Chesh and Derbys, **Olerenshaw** (scarce) in Staffs and Warwicks, and **Ollerearnshaw** in WRYorks. See also **Ravenshaw** and **Wrench**.

Olliff(e), *see* **Oliff**.

Oman(d)/Omond F From an ON first-name meaning 'great-grandfather protector', or (losing an *H*-) 'high protector' OE. Uncommon surnames, found mainly in Scotland.

O'Neil(l) F Irish: descendant of **Neill**.

Onion(s)/Anyan/Anyon/Ennion/Eynon F/O Welsh: from the first-name *Einion*, probably from Latin *Annianus*, from the family name *Annius*, adopted in OW and fathered on to such Welsh words as *anian* 'nature/genius' and *einion* 'anvil'. There was an early Welsh St *Einiawn*. See also **Beynon**. As an English surname, **Onion(s)** can alternatively be an occupational term for a seller of onions OF. The surname **Onion** is widespread, strong in Notts; **Onions** is found mainly in the West Midlands, **Anyan** in Lincs, **Ennion** in Chesh and Lancs, and **Eynon** in South Wales. See also **Kenyon**.

Onley P Place-name in Northants OE 'lonely glade'; the surname is found in Northants itself, and in other scattered localities.

Onn ?P Cottle would derive this scarce monosyllabic surname from a place-name in Staffs OW '?kiln' or '?ash-trees', but it is a Lincs surname, truly of unknown origin. Perhaps the first-name Owen is involved?

Openshaw P Place-name in Lancs OE 'unenclosed wood'.

Oram, *see* **Orme**.

Orbell F/N Reaney rejects the idea that the female Scottish first-name *Arabella* is the source here, preferring instead to opt for a nickname from Latin *arabilis* 'easy to be entreated'. Other theories as to the origin of this uncommon East Anglian surname arise from the fact that *Orbel(l)* is Dutch and Flemish for 'one ear-ring', a 'trademark' worn by Flemish weavers in mediaeval times.

Orchard T/P/O Dweller at an orchard OE, or from a place-name in Devon and Somerset OE 'orchard' and also in Dorset OW 'edge of the wood'; or an occupational term for a fruit-grower. Chiefly a surname of south-west England.

Ord(e) F/P From the Germanic first-name *Ort* ('point [of a sword]'), or from an OE place-name in Northd with the same meaning, referrring to a spit or projecting ridge. A surname of the north-east of England.

Ore P Place-names *Ore* and *Oare* in various southern counties OE 'flat-topped hill', though this is mainly a surname of the Midlands, especially Staffs.

Orford P Place-name in Lancs/Lincs/Suffolk OE 'upper ford/ford by the flat-topped hill'; a surname found mainly in Lancs and in East Anglia. Readily confused with/a variant of **Offord**.

Orgill N Nickname for a person exhibiting a great deal of pride OF. Chiefly a Derbys/Staffs surname.

Orlebar P Place-name in Northants, now *Orlingbury*, formerly *Orlebere* OE, of uncertain etymology, perhaps 'pasture/wood/hill/fort of the family of *Ordla*'. A very scarce surname, marginally more common in Beds and Northants than elsewhere.

Orme/Oram F From an ON first-name *Ormr*, meaning 'snake, dragon'. **Orme** is a surname of the Midlands and the northwest; **Oram**, more widely scattered, could alternatively be derived from an unidentified place-name ending in *-ham*.

Ormerod, *see* **Ormrod**.

Ormiston P Place-name in East Lothian and Roxburghshire, Scotland ON and OE '*Ormr*'s farm' (see **Orme**).

Ormond(e) F Irish: Anglicized form of Gaelic **O'** [descendant of] **Ruaidh** ('red'), altered by folk etymology so that it resembles *Ormond*, a regional name in East Munster. Also found in Lancs and in other parts of England, Scotland and Wales.

Orm(e)rod P Place-name in Lancs ON and OE '*Ormr*'s clearing' (see **Orme**).

Ormsby P Place-names: *Ormsby* in Lincs and NRYorks; *Ormesby* in Norfolk ON '*Ormr*'s farm' (see **Orme**).

Orrell P Place-name in Lancs OE 'hill where ore is found', and a Lancs surname.

Orrick/Orridge F From an OE first-name *Ordric* ('sword/spear-power'). **Orrick** is mainly found in Co Durham and Northd, **Orridge** in Derbys. A girl by the name of

'*P. Orridge*', born in Chesterfield, Derbys, in 1894, must have gone through life explaining to people that she was not some kind of breakfast cereal…

Orton P Place-name in several counties, the first element of which varies and is often hard to determine. The second element is OE *tun* ('settlement, enclosure'). A surname of the Midlands and the north, especially strong in Leics. *John Kingsley ('Joe') Orton (1933–1967), playwright, was born in Leicester.*

Orwell P Place-name in Cambs OE 'spring by the point'; a scarce surname with a presence in Staffs and elsewhere. *The novelist and political writer Eric Arthur Blair (1903–1950) adopted the pseudonym of George Orwell.*

Orwin F From an OE first-name meaning 'boar friend'. Mainly a surname of the Midlands and the north.

Osbaldiston/Osbaldeston/Osbaldstone/Osbildston P Place-name *Osbaldeston* in Lancs OE '*Osbald*'s farm/village'. **Osbaldiston** and **Osbildston** (very scarce) are found mainly in Chesh, and **Osbaldeston** in Lancs.

Osbaston/Osbeston/Osbiston P Place-name *Osbaston* in Leics, Salop and Montgomeryshire ON and OE '*Osbern*'s farm/village'. Reaney considers **Osbiston** to be a variant on the surname **Osbaldiston**, but since the three variants listed here are principally found in Derbys, then *Osbaston*, from the neighbouring county of Leics, is a more likely origin.

Osbildston, *see* **Osbaldiston**.

Osbiston, *see* **Osbaston**.

Osborn(e)/Osbourn(e)/Osburn F From an ON first-name *Asbjorn* ('god-bear'), reinforced after the Conquest by the Norman *Osbern*. **Osborne**, the commonest form, is the family name of the Dukes of Leeds. These are widespread surnames, though **Osburn** is found mainly in WRYorks. *John Osborne (1929–1994), dramatist, was born in London; his father was of*

South Wales extraction and his mother was a Cockney.

Oscroft P Place-name in Chesh OE 'croft with oxen'. A scarce surname found principally in Notts.

Osgathorp(e) P Place-name in Leics ON 'Osgod's farm'. A scarce surname, with a presence in WRYorks.

Osgerby P Place-names: *Osgodby* in Lincs (three such), ERYorks and NRYorks; *Osgoodby* in NRYorks ON 'Osgod's farm'. Chiefly a Lincs surname.

Osgood/Hos(e)good F From an ON first-name *Asgautr* ('God' plus the tribal name '*Gaut*'). For the added *H-* of Hos(e)good, compare **Osmer/Hosmer**. Osgood is principally a Hants surname; Hosgood and Hosegood are found mainly in Devon. *Peter Osgood (1947–2006), Chelsea and England footballer, was born in Windsor, Berks.*

Osler O Occupational term for a bird-catcher, poulterer OF (compare Modern French *oiseau*, a bird). Chiefly a Norfolk surname.

Osman(t), *see* Osmund.

Osmer/Hosmer F From an OE first-name *Osmaer*, meaning 'god-fame'. For the added *H-* of Hosmer, compare **Osgood/Hosgood**. Osmer and Hosmer are both very scarce Kent surnames.

Osmon(d)/Osmont, *see* Osmund.

Osmotherley P Place-name in Lancs and NRYorks ON and OE 'Osmund's mound/clearing'. A very scarce Cumbd surname.

Osmund/Osman(t)/Osmon(d)/Osmont F From an ON first-name *Asmundr*, meaning 'god-protector', reinforced after the Conquest by the Norman *Osmund*.

Ostler/Horsler O Occupational term for an innkeeper, a keeper of lodgings OF. Horsler is a very scarce Beds variant.

Ostridge O A place-name origin would seem likely here, but Cottle derives such a surname from an occupational term for a hawker, falconer OF, ultimately from a

Latin word meaning 'of *Asturias* (Spain)'. No connexion with *ostrich*, though thanks to folk etymology a smattering of individuals have borne the surname **Ostrich**. **Ostridge** is a very scarce Berks surname.

Oswald F From an OE first-name, meaning 'god-power', later fused with the ON *Asvaldr*. Its popularity was established by a seventh-century sainted King of Northumbria.

Othen F From an OE first-name *Odin/Woden*, meaning 'divine frenzy, prophecy'. A very scarce Hants surname.

Ott, *see* Oade.

Ottaway, *see* Ottewell.

Otter F/O/N From an OE first-name *Ohthere*, from ON 'dread-army'; or an occupational term for an otter-hunter, or a nickname for a person bearing some resemblance to an otter. Strongest in Lincs.

Ottewell/Ottaway/Otterwell/Ottewill/Ottoway F From one of two Norman first-names: *Otoïs* ('prosperity-wide/wood') or *Otewi* ('prosperity-war'). **Ottewell** is a Derbys surname; **Ottaway** is found mainly in Kent and Surrey, **Otterwell** in Suffolk, **Ottewill** in Kent and **Ottoway** in Middx and Surrey.

Ottoway, *see* Ottewell.

Oughtred F From an OE first-name meaning 'dawn/dusk counsel'. A Co Durham/NRYorks surname.

Outhwaite P Place-name in Lancs ON '*Ulf*'s clearing'. One family of this name, well known as rope-makers in the Wensleydale (NRYorks) town of Hawes, can trace its origins back to a John **Outhwaite**, who settled at Stalling Busk in the 1730s. Parish register entries for this family include spelling variants of the surname such as **Outhwayt** and **Outhett**.

Outlaw N Nickname for an outlaw, one who was beyond the law ON. A surname found mainly in East Anglia, but also well established in the USA.

Outridge, *see* **Utteridge**.

Ovenden P When most, if not all, surname scholars agree that the source of this surname must be the place-name *Ovenden* in WRYorks OE '*Ofa*'s valley', it's time to stand back and take stock. Bardsley cites a reference to Richard **de Ovenden** in a Yorks poll tax of 1379, and Reaney notes that a John **de Ovenden** appears in the Wakefield Court Rolls in 1277; such men may well have acquired their surname or byname from the township of *Ovenden*, but this is not the whole story. George Redmonds quotes the example of Lawrence **Wolfenden**, who was living in *Ovenden* in 1559, and who was soon being referred to as 'Lawrence **Hovenden**', his surname and his place of abode having become confused (see **Wolfenden**). Hanks and Hodges offer *Ovingdean* in Sussex OE 'valley of the people of *Ufa*' as another possible source of the surname **Ovenden**, and this certainly brings us closer to the county of Kent, which is where the overwhelming majority of **Ovenden**s were living by the time of the 1881 census. But why look for complications here? The place called *Ovenden* in Ulcombe, Kent (originally spelt with an initial *H*-) OE '?*Hov(i)*'s/ enclosure/dwelling pasture' will surely be the principal source of the surname in that county? The related but much scarcer surname of **Hovenden** could be found mainly in Kent and in Surrey in 1881.

Ovens T Dweller at the oven/furnace OE. A scattered surname.

Over T/P Dweller at the river-bank/hillslope OE, or from a place-name *Over* with a similar meaning in various counties, including Cambs, Chesh, Derbys and Gloucs, or which contain such an element, including *Littleover* and *Mickleover* in Derbys.

Overal(l) T Dweller at the upper hall OE. Found chiefly in Essex.

Overbury P Place-name in Worcs OE 'upper earthwork'. A Gloucs/Warwicks/Worcs surname.

Overend T Dweller at the 'upper end' of a place or at the 'end of the slope' OE. A WRYorks surname.

Overton P Place-name in several counties OE 'upper settlement' or 'settlement on a river bank' (places so-named in Lancs and NRYorks being so situated). A surname found in a swathe from East Anglia to Lancs, especially strong in Lincs. '*Crispy Ann* Overton', who appears in the 1841 census for Wainfleet St Thomas, Orby, Lincs, sounds as if she might be quite a tasty young woman?

Overy T/P Dweller beyond the river/island OE, or from a place-name with the same meaning, such as *Overy* in Oxon (situated over the Thame from Dorchester). Strongest in Kent.

Owen(s) F From the Welsh first-name *Owain*, probably connected with the name *Ewan*, and developed from the Latin *Eugenius* (*Eugene*).

Oxberry/Oxborough/Oxborrow/ Oxbrow/Oxburgh/Oxbury P Place-name *Oxborough* in Norfolk OE 'fort/ manor where oxen are kept'. **Oxberry** is found chiefly in Co Durham/York; **Oxborough** in Norfolk; **Oxborrow** in Suffolk; **Oxbrow** (very scarce) in Essex; **Oxburgh** (also very scarce) in Devon/Lancs/Lincs/ Norfolk; **Oxbury** in Norfolk/NRYorks.

Oxby T Dweller at an ox farm OE and ON; readily confused with/a variant of **Oxberry**.

Oxenham P Cottle speaks of the place-name *Oxenholme* in Westmd OE and ON 'water-meadow/island with oxen', but this is principally a Devon surname, and the village of *Oxenham* in that county OE 'water-meadow with oxen' must be the point of origin in most cases.

Oxford P Place-name *Oxford* in the county of that name OE 'ford for oxen'. A very scarce scattered surname.

Oxley P Place-name in various counties, including Staffs OE 'clearing/field for oxen'. Principally found in northern counties of England, very strong in WRYorks.

Oxnard O Occupational term for a herder of oxen OE. A Co Durham/Northd surname.

Oxton P Place-name in Chesh, Notts and WRYorks OE 'place/farm where oxen are kept'. An uncommon Chesh/Lancs surname.

Oyler O Occupational term for a dealer in, or extractor of, oil (such as linseed) OF. Principally a Kent surname.

Ozanne F/N From a Hebrew feminine first-name *Hosanna* ('?Save now'/'?Save, pray'), or possibly given to a child born or baptized on Palm Sunday, when hosannas were sung. A Guernsey surname.

Pace/Peace N Nickname for a peaceful, mild-mannered person ME *pace*. Readily confused with/a variant of **Pash** and the like (see **Patch**). See also **Pease**, under **Peascod**.

Pacey, *see* **Pacy**.

Pack, *see* **Patch**.

Packer O Occupational term for a woolpacker ME.

Packman/Pakeman O Occupational term for a packman, hawker, pedlar ME, or for the servant of a man called **Pack**. **Packman** is chiefly a Kent surname; **Pakeman**, quite scarce, is found in Derbys and elsewhere.

Packwood P Place-name in Warwicks OE '*Pacca*'s wood'. Most commonly found in Warwicks and Worcs.

Pac(e)y P Place-name *Pacy* in Eure, France OF, from a Roman first-name *Paccius*, plus a suffix. The surname has a strong presence in Lincs.

Padbury P Place-name in Bucks OE '*Padda*'s fort' or 'fort with toads/frogs (to which *Padda*'s name may be related)'. Chiefly a Warwicks surname.

Paddison, *see* **Patrick**.

Paddock T/N Dweller at a paddock, enclosure OE *pearruc*; or a nickname for a person bearing some resemblance (oh, dear…) to a toad or frog ON. Strongest in Salop. Readily confused with/a variant of **Puttock** and the like.

Paddon P Place-name in Devon OE '*Peatta*'s farm', and a Devon surname.

Padfield P There is a place called *Padfield* in Derbys OE '*Padda*'s field' or 'field with toads/frogs', but this is very largely a Somerset surname.

Padget(t), *see* **Page**.

Padley P Place-name in Derbys OE '*Padda*'s clearing' or 'clearing with toads/frogs'. Chiefly a Lincs/WRYorks surname.

Pagan ?F A surname of uncertain origin, found mainly in the north of England and in Scotland. Possibly a late variant of the ME first-name *Payne*.

Page/Paige O Occupational term for a young servant, a page OF; **Padget(t)/ Paget(t)** are diminutive forms. Of **Paget**, Cottle says: 'This immature surname was no bar to promotion; it is the family name of the Marquesses of Anglesey'. **Paige**, an uncommon variant, is found mainly in Devon.

Paget(t)/Paige, *see* **Page**.

Pailthorp(e), *see* **Palethorpe**.

Pain(e)/Pane/Pannel(l)/Payn(e) F From a ME first-name *Pain(e)/Payn(e)*, originally OF from Latin, meaning 'villager, country-dweller', but later 'pagan'. Theories that such a first-name was given to children baptized late, or to backsliding Christians, may be too fanciful, and this was a popular name in early mediaeval times. **Pannell**, a diminutive form found chiefly in southeast England, was borne by two Normans who left their names at Littleton *Pannell*,

Wilts, and Newport *Pagnell*, Bucks. **Pain** and **Paine** are chiefly found in southern counties of England; **Pane** and **Payne** are more widespread. A female child born in Hackney, London, in 1901, bore the unfortunate name of *'Constant* **Pain***'. Thomas Paine (1737–1809), revolutionary and author of* Rights of man, *was born in Thetford, Norfolk, to a Quaker father and an Anglican mother.*

Painter o Occupational term for a painter (of stained glass, etc.) OF. See also **Paynter**.

Paish, *see* **Patch**.

Paisley P Scots: place-name *Paisley*, Glasgow, British or Gaelic 'church, cemetery', from Latin *basilica*, or British '?pasture slope'. *Rev. Ian (Richard Kyle) Paisley, Northern Irish politician, was born in Armagh, Co Antrim, in 1925, the son of an Independent Baptist minister father and a Scottish mother.*

Pakeman, *see* **Packman**.

Pakenham P Place-name in Suffolk OE '*Pacca*'s homestead', but a scarce scattered surname, borne by the Earls of Longford.

Palethorpe/Pailthorp(e) P Although the place-name *Pallathorpe* in Bolton Percy, WRYorks OE 'settlement with toads/frogs' was called *Pailthorpe* in 1591, **Palethorpe** is largely a Notts surname (**Pailthorp(e)** being much scarcer), and the village of *Perlethorpe* in that county ON '?settlement held by the Peverel family' is a much more likely point of origin, and is still referred to locally as *Palethorpe*, one of its former names. **Parlethorpe** was a common spelling of such a surname in the sixteenth century. For a detailed study of this surname, see *Searching for surnames* by John Titford (2002).

Palfrey/Palframan/Palfreman/Palfreyman o Occupational term for a man charged with looking after palfreys (saddle-horses) OF. **Perfrement** very scarce, may be a variant of **Palfreyman**. **Palfrey** is a Devon/Somerset/Suffolk surname; **Palframan** and **Palfreman**, both scarce, can be found in WRYorks and elsewhere; **Palfreyman** belongs to Derbys and WRYorks.

Palgrave P From *Great Palgrave* in Norfolk OE '?*Poecga/Pacca*'s grave/grove'/'?the grove where pegs or stakes are made' or *Palgrave* in Suffolk OE '*Palla*'s grove'/'grove of the ledges'/'grove where stakes are obtained'. A family bearing such a surname (originally **Pagrave**) has long been prominent in Norfolk, and there have been **Palgrave**s in Suffolk from at least as early as the fourteenth century. *Francis Turner Palgrave (1824–1897) has been well known to generations of schoolchildren and poetry-lovers as the compiler of* The golden treasury, *first published in 1864, while his father Sir Francis Palgrave (1788–1861), a highly regarded historian and mediaevalist, was Deputy Keeper of the Public Records. But there would be little point in trying to trace the Palgrave ancestry of Sir Francis, because, quite simply, he doesn't have any. Born in London in 1788, he was the son of a Jewish stockbroker called Meyer Cohen, but changed his name – and his religion – in 1823, when he married Elizabeth Turner of Great Yarmouth, whose mother's maiden name was Palgrave.*

Palin, *see* **Hayling**.

Pallant P There is a district called *The Pallant* in Chichester, Sussex OE 'palace, palatinate', owned as an ecclesiastical 'peculiar', with palatine rights, by the Archbishop of Canterbury, but the surname **Pallant** belongs mainly to Suffolk.

Pallis(t)er/Palser o Occupational term for a paling-/fence-maker OF. **Palliser** is a surname of NRYorks; **Pallister** is more common in Co Durham; **Palser** is found chiefly in Gloucs and Warwicks. *Gary Pallister, Middlesbrough, Manchester United and England soccer player, was born in Ramsgate, Kent, in 1965.*

Palmer N A nickname applied to a palmer OF, a pilgrim who had brought back a palm-branch from the Holy Land. Family name of the Earls of Selborne.

Palser, *see* **Palliser**.

Pamplin/Blamphin/Plampin o Occupational term for a baker, from OF *blanc pain* ('white bread'). A member of the **Pamplin** family who emigrated to the USA had a village named after him; in its heyday the *Pamplin* Clay Pipe Factory in *Pamplin*, Virginia, was the largest such factory in the world. **Pamplin** and **Plampin** are found chiefly in Essex; **Blamphin**, very scarce, belongs to Lancs.

Pane/Pannell, *see* **Pain**.

Pankhurst F/P Traditionally said to be a variant of the first-name *Pentecost*, made to resemble a place-name. But as the surname is found mainly in Kent, Surrey and Sussex, the place-name *Pinkhurst*, found in Surrey and Sussex (*Penkehurst* in 1565), said to be derived from the *Pentecost* first-name, is likely to be the point of origin. *The surname Pankhurst will forever be associated with the suffragette movement. Christabel Harriette Pankhurst (1880–1958), (Estelle) Sylvia Pankhurst (1882–1960) and Adela Constantia Mary Pankhurst were born in Manchester, the daughters of Richard Marsden Pankhurst (1835/6-1898), a radical barrister originally from Stoke-on-Trent, Staffs, and his wife Emmeline, née Goulden (1858–1928), a suffragette leader born in Hulme, Lancs.*

Pannier(s) O Occupational term for a maker/user of panniers OF. Both **Pannier** and **Panniers** are very scarce Herefords surnames.

Pant(h)er O/T Occupational term for an official in charge of the pantry, or of distributing bread to the needy (compare Modern French *pain*, bread) OF; or a dweller at a house bearing the sign of a panther OF. **Panter** is most commonly found in Bucks and Northants, **Panther** (scarce) in Northants.

Panton P Place-name in Lincs OE '?hill farm'.

Pape, *see* **Pope**.

Papworth P Place-names *Papworth Everard* and *Papworth St Agnes* in Cambs OE '*Pap(p)a*'s enclosure', and a Cambs/Hunts surname.

Paradice/Paradise T Dweller by the garden, pleasure-ground OF, ultimately from an Avestic (ancient Persian) word meaning 'formed around' – that is, an enclosure. Very scarce West Country surnames.

Paramor(e)/Paramour N Nickname for a sweetheart, lover OF (literally 'with love'); not an opprobrious term in ME. **Paramor** and **Paramour** are Kent surnames; **Paramore** is most commonly found in WRYorks. *Norrie Paramor (1914–1979), the record producer and composer who did much to build the career of the singer Cliff Richard, was born in London.*

Pardoe/Pardew/Pardow/Pardue/Pard(e)y N Nickname for a person whose favourite oath was '*Par dieu!*' OF 'By God!'. The variant **Perdue** has been respelt as if meaning 'lost' OF. **Pardoe** is strongest in Worcs, **Pardew** in Devon, **Pardow** (very scarce) in Staffs, **Pardey** and **Pardy** in southern and south-west counties of England. **Perdue** is scarce and scattered.

Pardon O Probably a shortened form of the word *pardoner* OF, a licensed seller of indulgences (remissions of punishment due for sins); the pardoner in Chaucer's *Canterbury Tales* was the most reviled of the pilgrims. A widespread surname, commonest in Norfolk.

Pardow/Pardue/Pard(e)y, *see* **Pardoe**.

Parfett/Parfit(t) N Nickname for a person (probably an apprentice) who was perfect, complete, highly trained OF. For the relationship between *-ar-* and *-er-* see **Armistead**. The variant **Perfect** results from a pedantic Latinized respelling.

Parget(t)er/Pargiter O Occupational term for a plasterer OF. Late in the English Middle Ages such work became highly decorative, as can be seen on house fronts in Essex and Suffolk. Fairly scarce scattered surnames.

Parham P Place-name in Suffolk and Sussex OE 'homestead where pears grow'. A south-of-England surname.

Paris/Par(r)ish P From the city of *Paris* in France OF (from Gaulish, referring to the tribe known as *Parisii*). 'The illiterate *-sh* is like the common pronunciation of *liquorice* as *liquorish'* (Cottle). Parish foundlings were sometimes given the name of **Parish**. **Paris** is found mainly in the south of England, especially Hants; **Parish** and **Parrish** are widespread.

Park(e)(s) T/O Dweller at the park, enclosure, thinly wooded land kept for beasts of the chase or from Germanic; or an occupational term for someone who worked in such a place. **Parks** is a later form of **Parkes**, losing the inflexional *-e-*. **Perks** is possibly a variant, but see **Peter**. **Park** is most common in northern England and in Scotland; **Parke** and **Parks** can be found further south; **Parkes** is very strong in the West Midlands (especially Staffs), but also has a presence in Derbys, WRYorks and elsewhere. See also **Parrock**.

Parker O Occupational term for a keeper/ranger/gamekeeper employed in a park. A very common surname. The family name of the Earls of Macclesfield and of Morley.

Parkes, *see* **Park**.

Parkhouse T/P Dweller at a house/lodge in a park OF and OE (for which see **Park**); or from a minor place-name with the same meaning, such as *Parkhouse* in Washfield, Devon, in which county the surname is mostly found.

Parkin/Parkinson, *see* **Peter**.

Parkman O Occupational term for a keeper of a park OF and OE (for which see **Park**). An uncommon West Country surname.

Parks, *see* **Park**.

Parkyn, *see* **Peter**.

Parley P Place-name in Dorset, Hants OE 'clearing/field where pears grow'. The surname is very scarce in England, most common in Aberdeenshire, Scotland.

Parme(n)ter/Parmi(n)ter O Occupational term for a tailor OF, ultimately from Latin *paro* ('prepare'). There is a church named St Peter Parmentergate in Norwich. *Potage Parmentier* is named after an eighteenth-century French potato-grower of that name. A surname found chiefly in

southern/south-western counties of England and in East Anglia.

Parnall/Parnell/Parnwell/Pennell/Purnell F From the ME female first-name *Parnell* (Latin *Petronilla*, the name of a Roman martyr mythically said to be St Peter's daughter). Usually abbreviated in England to *Pernel*, thence *Parnel*. 'For some reason, it came to mean "priest's concubine" or even "prostitute" ' (Cottle). **Parnall**, scarce, is found mainly in Cornwall, **Parnwell** in Cambs, **Pennell** in Kent and **Purnell** in Gloucs; **Parnell**, more widespread, is the family name of the Barons Congleton.

Parr P/F Place-name in Lancs OE 'enclosure'; or, rarely, a variant of **Peter**. 'The claim of Thomas **Parr** (died 1635) to have lived to be 152 is not now accepted' (Cottle). *Catherine Parr (1512–1548), Queen of England and sixth consort of Henry VIII, was the daughter of Sir Thomas Parr of Kendal, Westmd, and his wife Maud Green.*

Parratt, *see* **Parrot**.

Parrell, *see* **Peter**.

Parrett, *see* **Parrot**.

Parrish, *see* **Paris**.

Parritt, *see* **Parrot**.

Parrock T Dweller at a paddock, enclosure OE, of the same ultimate Germanic origin as **Park**, to which form the surname is sometimes contracted. A scarce West Midlands surname.

Parrot(t)/Parratt/Parrett/Parritt/Perret(t)/Perrot(t) P/F Place-names *North Perrot* (Somerset) and *South Perrott* (Dorset), which stand on the river *Parret* (origin unknown); or, in some spellings, a diminutive form of the first-name *Peter* (see **Peter**). In the event, the bird called a *parrot* gets its name from *Peter*. It had to happen, of course: on 21 June 1778 Mr and Mrs **Parrot** took their baby girl for baptism in the parish church at Luddington, Lincs, and gave her the name *'Polly'*.

Parry F Welsh, 'son of *Harry*' (*ap Harry*).

Parsley/Parsloe/Parslow N/T Nickname, literally 'cross/pass the water' OF *pass-* and *l'eau*, perhaps used for a person who travelled abroad as a merchant or as a pilgrim, or who lived across a stream or river from a village or settlement. Compare **Passmore**. **Parsley** is found mainly in south-west England and in East Anglia, **Parsloe** and **Parslow** (both scarce) in Gloucs.

Parsons O/T Occupational term for a parson's servant/man, incorporating the possessive *-s*. The word *parson* is OF, with the same Latin origin as *person*; for the relationship between *-ar-* and *-er-* see **Armistead**. 'Much less likely to be "son of" than "servant of", since the former would show a notorious bastardy' (Cottle). Or a dweller at the parson's house/parsonage. The surnames **Parson** and also **Person** (mostly found in Lancs) are known to exist, though are far scarcer than **Parsons**, which is in evidence mainly in southern and south-western counties of England and along the Severn valley. **Parsons** is the family name of the Irish Earls of Rosse.

Partridge N/O/T Nickname for a person bearing some resemblance to a partridge (favouring bright clothes, strutting?) OF; or a hunter of/dealer in partridges, or a dweller at the sign of the partridge. A widespread surname, strong in Devon, Middx, Staffs.

Pascall/Pascoe/Pash(e), *see* **Patch**.

Pashley P There is a place-name *Pashley* in Sussex OE '*Pæcca*'s clearing', but this is principally a WRYorks surname. There is a *Pashley* Green in WRYorks, though the first-known reference to it dates from as late as 1771. Alternatively, **Pashley** may be readily confused with, or be a variant of, **Parsley**?

Pask(e)/Paskin(s), *see* **Patch**.

Passmore N Nickname for a person who frequently travelled over, or who knew the best way across, a fen or marsh ME. Compare **Parsley**. **Passmore** is chiefly a Devon surname.

Patch/Pack/Paish/Pasco(e)/Pash(e)/ Pask(e)/Paskin(s) N/F   Such surnames have at their root a term denoting 'Easter' – from Hebrew (a word for the Passover) via Greek, via Latin *pascha/pascua* – which is still in evidence in the *paschal* lamb, Easter *pace-egg* traditions and the Modern French *pâques* ('Easter'). Some of these surnames refer to a child born or baptized at Easter; others, such as *Pascal* (*Paschal* was a ninth-century sainted pope), have arrived by way of first-names with the same origin. See also **Pace** and **Paxman**. Nearly all these surnames belong to southern counties of England and/or the West Country (**Pasco(e)** is Cornish); but **Pask** is found principally in Lincs. **Paskin** and **Paskins** are both very scarce, but whereas the former is found chiefly in Staffs, the latter has its main presence in south-of-England coastal counties.

Pate N/F   Nickname for a man with a bald pate/head ME; **Paton/Patten/Patton/ Pat(t)erson/Pat(e)y/Patti(n)son** are diminutives. Or a diminutive of the first-name *Patrick* (see **Patrick**). Given former (and present) regional pronunciation patterns, **Pate** can readily be confused with **Peat**. **Pate** is primarily a Lancs surname, though **Patey** and **Paty** are found much further south; **Paton/Patton/Pat(t)erson/Patti(n)son** are strongest in north-east and north-west England and in Scotland. See also **Pateman**. *The earliest known male-line ancestor of the American General George Patton (1885–1945) was Robert Patton, who arrived in Virginia from Scotland during the eighteenth century.*

Pateman O Occupational term for a servant of a man called **Pate**.

Paternoster O/N Occupational term for a maker or seller of rosaries, from Latin *Pater noster* ('Our Father'), the opening words of the Lord's Prayer used to describe a particular rosary bead. Reaney has shown how such a surname could be applied not only to dealers in rosaries but also to those who held land by the service of repeating the Lord's Prayer for the souls of benefactors. Alternatively, a nickname for a super-pious individual. A scarce surname, strongest in Suffolk.

Paterson/Patey/Paton, *see* **Pate**.

Patrick/Paddison/Pattrick F From the first-name *Patrick*, Latin *Patricius* ('patrician, aristocratic'), made popular thanks to *St Patrick*, the fifth-century Romano-Briton who became the Apostle of Ireland. As a first-name, favoured chiefly in northern England, Scotland and Ireland, though the surname **Patrick** is rather more widespread. **Pattrick** is much scarcer, and **Paddison** ('son of *Patrick*') belongs almost exclusively to Lincs. **Peden** is a Scots Gaelic variant. See also **Pate**.

Patten O Occupational term for a patten/clog-maker OF; or readily confused with/a variant of **Patton** (see **Pate**). A scattered surname.

Patterson/Patti(n)son/Patton, *see* **Pate**.

Pattrick, *see* **Patrick**.

Paty, *see* **Pate**.

Paul(e)/Paulson/Pawle/Pawley/Pawlin(g)/Polson/Powley/Powling F From the first-name *Paul*, Latin *Paulus* ('small'), the name taken by Saul of Tarsus following his conversion on the road to Damascus. Formerly pronounced *Pole* or *Pool*, it was not a common first-name in mediaeval England, and was rarely favoured when it came to the dedication of churches (except in conjunction with St Peter). **Pawley**, **Pawlin(g)**, **Powley** and **Powling** are diminutives. **Paul** is widely scattered throughout England and Scotland; **Paulson** ('son of *Paul*') is mainly a Notts surname, though **Polson** is Scottish; **Pawley** is most commonly found in Devon/Leics, and **Powley** in Norfolk; **Pawle**, **Pawlin**, **Pawling** and **Powling** are scarce variants. See also **Paull**, **Pawlett**, **Pole**, **Pollard**, **Pool**, **Powel** and **Quail**. *John Polson (1825–1900), a cornflour manufacturer who developed a process for manufacturing edible starch and who made the family business of Brown and Polson a household name, was born in Paisley, Scotland.*

Paulet(t), *see* **Pawlett**.

Paull P Cornish: from the place-name *Paul* ('St Paul's church') near Mousehole, and a Cornish surname; or readily confused with/a variant of **Paul**.

Pauncefoot, *see* **Ponsford**.

Pav(i)er/Pavio(u)r O Occupational term for a paviour, a pavement-layer OF. **Paver** is principally a WRYorks surname; **Pavier**, **Pavior** and **Paviour** are more widely scattered.

Pawle, *see* **Paul**.

Pawlett P There is a place-name *Pawlett* in Somerset OF 'stream with poles/stakes', but as neither **Pawlett** nor **Paulet** nor **Paulett** are Somerset surnames, they are more likely to be derived from a diminutive of the first-name/surname **Paul**.

Pawley/Pawlin(g), *see* **Paul**.

Paxman ?N/O This is a very scarce East Anglian surname, and the historian Andrew Phillips maintains that the surname **Paxman** was invented by Roger Packsman, a successful and ambitious businessman in Suffolk in the fourteenth century who wished to be known as a 'Man of Peace'. It is just as likely to mean 'Servant of a man named **Pask**' (see **Patch**). *The British television journalist Jeremy Paxman was born in 1950 in Leeds, WRYorks, and was brought up in Yorks and Worcs. A man by the name of Thomas Paxman, seemingly Jeremy's direct ancestor, is known to have migrated with his family from Framlingham, Suffolk, to Farnworth, Lancs, in the nineteenth century.*

Paxton P Place-name in Cambs and in Berwickshire, Scotland OE '*Poecc*'s settlement'. An English/Scottish surname, strongest in Co Durham. *Sir Joseph Paxton (1803–1865), the architect and landscape gardener who was responsible for Crystal Palace and for many of the finest features in Chatsworth Estate, Derbys, was born in Milton Bryant, Beds, the son of an agricultural labourer.*

Paybody, *see* **Peabody**.

Payn(e), *see* **Pain**.

Paynter T Dweller at an end of land, Cornish *pen-dyr*; a Cornish surname. See also **Painter**, and compare **Pender**.

Payton, *see* Peyton.

Peabody/Paybody ?N A distinctive surname of uncertain meaning. Cottle tackles it thus: '?Having the body of a gnat OE *peo*; this makes a kind of sense, but doesn't satisfactorily explain **Paybody** (which looks equally like "peacock-body") or Bardsley's **Pyebody** in the early 1600s (which looks like "magpie-body" OF and OE) – unless *Pyebody* was from OE *pie*, the alternative form of *peo*'. In short, no-one is any the wiser. Maybe this was a nickname for a showy dresser, from ME *pe* ('peacock')? Both **Peabody** and **Paybody** (scarce) are South Midlands/Midlands surnames. *Peabody Buildings, found throughout London and managed by the Peabody Trust, owe their origin to the American banker George Peabody (1795–1869), who was born in Danvers (later renamed Peabody), Massachusetts, USA.*

Peace, *see* Pace.

Peach/Petch O/N Occupational term for a grower or seller of peaches OF (that is, a *Persian* apple); **Peach** and **Petch** may also be derived from the OF word *peche* ('sin') – Modern French *péché*. Readily confused with/a variant of **Peachey**. **Peach** is chiefly a South Midlands/Midlands surname, strongest in Derbys; **Petch** can be found in Lincs, Suffolk and northern England.

Peachey/Petchey N Nickname applied mockingly or in earnest to a sinful person OF *peche* ('sin') – Modern French *péché*. Readily confused with/a variant of **Peach**. **Peachey** is most commonly found in Cambs, **Petchey** in Essex.

Peacock(e)/Pocock N/T Nickname for a person who strutted like a peacock OE, dressed in a flashy fashion, won the peacock-prize in athletics, or lived at the sign of the peacock. **Pee** can be a variant of **Peacock** or of **Peter**. See also **Poe**. **Peacock** has a strong presence in the north and north-east of England, while **Pocock** belongs to the south. *Thomas Love Peacock (1785–1866), satirical novelist, was born at Weymouth, Dorset, the son of Samuel Peacock, a London glass merchant with family roots in Taunton, Somerset, and his wife Sarah, née Love.*

Peagram/Peagrim, *see* Pilgrim.

Peak(e)/Peek(e) T Dweller by a hill or peak OE. The *-e* of **Peake** and **Peeke** may be evidence of the use of the dative following a lost preposition. **Peake**, the family name of the Viscounts Ingleby, is strongest in Staffs; **Peak** is a distinctively Lancs surname; **Peek** and **Peeke** are found mainly in Devon. Readily confused with/a variant of **Pick**. *Mervyn (Laurence) Peake (1911–1968), artist and writer, was born in China. Both his father Ernest Cromwell Peake (a doctor) and his paternal grandfather Philip George Peake (born in 1843 at Barton-under-Needwood, Staffs) were Congregational missionaries... The English biscuit company of Peek Frean was founded in 1857 by James Peek, a City of London tea merchant, and George Hender Frean.*

Pear O/T/N Occupational term (also **Pearman**) for a grower or seller of pears, or a dweller near a pear tree ME; or a nickname for a peer/companion OF. See also **Pears**, under **Peter**.

Pearce, *see* Peter.

Pearl(e) O/N Occupational term for a trader in pearls OF, or a nickname for a person resembling a pearl in some way. **Pearl** is strongest in south-east England and East Anglia; **Pearle** is a scarce variant.

Pearman, *see* Pear.

Pears(e), *see* Pear and Peter.

Pearson, *see* Peter.

Peart N/P Scholars disgree on the origin of this surname. Cottle says that it is a nickname for a beautiful/smart/intelligent/adroit/cheeky/lively person OF; Hanks and Hodges suggest that it might be derived from the place-name *Pert*, near Montrose in Scotland (Pictish or Celtic, 'wood, copse'), though this is chiefly a Co Durham, not a Scottish, surname.

Peascod/Peas(e)good/Pescod ?O/N Possibly an occupational term (literally 'pea pod' OE), for a seller of peas, or a nickname for a person of little worth. But see **Pusey**.

Variant spellings of this scarce surname belong to different parts of the country: **Peascod** is found chiefly in Cumbd; **Peasgood** in Lincs; **Peasegood** in WRYorks and **Pescod** in Co Durham. **Pescott**, probably a variant (though readily confused with **Prescott**?), is found mainly in Hants, Surrey and Sussex. **Pease**, which probably carries similar meanings and is mostly found in WRYorks, is the family name of the Barons Daryngton, Gainford and Wardington. It can readily be confused with, or be a variant of, **Pace/Peace**.

Pease, *see* **Peascod**.

Peasley T Dweller at a clearing/field where peas grow OE, or from a minor place-name with the same meaning. A scarce scattered surname.

Peat(e)/Peet F/N **Peat(e)/Peet** can clearly be a shortened form of **Peter**, but could also be a nickname – 'pet, darling, pampered person' ME, related to the northern use of *peat* for a spoiled girl/poppet. Cottle says that such a name was once common in Yorks and Scotland, and that from Yorks it reached Montgomeryshire in and before the seventeenth century, thence to the Brecknocks, changing to **Pate**. Indeed, given former (and present) regional pronunciation patterns, **Peat(e)** can readily be confused with **Pate**. **Peat** is particularly in evidence in Derbys, **Peate** in Salop and **Peet** in Lancs.

Peckham P Place-name in Kent and London OE 'homestead by a hill'. Particularly strong in Hants.

Peddar/Pedder/Pedlar/Pedler O/N Occupational term for a pedlar, hawker OF; but **Pedlar** and **Pedler** may sometimes be a nickname for a fast runner OF *pie de lievre* (literally 'foot of hare').

Peden, *see* **Patrick**.

Pedlar/Pedler, *see* **Peddar**.

Pedley N Nickname for a stealthy person OF *pie de leu* ('wolf's foot'). Strongest in Staffs. See also **Pellew**.

Pee, *see* **Peacock** and **Peter**. A West Midlands surname.

Peebles P Place-name in Scotland: British, with the English plural *-s*, meaning 'tents, shielings'.

Peek(e), *see* **Peak**.

Peel N/T Nickname for a man who was tall and thin, from OF *piel* ('pole') – that is, 'as thin as a rake'; or a dweller by a stockade, palisade, castle OF, in particular one of the massive towers and fortified houses of the Scots Border. A northern surname. *John Peel (1776–1854), the huntsman 'with his coat so gay/grey' who was the eponymous hero of his very own folk-song, was born in Caldbeck, Cumbd; in 1797 he eloped with a local girl named Mary White and the couple were married at Gretna Green, seventeen miles to the north. In 1977 the Peel family grave at Caldbeck was damaged by anti-hunt protesters.* For the English disc jockey known as John Peel, *see* **Ravenscroft**.

Peers, *see* **Peter**.

Peet, *see* **Peat**.

Peever/Peover O/P Occupational term for a pepperer, a pepper-seller OF; or from the place-names *Nether* and *Over Peover* (pronounced *Peever*), on a Chesh river named *Peover Eye* (British, 'bright'). Scarce Chesh surnames.

Pegg(e) O/N/F Occupational term for a maker or seller of pegs ME from Germanic, or a nickname for a person with a peg-leg; *Peg* and *Peggy* are also well-known diminutives of the first-name *Margaret*. **Pegg** and **Pegge** are both principally Derbys surnames.

Pegler/Peglar O Occupational term for a peggler, rough mender, patcher, clumsy workman. Chiefly a Gloucs surname in both spellings.

Pegram/Pegrum, *see* **Pilgrim**.

Peirce/Peirs(e), *see* **Peter**.

Pell O/T/F Occupational term for a dealer in pelts, a fellmonger OF (compare **Pelter**); or a dweller by a creek or stream OE *pyll* (compare **Pill**); or from the first-name *Peter* (see **Peter**). **Pelly** is a diminutive form. Chiefly a Lincs/Northants surname. See also **Pellew**.

Pellew/Pellow(e) T/N Cornish surnames of uncertain origin: perhaps from Cornish *pell* (an adjective meaning 'far off') or from *pelyow* ('balls'), used to describe a rotund person. Possibly also connected with the surnames **Pell** and **Pedley**, and an Anglo-Norman origin ('**Pelleu**') has also been claimed. The *Pellew* group of islands in the Gulf of Carpentaria, Australia, were named in the early nineteenth century after Sir Edward **Pellew**, later Admiral Viscount Exmouth, who had Cornish origins.

Pelling P/F Place-name *Peelings*, Sussex (*Pellinges* in Domesday Book) OE '?(the home of) *Pydel*'s people'; or Welsh, 'son of *Heilyn*' (*ap Heilyn*). Chiefly a Sussex surname. See **Hayling**.

Pelly, *see* **Pell**.

Pelmear, *see* **Polmear**.

Pelter O Occupational term for a skinner, fellmonger OF. Compare **Pell**. A scarce Cumbd surname.

Pember P Cottle derives this surname from *Pamber* in Hants, (formerly *Penbere*) OE 'mound/grave/pasture with a pen/enclosure', but it belongs to Herefords, and is very likely a shortened form of the surname **Pembridge**.

Pemberton P Place-names in Lancs OW and OE 'barley hill/head settlement'.

Pembridge P Place-name in Herefords OE 'bridge at the pens/enclosures', or OW and OE 'bridge by a hill'. Found chiefly in Herefords and in Monmouthshire. See also **Pember**.

Penberthy P Place-names *Penberth* and *Penperth*, Cornwall, Cornish *pen-perthy* 'end of bushes'.

Pender T Principally a Cornish surname, from Cornish *pen-dyr* ('a head of land') – compare **Paynter**; elsewhere it may be a variant of **Pinder**.

Pendegrast/Pendergast/Pendergrest, *see* **Prendergast**.

Pendle P The hill-name *Pendle* in Lancs OW and OE 'hill hill', (tautological) would be an oh-so-obvious point of origin here, but in the event this is a surname found mainly in East Anglia, and some minor place-name in that area is probably the true source.

Pendlebury P Place-name in Lancs, from the hill-name *Pendle* (see **Pendle**) and OE 'fort/manor'. Unlike **Pendle**, **Pendlebury** is a Lancs surname.

Pendleton P Place-name (two such) in Lancs, from the hill-name *Pendle* (see **Pendle**) and OE 'enclosure, settlement'. Unlike **Pendle**, **Pendleton** is a Lancs surname.

Pendock/Penduck P Place-name *Pendock* in Worcs OW 'barley hill' or 'top of the barley field'. Scarce Gloucs surnames.

Pendry, *see* **Penry**.

Penduck, *see* **Pendock**.

Penebridge, *see* **Petherbridge**.

Penfold, *see* **Pinfold**.

Pengell(e)y/Pengill(e)y P Place-name *Pengelly* (many such) in Cornwall, Cornish *pen kelly* 'top of the wood, chief wood'. Cornish surnames.

Penhaligon P Place-name *Penhaligon*, Cornwall, Cornish *pen-helygen* 'end/top of willow-tree'. *David Penhaligon (1944–1986), the popular Liberal Party Member of Parliament whose career was cut short when he was killed in a car crash, came from Truro in Cornwall… Susan Penhaligon, British television actress, was born in Manila, Philippines, where her father was working for the Shell Oil Company.*

Penketh P Place-name in Lancs OW 'top/end of the wood', and a Lancs surname.

Penn O/P Occupational term for a shepherd, one who herded sheep into a pen OE *penn*; or from the place name *Penn* in Bucks, Staffs and elsewhere OE 'pen, enclosure, fold' or OW 'hill'. *William Penn (1644–1718), the English Quaker after whom the American* state of Pennsylvania was named, came from a family with its roots in Gloucs; his father Admiral William Penn was born in Bristol in 1621.

Pennant P Place-name in five Welsh counties, Welsh 'top of the valley, high valley'. A scarce surname, with a presence in Lancs and Northants.

Pennebridge, see Petherbridge.

Pennefather, see Pennyfather.

Pennell, see Parnall.

Penney, see Penny.

Pennicott, see Petticoat.

Pennington P Place-name in Cumbd, Hants, Lancs (near Ulverston) OE 'farm paying a penny rent' (or the owner may have had *Penny* as a nickname); but *Pennington*, Lancs, (near Leigh) is OE '?*Pinna*'s people's farm'. Mainly a Lancs surname.

Penny/Penney N/F Nickname from a penny coin OE; it was once of no mean value, and the surname may have been applied to a wealthy person. *Penny* was also used as a first-name. **Penny** is the family name of the Viscounts Marchwood. Both surnames are scattered and widespread, **Penny** being much in evidence in Hants and Somerset.

Pennycuick P Scots: from a place-name *Penycuick* in Midlothian OW 'hill of the cuckoo'. A scarce Lanarkshire/Midlothian surname.

Pennyfather/Pennefather N Nickname for a miser (literally 'penny-father') OE. Scarce scattered surnames.

Penrith P Place-name in Cumbd OW 'chief ford'. A scarce north-of-England surname.

Penrose P Place-name in various counties, including several in Cornwall and Wales, Celtic 'top/end of the heath'. One family of **Penroses** became prominent Irish Quakers.

Penruddock P Place-name in Cumbd OW '?little-ford headland', but a scarce Wilts

surname. *John Penruddock (1619–1655), Royalist leader of Penruddock's Rebellion, was the son of Sir John Penruddock of Compton Chamberlayne, Wilts.*

Penry/Pendry F Welsh, 'son of *Henry*' (*ap Henry*).

Pentecost/Penticost N Nickname for a person born at Whitsuntide OF *pentecost*, ultimately from Greek (being the fiftieth day after Easter Sunday). Surnames of south-east and south-west England. See also **Petticoat**.

Pentland P Scots: from the *Pentland* Hills in the Lowlands ON 'land of the Picts', rather than from *Pentland* Firth. Very strong in Co Durham, but otherwise scattered throughout England and Scotland.

Penton P From one of a group of villages in Hants so-called OE 'farm paying a penny rent', and still a Hants surname.

Pentreath P Cornish place-name *pen-treth* ('head of the ferry/beach'). 'Dolly Jeffery née **Pentreath**… is always (wrongly) claimed to have been the last speaker of Cornish before its fortunate recent revival' (Cottle).

Penybridg, see Petherbridge.

Peover, see Peever.

Peploe/Peplow P Place-name *Peplow* in Salop OE '?pebble hill'. Yet **Peploe** is strongest in Surrey, **Peplow** in Staffs.

Pepper O/N Occupational term for a pepperer, a dealer in pepper/spice OE, or a nickname for a man with a peppery temper. A widespread surname. See also **Piper**. Charmingly enough, the author of a book published in Pennsylvania in 1895 under the title *Spices from the Lord's garden* was Rev. E. I. D. **Pepper**. And what might friends and relations have said when they heard of the birth of '*Agnes Etta* **Pepper**' in Ipswich, Suffolk, in 1881? Would they have exclaimed 'Oh, did she?', or some such?

Peppercorn O/N Occupational term for a seller of peppercorns OE, or a nickname for a tiny man, or for one who paid a nominal 'peppercorn' rent, or who had a violent peppery temper. A scarce Cambs/Kent/Middx surname. *The London and North Eastern Railway locomotive engineer Arthur Henry Peppercorn (1889–1951) was born in Leominster, Herefords, the son of Alfred Thomas Peppercorn, a clergyman who had been born in 1845 in Eaton Socon, Beds.*

Pepperell N/P Cottle states that the origin here is a nickname derived from a diminutive form of the word *pepper*, applied to a man who was tiny, black-haired or bad-tempered, and that it was early used as a first-name. Yet this is principally a Devon surname, in which county it must be closely associated with the village of *Peppershill* in Werrington, where William **Pipard** appears in the Lay Subsidy return for 1333. The variants **Peverall**, **Peverell** and **Peverill** are all scarce, and of uneven geographical distribution.

Peppett/Peppiatt/Peppiett, *see* Peppin.

Peppin/Pippin F From a Germanic first-name *Pepin*, derived from a verb meaning 'to tremble'; the name of several early Frankish kings, including Charlemagne's father. A nominative form was *Pepis* (see **Pepys**). **Peppin** is a scarce Somerset surname; **Pippin**, more common and more widespread, also belongs mainly to the south-west. **Peppett/Peppiatt/Peppiett** are diminutives.

Pepys ?F/O Both the surname **Pepys** and its usual pronunciation ('peeps') have become famous thanks to the diarist Samuel **Pepys** (1633–1703), who was born in London into a family that had connexions with the **Pepys** family of Cottenham, Cambs. Manorial records for Cottenham include references to the **Pepys** name from as early as the year 1290, though the direct male-line ancestry of the **Pepys** family, Earls of Cottenham, can only be traced with certainty back to the early sixteenth century. The meaning of the surname seems to have eluded compilers of the earliest surname dictionaries. Mark Antony Lower in *Patronymica Britannica* (1860) says that a reference to **Pepis** in the Hundred Rolls shows the

name to be 'ancient in nearly its present form', but adds that 'the etymon has not occurred to me'. Bardsley can offer little further help, except to suppose that it might be a baptismal name: 'Like Mr Lower, I give up this surname in despair. Probably it is of easy solution, but I cannot at present come to any safe conclusion'. Cottle is more confident: '**Peppin**: Germanic [first-name], *Pepin* from verb meaning "tremble"... a nominative form was *Pepis* (whence **Pepys**...)'. Hanks and Hodges agree: '**Pepys**: from the Old French personal name *Pepis*, oblique case *Pepin*, introduced to Britain by the Normans'. So the mystery might have been solved – except that we might feel the need to explain the alias used by William **Pepyr** 'or **Pepis**', who had given a garden in the Barnard's Inn area of Holborn, London, to John Whittokesmede and his daughter Agnes in the year 1439 (referred to in *Early Holborn and the legal quarter of London* by E. Williams, 1927, item 1065). Could William's surname of **Pepyr** have been used originally as a byname by a seller of pepper? By the late nineteenth century, **Pepys** had become a scarce surname.

Perceval/Percival F/P From the first-name *Perceval*, of uncertain origin (becoming associated with OF 'pierce valley, rush through the valley', which Cottle says was 'invented by the twelfth-century poet Crestien de Troyes as the name of his hero, who became bound up with the Grail legend'; or possibly from the place-name *Perc(h)eval* in Calvados. A Lancs surname in both spellings. *The hapless Spencer Perceval (1762–1812), who as Prime Minister of England was assassinated in the House of Commons, belonged to the Irish family of Perceval, Earls of Egmont.*

Percy P From the place-name *Perci-en-Auge* in Calvados, or from other place-names in Calvados and Manche (*Perci/Percy*), from a Latin first-name *Persius*. Not an abbreviation of **Percival**, though often taken as such. **Pursey** is a variant. The **Percy** family, Dukes of Northumberland, descend from the Conqueror's companion William **de**

Perci, who took his name from *Perci-en-Auge*.

Perdue, *see* **Pardoe**.

Peregrine, *see* **Pilgrim**.

Perfect, *see* **Parfett**.

Perfrement, *see* **Palfrey**.

Perkin/Perks, *see* **Peter**.

Perrebridge, *see* **Petherbridge**.

Perret(t), *see* **Parrot**.

Perrin(g), *see* **Peter**.

Perriton P Cottle speaks of place-names such as *Periton/Piriton/Puriton/Pyriton* OE 'pear tree farm' in seven counties 'in the triangle Essex, Worcs, Somerset', though this is almost entirely a Devon surname. *Perriton* Farm in Whimple, Devon, was very probably named after a person, rather than vice versa.

Perrot(t), *see* **Parrot**.

Perry/Pirie T/F Dweller near a pear tree OE; or Welsh, 'son of *Henry*' (*ap Herry*). Compare **Parry/Penry**. **Perry** is a widely scattered surname, particularly strong in Staffs; **Pirie** belongs to Banffshire, Scotland. *(Douglas Alastair) Gordon Pirie (1931–1991), athlete, was born in Leeds, Yorks, where his Scottish father was working as a cable telegraphist.*

Person, *see* **Parsons**.

Pertuce, *see* **Pertwee**.

Pertwee/Pertuce P Place-names *Pertuis/Pertus/Pertuy/Perthuis* in France, from OF *pertuis* 'ravine, pass, cave'. So there's nothing 'twee' about **Pertwees**. In his biography *Moon boots and dinner suits* (1984) Jon **Pertwee** (1914–1996), the third actor to play *Doctor Who* in the television series of that name, has this to say about the **Pertwee** surname: *'Pertwee is of French Huguenot extraction. According to our family tree, researched by a French priest, one Abbé Jean Perthuis de Laillevault, and my cousin the late Captain Guy Pertwee RN, the original family of Perthuis de Laillevault were directly descended from the Emperor Charlemagne... The head of* the family is Comte Bernard de Perthuis de Laillevault who fought with the RAF during the last war and is now a celebrated painter of murals. After the Huguenot purge of 1685, the refugees fled to many countries including England where they settled mainly in Suffolk and Essex... Due to the inability of the English to pronounce Perthuis any other way than Pertwiss, it was subsequently changed to Pertwee'. Being a true enthusiast for such things, Jon **Pertwee** carefully filed away genuine examples of the way in which his name has been interpreted over the years, including: *Tom Peetweet; Jon Peterwee; Jon Peartree; Mr Twee; Mr Pardney; Mr Bert Wee; John Peewee; Mr Pickwick; Miss Jane Partwee; Master J Peewit; Mr Pertweek; Joan Pestwick; J Pertinee; John Between; J Parpertwuwe* – and even, in New York, *Jan Putrid*.

Pescott, *see* **Peascod**.

Pestell O Occupational term for one who used a pestle OF (and mortar), a druggist, spicer. An uncommon surname, mostly found in Norfolk.

Pester O Occupational term for a baker OF. A surname of south-west England, especially Somerset. *Col. John Pester (1778–1856), active in the service of the Bengal Army for many years, was baptized on 8 September 1779 in Odcome, Somerset.*

Petch, *see* **Peach**.

Petcher O Occupational term for a fisherman OF. A very scarce surname, found chiefly in the inland counties of Leics and Warwicks.

Petchey, *see* **Peachey**.

Peter(s)/Parkin/Parkinson/Parkyn/ Parr/Parrell/Pearce/Pears(e)/Pee/ Peers/Peirce/Peirs(e)/Pell/Perkin(s)/ Perks/Perrin(g)/Peterson/Pether/ Petre/Pierce/Piers/Pierse/Pierson/ Pither(s) F A group of surnames derived from the first-name *Peter*, with its origins in a Greek version of the Aramaic name *Cephas* ('stone, rock'), bestowed by Jesus on Simon the brother of Andrew. 'Whatever setbacks the first-name received from the unpopular Peter's Pence and the Reformation, it was brought back to tiresome popularity by *Peter Pan* in 1904' (Cottle). Variants such as *Piers*, the usual form of the first-name in mediaeval England (compare the French *Pierre*), together with associated pet-forms and diminutives, have led to the creation of a number of related surnames. For those containing the element *-ar-*, see **Armistead**. **Perks** can (in principle) alternatively be a variant of **Park(e)s**, and **Pee** of **Peacock**. Some variants of **Parrot** can be derived from *Peter*. See also **Peat(e)** and (for **Pears**) **Pear**. **Pearson** is the family name of the Viscounts Cowdray. Some of the surnames in this group are particular to certain geographical regions: **Parkyn** belongs to Cornwall; **Peter** is found in that county but also in Scotland; **Peirce** is strongest in Kent, **Perks** in Staffs and Warwicks, **Perring** in Devon, **Pether** in Middx and Oxon, **Pither** in Berks and Hants. Others have an unusual distribution: **Peterson** is found in Lancs but also in the Shetland Islands; **Perrin** has a presence in both the south-east and north-west of England, and **Petre** (a surname borne by a well-known Roman Catholic family) in Essex and Middx, but also in Cumbd; **Parrell** occurs in both Lancs and Surrey. For the rest, most (**Parkin**, **Parkinson**, **Parr**, **Pears**, **Pearson**, **Perkin**, **Pierce**, **Piers**) are principally surnames of the North, while **Pearce** and **Pierse** are commoner in the South. **Pierson** can be found in clusters in both north and south-east England, while **Peters** is more widespread than many others in the group.

Pethebrige/Pethibridg/Pethibridge, *see* **Petherbridge**.

Petherbridge/Pethybridge P Place-name *Pethybridge* in Devon OE '*Pyd(d)a/Pidda*'s bridge'. Devon surnames, with known variants **Pethibridge**, **Perrebridge**, **Pithebridge**, **Pethibridg**, **Pethebrige**, **Penybridg**, **Pennebridge**, **Penebridge** and others.

Petre, *see* **Peter**.

Petrie/Petry F Scots Gaelic forms of **Peter** or **Patrick**.

Pett P Place-name in Sussex OE 'pit'. Mainly a Kent/Middx surname. Readily confused with/a variant of **Pitt**.

Pettengale/Pettengell/Pettengill, *see* **Pettingale**.

Pettet(t), *see* **Pettit**.

Petticoat P A charming surname which is first recorded in Maryland, America, in the late seventeenth century, and which probably has its origins in an English surname such as **Pennicott**, adapted by folk etymology until it resembled something cosily familiar. **Pennicott**, **Pennicod**, **Pennycod**, **Penicod**, **Pennicut**, **Pennicud**, **Penneycad** and the like are mainly encountered in the south of England, being especially prevalent in Sussex, Devon, Cornwall and Surrey. In Sussex it developed into (or was even derived from) the surname **Pentecost**. The name might have its origin in the place-name *Pennicott* in Devon OE '*Pinna*'s cottage' or in one of the settlements called *Pencoed* or *Pencoyd* OW 'wood's end'. The surname continued to be unstable in America, where it can be found as **Pettic(h)ord**, **Peddycoart**, **Ped(d)icord**, **Pedicot**, **Peddycourt**, **Peddycord** and **Peddicoat**. For a detailed study of this surname, see *Searching for surnames* by John Titford (2002).

Petticrew, *see* **Pettigrew**.

Pettifer/Pettifor(d)/Pettipher/Potipher N Nickname for a man with a false limb, or for a tireless walker OF (literally 'foot of iron'). Chiefly found in South Midland counties of England (**Pettipher** is largely restricted to Warwicks), though **Potipher** is a scarce Essex surname.

Pettigrew/Petticrew/Petticrow N Nickname for a dwarf OF (literally 'little growth'). A Scottish surname in whatever spelling, commonest in Ayrshire and Lanarkshire.

Pettingale/Pettengale/Pettengell/Pettengill/Pettingall/Pettingell/Pettingill P/O A person from *Portugal*, or who had business interests there, from Latin *Portcale*, originally applied to the port of Cale, a city of old Lusitania, west of Oporto.

These are surnames chiefly found in eastern counties of England.

Pettipher, *see* Pettifer.

Pettit(t)/Pettet(t)/Petty N Nickname for a small person OF. **Petty** carries no sense of 'meanness'. **Pettit** and **Pettet** are mainly found in the south-east of England, **Petty** in WRYorks.

Peutherer O Occupational name for a pewterer OF. A very scarce Scottish surname.

Peverall/Peverell/Peverill, *see* Pepperell.

Peyton/Payton P Place-name *Peyton*, Sussex OE '*Poega*'s settlement', or from another similar minor place-name. A scattered surname in both spellings.

Pharaoh, *see* Ferrar. No connexion with the Egyptian king.

Phasey, *see* Vaisey.

Phelp(s), *see* Philip.

Phemister, *see* Femister.

Phibbs, *see* Phipps (under Philip).

Philcox, *see* Philip.

Philip F From the Greek first-name *Philippos* ('fond of horses'), borne by one of the apostles. 'The first-name lost face in England when Philip II was King Consort of Bloody Mary and national enemy of Good Bess; the present Consort has revived its popularity' (Cottle). Whence many surnames, some from pet-forms or diminutives, containing the elements *-ll-* or *-pp-*, and beginning *Phil(p)-, Phelp-, Phip-, Pip-*. **Phelps** and **Phipps** are largely found in Gloucs, **Philpot(t)** in Kent (*see also* **Pott**), **Phippen** in Somerset, **Phill** and **Philp** in Cornwall, and **Philcox** in Sussex. Most of the other variants are widespread, though **Flippance** ('son of *Philip*') is a very scarce Wilts surname. **Phillips**, by far the commonest surname of the group, is the family name of the Viscounts St Davids, the Barons Milford, and the Barons Strange of Knockin. **Phipps** is the family name of the Marquesses of Normanby.

Phill, *see* Philip.

Phillimore, *see* Finnemore.

Philp(s)/Philpin/Phil(l)pot(t)(s), *see* Philip.

Phimister, *see* Femister.

Phin(n)imore, *see* Finnemore.

Phipp(s)/Phippen/Phippin, *see* Philip.

Phizacklea, *see* Fazakerley.

Phoenix, *see* Fenwick.

Physick O Occupational term for a doctor, one who practised physic OF. Largely a Devon surname, but found also in Lancs. **Visick** is a Cornish variant.

Phythian, *see* Vivian.

Pick O Occupational term for a person who made or used picks/pickaxes ME. Mainly a Leics/Lincs surname. Readily confused with/a variant of **Peak**.

Pickard P/F Place-name *Picardy*, France OF. Also known to have been used as a first-name. Very strong in WRYorks. **Pitcher** is a variant.

Pickavance N Nickname (for an energetic, enterprising person?), literally 'prick/spur forward' OF. A scarce Lancs surname.

Pickbourne/Pickburn P Place-name *Pickburn* in WRYorks OE 'pike stream'. Principally a Notts surname in both spellings.

Pickering P Place-name in NRYorks, from an OE tribal name *Piceringas*. Widespread in the north; very strong in Lancs.

Pickersgill P Place-name in WRYorks ME and ON 'footpad's ravine'. *William Pickersgill (1861–1928), railway engineer, was born in Crewe, Chesh, where his father John G. Pickersgill (born in Burnsall, Yorks) was working as an engine fitter.*

Pickett, *see* Pigott.

Pickles T/P Dweller at the *pightle*, little enclosed field ME; or (as George Redmonds suggests) from one of two places called *Pikedlee* in Thornton, Yorks. *Wilfred Pickles*

(1904–1978), English actor and radio presenter, a professional Yorkshireman famous for his catchphrase '…and to all in the north, good neet…', was born in Halifax.

Pickup P Place-name in Lancs OE 'hill with a peak', and a Lancs surname. 'Despite its saucy sound, ten people answer to it in the London telephone directory' (Cottle).

Pickwell P Place-name in Leics OE 'spring/ stream by the peak(s)'. A Lincs surname.

Pickwick P Place-name *Pickwick*, Wilts OE 'sharp point (of land) dairy farm'. In the thirteenth century both the place and the bearers of the name bore spellings such as **Pykewyk(e)/Pikewik(e)**. Charles Dickens's character Mr **Pickwick** is bound to spring to mind here. In the year 1695 a young child was found abandoned in *Pickwick*, Wilts, and was baptized 'Moses **Pickwick**' accordingly. His grandson Eleazer **Pickwick** (c.1749–1837) became a wealthy stagecoach proprietor in Bath, serving as mayor of the city in 1826, and it was the name of his cousin, another Moses **Pickwick**, whose name Dickens's character Sam Weller saw emblazoned upon a London to Bath coach. The surname is a scarce one, found principally in Somerset, though William Samuel **Pickwick** was a well-known lawyer in Jamaica during the early years of the twentieth century.

Picton P Place-name in Chesh, NRYorks and elsewhere OE 'place by a pointed hill' or '*Pica*'s place'. Strongest in Lancs and in Pembrokeshire, Wales.

Piddock/Pidduck, *see* **Puttock**.

Pidge(o)n O/N/F Occupational term for a hunter of wood pigeons OF; or a nickname for someone easily plucked/swindled; or from ME *Pet(y)jon* ('little [OF *petit*] John'). **Pidgeon** is largely a Devon surname; **Pidgen**, very scarce, is found in Dorset and elsewhere. *The actor and singer Walter Pidgeon (1897–1984), though he made his career in the USA, was born in St John, New Brunswick, Canada.*

Pierce, *see* **Peter**.

Pierrepo(i)nt P Place-name in a number of regions of France – Calvados, Manche, Seine-Maritime OF *Pierrepont* ('stone bridge'). Chiefly a Notts surname. *Albert Pierrepoint (1905–1992), the best-known member of a family of public executioners (but who later fought for the abolition of the death penalty), was born in North Bierley, Bradford, WRYorks. In 1946 he became the landlord of a public house in Manchester, which he named 'Help the Poor Struggler'.*

Piers, *see* **Peter**.

Pigg O/N Occupational term for a keeper of pigs OE, or a nickname for a person who resembled a pig (in appearance and/or characteristics?). A Co Durham/Northd surname.

Pig(g)ott/Pickett F From the ME/OF firstname *Picot/Pigot*, a diminutive of the Germanic *Pic*. See **Pike**. **Pigott** is strongest in WRYorks, **Piggott** in both south-east and north-west England, and **Pickett** in Middx, Surrey and Wilts.

Pike T/O/N/F A surname with several possible origins: dweller by a peak, point, hilltop OE; a man who fished for pike OE, a fishmonger who sold them, or a person with the predatory instincts of such a fish; a maker or user of a pike, pickaxe OE or a soldier armed with a pike (a pikeman); a nickname for a person bearing some resemblance to a woodpecker OF *pic* (perhaps bearing a pointed nose?); or a nickname for a tall/lanky man ON *pik*; or from a Germanic first-name OF/ME *Pic* ('pointed'). Chiefly a West Country surname, strong in Devon.

Pilcher O/N Occupational term/nickname for a person who made/wore *pilches* OE with an *-er* suffix. A *pilch* was at first an outer garment of skin with the hair attached (compare *pelt*), later of leather or wool. A Kent surname.

Pile T Dweller by a post or stake, perhaps one with special significance OE. Chiefly a Devon surname.

Pilgrim/Peagram/Peagrim/Pegram/ Pegrum/Peregrine N/F Nickname used for a person who had been on a pilgrimage to the Holy Land, to a European shrine such as that at Santiago di Compostella, or to the tomb of St Thomas à Becket at Canterbury ME from OF. *Pilgrim* is also known to have been used as a first-name. **Peregrine** is found mainly in South Wales; all other spellings of the surname belong mainly to Essex.

Pilkington P Place-name in Lancs OE '*Pileca*'s farm', and a Lancs surname.

Pill T/N/P Dweller by a creek, stream OE; or from a place-name *Pill* in Monmouthshire, Pembrokeshire, Somerset, with the same meaning; or a nickname for a small tubby person OF. In Cornwall (where the surname is mostly found): possibly from Cornish *pyl* ('hillock') or from a minor place-name. **Pillar**, a Devon surname, could be a variant, though it could alternatively be a nickname for a robber, plunderer, pillager OF *pilleur*.

Pillar, *see* **Pill**.

Pilley P Place-name in Hants, WRYorks OE 'stake/shaft/pile-wood/clearing', and found in both these counties.

Pilling P A place and river name in Lancs, etymology uncertain, though OE *pyll* is a 'tidal creek'. Mainly a Lancs surname.

Pillinger O Occupational term for a baker OF (compare Modern French *Boulanger*). Chiefly a Gloucs/Somerset surname. **Bollinger** (forever associated in France with high-quality champagne) and **Bullinger** are much scarcer variants. See also **Pollinger**.

Pilton P Place-name in Devon, Rutland, Somerset OE '?place by a creek' and in Northants OE '*Pileca*'s farm'. A scarce surname, found mainly in Somerset.

Pim(m)/Pym(m) F From the mediaeval female first-name *Pymme/Pimme*, shortened forms of the Greek *Euphemia*. Mainly West Country/South Midlands surnames, though the diminutives (with OF suffixes) **Pimblett/Pimblott/Pimlett/Pimlott** belong mainly to Chesh/Lancs. *John Pym (1584–1643), politician, came from a family*

long-settled in the manor of Brymore, Somerset... The gin-based cocktail known as Pimm's was first produced in 1823 by James Pimm, a farmer's son from Newnham, Kent.

Pimblett/Pimblott/Pimlett/Pimlott/Pimm, *see* **Pim**.

Pinch, *see* **Pink**.

Pinchard, *see* **Pincher**.

Pinchbeck P Place-name in Lincs OE '?minnow/finch stream', and a Lincs surname. 'Christopher **Pinchbeck** (died 1732) invented a nasty alloy that looked like gold, and debased the name to the meaning *spurious*' (Cottle).

Pincher/Pinchard/Pinker ?N Possibly a nickname for a grumbler, fault-finder, haggler, tight-fisted person ME *pinch(en)*, from OF *pincier* ('to pinch'). **Pinchard** can readily be confused with or be a variant of **Punchard**. **Pinker** is a possible variant. **Pincher** is strongest in Staffs; **Pinchard**, very scarce, in Devon/Somerset.

Pinches ?N Possibly a variant of **Pink**. In a comprehensive study included in *The family of Pinches* (1981), John Harvey **Pinches** considers various possible origins for the surname, including a *Pynsach/Pinches* family from Aberdeen and the outside possibility that **Pinches**, a Shropshire surname, might be derived from the Welsh **Ap Innes/Johannis** ('son of *John*'). The Land Revenue Miscellaneous Books in the National Archives include references to a place in Pembrokeshire, Wales, known variously as *Pinches* and *Pyncheston*, in 1592.

Pinckney, *see* **Pinkney**.

Pincott P Place-name *Pincott* in Gloucs OE '*Pinna*'s cottage'. This place was *Pynecote/Pynekott* c.1220, and may then have been pronounced with the -*i*- long. By the late nineteenth century this and similar surnames were widespread throughout England (and elsewhere, including Australia). Forms such as **Pinkett**, **Pencott** and **Penkett**, which might appear to be variants, may have a different source.

Pindar/Pinder O Occupational term for an impounder of stray animals OE. **Pindar** is found mainly in Lincs/WRYorks, **Pinder** in the north of England and especially in WRYorks. See also **Pender**. *Peter Pindar was the pseudonym adopted by the Devon-born poet and satirist John Wolcot (1738–1819).*

Pine T/N/P Dweller near a pine tree or in a pine wood; or a nickname for a person as tall and thin as a pine OE; or from a place-name in Calvados and elsewhere with this feature. For the hyphenated surname **Pine-Coffin**, see **Coffin**.

Pinfold/Penfold T/O Dweller at the pin-fold/pound, or an occupational term for the man in charge of it (compare **Pindar**). **Pinfold** is found mainly in the South Midlands, **Penfold** in the south-east.

Pink/Pinch/Spink(e)(s) N Nickname for a person as chirpy as a chaffinch OE *pinc(a)*. See also **Finch**. **Pinker** is a possible variant. **Pink** is found mainly in Hants, **Spink** in WRYorks, **Spinks** in Norfolk and **Pinch** in Cornwall. **Spinke** is a very scarce widely scattered surname. *The company of Spink, which has a particular expertise in the sale of coins and medals, was founded in Lombard Street, London, by John Spink in 1666.*

Pinker, *see* **Pincher** and **Pink**. A Gloucs surname.

Pinkney/Pinckney P Place-name *Picquigny* (Germanic) in the Somme, France. **Pinkney** is a surname of north-east England; **Pinckney** (very scarce) is found in Hants and Wilts.

Pinn O Occupational term for a pin(-maker) OE. A Devon surname.

Pinney P Place-names in Devon: *Penhay* OE 'enclosure with a pen/fold'; *Pinhay* OE 'enclosure with a pound/pond/?dam'; *Pinhoe* (etymology uncertain: ?British and OE 'head/top/end projecting ridge of land'). A Devon/Somerset surname.

Pinnock P/N Place-name in Gloucs OE 'small pen/fold' or OW 'small hill'; or a nickname from a ME word for a hedge-sparrow. Strongest in Northants.

Pipe T/P Dweller by a water-pipe, conduit, stream OE; or from the place-name *Pipe* in Herefords, with the same meaning (or 'elongated strip of land') – though the surname is most commonly found in Suffolk; or a variant of **Piper**.

Piper O Occupational term for a player on the pipe/fife OE. 'But sometimes absorbing **Pepper** since Peter **Piper** in the jingle was surely a pepperer' (Cottle). See also **Pipe**.

Pippin, *see* **Peppin**.

Pirie, *see* **Perry**.

Pitcairn P Scots: place-name in Perthshire, Gaelic 'croft/field of the cairn'. The South Pacific island is named after Robert **Pitcairn**, the midshipman who first sighted it in 1767.

Pitcaithl(e)y/Pitke(a)thly P Place-name *Pitkeathly*, Perthshire, Scotland, ?Pictish and Scots Gaelic 'share belonging to *Cathalan*'.

Pitcher O Occupational term for one who sealed ships' seams with pitch, a caulker OE; or a variant of **Pickard**.

Pitchford/Pitchforth P Place-name in Salop OE 'ford near a source of pitch' (a bituminous well). **Pitchford** is a Salop surname, though **Pitchforth** is found mainly in WRYorks, where it can be found spelt **Pichforthe**, **Pitchworth** and even **Pickforke**.

Pithebridge, *see* **Petherbridge**.

Pither(s), *see* **Peter**.

Pitke(a)thly, *see* **Pitcaithly**.

Pitman, *see* **Pitt**.

Pitney P Place-name in Somerset OE '*Pytta/Peota*'s island'. The surname is most commonly found in Sussex. *Gene Pitney (1940–2006), American singer and songwriter, was born in Hartford, Connecticut. A James Pitney was living in Ipswich, Massachusetts, as early as 1639.*

Pitt(s) T/P Dweller in a pit/hollow/excavation OE, or from a place-name with the same meaning, such as *Pitt* in Hants or *Pett* in Sussex. **Pitter** (mainly Hants),

Pit(t)man (mainly Somerset and the south of England), **Putman** (south of England) and **Putt** (Devon) are variants. **Pitt** is widespread; **Pitts** is strong in WRYorks. Readily confused with/a variant of **Pett**. *William Pitt ('the elder'), First Earl of Chatham (1708–1778), British Prime Minister, was the son of Robert Pitt of Boconnoc, Cornwall, and his Irish wife Harriet Villiers.*

Pittaway ?P A surname of uncertain origin; Cottle suggests the place-names *Poitevin* in France and *Pitway* in Somerset OE '?track in a hollow'. Most commonly found in the South and West Midlands, strongest in Warwicks.

Pitter/Pittman, *see* Pitt.

Pittock, *see* Puttock.

Pitts, *see* Pitt.

Pittuck, *see* Puttock.

Pizer, *see* Poyser.

Piz(z)ey/Pizzie, *see* Pusey.

Place/Plaice/Pleace/Please/Pleass
T/O/N Dweller at a town square, marketplace, manor-house OF, or near a quickset hedge OF; or an occupational term for a fishmonger who sold plaice OF *plaise* or other flat-fish; or even used as a nickname for a person as thin as a plaice. **Place** is generally a north-of-England surname; **Plaice**, very scarce, can be found in Norfolk, **Pleace/Please** in Devon and **Pleass** in Somerset.

Plain T/N Dweller at an open tract of land, a flat meadow OF; or a nickname for a candid, frank person OF. A scarce Norfolk surname.

Plaistow P Place-name in several counties (spelt variously -*ai*, -*ay*-, -*ey*-) OE 'sportsground (literally 'play-place'). 'The one in West Ham has now lost the atmosphere of the village green' (Cottle). Chiefly an Essex surname. See also **Plaster**.

Plampin, *see* Pamplin.

Plant T/O/N Dweller at an enclosure, plantation OF; or an occupational term for a gardener OF *plante* ('cutting, shoot'), or a nickname for a delicate person, or a sprig/ young offspring. A surname of the Midlands and the north.

Plaster O/P Occupational term for a plasterer OF, or a variant of **Plaistow**. An uncommon surname, with a presence in Somerset and elsewhere.

Plater O Occupational term for a pleader, advocate OF, or for a plate-armour maker OF. Chiefly a Bucks/Middx surname.

Platt(s) T/N Dweller on a plot of flat level ground OF *plat* ('flat') or by a plank footbridge ME (as in *Platt Bridge*, Lancs); or a nickname for a thin man. **Platt** is found chiefly in Chesh/Lancs, **Platts** in WRYorks. *David Platt, soccer player for England, was born in 1966 in Oldham, Lancs.*

Player O Occupational term for a successful athlete or for an actor or musician OE. Most common in southern counties of England. *John Player (1839–1884), tobacco manufacturer, was born in Saffron Walden, Essex, but moved to Nottingham when he was in his early twenties.*

Playford P Place-name in Suffolk OE 'ford where sports are held'. Chiefly a Norfolk surname. *John Playford (1622/3-1686/7), who published* The English dancing master *in the 1650s, was born in Norwich, Norfolk.*

Pleace, *see* Place.

Pleasance F/P From the mediaeval female first-name *Plaisance* OF 'pleasant(ness)'; or from the Italian city of *Piacenza* (Latin *Placentia*). The word is found in the early fifteenth century for the fine linen or gauze made there. The surname **Pleasance** has an oddly scattered distribution, but is strongest in Suffolk. *The actor Donald Pleasance (1919–1995) was born in Worksop, Notts, though because his father worked on the railways he had a very peripatetic childhood.*

Please/Pleass, *see* Place.

Plenderleith/Plenderleath P From the place-name *Plenderleith* in Roxburghshire, Scotland, of uncertain etymology. A Scottish surname.

Plew(e)(s)/Plewis T Dweller at the plough

(land) OE; *plough(land)* was a term used in northern and eastern England for the area able to be tilled by one plough-team of eight oxen in a year (southern and south-western *hide*). The three forms Plew/ Plewes/Plews are chiefly found in northern England and south-east Scotland, but Plewis is a very scarce Kent surname.

Plimpton P Place-name *Plympton* in Devon OE 'plum-tree farm'. Yet by the late nineteenth century this was an oddly scattered surname, with almost no presence in the county of Devon. For comparison, see Plimsoll.

Plimsoll ?P The exact meaning of this distinctive surname is unknown, though the air is thick with kites flown by surname scholars. Bardsley is tentative in his suggestion that Plimsaul/Plimsoll might come from a parish near Chester called *Plemonstall* ('From Plimstall to Plimsoll would be an easy stage. I have no certain proof of this'). Henry Harrison in his *Surnames of the United Kingdom* (1918) repeats the same theory, adding the information that 'a form of this name AD 1326-7 was Pleymundestowe; a Plegmund was Archbishop of Canterbury AD 890-914'. Reaney is convinced that Plimsoll is a Huguenot surname, saying that 'several refugees of this name came from Brittany to southern England after the revocation of the Edict of Nantes, one of them to Bristol'. None of these theories takes account of the fact that Plimsoll is predominantly a Devon surname, and that it can be found there before the Edict of Nantes was revoked in 1685. It is not featured in David Postles' *The surnames of Devon* (1995), and no-one of this name appears in Subsidy Rolls for Devon in 1332 or 1524-7, but there are Plimsoll/Plymsholes in Bideford and in Alphington parish records from as early as the 1660s, and the Hearth Tax return for 1674 lists a John Plymsole of Crediton, who was too poor to pay the tax on his single-hearth dwelling. In the same year the will of Robert Plimpshole of Cheriton Bishop was proved in the local probate court. Given the fact that Plim and Plymbe are also Devon surnames (see

Plimpton), and that the river *Plym* and settlements such as *Plymouth*, *Plympton*, *Plymtree* and *Plymstock* are to be found in that county, it is tempting to suggest that the Plimsoll surname may have some kind of place-name origin. Just as Ingerson is a known variation on the surname Ingersoll, so a certain Richard Plymson, who married Agnis Mills in Exeter in 1695, is almost certainly a Plimsoll in disguise. *Samuel Plimsoll (1824–1898), born in Bristol, was elected Liberal MP for Derby in 1868. In 1876, thanks to his tireless efforts, an amendment to the Merchant Shipping Act of 1871 was passed whereby a 'Plimsoll line' was to be marked on ships to prevent overloading. Gym shoes of a distinctive design which originally carried a horizontal coloured band resembling a Plimsoll line, acquired the nickname of 'plimsolls' accordingly.*

Plomer, *see* Plummer.

Plomley, *see* Plumley.

Plott T Dweller on a plot (of ground) OE. A very scarce scattered surname.

Plowden P Place-name in Salop OE 'valley where sports are held' (compare Playford). A very scarce scattered surname. *Edwin Noel Auguste Plowden, Baron Plowden (1907–2001), compiler of the Plowden Report on primary school education, was born in Strachur, Argyll, though the Plowden family, Roman Catholics, had long been established in Shropshire.*

Plowman O Occupational term for a ploughman, or for a plowright OE. See Plowright. *Plow*, the American spelling of the English word *plough*, reflects its present pronunciation accurately enough, but no longer bears witness to its former guttural quality. Strongest in Hants, Northants and Surrey.

Plowright O Occupational term for a plough-maker OE. Compare Plowman. A scattered surname, strong in Lincs. *Dame Joan Plowright, the actress who became the third wife of Lord Laurence Olivier, was born in 1929 in Brigg, Lincs.*

Pluckrose N Nickname for a person fond

of picking or plucking roses OE and OE; Reaney suggests that it might refer to a rose paid for land tenure, in lieu of rent. A scarce Essex/Middx surname.

Plum(b) T/O Dweller by a plum tree OE; or an occupational term for a worker in lead OF. Compare **Plummer**.

Plumbley, *see* **Plumley**.

Plumer, *see* **Plummer**.

Plumley/Plomley/Plumbley P Place-names *Plumley* in Chesh, Hants, and *Plumbley*, Derbys OE 'clearing/field where plums grow'. **Plumley** is found mainly in southern and south-western counties of England, strongest in Somerset; **Plomley**, very scarce, can be found in Kent, and **Plumbley** in Lancs and in the Isle of Wight. *(Francis) Roy Plomley (1914–1985), the radio broadcaster who invented and presented Desert island discs, was born in Kingston upon Thames, Surrey.*

Plummer/Plomer/Plumer T/O Dweller by a plum tree OE (compare **Plum**); or an occupational term for a dealer in feathers OE *plume* ('feather') or for a worker in lead, a plumber OF. *The Canadian film, television and stage actor (Arthur) Christopher (Orme) Plummer was born in 1929 in Toronto.*

Plumpton P Place-name in various counties OE 'plum-tree farm'. Commonest in Lancs.

Plumtree T/P Dweller by a plum tree OE, or from the place-name *Plumtree*, with the same meaning, in Notts. Chiefly a Lincs surname. **Plumptre** (an exceptionally scarce variant) is the family name of the Barons Fitzwalter.

Poad/Poat(e) N Nickname for a person bearing some resemblance to a toad OE – the imagination boggles... Not common in any spelling: **Poad** is mainly a Cornish surname; **Poat** is found in Cornwall, but also in Devon and Sussex; **Poate** belongs to Hants.

Pobjoy/Pobgee/Popejoy/Popjoy N Nickname for a person who never stopped

taking or who wore brightly coloured clothes, from OF (originally Arabic) *papageia*, a popinjay, parrot; or used of someone who excelled at the sport of shooting at a wooden parrot on a pole. All variants are scarce: **Pobjoy** can be found in Somerset (especially in the town of Frome) and in Wilts; **Pobgee** in Surrey; **Popejoy** and **Popjoy** in Wilts.

Pocklington P Place-name in ERYorks OE 'The settlement of *Pocela*'s people'. Chiefly a Lincs surname. See also **Pollington**.

Pocock, *see* **Peacock**.

Podmore P Place-name in Staffs OE 'toad moor'. Chiefly a Staffs surname.

Poe/Pow(e) N Nickname for a person bearing some resemblance to a peacock ME *po*, ON *pá*. See **Peacock**. **Pow(e)** could alternatively be Welsh – 'son of Howe (Hugh)' (*ap Howe*) – though it would appear to have an insignificant presence in the Principality itself. **Poe** belongs mainly to the north of England, **Pow** to Somerset (though it also features fairly strongly in East Lothian, Scotland) and **Powe** to Devon. *The American author Edgar Allan Poe (1809–1849) was born Edgar Poe in Boston, Massachusetts, but was raised by the Allan family in Richmond, Virginia and in England. The Poe family were of Scots-Irish descent.*

Pogson/Poxon F From the mediaeval first-name *Pogg(e)*, a variant of *Mogg(e)*, diminutive of *Margaret*; compare the more modern English pet-form *Peg(gy)*. **Pogson** is strongest in WRYorks, **Poxon** in Leics and Staffs.

Points/Poyntz F/P From the Norman first-name *Ponc(h)e/Pons*, ultimately from the Roman *Pontius*, which *Pontius* Pilate did little to popularize; or from the place-name *Ponts* in Normandy OF ('bridges'). See also **Punchard**. Both **Points** and **Poyntz** are scarce and scattered, the latter being found mainly in South Wales.

Pole T Dweller at a pool OE (and the surname is frequently pronounced 'Pool'), the final -*e* exhibiting the use of the dative after a lost preposition; or a variant of **Paul**.

Almost inevitably, a child born in Leicester in 1904 was called '*May* **Pole**'. *Cardinal Reginald Pole (1500–1559), Archbishop of Canterbury, was probably born at Stourton Castle, Staffs.*

Polglase/Polglaze P There are places called *Polglase/Polglaze* in no fewer than twelve parishes in Cornwall: Cornish 'blue/green/grey pool' (the adjective coming second).

Polkinhorn(e)/Polkinghorn(e) P Cornish: from a place-name meaning '*Kenhoern*'s pool'.

Pollard N/F Nickname for a person with a big head or a cropped head ME *poll* ('head') plus the pejorative suffix *-ard*; or a pejorative variant of **Paul**.

Pollinger T Dweller by a polled tree ME *pollenger*; or a variant of **Pillinger**. A scarce surname, found mainly in Gloucs.

Pollington P It would be all too easy to assume that this surname must always be derived from *Pollington* WRYorks OE 'farmstead associated with a piece of ground called *Pofel* [low-lying land?]', referred to as *Pouilgleton* in the twelfth century, or even from *Pocklington* ERYorks OE '*Pocela*'s farm', which was *Poclinton* in Domesday Book, 1086. There are certainly thirteenth-century references to the surname in Yorks, and William **de Pollinton** appears in an Assize Roll for that county in the year 1219. George Redmonds has found references to **Pollington**s in Yorkshire covering the years 1250 to 1508. Yet by the time parish registers began to be kept consistently in the sixteenth century, the story has changed: by then **Pollington** was predominantly a Sussex surname, also found in Berks and elsewhere in the south of England, and probate records for Hants make reference to Thomas **Pollington** of Linkenholt in the year 1574. Thereafter **Pollington**s and **Pullington**s are constantly in evidence in Hants, as in Sussex. It is tempting to suppose that the origin here might be the Sussex place-name *Poling* OE 'people by the *pal* or stake', possibly referring to a palisade, which was *Paling(e)/Palyng* in the four-

teenth century. The Subsidy Rolls for Sussex, 1524–1525, would seem to give weight to this theory: listings for Warnham in the Hundred of Steyning include both a Stephen **Polyngton** and a John **Polyng**. At the time of the 1881 census **Pollington**, while scarce, was still a predominantly Sussex surname, and only a mere handful of **Pollington**s were living in Yorks. In 1881 the surname **Pollinton** can also be found: exceptionally scarce, it belongs to ERYorks; **Pollintine**s, meanwhile, are restricted to Suffolk and Middx, and **Pollentine**s to Lancs, Middx, Norfolk and Suffolk. In the early seventeenth century Alexander **Pollington** of Lombard Street in the City of London, Citizen and Harberdasher, whose father had held 120 acres of land in Slaugham, Sussex, purchased an estate in Antigua, West Indies, which he named '*Pollington*'s'. Present-day **Pollington**s have to get used to their surname being misheard as **Pockington**, **Bollington**, **Pillington**, **Pollerton**, **Hollington**, **Bonington** and **Collinson**; such is the case with Chris **Pollington** of Anderton, Chorley, Lancs, whose own geographically mobile maleline ancestors moved from Havant in Hants to Otley, Yorks, to Boston, Lincs, and to Leeds before settling down in Lancs. See also **Pocklington**.

Pollit(t) F From a mediaeval first-name derived from the Greek *Hippolytus* ('letting horses loose'); in Greek legend this was the name of the son of the Amazon Queen *Hippolyta*, but the use of the first-name stems from a Roman saint, martyred AD 252. Almost exclusively a Lancs surname.

Pollock P Scots: from a place-name in Renfrewshire, Gaelic '?pool in a field'. Family name of the Viscounts Hanworth.

Polmear/Pelmear/Polmeer P Place-name *Polmear* in Cornwall, Cornish *polmur* 'big pool'.

Polson, *see* **Paul**.

Polyblank N Nickname for a person with white hair OF *poil blanc*. A scarce Devon surname.

Pomeroy/Pomery P From one of a number of places in France called *La Pommeraie/Pommeraye* ('apple orchard'). **Pomeroy** is principally found in Devon, where one family of this name lived for over five hundred years at Berry Pomeroy castle; the variant **Pomery** belongs more to Cornwall than to Devon. **Pomeroy** is the family name of the Viscounts Harberton.

Pomfret/Pomphrett/Pontefract P
Place-name *Pontefract* in WRYorks OF *pont freit*, from Latin *Pons fractus* ('broken bridge'); the spelling represents the Latin form, while the usual pronunciation, '*Pomfret/Pumfret*', reflects the French version. The surname **Pontefract** belongs to WRYorks, though **Pomfret** is found mainly in Lancs, and **Pomphrett** in Essex. **Pomfret** can be readily confused with, or be a variant of, **Pumfrey**.

Pomphrey, *see* Pumfrey.

Pond/Ponder T Dweller by a pond ME. Readily confused with/a variant of **Pound**.

Ponsford P Place-name in Devon OW and OE 'ford of the river *Pont*', and principally a Devon surname. **Pauncefoot** (commonly pronounced '*Pouncefoot*') is a very scarce variant.

Ponsonby P Place-name in Cumbd OF and ON '*Puncun*'s farm'. The surname is usually pronounced '*Punsonby*'. One branch of the Ponsonby family has been prominent in Ireland since the seventeenth century, and this is the family name of the (Irish) Earls of Bessborough and of three Barons.

Pont T Dweller by the bridge OF. A scarce surname mainly found in Sussex.

Pontefract, *see* Pomfret.

Pontifex N Nickname, from Latin, for a person who behaved as if he were a pontiff/bishop/pope (literally 'bridge-maker'), or who had played such a part in a play. A scarce Middx/Surrey surname.

Ponton P There are places called *Ponton* in Lincs OE 'hill farm', but this is a scattered surname found largely in the north-east of England and particularly in Midlothian, Scotland. The name of Wilielmus **de Ponton** is recorded in Ayr in 1305-6, and **Ponton**, like **Graham** and **Lindsay/Lindsey**, may well have its origins in a Lincs place-name which became established in Scotland as a surname.

Pook N Nickname for a person resembling a goblin, water-sprite, elf, puck OE. Mainly a Devon surname.

Pool(e) T/P Dweller by a pool OE, or from one of a number of place-names with the same meaning; or a variant of **Paul**. Readily confused with/a variant of **Powel**. Both **Pool** and **Poole** are widespread. See also **Poolman**.

Poolman T Dweller by a pool OE and OE. A very scarce Wilts surname.

Poor(e), *see* Power.

Pope/Pape N Nickname for someone who adopted the manners of a pope or had played such a part in a pageant OE *papa*, from Greek *pappas* ('father') via Latin *papa* ('bishop, pope'). **Pope** is strongest in the south and south-west of England; **Pape** can be found from Lincs/Yorks northwards. *The poet Alexander Pope (1688–1744) was born in Plough Court, London, the son of a linen merchant of the same name and his wife Edith Turner (from Yorks).*

Popejoy, *see* Pobjoy.

Popham P Place-name in Hants OE '?pebbly homestead'. A Devon/Somerset surname.

Popjoy, *see* Pobjoy.

Pop(p)le T Dweller by a poplar-tree OE. 'In late ME a word of unknown etymology means "cockle, darnel, tares, charlock", but this and OE *popel* "pebble" are far less likely as surnames' (Cottle). **Popple** is strongest in Lincs, **Pople** in Somerset.

Popplestone N Nickname from the word 'pebble' OE *popelstân*. A Devon surname.

Poppleton P Place-name in WRYorks OE 'pebbly farm', and a WRYorks surname.

Popplewell P There are several places so-called in WRYorks OE 'pebbly spring/ stream', and this is a WRYorks surname.

Porch T/O Dweller/worker at a porch OF. An early instance of the name recorded in Somerset in the late thirteenth century is *atte Porche*, and this is a Somerset surname.

Porcher O Occupational term for a pig-keeper OF *porch(i)er* (compare the word *pork*). A scarce surname, mainly found in Norfolk.

Port T/O Dweller at, or controller of, a town gate OF *porte*; or a dweller at a port or harbour OE *port*. The earliest recorded instances are *de la Port(e)*. 'A name early eminent in Herefords and Derbys, where the family founded Repton School (with the punning *porta* in its motto)' (Cottle). Yet the surname is most commonly found in Kent and Surrey.

Portbury/Potbury P Place-name *Portbury* in Somerset OE 'fort/manor by the harbour'. A Devon surname in both spellings.

Porter O Occupational term for a gate-keeper, door-keeper, carrier or porter OF. *William Sydney Porter (1862–1910), the American short story writer born in Greensboro, North Carolina, adopted the pen-name of 'O Henry'.*

Portman O Status term for a townsman, burgess OE. Chiefly a West Midlands surname, strongest in Worcs.

Portsmouth P Place-name in Hants OE 'mouth of the harbour'. An uncommon surname, chiefly found in Hants.

Posnett, *see* **Postlethwaite**.

Postle N Nickname, 'apostle' OF, perhaps from taking such a part in a play, or from excessive piety. A Norfolk surname.

Postlethwaite P A field-name in Millom, Cumbd, of uncertain etymology. It may be ON 'apostle's clearing', but has no known religious associations. **Postlethwaite** is strongest in Lancs; **Posnett** is seemingly a variant, but is principally found in Leics. *The actor Peter William ('Pete') Postlethwaite*

was born in Warrington, Chesh, (formerly Lancs) in 1945.

Poston T/O Dweller at/keeper of a postern-gate OF. A scattered surname, strongest in the West Midlands and the north-west.

Potbury, *see* **Portbury**.

Pothecary/Potticary O Occupational term for a spicer, druggist, apothecary OF (ultimately from a Greek word for a place where one 'puts things away'). That is, in the immortal words of Shelley Klein, author of *The concise dictionary of surnames* (2004): 'Keeper of a drug store'. Compare **Prentice** as a surname for an apprentice. West Country surnames, strongest in Wilts.

Potipher, *see* **Pettifer**.

Potkin(s), *see* **Pott**.

Pott(s) T/O/F Dweller near (or even *in…?*) a hole, pit, pothole OE; or occupational term for a potter, a maker of pots OE; or from the first-name *Philip*, via *Philpot* (see **Philip**), in which case **Potkin/Potkin(s)** (very scarce, mainly Suffolk) are diminutive forms. **Pott** is found in both the south-east and the north-west of England, and is particularly strong in Chesh; **Potts** belongs mainly to the north and the north-east.

Pottenger, *see* **Pottinger**.

Potter O Occupational term for a potter, one who made crockery, metal pots, and even bells OE. A widespread surname, very strong in Lancs.

Potterton P Place-name in WRYorks OE 'potters' place', though the surname has a wide and unpredictable distribution. *The Potterton Company, manufacturers of boilers, was founded in Balham, London, in 1850 by Thomas Potterton.*

Potticary, *see* **Pothecary**.

Pottinger O Occupational term for a maker of soup, broth, pottage OF. 'The *-n-* (as in **Massinger**) is a slovenly adenoidal English insertion' (Cottle). **Pottinger** is widely scattered, strong in the Orkney and Shetland Islands; **Pottenger** belongs to Somerset.

Potts, *see* Pott.

Poulter o Occupational term for a poulterer OF. A scattered surname. The Worshipful Company of Poulters of the City of London was granted its charter in 1504.

Poultney, *see* Pountney.

Poulton P Place-name in Chesh, Gloucs, Kent, Lancs OE 'settlement at a pool'.

Pound T/O Dweller at, or official responsible for, a pound, pinfold, enclosure for stray cattle OE. Readily confused with/a variant of Pond.

Pountney/Poultney P Place-name *Poultney*, Leics OE '*Pulta*'s island', which was spelt *Pontenei* in Domesday Book, being subject to the usual Norman French substitution of -*n*- for OE -*l*. The surnames **Pountney** and **Poultney** both belong principally to the West Midlands. *Pulteney Bridge, Bath, famous for having shops on both of its sides, was built in 1773 for William Pulteney, whose wife Frances had inherited Bathwick, across the river Avon from Bath itself… The now-lost City of London Church St Laurence Poultney/ Pountney took its name from its principal benefactor, the draper and Lord Mayor Sir John Poultney or Pountney. Built in the fourteenth century, the church perished in the great fire of London in 1666.*

Poupard/Poupart N Nickname for a chubby child OF. Scarce south-east-of-England surnames. *Poupart's Jam Factory, built in Twickenham in 1911, was demolished in 2008.*

Povah, *see* Povey.

Povey ?N Of uncertain origin, perhaps from a Herefords/Gloucs/Wilts dialectal word for a barn-owl, which is 'puffy' in appearance, though the surname, widely scattered from Kent to Lancs, is strongest in Staffs. **Povah**, probably a variant, is strongest in Denbighshire, Wales.

Pow, *see* Poe.

Powdrell/Powdrill, *see* Putterill.

Powe, *see* Poe.

Powel(l)/Powle(s) F Welsh, 'son of *Hywel/ Howell*' (*ap Hywel*) – see **Howel**; or a variant of **Paul**. Commonly pronounced '*Pole*'. Readily confused with/a variant of **Pool**. *Sir Robert Baden-Powell, first Baron Baden-Powell (1857–1941), army officer and founder of the Boy Scouts and Girl Guides, was born in London, the son of Rev. Baden Powell (himself the son of another Baden Powell of Langton, Kent) and his wife Henrietta Grace Smyth.*

Power/Poor(e) N/P Nickname for a poor person OF; or a variant of *Pohier*, used to describe a person from *Pois* in Picardy. **Power** is largely an Irish surname; **Poor** is found mainly in southern counties of England. *The firm of Powers, whiskey distillers, was founded in 1791 by James Power, a Dublin innkeeper… The stage and film actor Tyrone Power (1914–1958), born in Cincinnati, Ohio, was the son of one Tyrone Power and the great-grandson of another. All were members of a family which had roots in Waterford, Ireland, but which flourished in London in the nineteenth century as soldiers, engineers and actors. Tyrone Power the actor had broader family connexions with Sir Tyrone Guthrie, Evelyn Waugh and (Lord) Laurence Olivier.*

Powley/Powling, *see* Paul.

Pownall P Place-name in Chesh OE '*Pohha*'s nook'. A Chesh/Lancs surname.

Powtrell, *see* Putterill.

Poxon, *see* Pogson.

Poyner o Occupational term for a boxer, fighter, one who was good with his fists OF. Mostly found in the West Midlands.

Poyntz, *see* Points.

Poyser/Pizer/Poyzer o Occupational term for a person charged with overseeing weights and measures, a superintendent of a public weighing-machine OF. Variants such as **Peyzer**, listed by Hanks and Hodges, appear not to have survived into modern times. **Poyser** is a surname of the Midlands and the north, and **Pizer** of ERYorks; **Poy-zer**, very scarce, can be found in Notts.

Prall P Place-name *Prawle* in Devon OE 'look-out hill' (compare the word *pry*), but chiefly a Kent surname.

Pratt N Nickname for a smart, cunning, astute person OE *proett* ('trick'). A wide-spread surname, the family name of the Marquesses Camden.

Preater O A learned translation (Latin *praetor*) of the occupational term *reeve* (see **Reeve**). A scarce Gloucs surname.

Precious F/N From a Latin female first-name meaning 'precious, valuable'; or a nickname given to a particularly valuable member of a community OF *precios*. A scarce Yorks surname.

Predith/Preddy, *see* **Preedy**.

Preece P/F Place-names *Preese/Prees* in Lancs and Salop ow 'brushwood, covert'; or a variant of **Price**.

Preedy F/O Welsh: from the first-name *Pre-dyr/Peredur*, borne by one of the knights of the Round Table, but *ap redith* ('son of *Mer-edith*'), giving **Predith**, **Preddy** and **Priddy**, must also be a possibility; or an occupational term for a bard, Welsh *prydudd*. Read-ily confused with/a variant of **Priddy**.

Preen ?P Probably from place-names such as *Church Preen* or *Holt Preen* in Salop OE '(hill shaped like a) brooch'. A Gloucs/ Salop surname.

Prendergast/Pendegrast/Pendergast/ Pendergrest/Prendergrass P There is such a place-name near Haverfordwest, Pembrokeshire, Wales, (though early forms are lacking) and a later *Prenderguest* Farm in Berwickshire, Scotland. But the ori-gin of this distinctive name, with its many variants, could be a now-lost place in Flan-ders called *Brontegeest/Prentogast*, taken as a personal name to Normandy by Flemish settlers (Hanks and Hodges). Mostly a Lancs surname in all spelllings.

Prentice/Prentis(s) O/N Nickname/occu-pational term for an apprentice OF, one which followed a man into adult life. Com-pare **Pothecary** as a surname for an apo-thecary. **Prentice** is found mainly in East Anglia, but also has a very strong concen-trated presence in Lanarkshire, Scotland; **Prentis**, scarcer, can be found in the south-east of England but also in WRYorks; **Prentiss**, scarcer still, belongs to Kent.

Presbury, *see* **Prestbury**.

Prescot(e)/Prescod/Prescott/Priscott P Place-name in Gloucs, Lancs, Oxon OE 'priests' cottage/manor'. Principally Lancs surnames, except the scarce **Prescod**, which has a limited presence in Co Durham, and **Priscott**, which is found in Somerset and in Devon, in which county it could in prin-ciple be derived from one of a number of place-names: *Prescott* (four such), *Priestacott* (two such), *Prestacott* (two such) or *Prista-cott*. Readily confused with/a variant of **Pes-cott** (see under **Peascod**)?

Presley, *see* **Priestley**.

Press/Prest, *see* **Priest**.

Prestbury P Place-name in Chesh, Gloucs OE 'priests' manor'. Scarce surnames: **Pre-stbury** is found chiefly in Staffs, **Presbury** in Derbys.

Prested P Place-name in Essex OE 'place where pears grow (literally "pear place")'. A very scarce surname found in Middx and Surrey.

Prestige, *see* **Prestwich**.

Preston P Place-name in two dozen coun-ties (most notably in Lancs, where the sur-name is at its strongest) OE 'priests' place/ farm'. Family name of the Viscounts Gor-manston.

Prestwich/Prestige P Place-name in Lancs OE 'priests' farm, parsonage'. '**Pres-tige**, a corruption of **Prestwich**, as if to make it *very* superior' (Cottle). **Prestwich** is a Lancs surname; **Prestige** is scarce and scattered.

Prettijohn, *see* **Prettyjohn**.

Pretty/Prettyman N Nickname for a fine,

smart person, or for one who was crafty (compare **Pratt**) OE. **Pretty** is widespread; **Prettyman** is found chiefly in Suffolk.

Prettyjohn/Prettijohn F A scarce Devon surname, explained thus by Cottle, echoing Reaney: 'From "Prester **John**" (first element *prestre* "priest" OF), the mythical Christian priest-king who ruled over an incredible area, at the fringe of the known world, for an incredible time. His fame began in the twelfth century, and even in the fourteenth century Mandeville claimed to have found him emperor of India'.

Prettyman, *see* **Pretty**.

Prew/Prewett, *see* **Prowse**.

Price/Pryce F/O Welsh: 'son of *Rhys*' (*ap Rhys*). See **Rhys**. The *-y-* of **Pryce** is not an affectation, but is nearer to the original. Very common throughout Wales, along its border and in the south-west of England. Reaney suggests an alternative source, from the word 'price' OF *pris*, for a fixer of prices. Desmond Holden remarks that following the establishment of the Hanoverian dynasty with George I in 1714, various German immigrants who made their way to the British Isles made use of the **Price** surname because *Prussia* was their homeland. See also **Preece**.

Prichard, *see* **Pritchard**.

Prickett, *see* **Pryke**.

Priddy P Place-name in Somerset OW 'earth house', the hilltop village where the boy Christ is said to have walked. Mostly found in the south and south-west of England. Readily confused with/a variant of **Preedy**.

Pride/Pryde N Nickname for a person exhibiting pride OE. **Pride**, a very scattered surname, is strongest in Gloucs and Notts; **Pryde** is found in the Scottish counties of Fife and Midlothian.

Prideaux P Place-name in Cornwall, originally *Pridias*, perhaps from Cornish *prytyas* ('clay covered'). Both the place-name and the surname have been Frenchified to

resemble *près d'eaux* ('near waters'); the pronunciation would originally have been '*Priddux*', but later '*Pridoh*', in the French fashion. All is explained in *Prideaux: a west-country clan* by R. M. Prideaux (1989). Compare **Cordeaux**. Many prominent/eminent men have borne this surname, including John **Prideaux** (1578–1650), Bishop of Worcester, who was born in Stowford, Devon.

Pridham, *see* **Prudhomme**.

Priest/Press/Prest O/N Theoretically an occupational term for a priest OE, going back to *presbyter*, the Greek word for 'elder' which occurs in the epigram 'New Presbyter is but old Priest writ large'. Priests were supposed to be celibate, but are known to have fathered bastards. Or a nickname used (literally or sarcastically) for someone who resembled a priest in demeanour, or an occupational term for one who worked for a priest. **Priest** and **Press** are widespread, the former being strongest in Staffs; **Prest** is a northern surname.

Priestley/Presley P Place-name in Beds, Herts, WRYorks OE 'priests' wood/clearing'. This is very strongly a WRYorks surname, and George Redmonds favours a spot called *Priestley Green* in Hipperholme, WRYorks, as the origin of the **Priestley** name as found in great profusion in the Calder Valley. **Presley** is more widespread. *Joseph Priestley (1733–1804), scientist, Unitarian minister and polymath, was born at Birstall Fieldhead, near Leeds WRYorks… John Boynton ('J. B.') Priestley, writer, was born in Bradford WRYorks… Elvis Aaron Presley (1935–1977), musician and singer, was born in Tupelo, Mississippi. He had several interesting ancestors, including a number of Scots-Irish and a Cherokee Indian called 'Morning White Dove' (1800–1835), but at present his paternal line, featuring one illegitimate birth in 1896, can be traced back no further than David Pressley, a Anglo-Irishman who settled at New Bern, North Carolina, in 1740. Some researchers have taken a different line of attack, highlighting the marriage of Andrew Presley and Elspeth Leg in Lonmay, Aberdeenshire, Scotland, in 1713; their son Andrew is then said to have emi-*

grated to America in 1745, the year of the Jacobite Rebellion.

Prime/Prin(n)/Pring N/F Nickname used to describe someone who was 'first', or 'fine, delicate' OF, or possibly from a first-name with the same meaning. **Prime** is strongest in Cambs; **Prin/Pring/Prinn** are largely surnames of Cornwall/Devon.

Primrose P Scots: place-name in the parish of Dunfermline, British *pren rhos* 'tree of the moor'. Both the place-name and the surname have acquired their present form thanks to folk etymology, to accord with the name of the flower. Family name of the Earls of Rosebery.

Prin, *see* **Prime**.

Prince N/O Nickname for a person who behaved like a prince or who played such a part in a pageant; or an occupational term for someone who worked in a prince's household OF *prince*, ultimately from Latin *princeps* ('first, chief'). Strongest in Lancs.

Pring, *see* **Prime**.

Pringle P Scots: place-name in Roxburghshire ON *'Prjonn*'s ravine'. Principally a surname of Scotland and of the north-east of England. *The luxury knitwear firm of Pringle was established by Robert Pringle in the Scottish borders in 1815.*

Prinn, *see* **Prime**.

Prior/Pryer/Pryor N/O Nickname for a person who behaved like a prior, the superior officer of a religious house ME *prior* (from Latin). In principle such a person should not also have been the head of an ordinary family (though some were), and the surname must often have been derived from an occupational term for one who served in a prior's household. Cottle claims that **Pryer** is 'an unpleasant Norfolk form of **Prior**', but in the event it is chiefly a Kent surname. **Prior** is widespread, strongest in south-east England and East Anglia; **Pryor** is chiefly found in Cornwall.

Priscott, *see* **Prescot**.

Priston P Place-name in Somerset OW and

OE 'place in the copse/brushwood'. A scarce surname, mainly found in Devon (where in principle it could alternatively be derived from one of a number of places called *Preston*).

Pritchard/Prichard F Welsh, 'son of *Richard*' (*ap Richard*). A surname which is common throughout Wales in both spellings, though **Prichard** is particularly strong in Caernarvonshire. **Pritchett** can be a variant, but see **Pryke**.

Pritchett, *see* **Pritchard** and **Pryke**.

Privett P Place-name in Hants and Wilts OE 'privet (copse)'. Principally a Hants surname.

Probert/Probin/Probyn F Welsh, 'son of *Robert/Robin*' (*ap Robert/Robin*). **Probin** is more common along the English border with Wales than in the Principality itself.

Procter/Prockter/Proctor O Occupational term for a steward, agent, tithe-collector, attorney in a spiritual court, one licensed to collect alms for lepers or enclosed anchorites OF from Latin *procurator* (also the ultimate origin of *procurer*). North-of-England surnames.

Proffitt/Profit N Nickname, 'a prophet' OF, either for a fortune-teller or for one who had acted as an Old Testament prophet in a mystery play. **Proffitt** is found mainly in Staffs; **Profit**, scarce, in Lancs and in Flintshire, Wales.

Proger F Welsh, 'son of *Roger*' (*ap Roger*).

Prosser F Welsh, 'son of *Rhosier (Roger)*' (*ap Rhosier*).

Prothero(e)/Prydderch F Welsh, 'son of *Rhydderch (Roderick)*' (*ap Rhydderch*).

Proud(e)/Prout(e) N Nickname for a proud, haughty man OE *prud/prut*. The *-e* in **Proute** could be a relic of a weak adjective following a lost definite article. **Proud** and **Proude** are chiefly northern surnames, the former being strongest in Co Durham; **Prout** belongs to Cornwall and Devon.

Proudfoot N Nickname for a person with a

proud or haughty gait OE. Stronger in Scotland than in England.

Prouse, *see* Prowse.

Prout, *see* Proud.

Provost/Provis O Occupational term for a provost, steward, head of one of a number of establishments, including those of a religious nature (and hence nominally celibate...) OF. It may sometimes have absorbed the Huguenot surname **Prevost**, of the same meaning. **Provost** is a scarce surname found in both Cambs and Lancs; **Provis** is strongest in Cornwall.

Prowse/Prew/Prewett/Prouse/Pruett N Nickname for a valiant, doughty person OF; Cornish: from *Map-ros* ('son of heath'). **Prowse** is a Cornwall/Devon surname; **Prew**, scattered, is strongest in Warwicks; the diminutives **Prewett** and **Pruett** are found mainly in Gloucs; **Prouse** belongs principally to Devon.

Prudham, *see* Prudhomme.

Prudhoe P Place-name in Northd OE ('*Pruda*'s ridge'). A Co Durham/Northd surname.

Prudhomme/Pridham/Prudham N Nickname for a wise/honest/expert man OF. **Purdham** is a variant arrived at by metathesis. **Prudhomme** is a Lancs surname, **Pridham** belongs to Devon and **Prudham** (very scarce) to Cumbd. *Pridhamsleigh* in Devon takes its name from a family called **Prodhomme**.

Pruett, *see* Prowse.

Pryce, *see* Price.

Prydderch, *see* Protheroe.

Pryde, *see* Pride.

Pryer, *see* Prior.

Pryke O/N Occupational term for a maker of instruments with a point OE *pric* ('point, prick'), or a nickname based upon a word used to describe a stag in his second year (having straight and unbranched horns) OE.

Prickett is a diminutive form, as is **Pritchett** (but see **Pritchard**).

Pryor, *see* Prior.

Puckle N Nickname: 'little puck/elf/goblin' OE *pucel*. A scarce Kent/Surrey surname.

Puddephat(t)/Puddefoot/Puddifoot N Nickname for a man with a fat stomach, literally 'bulgy vat/barrel' OE. Surnames found chiefly in Beds, Bucks and Herts.

Pudsey P Place-name in WRYorks OE '*Pudoc*'s island/river-meadow'. A scarce ERYorks surname.

Pugh F Welsh, 'son of *Hugh*' (*ap Hugh*).

Pugsley P Place-name in Devon, probably OE '*Pocg*'s clearing'. A Devon surname; 'J. Pugsley and Son, Drapers, Silk Mercers, Costumiers, Milliners, Tailors, Outfitters and Complete House Furnishers' were operating out of grand four-storey premises at 21 High Street, Ilfracombe, Devon, in the early twentieth century.

Pulford P Place-name in Chesh OE 'pool ford, ford by a pool'. Strongest in Chesh and Lancs, but with a significant presence in Suffolk.

Pulham P Place-name in Dorset and Norfolk OE 'homestead/river-meadow by a pool'. A scattered surname, strongest in Suffolk.

Pullen/Pullan/Pullin O/N Occupational term for a breeder of colts OF *poulain*, or a nickname for someone as wild and frisky as a colt. **Pullen** is found chiefly in south-east counties of England, **Pullan** in WRYorks and **Pullin** in Gloucs.

Pullman/Pulman T Dweller by a pool OE. **Pullman** is found mainly in south-east and south-west counties of England; **Pulman** is particularly strong in Devon. *The Pullman sleeping car, synonymous with luxury railway travel, was invented by George Pullman (1831–1897), who was born in Brocton, New York.*

Pulteney, *see* Pountney.

Pulvertaft, *see* Pulvertoft.

Pulvertoft P   A practically extinct Lincs surname of uncertain origin, probably derived from a now-lost place-name meaning *Pulver* (a stream-name) plus ON 'homestead'. A family named **Pulvertoft(e)** was well established at Swineshead and elsewhere in Lincs by the sixteenth century, and the surname **Pulvertaft** first appears in Co Cork, Ireland, in the mid eighteenth century.

Pumfrey/Pomphrey/Pumphrey   F   Welsh, 'son of *Humfrey*' (*ap Humfrey*). Readily confused with/a variant of **Pomfret**.

Punchard/Puncher/Punshon   F   Firstname from an OF (Norman dialect) diminutive of *Pontius*, meaning 'man from *Pontus*' (the Asia Minor province at the east end of the Black Sea). See also **Points**. Readily confused with/a variant of **Pinchard**. **Punchard** is found in Suffolk, but also in Devon, **Puncher** in Essex and **Punshon** in Co Durham.

Punter T/O   Dweller at a bridge, or an occupational term for a bridge-keeper OF. Compare Modern French *pont* ('bridge'). A surname of southern England.

Purcell O/N   Occupational term for a keeper of pigs, or a nickname with the sense of 'piglet' OF. Strongest in Lancs.

Purchas(e)/Purkess/Purkis(s) O   Occupational term for an official charged with purchasing provisions for an establishment such as a monastery OF – though Cottle takes a different tack: 'pursuit, chase, hunting, pillage... eventually used for couriers'. **Purchase** is strong in the West Country, particularly Somerset; **Purkiss** belongs principally to Essex, and **Purkess** (very scarce) to Hants. **Purkis** is found chiefly in southern counties of England and in East Anglia. *Samuel Purchas, geographical writer and Anglican clergyman (c.1577–1626), was baptized on 20 November 1577 at Thaxted, Essex, the son of George Purcas [sic] and his wife Ann.*

Purday/Purdey, *see* Purdy.

Purdham, *see* Prudhomme.

Purdy/Purday/Purdey/Purdie N   Nick-name for a person whose favourite oath was '*p(o)ur dieu!*' OF ('by God!'). **Purdie** is a variant mainly found in Scotland. *The firm of James Purdy and Sons, gunmakers, was established in London in 1814.*

Purkess/Purkis(s), *see* Purchas.

Purley P   Place-name in Surrey OE 'pear-tree clearing/field'. A very scarce Essex/Middx surname.

Purnell, *see* Parnall.

Purseglove, *see* Pursglove.

Purser O   Occupational term for a maker or seller of purses or pouches OE, or for an official in charge of expenditure. By the fifteenth century the word was being applied to a ship's officer in charge of accounts and provisions. Strongest in Beds.

Pursey, *see* Percy.

Purs(e)glove N/P   Cottle makes a bold stab at this distinctive surname, saying that it is possibly a nickname applied to a person who wore a glove with a purse in it OE – though he admits that no such word is mentioned in any dictionary. The truth must lie elsewhere: this is exclusively a Derbys surname, and seventeenth-century Hearth Tax records for that county include individuals with the surnames **Pureslove**, **Purslove**, **Purslowe** – and just one **Pursglove** (Robert **Pursglove** of Edale). All of this points us in the right direction: **Pursglove** will almost certainly have arisen as a surname when folk etymology, favouring the familiar word 'glove' (or 'love'), got to work on a place-name such as *Purslow*, Salop OE '*Pussa*'s tumulus', which has also given rise to the Salop surname **Purslow**. For a similar process, see **Spendlove**.

Purves/Purvis ?O   Possibly an occupational term for a purveyor or caterer in a religious or other establishment OF. Usually pronounced with two syllables, whatever the spelling. Principally surnames of the north-east of England.

Pusey/Piz(z)ey/Pizzie P   Place-name *Pusey* in Berks OE 'island where peas grow' (or, rather, the original singular *pease* as in *pease pudding*). A gravestone in Pusey, Berks, churchyard (formerly legible, but maybe no longer so) throws some interesting light on the relationship between **Pusey** and other related surnames: 'Richard **Pusey**, alias **Peasey**, **Pescod**, **Pecod**... died most comfortably Augt 2^d 1653, aged 34'. **Pusey** is mainly a Bucks surname; **Pizey**/**Pizzey** and **Pizzie** are more randomly scattered. *Edward Pusey (1800–1882), a leader of the Oxford Movement, was the son of Philip Bouverie (son of Jacob Bouverie, first Viscount Folkestone), who had assumed the surname Pusey in 1784 when he inherited extensive property in Pusey, Berks.*

Putman, *see* Pitt.

Putnam P Place-name *Puttenham* in Herts, Surrey OE '*Putta*'s homestead'.

Putt, *see* Pitt.

Puttack, *see* Puttock.

Putterill/Powdrell/Powdrill O/N Occupational name for a keeper of colts OF *poutrel*, or a nickname for someone as frisky as a colt. The main line of a prominent Roman Catholic family bearing the associated surname of **Powtrell** (formerly also **Powth(e)rell** and other variants), once well established in West Hallam, Derbys (though with its origins in the neighbouring county of Notts), had died out by the late seventeenth century. These are scarce surnames: **Putterill** and **Powdrill** are found mainly in Leics; **Powdrell** in ERYorks.

Puttick, *see* Puttock.

Puttock/Piddock/Pidduck/Pittock/ Pittuck/Puttack/Puttick/Puttuck N Nickname for a greedy eater OE 'kite' (the bird). Mostly Kent/Surrey/Sussex surnames. Readily confused with/a variant of **Paddock**.

Pyatt, *see* Pye.

Pye N/T/O/F Nickname for a person as talkative or as light-fingered as a magpie OF *pie*, a bird which only acquired the *Mag-* element in its name (a diminutive of *Margaret*) in the seventeenth century (compare *Robin Redbreast*, *Tom Tit*, *Jenny Wren*, *Jackdaw*, *Polly Parrot*, the dialectal *Nettle Peggy* [greenfinch], and so on...); or a person who lived at the sign of the (Mag)pie; or an occupational term for a baker or seller of pies ME; or Welsh, 'son of *Hugh*' (*ap Hugh*). Very strong in Lancs, rare in Wales. **Pyatt** (chiefly Staffs) is a diminutive.

Pym(m), *see* Pim.

Quaif(e) O/N Occupational term for a maker of skullcaps, or a nickname for someone who wore one OF (compare the word *coif*). A scarce Kent/Surrey surname.

Quail(e)/Quayle N/F Nickname for a person bearing some resemblance to a quail OF – 'a bird with a reputation for timidity and lasciviousness (not an attractive combination)' (Cottle). Irish and Manx: Anglicized and abbreviated form of Gaelic **Mac Phoil** ('son of *Paul*'). *Sir Anthony Quayle (1913–1989), actor and director, was born near Southport, Lancs, to a family with Manx origins… James Danforth ('Dan') Quayle, former Vice-President of the USA, born in Indianapolis, Indiana, also had Manx roots; his great-grandfather Robert Quayle (1853–1922, son of John Quayle), who was born in Douglas, Isle of Man, married in Chicago in 1886.*

Quaintance N Nickname for an acquaintance, companion OF. A very scarce Devon surname.

Quainton P Place-name in Bucks OE 'Queen's manor'. A very scarce Oxon surname.

Qualtrough F Manx: Anglicized and abbreviated form of **Mac Ualtair** ('son of *Walter*'). See also **Walter**.

Quant N Nickname for a clever, smart, crafty, unusual/eccentric person OF *cointe*, ultimately from Latin *cognit-*, with the sense of 'knowing' (compare the word *quaint*). Chiefly a Devon surname. *Mary Quant, fashion designer, was born in Kent in 1934 to Welsh parents.*

Quantick/Quantock P From the *Quantock* Hills in Somerset, British hill name *Cantuc* and OE *dun* ('hill'). Scarce surnames: **Quantick** belongs mainly to Devon, **Quantock** to Somerset.

Quantrell/Quantrill N Nickname for a fop, dandy OF. Principally Norfolk surnames.

Quarmby, *see* **Wharmby**.

Quarrell O/N Occupational term for a maker of crossbows/bolts/arrows OF; or a nickname for a trouble-maker OF *querel* ('complaint'). For the relationship between *-ar-* and *-er-* see **Armistead**. An unevenly scattered surname.

Quarrie/Quarry T/O/N/F Dweller by, or worker at, a quarry OF; or a nickname for a square-built, stocky man OF; Manx: an abbreviated form of **Mac Guaire** ('proud/ noble'). **Quarry**, an uncommon surname, is strongest in Staffs; **Quarrie** is found mainly in Lancs and the Isle of Man.

Quarrington P Cottle's reference to such a place-name in Co Durham and in Lincs would seem to be irrelevant; this is predominantly a (scarce) Kent surname, and the origin is likely to be the settlement called *Quarrington* in Mersham in that county, which is of uncertain etymology.

Quarry, *see* **Quarrie**.

Quartermain(e)/Quarterman N Nickname: 'four hands' OF. Applied to a person who wore chain-mail gloves, or who worked so hard he appeared to have two pairs of hands. Surnames found in scattered pockets in the south of England, especially Oxon. *Allan Quartermain is a fictional character in H. Rider Haggard's* King Solomon's mines *and in various associated works, one of which is entitled* Allan Quartermain.

Quayle, *see* Quail.

Queenborough P Cottle's reference to such a place-name in Kent would seem to be irrelevant; this is predominantly a (scarce) Leics surname, and the origin is likely to be the settlement called *Queniborough* OE 'The Queen's borough' in that county.

Quen(n)ell F From an OE female first-name meaning 'woman-battle'. Most commonly found in the south of England.

Quested ?P A surname of uncertain origin; place-names in Suffolk and Essex have been suggested, though this is predominantly a Kent surname, and *Whetste(a)d* in that county OE '?wheat settlement' may possibly be the place of origin.

Quick N/T/P Nickname for a quick, lively, agile person ME *quik* (also the origin of the surname **Quicke**); or a dweller beside vegetation such as quitch, couchgrass or a quickset hedge; or dweller at a dairy farm OE *cu-wic* (there are places called *Cowick* in WRYorks and *Cowick* Barton, Devon, with the same meaning). Cornish: dweller by a wood or village (*gwyk*) or from a minor place-name with this meaning. Strongest in Devon and Cornwall.

Quicke, *see* Quick.

Quickfall P Cottle derives this from a place-name *Wigfield*, formerly *Wigfall*, in WRYorks OE. The first element can be 'horse/steed/beetle'; the second is 'place where trees have been felled'. An uncommon Lincs surname.

Quiddington P Place-name *Quidhampton* in Hants OE 'settlement of the *Cweadhoeme*, the inhabitants of *Cweadham*' and in Wilts OE 'dirt/dung farm'. A scarce Kent/Surrey surname.

Quiggin F Manx: Anglicized and abbrevi-

ated form of **MacUigeann**, 'son of *Uige*' ('knowledge, skill, ingenuity'). *William* **Quiggin** *was already running a well-established confectionery business on the Isle of Man when Prince Albert paid a visit in 1845, at which time William's daughter proudly presented the Prince with a special gift in the form of the first ever recorded stick of lettered rock, bearing the words: 'Welcome Prince Albert to Mona'. In 1872 one of the four sons of William* **Quiggin** *moved to Kendal, Westmd, where he developed the world-famous Kendal Mint Cake, which is still made to a secret family recipe.*

Quigley F Irish: Anglicized form of Gaelic O' [descendant of] **Coigligh** ('?untidy').

Quiller ?F A surname which seems to have defeated most writers on the subject. Wild stabs at a meaning include: a maker of spoons or ladles; a nickname derived from a term used for a fledgling bird; a maker of quill pens; a person who washed up the escuelles, porringers and bowls; a dresser of quilled ruffs and collars (yet ruffs came into use after the period of surname-formation); or an occupational term (or a nickname?) for a 'queller' (that is, a 'killer'). Given the fact that this is primarily a Cornish surname with some spill-over into Devon, the true source must surely lie elsewhere. Since the Manx **Quilliam** is a shortened form of **MacWilliam** and the Scots and Irish **Quill** or **Quillan** mean **MacCuill** (son of *Coll*), then it must at least be possible that **Quiller** has a Celtic patronymic origin, probably with the meaning 'Son of *William*', or the like. *The eminent man of letters Sir Arthur Quiller-Couch (1863–1944), known universally simply as 'Q', whose entry in the* Dictionary of National Biography *begins by describing him simply as a 'Cornishman', was born in Bodmin. It is said that both his Quiller and his Couch ancestors had been settled in Polperro, Cornwall, for several generations. See also* **Couch***; for a detailed study of the surnames Couch and Quiller, see* Searching for surnames *by John Titford (2002).*

Quilliam F Manx: 'son of *William*'.

Quilter O Occupational term for a maker of

quilted mattresses/coverlets/garments OF. An Essex/Middx surname.

Quin(n) F Irish: Anglicized form of Gaelic **O'** [descendant of] **Cuinn** ('chief'). Cottle maintains that **Quin** is more Protestant than the Roman Catholic **Quinn**.

Quinc(e)y P Place-names in France: *Cuinchy* (Pas-de-Calais) and various places named *Quincy*, consisting of a first name from the Latin *Quintus* 'fifth (-born)' plus a Gaulish place-name suffix. The surname is found especially in Lincs and Northants. *The English writer Thomas De Quincey (1785–1859), born in Manchester into a family of Norman origin, added 'De' to his surname.*

Quine F Manx: abbreviated form of ON **Mac** ['son of'] **Sveinn** ('boy/page/servant'). An Isle of Man/Lancs surname.

Quinn, *see* **Quin**.

Quinney F Manx: abbreviated form of ON **Mac** ['son of'] **Coinne** ('fair one'). A surname also found in some numbers in Warwicks.

Quinton P/F/N Place-names in Gloucs, Northants, Worcs and elsewhere OE 'Queen's manor'; or from an OF (from Latin) first-name *Quentin/Quintin*, meaning 'fifth (-born)'; or from one of a number of places in northern France (for example in Manche, Somme), named in honour of St *Quentin* of Amiens, who was martyred in the third century; or a nickname for someone who tilted at a 'quintain' post OF. Generally a surname of the south of England and of East Anglia.

Quirk F Irish or Manx: Anglicized form of Gaelic **O'** [descendant of] **Cuire** ('heart/tuft of hair'). *Sir Randolph Quirk (Lord Quirk), an academic yet popular writer on linguistics, was born in 1920 at Lambfell, Isle of Man, where his family had lived for several generations.*

Quy P Place-name in Cambs OE 'cow island'. An uncommon Essex surname.

R

Rabbit(t)s/Rabbatts/Rabbetts F From the Norman first-name *Radbode/Rabbode*, Germanic 'counsel messenger'; or a variant of **Robert**.

Rabson, *see* **Robert**.

Raby P Place-name in Chesh, Cumbd, Co Durham ON 'landmark/boundary farm'. Found mainly in the north of England, strongest in Lancs.

Rackcliffe, *see* **Ratcliff**.

Rackham P There is such a place-name in Sussex, under *Rackham Hill* OE 'homestead by (a hill resembling) a hayrick', but this is chiefly a Norfolk/Suffolk surname. *Arthur Rackham (1867–1939), book illustrator, was born in London, one of twelve children.*

Rackliff(e), *see* **Ratcliff**.

Rackstraw/Rakestraw/Rexstrew N This gives every appearance of being a nickname from OE, perhaps referring to a stingy person who raked up every last scrap, even of straw. There is a place called *Rakestraws* in Longwood, WRYorks (spelt *Rake Straw* in 1771). **Rackstraw**, scarce, is mainly found in the Home Counties; **Rakestraw** belongs to Lancs and **Rexstrew** (very scarce) to WRYorks. A certain '*Virgin* **Rackstraw**' died in Wycombe, Bucks, in 1896.

Radbourne/Radburn P Place-names: *Radbourne*, Derbys; *Radbourn*, Warwicks OE 'reedy stream'. **Radburn** is strongest in Warwicks, but **Radbourne** is a scarce Berks surname.

Radcliff(e)/Radclyffe, *see* **Ratcliff**.

Raddon P Place-names in Devon OE 'red hill', and a Devon surname.

Radford/Radforth/Redford/Retford P From one of such place-names, of which there are several in England, all OE 'red (from the colour of the nearby soil) road', or 'riding road' (one that can be passed through on horseback). Referring to the not-dissimilar **Ratford**, Cottle speaks of a farm so-called in Sussex, but this is a scarce surname found predominantly in Essex. *(Charles) Robert Redford, Academy Award-winning actor and director, was born in 1936 in Santa Monica, California, USA, to a Scottish/Irish family.*

Radge P Place-name in Devon (*Radersh* in 1238) OE 'red stubble-field', but this rare surname is found mainly along the north-east coast of England.

Radley P Place-name in Berks OE 'red clearing'.

Radnage/Radnedge P Place-name in Bucks OE '(at) the red oak', the *-n-* representing a weak dative singular after a lost preposition and definite article, and the original *k* sound palatalized in the dative. **Radnage** is mainly found around the Severn estuary, in Monmouthshire and Somerset; **Radnedge** is chiefly a Somerset surname.

Radstone P Cottle mentions the place-name *Radstone* in Northants OE 'rood-stone [that is, stone cross]', but this is almost exclusively a Devon surname, where the origin will very probably be *Radstone* in that county OE '*Ruddoc*'s farm'.

Radway P Place-name in Warwicks OE

'way/road fit to ride on' (as with **Rodway**). A surname found mainly in Wilts and Gloucs.

Radwell P Place-name in Beds, Herts OE 'red spring/stream'. Strongest in Hunts and Bucks.

Rae, *see* **Ray**.

Rafe/Raff, *see* **Ralf**.

Rafferty F Irish: Anglicized form of Gaelic O' [descendant of] **Rabhartaigh/Robhartaigh** ('one who wields prosperity'). Chiefly found in Ulster.

Raffle(s) F/P Hanks and Hodges believe that **Raffle** is from the first-name *Raphael*. **Raffle** is a surname of north-east England, and **Raffles** of Cumbd; G. F. Black derives the latter from the place-name *Raffles* in Dumfriesshire, Scotland, and among the examples of the surname variants he quotes is one which is spelt '**Raphael**'. *Sir (Thomas) Stamford (Bingley) Raffles (1781–1826), colonial governor and founder of Singapore, was born aboard his father's ship, the West Indiaman Ann, off the coast of Jamaica. The male-line ancestry of this family is said to go back to Beverley, ERYorks, where a John Raffles was mayor during the late sixteenth century. The family eventually moved to Berwick-on-Tweed, and it was from there that Sir Stamford Raffles' great grandfather moved to London to work in the Prerogative Office in Doctors' Commons.*

Raggett F/N/T/P From an OF first-name *Ragot/Raguet*, from Germanic (a diminutive of 'counsel'); or a nickname for a ragged, shaggy, unkempt person ME, or perhaps a dweller near a gate for roe-deer OE; there is a place-name *Rogate* (*Ragat* in 1229) in Sussex. Chiefly found in south-east England, strongest in Surrey.

Raikes, *see* **Rake**.

Rain(e)/Rain(e)s F/N/P/T From a shortened form of any one of a number of Germanic first-names (*Raymond, Reynold* and the like) of which the first element is *ragin* ('counsel'), or from the mediaeval female first-name *Reine* OF 'Queen' or a nickname

from some resemblance to a frog OF *raine* (the imagination boggles…); Scots: from the place-name *Raine*, Aberdeenshire, Gaelic *rath chain* ('tax ford'). Cottle adds two other possibilities: '[dweller by a] strip of land, boundary, Co Durham dialect *rain*, or from *Rennes/Reims* (from Gaulish tribes *Redones/Remi*)'. **Rain** and **Raine** are chiefly found in north-eastern England, strongest in Co Durham; **Rains** and **Raines** are widely scattered throughout England.

Rainbird F From an OF first-name (from Germanic) meaning 'power bright'. Mainly found in Essex and surrounding areas.

Rainbow F From an OF first-name *Rainbaut* (from Germanic) meaning 'power bold', 'respelt to look like a phenomenon' (Cottle). Also found as **Raybould**. **Rainbow** is strongest in Warwicks, **Raybould** in Staffs and Worcs.

Raine(s), *see* **Rain**.

Rainey/Rean(e)y/Rennie F From diminutives of first-names such as *Reynold* or *Randolf*, containing the Germanic element *rand* '(shield) rim' (compare **Rand**) or *ragin* 'counsel' (compare **Rain**). **Rainey** is commonest in Somerset, **Reaney** in WRYorks, **Reany** (scarce) in various northern counties of England, **Rennie** in Scotland.

Rain(s)ford P Place-name *Rainford* in Lancs OE '*Regna*'s ford'.

Rains, *see* **Rain**.

Rainsford, *see* **Rainford**.

Raisbeck/Reasbeck P Place-name *Raisbeck* WRYorks ON 'roe-buck brook'. **Raisbeck** had become a strongly Co Durham surname by the late nineteenth century, at which time **Reasbeck**, much scarcer, belonged to WRYorks. One family of **Raisbeck**, originally from Teesdale, moved first to the Isle of Man, then to Arkengarthdale (NRYorks), thence to Wisconsin, USA.

Rake/Raikes/Reakes T/P Dweller at the narrow/rough path/valley OE (originally 'throat'); or from a place-name *Rake* in

Lancs, Staffs, Sussex, or *Raikes* in Surrey, WRYorks, with the same meaning. **Rake** is a south/south-west of England surname; **Raikes**, scarce, is widely scattered; **Reakes** belongs to Somerset.

Rakestraw, *see* **Rackstraw**.

Raleigh/Rawley P Place-names: *Raleigh*, Devon: one in Pilton OE '?red clearing' (but the first element may be OE 'roe [deer]'), another in Northam OE '?clearing where rye grows'. Both these place-names have traditionally been pronounced '*Rawley*', as has the surname. *Rayleigh*, Essex OE 'clearing where rye was grown/roe deer clearing'. By the late nineteenth century both **Raleigh** and **Rawley** had become sparsely scattered throughout England and Scotland. *Sir Walter Raleigh (or Ralegh) (1554–1618), courtier, explorer and author, was born near East Budleigh, Devon… It was in 1886 that three men (Woodhead, Angois and Ellis) began making bicycles in Raleigh Street, Nottingham; the Raleigh Bicycle Company was officially established two years later.*

Ralf(e)(s)/Rafe/Raff/Ralph(s) F From *Radulf/Raulf*, a Germanic first-name, Normanized, meaning 'advice wolf'. The *-ph* spelling is now much commoner for both the first-name and the surname; in some social circles the old vernacular pronunciation '*Rafe*' has become 'superior', and the spelling-pronunciation vulgar. The form *Raoul* is from Parisian French, whence surnames, some patronymic, such as **Ralling(s)**, **Rallis(on)**, **Rawle** (chiefly found in Somerset/Devon), **Rawlence**, **Rawles** (belonging to Dorset), **Rawlin(g)(s)**, **Rawlingson**, **Rawlins(on)**, **Rawlison** and **Rawson**. Bardsley observed that some of the many **Rawlinsons** in Cumbd and Furness, Lancs, must be the same as **Rowlandson**, which is there pronounced *Rawlandson*. Many of the surnames derived in some way from **Ralf** can all-too-easily be intertwined with those emanating from **Relf**, **Roland**, **Rolf**, **Rowe**, **Rowland** and **Ryland**.

Ralling(s)/Rallis(on)/Ralph(s), *see* **Ralf**.

Ramage N Nickname for a wild person/a free spirit, literally OF 'living in the branches', a hawking term. A Scottish surname, mainly found in Midlothian and surrounding areas.

Ramm N Nickname from 'ram' OE, applied to a person exhibiting sexual aggressiveness, or who had won the ramprize at wrestling, or who lived at the sign of the zodiacal ram. Chiefly a Norfolk surname.

Ramount, *see* **Rayment**.

Rampton P Place-name in Cambs and Notts OE 'ram farm', but a southern surname, strongest in Hants.

Ramsay, *see* **Ramsey**.

Ramsbottom/Ramsbotham P Place-name *Ramsbottom*, Lancs OE 'wild-garlic valley' (more probable than OE 'ram's/rams' valley'). **Ramsbotham** is the family name of the Viscounts Soulbury. How touching it is to find that a child born in Dewsbury, Yorks, in 1855, was named '*Wonderful* **Ramsbottom**'.

Ramsdale P Place-name in more than one county OE 'wild-garlic valley'. Principally a Lancs surname.

Ramsden P Major and minor place-name in various counties OE 'wild-garlic valley'. A surname mostly found in Yorks, where the origin is likely to be *Ramsden* in Catworth (parish of Kirkburton). *Harry Ramsden (1888–1963) established a fish-and-chip shop in a wooden hut in White Cross, Guiseley, near Leeds, WRYorks, in 1928. The brand which bears his name now operates worldwide.*

Ramsey/Ramsay P Place-name *Ramsey* in Essex, Hunts OE 'wild-garlic island'. **Ramsay** is a Scots form, the Scots family being descended from a twelfth-century settler from Hunts – compare the Scottish families of **Graham** (from *Grantham*, Lincs) and **Lindsay** (from *Lindsey*, Lincs). **Ramsay** is the family name of the Earls of Dalhousie. *(Arthur) Michael Ramsey (1904–1988), who served as the one hundredth Archbishop of Canterbury (1961–1974), was born in Chesterton, Cambs.*

Ramshaw P Place-name in Co Durham; OE

'wood/copse with rams'; or a variant of **Ravenshaw**. Almost exclusively found in Co Durham and Northd.

Ranald, *see* **Ronald**.

Rand F/T/P From the ME first-name *Rand(e)*, a shortened form of one of the various Germanic names (such as *Randolph*) containing the element *rand* '(shield) rim' (compare **Rainey**); or a dweller at a border, the untilled margin of a field, a strip of land on a river-bank OE, or from a place-name with the same meaning, such as *Rand*, Lincs or *Rand Grange*, NRYorks. **Randall/ Randell/Randle/Randoll/Rendall/Rendell/ Rendle/Rendol** are diminutives of **Rand** in the first definition given here, with an OF suffix *-el*, though **Rendall/Rendell/Rendle/Rendol** could alternatively be diminutives of **Reynold** in its **Rennell** form, with the addition of a *d-* glide. **Ransom** (a surname of the south and east of England) is 'son of **Rand**', with *-son* becoming *-som* by folk etymology. **Rand** is mainly found in Essex and surrounding areas; **Randall** is very widespread everywhere in England except the extreme north; **Randell** belongs mainly to the English South and Midlands; **Randle** is particularly strong in Warwicks; **Randoll**, very scarce, can be found in Sussex; **Rendall** is at its strongest in the Orkney Isles and in south-west England; **Rendell** and **Rendle** are chiefly found in south-west England; **Rendol**, a very rare surname, is generally confined to Gloucs. *Ruth (Barbara) Rendell, best-selling mystery and psychological crime writer, was born in London 1930, and educated in Loughton, Essex.*

Randall/Randell/Randle/Randoll, *see* **Rand**.

Randolph F From a Germanic first-name, Normanized, meaning 'shield wolf', probably absorbing Germanic 'raven wolf'. One source of **Rand** and its many variants. **Rankin(e)** and **Ranking** are diminutives. The surname **Randolph** is widely scattered throughout the south of England. For **Rankin**, see also Hank B. Marvin, under **Mervin**.

Rank N Nickname for a strong, exultant, proud person OE. Mainly found in Essex,

and on the Yorkshire coast. *(Joseph) Arthur Rank (1888–1972), born in Drypool, near Kingston upon Hull, ERYorks, established a flour-milling company which eventually became Rank Hovis McDougall, and a film production company, the Rank Organisation.*

Rankin(e)/Ranking, *see* **Randolph**.

Ransford T/P Dweller at a ford for rams, or at a ford where wild garlic grows OE. Reaney also suggests a place-name origin, from *Ram's Fold Farm* in Lurgashall, Sussex OE 'ram's fold'. The surname is widely scattered throughout England.

Ransom, *see* **Rand**.

Raper, *see* **Roper**.

Rapkin(s)/Rapson, *see* **Robert**.

Rasberry, *see* **Raspberry**.

Rasen P Place-name in Lincs OE 'plank (?-bridge)', and a mainly Lincs surname.

Rash T Dweller at an ash tree, from a misdivison of ME *atter ashe* ('at the ash'). Mainly found in East Anglia, strongest in Suffolk.

Raspberry/Rasberry ?P Cottle confidently states that such surnames are derived from a place called *Ratsbury* in Devon OE 'red (land with) brushwood', and that there is 'no connection with the fruit.' Both assertions may be wide of the mark. No such surname appears in the Devon Lay Subsidy of 1332, though by the sixteenth century variants of it can be found in a limited number of parishes in Lincs, London, Middx, Staffs and Yorks, but it would seem to have been unknown in Devon or elsewhere in south-west England. Spelling variations eventually multiplied, to include: **Raasby**, **Raisbury**, **Raiseby**, **Rasbe**, **Rasbeary**, **Rasbery**, **Rasberry**, **Rasbey**, **Rasbury**, **Rasby**, **Rasebury**, **Rashbury**, **Rassberry**, **Rausbery**, **Rausbrey**, **Rawsby**, **Raysby**, **Raysbye**, **Reisbury**, **Resbarie**, **Resberie**, **Reseberry** and **Ressberry**. As if the surname itself were not charming enough, Thomas **Rasberry** and his wife Elizabeth went one stage further when they took their daughter *Pleas-*

ant **Rasberry** for baptism in Colchester, Essex, on 15 May 1796. This was a more felicitous first-name, we may say, than that bestowed on *Uriah* **Rasbury**, baptized in Stepney in 1721. By the time of the 1881 census, **Raspberry**, **Rasberry** and **Raisby** could be found in Norfolk, while **Raspbury** had a very limited presence in ERYorks. For all that, over the centuries these have been more prolific surnames than might be supposed.

Rastel(l) O Occupational term for a dealer in/user of rakes OF *rastel*, though a connection with **Restler** should perhaps not be discounted. **Rastel**, exceptionally rare, can be found in Northants; **Rastell** belongs mainly to Gloucs.

Rastrick P Place-name in WRYorks ON 'stream/ditch at a resting-place' (though Ekwall prefers OE 'stream with a plank-bridge').

Ratcliff(e)/Rack(c)liff(e)/Radcliff(e)/ Radclyffe/Ratliff(e)/Redcliff(e)/Red-clift P From one of a number of English place-names such as *Ratcliff(e)*, *Radcliffe*, *Redcliff(e)* or *Radclive*, all of which are OE 'red cliff/slope'. **Radcliff** is a widely spread surname; **Ratcliffe** and **Radcliff** are strongest in Lancs; **Rackcliffe**, very scarce, is chiefly found in Co Durham; **Radcliffe** belongs mainly to the north-east of England and the Isle of Man, **Radclyffe** to Dorset and **Ratliff** to Suffolk. **Ratliffe** is sparsely scattered around England.

Ratford, *see* Radford.

Rathbone ?P/N A surname of uncertain origin; place-names such as *Radbourne*, Derbys and *Radbourn*, Warwicks, have been suggested, but in principle **Rathbone** could be from a nickname, OE *hrathe-bana* ('quick killer'). A surname found mainly in the north-west of England. *(Philip St John) Basil Rathbone (1892–1967), actor, famed for portraying Sherlock Holmes in fourteen movies between 1939 and 1946, was born in Johannesburg, South Africa. His family fled to England when his father was accused of being a British spy.*

Ratley P Cottle mentions the place-name *Ratley* in Warwicks OE '?*Rota*'s wood/clearing', but the surname is widely scattered around the south-east of England, where the origin could be the settlements known as *Upper* and *Lower Ratley* in Hants.

Ratliff(e), *see* Ratcliff.

Rattenbury P Apparently from an unidentified place-name, OE 'rat-infested fort/hill/mound'. The surname is mainly found in Devon, where there is a place called *Ratsbury* OE 'red brushwoood land'.

Ratter O/P In principle this could simply be an occupational term for a rat-catcher OF, but it occurs mainly in the Shetland Isles, and both there and in the Orkneys and in northern Scotland it will be from *Rattar Brough*, Dunnet, Caithness ON 'red headland'.

Rattray P Scots: place-name in Aberdeenshire and Perthshire, Gaelic/British 'circular fort' and Welsh 'dwelling/village'.

Raven N/F/T Nickname suggesting some similarity to a raven OE or ON (also used as a first-name); or a dweller at the sign of the raven. Widely scattered throughout England, strongest in East Anglia.

Ravenhill P Cottle refers to a place called *Ravenhill* in NRYorks (an invention of his own?) OE 'hill with ravens', but this surname is mainly found in Gloucs, where there is a *Ravenshill* with the same OE meaning. For that matter, there is a *Ravenhill* in Glamorgan, South Wales...

Ravenscroft P Place-name in Chesh OE '*Hroefn*'s paddock'. A Chesh/Lancs surname. A pedigree of the Harden family of Flintshire, Wales, begins with a certain Harri **Ravenscroft**, who married the daughter and heir of Raff Holland and thus acquired land in Bretton in that county, and one prominent gentry family of **Ravenscrofts** who were settled in Horsham, Sussex, can trace its origins to George **Ravenscroft**, a sixteenth-century migrant from Bretton. *The disc jockey and radio presenter John Peel (1939–2004) was born John Robert Parker Ravenscroft in Heswall, Chesh,* the son of a cotton merchant… The firm of Ede and Ravenscroft, which specializes in the manufacture of legal, academic and clerical wear, and whose business has received a boost in recent years from the proliferation of award ceremonies at new British universities, can trace its origins back to a family named Ede, who were well established as robe-makers in London at the close of the seventeenth century. Thomas Ravenscroft, a wig-maker from Shropshire, had moved to London in 1726, and in the late nineteenth century Joseph Webb Ede married Rosanna Ravenscroft, daughter of Burton Ravenscroft, also a wig-maker. In due course the Ede robe-makers and the Ravenscroft wig-makers joined forces, and the firm's name was eventually changed to Ede and Ravenscroft in 1921.

Ravensdale P Place-name in Derbys, Notts, Staffs OE or ON '?*Hraefn/Hrafn*'s valley'. A surname of the Midlands and the north-west.

Ravenshaw/Renshall/Renshaw P Place-names: *Ravenshaw*, Co Durham, Warwicks; *Renishaw*, Derbys OE 'raven wood/grove'. One theory has it that **Renshaw** can be an abbreviated form of **Ollerenshaw** (see **Ollerenshaw, Wrench**). See also **Ramshaw**. **Ravenshaw** is mainly found in Salop and surrounding areas, **Renshaw** and **Renshall** (very scarce) in Lancs.

Raw, *see* **Rowe**.

Rawbone N Nickname for a runner, from OE 'bone (leg) like a roe (deer)'. Mainly found in the South-West Midlands, strongest in Warwicks.

Rawcliff(e) P Place-name *Rawcliffe* in Lancs, NRYorks and WRYorks OE/ON 'red' and OE 'cliff'. A Lancs surname.

Rawdon P Place-name in WRYorks OE '?red hill'.

Rawle(s)/Rawlence, *see* **Ralf**.

Rawley, *see* **Raleigh**.

Rawlin(g)(s)/Rawlingson/Rawlins(on)/Rawlison, *see* **Ralf**.

Rawnsley P George Redmonds, referring to an article which appeared in the *Transactions of the Halifax Antiquarian Society* in 1943, says that this WRYorks surname comes from a locality in Barkisland formerly called *Rawnsleycliffe*, but now known simply as *Cliff*. The -*ley* suffix was originally -*law*, so the place-name means 'raven hill or mound'. The place-name *Rawnsley* in Staffs will only rarely, if ever, have given rise to the surname.

Rawson, *see* **Ralf**.

Rawsthorn(e)/Rawstorn(e)/Rawstron/Rostron P Place-name in Chesh, now *Rostherne* ON and ON/OE '*Rauthr*'s thornbush'.

Ray N Nickname from 'king' OF, for the same reasons as the surname **King** was used; or from some resemblance to a (female) roe deer (timidity?) OE. The Scottish surname **Rae** is probably a variant. See also **Rowe** and **Roy**. Readily confused with/a variant of **Rea, Rew, Roe, Rowe, Rye**.

Raybould, *see* **Rainbow**.

Raydon P Place-name in Suffolk OE 'hill where rye grows', though the surname is most commonly found in Surrey.

Rayment/Ramount/Raymond/Raymont F From a Germanic first-name, Normanized, meaning 'might/counsel protector'. **Rayment** is mainly found in Essex and surrounding areas, **Ramount** (exceptionally rare) in Lancs, **Raymond** in southern England and South Wales, and **Raymont** in Devon. See also **Redmond**.

Rayne(s), *see* **Rain**.

Rayner/Raynor F From the Germanic first-name (Normanized) *Rainer*, meaning 'might/counsel army'. **Rayner** is found in East Anglia, but is commonest in WRYorks; **Raynor**, scarcer, is also a WRYorks surname. See also **Renner**.

Rea/Ree T Dweller (at) the stream/river OE. Readily confused with/a variant of **Ray, Rew, Roe, Rowe, Rye**. **Rea** is a scattered surname, commonest in Worcs; **Ree** is widely distributed throughout England and Scotland. *Christopher Anton ('Chris') Rea, the singer-songwriter from Middlesbrough, NRYorks, was born in 1951.*

Reace, *see* Rhys.

Read(e)/Reed/Reid N/T/P Nickname for a person with red hair or a red face OE, the *-e* of **Reade** indicating the use of a weak adjective after a lost definite article; or a dweller at a woodland clearing OE (also the origin of **Ride**, a surname mainly found in Derbys, and compare **Rhodes**); or from place-names such as *Read*, Lancs OE 'roe headland'; *Rede*, Suffolk OE 'reedbed'; *Reed*, Herts OE 'brushwood'. **Reid** is a Scots/Northern Irish form.

Reader/Readman/Reedman O Occupational term for one who thatched houses with reeds ME. **Reader** is mainly found in Kent, **Readman** in NRYorks and **Reedman** in Northants. *Ralph Reader (1903–1982), originator of the Scouting Gang Show, was born in Crewkerne, Somerset.*

Reading/Redding/Ridding/Riding T/P Dweller in a clearing OE *ryding* (compare the verb *to rid*); or from the place-name *Reading* in Berks OE 'the family/folk of *Read(a)*'. *Riddings* in Derbys and *Riding* in Northd also share this latter derivation. **Reading** is mainly found in Warwicks, **Redding** (widely scattered) in Middx, **Ridding/Riddings** in the Midlands and the north and **Riding** in Lancs.

Readman, *see* Reader.

Readshaw/Redshaw/Reedshaw P Clearly a place-name origin lies behind this surname, which can be found in early parish register entries in north and northeast England, written down in various forms such as **Readshaw**, **Reedshaw**, **Redshaw**, **Ridshaw** and **Rudshaw**. Bardsley, speaking of **Redshaw**, says: 'Local, "at the red shaw", from residence beside the shaw or wood of a red soil… I cannot find the spot'. Bardsley may have given up far too easily here, leaving Reaney to make the not unreasonable supposition that such surnames come from a specific place in WRYorks called *Redshaw Gill* OE 'red copse' in Blubberhouses. As to other

place-names in WRYorks: the first-known reference to *Reedshaw (Moss)* ('reedy copse') in Cowling dates from as late as the seventeenth century, and the earliest mention of *Reedyshaw* (also 'reedy copse'), a now-lost place in the area of Soyland, is from 1485, the year of the Battle of Bosworth.

Ready N Nickname for a prompt, quick, opportunistic person OE. Mainly found in Lancs.

Reagan, *see* Regan.

Reakes, *see* Rake.

Realf(f), *see* Relf.

Rean(e)y, *see* Rainey.

Rearden/Reardon, *see* Riordan.

Reasbeck, *see* Raisbeck.

Reaveley P Place-name in Northd OE 'the reeve's wood/clearing' or OE '?rough clearing'. A Northd/Co Durham surname.

Reaves, *see* Reeves.

Redcliffe/Redclift, *see* Ratcliff.

Redding, *see* Reading.

Reddish P Place-names: *Reddish* in Chesh and Lancs; *Redditch* in Worcs OE 'reedy ditch'. Strongest in Notts.

Redfe(a)rn P Place-name *Redfern*, Lancs OE 'red bracken'.

Redford, *see* Radford.

Redgewell P Place-name *Ridgewell*, Essex (still pronounced with an *-e-*) OE 'reedy spring/stream', and an Essex surname.

Redgrave P Place-name in Suffolk OE 'reedy ditch/digging'. A Norfolk/Suffolk surname. *Sir Michael (Scudamore) Redgrave (1908–1985), stage and film actor, was born into an acting family in theatrical lodgings at St Michael's Hill, Bristol, Gloucs.*

Redland P There is a place so-called in Gloucs OE 'cleared (literally "ridded") land', but the surname is mainly found in Co Durham and in the Orkney Isles, where it is derived from *Redland* in the parish of Stromness.

Redman/Redmayne P/O Place-name *Redmain* in Cumbd OE '?red cairn', though Cottle suggests 'reed man' (a cutter or thatcher) as another possibility. Strongest in WRYorks. Readily confused with/a variant of **Redmond**. *The actress Amanda Redman was born in 1959 in Brighton, Sussex, her father was from Yorkshire, her mother from Sussex.*

Redmile P Place-name in Leics OE 'red earth' (compare the word *mould*). An East Midlands surname, strongest in Lincs and Notts.

Redmond F Irish version of **Raymond** (see **Rayment**). Readily confused with/a variant of **Redman**.

Redshaw, *see* **Readshaw**.

Redwood N A nickname for a blazingly angry, crazy man OE (literally 'red-mad'). The redwood tree has too late a name to figure here, and no place-name *Redwood* can currently be located, but a minor or lost place with the meaning OE 'cleared wood' is possible. A surname which is scattered around the south of England, strongest in Devon and Somerset. *John (Alan) Redwood, Conservative Party politician, former challenger for the leadership of his party (and far too phlegmatic to be 'red-mad'), was born in Dover, Kent, in 1951.*

Ree, *see* **Rea**.

Reece, *see* **Rhys**.

Reed, *see* **Read**.

Reeder/Reedman, *see* **Reader**.

Reedshaw, *see* **Readshaw**.

Reeman, *see* **Rye**.

Rees(e), *see* **Rhys**.

Reeve O Occupational term for a reeve, chief magistrate, bailiff, overseer OE (compare *sheriff*, a 'shire reeve'). See also **Preater**.

Reeves/Reaves O/T Servant/son/dweller at the house of **Reeve**; but Reaney found a reference to a man living in Worcs in 1327

called **atte Reuese**, which is a misdivision of ME *atter evese*, 'at the edge' (?of woodland), from OE singular *efes* (compare the word *eaves*). See also **Preater**.

Re(a)gan F Irish: Anglicized form of Gaelic O' [descendant of] **Riagain** ('?impulsive'). Readily confused with/a variant of **Ryan**. *The former American President and one-time actor Ronald (Wilson) Reagan (1911–2004) was born in Tampico, Illinois; his great-grandfather Michael Reagan was born in Ballyporee, Co Tipperary, in 1829.*

Reid, *see* **Read**.

Reilly F Irish: Anglicized form of Gaelic O' [descendant of] **Raghailleach** (of unknown origin). See also **Riley**.

Relf(e)/Realf(f)/Relph F From the OF first-name *Riulf* (Germanic, Normanized), meaning 'power-wolf'. Readily confused with surnames derived from **Ralf**, **Roland**, **Rolf**, **Rowe**, **Rowland** and **Ryland**. **Relf** is a Kent/Sussex surname; **Relph** has a presence in both the south-east of England and in the north.

Rem(m)ington, *see* **Rimington**.

Rendall/Rendell/Rendle/Rendol, *see* **Rand**.

Renfrew P Scottish place/county-name *Renfrew* OW 'point of current'. The surname has continued to be most commonly located in the county which gave rise to it.

Rennell(s), *see* **Reynold**.

Renner O Occupational term for a runner, messenger ON plus suffix, or a variant of **Rayner**. A Northd surname.

Rennick, *see* **Renwick**.

Rennie, *see* **Rainey**.

Rennison/Renowden, *see* **Reynold**.

Renshall/Renshaw, *see* **Ravenshaw**.

Renton P Place-name in Berwickshire, Scotland OE '*Regna*'s farm'. Mainly found in northern England and southern Scotland.

Renwick/Rennick P Place-name in Cumbd (commonly pronounced 'Rennick') OE 'Hroefn's dairy-farm'. Mainly found in northern England and southern Scotland.

Restler O Occupational term for a wrestler OE. At one time the w- was present in both spelling and pronunciation. This was not a gentlemanly sport – Chaucer's Miller was good at it, but so, too, was his absurd Sir Thopas. A very rare surname, found in Surrey. Compare **Rastel**.

Retallack/Retallick P Both are place-names in Cornwall, Cornish res-talek 'ford at the base of a short, steep slope'.

Retford, see **Radford**.

Retter O Occupational term for a net-maker OF or for one who soaked flax in preparation for its being made into linen ME. Principally a Devon surname.

Revel(l)/Revill(e) N Nickname for a boisterous, rebellious person OF revel ('sport, revelry, rebellion, insolence'). **Revel** is widely scattered throughout the United Kingdom; **Revell** occurs mainly in the east of England, being strongest in Kent and East Anglia; **Revill** is principally a WRYorks surname; **Reville** is sparsely scattered around England. Hugh Revell from Northants was the first Englishman to hold the post of Master of the Hospitaller Knights of St John of Jerusalem (1258–1277).

Reveley, see **Reaveley**.

Revell, see **Revel**.

Revere, see **Rivers**.

Revill(e), see **Revel**.

Rew P Place-names Rew/Rewe in Dorset, Devon, Isle of Wight OE 'row (of houses/cottages)', or '?hedgerow'. Mainly found in Devon. Readily confused with/a variant of **Ray, Rea, Roe, Rowe, Rye**.

Rex A surname which remains obscure, since none of the following explanations seems to be wholly convincing: a nickname 'king', from Latin; a variant on the first-name Richard (via Ricks/Rix); a topographical term 'rush(es)' (Dorset/Somerset/Devon dialect rix/rex). A surname of south-west England and of Yorkshire.

Rexstrew, see **Rackstraw**.

Reynold(s)/Rennell(s) F From a Germanic first-name introduced into England by Scandinavian settlers as Rögnvaldr, and later by the Normans as Reinald/Reynaud, meaning 'might/counsel-power'. The first-name Reginald is cognate. Hence several other surnames beginning with Ren-. **Reynolds, Reynoldson** and **Rennison** are 'son of **Reynold**'. Cottle says that the scarce Cornish surname **Renowden** (OF Renaudon) is a diminutive of **Reynold**, but the jury must remain out on such a claim.

Reynoldson, see **Reynold**.

Rhodes/Rhoad(e)s T/P Dweller by or in a woodland clearing OE rod (the -h- is intrusive, based on the well-known Greek island or its knights), but Rhodes, with the same meaning, is the name of two estates in Lancs. **Rhodes** is strongest in Lancs and WRYorks, and **Rhoades** in Lincs. **Rhoads** is scarce and scattered. See also **Roads, Rodd, Royds**. Cecil John Rhodes (1853–1902), famous for his commercial and political activities in South Africa during the reign of Queen Victoria, was born in Bishop's Stortford, Herts, where his father was then vicar. The Rhodes family had lived in North London for generations, and can be traced back at least as far as William Rhodes, who was living in the St Pancras area in the 1760s.

Rhys/Reace/Reece/Rees(e)/Rice F From the OW first-name Ris ('fiery warrior'). **Reese**, the commonest spelling, was reckoned by H. B. Guppy to account for over three per cent of the people of South Wales in the early twentieth century. **Reese** is rarer, **Reace** much rarer still. See also **Price**. **Rhys** is the family name of the Barons Dynevor.

Ribton P Place-name in Cumbd OE 'place where ribwort/hound's-tongue grows'. A sparsely scattered surname, found both in Lancs and in the south-east of England.

Rice, see **Rhys**.

Rich N/F/T Nickname for a wealthy person OE *or*, ironically, for a poor one; or a diminutive of **Richard**; but those who were *atte* **riche** lived by a stream OE. **Riches** is usually 'son of **Rich**'. **Rich** is widely scattered around England, strongest in the south; **Riches** is chiefly a Norfolk surname.

Richard(s)/Diccox/Dick(s)(son)/ Dicken(s)(son)/Dickin(s)(son)/Diggens/Diggins/Diggle(s)/Dix/Dixey/ Dixie/Dixon/Hedgecock/Hedgecoe/ Hick(s)/Hickmott/Hicks(on)/ Higgen(s)/Higgins(on)/Higgs/Higson/ Hiscock(s)/Hiscoke/Hiscott/Hiscox/ Hiscutt/Hiskett/Hitch/Hitchcock/ Hitchcoe/Hitchcott/Hitchcox/Hitchmough/Hix/Hix(s)on/Ick(e)(s)/ Richardson/Richey/Richie/Rick(s)/ Rickard(s)/Ricket(t)(s)/Rickson/Rigden/Ritchie/Ritson/Rix(on) F From a Germanic first-name *Richard* ('powerbrave/strong'), made popular by the Normans, which has spawned many related surnames thanks to its pet-forms *Hick*, *Hitch* (both now obsolete), *Dick*, *Rick* and the like. An alternative meaning for the surnames **Dixey/Dixie** is sometimes offered – that they can be derived from the Latin for 'I have spoken', being the opening of the thirty-ninth psalm, and thus a nickname for a chorister; this sounds incredible, but is supported by the French surname **Dixi**. The **Rick/Rix**-type surnames may alternatively refer to a dweller by rushes OE (West Saxon *rix*); **Hiskett** may sometimes be a variant of **Heskett**, and **Hicks(on)** and **Hixon** can be from the place-name *Hixon* in Staffs OE '*Hyht*'s hill'. **Hedgecock** and **Hedgecoe** have been given an ornithological look by the process of folk-etymology; for the element *-cock(s)* and *-cox* in these and the like surnames, see **Cock**. See also **Hedghog**, **Pritchard** and **Rich**. **Higgen(s)/Higgin(s)** (widely scattered within England), **Eakin** (very scarce, found in Salop and elsewhere – *see also* **Ead**) and **Egan** (strongest in Lancs) are from *Higg*, a voiced form of *Hick*, but in Ireland **Higgen(s)/Higgin(s)** commonly represent an Anglicized variant of the Gaelic **O'** [descendant of] **hUiginn** ('Viking'). **Hickmott/Hitchmough** is *Hitch*

(*Richard*)'s brother-in-law, or some similar relationship ME (compare **Watmore/Watmough** and **Maw**). The spelling **Dickson** is most commonly found in Scotland, but in the north of England its respelling **Dixon** is much more usual; **Dickinson** is also most frequently encountered in northern counties; **Higgs** is widely scattered, though rarely found north of Yorks; **Hitchcock** is not commonly present outside the southeast/south-west of England and East Anglia; **Richards** belongs mainly to the south-east/south-west/north-west of England, the West Midlands and South Wales, whereas the distribution of **Richardson** (south-east and northern counties of England, especially Lancs) is very different. **Ritson** is a far-north-of-England contraction of **Richardson**. **Rickard** is strongly Cornish, while **Rickards** is more evenly spread. **Rigden** is almost exclusively a Kent surname, and **Ritchie** is Scottish. **Dixon** is the family name of the Barons Glentoran;. **Richards** is the family name of the Barons Milverton. *Guy Stuart Ritchie, British film director and ex-husband of Madonna, was born in Hatfield, Herts, in 1968... Alfred Hitchcock (1899–1980), film director, was born in Leytonstone, Essex, the son of William Hitchcock, a grocerer and poulterer, and his wife Emma Jane Whelan... David Icke [pronounced 'Ike'], footballer/sports commentator/New Age visionary/conspiracy theorist, was born in Leicester in 1952. It is his firm belief that the world is ruled by a secret group called the 'Illuminati' or 'Global Elite', a race of reptilian humanoids; according to this theory, both Queen Elizabeth II and George W. Bush are reptilian.*

Riches, *see* **Rich**.

Richey/Richie, *see* **Richard**.

Richmond P There are various places called *Richmont* OF 'splendid hill' in northern France; this name was borrowed for *Richmond*, NRYorks, in the eleventh century, but *Richmond* in Surrey, formerly *Sheen*, was named in honour of King Henry VII, Earl of Richmond, and so is too late to have given rise to the surname. This scenario is borne out by the distribution of the **Rich-**

mond surname, which is primarily found in the north of England.

Rick/Rickard(s), *see* Richard.

Rickerby P Place-name in Cumbd '*Richard*'s (ON) farm'. A surname of the far north of England.

Ricket(t)(s), *see* Richard.

Rickman O Occupational term for a servant of a man called *Richard*.

Ricks/Rickson, *see* Richard.

Rickward/Rickwood F From the Germanic/Norman first-names *Richold* 'power-rule' or *Richward* 'powerful guardian'.

Riddett T Dweller at a clearing with reeds OE. A Hants/Isle of Wight surname. Readily confused with/a variant of **Rideout**.

Ridding, *see* Reading.

Ride, *see* Read and Ryde.

Rideout, *see* Ridout.

Rider O/T Occupational term for a rider/knight/cavalryman; or a dweller at a woodland clearing OE *ried/ryd*. Cottle considers **Ryder** (the family name of the Earls of Harrowby) to be a 'commoner but affected spelling of **Rider**'. **Rider** is widely scattered throughout England; **Ryder** is very strong in Lancs.

Ridge T Dweller at a ridge, long hill OE. **Rigg/Riggs** are northern forms.

Ridg(e)way T/P Dweller at an ancient hilltop track OE, or from a minor place-name with the same meaning. **Ridgway** is chiefly a north-west-of-England surname, strongest in Lancs; **Ridgeway** is more widely scattered.

Ridg(e)well P Place-name *Ridgewell* in Essex OE 'reedy stream'. An Essex surname in either spelling.

Riding, *see* Reading.

Ridler O Occupational term for a sieve-maker OE, or for one who riddled or sifted corn, or sand and lime (for making mortar). Mainly found in Gloucs.

Ridley P Place-name in: Chesh, Northd OE 'channel clearing'; Essex, Kent OE 'reedy clearing'. Strongest in Northd and Co Durham. *Nicholas Ridley (1502–1555) was born near Willimontswick, Northd, to a local gentry family. As Bishop of London he was burned at the stake for supporting the accession of Lady Jane Grey.*

Rid(e)out N ?Nickname from OE 'ride out', for a rider, messenger. 'From some lost joke' (Cottle). Readily confused with/a variant of **Riddett**. **Ridout** is found across southern England; **Rideout** is strongest in Dorset.

Rigby P Place-name in Lancs ON 'ridge farm'. A common Lancs surname. *Eleanor Rigby (1895–1939) is said to have been the inspiration behind the Beatles' song of the same name. John Lennon and Paul McCartney allegedly used to sunbathe near her grave in St Peter's Parish Church, Woolton, Liverpool, Lancs.*

Rigden, *see* Richard.

Rigg(s), *see* Ridge.

Rigglesford, *see* Wriglesworth.

Rigmaiden P Name of a farm, *Rigmaden,* in Westmd ON and OE 'maiden's ridge', the possessive being placed second in the Celtic manner. A very scarce Lancs surname.

Riley P Place-name *Ryley*, Lancs OE 'clearing with rye'; or a variant of **Reilly**. Principally a north-of-England surname.

Rimell/Rymell/Rymill F From an OE female first-name meaning 'border battle'. **Rimell** is mainly found in Gloucs and surrounding areas, **Rymell** in Warwicks and **Rymill** in Oxon.

Rimer, *see* Rymer.

Rim(m)ington/Rem(m)ington P Place-name *Rimington* in WRYorks OE 'place on a river-bank/ridge/boundary' (compare the word *rim*). **Rimington** and **Rimmington** are found mainly in WRYorks; **Remington**

and **Remmington** (very scarce) are widely scattered throughout England.

Rimmer, *see* Rymer.

Rimmington, *see* Rimington.

Ring O/N/T Occupational term for a maker of rings (for ornamental/utilitarian purposes) OE; or a nickname for one who ostentatiously wore a ring; or a dweller by a stone circle or some ring-shaped topographical feature. A surname of south-east England. Compare **Ringer**.

Ringer O/F Occupational term for a bell–ringer, or for a maker of rings (see **Ring**) OE, though Reaney suggests also a 'wringer (of ?cheese)' OE; or from an OF (from Germanic) first-name *Reinger/Rainger* 'counsel-spear', introduced by the Normans. Chiefly a Norfolk surname.

Ringstead P Place-name in: Dorset OE 'site with a salt-pan'; Norfolk, Northants OE 'site with a ?stone circle or circular earthwork'. This scarce surname is found almost exclusively in Norfolk.

Ringwood P Place-name in Hants OE 'border/boundary wood' and in Essex OE '?marsh in a curve/ring'. The surname is most commonly found in Norfolk.

Riordan/Rearden/Reardon F Irish: Anglicized form of Gaelic **O'** [descendant of] Rioghbhardain ('Royal bard').

Ripley P Place-name in various counties, including Derbys, Hants, Surrey, WRYorks OE 'wood/clearing shaped like a strip'. Strongest in WRYorks

Ripper O Occupational term for a maker or user of baskets ON. Found mainly in eastern England and in Cornwall.

Rippingale P Place-name in Lincs ON and OE 'the nook/recess of the *Hrepingas*'. Chiefly an Essex surname.

Rippon P Place-name *Ripon* in NRYorks, based on *Hrypum,* the dative plural of an OE tribal-name. 'The tribe recurs at *Repton* and *Ripley*, but the meaning of their name is

obscure' (Cottle). Mainly found in northern England, especially in Co Durham.

Risborough P There are place-names *Monks Risborough* and *Princes Risborough* (*King's Rysburgh* in 1290) in Bucks OE 'hill(s)/mound(s) overgrown with brushwood', but this rare surname is found equally in Norfolk and in Co Durham (where there is a place-name *Risebridge* OE '*Hrisa*'s bridge').

Risby P Place-name in various counties, including Lincs, Suffolk, ERYorks ON 'brushwood settlement'. Chiefly a Norfolk and Suffolk surname.

Riseley P Place-name in Beds, Berks OE 'brushwood clearing'. Readily confused with/a variant of **Risley**. Sparsely scattered throughout central England and South Wales.

Rishton P Place-name in Lancs OE 'place where rushes grow', and a Lancs surname.

Rishworth, *see* Rushforth.

Risley P Place-name in Derbys and Lancs OE 'brushwood clearing'. Readily confused with/a variant of **Riseley**. An unevenly scattered surname.

Ritchie/Ritson, *see* Richard.

Rivers P From one of many places in France called *Rivière(s)* OF 'river-bank(s)'. *The American patriot and craftsman Paul Revere (1735–1818), born in Boston, Massachusetts, USA, descends from a Huguenot family once called De Revoire or Rivoire.*

Rix(on), *see* Richard.

Roach/Roch(e) T/P Dweller by a rocky outcrop OF *roche* ('rock'), or from a place-name with the same meaning such as *Roche* in Cornwall or *Roch* in Lancs. **Roach** is widely scattered, most common in south-west England and in Lancs; **Roch** has a significant presence in Pembrokeshire, South Wales, and **Roche** in Lancs. **Roche** is the family name of the Barons Fermoy.

Roadnight O Occupational term for a

mounted servant OE. Most commonly found in Warwicks.

Roads T Dweller at a clearing OE; compare **Ridding**, etc. (under **Reading**), and **Ride** (under **Read**). There are place-names *Road* in Somerset and *Roade* in Northants OE 'clearing'. Chiefly a Bucks surname. See also **Rhodes, Rodd, Royds**.

Roan P/F From the place-name *Rouen* in Seine-Maritime, France OF. Irish: a variant of **Ruane**, an Anglicized form of Gaelic **O'** [descendant of] **Ruadhain** ('red' [diminutive]). A surname widely scattered across the north of England.

Roantree, *see* **Rowntree**.

Robart(s)/Robb/Robbins/Robens, *see* **Robert**.

Robert(s)/Dabb(s)/Dabinett/Dobb(s)/ Dobb(i)e/Dobbin(g)(s)/Dobbi(n)son/ Dobby(n)/Dobson/Hobb(e)(s)/ Hobbins/Hobbis/Hobday/Hobson/ Hopkin(s)/Hopkinson/Hopson/ Nabb(s)/Nobb(s)/Rabbatts/Rabbetts/ Rabbit(t)s/Rabson/Rapkin(s)/Rapson/ Robart(s)/Robb/Robbins/Robens/ Robertson/Robeson/Robey/Robin(s)/ Robinson/Robjohn/Roblett/Roblin/ Robson F From a Germanic first-name *Robert* 'renown-bright/famous', made popular by the Normans, which has spawned many related surnames thanks to its pet-forms *Dobb, Hobb, Nobb* and *Rob* (though *Bob* is a later pet-form). '*Dobbin*' was a name commonly applied to an old draught-horse. **Dabinett** (scarce, Somerset), **Roblett** (very scarce, Herts) and **Roblin** (very scarce, South Wales) are diminutive forms. **Robjohn** (very scarce, ERYorks) is a variant of the OF *Robion*. **Dobbie** and **Dobby** are mainly Scots; **Dobson, Hobson** and **Robson** are surnames of northern England, the latter being particularly strong in the north-east; **Hobbs** is found chiefly in the south of England and the South Midlands; **Hobbes**, much scarcer, belongs to the south-east; **Hopkins** is very common in South Wales, despite its Flemish suffix; **Rapson** belongs to Cornwall, **Rabson** to Kent and Sussex, **Rapkin** and **Rapkins** to Surrey; **Roberts** is

widespread, strong in North Wales and Lancs in particular; **Robertson** is chiefly a Scots surname. **Nabb** (rhyming with the pet-form *Rab*) is a scarce Lancs form. See also **Probert** and **Robey**. **Hopkinson** is the family name of the Barons Colyton. **Roberts** is the family name of the Barons Clwyd. Full marks must go to the parents of a son, born in Wortley, Yorks in 1888, called '*Crusoe* **Robinson**'. *Thomas Hobbes (1588–1679), philosopher, was born to a prosperous family of clothiers in Malmesbury, Wilts... Sir (Philip) Anthony Hopkins, Academy Award-winning actor, was born in Margam, Port Talbot, Wales, in 1937; his mother was distantly related to the Irish poet W. B. Yeats... Paul Leroy Robeson (1898–1976), born in Princeton, New Jersey, USA, achieved transatlantic fame as an actor, singer and political activist.*

Robertson/Robeson, *see* **Robert**.

Robey P Place-name in Co Durham ON 'landmark/boundary farm', the same origin as the surname **Raby** (and also **Roby**, with which **Robey** could readily be confused); but in Scotland this is a diminutive of **Robert**. *Sir George Robey (1869–1954), music-hall comedian, was born in London as George Edward Wade; when he saw the name of a Birmingham firm called 'Roby' misspelled as 'Robey', he liked the look of it and adopted it as his own.*

Robin(s)/Robinson/Robjohn/Roblett/ Roblin/Robson, *see* **Robert**.

Roby P Place-name in Lancs ON 'landmark/ boundary farm', with the same meaning as **Robey**, with which it could readily be confused.

Roch(e), *see* **Roach**.

Rochester P Place-name in Kent, British 'bridges at the stronghold'. One or two other minor places so-called may also have given rise to the surname – including *Rochester*, Northd (named after the Kent town?), which would account for the fact that it is most commonly found in that county and in Co Durham. Yet the variant

Rossiter is widely scattered throughout southern England, strongest in Somerset.

Rochford P Place-name in Essex and Worcs OE 'hunting dog's ford'. Mainly found in the north-west of England and in the West Midlands.

Rock T/P/O Dweller near a rocky outcrop ME *rocc* or at an oak tree ME 'atter oke', mis-divided; or from one of a number of places so-called, with either meaning, such as *Rock* in Northd ('rock') or *Rock* in Worcs ('at the oak'); or an occupational term for one who spun wool or who made distaffs ME *rok* 'distaff'. Readily confused with/a variant of **Rook**, and (in Ireland) **Rourke**. Compare **Rocker**. **Rock** is a scattered surname, strongest in Lancs and Staffs; the variant **Roke** is much more widely scattered, and infinitely scarcer.

Rockcliffe, *see* **Rockliffe**.

Rocker/Rooker T/O Dweller at the rock OE, or an occupational term for a maker of distaffs ME *rok*. Compare **Rock**. **Rocker** is a very scarce surname; **Rooker** is chiefly found in Warwicks.

Rockley P There is such a place-name in Wilts OE 'rook wood/clearing', but this is chiefly a Notts surname, and *Rockley* (with the same meaning), near Retford in that county, must be a major source.

Rock(c)liffe P Place-name *Rockcliff* in Cumbd OE/ON 'red' and OE 'cliff' (as with **Rawcliffe**). A scarce Lancs surname in both spellings.

Rodbourn(e) P Place-name *Rodbourne* in Wilts OE 'reedy stream'. **Rodbourn** is mainly found in Gloucs and surrounding areas, **Rodbourne** in Berks and Wilts.

Rodd P Place-name in Herefords OE 'clearing'. See also **Ridding**, etc. (under **Reading**), **Ride** (under **Read**), **Rhodes and Royds**. **Rodd**, mainly found in Devon and surrounding areas, is the family name of the Barons Rennell.

Roddam/Rodham P Place-name *Roddam*, Northd OE (dative plural of *Rod*, 'clearing').

A **Roddam** family has been at *Roddam Hall*, Northd, for centuries; there is a reference to William of **Roddam** in 1296, and Hanks and Hodges say that present-day bearers of this surname can be traced back to Sir John **Roddam**, who died in battle in 1461. The spelling of the surname of Yvo de **Rodham**, referred to in Assize Rolls for York in 1204, may suggest a different OE place-name origin, though it would almost certainly have carried the same pronunciation as **Roddam**. The **Rodham** spelling is the one used by Hillary Rodham Clinton, wife of former US President Bill Clinton, and a well-established politician in her own right, who was born in 1947 in Chicago, Illinois. By way of contrast with the **Roddam**s of *Roddam Hall*, who had served as Mayors of Newcastle-upon-Tyne and could count the distinguished Admiral Robert **Roddam** (1719–1808) as one of their own, Hillary Clinton's great-grandfather Jonathan **Rodham** was a colliery overseer in Oxhill, near Stanley, Co Durham. In 1881, at the age of 38, Jonathan (whose own grandfather, another Jonathan, had been born at Chester-le-Street, Co Durham, in 1779) made his way to the coalfields of Scrabton, Pennsylvania, where he later became a policeman and a florist. Both **Roddam** and **Rodham** are almost exclusively Northd/Co Durham/NRYorks surnames. Readily confused with/a variant of **Rodden**.

Rodden P There is such a place-name in Somerset OE 'roe bucks' valley', though this is primarily a surname of Lanarkshire, Scotland. Readily confused with/a variant of **Roddam**.

Roderick F From a Germanic first-name *Hrodric* ('fame-powerful'), brought to England by the Normans as *Rodric*; Welsh: an Anglicized form of **Rhydderch** ('red-brown' or 'famous').

Rodger(s)/Rodgerson, *see* **Roger**.

Rodway P Place-name in Somerset OE 'way/road fit to ride on' (as with **Radway**).

Roe N Nickname based upon some resemblance (speed, shyness?) to a roe (deer) OE, which in the north and Scotland remained **Rae**. Readily confused with/a variant of **Ray, Rea, Rew, Rowe, Rye**.

Roebuck N Nickname from OE 'roe buck', 'from some odd resemblance to the handsome animal' (Cottle). A popular WRYorks surname.

Rofe/Roff, *see* Rolf.

Roffey P Place-names: *Roffey* in Sussex OF 'deer fence' and *Roffy* in Essex OE '?rough enclosure'. A surname most commonly found in Surrey.

Roger/Dodge/Dodgeon/Dodgin/ Dodgshun/Dodg(e)son/Dodson/ Doidge/Dudgeon/Hodge(s)/ Hodgkin(s)/Hodgki(n)son/Hodgkiss/ Hodg(e)son/Hodson/Hotchkin(s)/ Hotchkiss/Rodger/Rodgers(on) F From a Germanic first-name meaning 'famespear', reinforced by ON *Hrothgar* and introduced into England by the Normans. **Hodge** (especially strong in Devon and Cornwall) and **Dodge** (largely found in Somerset) are pet-forms, and '*Hodge*' was commonly used as a nickname for a bucolic peasant. **Hodson**, usually a form of **Hodgson**, can alternatively mean 'son of *Odo*' (Germanic: 'riches'). See also **Proger, Prosser** and **Rudge**. Although **Hodgkin** can be found in the south-east of England (especially Kent) as well as in the Midlands, **Hodgkins** belongs almost exclusively to Staffs and Warwicks. As usual, variants ending in -*son*, such as **Dodgeson, Dodgson, Hodgeson, Hodgson, Rodgerson** (and also **Rodgers**), are principally found in the north of England. **Rodger** and **Roger** have a significant presence in Scotland, while **Rogers** can be found in counties stretching from Cornwall to Yorkshire. A touch of avian charm is in evidence in the firstnames of '*Stormy Petrel* Hodgson', who was born in Stepney, London, in 1892. *Charles Lutwidge Dodgson (1832–1898), better known as the writer Lewis Carroll, was born in Warrington, Chesh, to a family which was predominantly from northern England, with some Irish connexions… The American actor and singer Leonard Slye (1911–1998) took the* *stage-name of Roy Rogers; perhaps 'Rogers' seemed like a more mellifluous surname than his own, and/or perhaps he was attracted by the alliterative nature of his new moniker?*

Roke, *see* Rock.

Rol(l)and(s) F From the Germanic firstname *Rol(l)ant*, meaning 'fame-land', made popular throughout Europe thanks to Charlemagne's famed warrior. Readily confused with surnames derived from **Ralf, Relf, Rolf, Rowe, Rowland** and **Ryland**.

Roles, *see* Rolf.

Roley, *see* Rowley.

Rolf(e)(s)/Rofe/Roff/Roles/Roll(e)(s)/ Rollo/Rolph/Rowles F From the ME (from Germanic) first-name *Rolf*, meaning 'famewolf', known especially in its ON form *Hrolfr*. Reaney lists its family of over two dozen surnames, admitting that several of them (such as **Rol(l)in(g)(s), Rollinson** and others) may have alternative origins, and referring in particular to confusion arising from variants of **Ralf** (to which we might add the possibility of a cross-over with a whole host of surnames derived from **Relf, Roland, Rowe, Rowland** and **Ryland**). See also **Ruff**. *John Rolphe (1585–1622), the Virginia colonist who famously married Pocahontas, was born in Heacham, Norfolk… Frederick William Rolfe (1860–1913), the writer who styled himself Baron Corvo, was born in Cheapside, London.*

Roll(e)(s)/Rol(l)in(g)(s)/Rollinson/ Rollo/Rolph, *see* Rolf.

Roman(s) F/P/N From the Latin first-name *Romanus* ('Roman'), borne by three saints, or a name applied to a person known to have come from Rome/Italy, or to have travelled there on a pilgrimage. **Rome** and **Room(e)** are variants, the latter reflecting an older pronunciation of **Rome**, giving point to Shakespeare's pun 'Rome indeed, and room enough' in *Julius Caesar*. **Roman** is widely scattered throughout England, though not common in the Midlands; **Romans** is mostly found in Gloucs and WRYorks, **Rome** in north-west England and Scotland, and **Roome** in Derbys.

Room is more widely distributed, while **Rumens**, possibly a variant, is restricted in the main to Kent and Sussex.

Rome, *see* **Roman**.

Romilly P Place-names *Remilly/Romilly/ Rumilly* in France OF from the male first-name *Romilius*, plus suffix. There is a place-name *Romiley* in Chesh OE 'roomy/ spacious clearing', but by the late nineteenth century the surname is mainly found in Surrey and Middx, and would appear to have Huguenot origins.

Romney P Place-name in Kent OE '?*Rumen*'s river', and principally a Kent surname. *George Romney (1734–1802), painter, was born in Dalton-on-Furness, Lancs, the son of a furniture-maker.*

Ronald/Ranald F Scots: Anglicization of the Gaelic first-name *Roonull*, a form of ON *Rögnvaldr*. Readily confused with, or variants of, various **Reynold**-type surnames. **Ranaldson** and **Ronaldson** are patronymic forms.

Ronson, *see* **Rowland**.

Rook(e)(s)/Ruck N/T/P Nickname for a person bearing some resemblance to a rook, the bird OE *hroc* (having black hair, etc.); or a dweller at the sign of the rook; or from a minor place-name. Readily confused with/a variant of **Rock/Roke**. Both **Rook** and **Rooke** are widespread, the former being particularly strong in Devon; **Ruck** can mainly be found in Gloucs and Kent.

Rooker, *see* **Rocker**.

Rookes, *see* **Rook**.

Room(e), *see* **Rome**.

Rooney F Irish: Anglicized form of Gaelic **O'** [descendant of] **Ruanaidh** ('champion'). At its strongest around Liverpool and Glasgow. *Wayne (Mark) Rooney, the England footballer who began his playing career (briefly) with Everton, was born in Liverpool in 1985 and brought up in Croxteth.*

Roope/Rooper, *see* **Roper**.

Roos(e), *see* **Rose** and **Rous**.

Root N/O Nickname for a cheerful, bright person OE; or an occupational term for one who played on the psaltery/rote OF (compare **Rutter**). Mainly an Essex surname.

Roper/Roope/Rooper O Occupational term for a rope-maker OE. Of **Raper**, a northern dialect form, Cottle says: 'One bearer had an unfortunate address in **Sabine** Road, London SW11'. **Roper** is strongest in WRYorks, and **Roope** in Cambs and East Anglia. **Rooper** is scarce and scattered, and **Raper** belongs to NRYorks and WRYorks. 'John *Tight* **Roper**' was born in Guisborough, Yorks, in 1898; maybe he joined the circus when he grew up? *William Roper (c.1495–1578), biographer of his father-in-law Sir Thomas More, came from an established Kent family who were Lords of the Manor of St Dunstan, Canterbury.*

Rosamond/Rosaman/Roseman F From the Germanic first-name *Rosemunde*, meaning 'horse-protection', mistaken in the Middle Ages for Latin *rosa munda* 'rose undefiled', used of the Virgin Mary.

Roscoe P Place-name in Lancs ON 'roe-buck wood'.

Rose N/T/F Nickname from the flower OF, used perhaps for someone with a rosy complexion; or dweller at a promontory/cape (Scots Gaelic), a wood (Irish and Scots Gaelic), a moor (Cornish and Welsh), or a place where wild roses grew; or dweller at the sign of the rose; or from the Germanic female first-name *Rose*, meaning 'fame-kind', occurring as *Rohesia* and giving rise to **Royce**, though the Clan **Rose** of Kilravock, the Barons **de Ros** (from *Roos* in ERYorks), and the place-name *Roose* in Lancs are from Gaelic or Welsh. **Rose** as a surname is also popular with the Jewish community. Readily confused with/a variant of **Ross**. Both **Rose** and **Royce** are well-scattered surnames; the variants **Roos** and **Roose** occur most frequently in Lancs and in Cornwall/Lancs respectively (but see also **Rous**). *Sir (Frederick) Henry Royce (1863–1933), the engineer and motor car designer of Rolls Royce fame, was born at Awalton, near Peterborough.*

Roseberry P Place-name *Roseberry Topping* in NRYorks, originally *Othenesberg* ON 'Odinn's hill', a centre of pagan worship. Most commonly found in Co Durham.

Rosedale P Place-name in NRYorks ON 'valley of horses', but mainly found in Chesh and Flintshire.

Roseman, *see* Rosamond.

Roseveare P There are two places so-called in Cornwall: the one near St Austell is 'big moor', the one near St Mawgan in Meneage is 'big ford'. In both cases the adjective *mur* ('great/big'), mutated to *veare*, comes second.

Rosewall P Place-name in St Ives, Cornwall, Cornish 'ford-?rampart'. *Kenneth Robert ('Ken') Rosewall, the former professional tennis player who won the Australian, US and French Open titles, was born in Melbourne, Australia, in 1934.*

Rosewarne P Place-name in Cornwall 'alder-tree heath'.

Rosier, *see* Rosser.

Rosomon, *see* Rosamond.

Ross P/F There are various places called *Ross* or *Roos(e)*, from Welsh *rhos* ('promontory/upland/moorland'), including *Ross on Wye*, Herefords, *Roos*, ERYorks, *Roose*, Lancs, *Ross*, Northd, and the Scottish county name *Ross*; or from *Rots* (Germanic '?clearing') in Calvados, France; or from the Germanic first-name *Rozzo* ('fame'), introduced to England by the Normans. Overall, a surname principally associated with Scotland. Readily confused with/a variant of **Rose**.

Rosser F From a Welsh first-name of unknown origin, though **Roger** may have become *Rhosiêr*; the *Ap-* form **Prosser** is much commoner. **Rosier**, most commonly found in Berks, is a possible variant.

Rossiter, *see* Rochester.

Rostron, *see* Rawsthorn.

Rotherham P Place-name in WRYorks, from the British river-name *Rother* plus OE

'homestead'. Mainly found in Lancs and WRYorks, though the apparent variants **Rudderham** and **Rudrum** are strongest in Norfolk.

Rothwell P Place-name in Lincs, Northants, WRYorks OE 'spring/stream in a clearing'. Found in Chesh and WRYorks, but especially strong in Lancs. See also **Rowell**.

Rotton/Roughton P Place-name *Roughton* in Lincs, and also in Norfolk (where it is pronounced '*Rawton*') OE 'place where the ground is rough', or 'rye farm'. Known or apparent variants include **Roton**, **Roughton**, **Raughton**, **Rauton**, **Wrauton** and **Wroton**. **Rotton**, scarce, can be found in Staffs and Surrey; **Roughton** belongs to the Midlands and South Midlands. Readily confused with/a variant of **Rowton**. *Johnny Rotten, born in 1956 in Finsbury Park, North London, with the name of John Lydon, achieved notoriety as a punk musician with the Sex Pistols.*

Roughead N Nickname for a person with a 'rough head' (of hair) OE. Mainly found in Northd and central Scotland.

Roughton, *see* Rotton.

Round N Nickname for a rotund, plump person OF. A West Midlands surname, strongest in Staffs and Worcs.

Rountree, *see* Rowntree.

Rourke F Irish: Anglicized form of the Gaelic first-name *Ruarc* ('?heavy rain shower'). See also **Rock**.

Rous(e)/Russ/Rust N Nickname for a person with red hair or a red face OF. One American family is known to have changed its surname from **Rust** to **Russ**. **Rous(e)** is commonly pronounced '*Roose*' (but see **Roos(e)**, under **Rose**). **Rowse** is a variant found in Cornwall/Devon. See also **Russell**. **Rous** is the family name of the Earls of Stradbroke. *The historian Alfred Leslie ('A. L.') Rowse was born in Tregonissey, Cornwall.*

Routledge ?P English and Scottish, of uncertain origin. It is tempting to believe that this predominantly Cumbd surname must have a place-name origin, but the settlement called *Routledge Burn* in that county would appear to have derived its name from the family of William **Retleche**/William **Routleth**, rather than vice versa. *The publisher George Routledge (1812–1888) was born at Brampton, Cumbd.*

Rover O/N Occupational term for a roofer OE; or a nickname for a person of shady character ME *rover* 'thief, pirate', but *not* applied as a name to a roamer, drifter, which is a more modern usage. Sparsely scattered around north-west and south-east England.

Rowan T/F Dweller by a rowan tree, mountain-ash ON; Irish: Anglicized form of Gaelic **O'** [descendant of] **Ruadhain** ('red' [diminutive]).

Rowberry, *see* Rowbrey.

Rowbotham/Rowbottom T/P Dweller in a rough valley OE, or from an unidentified place with the same meaning. Surnames of the Midlands and the north.

Rowbrey/Rowberry/Rowbury/Rubery P These surnames, and others like them, are from a group of place-names with first element *Ro-/Row-/Ru-* and the second element *-berrow/-borough* OE 'rough hill' in Devon, Somerset and Wilts. **Rowbrey**, rare, is found mainly in Herefords, **Rowberry** in Herefords and Worcs, **Rowbury** in Essex and Herefords and **Rubery** in Staffs.

Rowcliffe, *see* Rawcliffe.

Rowden/Rowdon P Place-name *Rowden* in Herefords, Devon, Wilts OE 'rough hill'. **Rowden** is found in many south and south-western counties of England; **Rowdon**, scarce, belongs mainly to Devon. In 1884 a man by the name of 'John Robert **Shittler**' (born in Wimborne, Dorset, in 1851) changed his surname to '**Rowden**'. And who can blame him?

Rowe T/F Dweller in a row (of houses/cottages), or by a hedgerow OE, the *-e* indicating a dative following a lost preposition; or from the mediaeval first-name *Row*, some-

times a short form of *Rowland* (and thus possibly in some cases connected with surnames derived from **Ralf**, **Relf**, **Roland**, **Rolf**, **Rowland** and **Ryland**). Readily confused with/a variant of **Ray**, **Rea**, **Rew**, **Roe** and **Rye**. The variant **Raw** is mostly found in northern England, strongest in NRYorks.

Rowell P Place-name in Devon OE 'rough hill' or OE 'roe bucks' hill'; or a variant of **Rothwell** (the place of that name in Northants being pronounced '*Rowell*'). Widely scattered, strong in Co Durham and Northd.

Rower O Occupational term for a wheelwright OF. Most common in Lincs.

Rowland P/F Place-name in Derbys and Sussex ON 'roe wood'; or a variant of **Roland** (and thus possibly in some cases connected with surnames derived from **Ralf**, **Relf**, **Roland**, **Rolf**, **Rowe** and **Ryland**). Ronson, **Rowlands** (chiefly a Welsh surname) and **Rowlandson** are 'son of **Rowland**'.

Rowlands/Rowlandson, *see* Rowland.

Rowles, *see* Rolf.

Rowley P Place-name in various counties (some pronounced '*Roe-ley*') OE 'rough wood/clearing'. Especially strong in Staffs.

Rowney P Place-name in Herts and elsewhere OE '(at) the rough enclosure', the *-n-* representing a weak dative singular after a lost preposition and definite article. Widely scattered throughout England and Scotland. *In 1783 two brothers, Thomas and Richard Rowney, having abandoned their wig-powder business, opened an artists' colour shop in London. Thomas's son George Rowney expanded the business, which eventually became a major supplier of artists' materials; having merged with the Daler Board Company, it now forms part of Daler-Rowney Ld, based in Bracknell, Berkshire.*

Rowntree/Roantree T Dweller by a rowan/mountain-ash tree ON and OE. Most common in Co Durham and Yorks. *Joseph Rowntree (1836–1925), born to a Quaker family in York, helped to establish the Rowntree family's chocolate manufacturing company.*

Rowse, *see* **Rous**.

Rowsell, *see* **Russell**.

Rowthorn P There is such a place-name in Derbys OE 'rough thorn-bush', but the surname is most common in Hants.

Rowton P Place-name in Salop and ERYorks OE 'rough(-soiled) place', though the surname is most common in Cambs and in the Midlands. Readily confused with/a variant of **Rotton**.

Roxburgh P Place-name in Roxburghshire, Scotland OE '*Hroc*'s castle/manor'.

Roxby P Place-name in NRYorks ON '*Rauthr*'s farm' and in Lincs ON '*Hrokr*'s farm'. A Co Durham surname.

Roy N Scots: nickname for a person with red hair, Gaelic *ruadh*; or a variant of **Ray**. Any connexion with the OF word for a king, from service in a royal household, or from acting such a part in a play, remains speculative. *Roy* was early used as a first-name.

Royal, *see* **Royle**.

Royce, *see* **Rose**.

Royden P Cottle mentions the place-name *Roydon* in Essex, Norfolk and Suffolk OE 'hill where rye grows', but the surname is mainly found in Chesh and also in Lancs, in which county there is a *Royton* OE 'rye enclosure'.

Royds T Dweller by or in a clearing OE (Yorks dialect version of *roads*, 'clearings'; compare Yorks '*oil*' for '*hole*'). The element *-royd/-rod* is also commonly found in place-names, giving rise to surnames such as **Murgatroyd**, **Ormerod**. See also **Rhodes**, **Roads**, **Rodd**.

Roylance, *see* **Ryland**.

Royle/Royal P Place-name *Royle* in Lancs OE 'hill with rye'. See also **Ryall**. **Royle** is a Chesh/Lancs surname; **Royal**, more widespread, is commonest in Norfolk. *The English football manager Joseph ('Joe') Royle was born in Liverpool in 1949.*

Royston P Place-name in Herts OE 'settlement at *Roys, Roheis/Roese*'s cross' and in WRYorks OE '*Hror*'s settlement'. The surname is mainly found in WRYorks.

Rubery, *see* **Rowbrey**.

Ruck, *see* **Rook**.

Ruckley P Cottle mentions a place-name in Salop OE 'rook wood', but the surname is mainly found in Somerset and surrounding areas, and the origin there could be *Rockley*, Wilts, with the same OE meaning.

Rudd/Rudkin N Nickname for a person with red hair or a ruddy complexion OE. See also **Rudge**. **Rudd** is strongest in Norfolk, **Rudkin** in Leics.

Rudderham, *see* **Rotherham**.

Ruddick/Ruddock/Rudduck N Nickname from some resemblance to a robin red-breast OE.

Rudge T/P/F/N Dweller near a ridge of land ME or from a place-name with the same meaning in Salop; or from a mediaeval first-name, a variant of *Roger;* or a nickname for a person with red hair or a red face (compare **Rudd**) OF. *Daniel Rudge (1840–1880) was a Wolverhampton-born engineer who built high-end bicycles and velocipedes. His manufacturing company achieved fame as Rudge Whitworth Cycles.*

Rudkin, *see* **Rudd**.

Rudrum, *see* **Rotherham**.

Ruff T/N/F Dweller on rough ground OE; or a nickname for a rough, hairy, violent person OE; or a variant of **Rolf**. 'Anyway, nothing to do with the fish, the bird, or the linen collar' (Cottle).

Rufford P Place-names: *Rufford* in Lancs and Notts, and *Rufforth* (formerly *Rufford*) in WRYorks OE 'rough ford'; yet the surname is most common in Suffolk, where the place-name *Rushford* OE 'the rushy enclosure' may have had a part to play? See also **Rushforth**.

Rugby P Place-name in Warwicks OE and ON '*Hroca*'s settlement'. Mostly found in Staffs and Co Durham.

Rugman T Dweller on a ridge OE *hrycg*, here in its south-west Midland form with -*u*-. Chiefly a Gloucs surname.

Rumball/Rumbell/Rumble/Rumbold F From a Norman first-name *Rumbald*, Germanic 'glory-bold', made popular through the precocious St *Rumbald*, or *Rumwald*, who packed a lot into a short life, having confessed himself a Christian at birth, demanded baptism, preached a sermon, and died aged three days...

Rumbelow T/P Dweller at 'three hills/barrows' OE, or from a minor place-name with the same meaning; the initial *th*- of *three* has been dropped, but the -*m*- of the dative used after a lost preposition remains. Desmond Holden makes mention of a district of Aston, Birmingham, which is referred to in 1461 as '*The Rumbelow*', and a place in Wednesfield, Staffs, which was *Thromelowe* in 1339 but *Romylowe* by 1420. The surname, in similar fashion, can be found in mediaeval records as **de Thrimelowe** and the like. Reaney has shown that the resemblance to a nonsense word used in a heave-ho song favoured by sailors is coincidental. Mainly found in East Anglia.

Rumens, *see* **Roman**.

Rump N Nickname for a person with prominent buttocks OE; also used for an 'ugly creature' in dialect. Not the happiest choice of meanings, but the surname has survived in Norfolk until modern times.

Rumsey P Place-name *Romsey*, Hants OE '*Rum*'s island', reflecting its original pronunciation. Yet the prominent occurrence of this surname in East Anglia might suggest an origin in places called *Ramsey* in Hunts (now Cambs) and in Essex OE 'wild garlic island'.

Rumsum P Place-name *Rumsam*, Devon OE '*Rum*'s homestead'; a very rare Cornwall/Devon surname.

Runciman O Occupational term for a man who looks after the nags/rouncies OF plus OE *man*. Don Quixote's jade was called *Rocinante*. An almost exclusively Scottish surname. *Walter Runciman (1870–1949), first*

Viscount Runciman of Doxford, a prominent Liberal politician, was born in South Shields, Co Durham.

Runcorn P Place-name in Chesh OE 'wide bay'. A scarce Chesh/Lancs surname.

Rundall/Rundle N/P Nickname for a plumpish, somewhat rotund person OF *rondel*; or from the place-name *Rundale* in Shoreham, Kent OE 'spacious valley'. **Rundle** is predominantly a Cornish surname, and there is a *Rundle Stone* off the Cornish coast.

Runnacles/Runnicles T Dweller at the rye fields OE. **Runnacles** is mainly found in Suffolk, **Runnicles** in Essex and Middx.

Runton P Place-names *East Runton* and *West Runton*, Norfolk OE '*Runi/Runa*'s settlement', though the surname is mainly found in ERYorks.

Rush T/F Dweller by a rush-bed OE. Irish: Anglicized form of Gaelic **O'** [descendant of] *Ruis* ('?wood'). Widely scattered throughout the east and north-west of England.

Rushbrook(e) P Place-name in Suffolk, OE 'brook in the rushes'. A surname of the eastern counties of England in both spellings.

Rushfirth, *see* **Rushforth**.

Rushforth P There are places called *Rushford* in Norfolk and Suffolk OE 'ford in the rushes'. These may have given rise to the surname **Rufford**, which is most commonly found in that part of the world, but we should look elsewhere for a likely origin for **Rushforth**, which George Redmonds links with **Rushworth**, **Rushfirth** and **Rishworth**, describing them as being variants of 'a prolific but complicated surname'. The origin lies in one of two WRYorks place-names, *Rishworth* 'rush enclosure' in Elland chapelry, and *Ryshworth* (formerly *Ryshforth*) in Airedale, which would have been pronounced '*Rushworth/Rushforth*' dialectally. The elements '*worth*' and '*forth/ford*' were regularly interchanged (compare **Titford**).

Rushmer(e)/Rushmore P Place-names *Rushmere* and *Rushmore* in various counties OE 'mere/lake with rushes'. A Norfolk/Suffolk surname in all spellings.

Rushton P Place-name in Chesh, Dorset, Northants, Salop, Staffs OE 'place/farm in the rushes'. Readily confused with/a variant of **Ruston**. Strongest in Lancs.

Rushworth, *see* Rushforth.

Ruskin F Probably a diminutive form of the mediaeval first-name *Rose*. A scarce Home Counties surname. *John Ruskin (1819–1900), art critic, was born in Brunswick Square, London; his grandfather John Thomas Ruskin (1761–1817) had moved to Edinburgh from London to establish a grocery business, but the Ruskins were essentially an English family.*

Russ, *see* Rous.

Russel(l)/Rowsell N An English, Scots and Irish nickname for a person with red hair or a red face OF. A diminutive of **Rous(e)**. **Russell** is the family name of the Dukes of Bedford (who were originally from Dorset) and of four other peers. **Rowsell** is most commonly found in Somerset.

Rust, *see* Rous.

Ruston P From one of a number of place-names, including: *East Ruston* and *Sco Ruston*, Norfolk OE 'farm in brushwood'; *Ruston*, NRYorks OE 'farm with ?roosts/perches/rafters'; *Ruston Parva*, ERYorks OE '*Hror*'s farm'. Readily confused with/a variant of **Rushton**. A widely scattered surname, most common in Yorks.

Ruth N Nickname for a person exhibiting, or in need of, pity ME *reuthe* from OE or ON. No connexion with the biblical name of *Ruth* the Moabite, which is not recorded as being used in Britain until after the Reformation. A scarce, unevenly scattered surname. *George Herman ('Babe') Ruth (1895–1948), legendary baseball player, was born in Baltimore, Maryland, USA, to German-American parents.*

Rutherford P Place-name in Roxburghshire, Scotland OE 'cattle ford'. This is a surname found as much in Co Durham and Northd as in Scotland, so the place called *Rutherford* in NRYorks (with the same meaning) could well be the origin in some cases.

Ruthven P Scots: a place-name found in various parts of Scotland, including Perthshire, ON 'red marsh' or Gaelic 'red river'. The surname is commonly pronounced 'Rithen', 'Rivven' or 'Roothven'. Family name of the Earls Gowrie.

Rutley P Place-name in Devon OE 'red cliff'. Widely scattered throughout southern England and Wales.

Rutter O/N Occupational term for a player on the rote, an early mediaeval stringed instrument OF (compare **Root**); or a nickname for a highwayman, ruffian OF. Widely scattered, but not common in the East Midlands or in the West Country.

Ryal(l)/Ryle P Various place-names such as *Ryal(l)*, *Ryhall*, *Ryhill* and *Ryle* OE 'hill/nook where rye grows' could give rise to such surnames. See also **Royle**. **Ryall** is a West Country surname; **Ryal** is oddly scattered, and **Ryle** is strongest in Co Durham.

Ryan F Irish: Anglicized form of Gaelic O' [descendant of] **Rian** (of uncertain meaning); or an abbreviation of **Mulryan**, an Anglicized form of Gaelic O' [descendant of] **Maoilriaghain** ('devotee of *St Riaghan*'). Readily confused with/a variant of **Regan**.

Rycott P There is a place-name *Rycote* in Oxon OE 'cottage in the rye', but this very rare surname is almost entirely restricted to WRYorks, where it could readily have been confused with, or been a variant of, **Rycraft/Rycroft**.

Rycraft/Rycroft T/P Dweller at a croft where rye grows OE, or from a place called *Rycroft* in various counties in the Midlands and the north of England, with the same meaning. Readily confused with/a variant of **Rycott**. **Rycraft**, a scarce surname, can be found in Northants; **Rycroft** belongs principally to Lancs and WRYorks.

Ryde P Place-name in Surrey and the Isle of

Wight OE 'stream'. Readily confused with/a variant of **Ride** (see under **Read**). A scattered surname.

Ryder, *see* **Rider**.

Rye T Dweller (at) the island, (at) the low-lying land OE or (at) the stream OE (**Reeman** and **Ryman** are variants); or a dweller on land where rye was grown OE. Readily confused with/a variant of **Ray**, **Rea**, **Rew**, **Roe**, **Rowe**. **Rye** is strongest in Kent, **Reeman** in Sussex, **Ryman** in the Cotswolds. *The company known as 'Ryman the stationer' can trace its origins back to 1893, in which year Henry John Ryman (born circa 1853) opened his first shop in Great Portland Street, London.*

Rylance, *see* **Ryland**.

Ryland(s)/Roylance/Rylance T/P Dweller on land where rye grows OE, or from places called *Ryland* or *Rylands*, with the same meaning. Readily confused with various surnames derived from **Ralf**, **Relf**, **Roland**,

Rolf, **Rowe** and **Rowland**. **Ryland** is most common in western England; **Rylands**, **Roylance** and **Rylance** in Lancs. *John Rylands (1810–1888), the man after whom the University of Manchester's famous library is named, became the city's first multi-millionaire, though he was born into a family of modest means in St Helens, Lancs.*

Ryle, *see* **Ryal**.

Ryman, *see* **Rye**.

Rymell, *see* **Rimell**.

Rymer/Rimer/Rimmer O Occupational term for a rhymer, poet, minstrel ME. **Rymer** is chiefly found in NRYorks; **Rimer** (scarce) in Northd, and **Rimmer** in Lancs. *The literary critic and historian Thomas Rymer (1642/3-1713), famous as the editor of Foedera, was the son of Ralph Rymer, Lord of the Manor of Brafferton, Yorks.*

Rymill, *see* **Rimell**.

S

Saban/Saben/Sabin(e)/Savin(s) F From an OF first-name *Sabin* (male) or *Sabine* (female), originally borne by an ancient tribe of central Italy. There were several saints named *Sabinus*, and a martyred Roman matron *Sabina*. 'An unfortunate first-name in view of the alarming experience of the Sabine women' (Cottle). **Saban** is found mainly in Essex and Herts; **Sabin** in Warwicks; **Savin** in Lancs, Kent and Oxon; **Savins** in Oxon. **Saben** and **Sabine** are scarce variants.

Sacheverell P From a place-name *Sault-Chevreuil* in Manche OF 'kid's leap'. A very scarce surname within the British Isles.

Sacker/Sackett/Secker O Occupational term for a maker of sacks or sack-cloth OE. **Sacker** and **Secker** are found in both Yorks and Norfolk; **Sackett** belongs to Kent.

Sackett, *see* Sacker.

Sadd N Nickname for a settled, serious, firm person OE *soed*, with the sense of 'sated, tired' (but not, originally, 'unhappy'). Chiefly a Norfolk surname.

Saddington P Place-name in Leics OE '?*Saegeat*'s settlement'. Mainly found in the East Midlands, strongest in Northants.

Sad(d)ler/Sadleir O Occupational term for a saddle-maker OE; **Sadler** is widely scattered throughout England and Wales; **Saddler** also has a presence in Scotland, and **Sadleir** is chiefly an Irish surname.

Saer, *see* Sayer.

Saffron O/N Occupational term for someone who cultivated the saffron plant; or a nickname for a person with yellow hair OF. Mainly found in Essex and Middx.

Sagar/Sager/Seager/Seeger F From a ME first-name *Soegar* ('sea spear'). See also **Sugar**. **Sagar** and **Sager** belong to Lancs, **Seager** to Kent. *Charles Seeger (1886–1979), musicologist, could trace his ancestry back to immigrants who arrived in America aboard the Mayflower. Members of the Seeger family had fought in both the Revolutionary War and the Civil War, and several of Charles's children by his wives Constance de Clyver Edson Seeger and Ruth Crawford Seeger – principally Pete Seeger, Mike Seeger and Peggy Seeger – inherited their father's love of music and of radical politics.*

Sage N Nickname for a wise man OF. Most commonly found around the Severn and Thames estuaries.

Sager, *see* Sagar.

Sailer O Occupational term for a dancer OF. Mainly found in Kent and Middx.

Sainsbury P Place-name *Saintbury* in Gloucs OE '?*Saewine*'s fort'. *John James Sainsbury (1844–1928), born in Lambeth, London, founded the Sainsbury's chain of stores and supermarkets.*

Saint N Nickname for a saintly or (excessively?) pious person OF. A widely scattered surname.

St Clair, *see* Sinclair.

St John P From one of a large number of places in France called *Saint-Jean*, with churches dedicated accordingly. The common pronunciation of such a surname as

'Sinjun' clearly displeases Cottle, who is not in favour of such 'fancy slurrings, available though not obligatory', which he deems to be 'all uglier than their originals, but none so distasteful as calling a training college, dedicated to the Blessed Virgin, Simmeries'. **St John** is the family name of the Viscounts Bolingbroke.

St Leger, *see* Salinger.

Sainty, *see* Sankey.

Salaman/Salamon(s)/Salman/Salmen/Salmon(d)/Salmons/Salomon(s)/Sammon(d)s/Solomon(s) F/N From the Hebrew first-name *Shelomo*, based on *shalom* ('peace') and popular in the form *Solomon*; sometimes used as a nickname for one considered to be as wise as Solomon, or who had played such a part in a play. No connexion with the fish, the salmon. *Alexander Elliot Anderson ('Alex') Salmond, Scottish politician, was born in 1954 in Linlithgow... When Cyril Barnet Salmon (1903–1991), a celebrated judge, was raised to the peerage in 1972, he acquired the intriguing title of Lord Salmon of Sandwich.*

Salathiel F From a Babylonian first-name, sometimes Hebraized to mean 'requested of God'; the father of Zerubbabel. A surname found chiefly in Glamorgan.

Salcombe P Place-names *Salcombe* and *Salcombe Regis*, Devon OE 'salt valley'. A scarce surname which has become more common in Gloucs than in Devon.

Sale O/T/P Occupational term for one who worked at a hall or manor house OE *soel* ('hall'); or a dweller by a sallow/willow tree OE (compare **Sallows**, **Seal**), or from a place-name with the same meaning, such as *Sale* in Chesh.

Salesbury, *see* Salisbury.

Salford P Place-name in Beds, Lancs, Worcs OE 'ford at the sallows/willows', and in Oxon, Warwicks, OE 'ford where salt was transported'. The surname is sparsely scattered throughout England. **Sawford**, commonest in Northants, is probably a variant.

Salinger/St Leger P Place-names in France: *Saint Léger*, Manche, and *Saint Léger aux Bois*, Seine-Maritime, both of which have churches dedicated to the seventh-century saint of that name. A very rare surname within the British Isles. **St Leger** is commonly pronounced '*Selinger*'. *The American author Jerome David ('J. D.') Salinger was born in 1919 in Manhattan, New York, to a Jewish father and a half-Scottish/half-Irish mother.*

Salisbury/Salesbury/Salusbury P Place-names: *Salisbury*, Wilts – the first element of which, Celtic *Sorvio*, of unknown meaning, was eventually changed to *Searo* (imitating an OE word for 'armour'), the second element being OE 'fort' – and *Salesbury*, Lancs OE 'willow fort'. **Salisbury** and **Salesbury** are most commonly found in the north-west of England; **Salusbury**, very scarce, has a presence in Denbighshire, North Wales.

Salkeld P Place-name in Cumbd OE 'sallow/willow wood'.

Salley P Place-name *Sawley* in WRYorks OE 'sallow/willow clearing' and in Derbys OE 'sallow/willow hill'. The surname is most common in Lancs and Notts.

Sallows T Dweller by a sallow/willow tree OE (compare **Sale** and **Seal**). Mainly found in Essex and surrounding area.

Salman/Salmen/Salmon(d)/Salmons/Salomon(s), *see* Salaman.

Salt/Sault O/P Occupational term for a salt worker/seller OE (compare **Salter**, **Salthouse**); or from a place-name in Staffs OE 'salt works/pit'. *Sir Titus Salt (1803–1876), textile manufacturer, politician and philanthropist from Morley, near Leeds, WRYorks, founded the model industrial village of Saltaire.*

Salter O Occupational term for a salt worker/seller (compare **Salt**, **Salthouse**) OE, or for one who played on the (stringed) psaltery OF. Widely scattered throughout southern England, strongest in Devon. See also **Soutar**.

Salthouse O/T/P Occupational term for a person employed at a salt-works or salt store OE (compare **Salt**, **Salter**); or a dweller at such a place, or from a place-name with the same meaning in Lancs, Norfolk, Salop. A Lancs surname.

Saltmarsh P Place-name in various counties OE 'salt marsh'. Mainly found in Essex and Kent.

Salton P Place-name in NRYorks OE 'enclosure at the sallows/willows', and strongest in that county.

Saltonstall P Place-name in WRYorks OE 'homestead in the sallows/willows'.

Salusbury, *see* Salisbury.

Salway/Selway/Salwey F From a mediaeval first-name *Salewi* OE 'good fortune-war'. **Salway** and **Selway** are strongest in Devon and Somerset; **Salwey** is a very scarce variant.

Sam(m)(s), *see* Samson.

Sambourne P Place-names: *Sambourn*, Warwicks, and *Sambourne*, Wilts OE 'sandy stream'. The surname is most common in WRYorks and Somerset.

Sambrook P Place-name in Salop OE 'sandy brook'. Mainly found in Salop and Staffs.

Sammon(d)s, *see* Salaman.

Sampford P Place-name in Dorset, Devon (three such), Essex (two such), Somerset (two such) OE 'sandy ford'. Readily confused with/a variant of **Sandford**. A scarce Essex/Herts surname.

Sample, *see* Semple.

Sampson, *see* Samson.

Samson/Sam(m)(s)/Sampson/Sansam/Sansom(e)/Sanson/Sansum/Sansun F/P From the Hebrew first-name *Shimshon* (a diminutive of 'sun'). Made popular thanks to a sixth-century Welsh bishop bearing such a name, who crossed to Brittany and was greatly venerated. An alternative origin, from one of the places called *Saint-Samson* in France, is also possible. **Sansom** and the like are the result of metathesis.

Samuel(s)/Samwell F From the Hebrew first-name *Shemuel* ('name of God'). **Samuel** is the family name of the Viscounts Bearsted.

Samways N Nickname for a stupid person OE (literally 'half-wise'). Mainly a Dorset surname.

Samwell, *see* Samuel.

Sanctuary T A person who lived near a shrine, or was known to have taken sanctuary in a church or monastery OF. Mainly a WRYorks surname.

Sandal(l) P Place-name in WRYorks OE 'sandy nook'. Readily confused with/a variant of **Sandell** or **Sendal**.

Sandbach P Place-name in Chesh OE 'sandy stream/valley', and a Chesh surname.

Sandbrook T Dweller at a sandy brook OE. Chiefly a West Midlands surname, strongest in Warwicks.

Sandell T Dweller at a sand hill/slope OE. Readily confused with/a variant of **Sandal** or **Sendal**.

Sandeman O 'Servant of **Alexander**' (as in **Sanders**). Most common in Angus, Scotland. *Albert George Sandeman (1833–1923), a noted port and sherry producer, was born at 31 Highbury Place, Highbury, Middx.*

Sander(s)/Sanders(on), *see* Alexander.

Sandford/Sandifer/Sandiford/Sandiforth/Sanford P Place-names *Sandford/Sandy Ford/Sandyford/Sandyforth* in various counties OE 'sandy ford'. **Sandford** is widespread; **Sandifer** is most common in Sussex and Hunts, **Sandiford** in Lancs, **Sandiforth** in WRYorks and **Sanford** in Devon. Readily confused with/a variant of **Sampford**.

Sandhurst P Place-name in Berks, Gloucs, Kent OE 'sandy hill/wood'. A rare surname, found mainly in Gloucs.

Sandifer/Sandiford/Sandiforth, *see* Sandford.

Sandison, *see* Alexander.

Sandon P Place-name in various counties OE 'sandy hill'. Sparsely scattered throughout England and Wales.

Sands P/F Place-name in various counties OE 'sands'. The variant **Sandys**, which retains the inflexional vowel of ME, is commonly pronounced '*Sands*'. In principle either variant could alternatively be derived from **Alexander**.

Sandwith P Place-name in Cumbd and WRYorks ON 'sandy ford'. A Cumbd surname.

Sandy P/F Place-name in Beds OE 'sandy island'; or from an ON first-name *Sand(i)* ('truth'/'sand'); or a variant of **Alexander**.

Sandys, *see* **Sands**.

Sanford, *see* **Sandford**.

Sanger/Sangster/Singer O Occupational term for a singer, chorister OE. **Sangster** was originally a female form (compare **Brewster**, **Webster**), but was later also used for males. **Sanger** is mainly found in the West Country, **Sangster** in Aberdeenshire, Scotland, and **Singer** in both Somerset and Aberdeenshire. *John Sanger (1819–1889), born at Chew Magna, Somerset, established a famous circus at Astley's Amphitheatre in London with the assistance of P. T. Barnum… Singer sewing machines take their name from the inventor Isaac Merritt Singer (1811–1875), born in Pittstown, New York. Whether the original surname of his father Adam, an immigrant from Saxony, was Reisinger, and whether he was of Jewish descent, has been a matter of much conjecture.*

Sanigar P Place-name *Saniger Farm* in Gloucs OE 'herdsman's wooded slope' or OE 'wooded slope with swans'. A rare surname, restricted almost entirely to Gloucs.

Sankey P Place-name in Lancs, so-called from a British river-name ('?holy/sacred'). Cottle says that 'the surname settled in Salop, where it was *Zanchey* as late as the 1670s', though by the late nineteenth century it could principally be found in Lancs. More recent research by the Australian genealogist Malcolm Sainty and others has linked the surnames **Sankey** and **Sainty**. *Ira D. Sankey (1840–1908), the American gospel singer and composer closely associated with the evangelist Dwight L. Moody, was born at Edinburgh, Pennsylvania, USA.*

Sansam/Sansom(e)/Sanson/Sansum/ Sansun, *see* **Samson**.

Sant, *see* **Saint**.

Sapcote P Place-name in Leics OE 'sheep-shelter'. Most commonly found in Yorks and Warwicks.

Sapper O Occupational term for a maker or seller of soap OE. Sparsely spread throughout the north-east and the south-east of England.

Sargant/Sarge(a)nt/Sarge(a)ntson/ Sarje(a)nt/Sarj(e)antson/ Sergeant(son)/Sergent(son)/ Serjeant(son)/Serjent O Occupational term for a servant, an officer of the courts, a tenant by military service below the rank of a knight OF. Modern English has retained the original -*ar*- pronunciation of the -*er*-element, as it has in *clerk*, *Derby*, etc. **Sargent** and **Sargeant** are widely scattered across southern England, with something of a presence elsewhere; **Sarjent** and **Serjeant** are scarce Lancs surnames; **Serjent** (very scarce) is found in Chesh; **Sarjeant** is widely scattered throughout England and Scotland. The patronymic forms **Sargentson/Sarjanston/Sergentson** (Lincs), **Sargeantson/Sarjeantson** (WRYorks) and **Sergeantson** (Staffs/ERYorks) are all scarce or very scarce. *John Sergeant (born 1944), known both as a journalist and as a plucky aspiring ballroom dancer, is the son of a missionary father and a mother of Russian origin.*

Sarson, *see* **Sayer**.

Satterl(e)y/Saturley P Place-name *Satterleigh* in Devon OE 'robbers' wood/clearing'. Cottle suggests that the spelling of the variant **Saturley** might be influenced by *Saturday*. **Satterley** and **Satterly** are Devon surnames; **Saturley**, scarce, belongs to Somerset.

Satterthwaite P Place-name in Lancs, ON 'shieling pasture'.

Saturley, see **Satterley**.

Saul F/T/P From the Hebrew first-name *Shaul* ('asked for [child]'), borne by a King of Israel and by St Paul at the time when he was persecuting Christians, and rarely used by mediaeval Christians as a first-name; or a dweller at a sallow/willow wood OE; or from a place-name in Gloucs with the same meaning; or derived from the OF word *salle* ('room, chamber'). See also **Sewell**.

Sault, see **Salt**.

Saun(d)by P Place-name *Saundby* in Notts ON 'farm with sandy soil'. A scarce Lincs surname in either spelling.

Saunders(on), see **Alexander**.

Sauter, see **Soutar**.

Savagar, see **Savager**.

Savage N Nickname for a wild, savage person (originally 'of the woods') OF. A widespread surname, strongest in Lancs.

Savager/Savagar/Savaker/Saveker/ Savigar P From one of several places called *Saint-Vigor* in Normandy, named after *St Vigor*, a sixth-century Bishop of Bayeux (to whom a church in Stratton-on-the-Fosse, Somerset, is dedicated). **Savagar**, **Savaker**, **Saveker** and **Savigar**, all rare, are found in Herefords; **Savager** is sparsely scattered around central and southern England and South Wales.

Savin(s), see **Saban**.

Sawbridge P/F Place-name in Warwicks OE 'bridge by the sallows/willows'; or from an OE first-name meaning 'sea/victory-bright' (one man so-named is commemorated in *Sawbridgeworth*, Herts). Manly a Leics surname.

Sawdon P Place-name in NRYorks OE 'sallow/willow valley'. An ERYorks and NRYorks surname.

Sawer, see **Sawyer**.

Sawford, see **Salford**.

Sawyer O Occupational term for a man who sawed wood OE. Cottle believes that the variant **Sawer** can alternatively be derived from an occupational term describing a sower of seed OE, though he admits that 'this seasonal job leaves the rest of his working year unaccounted for'. Readily confused with/a variant of **Sayer**. Compare **Sewer**. **Sawyer** is widely scattered throughout England; **Sawer** is mostly found in Suffolk.

Saxby P/N Place-name in Leics and Lincs (two such) ON '*Saksi*'s settlement'; or a nickname from OF for someone quick to take offence or to start a quarrel (literally 'draw-sword'), the ERYorks surname **Shakesby** being a variant with this same meaning. This nickname origin probably accounts for the significant presence of **Saxby** in Kent, where the settlement known as *Saxby's Hill* in Brenchley is almost certainly named after a person, not vice versa.

Saxon F From the mediaeval first-name *Saxon*, originally used for a person from Saxony. The Saxons were literally 'people of the *seax* (dagger/short-sword)'. Compare **Sayce**. A Lancs surname. Readily confused with/a variant of **Saxton** or **Sexton**.

Saxton P Place-name in Cambs, WRYorks OE 'Saxons' farm'. Chiefly a WRYorks name. Readily confused with/a variant of **Saxon** or **Sexton**.

Say(e) O/P Occupational term for a maker or seller of fine cloth known as *say* OF; or from the place-name *Sai* or *Say* in Orne OF (from a Gaulish first-name *Saius*). A Somerset surname.

Sayce P Term for a *Saxon*, Englishman OW (what the Scots call *Sassenach*). Compare **Saxon**, **Saxton**. Most commonly found in Salop.

Saycell, see **Cecil**.

Saye, see **Say**.

Sayer(s)/Saer/Sear(s)/Seare(s) F/O From a ME first-name *Saher/Seir* ('?victory-army') – see also **Sugar**; or an occupational term for an assayer (of metals), a food-taster OF, a maker of fine cloth known as *say* OF (see **Say**), or a reciter, professional story-teller, 'sayer' OE. **Sayer** can readily be confused with, or be a variant of, **Sawyer**. **Sarson** could in principle be 'son of **Sayer**' (or even **Sara**), but on taking a close look at a family of this name long-settled in Shackerstone, Leics, W. G. Hoskins notes that they were originally **Sarazins** (Roger **Sara**zin having been mentioned in a Pipe Roll dated 1203) or **Le Sarazin**, and that the surname, almost certainly a nickname meaning 'the saracen', was first recorded as **Sarson** in a Subsidy List of 1571. When the Crusaders returned home, several of them brought back captured Saracens (Syrian or Arab nomads) as servants. **Sayer** is a widespread surname, strongest in East Anglia; **Saer** is chiefly found in Carmarthenshire, Wales, **Sayers** in Sussex, **Sear** in Bucks, **Sears** in Kent, **Seare** (very scarce) in Surrey and **Seares** in Middx. *The company which made Sarson's vinegar ('Don't say vinegar… say Sarson's') was founded in 1794 by Thomas Sarson.*

Saysell, *see* **Cecil**.

Saywell, *see* **Sewell**.

Scaife N   Nickname for an awkward, crooked, wild person ON. A surname of the north of England, strongest in WRYorks.

Scale(s), *see* **Scholes**.

Scammell ?N/T/F   A surname of uncertain meaning; perhaps a nickname for a lean, scraggy person ME, a dweller at a *shambles* OE (a bench, stall, hence a meat/fish-market), or from a ME first-name *Skammel* ('short'). Yet for all their ON appearance, both **Scammel** (most common in Hants) and **Scammell** (chiefly found in Wilts) are surnames of the south of England.

Scandrett ?F   A distinctive yet mysterious Herefords/Warwicks surname, of uncertain origin. Cottle muses: 'Is it conceivably a diminutive of **Alexander**?'.

Scanlan/Scanlon/Scannell F Irish: Anglicized form of Gaelic **O'** [descendant of]

Scannail ('contention'). The will of a mariner known as 'John **Scanlan**, alias **Scantlin**', was proved in London in 1750. *Hugh Parr Scanlon, Lord Scanlon of Davyhulme (1913–2004), trade union leader, was born in Melbourne, Australia, but was mainly raised back in Manchester after his father had died.*

Scannell, *see* **Scanlan**.

Scarborough P   Place-name in NRYorks ON '*Skarthi*'s fortress'. Mainly found in Lincs and Yorks.

Scarf(e)/Scarff(e) N   Nickname for a person bearing some resemblance to a cormorant ON, or from an ON byname *Scarfi*, with the same meaning. **Scarf** and **Scarfe** are surnames of East Anglia and WRYorks; **Scarff** is strongest in Suffolk, and **Scarffe** in the Isle of Man. *The cartoonist and illustrator Gerald Scarfe was born in St John's Wood, London, in 1936.*

Scargill P   Place-name in NRYorks ON 'valley/ravine with mergansers (a species of diving duck)'. *Some years ago a newspaper cheekily proposed that the fiery trade union leader Arthur Scargill (born in 1938 in Worsbrough Dale, near Barnsley, WRYorks) might be distantly related to his arch-enemy Margaret Thatcher, former Prime Minister.*

Scarisbrick P   Place-name in Lancs, ON '*Skar*'s hill/slope'.

Scarlet(t) O/N   Occupational term for one who dyed or sold bright scarlet cloth OF, or who wore colourful clothes. **Scarlett** is the family name of the Barons Abinger.

Scarth P   Place-names: *Scarth Hill*, Lancs; *Ayton Scarth*, NRYorks ON; various other place-names include such an element, meaning 'gap, pass, cleft'; or from an ON byname with the same meaning (that is, 'hare lipped'). Chiefly a WRYorks surname, though the **Scarth** surname as found in the Orkney Islands is from *Scarth* in the Orcadian parish of Firth.

Scatliff(e) P   Place-names *Scaitcliffe* in Lancs OF and OE 'slate cliff'. A scarce Lincs surname in either spelling.

Scattergood N Nickname for one who scattered his goods/property widely ME and OE – that is, a prodigal or a philanthropist. Mainly a Midlands surname, strongest in Warwicks.

Schofield/Scholfield T/P Dweller at a hut in a field ON and OE (compare **Scholes**), or from a minor place-name with the same meaning. Principally a Lancs surname (but also with a presence in WRYorks) in either spelling.

Scholar T/O Dweller at a shieling with a hut ON (compare **Scholes**); or a scholar, one who could read and write ME (compare **Scully**). Given that **Scholar** is a surname mainly found in Cornwall, far from from ON influence, the latter origin will probably be the more usual one. **Scoular** and **Scouler** are Scottish variants.

Scholes/Scales T/P Dweller in a primitive hut ON, or from one of a number of places called *Scholes* or *Scales*, with the same meaning. *Scholes* is a Lancs surname; *Scales* can be found in both the north of England and in East Anglia. *Paul Scholes, Manchester United and England footballer, was born in Salford, Lancs, in 1974.*

Scholfield, *see* **Schofield**.

Scob(b)ie P Lost place-name in Perthshire, Scotland, Gaelic 'thorny place'. Readily confused with/a variant of **Scoby**.

Scoby P A NRYorks surname, presumably derived from a lost ON farm-name. Readily confused with/a variant of **Scobie**.

Score, *see* **Scorer**.

Scorer O/P Occupational term for a person who kept accounts ON, or who worked as a spy OF. Given the fact that this scarce surname is chiefly found in Co Durham, Cottle's reference to a place called *Score*, near Ilfracombe in Devon OE '?steep hillside', is probably of little relevance, though **Score** itself is a Dorset surname.

Scothorne/Scothern/Scottorn P Place-name *Scothern* in Lincs OE 'the Scots' thorn-tree'. Chiefly a Notts surname in all spellings. Readily confused with/a variant of **Scotton**.

Scotland P/F A person from *Scotland* (the second element of which is OE) – see **Scott**; or, more narrowly, from *Scotland(well)*, Kinross-shire, an important spring; or from a Norman first-name *Escotland*. Mainly found in central Scotland, the greatest concentration being in Kinross.

Scott P A person from *Scotland* (*see also* **Scotland**). The Scots came from Ireland, and are represented by the Highlanders and Hebrideans of Scotland, the Lowlanders being mostly of English stock, while the Orcadians and Shetlanders are Norse in origin. The name *Scot* is mysterious – Sir John Rhys linked it with Welsh *ysgwthr* ('cutting/carving') and made it mean 'tattooed' (as if the Picts were the 'pictured/tattooed' people). In south Scotland the surname **Scott** may be applied to a person of Gaelic origin; in northern England it will just mean 'from over the Border'. Those called **Scott** in the east of England, in Devon and elsewhere, may originally have been settlers from the far north, or have been so-called thanks to a personal name of a nickname type. See also **Scutt**. **Scott** is the family name of the Earls of Eldon.

Scotton P Place-name in Lincs, NRYorks and WRYorks OE 'Scots' farm'. Mainly found in the East Midlands, strongest in Leics. Readily confused with/a variant of **Scothorne**.

Scottorn, *see* **Scothorne**.

Scoular/Scouler, *see* **Scholar**.

Scrafield P Place-name in Lincs, ON and OE 'field near a landslide/scree'. Sparsely scattered throughout the East Midlands and South Yorks.

Scragg N Nickname for a lean, scraggy person ME. Most common in Chesh, Lancs and Staffs.

Scrimgeo(u)r/Scrimger/Scrimshaw/ Scrimshire/Scrymgeo(u)r/Skrimshire O Occupational term for a fencing-master OF (compare *skirmisher*). Such men were classed with rogues, vagabonds and actors, and forbidden to keep schools in the City of London, though one family named **Scrimgeour** or **Scrymgeour** held the title of hereditary standard-bearers of Scotland. **Scrimgeor** is a Perthshire surname; **Scrimgeour** belongs principally to both Angus and Perthshire, **Scrimshaw** to Lincs and Notts, **Scrimshire** to Lincs and **Scrymgeo(u)r** (very rare) to Angus. **Skrimshire** is scarce and scattered. **Scrymgeour-Wedderburn** is the family name of the Earls of Dundee.

Scrine T Dweller near a shrine OE *scrin*. A scarce Wilts surname.

Scriven(er)/Scrivenor O Occupational term for a writer, copier, scribe, clerk OF. The Worshipful Company of Scriveners, known to have been active since the fourteenth century, still arranges for apprentices to be placed with masters within the City of London to learn their trade. **Scriven** is mainly found in Dorset and Staffs, **Scrivener** in eastern England, and **Scrivenor** in Essex. *The family which eventually founded the American publishing house of Scribner can trace its origins back to Benjamin Scrivener, a seventeenth-century immigrant to Connecticut; the name was changed to Scribner in the second half of the following century, and the company itself was established in 1846.*

Scrut(t)on P Place-name *Scruton* in NRYorks ON and OE '*Skurfa*'s farm'.

Scrymgeo(u)r, *see* Scrimgeor.

Scudamore/Skidmore P From an unidentified place OE 'dung/shit moor'. One **Scudamore** family gave its name to *Upton Scudamore*, Wilts. '**Scudamore**... is **not** "shield of love" OF *escu d'amour* – despite the family motto *scuto amoris divini*' (Cottle). **Scudamore** has an uneven presence, being found along the Severn Valley, but also in south-east and in north-west England; **Skidmore** is particularly strong in Staffs.

Scull N/F Nickname for a bald-headed man ME, the shape of whose skull was thus much in evidence. Cottle suggests that the origin

may alternatively be an ON first-name *Skúli* ('protector/King'), as found in the place-name *Sculcoates*, ERYorks, but admits that the surname's significant presence in Bristol and elsewhere in the West Country does not suggest an ON origin.

Scullion O Occupational term for a lowly kitchen servant OF. Most common in Co Durham and Lanarkshire.

Scully F Irish: Anglicized form of Gaelic O' [descendant of] *Scolaidhe* ('scholar'). Compare **Scholar**.

Sculthorp(e) P Place-name *Sculthorpe*, Norfolk ON '*Skúli*'s settlement'. **Sculthorp** is a Northants surname; **Sculthorpe** is most commonly found in the East Midlands and in South Yorks.

Scutt O/N Occupational term for a scout, spy OF; or a nickname for a swift runner ME ('scut/tail of the hare'). Or a variant of **Scott**? A Sussex surname.

Seaborn(e)/Seabourn(e) F From an OE first-name meaning 'sea warrior'.

Seabridge, *see* Seabright.

Seabright F From an OE first-name meaning 'sea/victory-bright'. **Seabright** is sparsely scattered throughout England, Wales and Scotland. **Seabridge** is a scarce Staffs variant.

Seacole A surname of unknown origin and meaning, which has had something of a presence in Oxon and elsewhere over the centuries, masquerading as: **Secall**, **Seccull**, **Sechol(l)**, **Secole** and **Seekell**. Such surnames are rarely what they seem, and a division into 'Sea' and 'cole' will probably be of little help. Guesswork suggests that a maker of satchells or sickles might be involved, but a first-name could be the source, and **Seacole** doesn't sound unlike the German first-name/surname **Siegel**; even a connexion with **Sagar/Sager/Seager/Seeger** might not be out of the question? *The best-known person to bear the surname Seacole acquired it by marriage: Mary Jane Grant (1805–1881) was born in Kingston, Jamaica, the daughter of a Scottish soldier and the* *mixed-race proprietress of a boarding house for military personnel. In 1836 Mary Jane married one of her mother's resident guests, Edwin Horatio Hamilton Seacole, about whom little is known except that he was baptized in 1803 in Prittlewell, Essex, the son of Thomas and Ann Seacole, and that he is said to have been a godson of Lord Nelson. Edwin died soon after the wedding, and eventually Mary, under her new surname of Seacole, achieved great fame thanks to the nursing skills she displayed during the Crimean War and elsewhere. In his book* Suffolk (Massachusetts) *surnames (third edition, 1861), N. I. Bowditch, never one to let an interesting surname go by, says: 'Mrs Seacole was popular among the soldiers at the siege of Sebastopol; and among the London bankrupts of 1857 appears the same name; it is to be hoped, not of the same person'.*

Seacombe P Place-name in Chesh OE 'valley by the sea'. Mainly found in Lancs. Readily confused with **Secombe**.

Seaford P Place-name in Sussex OE 'ford by the sea'.

Seager, *see* Sagar.

Seagrave/Seagrief/Seagrove P Place-name *Seagrave* in Leics OE 'grove/ditch at the sheepfold/pit'. **Seagrave** is most common in Notts and surrounding counties; **Seagrief**, very rare, is found only in Middx and Essex, while **Seagrove** is widely scattered throughout England. *The English actress Jennifer Ann ('Jenny') Seagrove was born in 1957 in Kuala Lumpur, Malaysia; she moved to England at the age of nine to attend the Bristol Old Vic Theatre School.*

Seagrim F From an ON first-name meaning 'sea guardian'. A very scarce Kent/Somerset surname.

Seagrove, *see* Seagrave.

Seal(e)(s) T/P/O/N Dweller by a sallow/willow tree OE (compare **Sale**, **Sallows**), or from a place-name such as *Seal* in Kent or *Seale* in Surrey OE 'the hall'; or an occupational term for a maker of seals OF or of saddles OF; or a nickname for a person as large or clumsy as a seal, the mammal OE. The *-e* of **Seale** is

evidence of the use of a dative following a lost preposition. See also **Selman** and **Zeal**.

Sealey/Seal(l)y/Seeley/Selley N Nickname for a happy, blessed person OE (whence, later, by the belittling ways of speech, 'innocent, simple', and at length 'silly'). See also **Selman**. **Seely** is the family name of the Barons Mottistone and the Barons Sherwood.

Seaman(s)/Seamons/Semmence/Semmens/Semmons O/F Occupational term for a seaman OE (though the word could mean also 'Viking, pirate'); or from an OE first-name *Soemann*, with the same meaning. **Semmence** (Norfolk), **Semmens** and **Semmons** (West Country), all scarce, can alternatively be variants derived from **Simon**. **Seaman** is strong in East Anglia, with its ancient sea ports; **Seamons** is a Bucks surname. *David Seaman, who kept goal for the England soccer team on 75 occasions, was born in 1963 in Rotherham, WRYorks.*

Seamer P/F/O There are two places called *Seamer* in NRYorks OE 'lake-lake' (tautologically), and *Semer* in Suffolk OE 'sea mere', though the surname occurs mainly in Sussex; or from an OE first-name meaning 'sea-famous', or an occupational term for a seamer, tailor OE (compare **Simister**).

Seamons, *see* Seaman.

Sear(s)/Seare(s), *see* Sayer.

Searl(e)(s)/Serle/Serrell F From a Germanic first-name, Normanized as *Serlo* (connected with *armour* – hence 'defender'?).

Seath T Dweller near a pit, well, pool OE. Almost exclusively restricted to Kent and to Fifeshire, Scotland.

Seaton P Place-name *Seaton* in various counties, most being OE 'place by the sea'; but the two *Seaton*s in ERYorks are 'place by a lake' and *Seaton* in Rutland is OE '?Saega's place'. *Seaton* in East Lothian, Scotland, was long the home of the **De Say** family, from *Say* in Indre. The exact origin of the surname borne by the powerful Scottish family of **Seton**, once Earls of Eglinton and Winton, has never satisfactorily been determined.

Seaver(s)/Sever(s) F From a female OE first-name meaning 'sea voyage'. **Seavers** is strongest in WRYorks, **Sever** in Lancs and **Severs** in NRYorks.

Seaward, *see* **Seward**.

Sebastian F From the first-name *Sebastian*, from the Latin *Sebastianus* ('man from *Sebastia*'). Very scarce as a surname in the British Isles, though the diminutives **Basten**, **Bastian**, **Bastien** and **Basti(o)n** are found in Devon and elsewhere.

Seccombe, *see* **Secombe**.

Secker, *see* **Sacker**.

Sec(c)ombe P There are two places named *Seccombe* in Devon, both OE '*Secca*'s valley'. Readily confused with **Seacombe**. Devon/Cornwall surnames in either spelling, though **Secombe** has a limited presence in Northd. *Sir Harry Donald Secombe (1921–2001), born in Swansea, South Wales, achieved fame as a comedian, singer and generally cheerful chap.*

Secrett N Nickname for a discreet person, one who could be trusted to keep secrets OF. A very scarce East Anglian surname.

Seddon ?P Apparently from a place-name (unidentified); if so, the the second element is probably OE 'hill', while the first could be OE 'house, dwelling, seat' or ON 'shieling, hill pasture'. Mainly a Lancs surname. *Richard Seddon (1845–1906), Prime Minister of New Zealand, was born in St Helens, Lancs.*

Sedgebeer P There is a place-name *Sedgeberrow* in Worcs OE '?*Secg*'s grove', but this very scarce surname belongs to Somerset, which is home to *Sedgemoor*, and perhaps once contained a place named in the *Sedgeberrow* mould? See **Sedgemore**.

Sedgemore/Sedgemoor P From *Sedgemoor*, Somerset OE 'moor where sedge grows'. **Sedgemore** is a very scarce Devon surname; **Sedgemoor**, equally scarce, is

found only in Cornwall and in Glamorgan, South Wales. See also **Sedgebeer**.

Sedgewick, *see* **Sedgwick**.

Sedgley P Place-name in Staffs OE '*Secg*'s wood/clearing'.

Sedgman O Occupational term for a thatcher with reeds OE literally 'sedge man'. A Cornish surname.

Sedg(e)wick(e)/Sidg(e)wick P Place-name *Sedgwick* in Westmd ON and OE '*Sigg(e)*'s dairy-farm'. These are North Country surnames, so any connexion with *Sedgewick* in Sussex OE 'dairy-farm in the sedge/reeds/rushes' is unlikely.

Seed(s) O/F Occupational term for a dealer in seeds OE, or from a short form of an OE first-name beginning with *Sidu-* ('custom, morality, purity'). **Seed** is strongest in Lancs; **Seeds**, much scarcer, has a presence in the same county, but also in Derbys.

Seedall, *see* **Siddall**.

Seeds, *see* **Seed**.

Seeger, *see* **Sagar**.

Seel, *see* **Seal**.

Seeley, *see* **Sealey**.

Sefton P Place-name in Lancs ON and OE 'place in the sedge/rushes', and a Lancs surname.

Segrave, *see* **Seagrave**.

Selby P Place-name in WRYorks ON 'sallow/willow farm'. A surname of the English North and Midlands, but also found in the South-East.

Selden/Seldon P These two surnames, the first of which can be found in both Devon and Sussex, while the second belongs almost exclusively to Devon, might look like variants of the same name, but each might have a different origin. Hanks and Hodges refer to *Selden Farm* in Patching, Sussex OE '?willow valley', but there is also a place called *Seldon* in Devon OE 'house/hall hill'. *John Selden (1584–1654), lawyer* *and historical scholar, was born in West Tar-ring, Sussex.*

Selkirk P Place-name in the Scottish Borders ME 'hall church'. *Alexander Selkirk or Selcraig (1676–1721), the Scottish sailor whose experiences as a castaway on the island of Juan Fernandez acted as a model for Daniel Defoe's Robinson Crusoe, was born in Largo, Fife.*

Sell(s) T/O Dweller in a primitive shelter/hut of the sort occupied either by animals or by the man who tended them OE. **Sell** is mainly found in Middx and Essex; **Sells** is also a surname of south-east England. See also **Sellar**.

Sellar(s)/Seller(s)/Sillars O Occupational term for a cellarer, storeman, purveyor OF; or for a saddler OF; or for a dealer, hawker OE (that is, a man who would *sell* things). Or a variant of **Sell**. **Zeller**, with the initial *S*-voiced, is a very rare variant, sparsely scattered. *The comedian Peter Sellers, whose real name was Richard Henry Sellers (1925–1980), was born in Portsmouth, Hants, the son of William Sellers and his wife Agnes (Peg) Marks, who came from a Jewish family and was the great-granddaughter of the famous pugilist, Daniel Mendoza.*

Selleck, *see* **Sellick**.

Seller(s), *see* **Sellar**.

Selley, *see* **Sealey**.

Sellick/Selleck P Place-name *Sellake* in Devon OE '?sluggish stream'. The first recorded reference to a place called *Sellick* in the same county dates from only the early seventeenth century. There is also a place in Herefords called *Sellack* ow 'Saint *Suluc*'s church'. **Sellick** and **Selleck** could readily be confused with the German/Jewish surname **Selig** and its variants. Both **Sellick** and **Selleck** are principally Devon surnames, though the former can also be found elsewhere in the West Country and in counties bordering the Severn Valley. *Thomas William ('Tom') Selleck, the American actor best known for his starring role in the long-running television show Magnum P.I., was born in 1945 in Detroit, Michigan, USA, to a Ukrainian family.*

Sellman, *see* **Selman**.

Sells, *see* **Sell**.

Sellwood, *see* **Selwood**.

Sel(l)man/Sillman N/O Nickname for a blessed/happy person OE; or 'servant of **Seal/Sealey**'. **Selman** is most common in Gloucs and Wilts; **Sellman** is sparsely scattered throughout England; **Sillman** (scarce) is mainly found in Oxon.

Selth N Nickname for a prosperous, happy person OE. A scarce Kent/Surrey surname.

Selway, *see* **Salway**.

Selwin/Selwyn F/N From one of two ME first-names: *Seluein* ('[of the] woods', as in 'sylvan'); *Selewyne* ('hall-friend'); or possibly a nickname for a wild, savage person, a man of the woods. Principally a Gloucs surname in either spelling. *George Augustus Selwyn (1809–1878), Bishop of New Zealand and of Lichfield, after whom Selwyn College, Cambridge, was named, was born in Hampstead, North London.*

Sel(l)wood P *Selwood* is the name of a wood and a parish in Somerset OE 'sallow/willow wood'. Principally a surname of South-West England.

Selwyn, *see* **Selwin**.

Semmence/Semmens/Semmons, *see* **Seaman**.

Semper/Simper P Place-name *Saint-Pierre* (St Peter) in France OF. **Semper** is a Lincs surname; **Simper** is strongest in Wilts.

Semple/Sample P/N Place-names *Saint-Paul* or *Saint-Pol* (St Paul Aurelian) in northern France OF; or a nickname for a simple, modest person OF. **Semple** is principally a Scottish surname, strongest in Lanarkshire; **Sample** belongs to the north-east of England.

Sendal(l) O/N Occupational term for a producer or wearer of fine silken cloth OF *sendal*. **Sendal** is a very scarce scattered surname; **Sendall** is strongest in Norfolk. Readily confused with/a variant of **Sandal** or **Sandell**.

Senescall/Sensicle O/N Occupational term for an official or major-domo in charge of a large household OF (from Germanic), or a nickname for a person who behaved in an officious manner. The term *seneschal* was used for many years to describe a steward in charge of a manor. **Senescall** and **Sensicle** are rare Lincs surnames; related surnames with a different spelling are scarcer still.

Senhouse P From a place-name in Cumbd, now called *Hallsenna*, but formerly (e.g. in 1225) *Sevenhoues* OE and ON 'seven hills'. A very scarce Cumbd surname. One Cumbd family named **Senhouse** were prominent land holders and public officials in Barbados.

Senior O/N Occupational term for a lord (of the manor, etc.) OF; or a nickname for one who behaved as if he had such status, or for the elder of two men bearing the same first-name (in contradistinction to 'junior'). A common WRYorks surname, though it can be found throughout northern England.

Sennett/Sennitt, *see* Sinnett.

Sensicle, *see* Senescall.

Sergeant(son)/Sergent(son)/ Serjeant(son)/Serjent, *see* Sargant.

Serle/Serrell, *see* Searl.

Service/Servis O Occupational term for a brewer or ale-seller OF *cervoise*. **Service** is strongest in Lanarkshire, Scotland; **Servis**, very scarce, is widely scattered throughout England and Scotland.

Sessions P Place-name *Soissons*, a City in Aisne, northern France OF, named after a Gaulish tribe, known in Latin as the *Suessiones*. Strongest from Middx westward towards Gloucs. *John Sessions, the Scottish actor and comedian, was born John Gibb Marshall in 1953 in Largs, North Ayrshire.*

Setchfield P There is a place called *Secqueville-en-Bassin* in Calvados, France OF 'dry domain', but the surname is strongest in Cambs, and could be based upon a lost settlement in that county. Cottle says that 'there may be some falling-together with **Sedgefield**' – but that is a practically non-existent surname…

Seton, *see* Seaton.

Settatree T Dweller near a planted tree OE. An exceptionally scarce Kent surname.

Settle P Place-name in WRYorks OE 'seat, abode, eminence'. A Lancs/WRYorks surname.

Sevenoaks P Place-name in Kent OE 'seven oak trees'; Cottle assumes that the number seven in this case must have folklore significance. A scarce Kent surname.

Sever(s), *see* Seaver.

Sevier O Occupational term for a sieve-maker OE. A scarce surname, found mainly in Hants and Somerset.

Sewall, *see* Sewell.

Seward/Seaward/Sewart F/O From one of two ME first-names, *Siward* or *Seward* (OE *Sigeweard* and *Soeweard*), meaning 'sea/victory [compare **Sewell**]-guard', which eventually became intertwined; or an occupational term for a swineherd (sowherd) OE. Irish: Anglicized form of Gaelic O' [descendant of] **Suaird/Suairt**.

Sewart, *see* Seward.

Sewell/Saywell/Sewall F/P/N From the ME first-names *Siwal(d)* and *Sewal(d)* (OE *Sigeweald* and *Soeweald*), meaning 'sea/victory [compare **Seward**]-ruler'. But where individuals have been referred to as *de Sewell*, the origin is a place-name such as *Sewell* (Beds), *Sowell* (Devon), *Showell* (Oxon), *Seawell* and *Sywell* (Northants), all of which are OE 'seven springs'. Cottle suggests that the proverb 'Say Well is good, but Do Well is better' might have resulted in an associated nickname. **Sewell** is very widespread; **Saywell** is strongest in Kent and Notts; **Sewall**, scarce, can be found in places as far apart as south-east England and Lancs. A One-Name Society dedicated to the study of **Sewell** and its several variants, including **Saul**, has carried out intensive and extensive research on these and a number of related surnames. *Henry Sewell (1807–1879), first Prime Minister of New Zealand, was born in Newport, Isle of Wight, son of Thomas Sewell, steward of the Island, and Jane (née Edwards); he arrived in New Zealand in 1853, aboard the* Minerva.

Sexton O/F   Occupational term for a churchwarden OF (a corrupted form of *sacristan*). 'His demotion to grave-digger is comparatively modern' (Cottle). Irish: Anglicized form of Gaelic **O'** [descendant of] **Seastnain** ('?bodyguard/defender'). Readily confused with/a variant of **Saxon** or **Saxton**. Strongest in East Anglia and south-east England.

Seymour/Seymo(u)re P   Place-name *Saint-Maur-des-Fossés* in Seine, France, which has a church dedicated to this saint OF; or from one of two places called *Seamer* in NRYorks OE 'sea/lake-lake'. **Seymour** is the family name of the Dukes of Somerset and of the Marquesses of Hertford (who came from *Saint-Maur-des-Fossés* or from *Saint-Maur-sur-Loire* in Touraine).

Shacklady N   Probably a nickname for a libertine ME, one well able to 'shake' a lady, referring especially to someone who succeeded in making love to a woman of higher rank than himself (compare **Toplady**). A Lancs surname.

Shackleton P   Reaney and others have maintained that the origin here is a place named *Scackleton* in NRYorks, but George Redmonds has shown that the source is *Shackelton* in Wadsworth, originally *Shackletonstall* (compare *Heptonstall, Saltonstall*), and the surname has sometimes appeared in this longer version. The exact meaning of the 'Shackle' element in this place-name has been a matter of some debate. *The Antarctic explorer Ernest Shackleton (1874–1922), born at Kilkea House, Co Kildare, came from a prominent Irish Quaker family with its roots in Yorks.*

Shacklock O/N   Occupational term for a gaoler/jailer ME *shaklock* ('fetter'), or literally a 'shaker of locks'; Reaney considers that it might alternatively be a nickname

for a person 'with a habit (not unknown today) of shaking back his long hair'. The surname has had a long and varied history: Reaney's earliest reference is to Roger and Richard **Schakeloc**, mentioned in a Pipe Roll for Gloucs in 1187, followed by twelfth- and thirteenth-century examples from Lancs, Staffs and Yorks. Yet the surname had a presence in East Anglia, too: a Subsidy Return for Suffolk in 1327 mentions a William and Christopher **Schakeloc**, living in Ipswich, and a similar return for 1524 features a John **Shaklokke** of Gorleston; Thomas **Shacklowe** of Rockland appears in a late sixteenth-century Muster Return for Norfolk; the will of George **Shakeloke** of Fordham was proved in the Norfolk Archdeaconry Court in 1546, and a Norfolk land transaction dated 1 April 1536 names John **Shakelok** of 'Frikby'. By the late sixteenth century, parish register entries would seem to indicate that such a surname was then most in evidence in Lancs (though also found in limited numbers in Co Durham, Kent, Lincs, London, Northd, Notts and Yorks), but by the late nineteenth century **Shacklock** was very much a Notts surname, with something of a presence also in Derbys, Lancs and WRYorks.

Shadbolt, *see* **Shotbolt**.

Shade T/N   Dweller near a boundary OE (compare the word '*watershed*'); or a nickname for a thin man ME. Widely scattered thoughout southern England and southern Scotland.

Shadwell P   Place-name in various counties, including Middx OE 'shallow stream' and Norfolk/WRYorks OE 'boundary stream'. **Shatwell** is a mildly unfortunate Chesh variant. *Thomas Shadwell (c.1640–1692), a poet and playwright of debatable talent, was born in Norfolk, though his paternal grandfather George Shadwell was of Enville, Staffs.*

Shafto(e) P   Place-name in Northd OE 'boundary-post ridge'. *Robert (Bobby) Shafto/Shaftoe (1732–1797), a landowner and politician born at Whitworth, near Spennymoor in Co Durham, is probably the man* *immortalized in the well-known folk song and nursery rhyme, 'Bobby Shafto's gone to sea...'.*

Shakesby, *see* Saxby.

Shakeshaft N Nickname from OE for a person known for publicly brandishing a lance/spear, or – less gallantly – an intimate part of his anatomy. Compare **Shakespeare**. A Chesh/Lancs surname.

Shakespear(e) N Nickname for a person quick to take up arms OE or, in the delightfully euphemistic words of Hanks and Hodges, 'a bawdy name for an exhibitionist'. Compare **Shakeshaft**. *William Shakespeare (1564–1616) was born in Stratford-upon-Avon, Warwicks, and the surname can still be found predominantly in that and neighbouring counties. Robert Greene (died 1592), wishing to be nasty at a greater playwright's expense, parodied the name as 'Shake-scene'.*

Shallcross/Shawcross P Place-name *Shallcross* in Derbys OE 'cross with a shackle/fetter attached'. A gravestone in the churchyard of Wirksworth, Derbys, commemorates the life and good qualities of Philip **Shullcross**, 'once an eminent Quill-driver to the Attorneys in the town', who had 'an invincible attachment to dogs and cats' and who died on 17 November 1787.

Shallish, *see* Challis.

Shank(s) N Nickname for a person with long or ungainly legs OE. Compare **Cruikshank**, **Sheepshanks**. Shank is a scattered surname; **Shanks** belongs to north-east England and to Scotland.

Shanklin P Place-name in the Isle of Wight OE 'hill with a waterfall', though the surname, very scarce, has a presence in Pembrokeshire, Wales.

Shanks, *see* Shank.

Shanl(e)y F Irish: Anglicized form of the Gaelic first-name *Seanlaoch* ('old hero').

Shapcott T Dweller by a sheep shed/shelter OE. The surname is mostly found in Devon, though the earliest recorded reference to a place called *Shapcott* (later *Shapcott Barton*) in Knowstone in that county dates only from the sixteenth century.

Shapland, *see* Shopland.

Shapley P Place-name in Devon OE 'sheep clearing'; a Devon surname.

Shardlow P Place-name in Derbys OE 'cleft/notched mound'. The surname is mainly found in Derbys and surrounding counties.

Sharman, *see* Shearer.

Sharp(e) N Nickname for a sharp, keen, smart, quick individual OE; the *-e* of **Sharpe** could indicate a weak adjective after a lost definite article. Strongest in WRYorks in both spellings.

Sharples(s) P Place-name *Sharples*, Lancs. Probably OE 'steep pasture'. *Ena Sharples was the name of fictional character, well known as something of a battleaxe, who was featured in the long-running Manchester-based TV soap opera,* Coronation Street, *from 1960 to 1980.*

Sharrad, *see* Sherrad.

Sharwood, *see* Sherwood.

Shatwell, *see* Shadwell.

Shave P Place-name in Dorset and Somerset OE 'at the wood/grove'. Mainly found in southern England, strongest in Hants.

Shaw T/F Dweller by a copse, thicket, small wood OE. Irish and Scots: Anglicized form of various surnames derived from the Gaelic first-name *Sithech* ('wolf'). Family-name of the Barons Craigmyle. *The male-line ancestry of the writer George Bernard Shaw (1856–1950) can be traced back to William Shaw, a Protestant who had fought with William III's army in Ireland.*

Shawcross, *see* Shallcross.

Shea/Shee F Irish: Anglicized form of Gaelic O' [descendant of] **Seaghdha** ('fortunate').

Shean(e), *see* Sheen.

Shear(s)/Sheer N Nickname for a bright/beautiful person, or one with fair hair OE. Cottle, having impishly pointed out that

'Sheer is now applied mainly to silk stockings', toys with other possible meanings for these surnames: a shear-/scissor-maker OE; dweller at the division/boundary OE; dweller in the shire OE. Readily confused with/a variant of **Shere**.

Sheard/Sherd T Dweller by a gap, cutting, cleft between hills OE. Chiefly a WRYorks surname, though George Redmonds believes that it originated outside Yorks, possibly in Chesh.

Shearer/Sharman/Shearman/Sherman O Occupational term for a sheepshearer, or for one who cut superfluous nap off woollen cloth OE. **Shearer** is mainly a Scottish surname; **Sharman** and **Shearman** are to be found scattered throughout England, as is **Sherman**, though it can often appear as a respelt German-Jewish surname. *The Hollywood actress (Edith) Norma Shearer (1902–1983) was the granddaughter of James Shearer, born in Caithness, Scotland, in 1822, who emigrated to Montreal, Canada, in 1843 and founded a lumber company… Alan Shearer, who played soccer for Southampton, Blackburn Rovers and Newcastle United and captained the England team, was born in Newcastle-upon-Tyne in 1970… John and Edmund Sherman, sons of an Essex farmer, emigrated to North America in the 1630s; Roger Sherman (1722–1793), who signed the Declaration of Independence, was a descendant of John; William Tecumseh Sherman (1820–1891), the Civil War general who famously marched from Atlanta to the sea (and after whom the Sherman tank was named), was a descendant of Edmund.*

Sheargold, *see* **Shergold**.

Shearman, *see* **Shearer**.

Shearn T Dweller at a place known for its mud, filth, dung OE *scearn*, found as the first element in various place-names. Chiefly a Somerset surname.

Sheather O Occupational term for a maker of sword-sheaths OE plus an *-er* suffix. A scarce surname found mainly in Sussex.

Shebbeare P Place-name *Shebbear* in Devon OE 'grove where poles/shafts could

be got'. A very scarce surname, rare even in Devon itself.

Sheddon P Cottle refers to a lost hall-name in Mistley, Essex, now Old Hall, called in Domesday Book *Sciddinchou* OE 'hill-spur/rise of the shed-dwellers', but Hanks and Hodges say that this predominantly Scottish surname could be derived from *Sheddens*, Renfrewshire (first element obscure, followed by ME *den*, 'hollow').

Shee, *see* **Shea**.

Sheehan F Irish: Anglicized form of Gaelic **O'** [descendant of] **Siodhachain** ('peaceful'). See also **Sheen**.

Sheehy F Scots and Irish: Anglicized form of the Gaelic first-name *Sitheach* ('?mysterious, fairy-like'). A surname first established in Ireland by a branch of the Scottish **McDonnells**.

Sheen/Shean(e) T/P/N Dweller in/by the huts, sheds OE (a 'weak' plural in *-n*, as in *oxen*); or from a place-name with the same meaning: *Sheen*, Staffs; *East Sheen* and *West Sheen* (renamed *Richmond* in the early sixteenth century), Surrey; or possibly a nickname for a beautiful person OE. Readily confused with/a variant of **Sheehan**. **Sheen** is widely scattered around England and Wales, though not found in the far north or south-west. **Shean** and **Sheane** are scarcer variants. *The real name of actor Martin Sheen (born in 1940, Dayton, Ohio) was Ramon Gerardo Antonio Estevez; his mother, Mary Ann Phelan, had fled from Co Tipperary, Ireland, during the Irish War of Independence (her family having had IRA connexions), and her son Martin took his stage name from the Catholic archbishop Fulton J. Sheen. By his marriage to Janet Templeton, Martin Sheen had three sons and a daughter who chose acting as their profession: Charlie Sheen, Emilio Estevez, Ramon Estevez Jr and Renee Estevez.*

Sheepshanks N English and Scots: nickname for a person with legs like a sheep – that is, ungainly? OE: 'a bit of Yorks humour' (Cottle). A rare surname, most common in Lancs and WRYorks. The following entry appears in *Singular surnames collected by the late Edward D. Ingraham, Esq*, edited by William Duane (Philadelphia, 1873): '"William Sheepshanks, an estimable citizen of Philadelphia, while walking along the street on Tuesday, fell dead in a fit of apoplexy" – December 12, 1837. He was an Englishman with remarkably thick legs'.

Sheepwash P Place-name in Devon, Northd, Sussex OE 'place for washing/dipping sheep', but chiefly a Kent surname.

Sheer, *see* Shear.

Sheffield P Place-name in WRYorks OE '[river] *Sheaf* ("boundary") field' and in Berks OE 'shelter field' and in Sussex OE 'sheep field'. A surname which is widely scattered around England, though rare in the south-west.

Shefford P Place-name in Beds, Berks, OE 'sheep ford'. Chiefly a Wilts surname.

Sheldon P Place-name in various counties, including Derbys OE 'heathery hill with a shed', Devon OE 'shelf (steep-sided) valley' and Warwicks OE 'shelf (steep-sided) hill'. Chiefly a Midlands and northern surname, commonest in Staffs.

Sheldrake/Sheldrick/Sheldrike N Nickname for an ostentatious or vain person, from the bird, the sheldrake OE, noted for its bright, pied plumage. **Sheldrake** is chiefly an East Anglian surname, strongest in Suffolk; **Sheldrick** belongs to Cambs, Essex and Middx, **Sheldrike** (very scarce) to Essex.

Sheldrick/Sheldrike, *see* Sheldrake.

Shelford P Place-name in Cambs, Notts, OE 'ford in the shallows': 'it seems a good place to have one' (Cottle). A scarce south-east-of-England surname.

Shellabear, *see* Shillaber.

Shelley P Place-name in various counties, including Essex, Suffolk, WRYorks OE 'wood/clearing on a ledge/bank/plateau'; *Shelley* in Northd is OE 'clearing/field with a shieling'. The greatest concentration of

the surname is found in Staffs. *The poet Percy Bysshe Shelley (1792–1822) came from a Sussex family which took its name from a minor place-name in that county near Crawley.*

Shelton P Place-name in various counties OE 'place on a ledge/bank/plateau'. Readily confused with/a variant of **Shilton**. Strongest in Notts.

Shenfield P Place-name in Essex, OE 'beautiful/bright field'. The surname is most common in Suffolk.

Shep(e)ard/Shep(h)erd/Sheph(e)ard/ Sheppard/Shepperd/Shippard O Occupational term for a shepherd ('sheep-herd') OE. Patronymic forms include **Shep(h)erdson/Sheppardson/Shepper(d)son**.

Sheppey P Place-name in Kent OE 'island with sheep', but chiefly a West Midlands surname.

Sheraton P Place-name in Co Durham, probably ON and OE '*Skurfa*'s farm' (as in **Scruton**), and a Co Durham surname. *Thomas Sheraton (1751–1806), born in Stockton-on-Tees, Co Durham, gave his name to a distinctive style of furniture.*

Sherborn(e)/Sherb(o)urne/Sherburn P Place-name *Sherborne* in various counties, the best known being in Dorset OE 'bright stream'. In the thirteenth century there had been two prominent families with similar surnames: the **Sherborns** of the Lancs/Yorks border, and the **Shernborns** of *Shernborn*, near Hunstanton, Norfolk. Known spellings of the surname include: **Sherborn, Sherborne, Sherbourn, Sherbourne, Sherbon, Sherburn, Shereburne, Sheerburne, Shearburn, Sharborne, Shirburn, Shirborn, Shirburne, Shireborne, Shirebourne, Shireburne, Shurborne, Scireburn, Scyreburne, Schyrebourne, Shyreburne, Schirburn, Schireburne, Schyreburne, Scyrburne, Cherbron, Churborne**. *Charles William Sherborn (1831–1860), an artist best known for his bookplate designs, was born in London, the son of Charles Sherborn, an upholsterer from Newbury in Berks, and his wife Mary Bance.*

Sherd, *see* Sheard.

Shere P Place-name in Surrey OE 'the bright one'. Readily confused with/a variant of **Shear**.

Shergold/Sheargold N Nickname from OE 'bright gold', though R. S. Charnock associates the surname with *Sherwood Forest* in Notts, '*wood*' becoming '*gold*'. **Shergold** is mainly found in Wilts and surrounding counties; **Sheargold** (scarce) in Lancs and Staffs.

Sheriff(s)/Sherriff(s)/Shreeve(s)/ Shrive(s) O Occupational term for a sheriff ('shire-reeve') OE. The scarce variant **Sreeves** (which has a very limited presence in Middx and in Warwicks) is particularly distinctive because no dictionary word begins with the letters *sr-* (compare **Srawley**, a variant of **Shrawley**). **Sheriff** and **Sherriff** are widely scattered throughout England and Scotland; **Sheriffs** and **Sherriffs** are most common in eastern Scotland, strongest in Aberdeenshire and Angus; **Shreeve** belongs to Norfolk, **Shreeves** to Beds, **Shrive** and **Shrives** to Northants.

Sheringham P Place-name in Norfolk OE '?*Scira*'s people's homestead'. The 1881 census indicates that **Sheringham** was by then predominantly a Norfolk surname, having travelled hardly any distance from its place of origin. Not only that, but its scarcity would suggest that it has a single-family origin. Only those **Sheringham**s who belonged to the professional classes and had a career to pursue are known to have moved any significant distance from their East Anglian home. John Tempest **Sheringham** was a solicitor working in London during early Victorian times. His son John William **Sheringham** was Archdeacon of Gloucester, 1881–1902, and in turn his son William Archibald **Sheringham** became rector of Donington, Wolverhampton. *Edward Paul ('Teddy') Sheringham, who holds the record as the oldest footballer to have scored a goal in the Premier League, was born in Highams Park, London, in 1966.*

Sherlock N Nickname for a person with bright/fair hair OE. The surname has two principal centres, in north-west and south-east England.

Sherman, *see* **Shearer**.

Sherra(r)d/Sharrad/Sherratt ?N Surnames of uncertain origin, perhaps originally nicknames from an OE word meaning 'bright', with the addition of an OF suffix *-ard*. A scarce surname in all spellings, except for **Sherratt**, which is strongest in Staffs..

Sherriff(s), *see* **Sheriff**.

Sherwin N Nickname for a fast runner, one who could 'shear/cut the wind' ME. Mainly found in Derbys, Staffs and surrounding counties.

Sherwood/Sharwood P There are places called *Sherwood* in Yarnscombe OE 'bright wood' and in Feniton OE 'clear ford', Devon. *Sherwood* is also famously the name of a forest in Notts OE 'wood belonging to the shire'. The spelling **Sharwood** represents the older pronunciation; for the relationship between *-ar-* and *-er-* see **Armistead**. **Sherwood** is a widespread surname; **Sharwood**, much scarcer, can be found in Kent, Northants and Sussex. *The company of Sharwood's, famous for producing Asian foods, was founded in 1889 by James Allen Sharwood, who was born in Islington, North London.*

Shewell N Nickname for a person resembling a scarecrow OE. A Gloucs surname, found in the county as a place-name element at *Shewell Hill*, *Shewel Wood* and *Shewhill Barn/Coppice*. **Showell** can be a variant of **Shewell** or of **Shovel**.

Shield(s) O/P/T/F Occupational term for an armourer, a maker of shields OE; or from the place-names *North* and *South Shields*, Northd and Co Durham ME 'sheds, shelters'; or dweller at the sheds or the shallows of a river OE. Irish: Anglicized form of Gaelic **O**' [descendant of] **Siadhail** (of unknown derivation). **Shiels** is chiefly a Scottish variant.

Shiels, *see* **Shield**.

Shillabe(e)r/Shellabear/Shillibeer P

From a lost place-name in Meavy, Devon, OE '?grove on a ledge/bank'. Whence the early names for a London omnibus and a funeral coach, from their pioneer George **Shillibeer** (1797–1866), who was born in London. Surnames of Cornwall and Devon.

Shilling N Nickname from OE 'shilling': 'from rent, or from some lost joke' (Cottle). Mainly found in Kent and eastern England.

Shillington P In principle such a surname could be from the place-name *Shillington* in Beds OE '?hill of *Scyttel*'s people/the hill people', though all early forms of this place-name approximate (oh, dear…) to *Shitlington*. In the event this rare surname is mainly found in Lancs.

Shilston(e) P Place-name *Shilston* in Devon OE 'cromlech (literally shelf-stone)', and chiefly a Devon surname in either spelling.

Shilton P Place-name in various counties, including Berks, Leics, Oxon, Warwicks OE 'place on a ledge/bank/plateau'. Readily confused with/a variant of **Shelton**. *Peter (Leslie) Shilton, who won no fewer than 125 caps playing in goal for the England soccer team, was born in Leicester in 1949.*

Shingler O Occupational term for someone who covered a roof with wooden tiles ME (ultimately from Latin). Mainly found in Staffs and surrounding counties.

Shinn, *see* **Skinner**.

Ship(p) O/T Occupational term for a sailor OE (*see also* **Shipman**); or a dweller at the sign of the ship. Mainly found in Middx and in eastern England.

Shipley P Place-names in several counties OE 'sheep pasture'. *William Shipley (c.1715–1803), founder of the Royal Society of Arts, was born in London, son of Jonathan Shipley (from Leeds, WRYorks) and his wife Martha.*

Shipman O Occupational term for a sailor OE (like Chaucer's pilgrim) – hence also **Ship(p)** – or for a shepherd ('sheep man') OE. Most common in the south Pennines, strongest in WRYorks.

Shippam P Place-name *Shipham* in Somerset OE 'sheep farm'. The surname is mostly found in Sussex, though the earliest-known reference to the place-name *Shepham* in that county dates only from the late sixteenth century. *Alfred Ernest Cooper Shippam (1874–1947), meat and fish-paste manufacturer, was born in East Street, Chichester, Sussex.*

Shippard, *see* **Shepard**.

Shippen T/P Dweller at (or in the case of a cowman, *in*) a cattleshed OE; or from place-names in various counties with the same meaning, including *Shippen* in WRYorks and *Shippon* in Berks. **Skippon**, a rare Scandinavianized variant, is mainly found in Norfolk.

Shipperbottom, *see* **Shufflebottom**.

Shipperley T Dweller at a pasture with sheep OE (or a distortion of *Shippen*, cow house?). Mainly found in Beds and surrounding counties.

Shipston(e) P Place-name *Shipston on Stour* in Warwicks, OE 'place at a sheep-wash'. *In 1852 James Shipstone founded the Star Brewery in New Basford, Nottingham; the eventual demise of the 'Shippo's' brand was mourned by many, but something of a relief to others with sensitive palates…*

Shipton P Place-name in several counties OE 'sheep farm'; but *Shipton* in NRYorks and ERYorks are OE 'place in the hips/dog-roses', and *Shipton Lee* in Bucks is OE 'hill with sheep'. A widespread surname.

Shipwright O Occupational term for a shipwright, shipbuilder OE. A very scarce Middx/Home Counties surname.

Shirland P Place-name in Derbys OE and ON '?bright grove/grove where the shire-court meets'. A scarce Derbys surname.

Shirley P Place-names in various counties OE 'bright wood/clearing' (though the first element may sometimes be OE 'shire' as in **Shirland**). **Shirley**, originally a place-name, was adopted as a surname and became by turns a first-name for boys and then for girls. Family name of the Earls Ferrers.

Shirt T Dweller at a 'skirt', a detached 'shortened' piece of land OE. A Derbys surname.

Shitler, *see* **Shutler**.

Shobbrook/Shobrooke P Place-name *Shobrooke* in Devon OE 'goblin brook', and a Devon surname.

Shoebotham/Shoebottom, *see* **Shufflebottom**.

Shoemaker/Shoemark/Shumack O Occupational term for a shoemaker OE. Rare in any form: **Shoemaker** is a Glamorgan surname and **Shoemark/Shumack** are strongest in Somerset.

Shoesmith O Occupational term for a shoeing-smith, horseshoe-maker OE. Principally found in both Sussex and WRYorks.

Shooter/Shuter O Occupational term for a shooter/marksman/accurate archer OE plus *-er* suffix (compare **Shutt**). Readily confused with/a variant of **Shute**.

Shopland/Shapland P There is a place-name *Shopland* in Essex OE 'island with a shed/shop', though these are almost exclusively Devon surnames (**Shopland** occurring also in neighbouring Somerset), so an unidentified place-name in that county could well be the true source.

Shopper O Occupational term for a shopkeeper OE. Chiefly a Wilts surname.

Shore T/P Dweller by the (sea-)shore ME or by a steep bank OE; or from one of a number of minor place-names with the same meaning. 'The most famous bearer was Edward IV's mistress Jane **Shore**, who did *not* give her name to Shoreditch' (Cottle). Family name of the Barons Teignmouth.

Short/Shortt N Nickname for a short person OE. **Shorter** is a comparative variant.

Shorter, *see* **Short**.

Shorthouse/Shorthose N Nickname for a person who wore short boots/stockings OE (compare **Curtis**), or who had a short neck OE. **Shorthouse** is chiefly a Staffs surname; **Shorthose** can also be found in Derbys.

Shortman N Nickname for a short man OE. Mainly found in Gloucs and surrounding counties.

Shortt, *see* **Short**.

Shotbolt/Shadbolt O/N Occupational term/nickname for an archer OE (literally 'shoot-arrow'). **Shotbolt** can be found in Beds/Lincs, **Shadbolt** primarily in Herts and Middx.

Shotton P Place-name in various counties, including Northd OE 'hill of the Scots'/ 'place or farm of the Scots' and Co Durham (three such). Some of these may be OE 'place on a slope'/'steep hill'. Mainly a Co Durham surname, so the place called *Shotton* in Flintshire is an unlikely point of origin.

Shoulder ?N ?Nickname for a hunched or broad-shouldered person, from the OE word *shoulder*. Sparsely scattered throughout England.

Shouler, *see* **Shovel**.

Shovel(l)/Shouler/Shoveller/Showler O Occupational term for a maker or user of shovels ME. **Showell** can be a variant of **Shewell** or of **Shovel**. **Shovel** is found mainly in Devon, **Shovell** in Cornwall, **Shoveller** in Surrey and surrounding counties, **Shouler** in Bucks, **Showler** in Lincs and **Showell** in Warwicks. *The popular British admiral Sir Cloudesley Shovell or Shovel (1650–1707), who was born in Cockthorpe on the north Norfolk coast, famously perished in a disastrous shipwreck off the Scilly Isles.*

Showell, *see* **Shewell** and **Shovel**.

Showers N A nickname derived from the OE word *scufan* ('to thrust, push, shove'); Reaney suggests that it might have been used for a person of violent habits. A very scarce Somerset surname. *A significant number of men surnamed Showers played a prominent part in the Bengal Army during the early years of the nineteenth century. All were descendants of Colonel Samuel Howe Showers of* *the Bengal Infantry, who had been baptized on 8 June 1746 in Salem, Massachusetts, USA.*

Showler, *see* Shovel.

Shrapnel(l) N Nickname for a little dusky man OF *charbon* plus the diminutive suffix *-el*, corrupted via *Sharpnel*. **Shrapnel** is mainly found in Surrey and surrounding counties, **Shrapnell** in Wilts. *Henry Shrapnel or Shrapnell (1761–1842), army officer and inventor of the Shrapnel shell, was born in Bradford-on-Avon, Wilts. The actor John Shrapnel (born 1942, son-in-law of the actress Deborah Kerr) and his son Lex Shrapnel (born 1979, plays the part of Jamie Cartwright in the TV series* Minder) *belong to this same family.*

Shrawley P Place-name in Worcs OE 'clearing by a hill-recess'. A very scarce Staffs/Worcs surname. Of the even scarcer **Srawley** (found in Warwicks), Cottle points out that the spelling is truly exceptional, 'for no dictionary word begins with *sr-*'.

Shreeve(s)/Shrive(s), *see* Sheriff.

Shrimpton P A surname with a significant presence in Bucks, possibly derived from *Sherington* in that county OE '*Scira*'s farm', which was referred to as *Shrington* in the fourteenth century; the surname could have arisen thanks to folk etymology. *Jean Shrimpton, the former supermodel and actress, was born in High Wycombe, Bucks, in 1943.*

Shropshire P From the county name OE 'the shire belonging to *Shrewsbury*'. Chiefly found in Shropshire itself and in Staffs, though an American family of **Shropshires**, descended from a clergyman by the name of St John **Shropshire** (born 1663), an emigrant to Virginia, has its roots in Wilts.

Shuck/Shu(c)ker N Nickname for a man with something of the devil, fiend, goblin about him OE *scucca*. **Shuck** is most common in Worcs, **Shucker** in WRYorks and **Shuker** in Salop.

Shuckburgh P Place-name in Warwicks OE 'goblin/demon hill'. A very scarce West Country/South Midlands surname.

Shucker, *see* Shuck.

Shufflebottom/Shipperbottom/ Shoebotham/Shoebottom/ Shufflebot(h)am P Place-name *Shipperbottom* in Lancs OE 'valley of the sheep-wash/stream'. The distribution of such surnames is perhaps not quite what might have been anticipated: **Shufflebottom** and **Shufflebotham** can principally be found in Lancs, but also in Staffs; **Shipperbottom** belongs to Lancs, but **Shoebotham** and **Shufflebotam** to Staffs. **Shoebottom**, very scarce, has a presence in both Lancs and Warwicks.

Shuker, *see* Shuck.

Shumack, *see* Shoemaker.

Shute T/P Dweller at a strip/nook of land OE; or from one of a number of places called *Shute* or *Shoot*, with the same meaning, including *Shute* in Devon. Readily confused with/a variant of **Shooter**. Chiefly a Devon surname.

Shuter, *see* Shooter.

Shutler O Occupational term for a maker/user of shuttles (for weaving) OE plus *-er* suffix. **Shutler** is mainly found in the West Country, strongest in Somerset; **Shitler** is a scarce Dorset/Hants variant.

Shutt O Occupational term for a 'shooter' OE *scytta*, referring, no doubt, to a good archer (compare **Shooter**). Most common in Lancs/WRYorks.

Shuttle O/N Occupational term for a maker or user of shuttles OE; Reaney suggests that the swiftly alternating shuttle could have given rise to a related nickname, applied to a variable, flighty person. Mainly found in the south of England, strongest in Berks.

Shuttleworth P From one of several places so-called in Derbys, Lancs, WRYorks OE 'gated enclosure, sealed with a bolt/bar or *shuttle*'. *The influential educationalist and politician Sir James Phillips Kay-Shuttleworth (1804–1877), born James Phillips Kay in Rochdale, Lancs, married into the Shuttleworth family of Gawthorpe, Burnley, Lancs, which* *features weavers' shuttles on its armorial bearings.*

Sibley F From the mediaeval first-name *Sibley*, a form of the Latin *Sibilla*, from Greek *Sibylla*, 'one of the females acting as mouthpieces for the gods; later accepted as blessed with divine revelations, and admitted to the Christian heaven along with the Prophets (as on the Sistine Chapel ceiling)' (Cottle). William the Conqueror's son Robert married a *Sibylla*, and the first-name took root in England. **Sibson** ('son of *Sib'*) arises from a pet-form.

Sibson, *see* Sibley.

Sibthorp(e) P Place-name *Sibthorpe* in Notts OE and ON '*Sibba/Sibbi*'s outlying farm', though the surnames **Sibthorp** and **Sibthorpe** are most common in Middx and the Home Counties.

Siddal(l)/Seedall/Siddel(l)/Siddle P Place-names: *Siddall*, Lancs; *Siddall*, WRYorks; *Siddle*, NRYorks OE 'broad nook'. Readily confused with/a variant of **Sudell**?

Siddons, *see* Siddorn.

Siddorn/Siddons ?F ?From a female first-name derived from Greek *Sindon* ('linen shroud'), whence *Sidony* (in honour of Christ's winding-sheet). **Siddorn** is found chiefly in Chesh, **Siddons** in WRYorks. *The actress Sarah Siddons (1755–1831), née Kemble, acquired the surname by which she is best known as a result of her marriage to William Siddons.*

Sidebottom/Sidebotham P Place-name in Chesh OE 'wide valley'; 'Mispronunciations such as *siddibottARM* and *siddibottOME* shouldn't deceive *anybody*' (Cottle). **Sidebottom** is found mainly in Chesh, Derbys, Lancs and WRYorks, **Sidebotham** in Chesh and Lancs.

Sidg(e)wick, *see* Sedgwick.

Sidney P Place-names: *Sidney* in Surrey OE '(at) the wide island' or '(at) the wide well-watered land', the adjective retaining remnants of a weak dative ending, originally used after a preposition and definite article; *Sydney* in Chesh (two such) OE 'wide recess'. The place-name *Saint-Denis* in Normandy may (but may well not…) have given rise to the surname **Sidney**. *Sidney*, originally a place-name, then a surname, became a female first-name and then a male first-name (popularized, says Cottle, thanks to the Whig idolization of the political writer Algernon **Sidney**, or **Sydney**, 1623–1683). The **Sidney** family, Viscounts De L'Isle, which includes the poet Sir Philip **Sidney** (1554–1586) and others among its famous members, originally held land in *Sidney*, Alfold, Surrey. In 1788 the Australian city of *Sydney* was named after the politician Thomas Townshend, First Viscount **Sydney** (1733–1800).

Siev(e)wright O Occupational term for a sieve-maker OE. A Scottish surname in either spelling: **Sievwright** is mainly found in Angus, **Sievewright** in Aberdeenshire.

Siggers F Patronymic from an OE first-name meaning 'Victory-Spear'. Chiefly an Essex surname.

Siggins F Patronymic from an OE first-name meaning 'Victory'. Sparsely and unevenly scattered throughout England.

Sikes, *see* Sykes.

Silburn N Nickname for a blessed/happy child OE. Most common in Suffolk.

Silcock(s)/Silcox, *see* Sill.

Silk O/F Occupational term for a silk-weaver/-dealer OE; or from the mediaeval first-name *Silkin* (compare **Sill**). Widely scattered throughout England, but most common in Middx and Kent.

Sill F From the mediaeval first-name *Sill*, a shortened form of *Silvester*. Hence the patronymic forms **Sills**, **Silcock(s)** and **Silcox**.

Sillars, *see* Sellars.

Sillman, *see* Selman.

Silver O/N/T Occupational term for a silversmith OE; or a nickname for a rich man, or for one with silvery hair; or a dweller by a silvery stream, as in evidence in a place-name such as *Monksilver*, Somerset. A surname which is widely scattered throughout England, Scotland and Wales.

Silverstone P Place-name in Northants OE '*Soewulf*/*Sigewulf*'s settlement'. A scarce Essex/Lancs/Middx surname.

Silverthorn(e) P From an unidentified minor place-name OE 'silvery/whitish thorn-bush'. **Silverthorn** can be found around the Severn estuary, strongest in Monmouthshire; **Silverthorne** is chiefly a Dorset surname. In either spelling this surname also has a significant presence in a number of Wilts villages west of Salisbury Plain.

Silvester/Sylvester F From a first-name with its origins in the Latin *Silvester* ('forest-dweller'), borne by three popes. **Silvester**, a scattered surname, has a significant presence in Hants; **Sylvester** is strongest in Lincs.

Sim(m)(s)/Simco(e)/Simcock(s)/Simcox/Sime(s)/Simeon, *see* Simon.

Simington, *see* Symington.

Simister O Occupational term for a sempstress OE. In theory this would have been applied only to females (as with **Brewster**, **Webster** and so on), the male equivalent being **Seamer**, but in practice such a distinction was not always maintained. **Simister** is mainly found in Lancs and surrounding counties.

Simkin(s)/Simkiss/Simmance/Simmans/Simmens, *see* Simon.

Simmer(s), *see* Summer.

Simmins/Simmonite, *see* Simon.

Simon/Sim(m)/Sime/Simeon/Simkin/Simond/Simpkin/Sym(e)/Sym(m)   F
From the Hebrew first-name *Shim'on* ('?hearkening'); Cottle adds: '...or perhaps "little hyena"; ?influenced by a Greek word meaning "snub-nosed"; a pretty poor choice'. Found as *Simon* in the New Testa-

ment (*Simeon* in the Old Testament), and very popular in mediaeval times – less because of the Apostle St Simon Zelotes than as a result of its being the first name of the nicknamed St Peter. Potentially confused in Britain with Scandinavian forms of *Sigmund*. Whence many surnames beginning with *Sim-/Simm-/Simp-/Sym-/Symm-*. **Simes, Simmance, Simmans, Simmens, Simkins, Simkiss, Simmins, Simmons, Sim (m)on(d)s, Simonson, Simpkins, Simpkinson, Simpkiss, Simpson, Sim(m)s, Simson, Sinkinson, Symes, Symmons, Symms, Symondson, Sym(m)on(d)s, Syms** are all 'son of *Simon*', as are **Semmence, Semmens** and **Semmons** (but for these, *see also* **Seaman**). **Simco(e), Simcock(s)** and **Simcox** carry the *-cock* suffix with the sense of 'young lad'. The distribution pattern of **Simon**-type surnames varies considerably according to their precise form. Some (scarce or common as they may be) are widespread throughout Britain, while others (such as **Simmonds, Simmons, Simonds, Simons, Sims** and **Symonds**) are not usually found in the far north of England. Several have a particular presence in certain counties or regions: **Simkin, Simkins, Simkiss, Simpkiss** in Staffs (and **Simcocks, Simcox,** which also occur in Chesh); **Simpkinson** in Norfolk; **Simon, Simm, Simms, Simpkin** and **Sinkinson** in Lancs; **Simpkins, Symes, Symons** and **Syms** in the West Country; **Simonson** and **Symm** in the north-east. **Sim, Sime, Sym** and **Syme** are principally Scottish surnames; **Simpson,** a particularly common variant, is strongest in Lancs and WRYorks, while **Simmance, Simmans, Simmens** and **Simmins** are all scarce. **Simmonite** (which consists of a diminutive form of **Simon** with the addition of the OF suffix *-et*), also scarce, has a limited presence in WRYorks. *The actor and director Alastair (George) Sim (1900–1976) was born in Edinburgh, Scotland.*

Simond/Sim(m)on(d)s/Simonson,   *see* Simon.

Simper, *see* Semper.

Simpkin(s)/Simpkinson/Simpkiss/ Simpson, *see* Simon.

Simple N Nickname for a guileless, honest person OF. A very scarce Chesh surname.

Simson, *see* **Simon**.

Sinclair(e)/St Clair/Sinclar P Place-names in France: *Saint Clair sur Elle* in La Manche and *Saint Clair l'Evêque* in Calvados, with churches dedicated to a seventh-century Norman saint and a third-century Bishop of Nantes (from Latin *clarus* 'bright, shining'). Scotland is home to the great majority of **Sinclairs**, but **St Clair** has more of a presence in England. **Sinclair** is the family name of the Earls of Caithness and of four other peers.

Singer, *see* **Sanger**.

Singleterry ?O/P A very scarce surname of uncertain meaning, probably with a single-family origin. By the late nineteenth century there was a mere handful of **Singleterrys** and **Singletarys** in Cambs and Norfolk, though the first recorded instance of the surname yet found is that of the baptism of Joan **Singletary** at Surfleet, Lincs, in 1549. Yet **Singleterrys** are much thicker on the ground in America, most if not all being descended from Richard **Singletary**, who is known to have been in Salem, then in Newbury, Massachusetts, from as early as 1637 – a very early transatlantic immigrant indeed, who is said to have been a hundred and two years of age when he died in 1687. When a member of this family was granted five hundred acres of land in Berkley County, South Carolina, in 1703, his surname was split into two parts, and he is described as Richard **Single Terry**. Such a split might be unhelpful; could the surname rather have its origins in the word *swingletree*, used to refer to the crossbar on a plough to which the traces are fastened, dialectal variations of which include *single-tree*? A *single-horse tree* is sometimes used to define the stretcher on a plough by which one horse draws, yet in some dialects a *swingletree* was the stock over which flax is beaten, or the movable part of a flail. Was the original Mr **Singleterry** a ploughman, or a man who worked with flax or wielded a flail? Or could **Singleterry** be a corruption by way of folk etymology of a place-name such as *Saint Gaultier*, situated in the Département of Indre, within the basin of the river Loire, which was named after *Gautier*, abbot of Lesterps, who had founded a priory there? *Saint Gaultier* would be pronounced *San/go/teeay*, which is perhaps close enough to **Singleterry** to merit at least some serious consideration. For a detailed study of this surname, see *Searching for surnames* by John Titford (2002).

Singleton P There is such a place-name in Sussex OE 'farm in a burnt clearing' (compare the word '*singe*'), but this is predominantly a Lancs surname, and *Singleton* OE 'farm on shingle' or 'farm roofed with shingles' in that county is likely to be the source in most cases.

Sinkinson, *see* **Simon**.

Sinnamon, *see* **Cinnamon**.

Sinnett/Sinnott/Sennett/Sennitt F
From the ME first-name *Sinod*, OE *Sigenoth* ('victory-bold'). **Sionoid** is an Irish variant. **Sinnett** and **Sinnott** are both found in Lancs, the former also having a presence in Pembrokeshire, Wales; **Sennett** is scarce and scattered; **Sennitt** belongs to Cambs. *Mack Sennett (1880–1960), comedian and film director, was born Michael Sinnott in Richmond, Quebec, Canada, the son of Irish immigrant farmers.*

Sionoid, *see* **Sinnett**.

Sirett F From an OE first-name meaning 'victory counsel'. Mostly found in Bucks.

Sisley/Sisson(s) F From the mediaeval first-name *Sisley* or *Cecile*, a feminine form of the Latin *Caecilius* (see **Cecil**). St *Cecilia*, martyred with her equally chaste husband Valerian, is the patron saint of music. **Sisley** is found mostly in Kent, **Sisson** and **Sissons** in the north of England. *Alfred Sisley (1839–1899), English impressionist landscape painter, was born in Paris, France, to affluent English parents.*

Sitch, *see* **Sykes**.

Sixsmith O Occupational term for ?sickle-smith OE. Readily confused with/a variant of **Sucksmith**. Mainly a Lancs surname.

Sizeland/Syzling P Place-name *Sisland* in Norfolk (pronounced *Size*land) OE '*Sigeheah/Sige*'s land'. **Sizeland** is a Norfolk surname; **Syzling** also has a limited presence in WRYorks.

Sizer O Occupational term for a juryman, a sworn witness in an assize court OF. Mainly found in eastern England, strongest in Suffolk.

Skates, *see* Skeat.

Skeat(e)(s)/Skates N/F Nickname for a swift person ON, or from a first-name with the same meaning.

Skeffington/Skevington P Place-name *Skeffington* in Leics OE 'settlement of *Sceaft*'s people'. A scattered surname. Family name (usually combined with **Clotworthy** as a first-name) of the Viscounts Massereene and Ferrard.

Skegg N Nickname for a person with a beard ON. Strongest in Middx and Surrey.

Skelhorn ?P A place-name origin is likely: possibly *Skeleron* WRYorks OE 'shelf-of-land headland', though the first recorded reference to this place dates only from the late sixteenth century. *Skellorn Green* in Chesh is a place-name derived from a surname, rather than vice versa. Compare **Skillicorn**. A fairly scarce Chesh/Lancs/Staffs surname.

Skelston, *see* Skelton.

Skelton P Place-name in Cumbd, Yorks (six such) OE 'place on a bank/hill'. **Skelton** is chiefly a WRYorks surname. **Skelston**, which would appear to be a variant, is a scarce surname found in Notts, where there may be some confusion with the place-name *Selston* in that county, the precise etymology of which is uncertain. *The exact origins of the English poet John Skelton (c.1460–1529) remain shrouded in mystery, though several of his early poems feature the county of Yorkshire.*

Skene P Scots: place-name in Aberdeen-shire, Gaelic 'bush'. An Aberdeenshire surname.

Skevington, *see* Skeffington.

Skidmore, *see* Scudamore.

Skillicorn ?P A Manx surname of uncertain origin – perhaps from a now-lost place-name in Lancs (compare **Skelhorn**). A man named Adam de **Skillicorne**, who is known to have had a son called Edmund, living in 1400, is a direct ancestor of the **Skillicorn**s of Skinscoe, Kirk Lonan, Isle of Man. John **Skillicorne**, who died in 1478, held the manor of Presse and had lands in Newton, Warton, Preston and Lancaster.

Skinner O Occupational term for a skinner ON plus an -*er* suffix. **Skinner** is a prolific surname, though most common in the south-east of England and in Devon; the variant **Shinn** is found mainly in Norfolk.

Skipp, *see* Skipper.

Skipper O/N Occupational term: a master of a ship ME (from Dutch); an acrobat (or a nickname for one adept at leaping and jumping) ME; a basket-maker ON (with **Skipp** as a variant). **Skipper** is chiefly a Norfolk surname; **Skipp** is mainly found in Herts and Middx.

Skippon, *see* Shippen.

Skipsey P Place-name *Skipsea* in ERYorks ON and OE 'pool/harbour for ships'. Mainly found in north-eastern England.

Skipwith P Place-name in ERYorks OE 'sheep settlement', which was originally *Schipwic*; the first element was eventually Scandinavianized and the second was falsified to ON *with* ('wood'). One family called **Skipwith** is known to have moved from Yorks to Lincs in the thirteenth century, but by the late nineteenth century the surname, by then very scarce, was most in evidence in Surrey. The variant **Skipworth** is strongest in Lincs.

Skipworth, *see* Skipwith.

Skrimshire, *see* Scrimgeor.

Slack T/P/N Dweller in a hollow, a little shallow valley ON; or from one of a number of place-names with the same meaning; or a nickname for a slack, lazy, careless person OE. Strongest in Derbys.

Slade/Slader T/P Dweller in a valley, dell, strip of greensward between woods OE; or from one of a number of minor places called *Slade* with the same meaning. **Slade** is chiefly a surname of south and south-west England, strong in Somerset; **Slader** is mostly found in Devon.

Sladen P From an unidentified place-name, perhaps *Sloden* OE '?slough valley', in line with earlier spellings of the surname. Very much a Lancs surname.

Slader, *see* Slade.

Slape T Dweller at a slippery place OE or at a slipway/portage OE. A scarce south/south-west of England surname.

Slater/Slate/Slatter O Occupational term for one who covered roofs with slates, a slater OF plus -*er* suffix. **Slate** can readily be confused with/be a variant of **Sleight**.

Slaughter O/T/P Occupational term for a slaughterer/butcher ME; or a dweller in a slough, muddy place OE, or from a place-name with this meaning, such as *Upper* and *Lower Slaughter*, Gloucs; or dweller by a sloe-tree, blackthorn OE. Mainly found in the south-east, strongest in Surrey and Sussex.

Slay, *see* Slaymaker.

Slaymaker/Slay O/T Occupational term for a maker of *slays*, used in weaving to beat up the weft ME. **Slay** can alternatively refer to a dweller by a grassy bank or slope ME. Uncommon surnames, principally found in the Thames Valley.

Slee/Sleeman/Sleigh, *see* Sly.

Sleight/Slight P These two surnames belong principally to Lincs, and are probably variants one of the other, though there could readily be a cross-over with **Slate** (see **Slater**). For Hanks and Hodges, **Slight** can be a Scots surname from northern ME *sleght/slyght* ('smooth, sleek, slender, slim'), or an

English one from ME *sleghth* ('craft, cunning, dexterity, adroitness'). If a place-name origin were to be sought, Cottle's reference to *Sleight* in Dorset OE 'sheep-pasture' is probably less than helpful, but *Sleights* in NRYorks ON 'level fields' would merit some consideration.

Sleightholme P Place-name in NRYorks ON 'level (field) island', and a NRYorks surname.

Slight, *see* Sleight.

Slingsby P Place-name in NRYorks ON '*Slengr*'s farm'. Strongest in WRYorks.

Slipper O Occupational term for a polisher, sharpener (of blades) ME from OE adjective *slipor*. A Norfolk surname.

Slocomb(e)/Slocum P Place-names: *Slocum* in the Isle of Wight; *Sloncombe* in Devon OE 'valley where sloes grow'. **Slocomb** is chiefly a Hants surname; **Slocombe** is mainly found in Somerset and surrounding counties, and **Slocum** belongs to South Wales.

Sloley P Cottle makes reference to such a place-name in Norfolk and Warwicks OE 'wood/clearing where sloes grow', but this uncommon surname belongs to Devon, where the origin must be *Sloley*, in Shirwell in that county, with the same meaning.

Sloman, *see* Slow.

Sloper O Occupational term for a maker of 'slops' (loose clothes such as tunics, smocks and trousers) ME. 'Still used by old engine drivers of their overalls' (Cottle). A Wilts surname.

Slough, *see* Slow.

Slow T/P/N Dweller by a swamp, slough OE, or from a place-name with the same meaning, such as *Slough*, Berks; hence also the surname **Slough**. Or a nickname for a person famed for being slow of movement or of understanding OE. **Sloman** and **Slowman** are variants. Generally fairly scarce south-of-England surnames, **Sloman** being most prevalent in Devon.

Slowman, *see* **Slow**.

Sly/Slee/Sleeman/Sleigh N/T Nickname for a clever/cunning/crafty person ME. Cottle considers that **Slee** might alternatively refer to a dweller on a grassy slope OE. **Sly** has a significant presence in Wilts, **Sleigh** in Lancs and Staffs; **Slee** is mainly found in the south-west of England (especially in Devon) but also in the north. **Sleeman**, most common in Devon and Cornwall, can be a variant of **Sly**, but also possibly of **Slee**. *Major General Sir W. H. Sleeman, who held some of the highest civil and political appointments in India, was born in Stratton, Cornwall, in 1788, the son of Philip Sleeman, a yeoman farmer.*

Smail(e)(s), *see* **Small**.

Smalbridge, *see* **Smallridge**.

Smale, *see* **Small**.

Small(s)/Smail(e)(s)/Smale(s)/Smele N Nickname for a thin, slender (and, less often, small) person OE. **Smail** and its close variants are mainly found in the north of England and in Scotland; **Smale** is principally a Cornish surname, **Smales** is most common in Yorks and **Smele** (scarce) in Gloucs.

Smallbone(s) N/P It's tempting to assume that this might be a nickname for a person with small/skinny bones/legs OE, but since **Smallbone** belongs very much to southern counties of England, the now-lost place-name *Smalebourne* OE 'small stream' in Boxley, Kent, must merit some consideration as a possible source. The distribution of the variant **Smallbones** stretches up into the South Midlands.

Smallbridge, *see* **Smallridge**.

Smallcombe P A West Country surname, probably derived from one of the places in Devon called *Smallcombe* or *Smallacomb(e)* OE 'narrow valley'.

Smalldridge, *see* **Smallridge**.

Smalley P Place-name in Derbys and in Lancs OE 'narrow wood/clearing/field'. Most individuals called **Smalley** can count

the Lancs place-name as the point of origin of their surname.

Smallpage, *see* **Smallpeice**.

Smallpeice/Smallpiece T Dweller at a narrow allotment of land OE and OF, a common field-name. A very scarce Surrey surname in either spelling. **Smallpage** (found mainly in Lancs and WRYorks) is possibly a variant.

Smallridge/Smal(l)bridge/Small-dridge/Smaridge P Devon surnames, probably all derived from the place-name *Smallridge* OE 'narrow ridge' in that county.

Smallthwaite, *see* **Smorthwaite**.

Smallwood P Place-names in Chesh OE 'narrow wood'. A surname of the English Midlands and the north.

Smaridge, *see* **Smallridge**.

Smart N Nickname for a smart, brisk, prompt person OE. **Smartman** is a very scarce variant.

Smartman, *see* **Smart**.

Smeardon, *see* **Smerdon**.

Smeaton/Smeeton P Place-names: *Smeaton* in NRYorks, WRYorks, Midlothian (Scotland) and *Smeeton*, Leics, all OE 'place/farm of the smiths'. **Smeaton** is mainly found in northern England and in Scotland, **Smeeton** in the Midlands.

Smedley P The place-name *Smedley* in Lancs OE 'smooth field' would appear to be the point of origin for this predominantly Derbys surname.

Smee T/N Dweller at a smooth/level place OE; or a nickname for a smooth, polite, suave person. Mainly an Essex surname.> See also **Smeeth**.

Smeed, *see* **Smeeth**.

Smeeth P There is a place-name *Smeeth* in Kent OE 'smithy', and the variant **Smeed** is mainly a Kent surname, but **Smeeth** is as likely to be a variant of **Smith** or of **Smee**.

Smeeton, *see* **Smeaton**.

Smele, *see* **Small**.

Smerdon/Smeardon P Place-name *Smeardon* in Devon OE 'hill with rich pasturage' (literally 'butter hill'). These are Devon surnames, though **Smeardon**, closer to the place-name spelling, is much scarcer than **Smerdon**.

Smethurst P Place-name in Lancs OE 'smooth hill'.

Smith/Smither(s)/Smyth(e) O Occupational term for a metal-worker, blacksmith, farrier OE. A prolific surname which bears eloquent testimony to the long-standing importance of the metal trades within the British economy. 'The primate and patriarch of our surnames, its form unchanged for over a thousand years; forms with medial -*y*- and a final -*e* are usually both ignorant and affected, though the first may sometimes have been used for clarity next to the minim letter *m*, and -*e* may rarely represent [dweller at a] smithy... It is a frequent victim of hyphenation, either in a sincere effort to avoid ambiguity or in an insincere one to sound distingué; and it has recently gathered to itself many changed foreign surnames. Yet it remains primitive: a smith *smites*, and his honoured name rings down the ages like an anvil' (Cottle). At the latest estimate there were something like 600,000 individuals in England and Wales called 'Smith', and within the United Kingdom twelve people out of every one thousand bear such a surname. **Smith** is by far the commonest surname in England and Scotland, though **Jones** is ahead of it in Wales; it is also strongly represented in the USA and in Ireland. Within Britain, **Smith** is most concentrated in Aberdeenshire, Scotland; **Smyth** and **Smythe**, infinitely rarer, occur in scattered patches within England and Scotland; **Smither** and **Smithers** are generally found in south-east England, and **Smithson** ('son of the smith') is very strong in WRYorks. See also **Smeeth**. **Smith** is the family name of five peers. Given the number of **Smiths** around, many parents have tried desperately hard to give their offspring some kind of distinctive first name(s) in compensation, so

we have genuine historical examples such as: *Elizabeth Utterly* **Smith** (married in Glanford Brigg, Lincs, in 1865); *Hairy* **Smith** (born in Keighley, Yorks, c.1877); *Minehaha* **Smith** (featured in the 1881 census for Gravesend, Kent); *Queen Victoria* **Smith** (born in Rochford, Essex, in 1901); *Sexey Jane* **Smith** (died in Amesbury, Wilts, in 1898); and *Streaker* **Smith** (born in Easington, Co Durham, in 1845). *Many men by the name of 'John Smith' have achieved a significant degree of fame over the centuries. One of the best-known is John Smith (c.1580–1631), the soldier and colonial governor who was with a group of English would-be settlers at Jamestown, Virginia, in the early seventeenth century. Baptized at Willoughby by Alford, Lincs, he was the son of George Smith, a yeoman farmer whose family had come originally from Crudley in Lancs... The Smithsonian Institution in Washington DC, USA, was founded thanks to a bequest from the English chemist James Smithson; born James Lewes Macie, the illegitimate son of Hugh Smithson Percy, Duke of Northumberland, he inherited a fortune from his mother, Elizabeth Macie.*

Smither/Smithson, *see* **Smith**.

Smithwhite, *see* **Smorthwaite**.

Smollett N English and Scots: a nickname for a person with a small/narrow head OE, or one of limited intelligence. A very scarce surname. *The writer Tobias (George) Smollett (1721–1771), who was born near the village of Renton, Dunbartonshire, Scotland, and who was the grandson of the Scottish politician Sir James Smollett (c.1648–1731), claimed that his family 'were originally Malet or Molet and came from Normandy with the Conqueror'. But then so did half the population of the British Isles, according to one legend or another... But at least such a story avoids the unfortunate charge of 'limited intelligence...'.*

Smorfit/Smorthit, *see* **Smorthwaite**.

Smorthwaite/Smallthwaite/Smithwhite/Smorfit/Smorthit/Smurthwaite P Place-names: *Smorthwaite* (*Smeretwayt* in 1379) in Sedbergh, WRYorks; *Smaithwaite* (two such) and *Smallthwaite* (two such, but possibly of late origin) in Cumbd.

And a place called *Smerthwayt* was recorded in Guiseley, WRYorks, in 1323. All are ON 'small clearing', or OE and ON 'smooth clearing'. George Redmonds found an example of a man surnamed **Smurthwaite** being referred to as **Smoothways**, c.1660. These are scarce or very scarce surnames in any spelling, and can principally be found in the following counties: Essex and NRYorks (**Smorthwaite**); Lancs (**Smorthit**, and **Smallthwaite**, which is also found in Chesh); Co Durham (**Smithwhite** and **Smurthwaite**); ERYorks (**Smorfit**).

Smyth(e), *see* **Smith**.

Snaith, *see* **Snead**.

Snape P Place-name in: Devon, Suffolk, Sussex, Wilts OE 'boggy patch'; Lancs, Notts, NRYorks WRYorks ON 'poor pasture'. Overwhelmingly a Lancs surname.

Snare N/T Nickname for a swift person OE or ON; or dweller near (or a user of?) an animal snare, trap OE. An East Anglian surname.

Snawdon, *see* **Snowden**.

Snead/Snaith/Sneath/Sneyd P Hanks and Hodges yoke these together as variants of the same surname, which in fact would seem not to be the case, though the various place-names from which each is derived have the same meaning: 'piece of detached land' OE *snoed*, ON *sneith*. Place-names which merit consideration here include: *Snead* farm and common in Worcs; *Upper Snead, Lower Snead, Snead Common* (near Mamble), *Snead Coppice* (near Wenlock) and *Snead Hamlet* (near Bishop's Castle) in Salop; *Snead* in Montgomeryshire, Wales; *Snaith* in WRYorks; *Sneath Common* in Norfolk; *Sneyd* in Staffs. The distribution pattern of such surnames suggests that each might have had a separate place-name origin: **Snead** is mainly found in the West Midlands and in east-central Wales; **Snaith** in Co Durham and Northd; **Sneath** in Lincs; **Sneyd** in Staffs. A family called **Sneyd** (pronounced '*Sneed*') built a substantial house for themselves at Keele in Staffs during the sixteenth century; their country estate was eventually acquired by Keele University.

Snedden/Sneddon, *see* **Snowden**.

Snelgrove P From an unidentified place-name OE 'snail copse'. South/south-west of England surnames.

Snell N/F Nickname for a bold, brisk person OE (compare the German word *schnell*, 'quick'), and known to have been used as an OE first-name. **Snelling** and **Snelson** are variants, but although the latter can be 'son of **Snell**', its strong presence in Chesh suggests that the place-name *Snelson* in that county OE '*Snell*'s farm' will usually be the point of origin. **Snell** is chiefly found in Cornwall and Devon, **Snelling** in southeast England and in East Anglia.

Snellgrove, *see* **Snelgrove**.

Snelling/Snelson, *see* **Snell**.

Sneyd, *see* **Snead**.

Snook(s) T/N Dweller at a projecting, pointed piece of land OE; or a nickname for a person with a prominent, pointed nose. **Snook** belongs to southern counties of England; **Snooks** is more scattered.

Snow N Nickname for a person with snow-white hair or skin OE.

Snowball N A charming but mystifying surname: perhaps from a nickname for a man with a snowy patch or bald spot on his head ME or for a tonsured monk, perhaps? Robert Albert **Snowball** of Fakenham in Norfolk tells the story of his grandmother, who threatened to push him up the chimney when he was naughty, saying that the young boys who climbed up chimneys to clean them were called 'snowballs', and that therein lay the origin of the surname... Chiefly a Co Durham/Northd surname.

Snowden/Snawdon/Snedden/Sneddon/Snowdon P Place-names: *Snowden* in WRYorks; *Snowdon* (two such) in Devon OE 'snow hill, hill where snow lies long'. **Snowden** is a northern surname, strongest in WRYorks (where early instances include the spellings **Snauden** and **Snawdon**); **Snawdon**, very scarce, belongs to Devon, and **Snowdon** to Co Durham and Northd. **Snedden** and **Sneddon** are Scottish and scarce.

Snuggs N Some kind of a nickname, possibly used for the son of a snug, neat, trim, cosy, comfortably-off person ME? 'Snug the Joiner in *A Midsummer Night's Dream* had a name appropriate to his skill' (Cottle). A scarce south-of-England surname.

Soame(s) P Place-name *Soham* in Cambs and Suffolk OE 'homestead on a lake'. **Soame** belongs mainly to Norfolk, **Soames** to Kent. *(Arthur) Nicholas (Winston) Soames, a British Conservative politician, grandson of Sir Winston Churchill, was born in Croydon, South London, in 1948.*

Soan(e) N Nickname/epithet applied to a 'son' OE, often used to mean 'junior'. Cottle points out with glee that **Soan(e)s** means 'son of the son'.

Soar P/N Dweller by the river *Soar* in the English Midlands; or a nickname for a person with chestnutty, reddish-brown hair OF (compare **Sorrel**). Mainly a Derbys/Notts surname.

Softley P Place-name in Co Durham OE 'soft/spongy hill'. Found in Co Durham and Northd, yet strongest in Norfolk.

Solomon(s), *see* **Salaman**.

Somer, *see* **Summer**.

Somerby/Summerbee P Place-names in Lincs, Leics ON 'farm used in summer'. Exceptionally scarce in either spelling, **Summerbee** having something of a presence in Hants. *Mike Summerbee, England football player, was born in 1942 in Preston, Lancs.*

Somerfield, *see* **Summerfield**.

Somerlad, *see* **Summerland**.

Somers, *see* **Summer**.

Somerscales/Summerscale(s)/Summerskill T/P Dweller in a shelter used only in the summer months ON; or from *Sum-merscales* in Hazlewood, WRYorks, with the same meaning. The first-known bearer of such a surname is Robert de **Somerscales** of Hazlewood, late thirteenth century. By the late nineteenth century **Somerscales** was a very scarce surname, found in Surrey and in ERYorks, but **Summerscales** and **Summerskill** were still firmly rooted in WRYorks. *Dr Edith Summerskill (1901–1980), Labour Party politician, was born in London; Dr Shirley Summerskill (born 1931), also a Labour Party Member of Parliament, is her daughter by her marriage to Dr E. J. Samuel.*

Somerset P From the county name *Somerset* OE 'dwellers at the summer settlement'. Oddly enough, the surname is most commonly found in WRYorks.

Somerton P Place-name in several counties OE 'farm/settlement used in summer'.

Som(m)erville P/F A Scottish surname in either spelling, probably from a place-name in France, such as *(Graveron) Sémerville,* in Nord. The surname was brought into Scotland by Walter **de Somerville** in the twelfth century. Irish: Anglicized form of Gaelic **O'** [descendant of] **Somachain** ('tubby person'), which also gave rise to the surname **Summerly**. See also **Summerfield**.

Sommer, *see* **Summer**.

Sommerlad, *see* **Summerland**.

Sommers, *see* **Summer**.

Sommerville, *see* **Somerville**.

Soothill/Suttill/Suttle P/N Place-names *Nether/Upper Soothill* in Dewsbury parish, WRYorks OE 'soot hill' (?hill with black soil, ?hill where charcoal is burnt); or a nickname for a subtle, smart, crafty, insidious person OF. Surnames of WRYorks, with a long history in Halifax.

Soper O Occupational term for a soap-maker/-seller OE. Largely a Devon surname. *Rev. Donald (Oliver) Soper (1903–1998), a prominent Methodist minister, socialist and pacifist, was born in Wandsworth, London.*

Sopwith P From an unidentified place-name; there is a *Sopworth* in Wilts OE '*Soppa*'s enclosure', but this is very strongly a Northd surname, and the origin may be the settlement now called *Soppit* OE '?path along which drainage runs' in that county, which in the fourteenth century was *Soppeth*. Cottle quotes a correspondent, writing in the 1970s, who said: 'Until my grandfather's time no Sopwith ever came south of Durham that I know of'. *Thomas Sopwith (1803–1879), surveyor and engineer, was born in Newcastle-upon-Tyne, Northd… Sir Thomas Octave Murdoch ('Tommy') Sopwith (1888–1989), the English aviation pioneer who was also a celebrated yachtsman, was born in Kensington, West London.*

Sorrel(l)/Sorrill N Nickname for a person with chestnutty, reddish-brown hair OF (compare **Soar**). **Sorrel** is sparsely scattered throughout England and Scotland, and **Sorrill** within England only; **Sorrell** is an Essex/Middx surname.

Sotheby/Sotherby/Suddaby T A person who lived in the southern part of a settlement ON. A significant family group of **Sothebys** had lived in Pocklington and Birdsall Hall, ERYorks, but by the late nineteenth century the surname had become very scarce, with a minimal presence in the south-west of England; **Sotherby**, almost as scarce, could then be found in the north-west. **Suddaby** is an ERYorks variant. *When Samuel Baker died in 1778 he left his auctioneers' business to his partner George Leigh and his nephew John Sotheby. In the course of time Leigh and Sotheby became a world-famous fine-art auction house… George Sotheby of the Bombay Civil Service, son of William Sotheby of Sewardstone, Essex, was killed at the battle of Sitabuldi in 1817 at the age of thirty.*

Sotheran/Sotheron, *see* **South**.

Sotherby, *see* **Sotheby**.

Sourbutts, *see* **Sowerbutts**.

Soutar/Sauter/Sout(t)er/Suter O Occupational term for a shoemaker, cobbler OE; or variants of **Salter**. **Suter** belongs to southern counties of England, and **Sauter** to Kent, but **Soutar**, **Souter** and **Soutter** are chiefly Scottish surnames.

South/Sotheran/Sotheron/Southern/Sowman T A newcomer from the south, or a dweller to the south of a given settlement OE. The fully pronounced *-r-* in **Sotheran/Sotheron**, indicated by the added glide-vowel, is characteristic of the North Country, but is missing in **Southern** and the like. **South** is scattered throughout England, but rare in the far north or the south-west; **Sowman** is an Essex/Suffolk surname.

Southall P Place-name in various counties OE 'south nook'. A strongly Midlands surname, so *Southall* in Middx is perhaps rarely the source.

Southam P Place-name in Gloucs and Warwicks OE 'homestead to the south'. Chiefly a South Midlands surname, strongest in Warwicks.

Southcombe P Place-name (several such) in Devon OE 'south valley', and a Devon surname.

Southcott P Place-names in various counties, including *Southcot* and *Southcott* in Cornwall and Devon OE 'southern cottage'. A Devon surname. *Joanna Southcott (1750–1814), a self-described religious prophetess and writer, was born in Taleford, near Ottery St Mary, Devon.*

Southerland, *see* **Sutherland**.

Southern, *see* **South**.

Southey P Place-name in various counties, including *Southey* in Devon, WRYorks, *Southey Green* in Essex and *Southey Wood* in Northants, all OE 'southern enclosure'. Mainly a surname of southern England. *The English Romantic poet Robert Southey (1774–1843) was born in Wine Street, Bristol, to a family with roots in Somerset.*

Southgate/Suggate/Suggett/Suggitt T/P Dweller at the south gate of a town, or from a place-name such as *Southgate* in Middx and in Norfolk OE 'south gate'. **Southgate** and **Suggate** are East Anglian surnames; **Suggett** is strongest in ERYorks, and **Suggitt** in all three Ridings of Yorks.

Southwell T/P Dweller at the south spring/ stream, or from a place-name with the same meaning, such as *Southwell* in Dorset and in Notts (the latter never quite being able to decide whether it should be pronounced as spelt, or as '*Suthell*'). A scattered surname, found in strength in both northern and southern counties of England.

Southwick P Place-name in various counties OE 'southern dwelling'. Strongest in ERYorks.

Southwood T/P Dweller at the southern wood OE, or from a place-name with the same meaning in various counties. Readily confused with/a variant of **Southworth**.

Southworth P Place-name in Lancs OE 'southern enclosure', and a Lancs surname. Readily confused with/a variant of **Southwood**.

Soutter, *see* **Soutar**.

Sowden P/N Place-name in Devon, OE 'south hill/south of the hill'; or a nickname for someone who behaved like a sultan OF (from Arabic), or who played the part of Head Saracen in a play. Found in the south-west and in WRYorks. **Sowdon** may be a variant, though its distribution pattern (scarce, scattered) is different, and some confusion with **Sowton** must always be a possibility.

Sowdon, *see* **Sowden**.

Sowerbutts/Sourbutts T Dweller at an end-piece of the common field ME (from Low Latin *butta*), frequently consisting of coarse, worked-out or acid soil. There are fields called *Sour Butts* in Derbys, Westmd and elsewhere, though **Sowerbutts** and **Sourbutts** are almost entirely Lancs surnames. *Bill Sowerbutts (1911–1990), stalwart of the radio programme* Gardeners' Question Time, *was born in Ashton Moss, Lancs.*

Sowerby P Place-name in various northern counties ON 'farm in the mud/marsh'.

Sowman, *see* **South**.

Sowton P Place-name in Devon OE 'southern farm'. Mainly found in Devon and surrounding counties. Readily confused with/ a variant of **Sowden**.

Spackman, *see* **Speakman**.

Spaight, *see* **Speight**.

Spain P Place-names in France: *Épaignes* in Eure (once occupied by a colony of Spaniards); *Espinay* in Brittany OF 'thorn bush'; or, more rarely, referring to a person from Spain, Latin *Hispania*. Sparsely scattered throughout England, strongest in Kent.

Spalding P Place-name in Lincs OE 'the *Spaldingas*, people of the district called *Spald*', a tribe also commemorated at *Spaldington* and *Spalding Moor*, ERYorks. Strongest in East Anglia, but also present in Scotland, whence it was taken in the thirteenth century.

Spark(e)(s) N Nickname for a sprightly, lively person ON, though Bardsley claims that there is a connexion with the word 'sparrowhawk' (see **Sparrowhawk**). Metathesis has given rise to variants such as **Spragg(e)** and **Sprague** (in which a voiced consonant has replaced the unvoiced -*k*-), **Sprake** and **Sprackling** (a diminutive form, mostly found in Dorset). See also **Spratling**. Fittingly enough, an author named R. A. **Sparkes** wrote a book called *Electronics for schools* (1972). *The novelist Muriel Spark, née Camberg (1918–2006) was born in Edinburgh to a Jewish father and an Anglican mother. In 1937 she married Sidney Oswald Spark and soon followed him to Rhodesia.*

Sparrow N Nickname for a sparrow-like person (chirpy, bouncy?) OE. Scattered throughout England, but strongest in the east.

Sparrowhawk N Nickname based upon some resemblance to a sparrowhawk, the bird of prey OE and OE. Cottle found an example of its being hyphenated: **Sparrow-Hawk**. See also **Spark**. Mainly found in Kent and surrounding counties.

Speak(e), *see* **Speight**.

Speakman/Spackman N/O Nickname or occupational name for a spokesman OE. **Speakman** belongs principally to Lancs; **Spackman**, a south-of-England surname, is most common in Wilts.

Spear(e)/Speir(s)/Spier(s) O/N Occupational term for a maker or wielder of spears OE; or a nickname for someone as thin as a spear. Cottle considers that **Speer/Spier** might alternatively refer to a watchman (a '*spier*') OF.

Speck, *see* **Speight**.

Speed N Nickname for a prosperous, successful person OE, or for a swift runner ME. A surname which can be found scattered across northern England and eastern Scotland. *John Speed (1552–1629), historian and cartographer, was born at Farndon, Chesh.*

Speer, *see* **Spear**.

Speight/Spaight/Speak(e)/Speck/Speke N/P Nickname based upon some resemblance to a woodpecker ME (noisy, wearing bright apparel?). There is a place-name *Speke* in Lancs OE 'brushwood, twigs'. **Speight** is strongest in WRYorks; **Spaight** and **Speke**, both scarce, belong principally to Lancs; **Speak** is a Lancs/WRYorks surname, **Speck** is found chiefly in ERYorks, and **Speake** in Salop. *Johnny Speight (1920–1998), the scriptwriter responsible for many classic British TV sitcoms, was born in Canning Town, East London.*

Speir(s), *see* **Spear**.

Speke, *see* **Speight**.

Spellar/Speller/Spel(l)man O Occupational term for a speaker, discourser, narrator OE (one who 'spells it out'). **Spellar** and **Speller** belong to the south-east of England, **Spelman** and **Spellman** generally to the north (though some **Spelmans** are to be found in East Anglia).

Spence, *see* **Spencer**.

Spenceley/Spensley P A place-name origin is clearly at work here; probably '*Low Spenceley/Spenselay* in Whitaside in Grinton' referred to in sixteenth-century pro-

bate records for Swaledale, NRYorks. At that time many **Spenceleys/Spensleys** can be found in Reeth in Swaledale in particular. By the late nineteenth century **Spenceley** was principally a Yorks surname; **Spensleys** were found chiefly in NRYorks and Co Durham, and the earliest-known person to have borne this surname is Thomas **Spensley** of York (1477). Several **Spensleys** emigrated from the Dales to North America during the nineteenth century. See also **Spendlove**. *Brothers Joseph Winfred (1865–1908) and Frederick (1872–1947) Spenceley, highly acclaimed bookplate artists, were both born in Boston, Massachusetts.*

Spencer/Spence/Spenser O Occupational term for a house steward, butler, one who looked after the pantry or larder known as the '*spence*' OF, and who '*dispensed*' provisions from there. Compare **Spender**. **Spens** is a Scottish variant. *The Spencer family, rich farmers in Northants from the fifteenth century onwards, prospered to such an extent that they became Earls of Sunderland and Earls Spencer, and – through the female line – Dukes of Marlborough (the Spencer-Churchills). Sir Winston Churchill and Diana, Princess of Wales (formerly Lady Diana Spencer) belonged to the family group as a whole… The poet Edmund Spenser (?1552–1599) was born in London, though it has been said that his family came from Burnley, Lancs.*

Spender O/N Occupational term for a steward in charge of supplies in a large house or monastery OF (compare **Spencer**); or possibly a nickname for a waster, squanderer OE. Sparsely scattered across the South and West Midlands. *The poet Sir Stephen (Harold) Spender (1909–1995) was born in London to a family which had long been settled in Bath, Somerset.*

Spendlove/Spend(e)(i)low/Spen(d)luff/Spindelow N/P The simple explanation for this surname – that it was a nickname for a person who spread love around, or who wasted it by over-use – may be accurate. However, a place-name origin is also a possibility, especially if we consider the variant **Spend(e)low**. The suffix -*low* (OE *hloew, hlaw*), meaning 'rising ground'/ '(burial) mound', is commonly found in place-names, so *Spellow*, Lancs, is '?*Spila/ Spileman*'s mound'. Of more immediate relevance, given the prevalence of **Spendlove**-type surnames in Derbys, is the presence in that county of place-names such as *Spellow* (Brassington) OE 'hill where speeches were made', and field-names such as *Spellow Cross* (Newton Solney), later corrupted to 'Sparrow Cross', and the thirteenth-century *Le Spenelowe* OE '? clasp/buckle mound' (Eaton and Alsop). So **Spendlove** may have as little to do with spending love as the Derbys surname **Purs(e)glove** has to do with purses or gloves. The use of the preposition 'de' in the name of Hugh **de Spendlove**, mercer, who was made a Freeman of the City of York in 1388, would also suggest a place-name origin, unless it represents a mere slip of the pen. Various York records also feature the surnames **Spendeluf** (1415), **Spenlowe** (1433), **Spensley** (1477) and **Spendlay** (1521). George Redmonds has found examples of the name **Spendlowe/Spendluff** giving way to **Spencley** and **Spendley** in succeeding generations of the same Yorkshire family. The surname **Spencley**, including a range of variants of the same name (**Spencelay**, **Spensley**, etc.) is much in evidence in sixteenth-century probate records for Swaledale, where we also find references to the hamlet of *Low Spenceley/ Spenselay* in Whitaside in Grinton. A surname such as **Waddilove**, with its variant **Waddilow**, bears comparison with **Spendlove/Spend(e)low**, and the possibility that the final element *-low* might be derived from the French word *loup*, meaning a wolf, should never be discounted. Walter **Spendlove** alias Alsop of Highedge (Heage), Derbys, a former Yeoman of the Guard who made his will in 1613, is said to be descended from a certain John **Spendlove**, who was living in the same village in the early fifteenth century. **Spendlove**, the commonest variant of this surname, is strong in Derbys; **Spendlow**, very scarce, can be found in Norfolk and Lincs; **Spendilow** is mainly a Staffs surname.

Spens/Spenser, *see* Spencer.

Spensley, *see* Spenceley.

Spib(e)y, *see* Spivy.

Spicer/Spice O Occupational term for a spice-seller, grocer, druggist OF. **Spicer** is scattered throughout the south-east, strongest in Middx and Kent; **Spice** is a Kent surname.

Spick(er)nell O Occupational term for a sealer of the monarch's writs in Chancery ME *spigurnel*, from Anglo-Latin. A Hants surname in both spellings.

Spier(s), *see* Spear.

Spiller O/N Occupational term for a jester or tumbler ME; or a nickname for a waster, parasite OE. A West Country surname, strongest in Somerset.

Spilsbury P Place-name *Spelsbury* in Oxon OE '*Speol*'s fortified place', though the surname is mainly found in Staffs and surrounding counties. *Sir Bernard Henry Spilsbury (1877–1947), the forensic pathologist whose cases included the Dr Crippen and the 'Brides in the bath' murders, was born in Leamington Spa, Warwicks.*

Spindelow, *see* Spendlove.

Spindler O Occupational term for a spindle-maker OE. A Suffolk surname.

Spink(e)(s), *see* Pink.

Spinney T Dweller at a copse or spinney OF *espinei*. Principally found in Dorset, the county which was home to a dynasty of **Spinney** clockmakers, descendants of Thomas **Spinney** of Winterborne Stickland, who died in 1709.

Spital/Spittal(l)/Spittle T/O Dweller/ worker at a hospital or lodging house ME (having lost the *ho-* of OF). Cottle toys with the idea that what he calls the 'unhygienically-named place-name *Spital in the Street*, Lincs' might have given rise to such surnames, but their distribution pattern is against him: **Spital**, very scarce, is found in NRYorks; **Spittal** is Scottish; **Spittall** is thinly scattered throughout England and Scotland; **Spittle** belongs to Staffs.

Spittlehouse T Dweller at a hospital house OF and OE. Chiefly a Lincs/Notts surname.

Spiv(e)y ?F/N For Reaney this surname is derived from a ME first-name *Spivey*. In *The place-names of the West Riding of Yorkshire* (vol 3, 1961) A. H. Smith, faced with the need to explain place-names such as *Spivie Holme* and *Spivey Row*, notes a reference to Thomas **Spyvy** in 1383, and believes that the surname might be connected with the dialectal words *spiff(y)*, *spiffing* or *spiving* ('fine, smart'); essentially George Redmonds is of the same mind, and says that much of the early history of the surname can be found in Lofthouse (near Wakefield) and in Sowerby. **Spiby** and **Spibey** would seem to be variants, though they belong principally to Lancs, unlike **Spivy** and **Spivey**, which are WRYorks surnames.

Spode P Place-name *Spoad* in Salop, of uncertain meaning ?OE *spadu* 'spade (-shaped field)'. A Staffs surname. *Josiah Spode (1755–1827), English potter and merchant, was born in Stoke-on-Trent, Staffs, the son of Josiah Spode senior, who had established the Spode pottery factory there.*

Spofford/Spofforth P Place-name *Spofforth* in WRYorks OE 'ford at a spot/plot of land', which was *Spoford(e)* in Domesday Book, later *Spotford*, and *Spoufford* in 1546, though it would seem unlikely that this settlement gave rise to the very scarce surname **Spufford**, which belongs principally to Beds and by the late nineteenth century could be found in Beds/Bucks/Herts; **Spuffard** at that period was restricted to Bucks and Middx.

Spong T Dweller at a long narrow strip of ground ME, 'later East Anglia–Leics–Northants dialect' (Cottle), though the surname is mainly found in Middx and Surrey.

Spooner O Occupational term for one who made or fitted roofing-shingles ME plus -*er* suffix, but also possibly a maker of spoons. David Hey sums up the situation thus: 'In southern England a spooner made roofs with wooden shingles, but in the north he made spoons out of wood or horn'. The surname is mainly found in eastern and north-western England. '*Spoonerisms* take their name from the Rev. W. A. **Spooner** (died 1930), something of whose spirit was upon me just now when I nearly invented the melancholy trade of "roofer with shingles"' (Cottle). Rev. Spooner, Warden of New College, Oxford, who was far from the buffoon he is sometimes made out to be, was born at Grosvenor Place, London. On one occasion he is said (apocryphally?) to have upbraided a student in the following terms: 'Sir, you have *tasted* two whole *worms*, you have *hissed* all my *mystery* lectures, you have been caught *fighting* a *liar* in the quad; you will leave Oxford by the next *town drain*'.

Spottiswoode P Place-name in Berwickshire, Scotland, of which the second element is ME *wode* ('wood'), the first being apparently a personal name. A surname which has travelled far and wide, carried by Scots settlers into the far reaches of the old British Empire. *Alexander Spotswood (c.1676–1740s), English army officer and Governor of Virginia, was born in Morocco, where his father was surgeon to the garrison; his great-grandfather was John Spottiswoode (1565–1639), Archbishop of St Andrews, and the family's deeper ancestry leads back to King Robert II of Scotland... George Edward Eyre and William Spottiswoode (1825–1883) achieved fame as official printers to Queen Victoria.*

Spowage A distinctive surname, one which has been ignored by compilers of surname dictionaries, and which seems determined to elude capture. The suffix -*age* is a familiar enough element in place-names, though no place called *Spowedge*, *Spowich* or the like comes readily to hand; it might alternatively suggest a French origin, but no such name is featured in French surname dictionaries. The existence of an obscure and now obsolete dialect term *spouch* (used of wood which is sappy), which is confined to Norfolk and Suffolk, may only be of passing interest. One theory has it that the origin may be a topographical term for a man who dwelt in a place where a plant known as 'spurge' (OF *espurge*), characterized by an acrid milk juice possessing medicinal properties, grew in abundance. The surname **Spurge** can be found in parish register entries as early as the sixteenth century in Berks, Essex, London, Leics, Norfolk and Surrey. But **Spowage** is a different kettle of fish: by the time of the 1881 census, it was very much a Notts surname, a concentration reinforced by an examination of parish register entries, where Notts predominates once again, putting a handful of Derbys and Yorks references in the shade. The earliest such entry which comes to light is that for a baptism of Alice, daughter of Thomas and Jane **Spowage**, baptized in East Bridgford in 1672. This poses a problem: either the **Spowage**s of Notts are **Spurge**s who have moved north and changed their name in the process, or they are immigrants, possibly from mainland Europe, who have brought their unusual surname with them. No **Spowage**s appear in the Protestation Returns for Notts in 1641/2, nor in subsidy lists for that county in 1689, nor in Notts marriage licences, 1590–1754. Meanwhile, alternative spellings include **Spouge** (eighteenth- and nineteenth-century parish register entries in Notts) and **Spouage** (nineteenth-century Notts marriage licences, together with three individuals named in the 1881 census – two in Derbys, one in Lincs). The fact that five individuals in the 1881 census named **Spourge** are living in Notts (four) and Derbys (one) might take us back to a **Spurge** surname after all? **Spowage**s alive today have the good fortune to be the proud possessors of an intriguing surname, but the bad fortune to be uncertain as to its exact origins.

Sprackling/Spragg(e)/Sprague/Sprake, *see* Spark.

Sprat(t) N Nickname for a person of small stature, perhaps a mere 'sprout' or 'young shoot' OE *spryt*. Readily confused with/a variant of **Sproat**. See also **Spratling**. Both **Sprat** and **Spratt** are scattered surnames.

Spratling N A diminutive of **Spratt**, or a variant of **Sprackling** (see **Spark**). A Kent/Somerset surname.

Spratt, *see* Sprat.

Spray N Nickname for a lanky thin person, a mere twig ME (compare **Sprigg**). Chiefly a Notts/Derbys surname.

Spreckley P Place-name *Spreakley* in Surrey OE 'clearing with shoots, twigs', its pronunciation perhaps influenced by ME (from Germanic) *spreckle* (a freckle, speckle). A surname which extends northwards from Northants to WRYorks.

Spriddell/Spriddle ?N A nickname based upon a diminutive of OE 'sprout, twig, peg, chip'? A Cornish surname in either spelling.

Sprigg(s) N Nickname for a lanky thin person, a mere twig ME (compare **Spray**).

Spring N Reaney derives this surname from the season ME, though the use of 'spring' in that sense is a late one; it could be a nickname for nimble and lusty youth, one with a spring in his step, from the OE verb *springan* ('to jump, leap') – compare **Springall**. See also **Springett**. Quite a prolific surname in the south-east quarter of England.

Springall N/O Nickname for a youth, stripling ME *springold, springald, springal(l)*, perhaps from the OE verb *springan* ('to jump, leap') (see **Spring**). But Reaney also makes reference to *springalde* ME 'catapult, ballistic engine', and in principle the surname could refer to a maker of these, or be a nickname for a belligerent person. See also **Springett**. A Norfolk surname.

Springer N/T Nickname for a jumper, leaper, lively person OE plus *-er* suffix; or a dweller by a spring or fountain ME. *The Yiddish word* shrpingen, *with the same meaning and origin, explains the use of the surname by Ashkenazi Jews – hence the TV 'celebrity' Jerry* **Springer**, *who was born in 1944 inside East Finchley tube station [sic], London, England, to Jewish refugee parents who had escaped from Nazi Germany.*

Springett N A diminutive of **Spring**, or a form of **Springall**. A south-east-of-England surname, strongest in Essex and Kent.

Springthorpe P Place-name in Cambs and Lincs OE 'settlement by a copse/spring'. Mostly found in the English Midlands and in WRYorks.

Sproat/Sprod/Sprot(t) F/N From an OE first-name *Sprot*, possibly meaning 'shoot, twig, sprout', though ME *sprote* (from Germanic) denotes freckles. Readily confused with/a variant of **Sprat**. **Sproat** and **Sprott** are strongest in the English/Scottish borders region, and **Sprot** in Northd, but **Sprod** belongs almost entirely to the Severn estuary, strongest in Somerset.

Sprunt N Nickname for a trim, smart, nimble person ME (from Germanic). A Scottish surname, mainly found in Perthshire and surrounding counties.

Spuffard/Spufford, *see* Spofford.

Spurgeon F Bardsley is convinced that the origin here is an 'old and long-forgotten Scandinavian personal name, *Sprigin*'. He describes **Spurgeon** as being a Norfolk surname, one which can be found in that county as early as 1273. 'The spelling of the surname is imitative, a copy of surgeon' – and, we might add, of 'sturgeon'. By the time of the 1881 census, **Spurgeon** had become chiefly an Essex surname, with a further healthy presence in Norfolk. Readily confused with/a variant of **Sturgeon**, a surname of neighbouring Suffolk. The Baptist preacher and religious writer Charles Haddon **Spurgeon** (1834–1892) was born in Kelvedon, Essex. The *Dictionary of National Biography* entry for him says that he 'came of a family of Dutch origin which sought refuge in England during the persecution of the Duke of Alva'. Fernando, Duke of Alva (1508–1582), the despotic Governor of the Netherlands, had certainly killed many thousands of Dutch men and women, and driven others into exile, and the Norfolk antiquary Walter Rye has this to say in his book *Norfolk families* (1912/1913): 'The late Judge Willis, when lecturing in 1903 on the "great" Spurgeon,

said he came out of Essex from a Boer family, but on my asking him for his authority he was unable to find it. Still it is not impossible, and Mr. Willis may have been right, for the first time I find the name in East Anglia is when John Spurgeon was party to a fine in Carbrooke [Norfolk], Michaelmas 6 Elizabeth 1564, and the Dutch had been arriving in Norwich in 1563 and 1579'. Known parish register entries for the surname **Spurgeon** date from as early as 1558 in Suffolk, 1562 in Norfolk and 1572 in Essex.

Spurrier/Spurr O Occupational term for a maker of spurs OE. There is a street called *Spurriergate* in York. **Spurrier** is found in south-west and south-east England, and along the Severn valley; **Spurr** is mainly a WRYorks surname.

Squibb N The word *squib* (probably imitative in origin) occurs early in the sixteenth century in reference to a firework, but it could also be applied to a lampoon or satirical attack (and to one who wrote such a thing?), and even used for a paltry, despicable fellow. *All of this is very unfair to two eminent genealogists who bore this Dorset surname: Arthur Squibb, Clarenceux King of Arms (1578–1650), was the son of William Squibb of Winterbourne Whitchurch, Dorset; his remote kinsman George Drewry Squibb, Norfolk Herald (1906–1978), was of Cerne Abbas, Dorset.*

Squire(s)/Squier(s) O Status or occupational term for a young gentleman attending a knight (and just below him in the social hierarchy), a shield-bearer OF. The term *squire* in the sense of a 'landed proprietor' is probably of too late a date to have had any influence on the surname. See also Swyer.

Squirrel(I) N Nickname for a person bearing some resemblance (large eyes? a good climber? hoarding instincts?) to a squirrel OF, ultimately from Greek 'shadow-tail', 'as if the creature used it for a parasol' (Cottle). Chiefly a Suffolk surname in either spelling. According to the *Squirrell Contact* website, most of the present-day bearers of the surname descend from a family living in and around Hitcham, Suffolk, in the seventeenth century.

Srawley, *see* Shrawley.

Sreeves, *see* Sheriff.

Stable(s) T/O/N Dweller/worker at a stable (formerly used as a shelter for cattle as well as for horses) OF; Cottle believes that such a surname might alternatively be a nickname for a reliable, steady, stable person OF. Surnames of the north of England.

Stac, *see* Stack.

Stace/Stacey, *see* Stacy.

Stack N/O Nickname for a hefty person, built like a haystack ON. Or maybe an occupational term for a haystacker? A scattered surname within England and Wales, found in Ireland as **Stac/Stak(e)**.

Stackhouse P Place-name in WRYorks, OE 'house at (or for) ricks', yet chiefly a Staffs surname.

Stac(e)y/Stace F From the mediaeval male first-name *Stace* (*Eustace*), with its origins in Greek/Latin, borne by several minor saints.

Staddon P Place-name in Devon (several such) OE 'steer (bullock) hill', and a Devon surname.

Stafford P Place-name in: Staffs OE 'ford by a staithe/landing-place'; Dorset (*West Stafford*) OE 'stony ford'; Sussex OE 'steers (bullocks) ford'; Devon (two such, with some etymological cross-over with *Stowford* OE 'ford marked by staves or posts'). Chiefly a surname of the English Midlands and North, strongest in Lancs.

Stagg N Nickname from OE *stagga*, male deer (is Cottle being coy in saying that 'various reasons suggest themselves'?), but used in northern dialects of ME for a young horse. Scattered across southern England, strongest in Somerset.

Stainburn P Place-name in Cumbd, WRYorks ON or OE, plus OE 'stony stream'. A WRYorks surname.

Stainer O Occupational term for a painter

or dyer OF. The Worshipful Company of Painter-Stainers is a London Livery Company. Strongest in Dorset and Hants.

Staines P Place-name in Middx OE '?(at) the (?mile-)stone'. A Middx/Essex surname.

Stainfield P There are two places so-called in Lincs, one near Lincoln OE (Scandinavianized) 'stony field', another near Haconby ON 'stony clearing'. A very scarce scattered surname.

Stainforth P From one of the places so-called in WRYorks OE (Scandinavianized) 'stony ford'. Mainly an ERYorks surname.

Stainton P Place-name in several northern counties OE (Scandinavianized) 'stony place/farm'. Readily confused with/a variant of **Standen**, **Standon**, **Stanton**, **Staunton** or **Stenton**.

Stak(e), *see* Stack.

Stallabrass/Stallebrass/Stallybrass ?P/N A fascinating surname of uncertain origin. A place-name origin would seem to be a possibility, but these surnames are not known to have been used with a preposition. Reaney supposes that there might be a first-name or nickname origin, but Cottle, having played with a nickname based upon 'stalwart arm' (ME *stalworth* and OF *bras*), calls such an option 'attractive but shaky'. **Stallabrass** is a Herts/Cambs surname; **Stallebrass** and **Stallybrass** are sparsely and unevenly scattered.

Stallan, *see* Stallion.

Stallard/Stallwood/Stallworthy/Stollard/Stollery/Stolworthy N Nickname for a stalwart, sturdy, brave person OE. **Stallard** is mainly found in Gloucs and surrounding counties, **Stallwood** in Bucks, **Stallworthy** in Surrey, **Stollard** in Middx, **Stollery** in Suffolk and **Stolworthy** in Norfolk.

Stallebrass, *see* Stallabrass.

Stallion/Stallan/Stallon N Nickname for a person bearing some resemblance to a stallion OF, 'for virility or lasciviousness' (Cottle). **Stallion** belongs mainly to

Middx, **Stallan** to Cambs and **Stallon** to Norfolk.

Stallwood/Stallworthy, *see* Stallard.

Stallybrass, *see* Stallabrass.

Stamford P Place-name in ERYorks, Lincs, Northants, Northd OE 'stony ford'. Readily confused with/a variant of **Stanford**.

Stamp P Place-name *Étampes* in Seine-et-Oise, France (ultimately *Stampae*, a pre-Roman name of unknown meaning). Widely scattered throughout England, strongest in Lincs. *The actor Terence (Henry) Stamp was born in Stepney, East London, in 1938.*

Stamper N/O Apparently derived from a nickname, from ME, applied to a person who used a pestle or rammer (or behaved like one?), or who was known for stamping his feet (even a treader of grapes?). Scattered throughout the north of England, strongest in Cumbd.

Stanbridge P Place-names: *Stanbridge* in Beds, Hants; *Stambridge* in Essex OE 'stone bridge'. A Beds surname.

Stanbury P Place-name *Stanborough*, Devon OE 'stone hill', and a Devon surname.

Standage, *see* Standish.

Standaloft N A nickname for a person who stood erect OE plus ON. A Lincs surname.

Standen/Standing P Place-name *Standen* in Berks, Lancs, Wilts, OE 'stony valley', and in the Isle of Wight OE 'stony hill'. **Standen** can be readily confused with, or be a variant of, **Stainton**, **Standon**, **Stanton**, **Staunton** or **Stenton**.

Standerwick P Place-name in Somerset OE 'dwelling on stony ground', and a Somerset surname.

Standeven N Nickname for a person who was upstanding, could act independently, 'stand straight' OE. Mainly found in WRYorks and surrounding counties. Compare **Standfast**.

Standfast N Nickname for a person who could stand his ground, be assertive/resolute OE. Most common in Somerset. Compare **Standeven**.

Standfield, *see* Stanfield.

Standidge, *see* Standen.

Standing, *see* Standen.

Standish/Standage/Standidge P Place-name *Standish* in Lancs OE 'stony enclosure/pasture'. **Standish** is a Lancs surname, though **Standage** and **Standidge** belong more to WRYorks. *Myles Standish (1584–1656), a military officer born at Ellan-bane in Lezayre parish on the Isle of Man, but of Lancs stock, sailed on the* Mayflower *as a military adviser.*

Standley, *see* Stanley.

Standon P Place-names in Hants, Herts, Staffs OE 'stony hill'. A surname found in places as far apart as Staffs and Surrey. Readily confused with/a variant of **Stainton**, **Standen**, **Stanton**, **Staunton** or **Stenton**.

Stan(d)field P Place-name *Stanfield* in Norfolk, Staffs OE 'stony field'. **Stanfield** is principally a northern surname, strongest in Lancs, but **Standfield**, much scarcer, is found mainly in Dorset.

Stanford/Staniford/Staniforth P Place-name *Stanford* in several counties OE 'stony ford'. Readily confused with/variants of **Stamford**.

Stanhope P Place-name in Co Durham OE 'stony valley'. Commonly pronounced 'Stannerp'. Family name of the Earls of Harrington.

Staniford/Staniforth, *see* Stanford.

Stanistreet/Stonestreet T Dweller at a paved (Roman) road OE. **Stanistreet** is mainly found in Lancs, **Stonestreet** in southern counties of England.

Stanley/Standley/Stanly P Place-name in several counties OE 'stony wood/clearing'. In recent times the popularity of *Stanley* as a first-name can be attributed to the fame of the explorer Sir Henry Morton

Stanley (1841–1904) – an ironic development, given the fact that this man was born John **Rowlands**, in Denbigh, Wales, eventually taking his new name after working for a Stockport (Chesh)-born New Orleans cotton trader called Henry Hope **Stanley**. **Stanley** is famously the family name of the Earls of Derby. **Stanley** is predominantly a Lancs surname; **Standley** and **Stanly** are more scattered.

Stannard F From a ME first-name *Stanhard* ('stone-hard'). A Suffolk surname.

Stanney P Place-name in Chesh OE 'stony island'. Sparsely scattered across northern England.

Stansfield P Place-name in Lancs and in WRYorks OE 'stony field'. A Lancs/WRYorks surname.

Stanton P Place-name in several counties OE 'stony place/farm', but *Stanton Harcourt*, Oxon, and *Stanton Drew*, Somerset, are named from prominent prehistoric stone monuments. Readily confused with/a variant of **Standen**, **Standon**, **Stainton**, **Staunton** or **Stenton**.

Stanway T/P Dweller at a stone (paved) road OE, or from one of a number of place-names with the same meaning. The reference will normally be to a Roman road. A Chesh/Staffs surname.

Stanwell P Place-name in Middx OE 'stony spring/stream', but chiefly a Lincs surname.

Stanwick/Stanwix P Place-names: *Stanwick*, Northants OE 'the rocking stone', *Stanwick St John*, NRYorks, and *Stanwix*, Cumbd (on Hadrian's Wall) ON 'stone walls'. Scarce in both spellings; **Stanwick** can be found in Co Durham, **Stanwix** both there and in WRYorks. *By the late nineteenth century there were no examples of the variant* **Stanwyck** *being used within Britain, but the Hollywood actress Barbara* **Stanwyck** *(1907–1990), whose real name was Ruby Catherine Stevens, acquired her stage-name in imitation of a stage actress by the name of Jane* **Stanwyck**.

Staple(s) T/P Dweller by a boundary pillar or post OE, or from a place-name with the same meaning, such as *Staple* in Kent or *Staple Fitzpaine* in Somerset. **Staple** is primarily a Dorset/Somerset surname; **Staples** is strongest in south-east England and in Lincs.

Stapleford P Place-name in several counties OE 'ford marked by a post'. Commonest in Leics.

Staplehurst P Place-name in Kent OE 'hill where posts could be cut'. A scarce Sussex surname.

Staples, *see* **Staple**.

Stapleton P Place-name in various counties OE 'place/farm with a pillar/post' (though the first element of the Herefords place-name may be OE 'steeple'). Widely scattered within England, and also found in Ireland.

Starbuck P Place-name *Starbeck* in WRYorks ON 'stream in sedge/bent-grass'. Strongest in Leics/Notts. *Samuel Starbuck of Nantucket and of Nova Scotia was a Loyalist during the American War of Independence… The international chain of coffee-houses known as Starbucks, established in Seattle, Washington, in 1971, was named after Starbuck, the first mate of the ship* Pequod *in Herman Melville's novel* Moby Dick.

Stark(e) N Nickname for a firm, tough, stiff, harsh person OE; 'no connection with *stark naked*' (Cottle). **Starkey/Starkie** are diminutives. **Stark** is commonest in Scotland, **Starke** in Middx and Norfolk, **Starkey** and **Starkie** in Lancs.

Starkey/Starkie, *see* **Stark**.

Starling N Nickname for a person bearing some resemblance to such a bird OE. It's hard not to agree with Cottle when he says that 'it is hard to see *why*'; unless it be a love for brightly coloured clothes, an ungainly waddling gait or a greedy, squabbling temperament? An east-of-England surname, strongest in Norfolk. Perhaps prone to be confused with **Stirling**?

Starr N/T A nickname from ME *sterre/starre* ('star'), 'for no obvious reason' (Cottle).

Hanks and Hodges suggest that such a name might have been applied to a person with a white patch of hair resembling the 'star' on a horse's forehead, but in principle it could refer to someone living at the sign of the star.

Start/Stert/Sturt P From a minor place-name *Start* or *Stert*, in Devon, Wilts and elsewhere OE 'promontory, hill-spur (literally "tail")'. For the relationship between *-ar* and *-er/-ur*, see **Armistead**. **Start** is widely scattered throughout England; **Stert**, very scarce, can be found around the Severn estuary; **Sturt** is strongest in Surrey and Sussex.

Startup N Nickname, literally 'jump up' (perhaps for a lively, active person?) ME (from Germanic) and OE. A Kent surname.

Statham P Place-name in Chesh OE '(at) the staithes/landing-place', exhibiting the use of a dative plural following a lost preposition.

Stather T/O Dweller/worker at a staithe (landing-place, wharf, embankment) OE. An ERYorks surname.

Staughton P Place-name in Beds, Hunts OE 'outlying farmstead', or 'dwelling built of logs' (compare **Stockton**). A scarce Hunts surname.

Staunton P Place-name in several counties OE 'stony place/farm', but *Staunton* on Wye, Herefords, is OE 'stony hill'. Readily confused with/a variant of **Standen**, **Standon**, **Stainton**, **Stanton** or **Stenton**. **Staunton** is found principally in Lancs and in Ireland (especially Co Mayo).

Staveacre T Probably a dweller at a plot of 'stavesacre' ME (from Latin, reproducing Greek *staphisagria* 'wild raisin', the seeds of which were used against vermin and as an emetic). A very rare Chesh/Lancs surname.

Staveley P Place-name in several Midland and northern counties OE 'wood/clearing where staves can be got'.

Stead P/N/O Place-name in WRYorks OE 'place/estate/farm'; or a nickname (also giving rise to the variant **Steed**) for a person resembling a steed, stallion, stud-horse OE (lusty, frisky, strong?) or an occupational term for someone who tended such beasts. Compare **Steer**.

Steadman/Ste(e)dman O Occupational term for farm-man or a groom/cavalryman (literally 'steed-man') OE (compare **Stead**). **Steadman** is widely scattered throughout England and Scotland, but generally not found in Wales or in the West Country; **Stedman** belongs to south-east England; **Steedman**, scattered, is commonest in Scotland.

Stear, *see* **Steer**.

Stearman O Occupational term for a man who looked after steers/bullocks OE (compare **Steer**), or for a steersman, skipper OE. Mainly a Norfolk surname.

Stearn(e)(s), *see* **Stern**.

Stebbing(s)/Stebbins/Stubbin(g)(s) T/P Dweller in a clearing OE *stybbing*, or from a place-name with the same meaning, or from *Stebbing* in Essex OE '*Stybba*'s people's place', or 'people dwelling at the tree stumps'. Chiefly East Anglian surnames, though **Stubbins** is commonest in Notts and Yorks.

Stedham P Place-name in Sussex OE 'homestead with horses'; a rare surname, found in Devon.

Stedman, *see* **Steadman**.

Steed, *see* **Stead**.

Steedman, *see* **Steadman**.

Steel(e) O/N Occupational term for a steel-worker OE; or a nickname for a man known for his firmness and reliability. Widespread throughout England and Scotland in both spellings.

Steen T/P Dweller near a prominent rock or stone (such as a hundred-stone) OE (compare **Stone**); or from a place-name such as *Stean(e)*, with the same meaning. 'The meaning *stone* applies even if the family origin is Dutch or German' (Cottle) – so compare **Stonhold**. Mainly found in north-west England, especially Lancs.

Steeples T Dweller near a high tower OE (but probably not near a church steeple, which is a later specific usage). A Derbys surname.

Steer/Stear O/N Occupational term for one who tended bullocks OE, or (perhaps with **Sterry** as a variant) one who was strong as an ox or of an unpredictable temper. See also **Stead** and **Stearman**. **Steer** and **Stear** are particularly in evidence in Devon; **Sterry** is a Gloucs/Suffolk surname. *Peter Sterry (1613–1672), Independent minister, was born in London, the son of Anthony Sterry (a cooper from Ruardean, Gloucs) and his wife Julia.*

Steggal(l)(s)/Steggell/Steggle(s), *see* Stile.

Stell, *see* Still.

Stenson P/F Place-name in Derbys (*Steineston* in 1206) ON '*Steinn*'s farm'; or a patronymic derived from **Stephen**.

Stenton P There is a such a place-name in East Lothian, Scotland OE 'stony place/farm', but this surname, which belongs principally to WRYorks, is quite likely to share its origins with the **Standen, Standon, Stainton, Stanton, Staunton** group.

Stephen/Steven F From the ME first-name *Stephen/Steven* (Greek *Stephanos* 'crown, wreath, garland'). Made popular thanks to the first Christian martyr. Those versions of the surname spelt with a -*v*- rather than a -*ph*- accurately imitate the voiced consonant which is the norm when the name is spoken aloud. **Stephens(on)**, **Stevens(on)**, **Stim(p)son** and **Stinson** are patronymic forms. See also **Stenson**. **Stephen** and **Steven** are mostly found in Scotland, **Stephens** in Cornwall, **Stevens** in southern counties of England and in the South Midlands, **Stephenson** and **Stevenson** in northern England and Scotland. The comically named '*Even* Stephens' was born in Llanwrthwl, Breconshire, Wales, in 1856. *The novelist, essayist and poet Robert Louis Stevenson (1850–1894), born in Edinburgh, was baptized 'Robert Lewis Balfour Stevenson', but changed his name while in his teens. To his family and friends he was always 'Louis'… The stage and television actor Robert Lindsay was born Robert Stevenson in Ilkeston, Derbys, in 1949.*

Stephens(on), *see* Stephen.

Stepney P Place-name in Middx OE '*Stybba*'s landing place'. A fairly scarce surname, found mostly in the south of England. *Alexander Cyril ('Alex') Stepney, a successful English goalkeeper who played for many years for Manchester United, was born in Mitcham, Surrey, in 1942.*

Stepto(e) ?N Presumably a nickname for a person known to tread lightly, from an OE word for 'tiptoe'. Bardsley favours a place-name origin but, as so often, laments the fact that he cannot 'find the spot' (which presumably contains a final element, *hoe*, as in *Prudhoe* OE '*Pruda*'s hill-spur', Northd). A surname of the south of England. *Patrick Christopher Steptoe (1913–1988), the obstetrician and gynaecologist who pioneered fertility treatment, was born in Oxford… The famous 1960s and 1970s television comedy series* Steptoe and Son, *featuring two rag-and-bone men living in the fictional Oil Drum Lane in London, was given a certain extra bite by the fact that its central father-and-son duo, played by Wilfrid Brambell and Harry H. Corbett, loathed each other offstage.*

Sterling, *see* Stirling.

Stern(e)/Stearn(e)(s) N Nickname for a stern, austere person OE. Forms ending in -*e* reflect the spelling of the OE adjective. The surname **Stern** (derived from 'star') has been reinforced in recent times by German-Jewish immigrants to the British Isles. **Stern** is the family name of the Barons Michelham. *Laurence Sterne (1713–1768), the English novelist and Anglican clergyman best known for his novel* The life and opinions of Tristram Shandy, *was born in Clonmel, County Tipperary, Ireland.*

Sterndale P Place-name in Derbys OE 'valley with stony ground', but principally a Lancs surname.

Sterry, *see* Steer.

Stert, *see* Start.

Steuart, *see* Steward.

Stevens(on), *see* Stephen.

Steward/Steuart/Stewart/Stuart   o
Occupational term for a steward, keeper of a household, seneschal OE; 'so to the Lord High Steward of Scotland, and on to a dynasty' (Cottle). The unvoicing of final -*d* to -*t* is a typically Scots custom. **Steward-son** and **Stewartson** are patronymic forms, while **Stuart** is perhaps a Frenchified respelling. Apart from the use of such surnames by the Kings and Queens of Scotland and England (Queen Anne being the last Stuart monarch to occupy the British throne), **Stewart** is the family name of the Earls of Galloway, and **Stuart** of the Earls Castle Stewart and the Earls of Moray.

Stewardson/Stewart/Stewartson, *see* Steward.

Stickells, *see* Stile.

Stickland P Place-name *Winterborne Stickland*, Dorset OE 'at the steep lane', and principally a Dorset surname.

Stickler T Dweller at a steep place or declivity OE plus -*er* suffix. The meaning 'moderator, umpire, mediator between combatants' (ME from Germanic) is first recorded as late as 1538, but may have existed in surname-forming days. A surname found chiefly around the Severn estuary.

Stickles, *see* Stile.

Stickley P From an unidentified place-name OE 'steep clearing' (compare **Stickland**) or perhaps 'clearing with sticks, branches' OE *sticca*. A possible source is *Stickley (Coppice)* in Dorset OE 'steep ridge'. Bardsley found a reference to *William atte Sticlegh* in Somerset, 1327–8. Like **Stickland**, this is a surname chiefly found in Dorset.

Stiff N Nickname for a physically rigid person, or for one who was steadfast, or tough, obstinate OE.

Stiggles, *see* Stile.

**Stile(s)/Steggal(l)(s)/Steggell/
Steggle(s)/Stickells/Stickles/Stiggles/
Style(s)** T Dweller at a steep incline OE *stigol* or at a stile OE *stigel* (both originating in the OE verb *stigan*, 'to climb'). Variants in *Steg/Stig-* have retained a voiced -*g*-, which is unvoiced to -*k*- in those beginning with *Stick-*. See also **Still**. **Stile** is mostly found in Devon; **Stiles** belongs to the south of England and to the South Midlands, **Style** to the south-east and south-west, and **Styles** to the south-east corner of England; all the **Steggal**-type variants are strongest in East Anglia, especially Suffolk; **Stickells** and **Stickles** belong to Kent, and **Stiggles** has a limited presence in Surrey. *Norbert Peter ('Nobby') Stiles, Manchester United and England football player, was born in Manchester in 1942.*

Still/Stell N/T Nickname for a quiet person OE; or a dweller by a fishing enclosure, fish-weir OE; or a short-vowelled form of **Stile**. **Still** is mostly found in south-east England and north-east Scotland, **Stell** in WRYorks.

Stillwell, *see* Stilwell.

Stilton P Place-name in Hunts OE 'place at a stile/ascent', though the cheese to which it gave its name is normally made elsewhere. Mainly found in Bucks and surrounding counties.

Stil(l)well T Dweller at a quiet spring/stream OE. Surrey/Sussex surnames.

Stim(p)son, *see* Stephen.

Stinchcombe P Place-name in Gloucs OE 'sandpiper/dunlin valley', and a Gloucs surname.

Stinson, *see* Stephen.

Stirk N/O Nickname for a person who resembled a bullock/heifer OE, or who tended such beasts. A WRYorks surname.

Stirling/Sterling P From the place-name *Stirling* in central Scotland (*Strivelin* in 1147), of uncertain etymology – perhaps derived from a river-name. Prone to being confused with **Starling**?

Stirton P There is such a place-name in

WRYorks OE 'farm on a Roman road', but this is predominantly a Scottish surname, strongest in Fifeshire, and may well have its origins in the place-name *Stirton*, near Cupar in that county.

Stob(b)art F From a mediaeval first-name, probably OE 'stump-strong'. A northern surname in both spellings, strongest in north-east England. *Edward 'Eddie' Stobart, transport entrepreneur, was born in Hesket Newmarket, Cumbd, in 1954.*

Stobbs, *see* **Stubbs**.

Stock(s) T/N/O Dweller by a tree-trunk, tree-stump, footbridge OE (compare **Stocking**); or a nickname for a stocky person, or an occupational term for a keeper of the village stocks or for one who felled or grubbed up tree-stumps. The surname reached its greatest eminence with the twelfth-/thirteenth-century St Simon **Stock**, who became head of the Carmelites. Readily confused with/a variant of **Stoke**; *see also* **Stoker**. Stock is mainly found in Essex and surrounding counties, and **Stocks** in WRYorks, while the variant **Stocker** is strongest in south-west England.

Stockbridge P Place-name in several counties OE 'tree-trunk/log bridge'. A surname of south-east England.

Stockdale/Stockdill/Stogdale/Stogdill P Essentially from a Cumb/NRYorks valley-name, with related place-names OE 'tree-stump valley', though some are possibly ON 'pillar valley' or OE 'outlying cattle-farm valley'. These are surnames of the north of England, especially WRYorks. George Redmonds says that the Yorks surname **Stockdale** can be found as **Stockden** (just as confusion is known to exist between **Ovendale** and **Ovenden**), but by the late ninteenth century **Stockden**, a scarce surname, was restricted almost exclusively to Gloucs.

Stockden, *see* **Stockdale**.

Stockdill, *see* **Stockdale**.

Stocker, *see* **Stock**.

Stockford T Dweller at a ford by a tree-stump OE. Mainly found in Oxon and surrounding counties.

Stocking T/P Dweller on ground cleared of tree-stumps OE (compare **Stock**), or from a place-name with the same meaning. **Stocking** can be found in isolated groupings in Middx, Norfolk and Staffs; **Stockings** belongs to Norfolk and Suffolk.

Stockings, *see* **Stocking**.

Stockland P Place-name in several counties OE 'land belonging to a religious house' or 'land having a tree-trunk, tree-stump, foot-bridge' (compare **Stock**). A rare Derbys surname.

Stockley P Place-name *Stockley* or *Stockleigh* in various counties OE 'clearing with tree-stumps' (compare **Stock**). A scattered surname, found in Dorset, Lancs and the West Midlands.

Stockton P Place-name in various counties OE 'outlying farmstead' or 'dwelling built of logs' (compare **Stock** and **Stoughton**). *Richard Stockton (1730–1781), of a family of New Jersey Quakers, was one of those who signed the Declaration of Independence.*

Stockwell P Place-name in South London OE 'tree-stump spring/stream, plank-bridge stream' (compare **Stock**). A scattered surname.

Stockwood P Place-name in Devon, Dorset, Somerset OE 'wood belonging to a religious house' or 'tree-stump wood' (compare **Stock**). Principally a surname of Glamorgan, South Wales. *(Arthur) Mervyn Stockwood (1913–1995), Bishop of Southwark (1959–1980), was born in Bridgend, Glamorgan.*

Stod(d)art/Stoddard/Stoddert/Stodhart/Stothard/Stotherd/Stothert O Occupational term for a stud-herd, one who bred or who kept horses OE (compare **Studd**). Surnames found principally in the north of England and in Scotland.

Stogdale/Stogdill, *see* **Stockdale**.

Stoke(s) T/P Dweller at a 'place', a religious site, a secondary (outlying) settlement OE *stoc*, or from a place-name with the same meaning. A scattered surname in both spellings. Readily confused with/a variant of **Stock**; *see also* **Stoker**.

Stoker P A variant of **Stock** or **Stoke**. A surname of the north-east of England.

Stokes, *see* **Stoke**.

Stokoe P Place-name *Stockhow* in Cumbd, of uncertain etymology; perhaps OE and ON 'tree-stump hill/barrow'. A Co Durham/ Northd surname.

Stollard/Stollery/Stolworthy, *see* Stallard.

Stone(s) T/P/O Dweller near a prominent rock or stone (such as a hundred-stone) OE (compare **Steen**); or from a place-name *Stone*, found in several counties; or an occupational term for a worker in stone. When a male child called '*Flint* **Stone**' was baptized on 12 September 1790 at Marsham, Norfolk, the creation of any such cartooon character lay very much in the future; the Rosetta Stone was acquired by the British Museum in 1802, and twenty-six years later a child named '*Rosetta* **Stone**' was taken for baptism at the City of London church of St Giles, Cripplegate.

Stoneham P Place-name in Hants OE 'stony homestead'. Chiefly a Kent/Middx surname. Readily confused with/a variant of **Stonham**.

Stonehouse T/P Dweller in a house made of stone OE (quite a luxury in mediaeval times), or from a place-name with the same meaning. Mainly found in NRYorks and surrounding counties. *John Thomson Stonehouse (1925–1988), a cabinet minister in Harold Wilson's government but best known as a confidence trickster who faked his own death in 1974, was born in Southampton, Hants.*

Stonelake P Place-name *Stanlake* in Devon OE 'stony stream'. A Devon surname, also found in significant numbers in Guernsey.

Stonestreet, *see* **Stanistreet**.

Stonham P Place-name in Suffolk OE 'stony

homestead'. A Kent/Sussex surname. Readily confused with/a variant of **Stoneham**.

Stonhold T/O A very scarce London/Essex surname. The **Stonhold**s, originally **Van Steenkolen** (probably based upon a Dutch word for 'coal', though the German surname **Steinkohl** [*Steenkuhl*], found especially in Hamburg, literally means 'stone pit'), have their origins in the Low Countries; known to have been worshipping at the Dutch Church in Austin Friars, London, as early as the 1690s, they were almost certainly Protestant refugees, driven from their homeland once the Edict of Nantes, which protected Huguenots and others, was revoked in 1685. For a detailed study of this surname, see *Searching for surnames* by John Titford (2002). See also **Steen**.

Stonor P Place-name in Oxon OE 'stony slope/edge'. Family name of the Barons Camoys.

Stoodley P Place-name *Stoodleigh* in Devon OE 'horse (compare the word "*stud*") clearing/pasture'. Mainly found in Somerset and surrounding counties, and with a strong presence in Jersey. Readily confused with/ a variant of **Studley**.

Stoppard/Stopford/Stopforth P Derived from a local pronunciation of the Chesh town of *Stockport* OE 'hamlet-market place'. **Stoppard** is found mainly in Midland counties of England, especially Derbys, and in the parish churchyard of Shirland in that county eighteenth-century graves for **Stoppard**s can be found alongside those for **Stopherd**s (the latter perhaps by analogy with *-herd* type surnames?). *The playwright Sir Tom Stoppard was born in Czechoslovakia in 1937 as Tomas Straussler. In 1945 his widowed mother Martha married a British army major named Kenneth Stoppard, from whom the boy acquired a new surname.*

Storer O Occupational term for an official in charge of provisions, one who stocked/furnished/catered/stored OF. An East Midlands surname, strongest in Derbys. See also **Storr**.

Storey/Story F From an ON first-name/

byname *Stóri*, meaning 'big'. Surnames of the north of England.

Stork N/T/P Nickname for a man with long spindly legs, like a stork OE; or a dweller at the sign of the stork; or from the place-name *Storkhill* (formerly *Storck/Stork[e]*) in ERYorks ?ON 'dried-out/drained land'. An ERYorks surname.

Storr P Place-name in Lancs, Yorks ON 'young trees, plantation', or a variant of **Storey**. A Lincs surname.

Story, *see* Storey.

Stothard/Stotherd/Stothert, *see* Stodart.

Stott N/O Nickname for a person bearing some resemblance to a bullock, steer, heifer, horse, nag OE, or an occupational term for a keeper of such beasts. A northern surname, strongest by far in Lancs. *The influential evangelical Christian leader John Stott was born in London in 1921. His physician father, Sir Arnold Stott, was the son of a cotton-spinner from Oldham, Lancs.*

Stoughton P Place-name in Leics, Surrey, Sussex OE 'outlying farmstead' or 'dwelling built of logs' (compare **Stockton**).

Stourton P Place-names in various counties OE 'place on the (river) *Stour*' (compare **Sturmer**). Readily confused with/a variant of **Sturton**. Family name of the Barons Mowbray, Segrave and Stourton (titles which have been united since the nineteenth century). The BBC news presenter Edward John Ivo ('Ed') **Stourton** (pronounced '*Sturton*'), born in Lagos, Nigeria, in 1957, is a member of this prominent Roman Catholic family.

Stout N/T Nickname for a bold, stately, stout person OF; or from an ON byname meaning 'gnat'; or a dweller by a squat hillock, stump OE. Particularly strong in Lancs and in the Orkney Islands.

Stove P The name of five farms in Orkney ON 'room, house', and an Orkney and Shetland surname.

Stow(e) P Place-names *Stow* and *Stowe* in several counties OE 'place, assembly-place, religious site', the final -*e* of *Stowe* being a trace of the OE dative inflection. Cottle points out that Harriet Beecher **Stowe**'s husband added a final -*e* to his surname after graduation.

Stowell P There are places so-called in Berks, Gloucs, Somerset, Wilts OE 'stony spring/stream', but the surname is strongest in Lancs.

Strachan/Strahan P Scots: place-name *Strachan*, near Kincardine, Gaelic '?little valley'. Commonly pronounced '*Strawn*'.

Strahan, *see* Strachan.

Straight N Nickname for a man who is upright in posture OE (literally 'stretched'). An Essex surname.

Strang, *see* Strong.

Strange/Stranger N Nickname for a newcomer, foreigner, a man from a distance OF. **Strange** is strongest in Wilts, **Stranger** in Devon (though with a significant presence in Guernsey).

Strang(e)ways P Place-name *Strangeways* near Manchester, Lancs OE 'strong wash/flow/current'. Rare in either spelling, marginally more common in Northd.

Stratford P Place-name in several counties OE 'ford on a Roman road'.

Stratton P Place-name in several counties OE 'place on a Roman road' (compare **Stretton**, **Sturton**). Chiefly a south/south-east of England surname. *Charles Sherwood Stratton (1838–1883), the diminutive-sized son of a Bridgeport, Connecticut, carpenter, achieved fame under the stage-name of General Tom Thumb.*

Straw O/N Occupational term for a dealer in straw OE, or a nickname for a person as thin as a straw, or who had straw-coloured hair. Chiefly a Derbys/Notts surname.

Strawbridge P Place-name in Devon (probably identical with *Stowbridge*, Dartmoor, referred to in 1532) OE 'market/assembly-place bridge'. A Devon surname.

Streat/Street/Strete T/P Dweller on the main street of a village (also **Streeter**), or from a place-name such as *Streat* (Sussex), *Street* (Somerset and elsewhere), *Strete* (Devon) OE 'Roman road'.

Streatley P Place-name in several counties OE 'wood/clearing on a Roman road'. An exceptionally scarce Berks surname. Compare **Streetly, Streetley, Strelley**.

Street/Streeter, *see* Streat.

Streetley P Place-name in Essex OE 'wood/clearing on a Roman road'. A rare Kent surname. Compare **Streatley, Streetly, Strelley**.

Streetly P Place-name in Cambs, Warwicks OE 'wood/clearing on a Roman road'. Mainly found in Kent. Compare **Streatley, Streetley, Strelley**.

Strelley P Place-name in Notts OE 'wood/clearing on a Roman road'. A very scarce Derbys surname. Compare **Streatley, Streetley, Streetly**.

Stretch N Nickname for a firm, severe, vehement, violent person OE *strec*. Chiefly a Chesh/Lancs surname.

Strete, *see* Streat.

Stretton P Place-name in several midland counties OE 'place on a Roman road'. Compare **Stratton, Sturton**.

Stribling, *see* Stripling.

Strickland P Place-name in Westmd OE 'land for bullocks/heifers'. Chiefly a Lancs surname.

Stringer O Occupational term for a bowstring-maker OE. Strongest in WRYorks.

Stringfellow N Nickname for powerful man/friend/chap OE and ON Chiefly a Lancs surname. *Peter Stringfellow, multi-millionaire businessman and club owner, was born in Sheffield, Yorks, in 1940.*

Stripling/Stribling N Nickname for a youth (?one as slim as a strip) ME, from Germanic, plus *-ling* diminutive. **Stripling** is mainly found in Essex/Middx, **Stribling** in Devon.

Strode P Place-name in Somerset OE 'marshland overgrown with brushwood' (compare **Strood, Stroud**), and a Somerset surname.

Strong N Nickname for a strong man OE, or sarcastically for a weak one. **Strang** is principally a Scottish form of the surname.

Strongitharm N Nickname for a person who was strong in the arm OE, a delightful dialectal rendition. A Lancs surname.

Strood P Place-name in Kent OE 'marshland overgrown with brushwood' (compare **Strode, Stroud**). A scarce Kent surname.

Strother, *see* Struthers.

Stroud P Place-name in Gloucs, Hants and Middx OE 'marshland overgrown with brushwood' (compare **Strood, Strode**). A south-of-England surname. *Robert (Franklin) Stroud (1890–1963), the convict who achieved fame as the 'Birdman of Alcatraz', was born in Seattle, Washington, USA, the son of parents of German or Austro-Hungarian descent.*

Stroulger/Strow(l)ger N/?O Nickname (occupational term?) for an astrologer, fortune-teller, Latin from Greek. East Anglian surnames.

Strudwick P From a place-name, possibly *Strudgwick Wood* in Sussex (formerly *Strodwick*) OE 'dairy-farm in bushy marshland'. Mainly found in Surrey and surrounding counties.

Struthers/Strother T/P Dweller on damp land OE, or from a place-name with the same meaning, such as *Struther* (Lanarkshire), *Struthers* (Fife) or *Strother* (Northumd). **Struthers** is a Scottish surname, strongest in Lanarkshire; **Strother** belongs to Northd.

Stuart, *see* Steward.

Stubbin(g)(s), *see* Stebbing.

Stubbs/Stobbs T/N Dweller at a clearing, a place with tree-stumps OE (compare **Stum-**

bles, **Such**), or a nickname for a short, stumpy man OE. **Stubbs** is found mainly in Chesh/Lancs/Staffs, **Stobbs** in Co Durham/Northd.

Studd T/O Dweller/worker at a stud farm OE (compare **Stodart**). Cottle adds: 'But Tengvik makes it a nickname: "gnat" OE *stût*, Normanized'.

Studley P Place-name in various counties OE 'stud farm wood/clearing'. Chiefly a West Country surname. Readily confused with/a variant of **Stoodley**.

Stumbles T Dweller near a tree-stump OE (compare **Stubbs, Such**). Chiefly a Devon surname.

Sturdee/Sturdy N Nickname for a brave, ferocious, hot-headed man OF (connected with Latin *turdus*, 'thrush', taken to be a mindless bird). **Sturdee** belongs to Devon; **Sturdy** to NRYorks and WRYorks.

Sturge/Sturges(s)/Sturgis F Seemingly from an ON first-name *Thorgils* '*Thor*'s hostage', with the addition of an initial '*S*'. **Sturge** is found mainly in Gloucs, **Sturgis** (scarce) in Middx, Northants and Wilts; **Sturges** and **Sturgess** are widely scattered. *Two prominent American film directors bore the surname Sturges: Preston Sturges (1898–1959), born in Chicago as Edmund Preston Biden, was adopted by Solomon Sturges, his mother's third husband; John Sturges (1911–1992) was born in Oak Park, Illinois.*

Sturgeon O/N Occupational term for a fishmonger, or a nickname for someone resembling a sturgeon, the fish OF ('But why?' Cottle asks in genuine bemusement). The first-known reference to *Sturgeon's Farm* in Writtle, Essex, dates from as late as 1777, though it is said to have been referred to before then as *Turges*, from a family so-called. **Sturgeon** is chiefly a Suffolk surname. Readily confused with/a variant of **Spurgeon**, which belongs to the neighbouring counties of Essex and Norfolk. The longest personal name in the bible was bestowed upon *Mahershalalhashbaz* **Sturgeon**, who was born c.1857 in Hessett, Suffolk.

Sturges(s)/Sturgis, *see* Sturge.

Sturmer P Place-name in Essex, Suffolk OE 'mere/lake formed by the (river) *Stour*' (compare **Stourton**). Mainly found in the eastern Home Counties, strongest in Essex.

Sturt, *see* Start.

Sturtivant/Sturtevant N Apparently a nickname for a hasty person ME 'start/leap forward' (from Germanic) plus OF. **Sturtivant** is a very scarce surname, found in pockets in Notts and Surrey; **Sturtevant** is even scarcer.

Sturton P Place-name in several counties OE 'place on a Roman road' (compare **Stratton, Stretton**). Readily confused with/a variant of **Stourton**. Scattered throughout the south-east quarter of England.

Stuttard, *see* Stodart.

Stutter N Nickname for a stutterer ME. Sparsely scattered throughout England, strongest in Surrey.

Stych(e) P Place-name *Styche* in Salop OE 'bit/piece/allotment of ploughland', and also a frequent element in Cambs/Essex field-names. Surnames of Staffs/Warwicks.

Style(s), *see* Stile.

Such/Sutch/Zouch T/N Dweller at a clearing, a place with tree-stumps OE (compare **Stubbs, Stumbles**); or a nickname for a short, stumpy man OE. Members of the **Zouch** family, once extensive landowners, gave their name to *Ashby de la Zouch*, Leics. **Such** is mainly found in the West Midlands, **Sutch** in Kent, Lancs and Middx. *David Edward Sutch (1940–1999), born in Hampstead, North London, was an English musician and politician who changed his name to 'Screaming Lord Sutch, Third Earl of Harrow' in honour of his favourite roll 'n' roll star, Screamin' Jay Hawkins, and founded the so-called Official Monster Raving Loony Party in 1983.*

Suckley P Place-name in Worcs OE 'wood/clearing with sparrows'. A surname of the north-west, strongest in Chesh.

Suckling N Nickname for a person resembling a suckling, an unweaned infant, either in appearance or in behaviour OE. Mainly found in Essex and surrounding counties. *The Cavalier poet Sir John Suckling (1609–1641), born in Whitton, Twickenham, Middx, came from a family with roots in Norfolk and Suffolk.*

Sucksmith O Occupational term for a ploughshare-smith OF and OE. Readily confused with/a variant of **Sixsmith**. A Lancs/WRYorks surname.

Sudbury P Place-name in various counties OE 'southern fort/manor'. A scattered surname.

Suddaby, *see* Sotheby.

Suddell, *see* Sudell.

Sudden N/P Nickname for an impetuous person OF; or from the place-name *Sudden* in Lancs OE 'southern valley'. Yet the surname is most commonly found in Berwickshire, Scotland.

Sud(d)ell T/P Dweller in a southern valley OE, or from a minor place-name with the same meaning. A Lancs surname in either spelling. Readily confused with/a variant of **Siddal**?

Suffield/Suffell/Suffill P Place-name *Suffield* in Norfolk and in NRYorks OE 'southern field'. **Suffield** is commonest in NRYorks, **Suffell** (scarce) in NRYorks and WRYorks and **Suffill** (also scarce) in ERYorks and NRYorks.

Suffolk P The county name *Suffolk* OE 'southern folk/people'. Most common in the Midlands, strongest in Leics and Warwicks.

Sugar(s) F From a ME first-name ?*Sigher/Soegar/Saher/Seir* (compare **Sagar**, **Sayer**). **Sugar** belongs mainly to Middx and Somerset, **Sugars** to Beds. *The entrepreneurial businessman Sir Alan Michael Sugar was born in Hackney, East London, in 1947, the son of a Jewish tailor.*

Sugden P Place-name in Salop and WRYorks OE 'swampy hill/valley'. A

WRYorks surname. Family name of the Barons St Leonards.

Suggett/Suggate/Suggitt, *see* Southgate.

Sullivan F Irish: Anglicized form of Gaelic **O'** [descendant of] **Suileabhain** ('eye-dark').

Summer/Simmer(s)/Som(m)er(s) N/O/F Nickname for a person with a sunny disposition, or having some connexion with the summer season OE; or an occupational term, a variant of **Sumner** or **Sumpter**. **Summers** and **Summerson** are patronymic forms. Irish: Anglicized form of Gaelic **O'** [descendant of] **Samhraidh** ('summer'). **Summer** is mostly found in Lancs; **Summers** is widely scattered throughout the British Isles; **Summerson** is strongest in Co Durham, **Simmer** in Norfolk, and **Simmers** in Aberdeenshire, Scotland.

Summerbee, *see* Somerby.

Summerell, *see* Summerill.

Summerfield/Somerfield T/P Dweller at a field used in the summer season OE, or from a minor place-name with the same meaning. Confusion between **Summerfield/Somerfield** and **Somerville** would seem to be inevitable.

Summerford T/P Dweller at a ford used in the summer season OE, or from a minor place-name with the same meaning. A scarce Home Counties surname.

Summerhay(e)s T/P Dweller at an enclosure used for beasts in summertime OE, or from a minor place-name with the same meaning. Principally a Somerset surname in either spelling.

Summer(h)ill/Summerell P From one of a number of minor places called *Summerhill/Summer Hill* OE 'summer hill' (hill facing south/used for summer grazing); 'The *-ell* could best be explained as south-eastern dialect (OE West Saxon *hyll*)' (Cottle). These are surnames found in Gloucs, whatever the spelling, though **Summerhill** also has a presence in Lanarkshire, Scotland, and **Summerell** in Somerset.

Summerland/Sommerlad F From an ON first-name *Sumarlithr/Sumarlithi* ('summer rover/warrior, a Viking'). The insertion of an *-n-* to make *land* is no doubt the result of folk etymology. A Scots Gaelic version has led to the surname **McSorley**, and M. A. Lower states that *Somerlad*, Thane of Argyle in the twelfth century, founded the Clan MacDonald. Cottle believes that a first-name *Somerlad* 'is still in occasional use'. **Summerland** is an East Midlands surname; by the late nineteenth century **Sommerlad** had a fragile and very restricted existence in Kent, Surrey and ERYorks, but has survived to the present day.

Summerly, *see* Somerville.

Summerscale(s)/Summerskill, *see* Somerscales.

Sumner O Occupational term for a summoner, an officer citing and warning people to appear in court OF. Perhaps not all were as seedy or thoroughly unpleasant as Chaucer's summoner in *The Canterbury Tales*? See also **Summer**. Chiefly a Lancs surname.

Sumpter/Sunter O Occupational term for a carrier, packhorse-man, muleteer OF *sometier*. See also **Summer**. **Sumpter** is found chiefly in Northants, **Sunter** in the north of England. *The variant Sumter had all but died out in England by the late nineteenth century, but has passed into history thanks to Fort Sumter in Charleston Harbour, South Carolina (named after General Thomas Sumter [1734–1832], whose father was an immigrant from Wales), which was the site of the skirmish which initiated the American Civil War.*

Sumption/Sumsion N Nickame for a person born or baptized on 15 August, the Feast of the Assumption (OF/Latin) of the Blessed Virgin Mary into Heaven. Surnames mainly found around the Severn estuary, strongest in Somerset.

Sunderland P Place-name in various counties, including the town in Co Durham OE 'separate land' (?private or ?away from the main estate); but *North Sunderland*, Northd, was originally OE 'southern land'. Chiefly a WRYorks surname.

Sunter, *see* Sumpter.

Supple N Nickname for a nimble/lithe person, or for one who was a compliant/adaptable person OF. Strongest in Lancs

Surgeon O Occupational term for a surgeon OF (ultimately from Greek *cheirourgia* 'handling, operating', applied even to crafts such as carpentry). A scarce surname found in Lanarkshire, Scotland.

Surrey P From the county name *Surrey* OE 'southern district'. Chiefly an Essex surname.

Surridge F/T/P From a ME first-name *Seric* ('sea-power'/'victory-power'); or applied to a person who had arrived from the south of a given settlement OF; or from the place-name *Surridge*, Devon OE 'southern ridge'. Mainly found in the eastern Home Counties, strongest in Essex. *Walter Stuart Surridge (1917–1992), cricketer and manufacturer of sporting equipment, was born at Herne Hill, London, within two miles of the Oval cricket ground.*

Surtees T Dweller on/by (OF *sur*) the (river) *Tees*, British '?boiling, fervent'. Predictably enough, a Co Durham/Northd surname. *John Surtees, former Grand Prix motorcycle rider and Formula One driver, was born in 1934 in Tatsfield, Surrey… The Surtees Society, dedicated to publishing documentary source material for the history of Northumbria, was founded in honour of the Durham-born historian Robert Surtees (1779–1834).*

Sussams F (Son of) of *Susan*, Hebrew 'lily', of which Cottle says: 'The embarrassing story of Susannah and the Elders in the Apocrypha has been no bar to the popularity of the first-name since the seventeenth century, but it was uncommon in the Middle Ages'. A Norfolk surname.

Sussex P The county name *Sussex* OE '(land of the) south Saxons'. An uncommon surname, strongest in Devon.

Sutch, *see* Such.

Sutcliff(e) P Place-name *Sutcliff*, near Brighouse, WRYorks OE 'southern cliff'. A prolific surname in parts of the West Riding, with an early presence in Hipperholme.

Suter, *see* Soutar.

Sutherland P The Scots county name *Sutherland* ON 'south land', which the Vikings thought of as being 'south' compared with Scandinavia, Orkney and Shetland. **Sutherland** is strongest in Caithness, though **Southerland** is a scarce Norfolk surname. *Graham Sutherland (1903–1980), a versatile and highly acclaiamed English artist, was born in Streatham, London… The Canadian actor Donald (McNichol) Sutherland was born in St John, New Brunswick, in 1935.*

Suttill/Suttle, *see* Soothill.

Sutton P From one of numerous places so-called in almost every English county OE 'southern/south-facing farm'. 'Often a settlement lying to the south of the main one, like Sutton Montis, Somerset, nestling at the southern foot of the conspicuous Cadbury Castle' (Cottle). Strongest in Lancs.

Swaddle P ?Place-name *Swaddale* in Derbys OE 'dale with a track/pathway' (compare the word '*swathe*'), or maybe from *Swaledale* in NRYorks OE and ON 'Valley of the river *Swale*', which is pronounced 'Swodil' locally. Chiefly a Co Durham surname.

Swaffer P Place-name in Kent (now *Swatfield Bridge*) OE 'track/pathway ford', being situated at the point where the road from Ashford to Hythe (formerly a simple pathway?) crosses a stream. A Kent surname.

Swaffield P There is a place called *Swafield* in Norfolk OE 'open country with a track' (compare the word '*swathe*'), but this is a Dorset surname.

Swain(e) F/O From an ON first-name *Sveinn* 'boy, servant'; or the same word used as an occupational term, sometimes for a swineherd, peasant. A surname which is found way beyond the old Danelaw in both spellings, though **Swaine** is at its strongest in WRYorks. The variant **Swayne** is chiefly found in Surrey and in Wilts. See also **Swan** and **McQueen**. **Swainson**, chiefly a

Lancs surname, can be 'son of **Swain**', or a variant of **Swainston**.

Swainston P Place-name in Co Durham ON and OE '*Sveinn*'s place'. Chiefly found in Co Durham, so *Swainston* in the Isle of Wight is unlikley to have contributed to the surname. See also **Swainson**, under **Swain**.

Swallow P/N Place-name in Lincs OE, named after the river *Swallow* ('whirlpool, rushing water'); or a nickname for a person bearing some resemblance to the bird, the swallow OE (graceful, speedy?). Mainly found in WRYorks and surrounding counties.

Swan(n) N/T Nickname for a person as graceful or as pure as a swan OE; or a dweller at the sign of the swan; or a variant of **Swain**, which was anglicized to **Swan** in Old English. **Swanson** (strongest in Caithness, Scotland) is 'son of **Swan**'. *The Hollywood actress Gloria Swanson (1897–1963) was born Gloria Mae Josephine Swanson or Svenson in Chicago, Illinois, the daughter of a Swedish American father and a Polish American mother.*

Swansborough P Cottle is pleased to point out that in the legend of King Havelock the Dane, his little sister is called *Swanborough*, but neither he nor Hanks and Hodges can identify a likely place-name origin here. Yet this is very largely a Wilts surname, and the source will almost certainly be *Swanborough Tump* OE 'barrow of the peasants' in Manninford Abbots, Wilts, the former meeting place for the Hundred of Swanborough. **Swansbury** is a rare Middx/Surrey variant.

Swansbury, *see* Swansborough.

Swanson, *see* Swan.

Swanton P Place-name in Kent and in Norfolk (three such) OE 'swineherds' place'; but chiefly a Somerset surname.

Swanwick P Place-name in Derbys and in Hants OE 'swineherds' dairy farm' (pronounced '*Swannick*'). Mainly found in Notts and surrounding counties.

Swart N Nickname for a 'swart', swarthy

person OE and ON. A very scarce surname, with a limited presence in Lancs and Middx.

Swatridge F From an OE first-name *Swetric* ('sweet power'), made to look like a place-name. A West Country surname, strongest in Somerset.

Swayne, *see* Swain.

Sweatman, *see* Sweet.

Sweet/Sweatman/Swe(e)tman N Nickname for a sweet, pleasant person OE, or, sarcastically, for someone exhibiting no such qualities. **Sweet** is a West Country surname, strongest in Somerset; **Sweatman** is widely scattered throughout England, though not generally found in the northeast; **Swetman** belongs to Staffs and Surrey, **Sweetman** to Lancs and Middx.

Sweetapple N A charming nickname for someone as sweet as an apple OE. Strongest in Dorset and Hants.

Sweeting N/F Nickname for an attractive person, a darling, sweetheart OE, and once used as a first-name. Most commonly found in WRYorks.

Sweetland T/P Dweller by a fertile/productive field OE, or from a place-name with the same meaning, such as *Sweetlands* in Devon. A surname of south-west England, strongest in Devon.

Sweetlove F From an OE female first-name, meaning 'sweet love'. Chiefly a Kent surname.

Sweetman, *see* Sweet.

Swetenham/Swetnam P Place-name *Swettenham* in Chesh OE '*Sweta*'s homestead' (the *-n-* being a sign of the possessive case). **Sweteneham** is most common in Lancs, **Swetnam** in Staffs.

Swetman, *see* Sweet.

Swetnam, *see* Swetenham.

Swift N Nickname for a swift, quick person OE. Most in evidence in the northern counties of England, strongest in Lancs and WRYorks.

Swinburn(e) P Place-name *Swinburn* in Northd OE 'pig brook'. *Algernon Charles Swinburne (1837–1909), the highly controversial poet of the Victorian era, was born at Grosvenor Place, London, though his paternal ancestry can be traced back to twelfth-century Northd, and his paternal grandfather had a country estate at Capheaton in that county.*

Swindell(s) ?P/O A surname of uncertain origin – possibly from a place-name such as *Swindale*, NRYorks OE 'wild boar valley', or a variant of **Swingler**? **Swindell** is most common in Derbys, **Swindells** in Chesh/Lancs. Most bearers of such a surname will pronounce it with a stress on the final syllable, thus avoiding any association with the word '*swindle*'. **Swindler** is (not surprisingly?) a scarce alternative, found in the Midlands and the north.

Swinden/Swindin P There are two places called *Swinden* in WRYorks, one in Langsett (Penistone), and another in Gisburn OE 'pig valley', and these are WRYorks surnames. Readily confused with/a variant of **Swindon**.

Swindlehurst, *see* Swinglehurst.

Swindler, *see* Swindell.

Swindon P Place-name in various counties, including Wilts OE 'pig hill'. A widely scattered surname, readily confused with/a variant of **Swinden**.

Swinfen P Place-name in Staffs OE 'pig marsh'. Mainly found in Warwicks and surrounding counties.

Swinfield P From an unidentified place-name OE 'pig/wild boar field', presumably in or about Leics, where this scarce surname is mainly found.

Swinford P Place-names *Swinford* and *Swineford* in several counties OE 'pig ford'. John of Gaunt's mistress Katherine **Swinford** (her married name) was ancestress of Henry VII and of the Ducal house of Beaufort. A scarce surname, mainly found in Gloucs.

Swinglehurst/Swindlehurst P From a place-name, possibly *Swinglehurst* in the

Forest of Bowland, WRYorks OE 'wild boar hill ridge'. A Lancs surname in both spellings.

Swingler O Occupational term for one who made, or used, a swingle OE *swingell* (a scourge/rod for beating flax, a flail). Mainly found in Leics and surrounding counties. See also **Swindell**.

Swinnerton P Place-name *Swynnerton* in Staffs OE 'farm by the pig ford'. A surname with a well-recorded and prominent history back to the twelfth century.

Swinscoe/Swinscow P Place-name *Swinscoe* in Staffs, on the outskirts of the town of Ashbourne, Derbys ON 'pig copse'. **Swinscoe** is mainly found in Notts and in the south Pennines; **Swinscow**, rare, has a limited presence in Lancs.

Swinton P Place-name in Lancs, NRYorks, WRYorks and in Berwickshire, Scotland OE 'pig farm'. A surname of the north of England and of Scotland (especially Fifeshire). 'An odd name for an Earldom', says Cottle, referring to a title held by the Cunliffe-Lister family.

Swinyard T/O Dweller/worker at a pig enclosure OE. Mainly found in Kent and surrounding counties.

Swire, *see* Swyer.

Swithenbank P From an unidentified place ME 'hillside cleared by burning'; there are place-names containing similar elements in WRYorks, and this is a WRYorks surname.

Sword/Sworder O Occupational term for a sword-maker OE. **Sword** is mostly found in north-east England and in Scotland (especially Angus); **Sworder** belongs to Herts and surrounding counties.

Swyer/Swire P/O From a place-name *Swyre* in Dorset OE 'neck, col, hollow on a ridge', or a variant of **Squire**. **Swyre** is chiefly a surname of the south coast of England, strongest in Dorset, but **Swire** belongs to Lancs/WRYorks.

Sycamore T Dweller by a sycamore tree OF (ultimately from Greek, with the meaning of 'fig-mulberry'). Mainly found in Essex and surrounding areas.

Sydenham P Place-name in Devon, Oxon and Somerset OE 'wide river-meadow', but the Kent place-name *Sydenham* is of later formation, having been *Chipeham* OE '*Cippa*'s homestead/enclosure' in the thirteenth century. The surname is strongest in Devon, Middx, Somerset.

Sydney, *see* Sidney.

Sykes/Sikes/Sitch T/P Dweller by the (boundary) stream, ditch or gully OE or ON; or from one of a number of minor place-names with the same meaning. The forms in *-k-* are northern, whereas the softer *-ch-* form **Sitch** (from OE only) belongs to Essex and Middx. The surname **Sykes** has been the subject of DNA analysis by Professor Brian **Sykes** of Oxford University. **Sykes** is a name principally found in WRYorks, being particularly prolific in Slaithwaite, and the word *syke* is very much a north-of-England topographical term. George Redmonds has found references to the **Sykes** surname in Flockton, near Huddersfield, as early as the 1280s, but a **Sykes** pedigree featured in *Ducatus Leodiensis* by Ralph Thoresby (revised by T. D. Whitaker, second edition, 1816) indicates (accurately or not, as the case may be) that a family of this name which eventually became well established in the West Riding could be traced back to a Richard **Sykes** of *Sykes-Dyke* near Carlisle, Cumbd. *The comic writer and actor Eric Sykes was born in Oldham, Lancs, in 1923.*

Sylvester, *see* Silvester.

Sym/Syme(s), *see* Simon.

Symington/Simington P There are two places called *Symington* in Scotland, one near Ayr and the other near Glasgow, Hebrew plus OE '*Simon*'s farm' (named, it is said, for a twelfth-century owner, Simon Lockhart). A Scottish surname in either spelling.

Symmons/Symms/Symondson/ Sym(m)on(d)s, *see* Simon.

Syzling, *see* Sizeland.

T

**Tabbe(r)ner/Tabberer/Taber(er)/
Tabor** o Occupational term for a drummer, a tabor-player (compare the word *'tambourine'*) OF; **Tabbe(r)ner** can alternatively be a variant of **Taverner**. **Tabbener**, **Tabberner**, **Tabberer** and **Taberer** are surnames of the English Midlands; **Taber** is strongest in Essex, **Tabor** in Cambs.

Tackley P Place-name in Oxon OE 'pasture for tegs (young sheep)'. A Middx/Surrey surname.

Tadd ?N ?A nickname for a person resembling a toad OE *tadde*. A surname of the south and south-west of England, strongest in Cornwall, Sussex and Wilts.

Tadlow, *see* **Tatlow**.

Tadpole A surname of unknown origin. The remarkable thing about **Tadpole** is not that there seem to have been so few examples of its use over the years, but that it was ever used as a surname at all. There is even a charming example of a female child named *Faithfull* **Tadpole**, who was baptized at St John the Evangelist, Dublin, on 11 November 1665. Anyone who is prepared to believe that a surname such as **Hedgehog** was first used of a man who resembled the animal of this name might have no problem in assuming that the first Mr **Tadpole** was a puny kind of a man or one who was always squirming around, like a diminutive tadpole. It would seem more likely that **Tadpole** was derived, by way of folk etymology, from a word such as *todpool* (a pool frequented by foxes), which itself might have been used to describe a topo-

graphical feature or even have acquired the status of a now-lost place-name.

Taffinder, *see* **Tavener**.

Taft, *see* **Toft**.

Taggart, *see* **McTaggart**.

Tailor, *see* **Taylor**.

Tainton P Various place-names could have given rise to such a surname, including *Bishops/Drews/Kings-teignton* in Devon OW and OE 'farm on the river *Teign*', and *Taynton* in Oxon (on a stream once called *Teign*), but **Tainton** is found chiefly in Gloucs, and the place-name *Taynton* in that county OE 'the farm of *Taeta*'s people' will be the origin in most if not all cases.

Tait N Nickname for a jolly, cheerful person ON; readily confused with **Tate**, but with a different origin, though both are principally Co Durham/Northd surnames.

Talbot(t) F The origin of such a surname is far from certain; Cottle suggests a Germanic first-name *Dalabod* (?dale/valley-offer/command), but is scornful of the suggestion that **Talbot** might have been derived from a sign-name, or from a nickname *taille-botte* 'cut-faggot' OF. Chetwynd-**Talbot** is the family name of the Earls of Shrewsbury.

Tal(l)boy(s) O/P Occupational term for a woodcutter OF (literally 'cut-wood'); or from a place-name *Taillebois* in Orne, Normandy OF 'copse wood'. Strongly represented in Gloucs in most spellings, though **Tallboys** is a rare Oxon surname.

Tall N Nickname for a decent, handsome, valiant, prompt person ME from OE – but not for one who was high in physical stature (a later meaning, which only became established in the sixteenth century). Strongest in Devon, but also scattered around eastern England.

Tallboy(s), *see* Talboy.

Tallemach, *see* Tollemache.

Tallentire P Place-name in Cumbd OW 'end of the land' (*-en-* representing 'the'). Mainly found in Cumb and Co Durham.

Tallon F From a Germanic first-name including the element *Tal-* ('destroy') – or '?dale/valley', as in **Talbot**? Chiefly a Lancs surname.

Talmadge, *see* Tollemache.

Tambling/Tamlin/Tam(b)lyn/ Tamplin(g), *see* Thomas.

Tancock F A diminutive of the first-name *Andrew*, with the addition of the *-cock* suffix ('young lad'). A Devon surname.

Tancred F From an OF first-name *Tancred* ('thought-counsel'), originally a Germanic name introduced into Britain by the Normans. It must have acquired some currency through being the first-name of a great Crusader. Sparsely scattered around England, strongest in Lancs.

Tandy F A diminutive of the first-name *Andrew*. Mainly found in Worcs and surrounding counties.

Tanguy/Tangye/Tingay/Tingey F From a Breton first-name meaning 'fire-dog', brought to England by Bretons after 1066, but reintroduced into Cornwall as *Tansys* at a later date. St *Tanguy* was an associate of St Pol de Léon. By the late nineteenth century **Tanguy** had become a rare Channel Islands surname, strongest in Jersey, while **Tangye** belonged to Cornwall. **Tank**, also Cornish, is probably a variant. **Tingay** and **Tingey** are most in evidence in East Anglia.

Tank, *see* Tanguy.

Tanner O Occupational term for a tanner OE. More often encountered in the Southern counties of England than in the North.

Tanton P There is a place called *Tanton* in NRYorks, Celtic and OE 'place on the (river) *Tame*', but the surname is strongest in Devon, where it could well be derived from *Tennaton* in Diptford OE '*Tun(n)a*'s settlement', which was *Tuneton* in 1244.

Taper O Occupational term for a maker or seller of tapers, candles, lamp-wicks OE. A rare Cornish surname.

Taplin, *see* Tapp.

Taplow P Place-name in Bucks OE '*Toeppa*'s burial-mound' (compare **Tapp**), though – like **Tatlow** – this is mainly a Derbys surname.

Tapp/Tapping F From an OE first-name *Toeppa*, of unknown meaning (compare **Taplow**). **Teape**, a scarce surname found in Middx and Surrey, may well be a variant, 'if John *Tepe* (Devon, 1273) were of the same linguistic origin as the *Tappa* who left his name at *Tapeley*, in Westerleigh, Devon' (Cottle). **Tapp** belongs chiefly to the south of England, though is also strong in Devon and in Northants; **Tapping** is a Bucks surname, the diminutive **Taplin** is mainly found in Hants and surrounding counties, and the patronymic **Tapson** in Devon. *The speciality paper-manufacturing firm of Wiggins Teape was founded in the City of London in 1761.*

Tapper/Tapster O Occupational term for a tapper (of casks), an ale-seller, inn-keeper OE with an *-er* suffix. **Tapster** is theoretically, but not exclusively, a feminine form (compare **Brewster**, **Webster**), and can also refer to a weaver or seller of carpets OF. **Tapper** is mainly found in Devon and surrounding counties, **Tapster**, very scarce, in Middx.

Tapping, *see* Tapp.

Tapscott P From a now-lost place-name OE '*Tapp*'s cottage'; this is primarily a Devon surname, though the place-name *Tascott* in that county would seem on the face of it to be too late to have given rise to a related surname.

Tapsfield P A scarce Kent surname, which could well be derived from *Toppesfield*, Essex OE 'open country of the hilltop'.

Tapson, *see* **Tapp**.

Tapster, *see* **Tapper**.

Tarbuck/Tarbock/Tarbox P Place-name *Tarbock* in Lancs OE 'thorn-bush brook'. **Tarbuck** is a Lancs surname, but the fact that **Tarbox**, by contrast, is mainly found in the Home Counties may possibly be explained by Cottle's statement that 'the mediaeval shepherd carried a tarbox full of tar as a salve for his sheep'. **Tarbock** is a very scarce variant. *The comedian Jimmy Tarbuck, father of the actress and television presenter Liza Tarbuck, was born in Liverpool in 1940.*

Tardif(f) N Nickname for a sluggish, tardy, lazy person OF *tardif*. Essentially French surnames, also found in limited numbers in Guernsey. Possibly related to the surname **Tordoff**?

Targett N/O Nickname for a person resembling a little round shield OF, or an occupational term for a user/maker of such objects. Mainly found in Wilts and surrounding counties.

Tarl(e)ton P Place-names: *Tarleton* in Lancs ON and OE '*Thorvaldr*'s settlement', and *Tarlton* in Gloucs OE '?place in the thorns'. **Tarlton** is a scattered surname; **Tarleton** is strongest in Derbys and Lancs.

Tarn T Dweller by a tarn, mountain pool ON. Strongest in Co Durham.

Tarr ?O/P A Devon/Somerset surname of uncertain origin: an occupational term for a man who tarred ships, or a mysterious place-name element?

Tarrant P/F From the river *Tarrant* which, like the *Trent*, is British but of unknown meaning (Ekwall guesses at 'trespasser, flooder'), and which is used as the first part of eight place-names in Dorset, and one in Hants, which are situated on its

banks. Irish: Anglicized form of Gaelic **O'** [descendant of] **Torain** ('hero'). A surname of southern England, strongest in Hants and Surrey. *Christopher John ('Chris') Tarrant, television and radio presenter, was born in 1946 in Reading, Berks.*

Tarry, *see* **Terry**.

Tarvin P Place-name in Chesh, on a river of that name, Welsh *terfyn* ('boundary'), from Latin *terminus*. For the relationship between *-er* and *-ar*, see **Armistead**. A rare surname, found mainly in Lancs.

Tash/Tesh T Dweller at an ash tree, the initial T- being a reduced form of ME *atte* ('at the'). **Tash** is chiefly found in Norfolk, **Tesh** in WRYorks.

Tasker O Occupational term for a task-worker, a piece-worker as opposed to a day-labourer, from Anglo-Norman French; or possibly a 'task-master', who assessed or regulated rates and prices. Scattered around England, Scotland, Wales and the Isle of Man, but strongest in northern England.

Tatam, *see* **Tatham**.

Tatchell, *see* **Tattersall**.

Tate F From an OE first-name *Tata*, of uncertain meaning (compare **Tatham**, **Tatton**). Readily confused with **Tait**, but with a different origin, though both are principally Co Durham/Northd surnames. *Sir Henry Tate, First Baronet (1819–1899), the sugar refiner of 'Tate and Lyle' fame and a benefactor whose good works included the establishment of the Tate Gallery in London, was born in Chorley, Lancs, the son of a Unitarian clergyman… Catherine Tate, comedian and actress, was born Catherine Ford in the Bloomsbury area of London in 1968.*

Tatem, *see* **Tatham**.

Tatford, *see* **Titford**.

Tatham/Tatam/Tatem/Tattam P Place-name *Tatham* in Lancs OE '*Tata*'s homestead' (compare **Tate**, **Tatton**). Chiefly WRYorks surnames, except for the scarce **Tattam**, which belongs to Bucks.

Tatlow P   From an unidentified place-name, of which the second element is OE 'mound'. There is a settlement called *Tadlow* in Cambs OE '*Tadda*'s mound', which would appear to have given rise to a related surname. Like **Taplow**, **Tatlow** is a surname most commonly found in Derbys (in which county there is a lost settlement of *Tadley* OE '?*Tada*'s/toad clearing'). Readily confused with/a variant of **Tetlow** (see **Tetley**).

Tattam, *see* **Tatham**.

Tatters(h)all/Tatchell/Tattershaw   P Place-name *Tattershall* in Lincs OE '*Tathere*'s nook'. **Tattersall** is strongest in Lancs, **Tattershall** in WRYorks, **Tatchell** in Dorset and Somerset, and **Tattershaw** (scarce) in Derbys. **Tortoiseshel(l)**, a charming surname which can also be found in the forms **Tortishell**, **Tortirshell**, **Tortershel(l)**, **Tortoishal**, **Tortyshell**, **Tortoiceshell**, **Tortorshall**, **Tortoischell**, **Dortishell**, **Tartershell**, **Tortoishall** and **Tortorsell**, and which had something of a presence in Staffs during the eighteenth and nineteenth centuries, will surely be a variant of **Tatters(h)all**, by way of folk etymology? At one point such a surname can be seen changing before our very eyes: Joseph **Tawtershell** married Anne **Wakefield** at St Werburgh's church in Derby in 1799, but is described as Joseph **Tartershell** and then **Tortershell** at the baptism of two of his children. *The human rights and gay equality campaigner Peter Tatchell was born in Melbourne, Australia, in 1952.*

Tatton P   Place-name in Chesh and Dorset OE '*Tata*'s settlement' (compare **Tate**, **Tatham**).

Taunton P   Place-name in Somerset ?Celtic and OE 'place on the (river) *Tone*' (compare **Toland**). A West Country surname, strongest in Wilts.

**Tave(r)ner/Taffinder/Tavender/
Tav(i)ner** O   Occupational term for a taverner, inn-keeper OF. **Taffinder**, with its unvoiced second consonant, is most common in WRYorks. See also **Tabbener**.

Taylerson/Taylorson/Taylour, *see* **Taylor**.

Taylor/Tailor/Tayler/Taylour O   Occupational term for a tailor OF (originally meaning a 'cutter'; compare **Talboy**). Although the occupational term is now spelt *tailor*, the scattered surname **Tailor** is infinitely rarer than the ubiquitous **Taylor**. **Taylerson** and **Taylorson** ('son of **Tayler/Taylor**') are northern variants. **Taylour** is the family name of the Marquesses of Headfort.

Tazewell N   A surname with a place-name look about it, yet it would appear to have originated in a nickname from OE for a person who could 'tease/toze well', one who was efficient at teasing cloth with a teasel. A surname mostly found in Somerset, where the use of teasels for straighteneing fibres in cloth was a common practice both before, and even after, the invention of metal-toothed 'cards' which served the same purpose. Compare **Tozer**.

Teacher O   Occupational term for one who offered instruction in a wide range of disciplines OE with an *-er* suffix. Sparsely scattered around England and Scotland, strongest in Lanarkshire. *William Teacher (1810/11–1876), a wine and spirit merchant who gave his name to Teacher's Whisky, is said to have been born in Paisley.*

Teague/Tighe F   Irish: Anglicized form of Gaelic **O'** [descendant of] **Taidhg** ('poet, philosopher'). Commonly pronounced '*Tie*'. See also **McTague**.

Teal(e)/Teall N   Nickname for a person resembling a teal, the bird ME, 'but why anyone should be nicknamed from a waterfowl is hard to say' (Cottle). Principally a WRYorks surname in all spellings.

Teape, *see* **Tapp**.

Tear(e) F   A Manx version of **McIntyre**.

Teasdale/Teasdall/Teesdale P   Regional name from *Teesdale*, Co Durham and NRYorks, Celtic and OE 'valley of the (river) *Tees*' (compare **Surtees**). Principally northern surnames, though **Teasdall** is very rare.

Tebb(oth)/Tebbet(t)/Tebbit(t)/Teb-but(t), *see* Theobald.

Tector O Occupational term for a plasterer, pargeter, stuccoer, from Latin. A Lancs surname.

Tedbury P Place-name *Tetbury* in Gloucs OE '*Tette*'s fortified place'. Chiefly a Devon surname.

Tee T Dweller at the river/stream OE *ea*, the initial *T-* being a reduced form of *atte* ('at the'). Chiefly a Hants surname.

Teesdale, *see* Teasdale.

Tegg O Occupational term for a shepherd, one who tended tegs/young sheep OE. A Berks surname.

Telfer/Telfair/Telford/Tolver   O/N
Occupational term for a cleaver or cutter of iron OF *taille-fer*, or used more particularly as a nickname for a powerful warrior who could pierce his enemy's armour. Compare **Tilford**. *Telford* in Salop was named after Thomas **Telford** the engineer (1757–1834), who was born in Dumfriesshire, Scotland, the son of a shepherd. **Telfer** is principally found in north-east England and in Scotland; **Telford** has an additional presence in Yorks; **Telfair** is a very scarce scattered variant, and **Tolver** is most common in Norfolk.

Temperley, *see* Timperley.

Tempest N Nickname for a person of stormy temperament, one prone to agitation, making a fuss OF. Mainly found in WRYorks and surrounding counties.

Temple(r)/Templar T/O Dweller/worker at one of the houses or temple's of the Knights Templar, the military and religious order founded to protect pilgrims to the Holy Land, which took its name from Solomon's Temple but was suppressed in 1312 for alleged vice and heresy. **Temple** was also bestowed upon foundlings taken for baptism at the Temple Church in London (which was built on land originally owned

by the Templars, and which has achieved yet more fame in recent times by being one of the locations featured in the novel and film *The Da Vinci Code*). **Temple** is principally a surname of the north and north-east of England; **Templar** is found both in the West Country and in Lancs; **Templer** has a significant presence in Devon, and **Templeman** ('servant/tenant of the Templars') is at its strongest in Lincs, Middx, Notts and Somerset.

Templeman, *see* Temple.

Templer, *see* Temple.

Templeton P Place-name in Ayrshire, Scotland ME 'Templars' settlement'. This is chiefly an Ayrshire and Lanarkshire surname, so places called *Templeton* in Berks, Devon and Wales have probably not contributed to its formation.

Tench N Nickname for a person resembling a tench OF, the fish, in some way (fat? sleek?). Chiefly found in north-west England, and at its strongest in Salop.

Tennant/Tennent O Status term for a tenant OF (literally a present participle: 'holding'), who held his land by virtue of owing service to his feudal overlord. His holding itself was a *tenement*, 'which in those days was not a tall block of slummy apartments' (Cottle). **Tennant** is the family name of the Barons Glenconner. Both **Tennant** and **Tennent** are mainly found in northern England and Scotland. *The company of Tennant Brothers, Sheffield brewers, acquired its name when brothers Edward and Robert Tennant took it over in 1840… The name of H. & R. Tennent, Glasgow brewers, reflects the fact that it was founded by Hugh and Robert Tennent in 1740… The actor David Tennant, well known above all for his role as the Doctor in the* Doctor Who *television series, was born David John McDonald, the son of Rev. Sandy McDonald, one-time Moderator of the General Assembly of the Church of Scotland, and his wife Helen. He chose the professional name 'Tennant' in honour of Neil Tennant, lead singer of the Pet Shop Boys. His Scottish and Northern Irish ancestry was featured in an episode of the TV series* Who do you think you are?

Tennison, *see* Denison.

Tenniswood, *see* Tinniswood.

Tennyson, *see* Denison.

Terry/Tarry/Torry F From a Germanic first-name *T(h)erry* ('people-rule'), introduced into Britain by the Normans and also well known in the form *Theodoric*. For the *-ar* element in **Tarry**, *see* Armistead. **Terry** is a well-established old Kent surname; **Tarry** is at its strongest in Northants, **Torry** in Lincs. *Joseph Terry (1793–1850), the confectioner after whom Terry's Chocolates are named, was born in Pocklington, Yorks.*

Tesh, *see* Tash.

Tester N Nickname for a person with a large or ugly head OF *teste* (modern French *tête*), ultimately from Latin *testa* 'pot'. A Sussex surname.

Tetford, *see* Titford.

Tetley/Tetlow P There is clearly a place-name at work here, of which the first element is probably an OE first-name such as *Toeta*, followed by *-ley* ('clearing') or *-low* ('mound'). George Redmonds says that some early **Tetleys** may derive their surname from *Tetley*, Lincs, but that many individuals so-named in WRYorks are named after **Tetlow**, Lancs. The surname **Tetlow** itself, commonest in Lancs, could in principle readily be confused with, or be a variant of, **Tatlow**. *Joshua Tetley (1778–1859), who gave his name to a famous brewery, was born at Armley Lodge, near Leeds, WRYorks.*

Tew P/N Place-names *Great Tew*, *Little Tew*, *Duns Tew* in Oxon OE 'row/ridge', or '?meeting-place, court'; Welsh: nickname for a fat person, Welsh *tew* ('plump'). Chiefly a surname of the English Midlands, strongest in Northants and Warwicks.

Thacher/Thacker, *see* Thatcher.

Thacker(a)y/Thackra(h)/Thack(w)ray P Place-names *Thackray* in WRYorks ON 'nook with thatching (-reed)', now under Fewston Reservoir. *Thackray Wood* in Cumbd is probably named after a person,

not vice versa. Mainly WRYorks surnames. Readily confused with/a variant of **Thackway**. *The novelist William Makepeace Thackeray (1811–1863), who came from a family with Yorks roots, acquired his first-names from an ancestor named William Makepeace, a sixteenth-century Protestant martyr.*

Thackham P Place-names: *Thatcham*, Berks and *Thakeham*, Sussex OE 'thatched homestead' or 'homestead where good reeds for thatching are to be had'. Chiefly a Herts surname.

Thackra(h)/Thackray, *see* Thackery.

Thackway P There are places called *Thackthwaite* in Cumbd and NRYorks ON 'clearing with (reeds for) thatching', though **Thackway** is chiefly a Herefords surname. Readily confused with/a variant of **Thackery**.

Thackwell P From an unidentified place OE '?spring/stream with (reeds for) thatching'. Mostly found in South Wales and along the Welsh/English border.

Thackwray, *see* Thackery.

Thain(e)/Thane O Status term for a thane, a tenant by military service OE (and in Scotland, eventually, clan chieftain and king's baron). **Thain** is mostly found in north-east Scotland, but **Thaine** belongs to Norfolk; **Thane** (scarce) is scattered throughout England.

Tharp, *see* Thorp.

Thatcher/Thacher O Occupational term for a thatcher OE. **Thacker** (commonest in Staffs) and **Theaker** (commonest in WRYorks) are ON forms. **Thaxter** (commonest in Norfolk) is theoretically, but not exclusively, a feminine form (compare **Brewster**, **Webster**).

Thaxter, *see* Thatcher.

Theaker, *see* Thatcher.

Thelwall/Thelwell P Place-name *Thelwall* in Ches OE 'pool by a plank (-bridge)'. Readily confused with/a variant of **Thirlwall**.

Theobald F From a Germanic first-name

meaning 'people-bold', the original *Theud-*
misrepresented as Greek *Theo-* ('God'). The
vernacular forms *Tebald* and *Tibald* helped
to give rise to a number of surnames beginning with *Teb-*, *Tib-*, *Tip-*, *Dib-* or *Dip-*,
including **Tebb(oth)**, **Tebbet(t)**, **Tebbit
(t)**, **Tebbut(t)**, **Tibb(s)**, **Tibball**, **Tibbatts**,
Tibbet(t)(s),   **Tibbins**,   **Tibbit(t)(s)**,
Tibble(s), **Tibbott(s)**, **Tibby**, **Tipp**, **Tippell**,
Tippett(s), **Tipping**, **Tippins**, **Tipple(s)**, **Tip-
son**, **Dibb(s)**, **Dib(b)le**, **Diboll**, **Dipple**,
Dyball, **Dybell**, **Dyble**, though some of
these could have developed via the first-
name *Tibb*, which was a contraction of
either the male *Theobald* or the female *Isabel*. **Theobald** is mainly an East Anglian surname, while **Theobalds** ('son of *Theobald*')
is found in limited numbers in Kent. The
geographical distribution of each of the
large number of other forms varies significantly according to spelling, and some are
very scarce. **Tidball** and **Titball** are rather
charming Devon variants, while **Tudball**
belongs mainly to Somerset; **Tippett** *is primarily a Cornish form, and the composer Sir
Michael (Kemp)* **Tippett** *(1905–1998), though
he was born in London, was of Cornish stock.*

Theodore F From a Greek first-name
meaning 'God's gift', made popular in England thanks to *Theodore* of Tarsus
(602–690), Archbishop of Canterbury and
biblical scholar. The famous dynastic name
of **Tudor**, a Welsh version of **Theodore**, is
still found chiefly within the Principality
itself.

Theophilus F From a Greek first-name
meaning 'dear to God'. In the bible, *Theophilus* was a friend of St Luke. A surname of
south-west Wales, strongest in Carmarthenshire.

Thetford P Place-name in Cambs, Lincs
and Norfolk OE 'people's (public) ford'.

Thew/Thow O Status term for a serf, slave,
thrall OE. **Thew** is chiefly a Northd surname;
Thow belongs to north-east Scotland.

Thewles(s)/Thewlis(s)/Thouless N Nickname for an ill-mannered, immoral person,
void of good qualities OE (though *thews* are
now 'muscles', not 'virtues'). **Thewles**,

Thewlis and **Thewliss** are mainly found in
WRYorks, **Thewless** in Surrey and **Thouless**
in Norfolk.

Thick N Nickname for a stocky, thick-set
person OE. A West Country surname,
strongest in Wilts.

Thickbroom P Place-name in Staffs OE
'thick broom (-brushes)'. Sparsely scattered
throughout central England, strongest in
Staffs.

Thimpson, *see* Tim.

Thin/Thynne N Nickname for a thin, slender person OE. A scarce surname, whatever
the spelling; **Thin** is mainly found in the
north of England; **Thynn** has a limited presence in Co Durham; **Thynne**, unevenly
scattered, is the family name of the Marquesses of Bath.

Thirkell/Thirkettle/Thirkill/Thirkle,
see **Thurkettle**.

Thirlby P Place-name in NRYorks ON
'thralls'/'serfs' farm', but a scarce Leics surname.

Thirlwall/Thirlwell P The settlement of
Thirlwall in Northd OE 'holed wall' (compare the word '*nostril*', 'nose-hole') is situated at a gap in Hadrian's Wall. Readily
confused with/a variant of **Thelwall**.

Thirsk P Place-name in NRYorks ON 'fen,
lake'.

**Thistlethwaite/Thistlethwayte/This-
tlewaite** P Place-names: *Thistlethwaite* in
Lancs; *Thistlewood* (which was *Thystelweit*
in 1241, *Thistlethwaite* in 1589, etc.) in
Cumbd OE and ON 'thistle meadow'.

Thistleton P Place-name in ERYorks,
Lancs, Rutland OE 'place in the thistles'.
Mainly a Lancs surname.

Thistlewaite, *see* Thistlethwaite.

Thistlewood P Hanks and Hodges mention a place called *Thistleworth* in Sussex
OE 'thistle enclosure', but the surname is
found chiefly in Lancs, Lincs and WRYorks,
and a more likely place-name origin must
be *Thistlewood* in Cumbd, so-called in the

eighteenth century, but formerly *Thystelweit*, etc. (see **Thistlethwaite**). *Arthur Thistlewood (1774–1820), the radical agitator who was a leader of the Cato Street Conspiracy, was baptized at Horsington parish church, near Horncastle, Lincs.*

Thoburn, *see* Thorburn.

Thoday ᴛ Dweller at the people's way/highway ᴏᴇ (compare **Tudway**). Chiefly a Cambs surname.

Thom, *see* Thomas.

Thomas ꜰ From a mediaeval first-name, with its origins in Aramaic 'twin'. The Greek version is *Didymus*, and the common pronunciation of *Thomas* in English, sounding an initial *T-* rather than *Th-*, is a result of French influence. *Thomas* was for long an unpopular first-name in England, since Thomas the Apostle (whose given name, according to Eusebius, was *Judah*) was renowned for having doubted Christ's resurrection, but it swept to popularity following the murder of Thomas **Becket** in 1170. Eventually, as *tomcat* and *tomboy*, it even became a generic term for males – perhaps in particular those who might engage in a spot of *tomfoolery*? *Thomas* has given rise to many surnames beginning with *Tom-* and *Thom-*, some making use of *-p-* as a labial glide. Diminutive forms include **Thom/Thoms** (mainly Scottish), **Thomassin** and **Thomazin** (both very scarce). Despite the fact that *Tam* is a Scottish form of *Thomas*, many surnames of the **Tambling**, **Tamlin**, **Tam(b)lyn** and **Tamplin(g)** type, all of which are double diminutives, some with labial glides *-p-* or *-b-*, are principally found in the south of England, with a strong presence in Cornwall. **Tonkin** is also Cornish; **Tom** and **Toms** are mainly found in that county but also in neighbouring Devon, while **Tonks** belongs to Salop, **Tunks** to Middx and Sussex, and **Tombs** to Gloucs and Worcs. **Thomas** on its own is far commoner than any of its numerous family, and is the pre-eminent surname of South Wales. Cottle shares with us the astonishing revelation that: 'In 1938 there were eighteen **Thomases** in the two hundred-odd boys at Cowbridge Grammar School, so that with the traditional numeration one of them was **Thomas** *Duodevicesimus*'. Forms ending in *-son*, such as **Thomason**, **Thomlinson**, **Thompson**, **Tomkinson**, **Tomlinson**, **Tompkins(on)**, **Tompson** and **Tomson**, are, as ever, found mainly in the north of England, while **Thomson** belongs largely, but not entirely, to Scotland. **Thompsett**, **Thomsett** and **Tomsett** (from the pet-form *Thomaset*, with a French suffix) are found mainly in Kent, as are **Tomkin** and **Tomlin**. **Tomes**, **Tomkins**, **Tomlins**, **Tompkin** and **Tompkins** are scattered variants, as are the much scarcer **Tampling**, **Thomerson**, **Thomes**, **Thomline**, **Thompkins** and **Tome**. **Tomison** belongs mainly to the Orkney Islands.

Thomason, *see* Thomas.

Thomassin, *see* Thomas.

Thomazin, *see* Thomas.

Thomerson, *see* Thomas.

Thomes, *see* Thomas.

Thomline, *see* Thomas.

Thomlinson, *see* Thomas.

Thompkins, *see* Thomas.

Thompsett, *see* Thomas.

Thompson, *see* Thomas.

Thoms, *see* Thomas.

Thomsett, *see* Thomas.

Thomson, *see* Thomas.

Thorburn/Thoburn ꜰ From an ᴏɴ first-name *Thorbjorn* '*Thor* [god of thunder]-bear' (compare **Thorold**, **Thurgar**, **Thurgood**, **Thurkettle** and **Thurstan**). Surnames of northern England and Scotland. **Thulbo(u)rn**, possibly a variant, is a scarce surname found in Cambs.

Thorley ᴘ There are places called *Thorley* in Herts and in the Isle of Wight ᴏᴇ 'thorn wood/clearing', but the surname is mainly found throughout north-west England (though it is strongest in Staffs), and a place-name such as *Thornley* (with the same meaning), in Lancs or elsewhere, is most likely to be the point of origin. Compare **Thornley**.

Thorn(e) T/P Dweller by a thorn bush OE, or from a place-name with the same meaning, such as *Thorne*, Somerset, or *Thorns*, Suffolk. The *-e* of **Thorne** represents the dative form.

Thornborough/Thornber/Thornburrow/Thornbury P Place-names *Thornborough* and *Thornbrough* in several counties, a complex of 'hill/mound covered with thorns' and 'fort/manor protected by thorns', all OE. **Thornborough** is mainly found in Warwicks and Westmd, **Thornber** in Lancs and WRYorks, **Thornburrow** in Westmd, and **Thornbury** in Gloucs and surrounding counties. Compare **Thornby**.

Thornby P Place-name in Northants, of the same origin as **Thornborough**, with a Scandinavianized *-by*; but the place-name in Cumbd is ON 'old farm'. Sparsely scattered throughout England, strongest in Kent and Lancs.

Thorncroft, *see* Thorneycroft.

Thorndike T/P Dweller at an embankment/ditch covered with thorns OE (though the second element could be ON), or from a place-name with the same meaning. Most common in Lincs and Suffolk. *The actress Dame (Agnes) Sybil Thorndike (1882–1976), whose married name was Casson, was born in Gainsborough, Lincs.*

Thorndycraft, *see* Thorneycroft.

Thorne, *see* Thorn.

Thornely, *see* Thornley.

Thorner T/P Dweller in the thorns OE plus an *-er* suffix, or from a place-name such as *Thorner* in WRYorks OE 'thorn slope', though this scarce surname is chiefly found in Dorset.

Thorney P Place-name in Cambs, Middx, Somerset, Suffolk, Sussex OE 'island with thorn-bushes', and in Notts OE 'enclosure

made by thorn-bushes'. A scattered surname.

Thorneycroft/Thorncroft/Thorndycraft/Thornicroft/Thornycroft T/P Dweller at an enclosed piece of land in the thorns OE, or from a place-name with the same meaning: *Thornycroft*, Chesh; *Thorney Crofts*, ERYorks; *Thornecroft*, Devon. Such surnames have a varied geographical distribution according to spelling: **Thorneycroft** is found mainly in WRYorks, **Thorncroft** in Middx and Kent, **Thorndycraft** (very scarce) in Kent, **Thornicroft** in Warwicks, **Thornycroft** in Chesh. *The politician (George Edward) Peter Thorneycroft, Baron Thorneycroft (1909–1994), who served a term as chairman of the Conservative Party (from 1975), was born in Dunston Hall, Staffs, to a family which had originally been Staffs ironmasters.*

Thornhill/Thornill P Place-name in several counties OE 'hill covered with thorns'. Strongest in Lancs in both spellings.

Thornicroft, *see* Thorneycroft.

Thornill, *see* Thornhill.

Thornley/Thornely P Place-name *Thornley* in Co Durham (two such), Lancs (two such) and the Isle of Wight OE 'clearing with thorns'; but the place-name in Kelloe, Co Durham, is OE 'mound/hill covered with thorns'. Compare **Thorley**. **Thornley** is a surname of the north of England, particularly strong in Lancs; **Thornely**, scarce, is found in Chesh and Lancs.

Thornthwaite P Place-name in Cumbd, Westmd, WRYorks ON 'clearing with thorns'. A northern surname.

Thornton P Ekwall counted thirty-odd places so-called, with a group of sixteen in Yorks, four in Lincs, three in Chesh and two in Lancs OE 'place in the thorns'. *The firm of G. E. Thornton & Sons, famous for its chocolate products, was founded by George Edward Thornton, who had spent his early years as a joiner and cabinetmaker in the Keighley area of Yorks during the 1870s.*

Thornwell T Dweller at a spring/stream in

the thorns OE. A rare South Midlands surname.

Thornycroft, *see* Thorneycroft.

Thorogood, *see* Thurgood.

Thorold F From a ME first-name *Turold*, ON '*Thor* [god of thunder]-rule' (compare **Thorburn**, **Thurgar**, **Thurgood**, **Thurkettle** and **Thurstan**).

Thoroughgood, *see* Thurgood.

Thorowgood, *see* Thurgood.

Thorp(e)/Tharp/Throp T/P Dweller at a farm (especially an outlying dairy-farm) or a village OE or ON (the *-e* of **Thorpe** possibly indicating the use of the dative after a lost preposition); or from one of several places called *Thorpe*, with the same meaning, of which there are more in the Danish-settled counties of the Midlands and north-east than in purely English areas. Forms such as **Thripp**, **Throp**, **Throop**, **Thro(u)p(e)** and **Thrupp** are a result of metathesis, and there are places called *Thrup* in Oxon and *Thrupp* in Berks and Gloucs. See also **Troup**.

Thorrington P Place-name in Essex OE 'place in the thorns/thornbushes'. Chiefly a Middx/Surrey surname.

Thouless, *see* Thewles.

Thow, *see* Thew.

Thrale/Thrall O Status term for a serf, villein OE from ON. Scarce surnames, with something of a presence in Notts.

Thrasher, *see* Thresher.

Threader O Occupational term for a maker or user of thread OE plus an *-er* suffix. Most common in the Home Counties, strongest in Beds.

Threadgill/Threadgo(u)ld/Treadgold O Occupational term for an embroiderer, one who would 'thread gold' OE. **Threadgill** is mainly found in eastern England (strongest in Cambs), **Threadgold** in the northwest and in Essex, **Threadgould** in Lincs and Yorks, and **Treadgold** in the South Midlands and Lincs.

Threlfall P Place-name in Lancs ON 'thrall's/serf's/slave's clearing [where trees had been *felled*]', and chiefly a Lancs surname.

Threlkeld P Place-name in Cumbd ON 'thrall's/serf's/slave's spring'.

Thresher/Thrasher O Occupational term for a thresher OE. Cottle ponders: 'What did he do for the rest of the year?'. Generally surnames of the south of England.

Thrift N Possibly an abstract nickname for a thrifty person ME (from ON), or a variant of **Firth**. Sparsely scattered throughout England and Scotland.

Thring P Place-name *Tring* in Herts OE 'slope with trees (literally "tree-hanger")'. Most common in the West Country, strongest in Somerset.

Thripp, *see* Thorp.

Throckmorton/Throgmorton P Place-name *Throckmorton* in Worcs OE 'farm/settlement at a pond/marsh with a drain'. The **Throckmortons** have long been a well-known Catholic family, and it is said that *Throgmorton Street* in the City of London was named after Sir Nicholas **Throckmorton** (or **Throgmorton**), a courtier and diplomat who died in 1571.

Throop/Thro(u)p(e), *see* Thorp.

Thrower O Occupational term for someone who turned raw silk into thread, or for a potter, who 'threw' pots OE plus an *-er* suffix. Chiefly a Norfolk/Suffolk surname. *Percy (John) Thrower (1913–1988), broadcaster and writer on gardening matters, was born in Little Horwood, Bucks.*

Thrupp, *see* Thorp.

Thrush/Thrussell N Nickname for someone who resembled a thrush or throstle OE, the bird, in some way (fine voice or whistle? cheerful?). **Thrush** can be found in both north and south-west England; **Thrussell** is a Herts surname.

Thulbo(u)rn, *see* Thorburn.

Thumb N Nickname for a person with a

deformed or missing thumb, or who was very small in stature (a kind of *Tom Thumb*) OE. Mercifully, a very scarce surname.

Thundercliff P Probably from a now-lost place called *Thundercliffe Grange*, WRYorks, formerly a grange of Kirkstead Abbey OE 'thunder cliff', so-called from the noise made by the monks' forges used for making iron (and not the dialectal 'th'under-cliff')? Chiefly an ERYorks surname.

Thurgar F From an ON first-name meaning '*Thor* [god of thunder]-spear' (compare **Thorburn**, **Thorold**, **Thurgood**, **Thurkettle** and **Thurstan**). Chiefly an Essex surname.

Thurgood/Thorogood/Thorough-good/Thorowgood F From a ME first-name *Thurgod*, from ON '*Thor* [god of thunder]', plus the ethnic name '*Gautr*' (compare **Thorburn**, **Thorold**, **Thurgar**, **Thurkettle** and **Thurstan**). A popular corruption was to **Thorough-good**, as if the surname meant 'thoroughly good' or 'good throughout', which it does not. **Thurgood** is most common in Essex/Herts, **Thorogood** and **Thoroughgood** in Essex, and **Thorowgood** in Middx.

Thurkettle/Thirkell/Thirkettle/Thirkill/Thirkle/Thurkle/Turkentine F From an ON first-name *Thorkell* '*Thor* [god of thunder]-(sacrificial)cauldron', introduced to northern parts of England by Scandinavian settlers, and to southern counties by the Normans, leading to what Cottle calls a 'ferocious' surname which 'descended by marriage to the gentle novelist Angela **Thirkell**, whose grandfather Burne-Jones was admittedly the uncle of Kipling and Baldwin'. Compare **Thorburn**, **Thorold**, **Thurgar**, **Thurgood** and **Thurstan**. See also **McCorquodale**, **Turtle**. **Tuttle** (a Norfolk surname) can be a variant. Cottle also believes that **Thirkell** and **Thirkle** as found in Cumbd, Yorks and north-east England are derived from **Threlkeld**. **Thurkettle** is strongest in Suffolk, **Thirkell** in Co Durham, **Thirkettle** in Norfolk and Suffolk, **Thirkill** in WRYorks, **Thirkle** (very scarce) in Northd, and **Thurkle** (also very scarce) in

Surrey. The distinctive variant **Turkentine**, found chiefly in Suffolk, is a diminutive form, to which have been added two OF diminutive suffixes, *-et* and *-in*.

Thurkle, *see* **Thurkettle**.

Thurley P Possibly from the place-name *Thurleigh* in Beds OE '(at) the wood/clearing', with *Thur-* reproducing the feminine dative singular of the definite article after a lost preposition. Mainly found in Essex.

Thurloe, *see* **Thurlow**.

Thurlow P Place-names *Great Thurlow* and *Little Thurlow* in Suffolk OE '?warriors'/assembly burial-mound', and mainly a Suffolk surname. **Thurloe**, a much scarcer variant, has a presence in ERYorks. *John Thurloe (1616–1668), secretary to the Council of State in Protectorate England and spymaster to Oliver Cromwell, was born in Essex, the son of Thomas Thurloe, rector of Abbess Roding, who is said to have come from Landbeach, Cambs… Edward Thurlow, Baron Thurlow (1731–1806), Lord Chancellor, was born at Bracon Ash, Norfolk, to a family with roots in Burnham Overy in that county.*

Thursby P Place-name in Cumbd ON '*Thori/Thuri*'s farm', and chiefly a Cumbd surname.

Thurstan(s)/Thursting/Thurston F/P From a ME first-name, from ON *Thorsteinn* '*Thor* [god of thunder]-stone' (compare **Thorburn**, **Thorold**, **Thurgar**, **Thurgood** and **Thurkettle**); or from **Thurston**, Suffolk ON and OE '*Thori*'s settlement'. **Thurstan** and **Thurstans** are mostly found in Staffs and Warwicks, **Thursting** (very scarce) in Surrey, and **Thurston** in East Anglia.

Thwaite(s)/Thwaytes/Twatt/Twite T/P Dweller by a clearing, meadow, piece of enclosed land ON, or from one of the places called *Thwaite* or *Thwaites*, with the same meaning, in Norfolk, Suffolk and the north of England. **Thwaite** and **Thwaites** are surnames of the north of England; **Thwaytes**, scarce, can be found in Westmd, and **Twite** in Norfolk. **Twatt** is from one of the places so-called in Orkney and Shetland; there were forty-eight individuals bearing such a surname in that region of the British Isles in the 1841 census.

Thynne, *see* **Thin**.

Tibb(s)/Tibball/Tibbatts, *see* **Theobald**.

Tibbenham/Tibenham P Place-name *Tibenham* in Norfolk OE '*Tibba*'s homestead'. Mainly a Norfolk surname in either spelling.

Tibbet(t)s/Tibbins/Tibbit(t)s/Tibble(s) /Tibbott(s)/Tibby, *see* **Theobald**.

Tibenham, *see* **Tibbenham**.

Ticehurst P Place-name in Sussex OE 'hill/ wood with kids', and a Sussex surname.

Tichbon/Tichbo(u)rne P Place-name *Tichborne* in Hants OE 'stream near where kids are kept'. Very scarce in all spellings, but by the late nineteenth century **Tichborne** (oddly enough) was at its strongest in Lancs. *In the celebrated nineteenth-century affair of the 'Tichborne claimant', an impostor named Arthur Orton claimed to be the missing heir of Sir Roger Tichborne (1829–1854), a member of a prominent Roman Catholic family with its roots in Hants.*

Tichener, *see* **Titchener**.

Tickle P Place-name *Tickhill* in WRYorks OE '*Tica*'s hill'. Most common in Chesh and Lancs.

Tickner/Ticknor, *see* **Titchener**.

Tidball, *see* **Theobald**.

Tidcombe P Place-name in Devon, Wilts OE '*Tida/Titta*'s valley'. Mainly found in Somerset and surrounding counties.

Tidd P There are place-names incorporating *Tydd* OE 'shrubs, brushwood' in Cambs and Lincs.

Tiddeman/Tid(i)man F/O From an OE first-name *Tideman* ('time/season-man'), or a status name for a tithingman (head of a frankpledge/tithing of ten householders). **Tiddeman** is most commonly found in Essex, and **Tidiman** in Middx. **Tidman** is sparsely scattered throughout England and South Wales.

Tideswell P Place-name in Derbys OE '*Tidi*'s spring' referred to locally as '*Tidsa*'. Chiefly a Staffs surname. See also **Tidwell**.

Tidey, *see* **Tidy**.

Tid(i)man, *see* **Tiddeman**.

Tidmarsh P Place-name in Berks OE 'marsh of the people'. Mainly found in Oxon, Warwicks and surrounding counties.

Tidwell P There are two places so-called in Devon OE '*Tudda*'s spring/the *Tiddy* (a Celtic stream-name) brook', but this predominantly WRYorks surname (though it has a minimal presence in Devon) is perhaps likely to be a corruption of **Tideswell** in many cases?

Tid(e)y N Nickname for a person of good appearance, worthy ME from Germanic. Surnames of south-east England.

Tiernan/Tierney/Kernan/Kiernan F Irish: Anglicized forms of Gaelic **O'** [descendant of] *Tighearnaigh* ('lord/master'). *Gene Tierney (1920–1991), the American film and stage actress once described by Darryl F. Zanuck as 'the most beautiful woman in movie history', was born in Brooklyn, New York, the daughter of Howard Sherwood Tierney, a wealthy insurance broker of Irish descent, and his wife Bella Lavina Taylor.*

Tiffany/Tiffen/Tiffin F From the mediaeval first-name *Tiffania*, from Greek *Theophania* 'the manifestation of God', occurring as French *Tiphaine* for girls born on the Feast of the Epiphany. Some surname dictionaries speak of a link with the male first-name *Stephen*. **Tiffany** is a WRYorks surname; **Tiffen** is widely scattered, most common in Suffolk and Cumbd; **Tiffin** belongs very largely to Cumbd. *The famous New York retail store of Tiffany and Co was founded by Charles Lewis Tiffany (1812–1902); his son Louis Comfort Tiffany (1848–1933) was an artist and designer who worked in the decorative arts and is best known for his work in stained glass… One of the first-known Tiffanys in America was Humphrey Tiffany, an inhabitant of Rehoboth, Massachusetts, who was was killed by a stroke of lightning while travelling between Swanzey* *and Boston on 15 July 1685... Tiffin's School, Kingston-upon-Thames, Surrey, was endowed in 1638 by two brothers bearing such a surname.*

Tigar F From a Germanic first-name meaning 'people-spear'. A sparsely scattered surname, found both in Middx and in ERYorks.

Tighe, *see* **Teague**.

Tiler, *see* **Tyler**.

Tilford P There is such a place-name in Surrey OE 'convenient ford/*Tila*'s ford', yet the surname is mainly found in WRYorks and surrounding counties. Compare **Telfer** and **Titford**.

Till F A diminutive of the first-name *Matilda*, for which see **Maud**. Whence double diminutives such as **Tillett/Tillott**, and also **Tillotson** ('son of **Till**'). **Till** is very strong in Staffs, **Tillett/Tillott** in Norfolk, and **Tillotson** in WRYorks. See also **Tilley** and **Tilling**.

Tillett, *see* **Till**.

Tilley/Tillie F/P/O A double diminutive of the first-name *Matilda* (see **Maud**, **Till**); or from a place-name such as *Tilley* in Salop OE 'clearing with branches/boughs', *Tilly* in Calvados and Eure (from a Latin first-name *Tilius*) or *Tilly* in Seine-et-Oise (from a Latin first-name *Attilius*); or an occupational term for a tiller of the soil OE plus *-er* suffix. **Tilley** is a scattered surname, strongest in Middx; **Tillie** belongs mainly to north-east England and Scotland.

Tilling(s) F A double diminutive form of a mediaeval male first-name, or of the female first-name *Matilda*, via **Till**.

Tillman O Occupational term for a tile maker OE or for a tiller of the soil, a farmer OE (compare **Tillyard**). Strongest in Kent.

Tillott/Tillotson, *see* **Till**.

Tillyard O/T Occupational term for a tiller of the soil, a farmer OE (compare **Tillman**). Cottle favours an alternative derivation: '(dweller by) a place with linden-trees OF

tillard'. A sparsely scattered surname, most common in Middx.

Tilton P Place-name in Leics OE '*Tila*'s farm'. A scarce surname, found in counties as far apart as Berks and Lancs.

Timberlake P From a lost place-name in Bayton, Worcs OE 'wooded stream'. H. Fox Talbot's suggestion in *English etymologies* (1847) that the source is 'Timber leg', a term for a wounded soldier with a wooden leg, is perhaps more noteworthy for its charm and originality than for anything approaching accuracy. **Timberlake** is principally a Home Counties surname; **Timblick** is a scarce Bucks variant. *The American pop singer and songwriter Justin (Randall) Timberlake, born in Memphis, Tennessee, claims (not surprisingly) that his distant male-line ancestry is English: 'I've had my genealogy studied... There was a British lad who was in a war, not sure which war, but he ran away from the war because he fell in love with an Indian girl...'. This may possibly be a reference to Lieutenant Henry Timberlake, who died in England in 1765 (though he claimed that he had been born in Virginia), who took part in the French and Indian War.*

Timblick, *see* **Timberlake**.

Timblin/Times, *see* **Tim**.

Tim(m)(s)/Timblin/Times/Timmins/ Timmis/Timmons/Tim(p)son F From an OE first-name of unknown form or meaning (possibly from *Dietmar*, almost certainly not from *Timothy*, which was a late arrival in Britain). The WRYorks variant **Timblin** contains a *-b-* glide, plus an OF suffix, *-lin*. **Timm** is mainly found in Lincs and in WRYorks, **Tims** and **Timms** in Oxon, **Times** in Lancs, **Timmins** and **Timmis** in Staffs, **Timmons** in northern England and in Scotland, **Timson** in Leics and **Timpson** in Northants.

Timothy F The first-name *Timothy* (Greek 'honouring God') was a late arrival in England, and Hanks and Hodges suggest that its use as a surname is by way of a variant of the Irish **Tomelty**, an Anglicized form of Gaelic **O'** [descendant of] or **Mac** [son of]

Tomhaltaigh ('glutton'). **Timothy** as a surname has something of a presence in England and also in South Wales.

Timperley/Temperley P Place-name *Timperley* in Chesh OE 'wood clearing' (where *timber* was obtained).

Timperon P Place-name *Tymparon (Hall)* in Cumbd, Irish *tiompan* (small, abrupt hill/standing stone) plus ME, from ON *runnr* (brake, thicket). A very rare Cumbd surname.

Tim(p)son, *see* Tim.

Tindal(l)/Tindell/Tindill/Tind(a)le, *see* Tyndale.

Tindsley, *see* Tinsley.

Tingay/Tingey, *see* Tanguy.

Tingle O/N/T Occupational term for a maker of pins or nails, or a nickname for a person as thin as a pin ME. Cottle toys with the idea that an alternative meaning could be: '(dweller on a) little farm, small estate OE, as at *Tincleton*, Dorset'. A Devon surname.

Tink(l)er O Occupational term for a tinker, an itinerant mender of pots and pans, or a metalworker ME.

Tinknell P Place-name *Tintinhull* in Somerset OE '*Tint*'s hill/a hill called, or at, *Tinten*/a clearing by fire on a hill', -*hull* being south-western dialect for -*hill*. A rare Somerset surname.

Tinniswood/Tenniswood P From an unidentified place-name OE '*Tynni*'s wood', though Bardsley claims that the source is *Tenniswood*, 'some small spot in co York... There can be no doubt that this is a sharpened form of *Denniswood*, i.e., the wood that belonged to *Denis* (compare **Tennyson**)'. **Tinniswood** is chiefly found in Cumbd, **Tenniswood** in NRYorks.

Tinsley/Tindsley P Place-name *Tinsley* in WRYorks OE '*Tynni*'s mound'. Chiefly Lancs surnames.

Tiplady, *see* Toplady.

Tipp/Tippell/Tippett(s), *see* Theobald.

Tipper O/N Occupational term for a maker of tips/ferrules/pendants/arrowheads ME, from Germanic. Or possibly a bawdy nickname along the lines of **Toplady**? See also **Topper**. Widely scattered throughout western and southern England.

Tipping/Tippins/Tipple(s)/Tipson, *see* Theobald.

Tipton P Place-name in Staffs OE '*Tibba*'s farm'. A Salop/Staffs surname.

Titball, *see* Theobald.

Titchener/Tichener/Tickner/Ticknor/ Titchner/Twiching(s)/Twitchen/ Twitchin T Dweller at a cross-roads or a fork in a road OE *twicen(e)*.

Titchmarsh P Place-name *Titchmarsh*, Northants OE 'marsh where kids are pastured'. Chiefly a Cambs surname. *Alan (Fred) Titchmarsh, ubiquitous television presenter, was born in 1949 in Ilkley, WRYorks.*

Titchner, *see* Titchener.

Titcomb(e) P Place-name *Titcomb* in Berks OE '?valley with tits/with a small rivulet'. Chiefly a Wilts surname.

Tite N ?Nickname for a swift, eager person ME from ON. Chiefly a Northants surname. Or a variant of **Titt**?

Titford/Tatford/Tetford/Totford/ Tutford P Said by many surname dictionaries to be from *Tetford*, Lincs OE '*Theod*'s ford' ('people's ford'), though genealogical evidence suggests that *Tetworth*, Hunts OE '*Tetta*'s enclosure' is a much more likely place of origin. William, son of Alured de **Tetford**, held land in Lincs in 1195, but in later centuries similar bynames/surnames are in evidence in Beds, Cambs and Hunts. However, in a different form the surname is encountered in the West Country from mediaeval times onwards, where it follows a pattern of vowel-change also observable in several place-names, whereby the surname **Totford** became **Tutford**, and finally (in the early seventeenth century) **Titford**. All **Titfords** alive today are descended from a small family group of **Tutfords/Tydworthes/Titfords** living in the village of Bratton, Wilts, in the sixteenth century, probably having arrived there from Beds. A snapshot of **Titford** entries featured in the birth, marriage and death indexes for England and Wales, 1837–1899, reveals how typical this surname is of one that has a single family origin and exists only in limited numbers. During this period there is an average of only two male births and one marriage per year. Over half of the marriages were in London and Middx, one-third in Somerset, Wilts and Hants, and the remainder almost entirely in the West Country. **Tatford** is an altered form found in Hants from the eighteenth century onwards, while **Titford** can readily be misspelled as **Tilford**.

Titler N Nickname for a person given to tittle-tattle, gossip ME, though Reaney cautiously adds *titlere* ME 'hound' as a possible alternative source. Sparsely scattered across England, most common in Surrey.

Titley P Place-name in Herefords ME '*Titta*'s wood/clearing'. Chiefly a Staffs surname.

Titmas/Titmus(s) N Nickname for a person as small as a titmouse ME and OE, a diminutive bird belonging to the tit family (no connexion with a *mouse*). A Herts surname in all spellings. *Frederick Titmuss (1898–1966), a footballer who played at fullback for Southampton and Plymouth Argyle and who also made two appearances for England, was born in Pirton, Herts.*

Titt N Nickname related to one of the meanings of 'tit' ME, from Germanic: the bird, a small horse, a young girl. A Wilts surname. Or possibly a variant of **Tite**.

Tobias/Tob(e)y/Tobin F First-name from a Greek form of the Hebrew *Tovya* '*Jehovah/ Yahweh* is good'. **Tobias** is found chiefly in Essex, Middx and Carmarthenshire, South Wales; **Tobin** (a diminutive form with the OF suffix -*in*) belongs to Lancs, and **Toby** to Devon, while **Tobey** is a scarce scattered surname.

Tod(d)(s) N/O Nickname for a person bear-

ing some resemblance to a fox (red-haired, sly, cunning?) ME, from ON. Cottle contends that such a surname could alternatively be a metonym for a foxhunter (compare **Todhunter**, **Todkill**, **Todman**). **Tod** is mainly found in Scotland, **Todd** in north and north-eastern England, and **Todds** in Lincs. *The actor Richard Todd was born Richard Andrew Palethorpe-Todd in Dublin, Ireland, in 1919, the son of a British army officer… The American theatre and film producer Mike Todd (1907/1909/1911–1958), one of several men to have taken on the real-life role of husband to Elizabeth Taylor, was born Avrom Hirsch Goldbogen in Minneapolis, Minnesota.*

Todhunter O Occupational term for a foxhunter (especially one employed by the parish) ME (from ON) and OE. Compare **Tod**, **Todkill**, **Todman**. Chiefly a Cumbd surname.

Todkill ?O/P It is tempting to assume that this surname could have been applied to a person adept at killing foxes (compare **Tod**, **Todhunter**, **Todman**). A much more likely point of origin would be the place-name *Todgill* ON 'fox ravine' in Cumbd, which includes a voiced '*g*' consonant rather than an unvoiced '*k*'. In general the place-name *Todgill* is first in evidence only as late as the seventeenth century, but a reference from the year 1279 to '*Tod Gill*' may well refer to the same place (see Robert Gambles: *Out of the forest: the natural world and the place-names of Cumbria*, 1989, p. 116). **Todkill** is a scarce surname, mostly found in Lincs, but with a presence in WRYorks. *Anas Todkill, a soldier who was employed as a servant by Captain Martin, was one of the first settlers of Jamestown, Virginia, during the early years of the seventeenth century… Thomas Todgill, who died before 1565, was the last Warden of the house of Grey Friars in Preston, Lancs, chaplain of Gray's Inn, London, and rector of Holy Trinity, Chester.*

Todman O Occupational term for a foxhunter ME (from ON) and OE. Compare **Tod**, **Todhunter**, **Todkill**. A surname of south-east England, strongest in Sussex.

Tods, *see* **Tod**.

Toft/Taft P Place-name *Toft* in several counties ON and late OE 'building-site, curtilage, homestead' (sometimes, as in *Piers Plowman*, 'hillock in flat surroundings'). **Toft** is chiefly found in Lancs, **Taft** in Derbys and Staffs. *The first-known male-line ancestor of William Howard Taft, twenty-seventh President of the USA, was Robert Taft or Taffe, an English emigrant who settled in Braintree, Massachusetts, in the 1670s.*

Tolady, *see* **Tolliday**.

Tol(l)and P There is a place called *Tolland* in Somerset, ?Celtic and OE 'land on the (river) *Tone*' (compare **Taunton**), yet this is chiefly a Lanarkshire, Scotland, surname, and might be a variant of **Toller**? *Gregg (Wesley) Toland (1904–1948), the Oscar-winning American cinematographer who famously created 'deep focus' photography for the film* Citizen Kane *(1941), was born in Charleston, Illinois.*

Toll/Towell/Towle T/F/P Surnames which can readily be confused one with the other, each of which may have a different point of origin. **Toll** in particular can refer to a dweller at a copse/clump of trees, from a southern and south-eastern dialect word of unknown origin (though the surname is mainly found in Norfolk); **Towell**, strongest in Devon, may have a similar origin, or be more closely related to **Towle**, which Reaney makes a pet-form of the ON first-name *Thorleifr/Thorleikr* 'Thor-game/play'; but since **Towle** is most commonly found in Notts, it's tempting to suppose that in some cases it might be a corruption of the place-name *Trowell* in that county OE '? spring by the tree', which was *Torwalle* in Domesday Book. Some confusion with **Toller/Towler** might be a possibility?

Tollady, *see* **Tolliday**.

Tolland, *see* **Toland**.

Tollemache/Tallemach/Talmadge O Occupational term for a wandering merchant, one who carried a knapsack OF *talemasche*. **Tollemache** is commonly pronounced '*Tollmash*'. **Tollemache** is evenly scattered throughout England,

though not found in the north-east. **Tallemach** and **Talmadge** are rare Surrey variants. *The Tollemache Family, Barons of Helmingham Hall near Ipswich, Suffolk, established and owned the Tollemache Brewery, later (from 1957) Tolly Cobbold, which now forms part of the Greene King brewery group... Norma Talmadge (1893–1957), one of the finest film stars of the silent era, was born in Niagara Falls, New York, the daughter of Frank Talmadge, a n'er-do-well alcoholic, and his wife Margaret ('Peg'). Norma's sisters Constance and Natalie also achieved fame as actresses.*

Toller O/P Occupational term for a toll-collector, tax-gatherer OE (also found in the forms **Towler/Tolman**, and see **Toland**); or from one of the place-names in Dorset with *Toller* OW river name 'stream in a hollow' as an element. Readily confused with **Toll** or one of its variants? **Toller** is a scattered surname, **Towler** is strongest in WRYorks, and **Tolman** in Devon.

Tollerfield/Tollfield, *see* **Turberville**.

Tolliday/Tol(l)ady ?N A surname of unknown origin. Possibly a variant on **Toplady**, avoiding the derogatory associations of such a name? Surname scholars have wrestled with such a name: Henry Alfred Long, author of *Personal and family names* (1883), says, '**Tolliday**. Born on St Olave's day, gives **Tully**, when English, Tooley Street [London] named from St Olave's church', while Ernest Weekley in *Surnames* (1916) admits to being perplexed: 'The Lincolnshire name **Tolliday** or **Tollady** is very puzzling. It may mean "Tolley the dey" or the "dey of Tolley"'. Leics Borough Records include the name of Richard **Tollidenoit** (Anglo-French, *toille de noit*, 'toil by night'); so was the first **Tolliday** the opposite of this, a toiler by day? Meanwhile, Rev. Henry Barber's dictionary of surnames makes a bold attempt to derive **Tollady** from *Tolladine* in Worcs – a stab in the dark which the author has the good grace to enter with a question-mark against it. Probable variants include: **Tolledy**, **Tolloday**, **Tol(l)aday**, **Toleday**, **Tollardy**, **Towleday** and **Tilledy**. For a detailed study of these surnames, see *Searching for surnames* by John Titford (2002). **Tolliday** is widespread geographically, though strongest in East Anglia in general and Cambs in particular.

Tollyfield, *see* Turberville.

Tolman, *see* Toller.

Tolver, *see* Telfer.

Tom(s)/Tombs/Tome(s)/Tomison/ Tomkin(s)/Tomkins(on)/Tomlin(s)/ Tomlins(on)/Tompkin/Tompkins(on)/ Tompsett/Tompson/Toms/Tomsett/ Tomson, *see* Thomas.

Tonbridge/Tunbridge P Place-name *Tonbridge* in Kent OE 'bridge by the town' (pronounced '*Tunbridge*'). Surnames of southeast England.

Tone/Toner, *see* Town.

Tong(e)/Tongue O/T/P/N Occupational term for a maker or user of tongs OE *tang(e)*; or a dweller at a tongue of land/ river-fork OE; or from a place-name so situated, such as *Tonge* in Leics or *Tong* in various counties; or a nickname for a person who had a deformity of the tongue, or who was a tongue-wagging chatterbox OE *tunge*. Mainly surnames of the north of England.

Tonkin/Tonks, *see* Thomas.

Toogood N Nickname for a person who was too good OE – applied literally or ironically. A Somerset surname. **Tugwood** is a Middx/Home Counties corruption.

Took(e)(y)/Tuckey F From an ON first-name *Tóki*, of uncertain origin – perhaps a short form of *Thorkell* (see **Thurkettle**). **Took** and **Tooke** are most common in Norfolk, **Tookey** in Kent and in the East Midlands, **Tuckey** in Northants. **Tooky** is a very scarce form, and **Tuck**, also probably a variant, is found mainly in southern counties of England and in East Anglia.

Toombs, *see* Tom.

Toop F From an ON first-name *Tópi/Túpi*, of uncertain origin, but probably including

the name of the God *Thor* as a first element. Chiefly a Dorset surname.

Tootal/Tootell, *see* Toothill.

Tooth N Nickname for a person with (at least one) strange or distinctive tooth OE: 'it must have protruded, or stood in ugly isolation' (Cottle). Most common in Staffs and surrounding counties. *The family of Lucas-Tooth acquired their double-barrelled surname when Robert Tooth (1844–1925), son of Edwin Tooth of Cranbrook, Kent, and Sarah (née Lucas), first adopted it by Royal Licence.*

Toothill/Tootal(l)/Tootell/Tootil(l)/ Tootle T/P Dweller by a hill used as a lookout place OE, or from one of a number of places named with such elements, such as *Toothill*, Hants. **Tuttle** (a Norfolk surname) can be a variant. **Toothill** is chiefly found in WRYorks; all other variants belong mainly to Lancs. *Tootal shirts take their name from Edward Tootal, who in 1842 joined an established clothing business in Manchester as a partner.*

Toovey, *see* Tovey.

Toozer, *see* Tozer.

Top(p) N From an OE byname *Topp*, or ON *Toppr*, which are effectively nicknames meaning 'tuft, topknot, forelock'. **Topping** is a Lancs variant. See also **Topper**.

Topcliff(e) P Place-name *Topcliffe* in NRYorks and WRYorks OE 'hilltop cliff'.

Topham P Place-name in WRYorks OE '?*Toppa*'s homestead', and chiefly a WRYorks surname.

Toplady/Tiplady/Toplass/Toplis(s) N Nickname for a libertine ME, one who was readily able to *tip* ladies over, or to be found *a-top* them, and referring especially to someone who succeeded in making love to a woman of higher rank than himself. The now-scarce surname **Toplady**, Cottle points out with glee, is 'sadly inappropriate to the author of *Rock of Ages*'. See also **Tolliday** and compare **Shacklady**, **Tipper** and **Tupper**. Many bearers of such surnames, mainly in Yorks and Co Durham, have retained the uncompromising **Tiplady**, while Notts has historically been home of most of the **Topladys**. **Toplass** is mainly found in Staffs, and the more euphemistically minded **Toplises** are almost all confined to Derbys, which is also home (along with Lincs) to most of the **Toplisses**. One **Tiplady** family with a proven history which goes back six hundred years was originally settled in Swaledale, NRYorks, thereafter having a presence in Askrigg and Gayle in Wensleydale. For a detailed study of these surnames, see *Searching for surnames* by John Titford (2002). *Augustus Montague Toplady (1740–1778), Anglican clergyman and hymn writer, was born in Farnham, Surrey, the son of an Irish army officer… (Francis) Percy Toplis (1896–1920), the confidence trickster and career criminal who achieved fame/notoriety as the 'monocled mutineer', was born in Newbold, Chesterfield, Derbys… William A. Toplis (1857–1942) was a highly regarded artist who lived on Sark, one of the Channel Islands.*

Toplass/Toplis(s), *see* **Toplady**.

Topp, *see* **Top**.

Topper T/O A surname of unknown origin, mainly found in Lancs. Cottle suggests: 'Perhaps for **Tupper**, or "one who lives on a hilltop" OE (but the element is rare)'. Reaney confines it to an occupational term for a person who put the *toppe* (the tuft of flax or tow) on a distaff, OE plus *-er* suffix. Or perhaps **Tipper** or **Top** are involved?

Topping, *see* **Top**.

Tordoff ?P A surname which has proved elusive, whichever of its known forms (including **Tordoff**, **Dordofe** or **Torder**) are taken into account. Possibly related to the surname **Tardif**? One theory, noted by George Redmonds, is of a Scottish origin: **Tordoff** appears as a byname in Dumfriesshire as early as the thirteenth century, perhaps being derived from *Torduff Point* on the Solway Firth. But the widely held belief that the **Tordoffs** of Yorks were originally soldiers fighting for Bonnie Prince Charlie who made their way north following his abandonment of the cause at Derby in

1745 fails to explain the existence of the surname in Bradford and Leeds, WRYorks, as early as the sixteenth century; thereafter it settled down solidly at Wibsey for over four hundred years. Even more far-fetched is the gem of surname history seriously confided to George Redmonds by a Bradford man many years ago: 'T'Tordoffs were from Russia, tha knaws; came 'ere during t'fost world war…'. A book entitled *The Tordoffs of North Bierley* by Rob Alexander was published in 1998.

Torr T/N Dweller at a hill, peak OE; or a nickname for someone resembling a bull, Anglo-Norman French *tor*. Particularly strong in the English Midlands, 'which would fit with a *tor* in the hills of Derbyshire' (Cottle).

Torry, *see* **Terry**.

Tortoiseshel(l), *see* **Tattersall**.

Toshach/Toshack, *see* **McIntosh**.

Totford, *see* **Titford**.

Totham P Place-name in Essex OE 'look-out homestead', and an Essex surname.

Tot(h)ill, *see* **Toothill**.

Totley P Place-name in Derbys (now South Yorks) OE '?*Tota*'s clearing'. A scarce WRYorks surname.

Tottenham/Tottingham P Place-name *Tottenham* in Middx OE '*Tota/Totta*'s homestead'. A scarce surname both in England (found mainly in southern counties) and in Ireland (where an Anglo-Irish family called **Tottenham** has been in Co Wexford from at least as early as the seventeenth century). **Tottingham**, also very scarce, has a limited presence in Herts. **Tottenham** is the family name of the Irish Marquesses of Ely.

Tottle, *see* **Toothill**.

Tough N/T/P Nickname for a tough, enduring, stubborn person OE. Scots: dweller on a hillside, Gaelic *tulach*, or from a minor place-name with the same meaning. In Scotland, where the surname is particularly in evidence in Aberdeenshire, it is generally pronounced '*Tooch*' (the *-ch* as in '*loch*').

Tout N/T Nickname from 'buttocks' ME (which Cottle helpfully points out is used twice by Chaucer in *The Miller's Tale*); or possibly from a hill so-shaped? Chiefly a West Country surname.

Tovey/Toovey F From an ON first-name *Tófi* (a diminutive form of names containing the divine name *Thor*). **Tovey** is mainly found in Gloucs and surrounding counties; **Toovey** is more common in the Home Counties and in south-east England.

Towell, *see* Toll.

Tower(s) T/O Dweller near a fortified tower OF; or an occupational term for a (white) leather-dresser OE. **Tower** is sparsely scattered across England, most common in Middx; **Towers** ('of/at the tower', or a plural) belongs mainly to Lancs.

Towle, *see* Toll.

Towler, *see* Toller.

Town(e)(s)/Tone/Toner/Towner T/O
Dweller at a place, farm, village, town (as opposed to an outlying settlement) OE *tun* (the same stem as in *-ton* place-names, and as in the modern English word '*town*'). The *-e* of **Towne(s)** indicates the use of the dative after a lost preposition, and **Towner/Toner** are OE plus an *-er* suffix. Reaney prefers to take **Towner** back to a Worcs name *le Tolnur* (1221), 'toll-/tax-gatherer' OE. **Town** is found mainly in WRYorks, **Towne**, **Towner** and **Townes** in south-east England, **Towns** in north-east England and Scotland, and **Toner** in Scotland. Thanks to the fame of the Irish Republican Theobald Wolfe **Tone** (1763–1798) and his distant kinsman the film actor Franchot **Tone** (1905–1968), the surname **Tone** is very often associated with Ireland, though the first evidence of its presence there dates from only the sixteenth century.

Town(s)(h)end T Dweller at the far end of a village/town OE. **Townsin** (most common in Berks and Northants) is possibly a cor-

ruption. **Townshend** is the family name of the Marquesses Townshend.

Towner, *see* Town.

Townl(e)y P Place-name *Towneley* in Lancs OE 'enclosure wood/clearing'.

Towns, *see* Town.

Towns(h)end, *see* Townend.

Townsin, *see* Townend.

Toy(e) N Nickname for a light-hearted person ME *toy* ('sport', 'play'). **Toy** is found in significant numbers both on the island of Alderney in the Channel Islands, and also in Cornwall; **Toye** is sparsely scattered around England and Scotland.

Tozer/Toozer O Occupational term for one who tozes, teases, combs, cards wool with teasels OE – a common enough practice before the invention of metal-tooth cards or carding machines were used for the same purpose. Compare **Tazewell**. **Tozer** is chiefly a Devon surname; **Toozer**, very scarce, can be found in the West Country and in South Wales and Monmouthshire.

Trac(e)y P Place-names *Tracy Bocage* and *Tracy-sur-Mer* in Calvados OF, from an owner called *Thracius* (Latin 'the Thracian'). Strongest in Lancs in both spellings. Irish: a variant of **Treacy**.

Trafford P Place-names in Chesh, Northants and Lancs OE 'ford in a valley (literally "trough")' or 'ford by a trap/snare' or 'ford on a street (a Roman road)'. The surname can certainly be found in these counties, but is at its strongest in Lincs.

Traherne, *see* Treharne.

Trainer/Trainor/Traynor O/F Occupational term for a trapper, a layer of snares OF. Irish: Anglicized form of Gaelic **Mac** [son of] **Threinfhir** ('champion'). **Trainer** is mainly found in the far north of England and central Scotland, strongest in Lanarkshire; **Trainor** and **Traynor** are chiefly found in Lancs.

Tranent P Place-name in East Lothian,

Scotland, British 'place in the dells/brooks'. A very scarce English/Scottish surname.

Tranmer P Place-name *Tranmere* in Chesh ON 'cranes'/herons' sandbank', yet chiefly a Yorks surname.

Trant N Nickname for a cunning, tricky person ME. Cottle claims that such a word is to be found in northern dialects, from Germanic, yet the surname belongs chiefly to Devon.

Tranter O Occupational term for a pedlar, carrier, waggoner OF from Low Latin *travetarius*. Mainly found in Staffs/Salop and surrounding counties.

Trapnell N Nickname for a person deemed to be 'too quick' OF (compare Modern French *trop*). Most common in Gloucs and Somerset.

Trapp O Occupational term for a person who set animal traps or snares OE. Sparsely scattered across southern England; rare in the north.

Tratton, *see* Tritton.

Travers T/O Dweller at a crossing, tollgate, tollbridge OF; or an occupational term for a tollkeeper or collector. Chiefly a Lancs surname in either spelling. *The radio presenter Dave Lee Travis, known as 'DLT', was born in Buxton, Derbys, but went to school in Manchester.*

Travis, *see* Travers.

Trayler/Traylor ?N Scarce Essex surnames of unknown meaning; perhaps a nickname for a huntsman hunting by the trail, a tracker, one who travels on foot, a footpad OF or OE?

Traynor, *see* Trainer.

Treac(e)y/Trac(e)y F Irish: Anglicized form of Gaelic **O'** [descendant of] **Treasaigh** ('fierce'). *Eric Treacy (pronounced 'Tracy') (1907–1978), Bishop of Wakefield and one of the finest railway photographers of his generation, was born in Willesden, London, and acquired his passion for railways while a pupil at the track-side school of Haberdashers'* *Aske's in Hampstead. Treacy's family had Irish origins, and his paternal ancestors included William de Tracy, one of the knights who murdered Archbishop Thomas Becket.*

Treadgold, *see* Threadgill.

Treasure N/O Nickname for a treasured person OF, or an occupational term for a treasurer (but perhaps for a miser?). Chiefly a Somerset surname.

Trebilcock P Place-name in Cornwall, Cornish and OE '?place/farm with cuckoo-haunted hillock' or '*Pilcok*'s place/farm'. The surname is commonly pronounced '*Trebilco*', with the stress on the second syllable.

Tredgett N Nickname for a mountebank/juggler OF. Chiefly an Essex surname.

Tredgold, *see* Threadgill.

Tredinnick P From one of a number of places in Cornwall so-called, Cornish 'fortified place/farm' or 'settlement covered in gorse/bracken'.

Tree T Dweller at a prominent tree OE, perhaps one used as a meeting-place. Mainly found in Kent and surrounding areas.

Treeby P Place-name *Treby* (pronounced '*Treeby*') in Devon OE '?dry curve/bend (in a river)', and a Devon surname.

Treeton P Place-name in WRYorks OE 'place in the trees'. A very rare and sparsely scattered surname. See also **Tritton**.

Trefusis P Place-name in Cornwall, Cornish '?place/farm at the entrenchments'.

Tregear P There are various places so-called in Cornwall, Cornish 'place/farm by a fort', or 'place/farm surrounded by a hedge'.

Tregellas/Tregelles P Place-names *Tregellas*, *Tregellast*, *Tregelles*, *Tregellis* in Cornwall, Cornish 'place/farm at the grove', or 'lost place/farm' or '*Celestis*' place/farm'.

Treglown/Tregloan P Place name *Treglohan* (*Tregeloghan* in 1270), Cornwall, Cornish '?place/farm with a hedge by the little lake'. The surname is commonly pronounced '*Treglone*', whatever the spelling.

Tregoning P There are various places so-called in Cornwall, Cornish '*Conan*'s place/farm'.

Treharne/Traherne F Welsh; from the first-name *Trahaearn*, literally 'most-iron', borne by a Prince of North Wales who was killed in 1081, and which has also given rise to related place-names. Several variant spellings occur, most of them rare, but almost all limited to South Wales.

Trelawn(e)y P Place-names *Trelawny*, *Trelawney*, *Trelawne* in Cornwall, Cornish '?place/farm of groves'.

Treleaven P Place-name in Cornwall, Cornish '?level place/farm'.

Tremain(e)/Tremayne P Place-name *Tremaine* in Cornwall, Cornish 'place/farm of the stone/monolith'. Cottle believes that some American bearers of such a surname were originally named **Truman**.

Trembath P Place-name in Cornwall, Cornish 'place/farm in a corner'.

Trembeth P Place-name *Trembleath* in Cornwall, Cornish 'place/farm of the grave'.

Tremelling P Place-name in Cornwall, Cornish 'mill place/farm'.

Tremenheere P There are various places so-called in Cornwall, Cornish 'place/farm at the long standing-stone'.

Trench T/P Dweller at a cut track, hollow walk, ditch, military excavation OF, or from the place-name *La Tranche* in Poitou, France, with the same meaning. A prominent **Trench** family first established itself in Ireland in the seventeenth century, and the double-barrelled **Chenevix-Trench**es have long played a significant role in Irish affairs.

Trenchard O Occupational term for a person noted for his skills in cutting – with a sword, cleaver, carving-knife or trenching-spade. Chiefly a Somerset surname. *Hugh Montague Trenchard, Viscount Trenchard*

(1873–1956), Chief of the Air Staff 1919–1929 and known as the 'Father of the Royal Air Force', was born in Taunton, Somerset.

Trenoweth P Place-names *Trenouth*, *Trenoweth*, *Trenowth* in Cornwall, Cornish 'new place/farm'.

Trent T/P Dweller on the banks of one of the several rivers called *Trent* (British, but of unknown meaning; compare **Tarrant**); or from *Trent* in Dorset, on a stream formerly called the *Trent*. The surname is strongest in Dorset.

Trentham P Place-name in Staffs, British and OE 'homestead on the (river) *Trent* (see **Trent**, **Tarrant**)'. A scarce Salop/Staffs surname, but also found in Devon.

Trerice/Trerise P There are various places called *Trerice* in Cornwall, Cornish 'place/farm by a ford' or '*Rys*'s place/farm'.

Trescothick P Place-name *Trescowthick* in Cornwall, Cornish *tre-scawek* 'homestead of elder grove'. *Marcus (Edward) Trescothick, the Somerset and England cricketer famed as a left-handed batsman, was born in Keynsham, Somerset, in 1975.*

Treseder/Tresidder P Place-name *Tresidder* (*Treseder* in 1327) in Cornwall, Cornish '*Seder*'s place/farm'.

Trethew(e)y P There are various places so-called in Cornwall, Cornish '*Dewi* (*David*)'s place/farm'.

Trethowan P Place-name *Trethowan* (*Trevewen* in 1295) in Cornwall, Cornish '?*Dewin*'s place/farm'.

Trett N Nickname for a shapely, handsome, neat person OF (ultimately from Latin *tract*: 'drawn out, slender'). Most common in Norfolk.

Tretton, *see* **Tritton**.

Trevail P There are various places called *Treveal(e)* in Cornwall, Cornish '?*Mael*'s place/farm'.

Trevellick P Place-name *Trevellack* in Cornwall, Cornish '?walled place/farm' or '*Elec*'s place/farm'.

Trevelyan P　Place-name in Cornwall, Cornish '?mill place/farm' or '?*Milian*'s place/farm'. *The historian George Macaulay Trevelyan (1876–1962) was born in Stratford-upon-Avon, Warwicks, to a family with Cornish origins.*

Trevor P/F　Place-name in various Welsh counties, Welsh *tre(f)-mawr* 'big village' (the adjective coming second). Irish: Anglicized form of Gaelic **O'** [descendant of] **Treabhair** ('industrious'). The use of *Trevor* as a first name is a more recent devlopement.

Trew, *see* **True**.

Trewartha P　Place-name in Cornwall, Cornish 'upper place/farm'.

Treweek P　Place-name *Treweeg* in Cornwall, Cornish 'place/farm in the wood/village'.

Trew(h)ella P　Place-names *Trewhella*, *Trewhela*, Cornish '?beetle place/farm' or '?highest place/farm'.

Trewen P　Place-name in Cornwall, Cornish 'white/fair place/farm'. Readily confused with/a variant of **Trewin**.

Trewhella, *see* **Trewella**.

Trewick P　Place-name in Northd OE 'dairy farm in the trees', and chiefly a Northd surname.

Trewin P　Place-name in Cornwall, Cornish 'white/fair place/farm'. Readily confused with/a variant of **Trewen**.

Trib(b)le N　A surname of unknown origin; perhaps a nickname for a person with a good treble voice OF, from Latin, cognate with *triple*. Most commonly found in Devon.

Trick/Tricker/Trickett N　Nickname for a trickster, cheat OF (Norman dialect). **Trick** is mainly found in Devon, **Tricker** in Suffolk and neighbouring counties, and **Trickett** in Lancs and WRYYorks.

Trickey P　Place-name in Devon; the second element is OE enclosure, the first element

(*Trike-* in 1238) is of unknown meaning. Chiefly a Devon surname.

Trig(g)(e)(s) N　Nickname for a faithful, trusty person ON *Triggr*, early used as a first-name. The distribution of **Trig(g)(e)s** varies according to spelling; the variant **Trigger** is a Devon surname.

Trigger/Trigges, *see* **Trig**.

Trimble, *see* **Trumble**.

Trimby P　Cottle refers to the place-name *Thrimby* in Westmd ON 'farm by a thornbush', but this is chiefly a West Country surname, strongest in Wilts.

Trindell/Trindle T　Dweller at a circle (of trees, stones, earthworks) OE. Scarce surnames, **Trindle** being most common in Worcs and Warwicks.

Trinder O　Occupational term for one who uses a spindle to braid or plait OE. Mainly found in Oxon and surrounding areas. *Thomas Edward ('Tommy') Trinder (1909–1989), the English stage, screen and radio comedian, was born in Streatham, South London.*

Trindle, *see* **Trindell**.

Tripe O　Occupational term for a producer/dresser/seller of tripe OF. A Devon surname. Readily confused with/a variant of **Tripp**.

Tripp(e) O/N　Occupational term for a dancer, or for a gangly, unco-ordinated person OF. Readily confused with/a variant of **Tripe**. **Tripp**, widely scattered, is most common in Somerset; **Trippe** is found chiefly in Hants; **Tripper** is a Lancs variant.

Tripper, *see* **Tripp**.

Trist O　Occupational term for a huntsman in charge of a hunting station OF. There would appear to be no link with the French adjective *triste* ('sad'). A Devon surname.

Triston/Tristram/Trustram F　From the Celtic first-name *Drystan* (connected with 'tumult, din'), which was modified by way of French *triste* ('sad') into *Tristan/Tristram*. The Atlantic island of *Tristan da Cunha* was named after a Portuguese admiral. **Tristram** is most common in Lancs and Staffs, **Tris-**

ton (very scarce) in Lancs, Middx and Surrey and **Trustram** (also scarce) in Herts.

Tritton ?F/P A surname which looks as if it would have a simple enough point of origin, but which nevertheless poses a few problems. Rev. Henry Barber in *British family names* (second edition, 1903) suggests that it either comes from a Dutch first-name *Tritten*, or is a variant of **Treeton**. **Treeton**, a very scarce scattered surname, would seem to be derived from *Treeton*, a place-name in WRYorks, but **Tritton**, by contrast, is overwhelmingly a Kent surname. There would appear to be no such place-name in Kent itself, but the neighbouring county of Sussex is home to a settlement called *Trotton*, which was *Traitone* in 1086, and *Tratton* in 1316 OE '?stepping-stone settlement'. The instability of the first vowel in such a place-name might make a development to the surname **Tritton** a possibility? Other surnames which might be related include **Tratton** (very scarce, found in Cornwall) and **Tretton** (scarce, found in Lancs and WRYorks).

Trivett ?N ?Nickname from the three-legged cooking-stand so-called OE (ultimately from Greek – compare *tripod*, or the Cambridge University *tripos*, candidates for which were originally subject to an oral examination while they sat on a three legged stool). One **Trivett** family featured such a stand on its armorial bearings (which proves little, of course, and could be by way of a pun). Or possibly a variant of **Tripp**, via a diminutive form such as **Tripet(te)**? An oddly scattered surname, strongest in Devon and Norfolk.

Troake/Troke T 'Dweller at the oak' OE, with ME *at ther oake* becoming *atter oake*, and then *troake*. **Troake** is mainly found in Devon and surrounding counties, **Troke** in Hants.

Trollope P From an early form of the place-name *Troughburn* in Northd, which was *Trollop* in 1352 ON and OE 'imp-(enclosed) valley'. The first recorded use of the word '*trollop*' to refer to a slut or slattern dates from as late as 1615 (compare **Trull**). The unfortunately named '*Silly* **Trollope**' was born in Doncaster, Yorks, c.1894. *The novelist Anthony Trollope (1815–1882) is descended from a family called Tro(w)lope which had held land in Co Durham since the fourteenth century; his distant kinswoman Joanna Trollope, also a novelist, was born in 1943 in her grandfather's rectory in Minchinhampton, Gloucs.*

Trott/Trotman/Trotter N/O Nickname for a person well known for trotting about the place, or more specifically an occupational term for a messenger OF. **Trott** can alternatively be a nickname for a hag, crone OF *trote*. **Trott** is widely scattered, strongest in Somerset; **Trotman** is very much a Gloucs surname, but **Trotter** belongs to northern England and Scotland.

Troubridge, *see* **Trowbridge**.

Troughton P Place-name *Troughton Hall*, Lancs OE 'hollow enclosure'. Strongest in Lancs. *Patrick Troughton (1920–1987), one of several actors to have played the leading role in the Doctor Who television series, was born in Mill Hill, London… John Troughton (c.1637–1681), the controversial Puritan minister and theologian who had been blinded by smallpox at the age of four, was born in Coventry, Warwicks.*

Trounce(r) O/N A maker, seller or user of cudgels OF (compare *truncheon*, and [?] the verb *to trounce*). **Trounce** is chiefly a Cornish surname; **Trouncer** is most common in Gloucs.

Troup(e) T/P A corruption, by metathesis, of **Thorp(e)** (compare **Thro(u)p(e)**). Scots: place-name *Troup* in Banffshire ME '?true hope'. **Troup** is very much an Aberdeenshire surname.

Troutbeck P Place-name in Cumbd and Westmd OE and ON 'trout stream'. This essentially Cumbd surname also had a significant presence in Chesh in the fifteenth century, but had become very scarce and scattered by the late nineteenth century. *Rev. John Troutbeck, English clergyman at Boston, was numbered amongst the Loyalists of Massachusetts during the American War of Independence… John Peel, known far and* *wide thanks to the song that celebrates his hunting exploits, 'lived at Troutbeck once on a day'.*

Trow, *see* True.

Trowbridge P Place-name *Trowbridge* in Wilts OE 'tree (wooden) bridge'. **Trowbridge** is mainly found in Wilts and Dorset; **Troubridge** is a very scarce scattered variant.

Trowel(l) P Place-name *Trowell* in Notts OE '?spring by the tree'. See also **Towle**, under **Toll**.

Trowse P Place-name in Norfolk OE 'wooden house', and a Norfolk surname.

Troy F Irish: Anglicized form of Gaelic **O'** [descendant of] **Troighthigh** ('foot soldier'). Within England, most common in Lancs.

Tru(e)body N Nickname for a faithful man OE and OE. Scarce Gloucs surnames.

Trubshaw P From an unidentified place-name. Cottle says that he would dearly love to make it OF and OE 'truffle wood', but that the dialect word *trub* is first instanced only very late – in 1668. In the event *trub* is more likely to be derived from a first-name such as *Truba*, or a metathetical variant of ON *thorp*, which as -*dorp* and -*trup* is a common element in German and Danish place-names. *Trub Smithy*, near Middleton, Lancs, is a fairly recent name for a settlement formerly known as *Smithy Ford*, but **Trubshaw** is a long-established Staffs surname, and the origin is likely to be *Trubshaw Cross* in Longport (near Burslem) in that county, where in 1949 a modern cross, replacing an ancient one, was erected in the centre of a traffic roundabout, bearing the inscription: 'Thomas *Trobbeschawe* was a juror at the great court of Tunstall held Tuesday, I Richard II, 4 May 1378'. Ward, in *The Borough of Stoke-on-Trent* (1843), says: 'We conceive that *Trubsharv* was the most ancient name of this locality, though now forgotten; for we find Thomas de *Trobeshawe*, one of the jurors of Tunstall Court, anno 27 Hen VI (1451)'. By the eighteenth century most **Trubshaws** were living in or near Great Haywood, Staffs, from where some indviduals migrated to

Leicester in the mid nineteenth century. *Ernest (Brian) Trubshaw, aviator, was born in Toxteth, Liverpool.*

True/Trew/Trow N/T/P Nickname for a trusty, faithful person OE (as in 'To thine own self be true' or 'Be true to me', which doesn't just mean 'Don't tell me lies'; compare **Trueman**); or a dweller by a prominent tree OE *treow*, or near a depression in the ground OE *trog*; there are places called *True* and *Trew* OE 'at the tree' in Devon, though these surnames are not generally found in that county.

Truebody, *see* Trubody.

Truelove N Nickname for a faithful lover, sweetheart OE. Most common in Warwicks.

Trueman/Truman N Nickname for a trusty/faithful man OE (compare **True**). **Trueman** is most common in north-west England and in Warwicks, **Truman** in Notts.

Trull P Place-name in Somerset OE 'ring, circle (?of stones/trees/earth)'. A surname which might well have been abandoned by some who originally bore it, thanks to an unfortunate later meaning of 'concubine, trollop' (compare **Trollope**). The German surname **Trull** (French **Trouillet**) is from a nickname for a devious or sly character OF *trouille*. In England, **Trull** is mainly found in Gloucs.

Truman, *see* Trueman.

Trumble/Trimble/Trumbull F From an OE first-name *Trumbeald* ('firm/strong-bold'). Readily confused with/a variant of **Turnbull**, by metathesis. *Baron (William) David Trimble, the politician who served as leader of the Ulster Unionist Party and as First Minister of Northern Ireland, was born in Bangor, Co Down, in 1944.*

Trump(er) O Occupational term for a trumpeter OF. **Trump** is a West Country surname, most common in Somerset; **Trumper** belongs to Herefords and Salop. *Donald John Trump, the American business executive, entrepreneur, television and radio personality and author, was born in Queens,*

New York, in 1946. He has Scottish ancestry on his mother's side, and his paternal grandfather, Frederick Christ Trump, emigrated from Germany to America in 1885.

Truscott P There is a place-name *Trescott* in Staffs, Celtic and OE 'cottages on (the stream once called) *Trysull*', but this is very largely a Cornish surname, where the origin is the place-name *Truscott* in that county, Cornish 'beyond/across (the) wood'.

Trustram, *see* Tristram.

Try N Nickname for a choice, excellent person ME (probably from an OF past participle). A Middx/Surrey surname.

Tubb F From a ME (from OE/ON) first-name *Tubbe*. There is probably no connexion with 'tub' ME in the sense of a barrel, and although **Tubman** could in principle be an occupational term for a tub-maker or cooper, it could simply be '*Tubbe*'s man/servant'. **Tubb** is mainly found in southern counties of England, but **Tubman** is a Cumbd/Westmd surname.

Tubman, *see* Tubb.

Tuck, *see* Took. Cottle maintains that it is 'certainly *not* related to **Tucker**' and adds that 'the fat Friar adds more mystery, since there weren't any friars in the reign of Richard I'.

Tucker O/N Occupational term for a fuller, one who fulled, teased and burled cloth ME (from a verb meaning 'maltreat'). Compare **Fuller** and **Walker**. Or a nickname for a generous or brave man, one who was 'all heart' OF *tout coeur*. Chiefly a surname of southwest England, especially strong in Devon, bearing witness to a great mediaeval cloth industry. **Tuckerman**, also a Devon surname, though much scarcer, is '**Tucker**'s man'.

Tuckerman, *see* Tucker.

Tuckey, *see* Took.

Tudball, *see* Theobald.

Tuddenham P Place-name in both Norfolk and Suffolk OE '*Tudda*'s homestead' (the *-en-*

being a sign of the genitive of a weak noun). Principally a Norfolk surname.

Tudor, *see* Theodore.

Tudway T Dweller at the highway ('people's way') OE; compare **Thoday**. Most common in Gloucs and Somerset.

Tuesley P Place-name in Surrey OE 'wood/ clearing dedicated to (the pagan god) *Tiw*' (his name also gives us *Tuesday*). A Surrey/ Sussex surname.

Tuff ?T ?Dweller by a tuft, clump of trees, grassy hillock ME (compare **Tuft**). Most common in Kent, but also found in north-east England.

Tuffley P Place-name in Gloucs OE '*Tuffa*'s clearing', and a Gloucs surname.

Tuft(s) T Dweller at the toft, curtilage, or at the tuft/cluster of trees or bushes (compare **Tuff**) (though the OE form began with *th-*). Cottle points out that 'a USA bearer (died 1815) was insensitively named Cotton **Tufts**'. Not common in either spelling; **Tuft** is found mainly in Staffs, **Tufts** in Norfolk.

Tugwood, *see* Toogood.

Tulloch/Tullock P Place-name in various Scottish counties, Gaelic 'hill, knoll, mount'.

Tullock, *see* Tulloch.

Tully F Irish: Anglicized form of Gaelic **O'** [descendant of] **Taithlagh** ('peaceable') or of **O'Maol Tuile** 'descendant of the devotee/servant of (St) *Tuile* ("will [of God]")'. See also **Flood**.

Tumman T/O A 'town-man' (villager) OE; or '*Tom*'s servant'. A Yorks surname.

Tunbridge, *see* Tonbridge.

Tunks, *see* Thomas.

Tunnah O Occupational term for a 'tunner', a maker or user of casks OE plus an *-er* suffix, slurred to *-ah*. A scattered surname, strongest in Denbighshire, Wales, and in Lancs and Northd.

Tunnard O Occupational term for a farm/

village herdsman OE and OE. A Lincs surname.

Tunnicliff(e) P Place-name *Tonacliffe* in Lancs OE 'enclosure on the banks of a stream'. Principally a Lancs surname, found also in Staffs.

Tunstall/Tunstell/Tunstill P From one of the many places called *Tunstall* OE and OE 'farm-site, farmstead', with the same meaning as **Dunstall**, and readily confused with it.

Tupholme P Place-name in Lincs ME and ON 'island with rams', and a Lincs surname.

Tupper O/?N Occupational term for a 'tupherd', one who herded rams ME. Cottle gives alternatives: 'rammer, a workman who beat and rammed with *tups*, from Germanic... but it may be a nickname as obscene as **Toplady**'. Mainly found in Sussex and surrounding areas.

Turberville/Turberfield P Distinctive Severn valley surnames, from the place-name *Thouberville* in Eure, France ON and OF '*Thorburn*'s place (Latin *villa*)'. Since Norman French names such as **Blonville** and **Grenville** were Anglicized to become **Blomefield** and **Greenfield**, a similar process could readily have turned **Turberville** into **Turberfield** (compare **Manderville/Manderfield**). Scarce Dorset surnames such as **Tollerfield**, **Tollfield** and **Tollyfield** might perhaps reflect another corruption of the ancient knightly name of **Turbeville**. Sir Pagan or Payne **Turbeville**, one of the Conqueror's companions, is featured on the Battle Abbey Roll, and **Turbevilles** were settled in the manor house at Bere Regis in Dorset for upwards of 550 years. It was the Dorset author Thomas Hardy who set this particular ball rolling. In the novel which bears her name, Tess **Durbeyfield** pays a high price for her poor father's ingenuous belief that he and Tess are members of the **D'Urbeville** family. Hardy is clearly fascinated by this theme of family names changing and falling from grace, and in essence what he has to say is accurate enough: 'There are many instances of the gradual decline of legitimate scions of the old knightly families. Their high-sounding names have undergone outrageous perversions and although they have inherited no worldly gear they own the same blood'.

Turk F/N/T From a mediaeval first-name, possibly from *Thorkell* (see **Thurkettle**); or a nickname for a rowdy, argumentative person OF *turc*, one who behaved as Turks were believed to behave; or applied to a person who had fought against the Turks or who lived at a house bearing the sign of a Turk. A surname found mostly in Kent and Sussex.

Turkentine, *see* **Thurkettle**.

Turley P Place-name in WRYorks OE 'round clearing', but a surname chiefly found in Staffs.

Turnbull N Nickname for a man deemed to to be strong enough to turn around a rampaging bull ME. Famously a surname of the England/Scotland border, strongest in Co Durham/Northd. Readily confused with/a variant of **Trumble**, by metathesis.

Turner/Turno(u)r O/N Occupational term for a turner, one who made small objects of wood, metal or bone OF, or for one who 'turned' in other ways, such as a turnspit, translator, maker of wooden wine-measures and ale-measures, or for a jouster (one who '*tourneys*'); or a nickname for a fast runner – one who could outstrip (or turn) a hare ME. **Turner** is a particularly prolific surname, and is the family name of the Barons Netherthorpe.

Turney P From one of a number of places in northern France called *Tournai*, *Tournay* or *Tourny*, consisting of the Gaulish first-name *Turnus*, plus a suffix. Chiefly a Bucks/Middx surname.

Turno(u)r, *see* **Turner**.

Turnpenny N Nickname for a profiteer, haggler, one who knew how to turn a quick penny OF and OE. A WRYorks surname.

Turpin F From a Norman French form of the ON first-name *Thorfinnr* (the God *Thor*, plus the race *Finnr*). Most common in Devon, but also found in Yorks and elsewhere. *Richard ('Dick') Turpin (1705–1739), highwayman, horse stealer and murderer, was born at the Blue Bell Inn in Hempstead, Essex (still standing), where his father was the publican. His attempt to hide his identity by adopting the name of Palmer having failed, he was hanged at York on 17 April 1739.*

Turpitt T Dweller at the turf/peat-pit OE. Most common in South Wales, strongest in Monmouthshire.

Turtle F/N From the ON first-name *Thorkell* (see **Thurkettle**); or a nickname for a person who was crippled in some way OF *tourtel* ('twisted, crooked'), or who was known for being gentle ME *turtel* ('turtle-dove' – which is what Paulina in *The Winter's Tale* means when she says: 'I an old turtle will wing me away to some withered bough...'). A widely scattered surname, most common in Lancs and in Middx. **Tuttle** (a Norfolk surname) can be a variant.

Turton P Place-name in Lancs ON and OE '*Thori*'s farm'. A Lancs/WRYorks surname, also found in the Midlands.

Turvey P Place-names in Beds OE 'turf island', and still strong in that county.

Turvill(e) P Place-name in Bucks and Gloucs OE 'dry field', but most common as a surname in Leics and Warwicks.

Tushingham P Place-name *Tushingham Hall* in Chesh OE '?homestead of *Tunsige*'s people', and a Chesh surname. *The film and stage actress Rita Tushingham was born in Liverpool, Lancs, in 1942.*

Tutford, *see* **Titford**.

Tut(h)ill, *see* **Toothill**.

Tuttle A variant of **Toothill**, **Thurkettle** or **Turtle**.

Tuttlebee P There are places called *Thirkelby* in ERYorks and NRYorks ON '*Thirkell*'s farm', but the scarce surname **Tuttlebee** is mainly found in Essex.

Twatt, *see* **Thwaite**.

Tweed(d)ale/Tweddell/Tweddle/ Tweedle P Dweller in the valley OE/ON of the river *Tweed*, British, of uncertain meaning, on the border between England and Scotland. The distribution of such surnames depends upon the spelling: **Tweedale** is mostly found in Lancs; **Tweeddale** in Lanarkshire, Scotland; **Tweddell** in Co Durham and Northd; and **Tweddle** in these two counties, but also in Chesh.

Twell(s), *see* **Atwell**.

Twelvetrees T Dweller by a group of twelve trees OE 'perhaps a round number for a clump' (Cottle). A Lincs surname.

Twemlow P Place-name in Chesh OE '(by) two hills', the *-m-* being a relic of the dative following a lost preposition. A Chesh/ Lancs/Staffs surname.

Twigden/Twigdon ?P A very scarce surname of unknown origin, principally found in Northants, but also in Leics, Hunts and elsewhere. It looks for all the world like a place-name, which could perhaps bear comparison with *Twigworth*, Gloucs, which is OE '*Twicga*'s enclosure'. *Twysden* in Kent, which has always maintained its '*s*', is probably not involved. *In the year 1633 the Rev Lawrence Washington, great-great-grandfather of the first American President George Washington, married Amphyllis, daughter and co-heiress of John Twigden of Little Creaton, Northants.*

Twigdon, *see* **Twigden**.

Twigg N Nickname for a thin person OE *twigge*. A surname of the Midlands and of northern England.

Twin(n) N Nickname given to one of a pair of twins OE. An east-of-England surname in both spellings, **Twin** being found mainly in Essex, **Twinn** in Cambs.

Twinberrow T ?Dweller between hills/burial-mounds OE. A Worcs surname.

Twineham/Twyn(h)am P There is a place called *Twineham* in Sussex OE 'between streams', and *Twinham* was the original name of *Christchurch*, Dorset, but the scarce surname **Twineham** belongs principally to ERYorks. By contrast, **Twynam** and **Twynham**, both scarce, are chiefly found in southern/south-western England and in Northants respectively.

Twining P Place-name *Twyning*, Gloucs OE 'between rivers', and a Gloucs surname. *Richard Twining (1749–1824), tea and coffee merchant, was born in London, the city to which his great-grandfather Daniel Twining, a weaver from Painswick, Gloucs, had moved at a time when the woollen industry was in decline.*

Twinn, *see* Twin.

Twiss P *Twiss* (evidenced in *Twiston*, Lancs, and elsewhere) is an OE place-name element meaning 'river-fork' (related to *twin*), and Bardsley derives **Twiss** from *Twiss Green* in Lancs. But it could readily be confused with, or be a variant of, **Twist**. Some members of the present-day **Twiss** family believe that their origins lie in a place called *Twizel* (also OE 'river-fork') in the English/Scottish border country, where individuals so-named were living during the thirteenth century (and from where they might have migrated to Lancs, giving *Triss Green* its name in the process?), and that the **Twiss** families living in Germany are descendants of English wool traders who had first settled in Rotterdam. **Twiss** has continued to be primarily a Lancs/Chesh surname.

Twist ?O A surname of uncertain origin, possibly an occupational term for a person who twisted threads into cord in the cotton industry, a 'twister' ME. Readily confused with/a variant of **Twiss**.

Twistleton P Place-names: *Twistleton*, WRYorks (situated at a narrow wedge of land formed where Kingsdale Beck meets the river Greta); *Twiston*, Lancs (which was *Twyselton* in the late thirteenth century) OE 'river-fork farm'. A family of **Twistleton**s has long been established in Craven, NRYorks, and a William of **Twyselton** held lands near Ingleborough in 1316. John **Twisleton** (writing in *Family Tree Magazine*, July 2007) has established certain relevant facts: that at the time when parish

registers were beginning to be kept in the sixteenth century, **Twistleton**s were concentrated in the parish of Giggleswick and east of Leeds; and that of a total of 541 **Twistleton** births, marriages and deaths recorded in England and Wales from 1837 to 1913, 38 per cent took place in Northants, 21 per cent in Craven and 12 per cent around London. We might add that at the time of the 1881 census, the surname **Twistleton**, very rare at that stage, had a presence in both Lancs and WRYorks. The family of **Twistleton-Wykeham-Fiennes** are Barons Saye and Sele.

Twitchell T Dweller at a river/stream-fork OE. The word *twitchell* is regularly used in the East Midlands to describe a narrow pathway between gardens, though the surname, scarce, is found mainly in Herts.

Twitchen/Twiching(s)/Twitchin, *see* Titchener.

Twite, *see* Thwaite.

Twopen(n)y N Nickname from OE 'two-penny' (two pence), from an amount of rent paid, or as a result of some lost joke. Mere guesswork would suggest that those bearing these Kent surnames would pronounce them as '*Tuppny*'. *The artist William Twopenny (1799–1873) came from a family that originally owned the estate of Woodstock Park, Tunstall, Kent.*

Twyford P Place-name found in several counties OE 'double ford'. Cottle speculates: 'the water must have forked, requiring two fords consecutively'. A scattered surname.

Twyn(h)am, *see* Twineham.

Tyas P An ethnic name used for a person from Germany or the Low Countries, Anglo-Norman French/Old High German. Chiefly found in WRYorks, where George Redmonds says that the early use of Christian names such as *Baldwin* and *Franco* by families bearing the surname **Tyas** suggests that they may have originated in Flanders.

Tydeman, *see* Tiddeman.

Tye T/P Dweller at an enclosure, common

pasture OE, or at an island (a misdivision of ME '*at(te) ye/ey*'); or from a minor place so-called. A widespread surname, strongest in Kent and Suffolk.

Tyldesley P Place-name in Lancs OE '*Til-weald*'s clearing', and a long-established Lancs surname.

Tyler/Tiler O Occupational term for maker or layer of tiles (on pavements, floors and [later] roofs) OE. **Tyler** is a widespread surname, commonest in south-east England; **Tiler**, much scarcer, is principally found in Kent.

Tyndale/Tindal(l)/Tindell/Tindill/ Tind(a)le/Tyndall P Regional name for a person who lived in *Tynedale*, the valley of the river Tyne, Celtic and OE; or from *Tindale*, Cumbd, situated on a tributary of the Tyne. These are generally surnames of the north of England and of Scotland, but **Tyndall** is chiefly found in Gloucs, where there may be a separate point of origin – perhaps related to the word *tyning*, used in south-western counties to refer to a fenced enclosure, from the OE verb *tynan* 'to enclose'? *William Tyndale (c.1494–1536), translator of the bible and martyr, was born in Gloucs, probably near Dursley, to a family related to the Tyndales of Northants, Essex and Norfolk (who may possibly have had ancestral roots in the Tyne valley?).*

Tyrwhitt P Place-name *Trewhitt* in Northd ON and OE '?resinous wood meadow'. By the late nineteenth century the surname (commonly pronounced '*Tirrit*') was chiefly to be found in Oxon. According to Wotton's *Baronetage*, one **Tyrwhitt** family of Kettleby, Lincs, can be traced back to Sir Hercules **Tyrwhitt**, who lived during the reign of King Henry I. The family arms – 'Gules, three tyrwhits (lapwings) or' – are allusive, and a legend arose that Sir Hercules was rescued from impending death by the cry of a flock of lapwings. All harmless fun? The well-known family of **Tyrwhitt-Drake** was formerly settled at Shardeloes, Bucks.

Tysoe P Place-name in Warwicks OE 'hill-spur dedicated to *Tiw* (a pagan deity)'. Mainly found in Beds and surrounding counties.

Tyson N A nickname for someone of a fiery temper OF; or a variant of **Dyson** (see **Dye**). A surname of the north of England, strongest in Lancs.

Tyte, *see* Tite.

Tytherleigh P Place-names *Tytherleigh* and *Tytherley* in Devon and Hants OE 'fragile/ young wood'. The surname **Tytherleigh** is mainly found in Somerset and surrounding counties.

U

Udall P Place-name *Yewdale* in Lancs OE 'yew valley'.

Ulph, *see* **Wolf**.

Ulrich, *see* **Woolrich**.

Umpleby P Place-name *Anlaby* in ERYorks ON '*Anlafr/Olafr*'s farm'. Compare **Oliff**. Chiefly a WRYorks surname.

Uncle(s) N/F Nickname for an avuncular man, one who behaved like an uncle OF; or from an ON first-name *Ulfketil* ('wolf-cauldron'), much corrupted. Most common in Middx and Herts.

Underdown T/P Dweller at the foot of a hill OE, or from a place so-called, such as *Underdown*, Kent. Chiefly a Kent surname. Compare **Underhill**.

Underhill T/P Dweller at the foot of a hill OE, or from a place so-called, such as *Underhill*, Devon. Chiefly a Devon/Staffs/Warwicks surname. Compare **Underdown**.

Underwood T/P Dweller at the edge of a wood ME, or from a place so-called in Derbys, Notts and elsewhere.

Unsworth P Place-name in Lancs OE '*Hund*'s enclosure', and a Lancs surname.

Unthank P Place-name in Cumbd (two such) and elsewhere, from an OE adverb meaning 'without leave, willy-nilly' – hence the place where squatters settled. Chiefly a Co Durham/NRYorks surname.

Unwin F From an OE first-name *Hunwine* 'bearcub-friend' or 'un-friend' ('enemy'). Mainly a surname of north-west England, but strong in WRYorks. *'Professor' Stanley Unwin (1911–2002), famous for having invented his own gobbledegook language known as 'Unwinese' ('Basic Engly Twenty-fido') was born in Pretoria, South Africa, his parents having emigrated there from the United Kingdom in the early 1900s.*

Upchurch P Place-name in Kent OE 'upper church', though the surname is chiefly found in Hunts.

Upcott P Place-names in Devon (four), Herefords and Somerset OE 'upper cottage/hut'. Chiefly a Devon surname.

Upcraft T Dweller at the upper croft (enclosed piece of land) OE. Mainly found in Norfolk and surrounding counties.

Uphill T/P Dweller at the 'upper hill' OE, or from a place-name with the same meaning, though *Uphill*, Somerset, is OE 'settlement above the hill or creek'. Mainly a Somerset/Wilts surname.

Upjohn F Welsh, 'son of John' (*ap John*). Sparsely scattered across southern England, most common in Dorset.

Uppington P Place-name in Wilts OE 'upper village' and in Salop (originally *Upton*) OE '*Uppa*'s estate'. Mainly found in Somerset and surrounding counties.

Upright ?N Probably a nickname for an erect, upstanding person OE. The meaning 'just, honourable' may have come too late to have affected the surname. Sparsely scattered throughout England; most common in Devon.

Upsall P Place-name in NRYorks ON 'upper hall/dwelling'. Chiefly a Lincs surname.

Upton P Place-names in nearly thirty counties from Cumbd to Kent, most of which are OE 'upper place/farm'. Family name of the Viscounts Templetown.

Urban F From a mediaeval first-name, from Latin, meaning 'citizen', made popular thanks to seven popes so-called.

Uren T/F Cornish: dweller by a swamp, *gwern*; or from a Brittonic first-name *Urbien/Urien* (*Urbgen* in OW), meaning '? town-born'. **Urien** is a much scarcer variant, as is the unfortunate **Urine**, which has something of a presence in Lancs.

Urien/Urine, *see* Uren.

Urmston P Place-name in Lancs OE '*Wyrm*'s town/village', and a Lancs surname.

Urpeth P Place-name in Co Durham OE 'aurochs' (wild ox) path'. A Northd surname.

Urquhart P Place-name in Inverness and elsewhere in Scotland OW 'on the wood/ wood-side'. Commonly pronounced '*Erkutt*'.

Urry, *see* Woolrich.

Ursell F From a first-name of Latin origin, meaning 'little bear' (the feminine form being *Ursula*). A Gloucs surname.

Urwin, *see* Irvin.

Usher O Occupational term for a doorkeeper, chamberlain, usher OF. A scattered surname, strong in Co Durham.

Ussell/Uzzell N Nickname for a person bearing some resemblance to a bird OF (compare Modern French *oiseau*). Very scarce West Country surnames.

Utteridge/Outridge/Uttridge F From an OE first-name *Uhtric* ('dawn-powerful'), with *-ric* modified so as to look like the place-name element *-ridge*. **Utteridge** is found mainly in Cambs and Norfolk, **Uttridge** in Cambs and Suffolk, and **Outridge** in south-east England.

V

Vacher O Occupational term for a cowman OF. Chiefly a Dorset surname.

Vail(e), *see* Vale.

Vaisey/Facey/Lenfest(e)y/Phasey/Vaizey/Voisey N Nickname for a playful, pleasure-loving (even wanton?) person OF *envoisié*. A surname which can be found in a large number of related forms (Reaney lists no fewer than twenty-eight), beginning variously with *F-*, *V-* and *Ph-*. **Lenfest(e)y**, an interesting rendering of the original French, is a Guernsey surname.

Valance, *see* Valence.

Vale/Vail(e) T Dweller in a valley OF. **Vale** is especially strong in Warwicks, **Vail** in Cambs and **Vaile** in Gloucs. **Vile(s)** can be a variant. Readily confused with/a variant of **Veal** and **Vial** (see under **Vidal**).

Valence/Val(l)ance P Place-name in Drôme, France, named after an individual with a name akin to *Valentine*. **Valance** and **Valence** are scarce widely scattered surnames; **Vallance** is particularly strong in Ayrshire.

Valentine F From a mediaeval first-name, Latin in origin, meaning 'strong, healthy'. 'Through a clash of dates, a pagan festival when lots were drawn for lovers was transferred to the feast-day of a third-century Roman martyr' (Cottle). Chiefly a Lancs surname.

Vallance, *see* Valence.

Vallis T/P Dweller in a valley OF, or from the place-name *Val(l)ois*, with the same meaning, in France, or from the province of

Valois. Alternatively, there is a place called *Vallis* ('valley') in Frome, Somerset, and this is primarily a Somerset/Wilts surname. Compare **Villis** (see under **Villiers**).

Vance, *see* Venn.

Vane, *see* Fane.

Vann, *see* Venn.

Varah, *see* Ferrar.

Varco(e), *see* Verco.

Varden/Vardon, *see* Verden.

Varker, *see* Verco.

Varley P In some cases, a variant of **Farley** (from one of a number of places so-called). *Varley* is also a place-name, of which there are examples in Devon OE 'clearing with ferns'. Yet this is predominantly a WRYorks surname; places such as *Varleys*, *Varley Field* and *Varley Lair* in that county take their name from the surname, not vice versa, and the consensus of opinion would indicate that the source of **Varley** is a place called *Verly* in Aisne, Picardy, from the first-name *Virilius*, plus a local suffix. For the relationship between the *-ar-* and *-er-* in such cases, see **Armistead**.

Varney, *see* Verney.

Varty, *see* Verity.

Vassall/Vassar O Status term for a vassal, servant OF, from Celtic. **Vassall** is a scarce Somerset/Severn Valley surname; **Vassar** is mainly found in Norfolk.

Vaughan N/F Welsh: nickname for a short man, a diminutive of OW *bach* ('little'), the guttural '*ch*' sound no longer being pronounced, though hinted at by the '*gh*' spelling. Irish: from one of various Gaelic names such as **O'** [descendant of] **Mochain** (*see also* **Mahon**), **O'Machain** or **O'Beachain**. **Vaughan** is the family name of the Earls of Lisburne.

Vause, *see* **Vaux**.

Vaux/Vause P/N From one of a number of places in France called *Vaux* OF 'valleys'; or in some cases a nickname for a false person, a liar OE/OF. **Vaux** is scattered throughout England and Wales, most common in WRYorks; **Vause** is more limited to Lancs and WRYorks.

Vavaso(u)r/Vavasseur O Status term for a feudal tenant next below a baron in rank OF *vavasour* (literally 'vassal of vassals'), or applied to a servant of such a man. One prominent Roman Catholic family of **Vavasors**, Baronets, was long settled at Haslewood, Yorks. A scarce surname in all spellings: **Vavasor** can be found in Devon, **Vavasour** in Lincs and **Vavasseur** in Kent. A family called **Vawser**, which was established in the fenland of Cambs by a migrant from Bawtry, WRYorks, in the seventeenth century, probably derives its surname from **Vavasour**. Another seemingly unlikely but well-documented metamorphosis of the **Vavasour** surname was through **Vavister** to **Bavister**.

Vawser, *see* **Vavasor**.

Veal(e) N/O/F Nickname for an old man (or the elder of two brothers) or for someone as docile as a calf OF; or an occupational name for a calf-herd OF. Yet these are mainly surnames of Cornwall and Devon, and G. Pawley White derives them from a Cornish first-name *Mael* or *Myghal*, also used as an element in various place-names. **Vile(s)** can be a variant. Readily confused with/a variant of **Vale** and **Vial(l)** (see under **Vidal**).

Vearncombe T/P Dweller in a bracken valley OE, or from a minor place so-called, with the same meaning. Chiefly a Somerset surname.

Veck/Vick O Occupational term for a

bishop (or for a bishop's servant), Anglo-Norman French *L'Eveske*, wrongly divided as *le vesk*, later **Veck** and **Vick**. Compare **Levick** and **Bishop**. **Veck** belongs mainly to Herts, **Vick** to Gloucs.

Vellacott P Place-name in Devon OE '*Willa*'s cottage'.

Venables P Place-name in Eure, France OF (?from Latin *venabulum* ['hunting area']). Strongest in Chesh, Lancs and Staffs. *Terry Venables ('El Tel'), former manager of the England football team, was born in Dagenham, Essex, in 1943.*

Venn/Fance/Fann/Fenn/Fenner/ Vance/Vann/Venning T/P Dweller at a fen, marshy ground OE; or from the place-name *Venn*, with the same meaning, of which there are several in Devon. A certain resemblance between some of these surnames and the word *venery* ('hunting' OF) might suggest an alternative meaning. **Venn** and **Venning** are south-western forms (compare **Fane**); **Fance** is a scarce Essex variant; **Vance** is strongest in both Lancs and Lanarkshire, Scotland; **Vann** is an East Midlands surname, strongest in Leics. **Venner**, probably a variant, is a Devon surname. *Fenner's cricket ground, one of the oldest in England, takes its name from F. P. Fenner, a noted batsman, who leased ground in Cambridge from Gonville and Caius College in 1846, and in 1848 sub-let it to the University Cricket Club.*

Vennall/Vennell T Dweller in an alley or lane OF. Scarce southern England surnames.

Venner/Venning, *see* **Venn**.

Venton P Place-name in Cornwall, Cornish *fenten* 'fountain, spring', with the initial *f*- voiced, and in Devon OE 'place/farm in a fen' (compare **Venn**). Or from a southern pronunciation of the place-name *Fenton*, in Devon and elsewhere (see **Fenton**). A surname of Cornwall and Devon.

Ventress/Ventris(s) N Nickname for an adventurous, daring person OF. **Ventress** and **Ventriss** are chiefly NRYorks surnames; **Ventris** belongs mainly to south-east England. *Michael Ventris (1922–1956), the archi-*

tect and classical scholar who deciphered the Mycenean 'Linear B' script, was born in Wheathampstead, Herts.

Verco(e)/Varco(e)/Varker F Cornish surnames, probably with the meaning of 'Mark's children'. *Sir Walter Verco (1907–2001), Norroy and Ulster King of Arms at the College of Arms, was born in Wandsworth, south-west London. His family, Cornish in origin, was of modest means, and his grandfather had migrated to London from Devon in the late nineteenth century.*

Verden/Varden/Vardon/Verdin/Verdon/Verdun P From one of various places in France called *Verdun* OF (?from Gaulish 'alder hill', compare **Verney** and **Vernon**). For the relationship between the *-ar-* and *-er-* forms of this surname, see **Armistead**.

Verity/Varty N Nickname for a truthful person OF, or for someone who played the part of *Truth* in a play. **Verity** is mainly found in WRYorks, **Varty** in Cumbd/Northd. For the relationship between the *-er-* and *-ar-* forms of this surname, see **Armistead**.

Verney/Varney P From one of a number of place-names in France, such as *St Paul du Vernay* in Calvados OF (?from Gaulish 'alder-tree', compare **Verden** and **Vernon**). For the relationship between *-ar-* and *-er-* (*Varney/Verney*), see **Armistead**. **Verney** is the family name of the Barons Willoughby de Broke.

Vernon P There are many places so-called in France, including *Vernon* in Eure OF (from Gaulish 'alder' plus a suffix, compare **Verden** and **Verney**), the home of William the Conqueror's companion Richard **de Vernon**. The use of *Vernon* as a first-name (as borne, for example, by Elvis Presley's father) is a more recent development. Family name of the Barons Lyveden and Vernon.

Verrier O Occupational term for a glassworker, glazier OF. Mainly found in Somerset and surrounding counties.

Vial(l)(s), *see* **Vidal**.

Vicar(s)/Vicary/Vickers/Vickery O Occupational term for a vicar OF, a clergyman having charge of a parish in the stead of a rector, or of a religious house to which the tithes were appropriated; or applied to a servant of such a man (who should in principle have been childless). **Vickers** may be readily confused with, or be a variant of, surnames in the **Vigars** group. **Vicar** is found mainly in Lancs, **Vicars** and **Vickers** in the north of England, **Vicary** in Devon, **Vickery** in Devon and Somerset, and **Vicarage** (probably a variant of **Vicary**) in Warwicks and Worcs. *The career of the eminent genealogist Sir Arthur Vicars (1862–1921), Ulster King of Arms, came to an ignominious end in 1908 following the theft of the insignia of the order of St Patrick (the 'Irish crown jewels') while they were in his official custody. Thirteen years later his country house at Kilmorna, Co Kerry, was set on fire by members of the Irish Republican Army and he was shot dead in the garden in front of his family and servants... Thomas Edward ('Tom') Vickers (1833–1915), steel maker and armamants manufacturer, was born in Sheffield into a family which had established a hugely profitable steel-making business. The Metropolitan Vickers Electrical Company was created in 1919.*

Vick, *see* **Veck**.

Vickers/Vickery, *see* **Vicar**.

Vidal(l)/Vial(l)(s) F From a mediaeval first-name *Vitale*, from Latin *Vitalis* ('living', vital'), borne by several early saints. **Vile(s)** can be a variant of **Vial(l)(s)**, and **Vial(l)** can readily be confused with, or be a variant of, **Vale** and **Veal**. *Gore Vidal, the American author and political commentator, was born in 1925 at West Point, New York, where his father was working as an aeronautics instructor. He was baptized with the Christian names Eugene Luther, but eventually took the surname of his maternal grandfather, Thomas Gore, a senator from Oklahoma, as his own first-name. Former Vice-President Al Gore is a distant cousin of Gore Vidal.*

Vidler N Nickname for a person with a face like a wolf OF *vis de leu*. Complimentary or not? Readily confused with/a variant of **Fidler**. Mainly found in Sussex and surrounding areas.

Vig(g)ars/Vig(g)ers/Vigo(u)r(s)/Vigrass/Vigu(r)s N Nickname for a vigorous, lusty person OF. Some of these variants may be readily confused with, or be variants of, **Vickers**. Surnames in this group have a distinctive geographical distribution according to spelling. Several have a presence in the two widely separated counties of Devon and Staffs; **Vigor** is found mainly in Sussex, **Vigors** in Glamorgan, South Wales, **Vigour** in Somerset, **Vigrass** in Staffs, **Vigus** in Cornwall and **Vigurs** in Devon and Surrey.

Vile(s), *see* **Vale**, **Veal** and **Vial** (under **Vidal**).

Villiers/Villis P From one of a number of places named *Vill(i)er(s)* OF 'part of an estate, farm, village', from Latin *villare*. *Villiers*, commonly pronounced '*Villers*', is the family name of the Earls of Clarendon (and formerly of the Dukes of Buckingham). The variant **Villis** is most common in Somerset (where it might have some connexion with **Vallis**?).

Vimpany N A nickname from OE, literally 'win-penny', perhaps from farming profitable land. A Gloucs surname.

Vincent/Vince/Vincett/Vinson F From a mediaeval first-name, from Latin *Vincentius* ('conquering'). *Vincent* was the name of a third-century Spanish martyr. **Vinson** is simply a variant of **Vincent**, with no sense of 'son of'. The diminutive form **Vince** is a surname of south-east England and East Anglia.

Vine/Viner T/O/P Dweller in, or worker at, a vineyard OF, or from a minor place so-called. 'The vine was cultivated in mediaeval England, even as wine was in the last century produced at Castell Coch, Glamorgan, by the mediaevalizing Marquis of Bute' (Cottle). A book published in New York in 1997 bearing the title *Winemaking from grape growing to marketplace* was, appropriately, written by Richard P. **Vine**. **Vine** is mainly found in Sussex (where wine is once

again being produced commercially); **Viner** is more widely spread across southern England.

Vin(n)icombe P Place-name *Vinnicombe* in Devon OE 'fenny/marshy valley'. Cornwall/Devon surnames.

Vinson, *see* **Vincent**.

Vinter/Vintin(n)er/Vintner O Occupational term for a vintner, wine-merchant OF. **Vinter** and **Vintner** (very scarce) can be found in Lincs, **Vintiner** and **Vintinner** in Beds.

Vipont/Vipond P Place-name *Vieuxpont* in Calvados, France OF ('old bridge'). Surnames of the north of England.

Virgin/Virgo(e) N An odd survival, a lack of virginity being a necessary prerequisite for procreation and the subsequent continuation of a hereditary surname. From OF, originally Latin *virgo* (genitive form *virginis*). Perhaps applied to a man who had played the Blessed Virgin in a mystery play (there being no actresses), or ironically for a lecherous person, one who was far from being a virgin. **Virgin** is mainly found in Somerset and surrounding counties, **Virgo** in Sussex and Gloucs, **Virgoe** in Surrey and Sussex.

Visick, *see* **Physick**.

Vivash N Nickname for a lively, vivacious person OF. Cottle considers but rejects 'the traditional place-name interpretation OE "five ash-trees", with *F*- voiced to south-western *V*-'. Most common in Hants.

Vivian/Fiddian/Fidgeon/Phythian/Vyvyan F From a mediaeval first-name *Vivian*, from Latin *Vivianus* 'living, alive', introduced to England by the Normans, and borne by a fifth-century martyr. Cottle calls **Vyvyan** 'an ostentatious form of **Vivian** that, before printing, had the excuse of greater legibility'. **Vivian** and **Vyvyan** are Cornish surnames, also present in Devon; **Fiddian** is mainly found in Warwicks and Worcs, **Fidgeon** in Essex and Warwicks, and **Phythian** in Lancs. **Vivian** is the family name of the Barons Swansea.

Vizard, *see* Wishart.

Voak, *see* Falk.

Voce/Voice/Voyce P From *Voise*, Eure et Loire, France. All the earliest occurrences of the **Voce** surname are '*de* **Voce**'. **Voce** is a Lancs/Notts surname; **Voice** is mainly found in Sussex, and **Voyce** in Gloucs. The reason why Mr and Mrs **Voce** gave their son Thomas (born in Bourne, Lincs, in 1842) the middle name of '*Dung*' must remain something of a mystery…

Vodrey P Place-names in France: *Vaudry* in Calvados, and *Vaudrey* in Jura, Germanic and Latin '?*Waldhar* (*Walter*)'s place'; but the Calvados place-name is locally thought to be OF *Val de Reuil* ('*Ralph*'s valley'). A very rare Staffs surname.

Voice, *see* Voce.

Voisey, *see* Vaisey.

Voke(s)/Vokins/Volk(e)s, *see* Falk.

Voller, *see* Fuller.

Voss, *see* Foss.

Vowell(s)/Vowels/Vowles, *see* Fowle.

Voyce, *see* Voce.

Voyle N Nickname for a bald person, Welsh *foel*, a mutated form of *moel* (both of which often figure in names of bald Welsh hills). A surname of South Wales.

Vyvyan, *see* Vivian.

W

Wackrill F From an OE female first-name meaning 'watchful-war'. Chiefly an Essex surname.

Waddell/Waddle P/F Scots: place-name *Wedale*, near Edinburgh ?Scots and ME 'mortgage/pledge-valley'; or a diminutive of **Wade**, with an OF suffix. **Waddell** is strongest in Lanarkshire, Scotland, and **Waddle** (much scarcer) in Co Durham. Readily confused with/a variant of **Wardle**. See also **Wathall**. Commonly pronounced (outside Scotland, at least) with the stress on the second syllable, to avoid any association with the verb 'to *waddle*'. *Christopher Roland ('Chris') Waddle, soccer player for England, was born in Heworth, Gateshead, Co Durham, in 1960.*

Waddilove F From one of two OE first-names: *Wealdtheof* ('power-thief'), with metathesis of the *-l-* and further corruption, or *Woeltheof* ('slaughter thief') – compare **Walthew**. **Waddilove** and **Waddilow** (a scarce variant, readily confused with/a variant of **Wadlow**) are mostly found in Lancs.

Waddilow, *see* **Waddilove**.

Waddington P There are places so-called in Lancs (formerly in WRYorks) and in Lincs OE 'the estate called after *Wada*'. Very largely a Lancs/WRYorks surname, so the place-name in Surrey OE 'hill where wheat grows' may not be of much relevance. *The firm of Waddingtons, publisher of playing cards and of board games such as Monopoly, was founded in the nineteenth century by John Waddington of Leeds and Wilson Barratt, initially as a printing business.*

Waddle, *see* **Waddell**.

Waddon P Place-name in Dorset and Surrey OE 'hill where woad grows' (woad continued in use as a blue dye among the English, long after the Britons stopped painting their bodies with it), and in Worcs OE 'hill where wheat grows'. A very scarce Somerset surname.

Wade F/T/P From the ME first-name *Wade*, from the OE verb *Wada* ('to go') – compare the word '*wade*'; or dweller at a ford OE, the *-e* reflecting the use of the dative after a lost preposition; or from a place-name in Suffolk, with the same meaning. A common surname, strongest in WRYorks. **Wadeson** ('son of **Wade**') is a scarce Lancs form. See also **Waddell**.

Wadey, *see* **Walthew**.

Wadley P Place-name in Berks OE 'woad/ *Wada*'s wood/clearing'. Strongest in Essex and Gloucs.

Wadlow P Place-name *Wadloo* in Cambs and a now-lost place-name *Wadlow* in Beds OE '?*Wada*'s hill/barrow'. A widely-scattered surname within eastern and central England. Readily confused with/a variant of **Waddilow** (see **Waddilove**).

Wadsworth/Wordsworth P Place-name *Wadsworth* in WRYorks OE '*Woeddi*'s enclosure'. **Wadsworth** is found mainly in Lancs and WRYorks; **Wordsworth**, less common, is chiefly a WRYorks surname. *The Romantic poet William Wordsworth (1770–1850), one-time Poet Laureate, was born in Cockermouth, Cumbd.*

Wafer O Occupational term for a waferer, a baker of sacramental bread and of thin, sweet cakes OF, Norman dialect from Germanic. Chiefly a Lancs surname.

Wager O Occupational term for a watchman ME *wacher(e)*. Chiefly found in Essex/Gloucs/Middx.

Waghorn(e) O/N Occupational term for a hornblower/trumpeter OE 'wield-horn', 'rather jocosely expressed' (Cottle); or an obscene nickname for a person who waved his 'horn' around in public – a 'flasher' (compare **Wagstaff**). Predominantly a Kent surname in either spelling. *Thomas Fletcher Waghorn (1800–1850), the naval officer who pioneered an overland route to India, was born in Chatham, Kent.*

Wagstaff(e) O/N Occupational term for an official (such as a beadle) who carried a staff of office OE 'wield-staff'; or an obscene nickname for a person who waved his 'staff' around in public – a 'flasher', in effect (compare **Waghorn**). Cottle found an example of a Middle English warrior who is seriously described in verse as '*wagging*' a weapon. R. S. Charnock makes the rather eccentric suggestion that the 'staff' element in **Wagstaff(e)** might be OE *stede* 'landing place', as found in place-names such as *Bickerstaff*. A long shot? **Wagstaff** is widely scattered across northern and central England, most common in Beds; **Wagstaffe** is mainly found in Lancs and surrounding counties.

Waight, *see* Wait.

Wailes, *see* Wales.

Wain(e)/Wayne O/T Occupational term for a maker of wains/wagons/carts OE, or for a carter. But Reaney cites a 1327 instance in Derbys of *Attewayne*, so it may sometimes be a sign-name. **Wain** is strongest in Derbys and Staffs, **Waine** (and the variant **Wainman**) in Lancs, and **Wayne** in Derbys and Lancs. *The poet, novelist and critic John Wain (1925–1994) was born in Stoke-on-Trent, Staffs… The American film actor John Wayne (1907–1979) was born Marion Robert Morrison (soon changed to Marion Michael Morrison) in Winterset, Iowa; the name 'John Wayne' was chosen for him at a Fox Studios discussion at which he was not even present.*

Wainford P Place-name in Norfolk and Suffolk OE 'ford for a wagon/cart' (see **Wain**). The surname is most common in Surrey.

Wainman, *see* Wain.

Wain(w)right O Occupational term for a maker of wains/wagons/carts OE (see **Wain**). **Wainwright** is strongest in Lancs and WRYorks, **Wainright** (much scarcer) in Staffs and WRYorks. *The American singer-songwriter, actor and humorist Loudon Wainwright III was born in 1946 in Chapel Hill, North Carolina, the son of Loudon Snowden Wainwright, Junior… Alfred Wainwright (1907–1991), famous for writing* Pictorial guide to the Lakeland Fells *(seven volumes, 1955–1966), was born in Blackburn, Lancs.*

Waistcoat, *see* Westcott.

Wait(e)(s)/Waight/Wayt(e)/Weight(s) /Whait(e)(s) O Occupational term for a watchman/'the watch', Anglo-Norman French. The *waits* were eventually also a body of musicians. The surname may sometimes have absorbed **Wheat**, and has taken bizarre forms in -*aigh*-, -*eigh*-, *Wh*-. **Wait** is widespread, strongest in Gloucs, Middx and Wilts; **Waite** is chiefly found in WRYorks, **Waits** (scarce) in ERYorks, **Waites** in Co Durham and ERYorks, **Wayt** (scarce) in Hants and Glamorgan, **Wayte** in East Anglia and the Midlands, **Waight** in southern counties of England, **Weight** in Gloucs and Surrey, **Weights** and **Whaite** in Lancs, **Whait** in Leics, **Whaites** in Norfolk and WRYorks and **Whaits** in Gloucs and Somerset. *Waitrose supermarkets owe their name to a fusion of the surnames of Wallace Waite and Arthur Rose, who opened a grocery store in Acton Hill, West London, in 1904.*

Wake N Nickname for a watchful, alert person OE/ON, or perhaps from an ON byname *Vakr*, with the same meaning. Strongest in Co Durham.

Wakefield P Place-name in Northants, WRYorks OE 'field for the (yearly) wake/festival'. A widespread surname.

Wakeford P From a now-lost place-name near Trotton, Sussex OE '*Waca*'s ford'. 'He, or his like, got around, grabbing also *Wakeham* and *Wakehurst* in Sussex' (Cottle). A surname of the south of England, strongest in Sussex.

Wakeham P Place-name in Devon and Sussex OE '*Waca*'s river-meadow'. Chiefly a Devon surname.

Wakeley, *see* Wakely.

Wakelin(g) F From the mediaeval first-name *Walquelin*, an Anglo-Norman French form of the Germanic *Walho*, with two OF suffixes. **Wakelin** is chiefly found in the English south-east, East Anglia and the Midlands, **Wakeling** in Essex/Middx. **Walklate** is a Staffs variant. **Wanklyn**, possibly a variant, is a scarce Herefords surname.

Wakel(e)y/Wakley P Place-name *Wakeley* in Herts OE '*Waca*'s wood/clearing', or OE 'field where the wake (annual festival) is held', yet **Wakeley** is strongest in Salop, **Wakely** in Dorset and **Wakley** in Devon.

Wakeman O Occupational term for a watchman OE. Cottle adds: 'Compare the motto on the exterior frieze of Ripon town hall: "Except Ye Lord Keep Ye Cittie, Ye Wakeman Waketh In Vain"; and the Mayor there was Wakeman until 1604'. Mainly found in Worcs and surrounding counties. *The musician Richard Christopher ('Rick') Wakeman, best known as the keyboardist for the progressive rock group Yes, was born in Perivale, London, in 1949.*

Wakley, *see* Wakely.

Walbrook P Place-name in London OE 'brook of the Welsh/serfs'. An exceptionally scarce surname, found in Somerset and Surrey.

Walby/Waudby/Wobey P Place-names: *Walby* in Cumbd OE and ON 'farm on the (Roman) wall', and *Wauldby* in ERYorks OE and ON 'farm in/on the wold'. **Walby** is a scattered surname, as much southern as northern. **Wobey** is a scarce Suffolk variant; **Waudby** is strongest in ERYorks.

Walcot(t) P There are places called *Walcot*, *Walcote* and *Walcott* in a number of English counties OE 'cottage(s)/shelter(s) of the Welsh/serfs'; but *Walcot*, Somerset, is OE 'cottage(s)/shelter(s) outside the (town) wall (of Bath)'. Sparsely scattered in both spellings; **Walcot** is most common in the north-west, while **Walcott** can be found throughout southern and eastern England. Readily confused with/a variant of **Woolcott**.

Wald/Waldman/Weld/Wold T Dweller at a forest, woodland; open upland; waste ground OE *w(e)ald*. Compare the Lincs and Yorks *Wolds*; the Kent and Sussex *Weald*; the Cots*wold*s. Scarce in all spellings: **Wald** can be found in the north, **Weld** in Kent, Lancs and Middx, **Wold** in Lincs and **Waldman** in Lancs.

Waldegrave/Waldgrave P Place-name *Walgrave* in Northants (*Waldgrave* in 1086) OE '*Old*'s grove', The surname is usually pronounced '*Walgrave*', in line with the more recent spelling of the place-name. Descendants of Sir Richard **Waldegrave**, speaker of the House of Commons in the fourteenth century, who came from Smallbridge, Suffolk, are now Earls Waldegrave. In more recent times, **Waldegrave** has become a scarce Lincs surname, while **Waldgrave**, very scarce, can be found in Hants.

Walden P Place-names in Essex, Herts, NRYorks OE 'valley of the Welsh/serfs'. A scattered surname of the English south and Midlands.

Waldgrave, *see* Waldegrave.

Waldman, *see* Wald.

Waldram/Waldren, *see* Waldron.

Waldo, *see* Walthew.

Waldron/Waldram/Waldren/Walrond F/P From a Germanic first-name meaning 'foreigner-raven'; or from the place-name *Waldron* in Sussex OE 'forest house'. **Waldron** is strongest in Devon, but also strong in Lancs and Staffs (and on the west coast of Ireland); **Waldram**

has a limited presence in Leics and Notts; **Walrond** is mainly found in Somerset and surrounding counties, and **Waldren** in Hants.

Wale F/N/T From a Germanic first-name *Walo* '?foreign' (compare the word '*Welsh*' and the surnames **Wales**, **Wallis**, **Waugh**, **Welsh**, **Welshman**); or a nickname for a choice, excellent, noble person ME; or a dweller on a ridge, bank OE (compare the word '*weal*').

Wales/Wailes P/N/F From the name of the Principality, properly called *Cymru*, but given the name *Wales* OE 'foreigner' by invading English tribes who had the effrontery to regard the indigenous inhabitants as being outsiders – compare *Cornwall* and the *wal*nut ('foreign nut'); or from the place-name *Wales* in WRYorks OE 'The Welshmen'; or from a nickname or a first-name with the same meaning (compare **Wale**, **Wallis**, **Waugh**, **Welsh**, **Welshman**). **Wales** is strongest in WRYorks; **Wailes**, scarcer, can be found in that county but also in north-east England.

Walford P Place-name in Herefords (near Leintwardine) and in Salop OE 'the ford by the spring'; in Herefords (near Ross) OE 'ford of the Welsh'; in Dorset OE 'unsteady ford'. The surname can certainly be found in Herefords, Salop and surrounding counties, but is at its strongest in Essex and Middx. Readily confused with/a variant of **Wolford**.

Walkden P Place-name in Lancs OE 'valley of the (stream called) ?*Wealce*' or OE '*Walca*'s valley'. A Lancs surname.

Walker O English and Scots: occupational term for a fuller OE, one who trampled cloth in a trough in the fulling process – originally a term used principally in the north and west of England (compare **Fuller** and **Tucker**); or from *Walker* in Northd OE and ON '(Roman) wall marsh'. A widespread surname, stronger in the north than in the south, and with an especially powerful presence in Lancs and WRYorks.

Walklate, *see* **Wakelin**.

Wall T Dweller beside a particularly conspicuous wall – a town wall, a ruined Roman wall, a sea wall OE; or dweller by a spring or stream, Northern ME. Compare **Wallbank** and **Waller**. **Walls** is 'of (at) the wall', or a plural. **Wall** has an especially strong presence in Lancs and Staffs (but also in Middx); **Walls** (scarcer) is chiefly found in Lancs. *The company of Wall's, known both for its sausages and for its ice-cream products, has a history stretching back to the year 1786, when Richard Wall set up shop as a butcher in St James's Market, London; in 1812 he received his first Royal Appointment, as 'Pork butcher to the Prince of Wales'.*

Wallace, *see* **Wallis**.

Wallbank T Dweller at a bank with a wall in it ME, or on the banks of a stream, Northern ME. Compare **Wall** and **Waller**. Strongest in Lancs.

Waller T/O/N Dweller at a wall, or at a spring/stream (compare **Wall**); or an occupational term for a salt-worker or salt-weller OE, or for a wall-builder OE; or a nickname for a good-tempered man OF (Norman dialect). Strongest in Middx and WRYorks.

Walley P Place-names: *Whalley* in Lancs, *Whaley* in Chesh OE 'clearing on a road'. A Chesh/Lancs/Staffs surname.

Walliams, *see* **Wooland**.

Wallinger F From a Germanic first-name '*Warin*-spear'. Mainly found in Beds and surrounding counties.

Wallington P Place-name in: Berks, Hants and Surrey OE 'place of the Welsh'; Norfolk OE '?place of the settlers by the wall'; Herts OE 'settlement of *Woedel*'s people'; Northd OE 'settlement of *Wealh*'s people'. Principally a surname of the south of England and the South Midlands.

Wallis P Term used for a foreigner – be it a Celt, Welshman, Breton or Scotsman, according to region, Anglo-Norman French *waleis*, OE *wealh*. Compare **Wale**, **Wales**, **Waugh**, **Welsh**, **Welshman**. **Wallis** is strongest in south-east England. **Wallace** is predominantly a Scots form, originally applied to Strathclyde Welshmen. *The Scottish patriot Sir William Wallace (c.1272–1305), probably born in Elderslie (Renfrewshire? Ayrshire?), was victorious at the Battle of Stirling, but was vanquished at the Battle of Falkirk. Legend has it that his descendants include Lech Wałęsa (born 1943), former President of Poland (1990 to 1995), the spelling of whose surname bears some similarity to 'Wallace', even if its pronunciation does not... The American author and screenwriter Irving Wallace (1916–1990) was born with the surname Wallechinsky in Chicago, Illinois. His daughter, the author Amy Wallace, retained her father's adopted surname, but his son, the writer and historian David Wallechinsky, reclaimed the original 'Wallechinsky'.*

Wallop P There are minor places so-called in Gloucs and Salop, together with *Nether Wallop, Middle Wallop* and *Over Wallop* in Hants OE 'stream valley'. A rare West Country surname, with a presence in Gloucs. Family name of the Earls of Portsmouth.

Walls, *see* Wall.

Walmer P Place-name in Kent OE 'pool of the Welsh/serfs' and in Lancs OE and ON '?mire/bog in a wood'. A very scarce surname.

Walm(e)sley/Walmisley P Place-name *Walmersley* in Lancs OE '?*Waldmer*/*Walhmer*'s wood or clearing'. **Walmsley** and **Walmesley** are mostly found in Lancs; **Walmisley**, very scarce, has a presence in Surrey.

Walpole P Place-name in Norfolk OE 'pool by a (Roman) wall' and in Suffolk OE 'pool of the Welsh/serfs'. Stronger in Norfolk than in Suffolk. *Robert Walpole, First Earl of Orford (1676–1745), commonly considered to be Britain's first prime minister, was born in Houghton, Norfolk; his son Horatio (Horace) Walpole (1717–1797) achieved fame as an author, politician and patron of the arts.*

Walrond, *see* Waldron.

Walsh(e), *see* Welsh.

Walsingham P Place-name in Norfolk OE 'homestead of *Woels*'s people'. Cottle adds:

'This pioneer's first-name is the OE version of the gloomy eponym of the Icelandic *Volsunga Saga*, father of Sigmund and Signy. Whether the surname ever means "one who has been on pilgrimage to Our Lady of Walsingham" is doubtful'. Chiefly a Herts/Middx surname.

Walter F From a Germanic first-name, Normanized as *Walt(i)er*/*Waut(i)er*, meaning 'rule-army/people', and usually pronounced '*Water*' in the Middle Ages. In modern times such a first-name is commonly shortened to *Wal, Wally* or *Walt*, but a much-favoured pet form in earlier centuries was '*Wat*', which became the origin of surnames such as **Watt** (chiefly found in Scotland, especially in Aberdeenshire and West Lothian), **Watkin** (Lancs, Staffs, WRYorks and Montgomeryshire, Wales) and **Watling** (Norfolk and Suffolk), which is not derived from the road called *Watling Street*, which means 'the road to St Albans'. '*Wat*' is also in evidence in place-names such as *Bridgwater*, Somerset ('*Walter*'s bridge'). Where names such as **Water/Waters** have been preceded by *de/atte*, the meaning will have been 'dweller beside a stretch of water, stream' OE. **Gwatkins** is a version of **Watkins**, from Welsh *Gwallter*. See also **Qualtrough, Waterman, Waterer** and **Whatman**. The surname **Walter**, of which Cottle says 'Its two most distinguished bearers bore the Duke of Monmouth (and was possibly Charles II's lawful wife) [i.e., Lucy Walter] and founded *The Times* [i.e., John Walter]', is mainly found in south-east and south-west England. **Water** is a scarce Lancs/Middx variant. Patronymic forms include **Walters** (widespread, very strong in Staffs and in Glamorgan, Wales), **Waters** (strong in Kent), **Waterson** (Lancs and elsewhere), **Watson** (chiefly northern England and Scotland), **Watters** (scarce, found in Cornwall, northern England, Scotland), **Watterson** (Isle of Man), **Watkins** (Gloucs, Herefords, South Wales), **Watkinson** (Lancs and WRYorks), **Watkis** (very scarce, Salop), **Watkiss** (Salop and Staffs) and **Watts** (widespread, thick on the ground). **Watson** is the family name of the Barons Manton.

The 1901 census for Shoeburyness, Essex, includes the name of an individual called '*Mineral* **Waters**'. *The engineer and scientist James Watt (1736–1819) was born in Greenock, Renfrewshire, Scotland… The Watersons, a group from Hull in Yorks who specialize in singing unaccompanied traditional English songs, originally comprised Norma, Mike and Lal Waterson and their cousin John Harrison; later line-ups have included Norma's husband Martin Carthy and their daughter Eliza.*

Walters, *see* **Walter**.

Waltham P Place-name in various southern and eastern counties of England OE 'homestead in/on a wold'. Strongest in Lincs.

Walthew/Waldo/Waltho F From the OE first-name *Woeltheof* ('battle thief' – one who stole victory at a time of conflict). Compare **Waddilove**. Or sometimes perhaps from the OE first-name *Wealhtheow* 'foreign servant/slave'. Cottle considers the very rare Notts surname **Watthey** to be a variant of **Walthew**, though it might in principle be related to **Wathall**. In Scotland there is evidence of a historically close relationship between the surnames **Walthere**, **Waitho**, **Watho**, **Waddic**, **Waldie**, **Waldy** and **Waldeve**, some of which have not survived into modern times. **Walthew** is chiefly found in Lancs, **Waldo** (very scarce, despite being the middle name of the American essayist Ralph Waldo Emerson) in Gloucs, **Waltho** in Staffs and **Wadey** (possibly a variant) in Sussex.

Waltho, *see* **Walthew**.

Walton P There are numerous places so-called throughout England, with a handful of distinct origins. The second element in each case is OE *tun* 'enclosure'. The first element can be: OE *wealh* 'Welsh/slaves/serfs'; OE *w(e)ald* 'wood/wold' (see **Wald**); OE *w(e)all* 'wall'; OE *woell(a)* 'spring, stream'. Strongest in Lancs/WRYorks.

Walwin/Walwyn F From an OE first-name meaning 'power-friend'; or a *W-* form of the first-name *Gawain* (see **Gavin**). **Walwin** is chiefly found in Somerset, **Walwyn** in Staffs.

Walwork P From an unidentified place-name, probably OE 'wall building/building of the Welsh'. A Lancs surname. Readily confused with/a variant of **Walworth** or **Woolworth**.

Walworth P Place-name in Co Durham, Surrey OE 'enclosure of the Welsh/serfs'. Mainly a Lancs/WRYorks surname. Readily confused with/a variant of **Walwork** or **Woolworth**.

Walwyn, *see* **Walwin**.

Wanbon P Place-name *Wombourn* in Staffs, probably OE 'at the winding stream'. An exceptionally scarce scattered surname.

Wanhill P From an unidentified place-name OE '?dark/lurid hill' (the word *wan* having changed its meaning over time). A rare West Country surname.

Wanklyn, *see* **Wakelin**.

Wann N Nickname for a pale, wan person ME. Found chiefly in Fifeshire, Scotland.

Want O/N/T Occupational term for a mole-catcher ME; or a nickname for someone resembling a mole in some way; or a dweller near a path or turning OE *went* (see **Went**). Mainly found in the south and east of England, strongest in Norfolk.

Wantling F From the female Welsh first-name *Gwenllian* ('fair-flaxen'). Chiefly a Staffs surname.

Warboys/Worboys O/P Occupational term for a forester, Anglo-Norman French ('guard-wood'); or from the place-name *Warboys* in Hunts (now Cambs) OE and OF '*Wearda*'s bush', once known for its strong connexion with witches. Chiefly a Cambs surname in both spellings.

Warburton P Place-name in Chesh, Lancs, WRYorks OE '*Woerburh*'s settlement' (*Woerburh* being a female first-name better known in the form *Werburgh*, borne by the former patron saint of Chester Cathedral). Chiefly a Chesh/Lancs surname. **Warbutton** is a scarce Lancs variant.

Warbutton, *see* **Warburton**.

Warcup P Place-name *Warcop* in Westmd ON and OE 'cairn/beacon/look-out hill'. An ERYorks surname.

Ward(e) O/T/F Occupational term for a guard, watchman OE; or dweller at or near a guard-house, prison, fortifications of a castle or town OE. The *-e* of **Warde** could indicate the use of a dative after a lost preposition: '(at) the fort'. Irish: Anglicized form of Gaelic **Mac an Bhaird** 'son of the bard'. **Ward** is the family name of the Earls of Dudley and the Viscounts Bangor.

Wardale, *see* **Wardle**.

Warde, *see* **Ward**.

Wardell, *see* **Wardle**.

Warden O/P Occupational term for a guard, warden, sentinel, Anglo-Norman French; or from one of a number of places so-called OE 'watch/look-out hill'. Strongest in Lancs.

Wardlaw, *see* **Wardlow**.

Wardle/Wardale/Wardell P Place-name *Wardle* in Chesh and Lancs OE 'guard/look-out hill'; or from *Weardale*, Co Durham, British and OE 'valley of the river *Wear*'. **Wardle** is strongest in Lancs, **Wardale** in Lincs, **Wardell** in Co Durham and in the three Ridings of Yorks. Readily confused with/a variant of **Waddell**.

Wardlow P Place-names in Derbys, Staffs OE 'guard/look-out hill'. The Scottish surname **Wardlaw** comes from one of a number of minor place-names with the same meaning. **Wardlow** is strongest in Lancs. **Warlow**, possibly a variant, has a presence in Gloucs, Lancs and south-west counties of Wales; *Warlow Pike* in Saddleworth, WRYorks, was *Harelowe* OE 'grey/boundary hill' in 1468.

Wardrobe/Wardrop(e)/Wardroper O Occupational term for an official of the wardrobe, a man in charge of the robes and clothes of a household, Anglo-Norman French. Not to be confused with a *garderobe*, Anglo-Norman French, which refers to a privy. **Wardrobe** is mainly found in ERYorks and surrounding counties, and **Wardrop** and **Wardrope** in central Scotland, strongest in Lanarkshire. **Wardroper** is sparsely scattered throughout England, though rare in the west.

Ware N/T/P Nickname for a wary, cautious, prudent person OE; or dweller near a weir, dam OE (compare **Wear**); or from a place-name *Ware* in Devon (five such), Dorset, Herts and Kent, with the same meaning. Strong in various counties in south and south-west England.

Wareham P Place-name in Dorset OE 'homestead at a weir', and a Dorset surname.

Wareing, *see* **Warin**.

Warfield P Place-name in Berks OE 'open land near the weir'. Chiefly a Somerset surname.

Warin(g)/Wareing/Wearing F From the Norman first-name *Warin*, from Germanic 'guard'. The *-g* in *Waring/Wareing/Wearing* is an excrescence, as is the odd *-e-* in **Wareing**. **Warin** can readily be confused with/be a variant of **Warne** or **Warren**. **Warin** is mainly found in Derbys and NRYorks, **Waring** in Lancs and WRYorks, **Wareing** and **Wearing** in Lancs, and the diminutive **Warnett** in Kent and Sussex. *The British rugby league coach and commentator Edward Marsden ('Eddie') Waring (1910–1986) was born in Dewsbury, Yorks.*

Wark P Place-name in Northd (two such) OE 'fortification'. Mainly found in Lanarkshire, Scotland, and surrounding counties. *The television journalist and presenter Kirsty Wark was born in 1955 in Dumfries, Scotland.*

Warleigh P Place-name in Devon OE 'wood/clearing by a river-bank' and in Somerset OE 'wood/clearing by a weir'. A very scarce surname, with a limited presence in Hants. Readily confused with/a variant of **Warley**.

Warley P Place-name in: Worcs (two such) OE 'cattle clearing/pasture'; Essex OE 'weir wood/clearing' or OE 'treaty/compact clearing'; WRYorks OE '*Werlaf*'s wood/clearing'. Strongest in ERYorks. Readily confused with/a variant of **Warleigh**.

Warlock, *see* **Werlock**.

Warlow, *see* **Wardlow**.

Warman O/F Occupational term for a chapman, merchant OE (literally 'wareman/goodsman'); or from the OE firstname *Woermund* ('faith/bond-protector'). Strongest in Kent and Middx.

Warmington P Place-name in Northants OE 'place/farm of the family/folk of *Wyrm*' and in Warwicks OE 'place/farm of the family/folk of *Woermund*'. Chiefly a Cornwall/Devon surname.

Warn(e) P/T Place-name *Warne* in Devon (*Wagefen* in the twelfth century) OE 'quaking marsh'. In both spellings the surname is strongest in Cornwall, where it can refer to a dweller by a swamp or by alder trees, Cornish *(g)wern*. Readily confused with/a variant of **Warin** or **Warren**. *Frederick Warne (1825–1901), founder of the publishing house which bore his name, was born in Westminster, London, and was the brother-in-law of the bookseller and publisher George Routledge (1812–1888). Frederick Warne's father, Edmund Warne or Warn, who came from Newent, Gloucs, carried a first-name much favoured in that family.*

Warner F From a Germanic first-name brought to England by the Normans as *Warnier* ('guard-army'); or an abbreviated form of **Warrener**. *Warner is a surname which exists in more than one European country, and the men who founded the famous Hollywood studio of Warner Brothers – Harry, Albert, Sam and Jack Warner – were the sons of Benjamin Warner (1857–1935), born in Warsaw, Poland, who emigrated to the USA in 1882… The 'other' Jack Warner (1895–1981), quintessentially English and famous for his central role in the TV series* Dixon of Dock Green, *was not really a 'Warner' at all. Born Horace John Waters in Poplar, London, he was the brother of comediennes Doris and Elsie Waters, who were famous in the 1930s and 1940s as 'Gert and Daisie'.*

Warnett, *see* **Warin**.

Warr O/N Occupational term/nickname for a brave soldier/warrior, Anglo-Norman French *werr(e)*. For the change from *-er* to *-ar*, see **Armistead**. Strongest in Dorset and Middx. The title of the Earls **de la Warr** preserves an older form, and the American state of *Delaware* was named after Thomas West, Baron **de la Warr** (1577–1618), former Governor of Virginia.

Warren T/O/P Dweller by/worker at a gamepark, Anglo-Norman French *warrenne*; or from the place-name *La Varenne*, Maine-et-Loire, France, Gaulish '?sandy soil/wasteland/game preserve'. 'The great family of **Warren**, still headed (albeit in France) by Reginald, Comte **de Warren**, was of immense power in England from the eleventh to the fourteenth centuries, with holdings in twelve counties, and their emphatic gold and blue check shield figures often in English civic heraldry' (Cottle). A widespread surname, particularly strong in Devon, Lancs, Middx and Surrey. Readily confused with/a variant of **Warin** or **Warne**. See also **Warrener**.

Warren(d)er O Occupational term for a warrener, a (game-)park-keeper OF. The *-d-* of **Warrender** is parasitic. **Warrender** is the family name of the Barons Bruntisfield. See also **Warner** and **Warren**.

Warrington P Place-name in Chesh (formerly in Lancs) OE 'place/farm at a weir'. A surname of the north of England, so *Warrington* in Bucks OE '?place/farm of the family/folk of *Wearda*' is less likely to be its source. *Rev. Percy Warrington (1889–1961), born in Newhall, Derbys, founded nine public schools and a theological college.*

Warsop P Place-name in Notts OE '*Woer*'s valley', and a Notts surname.

Warter P Place-name in ERYorks OE 'gallows' (literally 'felon tree'). A scarce ERYorks surname.

Warth P From the name of one of a number of minor places ON *vartha* ('beacon'). But the surname is mainly found in

WRYorks, so *Wath on Dearn* in that county ON 'ford' may be one source? See **Wath**.

Warton P Place-name in Lancs, Northd OE 'guard/look-out place'; and in Warwicks OE 'farm at the ?shaking tree' or 'farm in ?spongy ground'. Strongest in Lancs and Middx. Readily confused with/a variant of **Wharton**.

Warwick P Place-name in Warwicks OE 'dairy-farm at a weir/dam' and in Cumbd OE 'dairy-farm on a river-bank (the *Eden*)'. A scattered surname.

Washborne, *see* **Washbourn**.

Washbourn(e)/Washborne P Place-name *Washbourne* in Devon OE 'stream where washing is carried on' (compare **Washbrook**), and in Gloucs OE 'stream in alluvial land'. One prominent **Washborne** family was seated at *Little Washborne* OE '*Wassa*'s stream' in Overbury, Worcs, before the reign of King Edward III (1327–1377). One branch of this family (known variously as **Washbourne**, **Washborn**, **Washbourn** and even **Wishborne**) apparently lost much of its wealth during the Civil War, and Daniel **Washbourne** (1618–1702) moved to Gloucester, where he established a dynasty of Gloucs clock-makers. **Washbourn/Washbourne/Washborne** have continued to be principally Gloucs surnames. Readily confused with/a variant of **Washburn**.

Washbrook P Place-name in Lancs, Somerset, Suffolk OE 'brook for washing' (compare **Washbourn**). A scarce surname, strongest in Staffs and Warwicks. *Cyril Washbrook (1914–1999), Lancs and England cricketer, was born in Clitheroe, Lancs.*

Washburn(e) P In principle this scarce surname refers to a person living on the banks of the river *Washburn*, WRYorks OE '*Walc*'s stream', though by the late nineteenth century it is found principally in Chesh and Warwicks. Readily confused with/a variant of **Washbourn**. *George Washburn Lyon (born in 1820) established the Washburn Guitar Company in Chicago in 1883.*

Washer O Occupational term for a washer,

launderer OE plus an -*er* suffix. Strongest in Sussex.

Washington P Place-name in Co Durham and in Sussex OE 'place/farm of the family/folk of *Wassa*'. By the late nineteenth century the surname was not common, being found chiefly in the English North and Midlands, and in the 1960s/1970s Cottle was pointing out that 'there are only 150 telephonigerous ones in all Britain'. *George Washington (1732–1799), revolutionary army officer and first President of the United States of America, was born on his family's plantation near Pope's Creek, Westmoreland county, Virginia. His first-known Washington ancestor was William De Washington/Wessington, who had a grant of the manor of Washington, Co Durham, in the late twelfth century. According to the convoluted law which applies to English peerages, George Washington had a potential claim to the Barony of Kyme, which fell into abeyance in the year 1338.*

Wasp(e) N Apparently a nickname applied to a wasp-like person OE (sharp of character, narrow of waist?). Chiefly a Suffolk surname in either spelling.

Wass P Place-name in NRYorks ON 'fords' (compare **Wath**). A surname of the English Midlands.

Wastall/Wastell O/P Occupational term for a maker or seller of fine bread/cake OF; or from the place-name *Wasthills* in Worcs OE 'watch-tower'. **Wastall** is most commonly found in Kent, **Wastell** in Middx and Surrey.

Watcher O Occupational term for a watchman OE. Sparsely scattered around the south of England and South Wales. **Watchman** is a Co Durham variant.

Watchman, *see* **Watcher**.

Watchorn T Dweller at a watch-house/guard-house or at a horn-shaped hill OE. Chiefly a Leics surname.

Water(s) T/F Dweller beside water OE; or a variant of **Walter**. See also **Waterman**.

Waterall, *see* **Waterfall**.

Waterer O Occupational term for a water-seller or for one who watered land or beasts OE. Possibly confused with surnames from the **Walter** group?

Waterfall T/P Dweller by a waterfall OE, or from a place-name with the same meaning in Staffs, NRYorks, or from a now-lost place in Pontefract, WRYorks. Mainly found in Derbys and surrounding counties, as is **Waterall**, which may be a variant. The parish register of Norton, Derbys, includes the burial of 'Jane, wife of Robert **Watterhall**' on 26 December 1562, reflecting the fact that '*watter*' was (and still is) a widely used pronunciation of the word '*water*'.

Waterfield P Place-name *Vatierville* in Seine-Maritime, France OF '*Walter*'s settlement'. Strongest in the English Midlands. Compare **Waterlow**. *Robin Waterfield's antiquarian and second-hand bookshop was established in Oxford in 1972.*

Waterhouse T/P Dweller in a house situated near water OE, or from *Waterhouses* in Co Durham and Staffs, with the same meaning. Strongest in Lancs/WRYorks. *Keith Waterhouse, the novelist, newspaper columnist and TV scriptwriter, was born in 1929 in Leeds, WRYorks.*

Waterlow ?P This scarce surname, found in Lincs, Middx and elsewhere, looks for all the world as if it would have a place-name origin OE 'water-hill/burial mound', but the well-known **Waterlow** family of printers were of French Walloon descent. The family name was variously spelt **Vaterlo**, **Vaterlow**, **Waterlo**, **Waterloe/Waterlow/Watterlow**, and the records of the French Protestant Hospital of La Providence show that on 7 January 1718/19 'Samuel **Waterlow** est entré à l'Hôpital sur le Compte de l'Eglise de Londres'. This is possibly the same man as Samuel **Vatelet/Vattelet** of the Threadneedle Street Church in London, a tailor from Paris, who was granted denization in March 1681/2. A family called **Waterlow**, **Watrelo** or **Vaterlo** is known to have been worshipping at the Walloon Church in Canterbury, Kent, from at least as early as the mid seventeenth century. Sir

Sydney **Waterlow** (1822–1906), first Baronet, was Lord Mayor of London, 1872-3. Compare **Waterfield**.

Waterman O/T Occupational term for a water-carrier/seller OE, or for '*Wa(l)ter*'s servant'; or a dweller near water (see **Water**). Strongest in Hants, Kent, Middx. *Dennis Waterman, the actor best known for his performances in the television series* The Sweeney *and* Minder, *was born in 1948 in Clapham, London.*

Waters, *see* **Water**.

Waterson, *see* **Walter**.

Wates, *see* **Wait**.

Wath P Place-name in NRYorks, Westmd and WRYorks ON 'ford' (compare **Wass**). Readily confused with/a variant of **Warth**. The variant **Wathen** is '(at) the fords', exhibiting the use of a dative plural after a lost preposition. **Wath** is a very scarce scattered surname; **Wathen** is chiefly found in Gloucs.

Wathall P At least two place-names may have given rise to this scarce Derbys surname: *Warthall/Ward Hall* in Cumbd ON 'cairn/beacon hill', which was *Warthol* in 1256 and *Worthol* in 1279, and *Warthill* in NRYorks (with the same meaning), which was *Warthull* in 1330 and *Wathell* by 1574. The surname is now pronounced '*Wathall*', rather than '*Wat-hall*'. Or might **Wathall** be a shortened version of the Derbys surname **Waterall** (see **Waterfall**), or be related to **Watthey** (very scarce, found almost exclusively in Notts), or to the WRYorks surname **Wrathall**? The not-dissimilar Scottish surname **Wathell** is perhaps more likely to be a variant of **Waddell**, though a John **Wathell** married Elizabeth Poirce in Mells, Somerset, in 1584. Other early examples of such a surname are hard to come by, but Thomas, son of William **Wathall**, was baptized in Nantwich, Chesh, in 1598, Richard **Wathall** married Elizabeth Fletcher at All Saints, Derby, in 1599, and Alice **Watthall** and Thomas Noone were married at Evington, Leics, in 1618.

Wathen, *see* **Wath**.

Watkin(s)/Watkinson/Watkis(s)/ Watling, *see* Walter.

Watman, *see* Whatman.

Watmore/Watmough/Watmuff/ Whatmough F *'Watt (Walter)*'s relation by marriage', the second element having been used in ME for a variety of family relationships. George Redmonds takes the view that surnames of this type originated in Lancs. **Watmore** is strongest in Hants, but the other forms belong to northern England: **Watmough** (Lancs/WRYorks), **Watmuff** (WRYorks), **Whatmough** (Lancs). See **Whatmore**, and compare **Hitchmough** (under **Richard**) and **Maw**.

Watson/Watt(s), *see* Walter.

Watters/Watterson, *see* Walter.

Watthey, *see* Walthew and **Wathall**.

Watton P Place-name in Herts OE 'place/ farm where woad grows', in Norfolk OE *'Wade's* place', in ERYorks OE (Scandinavianized) 'wet hill', and in Devon (two such, one of which is OE 'farm in a ?wood'). Strongest in Staffs, Warwicks, Worcs.

Waudby, *see* Walby.

Waugh ?N A surname of unknown origin, perhaps from OE *walh*, applied to a foreigner, a Briton from the Strathclyde region? Compare **Wale**, **Wales**, **Wallis**, **Welsh** and **Welshman**. Most common in northern England and Scotland, strongest in Northd and Roxburghshire. *The writer Evelyn (Arthur St John) Waugh (1903–1966), perhaps best known for his novel* Brideshead revisited, *was born in West Hampstead, London; his father Arthur Waugh, from Midsomer Norton, Somerset, was the great-grandson of the Scottish Divine Dr Alexander Waugh (1754–1827), from Berwickshire. Evelyn's son Auberon (Alexander) Waugh (1939–2001) found fame as a journalist and author.*

Wavell P Place-name *Vauville* in Calvados and La Manche, Germanic and OF *'Walo* (see **Wale**)*'s settlement'. A Hants/Isle of Wight surname. *Archibald Percival, first Earl Wavell (1883–1950), Field Marshall and*

Viceroy of India, was born at Colchester, Essex, of a military family with roots in Hants. The explorer Arthur John Byng Wavell (1882–1916) was his cousin.

Way(e) T/P Dweller by a road or path OE; or from one of many minor places called *Way* (many such in Devon), with the same meaning. Chiefly a Devon surname in either spelling. **Waylett**, an Essex/Middx/ Surrey surname, could be a diminutive form, but might be a variant of **Willet**.

Waycott T/P Dweller at a cottage/cottages on the road OE, or from an unidentified place-name with the same meaning, probably in Devon, where this surname is most commonly found – though probably not from *Weycroft*, Axminster, which would appear always to have retained its *-r-*.

Waye, *see* Way.

Waylett F/T/P A variant of **Willet**, or a diminutive form of **Way**.

Waymark, *see* Wymark.

Waymouth, *see* Weymouth.

Wayne, *see* Wain.

Wayt(e), *see* Wait.

Weake, *see* Wick.

Wear/Were T/P Dweller at a weir, dam, fishtrap OE (compare **Ware**); or from the place-names *Weare* in Somerset or *Weare Giffard* in Devon, with the same meaning; or dweller beside the river *Wear*, Celtic ('?water') in northern England. **Wear** is strongest in Northd and WRYorks, **Weare** ('at the weir', the *-e* indicating the use of the dative after a lost preposition) in Gloucs and Somerset, and **Were** in Devon. See also **Weir**.

Weare, *see* Wear.

Wearing, *see* Warin.

Weather N/O/F Nickname for a person resembling a wether, a neutered ram OE (possibly a cuckold?), or an occupational term for one who tended such beasts. Cottle adds: from an OE first-name 'valiant army'. **Weather** is chiefly a Middx/Kent surname; **Weathers** ('son of **Weather**', or a plural) is mainly found in Lincs.

Weatherall/Weatherell/Weatherill/ Wetherald/Wetherall/Wetherell/ Wetherill
P Place-name *Wetheral* in Cumbd OE 'wether/ram nook' (compare **Weather**). These are predominantly surnames of Yorks and the north-east of England, though **Weatherall** has a certain presence in Notts, and **Wetherall** in Berks. *(Bruce) Bernard Weatherill (1920–2007), Baron Weatherill, former Speaker of the House of Commons, was born in London; following the Second World War he initially worked for his family business, Bernard Weatherill, tailors, of Dover Street, London.*

Weatherby, *see* Wetherby.

Weatherell, *see* Weatherall.

Weatherhead ?O/P Reaney takes this to be an occupational term for a herder of wether sheep OE (compare **Weather**), though G. F. Black's suggestion that the source may be a minor hill-name in Berwickshire, Scotland, is perhaps more convincing. **Weatherhead** can be found in Scotland and in northern England, strongest in WRYorks; **Wethered** may look like a variant, and Cottle claims that it is a WRYorks surname, but by the late nineteenth century it was very scarce and restricted to the counties of Berks, Bucks, Gloucs and Middx.

Weatherhogg O Occupational term for a man who tended male sheep (wethers/ rams) before their first shearing, with *hog* in the sense of 'young sheep' ME. Chiefly a Lincs surname.

Weatherill, *see* Weatherall.

Weatherley P There is a place called *Wedderlie* in Berwickshire, Scotland OE 'pasture for wethers/rams', though by the late nineteenth century the surname was found in both south-east and north-east England, but rarely in Scotland.

Weathers, *see* Weather.

Weaver O/P Occupational term for a

weaver OE with added *-er* suffix (compare **Webb**); or from the place now called *Weaver Hall* in Chesh, on the river *Weaver* OE *woefer* 'winding stream'. Strongest in the West Midlands and in north-west England.

Webb(e) O Occupational term for a weaver OE. The *-e* of **Webbe** reflects the *-a* or *-e* (masculine or feminine) endings of the OE noun. **Webber** and **Weaver** are later formations, and **Webster**, originally applied to females (compare **Brewster**, **Baxter**), was eventually more general in its use. *The American lexicographer Noah Webster (1758–1843) was descended from John Webster, who had emigrated from England to Massachusetts in the early 1630s and was one of the founders of Hartford, Connecticut.*

Webber, *see* Webb.

Webley P Place-name *Weobley* in Herefords OE '?*Wibba*'s clearing'. Chiefly a Gloucs surname.

Webster, *see* Webb.

Wedderburn P Scots: from a place so-called in Berwickshire OE 'stream where there were wethers/rams' (compare **Weather**). Strongest in Northd and Aberdeenshire.

Wedderspoon, *see* Witherspoon.

Wedlake/Widlake P These are West Country surnames, strongest in Devon, and a place-name in that county seem to be a likely source. There is a *Wedlake* in Petertavy and a *Willake* in Meavy OE 'wide stream', but the first known references to each only date from as late as the early sixteenth and mid eighteenth centuries respectively. **Wedlock** (sparsely scattered across the south of England and Wales) would seem to be a variant, though *Wedlock Farm* in Gumfreston, Pembrokeshire, was *Wideloke* OE 'wide enclosure' in 1362.

Wedlock, *see* Wedlake.

Wedmore P Place-name in Somerset OE 'hunting moor'. Chiefly a Gloucs/Somerset surname.

Weedon P Place-name in Bucks, Northants OE 'hill with a heathen temple'. An exceptionally scarce surname. Readily confused with/a variant of **Wheadon**. *Bert Weedon, best known as a guitar player, composer and tutor, was born in East Ham, Essex, in 1920.*

Week(e), *see* **Wick**.

Weekes, *see* **Wick**.

Weekl(e)y P Place-name *Weekley* in Northants OE 'wood/clearing by the dwelling-place'. Strong in Northants in both spellings. Cottle says: 'All honour here to Professor Ernest **Weekley** of Nottingham, that engaging and popular writer on surnames, whose wife ran away with D. H. Lawrence'. Amen. Weekley is a witty, entertaining writer on the subject.

Weeley P Place-name in Essex OE 'willow wood/clearing'. A very scarce Essex surname.

Weem(y)s, *see* **Wemyss**.

Weighell/Weighill P Place-name *Wighill* in WRYorks OE '?nook of land with a dairy farm'. Surnames of Co Durham and NRYorks.

Weight(s), *see* **Wait**.

Weir T/P/F English: a variant of **Wear**; Irish: Anglicized form of Gaelic **Mac an Mhaoir** ('son of the steward'), or of various Gaelic names based upon a translation/mis-translation of the word *core* ('weir'); Scottish: G. F. Black claims that this is a Norman surname derived from a number of places called *Vere* in Calvados, Manche, Eure-et-Loir and Orne ON *ver* ('dam') and can also represent an Anglicization of Gaelic **Mc-Amhaoir** ('son of the officer'). Family name of the Barons Inverforth.

Welborn(e)/Welbourn(e)/Welburn P Place-names *Welbourn* in Lincs, *Welborne* in Norfolk and *Welburn* in NRYorks OE 'stream from a spring'. **Welborn, Welborne, Welbourn** and **Welbourne** are chiefly found in Lincs and ERYorks, while **Welburn** is strong in all the Ridings of Yorks. Scarce variants include **Welbon** (ERYorks), **Wil-bourn** (Derbys), **Willbourn** (Essex), **Will-bourne** (Derbys, Kent) and **Willbond** (Leics/Notts).

Welby P Place-name in Lincs OE and ON 'farm by a spring' and in Leics, Old Danish and ON '*Ali*'s farm'. Strongest in Lancs and Lincs.

Welch, *see* **Welsh**.

Welchman, *see* **Welshman**.

Wel(l)come N/P Nickname for a well-liked or hospitable person (one who was welcome everywhere he went, or who was always happy to welcome visitors) OE or for someone who was 'well-combed', tidy OE; or from the place-name *Welcombe* in Devon and in Warwicks OE 'spring/stream valley'. **Welcome** and **Wellcome** are Sussex surnames. **Willicombe**, a Somerset surname, may be a variant of *Welcome*, but could be derived from some lost place OE 'willow valley', or from *Wilcombe* in Devon OE 'spring valley'. *The Wellcome Trust, the world's second-largest medical charity, was established by the pharmacist Sir Henry Solomon Wellcome (1853–1936). Born to a poor family in his grandfather's log cabin in Almond, Wisconsin, USA, he eventually made his home in England, becoming a British citizen in 1910. His private life was less successful than his business career: in 1916 he divorced his wife Syrie on the grounds of her adultery with the English writer Somerset Maugham.*

Weld, *see* **Wald**.

Weldon P Place-name in Northants OE 'hill with a spring/stream'. A surname which can be found scattered across northern England, strongest in Lancs/WRYorks. Readily confused with/a variant of **Welton**. *Fay Weldon, the novelist, short story writer, playwright and essayist, was born Franklin Birkinshaw in 1931 in Alvechurch, Worcs. Ronald Weldon was her second husband… Sir Huw Pyrs Wheldon (1916–1986), broadcaster and broadcasting executive, was born in Prestatyn, Wales.*

We(l)lfare N Nickname for a prosperous person, one who was 'faring well' OE.

Chiefly found in Sussex and surrounding counties in both spellings.

Welford P Place-name in Berks OE 'ford at the willows', in Northants OE 'ford over the stream' and in Warwicks OE 'ford at the springs/streams', but the surname **Welford** belongs chiefly to Co Durham and NRYorks, in which counties there would appear to be no places so-called.

Welham P From one of a number of places so-called in Leics OE 'homestead by the river', and in Notts and ERYorks OE *wellum* '(at) the springs', the latter exhibiting the use of a dative plural after a lost preposition. An Essex/Middx/Suffolk surname.

Well, *see* Wells.

Welland P Cottle's reference to the place-name *Welland* in Worcs, OW and OE 'land on the ?white river', may be something of a red herring here. There is a river *Welland* in Lincs, but the surname is found mainly in Devon (where there is a *Welland* OE 'wild/uncultivated land' in Bishop's Nympton), and in Surrey. *Colin Welland, English actor and screenwriter, was born in Newton-le-Willows, Lancs, in 1934.*

Wellbelove(d) N Nickname for a 'well-beloved' person OE. A very scarce surname, found in limited numbers in Middx and in Midlothian, Scotland.

Wellcome, *see* Welcome.

Weller T/O Dweller at the spring/stream OE (compare **Wellman** and **Wells**); or an occupational term for a salt-boiler OE. Primarily a south-east-of-England surname.

Welles, *see* Wells.

Wellfare, *see* Welfare.

Wellman T/F Man at the spring/stream OE (compare **Weller**, **Wells**); or a Norman version of **Gillman** (see **William**). Strongest in Dorset.

Wells/Welles T/P Dweller of (at) a well/spring/stream (or a plural); or from a place so-called, with the same meaning, such as *Wells* in Norfolk, Somerset. **Wells** is a common widespread surname; **Welles** (the *-es* of which preserves the older form of the inflection) is a very scarce surname found in limited numbers in south-east England. **Well** is a rare Lancs/WRYorks variant. See also **Weller** and **Wellman**. *The American director, producer, actor and writer (George) Orson Welles (1915–1985) was born in Kenosha, Wisconsin. One of his direct ancestors, John Alden, who was a cooper on board the Mayflower, is also an ancestor of Marilyn Monroe (aka Norma Jean Baker)… The novelist Herbert George ('H. G.') Wells (1866–1946) was born in Bromley, Kent, the son of Joseph Wells, a shopkeeper and professional cricketer whose father had been head gardener at Penshurst Place, Sussex, and his wife Sarah Neal.*

Wellstead T/P Dweller at the upper end of a stream OE; or possibly from the place-name *Wellshead*, Somerset. A Dorset/Hants surname.

Welsh P A person from *Wales*, a Celt, Briton OE *wealh* 'foreign'. 'Needless to say, the Welsh called and call themselves no such thing, and **Welsh** shows the point of view of the Anglo-Saxon invader' (Cottle). **Walsh** and **Walshe** can be variants of **Welsh**, but have become distinctively Irish surnames, from the Gaelic *Breathnach* ('British, Welsh'); within England they are strongest in Lancs. Compare **Wale**, **Wales**, **Wallis**, **Waugh**, **Welshman**. **Welsh** and **Welch** (a spelling still used by the *Welch Regiment*) are widespread surnames, strongest in Lancs. **Walsh** is the family name of the Barons Ormathwaite.

Welshman/Welchman P A Welshman OE; possibly applied in a more modern and restricted sense (to describe a man from present-day *Wales*) than is the case with **Welsh**. Compare **Wale**, **Wales**, **Wallis**, **Waugh**. Scarce in both spellings; **Welshman** has something of a presence in Hants, and **Welchman** in Gloucs and Somerset.

Welton P Place-name in Cumbd, ERYorks, Lincs (three such), Northants OE 'farm by a spring/stream'. Strongest in Norfolk and

Suffolk. Readily confused with/a variant of **Weldon**.

Wemyss P Scots: place-name *Wemyss* in Fifeshire, Gaelic (with English *–s* plural marker and with Scots *-ys* for the original *-es*) 'caves'. Generally pronounced '*Weems*'. Wemyss is strongest in Fifeshire; **Weems** and **Weemys** are scarce variants.

Wenden/Wendon P Place-names in Essex: *Wenden Lofts* and *Wendens Ambo* (*Ambo*, from Latin, meaning 'both the *Wendens*' – that is, *Great* and *Little Wenden*) OE 'winding (stream) valley'. Scarce Essex surnames.

Wenham P Place-name in Suffolk and Sussex OE '?tumulus/hill homestead/river-meadow'. Mainly found in Kent/Sussex and surrounding counties.

Wenlock P Place-name in Salop OW 'white/holy monastery'. Strongest in Staffs.

Wenn T/P Probably a dweller by a mound/hillock, or from an unidentified place-name OE 'wen, wart, tumour'. The early forms quoted by Reaney do not suggest a nickname origin. Most common in eastern England, strongest in Norfolk.

Wensley P Place-name in Derbys OE 'wood/clearing sacred to (the pagan god) *Woden*' or OE '*Vandal*'s wood/clearing', and in NRYorks, whence comes the famous *Wensleydale* cheese. The surname is certainly found in the north of England, especially Lancs, but is also strong in Somerset and in Devon, where it could perhaps have its origins in the place-name *Wansley (Barton)* in Roborough, Devon OE '*Want*'s clearing', or be a variant of **Winsley**?

Went T Dweller by a path OE *went* – as in *Four Wents/Four Wantz*, Essex (compare **Want**). An Essex/Herefords surname.

Wentworth P Place-name in Cambs and WRYorks OE '?*Wintra*'s enclosure' or 'enclosure occupied in the winter'. Yet by the late nineteenth century the surname was most commonly found in Middx and Surrey. *D'Arcy Wentworth (1762–1827), Australian physician and public servant, was born*

near Portadown, Co Armagh, Ireland, to a family which traced its male-line ancestry back to Wentworth Woodhouse, Yorks. His son William Charles Wentworth (1790–1872) achieved fame in Australia as a politician and landowner.

Were, *see* **Wear**.

Werlock/Warlock/Wherlock/Worlock N Nickname from an OE (?and ON) word meaning 'fiend, traitor, devil, monster, sorcerer, wizard'. For the *-ar* element in **Warlock**, *see* **Armistead**. **Worlock** is chiefly found in Gloucs, but in all other spellings this is a very scarce Somerset surname.

Wesley, *see* **Westley**.

Wesson, *see* **Weston**.

West T A newcomer from the west (compare **Western**)/dweller to the west of a village OE. A common and widespread surname. *Timothy (Lancaster) West, film, stage and television actor, was born in 1934 in Bradford, WRYorks, and is said to have a family connexion with the Earls de la Warr… Cicily Isabel Fairfield, the versatile writer and champion of women's suffrage better known as Dame Rebecca West (1892–1983) – a pen-name she took from Henrik Ibsen's play* Rosmersholm *- was born in London to an Irish father and a Scottish mother.*

Westacott, *see* **Westcott**.

Westall T/P Dweller at a western hall/nook OE, or from *Westhall* in Suffolk, with the same meaning. Strongest in Berks and Lancs.

Westborough P There are places so-called in Lincs and WRYorks OE 'western fort', but this is a very scarce Gloucs surname, and may have its roots in the place-names *Westbury-on-Severn* or *Westbury-on-Trym* in that county (see **Westbury**)?

Westbrook P Place-name in several counties (two such in Berks) OE 'western brook' or 'west of the brook'. Chiefly a Hants/Middx surname.

Westbroom P A now-nameless spot in Woolpit, Suffolk OE 'western place of broom/gorse/furze'. A very scarce Essex/ Middx surname.

Westbury P Place-name in Bucks, Gloucs, Hants, Salop, Somerset, Wilts OE 'western fort/manor'. Strongest in Warwicks. See also **Westborough**.

Westby P Place-name in Lancs, Lincs, WRYorks ON 'western farm'. Chiefly a Lancs surname. Readily confused with/a variant of **Westerby**.

Westcott/Westacott P Place-names *Westcot, Westcott, Westcote* in several southern English counties OE 'western cottage(s)/ hut(s)'. A Devon surname in both spellings. **Waistcoat**, a bizarre perversion, is a very rare Cornish surname. *Frederick John Westcott (1866–1941), born in Exeter, Devon, achieved fame as Fred Karno, the king of slapstick comedy.*

Westerby/Westoby P Place-name *Westerby* in Leics ON 'western farm' or ON '?west in/of the village'. **Westerby** (Lincs, WRYorks) is a scarcer surname than **Westoby** (Lincs and ERYorks). Readily confused with/a variant of **Westby**.

Western/Westren T A newcomer from the west OE (compare **West**). A Devon surname in both spellings.

Westfall T/N Dweller at a western clearing/ felling OE. Cottle suggests that it might alternatively be a nickname for a squanderer OF 'waste-straw', 'the owner of *Hartley Westpall*, Hants'. Chiefly a Lancs surname.

Westfield P Place-name in several counties OE 'western field'. Strongest in Lincs and Middx.

Westgarth T/P Dweller at a western enclosure OE, or from a place so-called in Chapel Allerton, WRYorks. Chiefly a Co Durham surname.

Westgate T/P Dweller at a west gate/west street OE/ON, or from one of a number of places so-called, with the same meaning(s). Chiefly a Norfolk/Sussex surname.

Westhall P Place-name in Suffolk OE 'western nook', but a scarce Lancs surname.

Westhead P Place-name in Lancs OE 'western hill/promontory', and a Lancs surname.

Westhorp(e) P There are various placenames of this ilk, including *Westrop* in Wilts and *Westrip* in Gloucs ON or OE 'western village'. Several variant spellings are known, all scarce or very scarce: **Westhorp** (Co Durham, Isle of Wight); **Westhorpe** (Middx, Norfolk); **Westhrop** (Surrey); **Westrip** (Essex, Surrey); **Westrop** (Essex, Middx); **Westrope** (Cambs); **Westrup** (Norfolk, Suffolk).

Westhrop, *see* **Westhorp**.

Westlake T Dweller to the west of a stream OE (see **Lake**). This is a Devon surname, and the two places so-called in that county, one in Ermington and the other in Dolton, would seem to have acquired their names from former owners – Richard **Bywestelake** and Henry **de Westlake** respectively, both of whom are mentioned in a Subsidy Return for 1333.

Westley/Wellesley/Wesley P From one of a number of places called *Westley* in Cambs, Salop and Suffolk, or *Westleigh* in Devon, Lancs, Somerset OE 'western wood/ clearing'. **Westley** is particularly in evidence in Northants and **Wesley** in Leics. By the late nineteenth century **Wellesley**, a scarce surname, could be found in Berks, Hants, and Lanarkshire, Scotland. *The Wesley family, Earls of Mornington, changed their surname to the older form 'Wellesley' in the late eighteenth century. Arthur Wellesley, Duke of Wellington (1769–1852), born in Dublin, the third surviving son of the first Earl of Mornington, is said to have been distantly related to John Wesley (1713–1791), the founder of Methodism.*

Westma(n)cott/Westmancote P Placename *Westmancote* in Worcs OE 'cottage(s)/ hut(s) of the western men (?Welsh)'. **Westmacott** is a scattered surname; **Westmancote**, very scarce, can be found in Gloucs and Worcs; **Westmancott**, even scarcer, has a limited presence in Gloucs.

Westmor(e)land P County name *West-*

morland OE 'district of the men living west of the (Yorkshire) moors'. Strongest in WRYorks in both spellings. *William C. Westmoreland (1914–2005), the US general who commanded military operations in the Vietnam War, was born in Spartanburg County, South Carolina.*

Westoby, *see* **Westerby**.

Weston/Wesson P *Weston* is a common place-name, found in most English counties OE 'western/west-facing farm' or 'to the west of the farm/village'. **Weston** is a prolific and widespread surname; **Wesson** is strongest in Leics and Middx.

Westover P Place-name in Hants, Isle of Wight, Somerset OE 'western bank/slope'. By the late nineteenth century the **Westover** surname was most in evidence in Kent and Middx. *Most Americans who bear the Westover surname are descended from Jonah Westover, born in Taunton, Somerset, England, in 1628, who died in 1708 in Simsbury, Connecticut, USA. When Charles Weedon Westover (1934–1990), born in Grand Rapids, Michigan, USA, decided to change his name in order to further his career as a singer and guitarist, he opted initially for 'Charlie Johnson', but finally for 'Del Shannon', under which name he achieved great success in the pop music world.*

Westren, *see* **Western**.

Westrip/Westrop(e)/Westrup, *see* **Westhorp**.

Westwood P There are various places so-called in several English counties; most are OE 'western wood', but *Westwood* in Kent is OE 'west of the wood (Blean Forest)'. Strongest in Staffs. *The English fashion designer Vivienne Isabel Westwood (married name, **Swire**) was born in 1941 in the village of Tintwistle, near Glossop, Derbys.*

Wetherald/Wetherall, *see* **Weatherall**.

Wetherby/Weatherby P Place-name *Wetherby* in WRYorks ON 'farm with wethers/rams'. **Wetherby** is strongest in WRYorks, and **Weatherby** in Lancs and Staffs.

Wethered, *see* **Weatherhead**.

Wetherell/Wetherill, *see* **Weatherall**.

Wetherspoon, *see* **Witherspoon**.

Wetmore P There is a place called *Wetmoor* in Staffs OE 'mere by a bend'. A scarce Gloucs surname, though the first-known reference to a place called *Wetmoor* in Horton in that county dates from as late as 1830.

Wetton/Whetton P Place-name *Wetton* in Staffs OE 'wet hill'. A surname chiefly found in nearby Derbys in both spellings.

Wexham P Place-name in Bucks OE 'homestead where (bees-) wax is found'. A very scarce surname, found in Middx.

Weyman/Weymont, *see* **Wyman**.

Weymouth/Waymouth P Place-name *Weymouth* in Dorset, Celtic (same as the river *Wye*) and OE 'mouth of the (river) *Wey*'. Chiefly a Devon surname in both spellings.

Whait(e)(s), *see* **Wait**.

Whale N Nickname for a large or clumsy person OE *hwal* ('whale'). A scattered surname, strongest in Middx and Wilts.

Whalebelly N Nickname for a person with a belly as fat as a whale's OE. 'A Norfolk surname which I was pleased to see on a butcher's shop in that county' (Cottle).

Whal(l)ey P Place-names: *Whalley*, Lancs, *Whaley*, Derbys OE 'wood/clearing by a hill'; *Waley*, Chesh OE 'wood/clearing by a road' (compare '*way*'). **Whaley** is strongest in WRYorks, **Whalley** in Lancs.

Wharf(e) T/P Dweller at a wharf, embankment OE, or at a bend, nook, corner ON; or from *Wharfe*, NRYorks, with the latter meaning. **Wharf** is strongest in Norfolk, **Wharfe** in WRYorks.

Wharmby/Quarmby P Place-name *Quarmby* in WRYorks ON '?farm with a quern/mill'. **Wharmby** is strongest in Lancs, **Quarmby** in WRYorks.

Wharton P Place-name in Chesh, Herefords OE 'place/farm on the (river) *Weaver* (*Woefer*)' (see **Weaver**); in Lincs OE 'beacon/ shore farm'; in Westmd OE 'wharf/embankment farm'. Cottle claims that 'Guppy's count of the surname in only Norfolk–Suffolk adds to the confusion' need not concern us; in the event the surname is strongest in Lancs, with a healthy presence in Chesh and Westmd, though is less common in Herefords and Lincs. Readily confused with/a variant of **Warton**.

Whatcott P Place-name *Whatcote* in Warwicks OE 'cottage(s) where wheat grows'. Chiefly a Gloucs surname.

Whatel(e)y/Whatley/Wheatley P Place-names in several counties, including: *Wheatley* in Co Durham, Lancs, Notts, Oxon, WRYorks; *Whatley* in Somerset; *Whateley* in Warwicks OE 'clearing/field where wheat grows'. **Whately** is strongest in Kent and Warwicks, **Whateley** in Warwicks, **Whatley** in Wilts, and **Wheatley** in Co Durham, Derbys, Middx, WRYorks. *Kevin Whately, the actor best known for his starring role in the television series* Auf Wiedersehen, Pet, *and for playing Sergeant Lewis in* Inspector Morse, *was born in 1951 in Newcastle-upon-Tyne and brought up in Humshaugh, near Hexham, Northd.*

Whatman/Watman F/O From a ME first-name *W(h)atman/Wheteman* (OE *Hwoetmann*) 'brisk/brave man'; or an occupational term for a servant of a man called *Wat(t)*, see **Walter**. **Whatman** is a Kent/Sussex surname; **Watman**, scarce, has a limited presence in Chesh and Lancs. *The name* Whatman *is famously associated with papermaking; James Whatman (1702–1759), from a family which had been in Kent since the fifteenth century, started life as a tanner, like his father, but eventually turned to making paper at Hollingbourne and at Turkey Mill, near Maidstone.*

Whatmore P Place-name *Whatmoor* in Salop OE 'damp moor' or 'moor in a bend'; or a variant of **Watmore**. Strongest in Staffs/ Worcs.

Whatmough, *see* **Watmore**.

Whatton P Place-name in Leics, Notts, OE 'wheat farm'. Strongest in Staffs.

Wheadon/Wheddon T/P Dweller at a wheat hill ('down') or valley ('dene') OE, or from *Wheddon* in Somerset, with the same meaning. Rare in both spellings; **Wheadon** can be found in Dorset/Somerset, **Wheddon** in Somerset/Warwicks. Readily confused with/a variant of **Weedon**.

Wheal(e)(s), *see* **Wheel**.

Wheat N/O Nickname for a brisk, brave person OE; or an occupational term for a grower/seller of wheat OE. Mainly found in Notts and surrounding counties. See also **Wait**.

Wheatcroft/Whitcroft P Cottle speaks of a place called *Wheatcroft (Farm)* in Devon, but the first-known reference to it dates only from 1809 ('*Whitcroft*'). **Wheatcroft** is primarily a Derbys surname, where the origin will almost certainly be the place called *Wheatcroft* in that county OE 'paddock where wheat grows'. **Whitcroft** is a scarcer Leics/Warwicks variant. *Harry Wheatcroft (1898–1977), the bewhiskered rose-grower who did much to popularize his favourite flower, was born in Sneinton, Notts.*

Wheatfill, *see* **Whitfield**.

Wheatley, *see* **Whately**.

Wheddon, *see* **Wheadon**.

Wheel(e)/Wheal(e)(s) O/T Occupational term for a wheelwright OE (compare **Wheeler** and **Wheelwright**); or dweller at a (water-)wheel. A surname with a significant presence in Essex in most spellings; **Wheels** ('of [at] the wheel') is a scarce Surrey variant.

Wheeler O Occupational term for a wheel-maker, wheelwright OE (compare **Wheel** and **Wheelwright**). A widespread and common surname, strongest in southern counties of England.

Wheelwright O Occupational term for a wheel-maker, wheelwright, OE (compare

Wheel and **Wheeler**). Most common in WRYorks.

Wherlock, *see* **Werlock**.

Whetton, *see* **Wetton**.

Whick(er), *see* **Wick**.

Whickham P Place-name in Co Durham OE 'homestead with a quickset hedge'. A very rare surname, readily confused with/a variant of **Wickham** or **Wykeham**.

Whimp, *see* **Wimpey**.

Whimpey, *see* **Wimpey**.

Whinnerah/Whin(e)ray P Presumably from the place-name *Whinneray* in Cumbd ?OE and ON 'pasture nook', though the earliest recorded reference to it (as *Wynwarrowe*) dates from as late as 1599. Compare **Wray**. Scarce in all spellings: **Whinnerah** can be found in Cumbd, **Whinray** in Lancs/WRYorks, **Whineray** in Lancs.

Whisker, *see* **Wishart**.

Whistlecraft/Whistlecroft T Dweller at the river-fork paddock OE *twisla croft*, an aspirate having been added in imitation of the word *whistle*. *Whistlecraft* is chiefly a Suffolk surname; *Whistlecroft* (rare) can be found in Lancs.

Whistler O Occupational term for a whistler, piper, flautist, OE. A very scarce scattered surname. *The American painter James McNeill Whistler (1834–1903) was born in Lowell, Massachusetts… The English artist Rex Whistler (1905–1944) was born in Eltham, Kent.*

Whit(t)aker/Wittaker P From one of a number of place-names, including *Whitaker* in Lancs, *Whitacre* in Warwicks OE 'white field' (compare the word '*acre*'), the whiteness being from chalk or liming (but see **Whitfield**); or *Whiteacre* in Kent, *Wheatacre* in Norfolk OE 'wheat field'. **Whitaker** is strongest in WRYorks, **Whittaker** and **Wittaker** in Lancs.

Whitamore, *see* **Whitmore**.

Whitbourn(e) N/P Nickname for a fair-

haired child/bairn OE; there are also places called *Whitbourne* in Herefords and Wilts OE 'white stream', but this rare surname is chiefly found in Surrey in both spellings. Readily confused with/a variant of **Whitburn**.

Whitbread O/N Occupational term for a baker/seller of white/wheat(en) bread OE; or a nickname for a man with a white beard OE (with metathesis of the letter -*r*-). Mainly found in the Home Counties, especially Beds/Essex/Middx. *Samuel Whitbread (1720–1796), an English Member of Parliament who was best known as a successful brewer, was born at Cardington, Beds, in 1742.*

Whitburn ?P Cottle's reference to a place so-called in Co Durham OE 'white stream' does seem rather less than helpful, given the fact that this is predominantly a Cornish surname. Readily confused with/a variant of **Whitbourn**.

Whitby P Place-name in NRYorks ON 'white settlement' and in Chesh OE 'white fortified place'. Chiefly a Chesh/Lancs surname.

Whitcher/Witcher O/T Occupational term for a maker of chests OE; or the suffix -*er* may indicate a dweller at the dairy-farm/wych-elm OE. Chiefly a Hants surname in either spelling.

Whitchurch P Place-name *Whitchurch* in several English counties OE 'white/whitewashed/stone-built church'. **Whitchurch** is strongest in Gloucs and Notts, **Witchurch** (much scarcer) in Gloucs alone.

Whitcomb(e) P From one of a number of places so-called, including *Whitcombe* in Dorset OE 'wide valley' and the Isle of Wight OE 'white valley'.

Whitcroft, *see* **Wheatcroft**.

Whitcutt P Place-name *Whitcott* in Salop OE 'white cottage(s)'. A rare Staffs surname.

White N/P Nickname for a person with white/fair hair or a pallid complexion OE – also **Whitt** (scarce, Notts), **Witt** (chiefly Hants) and **Witts** (chiefly Gloucs). But place-names with this element tend to have a different origin: *Great Whyte* in Ramsey, Hunts, was once *wiht* OE '?curve, bend (of river/road)' and *White* in Devon was *Wayte* OF 'look-out place'. **White** is a common and widespread surname, and the family name of the Barons Annaly. Sometimes also used by Scottish, Irish and Jewish people in place of a surname in their own language with the same meaning. Readily confused with/a variant of **Wight**. Patronymic forms include **Whiting** (widespread) and **Whiteson** (very scarce, WRYorks). Cottle is somewhat scathing about the Scottish variant **Whyte**: 'A form of **White**, altered to no purpose; *y*, as opposed to *i*, *did* have a usefulness in manuscripts, for clarity's sake, when it was used next to the minim letters *n m u w*; but that does not apply here'. See also **Whiteman** and **Whitson**.

Whitefield, *see* **Whitfield**.

Whitefoot N Nickname for a person with a noticeably white (or bent/club) foot OE or from a place called *Whit(e)ford* OE? Mainly found in Salop and surrounding counties.

Whitehead N/T Nickname for a person with white/fair hair OE; or dweller at a white top/eminence OE, of the same derivation. A widespread and fairly prolific surname, strongest in Lancs.

Whitehill P Place-name in Co Durham OE 'white hill' and in Oxon OE 'hill with a curved hollow'. An uncommon surname, mainly found in Lancs and in Lanarkshire/Renfrewshire, Scotland.

Whitehorn(e) P/N Hanks and Hodges speak of a place-name *Whithorn* in Wigtownshire, Scotland OE 'white house', which might seem unlikely as a source for such surnames, which are chiefly found in southern counties of England. Cottle is persuaded that early forms suggest a nickname from OE 'bright drinking-horn/trumpet'. *The distinguished journalist Katharine Whitehorn was born in London in 1928.*

Whitehouse T/P/N Dweller at a white (whitewashed or stone) house OE, or from a minor place-name with the same mean-

ing; or a nickname for a person with a white neck OE (compare **Halse**). Mainly found in Staffs and surrounding counties.

Whitehurst P Place-name in Staffs OE 'white/bright hill/wood', and chiefly a Staffs surname.

Whitelaw P From one of a number of places in the England/Scotland border region OE 'white hill'. *The Conservative Party politician William Stephen Ian ('Willie') Whitelaw, Viscount Whitelaw (1918–1999), was born in Edinburgh.*

Whitelegg N Nickname for a person with a noticeably white (or bent?) leg OE and ON. Chiefly a Chesh/Lancs surname.

Whiteley/Whitley P From one of a number of places called *Whiteley* or *Whitley* OE 'white clearing' (but see **Whitfield**). A surname of WRYorks in either spelling. Readily confused with/a variant of **Witley**. **Whiteley** is the family name of the Barons Marchamley. *(John) Richard Whiteley (1943–2005), who presented the TV show* Countdown *for no fewer than twenty-three years, was born in Bradford, WRYorks, to a family which owned a long-established textile mill.*

Whitelock, *see* **Whitlock**.

Whiteman/Whitman N/O/F Nickname for a person with white/fair hair or a pallid complexion OE (compare **White**); or an occupational term for a servant of a man called **White**. Cottle also notes the existence of a first-name *Hwitmann* OE 'white/ fair man'. A widespread surname in both spellings. *The American poet Walt Whitman (1819–1992) was a descendant of Joseph Whitman, an Englishman who settled in Connecticut in the mid to late seventeenth century.*

Whiter O Occupational term for a whitewasher OE. Cottle remarks: 'He must have been much in demand – Reaney reminds us that many big buildings (e.g. the White Tower, or Keep, of the Tower of London, and Corfe Castle) were so coloured; and some of the many place-names Whitchurch may have had whitewashed churches'. A very scarce Berks/Essex/Middx surname.

Whitesmith o Occupational term for a whitesmith, tinsmith OE; 'Trevisa, in his 1387 translation of Higden, says that all Europe likes and wants the "whyt metayl" of this land' (Cottle). Sparsely scattered throughout the United Kingdom, strongest in Argyllshire, Scotland.

Whiteson, *see* White.

Whiteway P Place-name in various counties in the West Country OE 'white road', used of a road with bright stones or situated on chalk or white clay. A Devon surname. *The Devon cider firm of Whiteway, owned by a family of that name for three generations, was eventually acquired by a conglomerate and closed down.*

Whitfield/Whitefield P Place-name *Whitfield* in several counties OE 'white field'. Not all necessarily mean 'chalky' or 'limed'; some scholars cite the dialect meaning of 'dry open pasture', and in some cases '*White*' may refer to land on which snow was wont to lie for a long time. **Whitfield** is strongest in Co Durham and Lancs, **Whitefield** (much scarcer) in Devon. **Whitfield** is the family name of the Barons Kenswood. *The comedy actress June (Rosemary) Whitfield was born in 1925 in Streatham, London.*

Whitford P Place-name in Devon, Worcs, Flintshire OE 'white ford'. Mainly found in Cornwall.

Whitgift P Place-name in WRYorks OE/ON and ON '*Hwita/Hwite/Hviti*'s dowry land'. A surname made famous thanks to John **Whitgift** (?1530/1531–1604), Archbishop of Canterbury and founder of a school in Croydon, Surrey, which bears his name, whose family had long held land at *Whitgift* itself. By the late nineteenth century the surname had all but vanished from sight.

Whiting, *see* White.

Whitley, *see* Whiteley.

Whitlock/Whitelock N/F Nickname for a

person with white/fair hair, locks OE; or from an OE first-name meaning 'elf/sprite/creature-play' (compare **Whitridge**). **Whitlock** is strongest in Hants/Middx/Northants, **Whitelock** in WRYorks.

Whitman, *see* Whiteman.

Whitmarsh P Place-names *Whitemarsh* and *Witmarsh* in Wilts OE 'white (?chalky ?shining) marsh'. Strongest in Hants/ Middx/Wilts.

Whitmer, *see* Whitmore.

Whit(e)more P From one of a number of place-names, such as *Whitmore*, Staffs, and *Whitmoor*, Devon OE 'white moor/mere'. **Whitmore** is a prolific and scattered surname; **Whitemore** is mainly found in Somerset, **Whittamore** and **Whittemore** in Beds, **Whitamore** in Cambs, and **Whitmer** (very scarce) in Surrey.

Whitney P Place-name in Herefords OE '*Hwita*'s island' (the -*n*- being a sign of the genitive of a weak masculine noun) or '(at the) white island' (the -*n*- being a sign of the dative of a weak adjective after a lost preposition and definite article). Strongest in Northants, and readily confused with/a variant of **Witney**, which is derived from a place-name in neighbouring Oxon.

Whitridge P/F Place-names: *Whitrigg*, Cumbd (three such, in Hutton-in-the-Forest, Torpenhow, Bowness) and *Wheatridge*, Northd ON/OE 'white ridge'; or from an OE first-name meaning 'elf/sprite/creature-ruler' (compare **Whitlock**). Strongest in Lancs.

Whitson F/T/P 'Son of **Whitt/White**'. Possibly also applied to a dweller near a white stone OE, or from a place-name with the same meaning, such as *Whitstone*, Cornwall, *Whitestone*, Devon or *Whitstones*, Worcs. No connexion with Pentecost, though **Whitson** is mainly found in Midlothian, Scotland, which has also been home to a small group of people bearing the remarkable surname of **Whitsunday**. But then, there is a place in Kent called *Whitsunden*…

Whitsunday, *see* Whitson.

Whitt, *see* White.

Whittaker, *see* Whitaker.

Whittall T Dweller at a white hall/nook/ hill OE. Chiefly a Salop surname. Readily confused with/a variant of **Whittell**, **Whittle**, **Whitwell**.

Whittamore, *see* Whitmore.

Whittell T Dweller at a white spring/ stream OE. Strongest in WRYorks. Readily confused with/a variant of **Whittall**, **Whittle**, **Whitwell**.

Whittemore, *see* Whitmore.

Whittingham/Whittenham P Place-name *Whittingham* in Lancs, Northd (where the pronunciation is -*nj*-) and East Lothian, Scotland OE 'homestead of the family/folk of *Hwita*'. **Whittingham** is strongest in Lancs and Staffs. **Whittenham**, apparently a variant, confuses matters by being chiefly a Hants surname.

Whittingstall P Place-name *Whittonstall* in Northd OE 'farmstead with a quickset hedge'; yet the surname is mostly found in Kent. *The celebrity TV chef Hugh Fearnley-Whittingstall was born in London, but brought up in Gloucs.*

Whittington/Wittington P From one of a large number of places called *Whittington*, being variously OE '(at the) white settlement', OE '*Hwita*'s settlement' or OE 'settlement of *Hwita*'s people'. **Whittington** is most commonly found in Middx/Surrey and along the south coast, with a strong presence on the Isle of Wight. **Wittington** is more widely spread, strongest in WRYorks. *Richard ('Dick') Whittington (1354–1423), the Lord Mayor of London and Member of Parliament whose memory is perpetuated thanks to the pantomime character who bears his name, was born in Pauntley, Gloucs, to a family with Staffs origins.*

Whittle P Place-name in Lancs, Northd OE 'white hill'. Chiefly a Lancs surname. Readily confused with/a variant of **Whittall**, **Whittell**, **Whitwell**.

Whittlesey P Place-name in Cambs OE '*Witel*'s island'. A scarce Cambs surname.

Whitton P Place-name in various English and Scottish counties OE '*Hwita*'s enclosure'. Strongest in Lancs, WRYorks and (especially) in Angus, Scotland. Readily confused with/a variant of **Witton**.

Whitty, *see* Witty.

Whitwell T/P Dweller at a white spring/ stream OE, or from one of many places so-called, with the same meaning. A widespread surname, most common in the north of England. Readily confused with/ a variant of **Whittall**, **Whittell**, **Whittle**.

Whitwham P Place-name in Northd OE or ON 'white corner/valley'. Chiefly a WRYorks surname.

Whitwood P There is a place so-named in WRYorks OE 'white wood', but this is a Norfolk surname.

Whitworth P Place-name in Co Durham, Lancs and elsewhere OE '*Whita*'s enclosure'. A surname of the north of England, strongest in Lancs but also strong in WRYorks. *Sir Joseph Whitworth (1803–1887), the engineer and entrepreneur best known for inventing several accurate measuring devices, was born in Stockport, Chesh.*

Whomsley P Place-name *Womersley* in WRYorks OE '*Wilmer*'s clearing'. A very scarce surname, found in limited numbers in Denbighshire, Wales, and in Notts.

Why(e), *see* Wye.

Whyatt, *see* Wyatt.

Whybrew/Whybro(w), *see* Wybar.

Whyman, *see* Wyman.

Whymer, *see* Wymer.

Whysall P Place-name *Wysall* in Notts OE 'hill-spur with a (heathen) temple'. Chiefly a Derbys surname. **Wysall** is a scarce Derbys/Notts variant.

Whyte, *see* White.

Wibrew/Wibrow, *see* Wybar.

Wich/Wych(e) ⊤ Dweller by a wych elm tree OE; or a palatalized form of **Wick**.

Wicher, *see* **Wick**.

Wick(e)/Wyke T/P Dweller at an outlying settlement, dairy-farm (or possibly a salt-works) OE; or from a place-name with the same meaning, such as *Wix* in Essex, *Wyke* in Dorset and Surrey, and *Week* in Devon. The *-e* of **Wicke** and **Wyke** can indicate the use of a dative after a lost preposition. In Scotland *Wick* can be ON 'creek, inlet, corner of land' (as in the town so-called in Caithness). **Wike** is a Lancs/WRYorks variant, with the *-i-* lengthened. There are several surnames containing the elements *Wich-*, *Wych-*, *Wik-*, *Wyk-* and *Week-*. **Weake** and **Week(e)** (together with its plural form **Weeks**, and also **Weekes**, which retains the inflectional *-e-*) can be variants of **Wick**, or be from a nickname for a weak, weedy person ME from ON. **Wick(e)s**, **Wykes** and **Wix** are 'of (at) the *wick*', or a plural. **Wicker** refers to one who lives or works at a dairy-farm, as does **Wicher** (a scarce Hants surname) and also **Whick(er)**, which contains what Cottle calls 'an erroneous and affected aspirate'. See also **Wich** and **Wicken**. *Alan (Donald) Whicker, the journalist and broadcaster best known for his travel reports, was born in Cairo, Eygpt, in 1921, but was raised in London. He once achieved the distinction of coming third in an Alan Whicker look-alike contest. 'Alan Whickers', sad to relate, has become Cockney rhyming slang for 'knickers'. Such is the price of fame…*

Wicken T/P Dweller at an outlying settlement, dairy-farm (or possibly a salt-works) OE (see **Wick**), with *-en* for OE *-um*, a dative plural after a lost preposition – or even 'dairy-farms', a weak plural in *-en* (as in *oxen*), extended to an OE strong noun; or from a place-name such as *Wyken* or *Wykin*, with the same meaning, found in counties as far apart as Essex and Salop. A Kent/Surrey surname.

Wicker, *see* **Wick**.

Wickham P Place-name in eight south-eastern counties of England OE 'home-stead/river-meadow with a *wick*' (see **Wick**), or simply OE 'manor, dwelling-place', especially one associated with a Romano-British town. As to the *Wickham* element in *Childs Wickham*, Gloucs, Ekwall suggests OW 'lodge in a plain/moor' or 'plain/meadow in a wood'. Strongest in Kent, Surrey and Sussex, and also particularly common in Co Wexford, Ireland. Readily confused with/a variant of **Whickham** or **Wykeham**.

Wickwar P Place-name in Gloucs OE and OF '*wick* (see **Wick**) belonging to the **de la Warre** family (see **Warr**)'. Chiefly a Leics surname.

Widdecombe/Widdicombe/Witha-combe/Withecombe/Withycombe P Place-name *Withycombe* in various counties, including Devon and Somerset OE 'willow (withe, withy) valley'. *Widdecombe* (Devon) Fair has achieved fame thanks to its being the title of a much-loved song (see **Cobleigh**). Principally a Devon surname, whatever the spelling. *Ann Widdecombe, outspoken and heterodox Conservative Party Member of Parliament, was born in 1947 in Bath, Somerset.*

Widdop/Widdup P Place-name *Widdop* in WRYorks OE 'wide valley', and a WRYorks surname in both spellings.

Widdow(e)s N 'Son of the widow(er)' OE, or a corruption of **Woodhouse**. **Widdows** can chiefly be found in Lancs and Oxon, **Widdowes** (very scarce) in Lancs, and the variant **Widdowson** in Derbys and Notts.

Widdowson, *see* **Widdows**.

Widdrington, *see* **Widrington**.

Widger F From an OE first-name meaning 'elf/sprite/creature-spear', or (Germanic) 'battle-army'. Cottle notes that a family of the latter origin left their name at *Broad-woodwidger*, Devon, in the twelfth/thirteenth centuries. Chiefly a Devon surname.

Widlake, *see* **Wedlake**.

Widley P Place-name in Hants OE 'willow

wood/clearing'. A very scarce scattered surname.

Widmer P Place-names *Widmere* in Bucks and *Widmerpool* in Notts OE 'mere/pool in the willows'. Sparsely scattered around southern and central England.

Wid(d)rington P Place-name in Northd OE 'settlement of *Wuduhere*'s people'. One prominent family of Northd **Widdrington**s suffered particularly mixed fortunes: Sir William **Widdrington** was raised to the peerage by King Charles I in 1643, but the fourth Baron was stripped of his titles following his support for the abortive Jacobite rebellion of 1715. Yet the surname itself refused to pass into oblivion, and was adopted during the eighteenth and nineteenth centuries by families formerly called Cook, Cooke, Jacson and Tingling, usually as a result of stipulations made in the wills of **Widdrington**s who otherwise would have seen their surname die out. By the late nineteenth century this had become a scarce Northd surname in either spelling.

Wigg N/O Nickname for a person bearing some resemblance to a beetle OE (compare the word '*earwig*'); or an occupational term for a maker of small fashion beads ME. **Wigg** is mainly found in the east and south-east of England, strongest in Norfolk/Suffolk; **Wiggs** ('son of **Wigg**'), scarce, can be found in south-east England.

Wigglesworth P Place-name *Wigglesworth* in WRYorks OE '*Wincel*'s enclosure'. A WRYorks surname. Readily confused with/a variant of **Wriglesworth**.

Wight N/T Nickname for a valiant, strong, nimble person ON *vigt* (the *-t* being the neuter inflection of the adjective); or dweller at a river- or road-bend OE *wiht* – but probably not from the *Isle of Wight*, which would seem to be British in origin. Strongest in north-east England and in Scotland. Readily confused with/a variant of **White**.

Wighton P Cottle refers to a place so-named in Norfolk OE 'dwelling-place', but this is a Scottish surname, strongest in Angus, and is probably derived from *Wig-*

town in Wigtownshire OE '*Wig/Wiga*'s settlement'. James **Wigtoun** of Dundee, Angus, had a precept of remission in 1492.

Wigley P Place-name in Derbys OE 'wood/clearing infested with beetles' (compare the word *earwig*) or '*Wi(c)ga*'s wood/clearing'. Mainly found in Derbys and surrounding counties, so *Wigley* in Hants is probably of little relevance. The first-name of *Lapidoth* **Wigley**, born in Wallingford, Berks, in 1846, was perhaps no more unusual than that of her siblings *Keturah, Philetus, Philiplus, Theophilius, Tryphena* and *Tryphosa*? *The Welsh politician Dafydd Wigley, former leader of Plaid Cymru, was born 'David' Wigley in Derby in 1943, but was educated in Wales.*

Wigmore P There is such a place-name in Herefords OW '?big wood/glade' (the adjective coming second), but the surname is mainly found in Berks, where a place now called *Wigmore Wood* (*La Wyde More* in 1249) OE 'wide marsh' in that county is likely to be the origin. *Wigmore Hall, London, stands in Wigmore Street, so-named in the early eighteenth century by Edward Harley, Earl of Oxford, after his family seat, Wigmore Castle, Herefords.*

Wignal(l) P Cottle makes reference to group of villages in Norfolk called *Wiggenhall* OE '*Wicga*'s nook', but this is a Lancs/WRYorks surname in both spellings, and the origin in most cases will be the place called *Wignal* in Croston, Lancs, which has the same origin/meaning.

Wigzell/Wigsell P From a place-name *Wigsell*, which Reaney confusingly says is in 'Salehurst, Kent'. In fact Salehurst is in Sussex, as is *Wigsell* OE '*Wicg*'s wood'. These are Kent/Middx/Surrey surnames, **Wigsell** being exceptionally rare.

Wike, *see* Wick.

Wilberforce/Wilberfoss P Place-name *Wilberfoss* in ERYorks OE '*Wilburh*'s ditch' (*Wilburh* being an OE female first-name meaning 'will-fortress'). An ERYorks surname in both spellings. *William Wilberforce (1759–1833), the noted politician and philan-*

thropist who played a major part in the abolition of the slave trade, was born in Hull.

Wilbourn, *see* Welborn.

Wilbraham P Place-name in Cambs OE '*Wilburg*'s homestead', but a surname of north-west England, strongest in Chesh.

Wilby P Place-name in various counties, inluding Norfolk OE and ON 'willow farm', Northants ON '*Vili*'s farm' and Suffolk OE 'willow circle/ring'. Strong in East Anglia, but strongest of all in WRYorks. Readily confused with/a variant of **Willoughby**.

Wil(l)cock(s)/Wil(l)cockson/Wil(l)cox/ Wilcoxson, *see* William.

Wild(e) N/T Nickname for a wild, undisciplined person; or dweller on wild, uncultivated land, from the same OE source. **Wild**, **Wilde** and the variant **Wildman** are strongest in Lancs, with an additional significant presence in WRYorks. The patronymic forms **Wilds** and **Wildes** are much scarcer, as are the variants **Wilder** and **Wilders**. See also **Wilding**. *Oscar (Fingal O'Flahertie Wills) Wilde (1854–1900), renowned as a playwright, novelist, poet, author of short stories and all-round sharp wit, was born in Dublin.*

Wildblood N Nickname for a rake, hooligan, one with 'wild blood' OE. Chiefly a Salop/Staffs surname.

Wildbore N Nickname for a person as ferocious or as proud as a wild boar OE, a creature that wasn't extinct in the north of England until the close of the Middle Ages. Mainly found in the East Midlands and along the course of the river Humber.

Wilde/Wilder(s)/Wildes, *see* Wild.

Wilderspin ?P A rare Cambs surname with a single-family origin. The first known reference to the surname occurs in the year 1701, when Archibald, son of John and Mary **Wilderspin**, was baptized at Swavesey, Cambs. 'Archibald' being a distinctively Scottish first name, the **Wilderspins** were probably **Witherspoons/Wetherspoons/ Wotherspoons** from Scotland (drovers travelling south on the 'Great North Road', per-

haps?) whose original surname proved too confusing for the parish clerk at Swavesey. Adam **Wytherpyn**, known to have been in Norfolk in 1273, and John **Wythspone**, found in Yorks in 1379, may have been earlier drifters away from their Scottish home? See **Witherspoon**. For a detailed study of this surname, see *Searching for surnames* by John Titford (2002). *Samuel Wilderspin (1791–1866) was joint-founder of the infant school system in England.*

Wildgoose N Nickname for a person bearing some resemblance to a wild goose OE. There was a Henry **Wildegos** in Shrewsbury, Salop, in 1201, but although this has become chiefly a Derbys surname, it is known to have been used in Scotland since at least as early as the fourteenth century, and John **Wildguse** was canon of Aberdeen in 1366. R. S. Charnock, writing in 1868, has convinced himself (but possibly no-one else?) that the origin is '*Wilgoss*, *Willgoss*, the Old German *Willigis* and *Wilgis* and the Anglo-Saxon *Wilgis*, a name which occurs in the genealogy of the Northumbrian Kings. It might translate: very warlike, or very strong...'. Nuff said?

Wilding F From an OE first-name *Wilding*, from OE *Wilde* ('savage') – see **Wild**. A Lancs surname.

Wildman, *see* Wild.

Wildridge, *see* Woolrich.

Wilds, *see* Wild.

Wildsmith O Occupational term for a wheel-smith OE, one who made the iron parts of wheels. Mainly found in WRYorks and surrounding counties.

Wileman/Wiles O/N Occupational term for a maker or user of snares/devices/ machines/traps OE; or a nickname for a devious person, who would trap or ensnare his victims. **Wileman** is chiefly found in Derbys, **Wiles** in Kent. **Wilyman**, probably a variant, is very scarce, with a limited presence in Lincs and elsewhere.

Wilford P Place-name in Notts and Suffolk OE 'ford in the willows'. Strongest in Leics.

Wilk(e)(s)/Wilkerson/Wilkie/Wilkin(s) /Wilking(s)/Wilkinson, *see* William.

Wilkshire, *see* Wiltshire.

Will(e) F/T A diminutive of **William**; or a dweller at a spring/stream OE (compare the word '*well*'). The *-e* of **Wille** indicates the use of the dative after a lost preposition. **Wills** ('son of **Will**') is the family name of the Barons Dulverton.

Willard F From an OE (or Norman from Germanic) first-name *Widelard*, meaning 'will/resolve-bold'; or a double diminutive of **William**, with an OF suffix. See also **Willet**.

Willat(t)s, *see* Willet.

Willbond, *see* Welborn.

Willbourn(e), *see* Welborn.

Willcock(s), *see* William.

Willcox, *see* William.

Wille, *see* Will.

Willen P Place-name in Bucks OE '(at the willows', exhibiting the use of the dative plural after a lost preposition; yet the surname, uncommon, can be found in places as far apart as Lancs and Norfolk.

Willet(t)(s)/Willat(t)s/Willitt(s)/Willott F Double diminutives of **William**. But all the surnames in this group could alternatively be reduced forms of **Willard**. See also **Waylett**.

Willey, *see* Wily.

Willgress/Willgrass N Nickname for a person bearing some resemblance to a wild pig OE and ON. A Norfolk surname in both spellings, **Willgrass** being very rare.

William F From an OF first-name, Germanic 'will/resolve helmet', brought into England by the Normans and soon exceedingly popular with all social classes. **William** is rare as a surname, but it has spawned many derivatives; unlike **Roger** or **Richard** it had only one abbreviated form in early times, *Wil(l)*, and the pet-form *Bill* came much later. The English surnames **Gillam**, **Gillem, Gillham, Gilliam, Gil(l)man, Gillum**

and the Welsh **Gwilli(a)m** (from *Gwilym*) are developments of the OF *Guillaume*. Patronymic forms include **Williams**, especially common in South Wales, and **Williamson**, a northern surname with a very strong presence in Lancs, and the family name of the Barons Forres. There are several diminutive/double diminutive variants, with or without patronymic indicators: **Wilcock** and **Willcock** (northern forms, featuring the familiar *-cock(s)/cox* ['young lad'] suffix); **Wilcocks/Willcocks** (Devon); **Wilcockson/Willcockson** (Derbys); **Wilcox** (scattered); **Wilcoxson** (scarce, scattered); **Willcox** (Somerset); **Wilk** (Staffs); **Wilke** (scarce, scattered); **Wilkerson** (East Anglia); **Wilkes** (Staffs); **Wilkie/Willkie** (Scotland); **Wilkin** (East Anglia); **Wilking** (scarce, Essex); **Wilkings** (scarce, Somerset); **Wilkins** (common, scattered); **Willkins** (Somerset); **Wilkinson** (prolific, northern); **Willkinson** (Lincs); **Wilks** (northern); **Willing** (Devon); **Willings** (Middx); **Willis** (very common, widespread); **Williss** (scarce, scattered); **Willison** (scattered). See also **Quilliam, Waylett, Wellman, Will, Willard, Willet, Willie, Willmett, Willock, Wilson, Wyatt**. *The energetic politician and radical John Wilkes (1725–1797) was born in Clerkenwell, London, the son of Israel Wilkes, a malt distiller, and his wife Sarah (née Heaton).*

Williams/Williamson, *see* William.

Willicombe, *see* Welcome.

Willie F/P A diminutive of **William**; or a variant of **Willey** (see **Wily**). Strongest in Somerset.

Willing, *see* William.

Willingale P Place-names *Willingale Doe* and *Willingale Spain* in Essex OE 'the nook of *Willa*'s people'. The second part of each name is based upon the byname/surname of a former owner. The churches of both places are situated in the same churchyard. A scarce Essex surname.

Willings/Willis(s)/Willison, *see* William.

Willitt(s), *see* Willet.

Willkie/Willkins/Willkinson, *see* William.

Willmett(s)/Willmitt/Wil(l)mot(t) F Diminutives of **William**. Whereas the common surname **Willmot** is Norman, Central French gives us the bird-name *guillemot*. **Wilmut** is a scarce Gloucs variant.

Willock F From the ME and OE first-name *Willoc*, a short-form of various compound names of which the first element '*Willa-*' means 'will, desire'; or an abbreviated form of **William**. **Willocks** and **Willox** are 'son of **Willock**'. **Willock** can be found scattered across England and Scotland; **Willocks** and **Willox**, both Scottish, belong to Angus and to Aberdeenshire respectively.

Willott, *see* Willet.

Willoughby P Place-name in Leics, Lincs (four such), Notts (three such) and Warwicks OE and ON 'farm in the willows'. Family name of the Earls of Ancaster and of the Barons Middleton. The surname is at its strongest in places as far apart as Surrey and WRYorks, and Cottle has sought to explain its significant presence in Cornwall: 'Mr J. L. Willoughby of Newton Ferrers has proved to me that the Cornish stock descend from Thomas **Wilbye** of Colchester, who got into paternity trouble, defected in 1647 to Cornwall, and there sired a race who were variously spelt **Willby/Wilaby/Willowby** and (in Illogan and Camborne registers alone) a dozen variant forms until 1728, when the present from settled down'. Readily confused with/ a variant of **Wilby**.

Willows T Dweller of/at the willow OE, or a plural. A long-established Lincs surname.

Wills, *see* Will.

Willson, *see* Wilson.

Wilmot(t)/Wilmut, *see* Willmett.

Wilsher(e)/Wilshire, *see* Wiltshire.

Wilson/Willson F/P 'Son of **William**'; or, much more rarely, from one of a number of place-names, such as *Wilson*, Leics ON and OE '*Vifill*'s farm/village'. **Wilson** is a surname which is found throughout Britain, with huge numbers in the north of England, and is the family name of the Barons Moran and of the Barons Nunburnholme. **Willson** is a less common variant, widespread, but still fairly prolific. Bearers of the surname **Wilson** have traditionally been referred to as '*Tug*', a nickname which arose when Admiral of the Fleet Sir Arthur Kynvet **Wilson** (1842–1921) sarcastically asked the captain of a battleship ordered to pull alongside whether he wanted a tug to help him complete the manoeuvre. *PC Denis 'Tug' Wilson, a tall and bewhiskered ex-Grenadier Guardsman who was once a familiar sight as he stood on duty in the Market Square ('Slab Square') in Nottingham, retired from the force in 1983.*

Wilton P From one of a number of places so-called. *Wilton* in Wilts (which gave its name to the county itself) is Celtic and OE 'place/farm on the (river) *Wylye* ("?tricky, liable to flood")'; another place so-called in Wilts and one in Somerset are OE 'place by a spring/stream'; *Wilton* in Cumbd, ERYorks, Herefords, Norfolk and WRYorks are OE 'place/farm in the willows'. Quite widespread, strongest in Cornwall.

Wiltshire/Wilsher(e)/Wilshire P The county name *Wiltshire*, derived from the town of *Wilton*, Celtic and OE 'place/farm on the (river) *Wylye* ("?tricky, liable to flood")', plus OE 'shire'. **Wiltshire** as a surname is strongest in Wilts itself. Of the Gloucs/Worcs variant **Wilkshire**, Cottle says: '…just a bad spelling of **Wiltshire**, even as many people nowadays say "*ekcetera*" for *etcetera*'; he is scarcely more complimentary about **Wilsher** (mainly Essex), **Wilshere** (mainly Beds) and **Wilshire** (mainly Gloucs and Middx), which he describes as being 'slovenly versions of **Wiltshire**'.

Wi(l)l(e)y/Wyley/Wylie P/N From one of a number of places called *Willey* in Chesh, Devon, Herefords, Salop, Warwicks OE 'willow wood/clearing', and in Surrey OE '(heathen) temple clearing' (*Whyly* and *Whiligh* in Sussex have the same origin); or from *Wylye*, Wilts, which stands on the river of that name (see **Wilton**). Cottle suggests that an alternative origin in some cases might be a nickname for a 'wily, tricksy' person ME. **Wylie** is a predominantly Scottish variant. See also **Willie**. **Willey** is the family name of the Barons Barnby.

Wilyman, *see* **Wileman**.

Wimbush P Place-name *Wimbish* in Essex OE '?*Wina*'s copse of bushes' or 'meadow/pasture reedy place', though in more recent times the surname is mainly found in Warwicks and surrounding counties.

Wimpenny, *see* **Winpenny**.

Wimpey An English surname of unknown origin, strongest in Devon, but also with deep roots in the town of Frome, Somerset. Possibly from an occupational term for a wimpler, a maker of wimples/veils OE? **Whimpey** (a scarce south-coast surname), and **Whimp** (found mainly in WRYorks) are possible variants 'Sir Elijah **Impey**, a well-known eighteenth century judge, had an illegitimate son who used this name [**Wimpey**], but it may simply have been selected as an existing surname approximating to his father's' (Hanks and Hodges). *The building firm of George Wimpey, Ltd, was founded by George Wimpey and Walter Tomes in Hammersmith, London, in 1880.*

Winborn(e) P Place-name *Wimborne* in Dorset OE 'pasture stream'. A scarce Sussex surname in both spellings.

Winch T/N References to such a surname/byname preceded by '*de*' lend force to the idea that it might be a topographical term for a person who lived at a place where pulleys/cranes/windlasses were used to haul boats out of the water OE; or, in cases where '*le*' is used in place of '*de*', a nickname for a person bearing some resemblance to a lapwing OE (literally 'leap-turner', from its flight). **Winch** is chiefly found in south-east England; the variants **Wink** and **Winks** are strongest in Suffolk and in WRYorks respectively.

Winchester P Place-name *Winchester*, the city in Hants, Romano-British and OE (from Latin *castra*) '*Venta*'s Roman site'. By the late nineteenth century the distribution of the surname had become somewhat bizarre: scattered throughout England and Scotland, it was strongest in south-east England and in north-east Scotland. *The Winchester rifle is named after its inventor Oliver F. Winchester (1810–1880), who was descended from John Winchester, an early seventeenth-century immigrant to the USA.*

Windeatt, *see* **Wingate**.

Windebank/Windibank/Windybank T Dweller on a windy hillside OE. Chiefly a Hants surname in all spellings. A Hearth Tax return of 1666/7 for the London wards of Farringdon Within and Without includes the name of a Mary **Winterbanke**, who was assessed for six hearths in the 'Precinct of White Fryars'. *Sir Francis Windebank (1582–1646), a politician who rose to become Secretary of State under Charles I, was born in Westminster to a family which had its roots in Lincs.*

Winder P/O Place-name in Cumbd, Lancs, Westmd (two), WRYorks ON 'wind-shelter' (compare **Windrum**); or an occupational term for one who wound or plaited (yarn, thread, etc.) OE plus suffix. A Lancs surname.

Windibank, *see* **Windebank**.

Windmill T Dweller in or near a windmill OE. Mainly found in the Home Counties, the West Midlands and Somerset.

Window(s) T/O Dweller at a house with some kind of prominent or distinctive window (such as an oriel) OE; or an occupational term for a glazier OE. Cottle suggests that **Windows** (or the Lancs surname **Windus**, and even the south-of-England **Windust**) might alternatively refer to a 'wind(ing)-house', a weaver's dwelling OE. Both **Window** and **Windows** are chiefly Gloucs surnames.

Windrum T Dweller at the 'wind shelters' ON, a dative plural (compare **Winder**). A scarce and scattered surname, found in Co Durham, Leics, Middx and Lanarkshire, Scotland.

Windsor/Winsor P Place-name *Windsor* in Berks, Devon, Dorset, Hants OE 'river-bank with a windlass/winch' (for pulling boats up). This has been the surname of the British Royal family since 1917, in which year it was decided that the name of Windsor Castle might appropriately be used for this purpose, replacing the all-too-German **Wettin** (of Saxe-Coburg-Gotha) at a time when the First World War was still raging. **Windsor-Clive** is the family name of the Earls of Plymouth. **Windsor** can be found scattered throughout England and Wales, but is rare in the east, West Wales and the far north; **Winsor** is largely a Devon surname.

Windus/Windust, *see* Window.

Windybank, *see* Windebank.

Wine(s)/Wyne(s) N Nickname, a 'friend' OE (compare **Winn, Winsley, Winslow**). **Wine** is strongest in Gloucs/Somerset, **Wines** in Somerset, and **Wyne** in Lancs and in Lanarkshire, Scotland. **Wynes** is scarce and scattered.

Winfield, *see* Wingfield.

Wing P Place-name in Bucks OE '*Wiwa*'s people' and in Rutland ON '?field'. A widespread surname, rarer in the north and west of England. A book published in New York in 1956 under the title *Natural history of birds* was written, appropriately enough, by Leonard William **Wing**.

Wingard, *see* Wynyard.

Wingate P Place-names: *Wingate* in Co Durham and Devon; *Wingates* in Lancs, Northd OE *windgeat* 'windy pass' (literally 'wind gate'). *Winnats* in Derbys, with its impressive steep pass, has the same origin. The variant **Windeatt** is closer to the OE original. **Wingate** can be found scattered throughout England and Scotland; **Windeatt** is a Devon surname; **Winnett** is a scarce variant. *Orde Charles Wingate (1903–1944), the charismatic and unorthodox army officer famous for leading his 3,000-strong force of Chindits against Japanese forces in Burma in 1943, was born in Naini Tal in the United Prov-*

inces, India, to a family with strong Plymouth Brethren connexions.

Wingfield/Winfield P Place-names *North* and *South Wingfield* in Derbys OE 'pasture-ground'; similar place-names in Beds and Suffolk have an obscure first element. Chiefly a Derbys surname in either spelling. Family name of the Viscounts Powerscourt. For **Winfield**, see also **Woolworth**.

Wink(s), *see* Winch.

Winn N/F Nickname, a 'friend' OE (compare **Wine, Winsley, Winslow**); or the remains of a two-element first-name beginning 'Friend-'. Strongest in WRYorks. Family name of the Barons St Oswald.

Winnett, *see* Wingate.

Winpenny/Wimpenny N Nickname for a money-grubber, one always eager to 'gain a penny' OE. Chiefly a WRYorks surname in both spellings.

Winser, *see* Windsor.

Winskell/Winskill P Place-names in Cumbd: *Winskill*, and *Winscales* (two such, one having given its name to the nuclear power plant, later renamed 'Sellafield') ON 'shelter from the wind'. Fairly scarce surnames of the far north of England.

Winslade P Place-name in Hants OE '*Wine*'s stream'. Chiefly a Somerset surname.

Winsley P Place-name in Wilts OE '*Wine*'s wood/clearing' (compare **Wine, Winn, Winslow**) and in WRYorks OE '*Wine*'s hill/mound'. Mainly a Devon surname. Readily confused with/a variant of **Wensley**.

Winslow P Place-name in Bucks OE '*Wine*'s burial-mound' (compare **Wine, Winn, Winsley**). A widely scattered surname. *Edward Winslow (1595–1655), one of the founders of the Plymouth Colony in North America, was born in Droitwich, Worcs.*

Winson, *see* Winston.

Winsor, *see* Windsor.

Winstanley P Place-name in Lancs OE '*Wynnstan*'s wood/clearing', and a Lancs surname.

Winston(e) F/P From an OE first-name meaning 'joy-stone'; or from one of a number of places called *Winston* or *Winstone*, derived from a variety of OE first-names plus OE *tun* 'enclosure' – though the second element in *Winstone*, Gloucs, is OE *stan* 'stone'. Reaney also shows how a name of this sound was used in Wales to render *Trewin* ('house of *Wyn*') as *Wynston*. The Churchill family have used *Winston* as a first-name for many generations, having acquired it thanks to an ancestral link with Sir Henry **Winston** of Standish, Gloucs, whose daughter Sarah married John Churchill of Mintern, Dorset, and was the mother of Sir Winston Churchill (born in 1620), whose son John became the first Duke of Marlborough. **Winston** is especially in evidence in Gloucs and in Glamorgan, Wales, **Winstone** in Gloucs and the (apparent) variant **Winson** in Derbys.

Winter(s) N Nickname for a person of a cold and frosty temperament, who had white hair, or who was born during an especially hard winter OE. A widespread surname in either spelling, **Winter** being particularly prolific. The variant **Wintour** is found chiefly in Gloucs.

Winterborn(e), *see* Winterbourn.

Winterbotham/Winterbottom   T/P
Dweller in a valley occupied only in winter OE. There are two places called *Winterbottom* in Chesh, one in Goostrey-cum-Barnshaw, the other in Mere, but the first recorded references to each date from as late as the nineteenth century, and such places are probably named from a former owner who bore the **Winterbottom** surname. **Winterbottom** is chiefly a Lancs surname; **Winterbotham** is more widespread, strongest in Derbys. *Sir Walter Winterbottom (1913–2002), the first person to be manager of the England football team (1946–1962), was born in Oldham, Lancs.*

Winterbourn(e)/Winterborn(e)/Winterburn P From one of a number of places called *Winterbourne* or *Winterborne*, or from *Winterburn* in WRYorks OE 'winter stream, stream dry in summer'. Cottle remarks that there is 'an amazing group of fifteen place-names (-*o[u]rne*), with sub-titles, in Dorset alone; eight more in Wilts; and others in Berks, Gloucs, Kent, WRYorks'. **Winterbourn**, **Winterbourne** and **Winterborne**, none of which are common surnames, can chiefly be found in Berks; **Winterborn** is strongest in Norfolk, and **Winterburn** in WRYorks.

Winterscale, *see* Wintersgill.

Wintersgill P From places in WRYorks called *Winterscale* and *Winterscales* ON 'winter hut'. **Wintersgill**, strongest in NRYorks and WRYorks, has been respelt to bring it in line with the word '*gill*' (a ravine), but although the surname **Winterscale** more closely resembles the original WRYorks place-names, by the late nineteenth century it had become a rare surname found mainly in faraway Devon.

Winterton P Place-name *Winterton* in Lincs, and also in Norfolk (which, appropriately enough, lies close to *Somerton*) OE 'farm used in winter' (though the first element may be the name of a proprietor who bore a name with the meaning of '*winter*'). A widespread surname, strongest in Leics. *The Conservative Party Member of Parliament Sir Nicholas (Raymond) Winterton was born in 1938 in Rugeley, Staffs.*

Winthrop P Place-name *Winthorpe* in Lincs OE '*Wina*'s settlement' and in Notts OE '*Wigmund*'s settlement', the surname being arrived at by metathesis. By the late nineteenth century the surname was scarce within England, and had an unusual spread, being strongest in Cumbd and Co Durham, but also in evidence in Kent. The scarce variants **Wintrop** and **Wintrup** could then mainly be found in Northd and in Roxburghshire, Scotland, respectively. *John Winthrop (1588–1649), who emigrated to America in 1629 and became the first Governor of the Massachusetts Colony, was born to a family of Suffolk gentry.*

Winton P Place-name *Winton* in NRYorks

and in East Lothian, Scotland OE '*Wine*'s enclosure'; in Lancs OE 'settlement with willows'; in Westmd OE '?pasture settlement'. The place-name *Winton* in Dorset is a modern coinage for an area of Bournemouth. The surname is strongest in Sussex, but is also well represented in various Scottish counties.

Wintour, *see* Winter.

Wintringham P Place-names: *Wintringham* in ERYorks, Hunts; *Winteringham* in Lincs OE 'homestead of the *Winter/Wintra*'s people'. Chiefly a Lincs surname.

Wintrop/Wintrup, *see* Winthrop.

Winyard, *see* Wynyard.

Wisdom N Nickname for a person known for his wisdom, knowledge – or perhaps for his occult powers OE. Abstract surnames of this kind are unusual, and some scholars have suggested a place-name origin, but it would appear that *Wisdome* and *Wisedom (Farm)* in Devon are named from previous owners, not vice versa. Compare the adjectival form represented in **Wise** and also **Wiseman**. Wisdom is mainly found in Surrey and surrounding counties. **Wisden**, a scarce Sussex surname, could well be a variant. *The internationally known comedian, singer and actor Sir Norman Wisdom was born in Marylebone, London, in 1915… John Wisden (1826–1884), a Brighton-born cricketer who played for Kent, Middlesex and Sussex, is now best known for having launched* Wisden Cricketers' Almanack.

Wise N Nickname for a person known for his wisdom, knowledge – or perhaps for his occult powers OE. Compare **Wisdom**, **Wiseman**. Sometimes found as a German/Jewish surname, from the German *weiss* 'white'. Wise is a widespread surname within England; the variant **Wyse** has a limited presence in south-east England, and in Fifeshire and other Scottish counties.

Wiseman N/F Nickname for a wise man OE, and also known to have been used as a first-name. Reaney shows that it could also be applied ironically to a man who was far from wise, or who was deemed to be a wiz-

ard or sorcerer. Compare **Wisdom** and **Wise**. Quite a prolific surname, scattered throughout both England and Scotland.

Wish P Place-name in Sussex OE 'marshy meadow'. Chiefly a Devon surname.

Wishart/Vizard/Whisker/Wisher/Wisker F From *Wiscard*, a Norman form of the OF first-name *Guiscard*, from ON elements meaning 'wise-hardy/brave', or including the OF suffix *-ard*. The variant **Vizard** constitutes a respelling through association with the word *vizard/visor* ('mask') OF, 'but meanings of *vizard* – "masked person, prostitute" – are fortunately too late to apply to the surname' (Cottle). **Wishart** is found mainly in north-east Scotland, **Vizard** in Gloucs, **Whisker** in ERYorks, **Wisher** (scarce) in Notts and **Wisker** (scarce) in ERYorks and Norfolk.

Wisher/Wisker, *see* Wishart.

Witcher, *see* Whitcher.

Witchurch, *see* Whitchurch.

Withacombe, *see* Widdecombe.

Witham P From one of a number of places so-called, including *Witham on the Hill*, Lincs, and *Witham*, Essex OE '?village on the bend'; *Witham Friary*, Somerset OE '*Wit(t)a*/the counsellor's homestead'; *North* and *South Witham*, Lincs, named after the river *Witham*, of uncertain etymology (first element Celtic '?forest'). Strongest in Essex and Middx, but with something of a presence in WRYorks.

Withecombe, *see* Widdecombe.

Witheridge P Place-name in Devon OE 'ridge with willows', and a Devon surname.

Witherington P Place-names: *Witherington*, Wilts OE 'willow-copse farm'; *Witherenden*, Sussex OE '*Wither*'s swine-pasture'. Yet this is mainly a Lancs surname, and there must be some confusion with **Withington**.

Witherspoon/Wedderspoon/Wetherspoon/Wotherspoon ?P Ancient Scots surnames of uncertain origin, perhaps from an unidentified place named with the elements ME *wether* 'wether/ram' and the dialectal *spong/spang* 'narrow piece of land'. See also **Wilderspin**.

Withey, *see* Withy.

Withington P Place-name in several counties, most (Chesh, Herefords, Lancs, Salop) being OE 'willow enclosure', though *Withington* in Gloucs is OE '*Widia*'s hill'. Largely a Lancs surname. Readily confused with/a variant of **Witherington**.

Withnell P Place-name in Lancs OE 'hill with willows', and a Lancs surname.

With(e)y T Dweller beside a withy/willow tree OE. Chiefly a Somerset surname in both spellings.

Withycombe, *see* Widdecombe.

Witley P Place-name in Worcs OE 'wood/clearing in the recess' and in Surrey OE '*Witta*'s wood/clearing'. A scarce surname, found in Middx and WRYorks. Readily confused with/a variant of **Whiteley**.

Witney P Place-name in Oxon OE '*Wit(t)a*'s island', the *-n-* indicating the genitive of the weak masculine name *Wit(t)a*. Strongest in Oxon. Readily confused with/a variant of **Whitney**.

Witt, *see* White.

Wittaker, *see* Whitaker.

Wittington, *see* Whittington.

Witton P Place-name in several counties, some being OE 'wood settlement', others OE 'settlement at a dwelling/salt spring'. A scattered surname, strongest in Staffs and WRYorks. Readily confused with/a variant of **Whitton**.

Witts, *see* White.

Witty/Whitty ?N/P Cottle believes that the origin here is a nickname for a wise, skilful person OE (as in *use your wits/have your wits about you*). Hanks and Hodges suggest an unidentified place-name OE 'white enclosure', or a nickname for a person with unusually pale eyes ME as the source. **Witty** is strongest in Co Durham, **Whitty** in Lancs.

Wix, *see* Wick.

Wobey, *see* Walby.

Wodehouse, *see* Woodhouse.

Woffenden/Woffendon/Woffinden/Woffindin, *see* Wolfenden.

Wogan F From a Welsh first-name *Gwgon/Gwgan*, 'little scowler', but a surname now very much associated with Ireland. *Thomas Wogan (c.1620-c.1669), parliamentary radical and regicide, was the son of John Wogan MP of Wiston, Pembrokeshire, Wales... Sir Michael Terence ('Terry') Wogan, television and radio broadcaster (not at all a little scowler), who was born in Limerick in the Republic of Ireland in 1938, has ancestral roots which go back to a Welsh family named* **Gwgon**.

Wold, *see* Wald.

Wolf(e)/Wolff/Woof(f)/Woolf(e) N/F Nickname for a person bearing some resemblance to a wolf OE, or from an abbreviated form of one of a number of Germanic compound names with this as a first element. Widely scattered surnames, in some cases brought to the British Isles by German/Jewish immigrants. The variant **Ulph** is chiefly found in Norfolk. *Charles Wolfe (1791–1823), author of the well-known poem 'The Burial of Sir John Moore at Corunna', was born in either Dublin or at Blackhall, Co Kildare, Ireland. His father Theobald Wolfe was first cousin to Arthur Wolfe, Viscount Kilwarden, the Lord Chief Justice of Ireland who was murdered in the Emmet rising, and it was from Theobald Wolfe that another relation, the Irish nationalist and political writer Theobald Wolfe Tone (1763–1798), derived his Christian name.*

Wolfenden/Woffenden/Woffendon/Woffinden/Woffindin P Place-name *Wolfenden* in Lancs OE '?*Wulfhelm*'s valley'. A WRYorks surname in all spellings, one which George Redmonds says can be found in over twenty different forms, many of them with *-dale* as a suffix. Not only that, but George has unearthed a reference in the West Riding Quarter Sessions to 'Joshua **Wolfenden** otherwise **Woffindale** otherwise **Ovenden** of Heckmondwike, Birstall' (1770). For further evidence of this **Wolfenden/Ovenden** inter-relationship, see **Ovenden**. *John Frederick Wolfenden, Baron Wolfenden (1906–1985), the educationalist and public servant who is perhaps best remembered for giving his name to the Wolfenden report, which recommended the decriminalization of homosexuality in 1957, was born in Halifax, WRYorks.*

Wolff, *see* **Wolf**.

Wolfit, *see* **Woolfit**.

Wolford P Place-name *Wolseley* in Warwicks OE 'watching-place for wolves', the OE element *weard* having been assimilated to OE *ford* 'ford'. Such a place would have been something of a necessity in a rural area where sheep were grazed or washed and where a wolf attack was always a possibility. A very scarce surname, found in Berks and elsewhere. Readily confused with/a variant of **Walford**.

Wolseley/Woolsey P Place-name *Wolseley* in Staffs OE '*Wulfsige/Wulfsi*'s wood/clearing'. **Wolseley** is a very scarce surname with a limited presence in Chesh and Derbys; **Woolsey** is strongest in Norfolk. Readily confused with/a variant of **Wolsey**.

Wolsey F From the OE first-name *Wulfsige* ('wolf-victory'). Strongest in Middx and Surrey, but also to be found in Lancs and elsewhere. Readily confused with/a variant of **Wolseley**. *Cardinal Thomas Wolsey (1470/1–1530), Archbishop of York and an all-powerful minister during the reign of King Henry VIII, was born to a family of modest means in Ipswich, Suffolk… The Wolsey textile company, originally established in 1756, adopted its present name in 1903 in honour of Cardinal Wolsey, who lies buried at Leicester Abbey, near the Wolsey factory… The Wolseley Sheep-shearing Machine Company Ltd (later Wolseley plc), which is now engaged in a wide range of industrial activities, was founded by an Irishman called Frederick York Wolseley in Sydney, Australia, in 1887. A former works manager at the company, Herbert Austin, began manufacturing cars in the 1890s and adopted the Wolseley name.*

Wolstencroft/Wolsoncroft/Wolston-croft/Wozencroft P Place-name *Woolstencroft* in Chesh OE '*Wulfstan*'s paddock'. **Wolstonecraft**, a spelling of the surname which is featured as its main form by Hanks and Hodges, has no presence in the British census of 1881. At that time **Wolstencroft** and **Wolstoncroft** were scarce surnames, found chiefly in Lancs; **Wolsoncroft** had a limited presence in both Chesh and Surrey, and **Wozencroft** in Radnorshire, Wales.

Wolstenholme/Woolstenhulme/Worsman/Worsnip/Worsnop P Place-name *Wolstenholme* in Lancs OE and ON '*Wulfstan*'s island'. **Wolstenholme** and **Woolstenhulme** are chiefly Lancs surnames; **Woosnam** is strongest in Montgomeryshire, Wales, **Worsman** and **Worsnop** in WRYorks, and **Worsnip** in both that county and also in Lancs. One family of Sheffield cutlers, originally called **Wolstenholme**, adopted the surname **Wostenholm** (dropping the first '*l*' and the final '*e*') in order to create a name which was more convenient for stamping on their knives. *Kenneth Wolstenholme (1920–2002), the football commentator who declared at the end of the 1966 World Cup final, 'They think it's all over… it is now!', was born in Worsley, near Manchester… The British professional golf-player Ian (Harold) Woosnam, nicknamed the 'Wee Welshman', was born in 1958 in Oswestry, Salop… Glyn Worsnip (1938–1996), the former actor and television presenter best known for his appearances on* That's Life! *and* Nationwide, *was born in Gloucs.*

Wolston P Place-name in Warwicks OE '*Wulfric*'s estate'. A very scarce surname, found in Surrey and elsewhere, readily confused with/a variant of the far commoner **Woolston** (or even **Woolton**).

Wolstoncroft, *see* **Wolstencroft**.

Wombwell P Place-name in WRYorks OE '*Wamba*'s spring/stream' or 'spring/stream in a hollow' (compare the word '*womb*'). Mainly found in Essex and Notts.

Wonfor P Place-name *Wonford* in Thornbury, Devon OE '?waggon ford'; but the first element in *Wonford*, Heavitree, Devon, is a stream-name. Chiefly a Kent surname.

Wonnacott P Place-name in Devon OE '*Wun(n)a*'s cottage', and a Devon surname. *Tim Wonnacott, the eternally-cheerful, cheeky and knowledgeable presenter of antiques programmes on television, was born in Barnstaple, Devon, in 1953.*

Wood T/O/N Dweller at or near a wood OE or an occupational term for one who worked as a woodman or forester. 'A surname as universal as woods were in medieval England' (Cottle). Rarely, a nickname for a mad, frenzied person OE (Shakespeare's 'wood within this wood' in *A Midsummer Night's Dream* means, rather, 'distracted, furious'). **Woods** is 'of/at the wood', or a plural. **Woodd** is a scarce WRYorks variant. **Wood** is the family name of the Earls of Halifax. See also **Woodey**.

Woodall, *see* **Woodhall**.

Woodard F/O From the ME first-name *Wodard*, meaning 'wood-hard/hardy'; or a contracted form of 'wood-herd' OE, an occupational term for one who tended swine feeding in a wood on acorns or mast. An East Anglian surname.

Woodbridge P Place-name in Dorset and Suffolk OE 'wooden bridge'. Chiefly found in the south of England and in the South Midlands.

Woodburn P From one of a number of places so-called in Northd and in Scotland OE 'stream in a wood'. Strongest in Lancs.

Woodbury P Place-name in Cambs, Devon, Somerset, Worcs, some being OE 'fort in a wood', others OE 'wooden fort' or OE 'old fort'. A Devon/Somerset surname.

Woodcock N/P Nickname for a person bearing some resemblance to a woodcock OE, a bird known for being something of a simpleton, and easily caught; or from one of a number of places in various counties called *Woodcott* or *Woodcote* OE 'cottage in/ by a wood'. **Woodcock** is strongest in Lancs and WRYorks.

Woodcraft/Woodcroft P Place-name *Woodcroft* in Gloucs, Northants OE 'paddock in/near a wood'. Most common in Beds in both spellings.

Woodd, *see* **Wood**.

Wooden P Place-name in Northd OE 'wolves' valley', though the surname, far from common, is chiefly found in Kent and Norfolk. Readily confused with/a variant of **Woodend**.

Woodend P Place-name in many counties OE 'end of the wood'. Chiefly a Lancs surname. Readily confused with/a variant of **Wooden**.

Woodey T Dweller at an enclosure in a wood OE, or possibly a variant of **Wood**. A scarce Gloucs surname.

Woodfall T/P Dweller at a (sheep)fold in a wood OE, or from the place-name *Woodfalls* in Wilts, with the same meaning (though Cottle seems to have located a place in Lancs called *Woodfall* OE 'clearing in a wood'). A scarce surname, with a presence in Middx, Surrey and Warwicks.

Woodford P Place-name in many English and Scottish counties, from Cornwall to Roxburghshire OE 'ford in/by a wood'. Yet the surname rarely encroaches into northern counties of England or into Scotland.

Woodfull N/F Nickname from OE 'wood-bird' (compare the word '*fowl*'), also known to have been used as a first-name. Chiefly a Warwicks surname.

Woodgate/Woodyatt T/P Dweller at a wood-gate, a gate leading into a wood OE, or from one of a number of places called *Woodgate*, with the same meaning. **Woodgate** is strong in Kent and in Suffolk, **Woodyatt** (much scarcer) in Herefords and Worcs.

Woodger, *see* **Woodyer**.

Woodhall/Woodall P From one of a number of places called *Woodhall* in England and Scotland (twelve in Yorks alone) OE 'hall in a wood, forest court-house', though one of the three places so-named in Worcs is OE 'spring in a wood'. **Woodall** is found mainly in the north of England and along the border with Wales; **Woodhall** is strongest in Lancs.

Woodham P From one of a number of places so-called in various English counties, including Essex (three such) and Surrey OE 'homestead in a wood'; Bucks OE 'river-meadow by a wood'; Co Durham OE '(at) the woods', exhibiting the use of a dative plural after a lost preposition. Strongest in Middx and Surrey.

Woodhead P From one of a number of places so-called in England and Scotland OE 'top of the wood'. Chiefly a WRYorks surname.

Woodhouse T/P/N Dweller at a house in a wood OE (or in a house made of wood?), or from one of several English and Scottish places so-called, with the same meaning, in WRYorks (a dozen such), Derbys, Notts, Lincs (several in each), and twelve other counties. Cottle also favours an alternative source – a nickname for a faun, satyr, troll, woodwose OE (see **Woodiwiss**). **Woodhouse** is strongest in Lancs and WRYorks, and the variant **Wodehouse** (much scarcer) in Middx and Norfolk. **Woodhouse** is the family name of the Viscounts Terrington, and **Wodehouse** of the Earls Kimberley. See also **Widdows**. *Sir Pelham Grenville ('P. G.') Wodehouse (1881–1975), the comic writer who created the character Jeeves the butler, was born in Guildford, Surrey, to a well-established gentry family.*

Woodhurst P Cottle mentions a place in Hunts called *Woodhurst* OE 'wooded hill' 'so-called after an adjoining area (now *Old Hurst*) had been cleared', but this is chiefly a Kent/Middx/Sussex surname, and the origin in most if not all cases is likely to be *Woodhurst* in Slaugham, Sussex.

Woodier, *see* Woodyer.

Woodisse, *see* Woodiwiss.

Woodiwiss/Woodisse N A distinctive surname which Cottle, associating it with one of the meanings of **Woodhouse**, says is derived from a nickname for a person bearing some resemblance to a faun, satyr, troll, woodwose/woodhouse OE *wuduwase*, or who played such a character in a play or pageant. The *wild man* was a frequent figure in pageants and heraldry, and the Barons **Wodehouse**, Earls of Kimberley, had as supporters to their arms two *woodwoses* (wild men covered in green hair, except where the flesh is visible in the face, elbows, knees, hands and feet). Hence there is a connexion with the Green Man of legend. Most early bearers of the **Woodiwiss** surname lived in the Derbys lead-mining settlements of Wirksworth and Bonsall, whence a branch was established later in Doncaster and in Barnsley, WRYorks. **Woodisse**, just as scarce a surname, has a limited presence in Staffs. *Sir Abraham Woodiwiss (1828–1884), railway contractor and philanthropist, born in Belper, Derbys, was descended from Henry Woodiwiss of Bonsall (born 1640). His son Abraham (1855–1912) served two terms as Mayor of Derby, in 1888/9 and 1901/2.*

Woodland T/P Dweller in woodland OE, or from one of a number of places so-called, from Co Durham to Devon, with the same meaning. Strongest in Kent, Middx and Somerset.

Woodleigh, *see* Woodley.

Woodley P From one of a number of places, such as *Woodleigh* in Devon and *Woodley* in Berks OE 'clearing/field in a wood'. **Woodley** is strongest in Berks, Devon, Middx and Surrey; **Woodleigh** is a very scarce variant.

Woodman T/O/F Dweller in a wood, or an occupational term for a woodman OE; or, more rarely, from the OE first-name *Wudumann*. Generally a south/south-west of England surname.

Woodmansey/Woodmansee P Placename *Woodmansey* in ERYorks OE 'woodman's lake', and chiefly an ERYorks surname. **Woodmansee** is a scarce Essex variant.

Woodroff(e), *see* Woodruff.

Woodrow P There are places so-called in Wilts and Worcs OE 'lane/row (of cottages) in a wood', but the surname is strongest in Norfolk.

Woodruff(e)/Woodroff(e)/Woodrup

T/N Dweller at a spot where the herb woodruff OE *wudurofe* (*Asperula odorata*) grew in some profusion; or a nickname for someone who smelt as sweet as woodruff, or who was known to have applied it as a perfume – or, ironically, for a smelly person who would have benefited from making liberal and regular use of it, but didn't. **Woodruff** and **Woodruffe** are strongest in Lancs, **Woodroff** in Middx, Surrey and Wilts; **Woodroffe** is a scattered surname, and **Woodrup**, scarce, belongs to WRYorks.

Woodrup, *see* Woodruff.

Woods, *see* Wood.

Woodstock P Place-name in Oxon OE 'place in the woods'. Mainly found in Middx and surrounding counties.

Woodthorpe P Place-name in Derbys, Leics, Lincs, Notts, WRYorks, OE 'settlement in a wood'. Strongest in Lincs.

Woodward O/F Occupational term for a wood-keeper, forester OE, or from the OE first-name *Wuduweard*, with the same meaning. A prolific surname, strongest in Lancs.

Woodyatt, *see* Woodgate.

Woodyer/Woodger/Woodier O Occupational term for a wood-hewer/cutter OE. **Woodyer**, far from common, is found in Lancs, but also in Middx and Surrey; **Woodger** is strongest in Surrey and surrounding counties, and **Woodier** in Chesh and Warwicks.

Woof(f), *see* Wolf.

Wookey P Place-name in Somerset OE 'snare, trap', and a Somerset surname.

Wool O/T/P Occupational term for one who worked in wool OE; or a dweller near a spring or stream ME *woll/wull*, a western/south-western dialectal form of OE *wiell(a)*, or from a place-name in Dorset, with the same meaning. A scarce south-of-England surname.

Wooland T Dweller on/beside curved or crookèd land(s) OE. There would appear to be precious few places so-called (though there are plenty of *Woodlands*), and even the related surname **Woolham**, despite appearances, doesn't have an obvious place-name origin. Reaney lists several variants of **Wooland**, including **Woollam(s)**; **Woolliams**, though it looks suspiciously like **Williams**, probably also belongs here. **Wooland** is a Devon surname; **Woolham** can be found in Salop and in WRYorks, and **Woollam** in Lancs and Salop. **Woollams** is scarce and scattered, and **Woolliams**, also scarce, can be found in Gloucs and Oxon. *The actor David Walliams, best known for his partnership with Matt Lucas in the television show* Little Britain, *was born David Williams, but found that there was another actor of the same name, so he adopted the invented form 'Walliams' (of which there are a mere three examples in the British census of 1881).*

Wool(l)ard, *see* Woolford.

Woolas(s), *see* Woolhouse.

Woolaway F From an OE first-name meaning 'wolf war'. A Devon surname.

Wool(l)combe P Place-names: *Woolcombe* in Dorset OE 'spring/stream valley', and *Woolacombe* in Devon, with the same meaning, or else OE '?wolves' valley'. A Devon surname in both spellings.

Woolcott/Woollacott P Place-name *Woolcot* in Somerset ME 'spring/stream cottage'. **Woolcott** is a scarce surname found in limited numbers in south-east England; **Woollacott** is strongest in Devon, and **Woolcock** is a fairly prolific Cornish variant. Readily confused with/a variant of **Walcot**.

Wooldridge, *see* Woolrich.

Wool(l)er O/P Occupational term for a worker/dealer in wool OE; or from *Wooler* in Northd, OE 'stream bank'. Strongest in WRYorks in both spellings.

Wooley, *see* **Woolley**.

Woolf(e), *see* **Wolf**.

Woolfit(t)/Wolfit/Woollatt F From the OE first-name *Wulfgeat* 'wolf-Geat' – *Geat* being the name of a tribe to which Beowulf belonged, commemorated in the title of the King of Sweden, *Rex Sveorum Gothorumque*, and in the *Goths*. **Woolfitt** (Lincs and Notts) and **Woolfit** (Lincs) are much commoner spellings than the exceptionally scarce **Wolfit**. **Woollatt** is chiefly found in Derbys, Herts and Notts. *The actor Sir Donald Wolfit (1902–1968), who originally bore the surname Woolfitt, was born in New Balderton, near Newark, Notts.*

Woolford F/P From a ME first-name *Wol(f)ward* (OE *Wulfweard*) 'wolf-guardian'; or from the place-name *Wolford* in Warwicks ME '?enclosure to protect against wolves'. See also **Woolworth**.

Woolgar/Woolger F From the OE first-name *Wulfgar* 'wolf spear'. Surnames of south-east England.

Woolham, *see* **Wooland**.

Woolhouse/Woolas(s) T Dweller at a building used for storing wool OE. **Woolhouse** is strongest in Northants, **Woolas** (scarce) in Lincs, ERYorks, WRYorks, and **Woolass** (even scarcer) in WRYorks and elsewhere.

Woollacott, *see* **Woolcott**.

Woollam(s), *see* **Wooland**.

Wooland P Place-name in Dorset OE 'pasture land'. Strongest in nearby Devon.

Woollard, *see* **Woolford**.

Woollatt, *see* **Woolfit**.

Wooller, *see* **Wooler**.

Woolley/Wooley P There are places called *Wooley* or *Woolley* in several counties, many of which are OE 'wood with wolves'; but *Wooley* in Northd is OE 'hill with wolves', and *Woolley* in Somerset is OE 'wood/clearing by a stream'. **Woolley** is strongest in the Midlands and in northern England, especially in Chesh, Lancs and Staffs; **Wooley**, less common, has a particular presence in Lancs.

Woolliams, *see* **Wooland**.

Woolman O Occupational term for a woolman/merchant OE. A scarce surname, strongest in Leics.

Woolmer P/F Place-names: *Woolmer Forest*, Hants; *Wolmer Farm* in Ogbourne St George, Wilts; *Woolmore Farm* in Melksham, Wilts OE 'mere/pool frequented by wolves'; or from a now-lost place-name *Wolmoor* in Ormskirk, Lancs OE 'moor frequented by wolves'. Cottle also suggests that an OE first-name meaning 'wolf famous' may be involved. **Woolmer** is chiefly found in south-east England, and **Woolmore** in Essex. *Robert Andrew ('Bob') Woolmer, the international cricketer and cricket coach who died in what initially appeared to be mysterious circumstances in March 2007, was born in 1948 in Kanpur, India (where his father was then playing Ranji Trophy Cricket), but he spent his early life in Kent.*

Woolmore, *see* **Woolmer**.

Woolner/Woolnough F From the OE first-name *Wulfnoth* 'wolf-boldness'. Chiefly a Suffolk surname in both spellings.

Woolnough, *see* **Woolner**.

Woolrich/Hurr(e)y/Ulrich/Urry/ Wool(d)ridge F From an OE first-name *Wulfric* 'wolf-powerful'. Cottle describes the variant **Hurr(e)y** as being *'Wulfric* ironed out by the Normans'. The *-ridge* element in **Woolridge/Wooldridge** (and in the apparent variant **Wildridge**, which can be found scattered across England and central Scotland, strongest in Fifeshire), a modification of *-rich* (from *-ric*), has the effect of making such surnames resemble a place-name. **Woolrich** is strongest in Chesh and Staffs, **Hurry** in Cambs, **Hurrey** in Lancs, **Ulrich** (scarce) in Middx and Surrey, **Urry** in the Isle of Wight, **Wooldridge** in Staffs and Worcs, and **Woolridge** in Staffs.

Woolsey, *see* **Wolsey** and **Wolseley**.

Woolstenhulme, *see* Wolstenholme.

Woolston(e) F/P From the ME first-name *Wol(f)stan*, OE *Wulfstan* 'wolf-stone', borne by an Archbishop of York who died in 1023 and by a canonized Bishop of Worcester who died in 1095; or from one of several places called *Woolston(e)* or *Wollston*, all of which consist of one of a number of OE first-names of which the first element is *Wulf-* 'wolf', followed by OE *tun* 'enclosure/settlement'. Strongest in Norfolk in both spellings. Readily confused with/a variant of **Wolston** and **Woolton**.

Woolton P Place-name in Lancs OE '*Wulfa*'s place/farm'. An uncommon scattered surname. Readily confused with/a variant of **Wolston** and **Woolston**.

Woolven/Woolvin F From an OE first-name meaning 'wolf-friend'. Chiefly a Sussex surname in both spellings.

Woolverton P From one of a number of place-names: *Wolverton* in Bucks, Hants, Warwicks, Worcs; *Woolverton* in Somerset; *Wolferton* in Norfolk; *Wollverton* in Salop. All have OE *tun* 'farm settlement' as the final element; the first element consists of one of a number of OE personal names beginning with *Wulf-* 'wolf'; the second elements vary, and are not always clear. Chiefly a Norfolk/Surrey surname.

Woolvin, *see* Woolven.

Woolward, *see* Woolford.

Woolworth ?P A surname of unknown origin. Given the fact that the surname/place-name elements *-worth* and *-ford* can readily become confused (rendering '**Titford**' out of '**Titworth**'), **Woolworth** could in principle be a variant of **Woolford**. But **Woolworth** is a scarce surname found mainly in Devon, where it could represent an abbreviated version of the cumbersome place-name *Woolfardisworthy* OE '*Wulfheard*'s farm', which was *Wollesworthye* in 1550 and is often referred to as '*Woolsery*'. Compare **Walworth**. *Frank Winfield ('F. W.') Woolworth (1852–1919), famous for having established the chain of 'five and ten cents' stores which bore his name, was born in Rod-man, New York, the son of John H. Woolworth, a farmer, and Fanny McBrier. His middle name of 'Winfield' was used as a brand-name for many of the products sold in Woolworth's stores.*

Woon T Dweller on downland, Cornish *gun*, or from a number of place-names in Cornwall containing this element. A Cornish surname.

Woosnam, *see* Wolstenholme.

Wooster, *see* Worcester. Mainly a Bucks surname.

Wootten, *see* Wootton.

Wootton/Wootten/Wotton P There are places called *Wootton* in at least fifteen counties, and *Wotton* can be found in Bucks, Gloucs and Surrey; all are OE 'place/farm by a wood'. **Wootton** is strongest in Staffs, **Wootten** in Wilts and **Wotton** in Devon.

Worboys, *see* Warboys.

Worcester/Wooster/Worster P Place-name *Worcester* OE and British 'Roman site (from the Latin *castra*) of the *Weogoran* tribe'. The Bishop of Worcester still signs his name '*Wigorn*'. **Worcester** is a rare surname, with something of a presence in Middx, Sussex and Warwicks; **Wooster** is mainly a Bucks surname, and **Worster** can be found in limited numbers in Middx and Surrey.

Worden P Place-name in Lancs OE 'weir valley' and in Devon OE '?enclosure'. Chiefly found in Lancs, but with a significant presence in Cornwall and Devon. **Worthen**, a very scarce Lancs surname, is probably a variant, though it could readily be confused with, or be a variant of, **Worthing** or **Worthy**.

Wordsworth, *see* Wadsworth.

Workman O/N Occupational term for a workman, builder OE, though Reaney says that during the middle ages *werkemanne* could refer to an ambidextrous person. Chiefly a Gloucs surname.

Worle P Place-name in Somerset OE 'wood-grouse wood'. A very scarce Kent/Somerset/Surrey surname.

Worlock, *see* **Werlock**.

Worm N Nickname for a person resembling a dragon, reptile, snake in some way OE. The 'worm' which young Lambton threw down a well in the famous song from north-east England was a serpent of some kind which grew to an enormous size and had 'great big googly eyes'. Chiefly an East Anglian surname.

Wormald P There are places so-called in Barkisland, Rishworth and Scammonden in WRYorks OE '*Wulfrun*'s well' (*Wulfrun* being a female personal name). Chiefly a WRYorks surname; George Redmonds traces its development from the place-name in Rishworth through examples of bynames/surnames such as: **de Wlfrun-welle/de Walronwalle** (thirteenth century), **de Wournewall** (fourteenth century), **Wormewall** (fifteenth century), **Wormall** (sixteenth and seventeenth centuries) and **Wormold** (seventeenth century).

Wormleighton P Place-name in Warwicks OE '*Wilma*'s herb garden'. Mainly found in Leics and surrounding counties.

Wormley P Place-name in Herts, Lincs, Surrey OE 'wood/clearing/field with worms (reptiles/snakes)'. A very scarce Kent/Yorks surname.

Worrall/Worrell P Place-name *Worrall* in WRYorks OE 'bog-myrtle nook'; the peninsula of the *Wirrall* in Chesh has the same origin, and could have given rise to such surnames. **Worrall** is chiefly a Chesh/Lancs surname; **Worrell** is widely and evenly scattered throughout England, as far north as Yorks.

Worsman/Worsnip/Worsnop, *see* **Wolstenholme**.

Worster, *see* **Worcester**.

Wort O Occupational term for a grower of vegetables OE. Mainly found in Hants and surrounding counties.

Worth T/P Dweller at an enclosure, fence, homestead OE, or from one of several places so-called in various counties, with the same meaning. A number of longer place-names include the element *-worth*. Strongest in Devon, but also much in evidence in northern counties of England. *The English comedian Harry Worth (1917–1989), born Harry Illingsworth in Tankersley, near Barnsley, WRYorks, used a shortened version of his surname as a stage-name.*

Worthen, *see* **Worden**.

Worthing T/P Dweller at an enclosure or homestead OE; or from one of a number of place-names such as *Worthen* in Salop OE 'enclosure settlement', *Worthing* in Norfolk OE 'the enclosure' or *Worthing* in Sussex OE '*Weorth*'s people'. A surname with a distinctive regional presence in South Wales and Herefords. Readily confused with/a variant of **Worthen** (see **Worden**) or **Worthy**.

Worthington P Place-name in Lancs and Leics OE '?*Wurth*'s people's place/farm', though the first element could be OE *worthign* 'enclosure'. Predominantly a Lancs surname. *William Worthington (1723–1800), born at Orton on the Hill, Leics, was responsible for founding the Worthington & Co Brewery in Burton upon Trent, Staffs.*

Worthy T/P/N Dweller at an enclosure OE *worthig*, or from one of a number of places so-called, with the same meaning, in Devon, Hants and elsewhere; or a nickname for a worthy person OE. A surname which is found throughout England, but which is strongest in Co Durham. Readily confused with/a variant of **Worthen** (see **Worden**) or **Worthing**.

Wortley P There are two places so-called in WRYorks: *Wortley* near Barnsley OE 'clearing/field with plants/vegetables' (compare the word '*wort*') and *Wortley* near Leeds OE '?*Wyrca*'s clearing/field'. Chiefly a WRYorks surname.

Worton P There are places so-called in various counties, most being OE 'vegetable/enclosure garden', but *Nether* and *Over Worton* in Oxon are OE 'place/farm/enclosure on a bank/slope'. Yet the surname is most in evidence in Staffs, in which county there is a place caled *Worston* OE '*Wifel*'s enclosure'.

Wotherspoon, *see* **Witherspoon**.

Wotton, *see* **Wootton**.

Wouldham P Place-name in Kent OE '*Wulda*'s homestead'. A very scarce surname.

Wozencroft, *see* **Wolstencroft**.

Wraight, *see* **Wright**.

Wraith/Wro(a)th N Nickname for a person with a violent temper, quick to show wrath OE *wrath*. **Wraith** is strongest in WRYorks, **Wroth** in Devon and **Wroath** in Cornwall.

Wrate, *see* **Wright**.

Wrathall P Presumably from a now-lost place-name, possibly OE 'nook where crosswort grows', or maybe related to **Wathall**? A WRYorks surname.

Wray P/N From one of a number of places called *Wray*, *Wrea* or *Wreay* in northern England ON *vra* 'nook/recess'. Cottle adds that the river- and place-name *Wray* in Devon is OE 'felon-stream', where convicted criminals were executed by drowning (compare **Wrayford**), and also suggests that the surname may alternatively be derived from a nickname for a twisted, crooked person OE (compare the word '*awry*'). **Wray** is strong in several northern counties, most in evidence in WRYorks; **Wroe** is a Lancs/WRYorks variant.

Wrayford/Wreford T Devon surnames, referring to a dweller at a ford on the river *Wray* OE 'felon-stream', where judicial drowning was permitted (see **Wray**). *Wrayford* may also have been used as an as-yet-unidentified place-name within the county.

Wreford, *see* **Wrayford**.

Wren(n) N Nickname for a person who bore some resemblance to a wren OE : 'it was tiny, but it was the King of birds – shrewd, towny, and a singer; on the whole, a nice name' (Cottle). **Wren** is a widespread surname; **Wrenn**, less common, is chiefly found in Sussex. *Sir Christopher Wren (1632–1723), architect, mathematician, astronomer and visionary, was born in East Knoyle, Wilts. His Wren ancestors came from Durham, though it is said that their earlier origins lay in Denmark.*

Wrench ?F/N/P A surname of uncertain origin, found chiefly in Chesh. Bardsley suggests a baptismal name; Reaney favours a nickname from OE *wrenc* 'wile, trick, artifice', and Lower has an elaborate theory that the surname **Ol(l)erenshaw** was corrupted to **Renshaw**, then to **Rench**, and finally to **Wrench**.

Wretham P Place-name in Norfolk OE 'homestead where crosswort/hellebore grows'. A very scarce Kent/Suffolk surname

Wride T/P/N Dweller by a bush, thicket OE, or at a twist/bend in a river OE; or from the place-name *Wryde* in Cambs, which carries the latter meaning. Reaney suggests that such a surname might alternatively be derived from a nickname for a 'twister' OE. Mainly found in Somerset and surrounding counties.

Wright(e)/Wraight O Occupational term for a craftsman who made ('*wrought*') almost any kind of useful object OE, though sometimes used specifically for a carpenter or joiner (see **Carpenter**). Words such as *wheelwright* and *playwright* are still in general use, but in previous times there were *cheesewright*s, *sievewright*s, *cartwright*s, etc. An exceptionally popular, widespread name, though most common in the north of England and with a presence in Scotland. **Wrightson** and **Wrixon** ('son of **Wright**') are at their strongest in Co Durham and in Dorset respectively. The spelling of **Wrate**, a very scarce variant found in Cambs, reflects what has long been a regional pronuciation of **Wright**.

Wrightson, *see* **Wright**.

Wrig(g)lesworth P Place-name in WRYorks, referred to as *Wridelsford* in the twelfth century, but now *Woodlesford* OE 'ford at the ?thicket'. A WRYorks surname. Readily confused with/a variant of **Wigglesworth**. In principle the very scarce surname **Rigglesford** could have the same origin (the elements -*worth* and -*ford* often having been confused in both place-names and surnames), though it is found mainly in Sussex; there is a place-name *Rigsford* in that county OE 'willow-tree ford', though the first recorded example of what was then referred to as *Wrygforde* dates only from the mid sixteenth century.

Wrigley P Place-name *Wrigley Head* in Lancs. The second element of *Wrigley* is OE *leah* 'wood/clearing'; the first element may be an OE personal name (as so often), or be from a topographical term from OE *wrigian* 'to bend/turn'. A Lancs surname, with an additional presence in WRYorks and elsewhere. *Wrigley's Chewing Gum takes its name from the company founded by William Wrigley, Jr (1861–1932), who was born in Philadelphia, Pennsylvania, USA... Ammon Wrigley (1861–1946), the dialect poet and folklorist, was born in Friarmere, Saddleworth, WRYorks.*

Wrixon, *see* Wright.

Wroath, *see* Wraith.

Wroe, *see* Wray.

Wroth, *see* Wraith.

Wyard, *see* Wyatt.

Wyatt/Whyatt/Wyard F From the mediaeval first-name *Wiot/Wyot/Gyot* (OE *Wigheard*, 'war-brave'), used by the Normans as a diminutive for both *Guy* (see **Guy**) and *William* (see **William**). *Famous members of the influential Wyatt family of Allington, Kent (whose roots lay in Yorks), include: Sir Henry Wyatt (c.1460–1536), politician and courtier, his son Sir Thomas Wyatt (c.1503–1542), poet and ambassador, and his son Sir Thomas Wyatt (c.1521–1554), soldier and rebel.*

Wybar/Whybrew/Whybro(w)/ Wibrew/Wibrow/Wyber/Wybrew/

Wybrow F From a ME female first-name *Wyburgh*, OE *Wigburh* 'battle-fortress'. Scarce or very scarce in all spellings: **Wybar** can be found in Lanarkshire, Scotland, **Whybrew** and **Wibrew** in Essex, **Whybro** and **Whybrow** in Cambs and Essex, **Wibrow** in Middx, **Wyber** in Midlothian, Scotland, **Wybrew** in Herts, and **Wybrow** in Essex, Middx and Surrey. **Wyber**, *see* **Wybar**.

Wyber, *see* Wybar.

Wybrew/Wybrew/Wybrow, *see* Wybar.

Wyburn F From an OE first-name meaning 'war hero' (a man of this name settled *Wybunbury*, Chesh). Cottle notes the fact that '*Wyburn*' is also – probably coincidentally – the local pronunciation of *Wythburn*, Cumbd, originally ON 'willow valley', though **Wyburn** as a surname is sparsely scattered throughout England and Scotland, strongest in Kent.

Wych(e), *see* Wich.

Wycherley P Place-name *Wycherley*, Salop (once a hamlet, now a hall) OE 'wych-elm wood/clearing'. An uncommon surname, found chiefly in Salop. *The playwright William Wycherley (c.1641–1716), though he was baptized in Whitchurch, Hants, belonged to a gentry family which had been settled at Wycherley Hall, Clive, Salop, since the year 1409... Ronald William Wycherley (1940–1983), born in Liverpool, achieved fame as a singer and songwriter under the name 'Billy Fury'.*

Wye P/F Place-name *Wye* in Kent OE 'at the heathen temple'; or a Norman dialect form of **Guy**. Strongest in Surrey. **Why** (Bucks, Surrey) and **Whye** (Leics, Surrey) would appear to be variants.

Wyke, *see* Wick.

Wykeham P Place-name in Hants, Lincs (three), NRYorks OE 'homestead/river-meadow with a *wick*' (see **Wick**), or simply a 'manor, dwelling-place', especially one associated with a Romano-British town. See **Wickham**. A very scarce Oxon surname.

Readily confused with/a variant of **Whickham** or **Wickham**.

Wylam P Place-name in Northd OE '(the settlement at) the fish-traps', exhibiting the use of a dative plural after a lost preposition. A Co Durham/Northd surname.

Wyley/Wylie, *see* Wily.

Wyman/Weyman/Weymont/Whyman F From the ME first-name *Wymund* (OE *Wigmund*) 'battle-protector'. **Wyman** is a scattered surname, strongest in Northants; **Weyman** is mainly found in Gloucs, **Weymont** (very scarce) in Essex, and **Whyman** in Kent.

Wymark/Waymark F From an Old Breton first-name *Wiumarch*, 'worthy (to have a?) horse', used for both males and females. Chiefly a Sussex surname in both spellings. Readily confused with/a variant of **Wymer**. *The actor Patrick Wymark (1926–1970) was born in Cleethorpes, Lincs, and spent his early life in neighbouring Grimsby.*

Wymer F From the OE first-name *Wymer*, 'battle-famous'. A Norfolk surname. **Whymer** is a very scarce variant. Readily confused with/a variant of **Wymark**.

Wyndham P Place-names: *Wyndham* in Sussex OE '?*Winda*'s water-meadow'; *Wymondham* in Leics and Norfolk OE '*Wigmund*'s homestead'. An uncommon surname, more southern than northern, and strongest in Wilts. Family name of the Barons Leconfield.

Wyne(s), *see* Wine.

Wyngarde, *see* Wynyard.

Wynn(e) N Welsh: nickname for a person with white/fair hair or a pallid complexion OW, a variant of **Gwyn**; or a variant of **Winn**. Strongest in Lancs in both spellings. **Wynn** is the family name of the Barons Newborough.

Wynyard/Wingard/Winyard/Wyngarde T/O Dweller at a vineyard, or an occupational term for a person who worked in one OE. A scarce scattered surname in all spellings, **Wyngarde** being particularly rare. *The actor Peter Paul Wyngarde, best known for playing the role of Jason King in two television series in the 1960s, was born in 1933 in Marseilles, France, where his father worked for the British Diplomatic Service.*

Wysall, *see* Whysall.

Wyse, *see* Wise.

Y

Yale T/P Dweller at a fertile upland, Welsh *iâl*, or from the place-name *Iâl* in Denbighshire, with the same meaning. Within the British Isles, the surname is strongest in Salop and Staffs, but also has a significant presence in America. *Two members of what would appear to be one extended family called Yale, founded by seventeenth-century immigrants from Plas Grono, near Wrexham, Denbighshire, made their mark in no uncertain terms in America: Elihu Yale (1649–1721) was an early benefactor to Yale University; Linus Yale (1821–1868) was the inventor of the Yale lock.*

Yalland, *see* Yolland.

Yandal(l)/Yandell/Yandle, *see* Yeandle.

Yapp N Nickname for a shrewd, smart (or possibly crooked/bent/deceitful?) person OE. Mainly found in Salop and surrounding counties.

Yarborough P Place-names *Yarborough* and *Yarburgh* in Lincs OE 'earth fort'. A hand in whist or bridge containing no card higher than a nine is named after a sporty Earl of **Yarborough**. Mainly found in Lincs and surrounding counties. On the face of it, the surname **Yerbury** could be a variant, though it is very largely a Somerset surname.

Yard(e) T Dweller at a particular piece of land. Cottle believes that such a surname is less likely to be from OE 'yard, enclosure' than from OE 'yardland, virgate (of varying size, commonly thirty acres)'. The *-e* of **Yarde** ('at the yardland') is from the dative form, used after a now-lost preposition.

Yard is mostly found in Somerset, **Yarde** (much scarcer) in Devon.

Yardley P Place-name in Essex, Northants, Worcs OE 'wood/clearing for getting sticks/spars/poles'; but the place-name in Bucks is OE 'clearing for ploughing'. Strongest in Staffs and Warwicks. *In 1620 a member of the Yardley family was granted a concession to manufacture soap for the whole of London. The famous firm of Yardley of London was founded by William Yardley in 1770.*

Yarnold, *see* Arnold.

Yarrow T/P Dweller at a place covered in yarrow OE, or beside a river so-called, British/Welsh/Gaelic 'rough (stream)'; or from *Yarrow* in Selkirkshire, Scotland, which stands beside such a river. A widespread surname throughout England, and also found in parts of Scotland.

Yarwood P From an unidentified place-name, the first element of which is probably '(river) *Yare*', from Welsh, the second being OE 'wood'. This is chiefly a Chesh/Lancs surname; places in Chesh called *Yarwood*, *Yeowood* or *Yewards* would generally seem to be of too late a date to have given rise to a related surname, though what is now *Yarwoodheath Covert/Farm* was *Yarwode* in 1384. *The comedian and impressionist Mike Yarwood was born in 1941 in Stockport, Chesh.*

Yate/Yeat(e)s T/O/P Dweller or worker (tollkeeper?) at a gate OE *geat* 'gate, gap', or from a place-name so-called with the same meaning; compare *Symonds Yat* ('*Simund*'s gate') in the Forest of Dean, on the river Wye. The surname **Yates** ('of/at the gate') is the commonest surname in this group.

Yaxley P Place-name in Hunts OE 'cuckoo's wood'. Principally a Norfolk surname.

Yeaman(s), *see* Yeoman.

Yeandel, *see* Yeandle.

Yeandle/Yandal(l)/Yandell/Yandle/ Yendall/Yendell/Yendle/Yendole ?T/P
A surname which seems reluctant to give up its meaning. Cottle suggests that it might be a derivative of the OE adjective *geandele* 'steep', while Reaney makes a tentative reference to the place called *Yen Hall* OE 'lamb nook/valley' in Cambs. Yet this surname in most of its various forms is centred upon the counties of Devon and Somerset (**Yeandel** being a scarce variant found in neighbouring Gloucs), so a minor place-name in the West Country might be the point of origin.

Yearling N Seemingly a nickname based upon an OE word for a yearling (a year-old animal, or one in its second year), though 'the reason for bestowal is obscure' (Cottle). Chiefly a Devon surname.

Yearnshaw, *see* Earnshaw.

Yearsley P Place-name in NRYorks OE 'boar's wood'. Chiefly a Chesh/Lancs surname.

Yeat(e)s, *see* Yate.

Yelland, *see* Yolland.

Yelverton P Cottle speaks of such a place-name in Norfolk OE '*Geldfrith*'s estate', but believes that *Yelverton* in Devon is too recent a place-name to be the origin of a related surname: 'It was *Elleford* ("*Ella*'s/ elder-tree ford" OE) in 1291, and the farm remained *Elfordtown*, but the Great Western Railway used the dialect form *Y-* on building its station there in 1859'. This may sound convincing enough, but it doesn't take account of the fact that the surname **Yelverton**, while scarce, is chiefly found in Devon, and that it could well have arisen from the very dialect form of the

place-name which the GWR mimicked in its 'new' spelling.

Yemm, *see* Eames.

Yendall/Yendell/Yendle/Yendole, *see* Yeandle.

Yeo T/P Dweller by a river, stream OE, or from a minor place-name or river-name with the same meaning. Chiefly a Cornwall/Devon surname. *The Conservative Party Member of Parliament for South Suffolk, Timothy Stephen Kenneth ('Tim') Yeo, who pronounces his surname 'Yo', was born in 1945 in Lewisham, London.*

Yeoland, *see* Yolland.

Yeoman(s)/Yeaman(s) O Status term for a yeoman, small freeholder (one step up from a husbandman) ME, though an earlier use of the word denoted a servant or attendant, occupying a rank between a sergeant and a groom, or between a squire and a page. **Yeoman** is a widespread surname, strongest in both Devon and NRYorks; **Yeomans** is mainly found in Derbys, and **Yeaman** in northern England, though at its strongest in Angus, Scotland. **Yeamans** is a very scarce variant. *Sir John Yeamans (c.1605-c.1676), a Barbados landowner who was later Governor of Carolina, came from a well-established Bristol family bearing the surname 'Yeamans' or 'Yeomans'.*

Yerbury, *see* Yarborough.

Yolland/Yalland/Yelland/Yeoland P
From one of a number of places called *Yolland, Yalland* or *Yelland* in Devon OE 'old (?long-cultivated) land'. Compare **Youlden**. **Yolland** is found chiefly in Devon, **Yalland** in Devon and Gloucs, **Yelland** in Cornwall and Devon, and **Yeoland** in Glamorgan, South Wales.

Yong(e), *see* Young.

Yorath/Yorwerth F From a Welsh first-name *Iorwerth* ('Lord-handsome'), which was in time supplanted by *Edward*, considered to be its equivalent. By the late nineteenth century **Yorath** and **Yorwerth**

could both be found in limited numbers in Glamorgan.

York(e) P From the city of *York*, originally British, Latinized as *Eburacum* ('?yew-tree place'), then mistakenly turned into OE *Eoforwic* (as if to mean 'wild-boar outlying settlement'), and finally Scandinavianized by the Vikings into *Iorvik* and then *Iork/York*. As a surname **York** and its variant **Yorke** are widespread, strongest in Northants. **Yorke** is the family name of the Earls of Hardwicke. *The film actor Michael York, whose real name is Michael Hugh Johnson, was born in 1942 in Fulmer, Bucks… Susannah York, English film, television and stage actress, was born Susannah Yolande Fletcher in London in 1942.*

Youens, *see* Ewan.

Youl, *see* Yule.

Yould N Nickname for an old person OE. A scarce Chesh surname.

Youlden/Youldon P Place-names *Youlden* and *Youldon* in Devon OE 'old (?long-cultivated) hill'. Compare **Yolland**. Devon surnames.

Youle(s)/Youll, *see* Yule.

Young(e)/Yong(e) N Nickname for a young person OE, or with the sense of the 'younger' or 'youngest' of two or more indi-

viduals bearing the same name. **Younger** (chiefly a Co Durham/Northd surname) can be a variant with the same meaning, but Reaney cites a 1364 Fleming whose name was from Middle Dutch *jonghheer* 'young nobleman'. The *-e* of **Younge** and **Yonge** could indicate the use of a weak adjective after a lost definite article. **Young** is the family name of the Barons Kennet. **Youngs** ('son of **Young**'), like **Youngman**, is an East Anglian surname.

Younger, *see* Young.

Younghusband O Occupational term for a young farmer/husbandman OE. Compare **Husband**. Chiefly a Cumbd surname.

Youngman N Nickname for a young man OE. Like **Youngs**, an East Anglian surname.

Youngs, *see* Young.

Yoxall P Place-name in Staffs OE '?nook the size of a yoke (of oxen – that is, fifty/sixty acres)'. Chiefly a Chesh surname.

Yule/Youl/Youle(s)/Youll N Nickname for a person born at, or having a special connexion with, Christmastide OE/ON. *Yule* was originally a twelve-day pagan festival. **Yule** itself is a surname mainly found in Aberdeenshire, Scotland, and surrounding areas, rare in England.

Z

Zeal(e) ᴘ From one of a number of places called *Zeal* in Devon ᴏᴇ *sele* (with initial *s*-voiced) '?hall/Manor-house'; or a variant of **Seal**. Chiefly a Devon surname in either spelling.

Zebedee ꜰ From a first-name meaning 'my gift', a Greek respelling of Hebrew, borne by the fathers of the apostles James the Great and John. A distinctive surname, mainly found in Wilts and surrounding counties.

Zeller, *see* **Sellar**.

Zouch, *see* **Such**.

PENGUIN REFERENCE LIBRARY

THE PENGUIN BOOK OF FACTS

EDITED BY DAVID CRYSTAL

'One of the greatest reference books ever published' *Independent on Sunday*

Funafuti is the capital of which south Pacific island? Which dog-toting film star's real name is Frances Gumm? How far is Brussels from Paris? *The Penguin Book of Facts* is the most comprehensive and authoritative general factbook available. Calling upon his famously encyclopaedic knowledge, David Crystal has compiled this international information bible with meticulous precision, layering fact upon fact in a logical order, from the beginnings of the universe to the World Water Skiing Union. It is not only the authoritative and infinite breadth of knowledge that sets this dictionary apart; Crystal has added an invaluable and comprehensive index that makes finding that elusive fact all the easier.

- Contains more facts than any other book of its kind and is illustrated throughout

- Includes contributions from over 250 experts

- This is the updated edition of *The New Penguin Factfinder*

ONLY PENGUIN GIVES YOU MORE

PENGUIN REFERENCE LIBRARY

THE PENGUIN DICTIONARY OF FIRST NAMES

EDITED BY DAVID PICKERING

What's in a name? Rather more than you might at first suspect, for names are steeped in history and myth and have much to tell us about our past, our beliefs – even our personality traits. Now fully updated for its second edition, with 150 new entries, *The Penguin Dictionary of First Names* is much more than just an inspiration for expectant parents. Each entry is a carefully researched mini-masterpiece in cultural and linguistic history, as David Pickering offers a wealth of information fitted for the twenty-first century reader. He takes a close look at over 5000 examples – ranging from the familiar to the comparatively obscure – drawn from all parts of the English-speaking world. No other book provides the same authoritative detail and quality of definition.

- Gives the meaning or origin of each name, its variants and diminutives

- Highlights names that have become popular from literature, films, culture and celebrities

- Shows how names have changed in use and popularity over time

- Lists the most popular girls' and boys' names from 1700 to the present, from *Siobhan* and *Iolanthe* to *Hayden* and *Sherlock*

- Examines trends and changing tastes in the twenty-first century

ONLY PENGUIN GIVES YOU MORE

PENGUIN REFERENCE LIBRARY

**THE PENGUIN DICTIONARY OF LITERARY TERMS
& LITERARY THEORY**

EDITED BY J. A. CUDDON

'Scholarly, succinct, comprehensive and entertaining … an indispensable work of reference' *The Times Literary Supplement*

Now over thirty years old, J. A. Cuddon's *The Penguin Dictionary of Literary Terms and Literary Theory* is a reference classic, a stunning survey of literature and theory that stands as the first port of call for any reader or student of literature. Consistently updated since, Cuddon's work illuminates the history and complexity of literature's movements, terms and major figures in relaxed, accessible prose. From *existentialism* to *caesura* to *doggerel*, the text ranges authoritatively over both high and low literary culture and theory, and is the primary reference source for anyone interested in writing or reading.

- Gives definitions of technical terms (*hamartia*, *iamb*, *zeugma*) and critical jargon (*aporia*, *binary opposition*, *intertextuality*)

- Explores literary movements (*neoclassicism*, *romanticism*, *vorticism*) and schools of literary theory (*feminist criticism*, *new historicism*, *structuralism*)

- Covers genres (*elegy*, *fabliau*, *pastoral*) and literary forms (*haiku*, *ottava rima*, *sonnet*)

ONLY PENGUIN GIVES YOU MORE

PENGUIN REFERENCE LIBRARY

THE PENGUIN HANDBOOK OF LIVING RELIGIONS

EDITED BY JOHN R HINNELLS

'Excellent ... This whole book is a joy to read'
The Times Higher Education Supplement

Religion is more relevant than ever. From Islam to fundamentalism to the Kabbalah, faith is never far from the headlines, making our understanding of it utterly crucial. *The Penguin Handbook of Living Religions* is designed with this in mind. Crammed with charts, maps and diagrams, it comprises lengthy enlightening chapters on all of today's major religions, from Hinduism to Christianity to Baha'ism, as well as additional essays on cross-cultural areas, such as gender and spirituality. Each chapter represents a book's worth of information on all twenty-first century religions, featuring detailed discussion of the history, culture and practices of each. Comprehensive, informative and compiled by a team of leading international scholars, it includes discussion of modern developments and recent scholarship.

- Explains the sources and history of the world's religions, from Buddhism, Christianity, Hinduism, Islam, Sikhism and Zoroastrianism to regional groups in Africa, China and Japan

- Describes different doctrines, practices and teachings, including rites of passage and specific rituals

- Explores the role of gender and diaspora in modern religion

ONLY PENGUIN GIVES YOU MORE

PENGUIN SUBJECT DICTIONARIES

Penguin's Subject Dictionaries aim to provide two things: authoritative complimentary reference texts for the academic market (primarily A level and undergraduate studies) *and* clear, exciting and approachable reference books for general readers on subjects outside the core curriculum.

Academic & Professional

ACCOUNTING
ARCHEOLOGY
ARCHITECTURE
BUILDING
BUSINESS
CLASSICAL MYTHOLOGY
CRITICAL THEORY
ECONOMICS
INTERNATIONAL RELATIONS
LATIN
LITERARY TERMS & THEORY
MARKETING (forthcoming)
MEDIA STUDIES
MODERN HISTORY
PENGUIN HUMAN BIOLOGY (forthcoming)
PHILOSOPHY
PSYCHOLOGY
SOCIOLOGY

Scientific, Technical and Medical

BIOLOGY
CHEMISTRY
CIVIL ENGINEERING
COMPUTING
ELECTRONICS
GEOGRAPHY
GEOLOGY
MATHEMATICS
PHYSICAL GEOGRAPHY
PHYSICS
PSYCHOANALYSIS
SCIENCE
STATISTICS

English Words & Language

CLICHÉS
ENGLISH IDIOMS
PENGUIN ENGLISH GRAMMAR
PENGUIN RHYMING DICTIONARY
PROVERBS
SYNONYMS & ANTONYMS
SYNONYMS & RELATED WORDS
ROGET'S THESAURUS
THE COMPLETE PLAIN WORDS
THE PENGUIN A–Z THESAURUS
THE PENGUIN GUIDE TO PLAIN ENGLISH
THE PENGUIN GUIDE TO PUNCTUATION
THE PENGUIN WRITER'S MANUAL
USAGE AND ABUSAGE

Religion

BIBLE
ISLAM (forthcoming)
JUDAISM (forthcoming)
LIVING RELIGIONS
RELIGIONS
SAINTS
WHO'S WHO IN THE AGE OF JESUS

General Interest

BOOK OF FACTS
FIRST NAMES
MUSIC
OPERA
SURNAMES (forthcoming)
SYMBOLS
THEATRE

Penguin Reference – making knowledge everybody's property